The R

# Mexico

written and researched by

**John Fisher, Daniel Jacobs, Zora O'Neill and Paul Whitfield**

with additional contributions by

**Richard Arghiris, Jason Clampet, Stephen Keeling and Caroline Lascom**

NEW YORK • LONDON • DELHI

www.roughguides.com

# Contents


## Colour section 1–24

Introduction ............................... 6
Where to go ............................... 9
When to go ............................. 12
Things not to miss ................... 14

## Basics 25–72

Getting there............................ 27
Getting around......................... 35
Accommodation....................... 42
Food and drink ....................... 44
Crime and personal safety ....... 49
Health ..................................... 51
The media............................... 55
Festivals.................................. 56
Sports and outdoor activities ............................... 58
Culture and etiquette ............... 59
Shopping ................................ 60
Travel essentials ...................... 61

## Guide 73–880

1. Baja California and the Pacific Northwest.........75–178
2. The north ...................179–238
3. The Bajío....................239–324
4. Northern Jalisco and Michoacán ................325–392
5. Mexico City and around........................393–538
6. Acapulco and the Pacific beaches .....................539–592
7. Veracruz.....................593–632
8. Oaxaca ......................633–694
9. Chiapas and Tabasco .....................695–774
10. The Yucatán...............775–880

## Contexts 881–948

History .................................. 883
Chronology ............................ 905
Ball-games and sacrifice: the pre-Columbian belief system ................................ 907
Environment and wildlife........ 913
Mexican music....................... 924
Books ................................... 934

## Language 949–960

Rules of pronunciation........... 951
Useful words and phrases ..... 951
Food and drink terms ............ 954
Terms and acronyms.............. 958
Art and architectural terms .... 960

## Travel store 961–966

## Small print & Index 967–984

**Mexican food and drink** colour section following p.264

**Festive Mexico** colour section following p.504

**Ancient Mexico** colour section following p.792




◀◀ The Zócalo, Mexico City ◀ Chac-mool statue, Cancún

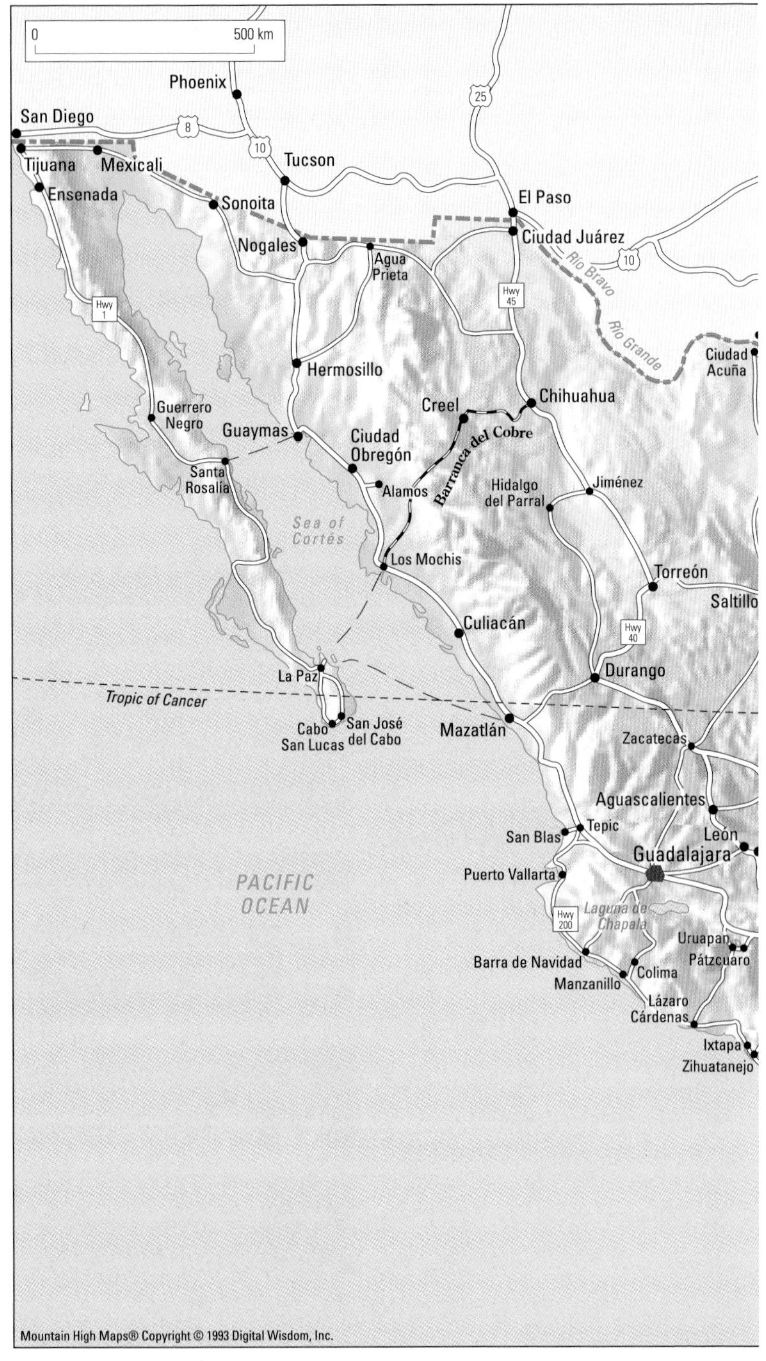

0
500 km
Phoenix
25
San Diego
8
10
Tijuana
Mexicali
Tucson
Ensenada
Sonoita
El Paso
Nogales
Ciudad Juárez
Agua
Prieta
Río Bravo
10
Hwy
45
Hwy
1
Río Grande
Ciudad
Acuña
Hermosillo
Creel
Chihuahua
Guerrero
Negro
Guaymas
Ciudad
Obregón
Barranca del Cobre
Santa
Rosalía
Alamos
Hidalgo
del Parral
Jiménez
Sea of
Cortés
Los Mochis
Torreón
Saltillo
Culiacán
Hwy
40
La Paz
Durango
Tropic of Cancer
Cabo
San Lucas
San José
del Cabo
Mazatlán
Zacatecas
Aguascalientes
San Blas
Tepic
León
Guadalajara
Puerto Vallarta
PACIFIC
OCEAN
Hwy
200
Laguna de
Chapala
Uruapan
Barra de Navidad
Pátzcuaro
Colima
Manzanillo
Lázaro
Cárdenas
Ixtapa
Zihuatanejo

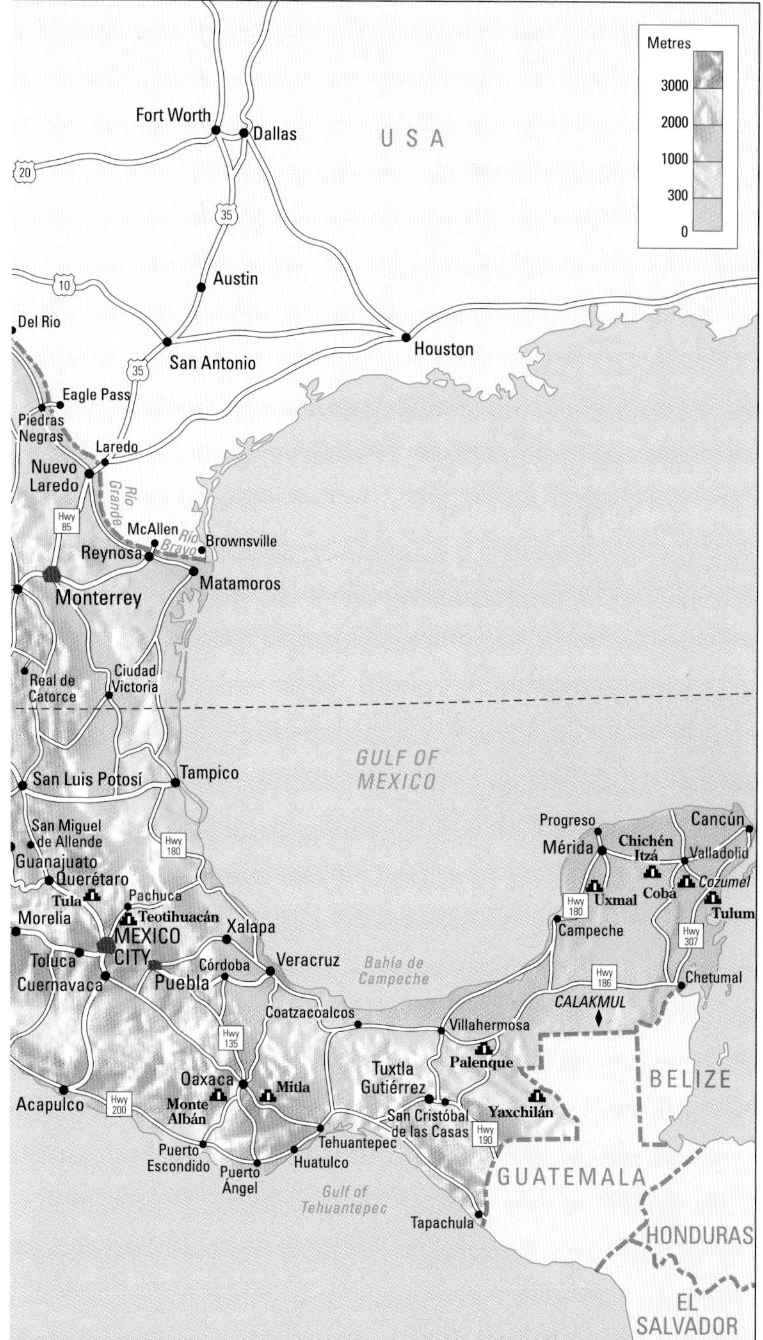
Metres
3000
2000
1000
300
0
USA
Fort Worth
Dallas
20
35
Austin
10
Del Rio
San Antonio
Houston
Eagle Pass
Piedras Negras
Laredo
Nuevo Laredo
Río Grande
Hwy 85
McAllen
Río Bravo
Brownsville
Reynosa
Monterrey
Matamoros
Real de Catorce
Ciudad Victoria
GULF OF MEXICO
San Luis Potosí
Tampico
San Miguel de Allende
Hwy 180
Guanajuato
Querétaro
Tula
Pachuca
Teotihuacán
Morelia
MEXICO CITY
Xalapa
Toluca
Cuernavaca
Puebla
Córdoba
Veracruz
Bahía de Campeche
Coatzacoalcos
Hwy 135
Oaxaca
Mitla
Monte Albán
Acapulco
Hwy 200
Puerto Escondido
Puerto Ángel
Huatulco
Tehuantepec
Gulf of Tehuantepec
Tuxtla Gutiérrez
San Cristóbal de las Casas
Hwy 190
Tapachula
Villahermosa
Palenque
Yaxchilán
CALAKMUL
Progreso
Mérida
Chichén Itzá
Cancún
Valladolid
Uxmal
Cobá
Cozumel
Tulum
Campeche
Hwy 307
Hwy 186
Chetumal
BELIZE
GUATEMALA
HONDURAS
EL SALVADOR

## Introduction to

# Mexico

**Mexico enjoys a cultural blend that is wholly unique: it's a patchwork of wildly different native American cultures, traditions brought by the Spanish five centuries ago and vast, modern industrial zones. Even the rapid change wrought by the "Mexican Miracle" has yet to erase the multitude of regional identities that make the country such a dynamic, constantly surprising place to travel.**

You can see different aspects of this blend even within a space as small as a few city blocks: on one sidewalk Maya women lay out their hand-made wares on colourful blankets, while on the next street teenagers skateboard to a soundtrack of *rock en español* in front of the heavy buttresses of a colonial cathedral, the legacy of the Catholic Church. Occasionally the mix is an uneasy one, but for the most part it works remarkably well. The people of Mexico reflect it, too: there are communities of full-blooded **indígenas**, and there are a few – very few – Mexicans of pure **Spanish** descent. The great majority of the population, though, is **mestizo**, combining both traditions, and, to a greater or lesser extent, a veneer of urban sophistication.

Despite the inevitable influence of the US, looming to the north, and close links with the rest of the Spanish-speaking world (an avid audience for Mexican soap operas), the country remains resolutely individual. The music that fills the plazas in the evenings, the buildings that circle around them, even the smells emanating from a row of taco carts: they all leave you without any doubt about where you are. The idea of "only in Mexico" – a thought sometimes had in awe, sometimes in exasperation, most often in simple bemusement – is rarely far from a traveller's mind.

The strength of Mexican identity perhaps hits most clearly if you travel overland across the border with the US, as the ubiquitous Popsicle vendors suddenly appear from nowhere, and the pace of life slows perceptibly.

Many first-time visitors are surprised to find that Mexico is far from being a "Third World" nation. If you're the type of traveller who gauges the level of "adventure" in terms of squalor endured, then you may be disappointed: the country has a robust economy, a remarkably thorough and efficient internal transport system and a vibrant contemporary arts and music scene. Adventure comes instead through happening upon a village fiesta, complete with a muddy bullfight and rowdy dancing, or hopping on a rural bus, packed with farmers all carrying machetes half their height and curious about how you've wound up going their way.

▲ Bahía Concepción, Baja California

## Fact file

- Bordering the US, Guatemala and Belize, Mexico is technically part of **North America**. The country covers an **area** of virtually two million square kilometres – about a quarter the size of the continental US and eight times the size of the UK – and has a **population** of more than 107 million. Well over 20 million live in the capital and its immediate vicinity in the Valley of México.
- Mexico is a country of tremendous geographical variety. The north is largely arid **semi-desert**, the south **tropical** and forested. The **volcanic mountains** of the centre rise to 5700m.
- The **economy** is growing rapidly, based on free-trade agreements with most countries in the Americas. Chief **exports** are oil and related products, silver (the world's largest source) and other metals and minerals, as well as manufactured goods produced using Mexican labour in the border zone.
- Mexico is a **federal republic**, with a presidential system loosely based on that of the US. A single party, the PRI, governed from the establishment of the modern constitution in 1917 until the conservative opposition party PAN won in an upset in 2000; the 2006 elections saw an even broader field of candidates.

### ¿Habla usted Nahuatl?

Spanish isn't *the* official language of Mexico – it's just *a* language, one of 63 legally recognized here. These other languages range from Nahuatl, spoken by more than 1.6 million people descended from the ancient Aztecs, to Kiliwa, kept alive by about fifty people in Baja California. All told, more than ten million people speak an indigenous language – a number second only to Peru. And this isn't even taking into account the numerous languages spoken by immigrant groups, many of whom have been in Mexico for a century or more: Old Order Mennonites converse in Plautdietsch (Low German), Lebanese families speak Arabic and the village of Chipilo, settled by Italians in 1882, has preserved an obscure Venetian dialect. You'll have to visit remote villages to hear Rarámuri, Chuj or Paipai, but in Chiapas and the Yucatán Peninsula, radio programs are broadcast in various Maya strains.

Don't worry, though: for the most part Spanish is still the *lingua franca*. Just don't be surprised if you meet people who speak it as a second language – just like you.

This is not to say Mexico is free of the hassles associated with "developing" countries, such as bribe-taking cops, dubious tap water and the like. And although the **mañana** mentality is largely an outsiders' myth, Mexico is still a country where timetables are not always to be entirely trusted, where anything that can break down will break down (when it's most needed) and where any attempt to do things in a hurry is liable to be frustrated. You simply have to accept the local temperament: work may be necessary to live but it's not life's central focus, minor annoyances really are minor and there's always something else to do in the meantime. Occasionally it can seem that there's incessant, inescapable noise and dirt. More deeply disturbing are the extremes of ostentatious wealth and grim poverty, most poignant in the big cities, where unemployment is high and living conditions beyond crowded. But for the most part, you'll find this is a friendly, fabulously varied and enormously enjoyable place in which to travel.

Physically, Mexico resembles a vast horn, curving away south and east from the US border, with its final tip bent right back round to the north. It is an extremely mountainous country: two great ranges, the Sierra Madre Occidental in the west and the Sierra Madre Oriental in the east, run down parallel to the coasts, enclosing a high, semi-desert plateau. About halfway down they are crossed by the volcanic highland area in which stand Mexico City and the major centres of population. Beyond, the mountains run together as a single range through the southern states of Oaxaca and Chiapas. Only the eastern tip – the Yucatán Peninsula – is consistently low-lying and flat.

# Where to go

For most visitors central and southeastern Mexico hold the bulk of the attraction. Many find the arid and sparsely populated north – a region heavily influenced by the neighbouring US and dominated by industrial cities such as **Monterrey** – relatively dull. The major exceptions are the shores and wilderness of **Baja California**, really destinations in their own right, and the **Copper Canyon**, with its spectacular rail journey. And the border cities can provide a bit of (sometimes sleazy) excitement.

It's in the highlands north of the capital that the first really worthwhile stops come, with the bulk of the historic colonial towns and an enticing spring-like climate year-round. Coming through the **Bajío**, the heart of the country, you'll pass the silver-mining towns of **Zacatecas** and **Guanajuato**, the historic centres of **San Miguel de Allende** and **Querétaro**, and many smaller places with a legacy of superb colonial architecture. **Mexico City** itself is a nightmare of urban sprawl, but totally fascinating, and in every way – artistic, political, cultural – the capital of the nation. Around the city lie the chief relics of the pre-Hispanic cultures of central Mexico: the massive pyramids of **Teotihuacán**; the main Toltec site at **Tula**; and **Tenochtitlán**, heart of both the Aztec empire and the modern capital. **Guadalajara**, to the west, is a city on a more human scale, capital of the state of **Jalisco** and in easy reach of **Michoacán**: between them, these states share some of the most gently scenic country in Mexico, where the thickly forested hills are studded with lakes and ancient villages. This area also has a reputation for producing some of the finest crafts in a country renowned for them.

▲ Paseo de la Reforma, Mexico City

▲ Great Pyramid of Cholula and Popocatépetl

South of the capital, the states of Oaxaca and Chiapas, home to some of the largest populations of pure indigenous groups, are mountainous and beautiful, too, but in a far wilder way. The city of **Oaxaca**, especially, is one of the most enticing destinations in the country, even following the protests of 2006, which occupied the central plaza for many months. It has an extraordinary mix of colonial and indigenous life, superb markets and fascinating archeological sites. **Chiapas** is probably still best known as the centre of the Zapatista uprising of the mid-1990s, though visitors are little affected these days, and the strength of indigenous traditions in and around the market town of **San Cristóbal de las Casas**, together with a number of lesser-known yet romantically tumble-down ancient Maya cities, continue to make it a big travellers' centre. It's typically the stop before the picturesque ruins of **Palenque**. East into the **Yucatán** there is also traditional indigenous life, side-by-side with a tourist industry based around the truly magnificent Maya cities – **Chichén Itzá** and **Uxmal** above all – and the burgeoning Caribbean resorts that stretch down the coast from **Cancún**. The capital of Yucatán state, **Mérida**, is a particular gem, both cosmopolitan and old-fashioned.

▲ Cathedral, Zacatecas

On the Pacific coast, where the surf is wilder and the scenery more rugged than in the Caribbean, **Acapulco** is just the best known of the beach destinations. Along the water to the north, hundreds of miles of relatively empty sand are broken up only by resort cities like **Mazatlán** and **Puerto Vallarta**; the south is even less developed, and the state of Oaxaca has some equally enticing shores. Few tourists venture over to the Gulf coast, despite the attractions of **Veracruz** and its mysterious ruins. The scene here is largely dominated by oil, the weather too humid most of the time and the beaches sometimes a disappointment. For music and general bonhomie, however, the city's central plaza is one of the country's finest.

## Mexico's markets

It's hard to beat the colour and bustle of Mexico's **markets**. Even if you've no intention of buying, half an hour is always well spent meandering through narrow aisles surrounded by heaps of perfectly ripe fruit and stacks of *nopal* cactus leaves (though stay away from the meat sections if you're at all squeamish). In small villages, like those around Oaxaca (see p.648), inhabitants still recognize one day of the week as the traditional market day, coming from miles around to sell their wares and stock up for the week ahead. The zócalo will come alive in the early morning, and return to its dozy ways only when all the day's transactions have been completed, usually in the mid-afternoon. Larger villages may have two or three official market days, but the rest of the week is often so busy it seems that every day is market day. In the cities, each *barrio* has its own vibrant market: especially noteworthy are Guadalajara's Libertad, Mexico City's enormous La Merced and Oaxaca's mercados Abastos and 20 de Noviembre. You'll soon find that each village or city's market has its own special character: while they primarily sell food, most will have a section devoted to artesanía, and in cities you'll sometimes find markets dedicated to goods like hammocks, mirrors and other handicrafts. For more info on markets and hints on bargaining, see Basics, p.61.

# When to go

▲ Palenque ruins

To a great extent, the physical terrain in Mexico determines the **climate** – certainly far more than the expected indicator of latitude. You can drive down the coast all day without conditions changing noticeably, but turn inland to the mountains, and the contrast is immediate: in temperature, scenery, vegetation, even the mood and character of the people around you. Generalizations, therefore, are difficult.

**Summer**, from June to October, is in theory the rainy season, but just how wet it is varies wildly from place to place. In the heart of the country you can expect a heavy but short-lived downpour virtually every afternoon; in the north hardly any rain falls, ever. Chiapas is the wettest state, with many minor roads washed out in the autumn, and in the south and low-lying coastal areas summer is stickily humid too. Along the beaches, September through mid-October is **hurricane season** – you'll usually get wet weather, choppy seas and mosquitoes, if not a full-on tropical storm. Late **winter** is the traditional tourist season, and in the big resorts like Acapulco and Cancún, December through April are the busiest months. Mountain areas, though, can get very cold then; in fact, nights in the mountains can be extremely cold at any time of year.

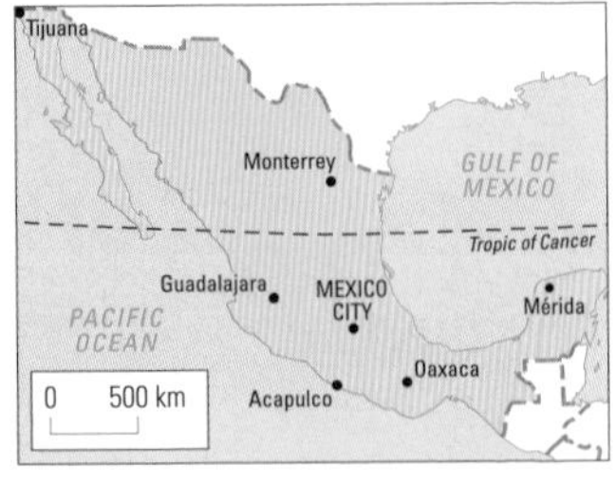


In effect, visitors come all year round – sticking on the whole to the highlands in summer and the coasts in winter. November is probably the ideal time to visit, with the rains over, the land still fresh and the peak season not yet begun. Overall, though, the climate is so benign that any time of year will do, so long as you're prepared for some rain in the summer, some cold in winter and the sudden changes which go with the altitude at any time.

## Average temperatures and rainfall

| | Jan | March | May | July | Sept | Nov |
|---|---|---|---|---|---|---|
| **Acapulco** | | | | | | |
| Max (°C) | 31 | 31 | 32 | 33 | 32 | 32 |
| Max (°F) | 88 | 88 | 90 | 91 | 90 | 90 |
| Min (°C) | 22 | 22 | 25 | 25 | 25 | 24 |
| Min (°F) | 72 | 72 | 77 | 77 | 77 | 75 |
| Rainfall (mm) | 13 | 5 | 0 | 203 | 279 | 15 |
| Rainfall (in) | 0.5 | 0.2 | 0 | 8 | 11 | 0.6 |
| **Guadalajara** | | | | | | |
| Max (°C) | 23 | 28 | 31 | 26 | 26 | 25 |
| Max (°F) | 73 | 82 | 88 | 79 | 79 | 77 |
| Min (°C) | 7 | 9 | 14 | 15 | 15 | 10 |
| Min (°F) | 45 | 48 | 57 | 59 | 59 | 50 |
| Rainfall (mm) | 13 | 8 | 25 | 178 | 178 | 13 |
| Rainfall (in) | 0.5 | 0.3 | 1 | 7 | 7 | 0.5 |
| **Mérida** | | | | | | |
| Max (°C) | 28 | 32 | 34 | 33 | 32 | 29 |
| Max (°F) | 82 | 90 | 93 | 91 | 90 | 84 |
| Min (°C) | 18 | 20 | 21 | 23 | 23 | 19 |
| Min (°F) | 64 | 68 | 70 | 73 | 73 | 66 |
| Rainfall (mm) | 25 | 13 | 76 | 127 | 178 | 25 |
| Rainfall (in) | 1 | 0.5 | 3 | 5 | 7 | 1 |
| **Mexico City** | | | | | | |
| Max (°C) | 22 | 27 | 27 | 24 | 23 | 23 |
| Max (°F) | 72 | 81 | 81 | 75 | 73 | 73 |
| Min (°C) | 6 | 10 | 13 | 13 | 13 | 9 |
| Min (°F) | 43 | 50 | 55 | 55 | 55 | 48 |
| Rainfall (mm) | 13 | 13 | 76 | 152 | 127 | 13 |
| Rainfall (in) | 0.5 | 0.5 | 3 | 6 | 5 | 0.5 |
| **Monterrey** | | | | | | |
| Max (°C) | 20 | 26 | 31 | 34 | 34 | 23 |
| Max (°F) | 68 | 79 | 88 | 93 | 93 | 73 |
| Min (°C) | 9 | 13 | 20 | 22 | 22 | 12 |
| Min (°F) | 48 | 55 | 68 | 72 | 72 | 54 |
| Rainfall (mm) | 25 | 25 | 51 | 76 | 102 | 25 |
| Rainfall (in) | 1 | 1 | 2 | 3 | 4 | 1 |
| **Oaxaca** | | | | | | |
| Max (°C) | 28 | 32 | 32 | 28 | 27 | 28 |
| Max (°F) | 82 | 90 | 90 | 82 | 81 | 82 |
| Min (°C) | 8 | 12 | 15 | 15 | 15 | 10 |
| Min (°F) | 46 | 54 | 59 | 59 | 59 | 50 |
| Rainfall (mm) | 51 | 25 | 127 | 203 | 279 | 51 |
| Rainfall (in) | 2 | 1 | 5 | 8 | 11 | 2 |
| **Tijuana** | | | | | | |
| Max (°C) | 20 | 21 | 23 | 27 | 27 | 23 |
| Max (°F) | 68 | 70 | 73 | 81 | 81 | 73 |
| Min (°C) | 6 | 8 | 12 | 16 | 16 | 10 |
| Min (°F) | 43 | 46 | 54 | 61 | 61 | 50 |
| Rainfall (mm) | 51 | 25 | 5 | 0 | 13 | 25 |
| Rainfall (in) | 2 | 1 | 0.2 | 0 | 0.5 | 1 |

# 35 things not to miss

*It's not possible to see everything Mexico has to offer in one trip – and we don't suggest you try. What follows, in no particular order, is a selective taste of the country's highlights: ancient ruins, vibrant cities and spectacular landscapes. They're arranged in five colour-coded categories to help you find the very best things to see, do and experience. All highlights have a page reference to take you straight into the guide, where you can find out more.*

**01 The Copper Canyon** Page **188** • Whether you take the awe-inspiring train ride here from the west coast or hike along the canyon floor, a visit to this vast chasm is the definite highlight of any trip to northern Mexico.

**02 Guanajuato** Page **277** • This gorgeous colonial town, sandwiched into a narrow ravine, is home to one of the country's finest Baroque churches, a thriving student scene and a relaxed café and bar culture.

**03 Hammocks** Page **793** • String a hammock from one tree to another and relax as locals do. Mérida, in the Yucatán, is one of the best places in the country to pick one up.

**04 Las Pozas, Xilitla** Page **319** • Built by English arts patron Edward James, this crumbling architectural experiment is a weird juxtaposition of modern concrete and timeless jungle.

**05 Turquoise waters and white-sand beaches** Page **111** • The Pacific coast around Bahía Concepción is classic picture-postcard material and a must for all beach lovers.

**06 Silver jewellery from Taxco** Page **523** • The town of Taxco, an interesting place in itself, offers the most exquisite silver products in the country.

**07 Football** Page **477** • Fan or not, you can't afford to miss out on the buzz generated by matches at Mexico City's Estadio Azteca, site of the 1970 and 1986 World Cups.

**08 The Zócalo, Mexico City** Page **413** • The eternal heart of the city, the capital's main plaza is surrounded by its oldest streets, its cathedral, Aztec ruins and the Palacio Nacional.

**09 Tula** Page **494** • The fantastic pre-Hispanic pyramid site of Tula, with its striking large statues atop the main pyramid, succeeded Teotihuacán as the Valley of México's great power.

**10 Lago de Pátzcuaro** Page **376** • Most famous for its Day of the Dead celebrations, the enchanting lake is a worthy destination year-round.

**11** **The Bonampak murals** Page **749** • Hidden deep in the forest until 1946, the ancient temples at Bonampak are home to the renowned paintings depicting vivid scenes of Maya life, including human sacrifice.

**12** **Coffee** Page **48** • Some of the country's best produce is grown in Veracruz state, and the coffee is no exception.

**13** **Palenque** Page **744** • This Maya site is remarkable not only for its distinct architectural style but also for its setting – surrounded by jungle-covered hills, right at the edge of the great Yucatán plain.

**14 Museo Nacional de Antropología** Page **440** • Mexico's best and most important museum, with an enormous collection of artefacts from all the major pre-Hispanic cultures.

**15 Nightlife in Playa del Carmen** Page **853** • Dance on the sand or in super-hip small clubs alongside stylish Mexico City weekenders and European expats in this Caribbean boomtown.

**16 Monarch Butterfly Sanctuary** Page **388** • Witness the amazing sight of millions of monarch butterflies settling on the landscape, turning it a vibrant orange, every year between November and April.

**17 Chichén Itzá** Page **819** • The most famous of the Maya sites, displaying eclectic styles. It's well worth staying nearby so you can see the sprawling ruins and complex carvings over a couple of days.

**19 Voladores de Papantla** Page **620** • An ancient religious ritual, this spectacle is now performed as much for tourists as it is for locals, but it's still breathtaking.

**18 Xochimilco** Page **460** • Punt around the canals, taking in the carnival atmosphere and dazzling colours while being serenaded by mariachi bands, then wander the streets of Xochimilco town and visit the flower and fruit market.

**20 Oaxaca markets** Page **648** • Any market in Mexico is a feast for the senses, but Oaxaca's are especially vibrant, with heaps of everything from fresh produce to some of the country's best-made and most imaginative textiles.

**21 Cenotes, Valladolid** Page **827** • Take a refreshing dip in these crystal-clear sinkholes, one of which has the roots of a huge alamo tree stretching down into it.

**22 Tulum** Page **864** • Looking out across the Caribbean from its clifftop setting, this important Maya spiritual and cultural centre is also one of the most picturesque of all the ancient sites.

**23 Museo Frida Kahlo** Page **454** • Politics, art and national identity combine at the home of Frida Kahlo and her husband Diego Rivera, two of Mexico's most iconic artists.

**24 Rodeo** Page **477** • If bullfights aren't for you, head to a rodeo instead; the ultimate *charrería* (cowboy) event, rodeos are just as good a traditional spectator sport.

**26 Upscale dining in Mexico City** Page **465** • In the capital's gastronomic temples, the country's top chefs blend traditional Mexican flavours, from hibiscus to chipotle, into refined new dishes.

**28 Mariachi** Page **473** • Probably the best known of all Mexican music styles, you'll find mariachi played the length and breadth of the country. In the evening, hundreds of bands compete for attention in a blur of silver-spangled finery and grand sombreros in Mexico City's Plaza Garibaldi.

**25 Calakmul** Page **792** • Still in the heart of the jungle and only partially restored, this is considered the biggest archeological zone in Mesoamerica, with a stunning seven thousand buildings in its central area alone.

**27 Sian Ka'an Biosphere Reserve** Page **867** • One of the largest protected areas in Mexico, this stunning bit of coastline comprises tropical forest, fresh- and salt-water marshes, mangroves and a section of the western hemisphere's longest barrier reef.

**29 El Tajín** Page **619** • Once the most important city on the Gulf coast, by the time of the Conquest it had been forgotten, and was only rediscovered by accident in 1785. Even now it remains one of the most mysterious archeological sites in Mexico – no one even knows who built it.

**30 Whale watching** Page **102** • From December to April, you can see some of the thousands of grey whales that have come to mate in the lagoons of Guerrero Negro, San Ignacio and Bahía Magdalena.

**31 The zócalo in Veracruz** Page **608** • One of the most enjoyable places in the republic to chill out. In the evening, the tables under the *portales* of the plaza fill up, and the drinking and marimba music begin.

**32 Acapulco's cliff divers** Page **584** • Watch the *clavadistas* plunge into the sea from precipitous cliffs – a spotlit-lit tourist display, but one requiring undeniable skill.

**34 Real de Catorce** Page **245** • This picturesque, ruined silver-mining town is a pilgrimage site for the Huichol people.

**33 The Rivera murals** Page **418** • Diego Rivera's work is inextricably linked with Mexicans' national identity, which is a particularly powerful theme in his classic murals at the Palacio Nacional in Mexico City.

**35 Diving** Page **854** • With water all around, Mexico has numerous fantastic diving opportunities: the coral reefs off Isla Cozumel provide some of the best.

# Basics

# Basics

Getting there ........ 27
Getting around ........ 35
Accommodation ........ 42
Food and drink ........ 44
Crime and personal safety ........ 49
Health ........ 51
The media ........ 55
Festivals ........ 56
Sports and outdoor activities ........ 58
Culture and etiquette ........ 59
Shopping ........ 60
Travel essentials ........ 61

# Getting there



**The quickest and easiest way to get to Mexico is to fly. Going overland from the US won't save you much money, if any, but becomes more convenient the nearer you live to the border.**

To some extent, airfares to Mexico depend on the **season**. Though ticket prices to Mexico City and other non-resort destinations show little, if any, fluctuation, fares to Mexico, especially the resort areas, are highest around Easter, from early June to mid-September and at Christmas and New Year. Prices drop during the "shoulder" seasons – mid-September to early November and mid-April to early June – and you'll get the best deals during the low season (November to April, excluding Christmas and New Year). Note also that flying at weekends may add to round-trip fares. The round-trip prices quoted here assume midweek travel.

Barring special offers, the best **airfares** carry certain restrictions, such as advance booking and fixed departure dates. You can often cut costs by going through a **discount flight agent**. Some agents specialize in charter flights, which may be cheaper than any available scheduled flight, but again with fixed departure dates. Agents may also offer special student or youth fares. Don't automatically assume that tickets purchased through a travel specialist will be cheapest, however – once you get a quote, check directly with the airlines and you may turn up a better deal.

### Packages and organized tours

Hundreds of companies – particularly in the US – offer good-value **package trips** to Mexican resorts, as do the tour arms of most major North American airlines. Packages are generally only available for the more commercialized destinations, such as Cabo San Lucas, Mazatlán, Puerto Vallarta, Acapulco, Ixtapa and Cancún, and travel agents usually only give you one or two weeks. In addition, literally hundreds of specialist companies offer **tours** of Mexico based around hiking, biking, diving, bird watching and the like. Remember that bookings made through a travel agent cost no more than going through the tour operator – indeed, many tour companies sell only through agents. See p.33 for information on tour operators.

## From the US and Canada

From most places in North America, flying is the most convenient way to reach Mexico. If you're willing to have your journey take a little longer, it is also possible to reach Mexico overland, via train, bus or car, or by water – several cruise lines make stops along the country's Pacific coast.

### By air

There are **flights** to Mexico from just about every major **US** city, with the cheapest and most frequent leaving from "gateway" cities in the south and west, especially Dallas, Houston, Los Angeles and Miami.

If you live close to the border, it's usually cheaper to cross into Mexico and take an **internal flight** (which you can arrange through your local travel agent). If it's a resort that you want, you'll probably find that one of the airlines offers an attractive deal including a few nights' lodging.

Aeroméxico and Mexicana fly direct to dozens of destinations in Mexico, and can make connections to many others; the bigger US airlines have connections to Mexico City and the more popular resorts. For the lowest-priced round trip to Mexico City in high season, expect to pay (including tax) around $420 out of Houston or Dallas, $515 from Miami, $435 from LA or $450 from New York. For a flight to Cancún, you'll be looking at around $375 from Houston or Dallas, $395 from Miami, $495 from LA or $355 from New York. There are

## Airpasses in Mexico

If you want to visit several destinations in a fairly short time (and even travel onwards to Central or South America), then there are a few **airpasses** worth considering – these can be especially useful if combined with the flexibility of an open-ended ticket.

The **Mexicana MexiPass** consists of prebooked and prepaid coupons for flights within Mexico, and between Mexico and the US or Canada, using Mexicana and Aeroméxico (including subsidiaries such as ClickMexicana), at discount prices. The pass is available to travellers from outside Mexico only, is valid for up to ninety days and costs the same from every supplier. You'll need to purchase a minimum of two coupons and book routes and dates in advance. Date (but not route) changes can be made without paying a penalty, provided space is available on the flight you want. Prices are for one-way flights, based on zones; they increase the further you fly and do not include domestic departure taxes (currently US$28 per flight). New York or Toronto to Mexico City, for example, is US$200; Mexico City to Acapulco is US$105; Mexico City to Cancún US$135; Oaxaca to Mérida US$165.

If you're travelling from outside the Americas and the Caribbean to Mexico and also want to fly to other parts of the American continent, then Hahn Air's **All American Air Pass** (Ⓦwww.allairpass.com) is worth thinking about. The pass links Mexico with all the major cities of North, Central and South America and the Caribbean. A routing New York–Mexico City–Guatemala City–San José–New York, for example, starts from US$763 plus tax, saving almost one-third on flying the same route without the pass. You could also omit a stage (Cancún to Guatemala City for example) and cover that by land if you want to, and the pass could include flights from as far north as Montréal or Seattle and as far south as Tierra del Fuego.

The potential permutations are mind-boggling, but it's easy enough to build a route online and see how much it will cost you before committing yourself.

direct flights to many parts of Mexico from numerous other US airports, but adding a feeder flight from any US or Canadian city to one of the main gateways should be straightforward.

There are few direct scheduled flights from **Canada** to Mexico, although Air Canada flies from Toronto and Montréal to Mexico City, and from Toronto to Cancún and Cozumel, and charter flights are plentiful in the winter. There's also currently a Japan Airlines flight from Vancouver to Mexico City en route from Tokyo. Your options expand greatly if you fly via the US. Typical lowest high-season round-trip fares to Mexico City are around C$800 from Toronto, Montréal or Vancouver. To Cancún, expect to pay C$800 from Toronto or Montréal, C$950 from Vancouver.

### By train

US passenger **train** services reach the border at El Paso, on the LA–Dallas line. El Paso is served by Amtrak's *Texas Eagle* (three times weekly from Chicago, St Louis, Little Rock and Dallas) and *Sunset Limited* (three times weekly from New Orleans, Houston, Tucson and LA). The journey takes seventeen hours from LA (US$92), nineteen from Houston (US$85), 28 from Dallas (US$100) and 51 from Chicago (US$135).

Arrivals on these services give you plenty of time to get across the frontier, have something to eat in Ciudad Juárez and get a bus on to Mexico City.

Check current timetables with Amtrak (Ⓣ1-800/USA-RAIL, Ⓦwww.amtrak.com).

### By bus

North American **bus** travel is pretty grim compared to the relative comfort of Amtrak, but you have a wider range of US border posts to choose from. Count on at least 45 hours' journey time from New York to a Texas frontier post (US$128), or at least twelve and a half hours from San Francisco to Tijuana (US$64) – and a further day's travel from either point to Mexico City.

Greyhound (ⓣ1-800/231-2222 or 1-214/849-8100, ⓦwww.greyhound.com) runs regularly to all the major border crossings. Some of their buses will also take you over the frontier to a Mexican bus station, which saves a lot of hassle. Greyhound agents abroad should be able to reserve your through tickets with their Mexican counterparts, which is even more convenient but involves pre-planning. Additionally, many Mexican bus companies cross the border into the US, so that you can pick up a bus to Mexico as far north as Houston or LA.

More countercultural, and arguably better value, are overland routes covered by Green Tortoise Adventure Travel (ⓣ1-800/TORTOISE or 1-415/956-7500, ⓦwww.greentortoise.com). Converted school buses provide reasonably comfortable transport and sleeping space for up to 35 people; the clientele comes from all over the world, and communal cookouts are the rule. Most tours depart from their San Francisco headquarters, but add-on journeys from Boston, New York and many points along the Pacific Coast are easily arranged on one of Green Tortoise's cross-country services.

## By car

Taking your own **car** into Mexico will obviously give you a great deal more freedom, but it's an option fraught with complications. Aside from border formalities, you'll also have to contend with the state of the roads, the style of driving and the quality of the fuel.

**Driving licences** from Australia, Canada, most European countries, Ireland, New Zealand, the UK and the US are valid in Mexico, but it's a good idea to arm yourself with an International Driving Licence – available to US citizens for a nominal fee from one of the motoring organizations listed on p.30. If you run afoul of a Mexican traffic cop for any reason, show that first; if they abscond with it you at least still have your own (more difficult to replace) licence.

As a rule, you can drive in Baja California, western Sonora and the Zona Libre (the border area extending roughly 25km into Mexico) without any special formalities. To drive elsewhere in Mexico, however, you must obtain a temporary **importation permit** (around US$30) from the Departamento de Migración (at the border). To make sure you don't sell the car in Mexico or a neighbouring country, you'll also be required either to post a cash bond, the amount of which will depend on the make and age of your vehicle, though it will be at least US$400 for a car less than four years old, or to give an imprint of a major credit card (Visa, MasterCard, Diners Club or American Express). This is done at Banjército, the Mexican army bank, which has offices at border posts specifically for the purpose. Plastic is obviously preferable, though it carries a US$16.50 fee, as you can only get a refund of a cash deposit at the same border post where you paid the bond – paying by plastic you can return via any border crossing you like. You'll need to show registration and title for the car, plus your driver's licence and passport, and you'll probably be asked to supply two photocopies of these as well as your tourist card. The permits are good for 180 days, during which you can drive your car out of Mexico and return, but there are penalties in force if you exceed the limit, including forfeiture of your vehicle. The necessary form can be downloaded from ⓦwww.banjercito.com.mx/site/tramiteitv_ing.jsp. More detailed information on importing a vehicle to Mexico can be found at ⓦwww.mexonline.com/drivemex.htm or ⓦciudadjuarez.usconsulate.gov/wwwhcarb.html.

With few exceptions, US **auto insurance** policies don't cover mishaps in Mexico, so you should take out a Mexican policy, available from numerous agencies on either side of every border post. Rates depend on the value of the vehicle and what kind of coverage you want, but figure on US$11 or so a day for basic liability (fourteen days' basic liability coverage for a US$10,000 vehicle is around US$110, with full coverage for around US$150). To arrange a policy before leaving the US, call Instant Mexico Insurance Services (ⓣ1-800/345-4701, ⓦwww.mexonline.com/instant1.htm); International Gateway (ⓣ1-800/423-2646, ⓦ216.55.132.138); Oscar Padilla Mexican Insurance (ⓣ1-800/466-7227, ⓦwww.mexicaninsurance.com); or Sanborn's Insurance (ⓣ1-800/222-0158,

Ⓦwww.sanbornsinsurance.com). The last is the acknowledged leader in the field.

To get discounts on insurance, it might be worthwhile joining a travel club, such as Discover Baja Travel Club (Ⓣ1-800/727-2252, Ⓦwww.discoverbaja.com) or Sanborn's Sombrero Club (Ⓣ1-800/222-0158, Ⓦwww.sanbornsinsurance.com). These clubs typically also offer discounts on accommodation and free travel advice. Annual dues are US$25–39.

The American and Canadian Automobile Associations produce road maps and route planners for travel to Mexico, and members may qualify for discounted insurance at affiliated border agencies, but their emergency/breakdown services do not cover you once you are inside Mexico.

### Motoring organizations

**AAA** US Ⓣ1-800/AAA-HELP, Ⓦwww.aaa.com.
**CAA** Canada Ⓣ1-800/267-8713, Ⓦwww.caa.ca.
**AA** UK Ⓣ0870/600 0371, Ⓦwww.theaa.com.
**RAC** UK Ⓣ0800/550 055, Ⓦwww.rac.co.uk.
**AAI** Ireland Ⓣ01/617 9999, Ⓦwww.aaireland.ie.
**AAA** Australia Ⓣ02/6247 7311, Ⓦwww.aaa.asn.au.
**NZAA** New Zealand Ⓣ0800/500 444, Ⓦwww.nzaa.co.nz.
**AASA** South Africa Ⓣ083/84322, Ⓦwww.aasa.co.za.

### Border crossings

There are some 35 **frontier posts** along the US–Mexico border. Many of them are only open during the day, and are more or less inaccessible without your own transport. For a full list, see Ⓦwww.mexico.us/bordercrossings.htm. The main ones, open 24 hours a day, seven days a week, are, from west to east:

**San Diego**, California–**Tijuana**, Baja California.
**Calexico**, California–**Mexicali**, Baja California.
**Nogales**, Arizona–**Nogales**, Sonora.
**Douglas**, Arizona–**Agua Prieta**, Sonora.
**El Paso**, Texas–**Ciudad Juárez**, Chihuahua.
**Laredo**, Texas–**Nuevo Laredo**, Tamaulipas.
**Brownsville**, Texas–**Matamoros**, Tamaulipas.

## By boat

If you want to **sail** to Mexico in your own boat, similar conditions apply to those in effect for motor vehicles (see p.29) – for further details, see Ⓦwww.tijuana.com/boatcrossing.

Alternatively, you could take a **cruise**. Several lines offer cruises on the Pacific coast, most popularly between LA and Acapulco, stopping at Los Cabos, Mazatlán, Puerto Vallarta and Zihuatanejo. Others ply the Caribbean side out of Miami, taking in Cozumel, Playa del Carmen and other Mexican destinations. Prices start at US$550 per person for a week-long cruise, plus airfare to the starting point, and go (way) up from there. Agencies specializing in cruises include those listed below.

### Cruiseboat contacts

**Carnival Cruise Lines** US & Canada Ⓣ1-888/CARNIVAL, Ⓦwww.carnival.com.
**Clipper Cruise Lines** Ⓣ1-800/325-0010, Ⓦwww.clippercruise.com.
**Cruise Adventures** US & Canada Ⓣ1-800/248-7447, Ⓦwww.cruiseadventures.com.
**Cruise World** Ⓣ1-800/228-1153, Ⓦwww.cruiseworldtours.com.
**Norwegian Cruise Line** US & Canada Ⓣ1-800/327-7030, UK Ⓣ0845/658 8010, Ⓦwww.ncl.com.
**Royal Caribbean Cruises** US & Canada Ⓣ1-866/562-7625, UK Ⓣ0800/018 2020, Ⓦwww.royalcaribbean.com.

## From the UK and Ireland

The only direct **scheduled flights** from the British Isles to Mexico are with British Airways, three times weekly from London Heathrow to Mexico City. Flying from anywhere else in Britain or Ireland, or to any

### Border formalities

**Crossing the border**, especially on foot, it's easy to go straight past the immigration and customs checks. There's a free zone south of the frontier, and you can cross at will and stay for up to three days. Make sure you do get your **tourist card** stamped and your bags checked, though, or when you try to continue south you'll be stopped after some 20km and sent back to complete the formalities. See "Entry requirements", on p.62, for more information.

other destination in Mexico, means you will have to change planes somewhere.

From **London**, British Airways' direct flights often work out to be very good value, especially in the high season. Good deals can also be found with a number of European carriers, which fly to Mexico via European hubs. Another possibility is to fly via the US and either continue overland or buy an onward flight once in the country. New York is usually the cheapest destination from London, but it's only halfway to Mexico City; for speedier connections, it's usually best to fly to Miami, Houston or Atlanta. LA and Houston are logical points from which to set off overland. Both of these cities, and Miami, also have reasonably priced onward flights to a number of Mexican destinations. **Prices** for scheduled return flights from London to Mexico City (including tax) range from £440 low season to £630 or more in high season.

From other British and Irish airports, you can either fly to London and pick up BA's direct flight there, or use an European airline such as Iberia or Lufthansa, changing planes at their hub cities (Madrid in the case of Iberia, Frankfurt with Lufthansa), or an American airline, changing planes in the US. For Mexican destinations other than the capital, Continental has the widest choice, with American Airlines not far behind.

**Charter flights** to Mexico are fairly common, flying from Gatwick, Birmingham, Glasgow or Manchester to Cancún, or occasionally Acapulco or Puerto Vallarta. Charter fares, sometimes under £400 in the low season, can also be very good value any time outside school holidays, though they can go as high as £800 in August, and your stay will probably be limited to one or two weeks. The best way to find out about charters is to call or log on to Sky Deals (ⓣ0800/9755477, ⓦwww.skydeals.com), who sell tickets for all the main operators, or My Travel (ⓣ0870/241 5333, ⓦwww.mytravel.co.uk), the main charter operator to Mexico.

If flying via the US, it's worth checking if your transatlantic carrier has an **airpass** deal for non-US residents – most major US airlines do – by which you purchase coupons at a flat rate for a certain number of flights in North America (with a usual minimum of three). Depending on the airline, the pass will usually also include one or more destinations in Mexico and Canada.

## From Australia, New Zealand and South Africa

The **high season** for flights to Mexico from the southern hemisphere is mid-June to mid-July and mid-December to mid-January, though prices do not vary vastly between seasons. There are no direct flights to Mexico from Australia, New Zealand or South Africa, so you will have to change planes somewhere en route.

From **Australia**, most options involve changing planes in Los Angeles. Your widest choice of flights is from Sydney, where you can fly with United via LA, LAN Chile via Santiago or Aerolineas Argentinas via Buenos Aires. All but the last are also available from Melbourne. Qantas flies from almost all Australian airports to LA, where you can continue to Mexico with Mexicana; you can also take an Air New Zealand/Mexicana combination, with an extra change of planes at Auckland. Prices start at around A$2000 (including tax) for the round trip.

From **New Zealand**, your choice is very similar: Air New Zealand, American Airlines or Qantas (via Sydney) from Auckland to LA, continuing with Mexicana; or United on both legs; or either LAN Chile via Santiago or Aerolineas Argentinas via Buenos Aires. From other New Zealand airports, you will probably need to change planes additionally at Auckland or Sydney. Prices start from around NZ$2600 return (including tax).

From **South Africa**, your most direct route is with Delta from Johannesburg via Atlanta, though European airlines such as Air France, Iberia, Lufthansa and British Airways will fly you via their respective hubs in Europe, with Lufthansa also offering flights out of Cape Town. Fares start around R14,000.

### RTW flights

If Mexico is only one stop on a longer journey, you might want to consider buying a **Round-the-World (RTW) ticket**. Some travel agents can sell you an "off-the-shelf" RTW ticket that will have you touching down in about half a

## Fly less – stay longer! Travel and climate change

Climate change is a serious threat to the ecosystems that humans rely upon, and air travel is among the fastest-growing contributors to the problem. Rough Guides regard travel, overall, as a global benefit, and feel strongly that the advantages to developing economies are important, as is the opportunity of greater contact and awareness among peoples. But we all have a responsibility to limit our personal impact on global warming, and that means giving thought to how often we fly, and what we can do to redress the harm that our trips create.

### Flying and climate change

Pretty much every form of motorized travel generates $CO_2$ – the main cause of human-induced climate change – but planes also generate climate-warming contrails and cirrus clouds and emit oxides of nitrogen, which create ozone (another greenhouse gas) at flight levels. Furthermore, flying simply allows us to travel much further than we otherwise would do. The figures are frightening: one person taking a return flight between Europe and California produces the equivalent impact of 2.5 tonnes of $CO_2$ – similar to the yearly output of the average UK car.

Fuel-cell and other less harmful types of plane may emerge eventually. But until then, there are really just two options for concerned travellers: to reduce the amount we travel by air (take fewer trips – stay for longer!), and to make the trips we do take "climate neutral" via a carbon offset scheme.

### Carbon offset schemes

Offset schemes run by Ⓦwww.climatecare.org, Ⓦwww.carbonneutral.com and others allow you to make up for some or all of the greenhouse gases that you are responsible for releasing. To do this, they provide "carbon calculators" for working out the global-warming contribution of a specific flight (or even your entire existence), and then let you contribute an appropriate amount of money to fund offsetting measures. These include rainforest reforestation and initiatives to reduce future energy demand – often run in conjunction with sustainable development schemes.

Rough Guides, together with Lonely Planet and other concerned partners in the travel industry, are supporting a **carbon offset scheme** run by climatecare.org. Please take the time to view our website and see how you can help to make your trip climate neutral.

**Ⓦwww.roughguides.com/climatechange**

dozen cities; others will have to assemble one for you, which can be tailored to your needs but is apt to be more expensive.

## Airlines, agents and operators

### Online booking

**Ⓦwww.expedia.co.uk** (in UK) **Ⓦwww.expedia.com** (in US) **Ⓦwww.expedia.ca** (in Canada)
**Ⓦwww.lastminute.com** (in UK)
**Ⓦwww.opodo.co.uk** (in UK)
**Ⓦwww.orbitz.com** (in US)
**Ⓦwww.travelocity.co.uk** (in UK) **Ⓦwww.travelocity.com** (in US) **Ⓦwww.travelocity.ca** (in Canada)
**Ⓦwww.zuji.com.au** (in Australia) **Ⓦwww.zuji.co.nz** (in New Zealand)

### Airlines

**Aer Lingus** Republic of Ireland Ⓣ0818/365 000, Northern Ireland Ⓣ0870/876 5000, Ⓦwww.aerlingus.com.
**Aero California** US Ⓣ1-305-446-9820, Ⓦwww.abstravel.com/aerocalifornia.
**Aerolineas Argentinas** Australia Ⓣ02/9234 9000, New Zealand Ⓣ09/379 3675, Ⓦwww.aerolineas.com.
**Aeroméxico** US and Canada Ⓣ1-800/237-6639, UK Ⓣ020/7801 6234, Australia Ⓣ02/9959 3922, New Zealand Ⓣ09/359 8397 or 8, South Africa Ⓣ011/791 2111, Ⓦwww.aeromexico.com.

**Air Canada** Canada ⓣ1-888/247-2262, ⓦwww.aircanada.com.
**Air France** US ⓣ1-800/237-2747, Canada ⓣ1-800/667-2747, UK ⓣ0870/142 4343, South Africa ⓣ0861/340 340, ⓦwww.airfrance.com.
**Air New Zealand** Australia ⓣ13 24 76, New Zealand ⓣ0800/737 000, ⓦwww.airnz.co.nz.
**Alaska Airlines** US ⓣ1-800/252-7522, ⓦwww.alaskaair.com.
**American Airlines** US and Canada ⓣ1-800/433-7300, UK ⓣ0845/7789 789, Ireland ⓣ01/602 0550, Australia ⓣ1300/650 747, New Zealand ⓣ0800/887 997, ⓦwww.aa.com.
**Aviacsa** US ⓣ1-800/758-2188, ⓦwww.aviacsa.com.mx.
**British Airways** UK ⓣ0870/850 9850, Ireland ⓣ1890/626 747, South Africa ⓣ011/441 8600, ⓦwww.ba.com.
**Continental Airlines** US and Canada ⓣ1-800/231 0856, UK ⓣ0845/607 6760, Ireland ⓣ1890/925 252, Australia ⓣ02/9244 2242, New Zealand ⓣ09/308 3350, ⓦwww.continental.com.
**Delta** US and Canada ⓣ1-800/221-1212, UK ⓣ0845/600 0950, Ireland ⓣ1850/882 031 or 01/407 3165, Australia ⓣ1300/302 849, New Zealand ⓣ09/379 3370, South Africa ⓣ011/482 4582, ⓦwww.delta.com.
**Iberia** UK ⓣ0870/609 0500, Ireland ⓣ0818/462 000, South Africa ⓣ011/7831 102, ⓦwww.iberia.com.
**JAL (Japan Air Lines)** Canada ⓣ1-800/525-3663, ⓦwww.jal.com or ⓦwww.japanair.com.
**LAN Chile** Australia ⓣ1300/361 400 or 02/9244 2333, New Zealand ⓣ09/977 2233, ⓦwww.lan.com.
**Lufthansa** UK ⓣ0870/837 7747, Ireland ⓣ01/844 5544, South Africa ⓣ0861/842 538, ⓦwww.lufthansa.com.
**Mexicana** US ⓣ1-800/531-7921, Canada ⓣ1-866/281-3049, UK ⓣ020/8492 0000, Australia ⓣ03/9699 9355, New Zealand ⓣ09/914 2573, South Africa ⓣ011/784 0985, ⓦwww.mexicana.com.
**Northwest** US ⓣ1-800/225-2525, ⓦwww.nwa.com.
**Qantas Airways** Australia ⓣ13 13 13, New Zealand ⓣ0800/808 767 or 09/357 8900, South Africa ⓣ11/441 8550, ⓦwww.qantas.com.
**South African Airways** South Africa ⓣ11/978 1111, ⓦwww.flysaa.com.
**United Airlines** US ⓣ1-800/UNITED-1, UK ⓣ0845/844 4777, Australia ⓣ13 17 77, ⓦwww.united.com.
**US Airways** US and Canada ⓣ1-800/428-4322, UK ⓣ0845/600 3300, Ireland ⓣ1890/925 065, ⓦwww.usair.com.

## Discount Agents

**ebookers** UK ⓣ0800/082 3000, Ireland ⓣ01/488 3507, ⓦwww.ebookers.com. Low fares on an extensive selection of scheduled flights and package deals.
**North South Travel** UK ⓣ01245/608 291, ⓦwww.northsouthtravel.co.uk. Friendly, competitive travel agency, offering discounted fares worldwide. Profits are used to support projects in the developing world, especially the promotion of sustainable tourism.
**STA Travel** US ⓣ1-800/781-4040, ⓦwww.statravel.com; UK ⓣ0870/163 0026, ⓦwww.statravel.co.uk; Australia ⓣ1300/733 035, ⓦwww.statravel.com.au; New Zealand ⓣ0508/782 872, ⓦwww.statravel.co.nz; South Africa ⓣ0861/781 781, ⓦwww.statravel.co.za. Specialists in independent travel; also student IDs, travel insurance, and more. Good discounts for students and under-26s.
**Trailfinders** UK ⓣ0845/058 5858, Ireland ⓣ01/677 7888, Australia ⓣ1300/780 212, ⓦwww.trailfinders.com. One of the best-informed and most efficient agents for independent travellers.
**Travel Cuts** Canada ⓣ1-866/246-9762, US ⓣ1-800/592-2887, ⓦwww.travelcuts.com. Canadian youth and student travel firm.
**USIT** Republic of Ireland ⓣ01/602 1904, Northern Ireland ⓣ028/9032 7111, ⓦwww.usit.ie. Ireland's main student and youth travel specialists.

## Tour operators

**Adventure Center** US & Canada ⓣ1-800/228-8747, ⓦwww.adventurecenter.com. Specializes in ecologically sound adventure travel, with a variety of Mexico trips.
**Adventures Abroad** ⓣ1-800/665-3998, ⓦwww.adventures-abroad.com. Canada-based travel planners providing small-group tours. Offers Mexico tours from seven to 23 days' duration.
**Adventure World** Australia ⓣ02/8913 0755, ⓦwww.adventureworld.com.au; New Zealand ⓣ09/524 5118, ⓦwww.adventureworld.co.nz. Adventure tours covering Mexico City and the Copper Canyon; Mexico's beach resorts; or a Mexico, Cuba and Guatemala combination.
**Backroads** US ⓣ1-800/GO-ACTIVE, ⓦwww.backroads.com. Hiking, biking and kayaking tours to Baja California and the Yucatán.
**Baja Expeditions** US ⓣ1-800/843-6967, ⓦwww.bajaex.com. Sea kayaking, whale watching, snorkelling and scuba diving, among other tours in Baja California.

**Bales** UK ⓣ0845/057 1819, ⓦwww.balesworldwide.com. Family-owned company offering upmarket nine- to fifteen-day tours, or tailor-made trips.

**Cathy Matos Mexican Tours** UK ⓣ020/8492 0000, ⓦwww.cathymatosmexico.co.uk. Wide variety of tailor-made tours, including colonial cities, beaches, sightseeing and archeology, whale watching and destination weddings.

**Ecosummer Expeditions** ⓣ1-800/465-8884, ⓦwww.ecosummer.com. Sea kayaking and whale watching in Baja California.

**Exodus** UK ⓣ0870/240 5550, Ireland c/o Abbey Travel ⓣ01/804 7153, US and Canada c/o G.A.P. (see below) ⓣ866/732-5885, Australia and New Zealand c/o Peregrine (see below), South Africa c/o Mask Expeditions ⓣ011/807 3333, ⓦwww.exodus.co.uk. Overland expeditions including a sixteen-day Ruta Maya tour in Mexico, Guatemala and Belize; two weeks in northern Mexico; or ten weeks across Central America.

**Explore Worldwide** UK ⓣ0870/333 4001, US c/o Adventure Center (see p.33) ⓣ1-800/227-8747, Canada c/o Trek Holidays ⓣ1-888/456 3522, Ireland c/o Maxwells Tours ⓣ01/677 9479, Australia c/o Adventure World (see p.33) ⓣ02/8913 0700, New Zealand c/o Adventure World (see p.33) ⓣ09/524 5118, South Africa c/o Shiralee Travel ⓣ028/313 0526, ⓦwww.explore.co.uk. Overland company offering a fifteen-day "Indian Mexico" tour (including visits to Guatemala and Belize – Yucatán extension also possible), or a sixteen-day Sierra Madre trek.

**Future Vacations** US ⓣ1-800/233-7260, ⓦwww.futurevacations.com. Vacation packages in Acapulco, Cancún, Cozumel, Los Cabos, Puerto Vallarta and other beach resorts, as well as Guadalajara and Mexico City.

**G.A.P. Adventures** US & Canada ⓣ1-800/708-7761, UK ⓣ0870/999 0144, ⓦwww.gap.ca. Guided adventure trips, some camping, mostly centred on the Yucatán.

**Global Exchange** US ⓣ1-415/255-7296, ⓦwww.globalexchange.org. Organization campaigning on international issues and offering "Reality Tours" to increase American travellers' awareness of real life in Mexico (especially Oaxaca and Chiapas) and other countries.

**Globus** US ⓣ1-866/755-8581, ⓦwww.globusjourneys.com. Escorted tours, including nine days in the Copper Canyon and eight days in the Yucatán.

**International Student Tours** Canada ⓣ1-888/472-3933, ⓦwww.istours.com. Student group-travel company offering resort packages to Cancún, Mazatlán and Puerto Vallarta.

**Majestic Mexico Tours** US ⓣ1-800/783-2485, ⓦwww.mexico-tours.com. A range of first-class cultural tours including Mexico's colonial cities, a Frida Kahlo tour of Mexico City, archeologial sites of the Yucatán and a week in Zacatecas.

**Mountain Travel Sobek** US and Canada ⓣ1-888/MTSOBEK, ⓦwww.mtsobek.com. Adventure trips including sea kayaking in Baja, exploring the jungle in Chiapas and a Copper Canyon hike in Chihuahua.

**Peregrine** UK ⓣ01635/872 300, Australia ⓣ1300/854 444 or 03/8601 4444, ⓦwww.peregrine.net.au. Trekking specialists with a wide range of tailored group and individual tours, including an eleven-day "Viva México" tour, or a two-week "Mexico in Depth" tour.

**Pleasant Holidays – Mexico** ⓣ1-888/825-9525, ⓦwww.4vacations.com/mexico. Getaways to various beach resorts including Acapulco, Cancún, Los Cabos, Mazatlán and Puerto Vallarta.

**S&S Tours** ⓣ1-800/499-5685, ⓦwww.ss-tours.com. Adventure tours of the Copper Canyon, whale watching in Baja California or colonial cities and monarch butterflies in Michoacán.

**South America Destinations** Australia ⓣ1800/337050 or 03/9725 4655, ⓦwww.south-america.com.au. Latin America specialists offering a range of Mexico tours, including a colonial cities tour, a Copper Canyon rail trip and a week in the Yucatán.

**South America Travel Centre** Australia ⓣ1800/655 051 or 03/9642 5353, ⓦwww.satc.com.au. Tours on offer include an eight-day Maya ruins tour (also visiting Monte Albán and Oaxaca), an eight-day colonial cities tour and a six-day Copper Canyon trip.
**Suntrek** US ⓣ1-707/523/1800, ⓦwww.suntrek.com. Two- to six-week overland adventure tours.
**The Adventure Company** UK ⓣ01420/541007, ⓦwww.adventurecompany.co.uk. Small-group, hotel-based tours including a fifteen-day "Realm of the Maya" tour in the Yucatán, Chiapas, Guatemala and Belize, and an eight-day "Mayans and Mexicans" family holiday in the Yucatán.
**Trek America** US ⓣ1-800/221-0596, UK ⓣ0870/444 8735, Australia and New Zealand c/o Adventure World (see p.33), ⓦwww.trekamerica.com. Small-group adventure trips, camping or staying at budget hotels across Mexico, with a choice of nine different tours.
**Trips Worldwide** UK ⓣ0117/311 4404, ⓦwww.tripsworldwide.co.uk. Friendly, experienced company with an inspired range of tailor-made itineraries to Mexico.
**Wilderness Travel** US ⓣ1-800/368-2794, ⓦwww.wildernesstravel.com. A ten-day "Mundo Maya" tour, or a week spent whale watching or sea kayaking in Baja California.
**Wild Oceans** UK ⓣ0117/965 8333, ⓦwww.wildwings.co.uk. Naturalist-led tours to observe whales (including blue whale research project), sea lions and other wildlife in the Sea of Cortés.
**World Expeditions** US ⓣ1-888/464-8735, ⓦwww.weadventures.com/us; Canada ⓣ1-800/567-2216, ⓦwww.worldexpeditions.ca; UK ⓣ0800/074 4135, ⓦwww.worldexpeditions.co.uk; Australia ⓣ1300/720 000, ⓦwww.worldexpeditions.com.au; New Zealand ⓣ0800/350 354, ⓦwww.worldexpeditions.co.nz. Offers a fourteen-day "Mayan World" tour in Chiapas and Guatemala, or a 22-day "Ancient Cultures of Aztecs and Mayans" trip including Oaxaca and Mexico City.

# Getting around

**Distances in Mexico can be huge, and if you're intending to travel on public transport, you should be prepared for some long, long journeys. Getting from Tijuana to Mexico City, for example, can take nearly two days nonstop. Although public transport at ground level is frequent and reasonably efficient everywhere, taking an internal flight at least once may be worthwhile for the time it saves.**

## By bus

Within Mexico, **buses** (long-distance buses are called *camiones*, rather than *autobuses*, in Mexican Spanish) are by far the most common and efficient form of public transport. There are an unbelievable number of them, run by a multitude of companies and connecting even the smallest of villages. Intercity services generally rely on very comfortable and dependable vehicles; remote villages are more commonly connected by what look

## Distance chart (in km)

| | Acapulco | Aguas-calientes | Cancún | Chihuahua | Ciudad Juárez | Durango | Guadalajara | Matamoros | Mérida |
|---|---|---|---|---|---|---|---|---|---|
| Acapulco | – | 889 | 1951 | 1732 | 2109 | 1281 | 859 | 1361 | 1647 |
| Aguascalientes | 889 | – | 2144 | 979 | 1356 | 417 | 250 | 819 | 1840 |
| Cancún | 1951 | 2144 | – | 3086 | 3463 | 2524 | 2174 | 2331 | 304 |
| Chihuahua | 1732 | 979 | 3086 | – | 377 | 632 | 1188 | 1097 | 2782 |
| Ciudad Juárez | 2109 | 1356 | 3463 | 377 | – | 1009 | 1565 | 1474 | 3159 |
| Durango | 1281 | 417 | 2524 | 632 | 1009 | – | 556 | 880 | 2220 |
| Guadalajara | 859 | 250 | 2174 | 1188 | 1565 | 556 | – | 995 | 1870 |
| Matamoros | 1361 | 819 | 2331 | 1097 | 1474 | 880 | 995 | – | 2027 |
| Mérida | 1647 | 1840 | 304 | 2782 | 3159 | 2220 | 1870 | 2027 | – |
| Mexico City | 390 | 514 | 1630 | 1456 | 1833 | 894 | 544 | 971 | 1326 |
| Monterrey | 1341 | 582 | 2349 | 790 | 1167 | 573 | 771 | 307 | 2046 |
| Nogales | 2572 | 1748 | 3855 | 769 | 635 | 1508 | 1698 | 2050 | 3551 |
| Oaxaca | 653 | 984 | 1702 | 1938 | 2315 | 1376 | 1026 | 1368 | 1398 |
| San Luis Potosí | 800 | 168 | 2043 | 1043 | 1420 | 481 | 344 | 651 | 1739 |
| Tampico | 863 | 575 | 1833 | 1307 | 1684 | 888 | 751 | 498 | 1529 |
| Tijuana | 3151 | 2504 | 4597 | 1532 | 1294 | 2087 | 2777 | 2629 | 4293 |
| Tuxtla Gutiérrez | 967 | 1389 | 1155 | 2331 | 2708 | 1769 | 1419 | 1764 | 851 |
| Veracruz | 711 | 898 | 1332 | 1808 | 2185 | 1279 | 929 | 999 | 1028 |
| Villahermosa | 1090 | 1283 | 861 | 2225 | 2602 | 1663 | 1313 | 1470 | 557 |

like (and often are) recycled school buses from north of the border.

There are basically two **classes** of bus, first (*primera*) and second (*segunda*), though on major long-distance routes there's often little to differentiate them. First-class vehicles have reserved seats, videos and air-conditioning, though an increasing number of second-class lines have the same comforts. The main differences will be in the number of stops – second-class buses call at more places, and consequently take longer to get where they're going – and the fare, which is about ten percent higher on first-class services, and sometimes a lot more. You may be able to get a discount with a student card, though it's unlikely. Most people choose first class for any appreciably long distance, and second for short trips or for destinations not served by a first-class bus, but you should certainly not be put off second class if it seems more convenient – it may even prove less crowded. Air-conditioning is not necessarily a boon – there's nothing more uncomfortable than a bus with sealed windows and a broken air-conditioner. The videos, mostly Hollywood action movies, in English with subtitles, aren't necessarily tasteful family viewing, and may contain violent scenes not suitable for children.

On important routes there are also **deluxe**, or **pullman**, buses, with names like Primera Plus or Turistar Plus and fares around thirty percent higher than those of first-class buses. They have few, if any, stops, waitress service and free snacks and drinks over longer distances, comfortable airline-style seating and air-conditioning that works – be sure to keep a sweater handy, as they can get very cold. They may also be emptier, which could mean more space to stretch out and sleep. Almost all pullman services have computerized reservations and may accept credit cards; these facilities are increasingly common with the larger regular bus lines too.

Most towns of any size have a modern **bus station**, known as the **Central Camionera** or **Central de Autobuses**. Don't let the word "central" fool you, as they are usually located a long way from the town centre. Where there is no unified terminus you may find separate first- and second-class terminals, or individual ones for each

| Mexico City | Monterrey | Nogales | Oaxaca | San Luis Potosí | Tampico | Tijuana | Tuxtla Gutiérrez | Veracruz | Villa-hermosa |
|---|---|---|---|---|---|---|---|---|---|
| 390 | 1341 | 2572 | 653 | 800 | 863 | 3151 | 967 | 711 | 1090 |
| 514 | 582 | 1748 | 984 | 168 | 575 | 2504 | 1389 | 898 | 1283 |
| 1630 | 2349 | 3855 | 1702 | 2043 | 1833 | 4597 | 1155 | 1332 | 861 |
| 1456 | 790 | 769 | 1938 | 1043 | 1307 | 1532 | 2331 | 1808 | 2225 |
| 1833 | 1167 | 635 | 2315 | 1420 | 1684 | 1294 | 2708 | 2185 | 2602 |
| 894 | 573 | 1508 | 1376 | 481 | 888 | 2087 | 1769 | 1279 | 1663 |
| 544 | 771 | 1698 | 1026 | 344 | 751 | 2777 | 1419 | 929 | 1313 |
| 971 | 307 | 2050 | 1368 | 651 | 498 | 2629 | 1764 | 999 | 1470 |
| 1326 | 2046 | 3551 | 1398 | 1739 | 1529 | 4293 | 851 | 1028 | 557 |
| – | 954 | 2242 | 482 | 413 | 473 | 2821 | 875 | 385 | 769 |
| 954 | – | 1743 | 1387 | 541 | 517 | 2322 | 1783 | 1018 | 1489 |
| 2242 | 1743 | – | 2707 | 1812 | 2076 | 817 | 3100 | 2577 | 2994 |
| 482 | 1387 | 2707 | – | 895 | 870 | 3303 | 547 | 369 | 841 |
| 413 | 541 | 1812 | 895 | – | 407 | 2568 | 1288 | 798 | 1182 |
| 473 | 517 | 2076 | 870 | 407 | – | 2839 | 1266 | 501 | 972 |
| 2821 | 2322 | 817 | 3303 | 2568 | 2839 | – | 1070 | 305 | 776 |
| 875 | 1783 | 3100 | 547 | 1288 | 1266 | 1070 | – | 765 | 294 |
| 385 | 1018 | 2577 | 369 | 798 | 501 | 305 | 765 | – | 471 |
| 769 | 1489 | 2994 | 841 | 1182 | 972 | 776 | 294 | 471 | – |



company, sometimes little more than bus stops at the side of the road. There is some form of baggage deposit (left luggage) office in every bus station – usually known as a **guardería**, **consigna** or simply **equipaje**, and costing about M$40–100 per item per day. Before leaving anything, make sure that the place will be open when you come to collect your bags. If there's no formal facility, staff at the bus companies' baggage dispatching offices can often be persuaded to look after your things for a short while.

Always check your route and arrival time, and whenever possible buy **tickets** from the bus station in advance to get the best (or any) seats; count on paying about M$60–75 for every 100km covered. There are very rarely problems getting a place on a bus from its point of origin or from really big towns. In smaller, mid-route places, however, you may have to wait for the bus to arrive (or at least to leave the previous stop) before discovering if there are any seats – the increased prevalence of computerized ticketing is easing the problem. Often there are too few seats, and without fluent and loud Spanish you may lose out in the fight for the ticket clerk's attention. Alternatively, there's almost always a bus described as *local*, which means it originates from where you are (as opposed to a *de paso* bus, which started somewhere else), and tickets for these can be bought well in advance.

Weekends, holiday season, school holidays and fiestas also overload services to certain destinations: again the only real answer is to buy tickets in advance. However, you could also try the cheaper second-class lines, where they'll pack you in standing, or take whatever's going to the next town along the way and try for a *local* from there. A word with the driver and a small tip can sometimes work wonders.

Terms to look out for on the timetable, besides *local* and *de paso*, include *vía corta* (by the short route) and *directo* or *expreso* (direct/nonstop – in theory at least). *Salida* is departure, *llegada* arrival. A decent road map will be extremely helpful in working out which buses are going to pass through your destination.

The legendary craziness of Mexican bus drivers is largely a thing of the past, and many bus companies have installed warning lights and buzzers to indicate when the driver is exceeding the speed limit (though these are often ignored by the driver). In recent years the government has been trying to improve the safety record through regular mechanical checks and also by keeping tabs on the drivers.

## By air

There are more than fifty airports in Mexico with regular passenger **flights** run by local airlines, plus several smaller airports with feeder services. The two big companies, both formerly state-owned and with international as well as domestic flights, are Aeroméxico and Mexicana, which between them connect most places to Mexico City, usually several times a day. Their monopoly is being challenged by a handful of smaller airlines such as Aviacsa, Aeromar, Aerolitoral and Aero California, which also cover most major destinations, as well as Mexicana's no-frills carrier ClickMexicana. The competition between the companies keeps prices steady and relatively low. Information about the independent operators can be difficult to find on the ground, but is available online and through travel agents.

Internal **airfares** reflect the popularity of the route: the more popular the trip, the lower the price. Thus the flight from Tijuana to Mexico City costs little more than the first-class bus, while the much shorter, but less popular flight from Tijuana to Chihuahua costs no less. Obviously, fares like the first are a real bargain, but even the more expensive routes can be worthwhile for the time they save. While the smaller airlines might be cheaper, the price of a ticket on a particular flight doesn't normally vary from agent to agent. There are few discounts, and it's usually twice as much for a round-trip as a one-way ticket.

Mexicana and Aeroméxico offer a multi-flight airpass, available only outside Mexico (see the box on p.28 for details).

### Domestic airlines

**Aero California** US ⓣ1-800/237-6225, Mexico ⓣ55/5207-1392, ⓦwww.aerocalifornia.com.
**Aerolitoral** Mexico ⓣ01-800/800-2376, ⓦwww.aerolitoral.com.mx.
**Aerolineas Mesoamericanas (ALMA)** Mexico ⓣ01-800/800-2562 or 333/ 3836-0770, ⓦwww.alma.com.mx.
**Aeromar** Mexico ⓣ01-800/237-6627 or 55/5133-1111, ⓦwww.aeromar.com.mx.
**Aeroméxico** Mexico ⓣ01-800/021-4010 or 55/5133-4010, ⓦwww.aeromexico.com (for contacts outside Mexico, see p.32).
**Aviacsa** US ⓣ1-800/758-2188, Mexico ⓣ01-800/AVIACSA or 55/5482-8280, ⓦwww.aviacsa.com.mx.
**Azteca** US ⓣ1-888/754-0066, Mexico ⓣ01-800/229-8322 or 55/5716-8989, ⓦaazteca.com.mx.
**ClickMexicana** Mexico ⓣ01-800/112-5425 or 55/2282-6262, ⓦwww.clickmx.com (outside Mexico, contact Mexicana).
**Interjet** Mexico ⓣ01-800/ 011-2345 or 55/1102-5555, ⓦwww.interjet.com.mx.
**Mexicana** Mexico ⓣ01-800/502-2000 or 55/5448-0990, ⓦwww.mexicana.com.mx (for contacts outside Mexico, see p.33).

## By rail

Mexico's railways were privatized in 1995, and since then, though more freight is carried by rail, all passenger services have been withdrawn bar two run especially for tourists. The first of these is the **Copper Canyon railway** in Chihuahua, an amazing scenic journey that rates as one of the country's top tourist attractions (see p.188). The other is the *Tequila Express* from Guadalajara to Amatitán, which carries tourists to the home of Mexico's most famous liquor (see p.355).

## By boat

**Ferries** connect Baja California with a trio of ports on the Pacific mainland: Santa Rosalía to Guaymas, and La Paz to Mazatlán and Topolobampo (for Los Mochis). For detailed information on schedules see ⓦwww.mexconnect.com/mex_/mexicoferryw.html. There are also smaller boats to islands off the Caribbean coast and Gulf coasts: from Chiquilá to Holbox, from Cancún to Isla Mujeres and from Playa del Carmen to Cozumel. Though not as cheap as they once were, all these services are still pretty reasonable: see the relevant chapters for current fares.

## By car

Getting your **car** into Mexico (see "Getting there", p.29) is just the beginning of your problems. Although most people who venture in by car both enjoy their trip and get out again with no more than minor incidents, driving in Mexico does require a good deal of care and concentration, and almost inevitably involves at least one brush with bureaucracy or the law.

**Renting a car** in Mexico – especially if done with a short, specific itinerary in mind – avoids many problems and is often an extremely good way of seeing quickly a small area that would take days to explore using public transport. There are any number of competing agencies in all the tourist resorts and major cities; the local operations usually charge less than the well-known names. Always check **rates** carefully to make sure they include insurance, tax and the mileage you need. Daily rates with unlimited mileage start around US$50/£30; weekly rates usually cost the same as six days. In some resorts mopeds and motorbikes are also available for short distances, but most of the large, international companies don't deal with them because of the high frequency of accidents.

Drivers from Australia, Canada, most European countries, Ireland, New Zealand, the UK and the US will find that their **licences** are valid in Mexico, though an international licence (available from the motoring organizations listed on p.30) can be useful, especially if your domestic one has no photo on it. You are required to have all your documents with you when driving. **Insurance** is not compulsory, but you'd be foolhardy not to get some sort of policy (see p.29 for more on motor insurance).

The government oil company, Pemex, has a monopoly and sells two types of **fuel**: Premium (leaded) and Magna Sin (unleaded), both of which cost slightly more than regular unleaded north of the border, at about US$2.50 per US gallon. Magna is increasingly available, in response to howls of outrage from US motorists who have ruined their engines using Premium.

Mexican **roads and traffic** are your chief worries. Traffic circulates on the right, and the normal speed limit is 40kph (25mph) in built-up areas, 70kph (43mph) in open country and 110kph (68mph) on the freeway. Some of the new highways are excellent, and the toll (*cuota*) superhighways are better still, though extremely expensive to drive on. Away from the major population centres, however, roads are often narrow, winding and potholed, with livestock wandering across at unexpected moments. Get out of the way of Mexican bus and truck drivers – if you signal left to them on a stretch of open road, it means it's clear to overtake. Every town and village limits the speed of through traffic with a series of *topes* (concrete or metal speed bumps) across the road. Look out for the warning signs and take them seriously; the bumps are often huge. Most people suggest that you should never drive at night (and not just for road safety reasons: see the box on p.40) – sound advice, even if not always practical. Any good road map should provide details of the more common symbols used on Mexican **road signs**, and SECTUR has a pamphlet on driving in Mexico in which they're also featured. One convention of note: the first driver to flash their lights at a junction, or where only one vehicle can pass, has the right of way – you're not being invited to go first.

Most large towns have extensive **one-way systems**. Traffic direction is often poorly marked (look for small arrows affixed to lampposts), though this is less of a problem than it sounds: simply note the direction in which the parked cars, if not the moving cars, are facing.

**Parking** in cities is another hassle – the restrictions are complicated and foreigners are easy pickings for traffic police, who usually remove one or both plates in lieu of a ticket (retrieving them can be an expensive and time-consuming business). Since **theft** is also a real threat, you'll usually have to pay extra for a hotel with secure parking. You may well also have to fork out over on-the-spot "fines" for traffic offences (real or concocted). In Mexico City, residents' cars are banned from driving on one day of every week, determined by their licence number (see box, p.397): the ban also applies to foreign cars, but rented vehicles are exempt.

Unless your car is a basic-model VW, Ford or Dodge (all of which are manufactured in Mexico), **spare parts** are expensive and hard to come by – bring a basic spares kit. Tyres in particular suffer on burning-hot Mexican roads, so you should carry at least one good spare. Roadside *vulcanizadoras* and *llanteros* can do temporary repairs; new tyres are expensive, but remoulds aren't a good idea on hot roads at high speed. If you have a breakdown on any highway between 8am and 8pm, there is a free mechanic service known as the **Ángeles Verdes** (Green Angels). As well as patrolling major routes looking for beleaguered motorists, they can be reached by phone on ⓣ078 or 01-800/987-8224, or by email at ⓔangelesverdes@sectur.gob.mx, and they speak English.

Should you have a minor **accident**, try to come to some arrangement with the other party – involving the police will only make matters worse, and Mexican drivers will be just as anxious to avoid doing so. If you witness an accident, you may want to consider the gravity of the situation before getting involved. Witnesses can be locked up along with those directly implicated to prevent them from leaving before the case comes up – so consider if your involvement is necessary to serve justice. In a serious incident, contact your consulate and your Mexican insurance company as soon as possible.

For more detailed advice on driving in Mexico, the Association for Safe International Road Travel produce a national report on Mexico, which can be downloaded for US$25 from their website, ⓦwww.asirt.org.

## Car rental agencies

**Alamo** US ⓣ1-800/462-5266, ⓦwww.alamo.com.
**Avis** US ⓣ1-800/230-4898, Canada ⓣ1-800/272-5871, UK ⓣ0870/606 0100, Ireland ⓣ021/428 1111, Australia ⓣ13 63 33 or 02/9353 9000, New Zealand ⓣ09/526 2847 or 0800/655 111, ⓦwww.avis.com.
**Budget** US ⓣ1-800/527-0700, Canada ⓣ1-800/268-8900, UK ⓣ0870/156 5656, Australia ⓣ1300/362 848, New Zealand ⓣ0800/283 438, ⓦwww.budget.com.
**Europcar** US & Canada ⓣ1-877/940 6900, UK ⓣ0870/607 5000, Ireland ⓣ01/614 2800, Australia ⓣ393/306 160, ⓦwww.europcar.com.
**Hertz** US & Canada ⓣ1-800/654-3131, UK ⓣ020/7026 0077, Ireland ⓣ01/870 5777, New Zealand ⓣ0800/654 321, ⓦwww.hertz.com.
**National** US ⓣ1-800/CAR-RENT, UK ⓣ0870/400 4581, Australia ⓣ0870/600 6666, New Zealand ⓣ03/366 5574, ⓦwww.nationalcar.com.
**Thrifty** US and Canada ⓣ1-800/847-4389, UK ⓣ01494/751 540, Ireland ⓣ01/844 1950, Australia ⓣ1300/367 227, New Zealand ⓣ09/256 1405, ⓦwww.thrifty.com.

## Hitching

It's possible to **hitch** your way around Mexico, but it can't be recommended – certainly not in the north. Lifts are relatively scarce, distances vast, risks high and the roadside often a harsh environment if you get dropped at some obscure turn-off. You may also be harassed by the police. Many drivers – especially truck drivers – expect you to contribute to their expenses, which you may think rather defeats the object of hitching. Quite apart from all this, hitching is not safe: robbery is common, and women in particular (but also men) are advised not to hitch alone. You should wait to know where the driver is going before getting in, rather than stating your own destination first, sit by a door and

### Banditry: a warning

You should be aware when driving in Mexico, especially in a foreign vehicle, of the danger of **bandits**. Robberies and even more serious assaults on motorists do occur, above all in the northwest and especially in the state of Sinaloa. Robbers may try to make you stop by indicating that there is something wrong with your vehicle; they've also been known to pose as policemen, hitchhikers and motorists in distress, so think twice about offering a lift or a helping hand. On the other hand, there are plenty of legitimate police checkpoints along the main roads, where you must stop. Roads where there have been regular reports of problems, and where you should certainly try to avoid driving at night, include **Hwy-15** (Los Mochis–Mazatlán) and express **Hwy-1** in Sinaloa; **Hwy-5** (Mexico City–Acapulco) in Guerrero; **Hwy-75** (Oaxaca–Tuxtepec); **Hwy-57** (San Luis Potosí–Matahuela); and near the border, in particular on **Hwy-2** (Mexicali–Agua Prieta) and **Hwy-40** (Matamoros–Monterrey). The US embassy in Mexico advises never driving after dark.

## Addresses

In Mexico **addresses** are frequently written with just the street name and number (thus: Madero 125), which can lead to confusion as many streets are known only as numbers (C 17). Calle (C) means "street"; Avenida (Av), Bulevar (Blv), Calzada and Paseo are other common terms – most are named after historical figures or dates. An address such as Hidalgo 39 8° 120, means Hidalgo no. 39, 8th floor, room 120 (a ground-floor address would be denoted PB for Planta Baja). Many towns have all their streets laid out in a **numbered grid** fanning out from a central point – often with odd-numbered streets running east–west, even ones north–south. In such places a suffix – Ote (for *Oriente*, East), Pte (for *Poniente*, West), Nte (for *Norte*, North) or Sur (South) – may be added to the street number to tell you which side of the two central dividing streets it is.

keep your baggage at hand in case you need to leave in a hurry (feigned carsickness is one way to get a driver to stop). Particularly avoid areas frequented by *bandidos*, such as those listed in the box opposite.

That said, you may find yourself hitching to get to villages where there's no bus or to while away the time spent waiting for one, and you'll probably come across genuine friendliness and certainly meet people you wouldn't otherwise encounter. It does help if your Spanish will stretch to a conversation.

## Local transport

**Public transport** within Mexican towns and cities is always plentiful and inexpensive, though crowded and not particularly user-friendly. Mexico City has an extensive, excellent **Metro** system, and there are smaller metros in Guadalajara and Monterrey, but elsewhere you'll be reliant on **buses**, which pour out clouds of choking diesel fumes; often there's a flat-fare system, but this varies from place to place. Wherever possible we've indicated which bus to take and where to catch it, but often only a local will fully understand the intricacies of the system and you may well have to ask: the main destinations of the bus are usually marked on the windscreen, which helps.

In bigger places *combis* or **colectivos** offer a faster and perhaps less crowded alternative for only a little more money. These are minibuses, vans or large sport utility vehicles that run along fixed routes to set destinations; they'll pick you up and drop you off wherever you like along the way, and you simply pay the driver for the distance travelled. In Mexico City, *combis* are known as **peseros**.

Regular **taxis** can also be good value, but be aware of rip-offs – unless you're confident that the meter is working, fix a price before you get in. In the big cities, there are often tables of fixed prices posted at prominent spots. At almost every airport and at some of the biggest bus stations you'll find a booth selling vouchers for taxis into town at a fixed price depending on the part of town you want to go to – sometimes there's a choice of paying more for a private car or less to share. This will invariably cost less than just hailing a cab outside the terminal, and will certainly offer extra security. In every case you should know the name of a hotel to head for, or they'll take you to the one that pays the biggest commission (they may try to do this anyway, saying that yours is full). Never accept a ride in any kind of unofficial or unmarked taxi.

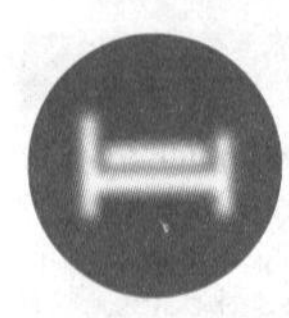

# Accommodation

**Finding a room is rarely difficult – in areas that are not overly touristy the cheap places to stay are usually concentrated around the main plaza (the zócalo), with others near the market, train station or bus station (or where the bus station used to be, before it moved to the outskirts of town). In bigger cities, there's usually a relatively small area in which you'll find the bulk of the less expensive possibilities. The more modern and expensive places often lie on the outskirts of towns, accessible only by car or taxi. The only times you're likely to have big problems finding somewhere to stay are in coastal resorts over the peak Christmas season, at Easter, on Mexican holidays and almost anywhere during a local fiesta, when it's well worth trying to reserve ahead.**

## Hotels

Mexican hotels may describe themselves as anything from *paradores*, *posadas* and *casas de huéspedes* to plain *hoteles*, all terms that are used more or less interchangeably. A *parador* is totally unrelated to its upmarket Spanish namesake, for example, and although in theory a *casa de huéspedes* means a small cheap place like a guesthouse, you won't find this necessarily to be the case.

All rooms should have an official **price** displayed, though this is not always a guide to quality – a filthy fleapit and a beautifully run converted mansion may charge exactly the same, even if they're right next door to each other. The only recourse for guaranteeing quality is seeing your room first – you soon learn to spot which establishments have promise. You should never pay more than the official rate (though just occasionally the sign may not have kept up with inflation) and in the low season you can often pay less. The charging system varies: sometimes it's per person, but usually the price quoted will be for the room regardless of how many people occupy it, so sharing can mean big savings. A room with one double bed (*cama matrimonial*) is almost always cheaper than a room with two singles (*doble* or *con dos camas*), and most hotels have large "family" rooms with several beds, which are tremendous value for groups. In the big resorts, there are lots of apartments that sleep six or more and include cooking facilities, for yet more savings. A little gentle haggling rarely goes amiss, and many places will have some rooms that cost less, so just ask (*Tiene un cuarto mas barato?*).

**Air-conditioning** (*aire acondicionado*) is a feature that inflates prices – it is frequently optional. Unless it's quite unbearably hot and humid, a room with a simple ceiling fan (*ventilador*) is generally better; except in the most expensive places, the air-conditioning units are almost always noisy and inefficient, whereas a fan can be left running silently all night and the

## Accommodation price codes

All the accommodation listed in this book has been categorized into one of nine **price codes**, as set out below. The codes normally refer to the price of the cheapest double room in high season.

1. M$150 and under
2. M$150–200
3. M$200–250
4. M$250–350
5. M$350–500
6. M$500–750
7. M$750–1100
8. M$1100–1500
9. M$1500 and over

draught helps to keep insects away. It might seem too obvious to mention, but be careful of the **ceiling fans**, which are often quite low. Don't stand on the bed, and keep well clear of them when removing any clothes from the upper body. In winter, especially at altitude or in the desert, it will of course be **heating** rather than cooling that you want – if there isn't any, make sure there's enough bedding and ask for extra blankets if necessary.

When looking at a room, you should always check its **insect proofing**. Cockroaches and ants are common, and there's not much you can do about them, but decent netting will keep mosquitoes and worse out and allow you to sleep. If the mosquitoes are really bad you'll probably see where previous occupants have splattered them on the walls. It is the same story for bedbugs around the bed.

### Campsites, hammocks and cabañas

There is not usually much alternative to staying in hotels. **Camping** is easy enough if you are hiking in the backcountry, or happy simply to crash on a beach, but robberies are common, especially in places with a lot of tourists. There are very few organized campsites, and those that do exist are first and foremost trailer parks, not particularly pleasant to pitch tents in. Of course, if you have a van or **RV** you can use these or park just about anywhere else – there are a good number of facilities in the well-travelled areas, especially down the Pacific coast and Baja.

If you're planning to do a lot of camping, an **international camping card** is a good investment, serving as useful ID and getting you discounts at member sites. It is available from home motoring organizations.

In a lot of less official campsites, you will be able to rent a **hammock** and a place to sling it for the same price as pitching a tent (around US$5/£3), maybe less, and certainly less if you're packing your own hammock (Mexico is a good place to buy these, especially in and around Mérida, Yucatán).

Beach huts, or **cabañas**, are found at the more rustic, backpacker-oriented beach resorts, and sometimes inland. Usually just a wooden or palm-frond shack with a hammock slung up inside (or a place to sling your own), they are frequently without electricity, though as a resort gets more popular, they tend to transform into sturdier beach bungalows with modern conveniences and higher prices. At backwaters and beaches too untouristed for even cabañas, you should still be able to sling a hammock somewhere (probably the local bar or restaurant, where the palapa serves as shelter and shade).

## Hostels

There are 28 official youth hostels in Mexico, charging around M$100 per person for basic, single-sex dorm facilities. A YH card is not usually necessary, but you usually pay slightly more without one. Rules are strict in some places (no booze, 11pm curfew, up and out by 9am) but others are open 24 hours and provide kitchen facilities, laundry, travel advice, Internet and other services. At holiday periods they're often taken over completely by Mexican groups. There's a comprehensive list of Mexican youth hostels on the HIM website (Ⓦwww.hostellingmexico.com), complete with addresses, phone numbers, prices, a location map and online booking services.

### Youth hostel associations

**In Mexico**

**Hostelling International Mexico (HIM)** República de Guatemala 4, Col Centro, México DF 06020 Ⓣ55/5518-1726, Ⓦwww.hostellingmexico.com.

**North America and overseas**

**US** Ⓣ1-301/495-1240, Ⓦwww.hiayh.org.
**Canada** Ⓣ1-800/663 5777, Ⓦwww.hihostels.ca.
**England and Wales** Ⓣ0870/770 8868, Ⓦwww.yha.org.uk.
**Scotland** Ⓣ01786/891 400, Ⓦwww.syha.org.uk.
**Ireland (Republic)** Ⓣ01/830 4555, Ⓦwww.irelandyha.org.
**Northern Ireland** Ⓣ028/9032 4733, Ⓦwww.hini.org.uk.
**Australia** Ⓣ02/9565-1699, Ⓦwww.yha.com.au.
**New Zealand** Ⓣ0800/278 299 or 03/379 9970, Ⓦwww.yha.co.nz.
**South Africa** Ⓣ021/788 2301, Ⓦwww.hisa.org.za.

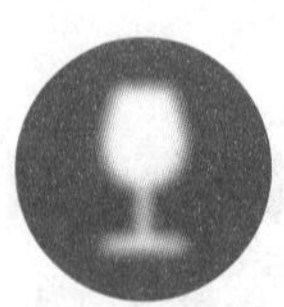

# Food and drink

**Whatever your preconceptions about Mexican food, if you've never eaten in Mexico, they will almost certainly be wrong. Food here bears very little resemblance to the concoctions served in "Mexican" restaurants or fast-food joints in other parts of the world – you certainly won't find chile con carne outside the tourist spots. Nor, as a rule, is it especially spicy; indeed, a more common complaint from visitors is that after a while it all seems rather bland.**

## Where to eat

Basic meals are served at **restaurantes**, but you can get breakfast, snacks and often full meals at cafés too; there are **takeout** and **fast-food** places serving sandwiches, tortas (filled rolls) and tacos (tortillas folded over with a filling), as well as more international-style food; there are establishments called **jugerías** (look for signs saying "Jugos y Licuados") serving nothing but wonderful juices (*jugos*), *licuados* (fruit blended with water or milk) and fruit salads; and there are **street stalls** dishing out everything from tacos to orange juice to ready-made vegetable salads sprinkled with chile-salt and lime. Just about every **market** in the country has a cooked-food section, too, and these are invariably the cheapest places to eat, if not always the most enticing surroundings. In the big cities and resorts, of course, there are international restaurants – **pizza** and **Chinese** food are ubiquitous. **Argentine** restaurants are the places to go for well-cooked, quality steaks.

As often as not, the food will come to you when you're travelling; people clamber onto buses (especially second-class ones) at every stop with baskets of home-made foods, local specialities, cold drinks or jugs of coffee. You'll find wonderful things this way that you won't come across in restaurants, but they should be treated with caution, and with an eye to hygiene.

## What to eat

The basic Mexican diet is essentially one of **corn** (*maíz*) and its products, supplemented by **beans** and **chiles**. These three things appear in an almost infinite variety of guises.

Mexican cooks use at least a hundred different types of **chiles**, fresh or dried, in colours ranging from pale green to almost black, and all sorts of different sizes (large, mild ones are often stuffed with meat or cheese and rice to make **chiles rellenos**). Each has a distinct flavour and by no means all are hot (which is why we don't use the English term "chilli" for them), although the most common, **chiles jalapeños**, small and either green or red, certainly are. Chile is also the basic ingredient of more complex cooked sauces, notably **mole**, which is Mexico's version of a curry, traditionally served with turkey or chicken, but also sometimes with enchiladas (rolled, filled tortillas). There are several types of *mole*, the two most common being the rather bland *mole verde*, and the far richer and more exciting **mole poblano**, a speciality of Puebla. Half of the fifty or so ingredients in this extraordinary mixture are different types of chile, but the most notable ingredient is chocolate – unless you hate chocolate, you should definitely try *mole poblano* at least once while you are in Mexico. Another speciality to look out for is **chiles en nogada**, a bizarre combination of stuffed green peppers covered in a white sauce made of walnuts and cream cheese or sour cream, topped with red pomegranate: the colours reflect the national flag.

**Beans** (*frijoles*), an invariable accompaniment to egg dishes – and pretty much everything else too – are usually of the pinto or kidney variety and are almost always served **refritos**, ie boiled up, mashed and "refried" (though actually it is the first time they're fried). They're even better if you can get them whole in some kind of country-style soup or stew, often with pork or bacon, as in **frijoles charros**.

**Corn**, in some form or another, features in virtually everything. In its natural state it is known as *elote* and you can find it roasted on the cob at street stalls or in soups and stews such as **pozole** (with meat). Far more often, though, it is ground into flour for **tortillas**, flat maize pancakes of which you will get a stack to accompany your meal in

### Salsa

Since so much Mexican food is simple, and endlessly repeated in restaurant after restaurant, one way to tell the places apart – and a vital guide to the quality of the establishment – is by their **salsa**. A restaurant with a superior salsa on the table will probably serve up some decent food, whereas a place that takes no pride in its salsa often treats its food in the same manner. To a certain extent you can tell from the presentation: a place that has grubby, rarely changed salsa dishes probably just refills them from a supermarket-bought can, and will not take the same pride in its food as a *casero* (home-cooking) restaurant that proudly puts its own salsa on the table in a nice bowl.

Frequently you will be served a variety of salsa and other sauces, including bottles of commercial hot sauce (Tapatío, Tabasco, Yucateco), but there should always be at least one home-made salsa among them. Increasingly this is **raw**, California-style salsa: tomato, onion, chile and cilantro (coriander leaves) finely chopped together. More common, though, are the traditional **cooked** salsas: either green or red, and relatively mild (though start eating with caution, just in case). The recipes are – of course – closely guarded secrets, but again the basic ingredients are tomato (the verdant Mexican tomatillo in green versions), onion and one or more of the hundreds of varieties of chile.

any cheap Mexican restaurant (in more expensive or touristy places you'll get bread rolls known as *bolillos*). Tortillas can also be made of wheat flour (*de harina*), which may be preferable to outsiders' tastes, but are rare except in the north.

Tortillas form the basis of many specifically Mexican dishes, often described as **antojitos** (appetizers, light courses) on menus. Simplest of these are **tacos**, tortillas filled with almost anything, from beef and chicken to green vegetables, and then fried (they're usually still soft, not at all like the baked taco shells you may have had at home). With cheese, either alone or in addition to other fillings, they are called **quesadillas**. **Enchiladas** are rolled, filled tortillas covered in salsa and baked; **enchiladas suizas** are filled with chicken and have sour cream over them. **Tostadas** are flat tortillas toasted crisp and piled with ingredients – usually meat, salad vegetables and cheese (smaller bite-size versions are known as *sopes*). Tortillas torn up and cooked together with meat and (usually hot) sauce are called **chilaquiles**; this is a traditional way of using up leftovers. Especially in the north, you'll also come across **burritos** (large wheat-flour tortillas, stuffed with anything, but usually beef and potatoes or beans) and **gorditas** (delicious fat corn tortillas, sliced open, stuffed and baked or fried). Also short and fat are **tlacoyos**, tortillas made with a stuffing of mashed beans, often using blue-corn flour, which gives them a rather bizarre colour.

Corn flour, too, is the basis of **tamales** – found predominantly in central and southern Mexico – which are a sort of cornmeal pudding, stuffed, flavoured and steamed in corn or banana leaves. They can be either savoury, with additions like shrimp or corn kernels, or sweet when made with something like coconut.

Except in the north, **meat** is not especially good – beef in particular is usually thin and tough; pork, goat and occasionally lamb are better. If the menu doesn't specify what kind of meat it is, it's usually pork – even steak (*bistec*) can be pork unless it specifies **bistec de res**. For thick American-style steaks, look for a sign saying "Carnes Hereford" or for a "New York Cut" description (only in expensive places or in the north or at fancier resorts).

**Seafood** is almost always fresh and delicious, especially the spicy shrimp or octopus cocktails which you find in most coastal areas (**coctél/campechana de camarón** or **pulpo**), but beware of eating uncooked shellfish, even *ceviche* (though the lime juice it is marinaded in does kill off most of the nasties). **Eggs** in country areas are genuinely free-range and flavoursome. They feature on every menu as the most basic of meals, and at some time you must try the classic Mexican combinations of **huevos rancheros** (fried eggs on a tortilla with red salsa) or **huevos a la mexicana** (scrambled with onion, tomato and chile).

### Vegetarian food

**Vegetarians** can eat well in Mexico, although it does take caution to avoid meat altogether. Many Mexican dishes are naturally meat-free and there are always fabulous fruits and vegetables available. Most restaurants serve vegetable soups and rice, and items like quesadillas, *chiles rellenos* and even tacos and enchiladas often come with non-meat fillings. Another possibility is **queso fundido**, simply (and literally) melted cheese, served with tortillas and salsa. Eggs, too, are served anywhere at any time, and many *jugerías* serve huge mixed **salads** to which grains and nuts can be added.

However, do bear in mind that vegetarianism, though growing, is not particularly common, and a simple cheese and chile dish may have some meat added to "improve" it. Worse, most of the fat used for frying is animal fat (usually lard), so that even something as unadorned as refried beans may not be strictly vegetarian (especially as a bone or some stock may have been added to the water the beans were originally boiled in). Even so-called vegetarian restaurants, which can be found in all the big cities, often include chicken on the menu. You may well have better luck in pizza places and Chinese or other ethnic restaurants.

## Meals

Traditionally, Mexicans eat a light breakfast very early, a snack of tacos or eggs in mid-morning, lunch (the main meal of the day) around 2pm or later – in theory followed by a siesta, but decreasingly so, it seems – and a late, light supper. Eating a large meal at lunch time can be a great way to save money – almost every restaurant serves a cut-price **comida corrida**.

**Breakfast** (*desayuno*) in Mexico can consist simply of coffee (see p.48) and *pan dulce* – sweet rolls and pastries that usually come in a basket; you pay for as many as you eat. More substantial breakfasts consist of eggs in any number of forms (many set breakfasts include *huevos al gusto*: eggs any way you like them), and at fruit-juice places you can have a simple *licuado* (see below) fortified with raw egg (*blanquillo*). Freshly squeezed orange juice (*jugo de naranja*) is always available from street stalls in the early morning.

**Snacks** mostly consist of some variation on the taco/enchilada theme (stalls selling them are called *taquerías*), but tortas – rolls heavily filled with meat or cheese or both, garnished with avocado and chile and toasted on request – are also wonderful, and you'll see takeout torta stands everywhere. Failing that, you can of course always make your own snacks with bread or tortillas, along with fillings such as avocado or cheese, from shops or markets.

You can of course eat a full meal in a restaurant at any time of day, but you'd do well to adopt the local habit of taking your main meal at **lunch time**, since this is when comidas corridas (set meals, varied daily) are served, from around 1pm to 5pm: in more expensive places the same thing may be known as the *menu del día* or *menu turístico*. Price is one good reason to go with comidas corridas: you'll usually get three or four courses for US$5/£3 or less (sometimes half that price), which can't be bad. More importantly, the *comida* is an affordable alternative to the budget traveller's staples of eggs, tacos and beans, as they include foods that don't normally appear on menus, such as home-made soups, stews, local specialities, puddings and elusive vegetables.

A typical comida will consist of "wet" soup, probably vegetable, followed by "dry" soup – most commonly *sopa de arroz* (simply rice seasoned with tomato or chile), or perhaps a plate of vegetables, pasta, beans or guacamole (avocado mashed with onion, and maybe tomato, lime juice and chile). Then comes the main course, followed by pudding, usually fruit, *flan* or *pudin* (crème caramel-like concoctions) or rice pudding. The courses are brought quickly, sometimes all at once, and in the cheaper places you may have no idea what you're going to get until it arrives, since there'll simply be a sign saying "comida corrida" and the price.

Some restaurants also offer set meals in the evening, but this is rare, and on the whole going out to **eat at night** is much more expensive.

## Drinks

The basic drinks to accompany food are water or beer. If you're drinking **water**, stick to bottled stuff (*agua mineral* or *agua de Tehuacán*) – it comes either plain (*sin gas*) or carbonated (*con gas*).

### Jugos, licuados and refrescos

**Soft drinks** (*refrescos*) – including Coke, Pepsi, Squirt (fun to pronounce in Spanish), and Mexican brands like apple-flavoured Sidral (which are usually extremely sweet) – are on sale everywhere. Far more tempting are the real **fruit juices** and *licuados* sold at shops and stalls displaying the "Jugos y Licuados" sign and known as *jugerías* or *licuaderías*. Juices (**jugos**) can be squeezed from anything that will go through the extractor. Orange (**naranja**) and carrot (**zanahoria**) are the staples, but you should also experiment with some of the more obscure tropical fruits, most of which are much better than they sound. *Licuados* are made of fruit mixed with water (**licuado de agua** or simply **agua de...**) or milk (**licuado de leche**) in a blender, usually with sugar added, and are always fantastic. **Limonada** (fresh lemonade) is also sold in many of these places, as are **aguas frescas** – flavoured cold drinks, of which the most common are **horchata** (rice milk flavoured with cinnamon) and **agua de arroz** (like an iced rice-pudding drink – delicious), **agua de jamaica** (hibiscus) or **de tamarindo** (tamarind). These are also often served in restaurants or sold in the streets from great glass jars. Make sure that any water and ice used is purified – street stalls are especially suspect in this regard. Juices and *licuados* are also sold at many ice-cream parlours – *neverías* or *paleterías*. The ice cream, more like Italian *gelato* than the heavy-cream US varieties, can also be fabulous and comes in a huge range of flavours.

## Coffee and tea

A great deal of **coffee** is produced in Mexico, and in the growing areas, especially the state of Veracruz, as well as in the traditional coffeehouses in the capital, you will be served superb coffee. In its basic form, **café solo** or **negro**, it is strong, black, often sweet (ask for it *sin azúcar* for no sugar), and comes in small cups. For weaker black coffee ask for **café americano**, though this may mean instant (if you do want instant, ask for "Nescafé"). White is **café cortado** or **con un pocito de leche**; **café con leche** can be delicious, made with all milk and no water (ask if it's "hecho de leche"). **Espresso** and **cappuccino** are often available too, or you may be offered **café de olla** – stewed in the pot for hours with cinnamon and sugar, it's thick, sweet and tasty. Outside traditional coffee areas, however, the coffee is often terrible, with only instant available (if you look like a tourist they may automatically assume you want instant anyway).

Tea (**té**) is often available too, and you may well be offered a cup at the end of a comida. Usually it's some kind of herb tea like **manzanillo** (camomile) or **yerbabuena** (mint). If you get the chance to try traditional **hot chocolate** ("the drink of the Aztecs"), then do so – it's an extraordinary, spicy, semi-bitter concoction, quite unlike the milky bedtime drink of your childhood.

## Alcohol

Mexican **beer**, or *cerveza*, is excellent. Most is light, lager-style *cerveza clara*, the best-known (but least flavourful) examples of which are Sol and Corona. Other examples are Bohémia, Superior, Dos Equis and Tecate, but you can also get dark (*oscura*) beers, of which the best are Negra Modelo, Indio and Tres Equis. Pacífico, originally from the west coast, is gaining popularity among the national brands. Try a *michelada,* a beer cocktail made by adding ice, lime and Worcestershire and Tabasco sauces to dark beer and rimming the glass with salt. The milder *chelada* is a light beer mixed with plenty of lime and salt, and both are refreshing on a sunny day.

You'll normally be drinking in **bars**, but if you don't feel comfortable – this applies to women, in particular (see opposite and p.60 for more on this topic) – you can also get takeout from most shops, supermarkets and, cheapest of all, *agencias*, which are normally agents for just one brand. When buying from any of these places, it is normal to pay a deposit of about thirty to forty percent of the purchase price: keep your receipt and return your bottles to the same store. Instead of buying 330ml bottles, you go for the 940ml vessels known as *caguamas* (turtles), or in the case of Pacífico, *ballenas* (whales).

**Wine** (*vino* – *tinto* is red, *blanco* is white) is not seen a great deal, although Mexico does produce a fair number of perfectly good vintages. You're safest sticking to brand names like Hidalgo or Domecq, although it may also be worth experimenting with some of the new labels, especially those from Baja California, which are attempting to emulate the success of their neighbours across the border and in many cases have borrowed American techniques and wine-makers.

**Tequila**, distilled from the cactus-like agave plant and produced mainly in the state of Jalisco, is the most famous of Mexican spirits, usually served straight with lime and salt on the side. Lick the salt and bite into the lime, then take a swig of tequila (or the other way round – there's no correct etiquette). The best stuff is aged (*añejo* or *reposado*) for smoothness; try Sauza Hornitos, which is powerful, or Commemorativo, which is unexpectedly gentle on the throat.

**Mescal** (often spelled mezcal) is basically the same thing as tequila, but is made from a slightly different of plant, the maguey, and is younger and less refined. In fact, tequila was originally just a variety of mescal. The spurious belief that the worm in the mescal bottle is hallucinogenic is based on confusion between the drink and the peyote cactus, which is also called mescal; by the time you've got down as far as the worm, you wouldn't notice hallucinations anyway.

**Pulque**, a mildly alcoholic milky beer made from the same cactus, is the traditional drink of the poor and sold in special bars called *pulquerías*. The best comes from the state of Mexico City, and is thick and viscous – it's a little like palm wine, and definitely an acquired taste. Unfermented *pulque*, called *aguamiel*, is sweet and non-alcoholic.

Drinking other spirits, you should always ask for **nacional**, as anything imported is fabulously expensive. **Rum** (*ron*), **gin** (*ginebra*) and **vodka** are made in Mexico, as are some very palatable **brandies** (brandy or coñac – try San Marcos or Presidente). Most of the **cocktails** for which Mexico is known – margaritas, piñas coladas and so on – are available only in tourist areas or hotel bars, and are generally pretty strong. **Sangrita** is a mixture of tomato and fruit juices with chile, often drunk as a mixer with tequila.

For drinking any of these, the least heavy atmosphere is in **hotel bars**, tourist areas or anything that describes itself as a "ladies' bar". Traditional **cantinas** are for serious and excessive drinking, have a thoroughly threatening, macho atmosphere and are usually closed to women; more often than not, there's a sign above the door prohibiting entry to "women, members of the armed forces and anyone in uniform". Cantinas are to some extent more liberal in big cities, but in small and traditional places they remain exclusively male preserves, full of drunken bonhomie that can suddenly sour into threats and fighting.

# Crime and personal safety

**Despite soaring crime rates and dismal-sounding statistics, you are unlikely to run into trouble in Mexico as long as you stick to well-travelled paths. Even in Mexico City, which has an appalling reputation, the threat of grievous bodily harm is not that much greater than in many large North American and European cities.**

Obviously there are areas of the cities where you wander alone, or at night, at your peril; but the precautions to be taken are mostly common sense and should be second nature. Travelling in the Zapatista-controlled areas of the state of Chiapas you will undoubtedly come across guerrillas and the army, but tourists are not targeted by either group, and you shouldn't encounter any trouble.

## Avoiding theft

**Petty theft** and **pickpockets** are your biggest worry in Mexico, so don't wave money around, try not to look too obviously affluent, don't leave cash or cameras in hotel rooms and do deposit your valuables in your hotel's safe if it has one (make a note of what you've deposited and ask the hotelier to sign it if you're worried). Crowds, especially on public city transport, are obvious hot spots: thieves tend to work in groups and target tourists. Distracting your attention, especially by pretending to look for something (always be suspicious of anyone who appears to be searching for something near you), or having one or two people pin you while another goes through your pockets, are common ploys, and can be done faster and more easily than you might imagine. Razoring of bags and pockets is another gambit, as is the more brutish grabbing of handbags, or anything left unattended even for a split second. **Mugging** is less common than pickpocketing, but you should steer clear of obvious danger spots, such as deserted pedestrian underpasses in big cities – indeed, avoid all deserted areas in big cities. When using ATM machines, use those in shopping malls or enclosed premises, and only in daylight when there are plenty of people around. **Robbery and sexual assault** on tourists by cab drivers are not unknown, and the US State Department advises its citizens against hailing a cab in the street in Mexico City (see p.397). Instead, phone for a radio cab or, failing that, take the next best option and get a cab from an official *sitio*. At night the beaches in tourist areas are also potentially dangerous.

When travelling, keep an eye on your bags (which are safe enough in the luggage compartments underneath most buses). Hold-ups of buses happen from time to time, and you may well be frisked on boarding to check for arms, since the bandits are most often passengers on the bus.

Drivers are likely to encounter problems if they leave anything in their car. The **vehicle** itself is less likely to be stolen than broken into for the valuables inside. To avoid the worst, always park legally (and preferably off the street) and never leave anything visible inside the car. Driving itself can be hazardous, too, especially at night (see box, p.40).

## Police

Mexican **police** are not well paid, and **graft** is an accepted part of the job. This is often difficult for foreign visitors to accept, but it is a system, and in its own way it works well enough. If a policeman accuses you of some violation (and this is almost bound to happen to drivers at some stage), explain that you're a tourist, not used to the ways of the country – you may get off scot-free, but more likely the subject of a "**fine**" will come up. Such on-the-spot fines are open to negotiation, but only if you're confident you've done nothing seriously wrong and have a reasonable command of Spanish. Otherwise pay up and get out.

These small bribes are known as *mordidas* (bites), and they may also be extracted by border officials or bureaucrats (in which case, you could get out of paying by asking for a receipt, but it won't make life easier). In general, it is always wise to back off from any sort of confrontation with the police and to be extremely polite to them at all times.

Far more common than the *mordida* is the **propina**, or tip, a payment that is made entirely on your initiative. There's no need to do this, but it's remarkable how often a few pesos complete paperwork that would otherwise take weeks, open firmly locked doors or even find a seat on a previously full bus. All such transactions are quite open, and it's up to you to literally put your money on the table.

Should a crime be committed against you – in particular if you're robbed – your relationship with the police will obviously be different, although even in this eventuality it's worth considering whether the lengthy hassles you'll go through make it worth reporting. Some insurance companies will insist on a police report if you're to get any refund – in which case you may practically have to dictate it to the officer and can expect little action – but others will be understanding of the situation. American Express in Mexico City, for example, may accept without a murmur the fact that your cheques have been stolen but the theft was not reported to the police. The department you need in order to *presentar una denuncia* (report the theft officially) is the Procuradoría General de Justicia.

The Mexican **legal system** is based on the Napoleonic code, which assumes your guilt until you can prove otherwise. Should you be jailed, your one phone call should be to your **consulate** – if nothing else, they'll arrange an English-speaking lawyer. You can be held for up to 72 hours on suspicion before charges have to be brought. Mexican jails are grim, although lots of money and friends on the outside can ameliorate matters slightly.

## Drugs

**Drug offences** are the most common cause of serious trouble between tourists and the authorities. Under heavy pressure from the US to clamp down on the trade, local authorities are particularly happy to throw the book at foreign offenders.

A good deal of **marijuana** (known as *mota*) – grown primarily in Guerrero ("Acapulco Gold"), Oaxaca and Michoacán (redder in colour, and generally considered the best), and to a lesser extent in other states – continues to be cultivated in Mexico, despite US-backed government attempts to stamp it out (at one time, imports of Mexican marijuana were so high that the DEA had crops sprayed with paraquat). Although cannabis is widely used, it remains strictly illegal, and foreigners caught in **possession** are dealt with harshly; for quantities reckoned to be for distribution you can wave goodbye to daylight for a long time. For possession of small quantities, you can expect a hefty fine, no sympathy and little help from your consulate.

Other naturally occurring drugs – Mexico has more species of psychoactive plants than anywhere else in the world – still form an important part of many indigenous rituals. **Hallucinogenic mushrooms** can be found in many parts of the country, especially in the states of Oaxaca, Chiapas and México, while the **peyote cactus** from the northern deserts is used primarily by the Huichol, but also by other indigenous peoples. The authorities turn a blind eye to traditional use, but use by non-indigenous Mexicans and tourists is as strongly prohibited as that of any other illegal drug, and heavily penalized. Expect searches and hotel raids by police if staying in areas known for peyote.

**Cocaine** trafficking is a national problem, as Mexico is a major staging post on the smuggling route from Colombian supply to American demand. Well-connected gangs involved in the trade – especially in Guadalajara, Ciudad Juárez and Tijuana – are often more powerful than the police and local government. Use of cocaine is also widespread and growing; **crack** is a blight in parts of the capital and in certain northern cities, approaching levels once seen in American cities. The best advice as far as this unpleasant trade goes is to steer as clear as possible.

In recent years many Americans have taken to travelling to the border region, especially Tijuana, to buy inexpensive **prescription drugs**. However, note that it is illegal to purchase controlled medicines such as Valium, Vicodin and codeine, in Mexico without a Mexican prescription. If caught, purchasers can spend anywhere from ten months to fifteen years in a Mexican prison. For information on controlled substances in Mexico, see Ⓦwww.cofepris.gob.mx/pyp/estpsic/es.htm (a list, in Spanish, of generic and brand names).

# Health

**Most travellers get through Mexico without catching anything more serious than a dose of Montezuma's Revenge. You will still want the security of health insurance (see p.64), but the important thing is to keep your resistance high and to be aware of the health risks linked to poor hygiene, untreated water, mosquito bites, undressed open cuts and unprotected sex.**

The lack of sanitation in Mexico is often exaggerated, and you'll never enjoy yourself if you're overly obsessive about it. That said, a degree of caution is wise – don't try anything too exotic in the first few days, before your body has had a chance to adjust to local microbes, and avoid food that looks like it has been on display for a while or not freshly cooked. You should always peel fruit before eating it. Avoid raw shellfish, and don't eat anywhere that is obviously dirty (easily spotted, since most Mexican restaurants are scrupulously clean). Salads are healthy, but think twice before eating them if you have a sensitive stomach. In general, keep an eye out for cleanliness of street stalls – beware of food that has been left out to breed germs rather than food that has been freshly cooked. For advice on water, see the box on p.52.

There are no required vaccinations for Mexico, but it's worth visiting your doctor at

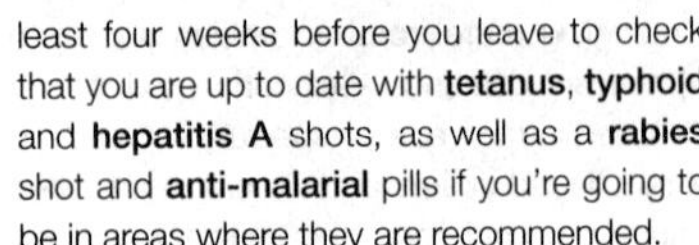

least four weeks before you leave to check that you are up to date with **tetanus**, **typhoid** and **hepatitis A** shots, as well as a **rabies** shot and **anti-malarial** pills if you're going to be in areas where they are recommended.

For comprehensive coverage of the sort of health problems encountered by travellers, consult the *Rough Guide to Travel Health* by Dr Nick Jones.

### Intestinal troubles

Despite all the dire warnings, a bout of **diarrhoea** (Montezuma's Revenge, or simply *turista* as it's also known in Mexico) is the only medical problem you're likely to encounter. No one, however cautious, seems to avoid it altogether, largely because there are no reliable preventive measures. It's caused by the bacteria in Mexican food, which are different from (as well as more numerous than) those found in other Western diets, and is compounded by the change in food intake and routine.

If you go down with a mild dose of the runs unaccompanied by other symptoms, this will probably be the cause. If your diarrhoea is accompanied by cramps and vomiting, it could be **food poisoning** of some sort. Either way, it will probably pass of its own accord in 24 to 48 hours without treatment. In the meantime, it's essential to replace the fluid and salts you're losing, so drink lots of water. If you have severe diarrhoea, and whenever young children have it, add oral **rehydration salts** – *suero oral* (brand names: Dioralyte, Electrosol, Rehidrat). If you can't get these, dissolve half a teaspoon of salt and three of sugar in a litre of water. Avoid greasy food, heavy spices, caffeine and most fruit and dairy products; some say bananas, papayas, guavas and prickly pears (*tunas*) are a help, while plain yogurt or a broth made from yeast extract (such as Marmite or Vegemite, if you happen to have some with you) can be easily absorbed by your body when you have diarrhoea. Drugs like Lomotil

#### What about the water?

In a hot climate and at high altitudes, it's essential to increase **water** intake to prevent dehydration. Most travellers, and most Mexicans if they can, stay off the tap water, although a lot of the time it is in fact drinkable, and in practice impossible to avoid completely: ice made with it, unasked for, may appear in drinks, utensils are washed in it, and so on.

Most restaurants and *licuaderías* use **purified water** (*agua purificada*), but always check; most hotels have a supply and will often provide bottles of water in your room. Bottled water (generally purified with ozone or ultraviolet) is widely available, but stick with known brands, and always check that the seal on the bottle is intact since refilling empties with tap water for resale is common (carbonated water is generally a safer bet in that respect).

There are various methods of **treating water** while you are travelling, whether your source is from a tap or a river or stream. Boiling it for a minimum of five minutes is the time-honoured method, but it is not always practical, will not remove unpleasant tastes and is a lot less effective at higher altitudes – including much of central Mexico – where you have to boil it for much longer.

**Chemical sterilization**, using either chlorine or iodine tablets or a tincture of iodine liquid, is more convenient, but leaves a nasty aftertaste (which can to some extent be masked with lime juice). Chlorine kills bacteria but, unlike iodine, is not effective against amoebic dysentery and giardiasis. Pregnant women or people with thyroid problems should consult their doctor before using iodine sterilizing tablets or iodine-based purifiers. Too many iodine tablets can cause gastrointestinal discomfort. Inexpensive iodine removal filters are available and are recommended if treated water is being used continuously for more than a month or is being given to babies.

**Purification**, involving both filtration and sterilization, gives the most complete treatment. Portable water purifiers range in size from units weighing as little as 60g, which can be slipped into a pocket, up to 800g for carrying in a backpack.

or Imodium plug you up – and thus undermine the body's efforts to rid itself of infection – but they can be a temporary stop-gap if you have to travel. If symptoms persist for more than three days, or if you have a fever or blood in your stool, seek medical advice (see "Getting medical help", p.55).

### Malaria and dengue fever

**Malaria**, caused by a parasite that lives in the saliva of female *Anopheles* mosquitoes, is endemic in some parts of Mexico. Areas above 1000m (such as the capital) are malaria-free, as are Cancún, Cozumel, Isla Mujeres and all the beach resorts of the Baja and the Pacific coasts. Daytime visits to archeological sites are risk-free, too, but low-lying inland areas can be risky, especially at night. The main risk areas are Chiapas, Tabasco, the Yucatán Peninsula, Oaxaca, Guerrero, Michoacán, northern Jalisco, Nayarit, Sinaloa and parts of Sonora, Chihuahua and Durango. Chloroquine (brand names: Nivaquin, Resochin, Avloclor, Aralen) is the recommended malaria prophylactic for travellers to Mexico; you need to start taking the pills one week before you arrive and continue for one month after you depart. Chloroquine is unsuitable for sufferers from various complaints such as epilepsy and psoriasis but daily proguanil (brand name Paludrine) can be used in its place. Consult a physician before beginning any course of medication; see Ⓦwww.cdc.gov/travel/regionalmalaria/camerica.htm for more information on malaria in Mexico.

If you go down with malaria, you'll probably know. The fever, shivering and headaches are like severe flu and come in waves, usually beginning in the early evening. Malaria is not infectious, but can be dangerous and sometimes even fatal if not treated quickly. If no doctor is available, take 600mg of quinine sulphate three times daily for seven days, followed on the eighth day (or sooner if the quinine isn't working at all) by three Fansidar (available from a local pharmacy) taken together.

The most important thing, obviously, is to avoid **mosquito** bites altogether. Though active from dusk till dawn, female *Anopheles* mosquitoes prefer to bite in the evening. Wear long sleeves, skirts or trousers, avoid dark colours, which attract mosquitoes, and put **repellent** on all exposed skin, especially feet and ankles, which are their favourite targets. Plenty of good brands are sold locally, though health departments recommend carrying high-DEET brands available from travel clinics at home. An alternative is to burn coils of **pyrethrum** incense such as Raidolitos (these are readily available and burn all night if whole, but break easily). Sleep under a **net** if you can – one that hangs from a single point is best (you can usually find a way to tie a string across your room to hang it from). Special mosquito nets for hammocks are available in Mexico.

Another illness spread by mosquito bites is **dengue fever**, whose symptoms are similar to those of malaria, plus a headache and aching bones. Dengue-carrying mosquitoes are particularly prevalent during the rainy season and fly during the day, so wear insect repellent in the daytime if mosquitoes are around. The only treatment is complete rest, with drugs to assuage the fever – and take note that a second infection can be fatal.

### Other bites and stings

Other biting insects can also be a nuisance. These include **bed bugs**, sometimes found in cheap hotels – look for squashed ones around the bed. **Sandflies**, often present on beaches, are quite small, but their bites, usually on feet and ankles, itch like hell and last for days. Head or body **lice** can be picked up from people or bedding, and are best treated with medicated soap or shampoo.

**Scorpions** are mostly nocturnal and hide during the heat of the day under rocks and in crevices, so poking around in such places when in the countryside is generally ill-advised. If sleeping in a place where they might enter (such as a beach cabaña), shake your shoes out before putting them on in the morning, and try not to wander round barefoot. The sting of some scorpions is dangerous and medical treatment should always be sought – cold-pack the sting in the meantime. **Snakes** are unlikely to bite unless accidentally disturbed, and most are harmless in any case. To see one at all, you need to search stealthily – walk heavily and they will usually slither away. If you do get bitten or stung, remember what the snake or scorpion looked like (kill it if you can do so without receiving more bites), try not to move the affected part (tourniquets are not recommended – if you do use one, it is *vital* to relieve it for at least ninety seconds every fifteen minutes), and seek medical help: antivenins are available in most hospitals.

## Altitude and heat problems

Two other common causes of health problems in Mexico are **altitude** and the **sun**. The solution in both cases is to take it easy. Especially if you arrive in Mexico City, you may find any activity strenuous, and the thin air is made worse by the high concentration of pollutants. Allow yourself time to acclimatize. If going to higher altitudes (climbing Popocatépetl, for example), you may develop symptoms of **Acute Mountain Sickness (AMS)**, such as breathlessness, headaches, dizziness, nausea and appetite loss. More extreme cases may include vomiting, disorientation, loss of balance and coughing up of pink frothy phlegm. The simple cure – a slow descent – almost always brings immediate recovery.

Tolerance to the sun, too, takes a while to build up: use a strong **sun screen** and, if you're walking during the day, wear a hat or keep to the shade. Be sure to avoid dehydration by drinking enough (water or fruit juice rather than beer or coffee and you should aim to drink at least three litres a day), and don't exert yourself for long periods in the hot sun. Be aware that overheating can cause **heatstroke**, which is potentially fatal. Signs are a very high body temperature without a feeling of fever, accompanied by headaches, disorientation and even irrational behaviour. Lowering body temperature (a tepid shower, for example) is the first step in treatment.

Less serious is **prickly heat**, an itchy rash that is in fact an infection of the sweat ducts caused by excessive perspiration that doesn't dry off. A cool shower, zinc oxide powder and loose cotton clothes should help.

## Hepatitis and other diseases

**Hepatitis A** is transmitted through contaminated food and water, or through saliva, and thrives in conditions of poor hygiene. It can lay a victim low for several months with exhaustion, fever and diarrhoea, and can even cause liver damage. The Havrix vaccines have been shown to be extremely effective; though expensive (around US$150/£80 for a course of two shots); protection lasts for ten years.

Hepatitis symptoms include a yellowing of the whites of the eyes, general malaise, orange urine (though dehydration can also cause this) and light-coloured stools. If you think you have it and are unable immediately to see a doctor, it is important to get lots of rest, avoid alcohol and do your best not to spread the disease. If medical insurance coverage is an issue, you can go to a pathology lab (most towns have them) to get blood tests before paying a greater amount to see a doctor.

More serious is **hepatitis B**, which is extremely contagious and passed through blood or sexual contact. A hepatitis B jab is recommended if you will be in contact with those with weaker immunity systems, for example, working around medical patients or with children. Ideally three doses are given over six months but if time is short, there are other options that take one to two months with a booster given after a year.

Typhoid and cholera are spread in the same way as hepatitis A. **Typhoid** produces a persistent high fever with malaise, headaches and abdominal pains, followed by diarrhoea. Vaccination can be by injection or orally, though the oral alternative is less effective, more expensive and only lasts a year, as opposed to three for a shot in the arm. **Cholera** appears in epidemics rather than isolated cases – if it's about, you will probably hear about it. Cholera is characterized by sudden attacks of watery diarrhoea with severe cramps and debilitation. The vaccination is no longer given, as it is ineffective.

Immunizations against **mumps**, **measles**, **TB** and **rubella** are a good idea for anyone who wasn't vaccinated as a child and hasn't had the diseases, and it's worth making sure you are covered for **tetanus**. You don't need a shot for **yellow fever** unless you're coming from a country where it's endemic (in which case you need to carry your vaccination certificate).

**Rabies** exists in Mexico and the rabies vaccine is advised for anyone who will be more than 24 hours away from medical help. The best advice is simply to give dogs a wide berth, and not to play with animals at all, no matter how cuddly they may look. A bite, a scratch or even a lick from an infected animal could spread the disease – rabies can be fatal, so if you are bitten, assume the worst and get medical help as quickly as possible. While waiting, wash any such wound immediately but gently with soap or detergent and apply alcohol or iodine if possible. If you decide to get the vaccination, you'll need three shots spread over a four-week period prior to travel.

### Getting medical help

For minor medical problems, head for a **farmacia** – look for a green cross and the Farmacia sign. Pharmacists are knowledgeable and helpful, and many speak some English. One word of warning however: in many Mexican pharmacies you can still buy drugs such as Entero-Vioform and Mexaform, which can cause optic nerve damage and have been banned elsewhere; it is not a good idea, therefore, to use local brands unless you know what they are. Note that the purchase of prescription drugs without a Mexican prescription is illegal; a US prescription will not suffice.

For more serious complaints you can get a list of English-speaking **doctors** from your government's nearest consulate. Big hotels and tourist offices may also be able to recommend medical services. Every Mexican border town has hundreds of doctors experienced in treating gringos (**dentists**, too), since they charge less than their colleagues across the border. Every reasonably sized town should also have a state- or Red Cross-run **health centre** (*centro de salud*), where treatment is free.

## The media

**If you can read and understand Spanish, you'll certainly find some interest in the Mexican media, though there's plenty of rubbish too. News is mostly local, and often heavily slanted towards the government, but there is an independent press, and if you pick and choose, you can sometimes find some interesting programmes on TV.**

### Newspapers

Few domestic **newspapers** carry much foreign news, and the majority of international coverage does not extend beyond Latin America. Papers are lurid scandal sheets, brimming with violent crime depicted in full colour. Each state has its own press, however, and they do vary: while most are little more than government mouthpieces, others are surprisingly independent.

Mexico has an English-language daily, the *Herald*, which is a Mexican edition of the *Miami Herald*. If you read Spanish, probably the best national paper is *Reforma*, with a good reputation for independence and political objectivity. Also worth a read is the left-wing *La Jornada*, which is quite daringly critical of government policy, especially in Chiapas (its journalists regularly face death threats as a result). The press has gradually been asserting its independence since the mid-1990s, tackling such subjects as human rights, corruption and drug trafficking, though journalists still face danger if they speak out, not only from shady government groups but also from drug traffickers. Reporting on links between the two is particularly dangerous. 2006 saw the murders of five Mexican journalists and one American, as well as the beating and harassment of journalists covering the confrontations between police and demonstrators in Oaxaca.

### Television

You can usually pick up a dozen channels in Mexico without cable or satellite. Four are run by the main **TV** company, Televisa, and another two by TV Azteca. Canal 22 tends to show cultural programmes, often rather dry. Canal Once is the most original and independent channel, and often has something quite interesting on, especially late in the evening. **Cable** and **satellite** are now widespread, and even quite downmarket hotels offer numerous channels, many of them American.

On Mexican TV you can watch any number of US shows dubbed into Spanish, but far and away the most popular programmes are the *telenovelas* – soap operas that dominate the screens from 6pm to 10pm and pull in millions of viewers. Each episode takes melodrama to new heights, with nonstop action and emotions hammed up to the maximum for riveted fans. Plot lines make national news, and *telenovela* stars are major celebrities, despite their ludicrously over-the-top acting styles.

### Radio

**Radio** stations in the capital and Guadalajara (among others) have programmes in English for a couple of hours each day, and in many places US broadcasts can also be picked up. If you have a short-wave radio, you can get the BBC World Service (check Ⓦwww.bbc.co.uk/worldservice for times and frequencies), the Voice of America (Ⓦwww.voa.gov) and at certain times, Radio Canada (Ⓦwww.rcinet.ca).

# Festivals

**Stumbling, perhaps accidentally, onto some Mexican village fiesta may prove to be the highlight of your travels. Everywhere, from the remotest Indian village to the most sophisticated city suburb, devotes at least one day annually to partying. Usually it's in honour of the local saint's day, but many fiestas have pre-Christian origins and any excuse – from harvest celebrations to the coming of the rains – will do.**

Details of the most important local fiestas can be found on pp.174–175 for Baja California and the Pacific Northwest; pp.234–235 for Monterrey and the north; pp.320-321 for Guanajuato and the Bajío region; pp.390-391 for inland Jalisco and Michoacán; pp.534-535 for Mexico City and the surrounding area; pp.590–591 for Colima, the coast of Jalisco and Guerrero; pp.630–631 for the state of Veracruz; pp.692–693 for Oaxaca; pp.770–771 for Chiapas and Tabasco; and pp.878–879 for the Yucatán Peninsula. In addition to these, there are plenty of lesser local festivals, as well as certain major festivals celebrated throughout the country. Traditional dances and music form an essential part of almost every fiesta, and most include a procession behind some revered holy image or a more celebratory secular parade with fireworks. The only rule is that no two fiestas will be quite the same.

**Carnaval**, the week before Lent, is celebrated throughout the Roman Catholic world, and is at its most exuberant in Latin America. It is the last week of taking one's pleasures before the forty-day abstinence of Lent, which lasts until Easter. Like Easter, its date is not fixed, but it generally falls in February or early March. Carnaval is celebrated with costumes, parades, eating and dancing, most spectacularly in Veracruz and Mazatlán, and works its way up to a climax on the last day, Mardi Gras (Shrove Tuesday).

The country's biggest holiday, however, is **Semana Santa** – Holy Week – beginning on Palm Sunday and continuing until the following Sunday, Easter Day. Still a deeply religious festival in Mexico, it celebrates the resurrection of Christ, and has also become an occasion to venerate the Virgin Mary, with processions bearing her image now a hallmark of the celebrations. Expect transport to be totally disrupted during this week as virtually the whole country is on the move; you will definitely need to plan ahead if travelling then. Many places close for the whole of Holy Week, and certainly from Thursday to Sunday.

**Secular Independence Day** (Sept 16) is in some ways more solemn than the religious festivals. While Easter and Carnaval are popular, this one is more official, marking the historic day in 1810 when Manuel Hidalgo y Costilla issued the Grito (Cry of Independence) from his parish church in Dolores, now Dolores Hidalgo, Guanajuato, which is still the centre of commemoration. You'll also find the day marked in the capital with mass recitation of the Grito in the Zócalo, followed by fireworks, music and dancing.

The **Day of the Dead** is All Saints' or All Souls' Day and its eve (Nov 1–2), when offerings are made to ancestors' souls, frequently with picnics and all-night vigils at their graves. People build shrines in their homes to honour their departed relatives, but it's the cemeteries to head for if you want to see the really spectacular stuff. Sweetmeats and papier-mâché statues of dressed-up skeletons give the whole proceedings a rather gothic air.

**Christmas** is a major holiday, and another time when people are on the move and transport is booked solid for weeks ahead. Gringo influence is heavy nowadays, with Santa Claus and Christmas trees, but the Mexican festival remains distinct in many ways, with a much stronger religious element (virtually every home has a Nativity crib). **New Year** is still largely an occasion to spend with family, the actual hour being celebrated with the eating of grapes. Presents are traditionally given on Twelfth Night or **Epiphany** (Reyes; Jan 6), which is when the three Magi of the Bible arrived bearing gifts – though things are shifting into line with Yankee custom, and more and more people are exchanging gifts on December 25. One of the more bizarre Christmas events takes place in Oaxaca, where there is a public display of Nativity cribs and other sculptures made of radishes.

# Sports and outdoor activities

**You'll find facilities for golf, tennis, sailing, surfing, scuba diving and deep-sea fishing – even horseback riding and hunting – provided at all the big resorts.**

**Sport fishing** is enormously popular in Baja California and the big Pacific coast resorts, while freshwater bass fishing is growing in popularity too, especially behind the large dams in the north of the country. The gentler arts of **diving** and **snorkelling** are big on the Caribbean coast, with world-famous dive sites at Cozumel and on the reefs further south. The Pacific coast has become something of a centre for **surfing**, with few facilities as yet (though you can rent surfboards in major tourist centres such as Acapulco and Mazatlán) but plenty of Californian surfers who follow the weather south over the winter. The most popular places are in Baja California and on the Oaxaca coast, but the biggest waves are to be found around Lázaro Cárdenas in Michoacán. A more minority-interest activity for which Mexico has become a major centre is **caving**. With a third of the country built on limestone, there are caverns in most states that can be explored by experienced potholers or spelunkers.

The Ministry of Tourism publishes a leaflet on participatory sports in Mexico, and can also advise on such things as licences and seasons.

## Spectator sports

Mexico's chief spectator sport is **soccer** (*fútbol*; see box, p.499). Mexican teams have not been notably successful on the international stage, but going to a game can still be a thrilling experience. The capital and Guadalajara are the best places to see a match and the biggest game in the domestic league, "El Clásico", between Chivas from Guadalajara and América from Mexico City, fills the city's 150,000-seater Aztec stadium to capacity. **Baseball** (*béisbol*) is also popular, as is **American football** (especially on TV). **Jai alai** (also known as **frontón**, or **pelota vasca**) is Basque handball, common in big cities and played at a very high speed with a small hard ball and curved scoop attached to the hand; it's a big gambling game.

Mexican **rodeos** (*charreadas*), mainly seen in the north of the country, are as spectacular for their style and costume as they are for the events, while **bullfights** remain an obsession: every city has a bullring – Mexico City's Plaza México is the world's largest – and the country's *toreros* are said to be the world's most reckless, much in demand in Spain. Another popular blood sport, usually at village level, is **cockfighting**, still legal in Mexico and mainly attended for the opportunity to bet on the outcome.

Masked **wrestling** (*lucha libre*) is very popular in Mexico, too, with the participants, Batman-like, out of the game for good should their mask be removed and their secret identity revealed. Nor does the resemblance to comic-book superheroes end in the ring: certain masked wrestlers have become popular social campaigners out of the ring, always ready to turn up just in the nick of time to rescue the beleaguered poor from eviction by avaricious landlords or persecution by corrupt politicians. For more on wrestling, see p.477.

# Culture and etiquette



**Mexicans are generally very courteous, and in some ways quite formal, and it is common, for example, to address people as señor or señora, while being too brusque can give quite a bad impression.**

Most Mexicans are also quite religious; you will often see little altars by the roadside, and many people cross themselves whenever they pass a church. It is wise to avoid open disrespect for religion unless you are sure of your company. While male travellers will find the country very easy-going, women may encounter a few difficulties arising from traditional Latin machismo that they would not expect at home.

## Homosexuality

There are no federal laws governing **homosexuality** in Mexico, and hence it's **legal**. There are, however, laws enforcing "public morality", which although they are supposed only to apply to prostitution, are often used against gays. 1997 saw the election of Mexico's first "out" congresswoman, the left-wing PRD's Patria Jiménez, and in 2003 the federal parliament passed a law against discrimination on various grounds including sexual preference. In 2005, however, a gay man from Tampico successfully claimed political asylum in the US after demonstrating the extent of persecution he faced in his hometown.

Nonetheless, there are a large number of gay **groups** and **publications** in Mexico – we've supplied two contact addresses below. The lesbian scene is not as visible or as large as the gay scene for men, but it's there and growing. There are gay bars and clubs in the major resorts and US border towns, and in large cities such as the capital, and also Monterrey, Guadalajara, Veracruz and Oaxaca; elsewhere, private parties are where it all happens, and you'll need a contact to find them.

As far as popular **attitudes** are concerned, religion and machismo are the order of the day, and prejudice is rife, but attitudes are changing. Soft-core porn magazines for gay men are sold openly on street stalls and, while you should be careful to avoid upsetting macho sensibilities, you should have few problems if you are discreet. In Juchitán, Oaxaca, on the other hand, gay male transvestites, known as *muxes*, are accepted as a kind of third sex, and the town even has a transvestite basketball team.

You can check the latest gay rights situation in Mexico on the International Gay and Lesbian Human Rights Commission website at Ⓦwww.iglhrc.org, and information on the male gay scene in Mexico (gay bars, meeting places and cruising spots) can be found in the annual *Spartacus Gay Guide*, available in specialist bookshops at home. As for **contacts** within Mexico: lesbians can get in touch with Grupo Lesbico Patlatonalli, Lopez Cotilla 996, Guadalajara, 44100 Jalisco (Ⓣ333/3825-0598, Ⓔpatlas@mail.udg.mx); while for gay men, CIDHOM (Centro de Información y Documentación de las Homosexualidades en México), Cerrada Cuauhnochtli 11, Col. Pueblo Quieto, Tlalpan, México DF 14040 (Ⓣ55/5666-5436, Ⓔcidhom_colso@yahoo.com.mx), can offer information.

## Sexual harassment and discrimination

**Machismo** is engrained in the Mexican mentality and, although it's softened to some extent by the gentler mores of indigenous culture, most women will find that a degree of harassment is inevitable.

On the whole, most hassles will be limited to **comments** (*piropos*, supposedly compliments) in the street, but even situations that might be quite routine at home can seem threatening without a clear understanding of the nuances of Mexican Spanish. It's a good idea to avoid eye contact – wearing sunglasses helps. Any provocation is best ignored – Mexican women are rarely slow with a stream of retaliatory abuse, but it's a dangerous strategy unless you're very sure of your ground, and coming from a foreigner, it may be taken as racism.

Public transport can be one of the worst places for harassment, especially groping in crowded situations. On the Mexico City Metro, there are separate women's carriages and passages during rush hours. Otherwise, if you get a seat, you can hide behind a newspaper.

Problems are aggravated in the big tourist spots, where legendarily "easy" tourists attract droves of would-be gigolos. Away from resorts and big cities, though, and especially in indigenous areas, there is rarely any problem – you may as an outsider be treated as an object of curiosity, and wherever you come across it, such curiosity can also extend to friendliness and hospitality. On the whole, the further from the US border you get, the easier things will become.

The restrictions imposed on drinking are without a doubt irksome: women are simply barred from most cantinas, and even in so-called "ladies' bars", "unescorted" women may be looked at with suspicion or even refused service.

### Tipping

At expensive restaurants in tourist resorts, waiters and waitresses are used to American tipping levels (15–20 percent), but elsewhere levels are more like those in Europe (10–15 percent). In mid-range and upmarket hotels, you will be expected to tip chambermaids (a few dollars, depending on the standard of the hotel and the length of your stay) and porters (ten pesos or a dollar is fine). It is not usual to tip taxi drivers, but small tips are expected by gas-station and car-park attendants and the bagboys at supermarkets (all of these will be happy with a few pesos of small change).

## Shopping

**The craft tradition of Mexico, much of it descended directly from arts practised long before the Spanish arrived, is still extremely strong. Regional and highly localized specialities survive, with villages throughout the republic jealously guarding their reputations – especially in the states of Michoacán, Oaxaca, Chiapas and the Yucatán. There's a considerable amount of Guatemalan stuff about, too.**

### Crafts

To buy crafts, there is no need these days to visit the place of origin – **craft shops** in Mexico City and all the big resorts gather the best and most popular items from around the country. On the other hand, it's a great deal more enjoyable to see where the articles come from, and certainly the only way to get any real bargains. The good stuff is rarely cheap wherever you buy it, however, and there is an enormous amount of dross produced specifically for tourists.

**FONART shops**, which you'll come across in major centres throughout Mexico, are run by a government agency devoted to the promotion and preservation of crafts – their wares are always excellent, if expensive, and the shops should be visited to get an idea of what is potentially available. Where no such store exists, you can get a similar idea by looking at the best of the tourist shops.

Among the most popular items are: **silver**, the best of which is wrought in Taxco, although rarely mined there; **pottery**, made almost everywhere, with different techniques, designs and patterns in each region; **woollen goods**, especially blankets, which are again made everywhere, and *sarapes* from Oaxaca – always check the fibres and go for more expensive natural dyes; **leather**, especially tyre-tread-soled *huaraches* (sandals), sold cheaply wherever you go; **glass** from Jalisco; **lacquerware**, particularly from Uruapán; and **hammocks**, the best of which are sold in Mérida.

It is illegal to buy or sell antiquities, and even more criminal to try taking them out of the country (moreover, many items sold as valuable antiquities are little more than worthless fakes) – best to just look.

### Markets

For bargain hunters, the **mercado** (market) is the place to head. There's one in every Mexican town, which on one day of the week, the traditional market day, will be at its busiest with villagers from the surrounding area bringing their produce for sale or barter. By and large, of course, mercados are mainly dedicated to food and everyday necessities, but most have a section devoted to crafts, and in larger towns you may find a separate crafts bazaar.

Unless you're completely hopeless at bargaining, prices will always be lower in the market than in shops, but shops do have a couple of advantages. First, they exercise a degree of quality control, whereas any old junk can be sold in the market; and second, many established shops will be able to ship purchases home for you, which saves an enormous amount of the frustrating bureaucracy you'll encounter if you attempt to do it yourself.

Bargaining and haggling are very much a matter of personal style, highly dependent on your command of Spanish, aggressiveness and, to some extent, experience. The old tricks (never show the least sign of interest, let alone enthusiasm; walking away will always cut the price dramatically) do still hold true; but most important is to know what you want, its approximate value and how much you are prepared to pay. Never start to haggle for something you definitely don't intend to buy – it'll end in bad feelings on both sides. In shops there's little chance of significantly altering the official price unless you're buying in bulk, and even in markets most food and simple household goods have a set price (though it may be doubled at the sight of an approaching gringo).

# Travel essentials

### Costs

The developed tourist resorts and big cities are invariably more expensive than more remote towns, and certain other areas also have noticeably higher prices – among them the industrialized north, especially along the border; Baja; and all the newly wealthy oil regions. Prices can also be affected by **season** and many hotels raise their prices during busy times of the year. Summer, Christmas and Easter are the peak times for Mexican tourists and areas like Acapulco and Cancún, which attract large numbers of overseas visitors, put their prices up during the high season. Special events are also likely to be marked by price hikes.

Nonetheless, wherever you go you can probably get by on US$300/£165 a week (you could reduce that if you hardly travel around or hitchhike, stay only on campsites or in hostels, live on basic food and don't buy any souvenirs, though this requires a lot of discipline); you'd be living well on US$600/£330.

As always, if you're **travelling alone** you'll end up spending more – sharing rooms and food saves a substantial amount. In the larger resorts, you can get apartments for up to six people for even greater savings. If you have an **International Student or Youth Card**, you might find the occasional reduction on a museum admission price, but don't go out of your way to obtain one, since most concessions are, at least in theory, only for Mexican students. Cards available include the ISIC card for full-time students and the Go-25 youth card for under-26s, both of which carry health and emergency insurance benefits for Americans, and are available from youth travel firms such as STA Travel. Even a college photo ID card might work in some places.

Most restaurant bills come with **fifteen percent IVA** (Impuesto de Valor Añadido, or Valued Added Sales Tax) added; this may not always be included in prices quoted on the menu. **Service** is hardly ever added to bills, and the amount you tip is entirely up to you – in cheap places, it's just the loose change, while expensive venues tend to expect a full fifteen percent. See p.60 for more on tipping.

## Disabled travellers

Mexico is not well equipped for people with disabilities, but it is improving all the time and, especially at the top end of the market, it shouldn't be too difficult to find accommodation and tour operators who can cater for your particular needs.

If you stick to beach resorts – Cancún and Acapulco in particular – and upmarket tourist hotels, you should certainly be able to find places that are wheelchair-friendly and used to having disabled guests. US chains are very good for this, with Choice, Days Inn, Holiday Inn, Leading Hotels of the World, Marriott, Radisson, Ramada, Sheraton and Westin claiming to have the necessary facilities for at least some disabilities in some of their hotels. The important thing is to check in advance with tour companies, hotels and airlines that they can accommodate you specifically.

You'll find that, unless you have your own transport, the best way to travel inside the country may prove to be by air, since trains and buses rarely cater for disabled people, and certainly not for wheelchairs. Travelling on a lower budget, or getting off the beaten track, you'll find few facilities. Ramps are few and far between, streets and pavements not in a very good state and people are no more likely to volunteer help than at home. Depending on your disability, you may want to find an able-bodied helper to accompany you.

## Electricity

Theoretically 110 volts AC, with simple two-flat-pin rectangular plugs – most North American appliances can be used as they are. Travellers from the UK, Ireland, Australasia, South Africa and Europe should bring along a converter and a plug adapter. Cuts in service and fluctuations in current do occur, and in cheap hotels any sort of appliance that draws a lot of current may blow all the fuses as soon as it's turned on.

## Entry requirements

Citizens of the US, Canada, the UK, Ireland, Australia, New Zealand and some Western European countries do not need **visas** to enter Mexico as tourists for less than 180 days. Other Europeans can stay for ninety days. Non-US citizens travelling via the US, however, may need a US visa (see opposite). Visitors entering by land are subject to a US$18.50 **entry fee**, which will be included in your ticket if arriving by air.

Visas, obtainable only through a consulate (in person or by mail), are required by nationals of South Africa and most non-industrialized countries, as well as by anyone entering Mexico to work, to study or for stays longer than six months. Business visitors need a Business Authorization Card available from consulates, and usually a visa too. Anyone under the age of 18 needs written consent from their parents if not accompanied by both of them (if accompanied by one, they need written consent from the other).

All visitors, regardless of nationality, need a valid **passport** and a **tourist card** (or FMT – *folleto de migración turística*). Tourist cards are free, and if you're flying direct, you should get one on the plane, or from the airline before leaving. A good travel agent should be able to arrange one for you, too. Otherwise, they're issued by Mexican consulates, in person or by post. Every major US city and most border towns have a Mexican consulate; tourist cards and vehicle import forms are also available from all AAA offices in California, Arizona, New Mexico and Texas. Finally, failing all these options, you should be able to get tourist cards at airports or border crossings on arrival. However, if they've run out, you'll have to twiddle your thumbs until the next batch comes in, and if your passport is not issued by a rich Western country, you may encounter difficulty in persuading border officials to give you a card at all; it's therefore preferable to get one in advance. Entering from Belize or Guatemala, it's not at all uncommon for border posts to run out of tourist cards, or for officials to (illegally) demand a fee for issuing them.

Most people officially need a passport to pick up their tourist card, but for US and Canadian citizens all that's required is proof of citizenship (an original birth certificate or notarized copy, for instance, or naturalization papers), along with some form of photo ID (such as a driver's licence).

A tourist card is valid for a single entry only, so if you intend to enter and leave Mexico more than once you should pick up two or three. On the card, you are asked how long you intend to stay. You should always apply for longer than you need, since getting an extension is a frustrating and time-consuming business. You don't always get the time you've asked for in any case: in particular, at Mexico's borders with Belize and Guatemala, you will probably only get thirty days (though they may give you more if you specifically ask), and entering via Chiapas state means you're likely only to get fifteen days (extensions unlikely). You may also be asked to show bank statements or other proof of sufficient funds for your stay, especially if you are not from a rich country.

A tourist card isn't strictly necessary for anyone who only intends to visit the northern border towns and stay less than three days (though you still need a passport or photo ID). In fact, the twenty-kilometre strip adjoining the US border is a duty-free area into which you can come and go more or less as you please; heading further south beyond this zone, however, there are checkpoints on every road, and you'll be sent back if you haven't brought the necessary documents and been through customs and immigration.

Don't lose the tourist card stub that is given back to you after immigration inspection. You are legally required to carry it at all times, and if you have to show your papers, it's more important than your passport. It also has to be handed in on leaving the country – without it, you may encounter hassle and delay.

Should you lose your tourist card, or need to have it renewed, head for the nearest **immigration department office** (Departamento de Migración); there are branches in the biggest cities. In the case of renewal, it's far simpler to cross the border for a day and get a new card on re-entry than to apply for an extension; if you do apply to the immigration department, it's wise to do so a couple of weeks in advance, though you may be told to come back nearer the actual expiration date. Whatever else you may be told, branches of SECTUR (the tourist office) cannot renew expired tourist cards or replace lost ones – they will only make sympathetic noises and direct you to the nearest immigration office.

## US visas

Non-US citizens travelling through the US on the way to or from Mexico, or stopping over there, may need a US visa. If there's even a possibility you might stop in the US, unless you are Canadian or from a country on the US visa waiver scheme (this includes Britain, Ireland, Australia, New Zealand, Singapore, the Netherlands, Denmark, Sweden, Norway and Germany), obtaining a visa in advance is a sensible precaution. You can expect to wait in line wherever you apply in person, but you can always apply by mail instead, provided you allow enough time (usually four weeks). For those countries on the visa waiver scheme, the plan only applies if you have a machine-readable passport; also, if your passport was issued after October 26, 2006, it must also have an integrated information chip (further details can be found on line at ⓦtravel.state.gov/visa/temp/without/without_1990.html). If your passport meets these conditions, you can use a visa waiver form available from travel agencies, the airline during check-in or on the plane; it must be presented to immigration on arrival. Be sure to return the part stapled into your passport when you leave the US: if it isn't returned within the visa expiry time, computer records automatically log you as an illegal alien. If re-entering the US by land from Mexico, you will need to have a form with you in order to be exempt from visa requirements, so make sure you get one in advance. Getting a US visa in Mexico will be a nightmare of waiting in line and frustration.

Many US airports do not have transit lounges, so even if you are on a through flight you may have to go through US immigration and customs. This can easily take two hours, so bear the delay in mind if you have an onward flight to catch.

## Mexican consulates and embassies abroad

The following all issue visas and tourist cards. To find the address of an embassy or consulate not listed here, see under "Representaciones" at Ⓦwww.sre.gob.mx.

### Australia

14 Perth Ave, Yarralumla, Canberra, ACT 2600 Ⓣ02/6273 3963, Ⓦwww.mexico.org.au.

### Belize

Corner of Wilson St and Newtown Barracks, Belize City Ⓣ223 0193, Ⓦwww.sre.gob.mx/belice; Santa Rita Hill, Corozal Ⓣ422 2049, Ⓔjjelectric@btl.net.

### Canada

45 O'Connor St, Suite 1500, Ottawa, ON K1P 1A4 Ⓣ1-613/233-8988, Ⓦwww.embamexcan.com; 2055 Peel, Suite 1000, Montréal, PQ H3A 1V4 Ⓣ1-514/288-2502, Ⓦwww.consulmex.qc.ca; 199 Bay St, Suite 4440, Commerce Court W, Toronto, ON M5L 1E9 Ⓣ1-416/368-2875, Ⓦwww.consulmex.com; 710–1177 W Hastings St, Vancouver, BC V6E 2K3 Ⓣ1-604/684-3547, Ⓦwww.consulmexvan.com.

### Cuba

Ave 7ma, no.1206 e/12 & 14, Reparto Miramar, Municipio Playa, Havana Ⓣ7/204 5446, Ⓔconsulmex@mexico.tdc.cu.

### Guatemala

2ª Avenida 7-57, Zona 10, Apartado Postal 1009 "A", Guatemala City Ⓣ2420 3433, Ⓦwww.sre.gob.mx/guatemala; 21 Av 8–64, Zona 3, Quetzaltenango Ⓣ7767 5542 to 4, Ⓔmexicoq@yahoo.com.mx.

### Ireland

43 Ailesbury Rd, Ballsbridge, Dublin 4 Ⓣ01/260 0699, Ⓦwww.sre.gob.mx/irlanda.

### New Zealand

111–115 Customhouse Quay, 8th floor, Wellington Ⓣ04/472 0555, Ⓔmexico@xtra.co.nz

### South Africa

1 Hatfield Square, 1101 Burnett St, Hatfield, PO Box 9077, Pretoria 0001 Ⓣ012/362 1380, Ⓔembamexza@mweb.co.za.

### UK

8 Halkin St, London SW1X 7DW Ⓣ020/7235 6393, Ⓦwww.mexicanconsulate.org.uk.

### US

2827 16th St NW, Washington, DC 20009–4260 Ⓣ1-202/728-1600, Ⓦwww.sre.gob.mx/eua; and in nearly 50 other US towns and cities, among them those in the border states listed below:

**Arizona** 1201 F Ave, Douglas, AZ 85607 Ⓣ1-520/364-3107, Ⓦwww.consulmexdouglas.com; 571 N Grand Ave, Nogales, AZ 85621 Ⓣ1-602/287-2521 or 3386, Ⓦportal.sre.gob.mx/nogales.

**California** 408 Heber Ave, Calexico, CA 92231 Ⓣ1-760/357-3863, Ⓦwww.sre.gob.mx/calexico; 1549 India St, San Diego, CA 92101 Ⓣ1-619/231-8414, Ⓦportal.sre.gob.mx/sandiego.

**Texas** 301 Mexico Blvd, Suite F-2, Brownsville, TX 78520 Ⓣ1-956/542-2051, Ⓦwww.sre.gob.mx/brownsville; 2398 Spur 239, Del Rio, TX 78840 Ⓣ1-830/775-2352, Ⓔconsulmexdel.titular@wcsonline.net; 2252 E Garrison St, Eagle Pass, TX 78852 Ⓣ1-830/773-9255 or 6, Ⓔconsulmxeag@sbcglobal.net; 910 E San Antonio Ave, El Paso, TX 79901 Ⓣ1-915/533-8555, Ⓦwww.sre.gob.mx/elpaso; 1612 Farragut St, Laredo, TX 78040 Ⓣ1-956/723-6369, Ⓦwww.sre.gob.mx/laredo; 600 S Broadway St, McAllen, TX 78501 Ⓣ1-956/686-0243, Ⓦwww.sre.gob.mx/mcallen; 127 Navarro St, San Antonio, TX 78205 Ⓣ210/227-1817, Ⓦwww.consulmexsat.org.

## Customs

Duty-free allowances into Mexico are three bottles of liquor (including wine), plus four hundred cigarettes or fifty cigars or 250g of tobacco, plus twelve rolls of camera film or camcorder tape. The monetary limit for duty-free goods is US$300. Returning home, note that it is illegal to take antiquities out of the country, and penalties are serious.

# Insurance

There are no reciprocal health arrangements between Mexico and any other country, so travel **insurance** is essential. Credit cards (particularly American Express) often have certain levels of medical or other insurance included, and travel insurance may also be included if you use a major credit card to pay for your trip. Some package tours, too, may include insurance.

Before paying for a new policy, it's worth checking whether you are already covered: some all-risks home insurance policies may cover your possessions when overseas, and many private medical schemes include cover when abroad. In Canada, provincial health plans usually provide partial cover for medical mishaps overseas, while holders of official student/teacher/youth cards in Canada and the US are entitled to meagre accident coverage and hospital inpatient benefits. Students will often find that their student health coverage extends during the vacations and for one term beyond the date of last enrollment.

After exhausting the possibilities above, you might want to contact a specialist travel insurance company, or consider the travel insurance deal offered by Rough Guides (see below). A typical travel insurance policy usually provides cover for the loss of baggage, tickets and – up to a certain limit – cash or cheques, as well as cancellation or curtailment of your journey. Most of them exclude so-called dangerous sports unless an extra premium is paid: in Mexico this can mean scuba diving, whitewater rafting, windsurfing and trekking, though probably not kayaking or jeep safaris. Many policies can be chopped and changed to exclude coverage you don't need – for example, sickness and accident benefits can often be excluded or included at will. If you do take medical coverage, ascertain whether benefits will be paid as treatment proceeds or only after a return home, and whether there is a 24-hour medical emergency number. When securing baggage cover, make sure that the per-article limit – typically under US$1000/£500 – will cover your most valuable possession. If you need to make a claim, you should keep receipts for medicines and medical treatment, and in the event you have anything stolen, you must make an official statement to the police and obtain a copy of the declaration (*copia de la declaración*) for your insurance company.

Rough Guides has teamed up with Columbus Direct to offer you **travel insurance** that can be tailored to suit your needs. Products include a low-cost **backpacker** option for long stays, a **short break** option for city getaways, a typical **holiday package** option and others. There are also annual **multi-trip** policies for those who travel regularly. Different sports and activities (trekking, skiing, etc) can be usually be covered if required.

See our website (Ⓦwww.roughguidesinsurance.com) for eligibility and purchasing options. Alternatively, UK residents should call Ⓣ0870/033 9988, Australians should call Ⓣ1300/669 999 and New Zealanders should call Ⓣ0800/55 9911. All other nationalities should call Ⓣ+44-870/890 2843.

## Internet

**Internet** cafés are easy to find in all the larger cities and resort destinations, and the level of service is usually excellent, although servers tend to crash with some degree of frequency. In smaller towns and villages, such facilities are still rare. Depending on where you are, Internet access can cost anything from M$5 to M$25 an hour. Major tourist resorts can be the most expensive places, and in these areas it's best to look for cheaper Internet cafés around the town centre and avoid those in the luxury hotel zones. Internet facilities in large cities are usually open from early morning until late at night, but in smaller towns they have shorter opening hours and may close altogether at weekends. Most home **email** accounts can be accessed from computers in Mexican cybercafés: if you don't already know how to do this, ask your service provider, or alternatively set up a free web-based account with Hotmail (Ⓦwww.hotmail.com) or Yahoo! (Ⓦwww.yahoo.com), which you can access from anywhere with an Internet connection.

## Laundry

*Lavanderías* (**laundromats**) are ubiquitous in Mexico, as the majority of households don't own a washing machine. Most *lavanderías* charge by the kilo, and for a few dollars you'll get your clothes back clean, pressed and perfectly folded, in less than 24 hours. Many hotels also offer laundry services that, although convenient, tend to charge by the item, adding up to a considerably greater cost.

## Living and working in Mexico

There's virtually no chance of finding temporary **work** in Mexico unless you have some very specialized skill and have arranged the position beforehand, and work **permits** are almost impossible to obtain. The few foreigners who manage to find work do so mostly in language schools. It may be possible, though not legal, to earn money as a private English tutor by simply advertising in a local newspaper or on notice boards at a university.

The best way to extend your time in Mexico is on a **study programme** or **volunteer project**. A US organization called AmeriSpan selects language schools throughout Latin America, including Mexico, to match the needs and requirements of students, and provides advice and support. For further information, call (from the US or Canada) ⓣ1-800/879-6640 or 215/751-1100, or see ⓦwww.amerispan.com.

Volunteers need to apply for a voluntary work visa (FM3), for which you will need to present a letter of invitation from the organization for whom you are volunteering.

### Study and work programmes

**AFS Intercultural Programs** US ⓣ1-800/AFS-INFO, Canada ⓣ1-800/361-7248 or 514-288-3282, UK ⓣ0113/242 6136, Australia ⓣ1300/131 736 or ⓣ02/9215 0077, NZ ⓣ0800/600 300 or 04/494 6020, SA ⓣ11/447 2673, international enquiries ⓣ1-212-807-8686, ⓦwww.afs.org. Intercultural exchange organization with programmes in over 50 countries, including Mexico.

**American Friends Service Committee** US ⓣ215/241-7295, ⓦwww.afsc.org. Summer volunteer work camps in Mexican villages for 18–26-year-olds. Spanish language skills required.

**Council on International Educational Exchange (CIEE)** US ⓣ1-800/40-STUDY or ⓣ1-207-533-7600, UK ⓣ020/8939 9057, ⓦwww.ciee.org. Leading NGO offering study programmes and volunteer projects around the world including Mexico.

**Earthwatch Institute** US ⓣ1-800/776-0188 or 978-461-0081, UK ⓣ01865/318 838, Australia ⓣ03/9682 6828, ⓦwww.earthwatch.org. Matches volunteers with scientists working on particular projects; recent programmes in Mexico have included restoring mango groves in Jalisco and searching for fossils in Guanajuato. It's not cheap: volunteers must raise US$1000–4000 (average about US$2000) for each one- to two-week stint as a contribution to the cost of research.

**Studyabroad.com** US ⓣ610/499-9200, ⓦwww.studyabroad.com. Language programmes, semester-long and year-long courses and internships.

**World Learning** US ⓣ1-800/257-7751 or 802/257-7751, ⓦwww.worldlearning.org. Its School for International Training (ⓣ1-800/336-1616, ⓦwww.sit.edu) runs accredited college semesters in Oaxaca, comprising language and cultural studies, homestay and other academic work.

## Mail

Mexican **postal services** (*correos*) are reasonably efficient. Airmail to the capital should arrive within a few days, but it may take a couple of weeks to get anywhere at all remote. **Post offices** (generally open Mon–Fri 9am–3pm, Sat 9am–1pm) usually offer a **poste restante/general delivery** service: letters should be addressed to Lista de Correos at the Correo Central (main post office) of any town; all mail that arrives for the Lista is put on a list updated daily and displayed in the post office, but is held for only two weeks. You may get around that by sending it to "Poste Restante" instead of "Lista de Correos" and having letter-writers put "Favor de retener hasta la llegada" (please hold until arrival) on the envelope; letters addressed thus will not appear on the Lista. Letters are often filed incorrectly, so you should have staff check under all your initials, preferably use only two names on the envelope (in Hispanic countries, the second of people's three names, or the third if they've four names, is the paternal surname and the most important, so if three names are used, your mail will probably be filed under the middle one) and capitalize and underline your surname. To collect, you will need your passport or some other official ID with a photograph. There is no fee.

**American Express** also operates an efficient mail collection service, and has a number of offices all over Mexico – most useful in Mexico City, where the address for the most central branch is: c/o American Express, Paseo de la Reforma 350, Planta Baja, Col Juárez, 06600 México DF. They keep letters for a month. If you don't carry their card or cheques, you have to pay a fee to collect your mail, although they don't always ask.

For personal mail, Mexican **addresses** begin with the street and house number. The number goes after the street name (Juárez 123 rather than 123 Juárez), and is followed if appropriate by the floor or apartment number (*planta baja* means ground floor). After that comes the *cólonia* (the immediate neighbourhood), then the town, then finally the zip code and the state (on one line in that order – in the case of Mexico City, "México DF" is the equivalent of the state).

Sending letters and cards home is also easy enough, if slow. Anything sent **abroad** by air should have an airmail (*por avión*) stamp on it or it is liable to go surface. Letters should take around a week to North America, two to Europe or Australasia, but can take much longer (postcards in particular are likely to be slow). Anything at all important should be taken to the post office and preferably registered rather than dropped in a mailbox, although the dedicated airmail boxes in resorts and big cities are supposed to be more reliable than ordinary ones. Postcards or letters up to 20g cost M$10.50 to the US and Canada, M$13 to the British Isles, Europe, South America or the Caribbean, M$14.50 to Australasia, Asia, Africa or the Pacific.

Sending **packages** out of the country is drowned in bureaucracy. Regulations about the thickness of brown paper wrapping and the amount of string used vary from state to state, but most importantly, any package must be checked by customs and have its paperwork stamped by at least three other departments, which may take a while. Take your package (unsealed) to any post office and they'll set you on your way. Many stores will send your purchases home for you, which is a great deal easier. Within the country, you can send a package by bus if there is someone to collect it at the other end.

**Telegram offices** (*telégrafos*) are frequently in the same building as the post office. The service is super-efficient, but international ones are very expensive, even if you use the cheaper overnight service. In most cases, you can get across a short message for less by phone or fax.

## Maps

Rough Guides, in conjunction with the World Mapping Project, produce a Mexico **map** on a scale of 1:2,250,000, with roads, contours and physical features all clearly shown, and printed on rip-proof, waterproof plastic. Obviously we recommend it. However, other reliable alternatives include those published by Collins (1:3,300,000), Geocenter (1:2,500,000) and Map Productions (1:3,300,000)

In Mexico itself, the best maps are those published by Patria, which cover each state individually, and by Guía Roji, who also publish a Mexican road atlas and a Mexico City street guide. Both makes of map are widely available – try branches of Sanborn's or large Pemex stations.

More detailed, large-scale maps – for hiking or climbing – are harder to come by. The most detailed, easily available area maps are produced by International Travel Map Productions, whose 1:1,000,000 Travellers' Reference Map series includes the peninsulas of Baja California and the Yucatán. INEGI, the Mexican government map-makers, also produce very good topographic maps on various scales. They have an office in every state capital and an outlet at Mexico City's airport. Unfortunately, stocks can run rather low, so don't count on being able to buy the ones that you want.

## Money

The Mexican **peso**, usually written $, is made up of 100 centavos (¢, like a US cent). Bills come in denominations of $20, $50, $100, $200 and $500, with coins of 10¢, 20¢, 50¢, $1, $2, $5 and $10. The use of the dollar symbol for the peso is occasionally confusing; the initials MN (*moneda nacional* or national coin) are occasionally used to indicate that it's Mexican, not American money that is being referred to. Prices in this book are generally quoted in Mexican pesos (M$). Note, however, that these will be affected by factors such as inflation and exchange rates. Check the Universal Currency Converter (ⓦwww.xe.com) for up-to-date rates. At the time of writing, one US dollar (US$) was worth approximately M$10.80, one pound sterling (£) approximately M$21.20 and one euro M$14.25.

Some tour operators and large hotels quote prices in US dollars, and accept payment in that currency.

### Carrying your money

The easiest way to access your money in Mexico is in the form of **plastic**, though it's a good idea to also have some back-up (cash or travellers' cheques). Using a Visa, MasterCard, Plus or Cirrus card, you can draw cash from **ATMs** in most towns and tourist resorts. By using these you get trade exchange rates, which are somewhat better than those charged by banks for changing cash, though your card issuer may well add a foreign transaction fee, and these can be quite high, often as much as five percent, so check with your issuer before leaving home. Local ATM providers may also charge a transaction fee, typically US$0.75. If you use a credit card rather than a debit card, note also that all cash advances and ATM withdrawals obtained are treated as loans, with interest accruing daily from the date of withdrawal.

It's wise to make sure your card is in good condition and, before you leave home, to check that the card and your personal identification number (**PIN**) will work overseas. Be aware that technical hitches at ATMs occasionally occur – though rare, it has been known for machines not to dispense cash but to debit your account anyway. Finally, take extra care when withdrawing money from ATMs, especially at night; it's best done with a friend beside you.

As far as other forms of money are concerned (the latter having the advantage that you can get them refunded if lost or stolen), the easiest kind of **foreign currency** to change in Mexico, obtaining the best rates, is **cash** US dollars. US dollar **travellers' cheques** come second. Canadian dollars and other major international currencies such as euros, pounds sterling (English notes, not Scottish or Northern Irish), Japanese yen and Swiss francs are a poor third, and you'll find it hard to change travellers' cheques in those currencies. Quetzales and Belize dollars are best got rid of before entering Mexico (otherwise, your best bet for changing them is with tourists heading the other way). It is a good idea to change other currencies into US dollars at home before coming to Mexico, since the difference in the exchange rate more than outweighs the amount you lose in changing your money twice. In some touristy places, such as Acapulco and Tijuana, US dollar bills are almost as easy to spend as pesos.

Although the **banks** have all been nationalized, each is run differently. The Banco Nacional de Mexico (known as Banamex) is probably the most efficient; Bancomer, almost as widespread, is also good, as is the smaller Banco del Atlántico. Banks are generally open Monday to Friday from 9.30am to 5pm, though often with shorter hours for **exchange**. The commission charged for currency exchange varies from bank to bank, while the exchange rate, in theory, is the same – fixed daily by the government. Generally, only larger branches of the big banks, plus some in tourist resorts, are prepared to change currencies other than dollars – and even then at worse rates than you would get for the dollar equivalent.

**Casas de cambio** (exchange offices) have varying exchange rates and commission charges; they also tend to have shorter queues, less bureaucratic procedures and more accommodating hours of operation than banks. The exchange rates are generally more favourable than at banks, but are always worth checking, especially if you're changing travellers' cheques. Occasionally, casas de cambio give rates for Canadian dollars, sterling and other currencies that are as good as those they give for US dollars, so again it's worth shopping around, especially if you intend to change a large sum.

If you're desperate, many hotels, shops and restaurants that are used to tourists are prepared to change dollars or accept them as payment, but rates will be very low. There isn't much of a black market in Mexico since exchange regulations are relatively loose, and it's not really worth bothering with unless it comes about through trustworthy personal contacts or you want to do someone a favour.

## Opening hours

It's almost impossible to generalize about **opening hours** in Mexico; even when times are posted at museums, tourist offices and shops, they're not always adhered to.

## Public holidays

The main **public holidays**, when virtually everything will be closed, are listed below. In addition, many places close on January 6 (Twelfth Night/Reyes).

| | |
|---|---|
| **Jan 1** | New Year's Day |
| **Feb 5** | Anniversary of the Constitution |
| **March 21** | Benito Juárez Day |
| **Late March/ early April** | Good Friday and Easter Sunday |
| **May 1** | Labour Day |
| **May 5** | Battle of Puebla |
| **Sept 1** | Presidential address to the nation |
| **Sept 16** | Independence Day |
| **Oct 12** | Día de la Raza/ Columbus Day |
| **Nov 1–2** | Day of the Dead |
| **Nov 20** | Anniversary of the Revolution |
| **Dec 12** | Virgin of Guadalupe |
| **Dec 24–26** | Christmas |

The **siesta** is still around, and many places will close for a couple of hours in the early afternoon, usually from 1pm to 3pm. The strictness of this is very much dependent on the climate; where it's hot – especially on the Gulf Coast and in the Yucatán – everything may close for up to four hours in the middle of the day, and then reopen until 8pm or 9pm. In central Mexico, the industrial north and highland areas, hours are more like the standard nine-to-five, and shops do not close for lunch.

More specifically, shops tend to keep fairly long hours, say from 9am to 8pm. Post offices are open Monday to Friday from 9am to 3pm and Saturday from 9am to 1pm, and the central post office in a large town will usually be open until 6pm weekdays. Banks are generally open Monday to Friday from 9.30am to 5pm.

Museums and galleries tend to open from about 9am or 10am to 5pm or 6pm. Many have reduced entry fees – or are free – on Sunday, and most are closed on Monday. Some museums may close for lunch, but archeological sites are open right through the day.

### Phones

Local **phone** calls in Mexico are cheap, and some hotels will let you call locally for free. Coin-operated **public phones** exist but internal long-distance calls are best made with a **phonecard** (sold at newsstands and usable in public phones on almost every street corner). Slightly more expensive, but less for international calls, are *casetas de teléfono*, phone offices now only found at bus stations and airports. Calling abroad with a phonecard or from a *caseta* is expensive. Some Internet offices offer **VOIP international calls**, which are much cheaper (typically M$2 a minute to the US or Canada, M$3 to the rest of the world), but the line will not be as good.

It is also possible to call **collect** (*por cobrar*). In theory, you should be able to make an international collect call from any public phone, by dialling the international operator (Ⓣ090). If you have a calling card from your home phone company, you can also use the person-to-person direct-dial numbers listed in the box below.

Calling Mexico from abroad, the **country code** is Ⓣ52. Mexican **numbers** consist of an area code (usually three digits, though Mexico City's, for example, is just Ⓣ55), followed by a number, usually seven digits, (though Mexico City's, for example, are eight digits). If dialling from abroad, you dial the area code immediately after the Ⓣ52 for Mexico. If dialling long-distance within Mexico, or from a mobile, you need to dial Ⓣ01, then the area code and the number. If dialling from a landline with the same area code, you omit it. The area code for toll-free numbers is Ⓣ800, always preceded by the Ⓣ01.

If you want to use your **mobile phone** in Mexico, you'll need to check with your phone provider whether it will work there, and how the calls are charged. Foreign mobile phones are unlikely to work in most of Mexico, even though there are several GSM providers, including Radiomovil (Telcel) and Pegaso Comunicaciones (Movistar). It is possible to

## Dialling codes

**Mexico long-distance** ⓣ01 + area code + number
**US and Canada** ⓣ001 + area code + number
**UK** ⓣ00 44 + area code (minus initial zero) + number
**Ireland** ⓣ00 353 + area code (minus initial zero) + number
**Australia** ⓣ00 61 + area code (minus initial zero) + number
**New Zealand** ⓣ00 64 + area code (minus initial zero) + number
**South Africa** ⓣ00 27 + area code (minus initial zero) + number

### Useful and emergency numbers

**National operator** ⓣ020
**International operator** ⓣ090
**Directory enquiries** ⓣ040
**Tourist information** ⓣ078
**Emergency** (general) ⓣ080
**Police** ⓣ060
**Fire** ⓣ068
**Ambulance** ⓣ065
**Green Angels** (tourist highway breakdown) ⓣ078

### Calling card numbers

**AT&T** ⓣ01-800/288-2872 or 001-800/462-4240
**BT** ⓣ01-800/123-0244
**Canada Direct** ⓣ01-800/123-0200 or 01-800/021-1994
**ekit** ⓣ 001-866/426-7530
**MCI** ⓣ001-800/674-7000
**Sprint** ⓣ001-800/877-8000

obtain a tri-band phone, which will cover local frequencies, but these can be pricey and generally, until GSM coverage is wider, it is better to rent a mobile while you are in the country. This is easy enough, costing around US$4.50–6 per day for a pay-as-you-go phone, with recharge cards widely available nationwide. For further information on using your mobile in Mexico, including a coverage map and list of overseas mobile phone companies with roaming agreements for Mexico, see ⓦwww.gsmworld.com/roaming/gsminfo/cou_mx.shtml.

## Photography

**Film** is manufactured in Mexico and, if you buy it from a chain store like Woolworth's or Sanborn's rather than at a tourist store, costs no more than at home (if you buy it elsewhere, be sure to check the date on the box, and be suspicious if you can't see it). Up to twelve rolls of film can be brought into Mexico, and spare batteries are also a wise precaution. Purchasing any sort of camera hardware, though, will be prohibitively expensive. Slide film is hard to come by, too.

## Senior travellers

Mexico is not a country that offers any special difficulties – or any special advantages – to **older travellers**, but the same considerations apply here as to anywhere else in the world. If choosing a package tour, consider one run by an organization such as Saga, Vantage or Elderhostel, which is specifically designed for over-50s.

Do remember that Mexico's high altitude, desert heat and tropical humidity can tire you out a lot faster than you might otherwise expect. As far as comfort is concerned, first-class buses are generally pretty pleasant, with plenty of legroom, though the videos (mostly Hollywood pap, or sometimes action movies) they show may not be entirely to your liking. Second-class buses can be rather more boneshaking, and you won't want to take them for too long a journey.

Most of the hotels we recommend in this book should more than meet your needs, and in general even relatively low-budget hotels are clean and comfortable. Remember that senior citizens are often entitled to **discounts**, especially when visiting tourist sights, but also on occasion for accommodation and transport, something which it's always worth asking about.

## Time

Four **time zones** exist in Mexico. Most of the country is on GMT–6 in winter, GMT–5 in summer (first Sunday in April till last Sunday in October), the same as US Central Time. Baja California Sur, Sinaloa, Nayarit and Chihuahua are on GMT–7 in winter, GMT–6 in summer (the same as US Mountain Time). Baja California is on GMT–8 in winter, GMT–7 in summer, the same as the US West Coast (Pacific Time); and finally, Sonora is on GMT–7 all year round, and does not observe daylight saving time.

## Toilets

Public toilets in Mexico can be quite filthy, and often there's no paper, although there may be someone selling it outside for a couple of pesos. Always carry some toilet paper with you: it's easy enough to buy in Mexico, but it's never there when you need it. Toilets are usually known as *baños* (literally bathrooms) or as *excusados* or *sanitarios*. The most common signs are "Damas" (Ladies) and "Caballeros" (Gentlemen), though you may find the more confusing "Señoras" (Women) and "Señores" (Men) or even symbols of the moon (women) and sun (men).

## Tourist information

The first place to head for **information**, and for free maps of the country and many towns, is the Mexican Government Ministry of Tourism (**Secretaría de Turismo**, abbreviated to **SECTUR**), which has offices throughout Mexico and abroad. It's always worth stocking up in advance with as many relevant brochures and plans as they'll let you have, since offices in Mexico are frequently closed or have run out.

Once you're in Mexico, you'll find tourist offices (sometimes called *turismos*) run by SECTUR, in addition to some run by state and municipal authorities; quite often there'll be two or three rival ones in the same town. It's quite impossible to generalize about the services offered: some are extremely friendly and helpful, with free information and leaflets by the cart-load; others are barely capable of answering the simplest enquiry. We have listed these in the relevant city and regional sections throughout the guide. You can also call SECTUR toll-free round the clock in Mexico at ⓣ078 or 01-800/903-9200, from the US or Canada on ⓣ1-800/44-MEXICO, or from the UK ⓣ00-800/1111-2266.

### Mexican tourist offices overseas

#### US

300 N Michigan Ave, 18th floor, Suite 1850, Chicago, IL 60601 ⓣ312/228-0517, ⓔchicago@visitmexico.com; 4507 San Jacinto, Suite 308, Houston, TX 77004 ⓣ713/772-2581, ⓔhouston@visitmexico.com; 1880 Century Park East, Suite 511, Los Angeles, CA 90067 ⓣ310/282-9112, ⓔlosangeles@visitmexico.com; 400 Madison Ave, Suite 11C, New York, NY 10017 ⓔnewyork@visitmexico.com; 5975 Sunset Drive, Suite 305, South Miami, FL 33143 ⓣ786/621-2909, ⓔmiami@visitmexico.com.

#### Canada

1 Place Ville Marie, Suite 1931, Montreal, PQ H3B 2C3 ⓣ450/871-1052, ⓔmontreal@visitmexico.com; 2 Bloor St W, Suite 1502, Toronto, ON M4W 3E2 ⓣ416/925-2753, ⓔtoronto@visitmexico.com; 999 W Hastings St, Suite 1110, Vancouver, BC V6C 2W2 ⓣ604/669-2845, ⓔvancouver@visitmexico.com.

#### UK

Wakefield House, 41 Trinity Square, London EC3N 4DT ⓣ020/7488 9392, ⓦwww.mexicotravel.co.uk.

### Government advisories

**US State Department** ⓦwww.travel.state.gov.
**Canadian Department of Foreign Affairs** ⓦwww.dfait-maeci.gc.ca.
**British Foreign & Commonwealth Office** ⓦwww.fco.gov.uk.
**Australian Department of Foreign Affairs** ⓦwww.dfat.gov.au, ⓦwww.smartraveller.gov.au.
**New Zealand Ministry of Foreign Affairs** ⓦwww.safetravel.govt.nz.

## Travelling with children

A minor under the age of 18 can enter the country with either their own passport or on the passport of a parent with whom they are travelling.

Travelling with younger kids is not uncommon – you will find that most Mexicans dote on children and they can often help to break the ice with strangers. The main problem, especially with small children, is their extra vulnerability. Even more than their parents, they need protecting from the sun, unsafe drinking water, heat and unfamiliar food. Chile peppers in particular may be a problem for kids who are not used to them. Remember too that diarrhoea can be dangerous for younger children: rehydration salts (see p.52) are vital if your child goes down with it. Make sure too, if possible, that your child is aware of the dangers of rabies and other animal-borne illnesses; keep children away from all animals and consider a rabies shot.

For touring, hiking or walking, child-carrier backpacks are ideal: they can weigh less than 2kg and start at around US$75/£50. If the child is small enough, a fold-up buggy is also well worth packing – especially if they will sleep in it while you have a meal or a drink.

One thing to be aware of, if you try to keep your children away from such things, is the level of on-screen violence typical of the movies shown on buses. You may wish to find seats away from the screen when travelling on long-distance bus journeys to avoid the level of gore that is likely to be shown.

# Guide

# Guide


1 Baja California and the Pacific Northwest ..................... 75–178

2 The north ..................... 179–238

3 The Bajío ..................... 239–324

4 Northern Jalisco and Michoacán ..................... 325–392

5 Mexico City and around ..................... 393–538

6 Acapulco and the Pacific beaches ..................... 539–592

7 Veracruz ..................... 593–632

8 Oaxaca ..................... 633–694

9 Chiapas and Tabasco ..................... 695–774

10 The Yucatán ..................... 775–880

# 1

# Baja California and the Pacific Northwest

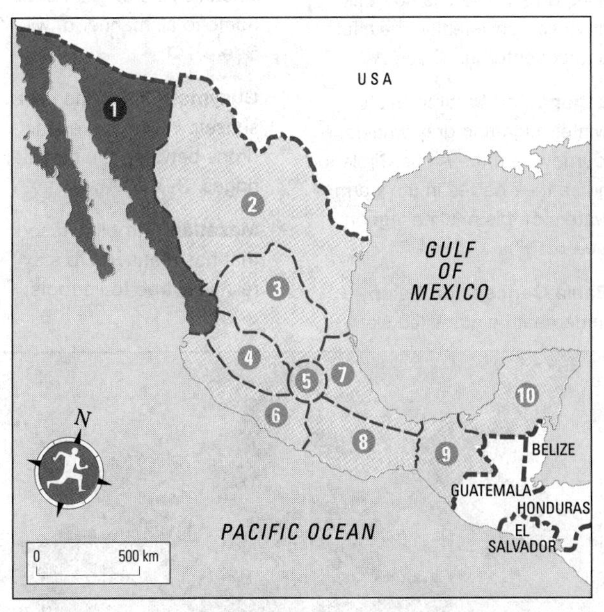

CHAPTER 1

# Highlights

* **Tijuana** No longer ruled by cheap souvenirs and sex tourism, TJ is on the cutting edge of cross-border culinary, musical and artistic innovation. See p.80
* **Valle de Guadalupe** Though still young, the wine industry here is rapidly maturing. See p.97
* **The Transpeninsular Highway** If you have the opportunity to travel the length of the peninsula, do so. There is no other drive so consistently beautiful and adventurous. See p.100
* **Laguna San Ignacio** Each winter migrating grey whales journey from the Arctic Circle to nurse their calves in the warm waters of this pristine lagoon. See p.107
* **Bahía Concepcíon** Camp underneath a star-filled sky and kayak alongside dolphins in these serene aquamarine waters. See p.111
* **La Paz** An amalgamation of the peninsula's best qualities: great restaurants, cheap rooms, vibrant street life and outdoor adventure opportunities aplenty. See p.115
* **Puerto Peñasco** Visit the massive Pinacate Biosphere Reserve, a fifty-kilometre-wide volcanic field of giant craters home to all manner of wildlife. See p.141
* **Guaymas** One of the best sunsets in Mexico, as the sun drops between the mountain ridges. See p.148
* **Mazatlán** A tropical resort that has managed to stay relatively true to its roots. See p.161

△ Marina, Guaymas

1

# Baja California and the Pacific Northwest

Mexico's **northwest** mainland is something of a bizarre – and initially uninviting – introduction to the country. Certain aspects of what you see here resonate as you travel south, yet in many ways it's atypical: at once fertile, wealthy and heavily Americanized, in parts it is also strikingly impoverished, drab and barren. The climate's not exactly welcoming, either – although the ocean and local conditions help produce one or two mild spots, summer temperatures can hit 50°C, while winter nights in the desert drop to freezing levels.

**Baja California**, on the other hand, is a destination in itself and only infrequently a part of trips to the rest of the country. Its plentiful devotees arrive in trucks and SUVs laden with outdoor gear, or in private boats and light planes that allow access to remote areas. Early in the year, visitors flock to the peninsula's west coast, near Guerrero Negro, to witness hordes of **whales** – participating in the longest-known mammal migration – congregating to calve. Further south, you'll find turquoise waters and white-sand beaches; most coastal towns in Baja California Sur offer fantastic opportunities for diving, fishing and kayaking, but **Loreto**, **La Paz** and the remote settlements on the **East Cape** are the standouts among them. All the way at the end of the peninsula, a booming resort industry in **Los Cabos** attracts crowds that fly in for week-long stays at self-contained hotels. It can be difficult to reach many of Baja's attractions – completely isolated beaches, prehistoric cave paintings, excellent fishing, snorkelling, surfing and windsurfing spots – without your own vehicle, but there is still plenty to see and do if you have to rely on public transport and stick to the more developed areas. Intra-peninsular **bus** lines connect Tijuana, Ensenada, La Paz and Los Cabos. There are also a number of **flights** that take advantage of deregulated airspace to link the major towns all the way down the coast.

Divided from Baja California by the Sea of Cortés, the **mainland** is an arid, sweltering expanse, particularly in the far north. Travellers who choose to enter Mexico here but bypass Baja California tend to stick rigidly to the highway – over 2000km of it from Tijuana to Tepic, where the main road finally leaves the coast to cut through the mountains to Guadalajara. On the whole, the best advice is to push through the northern part, at least, perhaps stopping at the shrimping port and burgeoning resort of **Puerto Peñasco**,

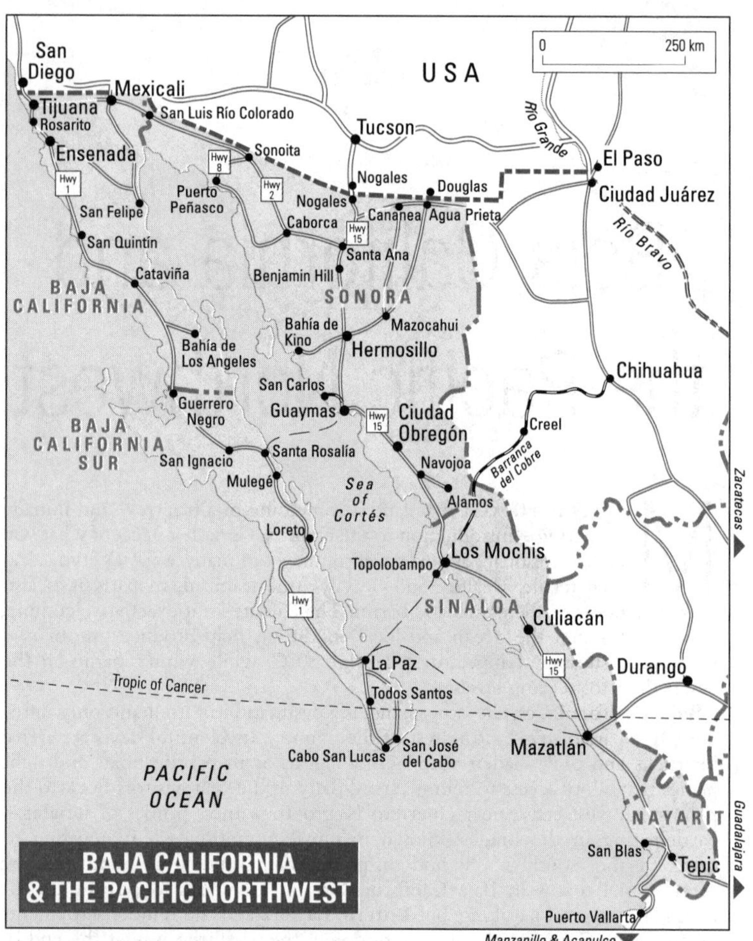




increasingly crowded with high-rise condominiums. You'll find quieter beaches as you head south, in **Bahía de Kino**, a quiet, largely residential settlement west of Sonora state capital **Hermosillo**, and in **San Carlos**, a small-scale resort with a golf course and swanky hotels close to the port of **Guaymas**. You might also consider heading inland, and visiting **Alamos**, once a silver-mining city and now a retreat for expats and artists, or **El Fuerte**, a colonial town rich in history. Continuing down the highway you'll pass through **Los Mochis**, the western terminus for the Copper Canyon railway (see p.188), and eventually cross the Tropic of Cancer, where there is a tangible change in the surrounding countryside – the land is greener and softer, the climate less harsh. Here you begin to come across places that can be regarded as destinations in their own right, including **Mazatlán** – part industrial port, part glossy resort – with its wealth of beaches, bars and fine seafood restaurants, and **San Blas**, a small, friendly town surrounded by steamy jungles and peaceful strips of sand.

If you're entering Mexico from the northwest with the intention of heading to the rest of the country, there's a straightforward choice of **routes**: down from Tijuana through the Baja California Peninsula and onwards by ferry from La Paz or Santa Rosalía; or around by the mainland road. While the mainland route is quicker if your only aim is to get to Mexico City, drivers should note that there have been numerous reports of assaults on motorists, especially between Los Mochis and Culiacán in Sinaloa. Not only is Baja's Hwy-1 safer, but the narrow strip of land that it traverses ranks as one of Mexico's most beautiful drives. It is worth noting, though, that you could be delayed for a day or two trying to get your car onto a ferry (see p.122) – book ahead if at all possible. If you're **driving** and planning to skip Baja California altogether, it's very much quicker to cross the border in **Nogales**, as Baja California entry points are quite busy. Even if you're coming from Mexico's west coast, you'll save considerable time by taking US highways via Tucson. You will, however, encounter numerous tolls, and over a long distance the costs can add up, but you always have the option of taking the free – *libre* – roads, which often parallel the toll roads. **Hitching** should be regarded here only as a last resort: beyond the normal dangers, the long-distance traffic moves fast and is reluctant to stop, and it's exceedingly hot and therefore dangerous if you get stranded by the roadside.

# The Baja California Peninsula

Seventeenth-century Spanish explorers first thought that the peninsula now called Baja California was an island. Even now, it maintains a palpable air of isolation from both the rest of Mexico and the other half of its original territory, just north of the border with the United States. Much of this remoteness can be attributed to geographical factors: the peninsula lies over 1300 kilometres west of Mexico City, and the sheer distances involved in traversing its length – it's over 1700 kilometres long – are not conducive to quick exploration. Though the Tijuana border crossing is the most trafficked port of entry in the world, a comparative few of the 130,000 who pass through the city each day venture further into Baja.

Outside of **Tijuana**, the peninsula is in many ways still in an embryonic stage. Its two states – Baja California in the north and Baja California Sur in the south – weren't designated until the second half of the twentieth century, and the **Transpeninsular Highway** – the first paved road connecting the north and south – wasn't completed until 1973. Development has proceeded in earnest since then, though it has largely been restricted to the areas that lie within easy reach of day-trippers from southern California and to Los Cabos, a prime destination for resort aficionados at the peninsula's southernmost point. Though the majority of visitors stick to the big towns in the north and the south, it's worth making a trip into the interior to see some of the peninsula's more interesting attributes – desert landscapes, lush oases and historic mountain treks.

## Driving distances

The **driving distances** below are for the major destinations or intersections along the Transpeninsular Highway and other primary paved roads. Times include necessary stops for petrol and army inspections.

| | | |
|---|---|---|
| **Tijuana to Mexicali** | 1hr 50min | (198km) |
| **Mexicali to San Felipe** | 2hr 15min | (195km) |
| **San Felipe to Ensenada** | 3hr 10min | (245km) |
| **Tijuana to Ensenada** | 55min | (109km) |
| **Ensenada to San Quintín** | 3hr | (190km) |
| **San Quintín to El Rosario** | 55min | (56km) |
| **El Rosario to Cataviña** | 1hr 50min | (123km) |
| **Cataviña to Parador Punta Prieta** | 1hr | (103km) |
| **Parador Punta Prieta to Bahía de los Angeles** | 45min | (69km) |
| **Parador Punta Prieta to Guerrero Negro** | 1hr 50min | (135km) |
| **Guerrero Negro to San Ignacio** | 1hr 30min | (146km) |
| **San Ignacio to Santa Rosalía** | 45min | (72km) |
| **Santa Rosalía to Mulegé** | 40min | (62km) |
| **Mulegé to Loreto** | 1hr 45min | (138km) |
| **Loreto to Ciudad Insurgentes** | 1hr 20min | (141km) |
| **Ciudad Insurgentes to La Paz** | 2hr 20min | (209km) |
| **La Paz to Todos Santos** | 45min | (77km) |
| **Todos Santos to Cabo San Lucas** | 55min | (77km) |
| **Cabo San Lucas to San José del Cabo** | 25min | (32km) |

# Tijuana

For a city that's not only northern Mexico's financial and cultural centre, but also one of the busiest tourist destinations in the world, **TIJUANA** doesn't try awfully hard to make a good initial impression. In many ways, the dust and dirt evident at first glance are a decent indication of its character. Decades of catering to its northern neighbour's vices and poor civic planning have taken their toll, and Tijuana's relative youth – it wasn't officially founded until 1889 – and prosperity are belied by cracked roads, endless graffiti and an air of indifference.

But if you can get past the grit and the tourist pandering near the border, you'll discover a place much smarter than it looks. Buoyed by the region's duty-free status and its legion of **maquiladora** assembly plants, Tijuana is among the wealthiest cities in the Mexican republic. This promise of available work has increased its population, and enterprising newcomers have breathed life into the city's restaurant industry, using cultural institutions like Centro Cultural Tijuana (CECUT) as a breeding ground for home-grown artistic and cultural movements. Downtown, beyond the areas where most tourists venture, the modern concrete and glass buildings wouldn't look out of place in southern California.

As gleaming and sophisticated as some parts are, though, to most travellers Tijuana will always be the definitive border town. Drinks and tchotchkes are readily available, and an almost round-the-clock trolley can take US visitors back home, sans sins, in under an hour. The main commercial drag, **Avenida Revolución**, or **La Revo**, caters exclusively to the hordes of day-trippers who make up the majority of the 40 million people passing through California's San Ysidro border crossing every year. La Revo and its surrounding streets brim with hundreds of tacky souvenir stands, cut-rate medical and dental offices, budget auto-repair shops and countless bars and restaurants. The prostitution and sex shows that made La Revo notorious throughout most of the last century have moved a few blocks to the north, although the tourist drag still has its share of insalubrious gentlemen's bars. And, as ever, Tijuana thrives on **gambling**. At the off-track-betting parlours throughout the city you can place money on just about anything that moves.

The fact that impressions of Tijuana are often formed solely along the well-worn track to and from La Revo is not entirely a result of a singular focus, however. Visitors on foot, who make up the vast majority of the tourist influx, often do get shaken down by both police and cabbies when they veer off Avenida Revolución – especially after drinking. Public transportation is confusing, and the city's fractured layout makes exploration daunting. That said, if you are able to break away, the payoff is hugely rewarding. A US$4 cab ride from the border can take you to any of the great nightclubs and restaurants around **Zona Río**, a tree-lined cultural and commercial district on the east side of town. Free of painted donkeys and other gimmicks, Zona Río offers the best glimpse of Tijuana's other life – one that has more in common with San Diego than the adult-themed carnival atmosphere of La Revo.

## Arrival and information

Entering Tijuana **by car** at either of the city's two border crossings – San Ysidro and Otay Mesa – is a simple affair that may not even require you to bring your car to a complete stop (see box, p.84). Once across the San Ysidro border, the road splits off into a series of right-hand exits to Playas de Tijuana and the scenic toll road; Calle 3a, which heads downtown; and Paseo de los Héroes into Zona Río. Streets are well marked – at times half a block in advance – and blue signs on lampposts identify the distance to prominent locations. A bit out of the way, Otay Mesa is typically used by drivers of passenger cars and RVs who don't mind driving a little further to avoid San Ysidro's long lines.

**Day-trippers** and **San Diego Trolley** passengers can park at Border Station Parking, 4570 Camino de la Plaza (US ⓣ619/428-6200; US$7) in San Ysidro and use the pedestrian route and walking bridge to reach downtown Tijuana.

Tijuana's long-distance bus station, **Central Camionera La Mesa** (ⓣ664/621-2982), is at Lázaro Cárdenas 15751, just north of Canal Alamar and the river and 8km east of the city centre. The smaller blue-and-white local bus marked "Centro" takes thirty minutes to the centre via Calle 2a (M$6). Mexicoach buses arrive at Terminal Turístico at Revolución at Calle 6 (ⓣ664/685-1470) and buses from Rosarito and Tecate drop you at the corner of Calle 1 and Madero. Buses from Ensenada and a small number of other cities in the peninsula's northwest arrive at Central de Autobuses de la Línea, adjacent to Plaza Viva Tijuana.

**Aeropuerto Internacional de Tijuana**, Camino al Aeropuerto, at Carretera Internacional (ⓣ664/683-2418 or 2118) 8km east of town, is simple for travellers to negotiate: there's only one terminal, and all services are contained in the kiosks that line its walls. Taxis to La Revo are about M$70. City buses (M$6) pick up passengers in front of the terminal; their destinations are posted near the door or written in soap on the front left-hand side of the windshield.

Of Tijuana's four very helpful **tourist offices**, two are right at the border – one for pedestrians (Mon–Thurs 9am–5pm, Fri & Sat 8am–5pm, Sun 8am–3pm; ⓣ664/683-4987) and the other for drivers (Mon–Thurs 8am–5pm, Fri & Sat 8am–7pm, Sun 8am–3pm; ⓣ664/683-1405); either is well worth a visit to pick

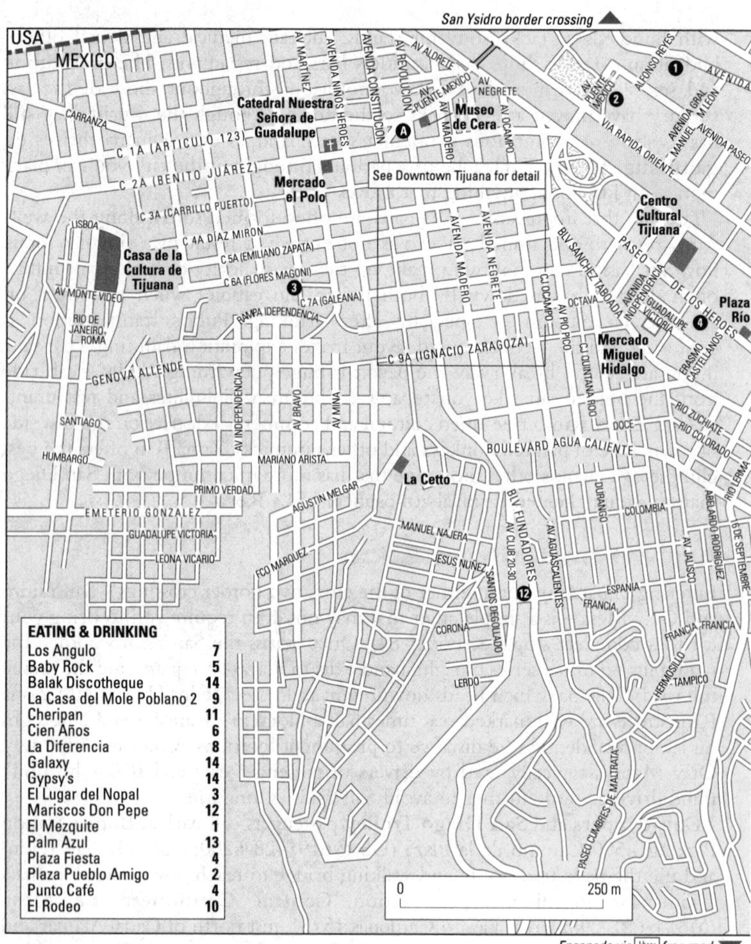


up a free map and some leaflets. The **main tourist office** is in the centre of downtown on Revolución between calles 3a and 4a (Mon–Thurs 10am–4pm, Fri–Sun 10am–7pm; ⓣ664/685-2210). There is also an outpost at the airport near luggage carousel E (daily 8am–3pm; ⓣ664/683-8244).

## Accommodation

Since a sizeable proportion of Tijuana's visitors leave before nightfall, the city offers fewer types of **accommodation** than one would expect. Many that do stay for any period linger only long enough to engage in vices or move quickly across the border, and there is no shortage of inexpensive options that cater to them. Therefore, a number of the low-end offerings should be avoided for safety reasons: none of the budget places along Calle 1a heading west from Revolución or north of Calle 1a (Zona Norte) is recommended – particularly not for lone women.

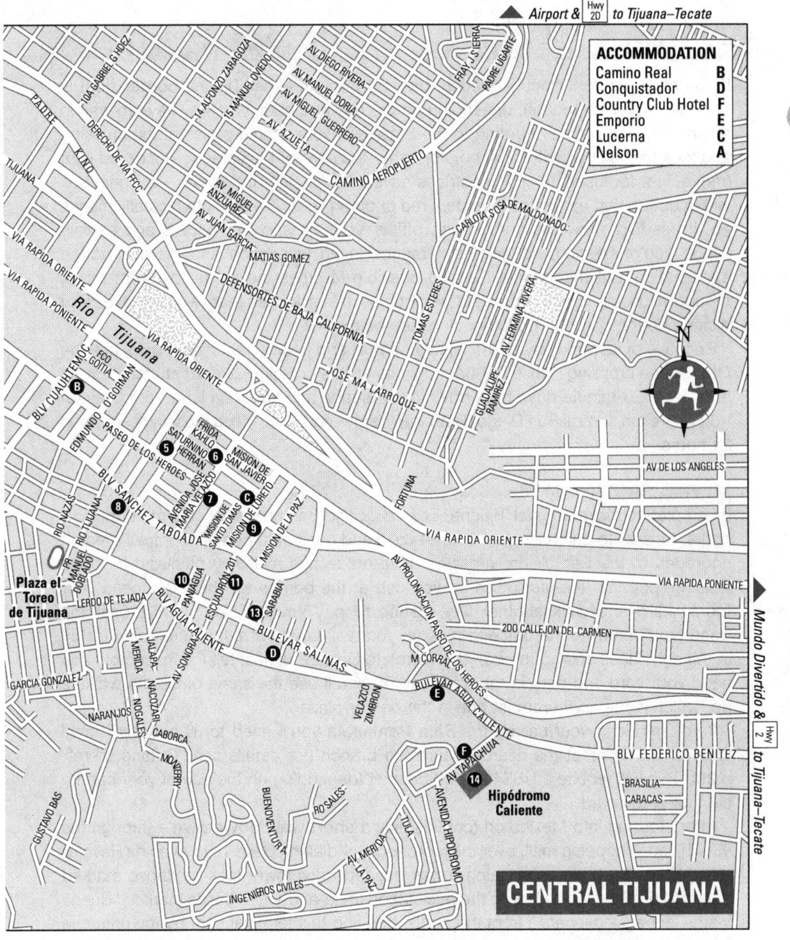


**Camino Real** Paseo de los Héroes 10305 ⓣ664/633-4000, ⓦwww.caminoreal.com/tijuana. The *Real*'s exterior walls are practically electric with colour, and the interior decoration – wood panelling and colours as bold as those outside – has more character than most chains. The 263 rooms are decked out with cable TV and bottled water. Live music and cocktails pull locals into the lobby bar, but there's also a tequila-centric cantina and a Mexican restaurant on site. ⑧

**Century Beach Resort** Km 25 Hwy-1D ⓣ664/631-3250, US ⓣ888/709-9985, ⓦwww.centurybeachresort.com. This resort, the first big one along the coastal route, is a Moorish-style gated community at the south end of Playas de Tijuana. Many of the hundred hotel rooms have private patios and views of the ocean. ⑥

**Conquistador** Agua Caliente 10750 ⓣ664/681-7955, ⓦwww.hotelconquistador-tij.com. The *Conquistador*'s two-storey white stucco building, red roof tiles, heavy wood furniture and tapestries may evoke a colonial era Tijuana never really had, but they give it character otherwise absent from the neighbourhood. Rooms open to the parking lot or the pool. ⑦

**Country Club Hotel** Agua Caliente and Tapachula 1 ⓣ664/681-7733, ⓦwww.bajainn.com. The best deal beyond the Zona Centro looks like its interiors were flash-frozen during the Rat Pack days and just recently thawed. Standard rooms are small yet

## Crossing the border at Tijuana

If you have the right documentation, passing through either Tijuana **border post** is normally a breeze, though, depending on the day and hour, you may have to wait in a very long line before returning to the States. Drivers should pause at the crossing and look to the adjacent signal box for either a green light (cleared to go) or red light (move right for inspection). Pedestrians have their version of this, too – a signal box with a button that generates a random red or green light. The red light typically means you'll need to show the immigration officer your passport or papers and explain where you're headed; sometimes it results in an inspection and more thorough examination, but this is rare. It's also possible to cross the border by shuttle bus, though it usually costs more and sometimes takes longer than walking over and picking up transport on the other side (see below).

Because of its proximity to the Tijuana airport and nearby factories, trucks use the **Otay Mesa** crossing. While US-bound waits at this crossing seldom stretch past an hour, it's a 25-minute drive from downtown Tijuana and about as long from Otay on I-805 to reach central San Diego. Both San Ysidro and Otay Mesa crossings are open 24 hours.

### Moving further into Mexico

If you plan to move on past Tijuana, Ensenada and San Felipe, or stay more than 72 hours, be sure to purchase your **tourist card** and get it stamped at *migración*; recent upgrades at the San Ysidro crossing have made this relatively painless. If you're walking, pop into the first office on your left at the border, tell them you need your tourist card and walk another fifty metres to pay your US$20 or M$210 at the Banamex. Return to the office to pick up your validated form. If you're driving, stay in the right lanes and go through the "Items to Declare" lanes, tell the inspectors you need your card and park in the adjacent lot. You'll use the same office the walkers do, which is the northernmost one in the border plaza.

If you're taking your car off the **Baja Peninsula** you'll need to fill out provisional importation forms at the nearby Banjercito branch (for details see "Getting there", p.29). This will require a US$400–800 deposit (depending on the age of your car) by cash or credit card.

After crossing into Mexico on foot, it's only a **short walk downtown** – through the Viva Tijuana shopping mall, over the footbridge, and along Calle 1a to Avenida Revolución. Alternatively you can catch a bus headed downtown (look for those marked "Centro" or "Revolución") or to the bus station (blue-and-white buses marked "Buena Vista/Central Camionera") from the public bus and taxi terminal right by the entrance to Viva Tijuana. There are also fixed-fare yellow taxis that stop between calles 2a and 3a on Madero and can take you to the Central Camionera for about M$50 after bargaining. Caliente's main off-track-betting parlour on Revolución offers a free van ride from the tourist information office, just next to the taxi stand. Mexicoach also operates a **shuttle service** between the border and Revolución, to Rosarito (M$50), Hipódromo's Plaza El Toreo (M$25) and the Bullring by the Sea (M$50).

appointed with TVs, desks and full baths, and – along with a good in-house restaurant and bar – look out onto the pool and golf course or across the street to the dog track. 6

**Emporio** Agua Caliente 11553 ⓣ664/622-6600, ⓦwww.hotelsemporio.com. This four-star stucco and glass hotel puts off vibes more akin to a resort than a business hotel. The 210 tastefully decorated rooms have the usual amenities you would expect from a hotel in this class, but the hip sushi bar and swank palm-lined pool and patio are a pleasant change of pace. 8

**Lafayette** Revolución 325 ⓣ664/685-3940. A spartan hotel well placed and well run, although street noise seeps in. Good prices for singles and better rates for groups that book blocks in advance. 4

**Lucerna** Paseo de los Héroes 10902 ⓣ664/633-3900, ⓦwww.hotel-lucerna.com.mx/tijuana/index.html. The six-storey main building and three annexes surround an outdoor pool with a mini waterfall. The best rooms, along with two restaurants and a bar, face this courtyard area. Every room has satellite TV, a balcony, coffee maker, a/c and purified water, as well as wireless Internet access for about M$120 per day. ⑦

**Nelson** Revolución 721 at C 1a ⓣ664/685-4302. Smack dab at the top of La Revo, this stucco palace can't be beat for location, but the street noise can be relentless at times. *Nelson* is one of La Revo's oldest hotels, so although the rooms have cable TV, they're otherwise quite dated and worn. ⑤

**Real del Mar** Km 19.5 Hwy-1D ⓣ664/631-3670, US ⓣ1-800/803-6038, ⓦwww.realdelmar.com.mx. An all-suite, resort-style hotel in Marriott's *Residence Inn* chain. The hotel looks down on the ocean from hills southwest of the city. Most of the guests who come here are looking for an out-of-town location for business meetings, aided by the excellent restaurant and the 18-hole, par 72 golf course. ⑧

**La Villa de Zaragoza** Madero 1480, at C 7 ⓣ664/685-1832, ⓦwww.hotellavilla.biz. This conveniently located US-style motel/hotel complex sits just to the east of the Jai Alai Frontón Palace. Choose from remodelled or older rooms, some with kitchenettes. A security guard watches over the parking lot. ⑥

## The City

If you're only in town to spend a few hours gawking at the city's historic tackiness, you need not wander far from the uninterrupted stream of bars, dance clubs, malls, markets and more or less permanent crowds on **Avenida Revolución** between calles 1a and 8a. When the frenetic activity and the lure of cheap souvenirs begin to pall, you'll do yourself a favour by heading east from La Revo to the **Zona Río**; the district's backbone, Paseo de los Héroes, is Tijuana's grandest boulevard and should be the first priority for visitors. Its tree-lined stretch contains the city's finest institutions, which frame a rich snapshot of Tijuana's non-tourist restaurant, shopping and nightlife scenes.

The prestigious **Centro Cultural Tijuana**, or CECUT, Paseo de los Héroes at Avenida Independencia (daily 10am–7pm; M$20; ⓣ664/687-9635, ⓦwww.cecut.gob.mx), opened in 1982 as the first – and last – in a proposed network

△ Centro Cultural Tijuana (CECUT)

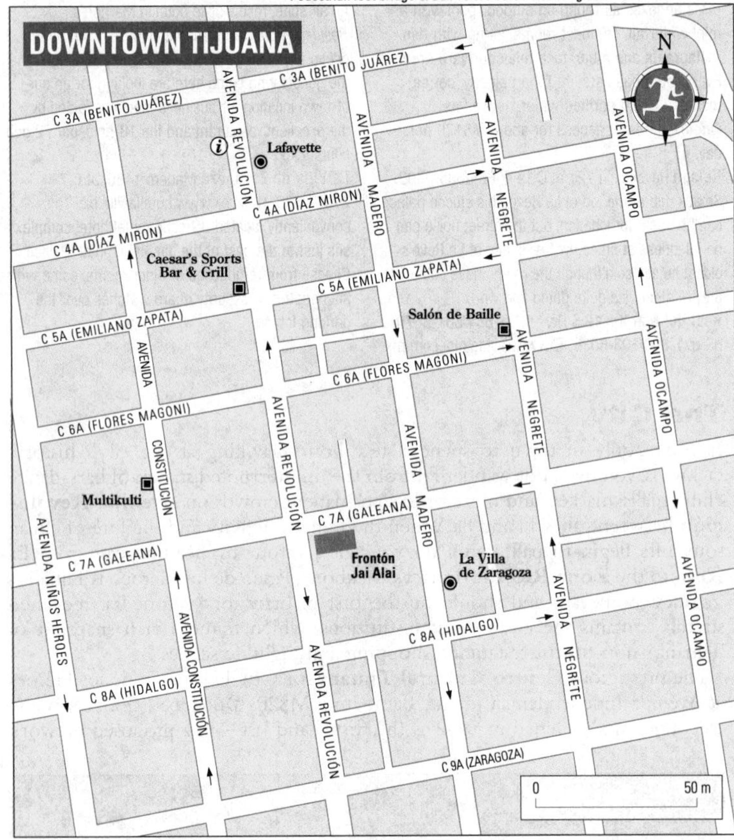


of regional cultural centres backed by the Mexican government. The centre is home to a major performance space, recital halls, a lobby for temporary visual art exhibits, an **Omnimax** movie theatre (the brown globe it is housed in gives the complex its nickname "La Bola"), an arts library, a garden, a bookshop and the **Museo de las Californias**. In addition to attracting performing groups, CECUT has ties with regional schools and universities and has its own drama school, the Centro de Artes Escénicas del Noroeste.

**Mercado Miguel Hidalgo**, Independencia at Guadalupe Victoria (daily 7am–7pm), is the city's largest outdoor market and the last real remnant of the zone's pre-spruced-up period. Early fears that it would be swept up in the demolitions that preceded the creation of Zona Río in the early 1960s were never realized, and the market has become one of the neighbourhood's most popular destinations. You can buy a little of everything at the colourful stalls that line its perimeter: produce, seafood, desserts, piñatas, toys and clothing are some of the more common goods on display. Some of the stalls double as restaurants, but if you can't find anything to your liking, there are a number of bakeries and fish taco joints along the nearby streets Guadalupe Victoria and Mina. The Mercado is within walking distance of the adjacent **Plaza del Zapato** (for cheap name-brand trainers) and the city's largest mall, the **Plaza Río**, Paseo de los Héroes 9698 (℗664/684-0402).

At Revolución's southern tip near Calle 11a, the avenue becomes Bulevar Agua Caliente as it makes a sharp turn east toward the bullring, and the racetrack that lends the Hipódromo neighborhood its name. **Hipódromo Caliente**, Tapachula 12027 (races Mon–Fri 7.45pm, Sat & Sun 2pm & 7.45pm; grandstand seating free, box seating M$110; ℗664/633-7300), was initially erected in 1929 for horse racing (Seabiscuit won the Caliente Handicap in 1938) and, in the smaller in-field track, dog racing. It now only features greyhound racing and off-track betting; horse races were eliminated in 1992 after a labour dispute, but in the departed jockeys' honour, track owner and current mayor Jorge Hank Rhon presents an annual race of greyhounds with costumed monkeys strapped atop their backs. If you want to watch the races from the racetrack's gentlemanly Turf Club bar (no phone; reserved ticket to races allows access, only open during race days), you must wear a jacket and be a man (or bring one along – women must be escorted). The city's other big draw is the nearby **Plaza El Toreo de Tijuana**, Avenida Santa María 221 (fights May–Oct Sun 4pm; box office ℗664/664-1510, Ⓦwww.bullfights.org), a prime site for outdoor concerts, rallies and other non-blood sport events, in addition to the seasonal bullfights. There's a box office open one hour before events, but you may also purchase tickets at a booth on Revolución and Calle 2a in front of the Hotel Lafayette or as part of package tours with Mexicoach at its office on the same street.

## Eating

The best by-product of Tijuana's population boom is its **vibrant restaurant scene**. Diners can sample regional specialities from throughout the country as well as indulge in successful Mexican variations on international cuisine. For the best meals, avoid **La Revo** almost entirely. **Zona Río** has the best selection of restaurants, with several sandwiched between Paseo de los Héroes and Sánchez Taboada. The options along Agua Caliente and Tapachula cater to the city's middle and upper classes.

**Los Angulo** Paseo de los Héroes 4449 ℗664/634-6027. The high palapa roof lends an element of grandeur to just about any type of outing. Dine on grilled, baked, stuffed or fried shrimps (M$100) and seafood dishes (M$70–120) with four hundred of your closest friends.

**Caesar's Sports Bar & Grill** Revolución 1071 ℗664/638-4562. Caesar Cardini first whipped up his eponymous salad here in 1924, and it is still prepared tableside with raw egg and garlic, Parmesan cheese, anchovies and hearts of Romaine lettuce (M$70) in an elaborate ceremony. The long, narrow space is predominantly a sports bar, albeit one that accents its many TVs with high ceilings, dark-wood wall panels and leather booths.

**La Casa del Mole Poblano 2** Paseo de los Héroes 10501 ℗664/634-6920. Dark chocolate and hot chiles flavour the Oaxacan sauce this restaurant uses to coat chicken legs and breasts (M$60) and other meat dishes. The lighting and decor are a pleasant surprise for a bargain spot, with waterfalls, plants and, on weekends, roving musicians.

**Cheripan** Escuadrón 201-3151 ℗664/622-9730, Ⓦwww.cheripan.com. Argentine grill famous for its succulent steaks (M$130), chops and extensive wine list, as well as the city's best chips, coated in parsley and garlic (M$30).

**Cien Años** José Maria Velazco 1407 ℗664/634-3039. This spot-of-the-moment has drawn notice for its use and adaptation of Aztec recipes. Gourmands swear by the corn fungus and marrow dishes (M$150–250); tamer items such as honey-roasted duck or chicken *mole* are available for the less intrepid.

**La Diferencia** Sánchez Taboada 10611-A ℗664/634-7078. Along with neighbour *Cien Años*, *Diferencia* has a more daring menu than most places in Tijuana, with satisfying takes on pre-Columbian meals. Unfamiliar dishes like beef-tongue strips with chiles, the Aztec delicacy crepes Cuitlacoche (an edible corn fungus) and cow-brain tacos (M$150–220) are made more appealing within a romantic setting complete with a courtyard and fountain.

**Gypsy's** Paseo del Centenario 9211, inside Plaza Pueblo Amigo ⓣ664/683-6006. This Spanish restaurant and bar is fronted by a mural of Salvador Dalí and opens onto a pedestrian mall. The tapas menu (M$20–50 per dish) is the perfect accompaniment to pitchers of sangria and well-made margaritas. Open late.

**Mariscos Don Pepe** Fundadores 688 ⓣ664/684-9086. Some would argue that the decor could use updating, but that might subtract from the inventive formula that helps Don Pepe churn out some of the most dependable, fresh and affordable seafood in town, including a ceviche starter that takes the place of the standard salsa and chips and jumbo shrimp wrapped in bacon.

**El Mezquite** Padre Kino 9970 ⓣ664/973-1242, ⓦrestaurantbarelmezquite.com. Large portions and its proximity to the border make this budget Mexican restaurant especially attractive to day-trippers. The menu (about M$80 per person) includes lamb, beef, fish and, on weekends, goat.

**Palm Azul** Salinas 11154 ⓣ664/6229773. If you missed or enjoyed the recreations in CECUT, you can dine surrounded by replicas of the peninsula's mysterious cave paintings, or on the large patio surrounding an open fireplace. Besides the atmosphere, the raw bar is the main draw, as are the daily seafood-centric specials like black sea bass (M$170–200). Closed Sun.

**El Rodeo** Salinas 1647 ⓣ664/686-5640. For a cowboy-themed restaurant, *Rodeo* has a lot in common with Korean barbecue. The signature parrilla grill (M$300 for two) is cooked tableside over charcoal and accompanied by a host of small plates that include pickled vegetables and cheese, beans, warm tortillas and potatoes.

## Nightlife

The rowdiest action in Tijuana is along **La Revo**, where numerous nightclubs pump out rock music and hip-hop for US visitors and the people who take advantage of them. Locals, visitors in the know and those who've outgrown beer bongs shun La Revo in favour of the clubs and bars clustered around the shopping areas of **Zona Río**, where the beats are louder, the clubs larger and the scene doesn't slow down until morning.

Discover smaller shows by picking up the free Spanish-language weekly *De Noche y De Día la Guía*, which covers current cinema, concerts and DJ events, as well as listings for clubs, cafés and restaurants. New editions can be found on Thursdays at most Café D'Volada outposts and other locations around town. The competing weekly *Bitácora* is available at many of the same places beginning Wednesdays as well as online at ⓦwww.bitacoracultural.com. Get tickets for bigger events through **Ticketmovil** (ⓣ664/681-7084; ⓦticketmovil.com.mx).

**Baby Rock** Diego Rivera 1482 ⓣ664/634-2404. The exterior and fake boulders say *Flintstones* but the inside is all lasers and techno beats. Cover starts around M$100; for an extra M$50 they'll park your car.

**Balak Discotheque** Oriente 9211, inside Plaza Pueblo Amigo ⓣ664/683-6244, ⓦwww.balak-disco.com. Tijuana's largest club doesn't skimp on anything, whether it's the sound system (it reportedly cost over US$1 million), its guests (Ricky Martin in his heyday) or the light system (blinding). The cover is typically a steep M$150–200 but free before 11pm.

**Galaxy** Oriente 9211, inside Plaza Pueblo Amigo. Dance club with regular appearances by respected touring DJs and local superstars like Nortec Collective.

**El Lugar del Nopal** Callejón 5 de Mayo 1328 ⓣ664/685-1264, ⓦwww.lugardelnopal.com. This café-cum-performance space is a gathering place for Tijuana's creative class, who turn up for exhibits, screenings and live music. Open Fri & Sat only.

**Multikulti** Constitución 13131 ⓔinfo@multikulti.org.mx. The gutted, open-air Bujazán Cinema now hosts small concerts, underground arts festivals and DJ events.

**Plaza Fiesta** Paseo de los Héroes 1001. Can't decide where to go? Locals often head here without a specific place in mind, preferring to wander between the bars and clubs until they find a scene that appeals to them. Standouts include *El Callejón* (ⓣ664/687-4953), *La Cantina* (ⓣ664/684-0705), *Monastario* (ⓣ664/634-1729) and *Sótano Suizo* (☎664/684-8834). Most spots are quiet before 11pm.

**Plaza Pueblo Amigo** Oriente 9211. Same idea as Plaza Fiesta, but with larger clubs. *Galaxy* and *Balak* (both above) get more attention, but *Paparazzi* (☎664/607-3441), *La Casa de la Trova* (☎664/638-4900) and the techno-meets-mechanical-bull-riding palace *Rodeo Santa Fe* (☎664/682-4967) are quite popular, too.

**Punto Café** Paseo de los Héroes 1001, inside Plaza Fiesta ☎664/634-1240. This trendy, low-key café with outside seating and magazines to flick through has an incredible range of coffees. A great staging ground for forays into Plaza Fiesta, *Punto* ditches the coffee-shop sheen around 11pm when the DJs begin playing house and lounge beats.

**Salón de Baile** C 6a, between Revolución and Madero. Don't be put off by the lurid paintings, this is the real thing: a traditional dance hall with an almost Caribbean feel, playing salsa, cumbia and *norteño*. Easy enough to spot – look for the big red star.

## Listings

**Airlines** Aeroméxico/Aerolitoral, Plaza Río ☎664/683-8444, 684-9268, ⓦwww.aeromexico.com; Aviacsa/Aeroexo, Plaza Guadalupe, Suite 6, Sánchez Taboada ☎664/622-5086 or 5024, ⓦwww.aviacsa.com; Mexicana, Diego Rivera 1511 ☎664/634-6545 or 6566 or 6593, ⓦwww.mexicana.com.mx (Mon–Fri 9am–6.45pm, Sat 9am–2pm); Aerolíneas Azteca, Paseo de los Héroes 10051 ☎664/633-9226, 634-7286, ⓦwww.aerolineasazteca.com (Mon–Fri 9am–7pm, Sat 9am–2pm).

**American Express** There's an office in Viajes Carrousel travel agency (Mon–Fri 9am–6pm, Sat 9am–noon) way out on Sánchez Taboada at Clemente Orozco, but their rates are poor.

**Banks and exchange** US dollars are accepted almost everywhere in Tijuana, but you do get a slightly better return on pesos. If you're visiting no further south than Ensenada there's really no reason to change your currency – you'll lose in the exchange rate whatever savings you'd get buying in shops. If you do change it's really no problem, with casas de cambio on virtually every corner. Most offer good rates – almost identical to those north of the border – though few of them accept travellers' cheques, and if they do, they charge a heavy commission. For cheques you're better off with a bank, most of which are on Constitución, a block over from Revolución. ATMs along both of these blocks dispense both dollars and pesos.

**Books** Sanborn's department store, at Revolución and C 8a, has books and magazines, some from across the border.

**Buses** There are constant departures with one company or another to destinations south down the peninsula along Hwy-1 from the Central Camionera. There are also multiple services a day to mainland cities, including Los Mochis, Mazatlán and Mexicali.

**Consulates** Australia/Canada, Germán Gedovius 10411-101 ☎664/684-0461; Germany, Cantera 400-305, Playas de Tijuana ☎664/680-2512; UK, Salinas 1500 ☎664/686-5320; US, Tapachula 96 ☎664/622-7400, ⓦwww.usembassy-mexico.gov/tijuana/Tijuana.htm.

**Hospital** Paseo de los Héroes 2507 ☎664/634-7002, 7001-3434.

**Internet access** The best Internet cafés are branches of SpaceBooth.com; one is at Revolución between C 2a and C 3a; the other at C 11a near Pio Pico. Both have good prices (M$20/hr) and serve coffee, drinks and snacks.

**Left luggage** Bags can be left at the Central Camionera (daily 6am–10.30pm), in lockers over the border in the Greyhound station (24hr) or next door at Pro-Pack (Mon–Sat 9am–6pm).

**Police** If you become a victim of crime, a rip-off or simply want to make a complaint, pick up any phone and dial ☎078.

**Post office** Negrete and C 11a (Mon–Fri 8am–4pm, Sat & Sun 9.30am–1pm), though to send international mail you're better off crossing the border.

**Telephones** The post office (see above) has long-distance phones, as does the Terminal Turístico, but you're better off crossing the border to make long-distance calls. Buy Telmex phonecards in any corner store to make local calls.

## Rosarito

If you want to escape the hectic pace and noise of Tijuana, head for **ROSARITO**, about 45 minutes' bus ride south on the old road to Ensenada. **Beaches** in Tijuana are invariably crowded and dirty, so Rosarito's longer and sandier beach is a good alternative and provides a more restful atmosphere during the week (and a better party scene on weekends). The hotels and condo developments that abut the beach are better value than those in the centre, making it worthwhile to stay out near the water. If at all possible, avoid visiting during March and April, when spring-breakers make the town difficult to bear for anyone who wishes to remain sober.



Until 1995 Rosarito was part of the city of Tijuana, but it became a municipality when local politicians realized that it was capable of generating its own tourism dollars. In the last ten years it has also become an attraction for movie aficionados who have come to see **Fox Studios Baja**, just south of town at Km 32.8 on the free highway to Ensenada. This bit of Hollywood-in-Mexico, originally created for the filming of *Titanic*, is now a massive full-time production facility that utilizes its seventeen-million-gallon ocean-front tank for water-based films (including *Pearl Harbor* and *Tomorrow Never Dies*). **Foxploration** tours are available every day but Monday and Tuesday (provided they are not filming). The *Titanic* model, created at 95 percent scale, has been disassembled, but much of the set is viewable in storage (Wed–Fri 9am–4.30pm, Sat & Sun 10am–5.30pm; M$90–120; ⓣ661/614-9444, US ⓣ866/369-2252, ⓦwww.foxploration.com).

## Practicalities

To **get to Rosarito** from Tijuana, **drive** south along either the toll or free road for 25km, or take a Mexicoach **bus** from the Terminal Turístico on La Revo. You can also take one of the *colectivo* taxis that leave from Madero between calles 4 and 5, or head for the old bus station at Madero and Calle 1, from where buses leave every hour or so; to **get back**, try flagging down a bus or *colectivo* on Juárez, Rosarito's main street.

The **main tourist office**, Km 28 Hwy-1, is a good twenty-minute walk from the centre (daily 9am–7pm; ⓣ661/612-5222). There is a smaller office (Mon–Fri 9am–noon & 2pm–5pm; ⓣ661/612-0200) inside a building shared with a hair salon on Hwy-1 2km south of the *Rosarito Beach Hotel*. Both offer brochures, maps and advice – the latter, though, is dependent on whether the friendly staff are on duty. The **convention** bureau has an office in the Centro Comercial Oceana Plaza on Juárez just across from *Señor Frog* (Mon–Thurs 10am–4pm, Fri & Sat 10am–7pm; ⓣ661/612-0396).

**Accommodation** prices are highest during spring break (March & April) and the week after Christmas, but drop considerably the rest of the year. Throughout the year it's advisable to reserve at least a week in advance if you plan on staying Friday or Saturday night. It's a short hike south of town, but the tiny rooms at the single-storey *Paraiso Ortiz*, Km 28 Hwy1 (ⓣ661/612-1020; ❹), in between *Rene's Sports Bar* and the southernmost tourist office, almost all have ocean views. Waterfront rooms and a restaurant/bar overlooking a native plant garden at *Pelicanos*, Cedros 115 (ⓣ661/612-5545, ⓦpelicanosrosarito.com; ❺), make up for rather lacklustre, frill-free rooms. The *Rosarito Beach Hotel*, Benito Juárez 31 (ⓣ661/612-0144, US ⓣ1-800/343-8582, ⓦwww.rosaritohtl.com; ❼), which gave the city its name, is now a mini-village with a spa, restaurants, bars, two pools, time-share apartments, a racquetball court, craft shops, liquor stores, a history museum and an Internet café. Many of the rooms have ocean views but are otherwise without charm; request an older room with garden view – they've managed to retain some character.

Along the single street behind the beach is a row of restaurants, cafés and bars, some of which are pretty good, in particular the **fish restaurants** and a couple of cafés that serve decent cappuccino and cakes. Party-goers flock to *Papas and Beer*, Coronado 100 (ⓣ664/612-0444, ⓦwww.papasandbeer.com), and nearby *Iggy's*, Coronado 11327 (ⓣ661/612-0537, ⓦwww.clubiggys.com), where

## Lobster town

Once not much more than a dusty roadside settlement between Rosarito and Ensenada at Km 42, **Puerto Nuevo** is nowadays known the length of the peninsula for its near-fanatical devotion to the local speciality that bears its name: Puerto Nuevo-style grilled Pacific lobster. Found off the coast and throughout the rest of the Pacific Rim, these lobsters don't grow as large as their Atlantic counterparts (actually, they're giant langoustines more closely related to shrimps) and they don't have claws, but they're just as delicious.

Choosing where to sample the revered dish is made easy enough by the town's one-way street plan, which juts to the west from Hwy-1. Though every one of the more than two dozen restaurants serves the lobsters the same basic way – grilled and split in half with beans, rice and warm flour tortillas – *Puerto Nuevo #2* (☎661/614-1454), directly to your south on the second block, and *Ortega's Patio* at the southwest corner of the grid (☎661/614-1320 or 0345) are consistently good bets. Expect to pay M$120 at the former and up to M$200 at the latter, which will also get you ocean views, low lighting and a wood-beam ceiling.

beach volleyball and knocking back as much Corona as possible are the order of the day.

If you're **continuing south** to Ensenada and beyond, you can pick up long-distance buses (at least hourly) at the autopista tollbooth 1km south of the tourist office, past the *Rosarito Beach Hotel*. The coast road down through Rosarito – now supplanted by the motorway to Ensenada – is an attractive drive, lined with seaside villas and condos.

# Ensenada and the road south

**ENSENADA**, just ninety minutes south of Tijuana by the toll road and sitting on Bahía de Todos Santos, is packed at weekends with both groups of partying southern Californians and crowds of cruise-ship passengers. Nevertheless, it remains far calmer, cheaper and smaller than Tijuana and is a good jumping-off spot for ecotourism destinations further south.

Spanish explorer Juan Rodríguez Cabrillo was the first European to pull into Ensenada's bay when he came ashore here in 1542. Failing to notice any inhabitants, he left four days later after naming the bay San Mateo. The next foreign visitor was Sebastián Vizcaíno, who arrived in 1602. He stayed long enough to rename the bay Ensenada de Todos Santos but, like his predecessor, didn't notice anyone on shore. The first Spaniard to stay for any length of time – at least long enough to notice the indigenous Kumai who fished regularly in the bay – was Franciscan Junípero Serra, who rode through in 1769 on his way from Loreto to San Diego.

By around 1870 Ensenada had developed into a supply point for missionaries working along the northern Mexican frontier. When gold reserves were discovered that year in nearby Real de Castillo, miners rushed in, but at the beginning of the twentieth century the mines closed and the population dwindled, leaving the town to revert to little more than a small fishing village. A renaissance came in the late 1930s with the rise of agriculture in the Mexicali Valley, and the port became a point of export for the produce. When the paved highway down from Tijuana opened some forty years later, American tourist dollars began to pour in. Today the city is a major port and fish-processing centre, as well as home to some industry, including one of Mexico's largest wineries.

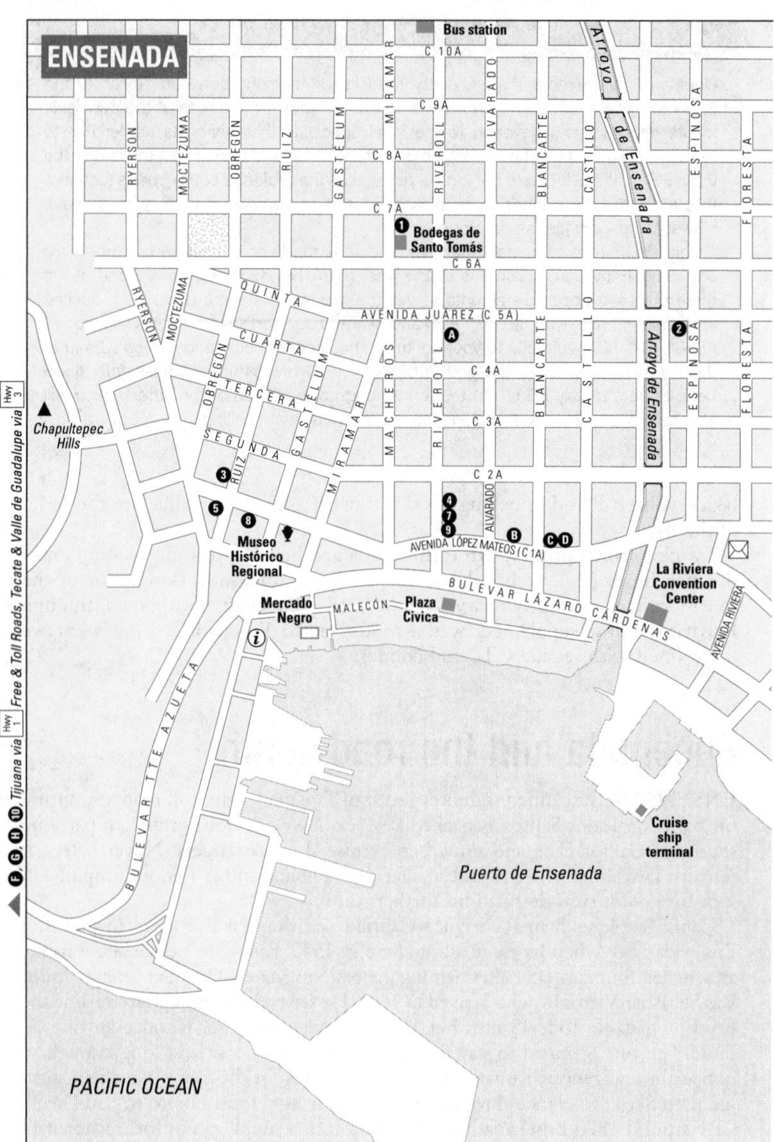


## Arrival and information

From the north, **arrival by car** is straightforward. Hwy-1, Hwy1D and Hwy-3 merge into one four-lane local road that, once downtown, becomes Bulevar Lázaro Cárdenas and runs along the waterfront. Entering town from the south is a bit messier. Hwy-1 approaches the city, becoming Avenida Reforma; to get downtown, turn left on Libramiento Sur.

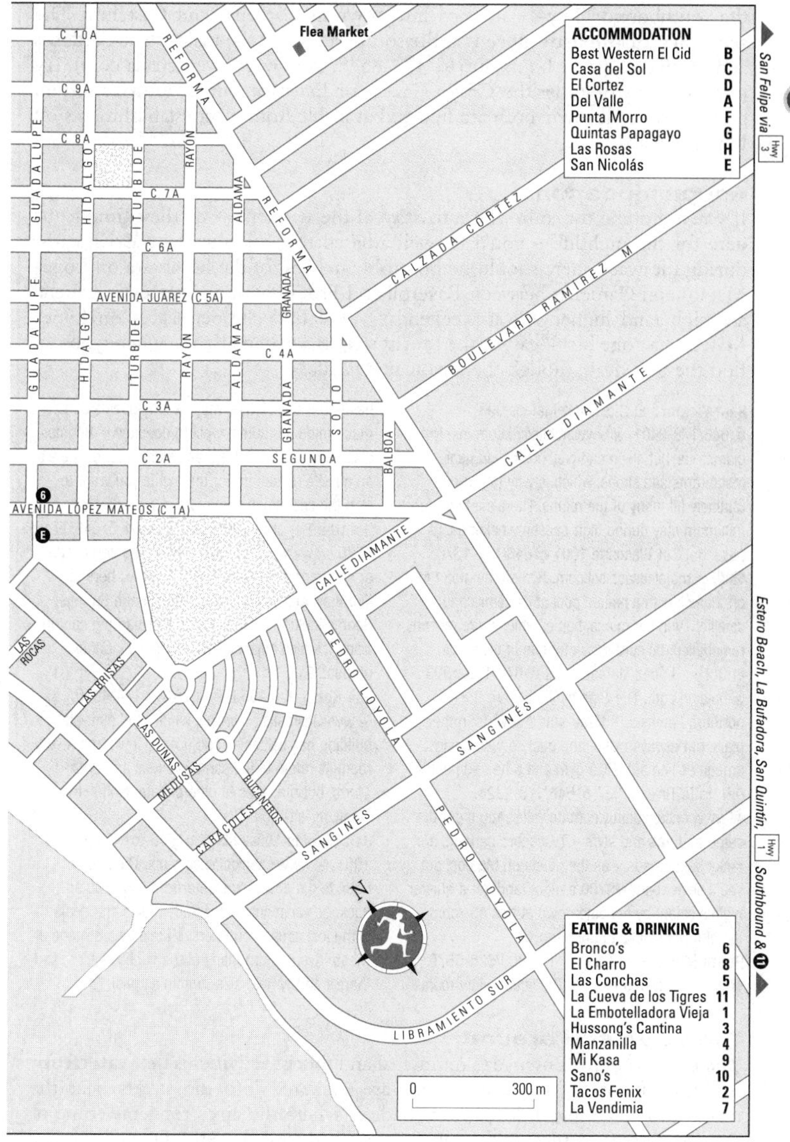


The long-distance **bus station** is at Calle 11a and Riveroll; to reach the bay, turn right out of the station and head down Riveroll. Buses from Tijuana arrive every two hours at a second, smaller station two blocks down on Riveroll between calles 8a and 9a.

The very helpful **visitor centre** (Mon & Tues 9am–5pm, Wed–Fri 9am–7pm, Sat & Sun 9am–5pm; ⓣ646/178-2411, ⓦwww.ensenada-tourism.com) is at the southbound Hwy-1 entrance into town at Cárdenas and Gastélum. The **secretary of tourism** office is at the southern end of the malecón at Cárdenas and Los Rocas (same hours; ⓣ646/178-8578, ⓦwww.enjoyensenada.com). Try to find a copy of either the *Gringo Gazette* or *Ensenada Tour* for information on goings-on about town; both are free and available from most establishments on López Mateos.

## Accommodation

If you're hoping for somewhere to **stay** at the weekend – the best time to be here for the nightlife – you'd be well advised to book ahead, or arrive early; during the week there should be no problem. Most of the hotels are on López Mateos and Cárdenas between Riveroll and Espinoza; though **rates** in general are high (and higher still at weekends), you'll find cheaper places on López Mateos. Just one block east of the tourist strip is a grubbier zone where you can find the best deals, though the area is not as safe.

**Best Western El Cid** López Mateos 993 ⓣ646/178-2401, ⓦwww.hotelelcid.com.mx. Not glamorous, but clean and well positioned near restaurants and shops, which is why tour groups routinely fill many of the rooms. There's a two-night minimum stay during high-season weekends. ❻

**Casa del Sol** Blancarte 1001 ⓣ646/178-1570, ⓦwww.motelcasadelsol.com. Two-storey motor inn off Mateos with a heated pool at its centre and satellite TV in the rooms, half of which were recently remodelled; be sure to ask for one of these. ❹

**El Cortez** López Mateos 1089 ⓣ646/178-1503, ⓦbajainn.com. The *Baja Inn* hotels are the northern Peninsula's three-star stalwarts: rather plain, but always clean, and packed with basic amenities like a/c, TV, a gym and a heated pool. ❻

**Del Valle** Riveroll 367 ⓣ646/178-2224, ⓦwww.ensenadahoy.com/delvalle/. You'll get the same features and style – TV, secure parking, a/c, tacky bedspreads – as the hotels on Mateos, but you'll save about M$200 a night (and get a quieter night's sleep) by bedding down at this 43-room motel three blocks to the north. ❹

**Punta Morro** Km 106 Hwy-1 ⓣ800/526-6676, ⓦwww.punta-morro.com. The ocean-view rooms have fireplaces, which may be why guests don't much mind the 30min walk to downtown. Rooms also have satellite TV, a/c and sitting areas. There's an on-site restaurant for the nights you want to skip the downtown commute. ❽

**Quintas Papagayo** Km 107.5 Hwy-1 ⓣ646/174-4575, ⓦwww.hussongs.com.mx. The two dozen or so charming one-storey bungalows here look like they were lifted out of 1950s Palm Springs. Rooms include kitchenettes and a parking spot in front. It's also adjacent to a *Hussong's Cantina* outpost. ❼

**Las Rosas** Km 105 Hwy-1 ⓣ646/174-4310, ⓦwww.lasrosas.com. This white- and pink-stucco building has balconies and ocean views from every room. It caters to the same clientele as *Punto Morro*, but manages to differentiate itself with a small, on-site spa. ❽

**San Nicolás** López Mateos 1536 ⓣ646/176-1901, ⓦwww.sannicolas.com.mx. The closest hotel to the downtown waterfront has popular package vacations that include meals and deals with local aquatic outfitters. Murals by a protégé of Diego Rivera adorn many of the public spaces, and there's an Olympic-size swimming pool. ❻

## The town and around

The focal point for Ensenada's municipal and tourist activities is the **waterfront** – almost all of the city's attractions are squeezed into the streets near the malecón. The six-block long promenade is where the city's residents come to see and be seen, gathering for sunset strolls and special events. During the day, the **Mercado Negro fish market** here is the centre of the action. Starting at 8am, over three dozen merchants begin selling the day's catches. The diversity of what's on display – from squirming eel to giant abalone – is staggering.

North of the malecón, Ensenada's downtown is shaped roughly as a narrow rectangle that runs northwest to southeast, corresponding to the parallel **Bulevar Lázaro Cárdenas** and lively **Avenida López Mateos** (or Calle 1a). On the latter you'll find scores of souvenir shops and outfits offering sport-fishing trips, as well as the bulk of the bars, hotels and restaurants – the majority

△ Mercado Negro fish market, Ensenada

of visitors come here to eat, drink and shop. If you want to branch out from these activities, you might pay a visit to the **Museo Histórico Regional**, at Gastélum off Mateos (Tues–Sun 9am–5pm; M$25 donation suggested; ⓣ646/178-3692), which documents what's known of the customs and plights of the area's pre-Columbian population as well as Ensenada's history. Pay attention to the small section devoted to the city prison, now home to the museum you're standing in. The Bodegas de Santo Tomás **winery**, one of the peninsula's largest, also offers tours and regular tastings in Ensenada, at Miramar 666 between calles 6a and 7a (tours daily 11am, 1pm & 3pm; free; ⓣ646/174-0836), as does the smaller Cavas Valmar, Ambar 810 (tours by appointment; free; ⓣ646/178-6405).

Although it enjoys an enviable position on the Pacific, Ensenada lacks good beaches, and to find a decent stretch of sand you'll have to head about half an hour south. As in other parts of Baja it can be difficult to get to many of the best beaches without your own transport; however, you can catch a local propane-powered "Brisa" bus from Macheros and Mateos (every 30min; M$8) to **San Miguel**, the closest surfing **beach** (rocky and not for beginners). The best **beaches** for swimming and sunbathing are at **Estero**, some 10km to the south and 2km off the main road. Occasional local buses run past these to the most startling attraction in the area, **La Bufadora** geyser. The combined action of wind, waves and an incoming tide periodically forces a huge jet of sea water up through a vent in the roof of an undersea cavern, in ideal conditions reaching 25–30m. Even though it's more than 20km off the main road and encircled by souvenir stands that rather spoil the atmosphere, it's worth a visit. To get there, take a micro from the Tres Cabezas park, on Costero at the bottom of Riveroll, to Maneadero and another from there, or a M$120–150 taxi ride from town.

From December to March, the California grey whale migration from the Arctic to the Peninsula's Pacific coast can be seen on daily **whale-watching tours** from Ensenada, which go to Bahía de Todos Santos, although what you'll see is as nothing compared to what you'll find in Baja California Sur. There are a half-dozen tour companies in the harbour that offer half-day excursions for about M$250 per person.

Ensenada itself hosts numerous events aimed squarely at the large US encampment in town, from sporting contests to food and wine festivals. The **Newport to Ensenada Yacht Race**, in April, is one of the largest international regattas in the world, with yachts leaving Newport, California, on a Friday afternoon and finishing in Ensenada a day later, when the partying commences and the town gets packed. April is also when the **Rosarito–Ensenada Bike Ride** draws thousands of cyclists here for the scenic eighty-kilometre "fun ride" from Playa de Rosarito to Ensenada, while off-road racing is the theme *du jour* during the Baja 500 (June) and the Baja 1000 (Nov). Culinary events kick off in August, when some of Peninsula's better vineyards host the ten-day **Fiestas de la Vendimia**, where tastings and wine-themed competitions and parties are held in the Valle de Guadalupe and in town; for information about tickets for the ten-day festival ask at the tourist office. The town celebrates **Independence Day** with a week of festivities.

## Eating and drinking

Even though fish is the big deal in town, you should sample the succulent local farm-raised beef at some point. Mateos has the largest share of straightforward **restaurant** options – be sure to steer away from the cavernous spaces promising every kind of Continental indulgence and instead look for those that smartly pair wines with their courses. **Dinner** hour for locals begins after 9pm, and reservations on weekends are recommended.

Ensenada offers many of the same **nightlife** opportunities for clubbing and drinking as Tijuana but within a smaller area and without the danger level of a border town (although you should still exercise caution).

**Abel's Bar** Lázaro Cárdenas at Riviera. Regional touring acts pack in dedicated crowds at this *cerveza*-fuelled 18+ bar for Spanish rock and alternative music.

**Bronco's** López Mateos 1525 ⓣ646/176-4900. The five blocks that separate *Bronco's* from the heart of the tourist district will save you a good M$100 on a steak (M$60). With spurs everywhere, the Wild West theme is over the top, but the spirit is genuine, and live bands on weekends add to the authenticity. Breakfast served.

**Capricho's Restaurant & Riedel Wine Bar** Ruiz 138 ⓣ646/178-3433. Local vintner favourite *Sé de Vino* has morphed into this more casual wine bar associated with the stemware company. The salads and small plates are good pre-dinner or late-night bites, when the bar is really humming.

**El Charro** López Mateos 475 ⓣ646/178-3881. Cheap, large and delicious portions of grilled rotisserie chicken and home-made guacamole are the popular choices in this rustic joint.

**Las Conchas** López Mateos 335 ⓣ646/175-7375. The best place in town to taste raw clams, oysters and cooked shellfish specialities matched with local wines. There's a sister restaurant and bar of the same name at Miramar 637.

**La Cueva de los Tigres** Acapulco and Las Palmas ⓣ646/176-6450. This somewhat hard to find all-day restaurant off Hwy-1 south of town is sought out in equal measure for its giant abalone and potent margaritas.

**La Embotelladora Vieja** Miramar 666 ⓣ646/174-0807. *Vieja*'s association with Santo Tomás Winery gives it an edge on rare and small-batch Baja wines – served by the glass and bottle – that are well-paired with the progressive Mexican-Mediterranean menu. Dinner only.

**Hussong's Cantina** Ruiz 113 ⓣ646/178-3210. Although it's a tourist destination with its own line of T-shirts, *Hussong's* is still an honest bar packed with locals and gringos alike. The floors are covered in sawdust, the bands are *norteña* and the drink of choice should always be the one invented here – a margarita.

**Manzanilla** Riveroll 122 ⓣ646/1750-7073, ⓦwww.rmanzanilla.com. The city's best restaurant is the unofficial home of local wine lovers and the region's growers. They come for the convivial dining room, with its exposed brick and wood beams, and the dishes, such as *añejo* rib-eye and whatever the chef's doing to fresh tuna that day, which never disappoint. Open Wed–Sun. Dinner only.

**Mi Kasa** Riveroll 87 ⓣ646/178-8211. This cafeteria opens to a busy breakfast crowd and finishes with family dinners. In three meals you can get a broad sampling of Mexican home cooking, from *huevos con nopales* (eggs with cactus) in the morning, to chicken in *mole* at lunch and deep-fried tacos or *menudo* (stewed tripe and peppers) at dinner, all for less than M$80.

**Sano's** Km 108 Hwy-1 Tijuana–Ensenada ⓣ646/174-4061. The portions are huge at this US-style steakhouse, which is why fillets (M$275) and chicken in plum sauce (M$210) aren't such a bad deal. Most of the wines are from the Valle de Guadalupe.

**Tacos Fenix** Espinosa at Juárez. This three-person outfit operates from a sidewalk next to the Ferreteria Fenix tyre shop, from which it has derived its name. The superb fish tacos are made to order and in your hands before they have time to cool.

**La Vendimia** Riveroll 85 ⓣ646/174-0969. Wine shop, bar and restaurant with tapas-style seafood dishes like marinated baby octopus and *bacalao* (salted cod).

## Listings

**Banks** Most are on Ruiz, a few blocks north of López Mateos.

**Books** The Bookseller, C 4a 240, at Obregón (Tues–Sat 10am–6pm), has a great selection of used books and magazines.

**Buses** The station at C 11a and Riveroll handles ABC and Águila long-distance buses between Ensenada and the mainland, as well as points further south and San Felipe. There are multiple services a day to destinations including Guerrero Negro, La Paz, Loreto and Mexicali.

**Car rental** Hertz, Riveroll and C 2a (ⓣ646/178-2982).

**Internet access** Try Equinoxio, at Cárdenas and Miramar (Mon 9am–10pm, Tues–Sat 8am–10pm, Sun 10am–9pm; M$20/hr), which has fast connections, many terminals and a full café; or Compunet, next to Hertz (Mon–Fri 9am–10pm, Sat & Sun 10am–9pm; M$15/hr).

**Post office** Club Rotario 93 and Mateos (Mon–Fri 8am–7pm, Sat 9am–1pm).

**Spanish courses** Baja California Language College, Riveroll 1287 (ⓣ646/174-1741, ⓦwww.bajacal.com).

## Valle de Guadalupe

The vineyards of the **Valle de Guadalupe** are so heavily drenched in hype that on first visit anyone but the most optimistic – or wine-soaked – visitor will be disappointed. A cynic would say the valley does a better job marketing its wine than making it, but the region is clearly on the right track, as illustrated by the growing number of vineyards that are experimenting with foreign vines and cross-breeding others. Small boutique wineries and epicurean-related ventures are riding on the coat-tails of the emerging industry, and farms that aren't devoted to grapes grow olives, raise organically fed cattle or turn their milk into artisanal cheeses. These places aren't in tourist brochures but their creations can be enjoyed at stellar restaurants like *Laja* in the valley and *Manzanilla* in Ensenada.

A total of 8600 acres in Valle de Guadalupe are currently devoted to wine production – about two-thirds that of Napa Valley in California. The villages of **San Antonio de las Minas** in the southwest and **Francisco Zarco** and **El Porvenir** in the northeast are the centres of the valley's production. To **reach the valley** from Ensenada, leave the city along Cárdenas and follow Hwy-1 through El Sauzal and exit on Hwy-3 towards Tecate, just prior to the beginning of the Hwy-1D toll road north of San Miguel. The vineyards and stores begin in about 10km, near the San Antonio de las Minas settlement. If you're coming southbound from Tecate on Hwy-3, wine country begins at Km 75 with two of the area's bigger landmarks, L.A. Cetto on the left side of the road and Domecq to the right. With a few exceptions, the valley's vineyards are located on dirt roads that branch off a 25km stretch of the main highway. Detailed signs direct visitors how to navigate the unmarked dirt roads that link the vineyards.

## Practicalities

Companies and epicurean groups in San Diego and Tijuana organize **day trips** to the valley that visit multiple vineyards and usually stop at a small museum connected to Bibayoff Bodegas, which offers an account of the region's history of emigration, from the Kumai to the Molokan Russians. The trips will shuttle you from either your hotel in Tijuana or across the border in the US. **Fees** run from M$800 for day trips to M$3000 for overnight tours that arrange lodging in Ensenada.

Although there are no hotels, there are a few small **inns** and **B&Bs**. Open year-round, *Adobe Guadalupe* (ⓣ646/155-2094, US ⓣ949/863-9776, ⓦwww.adobeguadalupe.com; ⑧) is a six-room inn on fifty acres. To get here, follow the main road into Francisco Zarco from Hwy-3 and turn north after 5.7km at the second stop sign in El Porvenir.

Of the few dining options in the valley, the best one – as well as one of the best on the entire peninsula – is *Laja*, Km 83 Hwy-3, Francisco Zarco (ⓣ646/155-2556, ⓦwww.lajamexico.com; Wed lunch only, Thurs–Sat dinner; reservations essential). Former *Daniel* and *Four Seasons* New York chef Jair Téllez, along with partner Laura Reinert, opened this prix-fixe destination restaurant in 2001, and it continues to draw eager diners with its changing, seasonally influenced menu – expect dishes like grouper with canellini beans, marinated Baja yellowtail or oven-roasted pig.

## The vineyards

Even though reservations are not required at any of the valley's wineries, it is best to call ahead everywhere before visiting, especially if you're coming in the warmer months (July–Sept).

**Bibayoff Bodegas** from Hwy-3, exit west at the sign to El Tigre, follow dirt road 4km and turn north, proceed 5.6km to Rancho Bibayoff ⓣ646/176-1008, ⓔbibayoff@telnor.net. The Russians were responsible for resurrecting the wine industry here, but this is the only Russian-run vineyard still open to the public. Bibayoff sells many of his grapes to other producers but keeps enough around to produce five estate wines, including a Nebbiolo and Colombard. Tours and wine tasting by appointment only.

**Cava de Don Juan** Km 28 Hwy-3, Valle de las Palmas ⓣ664/621-8190. Although technically outside Valle de Guadalupe (it's on the border of Tecate), Rancho Don Juan produces a Chenin Blanc and has a cellar store that's one of the better sources for local olive oil, preserves and honey. Daily 9am–5pm.

**Chateau Camou** from Hwy-3, follow main road into Francisco Zarco, turn north after 3km ⓣ646/177-2221, ⓦwww.chateau-camou.com.mx. Two hundred acres of vineyards surround the mission-style building housing a modern winery and small tasting room. From here Camou turns out 30,000 cases of Bordeaux, Zinfandel and a dessert blend of Chardonnay, Chenin Blanc and Sauvignon Blanc. Reservations required; some tours include lunch. Tours from M$50; no credit cards. Mon–Sat 8am–3pm, Sun 9am–2pm.

**Domecq** Km 73 Hwy-3, Francisco Zarco ⓣ646/155-2249, ⓦwww.vinos-domecq.com.mx. In 1972 Domecq was the first commercial winery to open in the valley, and it has steadily expanded from growing grapes for brandy to table wines and on to some smaller-batch, boutique wines. Like L.A. Cetto – with whom Domecq's wines make up eighty percent of the region's total output – its setup will be familiar to visitors used to California- and Australia-style vineyard tours. Its massive scale accounts for the fact that it processes grapes from three other regions in Mexico. The tasting area also includes a store with merchandise. Free wine tasting and tours. Mon–Fri 10am–4pm, Sat 10am–3pm.

**L.A. Cetto** Km 73.5 Hwy-3, Francisco Zarco ⓣ646/155-2264, ⓦwww.cettowine.com. Although the Cetto family has been bottling wine in Baja California since 1928, they didn't set up their current operation in the valley until 1974; they're now the largest producer of table wines in Mexico. If the gaggle of tour buses in the large parking lot aren't sufficient sign, a 15min drive through a few of Cetto's 2500 acres will give you some sense how large the operation is. For first-timers, Cetto offers a great introduction to the process through its free wine tours and tastings; it's also one of the few wineries to have food and a dining area. Daily 10am–5pm.

**Monte Xanic** from Hwy-3, follow main road into Francisco Zarco, turn north after 2.7km ⓣ646/174-6769, ⓦwww.montexanic.com. Thirty thousand cases of wine from estate-grown grapes roll out of Xanic every year, some with price tags north of M$1500. A portion of Xanic's land contains old-growth vines planted by Molokans a half-century ago, and the vineyard expertly uses this pedigree to enhance its boutique-wine claim. Its speciality is Bordeaux, but it also bottles Chenin Blanc and Syrah, the latter used for cheaper wines. Wine tasting and tours by appointment. Mon–Fri 9am–4pm, Sat 8am–noon.

## On to the 28th parallel

South of Ensenada, the topography around the highway shifts from suburban sprawl to farmland and then into curvy, hilly passes that are frightfully narrow, especially considering the number of large lorries moving through the area. Once you've dropped into the Santo Tomás valley below, the soothing sight of rows of grapevines stretches out before you. Almost the entire valley is farmed, although the water supply can only sustain about half of the area at a time, which explains why the other half lays fallow.

Sixty-five kilometres past Santo Tomás, just beyond Colonet, a road at Km 141 turns inland towards the **Parque Nacional San Pedro Martír**. The side road, unsurfaced but in good condition, winds almost 100km up into the sierra, which includes the peninsula's highest peaks at over 3000m – where it snows in winter. As you climb, the land becomes increasingly green and wooded, and at the end of the road astronomical observatories take advantage of the piercingly clear air. There are breathtaking views in every direction. Numerous poorly defined trails wind through the park, but again, there's no public transport and you need to be fully equipped for wilderness camping if you want to linger.

### San Quintín

**SAN QUINTÍN** is the first town of any size south of Ensenada, and even here, though there are a couple of big hotels, most of the buildings look temporary. There's no reason to stop here unless you are one of the many weekend fishermen destined for **Bahía San Quintín**, which is undeniably attractive, with five cinder-cone volcanoes as a backdrop to a series of small sandy beaches, and endless fishing (though not without a permit) and superb clam digging that draw campers and RV tourists. The closest of the beaches are some 20km from town, 5km from the highway, and there's no public transport to reach them.

**Buses** from Ensenada stop at **Lázaro Cárdenas**, 5km south of town. If you want a **place to stay**, try *The Old Mill* (US ⓣ1-800/479-7962, ⓦwww.oldmillbaja.com; ❹); exit west from Hwy-1 San Quintín–Punta Prieta directly across from the transformer station on the south side of Lázaro Cárdenas (there will be a sign for *Don Eddie's* motel at the turn-off) and follow directions to *Don Eddie's* until you see the marked turn-off to *The Old Mill*. The *Mill* has rooms ranging from doubles to suites and, although they're not exactly fancy, they're the most sought-after in town, both for their price and the hospitality of the owners. There are no TVs or a/c, which is just fine as most guests chat the evenings away outside or dine and drink at the adjacent restaurant and bar. On the highway in town, the sixteen-room *La Villa de San Quintín*, Km 190 Hwy-1 Ensenada–San Quintín (ⓣ616/165-1800, ⓔvillasanquintin@hotmail.com; ❹), is run by the family that owns Tijuana's *Hotel La Villa de Zaragoza*. The rooms, all of which have free high-speed Internet access, a/c, satellite TV and secure parking, are set 30m off the highway and behind the motel's restaurant. The

## The Transpeninsular Highway

Towns in Baja California have a tendency to describe their location as "only six hundred miles south of San Diego", as if a twelve-hour drive were a selling point. Elsewhere this might appear as lunacy, but on a peninsula whose furthest points are separated by over 1600km and linked by one paved road, the Transpeninsular Highway, it makes perfect sense.

Completed in 1973, the **Transpeninsular Highway** stands as one of North America's last great road trips. It's equal parts endurance and beauty, seclusion and camaraderie. What you're driving defines much of the experience: an RVer will encounter some of the peninsula's most long-term visitors; off-roaders will meet locals and visitors who trade tips on fixing flats; sedan drivers will commiserate about that great beach they just can't get to. Part of the thrill comes from the long spaces separating major towns, the narrow segments of highway that snake along precarious cliffsides and the animals and washouts that can block the road. But the biggest draw is the near-constant beauty of the desert, mountain, sea and ocean vistas and their illumination by brilliant blue skies and starry nights.

Before the Transpeninsular, Baja California was best known as the forbidding wilderness of the Baja 1000 auto race. Motorcycle, buggy and truck drivers started racing through the northwest in 1967 and they still flock to Ensenada every June (for the Baja 500) and November with the hope that they'll conquer the all-dirt track. The course isn't easy; it takes racers through the sierras San Pedro Martír, San Felipe and de Juárez, and the Laguna Salada – only half of the entrants make it across the finishing line.

*Hotel La Pinta*, Km 11 Hwy-1 (Ⓣ616/165-9008, Ⓦwww.lapintahotels.com/SanQuintin; ❻), is the luxury option, right on the beach 3km off the highway, some 8km south of Lázaro Cárdenas. There are also plenty of **camping** spots around the bay if you come equipped, and RV sites at the *Molino Viejo*. Should you need **Internet** access while in San Quintín, Internet Milenio has several computers (M$15) and is right on the Transpeninsular Highway at Km 195.

### El Rosario and Cataviña

Some 60km beyond San Quintín, the highway passes through **EL ROSARIO**, the original site of a Dominican mission. Founded in 1774, in 1802 the mission was forced by a shortage of water to move 3km downstream to **El Rosario de Abajo**, where you can see the ruins. Nowadays, however, the old mission site is little more than a BMX track for local kids, and definitely not worth getting off the bus for. El Rosario is primarily a staging point for excursions further south into the peninsula, and modern El Rosario de Arriba consists of just a couple of petrol stations, a few restaurants and small **motels**.

The recently remodelled *Baja Cactus Motel*, Km 55 Hwy-1 San Quintín–Punta Prieta (Ⓣ616/165-8850; Ⓦwww.bajacactus.com; ❸–❹) has relatively quiet rooms with satellite TV and wireless Internet access. It's conveniently positioned between the Pemex Station and *Mama Espinosa's* restaurant and cabañas (Ⓣ616/165-8770; ❹). *Espinosa's* is one of the oldest **restaurants** on the peninsula and serves as the unofficial town hall. Though famous, their lobster tacos are rather dry and expensive, but everything else – beef and pork tacos and big burritos – qualifies as the best food between here and Bahía de los Angeles. The ten-room *Motel Sinai*, Km 56.5 Hwy-1 San Quintín–Punta Prieta (Ⓣ616/165-8818; ❹), at the town's southern edge, is quiet and clean. If you're **driving**, it's absolutely necessary to fill up your tank here: there's no dependable pump until just north of the state border with Baja California Sur.

Beyond El Rosario, the road turns sharply inland, to run down the centre of the peninsula for some 350km to Guerrero Negro. This is where you head into Baja California proper – barren and god-forsaken. At times the road runs along the coast, but for the most part the scenery is dry brown desert, with the peninsula's low mountain spine to the left and nothing but sand and the occasional scrubby cactus around the road. It's a bizarre landscape of cactus – particularly yucca, *cirios*, unique to this area; and *cardones*, which can grow over 16m tall – and rock, with plenty of strange giant formations; much of it is protected within the **Parque Natural del Desierto Central de Baja California**. In the heart of this area is **CATAVIÑA**, comprising a dozen or so buildings strung along the highway, complete with a **hotel** and **restaurant**, *La Pinta* (Ⓣ646/176-2601, Ⓦwww.lapintahotels.com; ⑧). If you do stop, take time to look at some of the giant boulders; not far off the highway at Km 171, just before Cataviña, is **La Cueva Pintada**, a tiny cave beneath a huge rock decorated with ancient paintings that include circles, dots, sunbursts and stick figures. If you're driving through Cataviña, you may be able to fill your tank at the informal, itinerant roadside **fuel** station on the north side of the road (not the shuttered Pemex near *La Pinta*), though there's no guarantee. The petrol may be twice as expensive as in El Rosario, but that's the price you pay for not filling up when you should have.

## Bahía de los Ángeles

The turn-off for **BAHÍA DE LOS ÁNGELES**, a growing community on the Sea of Cortés, is about 100km further on from Cataviña at the Punta Prieta T in the road, followed by a 69km trip east along the recently resurfaced two-lane Hwy-6. Still a small place, the town sits on the eponymous bay, which teems with sea life and is hemmed in by contorted mountains. **Isla Ángel de la Guarda**, the largest island in the Sea of Cortés, dominates the bay and is the focus of the settlement's activities; it's the best place on the sea's northern coast for diving and kayaking trips. So far, there aren't any speciality operators in town, and any activity you'd like to indulge in – kayaking, fishing or off-roading – is typically arranged through the campground or motel you're staying at. If your hotel doesn't handle these directly, they'll direct you to someone who does.

There's an underdeveloped, frontier feeling in Bahía, and there's little here other than a few hotels, cafés and fishing boats. The one exception is the small bilingual **Museo de Naturaleza y Cultura**, two blocks west of the main drag (daily 9am–noon & 2–4pm; M$15 suggested donation). Its location is marked by a narrow-gauge locomotive, a relic of the gold and copper mines that first attracted Europeans to the area. Mining history and that of the local ranchero life is well covered, along with details of sea life in the bay.

Because of the difficulty in getting supplies to the bay, lodging and food are more expensive than you'd expect, but still cheaper than Ensenada or La Paz. Two of the better **places to stay** are just off crumbling asphalt roads on the north side of town. *Larry and Raquel's Motel on the Beach*, on La Gringa Road 3km north of the Hwy-6 junction (Ⓣ619/423-3454, Ⓔbahiatours@yahoo.com; ④), has nine rooms in a two storeys just 50m from the sea. The rooms are spare and clean, without phones or TVs, though the restaurant does have satellite TV, an Internet connection and some of the best fish tacos between Ensenada and San José del Cabo. *Camp Daggett's* (Ⓣ200/124-9101, Ⓦwww.campdaggetts.com; tent camping M$50, cabins ④), between *Larry's* and the town, is primarily an RV community, but they've reserved the beachfront for palapa-shaded plots for campers. There are also simple cabins with hot-water showers next to the restaurant.

## Ecotourism and Baja California Sur

The confluence of the **Colorado River**, the huge underwater canyons of the **Sea of Cortés** and the strong currents of the **Pacific Ocean** has created a plankton-wealthy environment in the waters around Baja that supports an extensive food chain and, in turn, an amazingly diverse aquatic culture. Inland, the combination of five mountain ranges, most notably the **Sierra de Juárez** in the north and the **Sierra de la Giganta** in the south, constitute the backbone of the peninsula and contain the petroglyphs of some of the peninsula's first inhabitants, dating back an estimated 1500 years. Inhospitable desert stretches away from these mountains to marshland, mangrove-lined rivers, coastal dunes and miles of untouched beaches.

With so many natural sights, **ecotourism** has become big business in Baja, particularly in the less developed southern portion of the peninsula, **Baja California Sur**, which stretches from Guerrero Negro nearly 1000km south to Cabo San Lucas at the bottom tip. One of the most exciting excursions here is to see the annual grey whale migration: from December to April, thousands of **grey whales** travel some 10,000km to mate and breed in the warm-water lagoons of Guerrero Negro, San Ignacio and Bahía Magdalena. San Ignacio is also the jumping-off point for trips to see the mountains and giant cave paintings of the Sierra de San Francisco. Further south, the tranquil aquamarine bays and islands of the Sea of Cortés near Mulegé, Loreto and La Paz offer the best **sea kayaking** in Mexico, and off the southern edge of the peninsula lives Cabo Pulmo, the only living **coral reef** on the western shore of North America. Home to hundreds of open-sea species, it is treasured among divers.

It would be quite easy to spend weeks exploring the local environment. However, as the tourist population expands each year, new tour companies crop up and it can be hard to sift through the marketing and understand exactly where to go. Listed below are some favourite activities and the best areas from which to embark.

### Whale watching

There are three main "sanctuaries" where you can see grey whales mating and breeding. Most whales congregate in **Ojo de Liebre** (see p.104), just off Guerrero Negro, where **tours** are plentiful and charge about M$550-650 for transportation to the lagoon, four hours of boat travel and lunch. Many people, though, prefer the lagoon near **San Ignacio** (see p.105), 150km south; here the town itself is also an attraction, as are the local birds, caves and mission church. The least-visited of the three sanctuaries is **Bahía Magdalena**, located near Ciudad Constitución, 140km south of Loreto and 216km north of La Paz – if you've bypassed Guerrero Negro and San Ignacio, then Bahía Magdalena is your last opportunity to view the whales within a sanctuary.

Most southern towns offer whale-watching tours as well, but keep in mind that these charge exorbitant prices for transportation to the west coast, where they will likely take you to one of the sanctuaries – a four-hour/M$400 whale tour could easily become a fourteen-hour/M$1300 affair from Loreto, La Paz or anywhere else further south. That said, many whales speed past the three sanctuaries and head further

There are other motels in town directly off the paved road, each offering a handful of basic rooms, along with attached restaurants and short walks to the shore. The forty rooms at *Villa Vitta* (Ⓣ200/124-9103, US Ⓣ619/454-6101, Ⓦwww.villavitta.com; ❹) are a bit worn, but the motel has a pool, Jacuzzi and boat ramp to keep you occupied. *Camp Gecko* (no phone, Ⓦwww.campgecko.com, Ⓔgecko@starband.net; campsites $M60, cabins ❸) is really bare bones, with beds and worn sheets in its cabins. *Camp Gecko* rents kayaks and snorkelling gear for M$30 per hour and can fill up your scuba tank; *Villa Vitta* does the same for its guests, along with anyone else on their side of the shore.

south along the coast; some even make the turn around the tip of the peninsula and into the Sea of Cortés. If you can't make it to one of the sanctuaries, you at least have the option of watching them from the shore, where you can see them pop up some 50m out: Todos Santos (see p.123) and the western side of Cabo San Lucas (see p.125) are particularly good for this. Tour operators running out of Guerrero Negro and San Ignacio are listed on p.104 and p.107, respectively.

### Cave-painting tours

Between Bahía de los Angeles and Loreto sits the **Sierra de San Francisco**, recently declared a World Heritage Site by UNESCO because of five hundred historic rock-art sites contained within it. Many of the famed sites are 45km north of **San Ignacio** (see p.107), so most people choose that town as their base for excursion. Tours are also a good option from **Guerrero Negro** in the north, and **Mulegé** in the south (see p.110); operators are listed with the relevant entries. Towns further south will have tours, but again, you will be paying exorbitant prices for the transportation costs north. The land is now also protected by the Instituto Nacional de Antropología e Historia (INAH), and they require you to be accompanied by a guide and to seek permission before setting out (tour companies/guides will help you with this). **Tours** generally last anywhere from five hours to several days; a five-hour tour will cost M$400–550 per person, depending on the length of your hike and transportation required from the tour. Having your own transportation will usually cut these costs in half.

### Sea kayaking

The waters around Baja are so picturesque and rich in marine life that nearly everyone will be drawn to try their hand at sea kayaking. It's as good a way as any to explore the bays, snorkel the ledges around the many islands and, for the more ambitious, to make your way down the coast. On the road south, the first real spot for even a novice to put in would be **Mulegé** (see p.110). There's no abundance of kayak-rental agencies in this area, but the few that exist have cornered the market and can offer you any related gear you could ever need. The standard open-top kayaks go for about M$300 per day, wet suit and fins another M$60 or so. Week-long packages bring the per-day price down to M$200, including the necessary VHF radio, optional wet suit and snorkel gear. **Loreto** (see p.113) and **La Paz** (see p.115) are also phenomenal options for sea kayaking. Trips to Isla del Carmen off Loreto and to Isla Espíritu Santo off La Paz pose more extended challenges and attract their share of experienced kayakers. Dozens of companies compete for business in each of these towns – see the relevant entries for details – so gear rental will always be reasonable, with half-day tours starting at around M$400 and full-day tours at about M$650. Some companies offer week-long all-inclusive kayak "safaris" that can creep up towards US$1000. **Los Cabos** (see p.123) also has its share of kayak adventures, but none as rewarding as in the north.

The **Pemex** station near the intersection with Hwy-6 has been known to close for long periods when petrol is not delivered; when this happens you can often find petrol by asking at one of the hotels – but don't depend on it.

## Guerrero Negro

Continuing on the main highway, there's little between Cataviña and the 28th parallel, where an enormous metal monument and a hotel mark the border of the states of Baja California and **Baja California Sur**; you'll have to set your watch forward an hour when you cross, unless Baja California is on **Daylight Saving Time** (April–Oct), in which case there's no change. **GUERRERO NEGRO**, just across the border, offers little in the way of respite from the heat and aridity that has gone before (winters, however, can find the town quite chilly). Flat and fly-blown, it's an important centre for salt production, surrounded by vast saltpans and stark storage warehouses. At most times of year you'll want to do little more than grab a drink and carry straight on. In January and February (and, peripherally, Dec & March–May), however, Guerrero Negro is home to one of Mexico's most extraordinary natural phenomena, the congregation of scores of **grey whales** just off the coast.

The whales, which spend most of their lives in the icy Bering Sea around Alaska, can be watched (at remarkably close quarters; the young are sometimes left stranded on the beaches) from an area within the **Parque Natural de la Ballena Gris**, which surrounds the **Laguna Ojo de Liebre**. The *laguna* is also known as **Scammon's Lagoon** after whaling captain Charles Melville Scammon, who first brought the huge potential of the bay to the attention of rapacious whalers in 1857. The town may have got its name from the *Black Warrior*, an overladen whaling ship that sank here a year later, but that's only the most popular of theories.

During the season there are organized **whale-watching trips**, and an observation tower that guarantees at least a distant sighting. Although talk turns every year to restricting numbers or banning boats altogether, there are currently more tours and **boat trips** than ever. If you can take one, then do so – it's an exceptional experience, and many visitors actually get to touch the whales, which sometimes come right up to bobbing vessels after the engines are switched off. Whale-watching trips are run from *Mario's* (see opposite); they charge around M$500 per person for a four-hour trip, including a complimentary drink or two. Malarrimo Eco-Tours (Ⓣ615/157-0100, Ⓦwww.malarrimo.com) also runs whale tours, as well as eight-hour tours to the Sierra de San Francisco to see cave paintings (Oct–Dec). If you are heading south, keep in mind that you will have two more opportunities to go whale watching: at San Ignacio and Bahía Magdalena.

To **watch the whales from the shore**, you'll need your own vehicle (preferably 4WD): head south from town until you see the park sign, from where a poor sand track leads 24km down to the lagoon. Midway there's a **checkpoint** where you must register your vehicle and its occupants, and at the park entrance a fee of around M$40 is charged. To see the whales you'll need to get up early or stay late, as they move out to the deeper water in the middle of the day.

## Practicalities

If you want to stay in Guerrero Negro, you can choose from numerous **hotels and motels** strung out along the main drag, Zapata. Perhaps the best is the *Malarrimo*, Zapata at Pipila (Ⓣ615/857-0250, Ⓦwww.malarrimo.com; ❺), to the right as you enter town, with clean rooms with TV, RV spaces and a good seafood restaurant. Further into town, the *Motel Las Dunas*, Zapata s/n at División del Norte (Ⓣ615/157-0650; ❹), is simple, clean and friendly, though sometimes a little noisy. You'll find much the same at *Las Ballenas*, Victoria s/n at Zapata (Ⓣ615/157-0116; ❸), which offers a dozen or so basic rooms with TV; or, on the north side of Zapata, there's the good but overpriced and almost antiseptic *Hotel El Morro*, Zapata s/n at Victoria (Ⓣ615/157-0414; ❹), whose rooms have fans and cable TV.

There are plenty of **restaurants** along the main street, though only a few ever seem to be open at any one time. *Malarrimo*, in the hotel of the same name, has good seafood and is another place to check about whale-watching trips; *El Asadero Norteño* serves meaty northern specialities; *Mario's* (☎615/157-0788), on the entrance to the highway, is good for breakfast and the basics; you can also try *Don Gus*, an agreeable place by the bus station where you can eat huge M$200 shrimp platters while gazing at one of the region's salt flats. Fresh produce can also be purchased from Supermercado La Ballena, on Zapata.

**Buses** from Guerrero Negro's bus station are irregular and often full upon arrival; buy your ticket at least a day in advance. The six services (one local) which head north to Tijuana (M$390), and the one to Mexicali, leave at night and early morning; the eight southbound services – two local, running all the way to La Paz (M$420) – depart either early in the morning or in the late afternoon and evening. The taxis at the stand in front of the blue and yellow Mercado Tianguis supermarket on Zapata adjust their rates depending on how long you'll have to wait for a bus – a ride to San Ignacio is about M$300 per person. A half-dozen **Internet** cafés (typically open Mon–Sat only; M$10–20/hr), such as Café Internet Las Ballenas, TechNet (open on Sun) and Cyber Guerrero Negro, line Zapata and the adjacent blocks between the *Malarrimo* and *Hotel El Morro*.

## San Ignacio

Leaving Guerrero Negro, the highway heads inland again for the hottest, driest stage of the journey, across the Desierto Vizcaíno. In the midst of this landscape, **SAN IGNACIO**'s appeal is immediate even from a distance. Gone are the dust and concrete that define the peninsula, replaced by green hues and a cool breeze; it's an oasis any desert traveller would hope for. In town, the central Plaza Ecotourismo plays hosts to concerts, festivals and children's soccer games, and is dominated by **San Ignacio de Kadakaamán**, a mission constructed of lava-block walls – carved out of the output from Volcan las Tres Virgenes to the east – over one metre thick.

The settlement was founded by the Jesuits in 1728, but the area had long been populated by the indigenous **Cochimí**, attracted by the tiny stream, the only fresh water for hundreds of miles. Underneath the surfaced road between the highway and town is the small dam that the settlers built to form the lagoon that still sustains the town's agricultural economy, mostly based on the Mediterranean staples of dates, figs, grapes, olives, limes and oranges. San Ignacio's **church**, built by the first arrivals and probably the best example of colonial architecture in the whole of Baja California, dominates the attractive, shaded plaza. Early missionaries were responsible, too, for the attractive palm trees that give the town its character.

In the bleak sierras to the north and south are numerous **caves**, many decorated with **ancient paintings**. Not much is known about the provenance of these designs, beyond the fact that they were painted at different periods and bear little resemblance to any other known art in this region of the world. A few of the murals were written about by eighteenth-century missionaries; at that time, the Cochimí Indians told them they were created by giants. Largely ignored until the 1960s, when an amateur archeologist named Harry Crosby started exploring them, it's really been within the last fifty years that the paintings have been subjected to examination. A 2003 study backed by the National Geographic Society concluded that the designs in the Sierra de San Francisco region were about 7500 years old – predating the Aztecs and any other known Mexican society. This finding has sparked more interest in the paintings and has led to the discovery of hundreds of previously unknown sites.

△ Whale watching, Laguna San Ignacio

The cave paintings are extremely hard to visit, reachable only by tracks or mule paths and almost impossible to find without a guide (which is also a legal requirement for visits). If you're determined, join one of the **tours** arranged from the hotels in town or through any of the operators listed in the box opposite, though all can be pricey.

At the beginning of the year, the same places also organize **whale-watching trips** (again, see box opposite) to the nearby Laguna San Ignacio, considered by some to be a better place to spot the animals than Guerrero Negro. The waters of the town's lagoon attract hundreds of species of birds to San Ignacio, which nest in its environs; in fact, if you stay overnight, you can't help but notice that the birds and frogs between them produce a rainforest-like soundtrack, a rather surreal feeling in the middle of a desert. For a nominal fee, informal **bird-watching tours** can be arranged at *Rice & Beans* (see below).

## Practicalities

The centre of San Ignacio lies almost 3km off the main highway, where all the **buses** stop. Upon arrival you may be lucky enough to pick up a taxi; otherwise it's a thirty-minute walk down the road through the palms. The stop is actually San Lino, a little settlement anchored by the campground and restaurant *Rice & Beans,* just west of the intersection along a road parallel to the highway (Ⓣ615/154-0283; ❺). There are old but clean rooms here, with hot showers, and outside, plenty of space to **camp** (M$50 per car and all passengers, M$110 if you want to use the showers). Camping at *Ignacio Springs Bed and Breakfast* on the northern side of Río San Ignacio (Ⓣ615/154-0333, Ⓦwww.ignaciosprings.com; ❺ includes breakfast and kayaks) is a rather glamorous and comfortable affair. The well-appointed yurts have queen-size beds, tile floors, a/c and patios; some even have their own bath. Guests have use of kayaks and easy access to the only espresso in town. If you can get in, the most enjoyable rooms in town are at the three-room *Casa Lerré* guesthouse, Madero s/n (Ⓣ615/154-0158, Ⓦwww.prodigyweb.net.mx/janebames/index.html; no credit cards, ❹). You can't miss the bright blue exterior, and even if you don't stay here you wouldn't want to miss the little bookshop and the years of local wisdom packed in it. The rooms themselves are clean and brightly painted, and look out on a courtyard, which has chickens.

For **food**, *Restaurant Chalita* on the central plaza has *chiles rellenos* and locally raised beef. *Rene's*, just past the plaza on La Correa, serves *desayuna* to gringos' liking (scrambled eggs and French toast) along with *chilaquiles* and *huevos rancheros*.

There are **no banks** in town, few places accept credit cards and people are reluctant to take travellers' cheques – it's best to come with a supply of cash. There is **Internet** access, though, on the north side of the plaza at Internet Café & Tour Service. The Tienda Nuevos Almacenes Mesa general store, on the main road one block north of the square, sells hats, drinks, maps, machetes, camping gear and anything else you'd need before heading down to the lagoon or into the Sierra de San Francisco.

## Tours and trips from San Ignacio

### Whale watching

Although whales are most in evidence in January and February (recent censuses have counted between 300 and 600 at one time), **whale-watching** tours are offered from December to April. Ecoturismo Kuyima (ⓣ615/154-0070, ⓦwww.kuyima.com), in town, opposite the mission, is the best **tour operator** of all, but you could also try El Padrino and Antonio Aguilar Eco Tours (ⓣ615/154-0089 or 0059, ⓔelpadrino@prodigy.net.mx), on the road between the river and plaza, directly opposite the *La Pinta* hotel. Kuyima charges about M$400 all-inclusive, while El Padrino charges a flat rate of M$1200 for up to six people, lodging not included. Most tours provide transportation, but if you have your own you can cut your expenses considerably – although the dirt road to Laguna San Ignacio from San Ignacio can be tough on a small car – and you can hire a guided *panga* when you arrive from any number of local guides, which should run to about M$300 per person for about three hours. Ecoturismo Kuyima (see above) has a **camp** at the lagoon, with tents and clean palapas with solar power, plus they serve food. It's possible to visit and return in one day, but it's better to stay the night (④ all-inclusive) as the whales are best seen in the early morning when they venture into the shallow waters.

### Rock art

**Rock-art tours** from San Ignacio focus on the area of Sierra de San Francisco about 45km north of San Ignacio, where nearly five hundred sites exist across around 11,000 square kilometres; tour operators also run cave-painting tours that begin in San Ignacio and usually pass through the little town of San Francisco de la Sierra and head for the easily accessible Cueva del Ratón, or remoter ones such as the Cueva Pintada and Cueva de las Flechas in Canón San Pablo, which require a minimum of two days. Tours are fairly expensive, so if you want to save some cash you can arrange a mule trip at Sierra de San Francisco. However, you will need your own transport to get there: at Km 118, 45km north of San Ignacio, you'll find a road heading east to San Francisco de la Sierra, and the first site is just over 2km further on. Note that you must always be accompanied by a guide and that you are required to get **INAH permission**, gained in San Ignacio from Cuco Arce, the INAH rep in San Ignacio (Mon–Sat 8am–3pm; ⓣ615/154-0215 or 0222); an easier alternative, though, is to stop at Ecoturismo Kuyima (see above) on the square and ask. Once you've got permission, sort out a guide and a mule and you'll be able to camp in the area – an excellent way to see a variety of paintings. Note that **flash photography** is not allowed in the caves.

## Santa Rosalía

The highway emerges on the east coast at **SANTA ROSALÍA**, which is also the terminal for the ferry to Guaymas. An odd little town, wedged in the narrow river valley of the Arroyo de Santa Rosalía, it was once a busy port used to ship copper from the nearby French-run mines of the El Boleo company (see box opposite). Nowadays, the mines are virtually exhausted and the smelters stand idle, though much of the equipment still lies around town, including parts of a rusting narrow-gauge railway. The government still claims to be developing a plan to employ modern techniques to extract the last of the ore from the five million tonnes of tailings, a move that would provide a much-needed financial boost to the community. To date, however, little real progress has been made on this front.

The town itself feels like nowhere else in Baja. Built by French miners, it has somewhat of a transient air, and many of its buildings look strikingly un-Mexican. Santa Rosalía does possess a certain charm that continually attracts tourists to break their trip along the peninsula. The streets are narrow and crowded, with the workers' houses in the valley, which feature low, angled roofs and hibiscus-flanked porches, resembling Caribbean dwellings, and grander colonial residences for the managers lining the hill to the north. Look out especially for the **church** on Obregón, a prefabricated iron structure designed by Gustave Eiffel and exhibited in Paris before it was shipped here.

### Practicalities

**Hwy-1** enters Santa Rosalía in both directions from along the coast, passing the harbour and the eastern border of the triangle-shaped **Parque Morelos**. Five avenidas – the main commercial drag Obregón, along with Constitución, Carranza, Sarabia and Montoya – run inland, crossing the numbered calles that intersect at right angles.

The **ferry terminal** lies two minutes' walk south of Parque Morelos; the ferry arrives from Guaymas in Sonora on Tuesday, Wednesday, Friday and Sunday mornings. The terminal also serves as the town's transport and **information** hub: **taxis** wait here and ABC and Águila **buses** use the parking lot to drop off and take on passengers. Bus riders are dropped here too, which makes it one of the few centrally located stations on the entire peninsula.

The best-value hotels will be just as you walk into the centre from the bus/ferry terminal. The *Hotel del Real*, Montoya at Calle Playa (Ⓣ615/152-0068; ❹), is on Parque Morelos, and has rooms with TV and a/c, as well as a plantation-style porch for morning coffee. The long-time backpacker's favourite *Blanco y Negro* (Ⓣ615/152-0080; ❸–❹), whose cheapest rooms share a bath, is just off the southwest corner of Plaza Juárez, four blocks in from the waterfront. The *Hotel Francés* (Ⓣ615/152-2052; ❻) is a beautiful colonial building on the hill to the north of town, and worth the little bit more for its relative luxury. *Las Casitas*, Km 195 Hwy-1 Santa Rosalía–Loreto (Ⓣ615/152-3023, Ⓦwww.santarosaliacasitas.com; ❺) is a short, ten-minute walk from downtown, but the excellent views of the sea from its hillside perch make the trip worthwhile. The large, ceramic-tiled rooms have modern amenities and large windows overlooking the water.

Sadly, no French **restaurants** remain as a reminder of the town's beginnings, but the *Panadería El Boleo* produces some of the best baked goods in these parts, even if the baguettes aren't as crisp as the real thing. Restaurants in general aren't up to much, though you can eat well enough at *Terco's Pollito*, Obregón at Calle Playa. Next to the *Hotel del Real* there's a wonderful morning place, which has

## Santa Rosalía's copper mines

While walking in the hills around Santa Rosalía in 1868, one José Villavicencio chanced upon a **boleo**, a blue-green globule of rock that proved to be just a taster of a mineral vein containing more than twenty percent copper. By 1880, the wealth of the small-scale mining concessions came to the notice of the **Rothschilds**, who provided financing for the French El Boleo Company to buy the rights and found a massive extraction and smelting operation. Six hundred kilometres of tunnels were dug, a foundry was shipped out from Europe, and a new wharf built to transport the smelted ore north to Washington State for refining. Ships returned with lumber for the construction of a new town, laid out with houses built to a standard commensurate with their occupier's status within the company. Water was piped from the Santa Agueda oasis 15km away, and labour was brought in: Yaqui from Sonora as well as two thousand Chinese and Japanese who supposedly found that Baja was too arid to grow rice and soon headed off to the Mexican mainland. By 1954, falling profits from the nearly spent mines forced the French to sell the pits and smelter to the Mexican government who, though the mines were left idle, continued to smelt ore from the mainland until the early 1990s.

If you fancy a short desert walk, pick a cool part of the day and make a circuit of what remains of the mining equipment and the tunnels that riddle the hills to the north. None of the mines is fenced, so take a torch and explore cautiously. Following Calle Altamirano from Eiffel's Iglesia Santa Bárbara, you reach the massive kilometre-long above-ground duct, built of furnace slag, which once conveyed fumes from the smelter to the hilltop stack. You can walk along the top of it to the chimney for a superb view of the town and surrounding desert. From here, choose one of the numerous paths that head away inland to a series of gaping maws in the hillside. You can return the same way or pick your way straight down to the town or, with enough time, continue among the low cacti on the mesa, working your way down to the top end of Santa Rosalía.

a good coffee and breakfast selection; they will prepare *huevos* any way you like them. Several inexpensive places are scattered along Obregón, many selling great fish and seafood tacos. Try *Hot Dogs Exquisitos* on Calle 6 just down from the *Hotel 6*, where you can enjoy a filling evening meal as you watch TV outside with the family who runs the joint. *Restaurant Regio*, on the highway just as you come into town, plays the role of local truck stop; they have tacos and quesadillas for M$10 apiece, as well as more expensive meals.

Both **banks** are on Constitución, and have ATMs: Bancomer changes cheques until noon, Banamex accepts only bills until 1pm. If you are heading south, note that Mulegé does not have a bank and this will be your last chance for money until Loreto. The **post office** is on Constitución at Calle 2, and there's a **phone** outside the *Hotel del Real*. There are a few places with **Internet** access: Café Internet Vision, on Calle 6 just off Obregón (Mon–Sat 10am–2pm & 4–10pm; M$15/hr), and its sibling Café Internet, on Obregón and Calle Playa (Mon–Sat 9am–9pm; M$15/hr).

## Mulegé and around

Some 60km to the south of Santa Rosalía lies **MULEGÉ**, a small village on the site of an ancient mission. Like San Ignacio, it's a real oasis: tucked into a lush valley, the village sits underneath myriad palms on the north bank of the Río Santa Rosalía. Roughly 960km south of the US border, Mulegé, a fruit-growing centre that's also popular with kayakers, has a definite feel of the tropics. The town is also one of the most peaceful and laid-back in Baja, helped in part by some superb beaches strung out along the coast to the south. Yet again you'll miss out on the best of them without your own transportation, but here hitching is at least a realistic possibility – many visitors commute to the beaches daily, particularly during the high season (mid-Oct to April).

There's not a great deal to see in Mulegé, though you could check out the unkempt **Museo Regional de Historia Mulegé** (Mon–Fri 9am–1pm; M$15 suggested donation), set on a hillside above town; head a couple blocks away from the centre towards the ocean, then follow the trail leading up the hill to the museum. Built nearly a hundred years ago, it is housed in a former prison known as the "prison without doors", as it allowed its inmates to work in town in the mornings and afternoons; some were even married in town. Visitors can enter the prison cells and view a number of local artefacts. The **Misión Santa Rosalía de Mulegé**, founded in 1705 and completed sixty years later, sits atop a hill overlooking the town. The church only opens for the occasional Mass, but it's still well worth the hike up for the spectacular view from above the palms. Follow Zaragoza south underneath the highway bridge until you see the dirt road that climbs to the mission.

### Mulegé practicalities

Part of Mulegé's charm comes from its narrow, one-way dirt streets that branch eastward from Hwy-1 and surround both sides of the estuary. Although it's difficult to find where you're going at first crack, the town's compact layout will keep you from wandering lost for too long. The streets' slimness prevents large trucks or cars with trailers from operating easily, or at all, in the town itself; scout your route ahead of time if you're driving in anything larger than an SUV. There are two **Pemex** stations in and around town: one in town on Avenida Martínez and another 2.5km south of town along Hwy-1. The **bus**

#### Activities and trips around Mulegé

Other than as a springboard for the beaches to the south, the main reason to stop at Mulegé is to go diving or take one of the **cave-painting tours** out to the Sierra de Guadalupe. This range boasts the densest collection of rock art in Baja (at least 700 paintings), as well as some of the most accessible, requiring as little as five hours for the round trip. Getting a group together to cut costs shouldn't prove a problem in high season, but you still need to shop around as the tours differ considerably. Expect to pay M$400 per person or half that with your own transportation. Overnight excursions are possible too, including a night at a 260-year-old ranch and two different cave locations. Otherwise, Ciro Romero can take you to the cave paintings (Ⓣ615/153-0481, Ⓔcirocuesta@yahoo.com.mx) for similar prices. Lastly, head to *Las Casitas* (see opposite), which also acts as an informal tourist office for information on other local attractions and tours.

For **snorkelling and diving trips**, head to Cortez Explorers (daily 4–7pm; Ⓣ615/153-0500, Ⓦwww.cortez-explorers.com) at Moctezuma 75-A; prices begin at M$700 per person. They also rent **mountain bikes** (M$200/day) and all-terrain vehicles (M$250/hr). A beginner's resort course costs M$1000, a snorkelling trip M$400 (including equipment). If you're qualified, you can also rent snorkel gear from them and go about it yourself: Punta Prieta – north of the lighthouse, a short walk from town – is still fairly unknown, even though it's really the only place you can dive or snorkel that can be reached by the shore (other spots must be accessed by boat). Follow Madero as it hugs the river, and before you reach the lighthouse you'll meet a dirt road; take a left and it will take you past an old hotel and a school before you reach Punta Prieta.

**stop** is at the triangle junction of Hwy-1 and Martínez, a good ten-minute walk southwest of downtown; to get to the centre, follow Hwy-1 to the right fork onto Martínez, then a second right onto Zaragoza and the plaza.

If you want to **stay** in Mulegé, you have a choice of either cheap and very basic *casas de huéspedes* or relatively upmarket hotels. The *Hacienda* (Ⓣ615/153-0021; ❹), on Madero just off the plaza, is the pick of the latter, with its small pool, pleasant courtyard and parking, though *Las Casitas*, Madero 50 (Ⓣ615/153-0019, Ⓔlascasitas1962@hotmail.com; ❻), the former home of Mexican poet José Gorosave, has its charms, with an orchard-like yard and dribbling fountains. Budget alternatives include the small, shaded *Casa de Huéspedes Nachita* (Ⓣ615/153-0140; ❷), a family-run place with the most laid-back staff you'll find in Baja, and the more comfortable *Manuelita* (Ⓣ615/153-0175; ❹), both of which are on Moctezuma, the left fork as you head into town from the highway. With slightly larger rooms, the somewhat musty *Canett* (Ⓣ615/153-0272; ❷) is on Madero beyond the church. For an altogether more peaceful stay, try *Hotel Mulegé* (Ⓣ615/153-0090; ❺), on the left as you head into town at Moctezuma 15. Just south of town on the east side of the Transpeninsular at Km 139, the luxurious *Serenidad* (Ⓣ615/153-0530, Ⓦwww.serenidad.com; ❼, closed Sept) has some great summer three-night-stay specials, and allows guests to fly into the private airstrip. **Campers** should head 1km south of the bus stop (or along the dirt road on the south side of the river from Mulegé) to *The Orchard* (Ⓣ615/153-0300, Ⓦwww.orchardvacationvillage.com; ❶–❸), where two can pitch a tent or rent a *casita* and guests can rent canoes on the Río Mulegé.

Mulegé doesn't offer a huge amount of **eating and drinking** options, but what's there is quite good. The majority of the North American long-stayers and a good many Mexicans gravitate towards the decent and reasonably priced restaurant and bar at *Las Casitas* (see above). You could also try *Los Equipales*, Moctezuma and Zaragoza, a mid-range steak and seafood place serving large portions – a steak complete with soup, salad and potatoes costs M$100; alternatively there's the less formal and cheaper *El Candil* on the plaza, another gringo rendezvous spot that does excellent breakfasts of fruit, eggs, ham, bacon, toast and potatoes for M$3. *La Palapa*, on the highway south and past the Pemex petrol station, also does great breakfasts. If you happen to be around on Sunday night, head to *Eduardo's*, Martínez s/n (Ⓣ615/153-0258), for some of the best Chinese food south of Mexicali; it's inexpensive, but be prepared to wait some time for service.

Mulegé has no banks, although *Rosario's Patio* serves as a **casa de cambio** with mediocre rates (Mon–Sat 9am–1pm & 4–8pm), on Moctezuma two blocks off the plaza; note that travellers' cheques are not widely accepted in town. If you're strapped for cash, try La Tienda, on Martínez, which primarily sells books, camera film plus diving and fishing accessories but also accepts payment by ATM cards. The owners are also a great source of local **information**. The small **post office** is also on Martínez, and outside it you'll find long-distance **phones**; there are also some at Padilla grocery store at Zaragoza and Martínez. If you find yourself staying for a few days and need a **laundry**, Lavamática Claudia, at Zaragoza and Moctezuma, washes, dries and folds your clothes for about M$40 per load. You can find a few **Internet** terminals with dial-up on Moctezuma, three blocks from the bus stop (Mon–Sat 9.30am–8pm & Sun 10am–2pm; M$20/hr).

## Bahía Concepción

There is good diving and fishing immediately around Mulegé, but the best beaches are between 10km and 50km south of town along the shore of **Bahía**

**Concepción**. The bay ranges from 3km to 6.5km wide, is 48km long and is enclosed on three sides and dotted with islands. The blue-green waters, peaceful bays and white-sand beaches are beautiful and relatively undeveloped – though you will at times find teams of RVs lining the waters – and it's a good place to break your journey for a day or so before travelling south. As far as **kayaking** goes, there are few places better than Bahía Concepción.

## Diving and fishing around Baja California

Nowhere in Baja California is more than 90km from either the Pacific Ocean or the Sea of Cortés, and both bodies of water support an abundance of **sea life**. The unmatched variety of marine environments in the Sea of Cortés make it one of the richest seas in the world, with over eight hundred species of fish and more than twice as many shellfish. Throughout the peninsula you'll see RVs and off-road vehicles laden with fishing tackle, dinghies and scuba gear headed for remote fishing camps or sheltered bays.

### Diving

The most popular **diving** areas in the north are **Islas Los Coronados**, off Tijuana, (but note that they are only served by organized trips from San Diego north of the border), and **Punta Banda** and **Islas de Todos Santos**, off Ensenada. In the south, where the waters are a good deal warmer and the fish dramatically colourful, the best dives are off the coast of **Mulegé** and **Bahía de Concepción**, **Loreto**, **La Paz** and **Los Cabos**. In the waters off San José del Cabo, the giant reef known as **Cabo Pulmo** offers the chance to dive amidst schools of hammerheads, whale sharks, tunas and sea lions; many proclaim it to be the peninsula's best diving spot. From August to November you'll find the ideal combination of water clarity and warmth.

Recent years have seen a dramatic increase in Baja's tourist numbers, especially in the south, and **dive shops** are plentiful once you cross the Baja California Sur line. Diving is not cheap, though, and having your own gear will cut costs in half. The average two-tank all-inclusive outing will cost you M$700–1000, and the prices generally increase the closer to Los Cabos you choose to dive. Many dive shops will offer something called a "resort" course for M$1000 – a basic introduction to scuba diving and guided shallow underwater dives, perfect for someone with zero experience. The more extensive Open Water Diver certification takes four or five days and will cost you at least M$3500, but this certifies you to dive in most waters of the world. Recommended **dive operators** for various locations are listed in the guide text.

### Fishing

**Fishing** in Baja can be spectacular, especially so in the south. The favourite holes have always been near **La Paz** and around **Cabo San Lucas**, the small fishing village of **La Playita** just east of **San José del Cabo**, and the rest of the **East Cape**, where the nearby Gordo Banks seamount produces more marlin, tuna, wahoo, sailfish and dorado than anywhere else in Mexico. Most large towns have established charters, while towns like Bahía de los Angeles offer cheaper, more rustic adventures. **Fishing charters** offer one of two services: either less formal fishing from a *panga* that can carry up to three anglers, or the giant marina-based fleets with boats that can accommodate up to six. *Pangas* charge anywhere from M$1500 to M$2000 for six hours, the larger boats upwards of M$4500, including food, drinks and gratuity. These trips generally begin at about 6am and last from five to eight hours. **Shore fishing** is an option almost anywhere in Baja, though as with fishing charters, a **fishing licence** is required. While fishing charters provide this, if you're on your own you will need to ask about them at the local tourist office. Tour operators are listed in the relevant town entries.

The best stretches of sand include **Playa Punta Arena**, at Km 118, then another 2km on a dirt road, where there are some basic palapa shelters to rent. **Playa Santispac**, some 5km further on, is right on the highway – despite the early stages of development and occasional crowds of RVs, it still has plenty of room to camp (for a fee) and enough life to make staying here longer-term a realistic option, though there are free open palapas to hang out under during the day if you just want to stop for a swim. **Posada Concepción**, just south of Santispac, shows the beginnings of Cabo-style development and has permanent residents; *EcoMundo* here, at Km 111 (no phone, www.ecomundobaja.com; camping M$100, palapas ❷), is an environmentally minded place offering standard palapa and tent accommodation, plus they rent out kayaks for a day or longer (from M$200/day, reservations a must). Facilities include a barbecue pit, an excellent little bookshop and a bar.

If you keep to the right on the *EcoMundo* road you'll pass around a bend and 1km thereafter arrive at the rather secluded *Playa Escondida* (no phone). Few trailers can make it over the hump, so the campground is more hospitable to tent campers. It is rustic (cold showers and outhouses) and there are no services.

Further south there are few facilities for anything other than camping: **Playa El Coyote**, where there's also a hot spring, and **Playa El Requesón**, another couple of popular, beautiful beaches, are the last and the best opportunities for this (M$50 for each). Note that there's no fresh water available at either, but locals drop by in the early morning and afternoon selling everything from water to fresh shrimps. Your other best bet is renting kayak, snorkelling or scuba equipment from the reputable Las Parras Tours in Loreto (see p.115).

## Loreto

**LORETO**, the next town down the coast, is far larger than Mulegé. The site of the earliest permanent settlement in the Californias, it was founded in 1697 as the head of the Jesuit missions to California. Later taken over by the Franciscans, in practice it served as the administrative capital of the entire territory for some 130 years until a devastating hurricane struck in 1829. More recently it has been a popular escape for fishing and diving enthusiasts, and nowadays it's enjoying something of a renaissance, boosted both by the development of Baja California Sur as a whole and the current generation of local and outside developers who are taking advantage of an infrastructure created in the 1970s and subsequently squandered by the tourism agency FONATUR (Fondo Nacional de Fomento al Turismo). It has natural assets, too: Mexico's largest marine park, **Parque Nacional Bahía de Loreto**, lies just offshore.

### Arrival, information and getting around

Loreto's **airport** (☎613/135-0454) is 5km south of town off Hwy-1, halfway between Nopoló and Loreto. Aeroméxico, Mexicana and Alaskan Air have desks here, and there are Hertz, Avis and National rental counters at the entrance. Taxi shuttles to downtown cost M$60–80; there's no regular bus service to or from the airport.

ABC and Águila **bus** lines use Loreto's bus station, Salvatierra and Paseo Pedro de Ugarte (☎613/135-0767), just in front of the baseball field. It's a fifteen-minute walk east along Salvatierra to the Plaza Cívica, and a further five minutes in the same direction to the beach. Though it's easy enough to get around town by foot there's a **local bus** system that runs along the major streets for a M$5 flat fee. Getting around via **taxi** is both easy and cheap. The stand at Salvatierra near the plaza serves both Sitio Loreto (☎613/135-0424) and Sitio Juárez (☎613/135-0915).

The English-speaking **tourist office** (Mon–Fri 9am–3pm; ☎613/135-0411) is located in the Palacio de Gobierno at Madero and Salvatierra, on the west side of the pedestrian Plaza Cívica. BBVA Bancomer, just across the street, has the **only ATM** between Santa Rosalía and Ciudad Insurgentes; the staff will change travellers' cheques Monday through Friday from 8.30am to 3.30pm. The **post office** is on Deportiva 13, just off Salvatierra on the way into town, behind the Cruz Roja building. More spots in town are adding wireless **Internet** access; if you have the right gear you can walk the streets and plop down on a bench with your laptop once you've picked up a signal. Established locations include Caseta Soledad Internet Café on Salvatierra just as it meets Hidalgo (Mon–Sat 8am–9pm & Sun 9am–1pm; M$30/hr), Ram 64 on Juárez (daily 9am–9pm; M$25/hr), and .Com Café, Madero at Salvatierra (Mon–Sat 9am–10pm; M$25/hr; ☎613/135-1847), which also has wireless access.

## Accommodation

Loreto has a wide range of **accommodation** available, from cute B&Bs to four-star resort-style hotels – waterfront lodging isn't limited to visitors with big bucks.

**Las Cabañas de Loreto** Moreles s/n, at the malecón ☎613/135-1105, Ⓦwww.lascabanasdeloreto.com. The four cabanas with a/c, kitchenette, TV and video are situated around a central, gated courtyard. Communal hammocks and a barbecue grill, as well as free WiFi access. ❻

**Coco Cabañas** Davis s/n, at Constituyentes ☎613/135-1729, Ⓦwww.cococabanasloreto.com. All eight cabanas surround a patio with a sunken pool and barbecue area. The rooms have kitchens and private baths but no TV. If you've caught your dinner in the sea, there's a cleaning area off the patio. ❻

**Iguana Inn** Juárez s/n, at Davis ☎613/135-1627. Another friendly, small inn near the centre of town. The owners live in the front house, guests stay in the four spotless cabañas situated around a gurgling fountain and courtyard in the back. The relatively modern rooms, with tile floors, a/c, TV and ceiling fans, have kitchenettes and private baths. ❹

**Inn at Loreto Bay** Misión de Loreto s/n, Nopoló ☎613/133-0010, Ⓦwww.innatloretobay.com. Built as a part of the *Camino Real* four-star chain, the *Inn* was bought up by the Loreto Bay developers who quickly remodelled the property to make the restaurant, bar, pool and all public spaces ecofriendly. The tiled rooms are large and have a/c, TV, private patios and sea views. In addition to a private beach, there's a giant pool with a swim-up bar at the centre of the property. ❽

**El Junípero** Paseo Hidalgo s/n ☎613/135-0122. *Junípero*'s location just off the plaza is its best asset; rooms are rather plain and sparse, but each comes with a/c and a private bath. ❺

**Oasis** C de la Playa s/n at Zaragoza ☎613/135-0211, Ⓦwww.hoteloasis.com. Opened in the 1960s, *Oasis* is a family-run affair whose palapa-covered buildings and a prime end-of-the-malecón location evoke a posh Gilligan's Island. The large rooms and suites have views of either the sea or pool, and all rooms have a/c and coffee-makers. Rooms with TV and phone are available on request, as are pre-departure fishing packages done in tandem with local partners. ❼

**Palmas Altas** Nicolas Bravo s/n, at Baja California ☎613/135-1429. The landscaped courtyard and pool add a bit of luxury to the otherwise bland surroundings. Rooms have TV and private bath but are otherwise rather bare. ❸

## The town and around

Neat and tidy, Loreto has a strong sense of history. The town is shaped roughly like a triangle pointing west from the malecón and the edge of the Sea of Cortés; all points of interest are near the wide end closest to the shore. Salvatierra turns into a pedestrian mall at Independencia and every building of note is along this six-block-long promenade to the sea, including the original mission church, the **Misión Nuestra Señora de Loreto Conchó**. Still standing, though heavily restored after centuries of earthquake damage, its basic structure – solid, squat and simple – is little changed. The inscription over the door, which translates as "The head and mother church of the missions of upper and lower California", attests to its former importance, as does the Baroque altarpiece originally transported here from Mexico City. Next door to the mission, in a former storage house and courtyard complex, stands the thorough and engaging **Museo de las Misiones** (Tues–Sun 9am–6pm; M$30; ⓣ613/135-0441). The museum chronicles the early conversion and colonization of Baja California in five rooms that are accessed via a covered walking path.

The city's greatest asset is the giant body of protected waters along its eastern shore. **Parque Nacional Bahía de Loreto** was established in 1996 to protect over 2000 square kilometres of the Sea of Cortés from overfishing, and it's become another superb place for **diving** and **kayaking**. Las Parras (ⓣ613/135-1010, ⓦwww.lasparrastours.com), at Madero 16, can set you up with gear for diving, kayaking and snorkelling. A two-tank dive will cost you M$800; a full eight-hour day of kayaking M$280. Dolphin Dive Center (ⓣ613/135-1914, ⓦwww.dolphindivebaja.com), Juárez between Mateos and Davis, has day-long package dive trips to Isla Coronados, Isla Danzante and other islands that include tanks, all gear, snacks, guide, boat and park fees, for M$950. They'll rent gear if you want to go out on your own and offer dive certification if you're a newbie (multi-day training for M$4000). Baja Outpost on the malecón (ⓣ613/125-1134, ⓦwww.bajaoutpost.com) does dive, snorkel and kayak trips, as well as package deals that include B&B-style rooms.

South of town, FONATUR's failed Cancún-like master plan for the new "town" of **Nopoló** has evolved into the **Villages at Loreto Bay**, the largest residential development by a foreign builder in Mexico. Loreto Bay's success, although providing a massive economic boost to the entire region, threatens to overwhelm the already limited water supply and upset the delicate desert ecosystem.

### Eating and drinking

Finding simple Mexican **food** is no problem at taco stands along Hidalgo or at fancier places around the plaza, notably the popular *Café Olé*, which does good-value breakfasts and *antojitos* – try the cinnamon rolls. *Tiffany's Pizza Parlour* on Hidalgo south of the plaza serves excellent, if pricey, pizza, though they are not always open in the off season. *Tío Lupe's*, a short walk down from *Tiffany's* on Salvatierra, offers a standard Mexican menu, but also has local seafood and a few Continental dishes. *La Terraza*, also on Hidalgo but closer to the malecón, cooks similar food, though it is somewhat cheaper and, as you may have guessed, has a terrace.

## La Paz

Everyone ends up in **LA PAZ** eventually, if only to get the ferry out, and it seems that most of the population of Baja California Sur is gravitating here, too. The outskirts are an ugly sprawl, their development outpacing the spread of paved roads and facilities. But the town centre, modernized as it is, has managed to preserve something of its quiet colonial atmosphere. You can stroll along the waterfront malecón, and, for a change, the beach in town looks inviting enough for a swim – though there are no guarantees on the cleanliness of the water.

The Bay of La Paz was explored by **Cortés** himself in the first years after the Conquest – drawn, as always, by tales of great wealth – but he found little to interest him and, despite successive military and missionary expeditions, La Paz wasn't permanently settled until the end of the eighteenth century. It then grew rapidly, however, thanks to the riches of the surrounding sea; for a time it was a major pearl-fishing centre. American troops occupied the town during the Texan war, and six years later it was again invaded, this time by the US freebooter William Walker in one of his many attempts to carve himself out a Central American kingdom; by this time it was already capital of the territory of California. He changed his mind and left by ship for the Ensenada area in the spring, but not without taking the former and current governors as hostages, as well as the town's archives.

The pearl trade almost completely dried up in the 1940s, a failure often falsely blamed on Japanese fishermen who supposedly poisoned the beds, but most likely due to a disease among the oysters. But since the 1960s La Paz has prospered; first because of the ferry service to the mainland, and then because of fly-in US fishermen attempting to emulate John Wayne and Bing Crosby, who dropped their own hooks in the sea from here. It's now fed by every sector of the peninsula's tourism: visitors from mainland Mexico, drivers on a Hwy-1 road trip, outdoor enthusiasts who kayak to the islands and Los Cabos tourists on day trips.

The best time to visit is from November to May, as summers can be unbearably hot. During the last week in February La Paz holds its **carnival**, with colourful parades and cultural events transforming the town; book ahead if you plan to come during this time. The event, which is less Río de Janeiro bacchanalia and more county fair, begins on Saturday at dusk with scores of themed floats parading down the malecón. You'll find a huge variety of live music played all over town till the wee hours, though the most interesting venues are the small bandstands at the end of the parade strip. Make reservations well in advance if you want to stay in La Paz during the carnival, as the town overflows with visitors.

## Arrival and information

**Car** and **bus** traffic from northbound Hwy-1 comes into the city via Calzada Forjadores; southbound Hwy-1 enters along Abasolo, which turns into the waterfront Obregón. If you're travelling between major cities in Baja California Sur, the bus is finally a viable option, especially from San José del Cabo – service is frequent and buses stick to schedule. Buses from there and everywhere else arrive at the modern **Central Camionera** along the busy malecón at Calle Independencia. The station serves ABC, Águila, Ejecutivo and EcoBaja lines, can help arrange tours, and even has Internet terminals available for a nominal cost (M$20/hr).

Getting a **taxi** is never difficult, especially if you use one of the many stands along the waterfront or on Plaza Jardín Velasco; there are stands on the malecón in front of *Hotel Perla* and *Seven Crowns* and on both sides of the cathedral on the plaza. They are metered, so make sure the cabby turns it on.

**Ferry** passengers arriving at Pichilingue (see box, p.122) are met by buses that drop off riders at the Central Camionera. Individual taxis are about M$95 to the city centre, while shared taxis cost M$30; negotiate the price ahead of time. La Paz has two main **marinas** that account for two-thirds of the private boat traffic: Palmira, Km 2.5 Carretera a Pichilingue (Ⓣ612/121-6159, Ⓦwww.marinapalmira.com) on the northeast end of the malecón, and La Paz, Topete 3040 (Ⓣ612/125-2112), to the southwest. The slips tend to operate near capacity, so make arrangements in advance of your arrival.

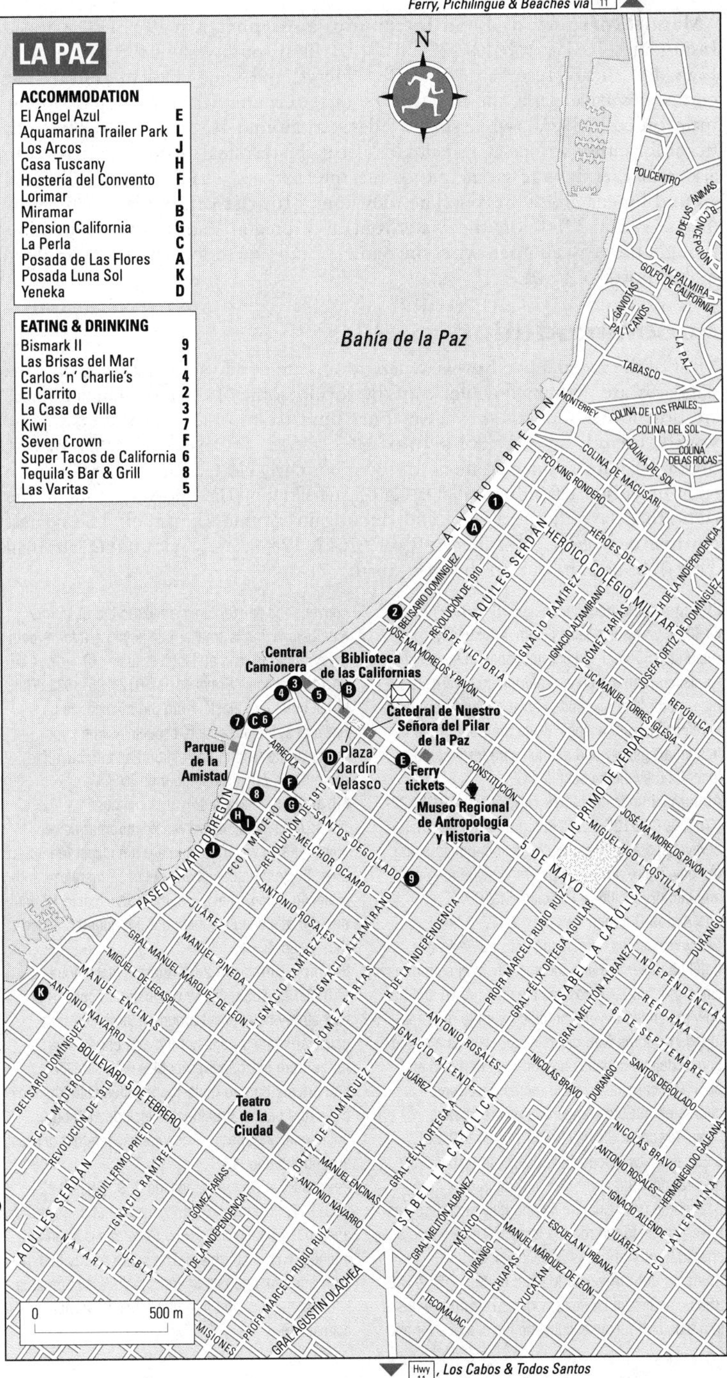
Ferry, Pichilingue & Beaches via Hwy 11
LA PAZ
N
ACCOMMODATION
El Ángel Azul E
Aquamarina Trailer Park L
Los Arcos J
Casa Tuscany H
Hostería del Convento F
Lorimar I
Miramar B
Pension California G
La Perla C
Posada de Las Flores A
Posada Luna Sol K
Yeneka D
EATING & DRINKING
Bismark II 9
Las Brisas del Mar 1
Carlos 'n' Charlie's 4
El Carrito 2
La Casa de Villa 3
Kiwi 7
Seven Crown F
Super Tacos de California 6
Tequila's Bar & Grill 8
Las Varitas 5
Bahía de la Paz
Central Camionera
Biblioteca de las Californias
Catedral de Nuestro Señora del Pilar de la Paz
Parque de la Amistad
Plaza Jardín Velasco
Ferry tickets
Museo Regional de Antropología y Historia
Teatro de la Ciudad
ÁLVARO OBREGÓN
PASEO ÁLVARO OBREGÓN
AQUILES SERDÁN
HERÓICO COLEGIO MILITAR
5 DE MAYO
ISABEL LA CATÓLICA
BOULEVARD 5 DE FEBRERO
LIC PRIMO DE VERDAD
CONSTITUCIÓN
POLICENTRO
MONTERREY
TABASCO
0 500 m
Airport & Ciudad Constitución
Hwy 11, Los Cabos & Todos Santos

**Manuel Márquez de León International Airport**, Km 10 Hwy-1 Ciudad Insurgentes–La Paz (Ⓣ612/122-2959), is 12km southwest of the city just off Hwy-1 Ciudad Insurgentes–La Paz. Hertz, Avis and Dollar **rental car** companies have desks in the airport's only terminal. Taxis to hotels on the malecón cost M$250, while shared rides start around M$80 a person; buy your ticket for either service at a small kiosk near the terminal's eastern exit. You can also rent cars downtown at one of the international chain agencies clustered around Pineda and Obregón. The most useful **tourist office** (daily 9am–8pm; Ⓣ612/122-5939) is on the waterfront at Obregón and 16 de Septiembre, though there is another with the same hours and information on Hwy-1, 5.5km north of town.

## Accommodation

Most of the inexpensive **hotels**, where rooms are good value by Baja California standards, are within a few blocks of the zócalo; some of the older fancier places are downtown too, but the newer ones tend to be out along the coast. The **youth hostel**, on Forjadores (Ⓣ612/122-4615; ❷), has reasonably priced, impersonal dorms, inconvenient for town but fairly close to the bus station; turn right up Jalisco, left along Isabel la Católica, following the one-way traffic to the right, then take the next right and right again, around 1km in all. The nearest **campsite** is *El Cardón Trailer Park* (Ⓣ612/124-0078, Ⓔelcardon@latinmail.com), about 2km out on the road north.

**El Ángel Azul** Independencia 518 Ⓣ612/125-5130, Ⓦwww.elangelazul.com. A tastefully restored 150-year-old courthouse with sparsely furnished rooms around a garden courtyard. The nine rooms and two suites have a/c and free wireless Internet access, while the front of the inn has an art gallery and a small café for breakfast, lunch and evening cocktails. ❼

**Aquamarina Trailer Park** Nayarit 10 Ⓣ612/122-3761, Ⓕ612/125-6228. Primarily used by small caravans, but with spaces for tent camping along the bay. There are hot showers, a swimming pool and laundry facilities. Camping M$100.

**Los Arcos** Obregón 498 Ⓣ612/122-2744, Ⓦwww.losarcos.com. Along with *La Perla*, this hotel has been serving the sport-fishing community since the 1950s. *Arcos* has steadily grown and has now expanded beyond an older wing to offer standard rooms with balconies as well as a collection of deluxe cabañas around the courtyard and pool. The cabañas and old rooms have more character, but the standard ones are cheaper. ❼

**Casa Tuscany** Nicolás Bravo 110 Ⓣ612/128 8103, Ⓦwww.tuscanybaja.com. The distinctive decorations that adorn the four bedrooms in this B&B come from Guatemala and Italy and all rooms have access to the rooftop terrace. There's also a shared library of books and videos. ❺

**Hosteria del Convento** Madero 85 Sur Ⓣ612/122-3508. The first of La Paz's two *casa de huéspedes* is in a blue and yellow building on the site of a former convent and has features similar to the *California* (see below), but is smaller and, if you ask for a room away from the road and lobby, quieter. ❷

**Lorimar** Nicolás Bravo 110 Ⓣ612/125-3822. This small hotel two blocks from the malecón is La Paz's best budget option, especially when you factor in the helpful desk staff. Each immaculate room has a private bath, but no TV. ❹

**Miramar** 5 de Mayo s/n, at Domínguez Ⓣ612/122-0672, Ⓦwww.hotelmiramarmexico.com. The views of the sea are the nicest feature at this 25-room hotel halfway between the plaza and malecón. Rooms have a/c, mini-bars, cable TV and decor that's been cleaned, but not updated, since the 1970s. ❺

**El Moro Suites** Km 2 Carretera a Pichilingue Ⓣ612/122-4084, Ⓦwww.clubelmoro.com. This two-storey hotel is set around a large central courtyard with a pool, hot tub and bar. Rooms range from inexpensive doubles with satellite TV and private bath to multi-room suites with kitchenettes and patios. Breakfast is included in some packages, and there's free wireless Internet access around the pool. ❻

**Pension California** Degollado 209 Ⓣ612/122-2896, Ⓔpensioncalifornia@prodigy.net.mx. The aged but wonderful *Pension California* is in an old building with a courtyard. The spare rooms all have bath and fan, and public areas include a communal kitchen, laundry and free high-speed Internet access. ❷

**La Perla** Obregón 1570, at La Paz ⓣ612/122-0777, ⓦwww.hotelperlabaja.com. Once the most popular place in town, this Spanish colonial gem is still a good deal. Tiled throughout, Western-style rooms have a/c, TVs and some bay views. There's also a playground for children, a pool and a gringo-packed restaurant. ❺

**Posada de Las Flores** Obregón 440 ⓣ612/125-5871, ⓦwww.posadadelasflores.com. Well-designed rooms with Mexican-Colonial chic decor, plush bath products and a mini-bar; you'll pay more here for the boutique hotel experience than it's worth, but the location on the malecón and the view from the attached second-storey restaurant are superb. ❽

**Posada Luna Sol** Topete 564, between 5 de Febrero and Navarro ⓣ612/123-0559, ⓦwww.kayakbaja.com. The location, along a residential block west of the marina, is a bit removed from the action, but the rooms – with artisan-tiled private baths, flat-screen TVs and a/c – break from the cookie-cutter hotel norm and the knowledgeable staff are excellent local resources. There's also secure, on-site parking. ❻

**Yeneka** Madero 1520 ⓣ612/125-4688, ⓔynkmacias@prodigy.net.mx. The funkiest hotel on the peninsula also bills itself as *Museo Posada Antiquario*. Folk art fills the two-storey courtyard and eccentric furniture decorates the comfortable, clean rooms, some of which come with a/c and TV. The helpful staff actually encourage you to negotiate your room rate (a/c will always be about M$70 more). ❹

## The town and around

There's not a great deal to see in La Paz itself and if you're staying for any length of time you should head for the beaches. If you're just hanging around waiting for a ferry, however, you can happily fill a day window-shopping in the centre – dozens of stores selling everything from clothes, cosmetics and varied bric-a-brac take advantage of the duty-free zone – and browsing around the market. The small **Museo Regional de Antropología y Historia**, 5 de Mayo and Altamirano (Mon–Fri 8am–6pm, Sat 9am–2pm; free; ⓣ612/122-0162), is also worth a passing look: exhibits include photos of cave paintings and an ethnological history of the peninsula. This is as good as Baja museums get, but it has no English labelling. More information on all aspects of Baja, some of it in English, is available in the Biblioteca de las Californias, opposite the cathedral on the zócalo, or at Libros Libros at Constitución 195.

### Baja California's ancestors

There's a growing body of knowledge that asserts Baja California's, and all of western North America's, **original inhabitants** were southern Asians and Pacific Islanders who arrived in North America by boat over fifteen thousand years ago. Remains found in the La Paz area, when put in context with similar remains found in the US state of Washington and in Chile, point to a wide dispersion of early settlers who have more in common with Australian aborigines than Aztecs or Apaches. This throws a spanner in the theory that all the descendants of modern Amerindians arrived from Siberia over the Bering Strait land bridge, something which pleases neither entrenched archeologists nor contemporary American Indians, who like to think *their* ancestors came first.

One of the primary archeological links is the similarity of the southern Asian skull type to these more recently discovered Paleoamerican remains. The remains of La Paz's Pericú tribe (which was wiped out completely by the mid-1700s), are like those of southern Asians but distinct from other Baja Californian tribes. This adds to the argument that two distinct native cultures existed side by side on the peninsula in relative isolation from other tribal groups and settlements on the mainland. Unfortunately, the research undertaken around La Paz can't be seen in any of its museums, though there is some information about the work at Loreto's mission museum (see p.115).

△ Malecón, La Paz

**Beaches** ring the bay all around La Paz, but the easiest to get to are undoubtedly those to the south, served by the local bus that runs along Obregón to the ferry terminal at Pichilingue. Decent ones are **Playa del Tesoro**, shortly before Pichilingue, and **Playa Pichilingue**, just beyond the ferry station. Both have simple facilities, including a restaurant. The best, however, is **Playa de Balandra**, actually several beaches around a saltwater lagoon with eight shallow bays, most of which are no more than waist deep: three buses leave the malecón from 10am daily and traverse the beach route, taking you here for M$35; the last bus back is at 5pm.

There are plenty of opportunities for fishing, diving and **boat trips** into the bay; just stroll along the malecón to find people offering the latter – **Isla Espíritu Santo** is a popular destination, as is **Los Islotes**, a small group of islands that hosts a colony of **sea lions**; also see "Listings", p.123, for details on specific operators.

## Eating and drinking

Wandering round La Paz you'll find dozens of places to **eat** – the seafood, especially, is excellent. There are numerous inexpensive local restaurants near the market, especially on Serdán and 16 de Septiembre, and around the zócalo.

**Bismark II** Altamirano and Degollado ⓣ612/122-4854. Excellent seafood – order the fresh catch grilled ($M75–110) – without having to pay inflated waterfront prices. Also runs a *taquería* of the same name towards the southern end of Obregón, with some of the best tacos in town.

**Las Brisas del Mar** Obregón at Colegio Militar ⓣ612/123-5055, ⓔlasbrisasdelmbcs@hotmail.com. When locals want to have a fancy night out, they come here for seafood and steaks. Prices are higher than other malecón spots – dinner for two with drinks will cost M$500 – but it's one of the few places with a wine list and without fluorescent lighting and fishing gear on the walls.

**Carlos 'n' Charlies** Obregón and 16 de Septiembre ⓣ612/122-9290. As everyone walks by during early evening and late night, it's more about the social scene here – and the drinks, too – than the food, a pan-Mexican hodgepodge of a menu. Two levels of outdoor space along Obregón give it the edge over other malecón pub-crawl stops.

**El Carrito** Obregón at Morelos ⓣ612/125-6658. Unpretentious and popular with locals who come for the *ceviche* and other great seafood, all reasonably priced.

**La Casa de Villa** Obregón and 16 de Septiembre ⓣ612/128-5742. The evening begins at happy hour at this multi-level dance club and pool hall with a split personality; sink the stripes indoors or head up to the roof deck for dancing amongst a mix of locals and visitors.

**Kiwi** Obregón at 5 de Mayo, ⓣ612/123-3282. Great local and regional cuisine for decent prices, with tables set right in the sand on the beach. Try the scrumptious stuffed fish fillet, a house speciality.

**Seven Crown** Obregón 1710 at Degollado ⓣ612/128-7787. This newly built minimalist hotel may have pricey rooms, but its stylish roof bar and restaurant, open to non-guests, have wonderful views of the water, with several small terraces for those seeking private sunset inebriation.

**Super Tacos de California** Esquerro, at Arreola. Seafood tacos and help-yourself salad stand; a lobster taco goes for M$260.

**Taquería Muello Hacienda** near Serfin bank, and a half-block from the malecón. Hugely popular taco stand; try the potato special.

**Tequila's Bar and Grill** Ocampo 310 ⓣ612/121-5217. Equally enjoyed by tourists and locals, *Tequila's* is one of the few places you can play pool while the kitchen cooks up what you've caught in the bay (M$40 per fish). There's a full seafood-centric menu for those who haven't been fishing, too.

**Las Varitas** Independencia 111 ⓣ612/125-2025. The city's premier live music club tends to be crowded even when there isn't a show. A second-storey covered balcony overlooks the street below and provides a temporary escape if the music starts going downhill. Cover M$40.

## Listings

**Airlines and flights** Aeroméxico ⓣ612/122-0091 or 0092, ⓦwww.aeromexico.com; for comprehensive flight details, contact the Viajes Perla travel agency, on the corner of 5 de Mayo and Dominguéz (Mon–Sat 8.30am–7.30pm & Sun 9am–2pm; ⓣ612/122-8666). The airport is 8km southwest of town, reached by an expensive taxi ride.

**American Express** Esquerro 1679, behind the *La Perla* hotel (Mon–Fri 9am–2pm & 4–6pm, Sat 9am–2pm; ⓣ612/122-8300).

**Banks** Most banks lie between the zócalo and the waterfront.

**Books** Libros Libros, Constitución 195, sells many English-language newspapers and books.

**Buses** Ten regular daily services head north, three going as far as Tijuana, 22 hours away (at 8am,

10am and 10pm), another to Mexicali (1pm). Buses leave roughly hourly (6.30am–6.30pm) for Cabo San Lucas and San José del Cabo; some are routed via Todos Santos, others take the eastern route direct to San José. The western route is quicker and more scenic as it follows the coast for quite a way below Todos Santos.

**Car rental** Most car rental agents have offices at the airport or on the malecón, including: Alamo ⓣ612/122-6262; Avis ⓣ612/122-2651; Budget ⓣ612/122-7655 or 123-1919; Dollar ⓣ612/122-6060; Hertz ⓣ612/122-5300; National ⓣ612/125-6585; and Thrifty ⓣ612/125-9696.

**Internet access** Several Internet joints line the malecón. Café Callejón, just in from the water on Callejón, has a restaurant and outdoor café (daily

## Moving on by ferry from La Paz

If you're planning to take the ferry from Terminal Pichilingue across the Sea of Cortés to Mazatlán or Topolobampo (the port for Los Mochis), you should buy tickets as far ahead of time as possible. You should also scour the Internet for updates to routes and schedules, as they change often and routes can close unexpectedly for months at a time. You may also find information about the infrequent services to other cities. In mid-2005, the state-run SEMATUR company ceded control of the long La Paz–Mazatlán route to Baja Ferries, which already ran the Topolobampo service, and TMC, a smaller, cargo-focused line.

### The routes

Baja Ferries leaves La Paz at 5pm on Tuesday, Thursday and Saturday and arrives in **Mazatlán** the next morning around 9am. *Turista* class seats start at M$250; for *cabina* it's M$650; *cabina* and *salón* M$950. TMC leaves La Paz every day at 5pm and arrives in Mazatlán at 8.30am the next day. The cheapest tickets start at M$570. There are four classes of service: *salón* class, which is a reclining seat, and three types of cabins – *turista* (four bunks, shared bath), *cabina* (two bunks, private bath) or *especial* (suite with private bath, sitting area and TV). There's rarely any problem going *salón* class (entitling you to a reclining seat), for which tickets are only available a day in advance.

Baja Ferries makes the journey to **Topolobampo** Monday to Friday at 4pm (arriving at 9pm) and Saturday at 11pm (arriving at 6am). *Salón* class seats are M$650; for *cabina* (four bunks with a private bath) it's M$1410. Cars are an additional M$970. The La Paz–Topolobampo route has two classes: *salón* (a reclining seat) and *cabina*.

### Getting tickets

Baja Ferries has a ticket office downtown at Morelos 720 (ⓣ612/125-7443, ⓦwww.bajaferries.com). Ferry schedules change frequently and it's always best to call ahead to check the schedule (toll free in Mexico ⓣ01-800/696-9600, US ⓣ1-800/884-3107). Tickets can be paid for with major credit cards. Bicycles go free. Tickets for the TMC ferry must be purchased in cash or with Visa and MasterCard at its counter at Terminal Pichilingue (ⓣ01-800/744-5050, ⓣ612/123-9226, ⓦwww.ferrytmc.com).

Before buying tickets, car drivers should ensure they have a permit to drive on the mainland. This should have been obtained when crossing the border into Mexico, but if not you may have some joy by taking your vehicle and all relevant papers along to the customs office at the ferry terminal a couple of days before you sail. If for some reason you've managed to get this far without having your tourist card stamped, you should also attend to that before sailing – there's an immigration office at Obregón 2140, between Juárez and Allende.

To get to Terminal Pichilingue catch a bus from the Central Camionera (hourly 8am–5pm; M$13), or take a taxi from town (M$200), and aim to arrive at the ferry three hours in advance of the departure time. According to signs at the terminal, it is illegal to take your own food on board, but since the catering is so poor, everyone does and nobody seems to mind. Try one of the *loncheros* by the docks for quesadillas, burritos and drinks to take along.

8.30am–10pm; M$10/hr). The Shark's Net, 16 de Septiembre and Aquiles Serdán, claims to be open 24 hours (M$15/hr).

**Laundry** La Paz Lava, Mutualismo 260 ⓣ612/122-3112 (daily 8am–midnight; M$20/load).

**Post office** Corner of Revolución and Constitución.

**Spanish courses** Se Habla La Paz, Madero 540 ⓣ612/122-7763, ⓦwww.sehablalapaz.com.

**Tours and activities** Baja Diving and Service, 1665 Obregón (ⓣ612/122-1826), offers good diving and snorkelling tours and courses. For decent kayak rental and snorkelling outings to nearby volcanic islands, or to the sea-lion colony at Los Islotes, try Baja Outdoor Activities (BOA), Madero and Campeche y Tamaulipas (ⓣ612/125-5636, ⓦwww.kayactivities.com), a 30min walk from downtown La Paz on the road to Pichilingue next to the *Hotel El Moro* (full- and half-day packages from US$30). Otherwise, operators include: Katun (ⓣ612/348-5609; ⓦwww.katun-tours.com), Juárez 1445 at Callejón, which runs mountain-biking and sea-kayaking trips; Scuba Baja Joe (ⓣ612/122-4006, ⓦwww.scubabajajoe.com), on Obregón and Ocampo, which offers competitively priced dive packages; Funbaja (ⓣ612/121-5884, ⓦwww.funbaja.com), Km 2.5 on the road to Pichilingue, which runs all kinds of aquatic outings; and The Cortez Club (ⓣ612/121-6120, ⓦwww.cortezclub.com), at Km 5 on the road to Pichilingue, which runs beginner's through to divemaster courses for PADI dive certification.

# Los Cabos and the eastern cape

The peninsula narrows to just a few dozen kilometres across at the Isthmus of La Paz, the informal northern border of the Cape – the land's end where the Pacific Ocean and Sea of Cortés come together in spectacular fashion. This isthmus is the only visual cue that separates the geography of the Cape region from the rest of the peninsula, though they were two distinct geological masses prior to colliding with one another a few million years ago.

In many ways, the Cape is still a land unto itself, driven largely by international investment into the southernmost tip of the peninsula. After running parallel for over 1300 kilometres, the ocean and sea meet dramatically at the sister towns of **Cabo San Lucas** and **San José del Cabo**, known collectively as **Los Cabos** – easily the most exclusive parcel of land in Baja California. Undeniably beautiful and home to the lion's share of the peninsula's lavish resorts, golf courses and oft-photographed beaches, the area carries a hefty price tag. It is also one of the fastest-developing regions in Mexico.

But Los Cabos is just a tiny part of the Cape. Many of its most remarkable areas still require a great deal of time and preparation to access. North of Los Cabos, the region is largely defined by three main roads: the fast new Hwy-19 runs straight up the Pacific coast from Cabo San Lucas and through increasingly posh **Todos Santos**; the older Transpeninsular Highway route trails north from San José del Cabo through the Sierra La Laguna, emerging for only one brief moment at the Sea of Cortés on its long journey to La Paz; and the third, most exhausting route along the **eastern Cape**. At the moment, the coastal towns between La Paz and San José are reached only via a dirt and sand road, despite years of highway planning to the contrary.

## Todos Santos

The farming town of **TODOS SANTOS**, located just north of the Tropic of Cancer, marks the halfway point between Cabo San Lucas and La Paz. It's also the closest thing to an exception to all the rules about the Cape region, with great beaches in easy reach, relatively affordable hotels and a bus service.

Founded in 1723 as a Jesuit mission, the fortunes of Todos Santos have risen and fallen ever since: at one time a successful farming community, it was destroyed by an eighteenth-century indigenous uprising and diseases introduced by European settlers, then gained (and subsequently lost) status as a major place for sugar-cane growing. In the 1970s, with the creation of the Transpeninsular Highway, throngs of surfers came in search of giant waves, followed in the 1980s by an artistic crowd, many of whom settled here. With the completion of Hwy-19 in the mid-1990s, the town became more easily accessed from La Paz and Los Cabos and now many drive here to experience some of the best **surfing** in Baja. There's also some great **whale watching** to be had from the shore: sit on any of the beaches in the winter months and you are bound to see several of the creatures.

Today, the pleasant, leisurely paced town is home to a thriving community of artists, and hosts a popular week-long **art festival** each February. There are plenty of galleries for you to check out, and if you feel like trying your own hand at being creative, you can join any of the local **workshops** that teach everything from writing to watercolours, pottery and even improvisational theatre. Check the local monthly publication *El Calendario* for details, or look in the bookshop on Juárez at Hidalgo, for *El Tecolote Libros* magazine. Take the historic house **tours**, offered occasionally, and learn about the people and events that have woven themselves into town lore; again, details are posted around town.

As for **beaches**, **Punta Lobos** and **San Pedrito** are among several strung out between here and Cabo San Lucas, the first few within a bumpy ten-minute ride west along any unmarked dirt road; several blocks west from the centre is a dirt road marked with a sign that reads "Aviso oficial" (if you can't find it, ask around), which brings you to the south edge of Punta Lobos. From here, the rest of the beaches line the coast for 10km south. Note that due to riptides, steeply shelving beaches and rogue waves, only **San Pedro** (also known as **Las Palmas**), beyond Punta Lobos, and **Los Cerritos**, 12km south (50m beyond Km 64), are safe for **swimming**.

## Arrival and information

The highway runs through the middle of Todos Santos at Calle Colegio Militar. Here, and on parallel Juárez, are the **bank**, shops, **post office** and telephones. El Tecolote on Hidalgo at Juárez has a great selection of new and used **books**. The **bus** will drop you at the corner of Colegio Militar and Zaragoza.

## Accommodation

**Cabañas Quiñones** Las Playitas 3km from the plaza; follow signs from Juárez and Topete ⓣ612/126-5113, ⓣ612/145-0219. Six palapa-covered cottages with tiny kitchens, large bedrooms, private bath and ocean-view patios. Also has limited laundry facilities. ④

**Hacienda Inn Todos Santos** signposted along a dirt road north of town ⓣ612/145-0073, ⓦwww.haciendainntodossantos.com. The lavish gardens, pool and Moorish domes are impressive, if out of place, at this near-luxury hotel with TV, a/c, fireplaces and a few rooms with kitchens; some rooms have ocean views. There's also a restaurant and laundry services – without your own transport, however, it's a bit far from town. ⑥

**Hotel California** Morelos, three blocks west of the main highway ⓣ612/145-0525, ⓔhotelcaliforniareservations@hotmail.com. An evening's stay at this gem might make it worth parting with some of those pesos you've been setting aside for a rainy day. The owners completed a beautiful restoration of the hotel in 2004, and the rooms are multicultural *mestizos* of Mexican and Moorish decor. There's a pool and restaurant, as well as ocean views from the top floor. ⑧

**Hotel Miramar** Mutualismo and Pedrajo, ⓣ612/825-0321. Basic rooms, some with sea views, a short walk from the beach but a little longer to the centre of town. The hotel has a laundry and pool. ④

**Motel Guluarte** Juárez at Morelos ⓣ612/825-0006. Still one of the cheapest places in town. Fifteen rooms with fridge and fan (some have a/c and TV). Also has a small pool and car park, and sits next to a nice little market. ❸

**Teampaty Surf Camp** Playa los Cerritos ⓦwww.todossantos.cc/ecosurfcamp.html. Rustic, bohemian campers and open sand for pitching a camp have made *Teampaty* the epitome of Todos Santos beach camping. Always book ahead, as guests have a habit of staying for a while. Tent camping ❶, trailers ❷

**Todos Santos Inn** Legaspi 33, between Topete and Obregón ⓣ612/145-0040, ⓦwww.mexonline.com/todossantosinn.htm. This US-expat-run inn is surrounded by many of the town's art galleries. The late nineteenth-century structure houses four elegantly decorated rooms and a garden patio. ❽

## Eating

**Places to eat** are mainly on Colegio Militar: you'll find street stalls around the bus-stop area and a couple of decent restaurants at the traffic lights a block away.

**Los Adobes** Hidalgo, between Juárez and Colegio Militar ⓣ612/145-0203. *Adobes'* peaceful desert garden dining room and adjacent café and WiFi hangout are its greatest assets – not the high-priced, over-done gourmet dishes. The café is open 9am–5pm; the restaurant for lunch and dinner.

**Café Santa Fe** Márquez de León s/n, on the plaza ⓣ612/145-0340. One of the Cape's best restaurants and hands-down Todos Santos's top spot, *Santa Fe*'s Northern Italian menu showcases locally grown ingredients and a stellar wine list that combines vintages from the Valle de Guadalupe and abroad. Dinner costs about M$700 a person, with wine, and tables are set inside an old hacienda or outside on the courtyard patio. Closed Tues.

**Caffé Todos Santos** Centenario 33, at Topete ⓣ612/145-0340. Decorated by local artists, this expat-run café does fine breakfasts, coffees, teas, muffins and bagels. Lunch and dinner are a few steps above deli fare.

**La Copa Wine Bar** Legaspi 33, at *Todos Santos Inn* ⓣ612/145-0040. Good by-the-glass selections as well as the town's most satisfying margaritas. Intimate and cosy, it's one of the few romantic hideaways in town.

**La Coronela** Morelos at Juárez, at *Hotel California*. Good, slightly highbrow Mexican cuisine – such as seared tuna – with a country slant, and tapas on a separate menu.

**Lonchería Carla** Hidalgo s/n, between Juárez and Colegio Militar. An open-air café with flavourful quesadillas and burritos for M$10 apiece.

**Mariscos Mi Costa** Colegio Militar s/n at Ocampo. Excellent seafood place with a relaxed atmosphere. Try the *sopa de mariscos* or shrimp *ceviche*; also serves decent tacos.

**Shut-up Frank's** Degollado s/n, between Rangel and Cuauhtémoc. The town's only sports bar, with great burgers and some traditional Mexican food.

**Tacos Chilakos** Juárez and Hidalgo. Cheap, easy and open-air, *Chilakos* is regarded as one of the best places for tacos on the peninsula.

# Cabo San Lucas

The bay of **CABO SAN LUCAS**, at the southernmost tip of Baja, was once a base for pirate vessels waiting to pounce on Spanish treasure ships. Even fifteen years ago, it was little more than a fishing and canning village occasionally visited by adventurous sports fishermen. Since then, it has earned a reputation for the marlin that can be caught here, and the bay is now full of sleek, radar-equipped fishing yachts. Multi-million-dollar second homes occupy the best vantage points, palms have been transplanted, golf courses have been laid, water has been piped in from San José and everywhere is kept pristine. It's more like an enclave of the US than part of Mexico, with almost all aspects of civilization geared to tourism – even a mammoth Wal-Mart has opened here, alongside Puerto Paraíso, an enormous mall on the marina, and future plans include an artificial island to sit in the bay, complete with restaurants and bars. Spending a day or two here can be fun; if you're looking to fish or dive, the allure will probably last a bit longer.

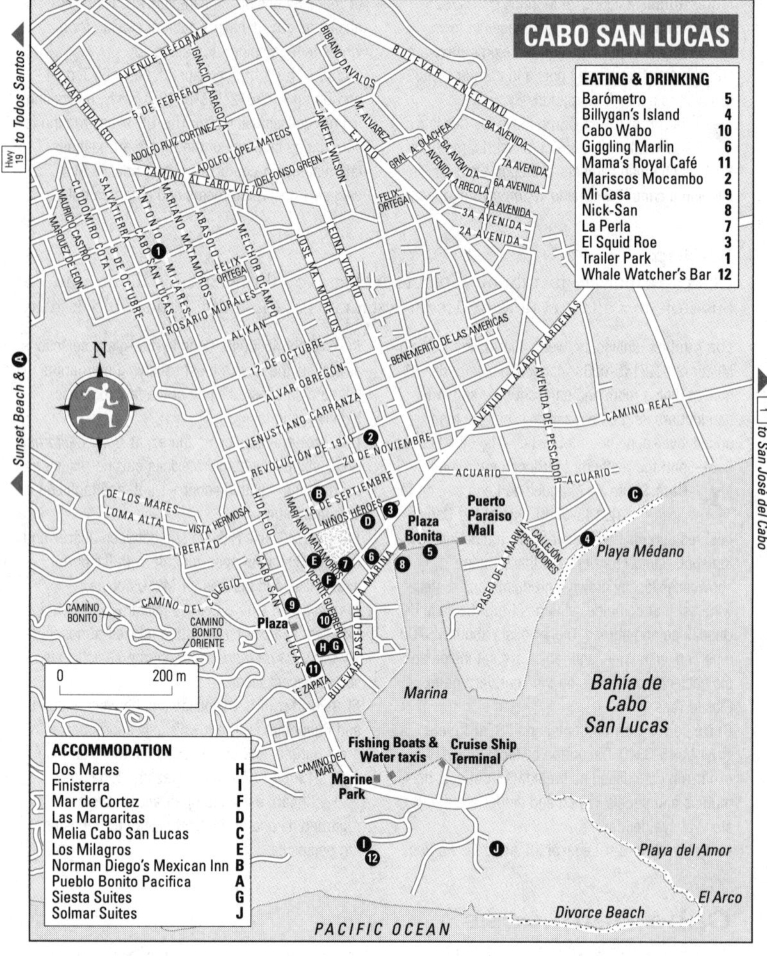


## Arrival and information

From Todos Santos, Hwy-19 ends northwest of Cabo San Lucas at Avenida Reforma before entering into a confusing warren of city streets – it's easier to take the less direct bypass road Bulevar Constituyentes (on some signs it is marked Calle Hidalgo) around Cabo's eastern edge and then double back into town via a right on Hwy-1. **Buses** into Cabo arrive at the station at Niños Héroes and Morelos (☎624/143-5020). Surprisingly, Cabo has **no official tourist office**, just dozens of places dishing out maps and drink coupons, and usually throwing in some time-share patter while they're at it. For information about **arrival by air**, see San José del Cabo, p.133.

## Accommodation

Most of the resorts occupy the prime real estate immediately around the marina, while downtown has a healthy selection of budget **accommodation**.

These places are not posh, but they have spirit and service common to B&Bs, and they're all less than a ten-minute walk from the action. Hotels on the marina will be noisier than downtown, but they're well suited for night owls. The resorts to the east of the marina empty out onto the active Playa Médano; those to the west have the beautiful but unswimmable Playa Solmar and the recently developed Sunset Beach at their doors.

**Dos Mares** Emiliano Zapata s/n, between Hidalgo and Vicente Guerrero ⓣ624/143-0330, ⓔhoteldosmares@cabotel.com.mx. Enjoying a good location right by the marina and close to the action, rooms here have TV as well as access to a tiny pool. Some studios have kitchens. ❺

**Finisterra** Marina s/n, at Playa Solmar ⓣ624/143-3333, ⓦwww.finisterra.com. This hotel on a towering hill isn't, as its name suggests, at Land's End, though it does have dramatic views of the Pacific Ocean. There are various room configurations available – it's part of many time-share programs – but all rooms have water views, TV, a/c and use of the pools and hot tubs. With the exception of the steep slope, it's an easy walk to the marina. ❼

**Mar de Cortez** Lázaro Cárdenas, between Guerrero and Matamoros ⓣ624/143-0032, ⓦwww.mardecortez.com. Colonial-style decor in a lovely planted setting with a mix of older and modern, larger rooms around a pool; some have terraces and all have a/c. Also has a good restaurant. ❺

**Las Margaritas** Plaza Aramburo 7 ⓣ624/143-6770, ⓔmargaritas@real-turismo.com. Smack in the middle of Cabo and stumbling distance from *El Squid Roe* (see p.129), the spacious rooms all have a/c, TV and kitchens, but no charm. ❼

**Melia Cabo San Lucas** Playa Médano s/n, off Paseo el Pescador ⓣ624/145-7800, USⓣ1-800/745-2226, ⓦwww.meliacabosanlucas.com. More South Beach, Miami, than Mexico, this style-heavy, substance-light resort has two pools and an outdoor bar scene that will disturb light sleepers. Many rooms have views of the water; inside they're outfitted with TV, a/c and WiFi. ❼

**Los Milagros** Matamoros 116 ⓣ624/143-4566, ⓦwww.losmilagros.com.mx. Tasteful, studio-like rooms with high-speed Internet connections, a small pool and a sun deck make this a real find, just a few blocks from the action. Reservations recommended. ❻

**Norman Diego's Mexican Inn** 16 de Septiembre and Abasolo ⓣ624/143-4987, ⓦwww.themexicaninn.com. The dirt road just outside the door gives a false impression of the comfort at this small B&B. Coffee and *postres* are served around the courtyard's fountain every morning and Mexican tile work, queen-size beds, a/c, TVs and DVD players adorn the rooms. ❻

**Pueblo Bonito Pacífica** Cabo Sunset Beach, off Via de Lerry ⓣ624/142-9696, US ⓣ1-866/585-1752, ⓦwww.pueblobonito.com. The scents of aromatherapy, multiple trickling water features and Pacific breezes create a sense of calm that can be matched only by a few of the hotels on the Corridor. *Pacífica* is a haul from downtown – across Pedregal and down a curvy road – but the free shuttles to and from sister properties on Playa Médano make getting back and forth easy. Rooms are modern, with wood panelling, high-thread-count sheets and private balconies. ❾

**Siesta Suites** Zapata s/n, between Hidalgo and Guerrero ⓣ624/143-2773, ⓦwww.cabosiestasuites.com. This expat-run establishment offers clean, studio rooms with TV, a/c, free local calls and close proximity to the marina, as well as a pool and restaurant. Weekly and monthly rates available. ❻

**Solmar Suites** Marina s/n, at Playa Solmar ⓣ624/143-3535, US ⓣ1-800/344-3349, ⓦsolmar.com. Old-school Cabo oceanfront resort with two heated swimming pools with swim-up bars, lap pool, fifteen-person Jacuzzi and the best sport-fishing fleet in Los Cabos. Rooms vary from predictable resort fare to fancy, but almost all have stunning ocean views. ❼

## The town and beaches

Cabo's **marina** is anchored by the open-air Puerto Paraíso mall. Although it's only half-occupied – which seems standard for any mall in Mexico – locals and visitors cruise its walkways, lounge on its steps and take coffee by fountains. West of the marina are some of the older resorts – *Solmar* and *Finisterra* – and to its east is **Playa Médano**, Cabo's swimming-safe beach. Médano and the sidewalks around the marina are busy with hawkers who constantly tout trips in glass-bottomed boats, fishing, water-skiing, paragliding or bungee jumping, and will rent anything from horses to off-road quad bikes to jet skis and underwater gear. Competition is fierce, prices fluctuate daily and places come and go, so shop

△ Cabo San Lucas marina

around. Scuba diving and snorkelling are perhaps the most rewarding of these activities, though the best sites (out towards *Finisterra*) can only be reached by boat. For gear rental, snorkelling trips and scuba courses, check out the many companies along Bulevar Marina, especially in the plazas. If it wasn't for the forbidding rocks and dangerous cliffs, you could easily walk from the marina southwest to **Playa del Amor** and the tip of the peninsula. The shore of "Lovers' Beach" has shrunk and severely diminished both its beauty and the amount of space free for swimming (see box, p.132). Del Amor does have a second beach on the Pacific side, though it's for looking only – the riptide will finish off any swimmers. From the safe side of Del Amor it's possible to swim in the direction of the marina to Pelican Rock, where the underwater shelf is home to schools of tropical fish. Experienced divers shouldn't miss the rim of a marine canyon, also off Playa del Amor, where unusual conditions at 30m create a "sandfall" with streams of sand starting their 2000-metre fall to the canyon bottom. The peninsula comes to its conclusion just over another pile of rocks from Del Amor. El Arco, the huge rock arch at *Finisterra* – Land's End, where the Sea of Cortés meets the Pacific – is an extraordinary place, with a clear division between the shallow turquoise seawater on the east and the profound blue of the ocean out to the west; a colony of sea lions lives on the surrounding rocks. It is possible for skilled climbers to walk over to El Arco from Playa Solmar and then Del Amor. Most people, though, opt for trips via water taxi or tour boat. The water taxi will cost a negotiable M$150.

## Eating, drinking and nightlife

For reasonably inexpensive **food**, head for Morelos and the streets away from the waterfront. The more touristy places – some of them the most expensive in Baja – cluster around the marina and along Hidalgo. At night, such places compete for partying patrons by offering **happy hours** (often 6–8pm) and novel cocktails. There's little difference between them; stroll along and take your pick.

**Barómetro** Puerto Paraíso Mall, west side ☎624/143-1466. There's a lounge scene at this sleek outdoor tapas and cocktail joint that straddles the marina's sidewalk; one side hangs cantilevered over the water. The menu includes a mix of appetizers and wood-fired thin-crust pizzas.

**Billygan's Island** Playa Médano s/n, at Paseo del Pescador ☎624/143-4830. One of the three beach bar-restaurants that caters to beach partygoers all day (8am–11pm). Breakfast, lunch and dinner are served right on the sand, and tropical drinks poured and consumed fairly nonstop.

**Cabo Wabo** Vicente Guerrero at Lázaro Cárdenas ⓣ624/143-1188. Rocker Sammy Hagar owns this boisterous club, which makes a popular tequila of the same name. Loud and lively, often with a heavy charge, but still a good place to hear live music – and if you're going here around a holiday, perhaps you can catch Sammy himself on stage.
**Giggling Marlin** Marina s/n, at Matamoros ⓣ624/143-1182. A Cabo institution, drawing an older set than other places on the strip. Mostly a place to drink and dance to Latin standards: chances of getting out without hearing *La Bamba* are slim.
**Mama's Royal Cafe/Felix's Fine Mexican & Seafood** Hidalgo at Zapata ⓣ624/143-4290, ⓦwww.felixcabosanlucas.com. Breakfast, lunch and brunch are served under the *Mama's* moniker, with dinner and drinks going by *Felix*; either way, this restaurant is cheaper (about M$150 per person) and better than most of what Cabo has to offer. Both menus are large, with two-dozen *huevos* choices in the morning and a dozen shrimp variations in the evening. The centrepiece is a three-dozen-strong salsa bar that sounds much hokier than it tastes.
**Mariscos Mocambo** Leona Vicario and 20 de Noviembre ⓣ624/143-6070. A palapa roof covers this unpretentious seafood restaurant popular with Mexicans and the fisherman crowd. *Mocambo* is known for its regional specialities, especially its grilled red snapper, and well-prepared *ceviche* and *cockteles*.
**Mi Casa** Cabo San Lucas at Lázaro Cárdenas ⓣ624/143-1933. This old Cabo joint has new Cabo prices in its otherwise low-key open-air restaurant decorated with handmade lanterns. The pan-Mexican menu – Yucatán-style baked fish, chicken in *mole*, Puerto Nuevo-style lobster – runs close to M$200 per entrée. Lunch time provides some decent deals.
**Nick-San** Marina s/n, Plaza de la Danza ⓣ624/143-4484. Plenty of restaurants in Baja will sell you raw fish without knowing what they're doing with it – *Nik-San* is the exception. In addition to the extensive selection of locally caught sushi and sashimi – try the tuna – the Indonesian-inspired lobster soup is especially tasty. Dinner for two M$900.
**La Perla** Lázaro Cárdenas, between Matamoros and Abasolo. Very inexpensive and surprisingly untouristy place right in the tourist zone; tortas, tacos and burgers for less than M$40.
**El Squid Roe** Lázaro Cárdenas s/n, at Zaragoza ⓣ624/143-0655. If you just want to go nuts, this Cabo classic should be your first stop; a wild party atmosphere where table dancing is allowed, if not encouraged. There's a full dinner menu of Tex-Mex dishes alongside cocktails such as the yard-long margarita. Open late.
**Trailer Park** Matamoros and Mijares ⓣ624/143-1927. Large platters of surf and turf for M$260 include some of the best budget shellfish and steak in the region.
**Whale Watcher's Bar** Marina s/n, at *Finisterra* ⓣ624/143-3333. They serve food here, but everyone comes for the stunning views of the Pacific Ocean. The bar is on the hotel's top floor – the highest point in Cabo – and lines up tables along its outdoor balcony and flush against sliding glass doors.

## Listings

**Airlines** For airport enquiries, call ⓣ624/142-0341. Airlines include: Aeroméxico ⓣ624/142-0397; Alaska ⓣ624/149-5800; Continental ⓣ624/142-3890; Mexicana ⓣ624/143-5352; and United ⓣ624/142-2880.
**Banks and exchange** There's an ATM, and the best exchange rates, at Bancomer (cheques cashed 8.30am–noon) on Lázaro Cárdenas at Hidalgo; after hours, several casas de cambio (one by *Giggling Marlin*; see above) offer decent rates until 11pm.
**Books** Libros Libros, Marina 20.
**Buses** Áquila ⓣ624/143-7878 or 7880. Buses leave hourly for Tijuana and the border (24hr; M$990) via La Paz (2hr 30min; MS$110).
**Car rental** Avis ⓣ624/143-4606 or 146-0201; Budget ⓣ624/143-4190 or 1522; Hertz ⓣ624/146-5088 or 142-0375; National ⓣ624/143-1414; and Thrifty ⓣ624/146-5030 or 143-1666.
**Consulates** US ⓣ624/143-3566; Canada ⓣ624/142-4333.
**Emergencies** Police ⓣ624/143-3997 or 142-0361; Hospital ⓣ624/143-1594.
**Internet access and phones** Cabomix, on Matamoros at Niños Héroes, has the best rates in town and also has phones (including Internet phone services); there are also several small Internet places near the old bus station at Zaragoza and 16 de Septiembre, as well as a number of good but expensive Internet providers along the strip, including Internet Services on Plaza Náutica.
**Post office** On Lázaro Cárdenas, east of the marina (Mon–Fri 9am–6pm).
**Tours and activities** Land's End Divers (ⓣ624/143-2200, ⓦwww.mexonline.com/landsend.htm), at A-5 in the marina, has good rates for their dive packages. Ecological snorkelling adventures are offered by Cabo Expeditions (ⓣ624/143-2700, ⓦwww.allaboutcabo.com/caboexpeditions.htm), in the *Plaza Las Glorias* hotel on the marina; they cost M$450 per person.

Pisces Fleet (Ⓣ624/143-1288, Ⓦwww.piscessportfishing.com), in the marina, run marlin-fishing trips (M$600–1000 per person). Solmar Fleet (Ⓣ624/143-3535), in the *Solmar Suites* hotel, is an equally established fishing fleet and has similar rates. Rancho Collins (Ⓣ624/143-3652), near Playa Médano, east of *Billygan's Island*, hires out horses at about M$350hr.



## The Corridor

The distinction between Cabo San Lucas and San José del Cabo blurs further each year as new resorts are erected along the **CORRIDOR** separating the two towns. Even with the construction, though, the Corridor is not packed with glass, steel and stucco eyesores but is a series of rolling and rocky hills, wide beaches, manicured golf courses and rather tame resorts hidden behind bougainvillea-covered gates. Many of the prime coastal spots have been occupied for decades, but new destinations are constantly being created while long-timers keep pace with multi-million-dollar makeovers. Each resort aims to be an end unto itself, with enough dining, drinking, relaxing and entertainment options to keep you from venturing out too often. Unlike downtown Cabo, Corridor resorts don't typically offer package meal plans, and a few days of carefree dining can result in staggering bills.

### Practicalities

The Corridor offers no real budget **accommodation**; the only way to get a bed under M$2500 here is to book a package trip ahead of time with an airline or consolidator. *Twin Dolphin*, at Km 12 Hwy-1 (Ⓣ624/145-8191, US Ⓣ800/421-8925, Ⓦwww.twindolphin.com; ⑨), may be one of the oldest hotels along the coast, but it's by no means rough around the edges. The 44 rooms are decorated in shades of white, have views of the water and include luxury bath products; there are no TVs or phones. Midway between Cabo San Lucas and San José del Cabo is *Las Ventanas al Paraíso*, Km 19.5 Hwy-1 (Ⓣ624/144-2800, US Ⓣ888/767-3966, Ⓦwww.rosewoodhotels.com; ⑨). Suites here – some with roof decks and private Jacuzzis – skip the Mexican craft style for John Pawson-like aesthetics. You're likely to run into a boldface tabloid name at either the *ceviche* bar or swim-up cantina. At *One & Only Palmilla*, Km 27.5 Hwy-1 (Ⓣ624/146-7000, US Ⓣ1-800/637-2226, Ⓦwww.oneandonlyresorts.com; ⑨), a US$75 million renovation has turned the property into one of the continent's best resorts.There isn't a bargain to be had, but you'll get unparalleled service and rooms that, even at their most basic, are first-class, as well as two pools, a beach and a spa. The cheapest option on the Corridor is the *Suites Terrazaz de Positano*, Km 4 Hwy-1 (Ⓣ624/143-9383, Ⓦwww.hotelpositano.net; ⑥), on the second floor of a shopping plaza. All eight suites look out onto the sea and have kitchenettes, TV and a/c, and the owners gladly prepare custom Italian dinners.

The region's best **restaurants** are in the resorts along the Corridor. But, like the resorts, price tags are exorbitant, and you'll still need to pay extra if you're not staying on site. If you're going to splash out at one Corridor restaurant, it should be at *Agua*, Km 27.5 Hwy-1, at *One & Only Palmilla*. Skip the wine and let the chef pair a tasting menu of Mediterranean-tinged Mexican dishes with flights of small-batch tequila; expect to pay about M$700 per person. For French haute cuisine, head to *Canto del Mar*, Km 21.5 Hwy-1 (Ⓣ624/144-2000), at the *Marquis Los Cabos* resort. Smoked duck with truffles and carrot and saffron pie are only a few of the interesting dishes.

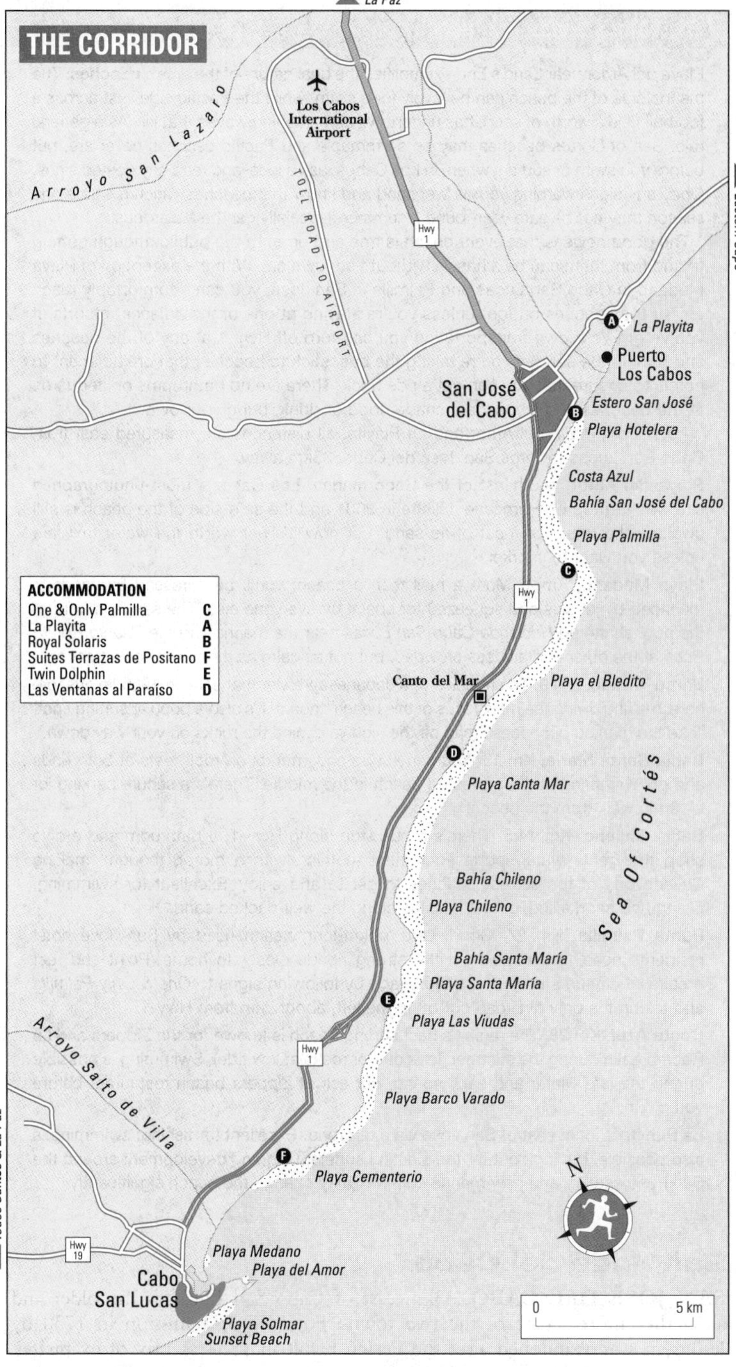
THE CORRIDOR
La Paz
Los Cabos International Airport
Arroyo San Lazaro
TOLL ROAD TO AIRPORT
Hwy 1
Eastern Cape
La Playita
Puerto Los Cabos
San José del Cabo
Estero San José
Playa Hotelera
Costa Azul
Bahía San José del Cabo
Playa Palmilla
ACCOMMODATION
One & Only Palmilla C
La Playita A
Royal Solaris B
Suites Terrazas de Positano F
Twin Dolphin E
Las Ventanas al Paraíso D
Canto del Mar
Playa el Bledito
Playa Canta Mar
Sea Of Cortés
Bahía Chileno
Playa Chileno
Bahía Santa María
Playa Santa María
Playa Las Viudas
Arroyo Salto de Villa
Playa Barco Varado
Playa Cementerio
Todos Santos & La Paz
Hwy 19
N
Playa Medano
Playa del Amor
Cabo San Lucas
Playa Solmar
Sunset Beach
0
5 km

## The cape's swimming beaches

Playa del Amor near Land's End exemplifies the dual nature of the area's **beaches**. The marina side of the beach can be lovely for a swim, while the Pacific side, just across a football field's worth of sand, has undertows and crashing waves that kill. As a general rule, Sea of Cortés beaches may be swimmable and Pacific beaches never are, but before you swim or surf anywhere in Los Cabos, ask a local and read any posted signs. Obey any signs warning you off wet sand and know that beaches which are safe one season may not be safe year-round – summer especially can be hazardous.

The good news is that every beach is free and open to the public, though getting to and from them can be a hassle without your own car. With the exception of Playa Médano in Cabo San Lucas and Palmilla in San José, you can't comfortably reach any of the beaches on foot unless you're staying at one of the adjacent resorts. If you've got your own transportation you can turn off Hwy-1 at any of the beaches and park in the sand; if you're taking the bus, stick to beaches that are adjacent to hotels to ensure that you can get a ride back. There are no bathrooms or lifeguards at the beaches and if you want shade, food or drink, bring your own.

Apart from Playa del Amor and La Playita, all distances are measured east from Cabo San Lucas towards San José del Cabo, 33km away.

**Playa del Amor**, southeast of the Cabo marina. Los Cabos's most-photographed site was torn up by Hurricane Juliette in 2001 and the safe side of the beach is still awaiting the return of most of its sand. For now it's not worth the water taxi fare unless you want to snorkel.

**Playa Médano**, Km 1. More a mall than a beach; you'll be harassed by vendors, menaced by jet skis and squeezed for space by everyone else. The sands in front of the now-shuttered *Hacienda Cabo San Lucas* near the marina and the *Pueblo Bonito Rosé* at the other end are less crowded, but not as calm as the out-of-town beaches.

**Barco Varado**, Km 9. The remains of a Japanese trawler that sank in 1966 lie offshore here, making diving the main focus of this beach, though it's also a popular surfing spot. Take the marked dirt access road off the highway; mind the rocks on your way down.

**Bahía Santa María**, Km 13. You can scuba and snorkel on rock reefs at both ends and go swimming at the protected beach in the middle. There's a secure parking lot a 10min walk from the beach.

**Bahía Chileno**, Km 14.5. There's a bus stop along Hwy-1, a bathroom and a dive shop that rents water-sports equipment (nothing with a motor, though), making Chileno one of the easiest beaches to get to and enjoy. Excellent for swimming, diving and snorkelling, or just relaxing along the well-packed sand.

**Punta Palmilla**, Km 27. Good, safe 1.5km-long beach used by San José hotel residents needing escape from the strong riptide closer to home. Point and reef breaks when surf's up. Access the beach by following signs to *One & Only Palmilla* and taking the only dirt-road cut-off to the left, about 2km from Hwy-1.

**Costa Azul**, Km 28. The region's best surfing beach is known for the Zippers and La Roca breaks during the summer (look out for rocks at low tide). Swimming is possible during the late winter and early spring, but ask at *Zippers* beach restaurant before you dip in.

**La Playita**, 2.5km east of San José via a dirt road. Excellent for fishing; swimming is also possible, but look out for the plentiful surfers. Ongoing development around the San José estuary and new marina complex may change the beach significantly.

## San José del Cabo

**SAN JOSÉ DEL CABO**, 33km east of Cabo San Lucas, is the older and altogether more sedate of the two towns. Founded as a mission in 1730 by Jesuits, it was abandoned after the Pericú revolt in 1734. A mix of ex-pirates, lapsed missionaries and drop-out miners began to repopulate the town in the early nineteenth century and turned the area into an agricultural centre and small port. Although frequently referred to as colonial, modern San José, like Cabo, is a product of late nineteenth-century construction and planning. No traces remain of its first settlement, and none of the buildings dates further back than the late 1880s.

## Arrival and information

**Los Cabos International Airport**, Km 42 Hwy-1 La Paz–Cabo San Lucas (Ⓣ624/146-5097), serves several Mexican and US West Coast cities, and a few US East Coast cities. It lies 19km north of downtown San José del Cabo and a further 32km from Cabo San Lucas.

Groups of licenced (and unlicenced) **taxi** drivers, time-share sellers and other opportunistic individuals greet all arrivals; give yourself a minute to collect your thoughts before accepting any offers and never get into a vehicle without negotiating a price beforehand. Taxis are the most expensive option into Los Cabos, costing at least to M$550 to San José, M$820 to Cabo and between M$600–660 for Corridor resorts.

If you're staying at a resort, find out ahead of time if they run a **shuttle**. Although few places provide free rides, the M$100 or so that many Cabo hotels charge is cheaper than a taxi or shared-ride van.

Beyond a resort shuttle, the cheapest options are the **shared-ride van** shuttles that run on a four-zone system and do not depart until full. If you're staying in San José (M$120) you'll get off the shuttle first, people going to Cabo (M$140) are dropped off last. If you're in a group of five people or more, you can book the entire van at M$700 for San José and M$930 to Cabo. For either option you'll do the booking inside the arrivals terminal.

**Car rental** agencies have kiosks in the arrivals section of each terminal but these only point you to the shuttle buses that run between the airport and the off-site pick-up. The fastest way from the airport to any other location is along a 19km toll road (M$26) that connects with Hwy-1 at Paseo de Los Cabos, right where San José begins to give way to the Corridor. This four-lane highway zips through grazing pastures, taking about a third of the time the free Hwy-1 takes to cover the same distance.

Avoid **changing money** at the airport, as the rates given here are among the worst in Mexico; you're much better off at the banks or ATMs at the airport or in town and the cost of your transportation and tips from the airport can be covered easily in US dollars. The **tourist office**, Mauricio Castro at Plaza San José (Ⓣ624/142-3310, Ⓦwww.loscabos.gob.mx), is quite far out on the highway, but they do offer helpful information on the Cabos area.

## Accommodation

It's difficult to tell where the Corridor ends and San José begins, except by your wallet – there is some more affordable lodging to be found in San José.

**Casa de Huéspedes Consuelo** Morelos s/n, at Colonia 10 de Mayo Ⓣ624/142-0643. Shared showers and stiff beds are the rule at San José's only guesthouse and cheapest non-camping option. ❸

**La Playita** Pueblo la Playa Ⓣ624/142-4166, Ⓦwww.laplayitahotel.com. A pleasant waterside alternative that's removed from the crowds, a three-storey hotel and restaurant with comfortable, spare rooms overlooking a small pool and an outdoor dining area. The hotel can arrange fishing trips for you and the restaurant will cook your catch. ❸

**Posada Señor Mañana** Obregón 1, at the plaza Ⓣ624/142-0462, Ⓦwww.srmanana.net. Run by a hospitable Swedish woman, offering spacious, palm-lined surroundings and charming, clean rooms with or without a/c. There's also a pool and large communal kitchen. ❺

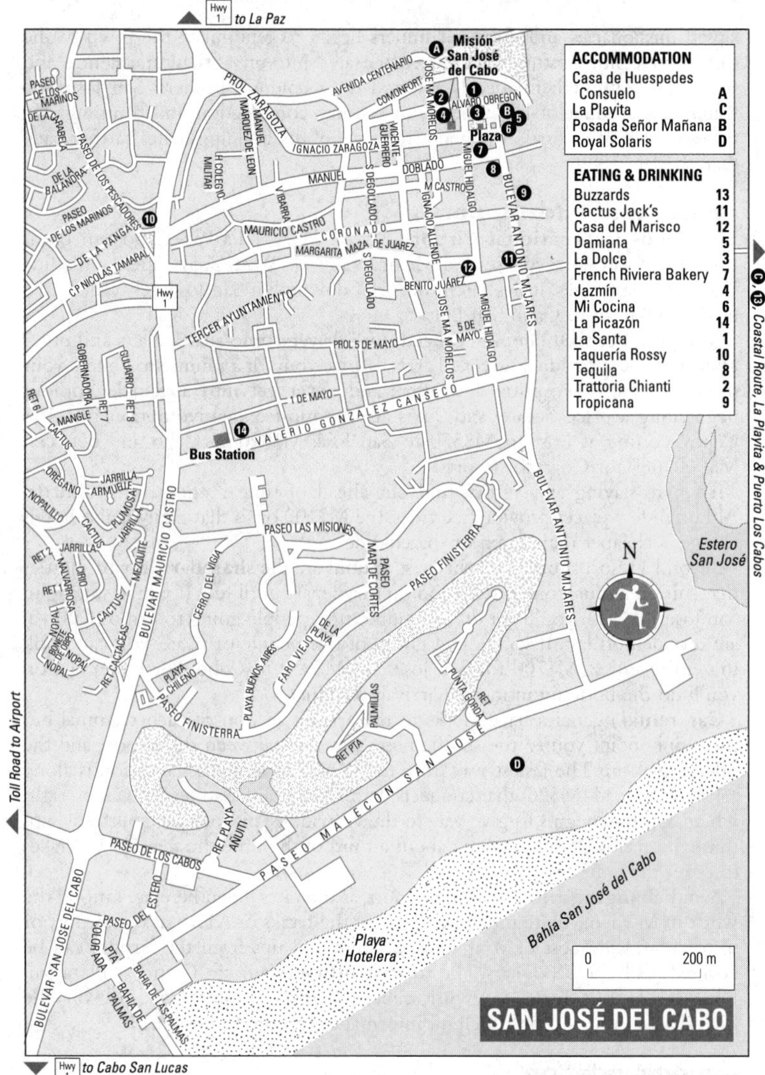


**Royal Solaris** Zona Hotelera San José ⓣ624/145-6800, ⓦwww.clubsolaris.com. Numerous pools, activities and some in-house childcare facilities make this a good spot for families – as does the all-inclusive deal. All rooms have balconies and at least partial views of the Sea of Cortés, which makes up for the dated decor. ⓽

## The town and around

Though increasingly hemmed in by shopping centres and resorts, the old **plaza** and the **Paseo Mijares** (which now leads to a modern hotel zone about 1km seaward) are still more or less intact, and there's a small local **museum** in the Casa de la Cultura. The numerous shops and restaurants that line the streets and shady courtyards are interesting enough, the latter offering a good variety of cuisine, but prices are high. Visitors, however, tend to come for the aquatic flora and fauna, for which most of the hotels can help arrange tours, guides and equipment, but you'd be wise to shop around.

Some 2km east is the lesser-known alternative **Pueblo La Playa** (**La Playita**), a hundred-year-old fishing village that offers numerous options for sport fishing; try Gordo Banks Pangas (ⓣ624/142-1147, ⓦwww.gordobanks.com). The waters at the seamount of Gordo Banks here house the highest concentrations of gamefish in the waters of Los Cabos. The **estuary** just northeast of town is halfway through its transformation from a home to hundreds of birds to one for foreign condo owners, golfers and boaters. The town celebrates its annual **festival** the third week in March – as good a time as any to visit.

## Eating, drinking and nightlife

There's a huge variety of upmarket **restaurants** downtown along Mijares, but it's more difficult to find places with local prices – look around Zaragoza and Obregón.

**Buzzards** East Cape Rd, 20min drive from San José ⓣ624/148-2415. If you're spending a day surfing on the eastern cape, this is one of the few places you can get a beer, margarita and a bite to eat. It closes by 9pm, but what surfer stays up that late?

**Cactus Jack's** Mijares at Benito Juárez ⓣ624/142-5601. Serves inexpensive Mexican breakfasts and seafood dishes off a large international menu, but the karaoke and big-screen TV here are the main draws for the locals.

**Casa del Marisco** Benito Juárez at Miguel Hidalgo ⓣ624/142-6350. Typical Mexican takes on seafood are augmented by pan-Asian takes like coconut shrimp in mango (M$180).

**Damiana** Mijares 8 ⓣ624/142-0499. The candlelit, bougainvillea-covered courtyard helps take the sting out of pricey takes on Mexican basics like *chiles rellenos* and *enchiladas suizas* (around M$350 per person). Dinner only.

**La Dolce** Mijares at Miguel Hidalgo ⓣ624/142-6621. Standard Italian cuisine, including wood-fired pizzas and pastas for relatively good prices (under M$100). Popular among tourists.

**French Riviera Bakery** Manuel Doblado at Miguel Hidalgo ⓣ624/142-3350. Its popularity has spawned fancier Corridor and Cabo outposts, but people keep coming to this original location just off the square for coffee, French pastries, cakes and both savoury and sweet crepes (M$60).

**Jazmín** Morelos, between Zaragoza and Obregón ⓣ624/142-1760. The best-value traditional Mexican food in town. Also has excellent breakfasts – perhaps the best *chilaquiles* on the Cape.

**Mi Cocina** Mijares 4, inside *Casa Natalia* ⓣ624/142-5100. The torch-lit atmosphere is captivating, and Chef Loïc Tenoux's French-influenced Mexican dishes are inspired. Charred *poblano* chiles stuffed with lamb share the menu with crayfish over couscous and a grilled Romaine Caesar salad. Dinner for two costs M$1200.

**La Picazón** Valerio Gonzalez s/n, next to the bus station ⓣ624/119-1859. All sorts of great inexpensive Mexican seafood specialities and *antojitos* served outside in a colourful, tropical setting. Try the *tacos del pulpo al mojo de ajo* – soft tacos with octopus cooked in garlic. Closed Sun.

**La Santa** Obregón 1732 ⓣ624/142-6767, ⓦwww.lasanta.com.mx. Wine bar and tapas joint that attracts a large contingent of locals in the hospitality industry and one of the few places in San José that's open past midnight. Closed Sun.

**Taquería Rossy** Hwy-1 at Manuel Doblado ⓣ624/142-6755. This storefront on the west side of Hwy-1 just before downtown San José is the lunch spot of choice for budget travellers and big spenders after fish tacos. Battered pieces of fillets, marlin, dorado and *carne asada* tacos go for less than M$10 each and cold Pacifico beer is M$25 a bottle.

**Tequila** Manuel Doblado 1011, between Mijares and Hidalgo ⓣ624/142-1155. The top choice in town, with a quaint garden atmosphere and attentive (overly attentive) waiting staff; overpriced wines and cigars.

**Trattoria Chianti** Obregón at Morelos. Serves excellent Italian food in a romantic courtyard setting; the pasta dishes and wood-fired pizza oven here make it a local gringo favourite.

**Tropicana** Mijares 38 ⓣ624/142-1580. A colonial-style restaurant with an attractive tiled, palapa-covered sitting area that's a popular choice. Serves excellent seafood, often with Cuban dancers providing entertainment.

### Listings

**Airlines** For airport enquiries, call ⓣ624/142-0341. Airlines include: Aeroméxico ⓣ624/142-0397; Alaska ⓣ624/149-5800; Continental ⓣ624/142-3890; Mexicana ⓣ624/143-5352; and United ⓣ624/142-2880.
**Banks and exchange** You'll find both ATMs and the town's best rates at Bancomer, on Zaragoza and Morelos (Mon–Fri 8.30am–4pm, Sat 10am–4pm), and Banamex, Mijares and Coronado (Mon–Fri 9am–4pm, Sat 10am–2pm).
**Books** Libros Libros, Mijares 41. Also sells English-language newspapers.
**Buses** Águila ⓣ624/142-1100. Buses to Loreto (6hr; M$330) via Cabo San Lucas (30min; M$20) and La Paz (3hr; M$120) leave hourly. Also serves Tijuana (24hr; M$1050).
**Car rental** Avis ⓣ624/142-1180 or 146-0201; Hertz ⓣ624/142-0375; National ⓣ624/142-2424; Quick ⓣ624/142-4600, ⓦwww.quickrentacar.com; Thrifty ⓣ624/142-1671.
**Consulates** Canada ⓣ624/142-4333.
**Emergencies** Police ⓣ624/143-3997 or 142-0361; hospital ⓣ624/143-1594.
**Internet access and phones** Espacio Internet, on Doblado five blocks west of the zócalo, across from the Coppola department store, has cheap rates (daily 10am–9pm; M$30/hr). Trazzo Digital Internet, off the zócalo, is more expensive, but has a much faster connection and reasonably priced international phone service (Mon–Fri 8am–9pm, Sat 9am–7pm; M$40/hr).
**Post office** On Mijares, on the way to the hotel zone from the beach (Mon–Fri 9am–6pm).
**Tours and activities** Lienzo Charro offers relatively inexpensive horseback tours to the surrounding mountains, while next door at Motosol shop (ⓣ624/143-9310, ⓦwww.atvsmotosol.com) you can book ATV tours to the beach and mountains for around M$500; head to the corner of Mijares and Cansesco. EcoTours de Baja also runs trips to nearby Santiago and Miraflores (ⓣ624/143-0775, ⓔcapeland@prodigy.net.mx). Aztec Surf (ⓣ624/146-9898, ⓦwww.aztecsurf.com), a 10min walk from the bus station down the Transpeninsular, rents boards for M$200/day, including rash guard, wax and a roof rack; they also offer lessons for M$450. Bajawild, on Obregón and Guerrero, has kayaks and snorkelling rental (ⓣ624/148-2222, ⓦwww.bajawild.com). The botanical garden/museum Cacti Mundo is now open on Mijares just north of the golf course, exhibiting 11,000 examples of the plant from all over Mexico (ⓣ624/146-9191; M$60, though students and seniors get a 50 percent discount).

## Los Barriles

The eastern cape is mostly known for its stunningly beautiful and largely undeveloped 120km of coastline between Bahía de los Muertos and San José's estuary. Within these few hundred kilometres there are only a handful of towns of note, along the water and inland. Ever since the Transpeninsular Highway's paving, developers have longed to transform this area into a resort area to rival Los Cabos in the south. So far, all they've done is clutter the unpaved roads – the only coastal roads here – with one billboard after another promising exclusive luxury enclaves and beautiful views of the sea.

The largest and most accessible resort is **LOS BARRILES**, a major **fishing** and **windsurfing** centre that takes advantage of the near-constant strong breeze in the bay. The wind, best in winter, is brilliant for experienced windsurfers (less so for beginners) and makes this a regular venue for international competitions. Hotels are expensive, and you almost certainly need to book in advance during high season in January and February; but you should be able to camp, either at one of the nearby trailer parks, or on the beach. Oddly, neither fishing nor windsurfing is easily arranged on the spot, and there's almost nowhere you can turn up and find an inexpensive room; *Hotel Palmas de Cortés* (ⓣ624/141-0050, US ⓣ1-800/368-4334, ⓦwww.bajaresorts.com/palmas.htm; ⑧) is the landmark **resort** here, well established and able to arrange activities and outings for you. Their room prices always include three meals, and they have good deals for groups. A block away, you can stop for a bite at *Tío Pablo's*, a US-expat-run restaurant with a mammoth menu of delicious burgers, fish and salads.

# The mainland

The extraordinary desert scenery first grabs your attention on the **mainland route through the northwest** of the country. Between Tijuana and Mexicali, especially, stretches a region of awesome barrenness. As you continue south through the states of Sonora and Sinaloa, the desert becomes rockier, which, along with the huge cacti, makes for some archetypal Mexican landscapes. Only as you approach Mazatlán does the harshness finally start to relent, and some colour creep back into the land.

Historically, this part of Mexico was little more favoured than Baja California. The first Spanish explorers met fierce resistance from a number of indigenous tribes – the Pima, Seri and Yaqui are still among the least-integrated of Mexico's peoples – and it wasn't until the late seventeenth century that the Jesuit missionary **Padre Kino** established a significant number of permanent settlements. During the dictatorship of Porfirio Díaz, new roads and railways were established, and after the **Revolution** these links were used to open the region to irrigation and development programmes, leading to considerable agricultural wealth. Today the big **ranches** of Sonora and Sinaloa are among the richest in Mexico.

## El Gran Desierto

If the peninsula of Baja California is desolate, the northern part of the state – to Mexicali and beyond into northern Sonora – is infinitely, yet spectacularly, more so. The **drive from Tijuana to Mexicali** is worthwhile for the views alone, as the mountains suddenly drop away to reveal a huge salt lake and hundreds of miles of desert below. This is **El Gran Desierto**, and it's a startlingly sudden change from the landscape that precedes it: the western escarpment up from Tijuana through **Tecate** (the small border town where the famous beer comes from) and beyond is relatively fertile and climbs deceptively gently, but the rains from the Pacific never get as far as the eastern edge, where the land falls away dizzily to the burnt plain and the road teeters between crags seemingly scraped bare by the ferocity of the sun. The heat at the bottom is incredible, the road down terrifying – the danger of its constant precipices proven by the piles of twisted metal at the bottom of so many of them. The more recent addition of the fast toll road has tamed the route somewhat, but it's still a fantastic trip. If you're travelling further into Mexico, you should consider a side trip to **San Felipe**, the northernmost town on the western coast of the Sea of Cortés, offering a good helping of kayaks and fish tacos.

### Mexicali

**MEXICALI** is hot – unbearably so in summer, though winter nights can drop below freezing – but despite its natural disadvantages it's a large, wealthy city, the capital of the state of Baja California and an important road and rail junction for the crossing into the States. It's also an increasingly important destination for Mexican migrants looking for work in the *maquiladoras*. While there may be an exotic ring to the name, there's nothing exotic about the place, and if you come looking for a movieland border town, swing-door saloons and dusty dirt streets, you'll be disappointed: you're more likely to run into a lobbyist or medical professional than a cowboy. The name of the town is a sweet-sounding hybrid of Mexico and California; its red-headed step-sibling, **CALEXICO**, is just across the border.

Though filled with some nice hotels, Mexicali is not a place where you'd choose to spend time (unless you're trying to pass a piece of legislation). It's really only valuable as a stop-off on the journey south, a daunting trip of at least nine hours on the bus to Hermosillo, the first place you might remotely choose to take a break, and a further hour and a half to the more appealing Guaymas. If you happen to be around during October you'll find a few cultural activities in town – live music, dance, street food and the like – taking place as part of the **Fiesta del Sol**; or at any other time of year you can fill an hour browsing the local history exhibits at the free **Museo Regional de la Universidad de Baja California**, on Reforma.

## Arrival and information

The Mexicali **border crossing** is open 24 hours and, except at morning and evening rush hours, is usually relatively quiet, with straightforward procedures. Remember to visit *migración* if you're travelling further on into Mexico. US Hwy-111 crosses the border at Calexico, California, at which point it becomes Bulevar Adolfo López Mateos and leads into Mexicali. It's an easy drive, as is entry along the well-maintained highways from Tecate, San Felipe and Sonora. Hwy-5 north from San Felipe becomes Bulevar Benito Juárez, the city's main north-south artery. Hwy-2 from Tijuana enters the city from the southwest.

Buses from Mexico arrive at the **Central Camionera**, at Anahuac and Calzada Independencia (Ⓣ686/557-2410). Buses from California and Arizona arrive at the Greyhound station in Calexico, 123 First St (Mon–Sun 5.30am–11.30pm; US Ⓣ760/357-1895); travellers are then shuttled across the border via waiting taxis arranged by the bus company.

**Aeropuerto Internacional de Mexicali**, Km 23.5 Mesa de Andrade (Ⓣ686/552-2148, Ⓦwww.aeropuertosgap.com.mx) lies 20km east of the city along a two-lane road branching off from the Mexicali–Los Algodones highway. Budget, Hertz and Alamo have **car rental** desks on the east side of the building. Buy tickets for shared taxis that leave every fifteen minutes from an enclosed booth near the departures gate; fares into Mexicali are M$250-400 depending on the zone.

There is a **tourist information booth** (daily 8am–7pm) opposite the vehicle entrance at the border, but it's not always open in the late summer, especially in the afternoon. The more helpful main office (Mon–Fri 8am–5pm; Ⓣ686/557-3276) is off Mateos at Camelias, in the Centro Cívico, the city's new municipal headquarters.

There are several **banks** and casas de cambio very close to the border – Bancomer, on Madero, is closest, and Banamex a couple of blocks up Madero near the **post office**. You can find **Internet** access at the Mexicali Café, López Mateos 485, at Morelos (Mon–Sat 9am–10pm; M$11/hr).

## Accommodation

Although not as expensive as Tijuana, Mexicali's **hotels** and **motels** charge higher rates than any other city in the state. You do tend to get more for the money, however: high-speed Internet access (via wireless or LAN) is cropping up everywhere, and the intense heat means that even the smallest motels have air-conditioning and a pool. The city's cheapest beds are near the border, but they're suspect even on a good day; if proximity to the border is what you're after, the Centro Cívico area is the nearest cluster of safe motels and hotels.

**Araiza** Benito Juárez 2220 ⓣ686/564-1100, ⓦwww.araizahoteles.com. Although it's relatively new, the *Araiza* looks dated with its blandly patterned bedspreads and heavy furniture. Still, the service is superb, and the pool and sleek lobby bar temporarily distract you from the fact you're in a brutally hot desert. ❼

**Del Norte** Madero 205 ⓣ686/552-8101, US ⓣ888/227-8504, ⓦwww.hoteldelnorte.com.mx. *Del Norte* is the one border hotel worth staying at. Its location just south of the border makes it the most pedestrian-friendly of hotels; you can walk to all the nearby restaurants and shops and use the adjacent taxi stand to get everywhere else. Rooms are clean, plus there's free coffee and an inexpensive breakfast buffet. ❺

**Hacienda del Indio** Fresnillo 101, at López Mateos ⓣ686/557-2277, US ⓣ866/218-0546, ⓦwww.hotelelindio.com. The palm-lined motor court and cast-iron railings add character to this two-star motel not far from the Centro Cívico. Rooms come standard with TV, a/c and phone. ❺

**Lucerna** Benito Juárez 2151 ⓣ686/566-4700, ⓦwww.hoteleslucerna.com. Though parts of it are identical to hotels of the same name in Tijuana and elsewhere, *Lucerna*'s two pools and well-shaded public areas speak to Mexicali's particular needs. Large bungalows in the courtyard are good for families, and the cheap rooms in the tower have balconies, satellite TV, coffee-makers and wireless Internet access. ❻

**Plaza** Madero 366 ⓣ686/552-9757, ⓕ686/554-0915. Centrally located budget motel has room service and a hair and nail salon. Rooms feature TV, bar, safe and a/c. ❺

**Siesta Inn** Justo Sierra 899 ⓣ686/568-2001, ⓦwww.hotelsiestainn.com. This two-storey business-oriented motor inn is smaller than its peers yet packs significantly more charm. There's a central pool and fountain, a decent enough restaurant and Internet access in all the rooms. ❺

## Eating

Don't miss an opportunity to dig into one of the city's many Chinese spots. *Dragon,* Libertad 990, at Centro Cívico, Mexicali's grandest Chinese restaurant, looks like a sixteenth-century imperial pagoda outside and a tricked-out dining hall inside. The Peking duck (M$120) is their signature dish. The white stucco walls, glass front and stained wood accents at *La Esquina de Bodegas*, Zaragoza at Calle L (ⓣ686/554-8919), an outpost of the San Tomás winery (see p.95), give it an exclusive on cool in the city. Wines are served by the glass (M$50) and can be paired with the pan-Mediterranean menu (starting at M$100). You can get very good, cheap food at two diverse locations. The first, *Hot Dogs Oscarin*, Benito Juárez at Normal, is dead by day and sleepy in the early evening, but after 9pm it comes alive with the smell of sizzling franks. The double-length outdoor grill serves up loaded hot dogs (from M$20) to walk-up or dine-in customers. Near the border at *Plaza de Cachanilla Food Court,* Mateos s/n between Larroque and Compresora, the US mall dining concept gets flipped, with local vendors instead of global chains selling fast-food versions of Mexicali Chinese,

### Moving on from Mexicali

Mexicali's **Central Camionera** (ⓣ686/557-2410; with guardería) is 4km from the border on Independencia at Anahuac, close to the new **Centro Cívico** development and not far off López Mateos. To get there, take a "Calle 6" bus from the local bus stand off Mateos. Altogether well over fifty buses a day head **south** (twenty to Mexico City), and there's at least one local service an hour to **Tijuana**. Golden State has an office at the station: three buses leave daily for Los Angeles via Palm Springs. On the other hand, you'll have far more choice, and save a few dollars, if you walk across the border to Calexico's Greyhound station. **Flights** to Mexico City and Acapulco leave daily from the airport 20km east of town.

fat tortas and non-mall staples like *birria* (a sort of barbecued goat or lamb stew) and *menudo* (a stew of tripe, hominy and peppers). Lunch from any of the counters shouldn't cost more than M$55.

## San Felipe

With so few places in northern Baja boasting a decent beach and reasonable public transport, the prospect of **SAN FELIPE**, a growing Sea of Cortés resort on a dead-end road 200km south of Mexicali, might seem attractive. In truth, its appeal is limited: the entire bay is strung with RV parks, and the dunes between here and the encircling folded ridges of the San Pedro Martír mountains reverberate to the screaming engines of dune buggies and balloon-tyred ATVs. If you're planning to continue south down Baja, then do just that. But San Felipe does have good swimming – at least at high tide – and if you are confined to the north, it's a good place to rent a catamaran or just relax for a day or so.

San Felipe first came to the attention of fishermen who, in the early 1950s, took advantage of the new tarmac road – built to serve the American radar station to the south on what is now called Punta Radar – to exploit the vast schools of tortuava, a species now fished onto the endangered list. Since the 1980s, the fishing village has grown to accommodate the November-to-April influx of holiday-makers from north of the border and college students on spring break. Apart from lying on the beach, you can rent **dirt bikes** and ATVs from a couple of places along the malecón (around M$250/hr), or **catamarans** (similar price; just ask along the beach wherever you see one), or indulge in a little **sport fishing**. Tours are arranged through a couple of places at the northern end of the malecón.

If the road through the cactus desert south of here to Hwy-1 ever gets improved to the point that it can be negotiated by low-clearance vehicles, this could become an interesting alternative route to southern Baja, but for the moment the hamlet of **Puertecitos**, 85km south (no public transport), is as far as ordinary cars can get – and even then with difficulty.

### Practicalities

**Buses** from Mexicali (4 daily; 3hr) and Ensenada (2 daily; 3hr 30min) arrive 1km inland: turn left out of the bus station and right down Manzanillo to get to Avenida Mar de Cortés, which runs parallel to the sea. At the junction, the **tourist office** (Mon–Fri 8am–7pm, Sat 9am–3pm, Sun 10am–1pm; ⓣ646/577-1155) gives out a map of the town but little else. North from here along Cortés there's a *farmacia* where you can **change money** (Mon–Fri 9am–6pm) and, beyond, a Bancomer but no ATM. The **post office** is on Mar Blanco just off Chetumal, five blocks inland. **Hotels** in San Felipe are not particularly cheap, though there are a couple of decent mid-range choices: the three-storey *La Hacienda de la Langosta Roja*, Chetumal 125 (ⓣ686/577-1608, US ⓣ1-800/967-0005, ⓦwww.sanfelipelodging.com; ❼), is the cleanest downtown hotel and has rooms overlooking both the sea and its popular restaurant. *Posada del Sol*, Mar de Cortés 238 (ⓣ686/566-9804, ⓦwww.posadadelsolbaja.com; ❹), has the cheapest rooms on the waterfront. While not posh, they're clean and come with refrigerators, satellite TV and a/c. At the south end of the malecón, the *Riviera*, Mar Báltico and Manzanillo (ⓣ686/577-1185, ⓦwww.geocities.com/rivieraservicios; ❻), is a family-friendly hotel with a pool and grills. Next door, the pink stucco *El Capitán*, Mar de Cortés 298 (ⓣ686/577-1303; ❼), is close to the water and has pool,

TVs and a/c. *San Felipe Marina* (ⓣ686/577-0820, ⓦwww.sanfelipemarina.net; ❽) is south of town on the road to Puertecitos, Km 4.5 Carretera San Felipe–Aeropuerto. With indoor and outdoor pools and beachfront waiter service, it's more luxurious than San Felipe's central hotels.

Not surprisingly, **seafood** is the staple diet here, with several restaurants and numerous stands selling shellfish cocktails along the front. Head for *The Bearded Clam*, the ill-named hole-in-the-wall at the northern end of the beachfront malecón, or *The Red Lobster* at *La Hacienda* hotel.

# East of Mexicali

Beyond Mexicali the road towards central Mexico trails the border eastwards, while the rail line cuts south around the northern edge of the Sea of Cortés; between them rises the Sierra del Pinacate, an area so desolate that it was used by American astronauts to simulate lunar conditions. Not far out of Mexicali you cross the border from Baja California into the state of **Sonora**; you'll have to put your watch forward an hour when you cross, unless Baja California is on Daylight Saving Time (April–Oct), in which case there's no change.

There's little to stop for on the road. You'll pass through **San Luis Río Colorado**, something of an oasis with a large cultivated valley watered by the Colorado River, and **Sonoita** (or Sonoyta), a minor border crossing on the river of the same name. Both are pretty dull, though they have plenty of facilities for travellers passing through. Past Sonoita the road splits: one leg heads south towards the coast of the Sea of Cortés and the town of Puerto Peñasco, while the other cuts inland before turning south and hitting the first foothills of the Sierra Madre Occidental, whose western slopes it follows, hugging the coast, all the way to Tepic. At **Santa Ana** this leg meets the southbound road from Nogales. Coming from Nogales, there's little to see; however, you do pass through the small town of **Magdalena**, where most buses stop briefly. Here there's a mausoleum containing the remains of **Padre Kino**. Kino, "Conquistador of the Desert", was a Spanish Jesuit priest who came to Mexico in 1687 and is credited with having founded 25 missions and converted at least seven local indigenous tribes to Catholicism. From Santa Ana, the highway cuts straight south, passing through several small towns on the way to Hermosillo.

## Puerto Peñasco

Not long ago, **PUERTO PEÑASCO** was little more than an inoffensive shrimping port, a mere handful of rudimentary houses. It was so unknown, in fact, that Al Capone used it as a secret base for his liquor-smuggling racket during Prohibition. In the past few years, though, the town has exploded into a resort area, and it is now filled with high-rise condominiums. As a major getaway for Arizona's beach-starved masses, Puerto Peñasco is tipped to become the next Cancún. And while this all-too-rapid transformation is bringing welcome economic growth, it is also wreaking ecological havoc, as construction work continues without regard to the environment.

### Arrival and information

There are good roads down here from Sonoita and east to Caborca, not far from Santa Ana. If you're taking the afternoon bus from Nogales or arriving in the evening by car, you should be able to catch a spectacular sunset on the way; the road itself is fairly flat, but is flanked on all sides by picturesque sierras that make for some unforgettable vistas. If you have your own vehicle you may fancy the detour, especially as it's quite easy to cut east to Caborca and rejoin the main road there. The three **bus stations** – Auto Transportes de la Baja California, Transportes Norte de Sonora and Albatros – are located a few kilometres outside town. One of the omnipresent white **taxis** (M$15 for a ride anywhere inside town) should get you to wherever you need to be.

The **Puerto Peñasco Convention and Visitors' Bureau** (Mon–Fri 9am–2pm & 4pm–7pm, Sat 9am–3pm; Ⓣ638/388-0444, Ⓦwww.cometorockypoint.com), on the corner of Juárez and Calle 11 (next to the Pemex station), has an ample assortment of flyers and glossy brochures. *Join us Here in Rocky Point* (Ⓦwww.JoinUsRP.com) and *The Rocky Point Times* (Ⓦwww.rptimes.com) are two English-language publications that have helpful information on the town, as well as many less useful pages of real estate advertisements. The latter has a book exchange in their offices at Pino Suárez 124.

## Accommodation

There isn't much cheap accommodation in Puerto Peñasco, with most options starting at around M$300. Many of the town's more reasonable hotels can be found around Calle 13, between Juárez and the colossal *Hotel Peñasco del Sol* on the water. Prices can double or triple at the weekends and high season, and even quadruple at spring break, Christmas and Semana Santa. Many **RV parks** front the beach along Matamoros, south of the port.

**Arizona Motel** Pino Suárez and C 17, near Plaza Las Glorias Ⓣ638/383-1059. Friendly staff at this fairly new motel in a quiet neighbourhood, offering clean, though somewhat cramped rooms with a/c and cable TV. Good access to the beach. ❻

**La Casa del Puerto** one block from the church in the old port Ⓣ638/383-6209. Tasteful studios and one-bedroom suites with Jacuzzi, sun deck, palapas and bar. A good deal for groups, the rooms here have luxurious touches, and prices drop slightly out of season. They also rent out kayaks and boogie boards at reasonable rates. ❼

**Hotel Peñasco del Sol** Paseo Las Glorias 1 Ⓣ01-800/614-9484, Ⓦwww.hotelrockypoint.com. There's no shortage of luxury lodgings in Puerto Peñasco, and this is but one, housing over 200 rooms, a pool, restaurant and spa facilities. It's also right on the beach. ❽

**Hotel Yuli** Pino Suárez and C 15 Ⓣ638/383-3289. It's often full, but the few rooms available are large and economical. Close to the beach and C 13. ❹

**Motel Peñasco** Encinas, between C 14 and C 15 Ⓣ638/383-3101. This budget motel offers large rooms with en-suite bathrooms, a/c and cable TV. A stone's throw from the action on C 13. ❺

**Posada La Roca** Primero de Junio 2, in the old port Ⓣ638/383-3199. This is the oldest building in town, frequented by Al Capone during Prohibition. A great budget option with cool, if plain quarters, and a cosy living room. Capone stayed in no. 10. ❺

## The town and around

Though the **Old Port** used to be the centre of town, tourist dollars are pushing development along the coast in both directions, and now the action is divided between the malecón and Calle 13 across the harbour. From the Old Port, the main Bulevar Juárez runs nearly parallel to the water before heading off towards Sonoita.

There are plenty of opportunities for **fishing**, **diving** and **sailing** here. Ocean-bound activities are best arranged in the Old Port; The Sun and Fun Dive Shop (Ⓣ638/383-5450, Ⓦwww.sunandfundivers.com), at Juárez and Contreras, rents fishing, scuba-diving and snorkelling gear, as well as skim and boogie boards. You can charter a vessel from Oceano Charters (Ⓣ638/383-5450) in the same building; they organize a variety of excursions including night dives and sunset cruises. Pampano's Landing (☎638/383-4419), across the street, is also an established operator. **San Jorge Island** is the most popular offshore destination, frequented by hordes of sea lions. If they're feeling up to it, and haven't been laid low by the daytime heat, you can swim with them. Otherwise, there are usually numerous dolphins frolicking around.

Even if you don't have the inclination to get in the water, a stroll on the beach at low tide, when tide-pools expose a plethora of sea-borne beasties including starfish, crabs, oysters and sea cucumbers, is good fun. The **Centro Intercultural de Estudios de Desiertos y Océanos** (CEDO; Mon–Sat 9am–5pm, Sun 10am–2pm), in Las Conchas residential zone, is the foremost authority on local wildlife, and currently researching the deleterious effects of development on regional ecology. It holds natural history lectures twice weekly (Tues 2pm & Sat 4pm; free) and runs expert-led tours to the estuaries, desert dunes, tide-pools, San Jorge Island and El Pinacate Biosphere reserve.

The region's most impressive natural attraction, **El Pinacate Biosphere Reserve** (Mon–Sat 9am–5pm), lies 52km north of Puerto Peñasco. NASA used this otherworldly expanse of volcanic cinder cones and craters, to train its astronauts for lunar landings. One of Pinacate's largest craters, "El Elegante", is 1km wide and 120m deep and can be seen from space. Camping is allowed by arrangement with the visitor centre at the edge of the park; permits are given on a first-come, first-served basis. For more information, check with the tourist office in town. Unfortunately, no public transport runs to Pinacate, so you'll have to fork out for a taxi or join an organized tour.

## Eating and drinking

Basic eateries line Calle 13, where liquor flows copiously and young gringo folk gather. More sophisticated dining can be had in the Old Port, where restaurants proliferate along and around the malecón. **Seafood stalls** are gathered at the end of Eusebio Kino.

**El Cabrón de Calle 13** at C 13 and Francisco Villa. A reliable open-air taco stand that serves up simple, cheap and tasty food.

**La Casa del Capitán** follow Juárez to Antonio's liquor store; from there you'll see the entrance to the path leading to the top of the mountain – it's a 15min walk to the top. One of the nicest restaurants in town, and with postcard-like views of the town and the sea, great for romantic dinners. They offer a full international menu, with a number of house seafood specialities, and live music at sunset.

**Flavio's** Malecón and Primero de Junio in the Old Port. Unpretentious place right on the boardwalk, favoured by residents for its excellent seafood and local prices.

**The Friendly Dolphin** Alcantan 44 in the Old Port. Local favourite with a full seafood menu and decent prices. Adorned with antique pictures of Mexico, the restaurant also serves on an outdoor patio upstairs. Occasionally one of the owners will play guitar and sing to the tables.

**Gamma's** C 13 right on the water, across from *Hotel Peñasco del Sol*. No-frills local joint that serves decent seafood, though not the place for a romantic dinner. Try the *ceviche*.

**JJ's Cantina** Cholla Bay. A beach-party seafood joint that does great fish. If you don't mind the American feel – monthly events include "Whiplash Racing" and "Bathtub Races" – it's an excellent place to watch the sun set over the bay.

**Lily's** Kino and Zaragoza. Standard Mexican fare at US prices. Popular with Americans and always buzzing, the patio seating is great for people-watching.

**Mario's Coffee** Juárez 10, at the entrance to the Old Port. Lovely little café that serves up excellent organic coffee from Chiapas.

**Sushi Sun** C 13 and Elias Callas. Locals swear by the sushi at this mid-range place. Specialities include tempura and Matsuri rolls, both made with local *camarones*. They also deliver.

### Listings

**Banks** There are several strung along Juárez.
**Buses** Services out of Puerto Peñasco are becoming more frequent, with daily routes to Hermosillo, Mexicali and Nogales.
**Internet access** Your best bet is the CiberChat café, C 13 at Encinas (daily 9am–11pm; M$10/hr).
**Laundry** There's a laundrette at Encinas 203 (Mon–Sat 8am–9pm, Sun 8am–4pm).
**Post office** Off Fremont, next to Proaset Realty (Mon–Fri 8am–3pm).

## Nogales

Compared to most of the frontier, **NOGALES** (its name means "walnut trees", though few are in evidence) is a reasonably pleasant town. Unlike Ciudad Juárez and Tijuana, Nogales is not part of a cross-border metropolis – the closest US city of any size is the somewhat distant university town of Tucson. Smaller and less frenetic than other cities along the boundary, it has a relatively low level of street hustling, vice and general nightlife options – though this is not to say these things do not exist. There's relatively little to do in Nogales; however, it's not a bad place in which to rest up and acclimatize for a day or two.

### Practicalities

Crossing the border (24hr) is straightforward; remember to have your tourist card stamped by *migración* if you're heading further south – there's also an office at the bus station where you can have this done. Immediately inside the border, the small **tourist office** (daily 9am–5pm; ⓣ631/312-0666) has a limited amount of local information and maps. Two main streets lead south from the border: Obregón, which eventually becomes the highway south, and Juárez. There are several **banks**, most with ATMs (some giving US dollars), and casas de cambio along López Mateos and Obregón, but if you want to make a phone call or send mail you're better off doing so across the border. You can use the **Internet** at Café Yajar, on Plaza Niños Heroes close to the church (daily 9.30am–8pm; M$20/hr).

There are plenty of **places to stay** close to the border, though none are particularly great value – accommodation in Nogales is pricier than in towns further from the border. Possibilities include the *Hotel San Carlos*, Juárez 22 (ⓣ631/312-1557, ⓕ631/312-1346; ❺), with a/c and free Internet access for guests; the *Olivia*, Obregón 125 (ⓣ631/312-4695, ⓔholivia@prodigy.net.mx; ❺), with a popular adjoining restaurant; and *Hotel Fray Marcos de Niza*, Campillo 91 (ⓣ631/312-1651, ⓕ631/312-1491; ❻), a slightly pricier option with fantastic decor. You'll find the cheapest lodgings east over the railway track, including *Hotel 47*, Buenos Aires 47 (ⓣ631/312-7489; ❹), though bear in mind that these places can be rough.

There are plenty of cafés and **restaurants** in town; *Café Olga*, on Juárez just across the border, is a Nogales institution. *Leo's Cafe*, at the corner of Obregón and Campillo, serves Mexican staples and seafood at reasonable prices. More upmarket options are *La Hacienda*, Obregón 142, which dishes up Mexican fare heavy on the beef, and elegant *La Roca*, Elias 91, the place to go for fine Sonoran cuisine and a romantic evening.

The main **bus station**, which is close to several smaller terminals, sits on the highway about 5km south of town – local buses (marked "Central Camionera") run from the border, or you can take a taxi, which will cost around M$70. Southbound departures from the camionera – which has all the usual facilities including long-distance phones and guardería – are frequent, going as far south as Guadalajara (26hr) and Mexico City (34hr). Albatros buses run to Puerto Peñasco four times daily from the TBC building, a couple of blocks north of the main terminal, past the fast-food restaurants. On the other side of the border, the **Greyhound** station is right by the customs office; buses leave every one or two hours (6.45am–6.45pm) for Tucson and Phoenix.



### Agua Prieta

To the east of Nogales lies another border crossing, **AGUA PRIETA**, just across from Douglas, Arizona. Still a quiet town that sees few tourists, it's gradually growing thanks to the *maquiladora* assembly plants on both sides of the border, and to new roads linking the town to **Janos** (for Ciudad Juárez and Nuevo Casas Grandes) and Hermosillo. Despite the fact that these roads are barely marked on many maps, they're paved highways, and Agua Prieta is thus on the only route from central Mexico to the Pacific between the border and Mazatlán; several buses a day run in each direction. If you're **staying** over, try the *Hotel Plaza* (Ⓣ633/338-9400, Ⓦwww.hotelplaza.com.mx; ⑥), Calle 6 and Avenida 1, or the *Hotel La Hacienda* (Ⓣ633/338-0621; ⑤), Calle 1 at Avenida 6, though you may find better value in Douglas, where there's a *Motel 6* (Ⓣ602/364-2457; ⑤), among other inexpensive motels.

## Hermosillo to Guaymas

South of Nogales, **Highway 15** traverses the Sonoran desert, passing parched landscapes of stoic cacti and thirsty-looking mesquite trees before reaching the state capital, **Hermosillo**. With a certain provincial charm, it's a relaxed, if unexciting, place to break a journey, but if you're really intent on spending a night in this particular stretch of Sonora, your best bet is to hit the region's beaches. **Bahía de Kino**, almost directly west from Hermosillo, where the desert plains meet the Sea of Cortés, offers low-key lodgings by the water's edge. Back on the highway, the next urban dwelling of any size is **Guaymas**, a further 138km south. It's a rough-and-ready port town without a shred of pretension, and the only reason to spend any time here is its inexpensive lodging.

### Hermosillo

From a distance, **HERMOSILLO**, the state capital of Sonora, is an odd-looking place. It's surrounded by strange rock formations and presided over, right in the centre, by a tall outcrop crowned by radio masts, surreally illuminated at night to resemble a giant, spiral snail-shell. Close up, though, Hermosillo is less fascinating – the boom of the last half-century has wiped out almost everything that might have survived of the old town. Some of the earliest organized **revolutionaries**, including General Alvaro Obregón, were locals, as were many of the early presidents of revolutionary Mexico: Obregón himself, Huerta, whom he overthrew, Plutarco Elías Calles and Abelardo Rodríguez. Though their many monuments and the streets named after them reflect pride in local history, today this is a thriving city and big ranching supply centre, with overflowing meat markets and shops full of tack gear and cowboy paraphernalia.

### Arrival and information

Although the city itself sprawls, **downtown** Hermosillo is relatively compact. The highway comes into town as Bulevar Eusebio Kino, known as Bulevar Rosales as it runs north–south through the centre of town. Crossing it, Bulevar Luis Encinas passes the **bus station** (ⓣ662/212-5952), 3km east of the centre, then leaves town to the west, past the airport towards Bahía de Kino (see opposite). Virtually everything you might want to see lies in the area bounded by these two, as well as Juárez and Serdán; the latter runs past the bottom of the distinctive hill known as the Cerro de la Campaña and is the main commercial street downtown.

To get downtown from the rather isolated **Central Camionera** (with guardería), take a "Ruta 1" microbus, a van (marked "Ranchito") or a "Multi-rutas" town bus across the main road. **Taxis** are rather expensive, costing a fixed M$55. From the **airport**, a short way out on the road towards Bahía de Kino, you can pick up one of the usual fixed-fare taxis.

The **tourist office** (Mon–Fri 8am–3pm & 5–7pm, Sat 10am–1pm; ⓣ662/217-0060, ⓦwww.visitasonora.com) is in the Edificio Sonora Norte, at Comonfort and Paseo Canal; they generally prove helpful, though they have little printed information and seem to come across few visitors.

### Accommodation

Nearly all the cheaper **hotels** in Hermosillo are strikingly poor value, but some very pleasant mid-range places cater to business people and the wealthy rancheros who come here for the markets. One budget favourite is the *Hotel Washington*, at Noriega 68 near Guerrero (ⓣ662/213-1183; ❷), with good-value rooms, excellent hot showers, a very helpful staff and free coffee in the lobby. Otherwise, the *Hotel Niza*, Plutarco Elías Calles 66, just off Serdán near the market (ⓣ662/217-2028; ❸), has a good location, but not great atmosphere. Much nicer, if you can afford them, are a couple of businesslike places down on Rosales: the solidly comfortable *Hotel San Alberto*, Serdán and Rosales (ⓣ662/213-1840; ❺), and the colonial-style *Hotel Suites Kino*, Pino Suárez 151, just off Rosales near the cathedral plaza (ⓣ662/213-3131, ⓦwww.hotelsuiteskino.com; ❺), which is really a motel but has all facilities including a pool. The most expensive hotels, and a number of motels, are almost all in the hotel zone, a long way from the centre on Kino.

### The town and around

While it's interesting enough to experience such a stereotypically Mexican town, there's no reason to stay here long; in any case, Hermosillo, spread out and car-oriented, is not geared to welcoming visitors, especially those without a vehicle. If you do have to, or want to, spend time here, head down to the **beaches** at Bahía de Kino (see opposite).

Short stays can be enlivened by strolling down Serdán past the market, and taking a look at the attractive plaza around the cathedral, across Rosales from the bottom of Serdán. Near here, you'll find the **Sonora Museum**, Jesús García Final, at the base of the Cerro de la Campana (Tues–Sun 9am–6pm; M$30), which houses exhibits charting the historical development of Sonora from the conception of the Earth to the construction of *maquiladora* plants. Alternatively, check out the **Centro Ecológico de Sonora**, an 88-hectare ecological preserve that is home to exotic fauna including lions, tigers and panthers. It's about 5km south on Bulevar Rosales (daily 8am–5pm; M$30; ⓦwww.centroecologico.gob.mx); take the "Luis Orcí" bus.

## Eating

Downtown Hermosillo is surprisingly short of decent **places to eat**: Serdán and the surrounding streets are lined with plenty of juice bars and places selling tortas and other snacks, but locals in search of fancier food tend to get in their cars and head for the restaurants situated on the main boulevards or in the hotel zone. There are several places on and around the plaza by the *Hotel Monte Carlo*: try the vegetarian restaurant and wholefood shop *Jung*, Niños Héroes 75 between Matamoros and Guerrero; or *La Fabula Pizza*, a branch of a chain at Morelia 34 between Matamoros and Juárez. *Rin-Rin Pizza*, just west of the *Hotel Washington*, is an option for cheaper but greasier pizza. *Xochimilco*, Obregón 51, a longstanding Hermosillo favourite, serves pricier Mexican fare, while *Mariscos Los Arcos*, Ocampo and Michel, is the place to go for seafood.

## Listings

**Banks and exchange** There are numerous casas de cambio on Serdán, and a handy Bancomer with ATM at Matamoros and Sonora, on the plaza a block from the *Monte Carlo* hotel.

**Buses** Almost all the intercity buses passing through Hermosillo are *de paso*, and at times it can be very hard to get on. However, TBC (depot outside the Central Camionera and left a few paces) runs a local service to Guaymas, Navojoa and, four times daily, to Alamos.

**Internet access** Try Contacto X, Niños Héroes and Guerrero (Mon–Sat 11am–11pm, Sun 1–8pm; M$15/hr), or visit Digital Graphics Internet Café, Noriega 136c (daily 9am–9pm; M$10/hr).

**Post office** At the corner of Serdán and Rosales.

**Travel agent** Turismo Palo Verde, inside the *Hotel San Alberto* (Ⓣ662/213-4701, Ⓔllamas50@hotmail.com).

# Bahía de Kino

Offering the nearest beaches to Hermosillo, **BAHÍA DE KINO**, 117km west, is a popular weekend escape for locals and increasingly a winter resort for Americans. There are two settlements around the bay: the old fishing village of **Kino Viejo**, a dusty collection of corrugated-iron huts, passed over by the fruits of development, and the younger **Kino Nuevo** – basically a single road strung with one-storey seafront houses, trailer parks and a couple of hotels and restaurants. There's really not a lot to it, but the beach is good, with miles of sand, and the offshore islets and strange rock formations make the sunsets particularly spectacular.

This whole area used to be inhabited by the **Seri** people, and there are still a few communities living round about: one such, on the offshore **Isla del Tiburón** (Shark Island), was relocated when the island was made into a wildlife refuge. You may come across Seri hawking traditional (and not-so-traditional) ironwood carvings along the beach in Kino Nuevo. The tiny **Museo de los Seris** (Tues–Fri 8am–6pm; M$5), on the plaza in the middle of Kino Nuevo, gives a little more information on Seri history.

**Buses** leave Hermosillo from a small Costa Expresso bus station on Sonora, a block and a half east of the *Monte Carlo*. There are about nine a day – hourly from 5.30am to 1.30pm, then every two or three hours up to 6.30pm – with more at busy weekends; they take around two hours.

There are several hotels in town, though none cater to anyone on a budget. If you are reasonably discreet and careful with your stuff, **camping** on the Kino Nuevo beach is a possibility. At the southern fringes of town, on the edge of Kino Viejo, you'll find *Posada del Mar Hotel* (Ⓣ662/242-0155; ❻), which has a pool. Further north, Sicilian-run *Hotel Saro* (Ⓣ662/242-0216; ❻) has big, new apartment-style rooms across from the beach; *Posada Las Aves*, Veracruz near

Nautla (Ⓣ662/242-0242; ⑥), a few kilometres away and two blocks inland, has a pool. *Kino Bay RV Park* lies at the northern edge of town (Ⓣ662/242-0216, Ⓦwww.kinobayrv.com) and offers full hook-up. Opposite it you'll find *Jorge's Restaurant*, one of a handful of places that dish up local **seafood**. Head south from *Jorge's* and you'll arrive at *El Pargo Rojo,* another popular and reputable eatery. *La Palapa del Pescador*, also offering quality fish dishes, lies at the other end of town, south of *Hotel Saro*.

## Guaymas

The next major stop on the road south is **GUAYMAS** – an important port that claims some proud history but has little to offer visitors. Like most ports, Guaymas is rough, dirty and vaguely depressing, and makes few concessions to tourism. There's a plaza where you can look out over the deep bay and scores of fishing boats at anchor, some crumbling old Porfiriano bank buildings and a dock that resembles a building site, complete with random piles of bricks, rubble and sand. Here and there are old boats, abandoned and disused, rotting in the salt air. The best thing about Guaymas is its sunset, one of the finest in Mexico – try to be here to see the sun sink behind the mountain ridges that surround the town. There are also some nice beaches just a short bus ride away.

### Arrival

Virtually everything that happens in Guaymas happens on Serdán, the main drag. Bringing southbound traffic from the highway into town from the west, it then leaves to the east for Ciudad Obregón via the docks, passing the now-defunct train station.

The **airport** is off the highway west of town, though you'll have to rely on taxis to get to the centre. Most people arrive by **bus**: Autobuses TUFESA (Ⓣ622/222-5453), Norte de Sonora (Ⓣ622/222-1271), Estrellas del Pacifico (Ⓣ622/222-4067) and Autobuses TAP (Ⓣ622/222-4533) are served by terminals on Calle 14 at Rodríguez, a couple of blocks off Serdán and within walking distance of all the action. **Ferries** from Santa Rosalía arrive at the docks 2km east of the centre, easily reached on local buses along Serdán.

### Accommodation

From the bus stations, Rodríguez leads towards the centre, the street numbers rising as you go. In the first block you pass what looks like a Venetian castle, but

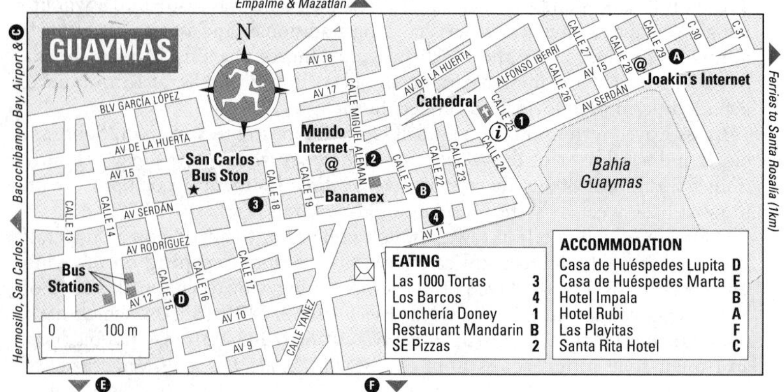

is in fact the town jail. The best of the budget **places to stay** in Guaymas is the *Casa de Huéspedes Lupita*, Calle 15 no. 125 (☎622/224-1945; ❶), opposite the prison and just a block from the bus stations. You'll pay a few dollars more for a/c and private bath. Nearby is their smaller sister hotel *Casa de Huéspedes Marta*, at Calle 13 and Avenida 9 (☎622/222-8332; ❶), with similar rooms and slightly higher prices. For a little more comfort, carry on into town and try the *Hotel Impala*, Calle 21 at Avenida 12, one block off Serdán (☎622/224-0922; ❸), an older place whose prices are inflated because it has had a face-lift, or the *Hotel Rubi*, Serdán and Calle 29 at the far end of the waterfront (☎622/224-0169; ❺), a better value for its simple, quiet courtyard rooms with private bath, TV and a/c. In the other direction, at Serdán and Mesa (aka Calle 9), the *Santa Rita Hotel* (☎622/222-8100, ⓔhotel_santarita@hotmail.com; ❹) is also worth a try (don't be confused by the more expensive motel of the same name). Perhaps the best place to stay is the comfortable motel–trailer park complex, *Las Playitas* (☎622/221-5196; ❷), which offers furnished cottages in a quiet spot overlooking the bay. It's out of town on the coast at nearby Las Playitas (see below); take a taxi, or the local bus.

### Eating

**Mercado Municipal**, a block off Serdán on Calle 20, sells fresh food good for picnics, but Guaymas has plenty of inexpensive, no-nonsense **places to eat**. On Serdán, between calles 17 and 18, and also at Calle 10, *Las 1000 Tortas* dishes out tasty tortas, tacos, quesadillas and comidas. Off to the right you'll find *Restaurant Mandarin*, a Mex-Chinese place in the *Hotel Impala*. Opposite Banamex, *SE Pizzas* also offer a great buffet deal: all-you-can-eat and a soft drink for M$30. *Lonchería Doney*, a popular local *comedor*, lies at the far end of Serdán, on the corner of Calle 25. To sample some of the town's best **seafood** head for *Los Barcos* on the seafront, Avenida 11 at Calle 20, with its huge palapa dining area.

### Listings

**Banks** Mostly on Serdán, including Bancomer at C 18, and Banamex at C 20. Both have 24hr ATMs.
**Buses** Many first-class buses on the Mazatlán–Hermosillo route stick to the main highway, skipping Guaymas. There are, however, second-class buses in both directions. TBC runs buses to Mazatlán, Alamos, Tucson and Phoenix.
**Ferries** Boats to Santa Rosalía in Baja California leave from the docks about 2km beyond Guaymas centre – just about any bus heading east on Serdán will take you there. There are currently four sailings a week (Mon, Tues, Thurs & Sat 8pm) and you buy tickets from the terminal (sales and reservations Mon–Sat 8am–3pm; ☎622/222-2324) or at the TNS bus station. Check the timetable and reserve in advance if possible; you must reserve if you plan to take a car across. Single fares for the 9hr crossing are M$550 for a reclining seat, M$750 sharing a simple four-berth cabin and M$2480 for a small car. Ferries may not sail if the wind is too strong.
**Internet access** Available at Mundo Internet, Serdán between C 19 and C 20, or at Joakin's Internet Café, C 28 off Serdán.
**Post office** Av 10 just off C 20 (C Miguel Alemán), which runs south from Serdán and round the side of the bay.
**Tourist information** A tiny booth is at Serdán and C 25, right across from the waterfront.

## Beaches around Guaymas

You may be told that there are beaches at **LAS PLAYITAS**, on the other side of Guaymas's bay. Don't believe it: the *Las Playitas* motel–trailer park has a pool and a good restaurant, but the beach is entirely wishful thinking. If you've a couple of hours to kill, though, it is interesting to take the bus out this way for the ride – you can stay on all the way and eventually it will turn round and head back home. You get to see the shipbuilding industry, the fish-freezing and processing centres and some fine views of the outer stretches of the wreck-strewn bay.

The best beach, and the one the locals use, is at **MIRAMAR**, an upmarket suburb on Bacochibampo Bay, a few kilometres north of Guaymas. On balance, this is your best bet for swimming, though there is more happening 16km further north at **SAN CARLOS** (also sometimes known as "Nuevo Guaymas" in an attempt to foster increased tourism), a town in the infant stages of becoming a larger resort geared towards a mainly retired clientele. You'll find a marina, a golf course and scores of villas and half-completed developments linked to the highway north by a long avenue of transplanted palms. There are some lovely looking bays here, but access to the shore is difficult, and most of the beaches you can reach are stony. As compensation you can rent all manner of **diving and fishing** gear or go on sightseeing **cruises** at Gary's (Ⓣ622/226-0049, Ⓦwww.garysdiveshop.com), about 1km south of the marina; they also have a fast broadband Internet connection upstairs, available every day except Sunday. If you want to **stay**, the *Totonaka RV Park* (Ⓣ622/226-0481, Ⓦwww.totonakarv.com; ❹) is as good a deal as any, on the right-hand side as you enter San Carlos; it also offers free Internet usage from its office. *Posada del Desierto Apartments* (Ⓣ622/226-0467, Ⓔpasadadesierto@yahoo.com; ❹) has inexpensive apartments, though the deals are much better if you have a group of three or more. Upmarket options include *Best Western Hacienda Tetakawi* (Ⓣ622/226-0220, Ⓦwww.bwtetakawi.com; ❼) with pool, restaurant and all the trimmings; and the *San Carlos Plaza* (Ⓣ622/227-0077, Ⓦwww.sancarlosplaza.com.mx; ❾), the most luxurious outfit in town, situated at Algodones, over the hill from San Carlos. There are some decent **eating** options: *Rosa's Cantina* on the main strip serves fine tortas and other Mexican dishes, and *JJ's* over the road does decent tacos. *Jax Snax*, a few doors down from Gary's, is open early and is good for breakfasts, hamburgers and pizzas. If you're in the mood for seafood, try *Charly's Rock* across from the *Totonaka RV Park*; the restaurant serves enormous lobsters and is also a good spot to have a drink and watch the sun go down. At the weekend, you can buy excellent sirloin steak at Santa Rosa Market for M$30.

**Buses** for Miramar and San Carlos leave Guaymas every thirty minutes or so from Calle 19 by the post office, but it's easier to catch them as they head up Serdán (try the corner of Calle 18). It can take up to an hour to reach San Carlos. To get to Las Playitas, hop on the bus marked "Parajes" from Calle Miguel Alemán; to get to Algodones from San Carlos, follow the strip that leads to the marina and its restaurants, or take a taxi.

## South to Alamos

There's little of interest along the main highway between Guaymas and the Sonora state border. **CIUDAD OBREGÓN**, founded in 1928 and named after the former president, has thrived on the agricultural development that accompanied plans to utilize the Río Yaqui – thanks to irrigation schemes and huge dams upriver, it's now a very large and uncompromisingly ugly town. There's the **Museo de los Yaquis**, in the indigenous town of Cócorit 7km north of the city, but apart from that about the only attraction is the town's cowboy clothing: locally produced **straw stetsons** are among the best and least expensive you'll find anywhere.

## The Yaqui

Between Guaymas and Ciudad Obregón lies the valley of the Río Yaqui, traditional home of the **Yaqui**, or Yoeme. Historically adept warriors, the Yaqui were among the fiercest and most independent of Mexican peoples. They resisted subjugation by the Toltec and Aztec empires, and defeated wave after wave of Spanish conquistadors. Preferring a peaceful existence, by the mid-seventeenth century they had forged a relationship with Jesuit missionaries, converted to Christianity and settled into eight towns along the Río Yaqui, Sonora.

However, in the early eighteenth century, the government began meddling in Yaqui–Jesuit relations, eventually expelling the Jesuits from Sonora. Civil unrest ensued, and the Yaqui instigated the first of many rebellions. Armed conflicts with various governments dominated Yaqui life for the next 190 years. They fought and lost their last major battle in 1927, but were granted official land rights by President Cardenas in 1939.

Today the Yaqui enjoy a degree of autonomy, though overall their cultural and political assimilation into the mainstream has been rapid. One surviving element of Yaqui culture is their religion, which constitutes a blend of Jesuit Christianity and pre-Columbian shamanism, whereby unseen spiritual worlds coexist with the world of people. Nature is a vital element in this cosmic order. Flowers, as the worldly manifestation of souls, are especially sacred. The **Danza del Venado**, or Deer Dance, is the most famous feature of Yaqui religion, performed mainly during Easter and Lent. Historically, the deer was vital to survival – its body provided food, clothing and tools. The ritual honouring of this most sacred animal is executed by highly trained performers who prepare for the role from early life. During its enactment, the dancer mimics the graceful movements of a deer, until at the climax he is struck by a symbolic arrow, falls to the earth and heroically struggles against death. The dance is said to symbolize the battle of good against evil.

**NAVOJOA**, too, is a rather dull farming town. It scores over Ciudad Obregón only because it serves as the jumping-off point for Alamos (see below). If you have some time to pass here, you could check out the **Museo Regional del Mayo** on Leona Vicario, between Morales and No Releccíón, with its small collection of historical and anthropological artefacts. Most **buses** (usually *de paso*) pull into either the TBC or Transportes de Pacífico stations, near each other around the junction of Guerrero and Calle No Reelección a couple of hundred metres away from the train station. Local buses to Alamos (hourly 6.30am–6.30pm) generally leave from either station. The TBC bus station is handy for a comfortable **hotel**, *Hotel Gema* a few blocks away at Allende 212 (Ⓣ642/422-0591; ❹). Unless it's necessary, though, you're better off heading straight through to Alamos.

## Alamos

A Spanish colonial town and national historical monument just five hours' drive from the US border and 50km southeast of Navojoa, **ALAMOS** hasn't escaped the notice of scores of Americans – predominantly artists and retirees – who have chosen to settle here over the last forty years or so, often renovating the otherwise doomed-to-decay colonial architecture. The expat community lives in near-complete social isolation from the local Mexicans, but the necessary economic interaction has at least prevented Alamos from going the way of so many other ex-mining villages in the region. A ride out to this patch of green makes a very pleasant respite from the monotony of the coastal road, and it's a

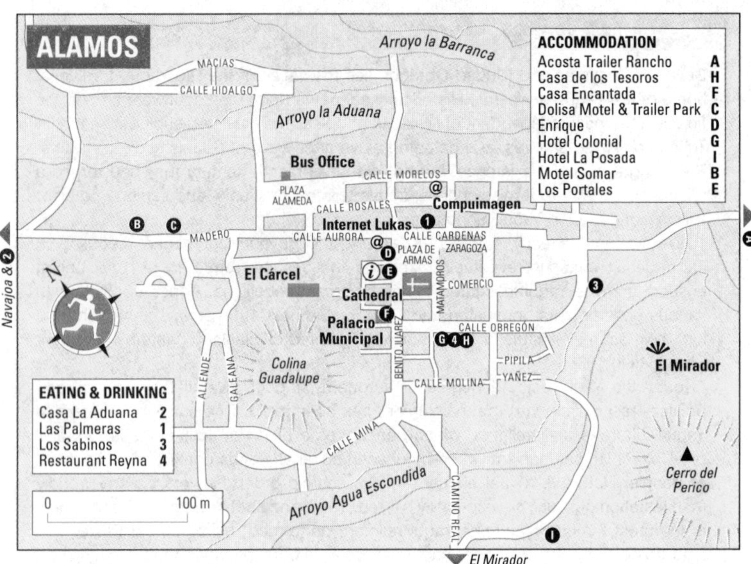


great place to do nothing for a while: a tour of the town takes no longer than a couple of hours, and there's little else to do but walk in the mountains (an exceedingly hot exercise in summer). The meeting of the Sonoran and Sinaloan deserts here at the foot of the Sierra Madre Occidental has created a fairly distinct ecosystem, home to a broad range of flora and fauna. In particular, this is a **bird-watching** mecca, boasting several hundred different species. Thousands of people descend upon Alamos at the end of January every year for the week-long Ortiz Tirado **music festival**, in honour of the late Dr Alfonso Ortiz Tirado, sometimes referred to as the "Mexican Pavarotti". Accommodation is usually booked solid at this time, so reservations are a must.

**Coronado** was the first European to pass through this area in 1540, spending most of his time trying to subjugate the Mayo and Yaqui, unaware that below his feet lay some of the richest **silver ore** in Mexico. When the ore was discovered in the late 1600s, Alamos became Mexico's northernmost silver-mining town; within a century it was a substantial city with its own mint, and the most prosperous town north of Guadalajara. Following Mexican independence, control of the area fell into the hands of the Almada family who, despite having initially productive mines, spent most of the nineteenth century protecting their property from political wranglings and petty feuds, and watching over the region's decline. The mint closed in 1896, and even the brief existence of a railway only served to help depopulate a dying town. Alamos languished until the 1940s, when an American, **William Levant Alcorn**, bought numerous houses here and set about selling the property to his countryfolk. A bank was built in 1958 and an airstrip opened, and a paved road from Navojoa was finished two years later. Today the population hovers around the 10,000 mark.

## Arrival and information

Hourly **buses** run to Alamos (6.30am–6.30pm; 1hr) from Navojoa, arriving at the bus station on Morelos by the Alameda. There is a **Bancomer**, with an ATM, across the park on Rosales. Follow Rosales east, then Juárez south to reach the Plaza de Armas, the cathedral and the enthusiastic **tourist office** (Mon–Fri 9am–1pm & 3–6pm, Sat & Sun 9am–1pm; ⓣ647/428-0450), in the same location as the *Los Portales* hotel – walk up to the hotel, and underneath the veranda is the tourist office. The **post office** is on the approach into town, opposite the *Dolisa Motel and Trailer Park*. There are a few places with **Internet** access; try Compuimagen, Morelos 37 (7.30am–11pm; M$10), or Internet Lukas, Madero 5 (8am–10pm; M$10)

**Moving on from Alamos**, there are six daily TBC buses (ⓣ647/428-0096) leaving for Navojoa, Guaymas and Hermosillo in the morning, returning in the late afternoon and evening.

## Accommodation

Low-cost accommodation in Alamos is hard to come by, but there are some beautiful, moderately priced hacienda-style places, with cool rooms ranged around orchid-draped courtyards. You'll pay ten to twenty percent less outside the high season (Nov–April). The town also boasts two **trailer parks**, both offering some rooms: *Dolisa Motel and Trailer Park* (ⓣ647/428-0131, ⓔdolisa@prodigy.net.mx; ⑤), a convenient though often crowded site at the entrance to town (open all year); and *Acosta Trailer Rancho*, about 1km east of town (Oct–April; ⓣ647/428-0246, ⓔranchoacosta@hotmail.com; ⑥), a secluded park with camping spots and a pool. To get there, follow Morelos east across the usually dry Arroyo La Aduana, then turn left at the cemetery.

**Casa de los Tesoros** Obregón 10 ⓣ647/428-0400, ⓦwww.tesoros-hotel.com. Just along from the *Casa Encantada*, up behind the cathedral, this eighteenth-century former convent now has a pool and tastefully decorated rooms, a/c for summer, fireplace for winter. ⑦

**Casa Encantada** Obregón 2 ⓣ647/428-0400, ⓦwww.tesoros-hotel.com. Attractive 300-year-old mansion with fully refitted rooms, some with a/c. Bookings are through *Los Tesoros* (see above), who own a total of three luxury hotels. Closed June–Sept. ⑦

**Enríque** Juárez, on the Plaza de Armas ⓣ647/428-1199. The only budget option in town is this slightly dilapidated hotel on the plaza with big colonial-style rooms. Only one room has a private bath. ④

**Hotel Colonial** Obregón 4 ⓣ647/428-1371, ⓦwww.alamoshotelcolonial.com. This elegant American-owned hotel offers ten sumptuous rooms, all decorated with antiques and furniture from around the world. There's a restaurant and a pool. ⑧

**Hotel La Posada** Follow signs from *Casa de los Tesoros* ⓣ647/428-0045. Wonderfully well-restored and tranquil mansion with a pool and some atmospheric ruins on site. Luxuriously furnished and one of the better upmarket options. ⑥

**Motel Somar** On the approach into town, near the *Dolisa Motel and Trailer Park* ⓣ647/428-0195. Basic, economical rooms in this rather empty and slightly ramshackle building. Rooms have bath and fan. ④

**Los Portales** Juárez, on the Plaza de Armas ⓣ647/428-0211. Splendid old hacienda formerly owned by the Almada family and currently owned by the Alcorns, with pleasant rooms around a broad stone courtyard, but no a/c or pool. ⑥

## The town and around

The town's focal point is its beautiful old arcaded **plaza** and elegant eighteenth-century **cathedral**. Opposite the arcade on the Plaza de Armas, the mildly diverting **Museo Costumbrista de Sonora** (Mon–Fri 9am–1pm & 3–6pm; M$10) illustrates the town's zenith through a mock-up of the mine and grainy photos of moustachioed workers (note that it's all done in Spanish, however). More interesting are the town's magnificent old Andalucian-style **mansions**, brooding and shuttered from the outside, but enclosing beautiful flower-filled patios. If poking your head through gaping doorways and visiting the restaurants or bars of houses converted into swanky hotels doesn't satisfy your curiosity, you can take an hour-long **house tour** (Sat 10am; M$110),

△ Cathedral, Alamos

which leaves from by the bank on the Alameda and visits some of the finest, predominantly American-owned, homes. You could also hire one of the informative, English-speaking **guides** who hang out in front of the tourist office (see p.153); they will walk you around the town and up to **El Cárcel**, a weathered stone jail that overlooks the town from Colina Guadalupe. The views alone are worth the trip, but you can also buy crafts woven by the tiny prison's handful of detainees. Guides may also take you to **El Mirador**, the best vantage point in town, from where you can see the whole of Alamos and beautiful vistas of the surrounding Sierra Madre.

### Eating and drinking

Most of the top **restaurants** in Alamos are at the town's fancier hotels: particularly good is the one at the *Casa de los Tesoros*. Right next door, *Restaurant Reyna* serves decent, economical home-cooked staples. On the plaza, *Las Palmeras* serves excellent Mexican food at very reasonable prices, and *Los Sabinos* (follow signs from *Los Tesoros*) is also highly recommended for steak. There are a number of run-of-the-mill cheaper places around the **market** that fronts onto the Alameda, and locals make for the roaming taco stand *Fortino's* when it lands in front of the cathedral at weekends. If you have your own transport, try *Casa La Aduana*, about 4km outside of town on the road to Navojoa; at the signpost for Aduana, take the dirt road for about 2km into the hills. It serves Spanish and French dishes with a Mexican twist.

## Into Sinaloa

Beyond Navojoa, Hwy-15 maintains its southbound course, soon crossing the state line into **Sinaloa**. The next place of any size is **Los Mochis**, an uninteresting destination in itself, but as the western terminus of the Copper Canyon railway, an important transportation hub. There are plenty of places to stay in Los Mochis should you need to spend a night, but many train passengers prefer to head inland to **El Fuerte**, a tranquil colonial backwater some two hours east. Back on Hwy-15, the city of **Culiacán** lies about 200km south of Los Mochis. Though it's the state capital, you'll find little to do here – most travellers choose to press on to the resort of Mazatlán.

### Los Mochis

**LOS MOCHIS** is another modern agricultural centre. Broad-streeted and rather dull, it's also a major crossing point for road, rail and ferry, and above all the western terminus of the incomparable **rail trip** between here and Chihuahua through the Barranca del Cobre (see box, p.159).

The various modes of **transport** into and out of this area are infuriating in their inability to connect – even the bus stations are on opposite sides of town – and the Los Mochis–Chihuahua route is now the only rail option. The ferry, meanwhile, leaves from the port at **TOPOLOBAMPO**, 24km away, and although the Chihuahua line goes there, the train doesn't carry passengers beyond Los Mochis. Again, see the box on p.159.

No matter how you arrange things, if you're planning to take the ferry or train you'll have little choice but to stay at least one night here – don't expect much excitement. The sweltering grid of streets that makes up Los Mochis has no real focus, but what there is of a **town centre** is on Hidalgo, between Prieto and Leyva. From the Tres Estrellas bus station, head right along Juárez and then, after

## Driving in Sinaloa

You should take particular care when driving in Sinaloa. The usual hazards are amplified (for more on these see p.40), especially around Culiacán, where there are some particularly hazardous stretches of Hwy-15 and there have been reports of robberies and attacks; the smooth new toll road that bypasses this is extremely expensive and is also said to be prey to bandits. More importantly, remote areas of the state are notorious **drug-growing** centres, and inquisitive strangers are not welcome, so stick to the main roads and don't even think about hitching here. For the same reason, there's an especially high concentration of checkpoints along the highways.

four blocks, left onto Leyva; from Pacífico turn left along Morelos and take the next left onto Leyva.

To kill some time you could take a look at the mildly diverting **Museo Regional del Valle Fuerte**, Obregón and Rosales (Tues–Sat 9am–1pm & 4pm–7pm, Sun 10am–1pm; M$15); or perhaps take a stroll around the **Parque Sinaloa**, at the corner of Rosales and Castro, with its small botanical collection. Alternatively, you could spend a whole afternoon exploring Topolobampo, a strange place on the coastline that appears almost Scandinavian with its green, deeply inset bays – there's water all around but the ocean itself is invisible and the ferry steams in through a narrow channel, appearing suddenly from behind a hill into what seems a land-locked lake. There are no beaches, unfortunately, but you might persuade a local fisherman to take you out for a ride round the bay and a swim off the boat. The Sociedad Cooperativa de Servicios Turísticos runs trips out to the offshore islands, some of which host colonies of sea lions, and if you're lucky you'll get to meet Pechocho, an amiable local dolphin. The beach favoured by locals is **Playa Maviri**, ten minutes by bus from Cuauhtémoc, between Zaragoza and Prieta.

### Arrival and information

The main first-class **bus station**, serving Elite, Futurama, Estrella Blanca and TAP, is at Castro and Constitución, south of the centre. The second-class Estrella Blanca and Norte de Sonora, as well as the first-class Tufesa, stations are clustered together on Degollado, between Juárez and Morelos. Transportes del Pacifico lies several blocks west on Morelos, near Zaragoza. All of these stations are within walking distance of most downtown hotels and restaurants. The **train station** is 3km from the centre; although there are frequent buses (marked "Colonia Ferrocarril") that depart for the train depot from outside the main bus station, you should allow at least an hour to get there in time for the 6am departure, and you can't rely on them to meet the late-evening arrival of trains from Chihuahua. **Taxi** fares in Los Mochis are a long-established rip-off, and while you should be charged around M$50 for a ride to the station, you might have a struggle to get this price. If you're aiming to catch an early morning train, try to gather a group of people and arrange in advance for a driver to pick you up. Normally, though, taxis are easy enough to find, especially around the bus stations and *Hotel Santa Anita* – the hotel also has a bus for guests only, connecting with the tourist trains.

Despite the number of visitors who come through Los Mochis on the way to the Copper Canyon railway, there are few concessions to tourism in Los Mochis. There is, however, a **tourist office** (Mon–Fri 9am–4pm; ⓣ668/816-2015, ⓦwww.vivesinaloa.com) in the Unidad Administrativa building at Allende and Cuauhtémoc.

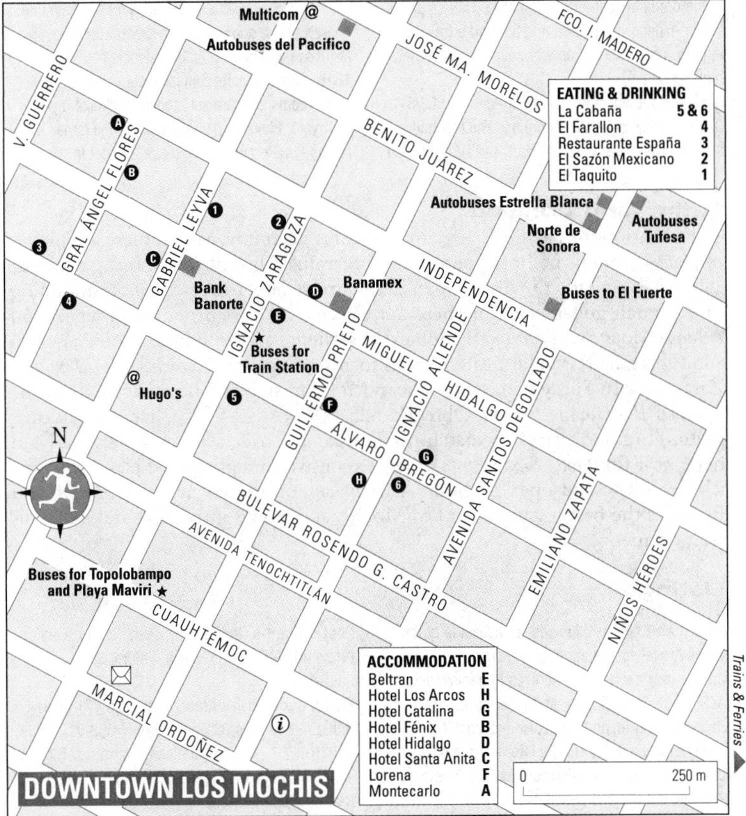




## Accommodation

Since they don't have to try too hard to attract customers – most people are simply stuck waiting for transport here – many of the **hotels** in Los Mochis are poor value, though some deals do exist.

**Beltran** Hidalgo and Zaragoza ⓣ668/812-0688, ⓦwww.losmochishotel.com. Clean, comfortable rooms, all with a/c and en-suite bathrooms. Tidy, professional and efficient, if uninspiring. ❺

**Hotel Los Arcos** Allende 534 Sur ⓣ668/817-1424. This is the cheapest option in town, although it's not the friendliest or most comfortable place. ❷

**Hotel Catalina** Obregón 48 ⓣ668/812-1240. All the rooms at *Catalina* are just acceptable, but the ones on the upper floors are a bit better than the rest, due to noise from a nearby bar. ❸

**Hotel Fénix** Flores 365 Sur ⓣ668/815-8948, ⓔhotelfenix@email.com. Clean, if slightly pokey rooms, compensated for by big-screen TVs in some of them. There's a reasonably priced café downstairs. ❹

**Hotel Hidalgo** Hidalgo 260 Pte ⓣ668/818-3453, ⓔhhidalgo@imm.megared.net.mx. Slightly more put-together than the other options of similar price, *Hidalgo* is worth the few extra pesos, especially for two or more (up to four) sharing. ❸

**Hotel Santa Anita** southwest corner of Leyva and Hidalgo ⓣ668/818-7046, ⓦwww.mexicoscoppercanyon.com. This is the luxury option in town, owned by the same people who operate many of the fancier lodges along the Copper Canyon rail line. Rooms are nice but bland, in the predictable international style. There's also a rather expensive restaurant, a bar and a travel agency. They often fill up with tour groups in the high season. ❻

**Lorena** Obregón, at the corner of Prieto ⓣ668/812-0239, ⓦwww.hotellorena.com.mx. The fifty mid-sized rooms at this hotel have a/c and TV, and if you ask nicely they will fix you a lunch for the train ride. There's also a good, cheap restaurant upstairs. ❹

**Montecarlo** Flores at Independencia ⓣ668/812-1818, ⓔsinaloanorte@infosel.net.mx. The plain, clean rooms here are set around a colonial-style courtyard. Make sure you get one of the larger rooms – their rooms vary in size, but not in price. ❹

### Eating and drinking

The situation for **eating** is as grim as that for accommodation: there are plenty of places around the hotels and the bus terminals, but nowhere really exciting, and hardly anywhere will be open if you arrive late. You're certainly not going to do much gourmet dining here. *La Cabaña*, on the corner of Obregón and Allende, does excellent tacos and burritos; there's a second branch on Zaragoza and Obregón. For light meals in clean surroundings, head to *El Sazón Mexicano*, Zaragoza 316 Sur, which serves cheap Mexican staples. The reliable Mexican-Spanish *Restaurante España*, Obregón 525 (ⓣ668/812-2335), has international pretensions and prices to match. *El Taquito*, just over a block up Leyva from here, near the *Hotel Santa Anita*, is less expensive though on the bland side, but it's clean, safe and open 24 hours. *El Farallon*, on the corner of Obregón and Flores, is the best restaurant in Los Mochis and has an intriguing and delicious seafood menu.

### Listings

**American Express** Services are available at the Viajes Aracely travel agent (see below).

**Banks and exchange** There's a Banamex with an ATM (Mon–Fri until 2pm) at the corner of Prieto and Hidalgo. Banorte, on Leyva, also has an ATM.

**Internet access** Try Hugo's Internet, just past Obregón on Leyva, or Multicom (daily 8.30am–9pm) by the Pacífico bus station.

**Post office** On Ordoñez, between Zaragoza and Prieto (Mon–Fri 9am–2pm & 4–6pm, Sat 9am–1pm).

**Travel agent** Viajes Aracely, Obregón 471 (Mon–Fri 8.30am–5pm, Sat 8.30am–2pm; ⓣ668/812-2084, ⓕ815-8787, ⓔventasaracely@viajesaracely.com), handles American Express needs and can help with train-related questions.

## El Fuerte

Founded in the sixteenth century, **EL FUERTE** is a tranquil, verdant backwater full of handsome colonial architecture and vivid local legends. It is here that the Río Fuerte emerges from the copper canyons, carrying water from a labyrinthine network of rivers, streams and tributaries. Located 75km east of Los Mochis on the railway line, El Fuerte makes an enticing alternative start (or end) to the Chihuahua-Pacifico train ride.

Aside from being "the gateway to the canyons", the town is an attractive destination in itself, rich in historical and natural diversions. The old **fort**, from which the town takes its name, supplies commanding views of the streets and surrounding countryside. Originally constructed to defend against local rebellions, it now houses the **El Fuerte Mirador Museum** (Tues–Sun 9am–5pm; M$5), where you'll find an array of historical artefacts and weathered old photos. Over 150 species of **birds** are supported by El Fuerte's green surroundings, best seen by boat at dawn when their activity is most intense. The region is home to several indigenous Mayo villages, where it is possible to witness traditional dances or purchase pottery and other crafts. Ancient **petroglyphs** depicting geometric and anthropomorphic shapes are also scattered throughout the area, most notably at the Cerro de la Máscara. Most hotels offer tours to any

## Moving on from Los Mochis

### Buses

The most comfortable **buses** depart from the first-class station on Castro and Constitución (☎668/812-5749). There are also several second-class terminals located on the other side of town: Autobuses Estrella Blanca (☎668/812-1757), on Juárez and Degallado; Transportes del Pacifico (☎668/812-0347), on Morelos; Tufesa (☎668/812-2222), on Zapata between Juárez and Morelos; and Autobuses Turísticos Azteca de Oro (☎668/812-9987), on Morelos. Finding a seat on second-class *de paso* buses can sometimes be a problem, but with departures north and south every thirty minutes or so you shouldn't have too long to wait. First-class buses cost M$300 to **Mazatlán**, M$570 to **Guadalajara**, M$90 to **Navojoa**, M$200 to **Guaymas**, M$280 to **Hermosillo** and M$700 to **Tijuana**. Second-class buses are usually around thirty percent cheaper, depending on the line. Buses to El Fuerte cost M$50 and depart several times daily from the station inside the Mercado Independencia, Independencia and Degollado.

### Trains

**Trains** are far less convenient than buses and their fares have increased significantly. Moreover, the only route currently open to passengers runs between Los Mochis and Chihuahua. Two trains leave for **Chihuahua** each day, the *Primera* (or *Estrella*, *Vista* or plain no. 73) at 6am (arrives Creel 3.30pm, Chihuahua 8.45pm) and the second-class *Económica* (or *Mixto* or no. 75) at 7am (arrives Creel 7pm, Chihuahua 1.30am), though they are usually subject to delays en route, especially on the second-class service. Also note that **Chihuahua time** is an hour ahead of local time in Los Mochis. Fares on the *Primera* are currently M$790 to Creel and M$1450 to Chihuahua; on the second-class train it costs M$390 to Creel and M$720 to Chihuahua. The **ticket office** at the station opens at 5am for same-day sales for both trains; tickets for the *Primera* can also be bought the previous day at Viajes Flamingo (☎668/812-1613, Ⓦwww.mexicoscoppercanyon.com), under the *Hotel Santa Anita* in town (see p.157), or at the Viajes Aracely travel agent (see opposite) or direct from Ferrocarril Chihuahua Pacifico (☎614/439-7212, Ⓦwww.chepe.com.mx).

### Ferries

Buses for the forty-minute journey to Topolobampo, from where the **ferries** leave, operate every fifteen minutes from Cuauhtémoc and Prieto (Mon–Sat), and Cuahtémoc and Allende (Sun). Departures for the 9–10hr **crossing to La Paz** are daily at 11pm; you can buy tickets as you board, but as ever it's safest to purchase tickets and check the timetable in advance. Currently, this route is covered only by Baja Ferries (Ⓦwww.bajaferries.com). Tickets cost M$680 for a reclining seat, M$760 for a cabin and M$1000 for a small car; they can be bought at Guillermo Prieto 105 on the corner of Morelos (☎668/817-3752), or at their offices at Topolobampo port (☎668/862-0503).

or all of these attractions; ask at the popular *Posada del Hidalgo*, enquire at the tourist office or speak to Chal at the *Hotel Río Vista* (see p.160). Otherwise, the best thing to do in El Fuerte is take it easy.

## Arrival and information

The **train station** is several kilometres out of town, and you'll need to arrange transit if you hope to catch the morning train. The pricier hotels should do this for you; otherwise you should scout around for a taxi near the plaza or market. **Buses** to El Fuerte (2hr; M$50) depart from Los Mochis several times a day from the station inside the Mercado Independencia, Independencia and

Degollado. They deposit you on Juárez, next to the town market, where you'll find **banks** with ATMs and the main plaza a couple of blocks away. There's a small **tourist information** booth (daily 9am–2pm) inside the Palacio Municipal, on the plaza, where there's also a **post office**. The town centre is small and easy to navigate, being focused on the plaza, with the Río Fuerte and old fort to the south. There's an **Internet** café, Cibercafé, at Degallado 209, also on the plaza.

## Accommodation

**Hotel El Fuerte** Monteclaros 37 ⓣ698/893-0226, ⓦwww.hotelelfuerte.com.mx. A beautiful 300-year-old hacienda with exquisite rooms and a Jacuzzi fed by illuminated waterfalls. Loads of colour, elegance and style make this the best luxury hotel in town. ❼

**Hotel Guerrero** Juárez 106 ⓣ698/893-1350, ⓔhotelguerrero@hotmail.com. This family-run place is a great budget option, with small but clean rooms around a tidy courtyard. All have bathroom and fan, and breakfast is included in the price. ❸

**Hotel Río Vista** Cerro de las Pilas ⓣ698/893-0413. Housed in the old fort stables, this pleasant hotel has excellent views over the Río Fuerte. There's a restaurant, a cooling-off pool and lots of rustic antiques. An appealing mid-range option. ❻

**Posada del Hidalgo** Hidalgo 101 ⓣ698/893-0242, ⓦwww.mexicoscoppercanyon.com. First-class service is provided by a small army of staff in this grand old hotel, the former home of the Almada family. There are spa facilities, restaurant, pool and plenty of quiet, leafy patios. ❼

**Posada Don Porfirio** Juárez 104 ⓣ698/893-0044, ⓦwww.donporfirio.cjb.net. Tranquil hotel with clean, bright rooms and a shady courtyard slung with hammocks. Ask the owners for a copy of *Legends of the City*, a small booklet that tells the history of this old place. ❹

**San José** Juárez 108 ⓣ698/893-0845. The cheapest place in town has small, basic rooms with fan; some have baths. ❶

## Eating and drinking

Economical *comedores*, **restaurants** and taco stands can be found on Juárez, close to the market. If you want to sample the town's culinary specialities, which include black bass and langostino, there are plenty of decent upmarket restaurants, mostly in the pricier hotels. Try *Posada del Hidalgo*, which has a 2-for-1 happy hour, or *Restaurant Diligencias* in *Hotel La Choza*. Slightly more economical is the *Mesón del General*, Juárez 202, which serves a range of seafood and steak dishes. For unpretentious, reasonably priced home-cooked fare, head to *El Supremo*, Constitución and Rosales.

# Culiacán

Some 200km south of Los Mochis, **CULIACÁN**, the capital of Sinaloa, is a prosperous city with a population of more than a million, surrounded by some of the richest arable land in Mexico. The city's outskirts are hopelessly ugly, but downtown it isn't so bad. There's a lot more life in the streets here, too, than in any of the city's near neighbours – probably thanks to the State University in the centre of town. Ultimately, however, Culiacán is a place of business and commerce, and outside of those interests there isn't much reason for visiting. Buses arrive at the brand new **bus station**, several kilometres southwest of the centre, and your best option is to take a fixed-price taxi into town from here. You'll find a small **tourist office** on the main plaza, on the second floor of the Edificio La Lonja (Mon–Fri 9am–5pm; ⓣ667/752-0620, ⓦwww.culiacan.com.mx); there's a big **Internet** café in the same building (M$10/hr). You could pass an hour or so inspecting the artwork in the **Centro Cultural**, or at local **beaches** at Atlata or El Tambor, about an hour away by bus, but all in all you'd be better off continuing to Mazatlán, 200km further south. In any case, once you get off the bus here, it's often extremely hard to get back on, as the majority of them are *de paso*.

For **hotels**, *Hotel San Francisco*, Hidalgo 227 Pte, just by the market (Ⓣ667/713-5863, Ⓔhotel_sanfco_cln@hotmail.com; ❺), is the best downtown choice, with TV and a/c in all the rooms. You could also try the *Hotel El Mayo* (Ⓣ667/715-2220; ❺), at Madero 730 away from the centre; the *Hotel Santa Fe* (Ⓣ667/715-1700; ❺), at Hidalgo 243 Pte; or the slightly more upmarket, modern and airy *Santa Fe II* (Ⓣ667/716-0140; ❺), Hidalgo 321 Pte.

There's **street food** aplenty round here, several pizza places and a curious abundance of sushi bars, but otherwise not too many restaurants in the centre. The terraced *Restaurant Santa Fe*, Hidalgo 317 Pte, isn't bad, while the *Agualoha*, Insurgentes 999 Norte, is favoured by the locals and is known for its steak *cabrería*, a regional speciality garnished with six different toppings and side dishes; or simply stick with the bus station's restaurant.

# Mazatlán

About 20km north of **MAZATLÁN** you cross the Tropic of Cancer. The transformation is sudden: while Culiacán lies in a temperate agricultural zone, Mazatlán is a tropical town with a humid airlessness about it.

Primarily, Mazatlán is a resort, and a burgeoning one at that, with hotels stretching further every year along the coast road to the north, flanking a series of excellent sandy beaches. But even as the new avenues of hotels may be entirely devoted to tourism, on the whole Mazatlán seems far less dominated by its visitors than Acapulco or Puerto Vallarta, its direct rivals. Most holiday-makers stay in the **Zona Dorada**, the "Golden Zone", and penetrate the town itself only on brief forays.

Mazatlán has been able to maintain much of its identity thanks in part to its status as Mexico's largest Pacific port. Also, with its location on a relatively narrow peninsula, the centre of town has preserved much of its old, cramped and traditional atmosphere. There are not many activities or sights in Mazatlán – you certainly wouldn't come here for the architecture – but it is a pleasant enough place and the separation of town and tourism means that you can find some remarkably good-value hotels on the streets just a few blocks inland. Mexican families mostly stay here, making the beachfront developments almost exclusively foreign preserves. There's an excellent bus service out along the coast road, so staying in town doesn't mean sacrificing the beach-bum lifestyle: with discretion, non-guests can use the hotel pools and the beaches in front of them. Remember to book accommodation well ahead if you are planning to be here around **Semana Santa**, when Mexicans descend on the city for massive celebrations.

## Arrival and information

The **bus station** lies on the main west coast route linking Tijuana and Mexicali in the north with Guadalajara and Mexico City in the south. The station has all facilities, including guardería and long-distance phones, and there are constant arrivals and departures to and from all points north and south. From the bus station, head up the hill to the main road and get on just about any bus heading to the right – they'll get you, by a variety of routes, to the **market**, very central and effectively the terminus for local buses. For the Zona Dorada, walk downhill from the bus station and catch a "Sábalo" bus heading to the right along the coast road.

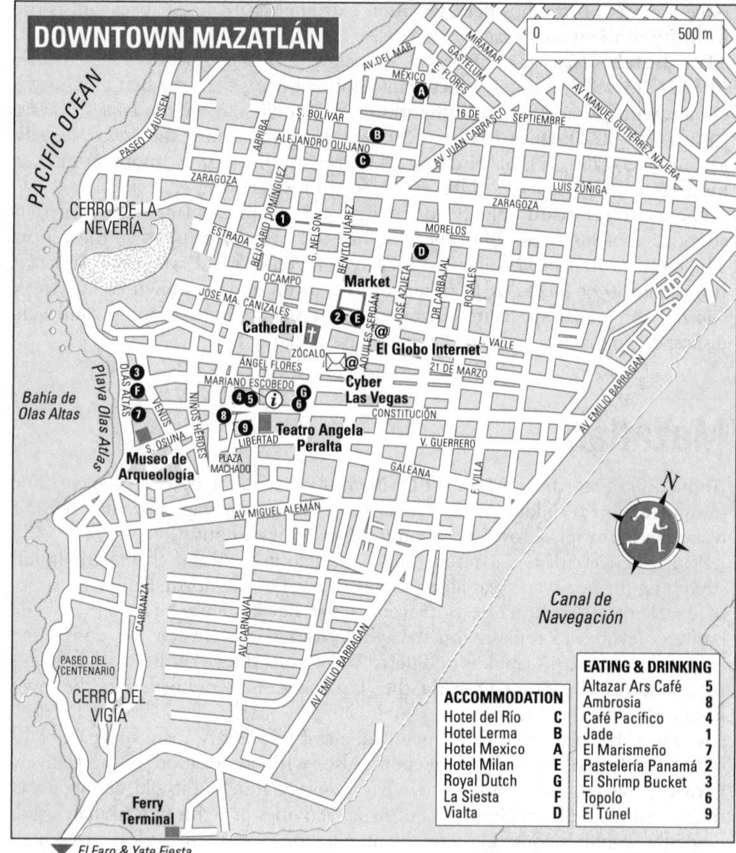


Arriving by **ferry** you'll be at the docks, south of the centre: there are buses here, but getting an entire ferry-load of people and their baggage onto two or three of them always creates problems. Taxis (M$30 to the old town) are in demand, too, so try to be among the first off the boat. If you do get stranded, don't despair: the 1km walk to the centre of the old town isn't too bad. Mazatlán **airport** is some 20km south of town, served by the usual system of fixed-price vans (M$220) and taxis (about M$200).

Downtown, you can walk just about everywhere, and the rest of the resorts are stretched out 15km along the coast road northwards – linked by a single bus route and patrolled by scores of taxis and little open *pulmonías* (they look like overgrown golf carts but are usually modified VW Beetles; cheaper than taxis as long as you fix the fare before getting in).

## Information

Mazatlán's **tourist office** (Mon–Fri 9am–5pm; Ⓣ669/981-8883, Ⓦwww.sinaloa-travel.com) is on the corner of Carnaval and Escobedo in the old town. The staff speak English and have plenty of information on local and state-wide diversions. In the Zona Dorada, commercial information booths pop up on almost every corner – most sell tours and condos, but some give friendly, free advice. If you have any trouble – theft, accident and so forth – seek help from the tourist **police** (Ⓣ669/914-8444). There are a couple of free English-language publications worth checking out if you're here for more than just a day: look for *Pacific Pearl* (Ⓦwww.pacificpearl.com) and *Mazatlán Interactivo* (Ⓦwww.mazatlaninteractivo.com), both of which contain useful information about events and attractions.

## Accommodation

Almost all Mazatlán's cheaper **hotels** are downtown, within a short walk of the market. There's also a small group around the bus station which are convenient for transport and beaches, but not in the most appealing part of town. Many have two classes of rooms, with and without a/c. The fancier hotels are all in the Zona Dorada, but even here some of the older places, and those on the fringes, can be real bargains out of high season or for longer stays.

If you're in a group, it's worth looking round for an **apartment**, as these are usually great value. **Trailer parks** tend not to last very long, occupying vacant lots and then moving north to keep ahead of development. Two of the more permanent sites are *Trailer Park Playa Escondida*, Playa Escondida (Ⓣ669/988-0077), in a quiet location almost at the end of the bus route, so probably safe from development for a few seasons (it also rents bungalows with kitchenettes; ④), and *Trailer Park Rosa Mar*, Camarón Sábalo 702 (Ⓣ669/983-6187), which is closer to the action.

### The old town

**Hotel del Río** Juárez and Quijano Ⓣ669/982-4430. Recently remodelled and very clean and tidy. A good deal for groups of four. ②

**Hotel Lerma** Bolivar, between Serdán and Juárez Ⓣ669/981-2436. Still the best deal in town. Sizeable, clean rooms around a very spacious courtyard with parking, and very hospitable staff. The café across the street has good, cheap breakfasts and comida corrida. ②

**Hotel Mexico** Mexico 201, at Serdán Ⓣ669/981-3806. Friendly, clean and close to the sea. Rooms can be a bit small. Ask for a room facing away from the noisy street. ②

**Hotel Milan** Canizalez 717 Ⓣ669/981-2673. Slightly faded, but clean. Rooms are not great value but they're right in the heart of downtown and there's a cheap restaurant downstairs. ④

**Royal Dutch** Constitución 627 Ⓣ669/981-4396, Ⓦwww.royaldutchCasadeSantamaria.com. Charming B&B with friendly and informative Dutch management. Rates include a full breakfast, coffee and tea, as well as an afternoon tea and pastries. Reserve at least two weeks in advance, as they are almost always full. ⑥

**La Siesta** Olas Altas 11, between Ángel Flores and Escobedo Ⓣ669/981-2640, Ⓦwww.lasiesta.com.mx. Lovely old hotel with private balconies and great sea views (worth the extra money); drawbacks are small rooms and noise from *El Shrimp Bucket* restaurant next door. ⑤

**Vialta** José Azueta 2006, about three blocks north of the market Ⓣ669/981-6027. Plain but acceptable rooms round a lovely courtyard; some with a/c. ②

### Near the bus station

**Emperador** Panuco, right opposite the bus station Ⓣ669/982-6288, Ⓔemperadorhotel@hotmail.com. Convenience is the main attraction, though rooms are clean and comfortable, with TV and a/c. ⑥

**La Fiesta** Esperanza 306 Ⓣ669/981-7888. Big, well-kept rooms, but fairly basic. ④

**Motel Acuario** Av del Mar 1196, near the Aquarium Ⓣ669/982-7558, Ⓕ669/981-7544. A short way down towards the Zona, the *Acuario*'s rooms are spartan, though there is a pool. ⑤

**Sands Hotel** Av del Mar 1910 Ⓣ669/982-0000. Facing the beach, straight down from the bus station. Comfortable, US-style motel with pool, slide and sea views; good value off season, when prices drop by over fifty percent. ⑦

**Santa María** Benemerito de las Americas Ⓣ669/982-2304. Uphill from the station. Big and functional, but with good rooms, all with TV. ④

### Zona Dorada

**Apartamentos Fiesta** Ibis 502 Ⓣ669/913-5355, Ⓦwww.mazatlanapartments.com. Well into the Zona off Playa Gaviotas, three blocks inland from the *Hotel Balboa Towers*. Great-value apartments set around a lovely, tranquil garden. Fishing and diving expeditions are organized by the management. ❷

**Del Real Suites** Av del Mar 1020 ⓣ669/983-1955, ⓦwww.delreal.com. Technically outside the Zona, this well-appointed hotel has large suites with kitchenettes, small suites and kitchenless rooms. Some rooms overlook the ocean. ❼

**Los Girasoles** Gaviotas 709 just next to the *Café Loma* ⓣ669/913-5288, ⓔmazatlanrental@hotmail.com. Huge, well-put-together rooms with kitchenettes on a quiet street off the strip. Pool and a/c. Prices are cut in half in the low season. ❼

**Inn at Mazatlán** Camarón Sábalo 6291 ⓣ669/913-5500, ⓦwww.innatmaz.com. This classy hotel–time-share complex oozes chic (or at least the Mazatlán equivalent thereof). Larger apartment units are excellent value for families or small groups. ❽

**Las Jacarandas** Av del Mar 2500, at entrance to the Zona ⓣ669/984-1177. Fading, but good-value hotel; some rooms with a/c and sea views, and there's a pool. ❹

**Motel Marley** Gaviotas 226 ⓣ669/913-5533, ⓦwww.travelbymexico.com/sina/marley. Comfortable units in small-scale place with great position right on the sand, and a pool. Pricey, but you won't find a place on the water for much less. ❼

## The town and around

As befits a proper Mexican town, Mazatlán's **zócalo** is very much the commercial heart of the city, harbouring the eclectic and somewhat gaudy cathedral, the post office, government offices, main bank branches and travel agencies. Always animated, it's especially lively on Sunday evening from 6 to 8pm, when there's a free *folklórico* show with singing and dancing.

Take time to stroll through the **market**, and have a look round the newly restored **Plaza Machado** in the other direction. Surrounded by fine nineteenth-century buildings, including the **Teatro Angela Peralta**, it often hosts interesting events or exhibitions. Just off the plaza on Constitución is the **Casa Machado**, a captivating museum depicting life in nineteenth-century Mazatlán (daily 10am–6pm; M$20). Lesser attractions include the small **Museo de Arqueología**, Sixto Osuna 76 (Tues–Sun 10am–1pm & 4–7pm; M$10), just a couple of blocks towards Olas Altas, and the **Aquarium** (daily 9.30am–6.30pm; M$60), just off Avenida del Mar halfway between town and the Zona Dorada.

There are also some great **views** of town from the top of the **Cerro del Vigía** or **Cerro de la Nevería**; unless you're feeling very energetic, take a *pulmonía* or taxi up. Likewise, the top of the **Faro de Crestón** at the southern edge of town is a good vantage point, though you'll have to walk up. If you feel the need to take in a **bullfight**, head to the **Plaza de Toros**, Rafael Buelna; fights are held most Sundays in the winter at 4pm, and cost about M$200.

### The beaches: Playa Olas Altas, the Zona Dorada and Isla de la Piedra

Right in town, **Playa Olas Altas** is a great place to watch the sun go down, but not the best place to swim – it's rather rocky and the waves tend to be powerful. Following the seafront drive from here around the jagged coast under the Cerro de la Nevería brings you to the **Mirador** – an outcrop from which local daredevil youths plunge into the sea. At a little over 10m, it's nowhere near as spectacular as the high-diving in Acapulco, but is exciting and dangerous nonetheless. You'll see them performing whenever there are enough tourists to raise a collection, generally starting at 10am or 11am – especially during the summer and Semana Santa – and again in the late afternoon (around 5pm) when the tour buses roll through.

To get to the **northern beaches** from here, you have to go back into the centre of town or continue all the way to **Playa Norte**, as the buses don't follow the coast round the Cerro de la Nevería. Though Playa Norte is

△ Playa Olas Altas, Mazatlán

perfectly adequate, it's worth heading even further north to the **Zona Dorada**. The sands improve greatly around **Sábalo**, a short way into the Zona, where the first of the big hotels went up. Where you go from here really depends on what you want – the beaches right in front of the hotels are clean and sheltered by little offshore islands (boats sail out to these from various points along the beach), while further on they're wilder but emptier. The more populous area does have its advantages – the beach never gets too crowded (most people stay by their pools and bars) and there's always a lot going on: water-skiing, sailing, parasailing, you name it. And if you get bored, there are the hotel pools and bars and any number of tourist watering holes and shops to pass the time. Among the dozens of artesanía markets and shopping malls, **Sea Shell City**, on Rodolfo Loaiza in the heart of the Zona, stands out as the kitschiest of all – a two-storey emporium of seashells that describes itself as a museum and is definitely worth a look.

If you ride the bus past all this, though, you eventually get to an area where there's far less development. Along the way you can see just how quickly Mazatlán is spreading, and assess progress on the new marina development by the *Hotel Camino Real*. Towards the end of the bus line, make sure you get off somewhere you can reach the beach – often the only access is through villa or condo developments with gates and security. **Buses** (marked "Sábalo") leave from the market on the Juárez side, and run up Avenida del Mar and right through the Zona to the last hotel, where they turn around. Those marked "Cerritos" can be picked up on Avenida del Mar at *Fiestaland* and run north up along Camarón Sábalo. If your goal is to reach a beautifully serene beach, stay on the bus in this direction to either Playa Cerritos or Playa Bruja; these beaches have become popular with local surfers and those interested in horseback riding with Ginger's Bilingual Horses on Playa Bruja (closed Sun; M$250/hr; ⓣ669/922-2026). There are also a few restaurants with great seafood, and the occasional spot for a post-beach drink. It is well worth enduring a few more minutes on the bus to reach these beaches.

Alternatively, south of the town centre, you can take a short and inexpensive boat trip (every 10min; 5am–7pm; M$20) from the beach next to the ferry docks to the **Isla de la Piedra** (or Stone Island), actually a long peninsula. There is a much more Caribbean feel here, with a very good palm-fringed beach that stretches for miles and is excellent for swimming, though you should keep an eye out for manta rays. It is possible to sleep out or sling a hammock on the terrace of one of the small restaurants – be sure to ask the owner first. Once a very basic community, the Isla is now included in many tour itineraries and can, at times, become crowded, especially on Sunday afternoons, when locals congregate for live music and dancing under the beach palapas. The *Yate Fiesta* three-hour **harbour cruise** also leaves daily (except Mon) from the ferry docks at 11am (☎669/982-3130; M$180).

## Eating, drinking and nightlife

As a rule, Mazatlán's more authentic and lower-priced **restaurants** are in the old town. For rock-bottom prices, seek out the noisy and hectic restaurants on the upper floor of the **market** on the corner of Melchor Ocampo and Juárez. All along the Playa Norte are shacks selling freshly prepared fish at good prices. You can come across bargains in the Zona, too, as long as you don't mind the menu being in English and the prices in dollars. The sheer number of tourists there means lots of competition and **special offers**; breakfast deals are often the best of all.

### The old town

**Altazar Ars Café** Constitución, on Plaza Machado. Serves burgers, tacos and other light fare. At night turns into a rock and blues club/bar, with live music every evening except Sunday.

**Ambrosia** Belisario Domínguez and Sixto Osuna, just off Plaza Machado. A wide selection of reasonably priced vegetarian Mexican dishes. Reservations recommended at weekends.

**Café Pacífico** Constitución 501, at Heriberto Frías. Mexican and European mix of styles in a pub with a selection of beers and liquors, snacks, sandwiches and coffee. A relaxing place to drink without the macho overtones of many Mexican bars. Open until 2am.

**Jade** Morelos and 5 de Mayo. About the only Chinese restaurant in the centre; not at all bad either.

**El Jardín** Right under the kiosk in the zócalo. Irregularly open café that does good coffee and breakfasts. Tables outside for watching the world go by.

**Machado** Sixto Osuna 34, in Plaza Machado. Come here for excellent fish tacos and a beer; the perfect place to watch the action in the Plaza Machado.

**El Marismeño** Olas Altas, a block down from *El Shrimp Bucket*. Probably the best seafood restaurant in this part of town, but no outdoor seating.

**Pastelería Panamá** Juárez and Canizales, on the corner opposite the cathedral. Fast-food style restaurant/cafetería, good for breakfast but not cheap.

**El Shrimp Bucket** Next to the *Hotel La Siesta*, Olas Altas 11, between Ángel Flores and Escobedo. One of the oldest and best-known restaurants in Mazatlán and apparently the original of the *Carlos n' Charlie's* chain. Now in bigger, plusher premises, it still has plenty of atmosphere and decent if increasingly pricey food.

**Topolo** Constitución 629, on the corner of Juárez. Popular new restaurant that offers slightly upmarket Mexican fare.

**El Túnel** directly across from the Teatro Angela Peralta. Perhaps the best Mexican food in all of Mazatlán, patronized by locals and tourists alike. Great specialities and coffee, but no beer (although you can bring your own). Open daily noon–midnight. Also has a branch in the Zona Dorada on Sábalo near the *Holiday Inn*.

### Zona Dorada

**Anthony's** Gaviotas L-39. A nice spot for some good Mexican food if you can bear the crowds in the surrounding area. Serves great seafood as well, and is reasonably inexpensive for the Zona Dorada.

**Los Arcos** Camarón Sábalo 1019, across from the *Holiday Inn* ☎669/913-9577. Locals flock here for some of the best seafood in the city.

**Arre LuLu** De las Garzas 18. A not-so-crowded alternative for seafood and cheap drinks; it also offers a traditional Mexican menu. You can get a complete breakfast of eggs, beans, tortillas, juice and coffee for under M$30.

**El Capitano** off Gaviotas, right on the beach. Large, open-air seafood restaurant overlooking the ocean. Serves shrimp, lobster and seafood platters.

**Casa Loma** Gaviotas 104 ☎669/983-5398. For that perfect romantic – and expensive – evening, this secluded restaurant in a colonial setting has far more atmosphere than the big hotels. Reservations are recommended. Closed late Aug to Sept.

**Fiestaland** Av del Mar and Buelna, at the far end of the coastal road. This bizarre, castle-like structure is a conglomeration of pricey nightclubs, discos and bars, of which *Valentinos* – a nightclub – is the most popular.

**No Name Café** Gaviotas, a few steps down from the Sea Shell Museum. This sports-themed restaurant, managed by a Chicago Cubs fan, does breakfast, beer, spare ribs and parties. Big-screen TVs show the day's action.

## Listings

**American Express** Camarón Sábalo, Plaza Balboa in the Zona Dorada (Mon–Fri 9am–1pm & 4–6pm, Sat 9am–1pm; ☎669/913-0600). Poor rates for cheques, but cardholders can receive mail.

**Banks and exchange** Citibank, Camarón Sábalo 1312, and Banamex, on Juárez at Ángel Flores by the zócalo, which has the longest hours (9am–2pm) and good exchange rates. Most places in the Zona accept dollars though often at a poor rate, so you may want to make use of Mazatlán's numerous casas de cambio.

**Car rental** Dozens of outlets, including: Budget, Camarón Sábalo 402 ☎669/913-2000; Express, Camarón Sábalo 610 ☎669/913-0800; and Hertz, Camarón Sábalo 314 ☎669/913-6060.

**Consulates** Canada, Playa Gaviotas 202, opposite *Hotel Playa Mazatlán* ☎669/913-7320; US (representative only), Playa Gaviotas 202 ☎669/916-5889.

**Internet access** The cheapest is located in the old town. Try El Globo Internet, Canizales 815 (10am–10pm; M$10/hr), or Cyber Las Vegas, corner

### Moving on from Mazatlán

#### Buses

The various **bus** companies operating from the main bus terminal are all owned by Grupo Estrella Blanca (☎1-800/507-5500) and include Futura, Transportes Chihuahuenses, Pacifico, Norte de Sonora and Elite. All have *de paso* services roughly hourly in both directions, beginning at 6.30am, and frequent local buses to **Culiacán** (M$150), **Los Mochis** (M$250), **Tepic** (M$150), **Guadalajara** (M$300) and **Durango** (M$300). There are also long-distance services to **Monterrey** (M$650), **Mexico City** (M$700) and **Tijuana** (M$680). To reach the bus station from downtown, take a "Sábalo" bus along the beachfront from Juárez near the market, then walk 300m along Espinoza.

#### Ferries

Baja Ferries run services to **La Paz** (Mon, Wed & Fri 3pm; schedule subject to change) from the port at Playa Sur, 1km southeast of the centre; catch the "Playa Sur" bus from Juárez. Information and **tickets** are available from their offices (☎669/985-0470) at the port: a *salón* class ticket (available on all boats) qualifies you for a reclining seat (M$770), a *turista*-class ticket gets you a space in a four-berth cabin (M$1000), *cabina* (M$1170) in a two-berth cabin; a small car will cost around M$2000, and bicycles go free. Prices include breakfast and dinner, though the food onboard isn't great; there are signs prohibiting bringing your own, though no one checks or seems to care. Travel agents in Mazatlán should also be able to arrange tickets.

#### Planes

Mazatlán **airport** (☎669/982-2399 or 2177) is 20km south of the city and only reachable by expensive taxi. Flights are run by Aero California (☎669/913-2042), Aeroméxico (☎01-800/021-4000), Alaska Air (☎669/981-4813), Continental (☎669/985-1881), Frontier (☎669/954-8038), Mexicana (☎669/913-0772) and American West (☎669/981-1184).

of Flores and Serdán (10am–8pm; M$10/hr). You will find many Internet places on the main drag in the Zona Dorada, though most are pricey, up to four times the cost of those in the old town (M$40–80/hr).

**Laundry** Lavafácil opposite the bus station by the *Hotel Fiesta*, and others at regular intervals throughout the Zona – in the Puebla Bonita complex, for example. There are also several downtown.

**Medical emergencies** Cruz Roja, Zaragoza 1801 (☎669/981-3690) runs free ambulance transport to local hospitals.

**Phones** You can make calls from any number of long-distance phones around the town (pick up a phonecard at a newsstand or kiosk).

**Police** ☎669/986-8126 or 066 for emergency assistance.

**Post office** Juárez and 21 de Marzo (Mon–Fri 8am–6pm, Sat 9am–1pm; ☎669/981-2121). They will accept your mail and hold it for ten days; have it sent to Lista de Correos, Administración Postal No. 1, Centro, Benito Juárez y 21 de Marzo, Mazatlán, Sinaloa, CP 82001, Mexico. There's another a post office inside the bus station, and a Post@Ship office in the Plaza La Lomita in the Zona Dorada.

**Spanish courses** Centro de Idiomas, Callejón Aurora 203 Pte (☎669/985-5606, Ⓦwww.spanishlink.org) is a well-established, award-winning Spanish language school. They offer reasonably priced courses in conversational Spanish, and can arrange homestays with Mexican families.

**Tours and activities** Any major hotel will be able to arrange a host of tours – nature, cultural and adventure – around the city and to the outlying islands or villages. The major operators include Ole (☎669/916-6288, Ⓦwww.oletours.com), Vista (☎669/986-8610, Ⓦwww.vistatours.com.mx) and Pronatours (☎669/916-6287, Ⓦwww.elcid.com). Jet skis, catamarans and boats can usually be rented on the beach with no prior arrangement necessary. You can rent scooters and ATVs for riding around town (though not on the beaches) from a number of places on Sábalo, including Pacific Moto Rent, Sábalo 414 (☎669/916-7048). Prices run from around M$100–250/hr. Mazatlán Surf Center, Sábalo near Gaviotas, will rent you a surfboard for M$300/day (☎669/913-1821).

**Travel agent** Turismo Coral, Zaragoza 618, between 5 de Mayo and Dominguez ☎669/981-3290, Ⓔturismocoral@mailcity.com. (Mon–Fri 8am–7pm, Sat 8am–2pm).

## Mazatlán to Durango

Leaving Mazatlán, you can either continue **down the coast** to **Tepic** and from there along the main road to Guadalajara or to more Pacific beaches at San Blas and Puerto Vallarta, or you can cut **inland to Durango** and the colonial cities of the Mexican heartland. This latter road, the first to penetrate the Sierra Madre south of the border, is as wildly spectacular as any in the country, twisting and clawing its way up to the Continental Divide (over 2500m). New vistas open at every curve as you climb from tropical vegetation through temperate forests of oak to the peaks with their stands of fir and pine. It can get extremely cold towards the top, so keep warm clothing on hand to cover the T-shirt and shorts you'll need for the first sweaty hour. Although it's little more than 300km long, the road is very slow, so reckon on at least six hours to Durango.

Popular with tours from Mazatlán, but otherwise quiet, **CONCORDIA**, 42km inland, is an attractive colonial town with a reputation for making robust wooden furniture, examples of which are found all over the region. The eighteenth-century Baroque **Church of San Sebastián**, overlooking the shady plaza, is unique in these parts but otherwise unexceptional, so you might as well press on towards the far grander edifices in the central highlands. For almost four hundred years, **COPALA**, a further thirty minutes on the bus towards Durango and a 1km walk down a side road, was Sinaloa's most important silver-mining town until 1933, when Charles Butter's processing plant closed, putting six hundred people out of work. Though the locals picked over the remains until the 1970s, the town's decline was already well advanced. The **jungle**, which has already engulfed the crushing mills and separation tanks, is nibbling at the edges of the village, which today largely relies on passing tourists from

Mazatlán for its survival. Once the day-trippers leave, however, the place takes on a languorous air, making it a relaxing, and cool, place to **spend a night** or two. The *Copala Butter Company*, Plaza Juárez (☎741/985-4225; ❷), has beautiful rooms with bath, and a balcony with views of the eighteenth-century church across the central plaza. It also offers **self-catering** bungalows (❹), which sleep up to four people. The restaurant here and the only other one in town, *Daniel's*, are both excellent and serve reasonably priced Mexican food, the latter in an open-air setting. Try the local speciality, coconut-banana cream pie.

## South of Mazatlán: Tepic

Below Mazatlán the main road steers a little way inland, away from the marshy coastal flatlands. There are a few small beach communities along here, and deserted sands, but on the whole they're impossible to reach without transport of your own, and totally lacking in visitor facilities once you get there. The first town of any size, capital of the state of Nayarit and transport hub for the area, is **TEPIC**.

Despite its antiquity – the city was founded by Hérnán Cortés's brother, Francisco, in 1544 – there's not a great deal to see in Tepic. It's appealing enough in a quietly provincial way, but for most travellers it's no more than a convenient **stopover** along the route to Guadalajara, or a place to switch buses for the coast. This is probably the best way to treat it, for while the surrounding country is beautiful, it's largely inaccessible. However, many anthropologists do make it into the mountains of Nayarit, homelands of the Huichol and Cora, whose vivid cultures are rich and interesting.

The eighteenth-century **cathedral**, on the zócalo, is worth a look, as is the small **Museo Regional** (Mon–Fri 9am–2pm & 4pm–7pm, Sat 9am–2pm; M$20), at the corner of México and Zapata, south from the zócalo, with a lovely collection of local pre-Columbian and Huichol artefacts. The **Museo de Los Cuatro Pueblos** (Mon–Fri 9am–2pm & 4pm–7pm, Sat 9am–2pm; free), at corner of Hidalgo and Zacatecas, has anthropological displays documenting the cultures of Nayarit's indigenous peoples. A couple of kilometres south on México, the **Ex-Convento de la Cruz de Zacate**, built in the sixteenth century to house a miraculous cross, has been restored for visitors. Plenty of places sell **Huichol artesanías**, including vibrant yarn paintings and bead statues, one of the best being upstairs at Casa Arguet, Amado Nervo 132. Alternatively, you can buy them directly from Huichol artists in the main plaza.

Tepic's **bus station** lies a couple of kilometres southeast of the centre on Avenida Insurgentes, but local buses shuttle in and out from the main road outside – to get into town, cross over it and catch one marked "centro". Transportes Norte de Sonora run hourly second-class buses to San Blas (M$40), as well as services to Mazatlán (M$110), Guadalajara (M$160), Los Mochis (M$300), Mexicali (M$750), Tijuana (M$820) and beyond. TAP also run comfortable first-class buses to all of those destinations.

The main **tourist office** is inconveniently located on the corner of Calz del Ejercito and México (Mon–Fri 9am–5pm; ☎311/214-8071, Ⓦwww.visitnayarit.com), although there are other branches in town, including on the corner of Los Insurgentes and México, on the corner of Amado Nervo and Puebla and inside the bus station. **Banks** are situated on and around the main plaza. If you need **Internet**, try the Ciber-cafe at Lerdo 23 Ote (8am–9pm; M$10/hr) or Conume Internet inside the Soriana shopping centre, opposite the bus station (10am–2pm & 4pm–8.30pm; M$10/hr).

### The Huichol

The **Huichol**, or Wixárika, are the most intensely mystical of Mexico's indigenous peoples. Dwelling in isolated mountain settlements around the borders of Nayarit, Jalisco, Zacatecas and Durango, they practise an extant form of pre-Columbian shamanism, having accepted only token elements of Spanish Catholicism.

For the Huichol, religion and ritual are central elements of daily life. The cultivation of maize, particularly, is bound with sacred rites and esoteric meaning. Animism – the belief that all objects are alive and imbued with spirit – is key to their enigmatic world view: rocks, trees, rivers and sky all have souls and there are as many gods as there are things in the world.

**Peyote**, a hallucinogenic cactus, is the most important and powerful god in their vast pantheon. Gathering and ingesting this plant is a major part of the ceremonial calendar, which includes an annual cross-country pilgrimage to the sacred desert around Real de Catorce to acquire supplies (see p.172). Grandfather Peyote is the teacher and guardian of the Huichol. He delivers sacred visions, heals the sick and guides the community.

Huichol artesanías are particularly striking and include vivid "**yarn paintings**" that are created by pressing lengths of yarn into wax. They represent peyote visions and are filled with vibrantly rendered snakes, birds, deer and other sacred animals, as well as gourd bowls and other ritually significant objects. Circular motifs usually symbolize peyote itself, or its flower. You can buy these paintings in Tepic and elsewhere.

If you're only staying for one night it's easiest to put up with the noise and stay by the bus station. Two cheap **hotels** with little to distinguish between them – the *Nayar* (Ⓣ311/213-2322; ❷) and the *Tepic* (Ⓣ311/214-7615, Ⓔhoteltepic@hotmail.com; ❷) – stand immediately behind the terminal on Martínez. In the centre, try the *Hotel Sarita*, Bravo 112 Pte (Ⓣ311/212-1333; ❶), north of the zócalo, or the *Cibrian*, Amado Nervo 163 Pte (Ⓣ311/212-8698, Ⓕ216-1461; ❸), slightly closer. For more comfort, the *Sierra de Alicia*, México 180 Nte (Ⓣ311/212-0322, Ⓦwww.hotelsierradealica.com.mx; ❺), and the luxurious *Fray Junipero Serra*, Lerdo 23 Pte (Ⓣ311/212-2211, Ⓦwww.frayjunipero.com.mx; ❼), right on the zócalo, are good choices. As for **food**, there's plenty of choice around the zócalo and on México: *Pat Pac's*, upstairs at México Nte and Morelos, is good, popular and reasonably priced, offering an excellent breakfast buffet and Mexican menu; *Café Diligencias*, México 29 Sur, is a good place to linger over a coffee; while *El Trigal*, corner of Zapata and Veracruz, serves decent vegetarian fare. Fancier restaurants, other than those in the hotels, are west of here, near the open spaces of the Parque La Loma: try for example *Roberto's*, Paseo La Loma 472 at Insurgentes, which offers seafood and international fare.

# San Blas

West of Tepic lies the coastal plain: sultry, marshy and flat, dotted with palm trees and half-submerged under lagoons teeming with wildlife. You have to go through this to reach **SAN BLAS**, as godforsaken a little town as you could hope to see – at least on first impression. It was an important port in the days of the Spanish trade with the Orient, wealthy enough to need a fortress to ward off the depredations of English piracy, but though it still boasts an enviable natural harbour and a sizeable deep-sea fishing fleet, almost no physical relic of the town's glory days remains.

Life in San Blas is extremely slow. The positive side of this is an enjoyably laid-back travellers' scene, with plenty of people who seem to have turned up years ago and never quite summoned the energy to leave. For such a small town, though, San Blas manages to absorb its many visitors – who come mainly in winter – without feeling overrun, submissive or resentful. During the summer it's virtually deserted, save for legions of ferocious sand flies, but at the beginning of February the city hosts its biggest festival in recognition of San Blas – the week-long fiesta often actually begins before and stretches long after its set dates. Do not come here without insect repellent or you will be eaten alive: it is bearable by day, but the mosquitoes descend en masse at dusk.

## Arrival and information

The majority of the **buses** serving San Blas arrive from Tepic, 65km east. The direct Mazatlán bus is permanently out of operation, though there are four daily services to/from Puerto Vallarta. Transportes Norte de Sonora run these and a daily bus to Guadalajara via Tepic.

The **bus station** is on Sonora at the northeast corner of the main plaza, right in the centre of town. Here Juárez crosses Heroico Batallón de San Blas, which runs 1km south to the town beach, Playa de Barrego. The very helpful **tourist**

**office** (Mon–Fri 9am–3pm; ⓣ323/285-0221 or 0005) is located inside the Governor's Palace on the main plaza.

## Accommodation

Part of the appeal of San Blas is that there's plenty of choice of budget **hotels**. Most places are on Juárez or Heroico Batallón. The town is especially well geared to small, **self-catering** groups: "bungalows" and "suites" are apartments with up to six beds, a small kitchen and usually (though you should check) some cooking equipment. Wherever you stay, make sure that the screens are intact and the doors fit; otherwise you'll be pillaged by biting insects.

The *Coco Loco* **trailer park** (ⓣ323/285-0055, ⓔloscocos@sanblasmail.com) is a shady and grassed camping area close to the beach, a kilometre down Batallón from the zócalo. There's also free camping on Playa de Barrego, but the bugs and the availability of good, cheap accommodation in town make this less than appealing.

**Casa María** Canalizo 67 ⓣ323/285-1057, ⓦwww.casamaria.sanblasmexico.com. Long-established and well-known cheapie with comfortable, clean rooms surrounding a courtyard filled with caged birds. ❸

**Garza Canela** Paredes 106, follow signs from Batallón ⓣ323/285-0112, ⓦwww.garzacanela.com. Comfortable, if plain, a/c rooms, pool, garden, and some kitchenettes. Rates include breakfast. Significant discounts during low season. ❽

**Hotel Bucanero** Juárez ⓣ323/285-0101. Good, clean rooms surrounding an airy courtyard and fountain. A good spot if you are looking for a hotel within a stone's throw of the action; a/c available for an additional charge. ❸

**Hotel Flamingos** Juárez 105 ⓣ323/285-0485, ⓦwww.sanblas.com.mx. The nicest place in town: sleek, classy rooms around the perimeter of a wonderful garden courtyard with pool and ping-pong table. ❼

**Hotel Morelos** opposite *El Ranchero* (no phone). Same family and setup as *El Ranchero* (without the kitchen), and just as comfortable and clean. ❸

**Posada Azul** Batallón, two blocks beyond *Casa María*. The cheapest in town. Basic, but safe and friendly. ❶

**Posada del Rey** Campeche 10, not far from the water ⓣ323/285-0123, ⓦwww.sanblasmexico.com/posadadelrey. Modern, plain and comfortable rooms with a/c and fans. Tiny pool and bar with views to the water. ❹

**Posada Portola** Paredes 118, two blocks northeast of the zócalo ⓣ323/285-0285, ⓦwww.bungalowsportola.com. Exceptional value with immaculate rooms and good kitchenettes. ❺

**La Quinta California** Batallón ⓣ323/285-0310, ⓦwww.quintacalifornia.com. Friendly management and good-value apartments set around a leafy, tranquil courtyard. Close to the beach, behind *El Herradero Cantina*, amongst the trees. ❸

**El Ranchero** Batallón at Michoacán ⓣ323/285-0892. Friendly in the extreme; rooms with or without bath include use of kitchen; beds in communal rooms at peak times. Having become a popular budget choice, it's often full in winter, and can be a bit noisy. ❸

**Suites San Blas** down by the beach ⓣ323/285-0505, ⓦwww.sanblasmexico.com/suitesanblas. Especially good value for groups or families – units for up to six people with (ill-equipped) kitchen in quiet spot with a pool. Slightly faded rooms, cheaper without a/c. ❺

## The town and around

Beyond lying on the pristine **beaches** to the south of San Blas or taking an excellent jungle-boat trip to **La Tovara springs** (see opposite for both), most visitors seem content to simply relax or amble about town. A more focused hour can be spent at **La Contadoría**, the ruins of a late eighteenth-century fort which, with the vaulted remains of a chapel, crown the Cerro de San Basilio near the river, a kilometre along Juárez towards Tepic (M$6). From here you get great views over the town to the ocean, where, according to Huichol legend, the small white island on the horizon is said to represent peyote. It marks the symbolic starting point of their annual pilgrimage to the central highlands, the actual start being on the **Isla del Rey**, the lighthouse-topped peninsula across the Estero del Pozo channel from San Blas. The pilgrimage begins approximately two weeks before Easter, with feasts and elaborate ceremonies centred around a sacred **cave** below the lighthouse. Remains of the cave can still be seen, though most of it was recklessly destroyed by the government in the 1970s to provide rock for a jetty. You can catch a **boat** across to the Isla del Rey from the landing stage at the end of Héroes 21 de Abril.

San Blas is also an excellent place for both **fishing** and **whale-watching** trips, the latter in the winter months. It is inexpensive as far as sport fishing goes, and M$800-1000 will get you a five- to seven-person boat for the morning, allowing you to trawl for yellowfin tuna, barracuda and others. You can spend half the morning fishing, half whale watching, and you're bound to do quite well on both fronts – when grey whales are in the area (Dec–April), they show up just about everywhere. There are a number of guides in town who'll take you out, but two of the best around are Abraham Murillo (aka "Pipila") and Antonio Aguayo. If they don't find you first, walk down Paredes past the *Garza Canela* until you come to the inlet and small harbour of fishing *pangas*; there's a good chance either Pipila or Antonio will be there, but if not any of the men fixing their nets can point you in the right direction.

### La Tovara and jungle boat trips

The **lagoons and creeks** behind San Blas are almost unbelievably rich in bird and animal life – white herons and egrets are ubiquitous, as are hundreds of other species that no one seems able to name (any bird here is described as a *garza* – a heron). The best way to catch a glimpse is to get on one of the three-hour boat trips into the jungle, the launch negotiating channels tunnelled through dense mangrove, past sunbaking turtles and flighty herons. The best time to go is at dawn, before other trips have disturbed the animals; you might even glimpse a cayman along the way. Most trips head for **La Tovara**, a cool freshwater spring that fills a beautiful clear pool perfect for swimming and pirouetting off the rope swing – if you're not put off by the presence of crocodiles, that is. Eat at the fairly pricey palapa restaurant or bring your own picnic.

**Trips** leave from the river bridge 1km inland from the zócalo along Juárez: get a group together for the best prices. Rates are fair and start at around M$300 for four, M$80 per extra person for three hours; M$400 for four and M$100 per extra person for four hours, including a trip to a crocodile farm. You may also want to consider negotiating something longer, giving more time for swimming and wildlife spotting en route. Shorter jungle boat trips leave from Matanchén (see below) but the longer boat ride from San Blas justifies the marginally higher cost.

### The beaches

As well as the fine beaches right in town, there are others some 4km away around the **Bahía de Matanchén**, a vast, sweeping crescent of a bay entirely surrounded by fine soft sands. At the near end, the tiny community of **Las Islitas** on the Playa Miramar has numerous palapa restaurants on the beach that serve up grilled fish and cold beers and, on the point, a group of beautifully situated but relatively expensive cabins for rent; if you can swing it, it's well worth staying at this remote outpost. At the far end lies **Aticama** (with more basic shops and places to eat) and the disappointing Playa Los Cocos, where erosion is steadily eating away at what was once a pristine beach. In between, acres of sand are fragmented only by flocks of pelicans and the occasional crab. There are plenty of spots where you can camp if you have the gear and lots of repellent, as well as a trailer park at Los Cocos. The waves here, which rise offshore beyond Miramar and run in, past the point, to the depths of the bay, are in the *Guinness Book of Records* as the longest in the world: it's very rare that they are high enough for surfers to be able to ride them all the way in, but there's plenty of lesser **surfing** potential – surfboards and boogie boards can be rented in Las Islitas or in San Blas for a few dollars.

You can walk from San Blas to Matanchén, just about, on the roads through the lagoons – it's impossible to penetrate along the coast, which would be much shorter. Considering the sweltering temperatures in this area, it's far easier to make the trip on one of the **buses** ("El Llano") that leave several times daily from the station, or by **taxi** (bargain fiercely).

## Eating and drinking

Seafood is big business in San Blas and you can buy it at beachfront palapas and street stands near the Tovara *embarcaderos*, as well as at the established

### Fiestas

**January**

**Ortiz Tirado Music Festival** (last week of Jan). Thousands descend upon Alamos (see p.151) for a week-long celebration in honour of Dr Alfonso Ortiz Tirado. Concerts, parades, cultural events and plenty of merry-making.

**February**

**Día de San Blas** (first week of Feb). The *feria* in San Blas (see p.170) starts on January 30 and ends a week or so later. Parades, fireworks and ceremonies.

**Carnaval** (week before Lent; variable Feb–March). Celebrated with particular gusto in La Paz (see p.115), Ensenada (see p.91) and Culiacán (see p.160). The best carnival in the north, though, is at Mazatlán (see p.161).

**March**

**Fiesta de San José** (March 19). Saint's day celebrations in San José del Cabo (see p.132) with horse races, cockfights and fireworks.

**April**

**Palm Sunday** (Sun before Easter). Dramatizations of biblical episodes in Jala, an ancient town between Tepic and Guadalajara.

**Semana Santa** (Holy Week). Observed everywhere. High points include Passion plays in Jala; processions and native dances in Rosamorada, north of Tepic on the main road; and pilgrimages and dances, including the renowned Danza del Venado (see box, p.151), in the Yaqui town of Cocorit near Ciudad Obregón.

**May**

**Día de la Santa Cruz** (May 3). Celebrated in Santiago Ixcuintla (see p.176), north of Tepic, with traditional dances.

**June**

**Día de San Juan** (June 24). Saint's day celebrations in Guaymas (see p.148) and Navojoa (see p.151), where there's a *feria* that carries on to the beginning of July.

**restaurants** in town. There's also plenty of fruit and other healthy offerings to cater for the tourists. At the beach most places close around sunset, and if you want to eat later you'll have to walk into town – a flashlight to guide your way is a worthwhile investment.

**El Cocodrilo** Juárez 1. A San Blas fixture with a great location on the zócalo. Travellers and locals alike come for the excellent if a bit pricey seafood, and to relax and drink long after the activity in the zócalo has died down.

**La Familia** Batallón 62. Reasonably priced and unpretentious place serving steaks and seafood. Family-run, as the name suggests.

**La Isla** Mercado at Paredes. A must, if only to admire the astonishingly kitschy decor: draped fishing nets festooned with shell pictures, shell mobiles and shell lampshades. Moderately priced meat and seafood dishes of average quality. Also known as *Chief Tony's*.

**McDonald's** Juárez 36. No relation to Ronald's place, this friendly restaurant just off the main plaza serves excellent, good-value meals. Breakfasts are particularly tasty; you'll often find a crowd of expats here to enjoy them.

**Mike's Place** Juárez 36 above *McDonald's*. Quiet drinking midweek but livens up on Friday and Saturday with dancing and anything from Latin to classic rock.

**La Tumba de Yako** Batallón at Querétaro. Kiosk run by the local surf team, popular for its banana bread and natural yogurt.

### July

**Romería** (first week of July). In Tecate (Baja California), extremely colourful, with cowboys, carnival floats and music.

**Día de Santiago** (July 25). Celebrated in Compostela (Nayarit), south of Tepic, where the men ride around on horses all day – the women take over their mounts the following morning and then do the same. Also boasts a fair with fireworks.

### September

**Independence Day** (Sept 16). Celebrated everywhere. Tijuana (see p.80) has horse and motor races, mariachi, dancing, gambling and fireworks, as does Ensenada (see p.91), while the much smaller crossing of Agua Prieta (see p.145) has a more traditional version of the same, with parades and civic ceremonies.

**Día de San Miguel** (Sept 28). A pilgrimage to Boca, a community located very close to Choix, on the railway from Los Mochis. There's dancing and a number of parades.

**Fiesta del Sol** (late Sept–early Oct). Music and arts commemorating the founding of Calexico (see p.138).

### October

**Día de San Francisco** (Oct 4). The culmination of a two-week fiesta in Magdalena (Sonora), attended by many Indians (Yaqui and Sioux among them) who venerate this missionary saint. Traditional dances.

### November

**Día de los Muertos** (Day of the Dead; Nov 2). Celebrated everywhere. Navojoa (p.151) has some of the more lively festivities.

### December

**Día de la Inmaculada Concepción** (Dec 8). Celebrated by the pilgrims who converge on Alamos (see p.151) and Mazatlán (see p.161), with parades, music and dancing.

**Día de la Virgen de Guadalupe** (Dec 12). In Navojoa (see p.151), the climax of ten days of activities comes with a procession. Tecate (Baja California) also has a lively and varied fiesta.

## Listings

**Banks and exchange** The Banamex on Juárez just east of the plaza cashes cheques (Mon–Fri 9am–2pm) and has an ATM, but is plagued by long queues, poor rates and an occasional lack of funds. You're better off changing money before you get here. If pushed, see if the Pato Loco store on Mercado and Echevarría will change cheques.
**Internet access** Try Café Net San Blas, on Juárez and Batallón (daily 9am–11pm; M$15/hr), around the corner from the creatively named *McDonald's* restaurant; Red.Com Cibercafe, Juarez 64 (10am–11pm; M$10/hr); or San Blas en Line, at *La Quinta California* (see p.172), a laid-back place with a coffeehouse feel, and a large collection of second-hand books.
**Post office** A block northeast of the bus station at Sonora and Echevarría.

## Around San Blas: Santiago Ixcuintla and Mexcaltitán

North of San Blas, from Hwy-15 you can take the turn-off for **SANTIAGO IXCUINTLA**, a market town where the only real interest lies in the **Huichol Centre for Cultural Survival and Traditional Arts** (approximately 1.5km from the central plaza towards Mexcaltitán at 20 de Noviembre and Constitución). This cooperative venture, aimed at supporting Huichol people and preserving their traditions, raises money by selling quality Huichol art and offering various classes; the centre is most active between November and May. From Santiago a road leads straight down to the coast and the **Playa Los Corchos**, a perfect stretch of sand lined with palm trees, by the mouth of the Río Grande de Santiago. Santiago has a few cheap hotels, but no other formal facilities – you might, however, find someone prepared to rent you a room in their house, or else space to sling a hammock under the veranda of one of the beach bars. You can reach Santiago by regular bus from both San Blas and Tepic.

North of Santiago, located on a lily-strewn lagoon and supporting only a few hundred habitants, is the extraordinary islet of **MEXCALTITÁN** – "House of the Mexicans" in Nahautl, which looks something like a very tiny version of Tenochtitlán, the Aztec capital before the Spaniards arrived. Indeed, the place is one candidate for the legendary Aztec homeland Aztlán, from which the tribe set out on their exodus to the Valley of México; the small **Museo del Origen** on the plaza (Mon–Fri 9am–2pm & 4pm–7pm, Sat 9am–2pm; M$15) addresses that hypothesis with a collection of archeological relics. Mexcaltitán sees very little tourism, but you should be able to find a guide to paddle you around the island and a room at the single **hotel**, *Ruta Azteca* (☎323/235-6020; ❸), offering four bare-bones rooms near the church. There's a handful of inexpensive **restaurants**, most specializing in seafood – try *Restaurante Xóchitl*, close to the *embarcadero*. If you're in the area around the end of June you should definitely try to visit the island fiesta, on June 28 and 29, when there are canoe races on the lagoons and rivers; be sure to make a reservation, too. To reach Mexcaltitán from Santiago, catch a *combi* from the station on Juárez, one block from the plaza (M$20). The journey takes about 45 minutes and is followed by a fifteen-minute boat ride across the lagoon (M$10).

# Tepic to Guadalajara: Ixtlán

Between Tepic and Guadalajara it's a long climb over the Sierra Madre, with an excellent toll road much of the way. **IXTLÁN DEL RÍO** is the first place you might be tempted to stop – the only other is Tequila (see p.354). Ixtlán was made famous by Carlos Castaneda's *Journey to Ixtlán*, which is attraction enough for a few, though it's hard to believe that many find what they're after, as this is an exceptionally unattractive little strip development along the highway, beset by constant traffic noise from huge trucks and permanent jams. What it does offer is plenty of hotels and restaurants: if you do want to **stay**, try the *Hotel Plaza Hidalgo*, Hidalgo 101 (☎324/243-2100; ❸), or the *Motel Colon*, Hidalgo 359 (☎324/243-3619; ❷). The *Río Viego*, very near the plaza, is a decent traditional Mexican **restaurant**.

Though it offers little spiritual diversion, Ixtlán does have one worthwhile attraction in its **archeological site**, Los Toriles (Tues–Sun 9am–6pm; M$30, free on Sun), a couple of kilometres east. The site is right by the highway and rail line: there are local buses, and second-class services on the main road should stop. Though not very impressive in comparison with the great sites in central and southern Mexico, this is one of the largest and most important in western Mexico, with numerous heavily restored buildings of plain, unadorned stone. Perhaps most striking is the sheer size of the place. What you can see is extensive, but the site in total is said to cover an area five times larger – and this is considered an "insignificant" culture of which relatively little is known. The site itself has a series of rectangular buildings forming plazas, each centring on an altar. The finest structure, and the most thoroughly restored, is an unusual circular temple ringed by a wall. The sides, which now slope out slightly, were originally vertical, so that the cylindrical building looked like a brazier. Circular temples like this are usually associated with **Quetzalcoatl** in his guise of Ehecatl, god of wind, but here the brazier shape may also refer to **Huehueteotl**, the Old God or god of fire. Outside the site it's easy to spot piles of stones in the farm at the back and odd humps in the surrounding fields; at one point the site fence cuts through an obvious mound.

# Travel details

## Buses

Services on the main highways south from Tijuana or Nogales are excellent, with constant fast traffic and regular express services, if you want them, from the border all the way to Mexico City. Be warned, though, that it can be hard to get a seat on *de paso* buses along the way, especially in Hermosillo, Culiacán and Los Mochis. Baja California has fewer services. Chief operators are Águila (Baja), Tres Estrellas de Oro – arguably the most reliable company – Transportes del Pacífico and Transportes Norte de Sonora (TNS), with dozens of second-class companies serving lesser destinations. For long distances and on the busiest routes you might consider one of the pullman services run by companies like Elite, with airline-style seats, drinks, video and icily effective air-conditioning. The following frequencies and times are for first-class services. Second-class buses usually cover the same routes, running ten to twenty percent slower. Keep in mind, too, that the Mexican bus service is always evolving and the number of departures can change overnight. The schedules below are approximate and should always be verified in person.

**Alamos** to: Navojoa (hourly; 1hr); Phoenix (1 daily; 13hr).

**Cabo San Lucas** to: La Paz via San José del Cabo (6 daily; 3–4hr); La Paz via Todos Santos (8 daily; 2hr); San José del Cabo (roughly hourly; 30min); Todos Santos (8 daily; 1hr).

**Ensenada** to: Guerrero Negro (7 daily; 8hr); La Paz (4 daily; 20hr); Loreto (4 daily; 15hr); Mexicali (4 daily; 4hr); San Felipe (2 daily; 3hr 30min); Tijuana (hourly; 1hr 30min).

**Guaymas** to: Hermosillo (every 30min; 1hr 30min); Los Mochis (every 30min; 5hr); Mexicali (every 30min; 11hr); Navojoa (every 30min; 3hr); Nogales (hourly; 5hr 30min); Tijuana (every 30min; 14hr).

**Guerrero Negro** to: Ensenada (7 daily; 8hr); La Paz (3 daily; 12hr); San Ignacio (7 daily; 3hr); Santa

Rosalía (7 daily; 4hr); Tijuana (7 daily; 10hr).

**Hermosillo** to: Bahía de Kino (13 daily; 2hr); Guaymas (every 30min; 1hr 30min); Mexicali (every 30min; 9–10hr); Nogales (hourly; 4hr); Tijuana (every 30min; 12–13hr).

**La Paz** to: Cabo San Lucas via Todos Santos (8 daily; 2hr); El Rosario (2 daily; 16hr); Ensenada (4 daily; 20hr); Guerrero Negro (4 daily; 12hr); Loreto (7 daily; 5hr); Mexicali (1 daily; 28hr); Mulegé (5 daily; 7hr); San Ignacio (3 daily; 9hr); San José del Cabo via eastern route (6 daily; 3–4hr); Santa Rosalía (5 daily; 8hr); Tijuana (1 daily; 22hr); Todos Santos (8 daily; 1hr).

**Los Mochis** to: El Fuerte (hourly; 2hr); Guaymas (every 30min; 7hr); Mazatlán (every 30min; 7hr); Navojoa (every 30min; 2–3hr); Tijuana (every 30min; 19hr); Topolobampo (every 15min; 40min).

**Mazatlán** to: Culiacán (every 30min; 4hr); Durango (12 daily; 6hr); Guadalajara (every 30min; 9hr); Los Mochis (every 30min; 7hr); Tepic (every 30min; 4hr); Tijuana (every 30min; 26hr).

**Mexicali** to: Chihuahua (1 daily; 19hr); Ensenada (4 daily; 4hr); Guadalajara (1 daily; 34hr); Guaymas (every 30min; 11hr); Hermosillo (every 30min; 9–10hr); Los Mochis (every 30min; 17hr); Mazatlán (every 30min; 24hr); Mexico City (1 daily; 40hr); Monterrey (1 daily; 29hr); San Felipe (4 daily; 3hr); Tijuana (every 30min; 3hr).

**Navojoa** to: Alamos (hourly; 1hr); Ciudad Obregón (every 30min; 1hr 30min); Guaymas (every 30min; 3hr); Los Mochis (every 30min; 2–3hr); Tijuana (every 30min; 17hr).

**Nogales** to: Agua Prieta (hourly; 3–4hr); Guaymas (hourly; 5hr 30min); Hermosillo (hourly; 4hr); Puerto Peñasco (4 daily; 5hr).

**San Blas** to: Guadalajara (1 daily; 7 hr); Puerto Vallarta (4 daily; 3–4hr); Santiago Ixcuintla (3 daily; 1hr); Tepic (hourly; 1hr 30min).

**Santa Rosalía** to: Guerrero Negro (7 daily; 4hr); La Paz (5 daily; 8hr); Loreto (8 daily; 3hr); Mulegé (8 daily; 1hr); San Ignacio (7 daily; 1hr); Tijuana (4 daily; 14hr).

**Tepic** to: Guadalajara (every 30min; 5hr); Mazatlán (every 30min; 4hr); Puerto Vallarta (hourly; 3–4hr); San Blas (hourly; 1hr 30min); Tijuana (every 30min; 30hr).

**Tijuana** to: Culiacán (every 30min; 22hr); El Rosario (4 daily; 6hr); Ensenada (hourly; 1hr 30min); Guadalajara (every 30min; 35hr); Guaymas (every 30min; 14hr); Guerrero Negro (7 daily; 10hr); Hermosillo (every 30min; 12–13hr); La Paz (1 daily; 22hr); Los Mochis (every 30min; 19hr); Loreto (4 daily; 17hr); Los Angeles (12 daily; 4hr); Mazatlán (every 30min; 26hr); Mexicali (every 30min; 3hr); Mulegé (4 daily; 15hr); Navojoa (every 30min; 17hr); El Rosario (4 daily; 6hr); San Ignacio (4 daily; 13hr); Santa Rosalía (4 daily; 14hr); Tepic (every 30min; 30hr).

## Trains

The only train in the region that carries passengers is the amazing Los Mochis–Chihuahua Copper Canyon railway (see p.188). One train with first-class carriages and another with second-class run in each direction each day. Remember that timetables are confused by the hour's difference between the region covered in this chapter and the rest of Mexico. The Los Mochis–Chihuahua *primera clase* train departs Los Mochis daily at 6am, the regular (second-class) *económica* train at 7am local time.

## Flights

Almost every town of any size has an airport, with flights, not necessarily direct, to Mexico City. Busiest are Tijuana, with half a dozen flights a day to the capital by a variety of routings and a couple direct to Guadalajara; La Paz, with flights to Mexico City and many towns along the mainland coast; and Mazatlán. Aero California is the biggest of the local operators, though Mexicana and Aeroméxico operate flights to major Mexican cities, often at prices little higher than the equivalent cost of the bus.

**La Paz** to: Guadalajara (1 daily); Los Angeles via Loreto (1 daily); Los Angeles direct (2 daily); Mexico City (1 daily); Phoenix (1 daily); San Diego (1 daily); Tijuana (2 daily); Tucson (1 daily).

**Mazatlán** to: Denver (3 weekly); La Paz (1 daily); Los Angeles (3 daily); Mexico City (4 daily); Tijuana (2 daily).

**San José** to: Houston (2 daily); Los Angeles (many daily); Minneapolis (1 daily); Salt Lake City (1 daily); San Diego (many daily); San Francisco (2 daily); Tijuana (2 daily).

## Ferries

Purchase tickets as far in advance as possible, thereby avoiding long queues during the busy summer months. All services are subject to change, so always check the schedule in advance.

**Guaymas** to: Santa Rosalía (8pm Mon, Tues, Thurs & Sat; 7hr).

**La Paz** to: Mazatlán (5pm Tues, Thurs & Sat; more during holiday periods; 18hr); Topolobampo (daily 3pm; 6hr).

**Mazatlán** to: La Paz (3pm Mon, Wed & Fri; more during holiday periods; 18hr).

**Santa Rosalía** to: Guaymas (9am Tues & Thurs, 8pm Fri & Sun; 7hr).

**Topolobampo** (Los Mochis) to: La Paz (daily 11pm; 6hr).

# 2

# The north

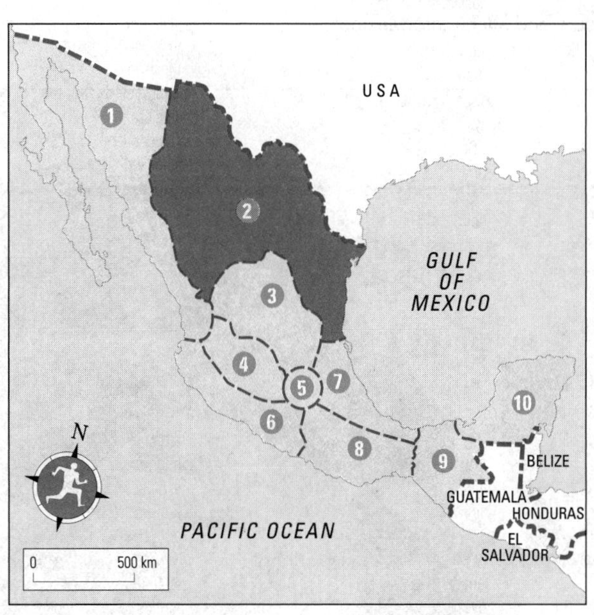
USA
1
2
3
4
5
6
7
8
9
10
GULF OF MEXICO
BELIZE
GUATEMALA
HONDURAS
EL SALVADOR
PACIFIC OCEAN
N
0
500 km

# CHAPTER 2 Highlights

* **Paquimé** Fantastic ruins that are more than worth the five-hour trip from Chihuahua. See p.187
* **The Copper Canyon railway** The journey through Chihuahua state's rugged canyons offers one of the world's most incredible train experiences. See p.188
* **Creel and the Sierra Tarahumara** For some great adventure and a look into Mexico's past, hike to the Rarámuri villages around Creel. See p.193
* **Durango** Star in your own Wild West duel at the John Wayne film sets of Villa del Oeste. See p.209
* **Monterrey** Art and culture reign in this bold, modern city, where superb museums and the bohemian Barrio Antiguo await. See p.224

△ Ruins, Paquimé

2

# The north



Rich in legends of the country's revolutionary past, Mexico's northern borderlands, known for their spirit and fervour, are perhaps best symbolized by unruly son and folk hero Pancho Villa. Harsh, barren and sparsely inhabited, the area is far less visited than the country's tourist-saturated southern states. This doesn't mean, though, that it is without points of interest. Rugged and untamed, the north is home to deserts, mountains, seamy frontier towns and modern cities, as well as a proud and hospitable people deeply rooted in ranching culture.

The region's principal natural attraction is the **Sierra Tarahumara**. Wonderfully wild, pristine and remote, the sierra conceals six awe-inspiring chasms known collectively as the **Copper Canyon**. Mexico's last surviving passenger locomotive, nicknamed "El Chepe", steers a phenomenal course right through its heart – one of the world's ultimate train rides. Archeological remains are also scattered throughout the north, including ancient petroglyphs and ruined Chichimec cities, all of which are thoroughly distinct from the Mesoamerican metropolises of the south. Most notable is the site of **Paquimé**, where a maze of adobe walls once housed an extensive and highly developed desert civilization.

The north promises urban appeal too. **Durango**, recently restored and more handsome than ever, offers a taste of colonial grandeur comparable to Mexico's heartland. Similarly attractive, **Chihuahua** boasts a wealth of nineteenth-century architecture, while historic **Parral** and laid-back **Saltillo** are quieter, low-key settings. The real draw, however, is **Monterrey**. Young, energetic and cosmopolitan, this modern city offers a host of cultural and artistic diversions.

Overland from the United States, Mexico's north is best accessed via **Ciudad Juárez** – a seething, sprawling border town notorious for its vice and squalor. Further east, a string of smaller, calmer crossings provide rapid access to the capital. The very shortest route south follows the Gulf coast. Hot, steamy and uncomfortable, this route is not especially recommended, but it does provide access to the fine beaches and archeological ruins of **Veracruz** (see Chapter 7).

## Border checks

Crossing the border, do not forget to go through **immigration and customs** checks. As everywhere, there's a free zone south of the frontier, and you can cross at will. Try to continue south, though, and you'll be stopped after some 30km and sent back to get your tourist card stamped (M$245).

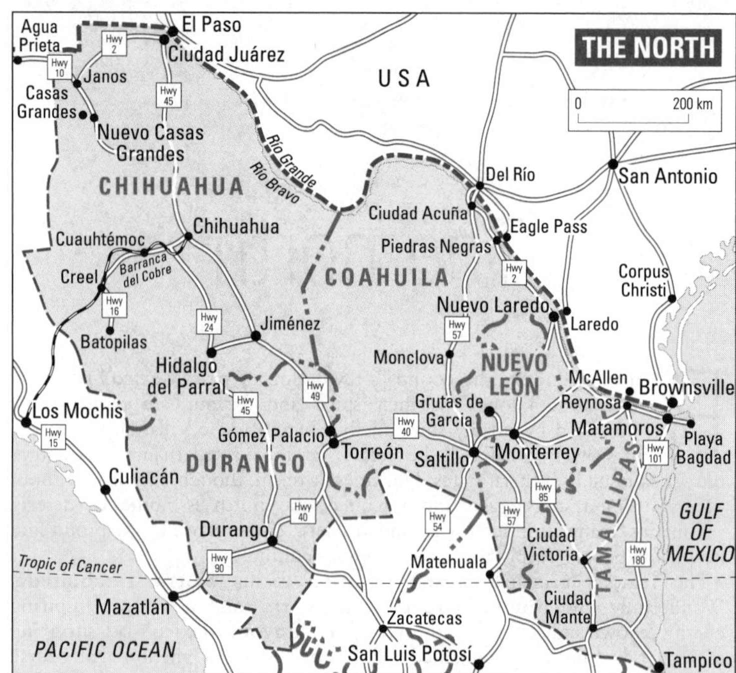


# The central corridor

**Ciudad Juárez**, the behemoth point of entry into Mexico's central corridor, offers little to detain most people heading south. If you have time, an excursion to the ruins at **Paquimé**, near Nuevo Casas Grandes, is worth the four-hour ride from the border, but those with less time should make for the rugged **Sierra Tarahumara** and the **Copper Canyon**. The town of **Creel**, on the Los Mochis–Chihuahua train line, is a great base for exploring the chasms and the many beautiful towns therein, such as **Batopilas**, which lies at the very bottom of a canyon. Allow plenty of time for exploring the Copper Canyon; it's likely to be the best part of your trip through northern Mexico. The city of **Chihuahua** is interesting for a day, though most travellers only pass through, coming for the train or to catch a bus south.

Rapid and efficient bus services run throughout the central area, the best of the main lines probably being Omnibus de México and Estrella Blanca, with Grupo Senda mounting a strong challenge as you head south. It can take as little as 25 hours to travel nonstop from the border to the capital.

# Ciudad Juárez

**CIUDAD JUÁREZ**, just across the border from El Paso, Texas, is possibly Mexico's nastiest border town. Vast, crumbling, dirty and riddled with visible social problems, Ciudad Juárez is also extremely confusing to find your way around and, at times, positively intimidating. Sadly, there's little doubt that the best thing to do on arriving is to leave again. In less than five hours you can reach Chihuahua or, rather closer, Nuevo Casas Grandes, the base for excursions to the archeological site at Casas Grandes.

Originally a small settlement on the Santa Fe Trail, known as Paso del Norte, Ciudad Juárez did have a brief moment of glory when Benito Juárez established his government here after he'd been driven out of the south by Maximilian – you can visit the **house** from which he governed, on Avenida 16 de Septiembre. The town changed hands frequently during the Revolution, most notably in 1913, when Pancho Villa, having stolen a train, managed to fool the local commander into expecting reinforcements and steamed into the middle of town with two thousand troops completely unopposed. Gaining access to the border and to arms from the north, this was one of the exploits that forged Villa's reputation.

In the past decade the city has gained notoriety as a playground for **violent crime**. According to Amnesty International, over four hundred women have been murdered in Ciudad Juárez and most of these cases remain unsolved. Much to the outrage of human rights groups, government nonchalance and police misconduct have hampered official investigations into the killings. The city's reputation is only worsened by its ties to organized crime. Ciudad Juárez is the base of operations for the infamous **Juárez cartel**, which manages a large share of cross-border trafficking of Colombian heroin and Andean cocaine. While the might of this ruthless drugs cartel has fallen in recent years, it remains one of the world's largest and most powerful criminal organizations.

## Arrival and information

Two downtown bridges serve one-way traffic in and out of Ciudad Juárez. Northbound vehicles cross the **Santa Fe bridge**, and southbound vehicles the **Lerdo bridge**. If you're on foot you can enter on either bridge, but it's best to walk in the same direction as traffic. If you're planning to venture deeper into Mexico, be sure to visit one of the immigration offices at the border to get your tourist card stamped.

Additionally, there are two bridges that serve two-way traffic. The **Cordova bridge** lies 2km east of the city centre on the edge of the **Pronaf zone**, an area of sheltered tourist development a world away from the sleazy machinations of downtown Juárez. East of here lies the **Zaragoza toll bridge**, well connected to the main highways and good for a speedy escape.

The city's **bus terminal** (Ⓣ656/613-6037) lies far from the centre at Flores and Borunda, and has services to both US and Mexican cities. Local buses depart regularly for downtown (and the border) and take around thirty minutes (M$4), though a fixed-price taxi can be quicker. To return to the bus station from downtown, catch a local bus from the corner of Guerrero and Villa near the market.

The Ciudad Juárez **tourist office** is inconveniently located in the **Pronaf zone** at Av de las Américas 2551 (Mon–Fri 9am–5pm, Sat & Sun 10am–2pm; Ⓣ656/611-3174, Ⓦwww.visitajuarez.com). The staff can provide details on rodeos, **charreadas** (April–Oct) and other local entertainment, as well as supply maps and information about attractions further south.

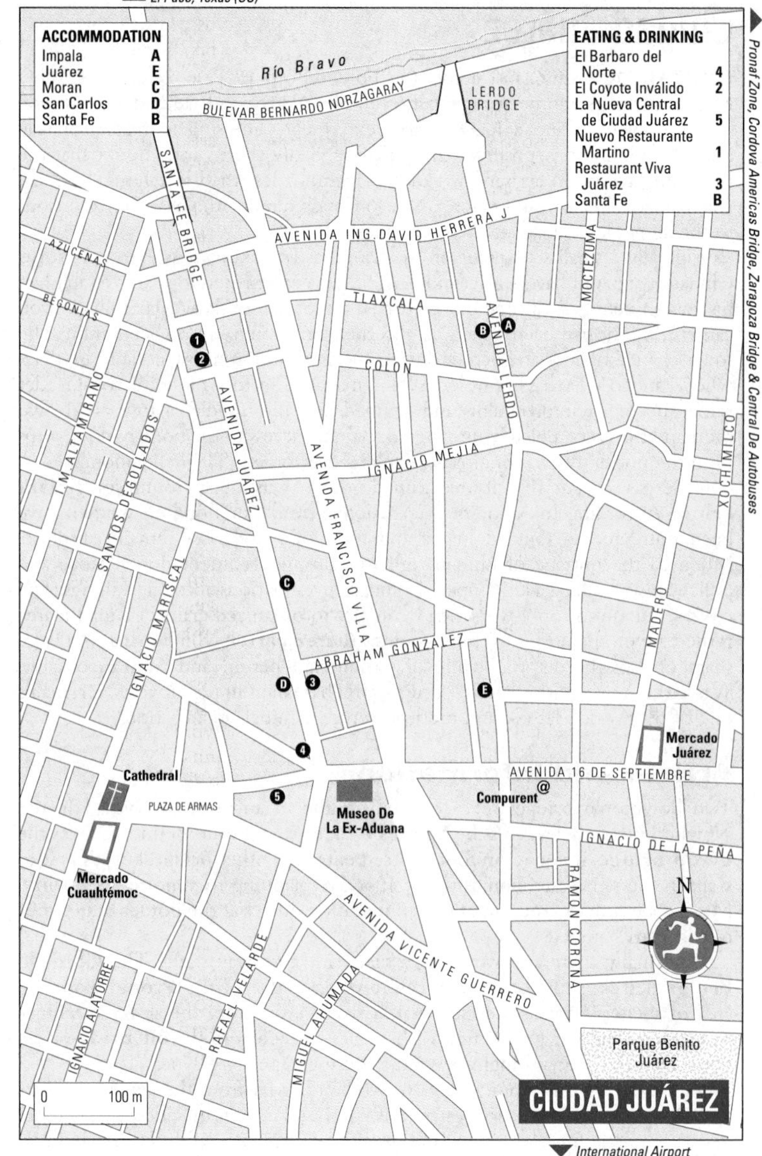


## Accommodation

None of the hotels in Ciudad Juárez is particularly good value by Mexican standards, so you might be tempted to stay across the border in El Paso, where the best **budget** choice is the *El Paso International Hostel*, 311 E Franklin St (T915/532-3661, Wwww.elpasohostel.com; dorms M$185). The helpful staff can give you information on the area, and sometimes runs tours to Juárez and around. Single **women** staying in Ciudad Juárez should take particular care to select a secure hotel, preferably one in the Pronaf zone.

**Hotel Colonial** Abraham Lincoln 1355 ⓣ656/613-5050, ⓦwww.hotelescolonial.com. Safely located in the Pronaf zone, this upmarket hotel offers large rooms with a/c, attentive service and a pool. ❼

**Impala** Lerdo 670 Nte ⓣ656/615-0431, ⓦwww.hotel-impala.com. A block from the border, this family-owned place is the nicest of the slightly pricier lodgings. Rates are the same for one to three persons and there is a good restaurant attached. ❺

**Juárez** Lerdo 143 Nte ⓣ656/615-0290. Some of the cheapest beds in town. If you're willing to sacrifice a/c and stay in a room on the roof, you can save a few bucks more. Rooms are tidy, though the building itself has seen better days. ❷

**Moran** Juárez 264 Nte ⓣ656/615-0862. Clean, basic rooms with discounted rates for stays of several days, should you be unfortunate enough to have to stick around. ❹

**San Carlos** Juárez 131 Nte ⓣ656/615-0419. Lightly dilapidated and fairly shabby for the price, but the rooms are clean and have en-suite bathrooms. ❸

**Santa Fe** Lerdo 675 Nte ⓣ656/615-1522, ⓦwww.hotel-santafe-juarez.com. Close to the border and opposite the *Impala*, this hotel has been recently remodelled and acquired by Best Western. Consequently, the rooms are new and tidy. There's also a decent restaurant downstairs. ❺

## The Town

If you decide to kill an hour strolling around the modest sights of downtown Juárez, be careful not to wander far off the main thoroughfares. Be especially vigilant in the city centre and around the **Santa Fe bridge**, a somewhat sordid locale where predatory hustlers, criminals and addicts predominate. Wandering after dark is not recommended.

Where 16 de Septiembre crosses Juárez, in the old customs building, the Aduana, there's a small, and mostly missable, **Museo Histórico** (Tues–Sun 10am–5pm; free), which traces the development of the town. A couple of blocks west of here on 16 de Septiembre you'll find a partly colonnaded square flanked by the cathedral and the seventeenth-century **Misión de Guadalupe**, around which the town grew up.

If you have more time, however, it's worth making for the **Museo de Arqueología del Chamizal** (Tues–Sun 10am–5pm; free) in the Parque Chamizal, east of the centre near the river, and the **Museo de Arte e Historia** (Tues–Sun 10am–5pm; free) in the Pronaf tourist zone – which also houses a huge, touristy craft market – not far from the bus station (local bus #8 runs there from the centre). Both museums offer limited introductions to Mexico; the former also has displays of some remarkable Paquimé pottery from the ruins at Casas Grandes (see p.187).

If you would like a guided tour of both Juárez and El Paso, the **border- jumper trolley** does just that, leaving hourly from the convention centre in El Paso (in the US ⓣ915/544-0062, ⓦwww.borderjumper.com; US$12.50). In El Paso itself, the **El Paso Museum of Art** (Tues–Sat 9am–5pm, Sun noon–5pm; free; ⓦwww.elpasoartmuseum.org) houses some five thousand European, North American and Mexican works of art from the fourteenth century onwards. You could also check out the murals painted by local youths and travellers alike, a couple of blocks west of the Greyhound station; what began as a vandalism problem is now positively encouraged by the town, and some of them are pretty good.

## Eating and drinking

**Places to eat** are plentiful around the centre and border area, although new arrivals should probably take it easy on the street food. The fancier options line

Juárez near the border. **El Paso** offers better value, however, and if you've been in Mexico some time, you may well want to rush across the border to the burger joints near the Greyhound station. The helpful staff at the *Camino Real* (see below) can also point you in the direction of any number of good restaurants within walking distance of the border.



**El Barbaro del Norte** Juárez 101 Nte. Popular economical restaurant that caters to carnivores with steaks, burgers, *cabrito* and rotisserie chicken.

**Camino Real** 101 S El Paso St, El Paso. Swanky hotel offering two restaurants: the casual and relatively inexpensive *Azulejos* specializes in Mexican fare, while the more international *Dome*, a dinner-only restaurant, serves nouvelle cuisine.

**El Coyote Inválido** Juárez 625 Nte. Bright and breezy budget taco house that stays open late and serves up hearty *chile relleno* burritos and filling breakfasts.

**La Nueva Central de Ciudad Juárez** 16 de Septiembre 322 Pte. Cavernous, cream-tiled and brightly lit place serving Mexican standards and basic Chinese specialities 24 hours a day.

**Nuevo Restaurante Martino** Juárez 643 Nte. Classy, popular restaurant with high prices and varied cuisine, though the majority of the menu is traditional Mexican.

**Restaurant Viva Juárez** Juárez 126 Nte, just before 16 de Septiembre (across from the *San Carlos* hotel). Good, inexpensive option for plain Mexican food.

**Santa Fe** Lerdo 675 Nte. Fairly priced hotel restaurant, serving enchiladas and sandwiches.

**The Tap** Kansas and San Antonio. One of the spots near the Greyhound station, it's a welcoming place with well-priced Mexican food and a jukebox playing *norteña*, classic rock and American country music.

## Listings

**Banks and exchange** It's easy enough to change money at casas de cambio and tourist shops along Juárez and 16 de Septiembre; most banks are also on 16 de Septiembre, and you'll find ATMs at nearly all of them. Many places accept dollars, but make sure you know the current exchange rate before you do any such deals.

**Car rental** Alamo, Paseo Triunfo de la República 2412 ⓣ656/611-1010; Budget, Paseo de la Victoria 2527 ⓣ656/648-1757.

**Consulate** US, López Mateos 924 Nte ⓣ656/611-3000.

**Internet access** The public library across the border in El Paso (Mon–Thurs 8.30am–8.30pm,

### Moving on from Ciudad Juárez

Ciudad Juárez is something of transportation hub, and its new **bus** station is busy with long-distance buses that connect cities in the north and centre of the country. The major lines are Omnibus (ⓣ01-800/011-6336, ⓦwww.odm.com.mx) and Estrella Blanca (ⓣ01-800/507-5500, ⓦwww.estrellablanca.com.mx). You should be able to pick up a first-class ride to any major city north of the capital. Destinations include: **Casas Grandes** (every 1–2hr; 4hr), **Chihuahua** (hourly; 5 hr), **Monterrey** (11 daily; 18hr), San Luis Potosí (every 1–2 hr; 20 hr), Zacatecas (hourly; 16hr) and Mexico City (every 1–2 hr). Second-class and *de paso* services are also prolific, and serve Baja California as well as all of the above.

International bus services are handled by Autobuses Americanos (ⓣ656/610-8529) and Greyhound (ⓣ01-800/710-8819). The latter runs an hourly shuttle bus to downtown **El Paso** (1hr 45min). Autobuses Americanos serves other US destinations, including Los Angeles (4 daily), Dallas (2 daily) and Santa Fe (4 daily).

**Flights** are handled by **Abraham González International Airport**, 18km from the centre of town on the Panamericana Highway (ⓣ625/633-0734). Several airlines serve Mexican and US destinations including: AeroCalifornia (ⓣ01-800/237-6225, ⓦwww.aerocalifornia.com), Aerolitoral (ⓣ01-800/800-2376, ⓦwww.aerolitoral.com), Aeroméxico (ⓣ01-800/237-6639, ⓦwww.aeromexico.com), Aviacsa (ⓦwww.aviacsa.com.mx) and Azteca (ⓣ01-800/229-8322, ⓦwww.aazteca.com.mx).

Fri & Sat 8.30am–5.30pm, Sun 1–5pm) has free Internet access. Walk north past the *Camino Real* hotel for about two blocks; it's on the corner of Franklin and Oregon. In Juárez, you can try Compu-Rent, 16 de Septiembre 372 at Lerdo (Mon–Sat 9am–9pm, Sun 10am–9pm; M$15/hr). **Post office** At the corner of Lerdo and Peña, one block south of 16 de Septiembre.



# Paquimé and Nuevo Casas Grandes

The only reason to stop in **Nuevo Casas Grandes** is to visit the nearby village of Casas Grandes and the adjacent archeological site of **Paquimé** (Tues–Sun 10am–5pm; M$40, free on Sun), the most important, and certainly the most striking, ruins in northern Mexico. Originally home to an agricultural community and comprising simple adobe houses (similar to those found in Arizona and New Mexico), it became heavily influenced by Mesoamerican, probably Toltec, culture. Whether this was the result of conquest or, more likely, trade, is uncertain, but from around 1000 to 1200 AD, Paquimé flourished. **Pyramids** and **ball-courts** were constructed, and the surrounding land was irrigated by an advanced system of **canals**. At the same time local craftsmen were trading with points both south and north, producing a wide variety of elaborate ornaments and pottery. Among the finds at the site (many of them are now in the National Museum of Anthropology in Mexico City) have been cages that held exotic imported birds, whose feathers were used in making ornaments; necklaces made from turquoise, semiprecious stones and shells obtained from the Sea of Cortés; and other objects of copper, bone, jade and mother-of-pearl.

Much must have been destroyed when the site was attacked, burned and abandoned around 1340 – either by a marauding nomadic tribe, such as the Apache, or in the course of a more local rebellion. Either way, Paquimé was not inhabited again, its people leaving their already depleted trade for the greater safety of the sierras. When excavation began in the late 1950s, there were only a few low hills and banks where walls had been, but by piecing together evidence archeologists have partly reconstructed the adobe houses – the largest of which have as many as fifty interconnecting rooms around an open courtyard or **ceremonial centre**. The foundations of the houses, which were originally two or three storeys high, have been reconstructed to waist-height, with an occasional standing wall giving some idea of scale.

To fully appreciate the sophistication of this civilization, it pays to first pop into the **Centro Cultural Paquimé** (Tues–Sun 10am–5pm; entrance fee included with site entrance), a beautifully laid-out, if thinly stocked museum, architecturally designed to mimic the ruins of the defence towers that once stood on the site. A large model of how Paquimé must have looked, interactive touch-screen consoles with commentary in Spanish and English and intelligent displays of artefacts aid interpretation. Modern examples of finds from the surrounding area – drums, dolls in native costume, ceramics and ceremonial masks – compete with the Paquimé artefacts, notably the beautiful pottery, its often anthropomorphic vessels decorated in geometric patterns of red, black and brown on a white or cream background.

## Practicalities

To **reach the site** you have first to travel 260km south of Ciudad Juárez through dusty chaparral and cotton country to Nuevo Casas Grandes. Travelling from Chihuahua is also an option, as buses for the five-hour journey depart regularly. Once in Nuevo Casas Grandes, take one of the frequent yellow buses ("Casas Grandes/Col Juárez") from the corner of Constitución and 16 de Septiembre to the plaza in Casas Grandes (about 15min), from where the site is signposted – it's a ten-minute walk.

Nuevo Casas Grandes itself is small and not especially interesting; if you leave Ciudad Juárez very early you can visit the site and continue to Chihuahua in the same day – a route that is longer but certainly more interesting than the main highway (though rains can take out the road south of Nuevo Casas Grandes). **Buses** arrive outside the adjoining Estrella Blanca and Omnibus de México offices on Obregón, just steps from the basic hotel *Juárez*, Obregón 110 (ⓣ636/694-0233; ❶), the town's only budget **accommodation**. The rooms can be grubby and the hot water sporadic, but the management is friendly. On the main street, a couple of blocks away, you'll find *Hotel Paquimé*, Juárez 401 (ⓣ636/694-1320, ⓔnpinon@paquinet.com.mx; ❹), which has clean rooms with cable TV. Best of all, however, is the amicable *Hotel Piñón*, Juárez 605 Nte (ⓣ636/694-0655, ⓔhotelpinon@prodigy.net.mx; ❺), a couple of blocks beyond *Paquimé* and boasting TV, reliable hot water, a swimming pool and even a small museum of Paquimé clay pots. The management occasionally offers tours of the ruins.

**Dining** in town is a fairly basic affair, with a number of *taquerías* dotted around. For more moderately priced fare, try *Dinno's Pizza* at the corner of Constitución and Minerva, which serves decent pizzas and an excellent breakfast buffet. Pricier restaurants line Juárez – the one inside *Hotel Piñon* is reputable, as is *Restaurant Constantino*. If you're on an ultra-tight budget, there's a supermarket on Urueta and Constitución. In Casas Grandes, you'll find a few eateries on the main square – *Paleteria y Neveria Mar y Sol* is good for tortas and ice cream, while *Restaurant Rosti Pollo* specializes, as the name suggests, in roast chicken.

If you need **Internet** access, there are a couple of places in Nuevo Casas Grandes on Juárez: Versailles and La Playa both charge about M$20 an hour.

# Los Mochis to Chihuahua: the Copper Canyon railway

The thirteen-hour **train trip** that starts on the sweaty Pacific coast at Los Mochis, fights its way up to cross the Continental Divide amidst the peaks of the Sierra Madre, then drifts down across the high plains of Chihuahua, is unquestionably one of the world's most extraordinary rail journeys. Breathtaking views come thick and fast as the line hangs over the vast canyons of the **Río Urique**. Chief of these is the awesome rift of the **Barranca del Cobre**, with a depth, from mountaintop to valley floor, of more than 2000m, and breadth to match – by comparison, the Grand Canyon is a midget. Scenically, however, there's no comparison with the great canyons of the southwestern US, and if you've visited them you may find the canyons here a little disappointing. Part of the difficulty is in getting a true sense of their size and beauty: there are none of the well-marked hiking tracks and official campsites that might tempt casual exploration north of the border, and serious hikers really need to devote the best part of a week to their endeavours.

The dream of the original builders – the Kansas City, Mexico and Orient Railway Company – was to carve a new route from the American Midwest to

Topolobampo on Mexico's Pacific coast, and in the early part of the twentieth century they made it right across the plains, only to be defeated by the sheer technical complexity of crossing the mountains. It's easy to see why. Only in 1953 did the Mexicans start work on the final link, an engineering feat demanding the construction of 73 tunnels and 28 major bridges that took a further eight years to complete.

Even when the bare mountain peaks here are snow-covered, the climate on the canyon floors is semitropical – a fact that the indigenous **Rarámuri** (also known as the Tarahumara), who were driven into these mountain fastnesses after the Spanish Conquest, depend on, migrating in winter to the warmth of

the deep canyons. The Rarámuri, whose population totals some 50,000, live in isolated communities along the rail line and in the stretch of mountains known as the Sierra Tarahumara, eking out an existence from the sparse patches of cultivatable land. Although their isolation is increasingly encroached upon by commercial forestry interests, ranchers and growing numbers of travellers, they remain an independent people, close to their traditions. Despite centuries of missionary work, their religious life embraces only token aspects of Catholicism and otherwise remains true to its agrarian roots – their chief deities being the gods of the sun, moon and rain. Above all, the tribe is renowned as runners: a common feature of local festivals are the foot races between villages that last at least one day and sometimes several on end, with the runners kicking a wooden ball ahead of them as they go.



## The route

The train timetable (see box, p.192) more or less dictates that you tackle the journey eastbound from the coast to the mountains; otherwise, you may well find yourself travelling along the most dramatic stretch of the line in the dark. The start of the journey is an inauspicious grind across the humid coastal plain, with passengers in the first-class, air-conditioned carriages settling back in their reclining seats while the rest just sweat.

The first-class cosseting becomes less of a benefit as the line breaks into the mountains and you start climbing into ever-cooler air. It was this section of the route that defeated the original builders, and, from the passenger's point of view, the bit you've been waiting for. For six hours, the train zigzags dizzily upwards, clinging to the canyon wall, rocketing across bridges, plunging into tunnels, only to find itself constantly just a few metres above the track it covered twenty minutes earlier. Eventually, you arrive at **Divisadero**, where there's a halt of about fifteen minutes to marvel at the view. At first it seems a perverse choice for a stop, with nothing around but the mountaintops and crowds of Rarámuri hawking their crafts and food (including delicious gorditas). But walk a little way down the path and you're suddenly standing on the edge of space, on the lip of a vast chasm. Below you are the depths of the **Barranca del Cobre** and, adjoining it, the Barranca de Balojaque and the Barranca de Tararecua. There are a couple of absurdly expensive places to stay here and a few bare-bones cheaper ones as well, but for most people it's all too rapidly back on the train, which clanks on for an hour to **Creel**, just past the halfway stage and, at 2300m, close to the highest point of the line. This is the place to stop if you want seriously to explore the Sierra Tarahumara and the canyons; it gives easy access into some remarkable landscapes, and boasts the only reasonably priced hotel options en route (see p.194 for details of accommodation in Creel and exploring the Sierra Tarahumara).

From Creel, the train takes a further six hours to reach Chihuahua – though beautiful, it's not a truly spectacular run. In fact, if the train timetable doesn't suit, there's no reason why you shouldn't take the **bus** from Creel to Chihuahua: it costs about the same as the second-class train fare, is quicker and covers much the same ground. East of Creel both bus and train begin to leave the Sierra Tarahumara behind as the route runs through gentle, verdant grazing land that wouldn't look out of place in some romantic Western film.

In many ways, this is pioneer ranching country, centred on the town of **CUAUHTÉMOC**, 70km from Creel and 130km from Chihuahua. This is also one of the chief centres for **Mennonites**, people you'll come across throughout northern Mexico – the men in bib-and-tucker overalls and straw stetsons, as often as not trying to sell the excellent cheese that is their main produce, and the

△ Copper Canyon railway

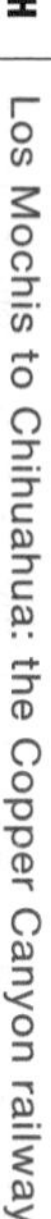



women, mostly silent, wrapped in long, black nineteenth-century dresses with maybe a dash of colour from a headscarf. The sect, founded in the sixteenth century by a Dutchman, Menno Simons, believe only in the Bible and their personal conscience: their refusal to do military service or take national oaths of loyalty has led to a long history of persecution. The Mennonites arrived in Mexico in the early twentieth century, having been driven from Frisia to Prussia, thence into Russia and finally to Mexico by way of Canada – each time forced to move on by the state's demand for military tribute or secular education. These days many are returning to Canada as impoverished emigrants, forced out of Mexico by limited land and a growing population – one lasting legacy is that they are credited with introducing the accordion to Mexican music. Among themselves the Mennonites still speak a form of German, although so divergent as to be virtually unintelligible to a modern German-speaker.

## Rail practicalities

The Copper Canyon line is operated by the Ferrocarril de Chihuahua al Pacífico (CHP), from which the train derives its affectionate nickname, "El Chepe". There are two daily services running in each direction: the first-class **Primera** (also known as *Estrella*), which is primarily a tourist service, and the second-class **Económica** (also known as *Mixto*), half the price but considerably slower and less comfortable. If you have the money, you're better off taking the *Primera* service, not only because it has air-conditioning and reserved, reclining seats, but also because the *Económica* tends to run late, so that particularly if you're travelling from Chihuahua out to the coast, you may pass many of the best sections in the dark. The *Económica* is also subject to seemingly random **cancellation**, but both services may be cancelled due to derailed freight trains, or landslides, which plague the track during the rainy season.

**Tickets** for the *Económica* can only be bought from the station on the morning of departure, but *Primera* tickets can be pre-booked either at the station or with any travel agency in Mexico City – reserve early to be sure of a first-class seat, especially from May to September and during Semana Santa. **Prices** for the whole journey from Los Mochis to Chihuahua have risen dramatically in the past few years – to nearly M$750 on the *Económica* and about M$1450 on the *Primera*. Tickets are available from travel agents or from Ferrocarril Mexicano direct (Ⓣ614/439-7212, Ⓦwww.chepe.com.mx).

It's advisable to break up the journey, not only to get the most out of it, but also because the trip, even travelling first class, is very exhausting. Section costs are based on a per-kilometre rate, so you'll pay hardly any more no matter how often you break the journey.

You'll save money by taking along your own **food and drink**, but it's not essential; both are available on the train (though not cheaply), and throughout the journey people climb on board or stand on the platforms selling tacos, *chiles rellenos*, fresh fruit, hot coffee and whatever local produce comes to hand.

## Divisadero and Cerocahui

**DIVISADERO**, where the train pauses briefly to take in the view, is famous for its one-hundred-mile panorama of the canyons. You'll find the stunning *Cabañas Divisadero Barrancas* (Ⓣ614/415-1199, Ⓦwww.hoteldivisadero.com; ❾) perched on the edge, but if you can't afford to stay, you can always dine in their restaurant for around M$200 a head. Alternatively, just grab a burrito from one of the many stands that serve the train during its fifteen-minute pause here. More luxury lodges lie 3km down the track at **Posada Barrancas**, including *Posada Barrancas del Mirador* (Ⓣ668/812-1613, Ⓦwww.mexicoscoppercanyon.com; ❾), which features great adobe-style rooms with balconies and fireplaces. *Posada Barrancas Rancho* (Ⓣ668/812-1613, Ⓦwww.mexicoscoppercanyon.com; ❾), run by the same company, has slightly cheaper rooms and no views, but prices can drop by a hundred dollars off season. Finally, there's the *Mansion Tarahumara* (Ⓣ614-415-4721, Ⓦwww.mansiontarahumara.com.mx; ❾), a rather surreal hotel resembling a fairy-tale castle, but sadly also lacking in views. Cheaper lodgings are also popping up, including *Los Portales Cabins* (Ⓣ635/578-3042; ❹) and *Díaz Family Cabins* (Ⓣ635/578-3008; ❹). Several **buses** a day run to Creel from Divisadero (1hr; M$30), the last one passing through at about 4pm; it's always worth checking the schedule for changes, though, so you don't get stuck. Otherwise, infrastructure is sparse.

### The CHP timetable

Currently the *Primera* and *Económica* travel daily in both directions, but always check to see if the service is running. The official **times** below are not entirely reliable, and trains (particularly the *Económica*) frequently run some hours late – check with your travel agent (or other train ticket vendors) for information on delays, which may affect your schedule. The *Primera* train is rarely, if ever, on time to connect with the La Paz ferry in Los Mochis.

| | *Primera* (no.73) | | *Económica* (no.75) | |
|---|---|---|---|---|
| Los Mochis | 6am | 8.50pm | 7am | 1.30am |
| El Fuerte | 8.30am | 6.10pm | 10.15am | 10.23pm |
| Bahuichivo | 12.27pm | 2.17pm | 12.45pm | 5.10pm |
| Divisadero | 1.45pm | 12.34pm | 4.55pm | 3.05pm |
| Creel | 3.24pm | 11.15am | 7.00pm | 1.20pm |
| Cuauhtémoc | 6.23pm | 8.15am | 10.35pm | 9.55am |
| Chihuahua | 8.45pm | 6am | 1.30am | 7am |

Another alternative base to Creel is the minuscule town of **CEROCAHUI**, accessed from **Bachuichivo**, about 50km west of Divisadero and 10km away on the rail line. Very much in the formative stages of tourist development, Cerocahui gives access to the **Urique** canyon system and a range of attractions including overlooks, waterfalls and disused mines. The four-hour drive to the bottom of the canyon is stunning, and the town of Urique at its conclusion marks the start (or end) of the popular two-day trek to Batopilas (see p.196). In Cerocahui, rather lovely and economical accommodation can be had at the Rarámuri-run *San Isidro Lodge* (Ⓣ635/456-5257, Ⓔsanisdrolodge@yahoo.com; ❹). For more pricey and luxurious quarters try the *Hotel Misión* (Ⓣ668/818-7046, Ⓦwww.mexicoscoppercanyon.com; ❻). Both hotels provide tours and should collect you from Bahuichivo station.

## Creel and the Sierra Tarahumara

Once nothing more than a rough-and-ready backwater, **CREEL** is rapidly metamorphosing into a tourist centre. Recently tagged by the Mexican government as a "magic town", a precious accolade reserved for the country's more enchanting locales, Creel has seen tourism all but replace logging as its main industry. Plans are under way to build an airport, Best Western has moved in, and, as the locals are proud to point out, the town has recently received smart new pavements. More than this, the *ejido* land (land collectively owned and maintained by indigenous communities) traditionally protected by law is now being sold off, one piece at a time. This is not to say that the town has become completely commercial; it still retains a good deal of its rural appeal, evidenced by its log cabins, unmarked dirt roads and traditionally attired Rarámuri and ranchers passing by on horseback. Beneath the facade of development, Creel is still the backward mountain town it's always been, and, stepping off the train, one has the sense of stepping into a scene from the Old West.

There isn't much to do in Creel itself, other than enjoy the refreshing, pine-scented mountain air, though the **Museo de la Casa de las Artesanías** opposite the plaza (Mon–Sat 9am–7pm, Sun 9am–1pm; M$15) is certainly worth a visit. It contains displays on Rarámuri culture that give intriguing insights into their archaic philosophy, most notably with a series of black and white photos revealing their vivid ceremonial and religious life. If you're in the market for handicrafts, the Jesuit mission shop **Artesanías Misión**, also by the plaza (Mon–Sat 9am–1pm & 3–6pm), has a host of wares including blankets, baskets, dolls, drums and violins – their artesanías lack the vibrancy of other Mexican crafts, but make up for it with rustic charm. The store's profits go to the mission hospital, so if you want to be sure that what you spend actually goes to the people who make the items, buy directly from the women who sell goods on the street; right outside the shop is the best place to look.

### Arrival and information

The train is obviously the way to **arrive** but, wonderful though it is, the vagaries of the timetable may induce you to catch one of the frequent daily buses that run between Creel and Chihuahua (M$200) – no great loss as the road pretty much follows the rail line. The train station and bus stops are all near the main plaza in the centre of town. Despite the droves of visitors to town, there's no official **tourist office** in Creel. To a great extent, that duty is fulfilled by Three Amigos Canyons Expeditions, López Mateos 46 (daily 9am–7pm). They can supply you with maps, information and advice regarding Creel and the Copper Canyon more generally. You'll find a branch of Santander Serfin

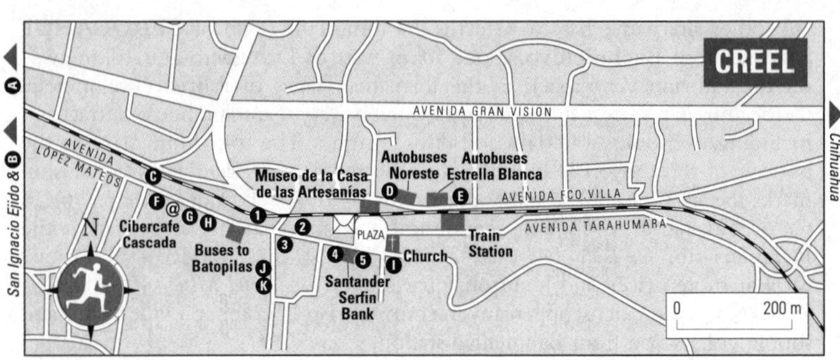


| ACCOMMODATION | | | | EATING & DRINKING | |
|---|---|---|---|---|---|
| Casa Margarita | I | Motel Cascada | G | The Lodge at Creel | F |
| Casa Valenzuela | C | Nuevo "Barrancas del Cobre" | E | Mi Café | 4 |
| Hotel Korachi | D | Parador de la Montaña Hotel | H | Pizza del Rey | 5 |
| Hotel Villa Mexicana | B | Sierra Bonita | A | Restaurant Lupita | 1 |
| The Lodge at Creel | F | Los Valles | K | Restaurant Veronica | 2 |
| Margarita's Plaza Mexicana | J | | | Tío Molcas | 3 |

**bank** on López Mateos (dollar and travellers' cheque exchange and cash advances Mon–Fri 9am–1.30pm). There's a **post office** on the main plaza, long-distance **telephones** all over town and a **laundry** (Mon–Fri 9am–2pm & 3–6pm, Sat 9am–2pm) in the two-storey house on Calle Villa, opposite the plaza. For **Internet**, you're best off at Compucenter, López Mateos 33 (daily 8am–9pm; M$20/hr). Cibercafe Cascada, also on López Mateos, has some less reliable machines (daily 8am–10pm; M$20/hr).

## Accommodation

The number of good **places to stay** in Creel grows every year, and most either meet the train with courtesy buses or dispatch small children to drum up business. Prices are rising in line with Creel's growing popularity; the cheaper places are on the edge of town. Alternatively, if you're in the market for something luxurious, take advantage of the courtesy buses that run to one of the **lodges** out in the nearby countryside.

**Casa Margarita** López Mateos and Parroquia 11 ⓣ635/456-0045. A Creel institution and the place for backpackers to meet, *Margarita*'s services run the gamut from tour guides to laundry. Breakfast is included in the price. Dorms M$100 (mattresses on the floor M$80). ❺

**Casa Valenzuela** López Mateos 68 ⓣ635/456-0104. Less backpacker-oriented than the *Casa Margarita* and extremely quiet. It's cheap, relatively clean, has hot water all day and feels like home. ❹

**Complejo Turistico Arareko** López Mateos ⓣ635/456-0126, ⓦwww.sanignacioarareko.tripod.com. If you fancy staying in more natural surroundings, this Rarámuri-run accommodation agency rents out basic cabins in the San Ignacio *ejido* and around Lake Arareco. ❹

**Hotel Korachi** just next to the bus station before the train station ⓣ635/456-0064. Bland, spartan and small rooms, with nicer, rustic cabins outside. It's still a decent alternative to either *Casa Margarita* or *Casa Valenzuela.* ❺

**Hotel Villa Mexicana** López Mateos, on the edge of town ⓣ614/421-7088, ⓦwww.vmcoppercanyon.com. Creel's only RV park offers full hook-up and a host of facilities including a communal kitchen. Its other accommodation ranges from cheap log cabins to luxury rooms. Hook-up M$250, cabins ❷, rooms ❻

**The Lodge at Creel** López Mateos 61 ⓣ635/456-0071, US ⓣ1-877/844-0409, ⓦwww.thelodgeatcreel.com. Creel's best-known luxury lodging, run by Best Western, offers cabin-style rooms with spa, sauna, Jacuzzi, and full restaurant. The wood-trimmed, rustic huts are ample and full of amenities, including coffee-makers, purified water and telephones. ❽

**Margarita's Plaza Mexicana** Elfida Batista Caro off López Mateos ⓣ635/456-0245, ⓦwww.hoteles-margaritas.com. The fancier sibling of *Casa Margarita* has spacious heated rooms set around a courtyard, each decorated with murals. Popular bar on site; again the price includes breakfast and dinner. Discounts are possible in the low season, depending on demand. ❻

**Motel Cascada** López Mateos 49 ⓣ635/456-0253, ⓕ635/456-0151. Motel-style inn with big, clean rooms around a central courtyard. There's karaoke in their bar on Fri and Sat. ❻

**Nuevo "Barrancas Del Cobre"** Francisco Villa 121, right across from the train station; look for the "Nuevo" sign ⓣ635/456-0042. Handsome log-cabin-style rooms that sleep up to four, complete with carpets, heaters and woody aromas. The rooms inside the main building are cheaper, more basic and less appealing. Rooms ❹, cabins ❼

**Parador de la Montaña Hotel** López Mateos 44 ⓣ635/456-0023, ⓦwww.hotelparadorcreel.com. Big, beautiful rooms with fireplaces in this tasteful upmarket hotel. A range of amenities are available, including restaurant, bar and children's play area. Rates include breakfast. ❼

**Sierra Bonita** Gran Visión, about 1km out of town ⓣ614/410-4015, ⓦwww.sierrabonita.com.mx. Perched on a hill overlooking Creel, this four-star hotel is one of the most luxurious in town. Its best rooms have a fireplace and Jacuzzi – perfect for unwinding after a hard, long day of hiking. ❼

**Los Valles** Elfida Batista Caro s/n, next to *Margarita's Plaza Mexicana* ⓣ635/456-0092, ⓦwww.hotellosvalles.tripod.com. This newly built motel off the main drag has small, clean rooms for decent prices; one of the better mid-range bargains in town. ❹

## Eating and drinking

**Restaurants** in Creel are all fairly similar, with the majority strung along on López Mateos and serving economical home-cooked fare. *Pizza del Rey*, on López Mateos near the plaza, serves reasonable enough pizzas, while nearby *Mi Cafe* at López Mateos 21 is popular with locals and does cheap tortas, burritos and burgers. A block away, *Restaurant Verónica* and *Restaurant Lupita* offer decent Mexican staples, the former having a very slight edge. Try their speciality, the "Norteño" – fried beef and vegetables topped with melted cheese. If you're craving steak, you could do worse than the *Lodge at Creel*, which serves quality American-style food at moderately high prices. *Tío Molcas* is currently the only **bar** in Creel that caters to tourists, although some backpackers are drawn to *Margarita's Plaza Mexicana*, which often has drink specials. The **cantinas** in Creel tend to be the preserve of locals, though if you behave discreetly you'll probably be free to frequent them.

## The Sierra Tarahumara

If you have the time and are reasonably fit, independent exploration of the sierra is both feasible and recommended. Whether you plan to see the sights of the sierra on your own or as part of a group, be sure to visit Three Amigos Canyon Expeditions, López Mateos 46 (ⓣ635/456-0179, ⓦwww.the3amigoscanyonexpeditions.com), the most professional and best-equipped outfit in town. They can advise on your trip, organize a well-priced tour or rent you vehicles; a five-person-capacity pick-up truck, with a cooler, maps and information costs about M$1300 a day, a well-maintained mountain bike M$165 a day (M$100/half-day) and a two-person moped is M$600 a day.

For anyone who wants to explore independently, the **San Ignacio ejido**, a Rarámuri land-owning cooperative on the edge of town, contains many of the attractions normally covered by tours. Get there by following López Mateos towards the highway, taking a left onto the dirt road and continuing past the cemetery and uphill into the pine forest (entrance M$15). A few kilometres from the gates you'll encounter the **San Ignacio Mission** and a series of otherworldly rock formations, including the **Valley of the Mushrooms**, which contains surreal structures closely resembling giant toadstools, and the **Valley of the Frogs**, with its squat amphibian-like boulders. The **Valley of**

**the Monks** lies 5km away, and has tall upright stones revered by the Rarámuri as symbols of fertility. Serene **Lake Arareco** is 8km from Creel, and a beautiful spot for fishing and camping.

Other highlights of the sierra include the **Recohuata hot springs**, 22km from Creel and within biking or riding distance. Here you can bathe in three pools of steamy, clean, sulphurous water. Note that the hour-long descent (and return) to the pools can be strenuous, and shouldn't be undertaken by the faint of heart. A shuttle of sorts does operate, though it has proved wholly ineffective in catering to crowds during busier times. **Cusárare falls**, 35m high and most impressive during the rainy season, also lies some 22km from Creel. The village of Cusárare, nearby, has a seventeenth-century Jesuit mission adorned with intriguing Rarámuri wall paintings. You can reach the falls by bike, or on the daily Batopilas bus (see Batopilas practicalities, opposite), though you'll have a long hike back to Creel if you don't stay overnight, which you can do either by camping or checking into the pricey *Sierra Lodge* (Ⓣ435/259-3999, Ⓦwww.coppercanyonlodges.com, reservations through Three Amigos; ❼). Hitching is certainly a possibility, though you are advised to exercise the usual precautions.

A bit further afield, **La Bufa**, a dwindling settlement overlooking the Río Batopilas, is reached via a spectacular and undulating mountain road that rises and falls through four different canyons. You're assured of some inspirational vistas, but you'll need a full day and either a guide or some form of motor-driven transport to reach them. You can catch the same scenery on the bus ride to Batopilas (see Batopilas practicalities, opposite), though taking the bus means you'll have to spend at least one night here. Furthest from Creel and actually outside the canyonlands is the famous 254m **Basaséachic Falls**, protected in the Parque Nacional de Basaséachic. Said to be the highest cascade in North America, it makes a long, but spectacularly rewarding day's excursion – about four hours' driving and two hours on foot.

If you're not up to strenuous activity, or have only limited time in Creel, an **organized tour** is the best way to see the canyons. These frequently require a minimum number of persons to run, so if your time is especially limited you should try the booth on the main plaza, or the more popular hotels like *Casa Margarita's* or *Hotel Parador*. Rates should be about the same between operators, but it's worth shopping around. Roughly speaking, a four-hour spin through the *ejido* should cost around M$165 (4-person minimum), a seven-hour trip to Recohuata spring is M$225 (6-person minimum), a full-day trip to La Bufa costs M$335 and a day-long trip to Basaséachic is around M$550 (6-person minimum). Find out if food is included with your tour and if there are any additional costs like museum entrance or toll fees before you set out. If you don't speak Spanish, check that your guide speaks English before parting with any money.

Hardcore adventure enthusiasts should contact Chito Arturo at Umárike Expediciones (Ⓣ635/456-0632, Ⓦwww.umarike.com.mx). A reputable guide with over ten years of experience, he can organize extensive backcountry hikes, **rock-climbing** lessons and biking and **canyoning** trips. A truly memorable way of exploring the canyons is on **horseback**, and if you want to be assured of animals that are cared for, speak to Norberto at El Adventurero on López Mateos (Ⓣ635/456-0557, Ⓦwww.ridemexico.com). Decent, professional tours start at M$120 for a two-hour ride through the *ejido* (2-person minimum).

## Batopilas

If you want to get a true idea of the sierra's size, a trip to isolated **BATOPILAS** is all but compulsory. Located 140km south of Creel, the town is accessible only via a nerve-wrenching six-hour drive on primitive dirt roads. The route rises and falls through four of the sierra's six canyons before commencing a final, convoluted descent to the floor of Batopilas canyon. Founded in 1632, the town emerged as a prosperous silver-mining centre, with production peaking in the nineteenth century under the auspices of the Batopilas Mining Company. By the early twentieth century, the surrounding mineral reserves were exhausted and the population had plummeted. For many years Batopilas was forgotten by the outside world – the town only received road connections in the 1970s and electricity in 1988. Today it's a peaceful, subtropical place with a population of about 800. Resplendent with bougainvillea, palm and citrus trees and strung along a single two-kilometre road by the Río Batopilas, it's a world away from the fresh pine forests of Creel. There are several worthwhile **hikes** here, leading to everything from Rarámuri villages to abandoned mines and waterfalls. The best of these go to the "Lost Cathedral", a huge mission church 7km away at **Satevo** that stands beautifully isolated in a desolate landscape of cacti and dust. A longer, two-day trek leads to the town of **Urique**, and can be easily organized with an operator in Creel (see p.195).

### Practicalities

**Buses** and vans leave Creel six times a week from *Hotel Los Pinos* on López Mateos (buses: Tues, Thurs & Sat 7.30am; vans: Mon, Wed & Fri 9.30am; both M$175). Tickets are available from the El Towi artesanía shop, next to the hotel. Return buses leave from outside the church in Batopilas at 5am, but always check for changes in the schedule. There is no official tourist office in Batopilas – Three Amigos in Creel (see p.195) can supply you with a map and other useful information. **Telephones** and a **post office** can be found on the main plaza in Batopilas, though public Internet facilities do not seem to have reached the town yet. Most importantly, there is no bank here, so be sure to bring enough pesos for your stay.

The cheapest **lodgings** are found at *Hotel Batopilas* (no phone; ❷), two blocks north of the plaza. *Casa Monse* (ⓣ649/456-9027; ❸), on the plaza itself, also has cheap rooms in a courtyard overflowing with plants, and an artesanía store attached. Next door you'll find *Juanita's* (ⓣ649/456-9043; ❹), which has large, clean rooms, and many quiet enclaves in which to relax. The best mid-range option is *Casa Real de Minas Aranasaina* (ⓣ649/456-9045; ❻), which has bright, beautifully decorated rooms around a central courtyard. The exquisite and very secluded *Copper Canyon Riverside* (ⓣ1-800-776-3942, ⓦwww.coppercanyonlodges; ❽) is the best place in town and only accepts advance bookings. **Dining** in Batopilas is fairly simple. *Restaurant Carolina* at the small Plaza de la Constitución, does decent and affordable home-cooked Mexican staples, as does *Casa Doña Mica* opposite. *The Swinging Bridge*, just off the main plaza, is the place for a cold beer, and also serves wine, steaks and seafood. *Quinto Patio*, inside *Hotel Mary's* near the church, serves standard economical fare including breakfasts.

If you decide to make the drive down the canyon on your own, be sure to leave early enough to arrive by sundown and make certain that the brakes on your vehicle are in top shape – you'll be using them for much of the descent. A more novel way of reaching Batopilas is by **bicycle**. Three Amigos in Creel (see p.195) offer a unique cycling tour where a pick-up truck follows you down with your luggage and a picnic.

## Guachochi

**GUACHOCHI**, about 170km south of Creel, is a somewhat unexciting ranching town, but it does provide access to the sierra's most remote and beautiful locale, the **Sinforosa Canyon**. Some of the hikes in Sinforosa are fairly hardcore – a trek along the canyon's length, for example, can take up to three weeks – while easier walks lead to stunning vantage points overlooking the valleys. There are various hot springs and waterfalls in the region; the most spectacular is **Rosalinda** with an 80m drop. Rarámuri culture is thriving around Guachochi, with several caves that have been inhabited since time immemorial – "the giants" cave is famous for an abnormally large human skeleton found inside it. **Norogachi**, 60km from Guachochi, is one of the last remaining Rarámuri ceremonial centres, especially renowned for the vivid celebrations that occur during Holy Week, when painted dancers perform exhausting routines for hours on end. You'll also find plenty of Jesuit missions in this area, most of which date from the seventeenth century.

The road to Guachochi takes in many of the same views as the route to Batopilas, with two Estrella Blanca **buses** leaving Creel daily (12.10pm & 5.30pm). If you catch the earlier one, you'll have time to make the connection to Parral, 190km away and another dramatic ride through mountain scenery. Additionally, there are direct buses to Chihuahua from the Estrella Blanca bus station, located in a pink building around a kilometre from the plaza, near where you'll find the Transportes Ballezanos station, which also runs several daily services to Parral.

There are plenty of **accommodation** options in Guachochi. Around half a kilometre from the plaza, you'll find *Hotel Melina*, Dominguez 14 (Ⓣ649/543-0255; ❺), with clean, comfortable rooms and an adjoining restaurant. *Hotel Mansion*, 20 de Noviembre 41 (Ⓣ649/543-0089; ❷), is a good budget option, while the slightly more upmarket *Hotel Chaparro*, Francisco Villa 1 (Ⓣ649/532-0210, Ⓕ649/543-0004; ❹), has cosy rooms with cable TV. Located on the highway and with good access to the canyon is *Los Cumbres Hotel* (Ⓣ649/543-0200; ❹). For **food**, be sure to try the town's speciality – fresh **trucha** (trout). *Los Adobes* on 20 de Noviembre is a great, if slightly expensive place for this. Economical staples can be had at *Multitortas*, at the corner of Dominguez and 20 de Noviembre, which serves burgers, burritos and sandwiches.

If you need to **change money** or withdraw cash, there's a branch of Scotiabank on Francisco Villa, and you'll find an **Internet** café at Aldana and Mateos, some blocks east of the plaza (M$10/hr).

## Chihuahua

You're unlikely to see any of the little bug-eyed dogs in **CHIHUAHUA**, the capital of the largest state in the republic. They do come from here originally, but their absence is presumably because the vicissitudes of a dog's life in Mexico are too great for so fragile a creature. Perhaps, too, because few could stand the fumes of this transport hub and industrial centre, which marshals the state's mineral and agricultural wealth.

Though the gloom in poor weather is generally depressing – and a stay of a night or two is ample for most – Chihuahua can have some appeal, with its colonial centre and suburbs of grandiose nineteenth-century Gothic-style mansions built when silver brought wealth to the region. This is also *vaquero* heartland and one of the best places in the country to look for **cowboy boots**: you're spoilt for choice in the centre, especially in the blocks bounded by Calle 4, Juárez, Victoria and Ocampo.

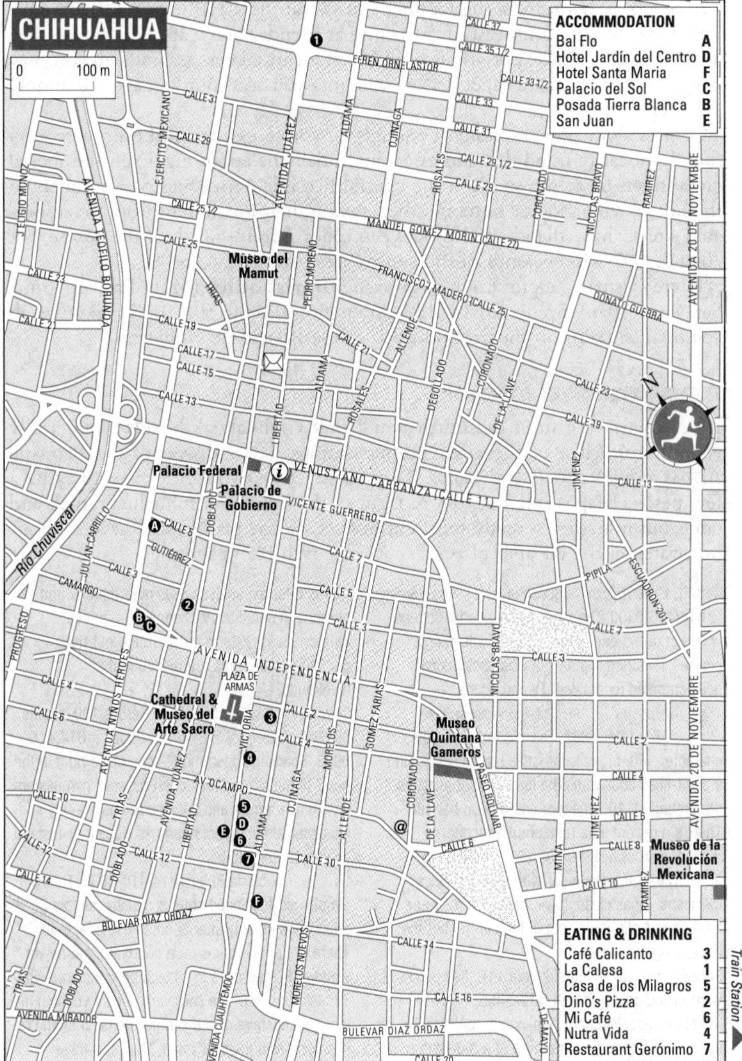


## Arrival, information and getting around

Transport in and out of Chihuahua is not well coordinated, frustrating the many travellers who come here only to take the Copper Canyon rail line. The **Central Camionera** (with guardería 9am–11pm and long-distance phone office) is miles out, near the airport on Juan Pablo II; local buses (M$4) from the main road outside run to and from Juárez in the centre, and there are plenty of taxis (M$60). From the **airport**, a fixed-fare system operates – buy your voucher as you leave the terminal.

Arriving by **train** from the Copper Canyon at the CHP station (Ⓣ614/439-7200), you're 2km southeast of the centre at Mendez and Calle 24. You can take a bus into the centre, but you'll probably want to take a taxi; indeed, you may have little choice, since eager drivers will grab you and your luggage the minute you step out.

Central Chihuahua is compact enough for you to **get around** everywhere on foot, but bear in mind that addresses can initially be confusing. Even-numbered cross streets lie to the south of the central Plaza de Armas and odd numbers to the north, with shop or hotel numbers taking their initial digit from the associated street; thus, Allende 702 is between calles 7 and 9 north of the centre, but Allende 607 will be south of the centre between calles 6 and 8.

There's a small, helpful English-speaking **tourist office** (Mon–Fri 9am–5pm, Sat–Sun 10am–5pm; Ⓣ614/429-3596 or 01-800/508-0111, Ⓦwww.ah-chihuahua.com) on the ground floor of the Palacio de Gobierno.

## Accommodation

If you're arriving from the north you'll find Chihuahua's **hotels** wonderfully economical. Most of the safe, cheaper options lie southwest of the Plaza de Armas along Victoria and Juárez. Those a street or two further west may be a few pesos cheaper still, but they're right in the heart of Chihuahua's small and tame, but nonetheless seedy, red-light district. All the places listed have 24-hour hot water; at the cheaper places, a/c is only available in summer.

**Bal Flo** C 5a 702, at the junction with Niños Héroes Ⓣ614/416-0300. The bunker-like exterior softens within to reveal one of the better middle-range choices, featuring slightly poky but exceptionally neat, carpeted rooms with TV and phone. ⑤

**Hotel Jardin del Centro** Victoria 818 Ⓣ614/415-1832. This old hotel has lots of character, with big colonial-style rooms set around a plant-filled courtyard. The less elegant quarters are around M$100 cheaper and a good bargain. There's a decent little restaurant attached. ④

**Hotel Santa Maria** Aldama 1212 Ⓣ614/410-3537. This hotel is popular with working-class Mexicans. It has clean, basic rooms with TV and bathroom. A slight way out of the centre, but the price is right. ①

**Palacio del Sol** Independencia 116, five blocks west of the centre Ⓣ614/412-3456, Ⓦwww.hotelpalaciodelsol.com. Top-notch, multistorey luxury hotel, though something of a monolithic eyesore; most of the large international-standard rooms offer expansive views over the city and come with satellite TV. Gymnasium, pricey cafeteria and restaurant/bar round out the package, and rooms are discounted at weekends. ⑦

**Posada Tierra Blanca** Niños Héroes 100, beside the *Palacio del Sol* Ⓣ614/415-0000, Ⓕ614/416-0063. Spacious, open motel-style place right in the heart of the city, with an open-air pool, gymnasium, on-site restaurant and bar. The rooms are tidy and spacious, although not nearly as elegant or tasteful as they pretend to be. ⑥

**San Juan** Victoria 823 Ⓣ614/410-0035. This simple, old-fashioned hotel is usually friendly, though the gloomy interior could use a face-lift. There are a few rooms off a courtyard and newer wooden-floored ones in a block behind, some with TV; ask for one of the courtyard ones if you can, as the ones upstairs give the vague sense that you're in a gymnasium locker room. They also have Internet for guests at M$10/hr. ①

## The Town

Chihuahua's centre of activity is the teeming **Plaza de Armas**, where its fine **cathedral** stands opposite a wonderfully camp statue of the city's founder in the very act of pointing to the ground, as if to say "Right lads, we'll build it here". The Baroque, twin-towered temple was begun in 1717 but took more than seven years to complete: work well worth it, though, since for once the interior detail is the equal of the facade. In a modernized crypt beneath the cathedral the small **Museo de Arte Sacro** (Mon–Fri 10am–2pm & 4–6pm;

△ Plaza de Armas, Chihuahua

M$15) displays some fine examples of Mexican religious art from the eighteenth century, notably a selection of sombre saints by Francisco Martinez and a collection of dark and forbidding images in which Christ is pushed, pulled, stabbed and punched.

Also on the Plaza de Armas is the imposing but relatively modern **Palacio Municipal**; follow Victoria down past this and you'll come to the Plaza Hidalgo, dominated by the **Palacio de Gobierno**. Now lined with bold murals of scenes from Mexico's colonial past painted by Aarón Piña Mora, this was originally a Jesuit college, and later converted to a military hospital after the expulsion of the Jesuits – Padre Miguel Hidalgo y Costilla and Ignacio Allende, the inspiration and early leaders of the Mexican War of Independence, were executed here in 1811, their severed heads sent for public display in Guanajuato. The site of the deed is marked (despite the fact that the building has been reconstructed several times since) and, by crossing the road to the adjacent Palacio Federal, you can visit the **Calabozo de Hidalgo**, at the corner of Juárez and Guerrero (Tues–Sun 9am–6pm; M$11), "Hidalgo's dungeon", where they were held beforehand. The museum has on display various relics of Hidalgo and the Revolution, including his pistol, chest, crucifix and a number of personal letters. A golden eagle marks the entrance.

Further north along Juárez, at Juárez and Calle 25a, you'll find the **Museo del Mamut** (Tues–Sun 10am–5pm; M$15), which has some fun expositions on local paleontology and geology. Among the museum's acquisitions are the fossilized remains of mammoths and giant anemones retrieved from the deserts of Chihuahua, which were underwater many million years ago. Most impressive is the huge whale skeleton suspended in mid-air.

More recent history is commemorated in Chihuahua's premier sight, the **Museo de la Revolución Mexicana**, Calle 10 3010 (Tues–Sat 9am–1pm & 3–7pm, Sun 9am–5pm; M$15), which occupies Pancho Villa's former home. This enormous mansion was inhabited, until her death in the early 1980s, by Villa's "official" widow (there were allegedly many others), who used to conduct personal tours; it has now been taken over by the Mexican army and put on a more official footing. The collection is a fascinating mix of arms, war plans and personal mementoes, including the bullet-riddled Dodge in which Villa was assassinated in 1923 and a funerary mask that clearly shows the bullet wound in his forehead. Quite apart from the campaign memories, the superbly preserved old bedrooms and bathrooms give an interesting insight into Mexican daily life in the early twentieth century.

The museum is some 2km east of the centre. To get there, walk along Ocampo, or take a bus (marked "Ocampo"), and continue two blocks past the huge church and two blocks to the left along Mendez. You may well want to break the journey at the extraordinarily elaborate **Museo Quinta Gameros** (Tues–Sun 11am–2pm & 4–7pm; M$22), at the junction of Calle 4 and Paseo Bolivar. Just the sort of ostentatious display of wealth that Villa and his associates were hoping to stamp out in their battle against the landed elite, the building was designed by a successful mine owner as an exact replica of a Parisian home. The interior is sumptuously decorated, with magnificent Art Nouveau stained glass and ornate woodwork, and, curiously, scenes from *Little Red Riding Hood* painted on the children's bedroom wall.

## Eating, drinking and entertainment

There's no shortage of good **places to eat** in Chihuahua, from basic cafés around the **market** (west of Juárez between calles 4 and 6), to taco stalls nearer the centre, to fancier steak houses and American burger restaurants around the main plazas. The southern end of Victoria has some of the best options, and tends to stay open late.

For traditional, back-slapping cantina **drinking**, pick one of the swing-door places at the southern end of Juárez, though take care. If you're after something a little more upmarket, rub shoulders with Chihuahua's more moneyed set at the bars and clubs along Juárez's northern reaches, close to its junction with Colón. Alternatively, you can always see a subtitled American **movie** (around M$65) at Cinema Revolución, where Doblado meets Neri Santos.

**Café Calicanto** Aldama 411. Popular restaurant with live Mexican music Tues–Sun. They serve meat-filled Chihuahuan specialities for around M$70. There's also an interesting vegetarian menu and various alcoholic coffees. Try the *beso de Santa*: coffee, milk, cognac, cinnamon and vanilla.

**La Calesa** Juárez 3300, at Colón ⓣ614/416-0222. One of Chihuahua's fanciest restaurants, all dark wood panels, crisp linen tablecloths, sparkling wine glasses and waistcoated waiters. Northern-style steaks are the house speciality. Expect to pay M$80 for *chiles rellenos de camarón* and up to M$145 for a massive plate of succulent *mariscos*. Bookings recommended at weekends.

**Casa de los Milagros** Victoria 810, opposite *Hotel Reforma*. Casual restaurant and bar comprising a beautiful colonial courtyard with fountain, surrounded by numerous small rooms. Here, Chihuahua's well-groomed meet for margaritas (M$30), one of 25 brands of tequila (M$10–50 a shot), real coffee and light snacks such as *quesadilla de flor de calabaza* (squash flower; M$40), burgers and salads.

**Dino's Pizza** Doblado 301, north of Independencia. Delicious pizzas made with an interestingly sweet dough (M$90 buys one big enough for two) and an excellent range of toppings. Also sandwiches and spaghetti dishes. Stays open late.

**Mi Café** Victoria 1000, almost opposite the *Hotel San Juan*. Reliable American-style diner with prices and quality both a little above average. The M$40 breakfast menu is in English and Spanish and extends from *norteño* and *ranchero* dishes to hotcakes and syrup. Come here later for burgers, sandwiches and steak and seafood mains.

**Nutra Vida** Victoria 420. Health-food place stocking delicious cinnamon-laced breads, juices and fruit cocktails. It also serves a reliable comida corrida and breakfast.

**Restaurant Gerónimo** at Aldama and C 10a. Clean and tidy place that lays on an excellent, if slightly pricey, breakfast buffet that includes fresh fruit, juices, eggs and a range of tasty *norteño* specialities.



## Listings

**Banks** Most banks are centrally located, and nearly all have ATMs, with branches on Victoria and Libertad around the Plaza de Armas.

**Buses** The Central Camionera (see p.199) has representatives from Estrella Blanca, Grupo Senda and Omnibus de México, plus Greyhound for buses to Denver, Los Angeles, Phoenix, Dallas and a few other US cities. Between the bus companies there are hourly buses to Juárez, frequent buses to Creel and a handful of buses for the five-hour jaunt to Nuevo Casas Grandes. The buses south are equally frequent, with hourly buses to Parral, at least ten buses daily to Durango, and services every other hour to Mexico City and Guadalajara.

**Internet access** You'll find a few terminals inside *Mi Café*, Victoria and C 6 (M$15/hr), and many more at Centro Ciber-Cafe, Coronado 421 (M$15/hr).

**Post office** Libertad 1700, behind the church (Mon–Fri 8am–5pm, Sat 9am–1pm).

**Telephones** There's a good long-distance phone booth in the pharmacy at Independencia 808, east of Aldama (Mon–Sat 8am–8pm), though you can easily find Telmex phone booths all over town.

**Trains** The only passenger train that serves Chihuahua is the Copper Canyon line (see p.188), from the CHP train station. You can catch the buses marked "Sta Rosa" or "Col Rosalia", which run along Ocampo. Get out a couple of blocks past the big church (impossible to miss) and walk a couple of blocks to the right down Mendez to the station. There are occasional cancellations so it's a good idea to visit the station ticket office a day ahead; it's even now possible to buy tickets the morning of departure, assuming you make it there early enough (Mon–Fri 6am–5.30pm, Sat & Sun 6am–12.30pm).

**Travel agent** Rojo y Casavantes, Guerrero 1207, at Allende ⓣ614/439-5858, ⓦwww.rojoycasavantes.com (Mon–Fri 9am–7pm, Sat 9am–1pm).

# South to Durango

Below Chihuahua sprawls a vast plain, mostly agricultural, largely uninteresting and broken only occasionally by an outstretched leg of the Sierra Madre Occidental. Freight trains cross at night and buses hammer through relentlessly; you'd be wise to follow their lead. At **Jiménez** the road divides, with Hwy-49 heading straight down through Gómez Palacio and Torreón, while Hwy-45 curves westwards to Durango. The nonstop route for Zacatecas and Mexico City is quicker, but if time is not your only consideration the Durango route offers far more of interest.

**Torreón** and **Gómez Palacio**, on the faster of the two routes, are virtually contiguous – there would be only one city were it not for the fact that the state border runs through the middle: Torreón is in Coahuila, Gómez Palacio in Durango. They're equally dull, modern towns anyway – both were devastated by heavy fighting in the Revolution. There's no need whatsoever to stop, though one consolation if you do is that they mark the start of wine-growing country, and you can sample the local produce (not the country's best) at various *bodegas*. On the longer route, **Durango** is the first of the Spanish colonial towns that distinguish Mexico's heartland, and while it's not quite as striking as some of those further south, it will certainly be the most attractive place you will have come to. That said, it's a good eight to ten hours on the bus from Chihuahua, so you might consider breaking the journey in **Hidalgo del Parral**.

## Parral



**PARRAL**, or "Hidalgo del Parral" as it's officially known, has a certain provincial and aesthetic charm, partly supplied by the vivid legends it sustains. You could do a lot worse than spend an afternoon exploring the streets of this pleasant, low-key city.

Parral is fixed in Mexican consciousness as the town in which Pancho Villa met his demise under a spectacular hail of hot lead in 1923. **The Museo Regional General Francisco Villa** on Juárez (Tues–Sun 10am–5pm; M$15), close to the spot where Villa's bullet-ridden vehicle came to a halt, commemorates the assassinated hero with displays of revolutionary effects, antique weapons, a small shrine and plenty of enigmatic old photos.

The town's history goes much further than this, however, having been established in the early seventeenth century as a silver-mining centre. The ramshackle spectre of **La Prieta mine** (Tues–Sun 10am–5pm; M$20), founded in 1629, overlooks Parral from a hill on the edge of town. It's now a regional museum containing heaps of old equipment, a disused tunnel and some very dilapidated buildings.

Mineral profits helped build some of the town's more impressive edifices, including the **Palacio Pedro Alvarado** (daily 10am–6pm; M$20), a restored mansion commemorating local mining magnate Don Pedro Alvarado. He was reputedly a close friend and business associate of Pancho Villa, which might explain why Villa's funerary car is parked inside the building. You'll find some excellent photos in this museum that chart the town's development.

Parral is also home to several striking churches. The **Catedral de San José**, one of the more interesting, houses the remains of the town's founder, Don Juan Rangel Viesma. Also worth a look is the **Iglesia de la Virgen del Rayo**, a few minutes' walk over the river. Legend has it this was constructed by an Indian on the proceeds of the gold mine he had discovered and worked in secret; the authorities tortured him to death in attempt to find the mine, but its location died with him.

### Practicalities

Parral's compact colonial heart is around twenty minutes' walk from the main **bus terminal** (daytime luggage storage) – turn left, then left again onto Independencia – or take a bus or taxi (M$20) from just outside. There are buses almost hourly to Durango and Chihuahua, as well as frequent services to Juárez and Torreón. The cheapest acceptable **hotel** in town by far is the basic, if slightly untidy, *Hotel Zaragoza*, Zaragoza 115 (Ⓣ627/522-6590; ❶), especially cheap for groups. If that's full, there's the clean and simple *Hotel Fuentes*, Maclovio Herrera 79 (Ⓣ627/522-0016; ❶). More comfortable and upmarket, *Hotel Acosta*, near the main plaza on Agustín Barbachano 3 (Ⓣ627/522-0221, Ⓕ627/522-0657; ❹), is a pleasant old establishment with excellent rooms that overlook the city, a rooftop terrace and 1950s atmosphere. For a touch of luxury only a stone's throw from the bus station, stroll to the *Hotel Los Arcos*, Dr Pedro de Lille 5 (Ⓣ627/523-0597, Ⓕ627/523-0537; ❺), where rooms faces a modern, plant-filled courtyard and come with satellite TV; there's also a restaurant. For **eating**, in the centre just off the plaza the bright and cheery 24-hour *Restaurant Morelos*, Coronado 22, serves *pozole de puerco* for M$45 and excellent *enchiladas suizas*, made with chicken, guacamole and green chile. If you've a taste for a torta or burger, stop off at the *OK Parral*, Independencia 47, on your walk from the bus station into town. The popular *Chagos* makes a good dinner spot, with filling, though slightly pricey, steaks; it's off Coronado. If you need a **bank**, a branch of Bancomer lies on the corner of Barbachano and Coronado, at the Plaza Principal. Ciber World is a good **Internet** spot at Bartolomé de las Casas 15 (near Juárez) and charges M$15 an hour, otherwise, try SMAC-Line at Mercaderes 80 (Mon–Fri 9.30am–1.30pm & 4–7.30pm; M$10/hr).

## Durango

Although the Sierra Madre still looms on the western horizon, the country around **DURANGO** itself is flat. Just two low hills mark out the city from the plain: the **Cerro del Mercado**, a giant lump of iron ore that testifies to the area's mineral wealth, rises squat and black to the north, while to the west a climb up the **Cerro de los Remedios** provides a wonderful panorama over the whole city. Officially named Victoria de Durango, the city, with its nearly 600,000 inhabitants, sits between these two hills in the Valle del Guadiana. Highways 45 and 40 intersect here, making it an important transport junction between the coast and the interior cities of Torréon, Saltillo and Monterrey, but the town is worth a visit of a day or two in its own right, with a national monument and beautiful colonial architecture. The people, too, are a charismatic and gregarious bunch whose hospitality comes as a charming respite from the north.

Durango's **fiesta**, on July 8, celebrates the city's foundation on that day in 1563 by Francisco de Ibarra. Festivities commence several days before and run right through till the fiesta of the Virgen del Refugio on July 22 – well worth going out of your way for, though rooms are booked solid.

### Arrival and information

Buses arrive at the **Central de Autobuses** (guardería, 7am–11pm) over 4km out of town; to get to town, take one of the off-white buses marked "Centro" or "Camionera" from in front of the station. These will drop you right at the Plaza de Armas near the cathedral. Facing the cathedral, turn left along 20 de Noviembre (as it runs into Florida) just past Independencia to reach the second-floor **tourist office**, Florida 1106 Pte (Mon–Fri 8am–8pm; ⓣ618/811-9677, ⓦwww.durangoturismo.com). Despite its compact, grid-plan centre, getting your bearings in Durango can initially be a little tricky, so it's as well to know that addresses south of Aquiles Serdán (two blocks north of the cathedral) are appended "Sur", and those west of Zarco (six blocks east of the cathedral) are tagged "Ote".

### Accommodation

There's no shortage of **rooms** in Durango, though you should book ahead if you want to visit during the fiesta. Most of the cheaper places are pretty grim; if price is your only concern, try around the market, though even here the better places charge heavily. If you're willing to spend a little more, Durango has a couple of very fine places worth splashing out on.

**Casablanca** 20 de Noviembre 811 Pte, at Zaragoza ⓣ618/811-3599, ⓦwww.hotelcasablancadurango.com.mx. Big, old-fashioned colonial hotel. Spacious and comfortable if unexciting. ❻

**Hotel California** Zarco 317 ⓣ618/811-4561. Budget hotel with rock-bottom rates and small, barely clean rooms to match. Close to the market and a 10min walk from the main plaza. ❶

# DURANGO

**ACCOMMODATION**

| | |
|---|---|
| Casablanca | D |
| Hotel California | C |
| Hotel Gallo | E |
| Hotel Plaza Cathedral | B |
| María del Pilar | F |
| Posada San Jorge | A |

**EATING & DRINKING**

| | |
|---|---|
| Los Canastos | 4 |
| Corleone Pizza | 1 |
| La Esquina del Café | 7 |
| La Fogata | 2 |
| Fonda de la Tía Chonda | 9 |
| Gorditas Gabino | 3 |
| Pampas | A |
| Samadhi Vegetarian | 5 |
| Sloan's Restaurant Bar | 6 |
| La Terraza | 10 |
| La Tostada | 8 |

Zoo (1km)
AmEx (1.5km) & Bus Station (3km)

Museo de las Culturas Populares
Museo de Arte Contemporáneo
Mercado Gomez Palacio
Cathedral
Sanborn's
Teatro Ricardo Castro
Museo de Cine
Café Internet
Plaza de Armas
Palacio de Gobierno
Casa de los Condes
Internet Gamar
Iglesia de los Remedios
Cerro de los Remedios
Parque Guadiana

HERNANDEZ
AYUNTAMIENTO
PEREYRA
COSTA
GÓMEZ PALACIO
BARCENA
BORREGO
HIDALGO
ELORREAGA
CASTANEDA
PALOMA
LAUREANO RONCAL
CUAUHTÉMOC
BRUNO MARTINEZ
JUÁREZ
GABINO BARREDA
APARTADO
REGATO
RAMIREZ
SALVADOR NAVA RODRIGUEZ
CONSTITUCIÓN
VICTORIA
MADERO
PASTEUR
PATONI
ZARCO
CORONADO
CANOAS
AQUILES SERDÁN
PORRAS
ZARAGOZA
INDEPENDENCIA
NEGRETE
VOLADORES
AVENIDA 20 DE NOVIEMBRE
FLORIDA
NOGAL
5 DE FEBRERO
PROGRESSO
CARLOS LEON DE LA PEÑA
PINO SUÁREZ
BACA ORTZ
MASCAREÑAS
CARLOS SANTA MARIA
ISAURO VENZOR
GRAL ENRIQUE CARROLA ANTUNA
ACEQUIA GRANDE
BULEVAR DOMINGO ARREITA
BLV DOLORES DEL RÍO
AV FANNY ANITUA
AV FERROCARRIL
PROL. GÓMEZ PALACIOS
PROL. CANOAS
AVENIDA UNIVERSIDAD
FRAY DIEGO DE LA CADENA
GRANADA
MORELOS
ALLENDE
BELISARIO DOMÍNGUEZ
MINA
LUNA
URREA
BRAVO
BULEVAR DE LOS REMEDIOS

0 500 m
N

**Hotel Gallo** 5 de Febrero 117 Pte ⓣ618/811-5920. Another budget option near the market. The dirt-cheap rooms are rudimentary and there's hot water only in the mornings and evenings. ❶

**Hotel Plaza Cathedral** Constitución 216, beside the cathedral ⓣ618/813-2480, ⓕ813-2660. Excellent value for such a charming, historic and centrally located hotel. Most of the rooms aren't as spacious as the grandiose stone corridors might suggest, but it's still a good deal considering its position right next to the cathedral. ❹

**María del Pilar** Pino Suárez 410 ⓣ618/811-5471. The rooms inside this pink building are all clean and tidy, come with private bath and phone and are a pretty good deal for your money. The management keeps a good stock of maps and other tourist information in the lobby. ❷

**Posada San Jorge** Constitución 102 Sur, at Serdán ⓣ618/813-3257, ⓦwww.hotelposadasanjorge.com.mx. The best of the pricier places, a gorgeous and recently remodelled hotel in a colonial house with a two-storey courtyard alive with caged birds and chatter from the attached Brazilian restaurant. Rooms, all with cable TV, are individually decorated in rustic fashion, with tiled floors, wood beams, bold paintwork and potted cacti. Prices drop by about M$200 off-season. ❻

### The Town

Almost all the monuments in downtown Durango cluster in a few streets around the Plaza Principal and the huge covered market nearby. On the plaza itself is the **cathedral**, its two robust domed towers dwarfing the narrow facade. It's a typical Mexican church in every way: externally imposing, weighty and Baroque, with a magnificent setting overlooking the plaza, and yet ultimately disappointing within, the interior dim and by comparison uninspired. Facing it from the centre of the plaza is a bizarre little two-storey bandstand from the top of which the town band plays on Sundays; underneath, a small shop sells expensive local crafts.

Following 20 de Noviembre down from the cathedral (stretching away to the left as you face it) brings you to the grandiose Porfiriano **Teatro Ricardo Castro**, with its elegant interior of marble floors and crystal chandeliers. Several blocks further on and next door to the tourist office at Florida 1106 is the **Museo de Cine** (Mon–Fri 9am–6pm, Sat & Sun 10am–6pm; M$5), a fairly interesting tribute to the films created around Durango, including over a hundred Westerns. You can view pictures of the sets, some old cameras and recording equipment.

Head back east on 20 de Noviembre and turn south onto Bruno Martínez, past the Teatro Victoria, and you come out in another plaza, its north side dominated by the porticoed facade of the **Palacio de Gobierno**. Originally the private house of a Spanish mining magnate, this was taken over by the local government after the War of Independence. The stairwells and walls of the two-storey, arcaded patio inside are decorated with murals by local artists depicting the state's history. On the east side of the square, an ancient **Jesuit monastery** now houses the offices of the Juárez Autonomous University of Durango.

From here 5 de Febrero leads back to the **Casa de los Condes**, the most elaborate of the Spanish-style mansions. Built in the eighteenth century by the Conde de Suchil, sometime Spanish governor of Durango, its exuberantly carved columns and wealth of extravagant detail are quite undamaged by time. History has given the mansion some strange functions, though: it was the seat of the local Inquisition for some time – and a more inappropriate setting for their stern deliberations would be hard to imagine – while nowadays it operates as a bank, having had a brief spell as a sort of upmarket shopping mall. A little further along 5 de Febrero, you reach the back of the **market**. It covers a whole block on two storeys and sells just about everything anyone could want, from medicinal herbs to farm equipment to food; it also holds a couple of *bodegas* upstairs that serve beer to a primarily local crowd.

Back at the plaza, you can stroll up Constitución, a lively shopping street with several small restaurants, to the little church and garden of Santa Ana, much more peaceful than the plaza for an evening *paseo*. On the east side lies the **Museo de la Cultura** (Tues–Fri 9am–6pm, Sat & Sun noon–6pm; M$10), an old converted mansion with separate rooms dedicated to local, native styles of weaving, ceramics, basketware and mask-making. Enthusiastic guides explain all, and there are often interesting temporary exhibitions.

### Parque Guadiana and Cerro de los Remedios

If you have kids in tow, or just fancy a break from bus diesel fumes, make for the prominent Cerro de los Remedios, 2km west of the city centre, or more particularly, **Parque Guadiana** on its northern flanks – take a bus marked "Remedios/Parque Guadiana" from outside the cathedral – a vast area of fragrant eucalyptus and shady willows, dotted with fountains and kids' playgrounds, and with a **miniature train** (Fri 3–7pm, Sat & Sun 11am–6pm; M$4). On the western side of the park, on Anillo de Circunvalación, is the **Zoológico Sahuatoba** (Tues–Sat 11am–6pm, Sun 10am–7pm; free), a collection of lions, tigers, hippos, monkeys and the like that's surprisingly well presented considering the free entry. Buses marked "Tierra y Libertad" come directly here from the corner of Serdán and Victoria.

The **Cerro de los Remedios**, rising immediately above the park and the zoo, is home to Durango's moneyed classes, and expensive modern homes are climbing inexorably towards the hilltop **Iglesia de los Remedios**, which commands a wonderful view over the entire city. The most direct way to walk up here from the city is to take the steps at the western end of Juan García.

### Eating, drinking and entertainment

It isn't difficult to find great **places to eat** in Durango, among them – and for no apparent reason – a proliferation of Italian restaurants. Your cheapest eating options are the stalls upstairs in the **market**, some of which serve excellent food. Adjacent streets, and those off the main plaza, are also good hunting grounds, but the greatest concentration of dining establishments is along the first six or so blocks of Constitución going north from the plaza, where both fashionable and more modest eating and drinking places fill the gaps between the boutiques. Apart from Sunday evening, when the streets around the plaza are blocked off for the weekly free **entertainment** – mainly *norteña* and *ranchera* bands – nightlife revolves around the restaurants. For **live music**, try *Sloan's* (see opposite). If you want to see a **film**, there's a multiplex cinema in the shopping centre just across from the bus station. You can buy **books** and magazines at Sanborn's, next door to the cathedral, which also has a café upstairs that serves good coffee and has an extensive menu, including a filling egg and pancake breakfast for M$45.

**Los Canastos** corner of Negrete and Victoria. Small health-food store with a good selection of nuts, dried fruit and other snacks.

**Corleone Pizza** Constitución 110 Nte, at Serdán. Buzzing family joint serving slightly sweet pizzas and an admirable range of cocktails.

**La Esquina del Café** the southwest corner of Nogal and Florida. Tiny coffee shop with real coffee (it's all they sell), something of an anomaly in northern Mexico.

**La Fogata** Cuauhtémoc at Negrete. Moderately priced restaurant, serving mostly Mexican food, though they have a full bar and a wide selection of choice steaks.

**Fonda de la Tía Chonda** Nogal 110. A Durango dinner favourite, the elegant interior is often packed with locals; serves very good traditional Mexican cuisine at high prices.

**Gorditas Gabino** Constitución 100 Nte. Bright, clean, economical restaurant serving steaks, tacos, burritos and burgers. They do a pretty decent *enchiladas rojas* for a few dollars.

**Pampas** in the *San Jorge* hotel. Its menu largely comprises Brazilian cuts of grilled steak, in something resembling *churrascuria*-style eating.

**Samadhi Vegetarian** Negrete 403 Pte. Small, brightly coloured joint, which serves a bargain veggie comida for M$20, yogurt, salads and vegetable-filled enchiladas.

**Sloan's Restaurant Bar** Negrete 1003. The Continental menu here is popular with Durango's upper class – steaks are their speciality. The bar and live music kicks off around 11pm at weekends.

**La Terraza** 5 de Febrero 603, on the first floor overlooking the plaza opposite the cathedral. Only worthwhile for drinks or a pizza if you can get a window seat to watch the world go by. Deafeningly loud *norteña* and mariachi music at night.

**La Tostada** Florida 1125. This pleasant, clean restaurant is popular with the locals. It serves affordable Mexican staples and good breakfasts too.

### Listings

**American Express** Operates from 20 de Noviembre 810 Ote (Mon–Fri 9am–7pm, Sat 10am–5pm; ⓣ618/817-0083), three blocks east of the post office; catch "Tecno" buses along 20 de Noviembre.

**Banks** There's a convenient branch of Bancomer right by the plaza at the corner of 20 de Noviembre and Constitución, in addition to several other banks nearby.

**Buses** Durango's bus station is well connected to points both north and south, with multiple services a day to destinations including Aguascalientes, Ciudad Juárez, Mazatlán, Mexico City, Monterrey, Parral and Zacatecas.

**Internet access** Durango has several inexpensive and good Internet cafés. Try Cafe Internet, 20 de Noviembre 1006 Pte (daily 8am–9pm, M$10/hr), or Internet GAMAR, Pino Suarez 609-A (daily 8am–9pm, M$6/hr).

**Laundry** There's a *lavandería* on Zarco at Negrete, where you can get three kilos washed and dried for M$30.

**Post office** Some twelve blocks east of the cathedral, at 20 de Noviembre 500-B Ote.

## Around Durango

The full title of Durango's tourist office is the **Dirección de Turismo y Cinematografía del Estado de Durango**. Until fairly recently they spent much of their time organizing the vast number of **film** units that came to the area to take advantage of its remarkably constant, clear, high-altitude light, its desert and mountain scenery (Westerns were the speciality) and the relatively cheap Mexican technicians and extras. Although only half a dozen movies have been shot here over the last decade, you can still see the remains of the permanent sets at Villa del Oeste and Chupaderos. The main road from Parral runs within a few hundred metres of the movie towns, so it's easy enough to get there by bus, and to flag one down when you leave – alternatively you get a pretty good, if fleeting, view as you pass by.

Parral-bound buses departing from Durango's main bus station will drop you 12km north at **Villa del Oeste** (Tues–Fri noon–7pm, Sat & Sun 11am–7pm; M$30; ⓣ618/112-2882, ⓦwww.villadeloeste.com), a kind of small theme park comprising the hundred-metre-long street of Bandido, which looks straight out of the Wild West until you realize the saloons and shops have been refashioned into a themed restaurant, music hall and a bar and grill. You can practise your horseback skills (M$90/hr), and on weekends there's a show featuring gun-slinging cowboys and cabaret girls (Sat 2.30 & 4.30pm; Sun 3.30, 5.30 & 7.30pm).

If all this sounds too cheesy, stay on the bus to the dusty village of **CHUPADEROS**, 2km further north, where the villagers have pretty much taken over a former set: the church and "Prairie Lands Hotel" are lived in, one house is a grocery store and the livestock exchange has been commandeered by Alcoholics Anonymous. A good way to link the two towns is to catch the bus out to Chupaderos, then follow the track past the lived-in

△ Villa del Oeste, Durango

church, across the train tracks and through scrubby, cactus-strewn desert 2km to a kind of back entrance to Bandido in Villa del Oeste, where you may or may not be charged entry. It is a particularly nice walk in the late afternoon, past the heat of the day.

An alternative day out is to head 35km south to **El Saltito**, a waterfall surrounded by bizarre rock formations, which has itself been a recurrent film location; the bus can drop you on the road 4km away. On any of these trips, watch out for **scorpions**: there's a genus of white scorpion unique to this area, which, though rare – the only place most people see one is encased in the glass paperweights on sale all over the place – has a sting that is frequently fatal.

On **leaving Durango** you face a simple choice: **west** to the Pacific at Mazatlán, over an incredible road through the Sierra Madre, which is itself a worthwhile journey; **east** towards Torreón, Saltillo and Monterrey; or **south** to Zacatecas (see p.257), among the finest of Mexico's colonial cities.

# Monterrey and the northeast

The **eastern border crossings**, from Ciudad Acuña to Matamoros, are uniformly dull – dedicated solely to the task of getting people and goods from one country to the other. In this they are at least reasonably efficient, with immigration officials on both sides well used to coping with mass cross-border traffic. In most cases, Mexican tourist cards are routinely issued at the border, while Mexican consulates in the Texan towns across the Río Grande can handle any problems. If you're entering the US as a non-US citizen, you might need a visa waiver, which can only be bought with exact US currency. You could also be subject to stringent security checks. There's a small toll to pay on the bridges: keep a selection of US coins for the turnstiles.

Once across the border, you're faced with the choice of pressing on south (invariably the best option) or choosing a suitable hotel from the dozens on offer. If you're eager to head on from the border towns of **Nuevo Laredo**, **Reynosa** or **Matamoros** there are frequent city bus services to the main bus stations, though you have to walk a few blocks to catch them. The bus stations in **Ciudad Acuña** and **Piedras Negras** are in town, within walking distance of the border crossing.

Once through the border towns, you could be forgiven for hot-footing straight to the Bajío (Chapter 3) or even Veracruz (Chapter 7), but you're talking at least twelve hours on the bus, and besides, it would be a pity to miss **Monterrey**, Mexico's industrial dynamo and home to a few essential sights. Neighbouring **Saltillo** is also worthwhile, if only as a pleasant place to break a long journey. Direct buses from the border to Monterrey, Mexico City and most of the major northern cities are frequent and efficient.

# The Lower Río Grande Valley: Ciudad Acuña to Matamoros

The **Río Grande**, known to Mexicans as the **Río Bravo del Norte**, forms the border between Texas and Mexico, a distance of more than 1500km. The country through which it flows is arid semi-desert, and the towns along the lower section of the river are heavily industrialized and suffer from appalling environmental pollution. This is the **maquiladora** zone, where foreign-owned assembly plants produce consumer goods, most of them for export to the US (see the box on p.220 for more on this). There are few particular attractions for tourists, however, and most visitors are here only for cheap bric-a-brac shopping or simply passing through on their way south.

## Ciudad Acuña and around

The smallest of the border towns, **CIUDAD ACUÑA** (setting of the low-budget Mexican thriller *El Mariachi* and its sequel, *El Regreso del Mariachi*) is quiet, relaxed and intensely hot. The main plaza has a small **museum** on one side, with a tiny collection of fossils and artefacts, in addition to rows and rows of deathly dull photographs of local dignitaries. Given that there's little to do in the town itself, the best idea is to press on south, unless you're drawn by the offerings around Acuña: water-sports enthusiasts are amply catered for at the **Presa Amistad**, a huge artificial lake straddling the border, while to the west the starkly beautiful mountains, canyons and desert of the interior of Coahuila state invite cautious exploration. The huge and scarcely visited **Parque Internacional del Río Bravo**, opposite Big Bend National Park in Texas, is a protected area offering superb wilderness, but you'll need a well-equipped vehicle to cope with the rugged terrain; there's no public transport, nor is there any real tourist infrastructure, though you might be able to wheedle

### Border checks

Crossing the border, do not forget to go through **immigration and customs** checks. As everywhere, there's a free zone south of the frontier, and you can cross at will. Try to continue south, though, and you'll be stopped after some 30km and sent back to get your tourist card stamped.



some information out of someone at Big Bend (Ⓣ432/477-2251, Ⓦwww.nps.gov/bibe).

Arriving over the bridge from Del Rio, Texas, the bus drops you at the **border** post, where there's a map of the town in the modern customs building, together with some limited tourist information. A full-fledged **tourist information** office is at Lerdo 110 where it meets Hidalgo (Ⓣ877/772-4692, Ⓔturismo_acuna@terra.com.mx). The **bus station**, at the corner of Matamoros and Ocampo, is just five blocks from the border and one from the plaza. Most shops and restaurants are glad to change your dollars at a fairly good rate for small amounts, but for proper exchange there's a choice of banks and **casas de cambio**. Of the **banks**, Bancomer, Madero 360, off Juárez, has a 24-hour ATM, as does Scotiabank at the corner of Guerrero and Madero. The **post office** is at Hidalgo 320, past Juárez. You'll pass several **hotels** as you walk down Hidalgo from the border: none is especially good value, but if you want to stay in the gaudy heart of town, try *San Jorge*, Hidalgo 165 (Ⓣ877/772-5070; ❹), which has tile, brick and stucco rooms with sparkling-clean bathrooms, or the more spacious *San Antonio*, at the corner of Hidalgo and Lerdo (Ⓣ877/772-5108, Ⓔhotelsanantonio@prodigy.net.mx; ❻). Also good for one night, especially if you're very tired, is the *Coahuila*, Lerdo 160, one block off Hidalgo (Ⓣ877/772-1040; ❷); if you're really low on funds, the less-than-spotless *Alfaro*, Madero 240, between Juárez and Lerdo (no phone; ❶), will do – here you might even be able to get in on a bingo game with some of the hotel's long-term residents out back.

The biggest **bars** and **restaurants** in Acuña – the ones which cater to dollar-toting border-crossers – are located around Hidalgo and Madero. Try the gargantuan early twentieth-century *Crosby's*, on Matamoros and Hidalgo, a restaurant/bar with a giant neon sign that screams for attention. Close by, at Hidalgo 245, you'll find *Amigos Pub*, which serves Mexican dishes and gallons of booze by night. Good-value **cafés** and *loncherías* line Matamoros – try *Las Cazuelas* at 44, where you'll find economical fare including tacos and enchiladas.

**Onward transport** is more frequent from towns further south, and it may be easier to head to Piedras Negras, ninety minutes away, and change **buses** there; however, there are a few daily services from Acuña to **Saltillo** (7hr) and **Monterrey** (8hr) via Monclova, and a couple to Mexico City and Torreón. In addition, El Águila buses go to **Guadalajara** (1 daily), **Zacatecas** (2 daily) and **Chihuahua** (1 daily). The airline-style Expresso Futura buses (a/c, reclining seats, toilets and videos) have one daily service each to Mexico City, Querétaro and San Luis Potosí.

## Piedras Negras and Monclova

Quaint, friendly and hassle-free, with the most laid-back immigration officers you're likely to encounter anywhere in Mexico, **PIEDRAS NEGRAS** is the ideal border town. The unpretentious main square is directly opposite the international bridge, and hotels and restaurants aren't far away. Nonetheless, there's no reason to stay longer than it takes to catch the first bus south, which traverses a parched plain before cutting through gaps in the mountains past **Monclova**, some four hours from Piedras Negras. Now little more than the site of a vast steelworks, Monclova can make a useful staging point, but you wouldn't go out of your way to visit.

Piedras Negras's extremely helpful **tourist office** (Mon–Fri 9am–5pm; ⓣ878/782-8424, ⓦwww.proturac.com), by the main square as you enter Mexico from the US, has free maps of the town and Eagle Pass on the other side, as well as of other cities in Coahuila. From the customs post, Allende runs straight ahead towards the bus station, while Hidalgo heads left past one of the longer-established **hotels**, *Hotel Santos*, Hidalgo 314 at the corner of Matamoros (ⓣ878/782-4775; ❹), though like almost all the others in town it seems to be suffering from years of neglect and border-town overpricing. Slightly nicer and more economical hotels can be found on Zaragoza, beyond the market square. These include the *Torreón*, Zaragoza and Dr Coss (ⓣ878/782-5043, ⓕ878/782-2984; ❸), which has plain, simple rooms; and the very similar *Hotel Reforma*, Zaragoza 507 Sur (ⓣ878/782-0390; ❸). Better still, stretch for the nearby and comfortable *Hotel Santa Rosa*, Guerrero 401 Ote, on the corner of Morelos (ⓣ878/782-0400; ❹), with bright rooms set around a plant-filled, tiled courtyard, or the luxurious Best Western-owned *Autel Río*, Padre de las Casas 121 Nte, at Teran (ⓣ878/782-7064, ⓔautelrio@prodigy.net.mx; ❻), with a TV in every room, a swimming pool and plenty of parking space; they also offer guests free Internet access in the lobby.

For a great introduction to cheap Mexican **food**, head straight for the *taquerías* around the market. If you want a cheapish sit-down meal, *Los Gitanos* on Zaragoza and Allende is popular with the locals and serves comida corrida. You could also check out *La Hacienda*, across from the *Autel Río*, which has a pricier buffet and dishes out Mexican fare. For **currency exchange**, head for one of the numerous stalls around the bus station, as rates here are generally very good; also try the market at Zaragoza 107. Bancomer (Mon–Sat 9am–5pm), one block from the main plaza on Morelos and Abasolo, has a 24-hour ATM.

The **bus station** (ⓣ878/782-7484) is a fifteen-minute walk from the main plaza along Allende. The main companies, Blancos and Águila, operate a decent second-class service, with frequent departures to all the major points south. Expresso Futura buses run to **Mexico City**, **Aguascalientes** and **Monterrey**, while Turistar Ejecutivo luxury buses serve **Mexico City**, **Monclova** and **Querétaro**. Frontera second-class buses have frequent departures to **Nuevo Laredo**, three hours away. The Coahuilense service to **Saltillo** takes around seven hours.

If you're headed **Stateside**, cross the border to Eagle Pass, Texas, and walk 200m north to the Greyhound station, which has four direct departures to San Antonio daily, and one a day to Dallas.

## Nuevo Laredo

The giant of the eastern border towns, **NUEVO LAREDO** is alive with the imagery and commercialism of the frontier. It doubles as the transport hub for the whole area, with dozens of departures to Mexico City and all major towns in the north. Cross-border traffic, legal and illegal, is king here, and both bridges from the Texan town of Laredo are crowded with pedestrians and vehicles 24 hours a day. The Mexican side greets you with insurance offices and sleazy

cantinas, while tired horses hitched to buggies wait dispiritedly for their next load of pasty, overweight tourists.

You'll do best to head straight out: the road **south from Nuevo Laredo** – towards the vibrant northern capital, Monterrey – at first crosses a flat, scrub-covered, featureless plain, but after an hour the scenery begins to improve as far to the west the peaks of the **Sierra Madre** rise abruptly. Easily the most noticeable plants are the giant yuccas known as **Joshua trees**; to the early settlers their upraised, spiky branches brought to mind Joshuas hands raised in supplication.

## Arrival, orientation and information

As a tourist entering or leaving Mexico, you'll take Puente Internacional no. 1; there's a small toll, payable in dollars or pesos if you're heading north, but in US currency only (US$0.35) when Mexico-bound. Despite the crush, immigration usually proceeds smoothly, though expect long queues crossing to the US in the mornings and on Sunday evenings.

Nuevo Laredo's huge **Central Camionera** (24hr guardería) is some distance south of town on Romo and Melgar, but battered city buses (marked "Puente"/ "Centro") run frequently between here, the border crossings and Plaza Hidalgo; it's about a 25-minute journey. Nuevo Laredo is served by buses from Monterrey (3hr) and Mexico City (15hr) day and night. Other buses come from and go to Saltillo, Ciudad Victoria, Guadalajara and Zacatecas; there are even a couple of services to Acapulco. Greyhound, Turismos Rapidos, El Espresso and Azabache all offer identically priced direct services between the Central Camionera and San Antonio, Austin, Houston and Dallas.

The **Nuevo Laredo International Airport** is a long taxi ride (about M$130) out of town. There's actually nothing international about it, as the only two (very expensive) flights available are between here and Guadalajara or Mexico City (both on Mexicana).

Coming from Laredo, head up Guerrero, past the curio shops and dozens of casas de cambio, and you'll find everything you're likely to need within seven or eight blocks of the border. Walk past the first square, **Plaza Juárez**, home to the cathedral and Nuevo Mercado de la Reforma craft market, and head for the main square, the palm-shaded **Plaza Hidalgo**, easily the most pleasant spot in the city. There are no pavement cafés on the plaza, which is a pity, but pretty much everything else you'd want is nearby.

The helpful **tourist office** (Mon–Fri 9am–3pm, Sat 10am–1pm; ⓣ867/712-7397, ⓦwww.nuevolaredo.gob.mx) is about twenty blocks from the border in the Palacio Federal just alongside Plaza Hidalgo; you may also be able to pick up leaflets and a useful map of the town from lobbies of the larger hotels, though theoretically these are for guests only. There are a few places to access the **Internet** in town, though none right near the border; try Cyberactivo, at Guerrero 1220, up on the third floor (Mon–Sat 9am–9pm, Sun 11am–6pm; M$10/hr). Buses to the Central Camionera (marked "Carretera") leave from outside the Palacio Municipal – which houses the **post office** – tucked around the back on Camargo. Bancomer and Serfin **banks**, both with ATMs, are around the corner at the junction of Reforma and Canales, which is also a good area to begin looking for a hotel if you need one.

## Accommodation

Although there's no shortage of inexpensive **hotels** in the city centre – especially along Hidalgo – many of them are extremely run down, and frequented by prostitutes and their clients, so check what you're getting very carefully before parting with any money. Nonetheless, against the admittedly low standard of hotels in Mexican border towns in general, Nuevo Laredo's are decent value and in reasonable condition. If you arrive late, however, you will likely find most of the cheaper rooms taken.

**Don Antonio** González 2435, at Camargo ⓣ867/712-1876. Clean and comfortable, but a step below *La Finca*. ❹

**Los Dos Laredos** Matamoros 108 ⓣ867/712-2419. Simple, plain rooms with bathrooms and fairly plentiful hot water, and evening accompaniment from the local clubs. Only one block from the border; turn right along 15 de Julio. ❶

**Fiesta** Ocampo 559 ⓣ867/712-4737. Relatively modern place with unrealized pretensions to grandeur but comfortable a/c rooms all with telephone, some larger and with TV. ❺

**La Finca** Reynosa 811 ⓣ867/712-8883. Modern motel-style place with a/c, TV-equipped rooms that are always clean and in good condition. Excellent value with ample parking. ❺

**Motel Romanos** Doctor Mier 2420, one block east from Plaza Hidalgo ⓣ867/712-2391. Decked out in substandard Grecian pillars, this hotel is somehow more reminiscent of a bawdy house than imperial Rome, but the beds are big and fit for an emperor. ❹

**Regis** Pino Suárez 3013 ⓣ867/712-9845. A good but pricier alternative if everything else is full. Don't be put off by the smell of urinal mints in the lobby: the rooms are adequate and don't share the same fine aroma. ❺

## Eating

There are plenty of decent places to **eat** around town: try the air-conditioned, reasonably priced and friendly *Café Almanza*, González 272, on the south side of Plaza Hidalgo, which serves decent Mexican fare and comida corrida. *Mi Tierra*, Matamoros 704, is a large, clean restaurant that has fairly economical steak and egg breakfasts. For something slightly more upmarket, *Mexico Tipico*, Guerrero 934, is a good place for dinner or an evening drink.

## Reynosa



A very easy border crossing and excellent transport connections combine to make **REYNOSA** a favourite point to enter Mexico. A sprawling industrial city filled with car repair shops and Pemex plants, it holds little to detain you, but the centre is compact, people are generally friendly and coming and going is simple. Crossing the international bridge over the Río Bravo from McAllen, Texas (US$0.25 coin-op pedestrian toll), don't forget to call in at the *migración* office (assuming you're headed south) and perhaps the small **tourist office** (Mon–Fri 9am–3pm; Ⓣ899/922-5184, Ⓦwww.tamaulipas.gob.mx), though don't expect too much enlightening information. The **bus station** is probably your first priority, and though buses do run into the centre and out again to the Central Camionera, it's easier simply to tackle the twenty-minute walk. Immediately off the bridge, head straight on along Lerdo de Tejada, which soon becomes Zaragoza, to the Plaza Principal, about five blocks down, where you'll find a couple of **banks** with ATMs. From here the bus station can be reached by following Hidalgo, the pedestrianized main street, for a few blocks and then turning left into Colón. Your best bet for **Internet** access is Cybertel, off the plaza at Zaragoza and Hidalgo, where upstairs you'll find a dozen new computers with fast connections (daily 10am–10pm; M$15/hr).

**Hotels** here aren't great value for your money, but *Hotel Avenida*, Zaragoza 885 Ote (Ⓣ899/922-0592; ❺), and the comparable *Hotel Internacional*, Zaragoza 1050 (Ⓣ899/922-2318, Ⓔexportadores@aol.com; ❺), both a five-minute walk to the centre from the border, are certainly comfortable enough, the latter having a slight edge. *Hotel Comfort*, Hidalgo 325 about six blocks south of the plaza (Ⓣ899/922-7955; ❷), has reasonable, if aging, rooms as well as some newer, pricier ones; *Hotel Estación*, Hidalgo 305 Sur, across from the *Comfort* (Ⓣ899/922-7302; ❶), is a less than appealing, and not wonderfully clean, introduction to Mexican hotels, but it's at least cheap. Opposite the bus station there's the luxurious *Grand Premier Hotel*, Colón 1304 (Ⓣ899/922-4850, Ⓕ922-1150; ❻).

There are a number of inexpensive **food stalls** and a Gigante supermarket by the bus station, as well as a well-stocked **market** on Hidalgo, midway between the train station and the plaza. For a proper meal, you can't fault *Café Paris*, Hidalgo 873 Nte, which serves great, inexpensive breakfasts (M$30) and comidas (M$70) in comfortable surroundings – occasionally someone wheels past a trolley full of cakes for your delectation.

For **moving on** from Reynosa, the Valley Transit Co operates buses between Reynosa and McAllen, Texas, roughly every fifteen minutes until 11.30pm (M$30). The nine-kilometre journey takes about forty minutes, including immigration. Autobuses Americana (Ⓣ899/922-0705) runs two services daily to Houston and San Antonio, with connections beyond, as does Greyhound. Buses to the rest of Mexico include services to Matamoros and Ciudad Victoria; Tampico, Tuxpán and Veracruz on the Gulf coast; and even an overnight bus to Villahermosa (24hr).

## Matamoros

**MATAMOROS**, across the Río Grande from the southernmost point of Texas, at Brownsville, is a buzzing little town with more history than the settlements strung out to its west. What began in the mid-eighteenth century as a cattle-ranching colony eventually became known – with the introduction of the port

of Bagdad – as "La Puerta México", and in the nineteenth century Matamoros (along with Veracruz) became the main port of entry for foreign immigrants. At the turn of the nineteenth century, rail lines from both sides of the border were directed through Matamoros, and again the city found itself as the necessary link in the trade crossroads. And since the passage of **NAFTA** in 1994, Matamoros has established itself as an important point for trade.

## Arrival and information

Stateside, the Brownsville **Chamber of Commerce**, two blocks from the border at 1600 E Elizabeth St (Mon–Fri 8am–5pm; in the US ⓣ956/542-4341, ⓕ504-3348), has leaflets on the valley of the Río Grande and a Matamoros-knowledgeable staff. The Matamoros **tourist office** (Mon–Fri 9am–7pm; ⓣ871/812-3630), right at the Mexican border post, is worthwhile for the latest Matamoros info, or for any destinations further south. Having paid your US$0.25 toll, walked across the bridge and dealt with immigration, you'll be wanting the casa de cambio at the border before boarding the fixed-price *peseros*, known here as "maxi taxis", which run frequently along Obregón to the centre and the **Central Camionera** (ⓣ871/812-2777; restaurant and guardería 6.30am–10.30pm), a long way south (look for "Centro" for Plaza Allende, "Puente Internacional" for the border or "Central" for the bus station). If heading into the Mexican interior, don't forget to have your tourist card stamped at the border.

## Accommodation

**Staying** in Matamoros is no problem. There are hotels in all price categories, including several good budget choices on Abasolo, the pedestrianized street between calles 6 and 11, a block north of Plaza Hidalgo. There are also a number of **more expensive** hotels in the same area; if you're in a large group, it can be worthwhile asking for a suite.

**Alameda** Victoria 91 ⓣ868/816-7108. Lovely, clean and well-furnished rooms with TV, either in the main hotel (M$235) or across the road where they are larger and newer, a/c affairs (M$360). A great deal for Matamoros. ❸–❹

**Autel Nieto** C 10 1508, between Bravo and Bustamante ⓣ868/813-0857, ⓔautelnieto@hotmail.com. Well-kept, carpeted rooms all with cable TV and telephone. There's a two-bedroom master suite that sleeps nine. Parking space and very kitschy lounge/lobby. ❺

**Chalet** near the bus station at Aguilar 7 ⓣ868/812-5975. Best bus-station hotel option with comfortable, clean quarters, all with en-suite bathrooms. There's also an Internet café attached. ❹

**Colonial** corner of C 6 and Matamoros ⓣ868/816-6606, ⓦwww.hcolonial.com. This is your best mid-range choice. Loaded with Mexican style and colour, the clean rooms are done in tile and brick, with small balconies. ❻

**Fiesta Gallo** very near the bus station at Aguilar 10 ⓣ868/813-4406. If you're only interested in a comfortable bed for the night, then this fits the bill. ❹

**Majestic** Abasolo 131 ⓣ868/813-3680. Best value among the budget hotels; the staff are friendly and rooms are clean, spacious and have ample hot water. ❸

**México** Abasolo, between C 8 and C 9 ⓣ868/812-0856. Simple, comfortable and the price is right. ❶

**Plaza Matamoros** at C 9 and Bravo ⓣ868/816-1696, ⓦwww.bestwestern.com/mx/hotelplazamatamoros. Best Western-owned; clean and safe, with somewhat predictable decor. Restaurant, parking and rooms with a/c and cable TV. ❼

**Plaza Riviera** corner of Morelos and C 10 ⓣ868/816-3998, ⓕ816-4299. Very comfortable refurbished hotel split into two buildings, though the rooms in one costs M$65 more for little apparent reason. Good value for the price: rooms are light and spacious and the hotel offers free Internet access for guests in the lobby. ❻

**Ritz** Matamoros 612 ⓣ868/812-1190. Comfortable a/c hotel, whose rates include buffet breakfast. There's a suite available for six people, plus plenty of safe parking, and it's about M$100 cheaper at weekends. ❻

**Roma** at C 9 and Bravo ⓣ868/813-6176, ⓦwww.hotelfroma.com. Nearly as nice as the Best Western across the street, and half the price. A considerable saving for groups of up to five. ❺

**San Francisco** C 10 between Abasolo and González ⓣ868/813-7110. Slightly insalubrious central budget hotel with shared showers. Be aware that it attracts its share of the one-hour crowd. ❷

## The town and Playa Bagdad

Matamoros's orientation is not all that difficult even for those with little experience of Mexican street grids. The streets around the centre, about 1.5km from the border crossing, are easily navigated: numbered streets run north–south and named streets run east–west. The busy but compact centre, focused on **plazas** Hidalgo and Allende and the **Mercado Juárez**, on calles 9 and 10, is a fairly stereotypical Mexican city centre. It's also a surprisingly youthful place, with a lively entertainment scene: the plazas and shopping streets seem to be almost entirely filled with teenagers, their numbers swollen by Americans dodging the Texan age limit on drinking.

If you've got an hour to kill, pop along to the **Museo Casa Mata**, Santos Degollado at Guatemala (Tues–Sat 8am–4pm, Sun 9am–2pm; free), which houses a collection of memorabilia from the Revolution and a selection of Huastec ceramics in a fort begun in 1845 to repel invaders from north of the border. When Zachary Taylor stormed in the following year, however, the building was still unfinished. Near the centre at the northeast corner of Abasolo and Calle 6, is the historic **Teatro de la Reforma**, originally built in 1864, and in 1881 the site of a festival honouring General Porfirio Díaz and his first four years as president (he would remain president until 1911). In 1992 the theatre was restored at the request of the town mayor, and now hosts drama and ballet performances, and various local entertainment.

**Playa Bagdad** (formerly "Playa Lauro Villar"), Matamoros's pleasant beach 35km east of town, was renamed after the US port of Bagdad, which stood at the mouth of the Río Grande and was at one point the only port supplying the Confederates during the Civil War. Clean (though watch out for broken glass) and pounded by invigorating surf, it offers the chance for a first (or last) dip in the surf off Mexico's Gulf coast, and is very popular at weekends with Mexican families, who gather in the shade of the palapas that stretch for miles along the sand. There are lots of **seafood restaurants**, but few actually seem to offer much worth eating, so most locals bring picnics or cook on the public barbecues. You'll need half a day to make a worthwhile trip out to the beach, though you can **camp** for free in the sandhills. To get there, take a *combi* marked "Playa" from the Plaza Allende, which drops you off in the car park by the Administración. It takes about an hour, and the office has showers (small charge) and lockers where you can safely store your clothes while you swim.



### Eating

Although most **restaurants** in Matamoros are fairly expensive – lots cater to cross-border trade – there are plenty of places for cheap, filling meals lining Calle 10 just off Plaza Allende, Calle 9 between Matamoros and Bravo, and a few *taquería* stands on the pedestrian *peotonál*, Abasolo.

**Caféteria Deli** Matamoros 82. Clean, bright restaurant serving a range of well-priced Mexican mains for around M$30.

**Caféteria Natalia's** C 5 between Abasolo and González, at Matamoros. Great diner-style place offering well-priced Mexican staples. Open until late, this makes a great pre-theatre stop if you're thinking of catching a performance at the *teatro* a block away.

**El Chinchonal** C 9 at Matamoros. A good lunch place serving a wide range of inexpensive home-cooked dishes. They close early, though, so don't plan to be eating here after about 4pm or so.

**Las Dos Repúblicas** C 9 off Abasolo. Nice colonial-style restaurant dishing up mammoth plates of tortillas, tacos, quesadillas and the like until around 7pm; everything on the menu costs about M$40.

**Los Feroles** Matamoros across from the *Ritz Hotel*. Though plainly decorated, it offers well-priced Continental dishes like cheese sandwiches (M$30) and steak fillets (M$70) as well as an excellent buffet breakfast (M$70).

### Listings

**Banks and exchange** There are branches of Bancomer at the corner of Matamoros and C 5, on the plaza itself, and Serfin (all operate Mon–Fri 9am–3pm). There are decent currency exchange facilities in the centre: head for Banorte, on Morelos between C 6 and C 7.

**Buses** The Central Camionera is well served by buses to the US and to the interior of Mexico. Greyhound has representatives in both Matamoros and Brownsville (in the US ☎956/546-7171), and has buses that cross the border to Brownsville for M$40, and they run all night. US-bound buses are frequent: Greyhound (cheaper than El Expresso) ventures to Houston (M$280), San Antonio (M$280) and Dallas (M$510), and offers brave souls a 48hr journey to New York (M$1430). El Expresso will take you to Miami for M$1600. Reynosa, Monterrey, Ciudad Victoria and Mexico City have frequent departures, and there is also a bus to Puebla. Heading west, Transportes Estrella de Oro serves Mexicali, Guadalajara and Mazatlán, while Autotransportes de Oriente covers the coast route, with buses to Tampico (7hr), Tuxpán (11hr), Veracruz (16hr) and Villahermosa (24hr).

**Internet access** There are a few places off lower Abasolo. Try Cybernet, Matamoros between C 5 and C 6 (Mon–Sat 10am–10pm, Sun 2–6pm; M$15/hr) or Cyber Soluciones, C 11 at Morelos (Mon–Sat 9am–9pm, Sun 10am–9pm; M$15/hr).

**Post office** In the Central Camionera.

## The coastal route

The eastern seaboard has so little to recommend it that even if you've crossed the border at Matamoros, you'd be well advised to follow the border road west

## NAFTA, Mexico and the maquiladora debate

**NAFTA** (North American Free Trade Agreement), or **TLC** (El Tratado de Libre Comercio) in Mexico, went into effect on January 1, 1994, and created the largest free-trade area in the world. The comprehensive agreement sought to improve virtually all aspects of trade between its three partners – Mexico, the US and Canada – with many trade duties immediately cut and the rest to be phased out by 2009. Ever since, however, the benefit of NAFTA has been widely contested and remains a hot subject for debate among the three countries involved.

At the epicentre of this debate sits Mexico's **maquiladora** programme, with the dramatic population increase and the host of environmental and humanitarian problems it has brought to Mexico's borderlands. The term *maquiladora*, from the Spanish *maquilar* (to perform a task for another), today refers to a Mexican corporation, entirely or predominantly owned by foreigners, which assembles products for export to the US or other foreign countries. Sometimes referred to as "production sharing" or "the global assembly line", the programme was originally touted as a win-win situation for all – foreign businesses could reduce overheads and enjoy larger profits, while Mexico could partake in foreign exchange while retaining its citizens. When NAFTA was passed in 1994, scores of US companies rushed to Mexican border towns. The *maquiladora* plants now employ millions of people in Mexico, about seventy percent of whom are located in the border area. After petroleum and tourism, the *maquiladora* programme is the third most important source of foreign exchange.

But the picture is not entirely rosy. In the richest-ever manifestation of US financial spillover (except, perhaps, the drug industry), Mexican migrants now crowd the border towns in search of employment, while the area continues to lack the necessary infrastructure to sustain such numbers. Many *maquiladora* workers are forced to dwell in shantytowns on city outskirts. Also, the cost of living on Mexico's border tends to be higher than in the southern states, further contributing to poverty problems.

Moreover, numerous **environmental studies** assert that *maquiladoras* have dumped everything from raw sewage to toxic metals into the local land. Children have been poisoned by toxins at dump sites, and defunct *maquiladoras* have left behind drums of hazardous waste. Lab samples from waterways in several border towns, too, have revealed abnormal deposits of **industrial chemicals**, petroleum and various industrial solvents. Sadly, there is little political will to improve the environmental damage that the *maquiladoras* are wreaking along the border. What's more, **abuse** of *maquiladora* workers has also entered the picture, and employees have come forth with horrific tales of unjust working conditions and treatment. This is particularly true of female workers, who are subjected to sexist and humiliating policies. While third-party coalitions have sprung up, hoping to improve the working and living conditions of workers, most *maquiladora* employees remain unaware of their rights; most unions are corrupt, and attempts to forge new, independent unions result in government opposition.

While Mexican policy-makers originally proclaimed the *maquiladora* industry as a necessary, temporary evil to aid Mexico's troubled economy, it now seems part of the backbone of the country's long-term economic strategy. And though Mexico has perhaps the strongest anti-NAFTA following of the three countries involved, pro-NAFTA devotees are equally abundant, especially in the north, where new fortunes can and have been made. Unfortunately for this new wealthy management class, Mexico is losing business at an alarming rate to other parts of the world with even lower-cost labour, especially China and Southeast Asia. The proposed FTAA (Free Trade Area of the Americas) would also give Mexico more labour competition for the North American market from smaller, impoverished Latin American nations. NAFTA and regional free trade remain hotly contested issues, but for the time being are here to stay.

to **Reynosa** and then cut down to Monterrey (see p.224). Unless you're determined to go straight down through Veracruz to the Yucatán by the shortest route, avoiding Mexico City altogether, there seems little point in following the coast. Even the time factor is less of an advantage than it might appear on the map – the roads are in noticeably worse repair than those through the heartland, and progress is considerably slower. Beyond Tampico, it's true, you get into an area of great archeological interest, with some good beaches around Veracruz, though these are probably best approached from the capital. Here in the northeast there's plenty of sandy beachfront, but access is difficult, beaches tend to be windswept and scrubby, and the whole area is marred by the consequences of its enormous oil wealth: there are refineries all along the coast, tankers passing close offshore and a shoreline littered with their discards and spillages. It's also very, very hot.

At the time of the Spanish Conquest this area of the Gulf coast was inhabited by the **Huastecs**, who gave their name to the region around Tampico and the eastern flanks of the Sierra Madre Oriental. Huastec settlement can be dated back some 3000 years; their language differs substantially from the surrounding native tongues, but has close links with the Maya of Yucatán. **Quetzalcoatl**, the feathered serpent god of Mexico, was probably of Huastec origin. At their most powerful between 800 and 1200 AD – just before the Aztecs rose to dominance – the Huastecs were still at war with the Aztecs when the Spanish arrived in the sixteenth century, finding them willing allies. After a successful campaign against Tenochtitlán, the Aztec capital, the Spanish, first under Cortés and later the notorious Nuño de Guzmán, turned on the independent-minded Huastecs, decimating and enslaving their former allies.

## Ciudad Victoria

**CIUDAD VICTORIA**, capital of the state of Tamaulipas, is little more than a place to stop over for a night. It's not unattractive but neither is it interesting, and while the surrounding hill country is a paradise for hunters and fishing enthusiasts, with a huge artificial lake called the **Presa Vicente Guerrero**, others will find little to detain them. The **bus station** (guardería daily 7am–10.30pm) is a couple of kilometres out of town and, if you arrive late, the *Hotel Colonial*, Articulo 123 no. 912 (Ⓣ834/316-7707; ❷), left out of the station and then first left, is shaded, cool and probably the cheapest place you'll find; avoid the noisy front rooms if you can. Local buses run frequently into the centre, where most of the town's facilities are concentrated around the zócalo, Plaza Hidalgo, but aside from the rather bland church, there isn't a whole lot going on. You've got several **hotels** to choose from here, including the excellent *Los Monteros*, Hidalgo 962 (Ⓣ834/312-0300, Ⓦwww.paginasprodigy.com/losmonteros; ❹), a lovely old colonial building with large rooms that are much cheaper than you might expect, and *Hostal de Escandón*, Juárez 143 at Hidalgo (Ⓣ834/312-9004; ❸), which offers good, clean rooms and meals for M$20 or so. Almost equally high standards and similar prices are maintained by a couple of places a block or so away: *Hotel Posada Don Diego*, Juárez 814 Ote (Ⓣ834/312-1279; ❸), has some nice large rooms, all with TV and a/c. For **food**, the main plaza has a few options serving typical Mexican food at good prices – a full plate of chicken with vegetables and rice costs about M$40. *Restaurant Los Candiles*, in *Hotel Sierra Gorda*, serves pricier Mexican fare, breakfasts and comida corrida at lunch time. You can check the **Internet** at *El Portal*, Hidalgo 990 (daily 8am–11pm; M$10/hr).

## Tampico

Along the 200km of road southeast from Ciudad Victoria to **TAMPICO**, the country's busiest port, the vegetation becomes increasingly lush, green and tropical – the Tropic of Cancer passes just south of Ciudad Victoria, and the Río Pánuco forms the border with the steamy Gulf state of Veracruz. As a treasure port in the Spanish empire, Tampico suffered numerous pirate raids and was destroyed in 1684. Rebuilding didn't begin in earnest until 1823, the date of the cathedral's foundation, and in 1828 Spain landed troops in Tampico in a vain and short-lived attempt to reconquer its New World empire. The discovery of oil in 1901 sparked Tampico's rise to prominence as the world's biggest oil port in the early years of the twentieth century.

Tampico's oil boom lasted into the 1920s, with many of the city's finer buildings constructed during this period of rapid economic growth. Today, following a decline in fortunes, the older parts of town have a slightly dilapidated feel, with peeling, ramshackle clapboard houses. Additionally, many *campesinos* and unskilled labourers have moved to town from the surrounding rural areas in search of work, contributing to a visible homelessness problem and adding to the air of decay.

### Arrival and information

Tampico's modern **bus station** (guardería 6am–midnight) is in an unattractive area some 10km north of the city, though waiting for buses here can be one of northern Mexico's little pleasures, as the waiting hall offers comfortable couches. To get downtown, take a bus, a rattling *colectivo* or one of the shared *perimetral* taxis (all M$4). Buses back to the camionera leave from the Plaza de Armas, at the corner of Olmos and Carranza. The grid-plan downtown area also centres on the Plaza de Armas, where the junction of Carranza and Colón marks the point at which the cardinal suffixes on street names change.

You'll find **tourist information booths** on both plazas, though these seem to be open quite irregularly. If you need a map, you could try asking in one of the swankier hotels. The **post office** at Madero 309 is easy to find, upstairs in the Correos building on the north side of the Plaza de la Libertad, and there are **banks** on the Plaza de Armas and all through the central area. Numerous **Internet** cafés line 20 de Noviembre near the plaza: try SCACT, Obregón 116 (daily 9am–11pm), or Club Mita Net, Carranza 106 (daily 8am–9pm), both of which charge M$10 per hour.

### Accommodation

One thing you can say for Tampico is that there's no shortage of **hotels**, though most are either expensive or very sleazy. Downtown, many of the cheaper hotels around the docks, train station and market area operate partly as brothels.

**Best Western Gran Hotel Sevilla** at the southwest end of the Plaza de la Libertad ⓣ833/214-2833, ⓦwww.bestwestern.com. Some of the sleek, wooden-floored rooms at this *Best Western* come with great views of the plaza. ❻

**Capri** Juárez 202 Nte ⓣ&ⓕ833/212-2680. One of the cheapest acceptable options downtown, centrally located about four blocks north of the plaza and with small, bright rooms. ❷

**Hotel La Central** Rosalio Bustamante 224 ⓣ833/217-0388. Opposite the bus station, this hotel has a complex tariff system but is probably the best deal in town. ❷

**Hotel Inglaterra** Díaz Mirón 116 ⓣ833/219-2857. On the Plaza de Armas, this is the most luxurious option in town, with a restaurant and a small pool. ❼

**Hotel Santa Helena** Rosalio Bustamante 303 ⓣ&ⓕ833/213-3507. Also opposite the bus station, the rooms here aren't as good value as those at *La Central*, but they do have a/c and TV, and there's a good, if pricey restaurant. ❺

**Impala** Díaz Mirón 220 Pte ⓣ833/212-0990, ⓕ212-2500. This aged hotel has been renovated and is now exceptionally clean, even elegant. ❻

**Posada del Rey** Madero 218 Ote ⓣ833/214-1024, ⓕ212-1077. Comfortable lodgings on the Plaza de la Libertad. The spacious rooms overlook the square; they can be a bit noisy. ❹

**Regis** Madero 605 Ote ⓣ833/212-0290. The rooms at the *Regis*, a five-minute walk from the plaza, are plain and high-ceilinged. There's a Chinese restaurant attached. ❺



## The town and around

Downtown, the city's dual nature is instantly apparent. Within a hundred metres of each other are two plazas: the grandiose **Plaza de Armas** – rich and formal, it is ringed by government buildings, the cathedral (built in the 1930s with money donated by American oil tycoon Edward Doheny) and the smart hotels; and the **Plaza de la Libertad**, which is raucous, rowdy – there's usually some form of music played from the bandstand each evening – and peopled by wandering salesmen. Ringed by triple-decker wrought-iron verandas, it has been spruced up in recent years to form an attractive square, almost New Orleans in flavour. Also worth a look is the **Casa de la Cultura**, formerly the town slaughterhouse and now home to an archeology and painting exhibition, with the second floor holding many of the town's archives and historical records. It's a bit of a hike to reach it (where Altamira runs into Hidalgo), so catch the "Águila" bus from the Plaza for M$4. To return, simply walk a block east until you reach Hidalgo, where you can jump on any number of buses headed into the centre.

Sadly, the docks pretty much cut off the centre of town from the water, so there's little to do here outside the centre, though you could head north to **Ciudad Madero**, Tampico's growing twin town, or onwards to **Playa Miramar**. The journey out is best made by bus or one of the lumbering 1970s Chevy *colectivos* (marked "Playa"; find them on Lopez de Lara, three blocks east of the Plaza de Armas), which will take you past the graceful arc of the new harbour-mouth bridge some 7km to the affluent, new and neatly planned suburbs of Ciudad Madero. Here it's worth calling in to see the Huastec artefacts at the small but excellent **Museo de la Cultura Huasteca** (Mon–Fri 10am–5pm, Sat 10am–3pm; free) in the Tecnológico Madero; get out at the Madero's central plaza, turn left along 1 de Mayo, and the museum is about 1km along, two blocks past the telecom tower. Playa Miramar, Tampico's town beach, lies a further 8km out (same buses and *colectivos*). Be warned that the water, extremely close to the refinery and the mouth of the river, is **heavily polluted**, and swimming is not recommended. That said, during the summer months, Semana Santa and weekends year-round, it seems that all Tampico is out here; at other times it's a little dispiriting with only a few run-down hotels, though there are a couple of little restaurants serving good fresh fish and offering showers for a small fee. This is also good **camping** territory, with a stand of small trees immediately behind the beach, and if you have your own transport you can drive miles up the sand to seek out isolation. In fact that's one other disadvantage out here – everyone insists on driving their cars around the beach, most local learners seem to take their first lessons here, and even the bus drives onto the sand to turn around.

## Eating

There are more than enough good **places to eat** to keep you happy for the day or so you might spend here. The town's gastronomical market, a block south of the Plaza de la Libertad, has numerous food stalls selling delicious seafood, especially crab.

**Comedor Silvina y Lorena** across from the bus station. Open 24hr, they serve unbeatable comidas whenever you're hungry.

**Elite Restaurante and Helados** Díaz Mirón 211 Ote. Offering a quiet haven in this noisy town, *Elite* does ice cream and good Mexican staples.

**Naturaleza** Aduana 107 Nte. Come here for buffet breakfasts and comida corrida lunches (8am–8.30pm). The same owners run the large health-food store next door.

**Super Cream "La Parroquia"** Olmos 201, at Altamira. This Tampico stand-by, a quick diner-style joint that serves fairly decent Mexican staples and ice cream, is clean and economical.

**La Troya** in the *Hotel Posada del Rey*. The best dining in town, if only for its location overlooking the Plaza de la Libertad. The menu itself consists of strong Spanish and seafood dishes.

## The road to San Luis Potosí

It is a seven-hour run from Tampico to San Luis Potosí (see p.250) – ideal for a sleep-over on a night bus you might think, but there are a couple of places along the way you could consider breaking the journey for. The town of **Río Verde**, surrounded by lush fields of maize, coffee and citrus fruit, is ringed by thermal springs and has the benefit of a small lake, the **Laguna de la Media Luna**, which is popular with snorkellers and divers. Still further east, the highway comes to **Ciudad Valles**, a busy commercial town some 140km from Tampico and the coast. The frequent **buses** to San Luis Potosí, Mexico City and Monterrey will set you back about M$390.

# Monterrey and around

The third-largest city in Mexico, capital of Nuevo León and the nation's industrial stronghold, **MONTERREY** is a contradictory place. While the vast network of factories, the traffic, urban sprawl, pollution and ostentatious wealth that characterize the modern city are relatively recent developments, the older parts retain an air of colonial elegance. The city's setting, too, is one of great natural beauty – ringed by jagged mountain peaks (which sadly serve also to keep in the noxious industrial fumes), the Cerro de la Silla, or "Saddle Mountain", dominates the landscape. But what makes Monterrey really outstanding is the abundance of modern architecture and the bold statuary sprouting everywhere, expressions of Mexico at its most confident. Even if they're not to your taste, there is nowhere better to set yourself up for the dramatic contrast of the colonial heartland to come.

In addition to the national and religious holidays, autumn in Monterrey sees a number of local festivals. There's the weekend-long brewery-sponsored **Fiesta de la Cerveza**, in early October, as well as the **Festival Alfonso Reyes**, with plenty of music and theatre, in the last week of October and the first week in November. The **Festival Cultural Barrio Antiguo** (Nov 15–25) is relatively new on the festival list but easily the city's favourite – cafés, galleries and restaurants open their doors to the masses of people strolling through the streets, with concerts, films, art exhibitions and the like.

## Arrival and information

Monterrey is the transport hub of the northeast, with excellent national and international connections. Flights from the rest of Mexico and from several points in the US (served by Continental, Delta and Northwest) arrive at **Mariano Escobedo International Airport** (Ⓣ81/8345-4434),

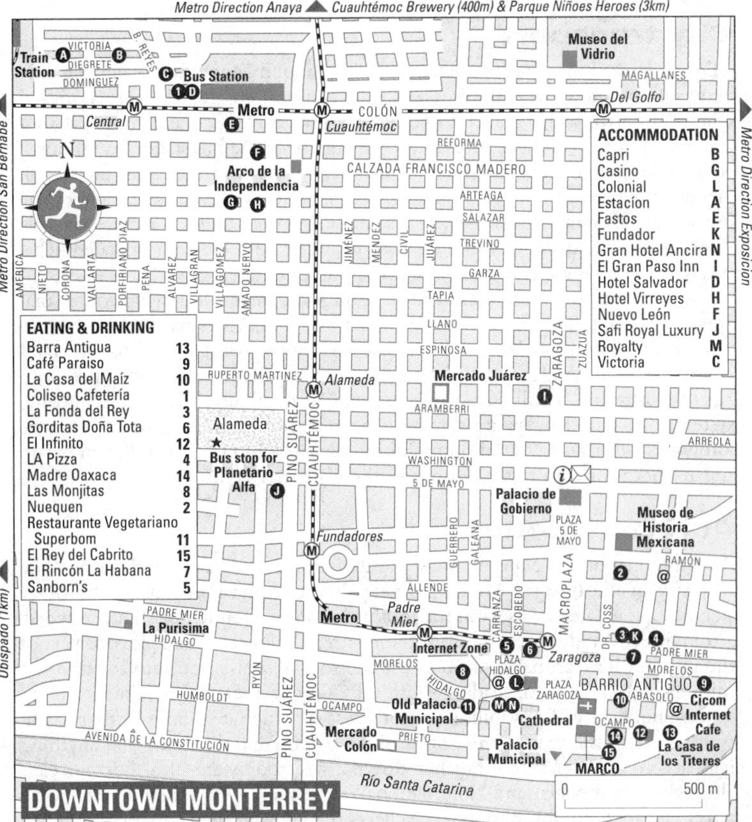


6km or so northeast of the city, only accessible by taxi for around M$225. On arrival you'll find pricey luggage storage and somewhere to change money.

Scores of **buses** pull into the enormous Central Camionera, northwest of the centre on Colón, complete with its own shopping centre, 24-hour guardería (though it is closed Fri 9pm–Sat 6.30am) and post office. To get from the **bus station** to the central Macroplaza, turn left towards the Cuauhtémoc metro station (see p.226) and take Line 2, or pick up a #1, #7, #17 or #18 bus heading down Pino Suárez and get off at a suitable intersection: Ocampo, Zaragoza or Juárez, for example. You can also get just about anywhere by **taxi** for M$30 or less; bargaining is generally in order here.

There's usually someone who can speak English at the helpful Infotur **tourist office**, Washington 648 Ote, inside the old Palacio Federal (Mon–Fri 9am–6pm; ⓣ81/8152-3333, ⓦwww.nl.gob.mx). They offer a wide variety of maps and leaflets – including the handy quarterly *Explore Monterrey* – and information on hotel prices and local travel agencies. For tourist information when dialling from outside Nuevo León, call ⓣ01-800/832-2200.

## City transport

Though limited in scope, the best way to get around Monterrey – and certainly between downtown and the bus and train stations – is to take the clean and efficient **metro**, which runs on two lines: Line 1 is elevated and runs east–west above Colón (you see it as soon as you emerge from the bus station); and Line 2 runs underground from the north of the city to the Macroplaza (at the station General I. Zaragoza), connecting with Line 1 at the Cuauhtémoc stop, right by the bus station. It's simple to use: tickets cost about M$4 per journey and are available singly or as a multi-journey card (at a small saving) from the coin-operated ticket machines. The system runs from around 5am until midnight.

The streets of Monterrey are almost solid with **buses**, following routes that appear incomprehensible at first sight. The city authorities have taken steps to resolve the confusion by numbering all the stops (*paradas*), having the fares written on the windscreen and occasionally providing the tourist office with **route plans**, but it still takes a fair amount of confidence to plunge into the system. The old clangers are slowly being replaced by more modern versions known as *panorámicos*, found on useful routes like #1, #17 and #18, which run north–south through town and out to the northern sights.

## Accommodation

Accommodation in Monterrey is possibly the worst value in Mexico. The majority of the **budget hotels** are near the bus station, mainly on the other side of Colón, safest crossed on the footbridge. Permanently noisy and crowded, a touch seedy and some way from the centre, it's not the most pleasant part of the city, but it's reasonably safe and the metro will whisk you into town in ten minutes. Amado Nervo, heading south off Colón immediately opposite the bus station, holds several possibilities, but it's best to penetrate a little further if you want to avoid the worst of the noise. Even so, you're unlikely to find anything half-decent under M$165. Further **downtown**, rooms are of a different class altogether, in modern and "international" hotels, all with a/c and many with pools. Geared up for business travellers, they lower their prices slightly at weekends. There's a good concentration in the so-called "zona hotelera" around Plaza Hidalgo.

**Capri** Victoria 1402 Pte ⓣ81/8375-0052, ⓕ8372-9164. Wonderfully gaudy *de paso* hotel that is normally the preserve of the one-hour crowd. It's heavily adorned with bright, fake flowers and has large rooms with telephones and cable TV. There's also a Jacuzzi. ❺

**Casino** Arteaga 816 ⓣ81/8372-0219. Another hourly rental, though it's relatively new and clean, with TV and a/c in the rooms. One of the better-value options among the bus-station hotels. ❻

**Colonial** Hidalgo 475 Ote ⓣ81/8380-6800, ⓦwww.hotelcolonialmty.com. Not quite luxurious, but fairly dignified nonetheless. It has spacious rooms, some with en-suite studies, but remains relatively poor value. ❻

**Estación** Victoria 1450 Pte ⓣ81/8375-0755. One of the nicest in the area with simple, comfortable and clean rooms arranged around a central courtyard. From the bus station turn right, then right up Bernardo Reyes for two blocks, then left onto Victoria. ❺

**Fastos** Colón 956 Pte, right opposite the bus station ⓣ81/8372-3250, US ⓣ1-800/839-2400, ⓕ81/8372-6100. Comfortable, modern hotel with large rooms all featuring a/c and satellite TV. Not bad value for Monterrey if you don't mind being so far from downtown. ❻

**Fundador** Montemayor 802 ⓣ81/8342-1694, ⓦwww.travelbymexico.com.mx. Colonial tile meets wood panelling. About the best value for money of all the hotels, and for now the only hotel in Barrio Antiguo, with comfortable and clean, if boring, a/c rooms, all with local TV. There's a fancy restaurant in the same building. ❺

**Gran Hotel Ancira** Hidalgo and Escobedo, on Plaza Hidalgo ⓣ81/8150-7000, US ⓣ1-800/333-3333, ⓦwww.hotel-ancira.com. Built as a grand hotel before the Revolution and full of period elegance, including a winding marble staircase, this is an outstanding (though very pricey, as rooms *start* at M$1600) upmarket option; owned and operated by Radisson. ⑨

**El Gran Paso Inn** Zaragoza 130 Nte ⓣ81/8340-0690, ⓦwww.elpasoautel.com. Decent mid-range option with winter rates and comfortable, if uninteresting rooms with cable TV and bath. It also has parking, a restaurant and a pool. ⑥

**Hotel Salvador** Villagran 1306 Nte ⓣ81/8374-5981, ⓕ81/8374-2545. Rooms are new and largish, with firm mattresses on hospital-bed frames, at this bus-station hotel. ④

**Hotel Virreyes** Amado Nervo 902 Nte ⓣ81/8374-6610. Another bus-station option that has clean and basic lodgings with fan and bathroom, but not much else. ④

**Nuevo León** Amado Nervo 1007 Nte ⓣ81/8374-1900. About the best value of several places on this street (but only just), and the cheapest rooms for lone travellers. Fans, TVs and cheap underground parking. ④

**Safi Royal Luxury** Pino Suárez 444 ⓣ81/8399-7000, ⓦwww.safihotel.com. Luxurious five-star hotel with expansive marble floors, elegant staircases and garden. The rooms are spacious, and there's a restaurant attached. ⑦

**Royalty** Hidalgo 402 Ote ⓣ81/8340-9800, US ⓣ1-800/830-9300, ⓦwww.royaltyhotel.com. Straightforward, middle-of-the-road business-style hotel with a/c rooms, cable TV, gym, Jacuzzi and a tiny pool. ⑥

**Victoria** Bernardo Reyes 1205 Nte ⓣ81/8375-6919. Slightly faded hotel that's a good bargain (though not the cheapest). Friendly, safe and only a block from the bus station, with some central rooms that aren't too noisy. From the bus station, turn right along Colón and then right onto Bernardo Reyes. ④

## The City

Most visitors' first impressions of Monterrey are unfavourable – the highway roars through shabby shantytown suburbs and grimy manufacturing outskirts – but the **city centre** is quite a different thing. Here, colonial relics are overshadowed by the office buildings and expensive shopping streets of the "zona comercial", and by some extraordinary modern architecture – the local penchant for planting buildings in the ground at bizarre angles is exemplified above all by the **Planetario Alfa** and the **Instituto Tecnológico**. The city in general rewards a day of wandering, but there are three places specifically worth going out of your way to visit – the old **Obispado**, on a hill overlooking the centre, the giant **Cervecería Cuauhtémoc** to the north and the magnificent **Museo de Arte Contemporáneo** (MARCO).

At the heart of Monterrey, if not the physical centre, is the **Macroplaza** (officially the Plaza Zaragoza, and sometimes known as the "Gran Plaza"), which was created by demolishing some six complete blocks of the city centre and opening up a new vista straight through from the intensely modern City Hall to the beautiful red-stone Palacio de Gobierno on what used to be Plaza 5 de Mayo. This is Mexican planning at its most extreme: when the political decision comes from the top, no conservationist or social considerations are going to stand in the way, especially as the constitution's "no re-election" decree makes every administrator determined to leave some permanent memorial. The result is undeniably stunning, with numerous lovely fountains, an abundance of striking statuary, quiet parks and shady patios, edged by the cathedral, museums and state administration buildings. There are frequent concerts, dances and other entertainments laid on; in the evenings people gravitate here to stroll, and to admire the laser beam that flashes out across the city from the top of the tall, graceful slab of orange concrete known as the **Faro del Comercio**.

The **cathedral**, with its one unbalanced tower, is a surprisingly modest edifice, easily dominated by the concrete bulk of the new **City Hall**, squatting on stilts at the southern end of the square. Opposite the cathedral, in the old City Hall, you'll find the **Museo Metropolitano** (Tues–Sun 10am–8pm; free) with its small art collection. Meanwhile, in the **Palacio de Gobierno** at the

△ Statuary, Monterrey Macroplaza

other end of the square is a room devoted to local history. Between the two lie the city's newest and most celebrated museums, the Museo de Arte Contemporáneo and the Museo de Historia Mexicana.

At the wonderful **Museo de Arte Contemporáneo**, or **MARCO**, at the junction of Zuazua and Ocampo by the cathedral (Tues–Sun 10am–6pm, Wed until 8pm; M$40, free on Wed; Ⓦ www.marco.org.mx), you're greeted by Juan Soriano's *La Paloma*, an immense sculpture of an obese black dove whose curvaceous lines stand in dramatic contrast to the angular terracotta lines of the museum building. It was built in 1991 to a design by Mexico's leading architect, **Ricardo Legorreta**, whose buildings are all highly individual but share common themes: visitors from the southwest of the US may recognize the style from various structures dotted around Texas, Arizona and New Mexico. Inside, none of the floors and walls seems to intersect at the same angle. The vast, at times whimsical, open plan centres on an atrium with a serene pool into which a pipe periodically gushes water: at the sound of the pump gurgling to life, you find yourself drawn to watch the ripple patterns subside. You might imagine that such a courageous building would overwhelm its contents, but if anything the opposite is true.

Apart from a couple of monumental sculptures tucked away in courtyards, there is no permanent collection, but the standards maintained by the temporary exhibits are phenomenally high. A key factor in this is undoubtedly the bias towards Latin American (particularly Mexican) artists, who are currently producing some of the world's most innovative and inspiring works. The quality art bookstore and fancy café are both worth visiting, but don't fail to stop by the lovely bar, right by the central pool.

Several blocks north of MARCO lies one of the city's best new museums, the **Museo de Historia Mexicana**, Dr Coss 445 Sur (Tues–Sun 10am–7pm; M$12, free on Tues), another bold architectural statement, though save for the double-helix staircase, a less successful one. All the ingredients appear to be there, though – displays on Mexico's ancient, colonial and modern civilizations, an extensive array of traditional costumes, interactive computer consoles and the story of the Revolution, along with associated paraphernalia. Should your patience with Mexican history wear thin, you might rent one of the roofed paddleboats (M$35/hr) below the museum's plaza to saunter about the huge fountain pool, or buy some bread and feed the schools of rather large fish which swim therein.

### Around the Macroplaza

West of the Macroplaza are smart shops, multinational offices and swanky hotels, centred on the little **Plaza Hidalgo** – a much more traditional, shady place, with old colonial buildings set around a statue of Miguel Hidalgo. The original Palacio Municipal, now superseded by the modern building, is here, acting today as an occasional cultural centre. Otherwise, the pavement cafés make a pleasant stop-off – though food is expensive. Pedestrianized shopping streets fan out behind, crowded with window-gazing locals.

Another part of the old centre survives to the east and has even grabbed the "**Barrio Antiguo**" tag, which seems appropriate for this increasingly gentrified district populated by chi-chi little galleries, appealingly laid-back cafés and, once the sun has gone down, the city's best nightlife opportunities. The city authorities are even playing ball, installing old-fashioned street lamps and taking measures to calm the traffic. There's usually a host of artistic goings-on here: check out the Centro Cultural Santa Lucía, Montemayor 510, for frequent photography, theatre and dance events, or have a glance at the bulletin boards posted in many of the local cafés and bars. There's also **La Casa de los Titeres** at Jardón 968 (Mon–Fri 9am–noon & 2–6pm, Sun 2–6pm; M$15; Ⓦwww.baulteatro.com). This small museum has a rather extensive and odd collection of puppets displayed behind glass. At 4pm on Sundays the owners put on a puppet show (M$55) based on anything from *Little Red Riding Hood* to García Lorca, which usually attracts a fair-sized crowd.

To the south is the dry bed of the Río Santa Catarina, now largely given over to playing fields, overlooked by the first slopes of the Cerro de la Silla, which rise almost immediately from its far bank.

Of Monterrey's two main **markets** – Juárez and Colón – the latter, on Avenida de la Constitución, south of the Macroplaza, is more tourist-oriented, specializing in local artesanía. Incidentally, the best of Monterrey's **flea markets** (*pulgas*; literally, fleas) is also held on Constitución: market days are irregular, but ask any local for details.

### El Obispado

The elegant and recently renovated **Obispado**, the old Bishop's Palace, tops Chepe Vera hill to the west of the centre, but lies well within the bounds of the city. Its commanding position – affording great views when haze and smog allow – has made it an essential target for Monterrey's many invaders. Built in the eighteenth century, it has served as a barracks, a military hospital and a fortress: among its more dramatic exploits, the Obispado managed to hold out for two days after the rest of the city had fallen to Texan general Zachary Taylor in 1846. The excellent **museum** inside (Tues–Sun 10am–5pm; M$30) records the city's long history with a little of everything: religious and secular art, arms from the War of Independence, revolutionary pamphlets and old carriages.

You get to the Obispado along Padre Mier, passing on the way the monumental modern church of **La Purísima**. Take the R4 bus, alighting where it turns off Padre Mier, then continue to the top of the steps at the end of Padre Mier and turn left; it's a ten-minute walk in all. Return to the centre using any bus heading east on Hidalgo.

## North of the centre

If you're thirsty after all this, head out to Monterrey's massive **Cervecería Cuauhtémoc** (Cuauhtémoc Brewery). This is where they make the wonderful Bohemia and Tecate beers you'll find throughout Mexico (as well as the rather bland Carta Blanca), and somehow it seems much more representative of Monterrey than any of the city's prouder buildings. Free guided tours of the brewery run almost constantly throughout the day, and you may be rewarded afterwards with free beer amidst strutting peacocks in the pleasant gardens outside – note the blackened tree trunks there which bear witness to the city's industrial pollution. Tours start across the road from the brewery at Alfonso Reyes 2202 Nte, 1km north of the bus station (Mon–Fri 10am–5pm, Sat 10am–3pm; free; English-speaking tours given, though only a few per day). Connected to the brewery is the **Salón de la Fama**, Sporting Hall of Fame, commemorating the heroes of Mexican baseball; entry is free. To get there take Line 2 to its northern terminus (General Anaya station) and walk 300m south.

Some 3km north of the brewery lies the vast **Parque Niños Héroes**, chiefly a gentle retreat from the city, best visited at weekends when the throng of Mexican families enjoying themselves goes some way towards masking the slightly run-down nature of the place. Among the semi-formal gardens and boating lake are minor sights (some have nominal entrance fees) such as a spherical aviary, a transport museum with vintage and classic cars and trucks, and the **Pinacoteca**, a small art gallery featuring mostly missable oils and sculpture by Nuevo León artists. The main attractions here are some fine pieces by Fidias Elizondo, notably the female nude *La Ola*.

Architecturally more compelling is the **Biblioteca Magna Universitaria**, Alfonso Reyes 4000 (Mon–Fri 8am–8pm, Sat 9am–8pm; free), in the northern end of the park but only accessible from the street. This is another fine example of the work of Ricardo Legorreta (see p.228), and though the design is completely different, the parallels to the MARCO building are strong. In fact, it sometimes feels more like an art gallery than a library, and does generally have a couple of modern works on display near the lobby. Like the MARCO, it is a constantly surprising building, with squares within circles and sudden courtyards, but with an overall sense of space and fun.

The park and library entrances can be reached on **buses** #17 and #18 from Padre Mier or on Cuauhtémoc outside the Cuauhtémoc metro station. To get back, take the same bus from Barragan on the western side of the park: the exits on this side are only sporadically open and you may have to make a long detour around the park.

For decades, glass production has been one of Monterrey's industrial strengths (for one thing, it has to provide all the beer bottles to the brewery), and to tap into the long history of Mexican glassware, pop along to the **Museo del Vidrio**, at the corner of Zaragoza and Magallanes (Tues–Sun 9am–6pm; M$15, free on Tues; Ⓦwww.museodelvidrio.com). A small but select display of pieces over the centuries and a mock-up of a nineteenth-century apothecary's only act as a prelude to the attic, where modern, mostly cold-worked glass sculpture is shown to advantage; Raquel Stolarski's *Homage to Marilyn* is particularly fine. To get there, take Line 1 to Del Golfo station, walk two blocks west and then two blocks north up Zaragoza.

## East of the centre

A new cultural development lies east of the centre, at the location of the city's old steel works. The serene **Parque Fundidora** (Ⓦwww.parquefundidora.org) is a surreal landscape of green parkland, industrial chimneys and processing plants, which have been converted into social spaces. Old warehouses contain the **Cineteca-Foteca**, a photo gallery and art-house cinema, and the **Pinacoteca**, which has art exhibitions and a media library. Many of the industrial structures are incorporated into children's playgrounds, and there's a theme park honouring the Latin American version of Sesame Street – **Plaza Sésamo**. Catch the metro (Line 1) to Parque Fundidora – the park lies south of the station across Madero.



### South of the centre

Like some vision from H.G. Wells's *The War of the Worlds*, the cylindrical form of the **Planetario Alfa**, Roberto Garza Sada 1000, 8km south of the city centre (Tues–Fri 3.30–8pm, Sat & Sun 11.30am–8pm; museum only M$40, museum and film M$84; Ⓦ www.planetarioalfa.org.mx), rises out of the ground at a rakish angle, providing an unusual venue for Omnimax films. If you've never seen one of these super-wide-vision movies before, or have kids to entertain, it may be worth the trip out here. Otherwise, the few science demonstrations and hands-on experiments aren't really worth the bother. If you do come, don't miss Rufino Tamayo's stained-glass opus, outside the main complex, in the Universe Pavilion. The only way to get here is on the **free shuttle bus**, which leaves from a dedicated stop at the western end of the Alameda on Washington. Times vary, but it runs roughly on the hour from 3pm to 7pm and also on the half-hour at weekends.

## Eating

Monterrey's **restaurants** cater to hearty, meat-eating *norteños*, with *cabrito al pastor* or the regional speciality *cabrito asado* (whole roasted baby goat) given pride of place in window displays. You'll find scores of tiny bars and rather sleazy places to eat near the bus station, especially at the little market just south of Colón; up here your best bet is to stick to one of the safer-looking fast-food joints. For fresh produce you could do worse than join the locals at the **Mercado Juárez**, north of the Gran Plaza on Aramberri. In the **centre** you can do a lot better, but you also pay more, especially at the dozens of places around the Gran Plaza.

**Barra Antigua** Constitución 1030. You'll find big plates and big screens in this restaurant that serves moderately priced Mexican fare, steaks and burgers, as well as beer, cocktails and tequila.

**La Casa del Maíz** Abasolo 870-B Ote, at Dr Coss. Airy, modern place taking its decorative cues from MARCO down the street, and serving unusual Mexican dishes, either with or without meat. Try the *memelas la maica*, a kind of thick tortilla topped with a richly seasoned spinach and cheese salsa. Closed Sun eve and all day Mon, opens at 6pm other days. Have a look at the funky *Akbal* (Maya for "night") *Lounge* upstairs.

**Coliseo Cafetería** Colón 235. Clean and cheerful 24hr place near the bus station, serving regular Mexican staples at low prices; quesadillas (M$25), bean tacos (M$20) and passable café con leche (M$7).

**La Fonda del Rey** Matamoros 816 Ote. Bright and cheery restaurant that does decent and economical Mexican staples.

**Gorditas Doña Tota** Escobedo near Morelos. This fast-food-like chain serves up delicious little gorditas for under a buck and has many outlets throughout the city. Beware, you might become a regular.

**El Infinito** Jardón 904 Ote. A surprising little find, with sofas and a small lending library (some English books), serving some of Monterrey's best espressos and lattes. Cakes and sandwiches, too, and a few times a month they have live acoustic music.

**LA Pizza** Matamoros 855. Simple takeout place. They do decent 12in pizzas for M$50 and 14in pies for M$65.

**Madre Oaxaca** Jardón 814 Ote. The speciality of this beautiful upmarket restaurant is Oaxacan cooking, the most delicious of Mexico's regional cuisines. Check this place out, especially if you can't get down south.

**Las Monjitas** Morelos 240 Ote. Waitresses dressed as nuns dish up Mexican steaks and a catholic selection of quality *antojitos*, including such house specialities as the *Father Chicken*, *The Sinner* and *Juan Pablo II*; the last is an artery-hardening combination of salami, pork, bacon, peppers, grilled cheese and guacamole. Beautiful *azulejos* on the walls make the slightly elevated prices worthwhile. There's a second branch a couple of blocks along at Escobedo Sur 913. Open daily 8am–11pm.

**Nuequen** Dr Coss 656. Renowned upmarket restaurant that specializes in Argentine cuisine, though they also have good Mexican and Italian dishes on the menu.

**Restaurante Vegetariano Superbom** Galeana 1018, between Hidalgo and Ocampo. Excellent vegetarian comidas (M$45), and an all-you-can-eat buffet (M$75) from noon until 5pm; mornings the food is à la carte. Closed Sat.

**El Rey del Cabrito** Dr Coss and Constitución. The best place in town for *cabrito* is this slightly unworldly restaurant, adorned with stuffed carnivorous animals and full of the delicious aromas of charcoal-grilled meat.

**Sanborn's** Morelos near the Plaza Hidalgo. As safe a bet as ever for sandwiches and snacks: great if your stomach's feeling homesick for more Continental-style fare.

## Nightlife

**After dark**, the place to head is the Barrio Antiguo, five square blocks of cobbled streets bounded by Dr Coss, Matamoros and Constitución. On Thursday, Friday and Saturday evenings (9pm–2am), the police block off the junctions, leaving the streets – especially Padre Mier and Madero – to hordes of bright young things surging back and forth in search of the best vibe. In the Barrio Antiguo, too, are a few late-closing **cafés**, which make the best destinations for a quieter evening. Alternatively, you could catch a wrestling match at the stadium opposite the bus station.

**Antropolis** Montemayor and Padre Mier. A dark, left-wing favourite among students and revolutionary types. It can sometimes get quite crowded and rowdy here, so don't wear your best clothes.

**Cadaques** Morelos 905. This minimalist, white-leather-clad lounge occasionally showcases European DJs for pricey covers. It's a good place to come for a quality cocktail.

**Café Iguana** Montemayor 927. Monterrey's best rock club. You'll find the patrons here similar to those at *Antropolis*. They play everything from techno to grunge, dress is casual and live bands occasionally perform.

**Café Paraiso** Morelos 958 Ote. Multi-roomed café and bar with local artwork on the walls, serving a fabulous range of coffees, delicious and huge tortas with fries (M$40) and fairly pricey drinks, though beers are two-for-one (M$30) round-the-clock.

**Dragonfly** Padre Mier 1094. Pop music, both the Mexican and US varieties, plays at this buzzing, jaunty nightclub.

**Kokoloco** Padre Mier 1102 Ote. Fun, popular disco with three different floors, featuring alternative vibes on the first, and pop and dance on the subsequent levels. There's also a loft space to chill out in.

**Loft** Morelos 870. This is the place to come if you're in the mood for hip-hop or rap.

**El Rincón La Habana** Morelos 887. The combination of Cuban food and live music is hard to resist (the music begins after 10pm), though they only open Thurs, Fri and Sat.

**Río Latino** at the eastern end of Padre Mier. Regularly staging live music, *Río Latino* currently plays host to the bilingual jet-set crowd. A very popular, if slightly pretentious venue, so dress to impress and try to act suave – at least for the doormen.

**La Tumba** Padre Mier 827 Ote. The main draw at this large, semi-outdoor bar is live acoustic music Thurs–Sat. Expect to hear anything from blues to jazz to rock. Open 5pm–2am. Cover M$20–50.

## Listings

**Airlines** Aero California ☎81/8369-0922; Aeroméxico ☎81/8343-5560; American Airlines ☎81/8342-9717; Continental Airlines ☎81/8369-0837.

**American Express** American Express, Washington 539 ☎81/8345-9412 (Mon–Fri 9am–6pm, Sat 9am–noon), holds clients' mail, and replaces and cashes traveller's cheques.

**Banks and exchange** You can change money at any of the several casas de cambio on Ocampo

## Moving on from Monterrey

You'll have no trouble getting a **bus** out of Monterrey at almost any time of day or night, to points all around the country. **Ciudad Juárez**, Mexico City, Guadalajara and **Mazatlán** are some of the major destinations served by the three big players: Grupo Senda, Omnibus and Estrella Blanca. The bus station is divided into six *salas*, or halls, each broadly serving different points of the compass; just ask at the first one you come to and someone will direct you to the right *sala*. Monterrey is also a good place to pick up transport into **Texas**: Transportes del Norte has direct connections with the Greyhound system with transfers in Nuevo Laredo; Americanos runs direct to San Antonio (7hr; M$365), Houston (10hr; M$490), Dallas (12hr; M$615), and Chicago (28hr; M$1675).

Monterrey's international **airport**, General Mariano Escobedo, is similarly well connected, with some three hundred **flights** a day. A plethora of lines, such as Aeroméxico, Aero California and Aviacsa fly out to a range of Mexican cities, including Mexico City, Cancún, Tijuana, Veracruz and Mérida. US destinations form around a fifth of all outbound destinations and include Houston, Dallas, Las Vegas and Los Angeles, among others.

between Zaragoza and Juárez (Mon–Fri 9am–1pm & 3–6pm, Sat 9am–12.30pm), and change traveller's cheques at banks (almost all with ATMs), most of which are on Padre Mier, right downtown – Banamex, Pino Suárez 933 Nte, which changes money until 1pm, is one example.

**Books** Sanborn's, on Morelos near the Macroplaza (daily 9am–10pm), holds a rather poor selection of English-language novels, though it does sell numerous magazines and some guides.

**Car rental** If you fancy renting wheels to get out to the sights immediately around Monterrey, or to explore the mountains, head for Plaza Hidalgo where all the main agencies have offices. Payless, Escodebo 1011 Sur (℡81/8344-6363, Ⓦwww.PaylessCarRental.com) has the best deal at M$725/day. Others include Advantage, Ocampo 429-A Ote (℡81/8345 7334); ALAL, Hidalgo 426 Ote (℡81/8340 7611, Ⓦwww.alal.com.mx); Budget, Hidalgo 433 Ote (℡81/8344 2948).

**Cinema** There's an MM Cinema on the corner of Escobedo and Ramon. Art-house films sometimes screen at the Cineta-Fototeca, Parque Fundidora.

**Consulates** Canada, ground floor, Zaragoza 1300, Zona Centro (Mon–Fri 9am–1pm & 2.30–5.30pm; ℡81/8344-3200); US, Constitución 411 Pte (Mon–Fri 8am–2pm; ℡81/8345-2120).

**Emergencies** Angeles Verdes (℡81/8115-0074); Cruz Roja (℡81/8342-1212); Cruz Verde (℡81/8371-5050); police (℡066 or ℡81/8343-0173); Hospital Muguerza, Hidalgo 2525 (℡81/8399-3400).

**Internet access** Facilities downtown at Internet Zone, Emilio Carranza 919, which has a card system letting you log in and out whenever you like. Also try K'Fé, Montemayor 713 at Allende in the Barrio Antiguo; it has a good connection and also houses a small cultural centre with art exhibitions and occasional poetry readings (Mon–Sat 11am–11pm; M$10/hr); in the same neighbourhood is CICOM, Abasolo 1017, which has private cabins and charges M$15/hr.

**Laundry** Antillón 237, between Matamoros and Sanchez.

**Photographic supplies** There are photo-developing places selling print film all over the place, but for specialist needs head for Photos de Llano, Padre Mier 565 (Mon–Sat 9am–8pm).

**Post office** In the Palacio Federal at the north end of the Macroplaza (Mon–Fri 8am–7pm, Sat 9am–1pm).

## Around Monterrey

After a day or two the bustle of Monterrey can get to you, but you can escape to the surprisingly wild and beautiful surrounding countryside. Without your own vehicle, however, getting around the sights in the vicinity can be awkward. An exception is a trip to the subterranean caverns of **Grutas de Garcia**, which, despite some impressive stalactites and stalagmites and an underground lake, have lost some of their appeal through overdevelopment. Only 40km west of Monterrey near the village of **VILLA GARCIA**, they are a popular outing from Monterrey, especially at weekends, when hundreds cram onto the funicular tram (M$50) from the village; you can walk from the end of the tram to the caverns in about thirty minutes. Buses run several times daily to Villa Garcia from outside the camionera, about a block and a half towards the train station; buy your ticket either from the Transportes Monterrey–Saltillo office or on the bus.

There's wilder country about 20km southwest of Monterrey in the **Parque Nacional Cumbres de Monterrey**, centred on the **Cañon de la Huasteca**, an impressive mountain ravine some 300m deep with vertical cliffs that have become a playground for committed rock climbers. Within it is **La Huasteca** "Ecological Park" (daily 9am–6pm; cars M$10, pedestrians M$1.50), with barbecue pits, picnic areas and a pool for children, all designed to cope with the weekend influx from the city.

The trip to the **Cascada Cola de Caballo** (Horsetail Falls), 35km south of Monterrey, is only really worthwhile after the rains – you can hire horses and burros to ride in the hilly Parque Nacional Cumbres de Monterrey, where there are views from the top of the falls and plenty of opportunities for hiking and camping. To get here by bus, take a Lineas Amarillas service to **El Cercado**, where *colectivos* wait to take you to the falls: once there, horse-buggy rides are available, and there are lovely swimming spots.

## Fiestas

### February

**Carnaval** (week before Lent; variable Feb–March) is at its best in the Caribbean atmosphere of Tampico (see p.222) – also in Ciudad Victoria (see p.221) and Monterrey (see p.224).

### March

**Festival de San José** (March 19). Celebrated in Ciudad Victoria (see p.221).

**Birth of Benito Juárez** (March 21). Ceremonies to commemorate Juárez's birth in Matamoros (see p.216).

### April

**Feria del Azúcar** (April 27). Celebrated in Ciudad Mante, south of Ciudad Victoria, with bands, dancing and fireworks.

### May

**Feria de La Raza** (May 2–5). In Monterrey (see p.224), music and arts culminating with Cinco de Mayo festivities held along Calle Juárez.

**Día de la Santa Cruz** (May 3). Tula, between Ciudad Victoria and San Luis Potosí, stages a fiesta with traditional dance. In Gómez Palacio (Durango), the start of an agricultural and industrial fair that lasts two weeks.

**Día de San Isidro** (May 15). Observed in Guadalupe de Bravos, on the border near Ciudad Juárez, with dances all day and parades all night. Similar celebrations in Arteaga, near Saltillo.

### June

**Día de San Antonio de Padua** (June 13). Marked in Tula by religious services followed by pastoral plays and traditional dances.

**Día de Santiago** (June 25). The start of a week-long fiesta in Altamira, near Tampico.

Another option is to head up to the **Mesa Chipinque**, a mountain plateau just 18km from Monterrey with famous views back over the city. Here again you can hire horses (from the enormously flash *Motel Chipinque*) to explore the hinterland. If you want an **organized trip** to the caves or falls, the Monterrey tourist office should be able to hook you up with a reputable guide, or for more extensive explorations of Nuevo León's natural locales, pick up a copy of *Aire Libre* – a useful booklet containing lists of adventure-tour operators. *Bakpak* is another good publication, but it's in Spanish only.



# Saltillo

**SALTILLO**, capital of the state of Coahuila, is the place to head for if you can't take the hustle of Monterrey. Lying just 85km to the southwest, down a fast road that cuts through the Sierra Madre Oriental and a high desert of yucca and Joshua trees, it's infinitely quieter, much smaller than Monterrey and, at 1600m above sea level, feels refreshingly cool and airy.

There's not a great deal to do here, but it's still a great place to stroll around, admire some beautiful buildings and soak up the colonial ambience. Two contrasting, and almost adjoining, squares grace the centre of town: the **Plaza**

### July

**Día de Nuestra Señora del Refugio** (July 4). Marked by dancing and pilgrimages in Matamoros (see p.216).

### August

**Feria de la Uva** (Aug 9). Exuberant festivities in Parras, between Saltillo and Torreón.

**Feria** (Aug 13). Saltillo (see above) begins its annual festival.

### September

**Feria** (Sept 11). Major festival on the border at Nuevo Laredo (see p.213).

**Independence Day** (Sept 16). Festivities everywhere, but the biggest in Monterrey (see p.224).

### October

**Feria** (Oct 25). Joint celebrations between the border town of Ciudad Acuña (see p.211) and its Texan neighbour Del Rio. Bullfights and parades.

### November

**Día de San Martin de Porres** (Nov 3). Fiesta with native dances in Tampico (see p.222).

**Feria de la Cultura Barrio Antiguo** (Nov 15–25). One of Monterrey's (see p.224) leading festivals; throngs of people come for music and food when the city's many cafés open to the street.

### December

**Día de la Virgen de Guadalupe** (Dec 12). A big one everywhere, especially in Guadalupe de Bravos; El Palmito (Durango), between Durango and Parral; Ciudad Anahuac (Nuevo León) in the north of the state; and Abasolo, near Monterrey. Monterrey (see p.224) itself attracts many pilgrims at this time.

Acuña, surrounded by crowded shopping streets, marks the rowdy heart of the modern city, while the old **Plaza de Armas** is formal, tranquil, illuminated at night and sometimes hosts music performances. Facing the Palacio de Gobierno across the Plaza de Armas, the magnificent eighteenth-century **cathedral** is one of the most beautiful in northern Mexico, with an elaborately carved churrigueresque facade and doorways, an enormous bell tower and a smaller clock tower. On the south side of the square the **Instituto Coahuilense de Cultura** (Tues–Fri 10am–7pm; free) often hosts diverting temporary exhibits by Coahuila artists.

The town's oldest streets fan out from the square, with some fine old houses still in private hands. One historical building worth seeking out is the carefully preserved old **Ayuntamiento** (town hall) on the corner of Aldama and Hidalgo. The walls of the courtyard and the staircase are adorned with murals depicting the history of the town from prehistoric times to the 1950s. Calle Victoria spurs west off the square, passing a few hundred metres of the city's major shops and cinemas, on the way to the **Alameda**, a shaded, tree-lined park, peopled with students looking for a peaceful spot to work – there are several language schools in Saltillo, as well as a university and technical institute; in summer especially, numbers of American students come here to study Spanish.

Saltillo is famous for its **sarapes**, and there are several small shops where (at least on weekdays) you can watch the manufacturing process – the best is tucked at the back of the artesanía shop El Sarape de Saltillo, Hidalgo 305 Sur (Mon–Sat 9am–1pm & 3–7pm). Sadly, the old ways are vanishing fast, and most now use artificial fibres and chemical dyes: all too many of those on sale in the market are mass-produced in virulent clashing colours.

Birders should head to **Museo de las Aves de México**, at the intersection of Hidalgo and Bolívar (Tues–Sat 10am–6pm, Sun 11am–7pm; M$10; Ⓦwww.museodelasaves.org), where you'll find a large collection of stuffed birds on exhibit throughout various themed rooms.

## Practicalities

City buses (marked "Centro/Camionera") run from Saltillo's main **bus station**, 3km southwest of the centre, to the cathedral on the Plaza de Armas, and onwards a couple more stops to the Plaza Acuña, right at the heart of things. The main tourist office is inconveniently located at Carranza 8520 (Mon–Fri 9am–5pm; Ⓣ844/432-3690, Ⓦwww.saltillomexico.org). There's a smaller office in a red-brick building a ten-minute walk north of the action at the intersection of Dr Coss and Acuña (Mon–Sat 9am–3pm; Ⓣ844/412-5122). Strategically positioned **maps of the city** – at the bus station and on both squares – help orientation. The **post office** is at Victoria 453, and there are long-distance **phones** and **banks** with ATMs all over the centre of town. At Padre Flores 159, Cyberbase has **Internet** access for M$10/hr (Mon–Sat 8am–10.30pm, Sun noon–8pm). In the centre try upstairs at Victoria 573 (Mon–Sat 9am–10pm, Sun 11am–10pm; M$10/hr).

Most of the better-value **hotels** are in the side streets immediately around Plaza Acuña, but have a tendency to fill up each night. Both *Hotel Jardín*, Padre Flores 211 (Ⓣ844/412-5916; ❸), and *Hotel Bristol*, Aldama 405 Pte (Ⓣ844/154-0134; ❷), are good-value budget places, the latter having the edge with cable TV. If you can spend a little more and want to savour some colonial splendour, have a look at the *Urdiñola*, Victoria 207 Pte (Ⓣ844/414-0940; ❺), with its tiled open lobby dominated by a wide staircase flanked by suits of armour, and fountains trickling amidst the greenery of the courtyard. If all these are full, you might try the unremarkable *Saade* at Aldama 397 (ⓣ844/412-9120, ⓔjrsade@prodigy.net.mx; ⑤).

**Restaurants** in Saltillo tend to close early, and the ones in the centre mainly cater for office workers and students. There are plenty of cheap places to eat around the **Mercado Juárez**, beside the Plaza Acuña, which is a decent market in its own right – tourists are treated fairly and not constantly pressed to buy. The *Café Victoria*, on Padre Flores just south of Plaza Acuña, is good for breakfasts, bulging tortillas and comidas corridas. At the western end of Victoria by the Alameda, *Terrazza Romana* serves up toothsome pasta dishes for around M$80 and fine pizzas for around M$90, while *El Conde*, the fast-food joint downstairs, dishes out single slices for M$10. If you're stocking up for a journey, pick up wholemeal bread, great carrot cake and the like from *Trigo Limpio*, Victoria 670; *Natura Es* across the street has good, healthy frozen yogurt for M$15 and up.

**From Saltillo** you can head **southeast to Zacatecas** or follow the direct route **to Mexico City** via San Luis Potosí, passing through Matehuala (with the possibility of branching off to the mountain ghost town of Real de Catorce) and Querétaro. Going through Zacatecas, though slower, gives you the chance to visit more of the beautiful colonial cities north of the capital.



# Travel details

## Buses

Services on the chief routes to and from the frontier (Ciudad Juárez–Chihuahua–Torreón/Durango and from the border to Monterrey–Saltillo–San Luis Potosí/Zacatecas) are excellent, with departures day and night. There are also direct services to Mexico City from just about everywhere. The best first-class lines are Omnibus de México (ⓦwww.odm.com.mx) and Grupo Senda (ⓦwww.gruposenda.com), both of which have online timetables. Estrella Blanca (ⓦwww.estrellablanca.com.mx), with its plethora of subsidiaries, often beats them for frequency of services and efficiency. What follows should be taken as a rough minimum.

**Chihuahua** to: Ciudad Juárez (at least hourly; 5hr); Creel (every 1–2hr; 4hr); Jiménez (roughly hourly; 3hr); Mexico City (every 2hr; 18hr); Nuevo Casas Grandes (11 daily; 4hr 30min); Zacatecas (hourly; 12hr).

**Ciudad Acuña** to: Monterrey (4 daily; 8hr); Piedras Negras (hourly; 1hr 30min); Saltillo (8 daily; 7hr).

**Ciudad Juárez** to: Chihuahua (at least hourly; 5hr); Durango (at least hourly; 16hr); Jiménez (at least hourly; 8hr); Mexico City (every 1–2hr; 24hr); Nuevo Casas Grandes (every 1–2hr; 4hr); Parral (at least hourly; 10hr); Torreón (at least hourly; 12hr); Zacatecas (hourly; 16hr).

**Ciudad Victoria** to: Matamoros (hourly; 4–5hr); Monterrey (hourly; 4hr); Reynosa (9 daily; 4–5hr); Tampico (hourly or better; 3hr).

**Creel** to: Batopilas (1 daily; 6hr); Chihuahua (14 daily; 4–5hr); Divisadero (7 daily; 1hr); Guachochi (2 daily; 3hr).

**Durango** to: Aguascalientes (20 daily; 6hr); Ciudad Juárez (at least hourly; 12–14hr); Fresnillo (15 daily; 3hr); Mazatlán (9 daily; 7hr); Mexico City (14 daily; 12–13hr); Monterrey (every 1–2hr; 9hr); Parral (9 daily; 6hr); Torreón (every 1–2hr; 4hr 30min); Zacatecas (roughly hourly; 4hr 30min).

**Guachochi** to: Chihuahua (5 daily; 7–9hr); Creel (2 daily; 3hr); Parral (6 daily; 4hr).

**Matamoros** to: Chicago (2 daily; 36hr); Ciudad Victoria (hourly; 4–5hr); Dallas (8 daily; 12hr); Houston (11 daily; 5hr); Monterrey (hourly; 4hr); Reynosa (every 45min; 2hr); San Antonio (8 daily; 6hr); Tampico (hourly; 7–8hr).

**Monterrey** to: Ciudad Victoria (hourly; 4hr); Dallas (4 daily; 12hr); Guadalajara (15 daily; 12hr); Houston (4 daily; 10hr); Matamoros (hourly; 4hr); Matehuala (hourly; 4–5hr); Mexico City (hourly; 12hr); Nuevo Laredo (every 30min; 3hr); Piedras Negras (12 daily; 5–7hr); Reynosa (every 30min; 3hr); Saltillo (constantly; 1hr 30min); San Antonio (5 daily; 7hr); San Luis Potosí (hourly; 7hr); Tampico (hourly; 7–8hr); Zacatecas (hourly; 6hr).

**Nuevo Casas Grandes** to: Chihuahua (hourly; 4hr 30min); Ciudad Juárez (every 1–2hr; 4hr).

**Nuevo Laredo** to: Acapulco (2 daily; 20hr); Austin (14 daily; 7hr); Chicago (2 daily; 36hr); Dallas (14 daily; 9hr); Guadalajara (5 daily; 14hr); Houston (9 daily; 7hr); Mexico City (10 daily; 15hr); Monterrey (every 30min; 3hr); Piedras Negras (8 daily; 3hr); Reynosa (8 daily; 4–5hr); Saltillo (8 daily; 4–5hr); San Antonio (hourly; 4hr); San Luis Potosí (14 daily; 12hr); Tampico (2 daily; 10hr); Zacatecas (6 daily; 8hr).

**Parral** to: Chihuahua (roughly hourly; 4hr); Durango (11 daily; 6hr); Guachochi (6 daily; 3hr 30min).

**Piedras Negras** to: Ciudad Acuña (hourly; 1hr 30min); Mexico City (3 daily; 18hr); Monterrey (8 daily; 5–7hr); Nuevo Laredo (10 daily; 3hr); Saltillo (12 daily; 7hr).

**Reynosa** to: Ciudad Victoria (9 daily; 4–5hr); Matamoros (every 45min; 2hr); Mexico City (6 daily; 14–16hr); Monterrey (every 30min; 3hr); Nuevo Laredo (9 daily; 4hr); San Luis Potosí (11 daily; 9–10hr); Tampico (hourly; 7hr); Zacatecas (10 daily; 9hr).

**Saltillo** to: Ciudad Acuña (14 daily; 7hr); Guadalajara (13 daily; 10hr); Matehuala (11 daily; 2hr 30min); Mazatlán (4 daily; 12hr); Mexico City (every 1–2hr; 12hr); Monterrey (constantly; 1hr 30min); Nuevo Laredo (every 1–2hr; 4–5hr); Piedras Negras (15 daily; 7hr).

**Tampico** to: Ciudad Victoria (hourly or better; 3hr); Matamoros (hourly; 7–8hr); Mexico City (every 1–2hr; 8hr); Monterrey (hourly; 7–8hr); Nuevo Laredo (2 daily; 10hr); San Luis Potosí (11 daily; 7hr); Veracruz (8 daily; 9hr).

**Torreón** to: Ciudad Juárez (at least hourly; 12hr); Zacatecas (10 daily; 6hr).

## Trains

The Copper Canyon railway (see p.188) is the big attraction in this region – the last remaining passenger train in Mexico.

## Flights

There are frequent flights from most of the major cities to the capital – Chihuahua, Monterrey and Tampico all have several a day. From Monterrey you can also fly to Guadalajara and Acapulco, and there are international services to Dallas, Houston, San Antonio and Chicago. From Ciudad Juárez and Nuevo Laredo you can get to the capital and Guadalajara.

# The Bajío

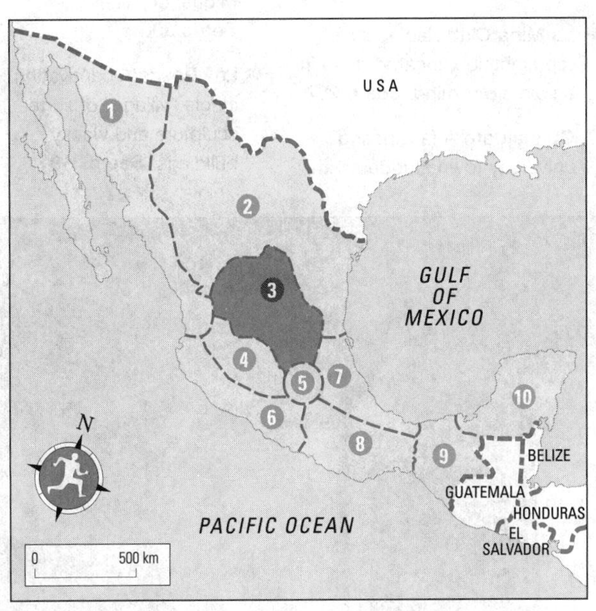
USA
1
2
3
GULF OF MEXICO
4
5
7
6
8
9
10
BELIZE
GUATEMALA
HONDURAS
EL SALVADOR
PACIFIC OCEAN
N
0
500 km

# CHAPTER 3 Highlights



* **Real de Catorce** Good hotels, excellent Italian meals and desert scenery make this semi-ghost-town perfect for relaxing extended stays. **See p.245**

* **Zacatecas** A glorious former silver town located high up in the northern deserts, packed with great museums and blessed with lively nightlife. **See p.257**

* **La Mina Club** Zacatecas's top nightclub, located deep in an old silver mine. **See p.267**

* **Guanajuato** A fascinating university town studded with fine museums and bustling with streetlife. **See p.277**

* **San Miguel de Allende** Gorgeous colonial town with beautiful hotels and great food: Mexico's most appealing gringo enclave. **See p.295**

* **La Gruta** Mineral hot springs in verdant surroundings just beyond the edge of San Miguel de Allende. **See p.306**

* **Las Pozas** A captivating jungle "village" of surreal sculpture and wacky buildings. **See p.319**

△ Real de Catorce

3

# The Bajío



Rugged and scattered with superb ancient towns, the twisting hills and beautiful, fertile valleys of the **Bajío** spread across Mexico's central highlands almost from coast to coast and as far south as the capital. This has long been the most heavily populated part of the country, providing much of the silver and grain that supported Mexico throughout the years of Spanish rule. As the country's colonial heartland, the legacy of Spanish architecture remains at its most impressive here, in meticulously crafted towns that – at their cores at least – have changed little over the centuries, while the surrounding land has been consistently developed, both agriculturally and industrially.

Mexico's broad central plateau narrows and becomes hillier as it approaches the Valley of México. Here in the Bajío proper – the states of Guanajuato and Querétaro – are its finest colonial cities, founded amid barren land and grown rich on just one thing: **silver**. Before the arrival of the Spanish, this was a relatively unexploited area, a buffer zone between the more civilized lands of central Mexico and the barbarian Chichimec tribes of the north. Though the Aztecs may have tapped some of its mineral wealth, they never exploited the area with the greed, tenacity and ruthlessness of the new colonists. After the Conquest, the mining cities grew rich, but in time they also grew restive under the heavy hand of control from Spain. The wealthy Creole (Spanish-blooded but Mexican-born) bourgeoisie were free to exploit the land and its people, but didn't control their own destinies and were forced to pay punitive taxes; lucrative government posts and high positions in the Church were reserved exclusively for Gachupines, those actually born in Spain, while the indigenous and poor *mestizos* were condemned either to landless poverty or to near-fatal labour. Unsurprisingly, then, the Bajío was ripe for revolution. This land is La Cuna de la Independencia (the **Cradle of Independence**), where every town seems to claim a role in the break with Spain. In Querétaro the plotters held many of their early meetings, and from here they were warned that their plans had been discovered; in Dolores Hidalgo the famous *grito* was first voiced by Father Hidalgo, proclaiming an independent Mexico; and from here he marched on San Miguel de Allende, picking up more volunteers for his armed rabble as he continued towards a bloody confrontation in Guanajuato.

Approaching the Bajío from the north you cross several hundred kilometres of semi-desert landscape punctuated only by the occasional ranch, where fighting bulls are bred, or defunct mining towns, such as the wonderfully strange semi-ghost-town of **Real de Catorce**, where decades of abandonment are gradually being reversed. Only then do you reach the colonial cities of **Zacatecas** and **San Luis Potosí** – both eponymous state capitals – that mark

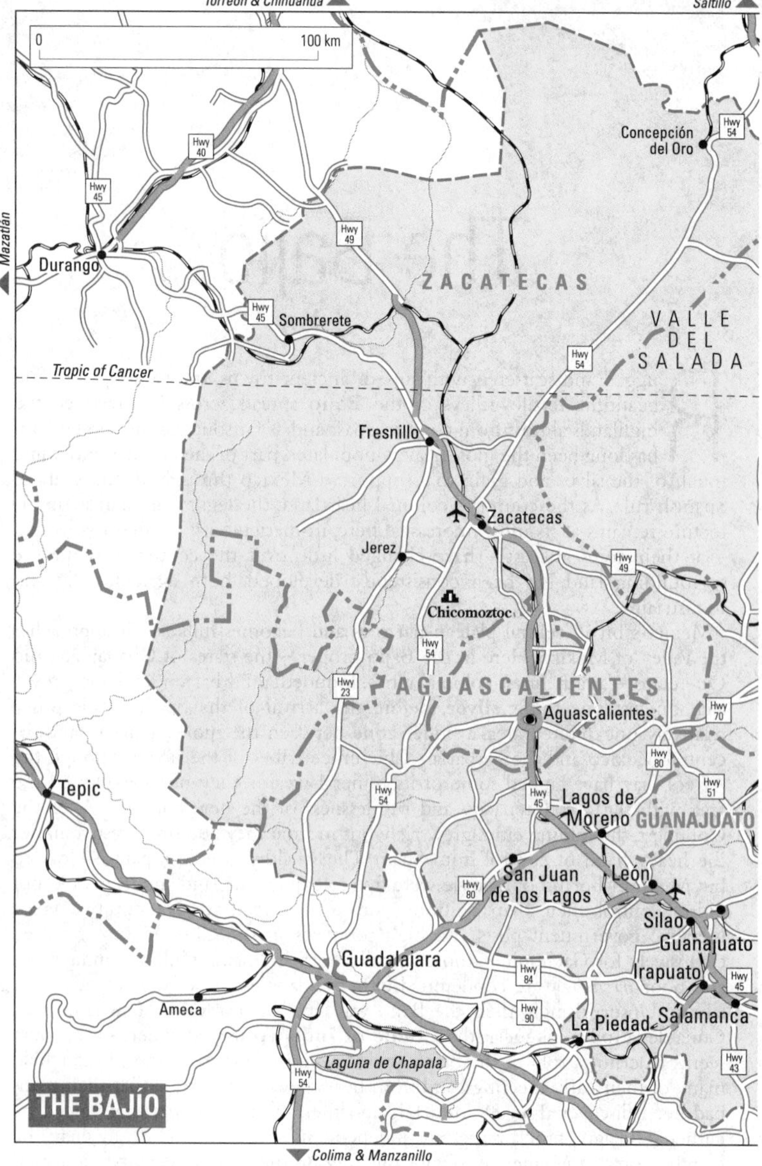




a radical change in landscape and architecture. Both are showcase examples of the region's architectural and historical heritage, sharing all the attributes of the towns further south. San Luis, a large modern metropolis, has its share of monuments, but Zacatecas is far more exciting, an oasis of culture and sophistication built in mountainous isolation on the bounty of the silver mines that riddle the landscape hereabouts. Some 300km south, beyond the modern town

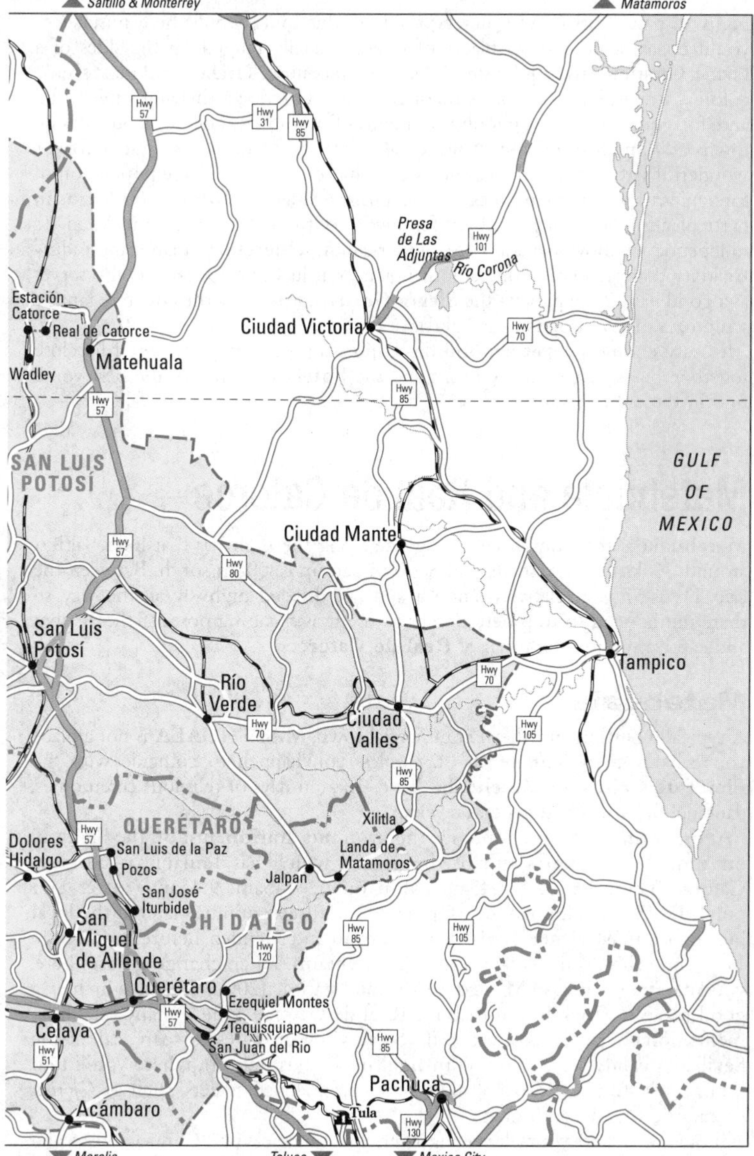


of **Aguascalientes**, you enter the green belt of the Bajío proper. Despite the widespread closure of its silver mines, this area continues to thrive, with centres of study, culture and tourism and thrusting modern cities benefiting from their proximity to the capital and the main transport routes.

If you're heading straight for Mexico City, you'll cut through the industrial cities of **León** – famous for its leather – and Irapuato before joining the highway past Celaya and Querétaro. Taking this route would be a mistake, as you'll bypass a number of places of interest: crazily ranged up the sides of a ravine, **Guanajuato** is quite simply one of the country's richest and most scenic colonial towns, with one of its finest Baroque churches, a thriving student life and, for good measure, a ghoulish museum of mummies. The gorgeous hillside town of **San Miguel de Allende** also has its advocates, as much for its wonderful setting as for the comforts of home, ensured by a large population of foreign artists, gringo retirees and language students. **Dolores Hidalgo**, in particular, is a point of pilgrimage for anyone with the least interest in Mexico's independence movement, as is, to a lesser extent, **Querétaro**, a large and industrial city that preserves a fine colonial quarter at its heart. Querétaro also serves as a good base for exploring the **Sierra Gorda**, particularly the concrete fantasy sculptures of **Las Pozas** near Xilitla.

It's easy enough to **get around** the Bajío – all the towns of interest lie close together, bus services are excellent and the **hotels** are some of the best you'll find in the entire country.



# Matehuala and Real de Catorce

**Matehuala** is the only place of any size along the highway that links Saltillo, around 260km to the north, and San Luis, around 200km south. Between the two, Hwy-57 is a relatively smooth and fast divided highway all the way, so there's little need to stop here except to use it as a staging post for the ancient and captivating mining town of **Real de Catorce**.

## Matehuala

A typically bustling, northern commercial town, **MATEHUALA** is not a place you're likely to be tempted to stay unless you happen to coincide with the **Fiesta de Cristo de Matehuala** (Jan 6–15), ten days of religious ceremonies, dancing, fireworks and general revelry.

At other times you may only see the main **bus station**, just off the highway on 5 de Mayo, 2km south of the centre, which has Tamaulipas buses to Catorce. These leave at 5.45am (Mon only), 7.45am, 9.45am (Sat & Sun only), 11.45am, 1.45pm and 5.45pm and call fifteen minutes later at the local bus station in Matehuala, corner of Guerrero and Mendez, before making the steep run (1hr 45min; M$45) into the mountains. When changing buses here, you may need the **ATM** next to the bus station (200m right), which is a good place to stock up on cash for Real de Catorce, where many establishments don't accept credit cards. If you've a few minutes to spare, call at the Sevillanas candy store (also 200m right of the bus station), where you'll find a huge selection of Mexico's best and most beloved sweets, such as *Glorias*, or caramels made with goat's milk.

Should you find yourself staying over, you can pick up "Centro" buses and taxis outside the main bus station, though if you don't have much luggage it's an easy enough walk, left then straight up 5 de Mayo and then left on Insurgentes when you've reached the centre – you can't miss the grey concrete bulk of the church a couple of blocks off the main plaza. The three main **hotels** are all within a block of the main plaza: *Hotel Alamo*, Guerrero 116 (ⓣ488/882-0017; ❸), is the cheapest and quite acceptable, though an extra M$60 is well spent at *Hotel Matehuala*, at the corner of Bustamante and Hidalgo, a block north of the plaza (ⓣ488/882-0680; ❹), where rooms surround a massive columned courtyard. Between the two, the new *Hotel de Valle*, Morelos 621 (☎488/882-3770; ④), offers spacious, clean rooms if astonishingly ugly decor. There are several pricier motel-style places out on the main road. Local **restaurants** include: the *Fontella*, close to the *Hotel Matehuala*, at Morelos 618, which does excellent comida corrida for under M$50; and the *Santa Fe*, Morelos 709, on the plaza, which is strong on seafood. The food at the main bus station is also surprisingly good.



## Real de Catorce and around

**REAL DE CATORCE** (or "Villa Real de Nuestra Señora de la Concepción de Guadalupe de los Alamos de los Catorce", to give it its full title), west of Matehuala, is quite an extraordinary place. With the hills around here once reckoned to be the second-richest source of precious metals in Mexico after Guanajuato, the main mines were founded in 1772, and at the height of its silver production early in the nineteenth century the town had 40,000

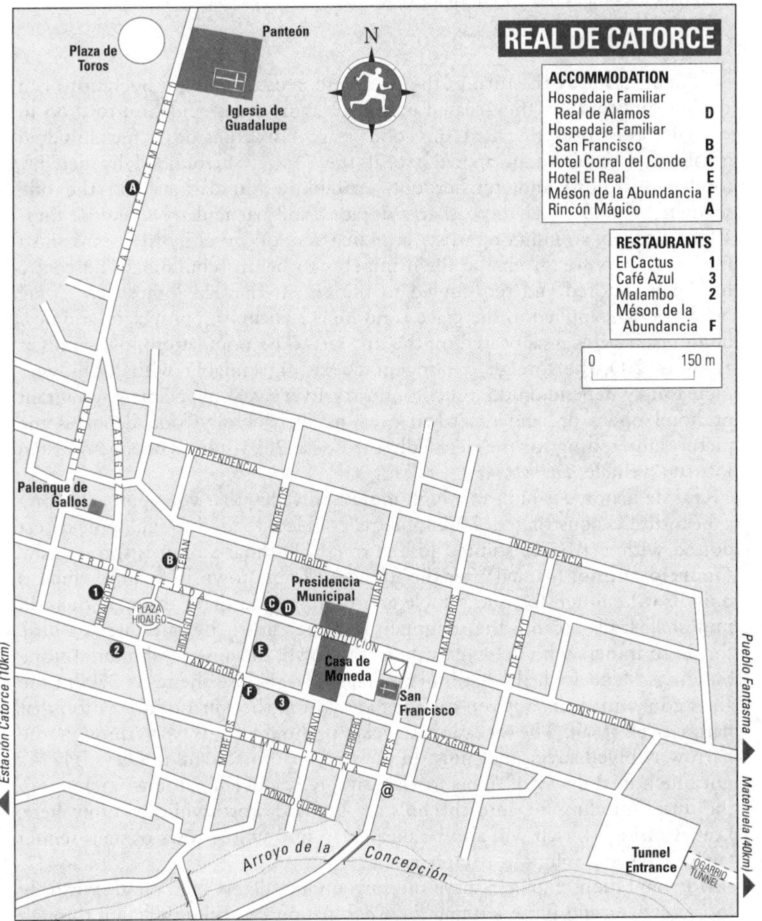

## Peyote: food for the Huichol soul

Since long before they were exploited for their silver, the mountains around Real de Catorce have been a rich source of **peyote**. The Huichol people (see box, p.170) traditionally make a month-long, four-hundred-kilometre annual pilgrimage from their homelands in northeastern Nayarit to gather the precious hallucinogenic cactus, which they regard as essential food for the soul. Once done on foot, nowadays the pilgrimage is mostly made by car, though the Huichol accord no less importance to their visit to Wirikuta, the flat semi-desert at the foot of the Sierra Madre Occidental. After the peyote "buttons" are collected, many are dried and taken away for later use, but some are carried fresh to their sacred site, Cerro Quemada (Burnt Hill), near Real de Catorce, for ceremonies.

Tales of achieving higher consciousness under the influence of peyote have long drawn foreigners, many of them converts of the books of Carlos Casteneda. Indeed, Real de Catorce only made it onto the tourist itinerary after it became a waystation on the hippy-druggy trail in the 1970s. New Agers continue to visit, but the hills around about have been picked clean and there are fears that over-harvesting may threaten the continued Huichol tradition.



inhabitants. But by the turn of the twentieth century mining operations had slowed, and in 1905 they ceased entirely, leaving the population to drop to virtually zero over the next fifty-odd years. For a period, a few hundred inhabitants hung on in an enclave at the centre, surrounded by derelict, roofless mansions and, further out, crumbling foundations and the odd segment of wall. Over the past few decades, and particularly since the mid-1990s, though, an influx of artists, artesanía vendors, wealthy Mexicans and a few foreigners has given the town impetus to begin rebuilding. The centre has been restored and reoccupied to the extent that the "ghost-town" tag once liberally applied to the place is no longer entirely appropriate, and new buildings have even appeared on the outskirts. The population now stands at around 1200, the foreign contingent coexisting amiably with locals who increasingly depend on the tourist industry. Every year or so a new restaurant or hotel opens up, and the town even made its Hollywood debut as the picturesque setting for the decidedly mediocre 2001 Julia Roberts and Brad Pitt star-vehicle *The Mexican*.

Real de Catorce is built in a high mountain valley that you approach along a beautifully constructed 25-kilometre cobbled road through semi-desert dotted with agave and stunted Joshua trees. The final 2.3km is through the **Ogarrio tunnel** (named after the founder's home town in Spain), which is only broad enough for one vehicle at a time. As you drive through, the odd mineshaft leads off into the mountain to either side – by one there's a little shrine to miners who died at work. In the town, the austere, shuttered stone buildings blend with the bare rocky crags that enclose them. At 2700m the air is cool and clean, but you can't get away from the spirit of desolation that hangs over it all. The occasional pick-up shoulders its way through the narrow cobbled streets, but most of the traffic is horses and donkeys. There's not much in the way of sights to visit: simply wandering around, kicking up the dust and climbing into the hills are big and worthwhile pastimes here. Lovers of high kitsch will also be pleased to find whole rows of stalls selling tacky icons and religious paraphernalia.

More ambitious explorers have the surrounding desert hill country virtually to themselves, and those looking for a destination can **hike** downhill through abandoned mine workings to the railway town of Estación Catorce, and its near neighbour Wadley, noted for its desert treats (see box opposite).

## Arrival and information

Most people arrive from Matehuala by **bus**. The bigger buses can't get through the Ogarrio tunnel, so you'll probably have to change buses at the eastern end for the run through the tunnel. These smaller buses drop you at a dusty parking lot at the tunnel's western end, from where it is a short walk down Lanzagorta to the town centre. When it comes time to leave, it always pays to ask about the latest bus timetables, but there are currently departures for Matehuala at 7.45am, 9.45am, 3.45pm and 5.45pm, and sometimes 11.45am (or you may choose to hike down to Estación Catorce and catch a bus from there: see p.250 for details).

Real has no tourist office, but before or during your stay you can get acquainted with the town by visiting the useful private **website** (Ⓦwww.realdecatorce.net). Day and overnight visitors from San Luis Potosí and Monterrey make the town much busier at weekends, Semana Santa and Christmas, when the better hotels put up their prices by around twenty percent. The town is also packed around the **Fiesta de San Francisco de Asís**, every weekend from the second Saturday in September to the fourth Sunday in October and for the entire week around October 4. At this time buses don't run through the tunnel and you either have to walk or ride one of the numerous horse-drawn carts for a few pesos.

Real is slowly dragging itself into the modern world and now has a single **ATM**, in the Presidencia Municipal on Constitución, and **Internet** access at La Quemada, at the corner of Reyes and Ramón Corona (daily 10am–8pm; M$20/hr).

## Accommodation

On arrival, as likely as not, you'll be accosted by a knot of small boys eager to carry your bags and guide you to their favoured *casa de huéspedes* in return for a small *propina*. Ensure you've some pesos handy, if you decide to follow their lead; if you're driving, don't be surprised if they hitch a ride on the bonnet of your car. You're not obliged to accept what they show you, but chances are you'll get a plain and small but clean **room**, which at least claims to have 24-hour hot water, for M$100–180: make sure there are plenty of blankets available as it can be very cold here at night. At the other end of the scale, Real is blessed with some wonderful hotels in converted **mansions**, often at very reasonable prices. There's little middle ground.

**Hospedaje Familiar Real de Alamos** Constitución 21 ⓣ488/887-5009. One of the better budget hostels, at the top end of the church square, with comfortable enough concrete-walled rooms and low prices for singles (M$100). ❷

**Hospedaje Familiar San Francisco** Terán 3, off Constitución (no phone). Fairly basic but clean and good-value rooms, especially rooms 6 and 7, which come with bathroom and a sunny terrace. ❷

**Hotel Corral del Conde** Constitución 17 ⓣ488/887-5048. *La Abundancia*'s main competition, this place comes in two parts. Rooms in the original portion have an elegantly rustic quality with stone walls, wooden beams and ageing furniture. The newer section across the road has more modern but equally comfortable rooms. They don't take reservations. ❻

**Hotel El Real** Morelos 20, behind the Casa de Moneda ⓣ488/887-5058, Ⓦwww.hotelreal.com. A charmingly converted old house with clean, airy rooms featuring native decoration, TVs (including videos and a video library), fireplaces and views galore. It's reputed to be haunted. ❻

**Mesón de la Abundancia** Lanzagorta 11 ⓣ488/887-5044, Ⓦwww.mesonabundancia.com. Located just past the church, this friendly hotel is the best of the lot, rebuilt from ruins and full of masks and huge stone-built rooms with beamed ceilings, rug-covered brick floors and ancient doors with their original hefty keys. Many rooms have small balconies and the suites (M$1200) are very spacious. ❻

**Rincón Mágico** Calle del Cementerio ⓣ488/887-5113. Nicely placed between the slightly scruffy *hospedajes* but half the price of the swanky joints, this small hotel has comfy rooms, some better than others and some with views down the plains. A restaurant/bar operates at weekends. ❹



## The Town

The single main street, **Lanzagorta**, runs down through the town past the 1817 **Church of San Francisco** (officially the Parroquia de la Inmaculada Concepción) with its square, shaded plaza and unusual removable wooden floorboards (for cleaning), and on down to the **Plaza Hidalgo** (aka Plaza de Armas), with its central bandstand. It's the church that attracts most Mexicans to Real, or rather the miraculous figure of St Francis of Assisi (known as Panchito, Pancho being a diminutive of Francisco) housed here. You'll soon spot the shrine by the penitents kneeling before it, but take time to head through the door to the left of the altar, where the walls are covered with hundreds of handmade *retablos* giving thanks for cures or miraculous escapes effected by the saint. They're a wonderful form of naive folk art, the older ones painted on tin plate, newer examples on paper or card or even photographs, depicting events that range from amazing to mundane – last-second rescues from the paths of oncoming trains, or simply the return of a stolen vehicle – all signed and dated with thanks to Panchito for his timely intervention. October 4, the saint's day, sees thousands of pilgrims crammed into Real, and the general festivities two weeks before and a week afterwards are also busy (see p.247).

Across the square, the **Casa de Moneda** is a magnificent old mansion with two storeys on one side and three on the other, thanks to the sloping site it was built on. This is where Real's silver was minted into coin, and as if to retain the memory there's a small silver workshop inside. Heading north out of town along

△ Retablos, Real de Catorce

Zaragoza, duck a few metres up Xicotencatl to the lovely old **Palenque de Gallos** (daily 9am–dusk; free), where cockfights were once held, then continue out along Zaragoza to the ruinous Plaza de Toros, opposite the **Panteón** (daily except Tues 9am–5pm, though hours depend on the gatekeeper's mood; free) where Real's dead lie covered by rough piles of dirt all around the decaying 1779 church. Peek inside to see its still-vibrant frescoes, which are going mouldy around the edges – just as they should be in a town like Real.



## Eating

**Eating** cheaply in Real de Catorce is easy, with numerous stalls and shops selling gorditas and tortas, mostly along Lanzagorta. Curiously, many of the best eateries in town are the **Italian**-oriented restaurants, many of which are connected to the main hotels.

**El Cactus** by the plaza. Does fine cannelloni and great tortas and stocks a huge range of fancy teas.

**Café Azul** Lanzagorta, next to *Mesón de la Abundancia*. Relaxed Swiss-run café serving good coffee, home-made cakes and sweet and savoury crepes (M$45).

**Malambo** corner of Zapata and Allende. Lovely, if pricey, restaurant with some outdoor seating around a tinkling fountain. The pizzas are good, but their signature light and flaky empanadas, served with a fresh salad (M$80), are excellent. For dessert don't miss the piping-hot apple and chocolate dumpling.

**Mesón de la Abundancia** (see p.247). The pick of the bunch. The Mexican and Italian food is superbly cooked and presented, and worth every peso: expect to pay M$150 for a full meal including a slice of torte and espresso. Credit cards accepted.

## Around Real de Catorce: Estación Catorce and Wadley

The specific sights in town are soon exhausted, but you could spend days here making forays out into the mountains all around, exploring any ruins you find, or heading downhill to the *altiplano* (high plain) of the desert below. One of the most relaxing ways to go is on **horseback**: horses are usually available around the Plaza de Armas and in front of the *Mesón de la Abundancia*, from where **guides** will take you out across the hills, perhaps visiting the Huichol ceremonial site of Cerro Quemada, though this can seem unpleasantly voyeuristic if any Huichol are around. Since your group will have to pay for the guide's time, better deals can be struck by rounding up a ready-to-go group, and then haggling hard. Midweek you should get something for around M$120–150 for three or four hours; prices are higher on weekends, when demand is higher. You really don't need any guidance for **short hikes**: just grab some water, food, good shoes and something to protect you from the sun and go. About the best nearby destination is the **Pueblo Fantasma** "Ghost Town", an extensive set of mine ruins reached in an hour or so by following the winding track uphill just to the left of the Ogarrio tunnel entrance as you face it.

The most rewarding unguided **longer hike** (12km one way; 3hr down, 4hr return; 850m ascent on way back) leads downhill from the Plaza de Armas (with the stables on your left), then forks right after 50m and follows a 4WD track towards the small dusty trackside town of Estación Catorce. You'll soon find yourself walking among mine ruins – you'll pass a dam built to provide water and power for the mines, and even a tall chimney from one of the smelters. After about an hour you get to the small village of **Los Catorces**, and beyond its cemetery, a second settlement known as **Santa Cruz de Carretas** (about 2hr from Real).

At this point you can turn around, knowing that you've had the best of the hike, but it is possible to continue to **ESTACIÓN CATORCE**, an hour further on. If the idea of hiking back seems too daunting, try flagging down the occasional vehicle, and be prepared to pay for your ride. A 4WD vehicle also plies the road a couple of times a day charging around M$40 for the journey. Its timing is erratic and dependent on numbers, though there is often one around noon: ask in Estacíon to find the vehicle. Estación Catorce itself is not a place to linger, though if you get stuck, there are a couple of fleapit hotels and a couple of places to eat, including a decent **restaurant**, located where **buses** depart, on the scruffy square by the rail tracks. Apart from local services to Wadley (at 10.30am, 4pm & perhaps a couple of others) all buses head north from here to Saltillo (8am, 2pm & 6pm; 4hr) and San Luis Potosí via Matehuala (6am, 7.30am & 2pm; 4hr).

Around 10km south of Estación Catorce along the asphalt road lies **WADLEY** (or Estación Wadley), a small dusty village that at first acquaintance seems even less appealing. It has, however, garnered a devoted following, chiefly for its proximity to a section of desert renowned for its abundant **peyote**. Most people rent a room for a few days, usually choosing a place with a kitchen as restaurants here are very limited: ask around and you should get something for around M$50 each per day, especially if you are staying a few days. There are a couple of **hotels** behind the station, notably *Hotel Monis*, Carranza 15 (☎488/881-8043; ❶), which has basic rooms either with or without bathroom. *Restaurante Central*, on the main road, has decent, basic meals and Internet access.

# San Luis Potosí

Situated to the north of the Bajío's fertile heartland, the sprawling industrial centre of **SAN LUIS POTOSÍ** owes its existence and architectural splendour to a wealth of mineral deposits. Though it can by no means equal the beauty of Zacatecas, it does have a fine colonial centre and an excellent contemporary art museum, and makes a good stop-off if you're heading south from Monterrey towards the Bajío proper. The city was founded as a Franciscan mission in 1592, but it wasn't long before the Spanish discovered rich deposits of gold and silver in the country round about and began to develop the area in earnest. They added the name Potosí (after the fabulously rich mines in Bolivia) in the expectation of rivalling the original, and though this was a thoroughly wealthy town, that hope was never fully realized. Unlike its erstwhile rivals, however, San Luis is still prosperous – most of the silver is gone but working mines churn out zinc and lead – with a considerable modern industrial base. As a result, San Luis, while preserving a little-changed colonial heart, is also a large and lively modern city.

## Arrival and information

Long-distance buses arrive at the main suburban **bus station** (officially Terminal Terrestre Potosina, with a pricey 24-hour guardería), around 3km east of the centre on Hwy-57; for downtown and the Alameda walk outside and board "Ruta 6". It appears to head out of town but doubles back: get off at the former train station (soon to be the town's railway museum) and walk from there. To return to the bus station, pick up "Ruta 6" from the northwest corner of the Alameda on Constitución.

For general information, head for the helpful **tourist office**, Othón 130, just off the Jardín Hidalgo (Mon–Fri 8am–9pm, Sat 9am–1pm; ☎444/812-9481,

# SAN LUIS POTOSÍ

Market (1 block)

Museo Taurino (500m), Bus Station (3km), F (3km) & G

6 (50m), 7 (100m), Zona Rosa (500m), 8 (500m), 9 (700m), 10 (1km) & Parques Tangamanga (4km)

I (400m)

0 — 300 m

N

University
La Compañia
Capilla de Loreto
PLAZA DE LOS FUNDADORES
Caja Real
Palacio de Gobierno
Palacio Municipal
JARDÍN HIDALGO
Cathedral
Casa de Othón
San Juan de Dios
Museo Federico Silva
JARDÍN DE SAN JUAN DE DIOS
Templo del Carmen
PLAZA DEL CARMEN
Buses to Main Bus Station
Museo Del Virreinato
Museo de la Mascara
Teatro de la Paz
Railway Museum
Alameda
Centro de Difusion Cultural
San José
Bellas Artes
PLAZA SAN AUGUSTÍN
Templo de San Augustín
CALLEJÓN DE LOZADA
Instituto de Cultura
PLAZA DE SAN FRANCISCO
Templo de San Francisco
Presbyterian Church
Templo del Tercera Orden
PLAZA DE ARANZAZU
Museo Regional Potosino
Sagrado Corazón

GONZALEZ ORTEGA
GONZALEZ BOCANEGRA
ARISTA
CARMONA
ALLENDE
ALVARO OBREGÓN
HIDALGO
MORELOS
ESCOBEDO
JUAN SARABIA
OTAHEGUI
XOCHITL
20 DE NOVIEMBRE
LOS BRAVO
LA PERLA
MANUEL JOSE OTHÓN
INDEPENDENCIA
VENUSTIANO CARRANZA
DIAZ DE LEON
FRANCISCO I. MADERO
ALDAMA
ITURBIDE
AGUSTIN DE ITURBIDE
VICENTE GUERRERO
UNIVERSIDAD
GUERRERO
5 DE MAYO
GALEANA
ZARAGOZA
ABASOLO
COMONFORT
OCAMPO
VALLEJO
VILLERAIS
PARRODI
CONSTITUCION

**ACCOMMODATION**

| | |
|---|---|
| Hotel Alameda | C |
| Hotel Anahuac | A |
| Hotel de Gante | E |
| Hotel Maria Dolores | F |
| Hotel Napoles | B |
| Hotel Panorama | D |
| Hotel Progreso | H |
| Hotel Sands | G |
| San Miguelito Hostal | I |

**EATING & DRINKING**

| | |
|---|---|
| La Abeja | 11 |
| Café Pacifico | 1 |
| El Callejón de San Francisco | 12 |
| La Cava del Gallego | 8 |
| Chaires | 2 |
| Club Play | 4 |
| La Corriente | 6 |
| Costanzo | 5 |
| Los Frailes Café | 13 |
| Hipo Campo | 7 |
| Imix | 9 |
| Luna Café | 14 |
| Osaka Sushi Bar | 10 |
| La Parroquia | 3 |

Ⓦ www.visitasanluispotosi.com.mx). They'll hand out a detailed **map** of the town. They can also fill you in on the city's **festivals**, the most exciting of which are the Día de la Asunción (Assumption; Aug 15), a religious festival with traditional dances outside the cathedral that coincides with the Feria de la Uva, the city's grape festival, and the Día de San Luis Rey (Aug 25), a huge fiesta enthusiastically enjoyed by virtually the whole town – a giant procession and fireworks follow.



## Accommodation

Apart from the new **hostel**, the cheapest **rooms** in San Luis are found in the slightly run-down area north of the **Alameda**. Places on the back streets can be quieter than those closer to the main plazas, where the **Jardín Hidalgo** is the focus. Even here, though prices are reasonable, there are few truly outstanding options, and for a little luxury you may prefer some of the more modern places around the long-distance bus station.

**Hotel Alameda** La Perla 3, behind the Pemex station on the north side of the Alameda Ⓣ 444/814-8901. Very basic and sometimes noisy, but clean and inexpensive. The best of a number of similar places in this area. ❷

**Hotel Anahuac** Xochitl 140 Ⓣ 444/812-6505, Ⓕ 814-4904. Bright, clean and cheery rooms make this friendly and comfortable hotel about the best in the Alameda area, provided you don't mind the photos emblazoned with scripture extracts. Safe parking. ❹

**Hotel de Gante** 5 de Mayo 140 Ⓣ 444/812-1492, Ⓔ hotel_degante@hotmail.com. Central, comfortable and spacious but with little atmosphere; chiefly of interest if you can get a room overlooking the Jardín Hidalgo. ❺

**Hotel Maria Dolores** Hwy-57, opposite the Central de Autobuses Ⓣ & Ⓕ 444/822-1882, Ⓦ www.hotelmariadolores.com. One of the swankiest of San Luis's hotels, all low-rise and set around attractive gardens studded with palms and swimming pools. Restaurants, bars and nightclubs fill ancillary buildings, and rooms, all with cable TV and minibars, mostly have direct access to lawns. There are almost always sizeable reductions from the rack rate if you ask. ❺

**Hotel Napoles** Juan Sarabiá 120 Ⓣ 444/812-8418, Ⓔ hnapoles@prodigy.net.mx. Modern and well-maintained business hotel with cable TV and phone in the carpeted rooms, and parking. One of the best in this price range. ❻

**Hotel Panorama** Venustiano Carranza 315, west of Plaza Fundadores Ⓣ 444/812-1777 or 01-800/480-0100, Ⓦ www.hotelpanorama.com.mx. Slick, upmarket business hotel – the plushest in the centre of town with pleasant breezy rooms, modern furniture, comfortable public areas, an outdoor pool, restaurant and sports bar. Pay the extra M$130 for the remodelled a/c rooms. ❻

**Hotel Progreso** Aldama 415, at Iturbide Ⓣ 444/812-0366. One of the best deals downtown, this old but well-maintained property displays some unusual details such as rare ceramic tiles. Rooms are plain, but with TVs. Ask for a streetside room, as some internal rooms are a bit poky, with poor ventilation. Breakfast available. ❹

**Hotel Sands** Km 423 Hwy-57, 100m east (right) of the Central de Autobuses Ⓣ 444/818-2436. Ⓦ www.hotelsands-slp.com.mx. Excellent-value hacienda-style motel set around a pool and shaded lawns. High-standard rooms all have cable TV, fans and adjacent parking. ❻

**San Miguelito Hostal** Fernando Rosas 530 Ⓣ 44/814-8382, Ⓦ mx.geocities.com/hostalsanmiguelito/. Brand new hostel fifteen minutes' walk south of the Plaza de Armas with comfortable dorms, Internet access and a good kitchen. Follow Vallejo off the southern edge of our map, continue 300m then turn right into Fernando Rosas. M$100 per person.

## The City

Despite its uninviting industrial outskirts, the centre of San Luis Potosí is calm and beautiful, set on a tidy grid of largely pedestrianized streets around a series of little colonial plazas. Chief among these is the **Jardín Hidalgo**, the old Plaza de Armas, surrounded by state and city government offices and overlooked by the cathedral. Northeast of the plaza, pedestrianized Avenida Hidalgo and the streets around it comprise the city's main shopping area; the department stores near the plaza give way to smaller, simpler shops as you approach the **Mercado Hidalgo**, a good place for souvenirs and fresh produce. Further north, the street stalls and stores become increasingly basic until you reach another, much larger produce and clothing market, beyond the main road that delineates the edge of the centre. Hidalgo's southern continuation, Zaragoza, is also traffic-free and heads through a more up-and-coming area, while to the west lies swanky Avenida Carranza, which, five blocks from Jardín Hidalgo, becomes a fully fledged *zona rosa*, the fancy restaurants and designer boutiques running for perhaps a kilometre to the leafy square of Jardín Tequis.



### Jardín Hidalgo and around

Though not the most elegant of the city's churches, the **cathedral** dominates the east side of the **Jardín Hidalgo**. It was built in the early eighteenth century, but successive generations have ensured that little remains of the original. Facing the cathedral across the square is the long facade of the **Palacio del Gobierno** (daily 8am–3pm & 6–9pm; free), with its balustraded roof. This, too, has been substantially refurbished over the years, but at least alterations have preserved the harmony of its clean Neoclassical lines. At the time of writing there was little to see inside, though once the current restorations are complete you should be able to see the Salón de Juárez, a suite of rooms occupied by Benito Juárez when San Luis became his temporary capital in 1863: head up either set of stairs and turn left. French troops supporting Emperor Maximilian soon drove him out, but Juárez returned in 1866, and in this building confirmed the death sentence passed on Maximilian. There's an absurd waxwork model of Juárez with the Princess Salm Salm, one of Maximilian's daughters, kneeling before him pleading for the emperor's pardon. He refused, "thus ending the short-lived empire", according to the state government's leaflet, "and strengthening, before all peoples and the entire world, Mexico's prestige as a liberty loving nation". Just behind the cathedral lies **Casa de Othón**, Othón 225 (Tues–Fri 10am–2pm & 4–6pm, Sat & Sun 10am–2pm; M$3), a pretty and well-tended museum, though a rather lifeless tribute to Manuel José Othón, San Luis' most famous poet, mainly comprising some of his furniture.

### East of Jardín Hidalgo: Plaza del Carmen, San Agustín and the Museo Federico Silva

Moving east along Othón, the **Templo del Carmen**, on little Plaza del Carmen, is the most beautiful and harmonious of all San Luis's churches. Exuberantly decorated with a multicoloured tiled dome and elaborate Baroque facade, it has an equally flashy interior: in particular, a fantastically intricate *retablo* attributed to eighteenth-century eccentric and polymath Francisco Tresguerras. Next door to the church is the **Museo del Virreinato** (Tues–Fri 10am–7pm, Sat & Sun 10am–5pm; M$3), a huge collection of artwork and artefacts from the Spanish colonial era.

A few steps south is the bulky, columned **Teatro de la Paz** (Tues–Sat 10am–2pm & 5–8pm; free for viewing), built in the nineteenth century under Porfirio Díaz and typical of the grandiose public buildings of that era, though its modern interior fails to live up to the extravagance of the exterior. Directly opposite the theatre, you'll find the **Museo Nacional de la Máscara**, Villerias 2 (closed for renovations at the time of writing; check with the tourist office), a compulsive and fascinating place with exhibits on everything from pre-Hispanic masks to costumes that are still worn for fiestas and traditional dances. Displays instruct (in Spanish) as to the meaning and continued significance of many of the dances. Also included are the so-called "giants of San Luis", eight enormous models representing four royal couples (from Africa, Europe, Asia and America), which are flaunted in the streets during the festival of Corpus Christi in May. Look out too for the funerary mask made from a skull, inlaid with a mosaic of turquoise and black stone. South of the museum, another magnificent Baroque exterior, that of the **Templo de San Agustín**, faces out onto the tiny Plaza San Agustín – there's little to offer if you venture inside, however.

If you trace your steps back to the Plaza del Carmen and this time head north out the plaza, you'll come to one of San Luis Potosí's highlights, the **Museo Federico Silva**, Jardín de San Juan de Dios (Mon–Sat 10am–6pm, Sun 10am–2pm; M$30; ⓣ444/812-3848, ⓦwww.museofedericosilva.com), which focuses on the works of Federico Silva, one of Mexico's most exalted sculptors. Transformed from a seventeenth-century convent into a contemporary sculpture museum, this relative newcomer to San Luis has already left its mark. The open spaces are a lovely synthesis of the ancient and modern, much like the works of Silva (now in his eighties) who has always striven to create modern interpretations of Mexico's pre-Hispanic forms. His blockish volcanic stone and steel forms dominate the galleries: some are vaguely human and others geometric abstractions – all are beautifully lit. Don't miss *Scriptum*, a huge weighty figure entirely filling a kind of crypt as if it were secreted deep within some Aztec pyramid.

### The Alameda and beyond

The **Alameda**, 300m east of the Jardín Hidalgo and ringed by heavy traffic, is typically crowded with strolling families, photographers, candy-sellers and people waiting for local buses. On its southern side, the modern **Instituto Potosino de Bellas Artes** (Mon–Fri 10am–1pm & 4–7.30pm) occasionally hosts art exhibitions and is usually worth sticking your head into. Nearby, the **Centro de Difusión Cultural** (daily 10am–2pm & 5–8pm; prices vary but usually under M$10) occupies a concrete building that looks like a modern church. It holds temporary exhibits of anything from modern art to stamp collections. The former train station, on the north side of the Alameda, is now in the process of being converted into a **railway museum**, though it's not yet known when construction will be complete.

Around a kilometre east of the Alameda lies the **Plaza de Toros**. If you're fascinated by "La Corrida" but would never attend, do so vicariously at the adjacent **Museo Taurino**, at the corner of Universidad and López Hermosa (Mon–Sat noon–2.30pm & 5.30–8pm; free), where, if you can rouse the custodian (buzz the second door on the right), you'll be shown ranks of dramatic promotional posters dating back to the glory days, elaborate blood-encrusted suits of lights and an array of stuffed bull heads, all of which are missing at least one ear.

### West of Jardín Hidalgo: Plaza de los Fundadores and Plaza de San Francisco

Immediately west of the Jardín Hidalgo, the paved **Plaza de los Fundadores** is a much larger and more formal open space. The area is fairly quiet, despite the fact that it's dominated by the enormous Neoclassical **State University**. Alongside the university are two small churches, the **Capilla de Loreto** and **La Compañía**, while the fine arcaded portals of the square continue around the corner into Avenida Venustiano Carranza. From here, Carranza heads west into the central city's densest concentration of quality restaurants, bars and clubs (see opposite).

There's more interest a block south along Aldama, where you can admire the ornate Baroque facade of the **Caja Real**, the old mint – one of the finest colonial mansions in San Luis. It is now owned by the university, which sometimes holds temporary exhibitions here: you can usually walk in and take a look during the day to see the gentle gradient of the stairway, which supposedly made it easier to lug boxes full of gold and silver up and down. Continuing south along Aldama you come to the quiet **Plaza de San Francisco**, a lovely, shaded area redolent of the city's colonial history. It's named after the Franciscan monastery whose church, the **Templo de San Francisco**, towers over the plaza's west side and features a magnificent ship's chandelier. The monastery itself now houses the **Museo Regional Potosino** (Tues–Sat 10am–7pm, Sun 10am–5pm; M$30, free on Sun), an excellent collection of pre-Hispanic sculpture and other archeological finds, displays of local Indian culture and traditions and articles relating to the history of the state of San Luis Potosí. In addition to a fine cloister, there's access, upstairs, to the lavish Baroque chapel, **Capilla de Aranzazú** – said to be the only chapel in Latin America located on an upper floor – with exceedingly rich and enthusiastically restored churrigueresque decoration. Inside and through the side chapels lies a miscellaneous collection of religious paintings and artefacts. At the back of the museum, the **Plaza de Aranzazú** is another pleasant open space.

At the southern end of the Plaza de San Francisco, two more tiny and elaborate churches, **Sagrado Corazón** and the **Templo del Tercera Orden**, stand side by side, with a small, plain 1894 National Presbyterian Church, terribly incongruous amid all this Baroque grandeur, facing them across Galeana.

### Parques Tangamanga

If urban life is getting you down, catch the "Ruta 32" or "Parques del Sur" from the Alameda to the green expanses of the **Parques Tangamanga I and II** (open daily 6am–6pm), around 2km west of the Jardín Hidalgo. Founded in the early 1980s, the parks still lack maturity, and there are great stretches that remain undeveloped, but they make a pleasant weekend outing nonetheless. **Parque Tangamanga I** has considerably more amenities and recreation options: the entire vast acreage is piped for music and offers picnic spots, fitness circuits and a couple of small lakes. Joggers, soccer players and cyclists come here, and you can rent **bikes** for M$40 an hour from a kiosk (daily except Mon). Parque Tangamanga I also has the added attraction of the **Museo de Arte Popular** (Tues–Fri 10am–2pm & 4–6pm, Sat 10am–2pm; M$2), a showcase museum-shop of local crafts, at the bottom of Tatanacho opposite the main park entrance.

## Eating, drinking and nightlife

The centre of San Luis has several **cafés** and simple **restaurants** offering good-value *menús del día*, though little that's more exciting. Local specialities to look out for include deep-fried enchiladas and *tacos Potosinos* (or *Huastecas*), dripping with salsa and cheese, and *cecina*, a thin cut of marinated and dried steak. The **Mercado Hidalgo** is home to a host of food stalls, but the place is too packed and noisy for anything other than a hurried snack.

For anything more than good, filling food in humdrum surroundings you're going to have to wander along Carranza (affectionately known as **La Avenida**) into what is effectively San Luis's *zona rosa*, starting half a kilometre west of Plaza Fundadores. This has also traditionally been the place to head for **nightlife**, which, at weekends anyway, is pretty lively, with many places staying open until the wee hours. Most of the nightclubs play a mix of the latest US and European club grooves and Latin beats, and generally charge little or no money to get in midweek and only a minimal entry at weekends: M$50 maximum, and less for women. In the last few years several new bars have opened up around the Plaza Aranzazú and many revellers start their evening off here before heading to La Avenida.



### Central San Luis

**La Abeja** Díaz de León 104, off Plaza Fundadores. Serves natural yogurts, fruit smoothies, health foods and vitamins.

**Café Pacífico** Los Bravo and Constitución, with another location around the corner. Come here for a potent mix of gossip, action and tasty Mexican food at moderate prices. Open 24hr, this very popular café-restaurant even has a nonsmoking section.

**El Callejón de San Francisco** Callejón de Lozada 1 ⓣ444/812-4508. Enchanting, quiet beam-and-stone restaurant, with a gorgeous rooftop terrace. *Antojitos* such as chicken fajitas and *tacos Potosinos* (both around M$80) compete for attention with succulent *arranchera* steaks (M$110). Reservations advised for dinner, especially at weekends. Closed Mon.

**Chaires** Jardín Hidalgo. Right on the plaza, *Chaires* is alive with families, friends and canoodling couples sipping java and tucking into elaborate pastries.

**Club Play** Carranza 333. San Luis's hottest nightspot and concert hall. The meat market begins after midnight.

**Costanzo** Carranza 325, at Plaza Fundadores. A confections chain, with all manner of tempting chocolates and sweet things in shiny paper. No seating, but there's a café next door.

**Los Frailes Café** Universidad 165. Youthful evening café with occasional live acoustic music at weekends.

**Luna Café** Universidad 155. Slightly more upscale than *Los Frailes* next door, offering gourmet coffees and cocktails.

**La Parroquia** Carranza at Plaza Fundadores. Comfortable middle-of-the-road café, where crusty rolls replace the traditional stack of tortillas. Excellent breakfasts and comida corrida – a firm favourite with local office workers.

### La Avenida

**La Cava del Gallego** Carranza 1040. No sign. Spanish-style bar that's fine for a quiet drink or as a place to practise your Spanish by discussing the football or the bulls on TV.

**La Corriente** Carranza 700, right at the start of the avenue. Lovely restaurant centred on a shaded courtyard and specializing in Mexican steak dishes (M$90–100) but also offering a wide range of enchiladas, *chilaquiles* and good comida corrida (M$60) at prices that are modest for this part of town.

**Hipo Campo** Carranza 725. Casual local hangout with fresh tortas, *aguas frescas* and rare sidewalk seating. Exceptionally clean.

**Imix** Carranza 1137. A small, dim and amiable bar with a trendy crowd and MTV on a big screen. There are often drink specials and no cover before midnight.

**Osaka Sushi Bar** Carranza 700. Reasonably priced sushi, *teppanyaki* and Mexican *botanas* (bar snacks), along with fairly pricey sashimi.

## Listings

**Banks and exchange** There are banks with ATMs all around the main plazas, including Banamex at Allende and Obregón, and several casas de cambio in the same area.

**Books and newspapers** The newsstands on Los Bravo, just off the Jardín Hidalgo, have a few English-language publications, and it might be worth trying Librerías Gonvil, Carranza 500 at Bolivar. Sanborn's, in the Plaza Tangamanga shopping centre, close to the Parques Tangamanga, has a slightly wider selection, though unless you are desperate it may not be worth the journey.

**Buses** Buses cover every conceivable route, with departures for Mexico City and Monterrey every few minutes, for Guadalajara, Tampico and the border at least hourly. Flecha Amarilla has excellent second-class services to Dolores Hidalgo (14 daily), San Miguel (every couple of hours) and Guanajuato (slightly less frequently). Northbound, there are very frequent services to Saltillo and beyond to the US border towns, most calling at Matehuala, where you change for buses to Real de Catorce.

**Emergencies** For general emergencies dial ⓣ066. For medical emergencies, the handiest clinic is Beneficencia Española, Carranza (ⓣ444/811-5694), or just call the Cruz Roja on ⓣ444/815-3635.

**Internet access** Several places, including Cibercafe La Paz, Guerrero 269 (daily 10am–10pm; M$10/hr), and Café Cibernetico, Carranza 416 (daily 10am–9pm; M$15/hr).

**Pharmacy** Farmacia La Perla, Los Bravo 240 at Escobedo (☎444/812-5922) and Farmacia Guadalajara, at Carranza 100, are always open.
**Post office** Morelos 235 (Mon–Fri 9am–4pm).

## South of San Luis Potosí

From San Luis most traffic heads south on Hwy-57 towards Mexico City, along a fast divided highway all the way. Unless you're in a crazy hurry, though, you should definitely spend time in Guanajuato, San Miguel and Dolores Hidalgo, some of the most fascinating towns in the whole of the republic. Hwy-70, the route east to Tampico and the Gulf of Mexico, can hardly compete for attraction, but it does run through a few towns of minor interest along the way and provides the easiest access to the fascinating sculpture garden at **Xilitla** (see p.319).

# Zacatecas

**ZACATECAS**, almost 2500m up and crammed into a narrow gully between two hills, packs more of interest into a small space than almost anywhere in Mexico and ranks, alongside Guanajuato, as one of the Bajío's finest colonial cities. Its beauty enhanced by the harshness of the semi-desert landscape all around, it remains much as the British Admiralty's *Handbook of Mexico* described it in 1905: "irregular", its streets "very narrow, steep, and frequently interrupted by stone steps" and "much exposed to winds blowing through the gorge". Those same winds still gust bitterly cold in winter, and even though many of the once cobbled streets are now paved and choked with traffic, the town is otherwise little changed.

The town is dominated by the **Cerro de la Bufa**, with its extraordinary rock cockscomb crowning the ridge some 150m above the city; at night it's illuminated, with a giant cross lit up on top. A modern Swiss cable car connects the summit with the Cerro del Grillo – a superb ride straight over the heart of the old town. From the Cerro de la Bufa itself, commanding views take in the entire city, from its drab new suburbs to the bare hills all around, pockmarked with old mine-workings. From this height, the city's sprawl isn't particularly inviting, but it's when you get down there, among the narrow streets, twisting alleys, colonial fountains, carved doorways and ornate churches, that the city's real splendour is revealed.

### Some history

It didn't take the conquistadors long to discover the enormous lodes of **silver** in the hills of Mexico's central highlands, and, after some initial skirmishes with the Zacateco Indians, the city of Zacatecas was founded in 1546. For the next three centuries its mines disgorged fabulous wealth, enriching both the city and the Spanish Crown; in 1728 the mines here were producing one-fifth of all Mexico's silver. Though bandits and local indigenous groups continuously preyed on the town, nothing could deter the fortune hunters and labourers from around the world – Spanish nobles, African slaves, German engineers, British bankers – drawn by the prospect of all that wealth. The end of the boom, when it came, was brought about more by the political uncertainties of the nineteenth century than by the exhaustion of the mines, some of which still

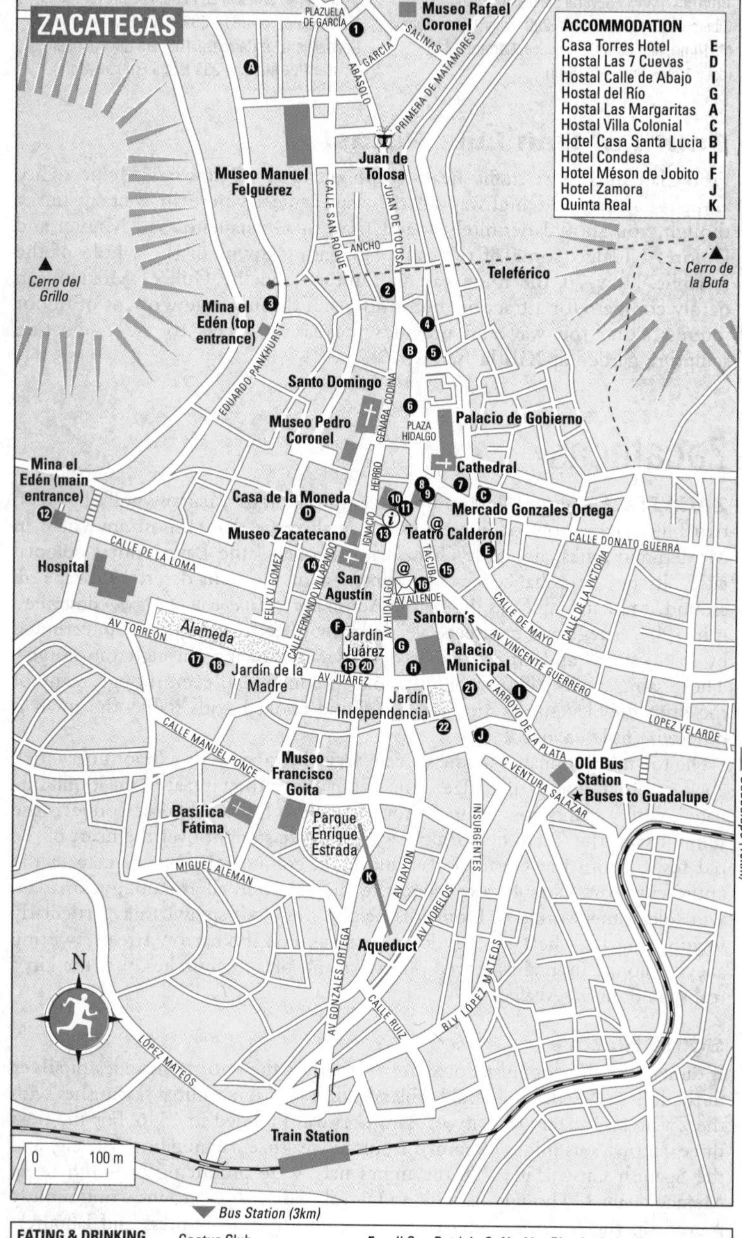


**EATING & DRINKING**

| | | | | | | | |
|---|---|---|---|---|---|---|---|
| Acrópolis | 8 | Cactus Club | 5 | Il San Patricio Café | 11 | Rincón de los Trovadores | 4 |
| Bar Botarel | K | Los Dorados de Villa | 1 | Mi Viejo | 14 | Rosticería el Pastor | 22 |
| Barekey | 3 | Garufa | 20 | La Mina Club | 12 | Todos Santos | 7 |
| Birrierias Jaramillo | 6 | Gaudí | 9 | La Plaza | K | El Tragadero | 19 |
| La Bodeguilla | 13 | Gorditas Doña Julia | 10, 15 & 17 | El Raspanieve | 2 | La Unica Cabaña | 21 |
| | | Hong Kong | 16 | El Recovero | 18 | | |

operate today. Throughout nearly a century of war, Zacatecas itself became an important prize: there were major battles here in 1871, when Benito Juárez successfully put down local rebels, and in 1914 when Pancho Villa's **División del Norte** captured the city, completely annihilating its 12,000-strong garrison. Today Zacatecas is booming once more, its business and light industry boosted by the increasing flow of traffic between Mexico and the US. The town's prosperity has ensured a strong vein of civic pride, and many of the old colonial buildings have been lovingly restored. The granting of UNESCO World Heritage status to the historic centre has helped maintain its rich and sophisticated air, and forced new growth south of town on the road towards Guadalupe. Lack of parking downtown has even forced university and government departments out to the modern developments, which are lent an increasingly Americanized feel by the presence of a Wal-Mart, multiplex cinemas and dozens of fast-food franchises.

## Arrival and information

Situated at one of northern Mexico's crucial crossroads, Zacatecas's modern **bus terminal** is a hive of activity both day and night. Four kilometres out of the centre, it lies south of the now-disused train station. There's a small 24-hour guardería. To get into town take "Ruta 8" (every few minutes 7am–9pm) or a taxi (around M$40). To return to the bus terminal, take "Ruta 8" (marked "Central"), which runs frequently along Fernando Villapando and past the Jardín Independencia. The *jardín* is probably the best place to get off the bus – wherever you're headed, you're almost certain to be able to get there from here, and it's within reasonable walking distance of most of the accommodation. From the **airport**, 27km north of town, take one of the official taxis into the centre for around M$200.

Barely marked, the **tourist office** is at Hidalgo 401, near the Teatro Calderón (daily 9am–9pm; ⓣ492/924-4047 or 01-800/712-4078, ⓦwww.turismozacatecas.gob.mx); it can provide a smattering of leaflets, a poor street map and informative, friendly advice. The staff will also provide guidance on Zacatecas's excellent **festivals**, of which there are many. For two weeks around Semana Santa the city celebrates the enormous **Zacatecas en la Cultura**, with daily events all over town including everything from high-quality Mexican rock acts and even a few foreign bands to folkloric dance, opera and ballet: most events are free. The **International Folk Festival** (late July–early Aug) is Mexico's top folk festival with around fifty nationalities represented, mostly performing in the plazas around the centre. It is closely flowed by **La Morisma** (weekend closest to Aug 27), when up to 10,000 people engage in mock battles in between Moors and Christians acted out on the Cerro de la Bufa. An import from Spain, where this type of stylized fighting is more common, Zacatecas's event is the best in Mexico. Zacatecas's principal fiesta is the **Feria de Zacatecas** (September, first two weeks), with bullfights (the fiercest fighting bulls in all Mexico are bred around Zacatecas) and plenty of traditional carousing. The activity happens at La Feria, 3km south towards Guadalupe.

## Accommodation

Once you're in the middle of town, finding somewhere **to stay** is no problem. Genuine budget hotels are rare and some of the mid-range places are unspectacular, but there are several hostels, and some excellent top-end places. If you've a little more money to spend, head straight for the superbly elegant establishments in the centre. Nights are cold in Zacatecas, so check that you have enough blankets.

It is worth noting that accommodation is hard to come by around Semana Santa, the week leading up to Easter, and during the main fiesta in late August and the first half of September.

**Casa Torres Hotel** Primero de Mayo 325 ⓣ492/925-3266, ⓦwww.hotelcasatorres.com. Quite unlike any other hotel in town, the rooms at this chic, modern place are tastefully decorated, with local artwork on the walls, and feature flat-screen TVs and climate control. Standard rooms are a bit small so you may want to step up to a junior suite (M$1380), or even a master suite (M$1509) with balcony and cathedral views. Breakfast (included) is served in the lovely top-floor restaurant/bar. ❼

**Hostal Las 7 Cuevas** Callejón de Lancaster 109 ⓣ492/925-4135. New and rather spartan hostel with communal cooking facilities, pleasant patios, dorms (M$100) and a few private rooms. ❸

**Hostal Calle de Abajo** Victor Rosales 160 ⓣ492/925-1255, ⓔhostal_calledeabajo@terra.com.mx. This friendly hotel on a quiet street has a dramatic arched entrance and antique reception desk. Rooms are simple but comfortable. ❺

**Hostal del Río** Hidalgo 116 ⓣ492/924-0035. Rambling colonial place full of character and right in the heart of things. All rooms are whitewashed and come with simple decor and TV. The basement rooms are cheaper, but most prefer the more spacious upstairs rooms, some of which sleep up to five (great for families). Unlimited purified water available. ❹

**Hostal Las Margaritas** Segunda de las Margaritas 105 ⓣ492/925-1711, ⓔlasmargaritashostal@hotmail.com. Attractive and welcoming hostel a short walk from the centre with comfortable six-bunk dorms (M$110 per person; M$90 with HI membership), doubles and twins. There's a great rooftop terrace with kitchen, a pool table downstairs, Internet access and laundry facilities. ❸

**Hostal Villa Colonial** Primero de Mayo and Callejón Mono Prieto ⓣ492/922-1980, ⓦwww.hostels-zacatecas.com. A dream hostel located in the thick of it and enthusiastically run by Zacatecan locals. Comfortable four-bed dorms (M$90 per person; HI members M$80), double and twin rooms (M$190) and very nice en-suite doubles in a separate building, some with their own kitchen (M$250). Extras include a sunny rooftop terrace, Internet access, cable TV, a book exchange and a genuinely sociable atmosphere. They also organize excursions to La Quemada, and English is spoken. ❷–❹

**Hotel Casa Santa Lucía** Hidalgo 717 ⓣ492/924-4900, ⓦwww.hotelcasasantalucia.com. Perhaps the best value of the middle to upmarket hotels, making attractive use of its beautiful ancient structure and providing comfortable rooms with high ceilings, big tiled bathrooms, exposed stonework and simple but tasteful decor. Breakfast is included, and there's a great terrace with views of the cathedral and La Bufa. ❼

**Hotel Condesa** Juárez 102 ⓣ492/922-1160, ⓦwww.hotelcondesa.com.mx. Remodelled hotel in a fantastic central location amid the action of the Jardín Independencia. The huge lobby exhibits old photos and the modern rooms come with TV and cherry furniture; some have bathtubs (M$700). Ask for a room with a view of the *jardín*. There's also a spiffy café and serviceable hotel bar. ❺

**Hotel Mesón de Jobito** Jardín Juárez 143 ⓣ492/924-1722, reservations 01-800/021-0040, ⓦwww.mesondejobito.com.mx. An entire colonial street on the city's most enchanting square has been converted into this superb luxury hotel. Pretty, plush and private, all rooms come with a/c, and some with Jacuzzis. There are two formal restaurants, and depending on the night, a lively bar – just what you'd expect in a top hotel. ❾

**Hotel Zamora** Plaza Zamora, at the top of Ventura Sálazar, by Jardín Independencia ⓣ492/922-1200. Cheap, central, no-frills option with TV and a shower over the toilet. ❸

**Quinta Real** Gonzalez Ortega, by the aqueduct ⓣ492/922-9104 or 01-800/457-4000, ⓦwww.quintareal.com. Gorgeous and outrageously luxurious hotel in the shadow of the colonial aqueduct that has beautifully incorporated what was once Zacatecas's bullring. Every comfort is taken to the extreme degree (there's even a "pillow menu"), and this is certainly a place worth saving up for, not to mention one of the most distinctive properties in the Americas. ❾

## The Town

Although you may find yourself tiring quickly if you're not used to the altitude, the most rewarding way to enjoy Zacatecas is by aimless wandering, particularly

△ Alleys, Zacatecas

in the cool of the evening, when the streets are full. This is a city of constant surprises, with narrow alleys crowding in on each other as they scramble about the steep-sided ravine, revealing a series of little plazas and glimpses of tiny hidden courtyards. In the beautifully preserved town centre the highlight is undoubtedly the ornate **cathedral**, from which all other main sights are within walking distance.

Though the cathedral is the formal heart of the city, and the adjacent **Plaza Hidalgo**, in front of the Palacio de Gobierno, is where formal events take place, life for locals revolves more around the **Jardín Independencia**. Just a few paces from the market and from the important junction of Juárez and Hidalgo, this is in effect the city's main plaza, where people gather in the evenings, hang out between appointments and wait for buses. West of the Jardín Independencia is the **Alameda**, a thin strip of stone benches, splashing fountains and a bandstand that makes a cool retreat from the heat of the day. Adjacent, you'll find the charming oasis **Jardín de la Madre**, distinguishable by its fountain featuring a beatific maternal figure and well-tended flora.



### The cathedral and around

Zacatecas's flamboyant **cathedral** is the outstanding relic of the city's years of colonial glory: built in the pink stone typical of the region, it represents one of the latest, and arguably the finest, examples of Mexican Baroque architecture. It was completed in 1750, its facade carved with a wild exuberance unequalled anywhere in the country. The interior, they say, was once at least its equal – furnished in gold and silver, with rich wall hangings and a great collection of paintings – but as everywhere, it was despoiled or the riches removed for "safekeeping", first at the time of Juárez's reforms and later during the Revolution; only the structure itself, with its bulky Doric columns and airy vaulting, remains to be admired. On each side of the cathedral there's a small plaza: to the north the formal Plaza Hidalgo, to the south a tiny paved *plazuela*, **Plaza Huizar**, which often hosts lively street theatre and impromptu musical performances.

The **Plaza Hidalgo** is surrounded by more colonial buildings. On the east side, the eighteenth-century **Palacio de Gobierno** was built as a home by the Conde Santiago de la Laguna and subsequently bought by the state government. In keeping with local fashion, a modern mural depicting the city's history embellishes the interior courtyard. Opposite, along with what is now the *Hotel Emporia*, lies the Palacio de Justicia, known locally as the **Casa de la Mala Noche**. According to legend, its builder, Manuel de Rétegui, was a mine-owner down to his last peso, which he gave away to a starving widow to feed her family. He then spent a long night of despair in the house ("la mala noche"), contemplating bankruptcy and suicide, until at dawn his foreman hammered on the door with the miraculous news that a huge vein of silver had been struck, and they were all to be rich.

On the other side of the cathedral, the **Mercado Gonzales Ortega** is a strikingly attractive market building, built at the end of the nineteenth century. It takes advantage of its sloping position to have two fronts: the upper level opening onto Hidalgo, the lower floor with entrances on Tacuba. Converted into a fancy little shopping mall, it's now filled with tourist shops and smart boutiques, as well as a superb wine store. On Hidalgo opposite the mercado, the **Teatro Calderón** is a grandiose nineteenth-century theatre. At the southern end of the mercado, broad steps help turn the little **Plazuela Goyita** into a popular place for street theatre.

### Santo Domingo, Museo Pedro Coronel and Museo Zacatecano

Climbing up from the west side of Plaza Hidalgo towards the Cerro del Grillo are streets lined with more mansions – some restored, some badly in need of it, but all deserted by the mining moguls who built them. The church of **Santo Domingo** stands raised on a platform above the plaza of the same name, just uphill from the Plaza Hidalgo – its hefty, buttressed bulk a stern contrast to the lightness of the cathedral, though it was built at much the same time. In the gloom of the interior you can just make out the gilded churrigueresque *retablos* in the chapels.

Next door, the **Museo Pedro Coronel** (daily except Thurs 10am–5pm; M$20) occupies what was originally a Jesuit monastery attached to the church. Pedro Coronel Rivera was a local artist, brother of Rafael Coronel (see p.264), who managed to gather an art collection that reads like a *Who's Who* of modern art: you'll find paintings here by Picasso, Kandinsky, Braque, Chagall, Dalí and Miró, among others, as well as lithographs by Calder and Moore, architectural drawings by Piranesi, Hogarth engravings and a separate room of Pedro's own paintings and sculptures. It's undeniably an amazing collection – astonishing that one person could create it – but it's not as good as the roll call makes it sound. With the exception of a few of the Mirós, these are mostly minor works, not particularly well lit or displayed. Some of the peripheral collections are more interesting, in particular the West African and Oriental art, and the Mexican masks – haunting death masks and some traditionally used in the Moors and Christians battles. Look too for the fine pre-Columbian antiquities, beautiful Buddhas and an ornate Japanese screen with ibises on six panels. The building itself served as a hospital, a barracks and a prison before becoming a museum, and one of the grimmer dungeons is also preserved as an exhibit.

Heading south along Ignacio Hierro you'll find the **Casa de la Moneda**, Zacatecas's mint in the days when every silver-producing town in Mexico struck its own coins. Further along you come to the **Museo Zacatecano**, Dr Hierro 301 (daily except Tues 10am–5pm; M$15), where some superb and wonderfully natural 1940s photos of the Huichol people lead to a room chock-full of some two hundred Huichol embroideries that incorporate an amazing range of geometric designs, as well as maize symbols, deer and butterflies, all executed in black, red and green (for death, life and prosperity respectively). It should come as no surprise that peyote features in a big way, usually depicted by eight diamonds, a logo strangely adopted by the VIPS chain of pharmacies and restaurants. Nothing is labelled, but one of the attendants may well give you an unbidden guided tour. Most of the rest of the museum is given to a display of religious iconography: a couple of hundred wonderful hand-painted *retablos*, including a couple of sixteenth-century examples, depicting just about every saint, martyr and apostle going.

Across the street lies the church of **San Agustín**, an early eighteenth-century temple that, after the Reform Laws, was converted into a casino, while the adjoining monastery became a hotel. It has been under restoration, on and off, for decades, and is currently undergoing a final push, after which it should reopen as a cultural centre.

### Museo de Arte Abstract Manuel Felguérez

Moving north along Juan de Tolosa, cut up a signposted alley to reach the **Museo de Arte Abstract Manuel Felguérez** (daily except Tues 10am–5pm; M$20), an extensive gallery imaginatively converted from a prison and its associated church. In places the cells have been turned into mini-galleries where the intimacy of the space draws you into the works. Elsewhere several levels of cells have been ripped out to leave huge rooms with floor-to-ceiling art viewed from steel walkways that gradually take you higher. Half of what's on show is by **Manuel Felguérez**, a native of Zacatecas state and an approximate contemporary of the Coronel brothers. Within the field of abstract art he is almost as highly regarded, though it can take a bit of effort to appreciate fully his work, particularly that of the early 1980s when he developed an obsession with male reproductive anatomy. He is perhaps most successful in his sculpture, notably 1995's *El Arco del Día*, a huge bronze tripod that looks like it has just landed in a side chapel off the church. Nearby, his huge canvas entitled *Retablo de los Mártires* is also particularly striking. Elsewhere within the museum there is work by the **Coronel brothers** and several other of Felguérez's Mexican contemporaries, as well as an excellent art bookshop, though almost everything is in Spanish.



### Museo Rafael Coronel

Pedro Coronel may have amassed a spectacular art collection, but his brother Rafael has a far more beautiful museum, the centrepiece of which is a huge collection of traditional masks, possibly the finest in Mexico. The wonderful **Museo Rafael Coronel** (daily except Wed 10am–5pm; M$20) occupies the ex-Convento de San Francisco on the north side of town. Founded in 1593 as a Franciscan mission (the facade is said to be the oldest in the city), it was rebuilt in the seventeenth century, only to begin deteriorating after the Franciscans were expelled in 1857 and finally suffer destruction during Villa's assault. The building and gardens have now been partially but beautifully restored, and the museum brilliantly integrated with the ruins. There are more than four thousand masks on display, which makes taking it all in a bit overwhelming. The masks trace the art's development in what is now Mexico from some very ancient, pre-Columbian examples to contemporary masks: often there are twenty or more variations on the same theme, and one little room is entirely full of the visages of Moors and Christians from the *Danza de los Moros y Cristianos*. As well as the masks, you can see Coronel's impressive collections of ceramics and puppets, the town's original charter granted by Philip II in 1593 and sketches and drawings connected with Coronel's wife Ruth Rivera, architect and daughter of Diego. There's also a bookshop and spiffy café. If you don't fancy the pleasant walk to or from town, several bus routes, including #5, #8 and #9, pass close by.

### The aqueduct and Museo Francisco Goitia

In quite the other direction, in the south of the city you can follow the line of the **aqueduct** that used to carry water to this area. Not much of it remains, but what there is can be inspected at closer quarters from the little **Parque Enrique Estrada** on Gonzales Ortega – the continuation of Hidalgo up the hill from the centre. At the back of the park, in what was once the governor's residence, stands a third local artist's museum, the **Museo Francisco Goitia** (Tues–Sun 10am–5pm; M$20). Goitia was one of Mexico's leading painters early in the twentieth century, and this enjoyable little museum houses a permanent exhibition of his work and that of more modern local artists (including Pedro Coronel), as well as hit-or-miss temporary displays and travelling art shows. Further behind the park sits the towering terracotta-coloured **Basílica Fátima**, which looks more impressive from a distance. There's not much historical significance here; it was only finished in 1975 and is one of the city's most recent large-scale constructions.

### Mina El Edén

The **Mina El Edén**, or Eden Mine (daily 10am–6pm; M$60, those under 12 and over 60 M$30), is perhaps the most curious and unusual of all Zacatecas's attractions. The main entrance to the old mine, from where you can explore some of the sixteenth-century shafts in the heart of the Cerro del Grillo, is in the west of the city, up a road behind the modern hospital. The super-rich mine

# Mexican food and drink

**Everyone has an idea what Mexican food is, but the reality can be both more and less. You almost certainly won't see the heaped plates of grilled meats accompanied by lashings of guacamole and sour cream so common in "Mexican" restaurants outside the country. Instead, you'll find a fabulous array of tasty treats that varies significantly from region to region. Even the basics – tortillas, chiles, beans – which can be quite boring on their own, appear in different guises depending on where you are. A plain tortilla can be transformed into a marvellous taco with a dab of salsa, some shredded *nopales* (cactus leaves) or a smear of *huitlacoche* (a kind of corn fungus).**

▲ Woman making tortillas

# Tortillas

More than anything else, **tortillas** are Mexico's staple food. These unleavened flatbreads accompany just about every meal – half a dozen will come in a basket wrapped in a cloth or in a special plastic container that keeps them just as warm but is a bit less elegant. If you run out, call for more: there's almost never a charge.

Most of the country eats **corn** tortillas. These are prepared from a *masa* (paste) of ground maize, salt and water which is pressed or patted flat by hand, then heated on a *comal*, a flat steel sheet. Corn tortillas are undoubtedly at their best – soft on the inside but with a slightly crisp exterior – when served fresh off the *comal*. In the northern states, however, tortillas are typically made with **wheat** flour and rolled rather than pressed. This method of preparation produces a much softer texture, and the milder wheat flavour is said to suit such northern dishes as *queso fundido* (melted cheese) and *carne asada* (grilled meat) better than corn.

# Chiles

**Chiles** have been cultivated in Mexico for over 5000 years, and there are now some 300 varieties used. Different types have distinct cultivation needs, so depending on where your travels take you, it's likely you'll see certain varieties more than others. Ranging from the size of matchsticks to that of large carrots and in colour from red and orange to green and black, they are equally varied in potency. The hottest is the **habanero**, some 25 times hotter than the more common **jalapeño**, which is traditionally grown around the Gulf Coast city of Xalapa in Veracruz state. Far less intimidating is the **poblano**, a large, mild chile used in dishes such as *chiles rellenos* and *chiles en nogada*.

▶ Chiles

◀ ◀ Stack of cactus leaves

# Chocolate

The Olmecs of the Gulf coast began mixing cacao beans in a bitter **chocolate** drink around 3000 years ago. By the time Cortés and the conquistadors reached New Spain in the early sixteenth century, the use of cacao had spread to the Aztecs, who consumed *chocoatl* cold and mixed with spices – this "drink of the gods" was said to be a favourite of Aztec emperor Moctezuma. Chocolate remains a popular drink in Mexico today (now with lots of added sugar), but its most distinctive use is in **mole poblano**, a thick sauce of chocolate and chiles that accompanies otherwise savoury dishes – particularly chicken. Though found all over the country, *mole* remains a speciality of Puebla in central Mexico, where the dish originated in the colonial era.

▲ Bowls of *mole*

## Salsa

Most first-time visitors don't realize how tame most Mexican fare actually is. The heat usually comes from one of several chile-based **salsas** supplied as condiments on the table. If you want your food to stay mild, go easy on the salsa. Even if you prefer things a bit spicy, it's worth tasting a little salsa before you go slopping it all over the place – they can be devilishly picante. For more on salsa composition, see the box on p.45.

# Tequila

You'll probably spend far more time in Mexico drinking beer rather than **tequila**. However, this distilled extract of the agave plant remains very much part of Mexico's national identity: though its manufacture is confined to the state of Jalisco and its immediate environs, tequila has become one of the country's most important exports. The spirit's well-entrenched reputation as a party-enlivener has earned it a pretty bad rap over the years, but that's beginning to change. While you can still buy a bottle of firewater for under M$100, connoisseurs are increasingly paying big bucks for sophisticated tipples, and thoughtful sipping is making inroads into the shot-glass tradition. For more on tequila styles and manufacture, see the box on p.356.

▼ Tequila

▲ Tropical fruit

# Mexican cuisine: a regional sampler

It's easy to think of Mexican food as one cuisine. In reality, while there are common themes, each region has its own excellent specialities.

**Baja California** In Baja, the sea is all around, so it makes sense that *mariscos* (seafood) and *pescado* (fish) dominate most menus – the fish taco is an eternal favourite. Bowls of *ceviche*, a delicious Peruvian import of raw fish marinated in lemon or lime juice, commonly grace tables. Northern Baja is home to Mexico's wine industry, and consequently a glass of wine with your meal is far more common here than elsewhere in the country.

**The north** Dining in the north, where the land is too dry to grow produce, tends to revolve around grilled meat: the *asado* (barbecue) is king. *Cabrito asado* (roast kid) is the classic dish, often served in gargantuan portions and accompanied only by tortillas and salsa. These basic ingredients combine into burritos and fajitas, dishes that have travelled north of the border to become what most of the world thinks of as "Mexican food".

**Central Mexico** With fertile valleys and highlands that receive enough rain to sustain agriculture, central Mexico is home to the widest range of local ingredients. This is the land of the avocado (and therefore guacamole) and the birthplace of tequila. Mexico's second city, Guadalajara, excels with its *birria*, a soupy stew, while coastal towns dish up huge plates of *camarones* (shrimps). Further south, Oaxaca is famed for its mild string cheese. Look out in Oaxaca, too, for *chapulines*, crunchy grasshoppers fried in chile and lime.

**The Yucatán** Influenced by the flavours of the Caribbean, an abundance of tropical fruits and the all-powerful burn of the *habanero* chile, Yucatecan cuisine is a world apart from that of central Mexico. The most celebrated dish is *cochinita pibil*, pork marinated in a *recado* made from garlic, chiles, black pepper, cumin, cinnamon, oregano and vinegar, then wrapped in plantain leaves and grilled.

produced the silver that gave Zacatecas its wealth, and though little is produced around the town now, Fresnillo, 60km to the north, has the world's largest silver mine, which sometimes produces seven tons of the precious metal a day.

The forty-minute guided tour (roughly every 15min; generally in frenetic Spanish, but ask if a bilingual guide is available) – which takes in only a fraction of the workings – involves a small train ride 500m into the mountain. Here a well-presented museum displays rocks from around the world (though mostly Mexico), including impressive geodes and fossilized ammonites and trilobites. You're then taken on a fairly sanitized look at the mine workings - subterranean pools, chasms crossed on steel bridges and scattered machinery, all complete with colourfully lit mannequins dressed as miners. Enthusiastic guides tell of the thousands of miners that died during the mine's four hundred years of operation. The high number of fatalities seems perfectly possible when you see level upon level of old galleries falling away for some 320m beneath you, inaccessible since the mine flooded when production stopped in 1966. The entire hill is honeycombed with tunnels, and in one of them a lift has been installed that takes you up to the slopes of the Cerro del Grillo, about 200m from the lower station of the cable car (you can also enter the mine from this end, though you may have a longer wait for a guide). It is also worth returning in the evening to dance the night away at *La Mina Club* (see p.267).

**To reach the mine**, take a bus from the Jardín Independencia up Juárez to the hospital (buses marked "IMSS"), or walk, taking in a pleasant stroll along the Alameda followed by a brief climb.

### The teleférico and Cerro de la Bufa

The lower station of the **teleférico** (cable car; daily 10am–6pm; M$24 each way; services can be disrupted by strong winds) is on the slopes of the Cerro del Grillo, near the back entrance to El Edén. Once you're used to the altitude, it's an easy climb up from San Agustín, or you can take bus #7 right to the door. Out from the station you pass right over the city centre – the views down on the houses are extraordinary. Most people make a return trip across the city from Cerro del Grillo to the top of the Cerro de la Bufa, but walking back down is no great strain.

At the summit of the **Cerro de la Bufa**, after you've taken in the superb panorama of Zacatecas and its surroundings, visit the little **Capilla del Patrocinio**, an eighteenth-century chapel with an image of the Virgin said to perform healing miracles, and stroll around the observatory, on the very edge of the crags. Also up here, the **Museo de la Toma de Zacatecas** (daily 10am–5pm; M$12), full of revolutionary arms and memorabilia, honours Pancho Villa's spectacular victory in the town, also commemorated with a dramatic equestrian statue outside.

Behind the statue a path leads to the top of the great crest of rock, from where there are yet more stupendous views. A second path to the right of the statue skirts around the base of La Bufa to the **Mausoleo de los Hombres Ilustres**, where *Zacatecanos* who have made their mark on history are buried, or at least have their memorials. There are still a few empty places, and it would be a magnificent place to end up – as close to heaven as you could wish, with great views while you're waiting.

## Eating

For a relatively small town, Zacatecas has a surprising number of good **restaurants**, pretty much all located in a small area around the centre, making it easy to walk around and pick something you fancy. There's a tolerably wide variety, but budget places are less abundant. For inexpensive tacos, tostadas and burgers, head away from the centre towards the old bus station: Ventura Sálazar is lined with places serving quick snacks. Another good hunting ground is the compact **market**, just north of the Jardín Independencia.

While in Zacatecas, you should sample *tuna*, the succulent green or purple fruit of the prickly pear cactus. In season they're sold everywhere, ready-peeled and by the bucketload, or you can go out into the country and can pick your own – if you do this, a pair of heavy gloves is a distinct advantage. Look out, too, for donkeys saddled with earthenware jars from which you can buy *aguamiel* (literally, honey water), the juice of the maguey cactus, which can be fermented to produce *pulque* (see p.471).



**Acrópolis** Mercado Gonzales Ortega. Very popular longstanding café serving excellent but quite pricey breakfasts from 8.30am, and ice cream, fruit juices, good coffee and main meals until 10pm. English menus are available.

**Birrierias Jaramillo** Hidalgo 729. Relaxed and friendly with family-style *birria* for M$30–50. A terrific place to sample this regional dish.

**La Bodeguilla** Callejón de San Agustín 103. Small, sophisticated, Spanish-style tapas bar with serrano ham on the bar and a smartish, student atmosphere. Prices are surprisingly low. It's a popular evening hangout, too.

**Los Dorados de Villa** Plazuela de García 1314 ⓣ492/922-5722. Cosy little restaurant a short walk from the centre with lovely tiled walls and exotic birds. Look out for pictures of "Los Dorados", the young followers of Pancho Villa. The excellent traditional menu mostly comprises *moles* and enchiladas that keep people coming back for more. Mains are M$50–60. Reserve in advance. Open daily from 3pm.

**Garufa** Jardín Juárez 135. Argentine restaurant specializing in gargantuan and super-succulent steaks imported from the pampas (M$140–200), along with much cheaper salads and pasta dishes, all of which are served in attractive rustic surroundings.

**Gorditas Doña Julia** Hidalgo 409. A one-trick pony, only serving gorditas (M$8–10 each) stuffed with either various cuts of meat, refried beans, shredded nopal cactus in a hot salsa or *mole* and rice, either to go or to eat in this cheerfully bright, open-fronted restaurant. Additional branches at Tacuba 110 and Torreón 601.

**Hong Kong** Allende 117. Attractive Cantonese restaurant and bar upstairs in the colonial surroundings of the bishop's former residence. All the expected foo yung, chow mein and fried rice dishes are here, mostly around M$50, and there's a daily special with several filling plates for M$85.

**Il San Patricio Café** Hidalgo 403. The best (Italian) coffee in town, and only a little more expensive than places selling far inferior brews. The extra couple of pesos are further justified by the peaceful courtyard setting, a choice of delicious cakes and a number of magazines to browse, some in English.

**Mi Viejo** Fernando Villapando 319. Intimate little café away from the bustle of town and with a great selection of coffees and sweet and savoury crepes, mostly around M$30. Closed Mon.

**La Plaza** inside the *Quinta Real* (see p.260). Pick of the bunch for an expensive, formal meal, if only for the setting overlooking the former bullring. Expect to spend around M$400 per person for a full meal of nopal stuffed with shrimp, chicken in a tamarind sauce, dessert, coffee and something from the wine list – which includes a good Mexican selection.

**El Raspanieve** Hidalgo 805. Traditionally from the neighbouring town of Jerez, *raspanieve* is ice cream served with crushed ice and mixed with fruit syrups, chocolate or burnt sugar coating. This popular parlour has been in operation since 1940, and has the sticky surfaces to prove it.

**El Recoveco** Torreón 513. One of the better bargains, with an all-you-can-eat buffet of over thirty dishes for M$65. Open daily 8.30am–7pm.

**Rosticería el Pastor** Independencia 14. The scent of wood-roasted chicken wafts to the street from this inexpensive, family-friendly joint. M$50 buys you a generous chicken dinner with all the fixings.

**El Tragadero** Juárez 232, by the Alameda. Inexpensive and reliable traditional Mexican restaurant with delicious and piquant *enchiladas Zacatecas* for M$35, with chicken M$40.

**La Única Cabaña** Jardín Independencia. Always alive with activity, this is one of the town's cheapest and most popular taco restaurants. Good, basic food served with a wide selection of salsas and beer at bargain prices in clean surroundings. Tacos are M$6, and a full chicken dinner costs M$45. Wonderfully fruity and thirst-quenching *aguas* are also sold to go. Try the sprightly *chía* flavour (a local herb, also famously grown on Chia Pets).

## Nightlife and entertainment

**Nightlife** in Zacatecas, especially at weekends while the university is in session, is quite lively, with much of the early evening action happening on the streets - there always seems to be some procession or a band playing, usually in the small plazas at either end of the Mercado Gonzales Ortega. On Friday and Saturday evenings (and sometimes Thurs and even Sun) you may well encounter a **callejóneada**, during which musicians – usually with several big drums and a brass section – promenade around the back alleys followed by whoever wants to tag along. There's often a donkey bearing carafes of tequila, and you may be offered some, though it is as well to come equipped with your own tipple. Tag on as you hear the procession go by, or head to the Plaza de Armas around 9pm to catch the start. Either way, a *callejóneada* is great start to an evening on the town, when you can visit some of the numerous bars and clubs that dot the downtown landscape.

**Bar Botarel** in the *Quinta Real* (see p.260). Gorgeous bar built under the seating of what used to be the bullring. Arrive soon after 6pm to get one of the intimate booths, from where you can look out at the plaza and the rest of the hotel. Prices are almost twice what you pay in other places, but nowhere else has the same sense of romance. Live music Fri and Sat until midnight.

**Barekay** Díaz Ordaz 717, by the lower cable-car station ⓣ492/922-7194. The main competition for *La Mina Club*, with great views over town. It is a little sterile, but is generally more popular with locals and isn't bad once it heats up after around 11.30pm. Entry typically M$100, M$50 for women.

**Cactus Club** Hidalgo 634. Lively and popular nightclub with pool and table football upstairs. Small cover charge for men on Fri and for all on Sat, but free on Wed when they have two-for-one drinks specials. Closed Sun.

**Gaudí** in the bottom portion of the Mercado Gonzales Ortega. Decent dance club that's packed at weekends, and particularly Thurs nights, when entry is free and beers only M$10. Normal cover M$20–30.

**La Mina Club** main entrance to Mina El Edén (see p.264) ⓣ492/922-3002. Zacatecas's major club, right in the heart of the mountain and accessed on the same train used in the mine tour. From 11pm it is pumping with Latin numbers, US and European dance tunes, but mostly cheesy electronic techno music. If you don't enjoy being trapped in an enclosed space, *La Mina* is not for you. Thurs–Sat 10pm–3am, reservations essential Fri and Sat; M$100 entry.

**Rincón de los Trovadores** Hidalgo 804. Very agreeable, mostly acoustic venue and bar where local musicians play every night except Mon (7pm–2.30am). The more exalted players come at weekends and there's a looser, jamming vibe earlier in the week. Bring your instrument if you have one.

**Todos Santos** Aguascalientes 235. Tucked into a tastefully decorated cellar, this is a modern take on the traditional cantina, but far more chic. There's usually an engaging mix of locals and visitors (women are certainly welcome), and entertainment is provided by roving minstrels.

## Listings

**American Express** Viajes Mazzocco, López Portillo 746, Plaza Commercial Zacatecas 2000 (Mon–Fri 9am–7pm, Sat & Sun 9am–2pm; ⓣ492/922-0859, ⓔviajesmazzocco@yahoo.com), and another smaller more central location in the *Hotel Casa Santa Lucía* (see p.260). They hold mail, cash and replace travellers' cheques and organize city tours (see p.268).

**Banks and exchange** Plenty of banks are situated along Hidalgo between Juárez and Allende, all with 24hr ATMs and offering currency exchange (Mon–Fri 9am–1pm).

**Books and newspapers** The best (though still limited) source of English-language books, magazines and papers is Sanborn's, Hidalgo 212.

**Buses** There are frequent long-distance bus services to all parts of northern Mexico, including hourly buses to Durango and Chihuahua, some of which push on through to the border at Ciudad Juárez. There are direct buses running to Torreón and Monterrey hourly and a couple daily to Mazatlán; you could also catch the first bus to Durango and get a connection to Mazatlán from there. Heading south, there are frequent buses to

Mexico City, either via Aguascalientes and León or through San Luis Potosí. If you're headed to Real de Catorce, you'll need to change at both San Luis Potosí and Matehuala: make an early start to be sure of getting there in a day.

**Emergencies** For general emergencies call ⓣ066. For tourist emergencies call ⓣ492/922-0180; open 24 hours a day 365 days a year. Cruz Rojo (ⓣ492/922-3005) handles medical emergencies.

**Internet access** Numerous businesses around town, mostly competitively priced at M$10–15 an hour. Try those at Tacuba 118 (daily 10am–10pm; M$7/hr), or Cyber Central, Hidalgo 304 (daily 10am–9pm).

**Laundry** Fast Clean, Fernando Villapando 203 (Mon–Sat 9am–7pm), has wash and dry for M$14 per kilo. Similar prices at El Angel, Aguascalientes 233 (daily 8am–8pm), but a minimum 3kg load.

**Post office** Allende 111 (Mon–Fri 8am–4pm, Sat 9am–1pm).

**Spanish courses** Fenix Language Institute, Ledezma 210 (ⓣ492/922-1643, ⓦwww.fenixlanguageinstitute.com) has courses starting weekly for around US$150.

**Travel agencies and tours** Several local agencies handle general travel requirements and offer tours of the city and to surrounding attractions: try Viajes Mazzocco (see "American Express"); and Operadora Zacatecas, Hidalgo 630 (ⓣ492/924-0050 or 01-800/714-4150), opposite the *Hotel Casa Santa Lucía*. All the bigger hotels stock leaflets detailing tours to Guadalupe (M$160) and to Chicomoztoc (M$200), among other destinations.

## Around Zacatecas: the Centro Platero de Zacatecas, Guadalupe, Chicomoztoc and Jerez

It's well worth basing yourself in Zacatecas to explore the immediate surroundings, not least the **Centro Platero de Zacatecas**, where the Zacatecan tradition of silver-working reaches is highest expression. Those with no interest in buying should definitely continue to **Guadalupe** – virtually a suburb of Zacatecas – to see the Convento de Guadalupe, a rich, sumptuously decorated monastery, rare in that it has survived the centuries more or less unscathed, and for that reason one of the most important such buildings in Mexico. Further out, the ruins of the great desert fortress town **Chicomoztoc** are by contrast quite unadorned, but enormously impressive nonetheless. You'll need to allow the best part of a day for either Chicomoztoc, or the pretty town of **Jerez**, a pleasant day out of town anytime but essential for the cowboy festival on Easter Saturday.

You can venture out to any of these places independently, though several travel agents in Zacatecas offer tours (see above).

### The Centro Platero de Zacatecas

Galleries in town sell stacks of jewellery, but the quality is often low and the designs unimaginative and poorly executed. There are good places to be found, but if you are serious about buying silver, or just want to see artisans at work, devote a couple of hours to visiting the **Centro Platero de Zacatecas** (Mon–Fri 10am–6pm, Sat 10am–2pm; free), located about 5km south of the centre in the former Hacienda de Bernárdez, within the exclusive gated community of Club de Golf de Zacatecas. "Ruta 11" from López Mateos outside the old bus station runs to the gate, where you can ask directions and walk the last kilometre; alternatively take a taxi to the door for M$50.

Within the ex-hacienda, students and recent graduates of the on-site silversmith school maintain a series of small workshops where you can see them creating original designs, many influenced by pre-Columbian images, or iconography associated with Zacatecas. Of course, everything is for sale, often at very reasonable prices, though the very best work commands a high price tag.

## Guadalupe

Local buses run out to **GUADALUPE**, 7km southeast of Zacatecas's centre, every few minutes from López Mateos outside the old bus terminal. Once there, you can't miss the enormous bulk of the **church**, with its dome and asymmetric twin towers. A flagged, tree-studded courtyard provides access to both the church (entered through the elaborate Baroque facade straight ahead) and the **monastery** (daily 9am–6pm; M$33, free on Sun), through a door on the right. The monastery, founded in 1704, is a vast and confusing warren of a place, with seemingly endless rows of cells opening off courtyards, stairways leading nowhere and mile-long corridors lined with portraits of monks and vast tableaux from the life of St Francis. There are guided tours in Spanish, but it's more enjoyable to wander alone, at your own pace, and possibly tagging on to a group for a few minutes when your paths cross. The monastery's two highlights are: the **Coro Alto**, the raised choir at the back of the church, with its beautifully carved and painted wooden choir stalls, and the **Capilla de Napoles**, whose Neoclassical domed roof is coated in elaborately filigreed gold leaf. Presumably, 150 years ago such sights were not altogether unusual in Mexican churches, though today it's the richest you'll see anywhere.

Though much of the former monastery is only partly restored, oil **paintings** cover every wall, and hang in rooms with rough tiled floors and whitewashed walls. Look particularly for the mid-eighteenth-century *Passion of Christ* series of oils by Zacatecan artist Gabriel José de Ovalle, who acknowledged the source of wealth of his patrons by featuring silver ornament and vessels in some of the paintings. One well-presented room is devoted to Baroque art, notably *La Anunciación* by Cristóbal de Villapando, one of Mexico's most important painters of the early eighteenth century.

Next door to the monastery, the **Museo de Guadalupe** (same hours; free) houses a marginally **interesting** transport exhibition with a reconstructed pre-Hispanic stone-wheeled cart, sumptuous horse-drawn carriages and nice bits of antique railway rolling stock. Occasionally this is moved out in favour of more diverting temporary exhibitions.

## Chicomoztoc

The ruins of **CHICOMOZTOC** (daily 10am–4.30pm; M$33), also known as **La Quemada**, lie some 40km south from Zacatecas on the road to Villanueva and Guadalajara. The scale of the complex isn't apparent until you're inside – from the road you can vaguely see signs of construction, but the whole thing, even the huge restored pyramid, blends so totally into the mountain behind as to be almost invisible. No two archeologists seem to agree on the nature of the site, its functions or inhabitants, even to the extent that many doubt it was a fortress, despite its superb natural defensive position and hefty surrounding walls. Most likely it was a frontier post on the outskirts of some pre-Aztec sphere of domination – probably the Toltecs – charged with keeping at bay the southward depredations of the Chichimeca. Alternatively, it could simply be the work of a local ruling class, having exacted enough tribute to build themselves these palaces and needing the defences to keep their own subjects out. Huichol legend seems to support the second theory: there was an evil priest, the story runs, who lived on a rock surrounded by walls and covered with buildings, with eagles and jaguars under his command to oppress the population. The people appealed to their gods, who destroyed the priest and his followers with "great heat", warning the people not to go near the rock again. Chicomoztoc was in fact destroyed by fire around 1300 AD and was never reoccupied;

even today, the Huichol, in their annual pilgrimage from the Sierra Madre in the west to collect peyote around Real de Catorce to the east, take a long detour to bypass this area.

In addition to the reconstructed temple, you'll see here a large hall with eleven pillars still standing, a ball-court, an extensive (if barely visible from the ground) system of roads heading out into the valley and many lesser, ruinous structures all listed for eventual reconstruction. Much of the restoration work is based on drawings produced over the course of ten years from 1825 by a German mining engineer, Carlos de Burghes. Copies are on display in the superb **museum** at the site (daily 10am–4pm; M$10), which makes a masterful job of bringing the place alive with a select display of artefacts, a detailed model of the area and several explanatory videos (in Spanish only).

Most visitors get to the site by car (it's a 30min drive along Ruta 54), but **getting to Chicomoztoc** is also easy enough by public transport, with Villanueva-bound buses leaving every thirty minutes or so from López Mateos outside the old bus station in Zacatecas. They're usually happy to drop you at the start of the two-kilometre access road (ask for "las ruinas"); the ride to this point takes about an hour, from where you've got a 25-minute walk to the entrance. To get back, hike to the highway and either flag down the first bus you see, or try to hitchhike while you're waiting. *Hostal Villa Colonial* also runs low-key **tours** (5hr; M$80) to La Quemada for its guests and anyone else who fancies joining them. They run whenever there are four people who want to go.

### Jerez

For an enjoyable day out of the city, consider a ride out to **Jerez** (formally Jerez de García Salinas), 50km southwest of Zacatecas, which is particularly lively on Sundays. It is a pleasant colonial country town gradually being populated by Canadian and US retirees, who appreciate the slower pace and lower altitude that translates into a warmer year-round climate. If you can, time your visit to coincide with the annual ten-day **Spring Festival**, celebrated around Easter with *charreadas*, bullfights, bands and much tequila drinking. The climax is the Easter Saturday procession when they burn an effigy of Judas. Festivities around the **Día de la Virgen de la Soledad** (Sept 8–15) are also worthwhile with an opportunity to catch the Danzas de los Matlachines.

At other times you'll have to make do with visiting the Porfiriano-era **Teatro Hinojosa**, on Jardín Hidalgo, and the attractive church of **Inmaculada Concepción** just nearby.

Buses to Jerez leave hourly from Zacatecas's Central de Autobuses, and take about an hour.

## Aguascalientes

The lively industrial town of **AGUASCALIENTES**, 100km south of Zacatecas, is an important and booming provincial capital with some fine colonial monuments in among its newer buildings. A couple of excellent **museums**, in addition, make this a good place to stop over for a day or two, especially when you take into account the town's reputation for some of the finest **fiestas** in Mexico – rarely a week goes by without celebration, or at least a band playing in one of the plazas at the weekend – and for the manufacture of excellent **wines** and **brandy**.

## Arrival, orientation and information

The **bus station** is around 4km south of the centre on the city's ring road (Avenida de la Convención), from where there's a frequent bus service into the **Plaza de Armas** ("Centro"), at the heart of town. To get back to the bus station from the centre, catch a bus marked "Central" from beside the cathedral on Matamoros.

In the Plaza de Armas and on the adjoining **Plaza de la República**, also known as the **Plaza de la Patria**, are all the important public buildings as well as the cathedral, government offices, fancier hotels and a handful of banks; many of the streets around here are pedestrianized, and most things you'll want to see are in easy walking distance.

The **tourist office** is also in the plaza, on the ground floor of the Palacio de Gobierno (Mon–Fri 9am–8pm, Sat & Sun 10am–6pm; ⓣ449/910-0051, ⓦwww.aguascalientes.gob.mx). The staff can give you information on the city's **festivals**, including the nearly two-centuries-old **Feria de San Marcos** (ⓦwww.feriadesanmarcos.com), famous throughout Mexico. Celebrated in the Jardín San Marcos from mid-April to mid-May, events include everything from bullfights and live music to film festivals and rides for kids (many of the events are free).

## Accommodation

**Budget** accommodation in Aguascalientes is located mostly around the market area, while some of the **hotels** on and around the Plaza de la Patría offer real luxury. During the *ferias* (mid-April to mid-May and the week around Nov 1), rooms are almost impossible to obtain at short notice and are likely to cost at least fifty percent more.



**Hacienda del Roble** 5 de Mayo 540 ⓣ & ⓕ449/915-3994. One of the best-value places in town; big, clean and relaxed, with friendly management, rooms with cable TV, and plenty of parking. ❺

**Holiday Inn** Nieto 102, on the Plaza Principal ⓣ449/916-1666, ⓔholidayinnags@prodigy.net.mx. Modern luxury hotel, offering bags of comfort though little soul. Some rooms have views over the plaza. ❼

**Hotel Colonial** 5 de Mayo 552 ⓣ & ⓕ449/915-3577. Comfortable hotel with car park and a small restaurant on site. All rooms with TV and phone, and the larger ones have big windows that let in plenty of light. ❹

**Hotel Don Jesús** Juárez 429 ⓣ449/915-5598. Basic, big, bare and very near the market, but fairly quiet and OK for the price, though you might prefer to pay the extra M$40 for a newer, carpeted room. ❷

**Hotel Gomez** Circunvalación, beside the bus station ⓣ449/978-2120. Not bad if you arrive late or plan to push on early. ❸

**Hotel Imperial** 5 de Mayo 105 ⓣ& ⓕ449/915-1650. Very faded elegance in a fine colonial building; it's well sited, overlooking the plaza, and particularly good if you can get a room with a balcony. ❹

**Hotel Maser** Juan de Montoro 303 ⓣ449/915-9662. Attractive and well-cared-for budget hotel with airy rooms around a central courtyard, and parking available. Rooms with TV cost M$30 more. ❷

**Hotel Posada de San Rafael** Hidalgo 205 ⓣ449/915-7761. Plain rooms with fans, TV and plenty of parking at a fair price. ❸

**Hotel Rosales** Guadalupe Victória 104 ⓣ449/915-2165. A bargain for the location, right by the north side of the plaza, with pleasantly furnished rooms around a central courtyard and 24hr hot water. ❸

**Hotel Señorial** Colón 104, south side of the Plaza Principal ⓣ449/915-1630. Simple carpeted rooms, but decent value for its location, particularly the corner rooms overlooking the plaza. ❹

## The City

Below the entire centre of Aguascalientes lies a series of mysterious and poorly understood tunnels and catacombs carved out by an unknown civilization. The Spanish initially referred to the place as La Ciudad Perforada (the Perforated City), then proceeded to build the current cluster of colonial buildings. These are arranged around the **Plaza de la Patría**, with its cathedral, and the **Palacio de Gobierno**, with its impressive murals. Fanning out from there are a few worthwhile museums, chief among them the **Museo José Guadalupe Posada**, dedicated to Mexico's most famous engraver.

### The Plaza de la Patría and around

The **Plaza de la Patría** is the place to start any exploration of Aguascalientes. In the centre of this enormous area is the **Exedra**, an amphitheatre-shaped space for performances, overlooked by a column topped with a Mexican eagle. Chief of the buildings here is the 1665 **Palacio de Gobierno**, a remarkably beautiful Neoclassical structure built from reddish volcanic rock, formed around an arcaded courtyard with a grand central staircase and decorated with four marvellous **murals** by the Chilean Oswaldo Barra Cunningham, who learnt his trade from Diego Rivera. The first of the murals, at the back on the ground floor, were painted in 1962, and others span the years following: the most recent (from 1992) are at the front of the building.

Next door, the modern **Palacio Municipal** is bland in comparison, while down the other side of the plaza, the eighteenth-century **cathedral** has been refurbished to reveal its full glory, in an over-the-top welter of gold and polished marble. The **Pinacoteca Religiosa**, in an annex, is well worth a look for its collection of eighteenth-century religious paintings, notably some by Miguel Cabrera.

Venustiano Carranza leads down beside the cathedral to the **Casa de la Cultura** (daily 7am–9pm; free), a beautiful old mansion given over to music and dance classes and the occasional exhibition. The notice board here is an excellent place to find out what's on around town, and in the patio there's a small café (see "Eating and drinking", p.275) – a tranquil spot to have a drink and a rest. A little further down, at Carranza 118, the **Museo Regional de Historia** (Tues–Sun 10am–7pm; M$30, free on Sun) chronicles local history, from a fossilized mammoth tusk and traditional crafts to the Revolution. There's also material on local composer and pianist Manuel Ponce, who in the first half of the twentieth century ranked alongside the three great muralists as Mexico's artistic culture took its place on the world stage. Escape from the sun by heading west on Carranza to the shady **Jardín de San Marcos**, a long, beautifully manicured park that runs down to the **Templo de San Marcos**. Turning left here you're on the pedestrianized **Paseo de la Feria**, which cuts through to López Mateos, its modern buildings a complete contrast to what went before. On your left is the **Casino de la Feria** with its giant palenque, where cockfights are staged – this is the site of the city's famous fiestas. Once very much the face of modern Aguascalientes, the area is looking a bit faded these days, and apart from the presence of a few swanky stores and a couple of restaurants there is little reason to hang around.

Heading back to the centre, follow **Calle Nieto** which is lined with boutiques selling one of the city's most recognized crafts: **lace**.

### South to the Museo José Guadalupe Posada

Though it only occupies a couple of rooms in a small building about 1km south of the centre, the **Museo José Guadalupe Posada** (Tues–Sun 11am–6pm;

△ Skeleton print, Museo José Guadalupe Posada

## Posada – the most Mexican artist

The frequently macabre work of **José Guadalupe Posada** will be familiar even if his name is not: Diego Rivera was not so wrong when he described the prolific Posada as "so outstanding that one day even his name will be forgotten". He was born a baker's son in Aguascalientes in 1852, and was later apprenticed to a lithographer. In 1888 he moved to the capital (having meanwhile lived in León for some time), and started to create in earnest the thousands of prints for which he soon became known. He mainly worked for the editor and printer Vanegas Arroyo, and his images appeared on posters and in satirical broadsheets that flourished despite – or more likely because of – the censorship of the Porfiriano era. Some of Posada's work was political, attacking corrupt politicians, complacent clergy or foreign intervention, but much was simply recording the news (especially disasters, which so obsess the Mexican press to this day), lampooning popular figures or observing everyday life with a gleefully macabre eye. Later, the events and figures of the Revolution, grotesquely caricatured, came to dominate his work.

Technically, Posada moved on from lithography to engraving in type metal (producing the characteristic hatched effect seen in much of his work) and finally to zinc etching, an extremely rapid method involving drawing directly onto a zinc printing plate with acid-resistant ink, and then dipping it until the untouched areas corroded. Although the *calaveras*, the often elegantly clad skeletons that people much of his work, are his best-known work, the museum devoted to him in Aguascalientes covers the full range of his designs. They all bear a peculiar mix of Catholicism, pre-Columbian tradition, preoccupation with death and black humour that can only be Mexican – and that profoundly affected all later Mexican art: Rivera and Orozco are just two of the greats who publicly acknowledged their debt to Posada.

M$10) is one of the main reasons to visit Aguascalientes. Indeed, the town is almost a place of pilgrimage for devotees of this influential printmaker, who is best known for his political satire and criticism of the Catholic Church. Rooms on three sides of a courtyard contain scores of nicely pressed lithographs, along with the original plates, contemporary photos and biographical information in Spanish. The museum occupies the former priest's house of the **Templo del Señor del Encino**, an elegant colonial church of pinkish stone with a pretty tiled dome. Amid the riotously gilded interior is the miraculous and much venerated "black Christ" of Encino – also depicted in stained glass above the main door. To get there, head east from the plaza and take the first right, Díaz de León, south for about seven blocks. In front of the church and museum there's a pleasant, quiet square, at the heart of a peaceful old neighbourhood.

### East to the Museo Aguascalientes and the baths

A few blocks northeast of the central plaza at the corner of Morelos and Primo Verdad, the **Museo de Arte Contemporáneo** (Tues–Sun 11am–6pm; M$10, free on Sun) is home to some of the most interesting and provocative art from the region, all changed every two months. What's more, all the works were created by artists under 35 years of age.

A couple of blocks further east you'll reach the over-the-top **Templo de San Antonio**, built around 1900 and featuring a muddled facade with some vaguely discernible Neoclassical elements. Inside, murals by local architect Refugio Reyes provide a blaze of colour. Opposite is the **Museo de Aguascalientes** (Tues–Sun 11am–6pm; M$10, free on Sun). Its art collection, mostly modern, is mainly of interest for its works by Saturnino Herrán, a local who was a contemporary and friend of Diego Rivera but who died young and never really achieved much recognition. Note his large stained-glass panel, and also rooms full of charcoal drawings, block prints and paintings by Gabriel Fernández Ledesma, another local son of some note.

You'll need to travel some 4km east from here to experience the **hot springs** that gave the city its name. They're located at the Centro Deportivo Ojocaliente (daily 7am–7pm; M$30), which is really just a outdoor swimming pool complex just outside town on the road to San Luis Potosí. A visit is only worthwhile if you're desperate for a swim: to get there, take "Ruta 12" along López Mateos.



## Eating and drinking

Ordinary **restaurants** are surprisingly thin on the ground in Aguascalientes, though all the large hotels on the plaza have their own. In addition, plenty of simple places along **Juárez** serve good, tasty barbecued chicken, and there are taco and seafood places in the **market** itself, between Juárez and 5 de Mayo at Alvaro Obregón; the smaller Mercado de Artesanías, on Obregón, doesn't have much in the way of decent crafts, but it does have more eating places without the frenzy of the main market. Fancier places to eat line **López Mateos**, especially just west of the centre towards the Paseo de la Feria. While you're in town you should try some of the local **wine** (not always easy except in the more expensive restaurants) or at least the **brandy**: San Marcos is the best known, made here and sold all over the republic.

**Los Antojos de Carranza** Carranza 301. Plenty of traditional, well-presented Mexican dishes, most under M$40, but more a place to stop in for a beer and top up on all manner of *botanas*. In the evening it is always thick with roving minstrels eager to serenade you.

**Los Arquitos Café** inside the Casa de la Cultura on Carranza. Serene spot for top-quality quiche, salads and that Mexican rarity, a strong espresso; not exactly cheap. Mon 4–9pm, Tues–Fri 10am–1pm & 4–9pm.

**El Cuarto de Arriba** Carranza 402. Cool student café offering mainly sandwiches and burgers, along with the obligatory cappuccino.

**Kiko's Merendero** Paseo de la Feria 132 (aka Arturo Pani), at Jardín San Marcos. More bar than restaurant, but food is served to soak up the drinks.

**Mitla Restaurante** Madero 222. Popular, old-fashioned Mexican restaurant that has been operating since 1938, with white-jacketed waiters serving a good selection of national and local dishes, including seafood and very reasonable comidas corridas. There's also an impressive M$65 Sun buffet.

**La Saturnina** Carranza 110. Lovely and colourful courtyard café that's great for breakfast, lunch or just coffee and cake.

## Listings

**Banks and exchange** Banamex and Bancomer are on 5 de Mayo on the north side of Plaza de la Patria, both with 24-hour ATMs.

**Buses** Aguascalientes is situated on Hwy-45 between Zacatecas and León, and there are hourly buses in either direction, many continuing as far as Chihuahua to the north and Mexico City to the south (via Irapuato and Querétaro). There are also slower services to Guadalajara and San Luis Potosí. For Guanajuato, you'll probably be quicker taking a bus first to León and getting a connection from there.

**Internet access** Very few places in the centre, but try the café at Juarez 111 (daily 10am–8pm).

**Post office** The main post office (Mon–Fri 8am–6pm, Sat 9am–1pm) is on Hospitalidad, a block north of the plaza and reached by following Morelos and then turning right.

## Around Aguascalientes: Lagos de Moreno and San Juan de los Lagos

Just 70km southeast of Aguascalientes, **LAGOS DE MORENO** lies at the intersection of the road from Mexico City to Ciudad Juárez and the route from Guadalajara to San Luis Potosí and the northeast. Though the town has always been a major staging post, surprisingly few tourists stop here now and, despite the heavy traffic rumbling around its fringes, it's a quiet and rather beautiful little town, with colonial streets climbing steeply from a small river to a hilltop monastery.

Cross the bridge by the bus station and head to your left along the stream, away from the choking fumes of the main road, and it's hard to believe you're in the same place. Whether you plan to stay a couple of hours or a few days, you'll want to head for the **zócalo**: in the streets around it are a massive **Baroque church** and a smattering of colonial mansions and official buildings, including a forbidding-looking jail that's still in use. The **Teatro José Rosas Moreno**, on the north side of the square behind the church, which opened in 1906 to stage opera performances, is worth a look for the beautiful mural on the dome depicting the Revolution and Independence, with local hero José Rosas Moreno, a famous writer of tales and fables, as the centrepiece. Once you've seen the centre, you might want to embark on the long climb up to the **Templo del Calvario**, a hillside church ten blocks to the north. The monastery is inhabited by monks, so you can't visit, and the church itself is tumbling down, but it's worth the trek for the **view**, especially at sunset.

There are several reasonable **hotels** near the zócalo. On the square itself, the red-painted and cavernous *Hotel París* (Ⓣ474/742-0200; ❷) has some basic but comfortable rooms and better remodelled affairs (❹). The slightly posher *Hotel Colonial*, Hidalgo 279 (Ⓣ474/742-0142; ❺), has pretty public areas and its own restaurant though the rooms are only average. Finally, *Hotel La Troje*, on the east side of the plaza (Ⓣ474/742-6677; ❹) has modern and reasonable rooms plus parking. The zócalo also boasts a few good **bars** and **places to eat**.

Getting to and from Lagos de Moreno could hardly be easier: there are **buses** at least every thirty minutes from Guadalajara, León, Aguascalientes, Zacatecas and Mexico City.

### San Juan de los Lagos

Some 45km southwest of Lagos de Moreno, on the road to Guadalajara, the old highway runs through **SAN JUAN DE LOS LAGOS**. From its outskirts, San Juan seems like just another dusty little town; in the centre, though, you'll find an enormous bus station surrounded by scores of hotels. This is thanks to the vast parish church and the miraculous **image of the Virgin** that it contains, making it one of the most important pilgrimage centres in Mexico. The site's busiest dates are February 2 (**Día de la Candelaria**) and December 8 (**Fiesta de la Inmaculada Concepción**), when the place is crammed with penitents, pilgrims, those seeking miraculous cures and others who are just there to enjoy the atmosphere. The celebrations build up for a couple of weeks beforehand, and spill over to several lesser events throughout the year, notably the first fortnight of August and the entire Christmas period. There's little chance of finding a room at these times and little point in staying long at any other, so it's best to treat San Juan de los Lagos as a day trip from – or stopover between – Lagos de Moreno and Guadalajara (less than an hour from the former, around three hours from Guadalajara).

# León

Heading south from Aguascalientes, most buses bypass Lagos de Moreno and head straight for **LEÓN**, a teeming, industrial city with a long history of excellence in **leatherwork**. This tradition is reflected in the scores of shoe factories and, in the centre, hundreds of shoe shops: it's a good place to buy hand-tooled cowboy boots, jackets, belts or just about anything else made of leather.

The area around the bus station, about 3km from the city centre, has the highest concentration of leather and shoe shops, most of which have very reasonable prices, although there are also some higher-class and more expensive boutiques. If you're changing buses in León it's well worth taking an hour to wander round the station's immediate vicinity. And even if you only spend ten minutes in the bus station you'll see stacks of shoeboxes being loaded into just about every waiting bus.

If you're determined to explore the town, stash your bag at the bus station's guardería and head for the partly pedestrianized Centro Histórico. In town, the linked **Plaza de los Fundadores** and **Plaza de los Martíres** are not at all what the rest of the city would lead you to expect – spacious, tranquil and elegant, with a fine eighteenth-century cathedral built by the Jesuits and a typically colonial palacio municipal. Little else survived a disastrous flood in 1883, but the plaza is surrounded by broad boulevards lined with shops, and there are a couple of other churches that deserve a look: the Baroque **Templo de los Angeles** and the extraordinary marble **Templo Expiatorio**, 500m southeast on Madero. The latter is particularly impressive, with its high-relief copper doors revealing a white Gothic interior illuminated by modern stained glass. You can also visit the crypt (Fri, Sat & Sun 10am & 1pm; M$5). The city's main festival is the **Feria de León** (Jan 10–20), a big agricultural and industrial fair that finishes with religious festivities on the Día de San Sebastián.

## Practicalities

To get into town from the **bus station**, walk left out of the station along Hilario Medina, pick up an articulated OptiBus ("Linea 1") headed to the right along López Mateos and get off at the "Centro Histórico" stop.

León also has the region's main **airport**, the nearest to both Guanajuato and San Miguel de Allende, with flights from all over Mexico and Houston, Dallas, LA, Chicago and more. On arrival, many just grab a cab direct to their destination, but there are also very infrequent buses and *colectivos* (around M$150) to León, and second-class buses ply the highway between León and Guanajuato; wave madly and you may be able to flag one down.

Should you need a place to stay here, you'll find a number of cheapish **hotels** in the streets immediately opposite the bus station: try the pleasant, clean TV and fan-equipped *Niza*, Nuevo Vallarta 213 (Ⓣ477/763-3557; ❹), or the simple but well-kept *Blanquita*, Tasco 150 at La Luz (Ⓣ477/763-1909, Ⓕ771-3303; ❷), which charges an extra M$30 for a TV. There are also several decent **places to eat**.

# Guanajuato

Shoe-horned into a narrow ravine, **GUANAJUATO** was for centuries the wealthiest city in Mexico, its mines pouring out silver and gold in prodigious

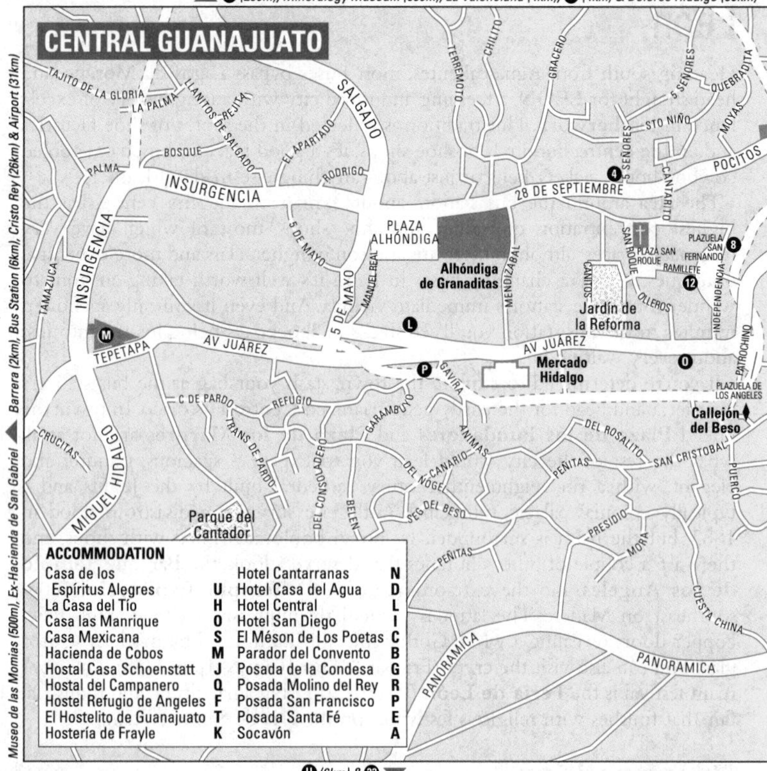


quantities. Today it presents a remarkable sight: upon emerging from the surrounding hills you come on the town quite suddenly, a riot of colonial architecture dominated by the bluff (and rather ugly) bulk of the university, tumbling down hills so steep that at times it seems the roof of one building is suspended from the floor of the last. Declared a UNESCO World Heritage Zone in 1988, Guanajuato is protective of its image: there are no traffic lights or neon signs here, and the topography ensures that there's no room for new buildings.

This is an extremely enjoyable place to visit: peaceful, yet with plenty of life in its narrow streets (especially during term time), lots of good places to eat and drink and plenty to see – it's never dull and always surprising. There's an old-fashioned, backwater feel to the city, reinforced by the students' habit of going serenading in black capes, the brass bands playing in the plazas and the town's general refusal to make any special effort to accommodate the flood of tourists – who thankfully never really manage to disturb the daily ebb and flow.

## Arrival and information

The **bus station** lies 6km west of the city. Regular local buses ("Centro-Central") shuttle into town in about fifteen minutes, usually terminating outside the Mercado Hidalgo, leaving you a ten-minute walk if you're staying close to the Jardín de la Unión. Alternatively, hop aboard one of the

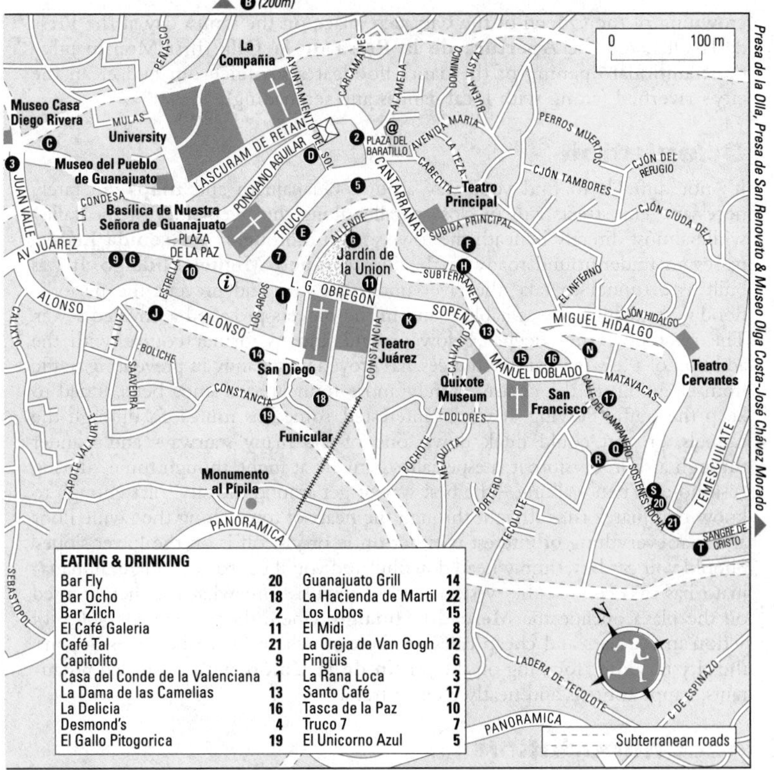


Panteón–Presa buses that run the length of town (partly through the tunnels) and ask to get dropped near the Jardín. Some local buses (marked "Presa") from the bus station run right through the tunnels and can drop you beside the Jardín. The nearest **airport** is 30km west of Guanajuato at Silao (closer to León; see p.277); taxis direct to Guanajuato should cost around M$300, and if you're prepared to schlep a few hundred metres from the airport out to the highway you can flag down second-class buses headed north to León or south to Guanajuato. **Drivers** will find Guanajuato's labyrinth of tunnels and prescriptive one-way streets confusing at first; you'll make your life easier by parking your vehicle and walking most places. The exception is a drive around the encircling Carretera Panorámica, which, as you would expect, has panoramic views of the district.

It's worth checking out the **tourist office**, Plaza de la Paz 14 (Mon–Fri 9am–7.30pm, Sat 10am–5pm, Sun 10am–2pm; ⓣ473/732-1574 or 01-800/714-1086, ⓦwww.guanajuato-travel.com), at least for the **free map**; there are also lots of private **information booths** throughout town offering tours and hotel reservations. You might also check out ⓦwww.guanajuatocapital.com, another useful website with information on the city. Guanajuato plays host to some excellent **festivals**, including the huge **Cervantino Festival** (see box, p.290), as well as the **Fiestas de San Juan y Presa de la Olla** (June 24), when fireworks, fairground rides and the crowning of the Queen of the City take place on the saint's day at the Presa de la Olla, and the **Apertura de la Presa de la Olla** (first Mon in July), the traditional opening of the dam's floodgates to sluice out and clean the city's riverbed (along with local dances and serenading).

## Orientation



It's not difficult to find your way around Guanajuato and **maps** are rarely necessary. The streets run in close parallel along the steep sides of the valley, while almost directly beneath the town's main thoroughfare, **Avenida Juárez**, passes an underground roadway: the **Subterráneo Miguel Hidalgo**. It was built as a tunnel to take the river under the city and prevent the periodic flooding to which it was liable – and in the process provided a covered sewer. The river now runs deeper below ground, and its former course, with the addition of a few exits and entrances, has proved very handy in preventing traffic from clogging up the centre entirely; more tunnels have since been added to keep the traffic flowing. If you're interested, some bus routes go through the tunnels, or you could duck down one of the many stairways and wander through a short section: it is especially dramatic at night, though fumey during rush hour. When walking – the best way to get around the city – it's enough to know that Juárez runs straight through the heart of town along the ravine floor and that everything of interest is either on it, or just off it on the lower slopes. Should you get lost, simply head downhill and you'll get back to Juárez. Guanajuato has two centres: the western end of town is somewhat rougher, focused on the plaza outside the **Mercado Hidalgo**, where there is always plenty of action in the bars and cheap cafés; to the east, where Juárez becomes Sopeña, the city is calmer, focusing on the **Jardín de la Unión**, with its shaded restaurants, happy tourists and neatly clipped trees.

## Accommodation

Guanajuato has an excellent selection of rooms at a wide range of prices. In the last couple of years there has been an explosion of **hostels**, and top-end places continually raise their standards. Rooms can be hard to come by during certain times of the year, especially on Mexican public holidays, at Christmas, Semana Santa and during the **Festival Internacional Cervantino** (two and a half weeks in Oct; see box, p.290). If your trip coincides with one of these holidays (see pp.320–321) it's worth trying to book a room several weeks, if not months, in advance. If you can get a room on such occasions, you'll pay a thirty-to-fifty percent premium on the rates quoted here, which are already fairly high by Mexican standards. By far the best place to stay in the centre of town is around the **Jardín de la Unión**, even if plaza-view rooms come with a sizeable premium and, at weekends, mariachi accompaniment until well past midnight. There are several budget options in the same area, which are generally preferable to the other main concentration of cheap hotels around the Mercado Hidalgo.

### Near the Mercado Hidalgo

**Casa las Manrique** Juárez 116 ⓣ473/732-7678, ⓕ732-8306. Eight large suites, very nicely decorated and all with TV, mini-bar and bathtub. No premium for those fronting the street with views over the town, but they're popular, so reserve early. ❻

**Hacienda de Cobos** Padre Hidalgo 3 ⓣ & ⓕ473/732-0143. Great-value hotel with a pool and comfortable, attractive motel-style rooms around a large central plaza. There's a restaurant on site and parking available, and a back entrance that means you're only a 5min walk from the market. Prices rise considerably during popular times. ❻

**Hotel Central** Juárez 111 ⓣ473/732-0080. The best of the cheap hotels around the Jardín Reforma, comprising simple rooms with TV and bathroom. ❸

**Posada San Francisco** Juárez 178, beside the market ⓣ473/732-2467. Central and large; the simple, spotless carpeted rooms all have private bathrooms. ❹

**Socavón** Alhóndiga 41-A ⓣ473/732-4885, ⓦwww.hotelsocavon.com.mx. A dark tunnel opens into the sunny courtyard of this small, friendly place that's well cared for and with attractive brick-ceilinged rooms, all with TV. A short walk from the centre but worth it – there's a restaurant and parking on site. ❻

## Jardín de la Unión and around

**La Casa del Tío** Cantarranas 47 ⓣ473/733-9728, ⓦwww.lacasadeltiohostel.com. Comfortable hostel with relatively spacious dorms and rooms, a small kitchen (free tea and coffee) and a nice roof terrace festooned with cacti. 15min free Internet access daily. Dorms M$100 per person. ❹

**Casa Mexicana** Sóstenes Rocha 28 ⓣ473/732-7393. Very good budget hotel/hostel with simple but tastefully decorated modern rooms, with or without bath. Often frequented by students at the associated language school. Everyone gets the use of a kitchen and rates are M$105 per person. ❸

**Hostal Casa Schoenstatt** Calle de Alonso 32 ⓣ473/733-9707. This hostel was only recently converted from a longstanding budget hotel. Very new and a bit bare, but looks promising. Dorms M$120. ❹

**Hostal del Campanero** Campanero 19 ⓣ473/734-5665, ⓦwww.hostaldelcampanero.3a2.com. Good-value hostel with dorms (M$80), private rooms (M$100 per person) and a separate two-room penthouse (M$300 per room) with its own kitchen and living area. There's no real kitchen but a Continental breakfast is served, and you get 15min free Internet access. ❸

**Hostel Refugio de Angeles** Cantarranas 38 ⓣ473/732-0793, ⓔinfo@rahostel.com. Welcoming hostel offering dorms with bathroom (M$100), private rooms either without (M$100 per person) or with bathroom (M$120), free Internet access, laundry, a good kitchen and a rooftop area with great views and a couple of hammocks. ❸

**El Hostelito de Guanajuato** Sangre de Cristo 9 ⓣ473/732-5483, ⓦwww.hostalitoguanajuato.com. Well-set-up hostel featuring comfy dorms with lockers, some private en-suite rooms (one with a small balcony), separate TV and quiet rooms, good kitchen and free Continental breakfast. There's also free Internet access and WiFi. Dorms M$135, ISIC cardholders M$125, HI members M$110. ❹

**Hostería del Frayle** Sopeña 3 ⓣ473/732-1179, ⓦwww.hosteriadelfrayle.com. This place, the nicest near the Jardín, is in a lovely colonial-style building right in the heart of things with bougainvillea-draped courtyards, spacious common areas and rooms that feature beautifully tiled bathrooms. Room quality varies, so look at a few first. ❼

**Hotel Cantarranas** Cantarranas 50, half a block from the Teatro Principal ⓣ473/732-5241, ⓦwww.hostalcantarranasgtocapital.com. A great, friendly and clean little place tucked away in the back streets. It doesn't look like much from the outside, but features a wonderful rooftop terrace with views of the Pípila (see p.284). Rooms have king-sized beds, and the suites all come with a kitchen stocked with utensils. There's even a three-room suite sleeping six. ❺

**Hotel Casa del Agua** Plazuela de La Compañía 4 ⓣ473/734-1974, ⓦwww.hotelcasadelagua.com. Lovely seventeenth-century building recently converted into a chic hotel on contemporary lines. There are just fifteen light and airy rooms, all very nicely appointed with spa bath and cable TV. ❼

**Hotel San Diego** Jardín de la Unión 1 ⓣ473/732-1300, ⓦwww.hotelerasandiego.com. Fine colonial warren of a place in the very centre with nicely tiled public areas and spacious carpeted rooms, all with satellite TV. There are great plaza views from its front rooms. ❽

**El Mesón de los Poetas** Positos 35 ⓣ473/732-0705, ⓦwww.mexonline.com/poetas.htm. A warren of very comfortable rooms (with cable TV) all painted in blues, yellows and reds, and lined with decorative tiles. Shady interior patios provide respite from the heat and noise of the day. Prices rise substantially from Jan to mid-March. ❼

**Parador del Convento** Calzada Guadalupe 17 ⓣ473/732-2524, ⓔparadordelconvento@hotmail.com. An attractive hotel on the slopes above the university, with decent rooms and nicer *cuartos rústicos*, which come with a balcony, more imaginative decor and a lot more space. ❻

**Posada de la Condesa** Plaza de la Paz 60 ⓣ473/732-1462. Central and cheap, but rooms (all with showers) are small and scruffy, and the loud nightclub next door can be a bit much. ❸

**Posada Molino del Rey** Padre Belaunzavan and Campanero ⓣ473/732-2223, ⓔmach1@avantel.net. At the east end of town, very reasonably priced with smallish but comfortable and quiet rooms around a courtyard. ❺

**Posada Santa Fé** Jardín de la Unión 12 ⓣ473/732-0084 or 01-800/112-4773, www.posadasantafe.com. Very comfortable old hotel right in the heart of the city, with interior and exterior rooms (M$1290), parking and a good rooftop terrace, though it leans heavily on its location. 7

### Outside the centre

**Casa de los Espíritus Alegres** Ex-Hacienda La Trinidad 1, Marfil, on the outskirts of town 473/733-1013, www.casaspirit.com. This enchanting B&B exudes charm and is decorated in a playfully sophisticated style with a riot of colour and a curious collection of Mexican skeleton folk art. Bedrooms and common spaces are comfortable and there's an honour-system bar for late-night patio tippling. 9



## The City

There must be more things to see in Guanajuato than in virtually any town of similar size: you'll find churches, theatres, museums, battlefields, mines and mummified corpses, to name but a few of the city's attractions. You'll need to take the bus to get to some of these places, but most are laid out along Juárez. If you start your explorations from the **Mercado Hidalgo** and walk east, you'll be able to see much of what Guanajuato has to offer in a day. Wandering through the maze of narrow alleys that snakes up the side of the ravine is a pleasure in itself, if only to spot their quirky names like Salto del Mono (Monkey's Leap) or Calle de las Cantarranas (Street of the Singing Frogs). Incidentally, references to **frogs** crop up everywhere around town – in sculpture, artesanías and T-shirts. The valley once had so many of the amphibians that the original name of the city was Quanax-huato, meaning "Place of Frogs".

### Mercado Hidalgo to the Plaza de la Paz

The first building of note as you head east up Juárez from where buses stop is the **Mercado Hidalgo**, a huge iron-framed construction reminiscent of British Victorian railway stations and crammed with every sort of goods imaginable. East of the market, to the left and through the **Jardín de la Reforma**, with its fountain and arch, you get to the lovely, quiet **Plaza San Roque**. A small,

△ Mercado Hidalgo, Guanajuato

irregular, flagged space, the plaza has a distinctly medieval feel, heightened by the raised facade of the crumbling church of **San Roque** that towers above. It's a perfect setting for the city's lively annual **International Cervantes Festival** (see box, p.290). The Callejón de los Olleros leads back down to Juárez, or you can cut straight through to the livelier **Plazuela San Fernando**, with its stalls and restaurants. Return to Juárez from here and you emerge more or less opposite the **Plazuela de los Angeles**. In itself this is little more than a slight broadening of the street, but from here steps lead up to some of Guanajuato's steepest, narrowest alleys. Just off the plazuela is the **Callejón del Beso** (20m up Callejón del Patrimonio and turn left), so called because at only a little over half a metre wide, it is slim enough for residents to lean out of the upper-storey balconies and exchange kisses across the street – naturally enough there's a *Canterbury Tales*-style legend of star-crossed lovers associated with it. To learn more, join one of the *callejóneadas* (see p.289) that pass this way, or engage the services of one of the small children who hang around eager to tell a tale. To experience one balcony firsthand, come in the evening and walk through the strategically located gift shop.

The **Plaza de la Paz** lies east of the Jardín de la Reforma, beyond a number of banks on Juárez. For a distance here, Juárez is not the lowest road – Alonso cuts down to the right, to rejoin Juárez a little further along. The Plaza de la Paz itself boasts some of the town's finest **colonial buildings**, among which the late eighteenth-century mansion of the Condes de Rul y Valenciana (then owners of the richest mine in the country) stands out as the grandest. It was designed by Eduardo Tresguerras, undoubtedly the finest Mexican architect of his time, and played host briefly to Baron Alexander von Humboldt, the German naturalist and writer, an event commemorated by a plaque. The **Casa de Gobierno**, a short way down towards the Jardín de la Unión (see below), is another fine mansion, this time with a plaque recording the fact that Benito Juárez lived there in 1858, when Guanajuato was briefly his provisional capital. On the far side of the plaza stands the honey-coloured **Basílica de Nuestra Señora de Guanajuato**, a Baroque parish church that houses an ancient image of the Virgin, patroness of the city. This wooden statue, which now sits amidst silver and jewels, was given to Guanajuato in 1557 by Philip II, in gratitude for the wealth that was pouring from here into Spanish royal coffers. At the time it was already old and miraculous, having survived more than eight centuries of Moorish occupation hidden in a cave near Granada in Spain.

### Around the Jardín de la Unión

From the Plaza de la Paz, you can cut up to the university, but just a short distance further east on Juárez is the **Jardín de la Unión**, Guanajuato's zócalo. It's a delightful little square – or rather triangle – set back from the street, shaded with trees, surrounded by cafés and with a bandstand in the centre from which the town band regularly plays in the early evening. This is the best time to sit and linger over a drink, enjoying the passing spectacle of the evening *paseo*.

Facing the Jardín across Juárez stands the Baroque church of **San Diego**, inside which are several old paintings and interesting chapels. One altar in particular is dedicated to the infant Jesus and mawkishly filled with toys and children's tiny shoes left as offerings. Next door is the imposing Neoclassical frontage of the **Teatro Juárez** (Tues–Sun 9am–1.45pm & 5–7.45pm; M$30, cameras M$30), all Doric columns and allegorical statuary. The interior of the theatre is fabulously plush – decked out in red velvet and gilt, with chandeliers and a Moorish proscenium – as befits its period. Built at the end of the nineteenth century, it was opened in 1903 by the dictator Porfirio Díaz himself.

Beyond the Jardín, Juárez becomes Sopeña, lined by fancy boutiques, restaurants and bars as far as the pretty pink church of San Francisco, which marks the Plazuela San Francisco. Here, too, is the **Museo Iconográfico del Quijote** (Tues–Sat 10am–6.30pm, Sun 10am–2.30pm; M$20, students free), an extraordinary little collection devoted entirely to Don Quixote. The museum contains mainly paintings of the don – including some by Pedro and Rafael Coronel – but also a couple of Dalí prints, a copy of a Picasso drawing, a Posada engraving of the hero as a *calavera*, an imposing sculpture by Federico Silva, murals, tapestries, sculptures, busts, miniatures, medals, plates, glassware, chess sets, playing cards, pipes and cutlery – you name it, it's here.

## Pípila

The **Monumento al Pípila**, a bulky statue on the hillside almost directly above the Jardín de la Unión, affords fantastic views of Guanajuato. From the viewpoint at its base you seem to be standing directly on top of the church of San Diego. It's an especially wonderful spot for the 45 minutes or so during which the sun sets behind the hills and the electric lights start to come on in town. The steep climb takes about twenty minutes going up and ten minutes coming down. There are several possible routes up through the alleys – look for signs saying "al Pípila" – including up the Callejón del Calvario, to the right off Sopeña just beyond the Teatro Juárez; from the Plazuela San Francisco; or climbing to the left from the Callejón del Beso. The signs run out, but if you keep climbing as steeply as possible you're unlikely to get lost. Along the way there are various viewpoints and romantic nooks. There's also a bus ("Pípila") that takes you round the scenic Carretera Panorámica, and the **Funicular** (Mon–Fri 8am–9.45pm, Sat 9am–9.45pm, Sun 10am–9pm; M$12 each way), a kind of cliff railway that whisks you up the steep valley side from behind the church of San Diego. Pípila was Guanajuato's own Independence hero (see opposite), and you can climb up inside his statue (daily 7.30am–8pm; M$2) to a point immediately behind his shoulder – from where you unfortunately can't see very much at all.

## Around the university

At the back of the Jardín de la Unión and a little to the north, the **Plaza del Baratillo** is a small, bustling space usually alive with students hanging out or busy at the Internet cafés. From here the Teatro Principal is down to the right, while if you follow the curve on round to the left you find the church of **La Compañía**. The highly decorated monumental Baroque church is just about all that's left of a Jesuit seminary founded in 1732; step inside to admire the unusually light interior afforded by the clear glass in the dome. At the back in the sacristy is a small museum or *pinacoteca* (Mon–Sat 10am–5pm, Sun 10am–2pm; M$10) with a few seventeenth- to nineteenth-century oils, including four images of saints by Miguel Cabrera.

The seminary was an educational establishment that eventually metamorphosed into the **State University**, now one of the most prestigious in Mexico. The university building is in fact quite modern – only finished in 1955 – but is designed to blend in with the town, which, for all its size, it does surprisingly effectively. There's not a great deal of interest inside to the casual observer, but wander in anyway: notice boards detail local cultural events, and there's often a temporary exhibition of some kind. Next door to the university building, the **Museo del Pueblo de Guanajuato** (Tues–Sat 10am–6.30pm, Sun 10am–2.30pm; M$15) is a collection of local art and sundry oddities, housed in the seventeenth-century home of the Marqués de San Juan de Rayas. It's an attractive building with a nice little Baroque chapel, where much of the decoration has been replaced by modern murals painted by one of the current standard-bearers of the Mexican muralist tradition, José Chávez Morado.

Positos leads west from the front of the university to the fascinating **Museo Casa Diego Rivera**, Positos 47 (Tues–Sat 10am–6.30pm, Sun 10am–2.30pm; M$15), which occupies the birthplace of Guanajuato's most famous son. For most of his life Rivera, an ardent revolutionary sympathizer and Marxist, went unrecognized by his conservative home town, but with international recognition of his work came this museum, in the house where he was raised until he was six. Until 1904, the Rivera family only occupied the lower floor, which is now furnished in nineteenth-century style, though only the beds and a cot actually belonged to them. The place is far bigger than it looks from the outside, and the extensive upper floors contain many of Rivera's works, especially early ones, in a huge variety of styles – Cubist, Pointillist, Impressionist – showing the influences he absorbed during his years in France and Spain. Although there are no major works on display, the many sketches and small paintings are well worth a look, particularly those showing his fascination with all things pre-Columbian. There's also a large temporary exhibition space that often captures major international exhibitions as they pass through Mexico.



### The Alhóndiga and the Museo de la Mineralogía

The **Alhóndiga de Granaditas**, the most important of all Guanajuato's monuments, lies west of the Museo Diego Rivera, more or less above the market. Originally a granary, later a prison and now a very good regional museum, this was the scene of the first real battle and some of the bloodiest butchery in the War of Independence. Just thirteen days after the cry of Independence went up in Dolores Hidalgo, Father Hidalgo approached Guanajuato at the head of his insurgent force – mostly peons armed with nothing more than staves and sickles. The Spanish, outnumbered but well supplied with firearms, shut themselves up in the Alhóndiga, a redoubtable fortress. The almost certainly apocryphal story goes that Hidalgo's troops could make no impact until a young miner, nicknamed **El Pípila** ("the Turkeycock"), volunteered to set fire to the wooden doors – with a slab of stone tied to his back as a shield, he managed to crawl to the gates and start them burning, dying in the effort. The rebels, their path cleared, broke in and massacred the defenders wholesale. It was a short-lived victory – Hidalgo was later forced to abandon Guanajuato, leaving its inhabitants to face Spanish reprisals, and was eventually tracked down by the royalists and executed in Chihuahua. His head and the heads of his three chief co-conspirators, Allende, Aldama and Jiménez, were suspended from the four corners of the Alhóndiga as a warning to anyone tempted to follow their example, and there they stayed for over ten years, until Mexico finally did become independent. The hooks from which they hung are still there on the outside walls.

Inside, there's a memorial hall devoted to the Martyrs of Independence and a **museum** (Tues–Sat 10am–6pm, Sun 10am–3pm; M$33, cameras M$30). On the staircases are **murals** by local artist José Chávez Morado (see p.287) depicting scenes from the War of Independence and the Revolution, as well as native folklore and traditions. The collection, mostly labelled in Spanish, spans local history from pre-Hispanic times to the twentieth century: the most interesting sections cover the Independence battle and everyday life in colonial times. The iron cages in which the rebels' heads were displayed are present, as are lots of weapons and flags and a study of Guanajuato's mining industry. There's also plenty of art, especially a wonderful series of portraits by Hermengildo Bustos; and don't miss the small artesanías section by the side door, which displays a bit of everything from fabrics and clothes to saddles and metalwork.

Only real rock enthusiasts will want to trek half a kilometre from here up Alhóndiga to the **Museo de la Mineralogía** (Mon–Fri 8am–4pm; free), which houses some 20,000 rock samples. The museum is in the "Escuela de Minas y Metalurgia" of the university, in a building on your left as you head out of town towards Valenciana: look for the broad set of steps about 400m past the *Hotel Socavón*.



### Museo de las Momias

Halfway up the hill going west along Juárez from the Alhóndiga, the ghoulish **Museo de las Momias** (daily 9am–6pm; M$50), holds a very different sort of attraction. Here, lined up against the wall in a series of glass cases, are more than a hundred mummified human corpses exhumed from the local public cemetery. All the bodies were originally laid out in crypts, but if after five years the relatives were unable or unwilling to make the perpetuity payment, the remains were removed. Over time many were found to have been naturally preserved, and the "interesting" ones are on display here – others, not properly mummified or too dull for public titillation, have been burned or transferred to a common grave. Some of the wasted, leathery bodies are more than a century old (including a smartly dressed mummy said to have been a French mining engineer) while others are relatively recent fatalities. The burial clothes hang off the corpses almost indecently – and some are completely naked – and the guides delight in pointing out their most horrendous features: one twisted mummy, its mouth opened in a silent scream, is the "woman who was buried alive"; another, a woman who died in childbirth, is displayed beside "the smallest mummy in the world". It's all absolutely grotesque, but not without a degree of macabre fascination. You can continue into the **Salón del Culto a la Muerte** (same hours; M$10), a house-of-horrors-style extension, with an array of holographic images, jangly motorized skeletons, a rusty old chastity belt and yet

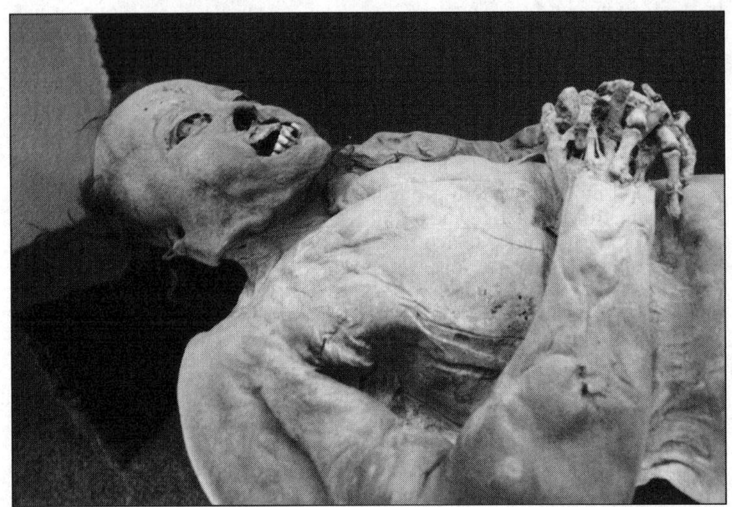

△ Museo de las Momias

more mummies. Fans of kitsch will be delighted with the hawkers outside selling mummy models and shards of rock in the shape of mummies. To get to the museum, either catch a bus ("Panteón" or "Momias") anywhere along Alonso or Juárez, or walk about 500m west of the Mercado Hidalgo along Juárez, then left into Calzada del Panteón.

### Presa de la Olla and the Museo Olga Costa-José Chávez Morado

East of the centre of town, Sangre de Cristo (later Paseo de la Presa) runs gradually uphill for a couple of kilometres through some of Guanajuato's fancier residential districts before ending up at the **Presa de la Olla** and the Presa San Renovato, two dams with small and rather unimpressive reservoirs. These are popular picnic spots, and you can rent rowing boats or sit out at a restaurant by the Presa de la Olla. A number of buses run out here (look for those marked "Presa"), heading through town on the underground street – a set of steps near the church of San Diego will take you down to a subterranean bus stop. Off Sangre de Cristo, Pastita runs northeast through the suburb of Pastita past a decayed section of an old aqueduct to the **Museo Olga Costa-José Chávez Morado** (Tues–Sat 9.30am–4pm, Sun 10am–3.30pm; M$15). The museum was formerly the Hacienda de Guadalupe residence and is where Mexican muralist Chávez Morado and his German painter wife spent much of their married life. He moved out and donated the building to the city of Guanajuato on his wife's death in 1993: her ashes fertilize a succulent prominently displayed on the patio outside. The house has been left largely as it was when they lived here, an eclectic mix of styles explained (in Spanish) by the guide: eighteenth-century majolica ceramics, seventeenth-century French chairs, Dutch porcelain, Iranian wall hangings and a fine collection of ex-votos. There's little of their work on show, but notice Morado's blue and white lamp, and his stained-glass windows – all blotches in red, yellow, blue and black – on the way up to the studio, now given over to temporary exhibitions. The museum is less than thirty minutes' walk from the Jardín de la Unión, or you can flag down any bus marked "Pastita" at the eastern end of town.

### Ex-Hacienda de San Gabriel de Barrera

If the crush of Guanajuato gets too much for you, head 2km west (either by foot or take any bus going to the Central de Autobuses) to the **Ex-Hacienda de San Gabriel de Barrera** (daily 9am–6pm; M$22, students M$15), a colonial home now transformed into a lovely little museum. The beautifully restored **gardens** of the hacienda range through a bizarre selection of international styles – including English, Italian, Roman, Arabic and Mexican – and make a wonderful setting for the house, which has been restored with a colonial look. Cool rooms evoke daily life among the wealthy silver barons of nineteenth-century Guanajuato, but include numerous fine pieces of furniture dating back several centuries: grand and opulent on the ground floor, rich in domestic detail upstairs. It's a great place to wander at your leisure and brings home the sheer wealth of colonial Guanajuato.

### La Valenciana

From close by the Alhóndiga on Calle Alhóndiga, buses ("Valenciana"; infrequent enough to make a short taxi ride a worthwhile investment) wind their way 4km uphill to the mine and church in **La Valenciana**. Near the top of the pass here, overlooking Guanajuato where the road to Dolores Hidalgo and San Miguel heads off north, you'll see the elaborate facade of the extraordinarily sumptuous **Templo de San Cayetano de Valenciana** church with its one completed tower. Built between 1765 and 1788, it's the ultimate expression of Mexico's churrigueresque style, with a profusion of intricate adornment covering every surface – even the mortar, they say, is mixed with silver ore. Inside, notice the enormous gilded *retablos* around the main altar and in each arm of the cross, and the delicate filigree of the roof vaulting, especially around the dome above the crossing.

The church was constructed for its owner, the Conde de Rul y Valenciana, who also owned La Valenciana **silver mine** – for hundreds of years the richest in Mexico, tapping Guanajuato's celebrated Veta Madre (Mother Lode). The mine still operates on a vastly reduced level, but exploitation continues apace with a clutch of ways to lure tourists to the associated silver shops, rock-sellers and restaurants. Beside the church, the original mine entrance now operates as the **Bocamina San Cayetano** (daily 10am–6pm; M$25), the name commemorating the saint who gets credit for the Mother Lode's discovery. Donning a hard hat fails to lend credibility to a brief tour of the upper 50m of tunnels, which end at a shrine to the mine's patron.

A visit to the excellent and expensive *Casa del Conde de la Valenciana* restaurant (see opposite), opposite the church, makes the journey up here much more worthwhile.

### Cerro de Cubilete and the statue of Cristo Rey

If you approached Guanajuato from León, you'll already have seen the huge statue of **Cristo Rey** crowning the 2661-metre **Cerro de Cubilete**, 20km west of the city. Variously claimed to occupy the geographical centre of the republic or just the state of Guanajuato, it seems a neat coincidence that it should be on the highest hill for miles. Nevertheless, the complex of chapels and pilgrims' dormitories is without question magnificently sited, with long views across the plains. At its heart is a twenty-metre bronze statue – erected in 1950 and ranking as the world's second largest image of Christ, just behind Rio de Janeiro's Cristo Redentor – standing on a golden globe flanked by cherubs, one holding a crown of thorns, the other the golden crown of the "King of Kings".

The easiest way to get up here is on one of the M$100 tours advertised all around Guanajuato, though you can do the same for less than half the price by nipping out to the Central de Autobuses and picking up one of ten daily Autobuses Vasallo de Cristo, which run up there in around thirty minutes.

## Eating

Finding something to eat in Guanajuato is easy – it's nearly impossible to walk more than a few yards down Juárez without passing some kind of café or restaurant. At the eastern end of **Juárez**, a whole series of very plain little places serve standard Mexican staples, many of them also offering inexpensive comidas corridas; the **university area**, too, has plenty of choice. Rather more adventurous, and cheaper still, are the stalls in the modern annex of the **Mercado Hidalgo**: two floors of delights (and horrors), where you're advised to take a careful look at what's on offer before succumbing to the frantic beckoning of the stallholders – some stalls are distinctly cleaner and more appetizing than others. Up around the **Jardín de la Unión**, the pricey outdoor restaurants are well worth visiting; in fact many people seldom stray from the excellent range of places all within five minutes' walk of each other along **Sopeña** and the surrounding streets.

**El Café Galería** Sopeña 10, right by the Teatro Juárez. Fashionable hangout with eating inside and a very popular outdoor terrace across the road where prices are high and the service slow.

**Café Tal** Temezcuitate 4. Great little café that roasts its own beans and consequently has some of the best coffee in town. They also have good fruit and yogurt breakfasts, a variety of teas and free WiFi.

**Casa del Conde de la Valenciana** at La Valenciana, 4km from town (see p.287). Beautifully set restaurant in the courtyard of a former hacienda with vines growing up the walls. The Mexican food is nicely prepared and presented, and you should leave room for the ice creams scooped out of the shells of the fruits they are flavoured with. Roughly M$200 for a full meal. Closed Sun.

**La Delicia** Plazuela de San Francisco 12. Eat-in *pastelería* with window seats that catch the afternoon sun.

**El Gallo Pitogorica** Constancia 10 ⓣ473/732-9489. One of Guanajuato's best restaurants, with a predominantly Italian menu, eclectic decor and a fabulous location high on the valley slopes right behind the San Diego church. Dine on prosciutto and melon followed by a tasty *arrabiata* as the sounds of the Jardín de la Unión waft up through the open windows. Around M$200 for a full meal.

**La Hacienda de Marfil** Arcos de Guadalupe 3 ⓣ473/733-1148. One of the city's best restaurants, with gorgeous garden dining, refined service and a mouthwatering international menu that changes seasonally. Set an evening aside, reserve ahead and don't expect much less than M$300 per person for a full meal.

**El Midi** Plazuela de San Fernando 41. A refreshing change from endless Mexican and Italian dining, this southern French place serves an excellent array of dishes from the Midi – among them quiches, terrines, salads and olive loaf – all self-served from a cold buffet and charged by weight (M$10/100g). Unless you're a glutton it works out very reasonably, and the coffee and desserts are excellent. Closed Sat.

**La Oreja de Van Gogh** Plazuela de San Fernando. Choose a starry night to sit outside at this relaxed restaurant on a pretty square away from the bustle of the Jardín de la Unión. Try the thick chicken stew served in a *molcajete* (M$80) or an arranchera steak (M$90). There's live acoustic music most nights.

**Pingüis** northeast corner of Jardín de la Unión. The best bargain in the Jardín: a little faded, but still a buzzing, friendly place good for breakfasts (around M$35), comidas corridas and a fair choice of Mexican and international main meals.

**La Rana Loca** Juan Valle 7. The slightly sterile atmosphere here won't encourage you to linger, but the food is great value, especially the comida corrida (M$30), and comes with a bottomless jug of *agua fresca*.

**Tasca de la Paz** Plaza de la Paz 28. Smart Spanish restaurant with outdoor tables, serving European delights such as *paella*, chicken in white wine and *jamón serrano*. Moderate to expensive.

**Truco 7** Truco 7. Beautiful little old-school café with a young, convivial atmosphere, comfy chairs and all manner of art covering the walls. Great, moderately priced breakfasts, comidas, salads, steaks and wonderful garlic soup with an egg poached in it. Ask for your cappuccino *sin miel* to avoid getting a dollop of corn syrup in it.

**El Unicornio Azul** Plaza del Baratillo 2. Tiny vegetarian restaurant selling whole-wheat breads to go and soya burgers and juices to have inside.

## Nightlife and entertainment

Home to a superb host of cafés and bars, Guanajuato is a great town in which to sit around and knock back a coffee or a bottle or beer or two. Things are especially busy at weekends, when refugees from the bigger cities, including Mexico City and León, come here to enjoy themselves. Most of the better places are close to the Jardín de la Union and the university, while the rougher **bars** and **clubs** are down on Juárez around Mercado Hidalgo, where the cantinas are generally reserved for men and prostitutes.

An excellent way to pass an hour or so is to follow one of the organized **callejóneadas** – walking tours that wind through the sidestreets and back alleys following a student minstrel group known as *estudiantinas*. *Callejóneadas* are aimed at Mexicans, so without fluent Spanish and some local knowledge you'll miss most of the jokes and risqué tales, but they're great fun all the same. It is possible to buy your own beer or wine and just tag along, but for the full experience you'll need a ticket. These can be bought (for around M$80) from

## Festival Internacional Cervantino

Usually referred to simply as the **Cervantino**, this two-and-a-half week festival (early to mid-Oct; ⓣ473/731-1150 or 731-1161, ⓦwww.festivalcervantino.gob.mx) is a celebration of all things to do with sixteenth-century Spanish author **Miguel de Cervantes**, though it is primarily about his most famous character and hapless romantic, Don Quixote. The festival has its foundations in the 1950s, when students performed **entremeses** – swashbuckling one-act plays from classical Spanish theatre – outdoors in Plaza San Roque. These still take place, and you don't need good Spanish to work out what's going on, as they're highly visual and very entertaining. There's a grandstand for which you have to book seats, but it's easy enough to join the crowds watching from the edges of the plaza for free. Groups of students will quite often put on impromptu performances outside festival times, so it's worth wandering up here in the early evening just to see if anything is happening, especially on Saturday nights. The Cervantino is now far larger, and during the festival the town, and just about every imaginable performance space, is alive with music and cultural events of every stripe – opera, dance, literature readings, music performances. You'll have to pay to get into many events, but there is almost always something free happening in the Plaza Alhóndiga. It is a great time to be here, though you'll need to book accommodation months in advance.

any of the information booths, at Juárez 210, or from the *estudiantinas* who hang around the Jardín de la Unión from around 6.30pm. They entitle you to a *porrón* (a kind of ceramic drinking vessel), which is topped up as you promenade. In high season, there's something happening most nights of the week, but at other times of the year Tuesday, Thursday, Friday and Saturday are your best bets, and the event usually kicks off around 8.30pm. *Callejóneadas* are also in full swing during the town's various **festivals** (see p.279), especially the Cervantino in October.

For a more sedate evening, Guanajuato also has a **cinema**, Cines Guanajuato, tucked up a side street behind the university. It shows first-run movies several times a day from around M$32 (Mon–Thurs M$22). On most Friday nights at 8.30pm you can watch the town turn out in its finery for the **Orquestra Sinfónica de la Universidad de Guanajuato**, at the Teatro Principal; it has an enviable reputation throughout Mexico and only costs about M$80.

### Bars and clubs

**Bar Fly** Sóstenes Rocha 30. Tiny, sociable bar with folk, jazz or acoustic music most nights from 9pm, and seldom any cover.

**Bar Ocho** Constancia 8. Youthful bar set up with sofas for intimate conversation, and a pool table upstairs. A good place to wind down after the clubs. The name is a play on the word *borracho*, Spanish for "drunk".

**Bar Zilch** Plaza del Baratillo. Great café and bar that's good for a drink any time but ideal for listing to live acoustic music, often jazz in the evening.

**Capitolio** Plaza de la Paz 62. One of the town's premier clubs. Come here to dance the night away. Don't expect the music to be anywhere close to cutting-edge, but it can be fun. Open Wed–Sat. M$50 cover.

**La Dama de las Camelias** Sopeña 34, opposite Museo Iconográfico. Great bar imaginatively decorated with evening dresses, high-heeled shoes and smashed mirror fragments. *La Dama* stays open until dawn and offers dancing most nights and great salsa late on Fri. Closed Sun.

**Desmond's** Positos 79. Intimate Irish pub and restaurant run by a long-time resident Irishman. Guinness is available, of course, and there's a different music style each evening, including Trad Irish on Wed. Open daily 2pm–midnight.

**Guanajuato Grill** Alonso 4. Guanajuato's other main club, fairly cheesy and usually packed with local teenagers doing very little but sweating and listening to the music.

**Los Lobos** Manuel Doblado 2. Dim and often crowded bar that resounds nightly to thumping rock classics. Cheap-ish beer.

**Santo Café** Campanero 4. Reached by a small bridge over a pedestrian alley, this quiet restaurant, café and bar is a favourite of intellectuals looking to wax philosophical over a drink.

## Listings

**American Express** Viajes Georama, Plaza de la Paz 34, operates as a travel agency (Mon–Fri 9am–8pm, Sat 10am–2pm; ⓣ473/732-5101, ⓔviajes_georama@hotmail.com), and also has all the usual Amex services.

**Banks and exchange** Banks can be found along Juárez: Bancomer at no. 9, Banamex on the Plazuela de San Fernando and a convenient branch of Banorte between the Plaza de la Paz and the Jardín Unión. Outside bank hours, try Divisas Dimas, an exchange office at Juárez 33 (daily 10am–8pm).

**Buses** Heading through the hills to Dolores Hidalgo couldn't be simpler, with half-hourly departures from a stop about 500m up Salgado towards La Valenciana (it is just past the Glorieta roundabout opposite *Hotel Socavón*). For other destinations, make for Guanajuato's Central de Autobuses (via local buses marked "Centro–Central" from Juárez), where there are regular services to Guadalajara, Mexico City, San Luis Potosí and Aguascalientes, and almost constant departures for León and San Luis de la Paz. There are relatively few buses direct to San Miguel de Allende, for which it's sometimes quicker to change in Dolores; if you have any problem getting anywhere else, head for León (see p.277), which is on the main north–south highway and has much more frequent services. Viajes Frausto, Juárez 10, close to the Jardín de la Unión (ⓣ473/732-3580), has the timetables, fares and booking facilities for all first-class companies operating from the bus station.

**Emergencies** Police ⓣ473/732-0266; Cruz Roja ⓣ473/732-0487; for emergency medical attention

### Learning Spanish in Guanajuato

Guanajuato has become a popular place to spend a couple of weeks learning Spanish – the only potential problem here is that there are so many other English speakers around you may get less Spanish practice than you had hoped. One way to avoid this is to **stay with a local family** (typically around M$180–220 a day), sharing meals with them and getting plenty of opportunity to try out your new language skills; schools will generally put you in touch with likely families. Classes with up to five students usually **cost** around M$60 an hour, and a little less if you're doing more hours per day. One-on-one tuition is around M$130 an hour. The following schools have a wide variety of programmes:

**Academia Falcon** Paseo de la Presa 80 ⓣ473/431-0745, ⓦwww.academiafalcon.com. Located just out of town, this is probably the best school overall, with a particularly strong range of specialist classes including Mexican music, mural painting and Mexican culture class; the last has an optional topic looking at local gay and lesbian culture. Classes start each Monday.

**Escuela Mexicana** Potrero 12 ⓣ473/732-5005, ⓦwww.escuelamexicana.com. Popular school in the heart of town offering everything from one-week beginners' courses to extensive advanced classes and an array of specialist courses in such subjects as culture, literature, politics and Mexican cooking. Their intensive "Spanish for Travellers" requires four hours of coursework a day and one or two weeks' commitment (US$220 per week, plus US$35 registration).

**University of Guanajuato** ⓣ473/732-0006, ⓦwww.ugto.mx. The Centro de Idiomas runs exchange programmes with universities around the world. They're aimed more at improvers than beginners, concentrating on Mexican and Latin American culture and costing US$600 for a four-week full-time programme. Students are encouraged to live with Mexican families but you have to find your own place.

visit Centro de Salud Urbano de Guanajuato, Pardo 5 (☎473/732-1467).

**Flights** Guanajuato state airport, 30km west, between Silao and León, has daily flights to major Mexican cities and the US. To get there, catch a second-class bus to León and get off as you pass the airport (or fork out M$300 or so for a taxi).

**Internet access** Numerous places around town, including a competitive concentration around Plaza Baratillo where M$10/hr is the norm. For those with laptops and PDAs, there's free WiFi at several cafés around the Jardín de la Unión.

**Laundry** Lavandería del Centro, Sopeña 26 (Mon–Sat 9am–8.30pm; ☎473/732-0436). M$50/3–5kg.

**Pharmacy** El Fénix, Juárez 106, near Plazuela de Los Angeles (Mon–Sat 8am–10pm, Sun 9am–9pm).

**Post office** Located at the eastern end of Positos, behind the Jardín de la Unión (Mon–Fri 9am–5pm, Sat 9am–1pm).

**Taxis** Linea Dorada ☎473/732-1026.

**Telephones** *Larga distancia* at Alonso 39, opposite *Casa Schoenstatt*.



# Dolores Hidalgo and around

Fifty kilometres or so from both Guanajuato and San Miguel de Allende, **DOLORES HIDALGO** is as ancient and as historically rich as either of its southern neighbours. This was Father Hidalgo's parish, and it was from the church in the main plaza here that the historic **Grito de la Independencia** ("Cry of Independence") was first issued in 1810 (see box, opposite). The town celebrates the event annually with the **Fiestas de Septiembre**, ten days of cultural and sporting events, music and fireworks, culminating with the Grito around dawn on the sixteenth.

Perhaps because of its less spectacular location or maybe because there is no university or major language school, Dolores hasn't seen a fraction of the tourist development that has overtaken other places in the Bajío. It's a good bet, though, for a one-night stopover, and if you can't find accommodation in Guanajuato or San Miguel, this is certainly the place to head; you'll get a better room here for appreciably less. True, there is less to see, but it's an elegant little town and thoroughly Mexican; it's busy, too, as it sits on a traditionally important crossroads on the silver route from Zacatecas.

Just a couple of blocks from the bus station as you walk towards the central plaza, the **Casa Hidalgo** (Tues–Sat 10am–5.45pm, Sun 10am–4.45pm; M$24, free on Sun), Hidalgo's home, has been converted into a museum devoted to his life, very much a point of pilgrimage for Mexicans on day trips. It's a bit heavy on written tributes from various groups to the "Father of Independence" and on copies of other correspondence he either sent or received – but it's interesting nonetheless and includes a few highlights such as his letter of excommunication from the Inquisition less than a month after the Grito. Continuing in the same direction, you come to a beautifully laid-out plaza, overlooked by the exuberant facade of the famous church, where a left turn takes you to the **Museo de la Independencia Nacional**, Zacatecas 6 (daily 9am–5pm; M$15, free on Sun). Inside, vibrant, graphic murals depict significant scenes from Mexican history from the Aztec perception of the world through to the life of Hidalgo. Don't miss the glass cabinets filled with record sleeves and cowboy boots that pay homage to the greatest *ranchera* singer of all time, José Alfredo Jimenez, another of Dolores's native sons, who died in 1973.

Besides a couple of other graceful churches, there's little else here but the attraction of the dilapidated old streets themselves. As you wander around, look out for the locally made **ceramics**. They're an ancient tradition and on sale everywhere. The bigger shops are near the Casa Hidalgo, but the best deals are found on the outskirts of town.

### The Grito de la Independencia

On the night of September 15, 1810, **Padre Miguel Hidalgo y Costilla** and some of his fellow leaders of the Independence movement, warned by messengers from Querétaro that their intention to raise a rebellion against the Spanish had been discovered, decided to bring their plans forward. At dawn on September 16, Hidalgo, tolling the church bell, called his parishioners together and addressed them from the balcony of the church with an impassioned speech ending in the **Grito de la Independencia**, "¡Mexicanos, Viva México!" This cry is now repeated every year by the president in Mexico City and by politicians all over the country at midnight on September 15, as the starting point for Independence Day celebrations. In 2006, protests in Mexico City's Zócalo against the alleged rigging of the year's presidential election made it unsafe for the traditional *grito*, and outgoing president Vicente Fox moved the commemoration to Dolores Hidalgo.

September 16 remains the one day of the year when the bell in Dolores Hidalgo's parish church is rung; however, the bell in place today is a copy of the original, which was either melted down for munitions or hangs in the Palacio Nacional in Mexico City, depending on which story you believe.

## Dolores Hidalgo practicalities

Dolores is connected to both San Miguel and Guanajuato by regular, rapid **buses** to and from the Flecha Amarilla terminal, on Hidalgo beside the river. Herradura de Plata also has a terminal a block away at the corner of Chiapas and Yucatán, from where buses run every thirty minutes south to San Miguel de Allende and Mexico City. There's little need to visit Dolores's small **tourist office** (daily 10am–4pm; Ⓣ& Ⓕ418/182-1164), on the main plaza by the church, but they can give advice on where to buy ceramics.

Finding a room is seldom a problem except during the week leading up to September 16, when the town is packed. The cheapest of the local **hotels** is *Posada Dolores*, Yucatán 8, past the Independence Museum and then left (Ⓣ418/182-0642; ❷), easily missed behind a small doorway. Some rooms are pretty basic, while others (❸) have been recently modernized. Slightly more upscale places are all good value: try the modern *Hotel Posada Hidalgo*, Hidalgo 15, near the bus station (Ⓣ418/182-2683, Ⓕ182-0477; ❺), which has a small gym and a sauna; *Hotel Caudillo*, Querétaro 8 (Ⓣ& Ⓕ418/182-0198; ❺), beside the church; and *Posada Cocomacan*, Plaza Principal 4 (Ⓣ418/182-6086, Ⓦwww.posadacocomacan.com.mx; ❺), with its cool interior, cable TV and some rooms overlooking the plaza.

You can also eat well around the plaza, notably at the **restaurant** at *Hotel Caudillo*, which does a M$65 comida corrida. For those with a sweet tooth, *Dulcería el Cubilete* is a wonderful candy store right next door that sells all sorts of sugary regional delicacies. The tiny restaurant adjacent to *Posada Dolores* serves heavenly tacos made with freshly pressed corn tortillas and comidas corridas for just M$28. Dolores Hidalgo is also home to the country's most unusual **ice cream** flavours: Mexicans come in droves to the Plaza Principal to lick scoops of creamy alfalfa, *mole*, *cerveza*, shrimp and avocado (fortunately most vendors let you sample before you commit to a full cone).

## East of Dolores: San Luis de la Paz, Pozos and San José Iturbide

If you carry straight on through Dolores, after 40km you hit the road between San Luis Potosí and Querétaro at **SAN LUIS DE LA PAZ**.

Though of little interest in itself, a minor road runs south from here, parallel to the main Hwy-57, through the intriguing half-deserted town of **Pozos**, 50km to the historic town of **San José Iturbide**. There are frequent bus services between the three towns, as well as south to Querétaro or San Miguel de Allende. San Luis de la Paz is the largest of this string of three small towns, a typically Mexican provincial settlement with one main street, a colonial plaza and horses tied up alongside farmers' pickup trucks outside the market. It's a good place to buy rugs and *sarapes* at reasonable prices, though most of what is made here is sent off to the markets in larger towns. If you need to stay, there are a couple of small, cheap hotels on the main street just up from the bus terminal.

### Pozos

Twenty minutes south of San Luis, the road to San José passes through what was once a rich and flourishing mining community called Real de Pozos. Now just known as **POZOS** (and officially, Mineral de Pozos), it is often referred to as a ghost-town, though in reality it is far from dead, with several hundred people living clustered around the gaping maw of half a church.

While you shouldn't expect swinging doors flapping in the breeze and tumbleweed gusting through the streets, you will find vast areas of crumbling masonry inhabited only by the odd burro. In the last decade or so the village has undergone a bit of a revival and is fast becoming a sub-colony of San Miguel de Allende – foreigners are buying up property and turning it into hotels and fine restaurants – though it is still early days yet.

A number of artisans have also moved in, some producing high-quality **pre-Columbian instruments** for sale – mostly drums, flutes, stone xylophones and slit gongs, and not cheap. The **Sala de Cultura**, on Ocampo (daily 10am–2pm & 4–6pm), is poorly marked and offers a lightweight introduction to the local culture. If you continue west from the main (and only) square, a vast area of harsh agave desert opens up, dotted with old mine shafts and perfect for a couple of hours' hiking: take water, sun screen and a hat and see where the road takes you.

If the prospect of moody walks isn't enough to entice you to **stay**, you might just be tempted by *Casa Mexicana*, Juárez 2 on the Plaza Principal (T442/293-0014, Wwww.casamexicanahotel.com; 7), an attractive five-bedroom B&B with exquisite and highly individual rooms set around an attractive garden, and with an on-site art gallery. Nicely prepared meals are also served to non-guests, or you could just drop in for a margarita. A step up, price-wise, is the *Casa Montana*, Plaza Principal 4 (T442/293-0032, Wwww.casamontanahotel.com; 7, suites 8) next door, which offers luxury accommodation (including Continental breakfast), lush terraces and a laundry list of amenities. They also have an art gallery, and can arrange for private tours and horseback-riding treks. It may be best to visit Pozos on a day trip from San Miguel de Allende (see opposite) if you're not able to secure a reservation at one of the two places to stay or if you've had enough of the town after a few hours' visit. In addition to the B&B restaurants, there are several **comedores** that sell tacos and comidas corridas sprinkled around the tiny town.

### San José Iturbide

Further south, **SAN JOSÉ ITURBIDE** is an immaculate town centred on a tidy plaza, chiefly distinguished by its behemoth Neoclassical **church**, dedicated to Agustín de Iturbide, a local opportunist who started the War of Independence as a general loyal to Spain – inflicting major defeats on

Morelos – only to change sides later. Having helped secure Mexico's Independence without any concomitant reform, he briefly declared himself emperor in 1822. The plaque reads, accurately enough, "from one of the few towns which have not forgotten you".

There's little reason to stay, but if you just fancy a night in a small ordinary Mexican town with good **accommodation**, then try the excellent *Hotel Los Arcos*, Plaza Principal 10, right by the church (Ⓣ419/198-0330, Ⓔsjiturbide@yahoo.com.mx; ❻), with large, modern, carpeted rooms. There's also the convenient, comfortable but basic *Hotel Posada Unión*, Callejón Olivera 10, two blocks along Allende near the temple (Ⓣ419/198-0071; ❹). The best meals in town are in the **restaurant** at *Los Arcos*, and there are good **snacks** and espresso at *Casas Viejas*, just steps away on the main plaza.

# San Miguel de Allende

Set on a steep hillside overlooking the Río Laja and dominated by red rooftops and domed churches, at first sight **SAN MIGUEL DE ALLENDE** seems little different from any other small colonial town. Its distinct character, though, is soon apparent: it's home to a very high-profile colony of artists and writers, fleshed out with less ambitious retirees from the US and by flocks of students drawn to the town's several language and arts schools. Like such a community anywhere, it's inward-looking, often pretentious and gossip-ridden, but it's also extremely hospitable and much given to taking newcomers under its wing. The town's increase in popularity in recent years, and in many ways the cause of the influx of **expats** and tourists, can be, in part, attributed to Tony Cohan's popular book *On Mexican Time*, which tells the story of a writer and his artist wife who abandon smog-ridden Los Angeles for a quieter life in San Miguel, where they restore an old house, learn the local lifestyle and are slowly seduced by the colonial city's unique charm. Now something like ten percent of the population are foreigners, some 10,000 of whom live in the vicinity more or less permanently, boosted by another 5000 or so who fly down to weekend here. The colonial centre remains relatively unchanged by the foreign presence, but the outskirts are now sprouting gated communities and even shopping malls.

There are many good reasons for the popularity of San Miguel – chiefly that it's a very picturesque town with a perfect climate and, for artists, good light throughout the year. What got it started, though, was the foundation in 1938 of the **Instituto Allende**, an arts institute that enjoyed an enormous boost after World War II when returning American GIs found that their education grants could be stretched much further in Mexico. With its reputation established, San Miguel has never looked back. For all its popularity, though, the town remains one of the most pleasant places you could pick to rest up for a while in comfort, with luxurious hotels (several of them excellent), great restaurants and some of the most vibrant nightlife in Mexico's interior. Having said that, you may find yourself blowing your budget in double-quick time.

There are few major sights, but the whole town (which has been a national monument since 1926, hence no new building, no flashing signs and no traffic lights) is crowded with old seigneurial mansions and curious churches. It was founded in 1542 by a Franciscan friar, Juan de San Miguel, and as "San Miguel El Grande" became an important supply centre for the big mining

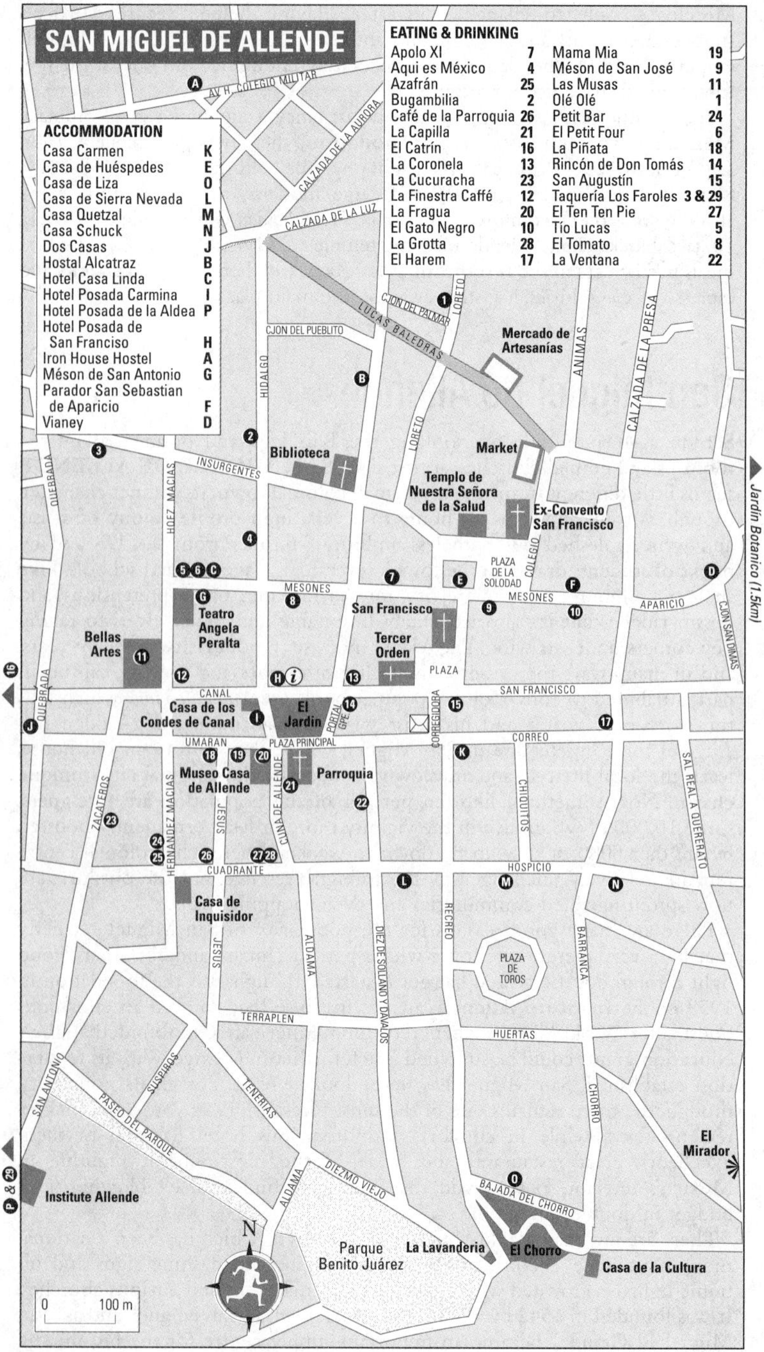
SAN MIGUEL DE ALLENDE
ACCOMMODATION
Casa Carmen K
Casa de Huéspedes E
Casa de Liza O
Casa de Sierra Nevada L
Casa Quetzal M
Casa Schuck N
Dos Casas J
Hostal Alcatraz B
Hotel Casa Linda C
Hotel Posada Carmina I
Hotel Posada de la Aldea P
Hotel Posada de San Francisco H
Iron House Hostel A
Méson de San Antonio G
Parador San Sebastian de Aparicio F
Vianey D
EATING & DRINKING
Apolo XI 7
Aqui es México 4
Azafrán 25
Bugambilia 2
Café de la Parroquia 26
La Capilla 21
El Catrín 16
La Coronela 13
La Cucuracha 23
La Finestra Caffé 12
La Fragua 20
El Gato Negro 10
La Grotta 28
El Harem 17
Mama Mia 19
Méson de San José 9
Las Musas 11
Olé Olé 1
Petit Bar 24
El Petit Four 6
La Piñata 18
Rincón de Don Tomás 14
San Augustín 15
Taquería Los Faroles 3 & 29
El Ten Ten Pie 27
Tío Lucas 5
El Tomato 8
La Ventana 22
AV H. COLEGIO MILITAR
CALZADA DE LA AURORA
CALZADA DE LA LUZ
LUCAS BALEDRAS
CJON DEL PALMAR
LORETO
CJON DEL PUEBLITO
HIDALGO
ANIMAS
CALZADA DE LA PRESA
Mercado de Artesanías
Market
Biblioteca
INSURGENTES
QUEBRADA
HOEZ MACIAS
Templo de Nuestra Señora de la Salud
Ex-Convento San Francisco
PLAZA DE LA SOLODAD
COLEGIO
MESONES
APARICIO
CJON SAN DIMAS
Jardín Botanico (1.5km)
Teatro Angela Peralta
Bellas Artes
San Francisco
Tercer Orden
PLAZA
CANAL
SAN FRANCISCO
Casa de los Condes de Canal
El Jardin
PORTAL GPE
CORREGIDORA
CORREO
UMARAN
PLAZA PRINCIPAL
Museo Casa de Allende
Parroquia
ZACATEROS
HERNANDEZ MACIAS
JESUS
CUNA DE ALLENDE
CHIQUITOS
SAL REAL A QUERETARO
CUADRANTE
HOSPICIO
Casa de Inquisidor
ALDAMA
DIEZ DE SOLLANO Y DAVALOS
RECREO
BARRANCA
PLAZA DE TOROS
TERRAPLEN
HUERTAS
SAN ANTONIO
SUSPIROS
TENERIAS
PASEO DEL PARQUE
CHORRO
El Mirador
DIEZMO VIEJO
BAJADA DEL CHORRO
Institute Allende
P & 29
N
Parque Benito Juárez
La Lavanderia
El Chorro
Casa de la Cultura
0 100 m

towns, and a stopover on the main silver route from Zacatecas. The name was later changed to honour **Ignacio Allende**, a native who became Hidalgo's chief lieutenant. The country hereabouts is still ranching territory, though is increasingly being taken over by the tourists and foreigners: attractions include hot springs, a nearby golf course, horse-riding at a couple of dude ranches and mountain biking.

## Arrival and information

San Miguel has a surprisingly poor bus service, but this is still the easiest way to arrive, perhaps expedited by a change at Guanajuato or Querétaro if you're coming from some distance. The **bus station** (with small guardería) is about 2km west of the centre, from where there are taxis and regular local buses (marked "Centro–Central") that run into town along Canal. San Miguel's nearest **airport** is near León (see p.277), from where Viajes San Miguel, Sollano 4 (ⓣ415/152-2537, ⓦwww.viajessanmiguel.com), runs a shuttle van (M$250 one-way; reserve in advance) meeting most flights. It also runs a M$550 shuttle service to the airport in Mexico City.

San Miguel's helpful **tourist office** (Mon–Sat 8.30am–8pm, Sun 10am–5.30pm; ⓣ415/152-0900, ⓦwww.turismosanmiguel.com.mx) is on the north corner of El Jardín (officially "Jardín de Allende" and also known as "Plaza Principal") at no. 8. As well as the usual racks of leaflets and maps, it can provide details of local art and language courses. For more information, pick up one of the free ad-driven booklets scattered around town, the weekly gringo **newspaper** *Atención San Miguel* (M$8; out Fri; ⓦwww.atencionsanmiguel.org), or, for really detailed coverage, consult *The Insider's Guide to San Miguel* by Archie Dean (M$200), available from the library or at Lagundi. The website ⓦwww.portalsanmiguel.com is also helpful.

San Miguel's calendar is full of **fiestas**, one of the best being the **Fiesta de San Antonio de Padua** (June 13), with a colourful parade for one of the town's patron saints, St Antony of Padua, involving a procession of crazily dressed revellers known as "Los Locos" (the Crazies). Bull-running in the main streets is the focus of the **Pamplonada** (third Sat in Sept). The most important fiesta of all is **San Miguel Arcángel** (Sept 29), two days of processions, concerts, traditional dancing, bullfights and ceremonies.

## Accommodation

Most of San Miguel's **hotels** are near the Jardín and, as with pretty much all other goods and services in town, have been made more expensive than in the rest of the Bajío by the large expat influence here. With the exception of a couple of **hostels**, budget lodging is hard to come by, but if you're prepared to pay a good deal more you can stay in one of dozens of places with gorgeous rooms set around delightful courtyards or gardens. Indeed, San Miguel must have Mexico's highest concentrations of boutique hotels and swish B&Bs. The pricier places that specifically cater to sun-seeking retirees from north of the border tend to charge more during the popular December–March high season; reasonably priced places adjust their rates upwards during Semana Santa and over the September fiesta season.

The city also offers **long-stay apartments**, which can work out to be economical; ask at the tourist office for details, or check notice boards around town or the back pages of the *Atención San Miguel* newspaper.

**Casa Carmen** Correo 31 ⓣ & ⓕ 415/152-0844, ⓦ www.infosma.com/casacarmen. Attractive and intimate hotel run by a US–Mexican couple. Comfortable and totally secure, with spacious and well-appointed rooms, each different. Rate includes breakfast and lunch (not Sun). 7

**Casa de Huéspedes** Mesones 27 ⓣ 415/152-1378. Quaint little second-floor hotel: friendly and relaxed, with clean, well-kept rooms – some with balconies – fluffy towels and fresh flowers. There are also rooms with kitchenette at no extra cost, and at M$150 the singles are an especially good deal. 4

**Casa de Liza** Bajada de Chorro 7 ⓣ 415/152-0352, ⓦ www.casaliza.com. One-of-a-kind B&B on Parque Benito Juárez. Each exquisite room is individually decorated with a variety of artwork. There's a pool, rambling patios, massage therapy and a bilingual staff. The gracious owners live by the "mi casa es su casa" motto and are all too happy to tell you about their most famous guest: Antonio Banderas. 9

**Casa de Sierra Nevada** Hospicio 35 ⓣ 415/152-7040, ⓦ www.casadesierranevada.com. Luxury hotel with spacious rooms around a beautiful colonial courtyard, built in 1580 and lush with greenery. The owners have now taken over half a dozen houses in the vicinity and have also opened an equally sumptuous outpost at Santa Elena 2, at the north end of Parque Benito Juárez. All guests have access to the hotel's lovely pool and classy restaurant. 9

**Casa Quetzal** Hospicio 34 ⓣ 415/152-0501, ⓦ www.casaquetzalhotel.com. Quiet, attractive hotel with six suites, all decorated in a casually elegant style. Some have kitchenettes, fireplaces and private terraces with rooftop views of the centre of town. 9

**Casa Schuck** Bajada de Garita 3 ⓣ 415/152-0657, ⓦ www.casaschuck.com. Splendidly styled and colourful hotel with antiques, amply sized rooms, small but beautiful pool, leafy nooks and personal touches. Welcoming owners make this one of San Miguel's best bets. 9

**Dos Casas** Quebrada 101 ⓣ 415/154-4073, ⓦ www.livingdoscasas.com. There's a beautiful balance of old structure and up-to-the-minute fittings in these two adjacent colonial homes gorgeously done up as a contemporary boutique B&B. With just five rooms, attention is personal and relaxed, and there's a dining room and chic wine bar on site. If you can, go for the rooftop suites (M$3650) with great town views. 9

**Hostal Alcatraz** Relox 54 ⓣ 415/152-8543, ⓦ www.geocities.com/alcatrazhostel/. Central and welcoming hostel with all the expected amenities, including kitchen, luggage storage, Internet access (free for HI members) and WiFi. There's also a new and slightly quieter annex down the street with identical rates and private en-suite rooms. Dorms M$100 per person. 4

**Hotel Casa Linda** Mesones 101 ⓣ 415/154-4007, ⓦ www.hotelcasalinda.com. Eclectic, inviting property with busy but attractive rooms, gym, Jacuzzi and video library. This lush oasis has loads of character and quiet charm. Breakfast included. 9

**Hotel Posada Carmina** Cuna de Allende 7, a few metres south of the Jardín ⓣ 415/152-0458, ⓦ www.posadacarmina.com. Large rooms with brick floors, high ceilings and white walls are set amid yet more colonial splendour around a beautiful courtyard; there are cheaper but still very nice rooms in an adjacent wing. A shade pricey for what you get, but you can't beat its location, one block from the Jardín and opposite the town's best restaurant, *La Capilla*, and the staff is gracious. 8

**Hotel Posada de la Aldea** Ancha de San Antonio 15 ⓣ 415/152-1022, ⓦ www.naftaconnect.com/hotellaaldea. Clean and comfortable a/c rooms all have modern amenities in this enormous hotel popular with Mexican tourists. There's a pool, tennis courts and parking, but its main virtue is being opposite the Instituto Allende. 7

**Hotel Posada de San Francisco** Plaza Principal 2 ⓣ 415/152-7213, ⓕ 152-0072. Ageing but comfortable rooms in a lovely and sedate colonial building at surprisingly reasonable prices for its location right on the Jardín. 7

**Iron House Hostel** Colegio Militar 17-D ⓣ 415/100-0292, ⓦ www.geocities.com/hostelsma. Small, friendly hostel about a 10min walk north of town in a quiet suburb. There's dorms, private rooms, a decent kitchen and free Internet access (with WiFi). Owner Ricardo is usually up for joining his guests for a night on the town, and on Tues and Wed leads free salsa lessons at *Mama Mia*. English spoken but Spanish encouraged. M$100 per person. 3

**Mesón de San Antonio** Mesones 80 ⓣ 415/152-0580, ⓔ mesondesanantonio@prodigy.net.mx. Modern and reasonably spacious carpeted rooms set around a small garden with a swimming pool; Continental breakfast included. The extra M$60 for a two-level suite is money well spent. 6

**Parador San Sebastian de Aparicio** Mesones 7 ⓣ 415/152-7084. Cool and tranquil, with simple rooms around a colonial courtyard. Ask for one of the larger rooms at no extra cost – a huge bargain. 4

**Vianey** Aparicio 18 ⓣ 415/152-4559. Modern and spotless rooms lacking character, but a decent fallback if others are full. 2

## The Town

Head first to **El Jardín**, the name by which San Miguel's **zócalo** is best known, which is within walking distance of almost everything you'll want to see and the main focus of activity in town. The **Instituto Allende**, south of the centre and a fairly easy walk from here, is an alternative hub, and an especially useful source of information for anyone who wants to stay in San Miguel longer than a couple of days.

Wherever you go in town, it seems that any place that's not a café or restaurant is operating as some kind of gallery or **artesanía** shop. The stores offer a bewildering array of top-notch goods from all over Mexico – prices are correspondingly high, some even bordering on extortionate. There are really too many quality places to be very specific, but as a starting point, try the streets immediately south and west of the Jardín.

### El Jardín

The most famous of the city's landmarks, **La Parroquia de San Miguel Arcángel** – the parish church – takes up one side of the Jardín. This gloriously over-the-top structure, with a towering pseudo-Gothic facade bristling with turrets and spires, was rebuilt towards the end of the nineteenth century by a self-taught Indian stonemason, Zeferino Gutiérrez, who supposedly learned about architecture by studying postcards of great French cathedrals and then drew diagrams in the dust to explain to his workers what he wanted. Inside, the patterned tilework of the floor, the *azulejos* along the walls and the pure semicircular vaulting along the nave exhibit distinct Moorish influences.

Opposite the church is a block containing the former **Palacio Municipal** and the **Galería San Miguel**, one of the most prestigious of the many galleries showing local artists' work. The remaining two sides of the square are lined with covered *portales*, under whose arches vendors of drinks and trinkets shelter from the sun, with a row of shops behind them. On the Jardín, too, are some of San Miguel's most distinguished mansions, all of them – like almost every home in San Miguel – built in the Spanish style. The **Casa de Don Ignacio de Allende**, on the corner of Allende and Umarán, was the birthplace of the Independence hero: a plaque notes *Hic natus ubique notus* – "here was born he who is famous everywhere". The house now operates as the **Museo Histórico de San Miguel de Allende** (Tues–Sun 9am–5pm; M$30, free on Sun), with two floors of fossils, pots and diagrams exploring Mexico's pre-Hispanic and colonial past, naturally concentrating on the San Miguel area. The collection is well presented but fairly small, and apart from a few nice fertility figures and an old apothecary, is mostly of interest to history buffs.

On the next corner, Hidalgo and Canal, you can see the **Casa de los Condes de Canal**, with an elaborately carved doorway and elegant wrought-iron grilles over the windows. Near here, too, just half a block down Umarán, is the **Casa de los Perros**, its central balcony supported by little stone dogs. Forbidding, even grim, from the outside, these mansions mostly conceal patios decked with flowers or courtyards with fountains playing.

### East and north of El Jardín

Leave the Jardín to the east and head uphill on San Francisco to where the streets seem less affected by outsiders – Spanish or *norteamericano*. The architecture is still colonial, but the life that continues around the battered

△ La Parroquia de San Miguel Arcángel

buildings seems cast in a more ancient mould. A block along San Francisco, the elaborate churrigueresque facade of the church of **San Francisco** contrasts sharply with its Neoclassical towers, tiled dome and plain interior, and quite overshadows the modest simplicity of its smaller neighbour, **Tercer Orden**. Behind and to the north, San Miguel's old market area has been refurbished to create the Plaza de la Soledad, complete with a huge equestrian statue of Allende. Here you'll find a little group of churches and chapels including the **Templo de Nuesta Señora de la Salud**, with its unusual concave facade topped by a scallop-shell pediment. To the left sits the **Templo del Oratorio de San Felipe Neri**, its Baroque facade showing signs of native influence – presumably the legacy of indigenous labourers – but the main interest lies in a series of paintings, among them a group depicting the life of St Philip Neri, attributed to Miguel Cabrera. One of its chapels, the **Santa Casa de Loreto** (entered from next door), is a copy of the Holy House at Loreto in Italy, and was put up by the Conde Manuel de la Canal; he and his wife appear as statues above their tombs in its gilded octagonal interior.

The town's **market** lies north of here and has managed to remain almost entirely traditional, with fruit, vegetables, medicinal herbs, pots and pans all on display, though little exists specifically for the tourist among the cramped tables with their low canvas awnings. Official market day is Sunday, but no one seems to have told the locals, and it's pretty busy all week. Behind the regular market along **Andador Lucas Balderas** lies the **Mercado de Artesanías**, full of the sort of stuff you see all over Mexico, though little of what's here seems especially good value. You'll find much more exciting goods in the many crafts shops around town.

From the Oratorio de San Felipe Neri you can head west along Insurgentes to the **Biblioteca Pública**, Insurgentes 25 (Mon–Fri 10am–7pm, Sat 10am-2pm; Ⓦ www.bibliotecasma.com), which lends a substantial collection of books in English (see "Listings", p.305, for more details). They also sell a number of cheap secondhand books – either duplicates or those deemed too lightweight for preservation in the library. Inside the library, the *Café Santa Ana* offers a quiet space to sit down and read.

## Bellas Artes

The Centro Cultural "El Nigromante" (also known as **Bellas Artes**) is on Hernández Macías, just one block downhill from the Jardín. Housed in the beautiful cloistered courtyard of the old **Convento de la Concepción**, it's an arts institute run by the state fine-arts organization, concentrating on music and dance, but to a lesser extent teaching visual arts, too. Mexicans can take courses here for virtually nothing; foreigners pay rather more. Around the courtyard there are various exhibitions, and several murals, including an entire room (now used for dance lessons and often inaccessible) covered in one by David Siqueiros that's devoted to the life and works of Allende. There's also the lovely *Las Musas* café (see p.303). The church of La Concepción, part of the complex, is nice, too, and notable mainly for its tall dome raised on a drum, again said to be the work of the untrained Zeferino Gutiérrez.

## Instituto Allende and around

The **Instituto Allende** lies down at the bottom of the hill following Hernández Macías south from La Concepción. On the way south, at the corner of Cuadrante, you pass the **Casa del Inquisidor**, Cuadrate 36, an eighteenth-century mansion with a particularly fine facade, and opposite, the old building that served as a jail for the Inquisition. The Instituto itself, on the edges of the old town, occupies a former hacienda of the Condes de la Canal – it was moved here in 1951 when the government recognized its success and it was accredited by the University of Guanajuato. It offers courses in all kinds of arts, from painting to sculpture to photography, in crafts like silverwork and weaving, and Spanish-language instruction at every level (see box, p.305), all within beautiful, park-like grounds. There's a café down here, too, and an office dealing with long-term accommodation and helping organize rides throughout Mexico and up to the US.



### Parque Benito Juárez, El Chorro and El Mirador

Ten minutes' walk immediately south of town, the refreshing, shaded **Parque Benito Juárez** was created out of the fruit orchards that belonged to many of the city's old families. The homes round about are still some of the fanciest in town. From here it's an uphill walk to **El Chorro**, the little hill whose springs supply the city with water, and the site of the town originally founded by Juan de San Miguel. Here you'll find **La Lavandería**, a series of twenty old-fashioned tubs where some locals still come to do their washing (and gossip). From the *lavandería* the Paseo del Chorro winds uphill to a series of seven former public bathhouses, which are now rooms in the **Casa de la Cultura**. To get the best views over town you'll have to climb higher (follow Bajada de Charro) to **El Mirador**, the viewing point on the road to Querétaro, where there's a little belvedere, a small café and San Miguel spread out below, with the broad plain and a ridge of mountains behind.

### Jardín Botánico

When you've had your fill of swanky cafés and artesanía shopping, consider spending a few hours at the **Jardín Botánico**, 1.5km northeast of town (daily dawn–dusk; M$30; Ⓦwww.laneta.apc.org/charco). Officially known as **El Charco del Ingenio**, it sprawls over the hill above town, just behind a suburb of some of San Miguel's finest new homes, almost all colonial in execution but with every amenity. The garden itself resembles almost any patch of northern Mexico desert (it is meant to), but comes heavily planted with various types of cactus, which has made it incomparably richer botanically than the surrounding desert. Around 10km of grassy paths wind through, some accessible to mountain bikes. If you're here around a full moon, enquire about the operation of the *temazcales*, ritual herb steam baths built within the garden.

Stroll beside the town's reservoir, and along a small canyon below the dam, being sure not to miss the glasshouse, marked "Conservatoir Solar" on the leaflet you get at the entrance (open 9am–4pm) where hundreds of species are raised ready for planting out.

To **get to** the Jardín Botánico, follow Homobono north from the market, walking steeply uphill taking the left turn when it forks. After ten minutes or so you reach one of the pedestrian entrances.

## Eating

Eating in San Miguel can be an expensive business; even local staples such as cappuccinos and margaritas are likely to cost half as much again as they would in, say, Querétaro. Though there are **restaurants** where you can get a standard comida or a plate of tacos for little more than you would pay elsewhere – the daytime *menú del día* is usually a good bet – you'll generally find yourself giving in to temptation and gravitating to places serving anything from sushi to fondue. These menus can be a tremendous relief for long-term travellers, with loads of stuff you may not have tasted for weeks and a surprising array of **vegetarian** options. The plentiful **cafés** are alive with students and expats who often seem to do little but hang out in such places all day – which is not a bad idea. The food quality is excellent, and with delicate gringo stomachs in mind, many places prominently advertise their assiduous use of sanitized water.

**Apolo XI** Mesones 43. Head upstairs here for ultra-casual, cheap *carnitas* (sold by the kilo) served on an open-air terrace. The hot and vinegary house pickles will curl your toes.

**Aqui es México** Hidalgo 28. Cheerful and attractive upstairs dining area with a wide range of Mexican favourites, though the best value is one of the two comidas corridas (M$45).

**Azafrán** Hernández Macías 97. Trendy new eatery featuring health-conscious gourmet dishes (many that actually taste good); its fun, somewhat nostalgic, decor gives a nod to the sleeker styles of the 1980s. Mains cost around M$170.

**Bugambilia** Hidalgo 42 ☎415/152-0127. Longstanding, charming courtyard restaurant. Tuck into beautifully prepared Mexican dishes such as warm goat's cheese topped with toasted almonds (M$70), followed by chicken in tamarind sauce (M$125) or *chiles en nogada* (M$160). There's usually live acoustic guitar music.

**Café de la Parroquia** Jesús 11. A great little place with seats inside or in the courtyard, justly popular with expats for breakfasts of hotcakes or yogurt and fruit (around M$40). Good Mexican food served as well – tamales, *chilaquiles* and the like for M$50–80 – and coffee all day long. Closed Mon.

**La Capilla** Cuna de Allende 10, steps from the Jardín ☎415/152-0698. San Miguel's most spectacular dining experience. Housed in what was once part of the town's main chapel, this lovingly restored two-storey restaurant has a thoughtful menu featuring international and local specialities made with seasonal ingredients and rooftop dining under the cathedral spires. *Estudiantinas* perform several times a week, and there's even a boutique selling hand-made chocolates in creative flavours such as peanut curry. It's not cheap but it's worth every peso. Reservations recommended. Closed Tues.

**El Catrín** Canal 154. Succulent BBQ served with organic veggies in a restored 1926 Pullman rail car. It's not cheap, but you're sure to rave.

**La Finestra Caffé** Plaza Colonial, opposite Bellas Artes. Another popular and relaxed breakfast café with sun streaming in through the windows, delicious *huevos a la cazuela* (eggs baked in a pot with a hot sauce and cheese) and good coffee and pastries all day.

**La Grotta** Cuadrante 5. Great pasta and pizza joint, now expanded to a cosy room with red-washed walls and kitchen pans hanging from the ceiling. The home-made pasta dishes (M$95) are great but no match for the crispy pizza and calzone. Also fresh salads and a small selection of *secondi piatti*.

**El Harem** Murillo 7. Arabic restaurant serving hummus with pita bread (M$25), lamb brochettes (M$55) and stuffed vine leaves. Coffee-ground "readings" a bonus. Closed Tues.

**Mesón de San José** Mesones 38. Lovely patio restaurant serving quality Mexican mains for M$80–100 and several cheaper vegetarian choices.

**Las Musas** in the Bellas Artes complex. Beautifully sited café away from the traffic noise, where students take a break over coffee, sandwiches, ice cream and croissants.

**Olé Olé** Loreto 66-A. Decked out in antique posters of bullfights, this festive spot features fajitas (beef, chicken or shrimp for M$70–115), but closes early at 9pm.

**El Petit Four** Mesones 99. Delightful little French *patisserie* with a few tables where you can tuck into a *pain au chocolat* or a slice of *tarte aux pommes* with your espresso. Superb raspberry tarts. Closed Mon.

**La Piñata** Umarán 10. Unpretentious and excellent-value café that's perfect for tacos, tostadas and tortas at a price unmatched around the Jardín, just a block away.

**Rincón de Don Tomás** Portal de Guadalupe, at the corner of San Francisco. Fantastic place for breakfast. Authentic Mexican dishes at wallet-friendly prices.

**San Augustín** San Francisco 21. Run by a retired Mexico City *telenovela* star, this pleasant restaurant is especially known for its sugary, fried *churros* eaten with a drink of chocolate – either sweet Spanish, semi-sweet French or Mexican, flavoured with cinnamon.

**Taquería Los Faroles** Insurgentes 178 and Ancha San Antonio 28-C. A few pesos buy amazingly delicious tacos at this local favourite. Try the *tacos* *al pastor* and be sure to sample the colourful array of home-made *salsitas*. Open 7.30pm–midnight. Closed Sun.

**El Ten Ten Pie** Cuna de Allende 21. Small café with walls covered in the work of local artists, serving good Mexican staples and an extensive M$70 comida.

**Tío Lucas** Mesones 103. Some of the most succulent steak in town – a New York strip, or beef medallions baked in red wine and served with peppers and Roquefort (M$160–220) – comes in generous portions and is served on a verdant patio to the strains of quality live jazz. The chicken and seafood dishes are equally memorable, and they serve excellent margaritas.

**El Tomato** Mesones 62, east of Hidalgo. Mostly healthy, mostly vegetarian place for lunch and dinner, with soya- and spinach-based burgers, exotic salad concoctions and a M$80 three-course *menú*.

**La Ventana** Sollano 11. Your best bet in town for a caffeine fix, this quiet coffee shop features dark roasts from Chiapas and all manner of java concoctions. Drinks also available to go from a street-front window.

## Nightlife and entertainment

San Miguel **nightlife** can become expensive. Prices are fairly high but the main culprit is the sheer range of things to do – a refreshing change in itself. Your best bet is to gather with everyone else in the Jardín to take the air, stroll around and check out what's going on. It is also worth seeing if there is anything on at Teatro Angela Peralta, Mesones 82 (ⓣ415/152-2200), which typically hosts **ballet**, **theatre** and occasional performances of **classical music**.

**Film** and **music festivals** pepper the year, kicking off with **Expresión en Corto** (third week of July; ⓦwww.expresionencorto.com), a week-long short-film festival that's rapidly gaining worldwide recognition. The quarter-century-old **Festival de Música de Cámara** (Chamber Music Festival; first two weeks in Aug; ⓣ415/154-8722, ⓦwww.chambermusicfestival.com) features a range of performances by internationally acclaimed musicians. The **Festival Internacional de Jazz & Blues** (last weekend of Nov) includes two shows nightly by international performers at the Teatro Angela Peralta.

### Bars and clubs

**La Coronela** San Francisco 2. Dependable cocktail lounge decorated with old Mexican cinema posters featuring 2-for-1 beers on Mon and Tues.

**La Cucaracha** on Zacateros, between Umarán and Pila Seca. Dim and fairly seedy late-night bar where Jack Kerouac and William Burroughs knocked back titanic amounts of booze in the 1950s. Though the location has changed since then, the spirit and tenor remain, with a great jukebox, cheap but very rough margaritas and plenty of off-beat company.

**La Fragua** Cuna de Allende 3, just off the Jardín. Terrific local stand-by featuring a tapas menu, an expansive cocktail lounge and live music Fri and Sat.

**El Gato Negro** Mesones 10. Tiny and hip swinging-door cantina (women welcome) absolutely plastered in photos of Marilyn Monroe – plus a couple of Jim Morrison and John Lennon. The drinks are cheap, and there's no cover. There's also an old-fashioned *pissoire*.

**Mama Mia** Umarán 8. Probably the most happening nightspot in town, with restaurant, superb terrace bar with great views over the rooftops and the adjacent after-hours *Mama's Bar*. You can count on good DJs, live bands and live salsa on Fri and Sat nights (midnight–3am). There are also free salsa classes on Wed nights.

**Petit Bar** at *El Market Bistro*, Hernández Macías 95. Just a couple of small rooms (one with sofas and imaginative decor) attached to this French restaurant. Low-cost drinks and sometimes poetry readings earlier in the evening. Closed Tues.

### Cinema

**Cine Gemelos** a couple of kilometres to the southeast of town by the Gigante supermarket. First-run movies on two screens. Tickets are around M$32.

**Hotel Villa Jacaranda** Aldama 53, at Terraplen ⓣ415/152-1015. The hotel hosts English-language movies every night at 7.30pm (M$75 including a drink and popcorn). A new film starts each Sat.

## Listings

**American Express** Viajes Vertiz, Hidalgo 1, just north of El Jardín (Mon–Fri 9am–2pm & 4–6.30pm, Sat 10am–2pm; ☎415/152-1856, Ⓦwww.viajesvertiz.com), will hold mail and reissue stolen or lost cheques, and cash them if they have enough money.

**Banks and exchange** Banamex, at the northwest corner of the Jardín on Canal; and Banorte, half a block east of Banamex along San Francisco. Casas de cambio include Dicambios, Juarez 1 at San Francisco (Mon–Fri 9am–4pm, Sat 9am–2pm, Sun 10am–2pm).

**Bicycle rental** See box, p.306.

**Books and newspapers** Purchase international weeklies and the Mexico edition of the *Miami Herald* (after midday for that day's) from newspaper vendors around the Jardín. Airport novels and weightier fiction, along with hardbacks, magazines and art supplies are all stocked by El Colibrí, Sollano 30 (Mon–Sat 10am–3pm & 4–7pm), a block or so south of El Jardín. There's a good stock of magazines, among other things, at Lagundi, Umarán 17 (Mon–Sat 10am–2pm & 4–8pm). Also Libros El Tecolote, Jesús 11, beside *Café de la Parroquia* (Tues–Sat 10am–6pm, Sun 9am–4pm).

**Consulates** US, Hernández Macías 72, opposite Bellas Artes (Mon–Fri 9am–1pm; ☎415/152-2357).

**Emergencies** General emergencies ☎415/152-0911; Cruz Roja ☎415/152-1616; police ☎415/152-0022.

**Internet access** Spiral Internet, Mesones 38 inside Meson de San José, charges M$10/hr.

**Laundry** Lavamagico, Pila Seca 5 (Mon–Sat 8am–8pm), offers a same-day service (M$46 for up to 4kg) if dropped off before noon.

**Library** The Biblioteca Pública, Insurgentes 25, allows visitors to borrow books after obtaining a library card (two passport photos and M$50; valid one year) and leaving a M$100 deposit.

**Pharmacy** Farmacia Agundis, Canal 26 (daily 9.30am–1am). English spoken.

**Post office and couriers** Correo 16 (Mon–Fri 8am–4pm, Sat 8am–noon). There are numerous express postal services, including DHL, at Correo 21 and opposite the post office.

### Learning Spanish in San Miguel de Allende

For many, the reason to come to San Miguel is to learn Spanish. Notice boards around town advertise private lessons, but most people end up taking one of the courses run by the main **language schools**, each of which offers a range of courses taught by professional Mexican teachers. Instruction is almost entirely in Spanish, with the focus on practical usage rather than academic theory. The best known is the Instituto Allende, though the others compete admirably on both price and quality. Students usually stay with a local family (count on US$18–23 a day for full board) to consolidate the instruction.

**Academia Hispano Americana** Mesones 4 (☎415/152-0349, Ⓦwww.ahaspeakspanish.com). Respected school running four-week Spanish immersion sessions (6hr/day; US$580) and more relaxed semi-intensive programmes (4hr/day; US$120/week), plus extension courses in Mexican history, literature and folklore.

**Instituto Allende** Ancha de San Antonio 20 (☎415/152-0190, Ⓦwww.instituto-allende.edu.mx). The most prestigious of the schools, the Instituto conducts university-credited four-week courses (starting the first Mon of each month), offering everything from one to four hours a day (US$11/hr) throughout the year at all levels. There are also intensive one-to-one classes (US$14/hr), less demanding monthly courses and special subject courses in topics such as Mexican history, ceramics, paper-making and photography, among others.

**Instituto Habla Hispana** Calzada de la Luz 25 (☎415/152-1535, Ⓦwww.mexicospanish.com). Runs month-long courses for US$450 with around twenty contact hours per week; alternatively, you can just do a week for US$120. They'll also organize homestays for around US$18 a day for a double, and US$22 for a private room.

## Around San Miguel: hot springs and Atotonilco

One of the easiest and most enjoyable outings from San Miguel is to spend a good part of the day at one of the **hot springs**, where the warm thermal waters are ideal for soaking your bones. There are numerous hotels and mini-resorts with geothermal pools all around the area, but the best and easiest to reach are clustered around 9km to the northwest of town on the road to Dolores Hidalgo. The most popular (certainly with San Miguel's wintering Americans) is **La Gruta** (daily 10am–6pm; M$80) right by the highway and with a series of outdoor mineral pools at different temperatures all surrounded by lawns and banana trees. There's even a little grotto you can swim into with an artificial waterfall, and a small and reasonably priced restaurant on site with snacks and M$45 fajitas. Around 500m before La Gruta, a side road leads just over a kilometre to **Escondido** (daily 10am–6pm; M$800), an equally appealing proposition, with small lily-filled lakes all around, cool outdoor pools and a series of small indoor ones linked by little tunnels and cascades. It can be quiet here midweek, but comes alive at weekends. Second-class **buses** to Dolores Hidalgo from San Miguel's bus station will all drop off on the highway near both sets of pools; to get back just flag down any bus you see.

A day at the hot springs can be conveniently combined with a worthwhile outing to **SANTUARIO DE ATOTONILCO** (easily confused with the larger Atotonilco el Grande in Jalisco state), 5km further in the same direction, then 3km down a side road. This is a dusty, rural indigenous community whose church has come to be a centre of pilgrimage for two reasons – it was founded by Padre Felipe Neri, who was later canonized, and it was from here that Padre Hidalgo, marching from Dolores to San Miguel, took the banner of the Virgin of Guadalupe that became the flag of the

### Tours and activities in and around San Miguel de Allende

The expat community in San Miguel runs a couple of tours that give interesting insight into the workings of the city. Several companies around town offer day trips and longer excursions to towns and sites of interest in the region; look for their posters if you're interested.

**Bici-Burro** Hospicio 1 ⓣ415/152-1526, ⓦwww.bici-burro.com. A range of van-supported tours, but most frequently to the Santuario de Atotonilco (5–6hr; M$600), or to Pozos (5–6hr; M$850). They'll also rent you a good hardtail machine for around M$300 a day and point you in the right direction.

**Coyote Canyon Horseback Adventures** ⓣ415/154-4193, ⓦwww.coyotecanyonadventures.com. Group and private riding trips, lessons and even moonlit excursions at a variety of levels at their ranch 16km southwest of town. All trips give a great introduction into charro life; they run half-day outings (US$75) as well as full-day (US$125) and overnight excursions (US$180). Full-day trips might also include hiking, camping and hot-air ballooning (US$180).

**Historic Walking Tour** (Mon, Wed & Fri 10am; M$100). Meet in the Jardín across from the Parroquia at 9.45am for a gentle stroll around town and a good deal of education. All the proceeds go towards medical care for underprivileged children.

**House and Garden Tour** (Sun noon; M$150). Starting from the Biblioteca Pública (see p.301), these tours typically visit three different homes – mostly owned by expat Americans. All money is donated to the public library.

Mexicans in the War of Independence. His comrade-in-arms Allende was married here, too. The six chapels of the church (now under extensive restoration but mostly open to the public), liberally plastered with murals and freely interspersed with poems, biblical passages and painted statues, demonstrate every kind of Mexican popular art, from the naive to the highly sophisticated. Direct **buses** ("Santuario") leave every hour from Calzada de la Paz in San Miguel and spend ten to fifteen minutes in Atotonilco, giving you just enough time for a quick look before the run back, when you can get dropped off at the hot springs.



## Querétaro and around

Most people seem to hammer straight past **QUERÉTARO** on the highway to Mexico City, catching sight only of the expanding industrial outskirts and the huge modern bus station. Yet of all the colonial cities in the Bajío, this is perhaps the most surprising, with a tranquil historical core that boasts magnificent mansions and some of the country's finest ecclesiastical architecture. Little more than two hours from Mexico City, and at the junction of every major road and rail route from the north, it's also a wealthy and booming city, one of the fastest-growing in the republic thanks to industrial decentralization and its close proximity to the capital. This vibrancy, along with a series of pretty plazas linked by narrow alleys all lined with restaurants and bars, makes Querétaro a wonderful place to spend a couple of evenings simply lingering over a meal, and perhaps seeking out some live music around the bars and cafés.

There are points of interest, too, in the surrounding hills of the Sierra Gorda, notably the small towns of **Bernal** and **Tequisquiapan**, and much more distant charms of Edward James's jungle "sculpture garden" at **Xilitla**.

### Some history

There's a history as rich and deep here as anywhere in the republic, starting before the Conquest when Querétaro ("rocky place") was an Otomí town subject to the **Aztecs**; many Otomí still live in the surrounding area. In 1531 the Spanish took control without much struggle and under them the town grew steadily into a major city and provincial capital before becoming, in the nineteenth century, the setting for some of the most dramatic events of Mexican history. It was here, meeting under the guise of Literary Associations, that the **Independence** conspirators laid their earliest plans. In 1810 one of their number, María Josefa Ortiz de Dominguez, wife of the town's Corregidor (or governor – she is known always as "La Corregidora"), found that her husband had learned of the movement's intentions. Although locked in her room, La Corregidora managed to get a message out warning the revolutionaries, thus precipitating an unexpectedly early start to the struggle for independence.

Later in the century, less exalted events took place. The **Treaty of Guadalupe Hidalgo**, which ended the Mexican–American War by handing over almost half of Mexico's territory – Texas, New Mexico, California and more – to the US, was signed in Querétaro in 1848, and, in 1867, Emperor Maximilian made his last stand here. Once defeated, he was tried by a court meeting in the theatre and finally faced a firing squad on the hill, the Cerro de las Campañas, just to the north of town. The same theatre hosted an important assembly of

## QUERÉTARO

| ACCOMMODATION | |
|---|---|
| La Casa de la Marquesa | H |
| Doña Urraca | B |
| Hotel Hidalgo | F |
| Hotel Plaza | D |
| Hotel Señorial | C |
| Jirafa Roja | I |
| K'angi Hostel | A |
| Méson de Santa Rosa | E |
| Posada La Academia | J |
| Posada Acueducto | K |
| Villa Juvenil | G |

| EATING & DRINKING | |
|---|---|
| 1810 | 12 |
| Alquimia | 7 |
| Barras Exprés Café | 3 |
| Café Amadeus | 5 |
| Café del Fondo | 15 |
| Café Tulipe | 13 |
| La Ferándula | 9 |
| Fonda del Refugio | 2 |
| El Globo | 14 |
| Marrón 86 | 10 |
| Ostionería Tampico | 4 |
| Padeco | 11 |
| Restaurant de la Rosa | 1 |
| San Miguelito | 6 |
| Thai Bar | 8 |
| La Viejoteca | 6 |

Museo de la Matemática
Jardín Corregidora
Teatro de la Republica
Casa de la Corregidora
Museo de la Ciudad de Querétaro
Santa Clara
Jardín Zenéa
San Francisco
Plaza de la Independencia
Museo Regional de Querétaro
Cathedral
Plaza de la Constitución
Palacio de Gobierno
Museo de Arte de Querétaro
Casa de los Perros
Buses to Main Bus Station
Alameda
Santa Rosa de Viterbo
Convento de la Cruz
Aqueduct Mirador
Mausoleo de la Corregidora
Aqueduct
Mariano Escobedo
15 de Mayo
Avenida Pasteur
Prospero Vega
Altamirano
16 de Septiembre
Avenida José Morelos
Hidalgo
Miguel
Andador 16 de Sept
5 de Mayo
Rio de la Loza
Carranza
Vicente Guerrero Norte
Balvanera
Ocampo
Madero
Allende Norte
Andador Libertad
Independencia
Norte
Avenida Pino Suárez
Juárez
Corregidora
Vergara
Pasteur
Reforma
Doctor Lucia
20 de Noviembre
Calzada de los Arcos
Ejército Republicano
21 de Marzo
Avenida General Arteaga
Zaragoza
Ezequiel Montes
Av Constituyentes
Avenida Pasteur
N
0 — 400 m
Cerro de las Campanas (1km)
Bus Station (5km)
5 (200m)

Revolutionary politicians in 1916, leading eventually to the signing here of the 1917 Constitution, which is still in force today.

## Arrival, orientation and information

Querétaro's massive **Central de Autobuses** lies 6km south of town and is one of the busiest in this part of Mexico, with three separate buildings: Sala A for long-distance and first-class companies, and salas B and C for shorter runs and second-class companies. Fixed-price **taxis** (buy a ticket from the kiosk) run from outside all terminals, and an endless shuttle of **local buses** ("Ruta 8" is the most convenient) runs to the centre from the end of Sala B. Buses generally don't enter the historic centre, so get off at Zaragoza, by the Alameda, and walk from there. This is also the spot to pick up services back to the bus station: #36 and others.

For all its sprawl, Querétaro is easy to find your way around once you get to the centre, since the core remains confined to the grid laid down by the Spanish: all tiny plazas interconnected by pedestrian walkways known as *andadores*. Local buses run anywhere you might want to visit, and taxis are cheap, but on the whole walking proves simpler. The main focus is the zócalo, the **Jardín Zenéa**, with its typical triumvirate of bandstand, clipped trees and bootshines. To the west lies the commercial centre with the bulk of the shops, but you'll probably spend much of your time to the east among the gift shops, restaurants and bars leading to the Plaza de la Independencia.

The **tourist office**, Pasteur 4 Nte (daily 9am–8pm; ⓣ442/238-5067, ⓦwww.venaqueretaro.com), offers free maps, and is also the starting point for hour-long town **trolley tours** (Wed–Sun 10am & 11am, noon, 4pm, 5pm & 6pm; M$50), which visit the main sights and might help you get your bearings.

## Accommodation

For **hotels**, head straight for the zócalo and the streets in its immediate vicinity. Streetside rooms may be noisy, but there's a fair selection of places in this area, three of them particularly gorgeous (and expensive). There are also several budget places, though the **hostels** are all a few hundred metres to the east towards the Convento de la Cruz. Where Querétaro trips up is in the mid-range, with few decent choices in the centre: if you can't stretch to the pricier places, go for the better rooms at, say, the *Hidalgo* or *Posada Acueducto*.

**La Casa de la Marquesa** Madero 41 ⓣ442/212-0092, ⓦwww.lacasadelamarquesa.com. Lovely old-fashioned hotel housed in a mansion with a gorgeous Moorish courtyard. The antique-furnished suites (M$2100–2900) are magnificent and this is where you should stay, though they also have slightly less luxurious rooms (M$1580) in a separate building across the road. Breakfast included. ❾

**Doña Urraca** 5 de Mayo 117 ⓣ442/238-5400 or 01-800/021-7116, ⓦwww.donaurraca.com.mx. An excellent and more modern alternative to the *Casa de la Marquesa*, this is one of the city's newest hotels and comes complete with heated outdoor pool and spa. Rooms (from M$2670) are named for birds and feature stone, wood and gorgeous natural-fibre linens. Packages including massage and spa treatments are surprisingly reasonable. ❾

**Hotel Hidalgo** Madero 11 Pte, just off Jardín Zenéa ⓣ442/212-0081, ⓦwww.hotelhidalgo.com.mx. Simple but clean rooms set around an open courtyard, all with bath and cable TV. Some of the larger rooms with balconies go for M$60 more. Good budget option. ❺

**Hotel Plaza** Juárez 23 Nte, on the Jardín Zenéa ⓣ& ⓕ 442/212-1138. On the zócalo; clean, but a touch faded and impersonal. All rooms with bath, TV and phone. ❹

**Hotel Señorial** Guerrero 10-A Nte ⓣ442/214-3700, ⓦwww.senorial-hotel.com. About the only decent mid-range place in the centre, with comfortable carpeted rooms, cable TV, WiFi, parking and some larger rooms with a/c for M$30 more. ❺

**Jirafa Roja** 20 de Noviembre 72 ⓣ442/212-4825, ⓔjirafarojahostel@yahoo.com.mx. Fun and youthful hostel with dorms, doubles and a nice rooftop terrace. M$120 per person. ❸

**K'angi Hostel** Altamirano 8 Nte ⓣ442/212-3324, ⓦwww.kangihostal.com.mx. Brand new hostel close to the centre with several dorms, relaxed communal areas, Internet access and a free Continental breakfast. There are no private doubles but they do have a single (M$180). M$140, ISIC cardholders M$125, HI members M$115.

**Mesón de Santa Rosa** Pasteur 17 Sur ⓣ442/224-2623, ⓦwww.mesonsantarosa.com. Superb luxury hotel, very quiet and beautiful, in an old colonial mansion on the Jardín Independencia and with a great restaurant to boot. ❽

**Posada La Academia** Pino Suárez 3 ⓣ442/224-2739. Clean and basic rooms are nothing special, though they are cheap and have TV. ❷

**Posada Acueducto** Juárez 64 Sur, at Arteaga ⓣ442/224-1289. Cheerily painted and well-cared-for hotel, right in the centre, with modern a/c rooms all with cable TV. The large suites (M$350) are particularly nice. ❹

**Villa Juvenil** (CREA) Ejército Republicano, behind the ex-Convento de la Cruz, about a 15min walk from the centre ⓣ442/223-3142. One of Mexico's better old-style sporting complex hostels; relatively helpful staff and clean, if cramped, single-sex dorms (no kitchen) and 24hr hot water, but an inconvenient 10.30pm curfew. M$30 per bunk.

## The City

The church of **San Francisco**, dominating the **Jardín Zenéa**, Querétaro's main square, was one of the earliest founded in the city. Its beautiful facade incorporates a dome covered in *azulejos* – coloured tiles imported from Spain around 1540 – but for the most part San Francisco was rebuilt in the seventeenth and eighteenth centuries. Adjoining it, in what used to be its monastery, is the **Museo Regional de Querétaro** (Tues–Sun 10am–7pm; M$33). This building alone is reason enough to visit, though the displays inside are well worth an hour or two. Built around a large cloister and leading back to a lovely chapel, it's far bigger than you imagine from the outside. Inside the exhibited items are eclectic: the keyhole through which La Corregidora passed on her news; early copies of the Constitution; the table on which the Treaty of Guadalupe Hidalgo was signed; and quantities of ephemera connected with Emperor Maximilian, whose headquarters were here for a while. There are also the more usual collections relating to local archeology, and a sizeable gallery of colonial art.

South of the museum lies the **Plaza de la Constitución**, formerly a market square now transformed into an attractive modern plaza with a central fountain that mimics the domed roof of the building on its south side. There's more to see a couple of blocks north of the Jardín at the **Teatro de la República**, which sits at the junction of Juárez and Peralta (Tues–Sun 10am–3pm & 5–8pm; free). A grand nineteenth-century structure, the theatre has played a vital role in Mexican history: here a court met to decide the fate of Emperor Maximilian, and here the 1917 Constitution was agreed upon. A small exhibition celebrates these events, though the main reason to go in is to take a look at the theatre itself. The guards sometimes let visitors slip in to hear the philharmonic orchestra practice for free.

### Around the Plaza de la Independencia

The little pedestrianized alleys that lead up to the east of the Jardín are some of the city's most interesting, crammed with ancient houses, little restaurants, art galleries and shops selling junky antiques and the opals and other semiprecious stones for which the area is famous. If you decide to buy, double-check the stones for authenticity. The first of several little plazas and almost part of the Jardín Zenéa is the **Jardín Corregidora**, another beautiful square, with an imposing statue of La Corregidora and several restaurants and bars where you can sit outside. The pedestrianized Andador Libertad runs past art galleries and boutiques from the Plaza de la Constitución to the **Plaza de la Independencia**, or Plaza de Armas, a very pretty, arcaded open space. In the middle of the plaza stands a statue of Don Juan Antonio Urrutia y Arana, Marques de la Villa del Villar del Aguila, the man who built Querétaro's elegant aqueduct, providing the city with drinking water. Around the square is the **Casa de la Corregidora**, now the Palacio Estatal (Mon–Fri 8am–9pm, Sat 8am–6pm; free). It was here, on September 14, 1810, that La Corregidora was locked up while her husband made plans to arrest the conspirators. She managed to get a message to Ignacio Perez, who carried it to Independence movement leaders Allende and Hidalgo in the towns of San Miguel and Dolores. The house is an attractive building, but there's not a great deal to see inside.

Immediately to the north, the **Museo de la Matemática**, 16 de Septiembre 63 Ote (Mon–Sat 10am–6pm; M$25), may appeal to visitors with an interest in geometry and mathematical phenomena, especially those who also have a good command of technical Spanish.

### The commercial centre: Avenida Morelos and around

While the city's more exciting restaurants and bars remain around the eastern plazas, the commercial centre of Querétaro lies west of the zócalo, on and around **Avenida Morelos**. This is where you'll find most of the shops, on formal streets lined with stately mansions. At the corner of Madero and Allende, the little Jardín de Santa Clara features a famous **Fountain of Neptune**, designed by **Francisco Eduardo Tresguerras** in 1797. Tresguerras (1765–1833) is rightly regarded as one of Mexico's greatest architects – he was also a sculptor, painter and poet – and was almost single-handedly responsible for developing a native Mexican architectural style diverging from (though still close to) its Spanish roots. His work, seen throughout central Mexico, is particularly evident here and in nearby Celaya, his birthplace. Beside the fountain rises the deceptively simple church of **Santa Clara**, once attached to one of the country's richest convents. Inside it's a riot of Baroque excess, with gilded cherubs and angels swarming all over the profusely decorated altarpieces.

Carry on west down Madero and you get to the **Palacio de Gobierno** and the **cathedral**, eighteenth-century buildings, neither of which, by Querétaro's standards, is particularly distinguished. Cut north along Guerrero, however, and you'll come to the **Museo de la Ciudad de Querétaro**, Guerrero 27 Nte (Tues–Sun 11am–7pm; M$5), which fills a huge colonial building with temporary exhibitions, predominantly contemporary painting, sculpture and photography. There's almost always something worth half an hour of your time.

### Convento de la Cruz

There's more to see a short walk east from the centre at the **Convento de la Cruz** (Tues–Sat 9am–2pm & 4–6pm, Sun 9am–4pm; visit by half-hour guided tour in English on request; small donation requested), built on the site of the battle between the Spanish and the Otomí in which the conquistadors gained control of Querétaro. According to legend, the fighting was cut short by the miraculous appearance of St James (Santiago – the city's full name is Santiago de Querétaro) and a dazzling cross in the sky, which persuaded the Indians to concede defeat and become Christians. The **Capilla del Calvarito**, opposite the monastery entrance, marks the spot where the first Mass was celebrated after the battle. The monastery itself was founded in 1683 by the Franciscans

△ Aqueduct, Querétaro

as a college for the propagation of the faith (Colegio Apostólico de Propaganda Fide) and grew over the years into an important centre for the training of missionaries, with a massive library and rich collection of relics. Because of its hilltop position and hefty construction, the monastery was also frequently used as a fortress. Functioning as one of the last redoubts of the Spanish in the War of Independence, it was Maximilian's headquarters for the last few weeks of his reign and he was subsequently imprisoned here to await execution. The convent's greatest source of pride is the **Árbol de la Cruz**, a tree whose thorns sprout in the shape of little crosses. The tree grew, so the story goes, from a walking stick left behind by a mysterious saintly traveller who slept here one night. It certainly does produce thorns in the form of crosses, and the monks, who appear very excited by the phenomenon, point out that an additional five percent of the thorns grow with extra spikes to mark the spots where nails were driven through Christ's hands and feet; look for the framed collection in the entrance foyer.

Come up to the monastery in the late afternoon, then wander 200m beyond along Ejército Republicano to the **Mausoleo de la Corregidora** (daily 9am–5pm; free), where the heroine's remains, along with those of her husband, are surrounded by statues of other illustrious *Querétanos*. Across the road a *mirador* provides a superb sunset view of the city's early eighteenth-century **aqueduct**, a beautiful 1.3-kilometre-long series of 74 arches up to 23m high, which once brought water into the city from springs nearly 9km away. Spotlit at night, it looks magnificent, especially as you drive into town. *Café Tulipe* and *Café Amadeus* (see p.314) are both a short stroll down the hill from here.

### Museo de Arte de Querétaro and around

A couple of blocks south of the Museo de la Ciudad lies the **Museo de Arte de Querétaro**, Allende 14 Sur (Tues–Sun 10am–6pm; M$20, free on Tues) occupying the former Palacio Federal, by the church of San Agustín. Originally an Augustinian monastery (it has also been a prison and a post office in its time), it is one of the most exuberant buildings in town. In the cloister, every surface of the two storeys of portals is carved with grotesque figures, no two quite alike, and with abstract designs. The sculptures, often attributed to Tresguerras though almost certainly not by him, are full of religious symbolism, which you should try to get someone to explain to you. The large figures supporting the arches, for example, all hold their fingers in different positions: three held up to represent the Trinity, four for the Evangelists and so on. The contents of the museum are good, with galleries devoted to sixteenth- and seventeenth-century European painting downstairs, along with temporary exhibition spaces usually featuring quality contemporary Mexican art. The collection of Mexican painting upstairs is mostly from the seventeenth and eighteenth centuries, with a room full of works attributed to Tresguerras and Manuel Cabrera and a fine series of nine (out of an original fourteen or fifteen) portraits of saints by Cristóbal de Villalpando.

A few metres south along Allende lies the **Casa de los Perros**, Allende 16 at Pino Suárez, a mansion named after the ugly canine gargoyles that line its facade. The church of **Santa Rosa de Viterbo** sits further out in this direction, at the junction of Arteaga and Montes. Its interior rivals Santa Clara for richness of decoration, but here there is no false modesty on the outside either. Two enormous flying buttresses support the octagonal cupola (remodelled by Tresguerras) and a blue and white tiled dome. The tower, too, is Tresguerras's work, holding what is said to be the first four-sided public clock erected on the American continent.

### Cerro de las Campañas

Further out to the west, and a little to the north, the gentle eminence of the **Cerro de las Campañas** ("Hill of Bells") commands wide, if less than scenic, views over Querétaro and its industrial outskirts. Maximilian and his two generals, Miguel Miramón and Tomás Mejía, faced the firing squad here. The hill is dominated by a vast stone statue of the victor of that particular war, Benito Juárez, glaring down over the town. In order to reach the summit, avoid the parts of the new university campus sprawling up one slope, follow Hidalgo west, turn right onto Tecnológico and then left after 400m onto Justo Sierra where there's the entrance to the neatly tended Parque Municipal del Cerro de las Campañas (daily dawn–dusk; M$1).

## Eating and drinking

There's plenty of good food in Querétaro, and some delightful places to sit outside amid the alleys and plazas east of the **Jardín Zenéa**. The **zócalo** itself has plenty of rather cheaper places while the Plaza de la Independencia has a refined air. In the last few years the dining and drinking torch has passed to 5 de Mayo, where a slew of new and chic places have opened up.

If you want to get together something of your own, head for the **market**, sprawled across several blocks just off Calzada Zaragoza, not far from the Alameda. While in Querétaro look out for a couple of **local specialities**, particularly a hearty lentil soup laced with chunks of dried fruit (usually just called "sopa regional"): it sounds odd but is delicious, though vegetarians won't appreciate the pork-broth base. Also try *enchiladas Queretanas*, tortillas fried in a chile sauce and stuffed with onions and cheese. In fancier places these may come topped with potatoes and carrots.

Evening entertainment tends to involve a couple of beers in one of the restaurants or an hour or two lingering in one of the cafés. To find more lively nightlife, head to the bars along 5 de Mayo and see where the night takes you. The bigger **clubs** are all out in the suburbs and fashions change rapidly, so ask around and follow the crowd (probably by taxi). Many have some sort of live music at weekends and charge M$50–100 to get in.

**1810** Jardín Independencia 62. Excellent sidewalk restaurant that does regional specialities to perfection. You'll have to take your chances with the live entertainment – sometimes relaxing jazz, though often cheesy crooners. Expect to pay M$60 for Mexican staples, M$80–150 for meat and fish dishes.

**Alquimia** 5 de Mayo 71. Sophisticated dim bodega with bottles racked up behind the bar and usually with the doors thrown open to the street. Perfect for a quiet beer or one of their delicious cocktails. Closed Sun & Mon.

**Barra Exprés Café** Andador 16 de Septiembre 40. A relaxed stop for a selection of crepes and some of the town's best coffee (unfortunately served only in paper cups). Closed Sun.

**Café Amadeus** at the corner of Calzada de los Arcos and Puente de Alvarado, halfway along the aqueduct. Munch on scrumptious tortes or fine breakfasts and *antojitos*, all to the strains of Mozart.

**Café del Fondo** Pino Suárez 9. This airy multi-roomed café serves bargain breakfasts from 7.30am – fresh juice, espresso and a plate of eggs, enchiladas or hotcakes for under M$25. There are also more substantial dishes available throughout the day, and good coffee and cakes until around 10.30pm. One room is often devoted to board games, most frequently chess.

**Café Tulipe** Calzada de los Arcos 3, near the west end of the aqueduct. A definite favourite for its predominantly Mexican but French-tinged menu – filet mignon for M$90 – plus delectable desserts. The delicious fondue and *caldo conde* (a black bean, cream and herb soup) are especially good.

**La Ferándula** Andador 5 de Mayo 16. The main club downtown, sometimes with live music. It's fairly quiet before 11pm.

**Fonda del Refugio** Jardín Corregidora, behind the statue. One of several decent places surrounding the Jardín. They serve food, but this is primarily a place to sit outside, drink and watch the world go by.

**El Globo** Corregidora 41. About the best *pastelería* in town, with lots of French pastries – croissants, *pain au chocolat* and so on – big sticky cakes and even their own brand of ice cream, all to take out.

**Marrón 86** Pasteur 9, Plaza de la Independencia. Prime real estate under the colonnades on the Plaza de Armas. Good for pasta dishes, stuffed baguettes and salads, but the coffee is really the highlight.

**Ostionería Tampico** Jardín Corregidora. Top-notch seafood at moderate prices, best selected from one of three daily comidas (M$65–85). Their seafood cocktails should be eaten the traditional Mexican way: with a squirt of ketchup.

**Padeco** Pasteur 17 Sur, Plaza de la Independencia. Superb restaurant serving predominantly Italian dishes (gnocchi M$95, steaks M$150) – in a beautiful garden setting.

**Restaurant de la Rosa** Juárez 24-A. The best place downtown for a simple but tasty *menú del día* for under M$50.

**San Miguelito** Andador 5 de Mayo 39. This unique spot has justly earned a reputation as one of the city's best restaurants, and you're guaranteed an impressive selection of delicious regional, national and international dishes in eclectic surroundings. Try the chicken in chipotle sauce or one of their fine steaks. Mains around M$110.

**Thai Bar** 5 de Mayo 56. Somewhat misnamed, this chic spot is primarily a bar mainly populated by sophisticated *Queretanos*. Closed Mon.

**La Viejoteca** Andador 5 de Mayo 39. Pricey piano bar in a large high-ceilinged room with interesting decor – everything from old jukeboxes to an entire wall of old pharmacy shelves – that's bustling most evenings and often has live music. Expect a M$60 cover towards the weekend.

## Listings

**American Express** Turismo Beverly Querétaro, Tecnológico 118 (Mon–Fri 9am–2pm & 4–6pm, Sat 9am–noon; ⓣ442/216-1500), has all the usual services. It's around 2km southwest of the centre, reached by buses running west along Zaragoza to Tecnológico, then 200m south.

**Banks and exchange** There are several banks around the Jardín Zenéa that will change currency (Mon–Fri 9am–3pm), and a couple of casas de cambio south along Juárez, such as Eurofimex at no. 58, beside *Posada Acueducto*.

**Books and newspapers** International weeklies can usually be found at the newspaper stands around the Jardín Zenéa and the Plaza de la

Independencia. Beyond that, Sanborn's, on Constituyentes, 2km southeast of the centre, have a wide range of magazines.

**Emergencies** For general emergencies call ⓣ066; Cruz Roja ⓣ442/229-0505.

**Internet access** There are several Internet places in the centre mostly costing M$10–12/hr, including those at Andador 5 de Mayo 33 and at Carranza 9.

**Laundry** Lavandería Verónica, Hidalgo 153 at Ignacio Pérez (Mon–Fri 9am–2.30pm & 4.30–8pm, Sat 9am–3pm), lies about 1km west of the centre. Also Servi-Clean, Independencia 49 near Convento de la Cruz (Mon–Fri 10am–2pm & 4pm–8pm, Sat 10am–3pm).

**Pharmacy** There are dozens of pharmacies around the centre, including the large Farmacia Guadalajara at Madero 32, just west of the Jardín Zenéa.

**Post office** Arteaga 5 (Mon–Fri 8am–6pm, Sat 9am–1pm).

**Spanish schools** Ole Centre for Spanish Language and Culture, Mariano Escobedo 32 ⓣ442/234-4023, ⓦwww.ole.edu.mx. Good-value Spanish courses in a town where you won't get too distracted talking English to all the foreign visitors.

## Around Querétaro

From Querétaro you can race straight into the capital on Hwy-57, and if you are not reliant on public transport, then there are a couple of places that might be visited en route: the ancient Toltec capital of Tula, and Tepotzotlán, with its magnificent Baroque architecture, both of which are covered in Chapter 5. But before charging south, consider exploring the towns around Querétaro, particularly **Bernal**, **Tequisquiapan** and **San Juan del Río**, where you could easily spend a pleasant few days exploring.

### Bernal

The pretty village of **BERNAL**, 45km east of Querétaro, hunkers under the skirts of the monolithic Peña de Bernal, a 450-metre-high chunk of volcanic rock that towers over the plains and is the third largest boulder of its kind in the world – after the Rock of Gibraltar and Rio's Sugarloaf. By wandering towards the rock you'll soon pick up a rough but clearly marked path about two-thirds of the way to the top (the ascent takes up to an hour, half that to get down), where there's a small shrine and long views stretching out below. Only appropriately equipped rock climbers should continue up the metal rungs to the summit, passing a memorial plaque to an earlier adventurer along the way.

At weekends, half of Querétaro seems to come out here, making for a festive atmosphere, but midweek it is an altogether more peaceful place: the mountain is likely to be deserted and you'll be about the only thing disturbing the lovely village plaza with its attractive church and terracotta-washed buildings, sumptuous in the afternoon light. Be forewarned, however, that many businesses are only open at the weekends and many more shut for the month of May.

The centre is ringed by narrow streets full of shops selling handicrafts, and there's even a small and sporadically open **tourist office** on Hidalgo, which runs west from the plaza, though there isn't much they can tell you that you can't discover for yourself in ten minutes. Also on Hidalgo is one of the nicest **places to eat**, in the shaded courtyard of *Mesón de la Roca*, at no. 5, serving moderately priced and well-presented Mexican dishes along with a M$70 comida corrida and, for the daring, grasshopper tacos (M$67). There are also several cheap *comedores*, and at weekends perhaps a dozen restaurants to choose from. Flecha Amarilla and Flecha Azul combine to offer hourly **buses** from Querétaro's bus station (Sala C) which drop you on the highway five minutes' walk from Bernal centre; it's worth remembering that the last bus back passes at around 6pm. It is also possible to continue to Tequisquiapan by taking a bus to the small town of Ezequiel Montes and changing there.

If you get stuck, or just fancy a night here (not a bad thing), there are clean, comfortable and excellent-value **rooms** at *Posada Peña*, Iturbide 3, behind the church (Ⓣ441/296-4149; ❸).

### Tequisquiapan

Some 20km north of San Juan, along a road lined with factories and workshops, **TEQUISQUIAPAN** ("Tequis" to locals), is a former Otomí village that developed in viceregal times primarily on account of its warm springs. Exclusive villas, all with beautifully tended walled gardens, are set around the central Plaza Santa María, itself ringed by arched *portales* on three sides and the church on the fourth, painted in soft tones of orange, red and azure. It is very popular with wealthy *chilangos* (residents of Mexico City) up from the capital, but has never really caught on with *extranjeros*. Although perfect as a weekend escape from the city, there's little to do other than bathe in your hotel pool, dine in one of many restaurants around the plaza and nose around the boutiques, some of which are cheap, many expensive and almost all of the highest standard. Like San Juan del Río, further south, Tequisquiapan has a big **crafts market** – especially active on Sundays – one block from the main plaza.

It is worth trying to time a visit to Tequisquiapan that coincides with one of the town's many **festivals**, including the **Feria del Toro de Lidia** (middle week of March), which features assorted bullfights, and the **Feria Internacional del Queso y del Vino** (late May and early June), a major wine and cheese festival. There's plenty of free food and drink and no shortage of other entertainment, including music and dancing. If you miss the festival and still have a taste for wine, Freixenet, the Spanish producer of bubbly, has a cava about 20km north at Carretera San Juan del Río km 40.5 (Sat & Sun 11.30am–1pm & 2–3pm; Ⓣ414/277-0147), with free twenty-minute tours and tasting.

Free town maps are available from the **tourist office** (Mon–Fri 9am–7pm, Sat & Sun 10am–8pm; Ⓣ414/273-0295, Ⓦwww.tequis.info) on the main square. When the attraction of artesanía-shopping begins to pall you'll probably want to press on, but if you decide to stay you can choose from the thirty-odd **hotels** packed into the tiny town, most ranged around bougainvillea-draped courtyards, many with pools fed by springs. There's nowhere you'd really call cheap, but you do get decent value for money. About the cheapest place in town is *Posada San Francisco*, Moctezuma 2 (Ⓣ414/273-0231; ❺), featuring comfortable rooms decorated with artesanías and with access to a lush garden. Ask for one overlooking the pool. It is a small step up to *Hotel La Plaza*, on the plaza at Juárez 10 (Ⓣ414/273-0005, Ⓦwww.tequisquiapan.com.mx/la_plaza; ❺), a perfect luxury hotel, very relaxed, with its own pool and some very attractive suites (❼). Though not quite the "ecological paradise" it claims to be, *Hotel El Relox*, Morelos 8 (Ⓣ414/273-0006 or 01-800/552-2173, Ⓦwww.relox.com.mx; ❽), does have luxuriant gardens and a multitude of outdoor and indoor private pools making this the best place in town. There's also a gym, sauna, massages (from M$320 for 40min), games areas and a selection of comfortable rooms and impressive suites.

For budget **eating** you can eat a M$30 comida at a cluster of *fondas* at the back of the market just off the east side of the main square. **Restaurants** abound, though many only really come to life at the weekend. The town is so small that you can walk around them all in ten minutes and see what appeals to you, though it is worth wandering along Morelos to *La Capilla*, an authentic

Italian restaurant serving delicious *arrabbiata*, seafood risotto and tiramisú, all at low to moderate prices (closed May).

Flecha Azul **buses** from Querétaro (Sala C; every 30min 6.30am–9pm) run direct to Tequisquiapan, and there's also a bus every half-hour from San Juan del Río (see below). From the bus station, turn right and walk the ten minutes into the plaza, passing an ugly concrete tripod said to mark the geographical centre of the country.



### San Juan del Río

Though **SAN JUAN DEL RÍO**, 50km south of Querétaro, looks like nothing at all from the highway, it is in fact a major market centre, and a popular weekend outing from both Querétaro and the capital. Among the goods sold here are **gemstones** – mostly local opals, but also imported jewels, which are polished and set in town – as well as baskets, wine and cheese. Once again, if you're going to buy gems, be very careful: it's easy to get ripped off. Other purchases are safer, though not particularly cheap on the whole. The best-known local wine is Hidalgo, a brand sold all over the country and usually reliable.

Direct buses from Querétaro (Flecha Azul from Sala B, among others; every 20min) take forty minutes to get to San Juan del Río's **bus station**, a couple of kilometres south of town. A local bus will run you up Hidalgo and drop you on a broad section of **Avenida Juárez**, where there's a central fountain, manicured trees and an attractive arcade on one side. Here you'll find an occasionally open **tourist kiosk**.

The Mercado Reforma and the twin central squares of the Jardín Independencia and Plaza de los Fundadores are a couple of long blocks north of Juárez, up Hidalgo, but there is more interest a couple of blocks south of Juárez at **Museo de la Muerte**, 2 de Abril 42 (Tues–Sun 10am–6pm; free), where the former cemetery, on a hill overlooking town behind the church of Santa Veracruz, conveys the different ways Mexicans express their connectedness with the dead. The fairly cursory displays of pre-Hispanic and Catholic rituals and beliefs won't detain you long.

If you decide that you'd like to stay a while to enjoy San Juan's unhurried atmosphere, take your choice of several good **hotels**, on or just off Juárez: the best is *Layseca*, very central at Juárez 9 Ote (Ⓣ427/272-0110, Ⓔhotellayseca@prodigy.net.mx; M$370), an old colonial house with nicely decorated rooms set around a beautiful open courtyard. In summer you might appreciate the pool at the friendly, pleasant and comfortable *Portal Royalty*, Juárez 20 Ote (Ⓣ/Ⓕ427/672-0038; ❺), where you should pay the extra M$60 for one of the upgraded rooms. For something simple and inexpensive, walk around the corner to *San Juan*, Hidalgo 4 Sur (Ⓣ427/272-4001; ❷). For something to eat, choose from several **restaurants** along Juárez, many with outdoor seating. There's tasty seafood at *Plaza del Mariscos*, at the corner of Juárez and Hidalgo, and a M$68 *menú del día* and good coffee, burgers and salads at *Finca Santa Vera Cruz*, Juárez 10.

## The Sierra Gorda and Xilitla

You'll need to set aside a couple of days to explore the hill country to the northeast of Querétaro, particularly if you're headed for the wonderful tropical fantasy world of **Las Pozas** at Xilitla. This is the **Sierra Gorda**, a remote and mountainous region where roads are winding and travel slow. There are bus services to most places, but this is an ideal region to explore by car, motorbike or even bicycle, though you'll need to be fit.

Apart from Las Pozas, the region's main attractions are the **Sierra Gorda missions**, five communities (each with an elaborate church) from the final phase of Mexico's Christianization in the mid-eighteenth century. The missions were founded by Spanish Franciscan **Frey Junípero Serra**, who'll be familiar to Californians – once his work in Mexico was complete, he continued evangelizing in the new missions there. He spent nine years in the Sierra Gorda working with, and gaining the trust of, the indigenous people. It is this rare synthesis of missionary and native creative efforts that earned the district UNESCO World Heritage status in 2003.

## Along Hwy-120

The main route from Querétaro towards Xilitla is Hwy-120, picked up at the small town of Ezequiel Montes. From there it twists its way through the mountains, climbing a couple of passes. The only major town along the way is **Jalpan**, in the heart of the Sierra Gorda, 120km northeast of Querétaro. Now the largest of the missions, it is an attractive colonial place centred on its church. This was the first such church in the area and its Baroque facade became a template for those to follow. On either side of its central panel are the Virgins of Pilar and Guadalupe, the patrons of Spain and Mexico. For more background on the missions and the indigenous people who built them, call at the **Museo Historic de Sierra Gorda**, on the square at Junípero Serra 1 (daily 10am–3pm & 5–7pm; M$10). Next door is the very comfortable *Misión Jalpán* (Ⓣ441/296-0165, Ⓦwww.hotelesmision.com.mx; ❼), and across the plaza you can **stay** at the *Hotel María del Carmen*, Independencia 8 (Ⓣ441/296-0328; ❺). The **bus station** is 1km northeast of town, but you can flag down buses as they pass through town.

### Edward James

Born in 1907 to a second-rank British aristocratic mother and American railroad millionaire father, **Edward James** may well have also been an illegitimate descendant of King Edward VII. He grew up cosseted by an Eton and Oxford education, and with no lack of money set about a life as a poet and artist. Meeting with only limited success, he turned his attentions to becoming a patron of the arts, partly in an attempt to prolong his waning marriage to a Hungarian dancer, Tilly Losch. Despite his bankrolling ballets that served as vehicles for her talent (notably those by George Balanchine's first company), she eventually left him, whereupon he retreated from London society to Europe. Here he befriended Salvador Dalí, and agreed to buy his entire output for the whole of 1938. As James increasingly aligned himself with the Surrealists, Picasso and Magritte also benefited from his patronage. Indeed, Picasso is reputed to have described James as "crazier than all the Surrealists put together. They pretend, but he is the real thing." During World War II, James moved to the US, where he partly funded LA's Watts Towers and made his first visit south of the border. After falling in love with Xilitla, he moved here in the early 1950s and experimented with growing orchids (which all died in a freak snowstorm in 1962) and running a small zoo. In his later years he was often seen with a parrot or two in tow as he went about building his concrete fantasy world. Aided by local collaborator and long-time companion **Plutarco Gastelum Esquer** and up to 150 workers, James fashioned Las Pozas, continually revising and developing, but never really finishing anything. He died in 1984, leaving his estate to Esquer and his family, though without making any provision for the upkeep of his work.

The other four missions – Landa, Tilaco, Tacoyol and Concá – are harder to visit without your own transport.

## Xilitla and Las Pozas

Travelling through the Sierra Gorda is a joy in itself, but really doesn't prepare you for the picturesque small town of **Xilitla**, sprawled over the eastern foothills some 320km northeast of Querétaro. With limestone cliffs all about it, it is a dramatic location, and at 600m, it is warmer than the Bajío and with a lusher feel. There are tremendous views over the surrounding temperate rainforest, which is thick with waterfalls, birdlife and flowers, particularly wild orchids. It is mainly of interest as a place to relax, though you might devote a few minutes to admiring the beautifully preserved interior of the sixteenth-century **Ex-Convento de San Agustín**, which overlooks the central plaza, Jardín Hidalgo.

The real justification for the lengthy journey to Xilitla is to visit **Las Pozas** (roughly 9am–6pm; M$30), some 2.5km east of town along a dirt road: head down Ocampo on the north side of the square, turn left and follow the signs. It is a pleasant walk downhill on the way there, or you can grab a taxi for around M$60. Here, English eccentric **Edward James** (see box opposite) spent the 1960s and 1970s creating a surreal jungle fantasy full of completely useless concrete buildings. Sprouting beside nine pools ("pozas") of a cascading jungle river you'll find a spiral staircase that winds up until it disappears to nothing, stone hands almost 2m high, thick columns with no purpose, a mosaic snake and buildings such as the "House With Three Stories That Might be Five" and "The House Destined To Be a Cinema". Only one is in any sense liveable, a hideaway apartment four storeys up where James spent much of his time. With so little complete, there are all sorts of unprotected precipices: take care.

Mildew now ages the concrete beyond its years, and in places it is crumbling away revealing the reinforcing steel beneath, but it all adds to the enchanting quality of the place. You could see everything in an hour or so, but plan to spend the better part of a day here bathing in the pools and just chilling out; best bring your own lunch.

Back in town, call at the **Museo Edward James**, behind the *Posada El Castillo* (nominally daily 10am–6pm, but actually open when they feel like it; M$30), which showcases James's life and particularly his work here. Photos of the construction are particularly worth perusing.

**Getting to Xilitla** isn't difficult, but it can be time-consuming. Eight twisting hours through the Sierra Gorda from Querétaro (7 buses daily), it's perhaps most easily accessed from the unexciting but sizeable town of Ciudad Valles (see p.322; hourly; 1hr 30min), some 60km north. There are also one or two services direct from Tampico and San Luis Potosí: all pull up outside one of two bus company offices close to Jardín Hidalgo. There's no tourist office, but everything else (including several **banks** with ATMs and the **post office**) is easy to find on the streets nearby. Here, too, you'll find several serviceable **restaurants**, and simple and clean accommodation.

*The* **place to stay** in Xilitla is *Posada El Castillo*, Ocampo 105, half a block down from the plaza (ⓣ489/365-0038, ⓦwww.junglegossip.com/castillo.html; no credit cards; ⑥), in the house where James lived when he wasn't ensconced in his hut or apartment at Las Pozas. His spirit still inhabits the eight highly individual guestrooms, designed by Esquer and harmoniously blending Mexican, English and Moorish styles. There's a lovely pool, meals are served and the hosts not only speak English but also have produced a documentary on James's life and work, which they screen for guests. If your budget can't stretch this far, stay at *Hotel Dolores*,

## Fiestas

The Bajío is one of the most active regions in Mexico when it comes to celebrations. The state of Guanajuato is especially rich in fiestas: the list below is by no means comprehensive and local tourist offices (and the state websites) will have further details.

### January

**Fiesta de Cristo de Matehuala** (Jan 6–15). Feria in Matehuala (see p.244).
**Feria de León** (Jan 10–20). Agricultural and industrial fair in León (see p.277).
**Día de San Sebastián** (Jan 20). The climax of ten days of pilgrimages in San Luis Potosí (see p.252) and León (see p.277).
**Natalicio del General Allende** (Jan 21). Parades and celebrations in San Miguel de Allende (see p.295).

### February

**Día de la Candelaria** (Feb 2). Major religious festival in San Juan de los Lagos (see p.276).

### March

**St Patrick's Day** (March 17). Now in San Miguel de Allende (see p.295).
**Batalla de las Flores** (Fri before Good Friday). Altar-building in Guanajuato (see p.277).
**Semana Santa** (Holy Week). Observed with a huge procession almost everywhere. See especially San Miguel de Allende (p.295), San Luis Potosí (p.250) and Guanajuato (see p.277).
**Zacatecas en la Cultura** (two weeks around Semana Santa). Enormous citywide celebrations of all strands of culture in Zacatecas (see p.259).
**Feria del Toro de Lidia** (middle week of March). Bullfights in Tequisquiapan (see p.316).
**Peregrinatión** (two Sun before Easter). Religious procession in San Miguel de Allende (see p.295).

### April

**Feria de San Marcos** (mid-April to mid-May). Huge, month-long fair in Aguascalientes (see p.271).
**Peregrinatión** (second Sun before Easter). Culmination of a week's celebration in San Miguel de Allende, with an overnight pilgrimage following an image of Our Lord of the Column from Atotonilco to the church of San Juan de Dios in San Miguel. The procession is greeted at dawn with rejoicing and fireworks.

### May

**Internacional Feria de Queso y Vino** (late May–early June). Tequisquiapan (see p.316).
**Festival de Súchil** (Wed after Corpus Christi). A very ancient fiesta in Juchipila, 100km southwest of Aguascalientes, with flowers and dances including the famous Jarabe Tapatío, the Mexican Hat Dance.
**Día de María Auxiliadora** (May 24). Fiesta lasting until the next Sun at Empalme Escobeda, 25km south of San Miguel de Allende, with traditional dances including that of Los Apaches, one of the few in which women take part.

### June

**Fiesta de San Antonio de Padua** (June 13). "The Crazies" are out in San Miguel de Allende (see p.297).
**Fiestas de San Juan y Presa de la Olla** (June 24). Fiesta in Guanajuato (see p.279).

## July

**Apertura de la Presa de la Olla** (first Mon in July). Festivities and dancing in Guanajuato (see p.280).
**Festival del Día de Santiago** (July 25). Stylized battles just outside Aguascalientes (see p.270).
**International Folk Festival** (late July–early Aug). Mexico's top folk festival in Zacatecas, with around fifty nationalities represented (see p.259).

## August

**Festival de Música de Cámara** (first two weeks of Aug). Chamber music festival in San Miguel de Allende (see p.304).
**Día de la Asunción** (Assumption; Aug 15). Religious and grape festivals in San Luis Potosí (see p.252) and Aguascalientes (see p.270). In Celaya, 45km east of Querétaro, it coincides with the Feria de la Cajeta, celebrating the syrupy confection made there.
**Día de San Luis Rey** (Aug 25). Festivities in San Luis Potosí (see p.252).
**La Morisma** (weekend closest to Aug 27). Massive mock battle between Moors and Christians in Zacatecas (see p.259).

## September

**Día de la Virgen de Remedios** (Sept 1). Lively fiesta in Comonfort, 25km south of San Miguel de Allende.
**Feria de Zacatecas** (first two weeks of Sept). Zacatecas's principal fiesta (see p.259).
**Fiesta de San Francisco de Asís** (second Sat in Sept to fourth Sun in Oct). Weekly pilgrimages to Real de Catorce (see p.247).
**Día de la Virgen de la Soledad** (Sept 8–15). Festival in Jerez (see p.270).
**Independence Day** (Sept 16). Celebrations everywhere, particularly in Dolores Hidalgo (see p.292) and San Miguel de Allende (see p.295).
**Pamplonada** (third Sat in Sept). Bull running in San Miguel de Allende (see p.297).
**Festival de San Miguel** (Sept 28–30). Mock battles at San Felipe (Guanajuato), near Guanajuato.
**San Miguel Arcángel** (Sept 29). San Miguel de Allende's most important festivities (see p.297).

## October

**Fiesta de San Francisco de Asís** (Oct 4). Final massive pilgrimage in Real de Catorce (see p.247).
**Festival Internacional Cervantino** (early to mid-Oct). Huge cultural and arts festival in Guanajuato (see box, p.290).

## November

**Día de los Muertos** (Day of the Dead; Nov 2). Celebrated everywhere.
**Fiesta de las Iluminaciones** (Nov 7–14). Religious festivities in Guanajuato (see p.277).
**Festival Internacional de Jazz & Blues** (last weekend in Nov). In San Miguel de Allende (see p.305)

## December

**Día de la Inmaculada Concepción** (Dec 8). A religious festival with a feria and traditional dancing in Dolores Hidalgo (see p.292) and San Juan de los Lagos (see p.276).
**Christmas Posadas** (Dec 16–25). These traditional parades are widely performed. Particularly good in Celaya, 45km west of Querétaro, and in Querétaro itself (see p.307) on Dec 23 when there's a giant procession with bands and carnival floats.

Matamoros 211 (Ⓣ489/365-0178, Ⓦwww.hoteldoloresxilitla.com; ❸), a modern and very clean hotel featuring rooms with TV and fan, some also with a/c and fine mountain views (❺). A pool is in construction. To get there, follow Hidalgo east from the main square for one long block, head straight across the road and down a long flight of stairs. At the bottom of the steps turn left. The cheapest rooms are at *Hotel Casa María Mercado*, Guerrero 103, tucked in behind the market (Ⓣ489/365-0049; ❷). They're all decent, clean and ranged around a modern central courtyard. Those on the top floor have more air and limited views.



### Ciudad Valles

There is no reason to spend any time in **Ciudad Valles**, a dull, small, sweaty city 60km north of Xilitla and pretty much at sea level. It is on the highway between San Luis Potosí and Tampico, and with a major bus station on the outskirts of town is the place to get buses to Xilitla (hourly 4am–5pm). You may be forced into a night here, something easily done at hotels around the bus station. None are incredibly cheap, but the best value is *Pizaño Zamora*, Luis Venegas 138 (Ⓣ481/381-3543; ❹) with a/c and TV. There are several modest restaurants nearby.

## Travel details

### Buses

**Aguascalientes** to: Guadalajara (roughly hourly; 6hr); Guanajuato (5 daily; 4hr); León (every 30min; 2hr); Matehuala (at least hourly; 2hr); Mexico City (hourly; 7hr); Querétaro (hourly; 6hr); San Luis Potosí (hourly; 2hr 30min); San Miguel de Allende (4 daily; 4hr 30min); Zacatecas (every 30min; 2hr).
**Ciudad Valles** to: Tampico (12 daily; 2hr 30min); San Luis Potosí (hourly; 4hr 30min); Xilitla (hourly 4am–5pm; 1hr 30min).
**Dolores Hidalgo** to: Guanajuato (every 20min; 1hr); León (every 20min; 2hr 45min); Mexico City (every 40min; 5hr); Querétaro (every 40min; 2hr 30min); San Luis de la Paz (every 20min; 1hr); San Luis Potosí (10 daily; 2hr 30min); San Miguel de Allende (every 20min; 50min).
**Guanajuato** to: Aguascalientes (4 daily; 4hr); Dolores Hidalgo (every 20min; 1hr); Guadalajara (5 daily; 6hr); León (constantly; 40min); Mexico City (7 daily; 4hr); Querétaro (8 daily; 3hr); San Luis de la Paz (5 daily; 2hr 30min); San Luis Potosí (10 daily; 3hr); San Miguel de Allende (10 daily; 1hr 30min).
**Lagos de Moreno** to: Aguascalientes (every 30min; 1hr 30min); Guanajuato (roughly hourly; 1hr 30min); Leon (every 15min; 1hr).
**León** to: Aguascalientes (hourly; 1hr); Guadalajara (hourly; 4hr); Guanajuato (constantly; 40min); Mexico City (hourly; 5hr); Querétaro (hourly; 2hr); Zacatecas (hourly; 4hr).
**Matehuala** to: Real de Catorce (4–5 daily; 2hr); Saltillo (hourly or better; 3hr); San Luis Potosí (every 30min; 2hr); Wadley (4 daily; 1hr 45min).
**Pozos** to: San José Iturbide (every 30min; 40min); San Luis de la Paz (every 30min; 20min).
**Querétaro** to: Aguascalientes (hourly; 5hr); Bernal (hourly; 1hr); Dolores Hidalgo (every 40min; 2hr); Guadalajara (hourly; 6hr); Guanajuato (6 daily; 3hr); León (hourly; 2hr); Jalpan (hourly; 5hr); Mexico City (every 10min; 3hr); Morelia (every 30–60min; 3hr); San Juan del Río (every 15min; 45min); San Luis Potosí (hourly; 2hr); San Miguel de Allende (every 40min; 1hr 15min); Tequisquiapan (every 30min; 1hr); Tula (9 daily; 2hr 30min); Xilitla (3 daily; 7hr); Zacatecas (hourly; 5hr).
**San José Iturbide** to: Pozos (every 30min; 40min); Querétaro (every few min; 1hr 10min); San Luis de la Paz (every 30min; 1hr).
**San Juan del Río** to: Mexico City (every 15min; 3hr 15min); Querétaro (every 15min; 45min); Tequisquiapan (every 20min; 30min); Tula (9 daily; 1hr 30min).
**San Luis de la Paz** to: Dolores Hidalgo (every 20min; 1hr); Guanajuato (10 daily; 2hr 30min); Pozos (every 30min; 20min); San José Iturbide (every 30min; 1hr).
**San Luis Potosí** to: Aguascalientes (hourly; 2hr 30min); Dolores Hidalgo (13 daily; 2hr 30min); Guadalajara (hourly; 5hr); Guanajuato (10 daily; 3hr); Matehuala (every 30min; 2hr 30min); Mexico City (frequently; 5hr); Monterrey (hourly; 7hr);

Nuevo Laredo (6 daily; 10hr); Querétaro (hourly; 2hr 30min); San Miguel de Allende (8 daily; 3hr); Tampico (4 daily; 7hr); Wadley (3 daily; 4hr); Zacatecas (10 daily; 3hr).
**San Miguel de Allende** to: Aguascalientes (2 daily; 4hr); Dolores Hidalgo (every 15min; 50min); Guanajuato (10 daily; 1hr 30min); Mexico City (every 40min; 4hr); Querétaro (every 40min; 1hr 15min); San Luis Potosí (8 daily; 3hr).
**Tequisquiapan** to: Mexico City (every 40min; 3hr 45min); Querétaro (every 30min; 1hr); San Juan del Río (every 20min; 30min).
**Xilitla** to: Ciudad Valles (hourly; 1hr 30min); Jalpan (every 30min; 2hr); Querétaro (8 daily; 7hr); San Luis Potosí (3 daily; 6–7hr); Tampico (7 daily; 4–5hr).
**Zacatecas** to: Aguascalientes (every 30min; 2hr); Chihuahua (hourly; 12hr); Ciudad Juárez (hourly; 16hr); Durango (hourly; 4hr); Guadalajara (hourly; 5hr); Jerez (hourly; 1hr); León (hourly; 4–5hr); Mazatlán (2 daily; 10hr); Mexico City (roughly hourly; 8hr); Monterrey (roughly hourly; 7hr); Nuevo Laredo (5 daily; 8hr); Puerto Vallarta (1 daily; 10hr); Querétaro (hourly; 6hr); San Luis Potosí (10 daily; 3hr); Tijuana (4 daily; 36hr); Torreón (roughly hourly; 6hr).

# Northern Jalisco and Michoacán

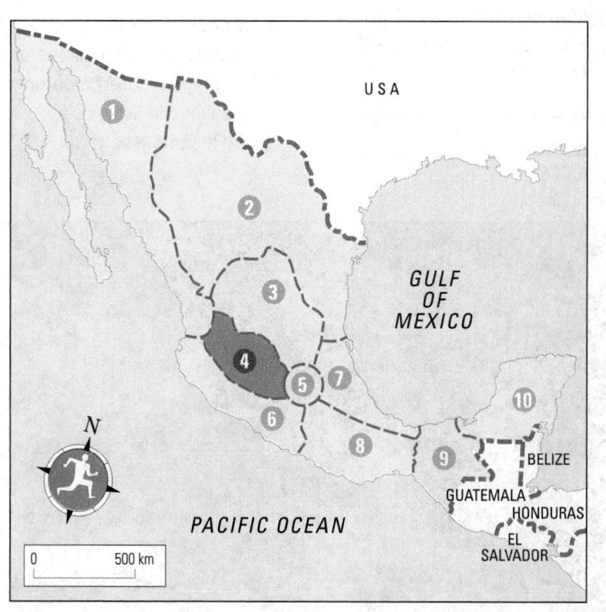

CHAPTER 4

# Highlights

- **Guadalajara** Experience the drama of mariachi music in Mexico's most "Mexican" city, the capital of Jalisco. See p.330
- **Tequila** Visit a tequila distillery and, more importantly, sample the legendary spirit in a café on the town's plaza. See p.354
- **Uruapan** Take in the cascading waterfalls and lush surroundings of the Parque Nacional Eduardo Ruíz. See p.364
- **Paricutín** Climb up this still-active volcano through an unearthly landscape. See p.368
- **Pátzcuaro** One of the best places in Mexico for seeing the spectacular and moving Day of the Dead celebrations. See p.370
- **Morelia** Enjoy dulces, wine and classical music in one of the cafés overlooking historic Morelia's central plaza. See p.380
- **Monarch Butterfly Sanctuary** See millions of the brightly coloured creatures blanket the fir trees around El Rosario. See p.388

△ Parque Nacional Eduardo Ruíz, Uruapan

# Northern Jalisco and Michoacán



Separated from the country's colonial heartland by the craggy peaks of the Sierra Madre, the stretch of land from Guadalajara to Mexico City through the semitropical states of **Jalisco** and **Michoacán** has an unhurried ease that marks it out from the rest of the country. Containing a complex landscape of lofty plains and rugged sierras, the area is blessed with supremely fertile farms, fresh pine woods, cool pastures and lush tropical forest.

Something of a backwater until well into the eighteenth century, the high valleys of Michoacán and Jalisco were left to develop their own strong regional traditions and solid farming economy. Wherever you go, you'll find a wealth of local commercial goods, both agricultural and traditionally manufactured items, from avocados to tequila, glassware to guitars. Relative isolation has also made the region a bastion of conservatism – in the years following the Revolution, the Catholic *Cristero* counter-revolutionary guerrilla movement enjoyed its strongest support here. More recently the region has gained some notoriety as the centre of a **drugs war**, as gangs struggle for control of the country's trade in illegal substances. This was gruesomely illustrated in 2006 in otherwise peaceful Uruapan, when mobsters invaded a nightclub and rolled five freshly severed heads onto the dancefloor. The drug lords aren't interested in law-abiding tourists, so there is no cause for alarm, though you may notice an increase in highway police checks.

Easygoing **Guadalajara**, Mexico's second city, is packed with elegant buildings and surrounded by scenic country. Outside the city, the land is spectacularly green and mountainous, studded with volcanoes and lakes, most famously **Laguna de Chapala**, where D.H. Lawrence wrote *The Plumed Serpent*. There are also some superb colonial relics, especially in the towns of **Morelia** and **Pátzcuaro**, although it's the latter's majestic setting and still-powerful Indian traditions that first call your attention. The indigenous culture still in evidence more than compensates for the paucity of physical remains from the pre-Hispanic era, though the ruins of **Tzintzuntzán** on Lago de Pátzcuaro are certainly impressive. Local **fiestas** – and there are many – are some of Mexico's liveliest, and the legacy of village handicrafts has survived since the earliest days of the Conquest.

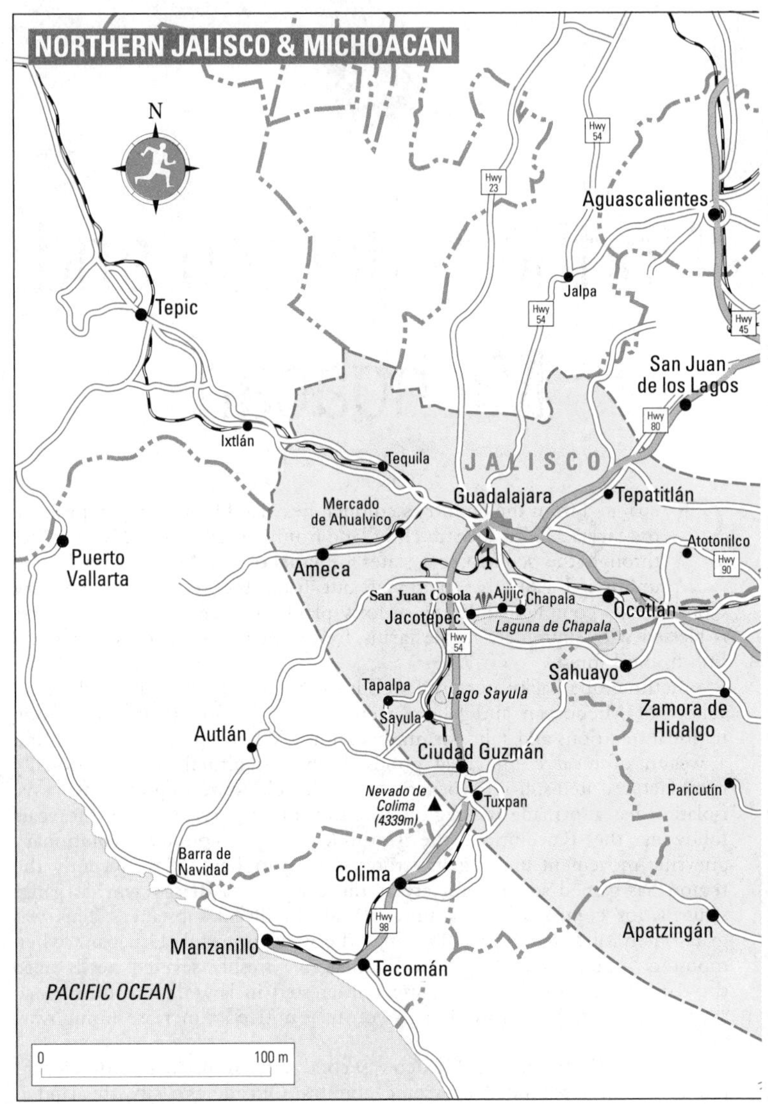


Jalisco and Michoacán are among the most serene states in the country: relaxing, easy to get about and free of urban hassle. Add the fact that Jalisco is the home of **mariachi** and **tequila** and you've got a region where you could easily spend a couple of weeks exploring without even beginning to

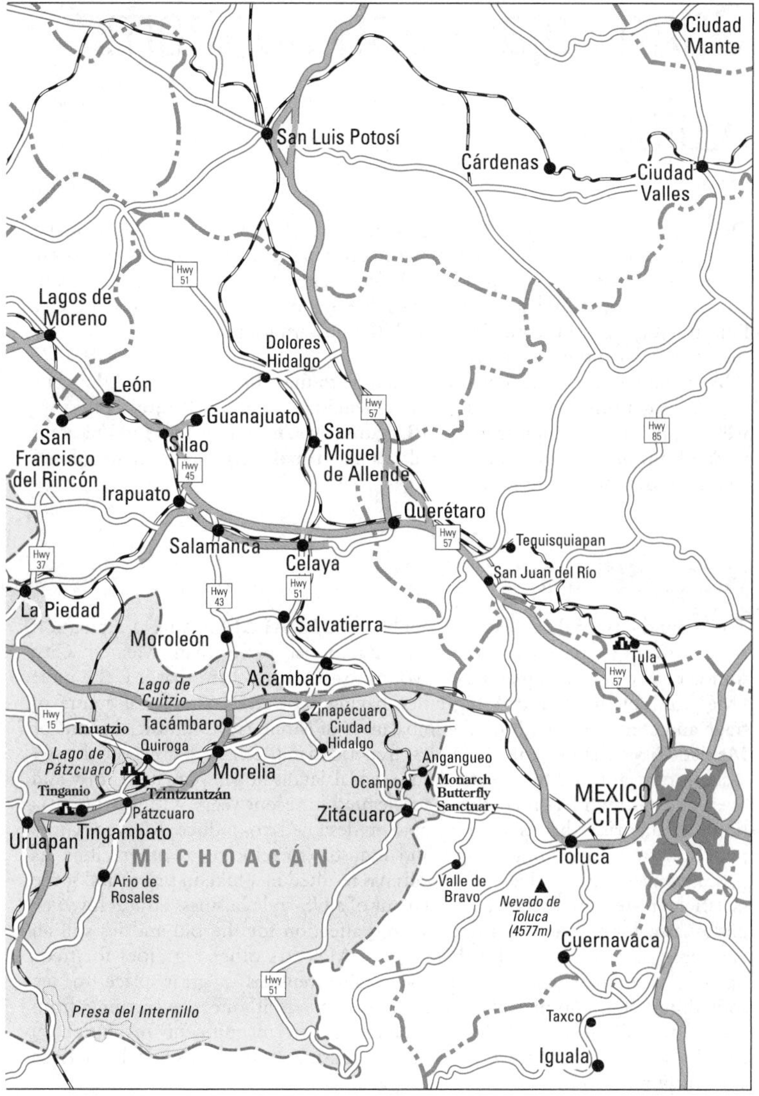


see everything. Overall, tourist numbers are pretty low except for in Pátzcuaro around the Day of the Dead, and winter weekends at the Monarch Butterfly Sanctuary.

# Guadalajara and northern Jalisco



Quite simply, **Guadalajara** dominates the state of **Jalisco**. Not only is it the capital city, but it's also the main attraction. If you spend any time in the region, you're inevitably going to spend much of it here; even if you wanted to avoid Guadalajara, you'd find it nearly impossible – a major transport hub, the city links the roads from the northwest with the onward routes to Mexico City and the country's central highlands.

To see only Guadalajara, however, would be to miss the real nature of the state, which, away from the capital, is green, lush and mountainous. **Tequila** offers . . . well, tequila. The tranquil scenery of **Laguna de Chapala** makes for a pleasant respite from the city; in mountain villages like **Tapalpa**, there's fresh air aplenty and life moves at a more sedate pace.

## Guadalajara

The second city of the Mexican Republic, **GUADALAJARA** has a reputation as a slower, more conservative and traditional place than Mexico City, somewhere you can stop and catch your breath. Many claim that it is the most "Mexican" of the country's big cities, having evolved as a regional centre of trade and commerce, without the imbalances of Monterrey's industrial giants or Mexico City's chaotic scale. Being less frenetic than the capital, however, doesn't make it peaceful, and by any standards Guadalajara is huge, sprawling, noisy and energetic. Growth has, if anything, accelerated in recent years, with the population on the rise thanks to a campaign designed to reduce Mexico City's pollution by encouraging people and industry to relocate to other cities. Its partial conversion to a sleek metropolis has resulted in a hike in prices and some sacrifice of Mexican mellowness in favour of a US-style business ethic. However, enthusiasm for the new has not replaced affection for the old and it's still an enjoyable place to visit, with the edge on Mexico's other big cities for trees, flowers, cleanliness and friendliness. It also remains a great place to see something of traditional and modern Mexico, as it offers everything from museums, galleries and colonial architecture to magnificent revolutionary murals by José Clemente Orozco to a nightlife scene enlivened by a large student population.

Parks, little squares and open spaces dot the city. Right downtown around the cathedral is a series of plazas unchanged since the days of the Spanish colonization. This small colonial heart of Guadalajara can still, especially at weekends, recall an old-world atmosphere and provincial elegance. The centre is further brightened by the **Plaza Tapatía**, which opens out the city's historical core to pedestrians, mariachi bands and street theatre. Around this relatively unruffled nucleus revolve raucous and crowded streets typical of modern Mexico, while further out still, in the wide boulevards of the new suburbs, you'll find smart hotels, shopping malls and office buildings.

## Some history

Guadalajara was founded in 1532, one of the fruits of the vicious campaign of Nuño de Guzmán at the time of the Conquest – his cruelty and corruption were such that he appalled even the Spanish authorities, who threw him into prison in Madrid, where he died. The city, named after Guzmán's birthplace, thrived, was officially recognized by Charles V in 1542 and rapidly became one of the colony's most Spanish cities – in part because so much of the indigenous population had been killed or had fled during the Conquest. Isolated from the great mining industry of the Bajío, Guadalajara evolved into a regional centre for trade and agriculture. The tight reins of colonial rule restrained the city's development, and it wasn't until the end of the eighteenth century, as the colonial monopolies began to crumble, that things really took off. Between 1760 and 1803 the city's population tripled, reaching some 35,000; a new university was established; and the city became famous for the export of wheat, hides, cotton and wool.

When Spain's colonial empire finally fell apart, Guadalajara supported Hidalgo's independence movement and briefly served as the capital of the nation. By the beginning of the twentieth century it was already the second largest city in the Republic, and in the 1920s the completion of the rail link with California provided a further spur for development. More recently, the exodus from Mexico City and attempts at industrial decentralization have continued to swell the urban area's population, which now tops eight million.

# Arrival

Guadalajara's **airport** is some 17km southeast of the city on the road to Chapala. Facilities include money exchange and car rental, and there's also the usual system of fixed-price taxis and vans to take you downtown (around M$170 for a car with up to four people – vouchers are sold inside the terminal and the ride takes 45min–1hr). A much cheaper bus service (every 15–30min 6am–9pm; M$10) heads from the junction of Enrique Diaz de León and Alenaia to the Central Vieja (see below), from where you can hop on another bus, or walk, to the centre.

Some 10km out in the city's southeastern suburbs, Guadalajara's **Central Nueva** (aka Camionera Nueva), is one of Mexico's largest **bus** terminals, comprising seven buildings strung out in a wide arc, with its own shopping centre (Nueva Central Plaza) and hotel (see "Accommodation", p.335). Very broadly, each building serves a different area, but since they're organized by bus company rather than route, it's not quite that simple – there are buses to Mexico City from just about every building, for example. Bus company staff are usually happy to tell you which company, and therefore which building, suits your needs. Local buses #616 and #644 ("Centro") and the slightly dearer (but faster) turquoise TUR bus stop outside each terminal; all three take you to Avenida 16 de Septiembre, within walking distance of the cathedral if not right past it. The last city buses between the terminal and the centre leave at around 10pm. A taxi downtown costs around M$80. For details of how to reach the terminal from the centre, and of long-distance buses running from it, see the box on p.334.

Some second-class buses from local destinations, including Tequila, Tapalpa, Ciudad Guzmán and the villages on the shores of Laguna de Chapala, as well as the airport service, use the **Central Vieja** (aka Camionera Vieja), the old downtown terminal, surrounded by cheap hotels and only a short bus ride (#174) up Calzada Independencia from the centre. If you're coming from somewhere only an hour or two away, it can be worth the slightly less comfortable second-class journey for the convenience of this much more central point of arrival. The two bus stations are connected by the #616 bus.

The **train station**, a couple of kilometres south of the centre at the bottom of Calzada Independencia is used only for the touristy Tequila Express (see box, p.355).

## Orientation

The centre of the old city is a relatively compact grid around the junction of **Morelos** and **16 de Septiembre**, by the huge bulk of the **cathedral**; east of here Morelos leads to the **Plaza Tapatía** and the **Mercado Libertad**, while to the west are busy shopping streets. **Juárez**, a couple of blocks south, is actually the main east–west thoroughfare in the centre, heading out to the west past the **university** (where it becomes Vallarta), and crossing avenidas **Chapultepec** and **Américas** in an upmarket residential area. Further west still, it crosses **López Mateos**, a main through route, which heads south past the **Plaza del Sol**, a shopping centre surrounded by big hotels, restaurants and much of Guadalajara's best, but most expensive, nightlife, and eventually heads out of the city as the main road towards Colima and the coast.

The main north–south arteries in the centre are the **Calzada del Federalismo**, along which the Tren Ligero, the city's metro, runs, and **Calzada Independencia**, which runs from the train station past the **Parque Agua Azul**, the old bus station, the market and Plaza Tapatía, and eventually out of the city to the **Parque Mirador**. Finally, **Revolución** leads off Independencia towards the southeast, to Tlaquepaque, the new bus station and Tonalá. If you fancy taking a **city tour** to get your bearings, try Panoramex (Ⓣ33/3810-5109, Ⓦwww.panoramex.com.mx; M$150 for 5hr, offered Mon–Sat).

CENTRAL GUADALAJARA
See Centro Histórico map
ACCOMMODATION
Hotel Canada F
Hotel Consulado C
Hotel Costa Brava E
Hotel Flamingos E
Hotel León D
Quinta Real A
Villa Ganz B
EATING & DRINKING
Casa Bariachi 4
La China Poblana 5
El Duende del Sacromonte 3
Goa 6
Los Itacates 1
Pierrot 2
La Trattoria 7
British Consulate
Canadian Consulate
Monumento Los Arcos
American Express
Centro Magno (Shopping Mall)
Minerva Circle
University of Guadalajara
Museo de las Artes
Templo Expiatorio
ICMNJ (Language School)
Institute de Artesanio Jalisciense
Parque Agua Azul
Centra Vieja (Old Bus Station)
Train Station for Tequilla Express
Washington
Santa Filomena
Unidad Deportiva
Sandi Bookstore
Plaza del Sol
0 1 km
N

**Useful bus routes**

All of these also run in the opposite direction: the #600 numbers are minibuses.

**#60** Calzada Independencia–Soccer stadium and bullring–Central Vieja
**#176** Centro–airport
**#275** Central Nueva –Tonalá–Tlaquepaque–Centro–Zapopan
**#603-A** Cabañas–Barranca de Huentitan
**#616** Central Nueva–Central Vieja–Centro
**#629** Centro–Morelos (westbound)/Pedro Moreno (eastbound)–Minerva Circle
**#639** Centro–Colonia Jalisco
**#707** TUR turquoise bus Central Nueva–Tonalá–Tlaquepaque–Centro–Zapopan
**Trolleybus Independencia** Centro–Soccer stadium and bullring–Zoo

## Information

The helpful state **tourist office** is at Morelos 102 (daily 9am–8pm; ⓣ33/3668-1600 or 3668-1601, ⓦvive.guadalajara.gob.mx), off Plaza Tapatía. In addition, there are information booths at the main bus station, the airport and inside the entrance of Teatro Degollado, as well as a free tourist information phone line from elsewhere in the country (ⓣ01-800/363-2200).

The best source of **listings** information is the *Acid* magazine section that comes with Friday's edition of Guadalajara's main newspaper, *Público*. The cooler cafes often have a copy lying around. If your Spanish isn't that great you'll miss out on the gallery and film reviews, but should still be able understand the restaurant and gig listings.

For something in English, opt for the weekly *Guadalajara Reporter* (ⓦwww.guadalajarareporter.com), which reflects the concerns and aspirations of the expat community both here and around Laguna de Chapala.

For details of **banks**, foreign exchange, **post offices**, **telephones** and much more, see "Listings", p.352.

## City transport

Guadalajara is a very big city, but getting around is not too difficult once you've got the hang of the comprehensive system of public transport. In the centre, most of the main attractions are within walking distance of each other, and elsewhere using public transport is relatively straightforward. Almost all **buses** are funnelled through the centre on a few main roads and have their destinations written on the windscreen. The sheer number of buses and the speed at which they move can make things slightly more difficult, however, especially at peak hours when you may have to fight to get on; if possible, get a local to show you exactly where your bus stops. Most bus rides cost M$4, though you'll pay twice that on the turquoise, air-conditioned TUR express routes.

The **Tren Ligero** (metro system), with one north–south and one east–west line, is designed for local commuters. You may not use it at all, though it can be handy for quick east–west travel across the centre. To ride, buy a one-journey token (M$4) from a machine on the platform.

**Taxis** are also reliable if you're in a hurry, and for a group they aren't usually too expensive as long as you establish a price at the outset; many downtown taxi ranks post a list of fixed prices. From the centre to the Plaza del Sol, Central Nueva or Zapopan should cost around M$80; it'll be around M$50 to

Tlaquepaque and M$160 to the airport. Fares are generally 25 percent higher after 10pm and before 6am.

The best way to get around, however, is **on foot** – Guadalajara's streets are even more pleasant if you appreciate them slowly.

## Accommodation

With a range of hotels to suit all budgets (as well as a couple of **hostels**) right in the *centro histórico*, there is little reason to stay elsewhere in the city. In this area you'll be able to walk to everything in the centre and have easy access to buses out to the outlying suburbs.

If you're looking for a budget option and the central places are all full, consider some of the **cheap hotels** around the old bus station or in the streets south of the Mercado Libertad. Both areas are noisy and none too appealing, though the hotels we've listed are fine.

Most of the more **expensive** business hotels tend to be a long way out to the west of the city, though you're almost certainly better off in the **luxury B&B**-style places downtown or in Tlaquepaque.

There's also Avenida López Mateos, 2km to the west of the centre, which is Guadalajara's **motel** row. This can be handy if you're driving and don't want to tackle the city. Finally, if you arrive late at night at the **Central Nueva** and all you want to do is sleep, try *Hotel Serena* (see p.336).

Unless otherwise noted, the establishments listed below are marked on the "Guadalajara: Centro Histórico" map (see p.338).

### In the centre

**Don Quixote Hotel** Héroes 91 ⓣ33/3658-1299, ⓕ3614-2845. Friendly, small hotel with rooms around a colonial-style courtyard. A little more characterful than some of the business hotels. ❻

**Hostel de María** Nueva Galicia 924 ⓣ33/3562-9520, ⓔhostaldemaria@prodigy.net.mx. Peaceful hostel in a quiet neighbourhood a short walk from the cathedral. Mostly eight-bunk dorms (M$150 per person, HI members M$125) plus a couple of private rooms. Free Internet access and a Continental breakfast included. ❹

**Hostel Guadalajara** Maestranza 147 ⓣ33/3562-7520, ⓦwww.hostelguadalajara.com. Very central and modern hostel (though in an old building) that's always alive with backpackers and language students. It suffers from street noise but compensates with Internet access, laundry and cooking facilities, private lockers and friendly staff who regularly organize nights out to interesting bars. A light breakfast is included and if you pay in advance you get four nights for the price of three. Dorms M$135, ISIC cardholders M$125, IYH members M$108. ❸

**Hotel de Mendoza** Carranza 16, at Hidalgo ⓣ33/3942-5151, ⓦwww.demendoza.com.mx. Attractive establishment in a refurbished colonial convent. Rooms come with all amenities (including in-room safe) and access to the nicest pool in the centre of town. A central location makes this an ideal base for sightseeing; it's quite popular with groups. ❽–❾

**Hotel Fénix** Corona 160 ⓣ33/3614-5714, ⓦwww.holahoteles.com.mx. Large, modern, four-star hotel with impeccable rooms right in the centre of things. Go for one on the upper floors with views of the cathedral, and opt in for the buffet breakfast at a slightly higher rate. ❼

**Hotel Francés** Maestranza 35 ⓣ33/3613-1190, ⓦwww.hotelfrances.com. Just off the plaza behind the cathedral, this beautiful colonial building, founded as an inn in 1610, is the most appealing of Guadalajara's more expensive hotels; it even has an ancient creaking elevator said to be the second ever installed in the city. Even if you're not going to stay, try to stop by for a superb margarita in the lobby bar. Sadly, the fairly drab rooms don't quite match the public areas and you might want to step up to a junior suite (M$819). ❼

**Hotel Hamilton** Madero 381 ⓣ33/641-6726. Clean and friendly, the *Hamilton* is very cheap and consequently a popular spot with backpackers and young Mexican couples. Rooms have private bath and TV costs few pesos extra. ❶

**Hotel Jorge Alejandro** Hidalgo 656 ⓣ33/3658-1051, ⓦwww.hoteljorgealejandro.com. Spotless rooms in a central hotel. Most rooms are carpeted, and there's Internet access and parking. Larger rooms are good for families or groups. ❹

**Hotel Posada San Rafael Inn** López Cotilla 619 ⓣ33/3614-9146, ⓦwww.sanrafael1.tripod.com. A pleasant, friendly little place in a prettily decorated old house. For those really on a budget, they have rooms with shared bath for a few pesos less. Some rooms are brighter than others, and Internet access is available. ④

**Hotel Santiago de Compostela** Colón 272 ⓣ33/3613-8880, or 01-800/365-5300, ⓦwww.santiagodecompostelagdl.com. Attractive hotel set around an enclosed courtyard decorated with Turkish rugs. Rooms are well appointed with a/c, carpets and cable TV, though the streetside ones can be noisy. All have a deep tiled bath but you may just prefer to use the rooftop pool, a lovely place to hang out through the middle of the day. ⑦

**Posada Regis** Corona 171 ⓣ& ⓕ33/3613-3026. Appealing ramshackle old building locked away from the world behind an iron gate, and with high-ceilinged rooms around a peaceful, covered courtyard. They also have small rooms on the roof (M$150 per person) that are ideal for one but acceptable for two. Internet access. ④–⑤

**Posada San Pablo** Madero 429 ⓣ& ⓕ33/3614-2811. With no sign, this place can be hard to spot, but once you get in you'll find clean rooms around a covered courtyard replete with flowers and birds. Ring the bell at the front door for entrance. ④

## Around the Mercado Libertad

**Hotel Ana-Isabel** Javier Mina 164 ⓣ33/3617-7920, ⓕ3617-4859. Simple but clean tiled rooms with TVs and parking nearby. Go for the quieter rooms at the back if possible. ③

**Hotel Chapala** José María Mercado 84 ⓣ33/3617-7159, ⓕ3617-3410. Around the corner from the *Ana-Isabel*, neat and basic, but a touch dark. ③

**Hotel Maya** López Cotilla 39 ⓣ33/3614-5454. Bare but decent rooms in vibrant pink come with TV and parking. It is a noisy area but a short walk to the centre. ④

## South of the centre: Calzada Independencia and the Central Vieja

**Hotel Canada** Estadio 77 ⓣ33/3619-4014, ⓕ3619-3110. One of dozens of hotels surrounding the old bus station, this large place is pretty good value with the bonus of the excellent *Restaurante Ottawa*, and some slightly nicer "suites" (M$330). Not to be confused with the *Gran Hotel Canada* around the corner. ④

**Hotel Costa Brava** Independencia 739 Sur ⓣ33/3619-2324 or 3619-2327. Friendly, new hotel. All rooms have TV. Those away from the road noise are a fraction more expensive. ③

**Hotel Flamingos** Independencia 725 Sur ⓣ33/3619-8764. Next door to the *Costa Brava*: bigger, plainer and cheaper. ②

**Hotel León** Independencia 557 Sur ⓣ33/3619-6141. Very basic place, but clean and perfectly serviceable with bath and 24hr hot water. A bargain. ①

## West of the centre: López Cotilla and the Zona Minerva

The establishments listed below are marked on the "Central Guadalajara" map (see p.333).

**Hotel Consulado** López Cotilla 1405 ⓣ33/3563-6465, ⓦwww.hotelconsuladogdl.com.mx. With its chic, modern entrance and minimal leather sofas this place is unlike almost everywhere else in town, though the comfortable rooms don't quite follow the style. There's free Internet, off-street parking and a bunch of good restaurants nearby. ⑥

**Quinta Real** México 2727 ⓣ1-800/362-1500, ⓦwww.quintareal.com. Gorgeous luxury hotel that's also well set up for business guests. The grounds are spacious and immaculately tended, and the suites come with neo-colonial styling and every amenity. ⑨

**Villa Ganz** López Cotilla 1739 ⓣ33/3120-1416, ⓦwww.villaganz.com. A gorgeous boutique hotel with nine suites, all impeccably decorated in soft tones, and with every luxury on hand. Common areas are so delightful you'll never want to step outside, though it is only a short walk to some great bars and restaurants. Rates start at US$240 and include Continental breakfast and "welcome cocktail". ⑨

## Near the Central Nueva

The establishment listed below is marked on the "Central Guadalajara" map (see p.333).

**Hotel Serena** Central Nueva, beside Sala 1 ⓣ33/3600-0910, ⓦwww.aranzazu.com.mx. Conveniently located by the Central Nueva, this hotel is modern and soulless, but has two pools and reasonably soundproof rooms with TV. ⑤

## Tlaquepaque

The establishments listed below is marked on the "Tlaquepaque" map (see p.345).

**Casa Campos B&B** Francisco Miranda 30-A. ⓣ33/3838-5296, ⓦwww.hotelcasacampos.com. One of the most charming places in town to lay

## Haciendas and overnight retreats

For a completely different perspective on Jalisco, consider staying at one of the numerous well-preserved **haciendas** within an hour's drive of Guadalajara. These destinations provide an easy, if somewhat pricey, overnight escape and a change of pace from the bustling city. They're ideal for those on shorter trips who want quickly and comfortably to experience a bit of the countryside, and learn a little about a different side of *Tapatío* lifestyle. The tourist office of Guadalajara (Ⓣ33/3668-1600, Ⓦwww.visita.jalisco.gob.mx) can provide information on these and other rural homes and relaxing retreats. You can also go directly to Ⓦwww.haciendasycasonas.com, which has links to almost a dozen places.

One particularly fine example is *Hacienda El Carmen*, 35km west of the city, Km 58 Carretera Gdl-Tala-Etzatlán (Ⓣ33/3633-1771, Ⓦwww.haciendaelcarmen.com.mx; ❽), which originated as a family-owned estate, became a convent in 1722 and retains a traditional feel in its current incarnation as a luxury hotel. Colonially styled accommodation encircles a patio garden, full spa and Aztec sweat lodge. There's also horseback riding and mountain biking on country roads, and nearby you'll find the archeological ruins of Guachimontones (Teuchitlán, 300–900 AD).

Other top haciendas in the area include: *Hostal Casona de Manzano* (Ⓦwww.casonademanzano.com), *La Casa de Los Patios* (Ⓦwww.lacasadelospatios.com) and *Hotel-Restaurante Mis Amores* (Ⓦwww.misamores.com).

your head, this beautifully remodelled colonial house comes with modern fittings, an understated elegance and a family of palm-size marmoset monkeys that have free rein in the garden. Rates include breakfast in the adjacent sleek modern restaurant *Sandwich & Friends*. ❼–❽

**La Casa del Retoño** Matamoros 182 Ⓣ33/3587-3989, Ⓦwww.lacasadelretono.com.mx. Neatly set away from the commercial bustle of Tlaquepaque, this modern B&B has eight cheery artesanía-decorated rooms and a sunny terrace and garden where you can eat a good Continental breakfast. ❻

**Donde el Indio Duerme** Independencia 74 Ⓣ33/3535-2189, Ⓦwww.indiosleep.com. Much more basic than everything else hereabouts, but with simple, clean rooms at a good price. ❷

**La Villa del Ensueño** Florida 305 Ⓣ33/3635-8792, Ⓦwww.villadelensueno.com. This "Villa of Dreams" is a delightful boutique hotel with spacious rooms all tastefully decorated and with lovely tiled bathrooms. A pool and assorted nooks make it a great place to hang out between shopping forays. Rates include a buffet breakfast. ❼

# The City

Any tour of Guadalajara inevitably starts at the **cathedral**. With the Sagrario, or sacristy, next door, it takes up an entire block at the very heart of the **colonial centre**, which is bordered by four plazas that form the shape of a Latin cross. The traffic, noise and bustle of the busiest commercial areas of downtown Guadalajara surround the plazas: to the east the crowds spill over into Plaza Tapatía, with its upmarket shops, and to the complete contrast of the old market beyond that; less modern shopping streets to the west are also busy.

Venture a little further out and the atmosphere changes again. Guadalajara's rapid expansion has swallowed up numerous communities: once-distinct villages are now barely distinguishable from the city all around. Heading **west**, the university area blends into chic suburbs and some of the city's most expensive real estate. **East**, Tlaquepaque and Tonalá are the source of some of the area's finest handicrafts. And finally to the **north**, Zapopan has a huge, much revered church and a museum of indigenous traditions, while the Barranca de Oblatos offers stunning canyon views and weekend picnic spots.

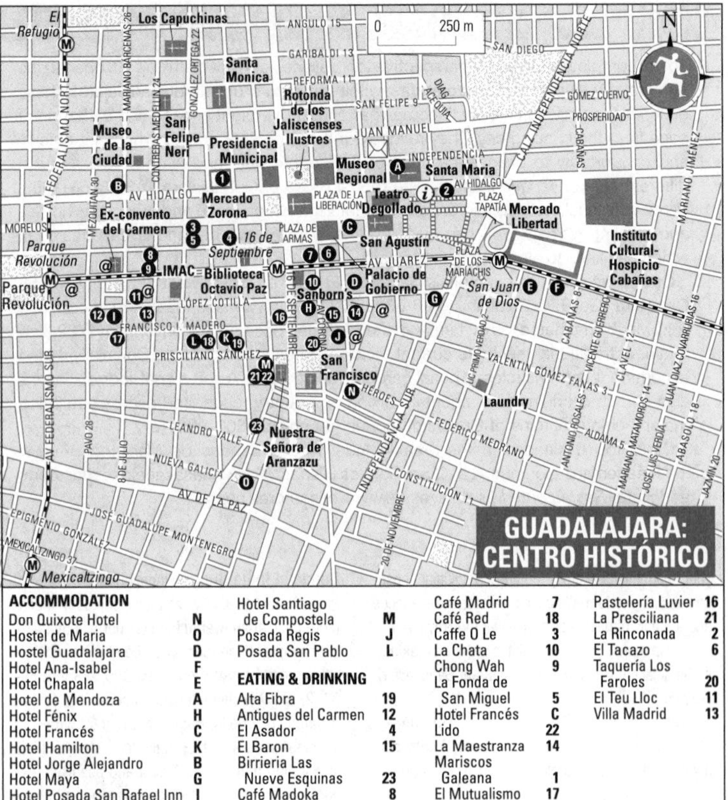


## The cathedral and around

With its pointed, tiled twin towers, Guadalajara's **cathedral** (daily 8am–8pm; free) is a bizarre but successful mixture of styles. Building work began in 1561 and didn't finish for over a century – since then, extensive modifications, which effectively disguise the fact that there was probably never a plan behind the original design, have included a Neoclassical facade and new twin yellow-tiled towers (the originals collapsed in an 1818 earthquake). The interior is best seen in the evening, when the light from ornate chandeliers makes the most of its rich decoration; the picture of the Virgin in the sacristy is attributed to the Spanish Renaissance artist **Murillo**.

Flanking the cathedral is a series of bustling plazas – Plaza Guadalajara, Rotonda de los Jaliscenses Ilustres, Plaza de la Liberación and Plaza de Armas. At weekends and on warm evenings these plazas are packed, the crowds entertained by an array of street performers and wandering musicians; there are frequently bands playing during the day, too. The **Plaza Guadalajara**, formerly known as the Plaza de los Laureles for all its topiaried laurel trees, faces the main west entrance of the cathedral. It is bordered to the north by the porticoed **Presidencia Municipal** (only built in 1952, though you wouldn't know it). On the north side of the cathedral lies the **Rotonda de los Jaliscenses**

**Ilustres**. This Neoclassical circle of seventeen Doric columns is the latest architectural expression of Jaliscan pride and commemorates the state's heroes. Around the cathedral and departing regularly from in front of the Museo Regional, Mercado de San Juan de Dios and the Jardín de San Francisco are *calandrias*, or elegant **horse-drawn covered carriages**. Most drivers are knowledgeable (and entertaining) city guides and charge around M$200 (for 1–5 people) for a forty- to fifty-minute tour.

## Museo Regional

Just north of the cathedral, the **Museo Regional** (Tues–Sat 9am–5.30pm, Sun 9am–4.30pm; M$33, free Sun) is housed in an eighteenth-century colonial mansion. Over time it's been a religious seminary, a barracks and a school; it's now a supremely elegant setting for an extensive and diverse collection. Downstairs, exhibits start with a section devoted to regional **archeology** and range from stone tools and the skeleton of a mammoth to the finest achievements of western Mexican pottery and metalworking. The peoples of the west developed quite separately from those in southern and central Mexico, and there is considerable evidence that they had more contact with South and Central American cultures than with those who would now be regarded as their compatriots. The deep **shaft tombs** displayed here are unique in Mexico, but were common down the Pacific coast in Peru and Ecuador. In the centuries before the Conquest, the Tarascan kingdom, based around Pátzcuaro (see p.370), almost came to rival the strength of the Aztecs – partly due to their more extensive knowledge and use of metals. The Aztecs tried, and failed, to extend their influence over Tarascan territory; it wasn't until after Cortés's destruction of Tenochtitlán that the Tarascans submitted relatively peacefully to the conquistadors.

Upstairs, along with rooms devoted to the state's **modern history** and ethnography, is a sizeable gallery of colonial and modern art. Most remarkable here is the large collection of **nineteenth-century portraiture**, a local tradition that captures relatively ordinary Mexicans in a charmingly naive style.

## Plaza de Armas and the Palacio de Gobierno

On the south side of the cathedral, the **Plaza de Armas** centres on an elaborate *belle époque* rotunda – a present from the people of France – where there's music (often the state band) Tuesday to Friday and Sunday evenings at 6.30pm. Dominating the eastern side of the square is the **Palacio de Gobierno** (daily 9am–8pm; free), recognizable by its Baroque facade with a clock surrounded by elements from the Aztec calendar. Here Padre Miguel Hidalgo y Costilla (the "father of Mexican Independence") proclaimed the abolition of slavery in 1810, and, in 1858, Benito Juárez was saved from the firing squad by the cry of "Los valientes no asesinan" – "the brave don't murder". The overwhelming reason to penetrate the arcaded courtyard, however, is to see the first of the great **Orozco murals**.

The main mural dates from 1937 and is typical of Orozco's work (see box, p.341) – Hidalgo blasts triumphantly through the middle, brandishing his sword against a background of red flags and the fires of battle. Curving around the sides of the staircase, scenes depict the Mexican people's oppression and struggle for liberty, from a pre-Conquest Eden to post-revolutionary emancipation. Upstairs in the domed Congress Hall a smaller Orozco mural (his last, painted just before his death in 1949) also depicts Hidalgo, this time as *El Cura de Dolores* (the priest from Dolores), legislator and liberator of slaves.

△ Orozco mural, Palacio de Gobierno

## Plaza de la Liberación

Back around the cathedral, the largest of the four squares is the **Plaza de la Liberación**, which lies between the cathedral and the **Teatro Degollado**, to the east. Modelled on La Scala in Milan, the theatre was built in the mid-nineteenth century and inaugurated in 1866 during the brief reign of

## José Clemente Orozco

**José Clemente Orozco** (1883–1949) was a member, along with Diego Rivera and David Siqueiros, of the triumvirate of brilliant artists who emerged from the Revolution and transformed Mexican painting into an enormously powerful and populist political statement, especially through the medium of the giant mural. Their chief patron was the state – hence the predominance of their work in official buildings and educational establishments – and their aim was to create a national art that drew on native traditions. Almost all their work is consciously educative, rewriting – or, perhaps better, rediscovering – Mexican history in the light of the Revolution, casting the Imperialists as villains and drawing heavily on pre-Hispanic themes. Orozco, a native of Jalisco (he was born in Zapotlan, now Ciudad Guzmán), was perhaps the least overtly political of the three; certainly, his later work, the greatest of which is here in Guadalajara, often seems ambiguous. As a child he moved to Guadalajara and then to Mexico City, where he was influenced by renowned engraver **José Guadalupe Posada** (see box, p.274) and where he painted murals from 1922 to 1927. Then followed seven years in the US, but it was on his return that his powers as an artist reached their peak, in the late 1930s and 1940s, above all in his works at Guadalajara's Hospicio Cabañas and the University of Guadalajara (see below and p.343).

Maximilian (see Contexts, p.892). It's an imposing, domed Neoclassical building with a Corinthian portico; look on the portico's pediment for a frieze depicting the Greek Muses. A programme of drama and concerts is still staged here, mostly in October during the fiesta, though also sporadically throughout the rest of the year. The impressively restored **interior** (viewing Tues–Sun noon–2pm; free) is notable for its frescoed ceiling, which illustrates scenes from the fourth canto of Dante's *Divine Comedy*.

On either side of the theatre are two small churches, **Santa María** and **San Agustín**, the only remains of a monastery that once stood here. San Agustín has a fine Baroque facade; relatively plain Santa María is one of the oldest churches in the city, built in the seventeenth century on the site of Guadalajara's first cathedral.

### East along the Plaza Tapatía: the Hospicio Cabañas

Behind the theatre is the beginning of the **Plaza Tapatía**, with its view all the way down to the Hospicio Cabañas, home to another set of Orozco's murals. Although the plaza was only constructed in the late nineteenth century (by demolishing some of the city's oldest neighbourhoods), it manages to look as if it has always been there. It takes its name from *tapatío* – an adjective used to describe anything typical of Guadalajara, supposedly derived from the capes worn by Spanish grandees (Guadalajarans themselves are often referred to as *Tapatíos*). Almost entirely lined with swish department stores and glossy office buildings, it's also dotted with modern statuary and fountains – an undeniably attractive place to wander and window-shop.

At its eastern end, the plaza opens out to a broad paved area full of wacky anthropomorphic **bronze sculptures**, the work of Guadalajara native **Alejandro Colunga**. Stretched, squashed and generally distorted human figures form chairs, their patinas rubbed shiny by thousands of tired shoppers and tourists.

Beyond the sculptures, the **Instituto Cultural-Hospicio Cabañas** (Tues–Sat 10am–6pm, Sun 10am–3pm; M$10, free on Sun, M$10 to bring in a camera) was founded as an orphanage by Bishop Juan Cabañas y Crespo in 1805 and took nearly fifty years to complete. Designed by Spanish architect

Manuel Tolsá, the Hospicio is a huge, beautiful and tranquil building, with no fewer than 23 separate patios surrounded by schools of art, music and dance; an art cinema/theatre; various government offices; and a small cafeteria. The chapel, the **Capilla Tolsa**, is a plain and ancient-looking structure in the form of a cross, situated in the central patio right at the heart of the building. Orozco's **murals**, in keeping with their setting, are more spiritual than those in the government palace, but you certainly couldn't call them Christian: the conquistadors are depicted as the Horsemen of the Apocalypse, trampling the native population beneath them. The Man of Fire – who leads the people from their dehumanizing, mechanized oppression – has a symbolic role as liberator, which is clearly the same as that of Hidalgo in the palace murals. In this case, he is a strange synthesis of Christian and Mexican deities, a Christ-Quetzalcoatl figure. There are benches on which you can lie back to appreciate the murals, and also a small museum dedicated to Orozco, with sketches, cartoons and details of the artist's life.

Almost alongside the Hospicio is the vast **Mercado Libertad** (locally known as Mercado San Juan de Dios), which Guadalajarans claim is the world's largest indoor market. Although the building is modern, much of what's inside is thoroughly traditional, and it's one of the few places in the city where you can still haggle over prices. Beyond the touristy souvenir stalls, you'll find *curanderas* offering herbal remedies, dried iguanas (for witches' brews) and the renowned Paracho guitars. There are also countless stalls selling all manner of regional food and vast piles of colourful fruit, vegetables, chocolate and spices and traditional leather goods from saddles to clumpy working boots. The market is huge, chaotic and engrossing, but before you buy crafts here, it's worth paying a visit to the **Instituto de la Artesanía** in the Parque Agua Azul (see opposite), or to the expensive boutiques in Tlaquepaque (see p.344), to get some idea of the potential quality and value of the goods.

Immediately southwest of the Mercado is the **Plaza de los Mariachis**, a place to return after dark to see Guadalajara's finest (see p.351).

### South of the Plaza de Armas: Parque Agua Azul

South of the Plaza de Armas, the churches of **San Francisco** and **Nuestra Señora de Aranzazu** face each other across 16 de Septiembre. San Francisco lies on the site of what was probably Guadalajara's first religious foundation, a Franciscan monastery established in the years just after the Conquest. The present church was begun in 1684 and has a beautiful Baroque facade. Aranzazu, by contrast, is entirely plain on the outside, but conceals a fabulously elaborate interior, with three wildly exuberant, heavily carved and gilded churrigueresque retables. The **Jardín de San Francisco**, which would be pleasantly peaceful were it not for the number of local buses rattling by, lies across from the two churches.

Several buses (marked "Parque Agua Azul") run down from past the Jardín de San Francisco to the **Parque Agua Azul** (Tues–Sun 10am–6.30pm; M$4). You couldn't really describe the park as peaceful: there's always some kind of activity going on and the green areas are permanently packed with kids enjoying the zoo, miniature train rides and playgrounds. An outdoor concert shell (*la concha*) hosts popular free performances on Sundays, and weekends see football games and constant crowds. Nonetheless, by Guadalajara standards, it's a haven of calm, especially during the week, and the entrance fee includes attractions such as a dome full of butterflies; exotic caged birds, including magnificent toucans; a palm house, also full of tropical birds; and a strange, glass-pyramid orchid house.

Perhaps the area's greatest attraction (and accessed from outside the park) is the **Instituto de la Artesanía Jalisciense**, Calzado González Gallo 20 (Mon–Fri 10am–6pm, Sat 10am–5pm, Sun 10am–3pm; free), a showcase for regional crafts that is as much a museum as a shop. Its collection is ambitious, with examples of all sorts of local crafts – furniture, ceramics, toys, glassware, clothing – of the highest quality. Many of the items are expensive, but are worth it when you consider the fine worksmanship.

### West of the Plaza de Armas

The area to the west of the cathedral is a great part of the city for aimless meandering. There has been far less modernization in this direction, and the busy shopping streets, many of them closed to traffic, turn up fascinating glimpses of traditional Mexican life and plenty of odd moments of interest. The small, general **Mercado Corona** is at Santa Monica and Hidalgo. A little further out, the university area is quieter than the centre, the streets broader, and there's also a younger atmosphere, with plenty of good restaurants and cafés. Still further in the same direction are expensive residential areas, interesting in their own way for the contrast to crowded downtown.

The "Ex-Templo de la Compañía", or the **Biblioteca IberoAmericana Octavio Paz** (Mon–Fri 9am–9pm, Sat 9am–5pm; free) – lies just west of the Plaza de Armas at the junction of Pedro Moreno and Colón. Originally a church, the building later became a university lecture hall, during which time the nineteenth-century Neoclassical facade was added and it was decorated with **murals** by **David Siqueiros** and **Amado de la Cueva**. Currently a library, it has dramatic crimson-hued murals depicting workers, peasants and miners in a heroic-socialist style that are open to visitors – they make an interesting contrast to Orozco's work. Outside there's an attractive little plaza, and the pedestrianized streets make a pleasant escape from the traffic, if not the crowds.

Immediately to the north of the *biblioteca* are several examples of the beautiful, little-known Baroque churches that stud Guadalajara. The closest is the **Templo de Santa Monica**, on Santa Monica between San Felípe and Reforma, with fabulously rich doorways and an elegant, stone interior. The nearby **Templo de San Felípe Neri**, San Felípe at Contreras Medellin, is a few years younger – dating from the second half of the eighteenth century – and more sumptuously decorated, with a superb facade and lovely tower. Both of these churches have extravagant rain-spouts, which take the form of dragons on San Felípe. A block along Gonzales Ortega, at the corner of Garibaldi, the **Templo de las Capuchinas** is, conversely, plain and fortress-like; inside, though, it's more interesting, with paintings and a lovely vaulted brick roof. Back south towards Juárez and the main drag, the **Museo de la Ciudad**, Independencia 684 (Tues–Sat 10am–5.30pm, Sun 10am–2.30pm; M$7), housed in a former convent, showcases the city's history through photos and artefacts.

Back on the main route west, at Juárez and 8 de Julio, the **Ex-Convento del Carmen** was one of the city's richest monasteries, but its wealth has largely been stripped, leaving an austere, white building of elegant simplicity. Modern art exhibitions, dance events and concerts are regularly staged here.

### The University and the Zona Minerva

The **University** is a fifteen-minute walk west along Juárez from the centre, but if you're heading any further this direction, you may want to take a bus or taxi (anything heading for the Plaza del Sol should pass all the areas below, or look for "Par Vial").

The Parque Revolución, immediately west of Federalismo (and the north–south Tren Ligero line), marks the start of the campus of the **Universidad de Guadalajara**. A couple of hundred metres on you can see more of **Orozco**'s major murals, among the first he painted in Guadalajara, in the **Museo de las Artes**, López Cotilla 930 (Tues–Fri 10am–6pm, Sat & Sun 10am–4pm; free). Head for the main hall (*paraninfo*) to see the frescoed dome and front wall. Again, the theme of the works fits the setting: the dome shows the glories and benefits of learning, while the wall shows the oppressed masses crying out for books and education, which are being denied them by fat capitalists and the military. Immediately south of the museum is the **Templo Expiatorio**, a modern neo-Gothic church modelled on Orvieto cathedral in Italy and featuring some innovative stained glass and an attractive altarpiece.

Beyond the university, Juárez changes its name to Vallarta, and the character of the street changes rapidly, too. Within ten blocks, around the major junction of Vallarta and Chapultepec, you find yourself in what could be a different city. The **Zona Minerva** – far quieter than the blocks to the east – is a place of broad avenues, expensive shops and pleasant restaurants. The best are a couple of blocks south along López Cotilla, an altogether more pleasant place to stroll than busy Vallarta.

Further west along Vallarta, the vast **Centro Magno** shopping centre has upscale shops and international fast-food restaurants, and makes an air-conditioned respite on a hot day. Opposite is an American Express office and the offices for a number of airlines, including American, Aero California, Mexicana and Aviacsa. Beyond Centro Magno, Vallarta crosses the major artery of López Mateos at the **Minerva Circle**, an intersection marked by a double triumphal arch. This Neoclassical **Monumento Los Arcos** (daily 8am–7pm; free) contains a colourful mural and stairs up to the roof, which has good views.

Most buses turn left at the Minerva Circle down López Mateos Sur towards the **Plaza del Sol**, a vast commercial development said to be one of the largest in Latin America. There's an enormous shopping centre, as well as administrative offices, and inside a couple of good cafés, an ice-cream parlour and, in the evenings, several nightclubs. Also on López Mateos are numerous big hotels and themed restaurants – all very much the modern face of suburban Mexico.

## San Pedro Tlaquepaque and Tonalá

The most celebrated of Guadalajara's suburbs, **TLAQUEPAQUE** (officially San Pedro Tlaquepaque) has traditionally been famous for its artesanías and its **mariachi** bands. Once a separate town some 5km southeast of the centre, it has long since been absorbed by urban sprawl, and most of its traditional crafts taken over almost entirely by chi-chi designer-furniture and jewellery stores. This said, some of the area's most desirable **crafts** – ceramics, glass, jewellery, textiles and more – are still to be found. Standards are high, but the stores are not intimidatingly exclusive and, though for the most part prices are high, there are usually some moderately priced goods, notably ceramics and glassware.

Tlaquepaque centres around a pleasantly laid-back main square complete with bandstand, on whose north side is the blockish church of **San Pedro**. To the west of the square, the three-domed **Nuestra Virgen de la Soledad** is an almost equally distinctive landmark. Along the square's south side runs Independencia, Tlaquepaque's main street. At the plaza's southeast corner you'll find **El Parian**, an enclosed plaza that is, in effect, the biggest bar that you've ever seen. Since most of the shops close down for a siesta, you have every excuse to hang out here for a couple of hours. There are actually a dozen or so separate

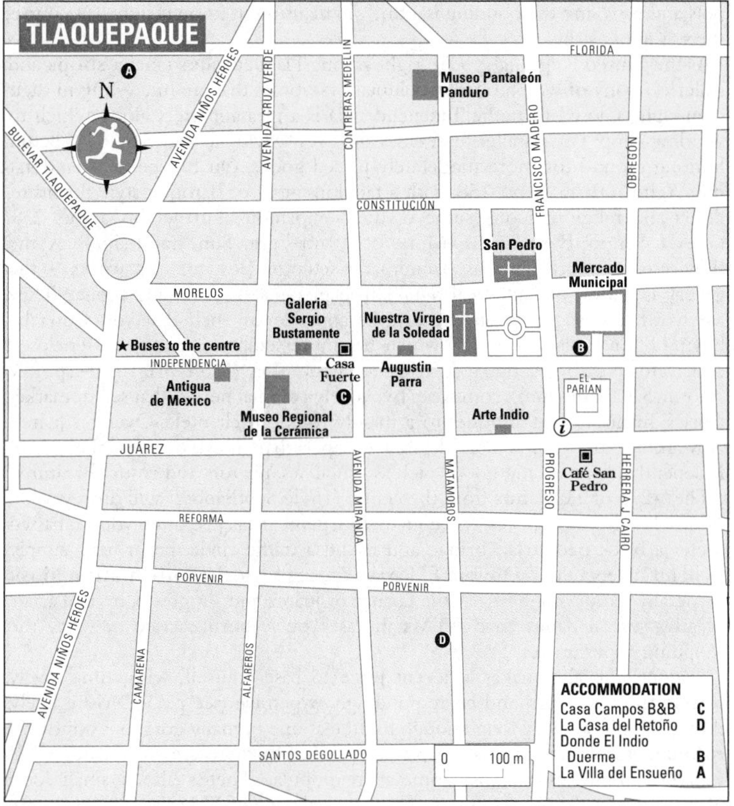


establishments around this giant courtyard, but since everyone sits outside, the tables tend to overlap and strolling serenaders wander around at random, it all feels like one enormous place. They all charge much the same, too, and offer the same limited range of food – basically *birria,* quesadillas and *queso fundido* – plus lots to drink: prices seem reasonable on the menu, but be sure to check the bill for added service charges. At the weekend, particularly Sunday afternoons, you'll see mariachi at its best here, when the locals come along and offer their own vocal renditions to the musicians' backing. On weekdays it can be disappointingly quiet (or pleasantly peaceful, depending on your fondness for mariachi).

For an insight into just how wonderful the local ceramics can be, visit the **Museo Pantaleón Panduro**, Princiliano Sánchez at Flórida (Tues–Sat 10am–6pm, Sun 10am–5pm; free), which was named after the father of Jaliscan ceramicists. Here you can see exemplary prize-winning pieces from the museum's annual ceramics competition (held each June). To learn something of the techniques used, visit the small **Museo Regional de la Cerámica**, Independencia 237 (Mon–Sat 10am–6pm, Sun 10am–4pm; free), which has displays of pottery not only from Tlaquepaque but from all over the state, especially Tonalá (see p.346). Beyond the individual works of some of the finest craftsmen, there's a traditional kitchen on display, complete with all its plates, pots and pans, and the building is a fine old mansion in its own right. Of course, there is also a store.

At the Museo Regional, you're right among Tlaquepaque's fancier **shops** and galleries, many of which occupy colonial-era houses that are interesting in their own right. Closed to traffic, Independencia is a pleasant street along which to window-shop. The parallel Juárez is a little less exclusive and may be a better hunting ground for more moderately priced goods. On Independencia, don't miss Agustín Parra, at no. 158, with a fabulous array of Baroque-style furniture, doors and religious icons, some of them enormous. Further up, at no. 238, Galeria Sergio Bustamante (Mon–Sat 10am–7pm, Sun noon–4pm) is the showcase for world-famous painter and sculptor Bustamente's works – the gallery is full of his fantastical figures in papier-mâché, resin and bronze. They are worth looking at, even if the price and size are such that you won't be buying. Don't miss the toilet, which has more sculpture in its own enclosed courtyard. Nearby, Antigua de México, at no. 255 (Mon–Fri 10am–2pm & 3–7pm, Sat 10am–6pm), comprises two lovely colonial houses that sell upmarket fabrics, furniture and antiques to a mainly Mexican clientele. Over on Juárez, Arte Indio, no. 130, is considerably cheaper than most of the galleries on Independencia, stocking goods such as crucifixes, mirrors and rustic furniture.



The #275 or TUR **bus** from the centre (16 de Septiembre) will drop you on Niños Héroes at the western end of Independencia, just after you've passed under a brick pedestrian bridge and round a traffic circle. From here, simply walk up Independencia toward El Parian. There's a **tourist information kiosk** (generally daily 9am–8pm) at the corner of Juárez and Progresso, by El Parian. Nearby, several banks have **ATMs** in case you've been carried away by the shopping experience.

Tlaquepaque also makes a decent place to base yourself, with some lovely **hotels**, mostly superb and correspondingly expensive (see p.336). More likely, though, you'll just stay long enough to dine at one of many gorgeous courtyard **restaurants**. We've listed a couple on p.350, but there are many more; just wander around and choose somewhere popular. There's also a small local **Mercado Municipal**; its entrance is the north side of El Parian.

### Tonalá

There's more of a workaday feel to **TONALÁ**, a ceramics manufacturing centre some 8km southeast of Tlaquepaque. Like that town, it was once an autonomous village, but that's where the similarities end. There are no pedestrian streets, far fewer designer home-furnishing stores and the emphasis is more on the crafts themselves. Goods are cheaper, too, especially if you go (as you should) for the animated **street markets** (Thurs & Sun roughly 8am–4pm), when Tonaltecas Sur is clogged with stalls selling all sorts of ceramic goods, glassware and handicrafts. Some are pretty good value, some are factory seconds, and others are just junk.

Specific sights are limited, but you might like to visit the **Museo Nacional de la Cerámica**, Constitución 104 (Mon–Fri 10am–5pm, Sat & Sun 10am–3pm; free), which has both contemporary and antique pots from every Mexican state. Mostly, though, Tonalá is about strolling and browsing, but if you've more than a passing interest in ceramics it is worth making for some specific **shops**. Start with Mis Amores, Tonaltecas Sur 80, which has all sorts of ceramics, papier-mâché and sheetmetal work including designs based on the works of Posada (see box, p.274), such as *La Catrina*, his famous skeleton woman with a huge floral hat. Close to Tonalá's central plaza, visit Galeria José Bernabe, Hidalgo 83, the place to come for superb and highly regarded *petatillo*,

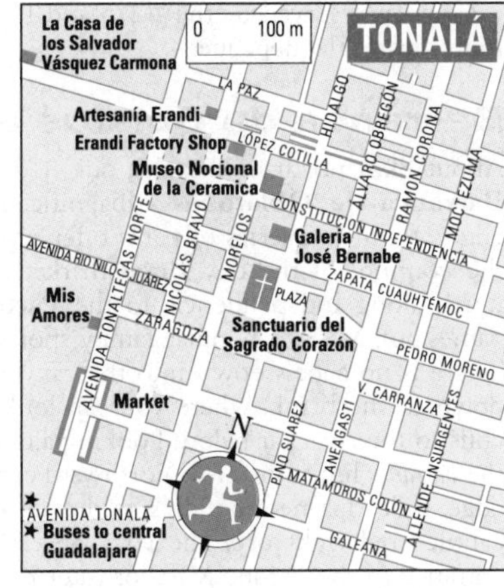


an intricate ceramic form with painted animals and flowers on a cross-hatched background. A few blocks further north at Artesanía Erandi, López Cotilla 118, you can head out the back of the shop to see artisans hand-painting plates. The plates are made at the factory virtually across the road, and they export all over the world. Moving west, you'll need to knock on the bright green door to gain access to La Casa de Salvador Vásquez Carmona, López Cotilla 328. Around the rear patio, Carmona shapes pots and bowls, hand-fires them, then paints the finished article. He'll show you his gallery complete with finished pots that have graced the covers of magazines and design glossies.

**To get to Tonalá** from the centre of town, take a #275 or TUR bus heading south on 16 de Septiembre. Get off at the corner of Avenida Tonalá and Tonaltecas Sur. Three blocks north you'll find the **tourist office**, Tonaltecas Sur 140, in the Casa de Artesanos (Mon–Fri 9am–3pm; ⓣ33/3284-3092), which gives out free maps and runs town tours. Bilingual tours can be arranged if you call a couple of days in advance.

## Zapopan

**ZAPOPAN**, some 7km northwest of the city centre, is the site of the **Basílica de la Virgen de Zapopan**, one of the most important churches in the city, much revered by the Huichol people. Pope John Paul II gave a Mass in the giant **Plaza de las Américas** in front of the church during a visit to Mexico in 1979; a statue commemorates the event. The Baroque temple houses a miraculous image of the Virgin: the 250mm-high figure was dedicated to the local Indians by a Franciscan missionary, Antonio de Segovia, after he had intervened in a battle between them and the conquistadors. Since then, it has been constantly venerated and is still the object of pilgrimages, especially on October 12, when several hundred thousand people gather early in the morning to march the Virgin back to the Basílica after an annual six-month tour of all the churches in Guadalajara. Crowds and assorted food vendors start arriving the night before, and the *portales* are choked with people bedding down to be ready for the procession's 4am start.

Beside the church, the small **Museo Huichol Wixarica de Zapopan** (Mon–Sat 10am–1.30pm & 3.30–6pm; M$5), an ethnographic museum, exhibits clothes and objects relating to Huichol traditions, as well as a photographic display of their modern way of life. They also sell Huichol crafts, including psychedelic yarn paintings (*cuadros de estambre*) and beadwork.

Just east of the Plaza de las Américas, the **Museo de Arte de Zapopan**, Andador 20 de Noviembre 166 (Tues–Wed & Fri–Sun 10am–6pm, Thurs 10am–10pm; M$20) is Guadalajara's most outstanding contemporary art gallery. Changing exhibitions cherry-pick the best talent from Mexico and abroad – painting, sculpture, photography, video installations, you name it.

Zapopan is served by the #275 and TUR **buses** at the opposite end of their routes from Tlaquepaque.

## Barranca de Oblatos and the zoo

About 8km north of the city, out at the end of Calzada Independencia, the **Barranca de Oblatos** is a magnificent 600-metre-deep canyon, along the edge of which a series of parks offer superb views and a welcome break from the confines of the city. Buses marked "Parque Mirador" (notably #60) run north along Independencia to the **Parque Mirador Independencia** (daily 7am–7pm; M$2), a popular family spot with picnic areas and excellent views. There is no access down into the canyon from here, but concrete paths wind down to the brink, where you can look gaze down past vegetated bluffs and cliffs to the river far below. Looking along the canyon it becomes evident how the *barranca* limits the city's northward expansion, as buildings come right to the edge. Indeed, a new building at the adjacent design and architecture school is cantilevered right over the void. Several good cafés and restaurants near the entrance to the Parque Mirador cater to student budgets.

About 1500m back down Independencia towards the city is the **Zoológico Guadalajara** (Wed–Sun 10am–6pm; M$42), which has superb canyon views from its northern end, along with a relatively well-kept selection of Mexican and international wildlife. Opened in 1988, the modern zoo also features an ecological centre that works to preserve a range of endangered species through education and reproduction initiatives. World-renowned artist Sergio Bustamante created the monkey sculptures that greet visitors at the zoo's entrance. Assorted entry packages also give access to a train ride through the zoo and a twenty-minute Masai Mara truck "safari" through an open area populated with African beasts.

The adjacent **Selva Mágica** (Mon–Fri 10am–6pm, Sat & Sun 10am–8pm; entry packages M$70–100) offers all manner of amusement park rides.

## Eating

As a rule, *Tapatíos* take their food seriously. Guadalajara boasts literally hundreds of **places to eat**, ranging from elegant restaurants to unpretentious cafés, and from *loncherías* (cafés with an emphasis on short orders) to *neverías* (with ice cream and fresh-fruit drinks). Don't pass up the **street vendors** either – their fresh tacos and bags of spiced fruit are delicious and make a cheap, healthy snack.

### Gastronomía Jalisciense: Tapatío specialities

While in Guadalajara, you shouldn't miss out on some of Jalisco's culinary specialities. The most celebrated is **birria**, stewed beef or mutton in a spicy, but not particularly hot, sauce, and served with tortillas or in tacos from street stalls, bars and in markets. **Roast goat** is another favourite, often seen in the markets along with a goat's skull (just in case you don't know what *chivo* means). **Pozole**, a stew of pork and hominy (ground maize) is also popular, and typically found as a restaurant special on Thursdays. Rarely seen much beyond the city limits, there's also **torta ahogada** (literally "drowned sandwich"), a bread roll stuffed with a filling of your choice (traditionally pork) then drenched with a thin, spicy salsa that soaks right through the bread. It's a bit messy, but extremely delicious. And then, of course, there's **tequila**, discussed more fully on p.356.

For basic meals, the mezzanine of the **Mercado Libertad** has seemingly hundreds of little stands, each displaying their own specialities. There's a more limited, but handier, selection at the **Mercado Corona**.

In the centre, your best choice is west of the cathedral, where traditional cafés and restaurants line **Juárez**. Though there are plenty of more **expensive** places round the centre, they tend to be rather dull: in the evenings, locals are far more likely to be found out in the suburbs. A good and relatively close hunting ground is **López Cotilla**, a few blocks west of the university.

### Downtown

**Alta Fibra** Sanchez 370, between Ocampo and Galeana. As the name suggests, *Alta Fibra* specializes in high-fibre foods; the menu isn't strictly vegetarian, but is low fat. Excellent-value comida corrida (M$35), and a range of other bargain dishes. There's also a wholemeal bakery next door. Closed Sun.

**El Asador** upstairs at Moreno 466. Pleasant, reasonably priced restaurant specializing in grilled meat, such as *carne asada* (M$65) and *arranchera* (M$95), or meat on a platter with heaps of salsa, *frijoles* and tortillas as accompaniment. Try for a table by the window.

**Birrieria Las Nueve Esquinas** Colón 384. Peacefully set on a quiet plaza, this little restaurant serves up traditional Mexican mutton dishes and does and excellent *birria de chivo* (goat stew; M$49 or M$69).

**Café Madoka** Gonzalez Martínez 78. Big, traditional café, operating since 1959 and serving tasty breakfasts (especially the *chilaquiles gratinados*), soups and *antojitos* (mostly around M$50). You can also just play a game of dominoes and sip a coffee; try the "Café Madoka Especial", served with a dollop of vanilla ice cream.

**Café Madrid** Juárez 264 near Corona. A smallish 1950s-style diner and coffee bar, good for moderately priced breakfasts (M$32), comidas corridas and sandwiches (8am–10pm). Try the *queso fundido* with chorizo (M$38).

**Cafe Red** Ocampo 218. Cool little café – there's a wall of images of Frida Kahlo. It's a nice spot to relax with a magazine and a coffee, grab lunch (baguettes M$25, salads M$25–30) or a cheap beer (M$10). Open afternoons and evenings until 11pm or midnight. Closed Sun.

**Caffe O Le** Donata Guerra 25. Intimate city café with good lattes and complex infusions (such as cherry, banana and Jamaica blossom). Also a wide range of cakes and breakfast and coffee combos for around M$30.

**La Chata** Corona 126. Excellent medium-priced Mexican dishes, including *mole* and *platillo jalisciense* (chicken with side snacks; M$67). Hugely popular with local families since 1942. Extensive breakfasts go from M$61 and a big jug of sangria costs M$85.

**Chong Wah** Juárez 558. Moderately priced Cantonese food to eat in or take away. Their buffet lunch is very reasonable at M$48.

**La Fonda de San Miguel** Donata Guerra 25 ⓣ33/3613-0793, ⓦwww.lafondadesanmiguel.com. In the heart of the *centro histórico*, this delightful restaurant is set in the courtyard of a former convent. The daytime tinkling fountain and caged birds are replaced at night by a constellation of pinprick lampshades in creative imitation of the night sky. Try the excellent *sopa de tortillas* (M$33), perhaps followed by the "Molcajete San Miguel" (M$90), a big stone mortar filled with a steaming stew of chicken, mushrooms, onions and cheese.

**Lido** Colón 294, at San Miguel Blanco. Spanish-style bar and restaurant, serving good, moderately priced Mexican *moles*, sandwiches, snacks and a M$50 set menu. Open 24 hours.

**Mariscos Galeana** Galeana 154, at López Cotilla. Seafood restaurant with prawn and octopus (M$55–95), among other delicious dishes; there's live music at lunch time.

**Pastelería Luvier** Colón 183. One of the best of many *panaderías* and *pastelerias* in the centre.

**La Rinconada** Morelos 86, at Callejón del Diable, Plaza Tapatía ⓣ33/3613-9914. In a glorious colonial setting, this moderately expensive restaurant serves seafood dishes (salmon with fine herbs or *pimiento verde* for M$89), US-style steaks (from M$135) and Mexican specialities. Their lunch buffet is good value at M$54.

**El Tacazo** Juárez 246. Fast, flavourful tacos; popular and cheap, though choices such as *lengua* (tongue) and *cabeza* (head) are not for the timid.

**Taquería Los Faroles** Corona 250. Popular taco and torta joint with a wide range of tacos served till midnight daily. It's a good place to have your first taste of *torta ahogada* (M$20), washed down with *horchata*.

**Villa Madrid** López Cotilla 551 at Gonzalez Martínez. Great *licuados*, fruit salads and yogurt, as well as sandwiches and salads.

### University and further out

**La China Poblana** Juárez 887. Reasonably priced, traditional Puebla dishes, including *mole* and *chiles en nogada*.

**Goa** López Cotilla 1520 ⓣ33/3615-6173. Guadalajara's only Indian restaurant, intimately lit and with Bollywood on the screen. Serves a range of excellent dishes, several straight out of the tandoor. Mains are mostly M$80 though several vegetarian options are only M$60. Closed Mon.

**Los Itacates** Chapultepec Nte 110, at Sierra ⓣ33/3825-1106. Traditional Mexican food (mains around M$50) with live-music evenings. Tables best booked in advance.

**Pierrot** Justo Sierra 2355 ⓣ33/3630-2087. The city's finest French restaurant, in gracious surroundings and with attentive but never intrusive service. The duck in orange sauce and chocolate mousse are both spectacular. Closed Sun evening.

**La Trattoria** Niños Héroes 3051 ⓣ33/3122-1817. The lively Italian restaurant is one of Guadalajara's best. *Segundi piatti* such as trout amandine and shrimp linguine go for around the M$130 mark. Evening reservations recommended.

### Tlaquepaque

**Café San Pedro** Juárez 81. Tlaquepaque's best coffee, with seating under the *portales* and a great range of teas and cakes.

**Casa Fuerte** Independencia 224 ⓣ33/3635-9015. Pleasant courtyard restaurant in a majestic mansion. Enjoy the live accompaniment, often mariachi, while you sample the likes of tamarind shrimp or salmon in caper butter.

## Drinking and nightlife

Traditionally the downtown area hasn't been that lively, but things are picking up, particularly southwest of the cathedral (along López Madero, Madero and Sanchez) and in the **Nueve Esquinas** quarter, three blocks further south, where Colon and Galeana meet. Most of the fashionable, younger-crowd *Tapatíos* tend to hang out in the distant moneyed suburbs – the **Plaza del Sol complex**, for example, houses a couple of clubs, as do many of the big hotels out that way. Any of them will knock a sizeable hole in your wallet. There are more clubs where Juárez becomes **Avenida Vallarta** (most of which enforce the "no jeans or sneakers" policy typical at Mexican nightspots). **Avenida López Mateos** has a number of trendy pubs with live music and a younger crowd. Some have open bars on certain nights of the week in exchange for a cover charge of around M$100 for men, M$50 or less for women.

Guadalajara has a reputation for being one of Mexico's gayest cities, and while that doesn't mean public displays of affection are widely accepted, there's greater freedom in the dozen or so bars and clubs that advertise their orientation with rainbow flags. Guadalajara's **gay quarter** is centred on the junction of Ocampo and Sanchez, about five blocks southwest of the cathedral. *La Presciliana* (see opposite) is a good place to start, and Spanish readers can check out what's going on at ⓦwww.gaygdl.com.

**Antigues del Carmen** Jacobo Galvez 45-B, at Juárez ⓣ33/3658-2266. Decent restaurant that spills out onto a shaded plaza where dancers of all ages (though mostly older couples) come to twirl elegantly to the strains of recorded Latin music until around 1am – *danzon* on Sat, bossa nova on Sun. No cover charge, but food and drink prices have an entertainment component built in. Alternatively, you can just hang out under the trees and listen for free.

**El Baron** upstairs at Corona 181. Traditional restaurant-bar with Latin music. There are usually live performances Wed–Sun. Daily 7pm–5am.

**Casa Bariachi** Vallarta 2221. Loud and colourful restaurant-bar decorated with giant piñatas and full of mariachi bands. Closed Sun.

**El Duende del Sacromonte** Pedro Moreno 1388, at the corner of Robles Gil. Lively bar worth visiting on Fri nights for its rumba and flamenco dancing.

**Hotel Francés** Maestranza 35. Piano-bar-style establishment in the courtyard of one of the centre's grander hotels. Come in the early evening (before 8pm) for happy-hour drinks typically accompanied by mariachi or piano-based trios.

**La Maestranza** Maestranza 179. Fairly straightforward drinking bar made all the more appealing by walls completely plastered with bullfight promo posters (plus a few bull's heads above the bar). DJs at weekends and moderately priced drinks.

**La Moresca** López Cotilla 1835, at De Cervantes Savedra. Lively late-closing restaurant and bar that makes a good spot for a bottle of house wine and a *bruschetta*.

**El Mutualismo** Madero 553. On Thurs and Sat nights this cavernous venue (normally a cantina) gets taken over by a Cuban band and everyone hits the dancefloor. Ceiling fans and wide-open windows give a suitably Cuban dancehall feel. Fri sometimes sees rock bands play. M$10 cover.

**La Presciliana** Sanchez 407. Dark and chilled-out gay bar (straights welcome) with casual drinking to Latin dance beats. A good place to kick the night off – then follow the crowds.

**El Teu Lloc** López Cotilla 570. The emphasis here is on drinking, but they also do very good pizza (M$50–65) and stuffed baguettes (M$45–50). There's a different house band every night, mostly acoustic, Latin, jazz and world music. Bands start around 9pm; things usually close down by midnight, so it's a good place to begin your night out.

## Entertainment

There's an impressive range of traditional Mexican and classical concerts, contemporary gigs, classic and modern film, theatre and opera performances and art exhibitions in town – you can see some kind of performance most nights of the week. Anyone on a tight budget should check out the **Plaza de Armas**, where there's usually something free happening. One thing no visitor to Guadalajara should miss is hearing mariachi in its hometown, specifically at the **Plaza de los Mariachis**.

Going to the **cinema** in Guadalajara is not particularly convenient, as suburban multiplexes have killed downtown movies. The big shopping centres such as Centro Magno and Plaza del Sol have the latest blockbusters, and we've also listed a couple of more convenient alternatives.

Several entertaining **festivals** take place throughout the year including: the highly animated **Día de San Pedro** in Tlaquepaque (June 29), with mariachi, dancing and processions; and the **Día de la Virgen de Zapopan** (Oct 12), an all-night fiesta capped with a massive early-morning procession that starts before dawn at the cathedral and finishes in Zapopan. Crowds and assorted food vendors start arriving the evening before, when there all sorts of music and the *portales* are choked with people bedding down for the 4am start.

In the autumn, everything cranks up to fever pitch for the **Fiestas de Octubre** (Ⓦwww.fiestasdeoctubre.com.mx), a month-long celebration when downtown Guadalajara comes alive with all manner of outdoor performances and bands, often free. Daily events include *charreadas* (rodeos), processions and fireworks, as well as all kinds of free entertainment – modern Mexican music performances are put on from noon till 10pm in the fairgrounds of the Benito Juárez auditorium.

### Live music

**Instituto Cultural Mexicano Norteamericano de Jalisco** Enrique Díaz de León 300 Ⓣ33/3825-5838, Ⓦwww.institutocultural.com.mx. Hosts classical music concerts and recitals year-round.

**Plaza de Armas** Regular free performances of Jaliscan music in the rotunda just south of the cathedral (Tues–Fri & Sun 6.30pm).

**Plaza Fundadores** Open area behind the Teatro Degollado that sometimes sees music or drama performances at weekends; often free.

**Plaza de los Mariachis** Guadalajara is the home of mariachi, and you shouldn't leave town without experiencing it. You needn't spend anything at all in the Plaza de los Mariachis, really a short pedestrianized street by the Mercado Libertad and the church of San Juan de Dios, where mariachi bands stroll between bars, playing to anyone prepared to cough up for a song. Players start arriving in the late afternoon but the best listening happens just after dark, when there are usually several bands. If they play for you personally, you'll have to negotiate a price before they start, probably around M$100 for one or two songs, but only M$200 for five. You'll also find mariachi bands out in Tlaquepaque.

**Teatro Degollado** This magnificent theatre in central Guadalajara hosts a regular programme of theatre and dance. Pick up details of events from the tourist office.

### Cinema

**Cineclub Alianza** Alianza Francesa, López Cotilla 1199 ⓣ33/3825-2140, ⓦwww.alianzafrancesa.org.mx/guadalajara. Occasional French films usually subtitled in Spanish.
**Cinépolis Centro Magno** Vallarta 2425. ⓣ33/3540-9090, ⓦwww.cinepolis.com.mx. The most convenient multiplex, around 3km west of downtown. Most movies dubbed in Spanish.
**Ex-Convento del Carmen** Juárez 638 ⓣ33/3030-1390. Alternative and classic movies, plus the occasional festival. Films usually shown in their original language. Tickets M$60.

## Sport

Jaliscans pride themselves on their equestrian skills, notably in the regular *charreadas* (**rodeos**) held every Sunday (from noon) at the Licenzo Charro de Jalisco, Dr Michel 577 near the Parque Agua Azul. For details call ⓣ33/3619-3232 or just turn up and expect to pay around M$35.

**Bullfights** are considered to be a sport for connoisseurs, and the cognoscenti watch the *corrida* at the city's largest bullring, the Plaza de Toros Nuevo Progreso (ⓣ33/3637-9982, ⓦwww.plazanuevoprogreso.com.mx), almost 4km northeast of the centre along Calzada Independencia. Fights occur several times in October, then on irregular Sundays until March (4.30pm; tickets M$50–300).

Almost opposite the bullring is the enormous Estadio Jalisco, where *Tapatíos* go to watch their favourite sport, **football**. It was a venue for matches at both the 1970 and 1986 World Cups, but is primarily the stadium for FC Guadalajara (Las Chivas; ⓦwww.chivascampeon.com) who play their home matches here (usually Sat night and Sun afternoon). Tickets start from as little as M$60, though for around M$250 you can get a really good seat. The city's two other top-division teams – Atlas (ⓦwww.atlas.com.mx) and Tecos (ⓦwww.tecos.com.mx) – also play here from time to time.

Buses #60, #62 and the Independencia trolley run up Calzada Independencia past the bullring and football stadium.

## Listings

**Airlines and flights** Several offices at Vallarta 2440, opposite Centro Magno, 3km west of downtown. Aerocalifornia, Vallarta 2440 (ⓣ33/3616-2525); Aeroméxico, Corona 196, at Madero (ⓣ33/2376-1180); American, Vallarta 2440 (ⓣ33/3688-5646); Continental, at the airport (ⓣ33/3688-5902); Delta, López Cotilla 1701 (ⓣ33/3630-3130); Mexicana, airport and Vallarta 2440 (ⓣ33/3615-3227); Taca, Vallarta 2440 (ⓣ33/3630-1235).
**American Express** Vallarta 2440, opposite Centro Magno ⓣ33/3818-2319 (Mon–Fri 9am–6pm, Sat 9am–1pm).
**Banks and exchange** There are numerous banks (all with ATMs) throughout the centre, including a cluster around Corona and Juárez. Virtually identical rates, faster service and longer hours are available in the dense cluster of casas de cambio around the corner of Maestranza and López Cotilla. After hours, the bigger hotels will usually change money at a considerably worse rate. Alternatively, try American Express (see above) or Thomas Cook, Circunvalación Agustín Yañez 2343-D ⓣ33/3669-5507.
**Books** You're better off looking for English-language books & magazines in Chapala and Ajijic (see p.357 and p.358), but you will find limited supplies at Sanborn's, Juárez between 16 de Septiembre and Corona, and at Vallarta 1600. Downtown, try Librería Gonvill, López Costilla and Guerra, which has a few novels. Way out west in Colonia Chapalita, Sandi Bookstore, Tepeyac 718, has a stack of books in English, including travel guides.
**Car rental** Agents can be found at the airport, as well as downtown, where they're concentrated on Niños Héroes near the *Sheraton* (not far from the Parque Agua Azul); these include Budget, Niños Héroes 934 (ⓣ33/3613-0027, or at the airport ⓣ33/3688-5531); Europcar, Niños Héroes 3070 (ⓣ33/3122-6979); Hertz, at the airport (ⓣ33/3688-5633); National, Niños Héroes 961-C (ⓣ33/3614-7175; Quick, Niños Héroes 954 (ⓣ33/3614-2247); and Thrifty, Niños Héroes 963-2 (ⓣ33/3121-7236).

## Moving on from Guadalajara

If you're heading to destinations within about 150km of Guadalajara, chances are you're best off heading to the **Central Vieja** (see p.332). Here you'll find **second-class bus** services to places such as Chapala, Ajijic, Tequila and Tapalpa. A few first-class services to these same destinations also leave from here, so it is worth looking around to see who offers the best deal.

All **long-distance buses** leave from the **Central Nueva**, way out in suburbia (see p.332). To get there from the centre, pick up the #616, #644, the faster TUR bus, or anything marked "Central Nueva" heading south along 16 de Septiembre. The more popular destinations seem to have buses from just about every building. In general, salas 1 and 2 serve destinations in **Jalisco**, Colima and **Michoacán**, plus **Pátzcuaro** and many of the premium services to Mexico City; Mexico City via **Morelia**; and many towns in the Bajío. Salas 3 and 4 have buses to the north and northwest, with services to Puerta Vallarta; the US border; and up the Pacific coast, plus points en route. Sala 5 is for eastbound services towards San Luis Potosí and Tampico, as well as some more local services; Sala 6 serves the Bajío, the northeast and many local second-class buses; and Sala 7 serves the north and northeast again, as well as Mexico City.

From the airport (see p.331) there are constant **flights** to Mexico City, as well as departures to most other Mexican cities and direct connections to many US, Canadian and Central American destinations.

**Consulates** Canada, *Hotel Fiesta Americana*, Local 30, Aurelio Aceves 225 (☎33/3615-5642); El Salvador, Guadalupe 4358, Colonía Camino Real (☎33/3121-8712); Honduras, Regidores 1114, Colonía Chapultepec (☎33/3817-4998); UK, Jesús de Rojas 20, Colonía Los Pinos (☎33/3343-2296); and the US, Progreso 175, Colonía Americana (☎33/3268-2100). The tourist office (see p.334) has a complete list of addresses for all consulates.
**Emergencies** The general emergency number is ☎066. The police station is way out to the east of the city, and it's easier to report a crime or accident at the Procuraduría de Justicia (Justice Department), Av la Paz 2873 (☎33/3688-5588).
**Internet access** There are several Internet cafés in central Guadalajara, many within easy walking distance of the cathedral. The strongest competition is west on Juárez around the Ex-Convento del Carmen, but prices vary little from M$12–15/hr. The places marked on our map are at: Maestranza 163, Paseo Degollado 90, Gonzalez Martirez 124, Juárez 642 and Juárez 679.
**Laundry** The closest laundry to the centre is at Aldama 125, off Independencia in a slightly rough area a few blocks south of the Mercado Libertad (Mon–Sat 9am–7pm).
**Markets and shopping** The giant Mercado Libertad may be the biggest of Guadalajara's markets, but every city barrio has its own. They include the very touristy Mercado Corona near the cathedral, and craft markets and upscale boutiques in Tlaquepaque and Tonalá. The flea market El Baratillo (Sun) is vast, sometimes stretching a mile or more along Javier Mina, starting a dozen blocks east of the Mercado Libertad. The city is also big on nutritionists, and health-food/aromatherapy stores; head for López Cortilla if you're after some Echinacea, green tea or muscle-building protein powder.
**Pharmacy** Farmacia Guadalajara, with several locations in the centre including Moreno 160 near Plaza Tapatía (open 24hr). There's another branch at López Cotilla 423 at Galeana (daily 7am–10pm).
**Phones** Dedicated phone offices have all but died out in Guadalajara. Either use a phonecard from one of the relatively quiet phones around Plaza Tapatía, or try one of the Internet places that do cheap VOIP calls.
**Post office** Venustiano Carranza 16 at the junction with Independencia (Mon–Fri 8am–7pm, Sat 9am–1pm).
**Spanish courses** Guadalajara makes a pretty decent place to learn Spanish, with several schools handily sited close to downtown. One of the most popular is IMAC, Donata Guerra 180 at Madero (☎33/3613-1080, Ⓦwww.spanish-school.com.mx) with a flexible schedule allowing short or long courses as well as special-interest classes in ceramics, guitar and flamenco, among other options, and homestay opportunities. Others worth considering are Guadalajara University's CEPE, Tomás V Gómez 125

(Ⓣ33/3616-4399, Ⓦwww.cepe.udg.mx) and the Instituto Cultural Mexicano Norteamericano de Jalisco Díaz de León 300 (Ⓣ33/3825-5838, Ⓦwww.institutocultural.com.mx).

**Travel agents** There are plenty of travel agents around the centre, including in the lobbies of all the big hotels, or head for American Express or Thomas Cook (see "Banks and exchange").

# Tequila and around

The approach to **TEQUILA**, some 50km northwest of Guadalajara, is through great fields of spiky cactus-like blue agave. It's from these rugged plants that the quintessentially Mexican liquor is produced in vast quantities at local distilleries. They've made tequila (see box, p.356) here since the sixteenth century, with the *indígenas* fermenting its precursor for at least 1500 years before that. It is this long and well-preserved legacy that earned Tequila and its surroundings UNESCO World Heritage status in 2006.

The town itself is a pretty enough little place, though its fine church and smattering of bourgeois mansions are somewhat overwhelmed by the trappings of thriving modern business. But no matter: you don't come here to sightsee, you come to drink, or at least to visit the distilleries. Easily the most popular and slickest operation in town is run by **José Cuervo**, which seems to have taken over several blocks immediately north of the main square. This is their La Rojeña factory, parts of which date back to 1758. Here you'll find **Mundo Cuervo** (Ⓣ01-800/006-8630, Ⓦwww.mundocuervo.com), which offers **tours** every hour (Mon–Sat 10am–4pm, Sun 11am–4pm; tours in English are at noon). The basic tour (45min; M$75), makes a quick turn through the factory, where you can taste the raw distillate, then continues to the barrel storage area, where you can try a little of the finished product. The extended tour (1hr 15min; M$100) takes in all this, gives you a chance to sit down and learn how to appreciate the qualities of the various tequilas and includes a margarita and

△ Tequila distillery

## The Tequila Express

One of the best ways to experience the Tequila region is to travel on the **Tequila Express** (@www.tequilaexpress.com.mx), one of only two train trips left in Mexico (the other being the longer Copper Canyon run; see p.188). It is undoubtedly touristy, but gives you ample chance to learn something of the process and see how the agave is harvested, and includes lunch accompanied by mariachi music and no shortage of samples. The train doesn't actually take you to the town of Tequila; rather it travels at a stately pace through blue agave fields and stops 15km short at the town of Amatitán, home to tequila-maker Herradura's ancient Hacienda San José del Refugio, where you can see them still making the fiery liquor along traditional production lines.

The Tequila Express is packaged as an all-in-one **day tour** (Sat, Sun and holidays 10.30am; M$770, kids 5–12 M$450, infants free). Tickets should be bought a few days in advance either through Ticketmaster (T33/3880-9099), from the Chamber of Commerce cashier department, Vallarta 4095 at Niño Obrero (T33/3880-9099), or from their downtown office at Morelos 395 (T33/3614-3145).

a visit to the old storage cellars – it's worth the few extra pesos. If you're interested in something a little less stage-managed but still informative, Sauza's **La Perseverancia** distillery, Mora 80, also offers tours (Mon–Fri 11.30am, noon, 3pm & 4pm; M$35; usually bilingual). To get there, head five blocks west of the plaza along Ramon Corona.

Across the street from the main entrance to Mundo Cuervo is the small but proud **Museo Nacional del Tequila** (Tues–Sun: April–Aug 10am–6pm, Sept–March 10am–4pm; M$15), where you can learn about the history of the popular drink and its crucial role in the town's development. They have a fine collection of tequila bottles (both ornate and primitive) and agave art.

When you enter town you'll probably be approached by people trying to get you to visit less-well-known **out-of-town distilleries** such as La Cofradia (@www.tequilacofradia.com). These trips can be a bit hit-or-miss, but when they're good, they can be wonderful experiences with far fewer people and a more personal touch. The factories are typically amidst the agave fields so you may also see something of the harvesting. Trips cost around M$60 and include a minibus ride out there. The serene Herradura distillery (Hacienda San José del Refugio: 50min tours Mon–Fri 9am, 10am, 11am, noon & 1pm) in the small town of **Amatitán**, 15km southeast of Tequila on the main road from Guadalajara, deserves a stop. The restaurant here offers a unique dining experience – gourmet food and gracious service in an early eighteenth-century hacienda.

## Tequila practicalities

It's easy enough **to get to Tequila** on regular Transportes Teocuitatlan **buses** from Guadalajara's Central Vieja bus station (Sala B; every 15min; 1hr 45min), or save a little time by picking up the same bus outside the Periférico Sur station, the southern terminus of the Tren Ligero line 1. Unfortunately, the bus is pretty slow and it can be rather uncomfortable to return to Guadalajara after a few too many tequila samples. A good alternative is to go on an **organized tour** such as the Tequila Express train (see box opposite) or the Mundo Cuervo's own Cuervo Bus (daily at 9.15 am; M$200), which leaves from the Central Vieja for a six-hour day trip.

Regular buses drop off passengers on the edge of Tequila, from where it is a one-kilometre walk along Sixto Gorjon to the main plaza and Mundo Cuervo.

## Making tequila

Visitors to Tequila are often surprised to hear that the town's eponymous spirit is more complex than its reputation lets on. As with alcoholic beverages considered more sophisticated, like champagne, **tequila** is subject to strictly enforced appellation rules: true tequila must be made from at least 51 percent **Weber blue agave** grown in the Zona Protegida por la Denomination de Origen – essentially all of Jalisco plus parts of Nayarit, Michoacán, Guanajuato and Tamaulipas. The balance can be made up with alcohol from sugar, but the better brews are usually one hundred percent agave, which gives more intense and flamboyant flavours.

The agave takes seven to ten years to reach an economically harvestable size. The plant is then killed and the spiky leaves cut off, leaving the heart, known as the **piña** for its resemblance to an oversized pineapple. On distillery tours you can see the hearts as they're unloaded from trucks and shoved into ovens, where they're baked for a day or so. On emerging from the ovens, the warm and slightly caramelized *piñas* are crushed and the juice fermented, then distilled, to a rough liquor.

Tequila isn't a drink that takes well to extended **ageing**, but some time in a barrel definitely benefits the flavour and smoothness. The simplest style of tequila, known as *blanco* or *plata* (white or silver), is clear, and sits just fifteen days in stainless steel tanks. The *reposado* (rested) spends at least two months in toasted, new white-oak barrels. The degree to which the barrels are **toasted** greatly affects the resulting flavours; a light toast gives spicy notes; a medium toast brings out vanilla and honey flavours; and a deep charring gives chocolate, smoke and roast almond overtones. If left for over a year the tequila becomes *añejo* (old), and typically takes on a darker colour. A fourth style, *joven* (young), is a mix of *blanco* with either *reposado* or *añejo*. While the nuances of tequila are slowly being explored by a select few, the benefits of oak ageing aren't appreciated by all – many still prefer the supple vegetative freshness of a good *blanco*.



Unless you work in the spirits business and are on a buying trip, there's little need to spend more than an afternoon in Tequila, but you can **stay** at the comfortable *Hotel Plaza Jardín*, José Cuervo 13 (Ⓣ374/742-0061, Ⓦwww.hotelplazajardin.com; ④) right on the main plaza, which has a nice rooftop terrace and its own restaurant and bar. More likely you'll just want a **meal**, best at *La Fonda Cholula*, a bright colourful place to eat right opposite Mundo Cuervo. They have nice shady rooftop seating and serve respectable chicken *mole* and *chiles en nogada* for M$70.

Visiting Tequila is particularly fun during one of its **fiestas**: the town celebrates the **Día de la Santa Cruz** (May 3) with mariachi and plenty of imbibing; and **La Señora de la Salud** (Dec 8), with rodeos, cockfights, fireworks and more drinking.

# Laguna de Chapala and around

At around 35km wide and 120km long, **Laguna de Chapala**, just over 50km south of Guadalajara, is the largest lake in Mexico. Its northern shore has long been a favourite retreat for *Tapatíos*, especially since the early years of the twentieth century when dictator Porfirio Díaz regularly spent his holidays here. Expats from north of the border, particularly Canadians, have also been appreciative of the lake scenery and even year-round temperatures. It is said that there are now around 30,000 living in and around Guadalajara, a sizeable proportion of whom have settled on the lakeside – particularly in **Chapala** and in the smaller village of **Ajijic**. Most of these snowbirds are retirees – during the 1990s, Laguna de Chapala was spoken of locally as being in the "gay 90s", the joke being that anyone who lived there was either gay or over 90. If you spend any time in the area, though, you may get the feeling that some of them regard themselves as writers or artists *manqués*, and have come hoping to pick up some of the inspiration left behind by **D.H. Lawrence**, who wrote the first draft of *The Plumed Serpent* here, as well as more recent inhabitants like Ken Kesey.

This mass expat presence has rendered the area rather expensive and in many respects somewhat sanitized and stratified – you'll see numerous real estate offices trying to sell lots in newly created gated communities, and as you'd imagine, English is spoken widely. There are even a couple of English-language magazines produced here: the *Lake Chapala Review* and the *El Ojo del Lago*. None of this, though, can detract from the allure of the deep-red sunsets over the lake. Whether the intense colour is actually the result of pollution is another matter entirely, and remains a hot-button topic with locals.

Indeed, environmental issues have been at the fore in recent years. The lake averages only eight metres deep, making it sensitive to fluctuating water levels. During the 1980s and 1990s the **lake level** dropped significantly when the government used its feeder rivers as a freshwater supply for Guadalajara and Mexico City – the lake receded so far that shoreline property was 2km from the water's edge. Things have improved markedly since 2003 thanks to heavier rainfall and the dedicated work of the 20,000-strong group Amigos del Lago de Chapala (Ⓦ www.amigosdelago.org). For the moment lake levels have returned to normal, but agricultural runoff has raised nitrate pollution to unsustainable levels and encouraged the growth of picturesque, but ultimately choking, rafts of **water hyacinth**. The *charales*, the fish for which the lake was once famed, are virtually gone.

Nonetheless, the lake remains popular, and on **weekends** and holidays day-trippers from the city help to create a party atmosphere, joining with yahoos to tipple and whoop it up late into the weekend nights. Panoramex (see p.332) runs a day trip to Chapala and Ajijic from Guadalajara (M$150). **Peak season** is November to April, which coincides with the arrival of seasonal snowbirds.

## Chapala

**CHAPALA** (Ⓦ www.chapala.com) on the northern shore of the lake, is a sleepy community most of the time, and has a quiet charm and relaxed pace that you can easily get used to. However, it becomes positively festive on sunny weekends, when thousands come to eat, swim or take a boat ride out to one of the lake's islands. Shoreline restaurants all offer the local speciality, *pescado blanco*, famous despite its almost total lack of flavour and lake-bottom origins, and street vendors sell cardboard plates of tiny fried fish from the lake, known as *charales*. Head to the left along the promenade, past streets of shuttered nineteenth-century villas, and you'll find a small **crafts market**. There's even a flat *ciclopista* (cycle path) running along the lakeside between Chapala and Ajijic for easy cycling and walking, with nice views of the lake; on a hot day it beats taking the bus.

If you're in the mood for a longer walk, you might consider heading up to the cross on the top of the hill overlooking the town: there's a path starting on López Cotilla between no. 316 and no. 318, across the street from *Hotel Candilejas* (see p.358).

### Practicalities

**Buses** leave the old bus station in Guadalajara for Chapala throughout the day (Sala A; every 30min; 6am–8.30pm). Be sure to get on one of the *directo* services, or you'll stop at every little village along the way. From Chapala, regular services run on to Ajijic (5min) and from there back to Guadalajara by a more direct route along the highway to the coast – you can hail them in the street. From the bus station, the main street, Madero, stretches six blocks down to the lakeside. The main square is halfway down, with Hidalgo, the road to Ajijic, branching off to the right after five blocks.

There is a **casa de cambio**, Lloyd's, across from the plaza; a **caseta telefónica** on the corner of Madero and Hidalgo; and at Madero 230-B, a **bookshop** stocking the *Miami Herald*'s Mexico edition, *USA Today*, a good number of international magazines and a few novels in English. The **post office** is a couple of blocks along Hidalgo, and there's a **laundry** on the corner of Zaragoza and López Cotilla. If you decide you want to spend more than a day here, Chapala does have some decent **places to stay**. *Casa de Huéspedes Las Palmitas,* Juárez 531, just behind the Mercado Municipal (ⓣ376/765-3070; ❸), is pretty basic, but about the cheapest place in town. Rooms are clean and have private baths. At *Hotel Candilejas,* López Cotilla 363 (ⓣ376/765-2279; ❹), a moderately priced hotel with tiled floors and arched brick ceilings just off the main square, guests are treated like members of the family. For a bit more, the *Villa Montecarlo* (ⓣ376/765-2120; ❻), on the outskirts of town, offers tennis courts, a pool, lake views and airy rooms. One of the nicest options in town is *Quinta Quetzalcoatl*, Zaragoza 307 (ⓣ376/765-3653, ⓦwww.accommodationslakechapala.com; no kids; ❼), where D.H. Lawrence wrote *The Plumed Serpent*. There's a wide assortment of gorgeous rooms, most with a Lawrence theme and private terrace.

For **places to eat**, *Café Paris*, Madero 421, has good breakfasts and reasonably priced comidas, as well as great booths for people watching. Under the *portales* of the main square, *Chabela's Fonda*, Paseo de los Ausentes 621, dishes out tasty *chilaquiles*. For a larger meal, try *Cazadores*, Ramon Corona 8 (ⓣ376/765-2162; closed Mon), which has been serving hearty, and somewhat pricey, surf-and-turf dinners amidst the faded elegance of a grand mansion since 1956. And for something completely different, *La Petite Belgique*, Encarnacion Rosas 8, is a cute little creperie that makes sweet and savoury crepes, Belgian waffles and good cappuccino. In addition to all these, there is also a row of fish restaurants competing for custom along the lakefront – most of the fish served is brought in from elsewhere, due to the lake's depleted stock and contamination.

## Ajijic

With its narrow cobbled streets, **AJIJIC**, 7km west of Chapala, has a decidedly more quaint atmosphere. Undeniably picturesque, it's even smaller, quieter and more self-consciously arty, with numerous little crafts shops. It may be a wonderful place to paint or retire, with a thriving expat social and cultural life, but as a visitor you're likely to exhaust its charms in a couple of hours. That's quite long enough to have wandered by the lake, seen the little art galleries, read the notice boards, eaten a good meal and perhaps visited the **Casa de Cultura**, on the north side of the plaza, which also hosts regular performances and year-round exhibitions of history, art and photography.

### Practicalities

The **bus** drops you either in the centre or on the Carretera Chapala, from where Colón runs six blocks southward to the lake, with the main square halfway along it. Many of the best places to stay and eat are within a couple of blocks of here. There's a high standard of **accommodation** in town, as well as **apartments** and **houses** to rent for longer stays; check out the notice boards in shops and galleries. One of the best picks in town is *Mis Amores*, Hidalgo 22 (Ⓣ376/766-4640, Ⓦwww.misamores.com; ⑦), Ajijic's answer to a contemporary boutique hotel, with tasteful decor, individual terraces shaded by banana trees and a warm proprietor. *La Nueva Posada*, Donato Guerra 9 (Ⓣ376/766-1444, Ⓦwww.mexconnect.com/mex/rest/nueva/posada.htm; ⑦), by the lake three blocks east of Colón, is an eclectically decorated, welcoming place with lovely gardens, a small pool and distant water views. The main building feels like a grand hotel; you can also opt for one of the separate villas. There's an excellent restaurant where breakfast (included) is served. *Hotel Italo*, off the main square at Guadalipe Victoria 10 (Ⓣ376/766-2221, Ⓦwww.hotelitalo.com.mx; ⑤), is a decent bet even though the bells of the church next door ring every hour – light sleepers will want to try elsewhere.

If you are **eating** on a tight budget, head for the makeshift family-run *sopes* stands around the plaza, where you can dine heartily for M$25. Many of the better restaurants cater to expat tastes, serving loads of salads and juices. One of the better examples is *The Secret Garden*, Hidalgo 12, with a relaxed and shady garden setting that's perfect for espresso and a muffin, or something from their healthy-leaning menu – stuffed white or whole-wheat baguettes (M$50), garden burger and salad (M$44), or vegetable lasagna (M$65). The restaurant in the *Hotel Italo* serves authentic pizza (large for M$80) and pasta, though you'll do well to go for the imaginative daily specials. For something special, visit *Nueva Posada* in the hotel of the same name, a lovely restaurant with obscured lake views, where you can sit down to *sopa Azteca* followed by lamb with jalapeño and mint jelly (M$140) or pork ribs (M$110), all done to perfection.

### San Juan Cosalá

Buses continue five kilometres west of Ajijic along Carratera Chapala towards **SAN JUAN COSALÁ**. On the lakeshore, 1km east of the village, you come upon a string of lakeside resorts offering visitors a chance to bask in natural thermal waters said to have healing properties. The *Hotel Balneario* (Ⓣ376/761-0222; Ⓦwww.hotelspacosala.com; ⑦), right beside the lake, is the cheapest and most popular, and the only one to offer day-trippers the use of its pools (M$110). The rooms are nothing special for the price, but the same applies to neighbouring establishments. Perhaps the best value is the adjacent and slightly pricier *Villa Bordeaux* (Ⓣ376/761-0494; Ⓦwww.hotelspacosala.com; ⑦), a spiffy hacienda-style hotel featuring a thermal pool, sauna, steam room and rooms each with a terrace overlooking the pool to the lake. Both places offer massages from M$150 for thirty minutes.

## South towards the coast

Some of the most delightful subalpine scenery in the country lies southwest of Laguna de Chapala, on the road to Colima. You'll miss much of it if you stick to the speedy toll road (Hwy-54), though even that has its exciting moments as it passes the so-called Zona de Montaña: the following places are all reached from the far slower, far more attractive, if bumpier, old road plied by second-class buses.

## Tapalpa

The town of **TAPALPA**, 130km southwest of Guadalajara, makes an ideal base for a few days of relaxation amid upland pastures and pine forests. It is reached via a steep, winding road off the old highway, which climbs continuously until it crests a 2300-metre ridge at El Balcón. If you're driving, stop here to check out the view back down the valley and to feel the near constant steady breeze, a phenomenon that drew World Cup paragliding events in 2002 and 2004.

Tapalpa, 10km further on, lies amid magnificent surroundings – ranch country and tree-clad hills that are often covered in a gentle mist. The town itself is a pretty little place, and, with a population of only around 14,000, there's a village feel to it, especially around the plaza. Here you'll find eighteenth-century wooden-balconied houses, encircling *portales* and two impressive **churches** – the larger with an unusually plain brick interior. On the outskirts little clusters of cabañas dot the woods luring upwardly mobile *Tapatíos*, and a fair bit of desirable real estate has sprung up in recent years.

One of the best things to do in Tapalpa is simply to walk along the country roads that fan out from the town into fresh-scented pine forests. There's good walking in almost any direction, with plenty of wildlife, especially birds, to spot; you can also hire **horses** (look for the signs) for the popular ride to the local waterfall. One especially pleasant hike is to **Las Piedrotas** (10km return; 2hr), which follows a decent but little used road towards Chiquilistlán (marked as you enter Tapalpa). It passes the romantic ruins of a *fábrica* – an old water-driven paper mill – and climbs towards a gorgeous valley of pasturelands, studded with wild flowers and with huge boulders that look as if they've been dropped from the sky. If you don't fancy walking both ways, get a taxi to drop you off (around M$60) and walk back.

Tapalpa is very much on the Guadalajara weekender circuit, so try to visit midweek when its old-world charm is little affected (although hotels remain rather pricey). Be warned that it's very cold in winter, and even the summer nights can become chilly. Locals brew their own mescal in the village, which may help warm you; it's sold from the barrel in some of the older shops and is extremely rough (but also very cheap).

### Practicalities

Second-class **buses** run from Guadalajara's old bus station (Sala B; hourly 6.30am–5.30pm; 3hr) to Tapalpa where they stop outside the ticket office at Ignacio López 10, two blocks south of the plaza. Four daily services go direct to Sayula (1hr) and Ciudad Guzmán (2hr), but many more pass by the junction of the main road (El Crucero, some 20km away); it's easy enough to catch a bus, or even hitch, down there, but if you do hitch, go during the day and leave yourself plenty of time. Locals consider the route dangerous after dark.

For most things, head for Tapalpa's main plaza, where several of the old buildings have been refurbished as restaurants and hotels, and there's even a **bank** with ATM. The municipal **tourist office**, on the north side of the plaza, does not seem to have fixed hours or a telephone, but is likely to be open at weekends. For the **Internet**, head to @ Rova, a cyber café and *pastelería* at Matamoros 7, in the little courtyard on the south side of the plaza. You can drink good coffee while you surf.

During the week you may be one of the few visitors, but all **rooms** are often taken at weekends and around the **fiesta** for the Día de la Virgen de Guadalupe (Dec 12), when Tapalpa attracts pilgrims from a wide area. *La Casa de Maty*, Matamoros 69 (☎343/432-0189; ❼), on the south side of the plaza, is the pick of the pricier places to stay in town, set around a beautiful plant-filled courtyard with a fountain. The comfortable, rustic rooms come with dark tiles, tasteful artwork and fireplace. At the *Villa de San José*, Cerrada Ignacio López 91 (☎343/432-0451, ⓔhotelvilladesanjose@yahoo.com.mx; ❻), one block southeast of the plaza, you'll find country-style charm in rooms with warm wooden floors. The owner of the property at 16 de Septiembre 33 rents several pleasant rooms (❻) on the roof of the house that have views over the town. Rates include Continental breakfast. The cheapest place in town is *Posada La Hacienda*, Raúl Quintero 120 (☎343/432-0193; ❹), half a block southeast of the plaza. The good-value rooms are spacious, and some have views of the surrounding countryside.

Numerous **restaurants** around the main plaza serve plain country food. Be on the lookout for places serving *poche*, a local wine made from an unusual concoction of pomegranate, peanuts, coffee and guava. It's also a good place to try *queso fundido*, as the farms hereabout produce good cheese – *Los Girasoles*, Obregón 110 (☎343/432-0458), a lovely little place just off the southwest corner of the plaza, serves it with chorizo and mushrooms. The balcony at *Paulinos*, on the north side of the plaza, is a nice spot to watch the town come awake over *huevos rancheros*, while the tables at *La Villa*, Raúl Quintero 93, are perfect for closing the day with a sundowner.

## Sayula and Ciudad Guzmán

Beyond the turn-off for Tapalpa, the old main road continues 12km south to **SAYULA** (the name chosen by D.H. Lawrence for the town on Laguna de Chapala in *The Plumed Serpent*) and then to the sizeable city of Ciudad Guzmán. Sayula itself has an interesting enough history – it was once fought over by indigenous tribes eager to control the production of salt from the nearby lake – but there's little to see, apart from a thriving market and some old convents that have been converted into basic **hotels**. If you're in the region around December 8, though, be sure to call in for the Día de la Inmaculada Concepción, a **fiesta** with traditional dances including the Danza de la Conquista, which partly re-enacts the Spanish Conquest. The **bus** stops at Portal Rayon 31, a block and a half from the pretty central plaza. Here you'll find *Hotel Díaz,* Portal Galeana 5 (☎342/422-0633; ❷), with an attractive courtyard but dark rooms. About five blocks towards the highway *Hotel Meson del Anima*, Avila Camacho 171 Ote (☎342/422-0600; ❹), has nicer rooms but less character.

Birthplace of José Clemente Orozco, **CIUDAD GUZMÁN** is a busy little city thoroughly steeped in local culture, with attractive colonnaded streets in the centre, though there seems little reason to stop except to break a journey. If you do visit, don't miss the pleasant **Museo de las Culturas de Occidente**, Dr Angel Gonzalez 21 (Tues–Sun 9.30am–5.30pm; M$24), off Reforma, a block west of the plaza. It's just one room, but there are some lovely figures and animals in the collection of local archeology, and often an interesting temporary display that may include early works by **Orozco**. The centre of the town's main plaza is a bandstand with a replica of Orozco's *Man of Fire* mural from Guadalajara (see p.342).

**Buses** stop at the new Central de Autobuses around 3km west of the town centre; it has good connections to Guadalajara and the coast. Local buses (#5a & #6b) stop outside and run to the plaza along Madero y Carranza, which becomes Reforma. As ever, almost everything of interest is on or around the plaza, where you'll find banks, phones and **places to stay**. The pick of places is *Hotel Zapotlan*, Federico del Toro 61, along the west side of the plaza

(Ⓣ341/412-0040, Ⓕ412-4783; ❹), which has a beautiful wrought-iron courtyard, comfy rooms and Continental breakfast. Rooms come with ceiling fans, which are very low in some rooms; watch your head. A block to the north, the *Hotel Flamingos*, Federico del Toro 133 (Ⓣ341/412-0103; ❷), has less character but is clean and quiet. The cheapest place to stay is the *Hotel Morelos*, off the northwest corner of the square at Refugio Barragán del Toscano 20 (no phone; ❶), whose rooms are very basic.

Back on the plaza are a few *taquerías* and a couple of **restaurants**, including the *Juanito*, at Portal Morelos 65, a few doors from the *Hotel Zapotlan*. One block to the south, the attractive *Los Portales*, at Refugio Barragán del Toscano 32, has delicious, reasonably priced breakfasts and Mexican main dishes in a Moorish courtyard. There are also good value tortas and *licuados* at *El Buen Sazon*, Reforma 22. You can have an inexpensive and healthy breakfast with cereal and fresh juice at the stands behind the church in the main square. The salty local cheeses are a treat and can be bought at the **market** near the stalls.

## The road from Ciudad Guzmán to Colima

Between Ciudad Guzmán and Colima, the drive becomes truly spectacular, through country dominated by the **Nevado de Colima** – at 4335m the loftiest and most impressive peak in the west, which is snowcapped in winter. The main highway slashes straight through the mountains via deep cuts and soaring concrete bridges, while the old one snakes above and beneath it as it switchbacks its way through the hills. Both have great views of the Nevado, at least when it's not covered by clouds. If you're on the old road, close your windows as you pass through **Atenquique**, a lovely if odorous hidden valley some 25km from Ciudad Guzmán, which is enveloped in a pall of fumes from a vast paper works. Not far from here, off the road and served by two buses an hour from Ciudad Guzmán, **Tuxpan** – not to be confused with Tuxpán in Veracruz (see p.622), where the exiled Fidel Castro plotted, organized and set off for the Cuban revolution - is a beautiful and ancient little town. It's especially fun during its frequent, colourful **fiestas**, including the Día de San Sebastian (Jan 20), with its many traditional dances; the Día del Señor de la Misericordia (last Sun in May), in honour of this miraculous and highly venerated image; and the Día de Santiago Apóstol (July 25), which is celebrated with fireworks.

# Northern Michoacán

To the southeast of Jalisco, **Michoacán** state is one of the most beautiful and diverse in all Mexico, spreading as it does from a very narrow coastal plain with several tiny beach villages, up to where the Sierra Madre Occidental reaches eastwards into range after range of wooded volcanic heights. Several of the towns, including the delightfully urbane capital, **Morelia**, are utterly colonial in appearance, but on the whole Michoacán's appeal is more rural than urban. The land is green and thriving – in **Uruapan** the lush countryside seems to press in on the town, and is certainly the main attraction – and throughout the state

## Vasco de Quiroga – the noble conquistador

When the Spanish arrived in Michoacán in 1519, they found the region dominated by the **Purépechan** people – whom they named **Tarascans** – whose chief town, Tzintzuntzán, lay on the shores of Lago de Pátzcuaro. The Tarascan civilization, a serious rival to the Aztecs before the Conquest, had a widespread reputation for excellence in the arts, especially metalworking and feathered ornaments. Though the Tarascans submitted peaceably to the Spanish in 1522 and their leader converted to Christianity, they did not avoid the massacres and mass torture that **Nuño de Guzmán** meted out in his attempts to fully pacify the region. Guzmán's methods were overly brutal, even by colonial standards, and elderly Spanish nobleman-turned-priest, **Vasco de Quiroga**, was appointed bishop to the area in an attempt to restore harmony. He succeeded beyond all expectations, securing his reputation as a champion of the native peoples – a reputation that persists today. He coaxed the native population down from the mountains to which they had fled, established self-sufficient agricultural settlements and set up missions to teach practical skills as well as religion. The effects of his actions have survived in a very visible way for, despite some blurring in objects produced for the tourist trade, each village still has its own craft speciality: lacquerware in Uruapan, guitars in Paracho, copper goods in Santa Clara del Cobre, to name but a few.

Vasco de Quiroga also left behind him a deeply religious state. Michoacán was a stronghold of the reactionary **Cristero** movement, which fought a bitter war in defence of the Church after the Revolution. Perhaps, too, the ideals of Zapata and Villa had less appeal here as Quiroga's early championing of native peoples' rights against their new overlords meant that the hacienda system never entirely took over Michoacán. Unlike most of the country, the state boasted a substantial peasantry with land it could call its own and therefore it didn't relate to calls for land and labour reform.

there is a very strong indigenous culture, matched only in the state of Oaxaca. This is largely thanks to Michoacán's first bishop, **Vasco de Quiroga** (see box above), one of the few early Spanish colonists to consider the native population as anything more than an expendable slave-labour force. The fruits of Quiroga's efforts are most clear in and around **Pátzcuaro**, the beautiful lakeside town that was his base. Here, and in the surrounding villages, traditional and introduced crafts – everything from weaving to guitar manufacturing – have flourished for centuries, and today this region is one of the most important sources of Mexican artesanías. Native traditions also draw large crowds to the lake for the **Day of the Dead** at the beginning of November, one of the most striking of Mexican celebrations.

However, despite its beauty and charms, Michoacán remains a region that people travel through rather than to. Morelia, Pátzcuaro, Uruapan and other towns lie conveniently near the major route from Guadalajara to Mexico City. You could easily spend several days in each, or weeks trying to explore the state fully, but even in a couple of days passing through you can get a strong flavour of the area. If you're doing so between mid-November and the end of March, the orange, black and white markings of the **monarch butterfly** may catch your eye as they sporadically float across your path. The creatures migrate here from around the Great Lakes region of the US and Canada every year to hibernate and reproduce, covering a formidable 4000km. Their image has been appropriated as a symbol of economic integration between the US and Mexico – look out for them on the side of taxis in Uruapan and Pátzcuaro.

# Guadalajara to Uruapan

From Guadalajara, the most direct route to Mexico City heads through the major junction of La Piedad and continues east towards Irapuato. If you can afford to dawdle a while, though, it's infinitely more rewarding to follow the slower, southern road through Zamora and Morelia, spending a couple of days in Uruapan and Pátzcuaro. From Uruapan, a good road slices south through the mountains to the Pacific coast at Lázaro Cárdenas (see p.570).

Leaving Guadalajara, you skirt the northeastern edge of Laguna de Chapala before turning south, heading into Michoacán and reaching **ZAMORA DE HIDALGO**, some 200km away. Zamora has little intrinsic interest. However, if you're planning to head straight down to Uruapan you may want to change buses here – you can catch a direct bus from Guadalajara to Zamora, where there's a frequent service to Uruapan. Although not much to go out of your way for, the town boasts several small restaurants and a market very close to the bus station. The old cathedral, unusually Gothic in style, is ruined and often closed, but you can while away some time on the pleasant grassy plaza in front.

If you're driving, there's no need to stop between Zamora and Uruapan, though you may want to pause a while in the village of **PARACHO**, 50km south of Zamora, which has been famous for the manufacture of **guitars** and other stringed instruments since Quiroga's time. Every building seems to house a workshop, a guitar shop or both. The guitars vary enormously in price and quality – many are not meant to be anything more than ornamental, but others are serious, handcrafted musical instruments. Though you'll find them on display and for sale in the markets and artesanía museums in Uruapan or Pátzcuaro, if you're really looking to buy, you should do it here at the source. Paracho also hosts a couple of fascinating **fiestas**. On Corpus Christi (the Thurs after Trinity, usually late May/early June) you can witness the **Danza de los Viejitos** (see box below). August 8 sees an even more ancient ceremony, whose roots go back to well before the Spanish era: an ox is sacrificed and its meat used to make a complicated ritual dish (*shuripe*) that is then shared out among the celebrants. This coincides with the music, dance and general jollity of the **Feria Nacional de Guitarra**, the National Guitar Fair.

## Uruapan and around

**URUAPAN**, they say, means "the place where flowers bloom" in the Tarascan language, though *Appleton's Guide* for 1884 tells a different story: "The word Uruapan comes from *Urani*, which means in the Tarasc language 'a chocolate cup', because the Indians in this region devote themselves to manufacture and painting of these objects." Demand for chocolate cups, presumably, has fallen since then, but whatever the truth, the modern version is certainly appropriate: Uruapan,

### The Dance of the Little Old Men

The **Danza de los Viejitos**, or the **Dance of the Little Old Men**, is the most famous of Michoacán's traditional dances. It is also one of its most picturesque, with the performers (usually children), dressed in baggy white cotton and masked as old men, alternating between parodying the tottering steps of the *viejitos* they represent and breaking into complex routines. Naturally enough, there's a lot of music, too. You'll see the dance performed at festive occasions all over Michoacán, but the finest expression is in Paracho (see above).

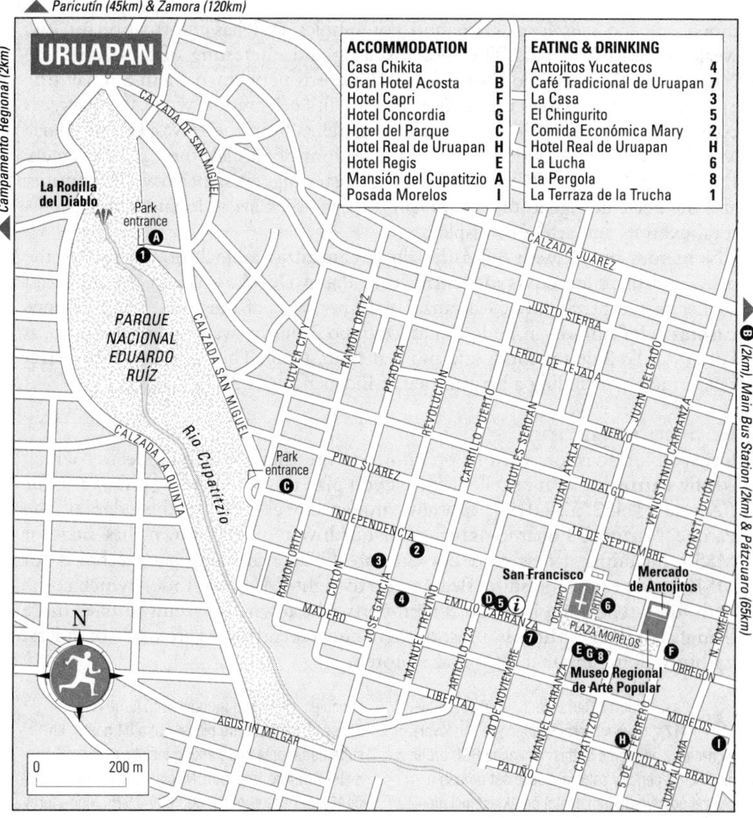




lower (at around 1600m) and warmer than most of its neighbours, enjoys a steamy subtropical climate and is surrounded by thick forests and lush parks.

It's a prosperous and growing town, too, with a thriving commerce based on the richness of its agriculture (particularly a vast export market in **avocados** and **macadamia nuts**) and on new light industry. To some extent these businesses have come to overshadow the old attractions, creating ugly new development and displacing traditional crafts, but Uruapan remains a lively place with a fine market, an abiding reputation for **lacquerware** and fascinating surroundings – especially the giant waterfall and "new" volcano of Paricutín (see p.368).

## Arrival and information

Most visitors arrive at Uruapan's modern **bus station**, the Central de Autobuses, 3km northeast of the centre; a local bus (marked "Centro") from right outside will take you down to the Plaza Morelos, the plaza in the heart of town, or back again from there. There's also a domestic **airport** with daily connections from Mexico City.

Uruapan's **tourist office** (Casa Regional del Turista), Carranza 20 (daily 9am–7pm; ⓣ452/524-0667), not only gives away a good **map** of town but also showcases and sells local crafts and comestibles, and has information on the wealth of local **festivals**. The most exciting and interesting of these are: Año Nuevo (Jan 1), when the Danza de los Viejitos is performed; Palm Sunday (the Sun before Easter), the culmination of a week's celebration when the *indígenas* collect palms from the hills and make ornaments from the leaves; Día de María Magdalena (July 22), when there's a processions of animals through the streets; Día de San Francisco (Oct 4), one of the year's biggest saint's day celebrations; and the Feria de Aguacate (Nov/Dec), a three-week avocado fair with agricultural exhibits and artesanía displays.

Numerous **banks** with ATMs lie along Cupatitzio, a block or so south of the plaza, and there are **casas de cambio** at Portal Degollado 15 in the northeast corner of the plaza and at Carranza 14-D, just west of the plaza. Long-distance **casetas telefónicas** can be found at Ocampo 3 on the west side of the plaza, at Portal Carillo 3 on the south side and at the bus station. There are several **Internet** cafés in town, including a bargain one at Independencia 33 (M$5/hr).

## Accommodation

Uruapan lures visitors with its proximity to breathtaking natural beauty, which is why **camping** is an excellent idea if you plan to stay in the area. *Campamento Regional* (ⓣ452/524-0197, ⓦwww.parquenacional.org), on the edge of the Parque Nacional Eduardo Ruíz, 3km northwest of downtown, has sites for M$50, including access to a cooking area. There are also basic cabañas for M$100 per person and suites sleeping up to eight (M$1000–1500), which come with full kitchen and bath, on the property. The town also seems to have more than its fair share of **hotels**, most of them conveniently sited around – or at least within walking distance of – Plaza Morelos.

**Casa Chikita** Carranza 32-A ⓣ452/524-4174, ⓦwww.casachikita.com. The lovely, high-ceilinged rooms at this appealing B&B are in a nineteenth-century colonial house set around a central courtyard. Continental breakfast included. ④

**Gran Hotel Acosta** Filomena Mata 325 ⓣ452/523-4564. Opposite the bus station, this is hardly an ideal spot, but if you're passing through it does offer clean, simple, reasonably priced rooms. ①

**Hotel Capri** Portal Degollado 10, at the eastern end of the plaza ⓣ452/524-2186. The action of the plaza often spills over into the lobby of this very basic hotel featuring fairly scruffy rooms with bath. It is, however, a much better bet than other hotels on the same block. ①

**Hotel Concordia** Portal Carillo 8 ⓣ452/523-0400 or 01-800/420-0400, ⓦwww.hotelconcordia.com.mx. Modern, clean and efficient: all rooms are pleasantly decorated, and with TV and phone. There's parking and a good breakfast buffet (extra M$55), but it is less characterful than the similarly priced *Regis*. ⑥

**Hotel Continental** Nicolas Bravo 33 ⓣ452/523-7362. Relatively quiet hotel with modern, clean rooms with TV and phone, parking facilities and a restaurant. ⑤

**Hotel del Parque** Independencia 124, near the Parque Nacional ⓣ452/524-3845. Best deal of the cheapies: clean and friendly, with large rooms (those at the front are nicest but a bit noisy), en-suite bathrooms and parking facilities. ③

**Hotel Real de Uruapan** Nicolas Bravo 110 ⓣ452/527-5900 or 01-800/000-7325. Nine-storey international style hotel with carpeted rooms, each with TV and phone. The executive rooms on the upper floors get the best views. ⑦

**Hotel Regis** Portal Carillo 12 ⓣ452/523-5844. Friendly place in a central location featuring characterful rooms with the accompaniment of twittering caged birds. Parking is available and some rooms overlook the plaza (though that makes them noisy). ⑥

**Mansión del Cupatitzio** at the north end of the Parque Nacional Eduardo Ruíz ⓣ452/523-2100 or 01-800/504-8793, ⓦwww.mansiondelcupatitzio.com. Uruapan's finest hotel, with superb service, a pool, a terrace restaurant and beautiful grounds full of all manner of flora. Located away from the fray, the hotel is conveniently adjacent to the entrance to the national park. ⑧

**Posada Morelos** Morelos 30 ⓣ452/523-2302. Secure, family-run hotel set around a pleasant courtyard. Clean and reasonably priced singles plus rooms for groups. There are also rooms without baths (①) for anyone really on a budget. Avoid rooms near the noisy street. ③

## The Town

The **Plaza Morelos**, a long strip of tree-shaded open space, is in every sense the heart of Uruapan. Always animated, it's surrounded by everything of importance: shops, market, banks, principal churches and many of the hotels. This is the place to head first, either to find a place to stay or simply to get a feel for the place. On the plaza, too, is the town's only overt tourist attraction, **La Huatapera**. One of the oldest surviving buildings in Uruapan, it has been exquisitely restored to house the fascinating **Museo Regional de Arte Popular** (Tues–Sun 9.30am–1.30pm & 3.30–6pm; free), an impressive display of crafts from the region, especially Uruapan's own lacquerware. Look out for particularly fine painted bowls from Quiroga and for the lacquerware from Pátzcuaro, with its gold inlay. The small courtyard and adjoining chapel were built by Juan de San Miguel, the Franciscan friar who founded the town itself, and later were adopted by Bishop Quiroga as a hospital and training centre. The carvings around the windows bear a marked Arab influence, as they were crafted by Christianized Moorish artisans from Spain (Mudéjares).

The wares shown in the museum are of the highest quality, and are worth close inspection if you plan to go out hunting for bargains in the market or in the shops around the park. The art of making lacquer is complex and time-consuming, involving the application of layer upon layer of different colours, with the design cut into the background. All too many of the goods produced for tourists are simply given a couple of coats (one for the black background with a design then painted on top), which is far quicker and cheaper but results in an inferior product.

The **Casa de la Cultura** (daily 8am–9pm; free), to the left of the museum on the north side of the plaza, hosts regular cultural events, exhibitions, concerts and dance performances. You'll find a bulletin board of upcoming events in the entryway. Between the museum and the Casa de la Cultura an alley runs down to the **Mercado de Antojitos**, a large open **market** section just half a block north of the plaza, where women serve up meals for stallholders and visitors alike at a series of long, open-air tables. Here you'll find the cheapest, and very often the freshest and best, food in town – this is a great place to sample the salty regional cheese, *adobada*. The rest of the market, with herb and fruit stalls but mostly clothes, shoes and CDs, sprawls along Corregidora and Constitución. Despite the variety of wares, for **native crafts** like pottery or wood furniture you're far better looking to the smattering of shops along **Independencia**, which leads up from the plaza to the Parque Nacional. At the top of this street are several small places where you can watch the artisans at work – some establishments are no more than a single room with a display of finished goods on one side and a worktable on the other, while others are more sophisticated operations. Opposite the entrance to the park is a little "craft market", mostly selling very poor souvenirs.

## Río Cupatitzio and the Parque Nacional Eduardo Ruíz

Just fifty acres on the northwestern edge of downtown and 1km from the plaza, the **Parque Nacional Eduardo Ruíz** (daily 8am–6pm; M$12), is far more compact than national parks you may be used to elsewhere, but this luxuriant and tropical city park is one of Uruapan's proudest assets. The Río Cupatitzio flows through in a little gorge, via a series of man-made cascades and fountains. The river springs from a rock known as *La Rodilla del Diablo* ("the Devil's knee"); according to legend, water gushed forth after the Devil knelt here in submission before the unswerving Christian faith of the drought-ridden population. Alternatively, it is said that the Devil met the Virgin Mary while out strolling in the park, and dropped to his knees in respect. *Cupatitzio* means "where the waters meet", though it's invariably translated as "the river that sings" – another appropriate, if not entirely accurate, tag.

Locals come here to stroll the cobbled footpaths betweens stands of banana plants, gaze at the cascades (particularly good during or just after rain), catch trout and eat at assorted restaurants and taco stands. There are two entrances, one at the end of Independencia (take a bus along here if you don't feel like walking), and one up by the *Mansión del Cupatitzio* hotel.

Some 12km south of Uruapan, the river crashes over the **waterfall of La Tzaráracua**, an impressive 25-metre plunge amid beautiful forest scenery. This is also a popular outing with locals, especially at weekends, and hence fairly easy to get to – take one of the buses (marked "Tzaráracua") from the south side of the plaza at Cupatitzio (hourly), or share a taxi. If it seems too crowded here, make for the smaller falls, **Tzararacuita**, about 1km further downstream.



## Eating and drinking

There are plenty of decent places to eat in town, though little that's truly spectacular. The best place to sample local delights at low prices is the **Mercado de Antojitos** (see p.367).

**Antojitos Yucatecos** Carranza 37. Mexican breakfasts and good-value comidas. Normally open to 11pm; closed Mon.

**Café Tradicional de Uruapan** Carranza 5. This Uruapan classic serves great breakfasts, superb local coffee, ice cream, cakes, *antojitos* and a decent range of herbal and fruit teas (including an intriguing piña colada). Airy window seating, but the interior is a bit darker. Definitely a place to relax, usually until 11pm.

**La Casa** Revolución 3. Charming courtyard café-cum-cocktail lounge that's good for a coffee during the day or a tequila in the evening, when it becomes a bit of a hangout.

**El Chinguirito** Carranza 32. Intimate lighting and a cave-like room set this place apart. Nip in for a margarita and one of their *entremeses* (Spanish tortilla or grilled mushrooms; M$40) or dine on fresh Caesar salad (M$75) and tasty pasta dishes (M$55–70). Popular for late drinks at weekends.

**Comida Económica Mary** Independencia 59. Wholesome home-style cooking at low prices. Perfect for breakfast and comidas corridas (M$33), though go elsewhere for your coffee.

**Hotel Real de Uruapan** Nicolas Bravo 110. Top-floor restaurant with a beautiful view. Reasonably priced evening meals and live music (Thurs–Sat). Expect the likes of avocado soup (M$30) followed by steak (M$90) or shrimp in garlic and chile (M$110).

**La Lucha** Garcia Ortiz 22. A small café serving only basic coffee and cakes, but it's a good place to sample the local hearty brews.

**La Pergola** Portal Carrillo 4, on the south side of the plaza. Popular restaurant serving a selection of regional and national dishes (M$45–80), a good comida corrida (M$60) and local coffee.

**La Terraza de la Trucha** at the upper entrance to the Parque Nacional Eduardo Ruíz. Simply a delight. Enjoy avocado cocktail (M$25), grilled *trucha* (trout; M$70) and heavenly *aguas frescas* while surveying the park's waterfalls and giant banana trees. Daily 9am–6pm.

## Paricutín

An ideal day trip from Uruapan, the "new" **Volcano of Paricutín**, about 40km northwest of town, gives you an unusual taste of the surrounding countryside. On February 20, 1943, a Purépecha peasant working in his fields noticed the earth rumble and then smoke. The ground soon cracked and lava began to flow to the surface. Over a period of several years, it engulfed the village of Paricutín and several other hamlets, forcing the evacuation of some seven thousand inhabitants. The volcano was active for eight years, producing a cone some 400m high and devastating an area of around twenty square kilometres. Now

△ Paricutín

there are vast fields of lava (mostly cooled, though there are still a few hot spots), black and powdery, cracked into harsh jags, along with the dead cone and crater. Most bizarrely, a church tower – all that remains of the buried hamlet of San Juan Parangaricutiro – pokes its head through the surface. The volcano wasn't all bad news, though: during its active life the volcano spread a fine layer of dust – effectively a fertilizer - on the fields that escaped the full lava flow, and drew tourists from around the world. It is still popular, especially on Sundays, when the upwardly mobile from Uruapan come out to play.

The volcano is visited from the small and very traditional Purépecha village of **Angahuan**, where the women still wear heavily pleated satin skirts with an embroidered apron and a shawl. On the **plaza**, the **church** warrants a second glance. Built in the sixteenth century, its doorway was carved in the largely Arab Mudéjar style by Andalucian artisans (Andalucia was the centre of fine arts in the Arab empire until the fall of Granada in 1492). The cross in the courtyard, on the other hand, is most definitely Mexican, complete with serpents, a skull and other pre-Hispanic motifs. In the street to the right of the church (as you look at it), across from the side gate of the courtyard, a door lintel has been turned into a kind of lava frieze of the volcano and church tower.

## Practicalities

To see much of Paricutín you really need to set aside a day. You'll want to leave Uruapan early (say 7am or 8am) so you get as much of the hiking as possible done in the cool of the day and catch the ruined church in the morning light. You'll also need to take **food and drink** as there is very little available in Angahuan.

By car, simply take the main road to Los Reyes and look for signs to Angahuan – there are many. By bus, hop aboard the Autotransportes Galeana/Ruta Paraíso service toward Los Reyes or Zicuicho from the Central de Autobuses in Uruapan (hourly 5am–7pm; about 30min; M$15). Alternatively, walk up to the

Glorieta roundabout at the junction of Calzada de San Miguel and Calzada Juarez and flag down the bus there. The bus climbs about 700m from Uruapan up through pines then drops you on the highway outside the village.

When you get off the bus in Angahuan you'll be besieged by boys and men offering to **guide** you or take you on **horseback**; it's not a bad idea to hire a guide, as the paths through the lava are numerous and can be difficult to follow. **Prices** fluctuate with demand, but you can probably expect to pay around M$250 for a guide for the day, plus another M$250 for each horse. If you just want to see the ruined church, a couple of hours will suffice; a return trip to the cone of the volcano will take about eight hours on either foot or horseback. The horse trail is easier than the walking trail, though it finishes at the base of the main cone, leaving you to tackle the final steep climb on your own.

It is a ten-minute walk from the bus stop to the plaza and church. From the plaza, turn right down Juárez for about 200m to an ornately carved wooden house on the left. Veer left here (not signposted) and head straight on for a kilometre to reach the **Centro Turístico de Angahuan** (daily 7am–8pm; M$8), which offers superb views of the volcano from its *mirador*, has a small museum on the creation of the volcano and local Purépecha culture and includes a decent restaurant. You can also **stay** here in concrete block cabañas (☎452/523-3934), each with an open fire. Most are set up for six (M$660) but there are some designed for three (M$350). There's also tent **camping** for M$40 per person.

## Tinganio

The small but pretty and well-restored pre-Hispanic ruin of **TINGANIO** (daily 9am–5pm; M$30) is roughly halfway between Uruapan and Pátzcuaro in a town that is now called **Tingambato**. The site was first inhabited around 450–600 AD and greatly expanded between 650 and 900 AD. Though the structures draw on several architectural styles, that of Teotihuacán is particularly evident, especially in the pyramid that dominates the religious area, overlooking a plaza with a cruciform altar. The adjacent ball-court shows Toltec design influence. Beyond the ball-court, an unexcavated pyramid lies under a grove of avocado trees. In the residential area just to the north, a sunken plaza with two altars and five stairways, each to a separate residence, is very much in the style of Teotihuacán, but the tomb under the largest residence (which the caretaker will open on request) has a false dome suggestive of Maya influence. Surrounded by beautiful countryside, the site is best appreciated from atop the pyramid. Except on Sundays, you are not likely to see many foreigners here. If you're going by car, take the *cuota* highway from Uruapan towards Pátzcuaro and take the Zirahuén exit and follow the *libre* road past Ajuno to Tingambato. It lies approximately 30km west of Pátzcuaro: buses between Uruapan and Pátzcuaro pass right by.

# Pátzcuaro and around

**PÁTZCUARO** is almost exactly halfway between Uruapan and Morelia, some 60km from both, yet strikingly different from either. Basically a village swollen by the tourist trade, Pátzcuaro is far more colonial than Uruapan and infinitely more Indian than Morelia, boasting both fine architecture and a rich indigenous culture. Add to that the fact that it sits by the shore of **Lago**

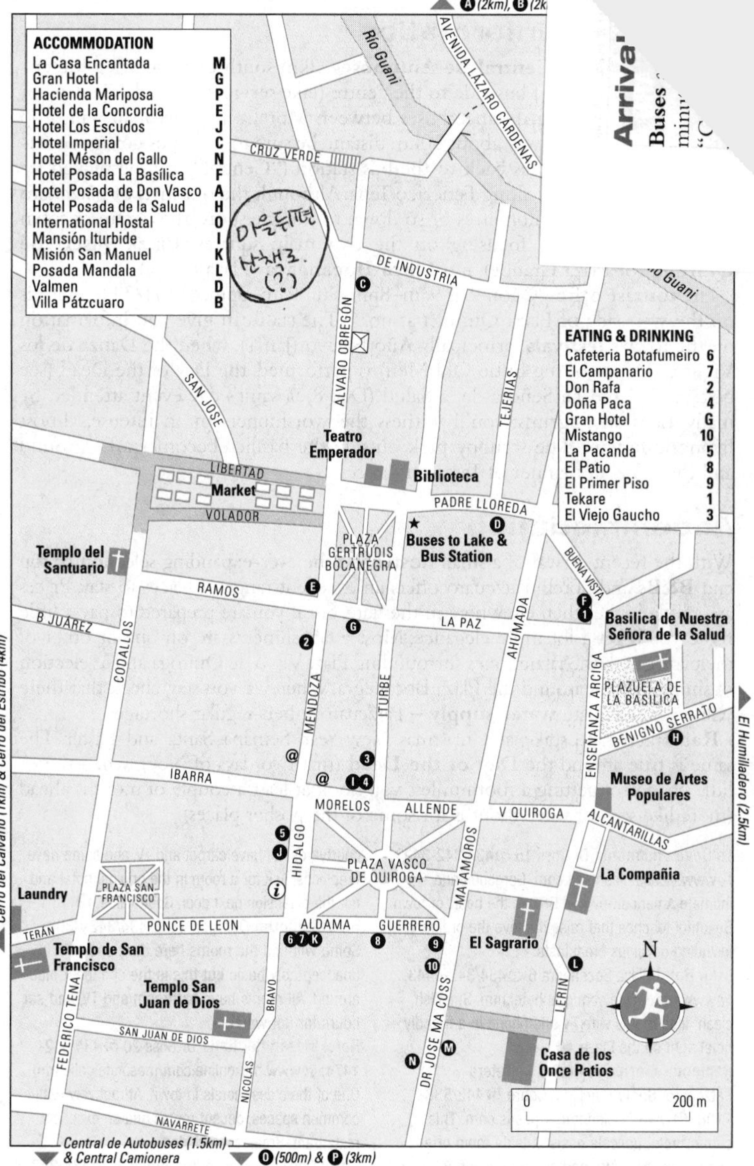


de **Pátzcuaro** (see p.376), probably the most beautiful lake in Mexico – and certainly the most photogenic, especially during Pátzcuaro's famed **Day of the Dead** celebrations (see box, p.376) – and it's hardly surprising that it attracts hordes of visitors. In the vicinity, you can take trips around the lake and to other, less developed villages, and see the site of **Tzintzuntzán**, one-time capital of the Tarascan kingdom.

## and information

…rrive at the **Central de Autobuses**, 2km south of town: it's a fifteen-…e walk or a brief bus ride to the centre (take services marked "Centro" or …ol Popular"). Long-distance buses between Morelia and Uruapan will drop you on the main highway about 10km distant: be sure to get a bus going specifically to Pátzcuaro. Buses back to the bus station ("Central") can be picked up in Plaza Bocanegra or along Federico Tena. Although the outskirts of Pátzcuaro straggle about three kilometres or so down to the lakeshore, the centre of town is very small indeed, focusing on the two main squares, **Plaza Vasco de Quiroga** (or Plaza Grande) and **Plaza Bocanegra** (Plaza Chica).

The **tourist office** (Mon–Sat 9am–8pm, Sun 9am–3pm; ⓣ434/344-3486) is on the west side of Plaza Quiroga at no. 1. The staff can give you information on the town's **festivals**, principally Año Nuevo (Jan 1), when the Danza de los Viejitos (Dance of the Little Old Men) is performed; the Day of the Dead (see box, p.376); and La Señora de la Salud (Dec 8), a saint's day event attended by many Tarascan pilgrims: you'll witness the worshippers in an intense, almost hypnotic fervour. The scrubby park outside the basílica becomes a fairground and there are all manner of Tarascan dances.

## Accommodation

With the recent arrival of a small **hostel** and the ever-expanding selection of top end **B&Bs** and hotels, Pátzcuaro offers an excellent range of places to stay. Prices are a little higher then elsewhere in the state, but if you are prepared to pay a little more you'll get a lot more elegance. Most establishments are on one or other of the plazas, with the ritzier ones surrounding Plaza Vasco de Quiroga and a selection of simpler places around the Plaza Bocanegra. Wherever you stay, check that there will be an adequate **water supply** – Pátzcuaro suffers regular shortages.

**Rates** generally spike at Christmas/New Year, Semana Santa and Easter. The same is true around the **Day of the Dead** (first two days of Nov), when there's little chance of getting a room unless you book at least a couple of months ahead (more like six to twelve months for some of the posher places).

**La Casa Encantada** Dr Coss 15 ⓣ434/342-3492, ⓦwww.lacasaencantada.com. Gorgeous and intimate American-owned B&B in the heart of town. Beautiful touches that raise it above the ordinary, including delicious breakfasts. ❼

**Gran Hotel** Plaza Bocanegra 6 ⓣ434/342-0443, ⓦwww.mexonline.com/granhotel.htm. Smallish, clean, tiled rooms with TV and phone in a friendly hotel right on the Plaza. ❺

**Hacienda Mariposa** Km3.5 Carretera Pátzcuaro–Santa Clara del Cobre ⓣ443/338-7198, ⓦwww.haciendamariposas.com. This comfortable, upscale oasis outside town offers pony treks, ecotours and superb cuisine in serene wooded surroundings. ❽

**Hotel de la Concordia** Plaza Bocanegra 31, ⓣ434/342-0003. Well-maintained, clean rooms, with bathrooms, secure parking and TV. ❹

**Hotel Los Escudos** Plaza Quiroga 73 ⓣ434/342-1290, ⓔhescudos@ml.com.mx. Beautiful colonial building with rooms around two flower-filled courtyards; all have carpet and TV, and some have fireplaces. Ask for a room in the original hotel and not the extension next door. Good value. ❻

**Hotel Imperial** Obregón 21 ⓣ434/342-0308. Some will find the rooms here dark and unacceptably basic but this is the cheapest place around. All rooms have bathroom and TV, and set hours for hot water. ❸

**Hotel Mesón del Gallo** Dr Coss 20 ⓣ434/342-1474, ⓦwww.mexonline.com/mesondelgallo.htm. One of the oldest hotels in town. Attractively rustic common spaces, decent rooms and an excellent restaurant. Breakfast included. ❻

**Hotel Posada La Basílica** Arciga 6 ⓣ434/342-1108, US ⓣ1-800/288-4282, ⓦwww.posadalabasilica.com. Up the hill opposite the basilica. Delightful rooms, some with fireplaces, in an eighteenth-century building with superb views of the town. All the expected amenities, including fireplaces, cable TV, phones and wireless Internet. ❽, master suite ❾

**Hotel Posada de Don Vasco** Lázaro Cárdenas 450, 2km north of town ⓣ434/342-0227, ⓦwww.bestwestern.com. This tastefully decorated hotel was built in 1938. Now a Best Western, it boasts a swimming pool, tennis court and gardens filled with fruit trees. All rooms are well appointed, though the "Colonial" rooms, with nicer decor and bathtub, are worth the extra M$100. 7–8

**Hotel Posada de la Salud** Serrato 9 ⓣ434/342-0058, ⓔposadadelasalud@hotmail.com. Behind the basilica, a short walk from the centre. Beautiful little budget hotel, peaceful and spotless and run by two sisters; some rooms have fireplaces. Probably the best value in town. 4

**International Hostal** Michoacán 43 ⓣ434/342 0975. Welcoming hostel with three rooms, each with a double bed and access to a common bathroom and kitchen. The showers are hot, the back garden private and the staff very helpful. Balconies have views over the town towards the lake. M$100 per person.

**Mansión Iturbe** Plaza Quiroga 59 ⓣ434/342-0368, ⓦwww.iturbide.com. Once a muleteer's house, this small luxury inn and architectural jewel is run by a mother–daughter team. There's a library, superb dining and attractive bedrooms with soaring ceilings and down duvets. Your fourth night is free if booked on arrival. 8

**Misión San Manuel** Plaza Quiroga 12 ⓣ434/342-1050. The great colonial front on this ex-convent hides a modern interior. Comfortable rooms, several with fireplaces. 5

**Posada Mandala** Lerin 14 ⓣ434/342-4176, ⓦwww.geocities.com/mandala_mex. This B&B near the Casa de los Once Patios has a groovy proprietor and comfortable rooms with handwoven grass mats and exquisite rooftop views. 4

**Valmen** Padre Lloreda 34 ⓣ434/342-1161, ⓦwww.mexonline.com/valmen.htm. Large, clean, tiled rooms with TV and bathroom, all around a plant-filled courtyard. A good budget option, though the candy-green walls won't be to everyone's taste. 3

**Villa Pátzcuaro** Lázaro Cárdenas, 2km north of town ⓣ434/342-0767, ⓦwww.villapatzcuaro.com. Great little hotel and RV park in spacious grounds with a small pool. Tent and RV campers (M$70 per person) have access to a kitchen. Tasteful rustic-style rooms are imaginatively decorated and very clean and come with breakfast. There are also a couple of self-contained houses for longer stays. Frequent buses from Plaza Bocanegra pass right outside. 5

## The Town

More than anywhere in the state, Pátzcuaro owes its position to Bishop Vasco de Quiroga, whose affection for the area's indigenous peoples led him to settle in the Purépechan heartland on the shores of Lago de Pátzcuaro. It was he who decided, in the face of considerable opposition from the Spanish in Morelia (then known as Valladolid), to build the cathedral here, where it would be centrally located. Although subsequent bishops moved the seat of power back to Morelia, the foundation had been laid for the community's continued success. Pátzcuaro enjoyed a building boom in the sixteenth century and has been of secondary industrial and political importance ever since. Throughout the centre are old mansions with balconies and coats of arms, barely touched since those early years. Today, quaint Pátzcuaro has developed into an upmarket and artistically inclined town with numerous boutiques. You can spend hours wandering around the beautiful – and expensive – arts, crafts and antique shops, aimed mainly at visitors from Mexico City and abroad.

### The plazas

Nothing much worth seeing in Pátzcuaro lies more than a few minutes' walk from **Plaza Gertrudis Bocanegra**, named after a local Independence heroine, and **Plaza Vasco de Quiroga**. The finest of Pátzcuaro's mansions are on the latter, especially the seventeenth-century **Casa del Gigante**, with its hefty pillars and crudely carved figures. Another nearby mansion is said to have been inhabited by Prince Huitzimengari, son of the last Tarascan king. Both are privately owned, however, and not open to visitors. There are more luxurious houses on the Plaza Bocanegra, but the most striking thing around here is the

**Biblioteca** (Mon–Fri 9am–7pm, Sat 10am–1pm), with its rough-hewn wooden barrel ceiling. The former sixteenth-century church of San Agustín, it has been converted into a library and decorated with **murals** by **Juan O'Gorman** depicting the history of Michoacán, especially Nuño de Guzman burning alive the leader of the Tarascans. O'Gorman (1905–82) possessed a prodigious talent, and is one of the muralists who inherited the mantle of Rivera and Orozco: his best-known work is the decoration of the interior of Chapultepec Castle in Mexico City. The paintings here couldn't be described as subtle, and he certainly ensures that the anti-imperialist point is taken. However, even O'Gorman manages to find praise for Vasco de Quiroga.



### The Basilica and El Humilladero

East of the Plaza Bocanegra, Quiroga's cathedral – the **Basílica de Nuestra Señora de la Salud**, or **Colegiata** – was intended by Quiroga to be Pátzcuaro's masterpiece, with space for 30,000 worshippers. A massive structure for such a small town, it was never completed, and the existing basilica, finished in the nineteenth century, is only the nave of the original design. Even so, it is often full, for local people continue to revere Quiroga: the first chapel on the left as you walk in the main entrance is the **Mausoleo de Don Vasco**, the doors typically closed and adorned with notes of thanks for his miraculous intervention. The church also possesses a miraculous healing image of the Virgin, crafted in a traditional Tarascan method out of *pasta de caña*, a gum-like modelling paste made principally from maize. Services here are extraordinary, especially for the town's patron saint, the Virgin de la Salud, on December 8.

A twenty-minute walk east along Serrato is **El Humilladero** ("the place of humiliation"), probably the oldest church in Pátzcuaro. It stands on the site where the last Tarascan king, Tanganxoan II, accepted Spanish authority – hence the humbling name. Such a tag may seem appropriate with hindsight, though a more charitable view suggests that Tanganxoan was simply hoping to save his people from the slaughter that had accompanied resistance to the Spanish elsewhere. The church itself, pretty enough, is often closed, so there's little to see.

### Museo de Artes Populares

The **Museo de Artes Populares**, at the corner of Quiroga and Lerin, south of the basilica (Tues–Sat 9am–7pm, Sun 9am–4.30pm; M$30, free on Sun), occupies the ancient Colegio de San Nicolas. Founded by Quiroga in 1540, the college is now devoted to a superb collection of regional handicrafts: local lacquerware and pottery; copperware from Santa Clara del Cobre; and traditional masks and religious objects made from *pasta de caña*, which, apart from being easy to work with, is also very light, and hence easily carried in processions. Some of the objects on display are ancient, others the best examples of modern work, and all are set in a very beautiful building. Almost opposite, the church of **La Compañía** was built by Quiroga in 1546 and later taken over by the Jesuits.

### Casa de los Once Patios

A short walk south of the art museum on Lerin, the **Casa de los Once Patios** (daily 10am–7pm, though individual stores may keep their own hours) is an eighteenth-century convent converted into a crafts showhouse, full of workshops and moderate to expensive boutiques. As its name suggests, the complex is set around a series of tiny courtyards, and it's a fascinating place to stroll through even if you can't afford the goods. You can watch restored treadle looms at work, admire the intricacy with which the best lacquerware is created and wander at liberty through the warren of rooms and corridors.

### Cerro del Estribo

The best views of Lago de Pátzcuaro are found east of town along the road to the Cerro del Estribo: head out along Terán past the Templo San Francisco. It is about a kilometre from here to the **Cerro del Calvario**, a tiny hill topped by the little **chapel of El Calvario**. You won't be able to see much from the chapel, so take the road to the right just before you reach it and continue on along a cobbled, cypress-lined avenue. You'll climb over 200m in the next 3km to a viewpoint with great vistas over Lago de Pátzcuaro and Janitzio. You can get a taxi out here from town, or if you're walking and don't fancy the road, look out for a parallel horse trail on the right.

From the viewpoint, 417 steps lead straight up to the very summit of **Cerro del Estribo** (Stirrup Hill), though the views are no better.

## Eating and drinking

Most of Pátzcuaro's hotels have their own **restaurants**, with fairly standard menus throughout: lots of reasonably priced, if unexciting, comidas corridas. Most of the establishments ringing Plaza Quiroga rely too heavily on their (admittedly excellent) location and the food is neither exceptional nor great value; they're better for a snack or coffee. Most of the more interesting places are tucked down side streets. Overall, cheap eats are hard to come by, but there are a few food stalls in the **market**, which is at its most colourful and animated on Friday, when the *indígenas* come in from the country to trade and barter their surplus. Most evenings you can also get basic food from the stalls set up in the Plaza Bocanegra.

One feature of virtually all menus in town is *pescado blanco*, a rather flabby whitefish from the lake, and *sopa tarasca* – a tomato-based soup with chile and bits of tortilla. For the best **fish**, head to the lake, where a line of restaurants faces the landing jetty. A decent *menú del día* goes for M$30–45.

Pátzcuaro isn't really a late-night kind of place. Most of the restaurants close up by around 9pm, and even the few **bars** close fairly early.

**Cafetería Botafumeiro** Plaza Quiroga 10. A relaxed place to sit out under the arches eating fresh cakes over a good coffee.

**El Campanario** Plaza Quiroga 12. Reasonably lively bar on the Plaza Quiroga, often with either a DJ or a couple of musicians playing in the corner.

**Don Rafa** Mendoza 30. A pleasant room decorated with old photos of Pátzcuaro makes a comfortable setting for very tasty three-course *menu del día* (M$55). Delicious fresh salsa on every table, and attentive service.

**Doña Paca** Plaza Quiroga 59, attached to the *Mansión Iturbe* hotel ⓣ434/342-0368. Come here for comfortable and elegant dining and a menu of reasonably priced regional dishes, including creative salads of local ingredients, triangular Purépechan tamales (*corundas*), hearty Tarascan soup, *churipo de carne* (beef stew) and fish with coriander sauce.

**Gran Hotel** Plaza Bocanegra 6. The streetside tables here catch the morning sun, making it one of the best spots in town for a hearty breakfast (M$55).

**Mistongo** Dr Coss 4. Inviting restaurant with pared-down traditional Mexican decor, serving the likes of *sopa tarasca* (M$35), fajitas (M$80) and pasta dishes (M$70–90).

**La Pacanda** Portal Hidalgo, Plaza Quiroga. Just a couple of wooden carts with metal tubs on ice serving superb ice cream and sorbets since 1905. Try interesting flavours like tequila, mandarin and tamarind.

**El Patio** Plaza Quiroga 19. Quite a chic little restaurant offering good coffee, reasonably priced breakfasts, *antojitos*, steaks, sandwiches and, of course, fish.

**El Primer Piso** Plaza Quiroga 29, ⓣ434/342-0122. This gourmet place serves a mixture of Tarascan, French and Italian flavours at tables upstairs overlooking the square. Expect the likes of palmetto and artichoke-heart salad (M$58) followed by fillet Roquefort (M$115) or chicken *nogada* (M$100).

**Tekare** Arciga 6, inside the *Hotel Posada la Basílica*. Try the house speciality, *kurucha urapiti* (battered whitefish with chiles). Great views of the town and beyond to the lake.

**El Viejo Gaucho** Iturbide 10. Relaxed restaurant with a loosely Argentine-influenced menu of steaks (M$120–160), pizza (M$70–100) and burgers (M$40). There's also a separate bar where live music (cover around M$25) is performed most evenings from around 8pm.

## Listings

**Banks and exchange** There's a bank on the north side of Plaza Quiroga and a couple more on Iturbe between the two plazas (all with ATMs). At the corner of Buena Vista and Ahumada near the *Hotel Valmen* there's a casa de cambio.

**Internet access** Numerous places all charging around M$12/hr. Try Meg@net at Mendoza 8 and Plaza Quiroga 67.

**Laundry** Lavanderia San Francisco, Terán 16, is in front of the Templo San Francisco (Mon–Sat 9am–8pm).

**Post office** Obregón 13 (Mon–Fri 8am–4pm, Sat 9am–1pm).

**Spanish courses** The Centro de Lenguas y Ecoturismo de Pátzcuaro, Navarette 50 (Ⓣ434/342-4764, Ⓦwww.celep.com.mx), offers assorted language classes. Homestays also available.

**Telephones** You can phone and fax from several *casetas* on the east side of Plaza Bocanegra, or at cardphones under Portal Hidalgo on the west side of Plaza Quiroga.

## Lago de Pátzcuaro and Janitzio

Apart from the beautiful town itself, Pátzcuaro's other great attraction is **Lago de Pátzcuaro**. It's around 4km (less than an hour's **walk**) down to the jetty (follow the "embarcadero" signs), while **buses** and minibuses leave from the Plaza Bocanegra. Those marked "Lago" will drop you right by the boats. The lake itself was once a major thoroughfare, but that role has declined since the completion of roads linking the lakeside villages a few years back. Most locals now take the bus rather than paddle around the water in canoes, but there is still a fair amount of traffic and regular trips out to the closest island, **Janitzio** (see opposite).

### The Day of the Dead around Lago de Pátzcuaro

The **Day of the Dead** (Nov 1, and through the night into the next day) is celebrated in spectacular fashion throughout Mexico, but nowhere more so than on Lago de Pátzcuaro, particularly the island of **Janitzio**. On this night, the locals conduct what is an essentially private meditation, carrying offerings of fruit and flowers to the cemetery and maintaining a vigil over the graves of their ancestors until dawn, chanting by candlelight. Death is thought to be a continuation of life, and this is the time when the souls of *muertitos* (deceased loved ones) return to the land of the living. It's a spectacular and moving sight, especially earlier in the evening as indigenous people from the surrounding area converge on the island in their canoes, each with a single candle burning in the bow.

Impressive and solemn though the occasion is, over the years the occasion has become somewhat marred by its sheer press of **spectators**, both Mexican and foreign. Thousands head over to tiny Janitzio, and from around 10pm on Oct 1 until around 3am the following morning you can hardly move, especially in the cemetery where the vigil takes place amid a riot of marigolds and candles. If you can manage it, stay up all night and return to the cemetery around 5am when it is quiet and the first hint of dawn lightens the eastern sky. Alternatively, head to one of the other lakeside communities marking the Day of the Dead – Tzurumutaro, Ihuatzio, Cucuchucho or Tzintzuntzán. There's no guarantee of a quiet and respectful vigil, but crowds will be smaller and the cemeteries no less amazing.

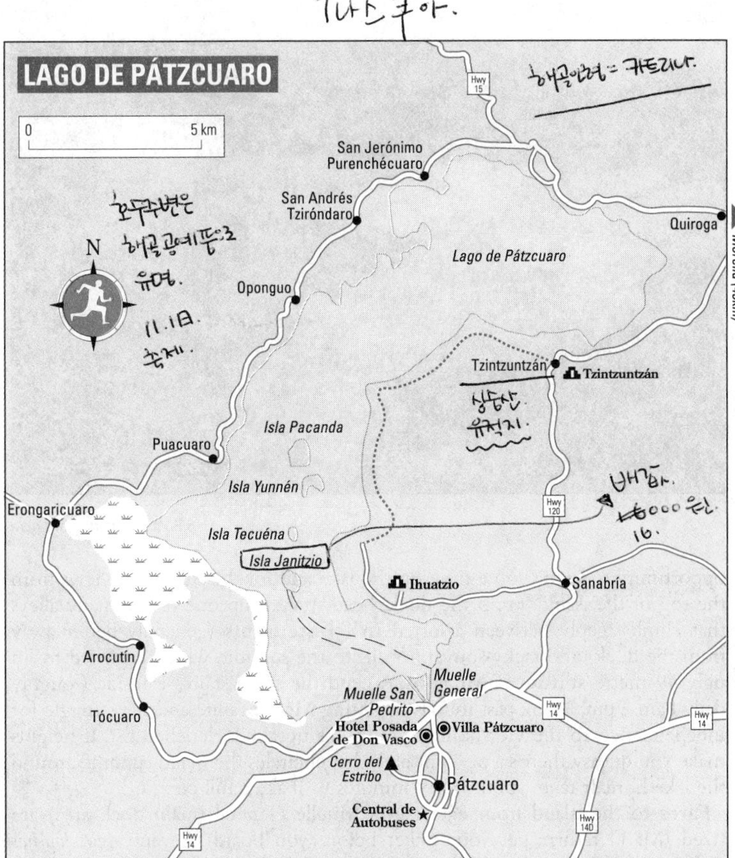


There isn't a great deal to see or do on the other islands in the lake, with the exception of **Isla Yuñuen**, where you can stay in the rustic *Cabañas de Yuñuen* (Ⓣ434/342-4473; ⑤), each with a small kitchen and TV. A boat makes trips to the island from the Muelle General in Pátzcuaro (the main dock area; around M$150 return for four people).

The lake's other draw is the chance to see and photograph the famous **butterfly nets** wielded by indigenous fishermen in tiny dug-out canoes. It is a long time since this was considered a viable means of gaining food, but a handful of nets are maintained to catch tourists. Occasionally a group of locals lurking in readiness on the far side of Janitzio will paddle into camera range when a sufficiently large collection of money has been taken.

## Janitzio

From a distance, the island of **Janitzio** looks quaint, but as you get closer it appears almost squalid. With fishing becoming ever less viable and with no land flat enough for agriculture, the conical, car-free island has found itself relying increasingly on the tourism industry – you'll be besieged by souvenir hawkers from the moment you arrive. Still, it is worth the journey if only for the

△ Boats, Lago de Pátzcuaro

opportunity to spend some time on the lake and for the expansive views from the top of the island. From the dock, head straight up one of the many alleys that climb steeply between assorted **fish restaurants** (generally better away from the dock) and tacky souvenir stalls to the summit, which crowned by an ugly 49-metre-**statue of Morelos**. Ascend the spiral staircase inside (roughly daily 8am–7pm; M$6), past murals depicting Morelos's life and the struggle for independence, to the viewpoint right by his upraised, clenched fist. If heights make you queasy, there's a pleasant path that encircles the island running around the lakeshore. It takes about thirty minutes to make a full circuit.

**Fares** to the island from Pátzcuaro's Muelle General (main dock area) are fixed (M$30 return; get your ticket before you board). Seventy-seat *lanchas* make the stately, if noisy, half-hour crossing (daily 7am–7pm; every 15min).

## Around Lago de Pátzcuaro

No visit to Pátzcuaro is complete without an excursion to the small lakeside villages, which, thanks to Vasco de Quiroga, each specialize in a different **artesanía**. **Getting around** the villages is fairly easy. Buses to Tzintzuntzán and Quiroga leave from the Central de Autobuses but can also be picked up on the highway close to the *embarcadero*. You can also take a *colectivo* from the Plaza Bocanegra to Ihuatzio, and another from there to Tzintzuntzán. Buses and *colectivos* then continue frequently to Quiroga.

### Ihuatzio

While they're no match for the ruins at Tzintzuntzán, further around the lake (see opposite), the older, pre-Tarascan ruins of **IHUATZIO** (daily 10am–6pm; M$24) are interesting in their own right and worth a peek if you have the time. Located around 12km north of Pátzcuaro, 4km off the Pátzcuaro–Quiroga road on a remote track that traverses a cow pasture, Ihuatzio was strategically placed near the shores of the Lago de Pátzcuaro and used for water defence and enemy lookout. The ruins are essentially divided into two sections, one older than the other: the first (900–1200 AD), is thought to have been constructed by the

Náhuatl, and the second dates from 1200–1530 AD, during the Tarascan occupation. Two fifteen-metre-high **squared-off pyramids**, once considered a sort of Plaza de Armas, are the main features of the site open to the public.

Buses (every 20min; M$6) to Ihuatzio leave from the Plaza Bocanegra in Pátzcuaro. You'll be dropped at the end of a cobblestone road and will have to walk 1500m to the site's entrance. On the walk, look for three vegetated hummocks which are the unexcavated ruins of *yácatas* (see below). To continue to Tzintzuntzán, hop on one of the frequent Quiroga-bound *colectivos* from the road where you were dropped off.



## Tzintzuntzán

The remains of **TZINTZUNTZÁN** (daily 9am–5.30pm; M$33), ancient capital of the Tarascans, lie 15km north of Pátzcuaro on the road to Quiroga. The site was established around the end of the fourteenth century, when the capital was moved from Pátzcuaro, and by the time of the Conquest the Spanish estimated that there were as many as 40,000 people living here, with dominion over all of what is now Michoacán and large parts of the modern states of Jalisco and Colima. Homes and markets, as well as the palaces of the rulers, lay around the raised **ceremonial centre**, but all that can be seen today is the artificial terrace that supported the great religious buildings (*yácatas*), and the partly restored ruins of these temples.

Even if you do no more than pass by on the road, you can't fail to be struck by the scale of these buildings and by their semi-circular design, a startling contrast to the rigid, right-angled formality adhered to by almost every other major pre-Hispanic culture in Mexico. Climb up to the terrace and you'll find five *yácatas*, of which four have been partly rebuilt. Each was originally some 15m high, tapering in steps from a broad base to a walkway along the top less than 2m wide. Devoid of ornamentation, the *yácatas* are in fact piles of flat rocks, held in by retaining walls and then faced in smooth, close-fitting volcanic stone. The terrace, which was originally approached up a broad ceremonial ramp or stairway on the side furthest from the water, affords magnificent views across the lake and the present-day village of Tzintzuntzán. Tzintzuntzán means "place of the hummingbirds"; you're unlikely to see one nowadays, but the theory is that there were plenty of them around until the Tarascans – who used the feathers to make ornaments – hunted them to the point of extinction. The ruins are around 1km from the village and are signposted "Zona Arqueológica" up a side road.

Down in the **village**, which has a reputation for producing and selling some of the region's best ceramics, you'll find what's left of the enormous **Franciscan Monastery** founded around 1530 to convert the Tarascans. Much of this has been demolished, and the rest substantially rebuilt, but there remains a fine Baroque **Templo de San Francisco** and a huge atrium where the indigenous people would gather for sermons. Vasco de Quiroga originally intended to base his diocese here, but eventually decided that Pátzcuaro had the better location and a more constant supply of water. He did leave one unusual legacy, though: the **olive trees** planted around the monastery are probably the oldest in Mexico, since settlers were banned from cultivating olives in order to protect the farmers back in Spain. The broad, veined trunks certainly look their age, and several only have a few living branches sprouting from apparently dead trees.

Tzintzuntzán has several good **fiestas**. The best are a week-long one starting on February 1, and Semana Santa (the week before Easter Sunday), when the Thursday sees the ceremony of Washing the Apostles' Feet, followed on Good Friday by further scenes from Christ's Passion acted out around town.

### Quiroga

**QUIROGA**, 8km northeast of Tzintzuntzán and around 25km from Pátzcuaro, is another village packed with craft markets, though the only genuinely local products seem to be painted wooden objects and furniture. This said, there's plenty of other good wares – leather and woollen goods in particular – in the daily handicrafts **market** which spreads on side streets in all directions from the main plaza.

Make an effort to come to Quiroga if you're in the area around the first Sunday in July, when the town celebrates the **Día de la Preciosa Sangre de Cristo** with a huge fiesta and a beautiful torch-lit procession behind a paraded image of Christ.

## Santa Clara del Cobre

Approximately 25km south of Pátzcuaro, via a country road over a pine-draped pass, lies **Santa Clara del Cobre**, long celebrated for the **copper crafts** on which it continues to thrive. There are no fewer than two hundred family-run studios (*talleres*) and shops, many of which line the quaint town's arcades and side streets selling everything from cheap bracelets and thimbles to hammered sinks and sparkling *carnitas* caldrons.

Much more of the metal is on display at the town's **Museo del Cobre**, Morelos 263 at Pino Suárez (Tues–Sat 10am–3pm & 5–7pm, Sun 10am–4pm; M$2), which exhibits a small but impressive collection of decorative and utilitarian copper crafts. Sadly, only a handful of these intricate old designs are still being incorporated into the production of modern goods. The annual **Feria Nacional del Cobre** (Copper Fair), combined with the **Fiesta de la Virgen del Sagrario**, is held in Santa Clara del Cobre from August 6 to 17. Festivities include exhibits and sales of hand-worked copper, music and dance.

While the town is a quick day trip from Pátzcuaro, you may be moved to spend the night, if not to shop, then to enjoy the clear vistas and mountain air. *Hotel Oasis* (☎434/343-0040; ④) is serviceable and centrally located on the main plaza. Be sure to ask for a room with mountain views. Restaurant *El Portal*, Portal Matamoros 18, overlooks the main plaza and serves good breakfasts (M$35) and comidas corridas (M$45) along with hamburgers (M$15). Driving time to Santa Clara del Cobre from Pátzcuaro is about twenty minutes (follow signs for Opopeo), taxis cost M$80, and buses (Autobuses Purhépechas; M$7; bound for Ario de Rosales) leave the central station in Pátzcuaro every thirty minutes throughout the day for the thirty-minute trip.

# Morelia

The state capital, **MORELIA**, is in many ways unrepresentative of Michoacán. It looks Spanish and, despite a large indigenous population, it feels Spanish – with its broad streets lined with seventeenth-century mansions and outdoor cafés sheltered by arcaded plazas, you might easily be in Salamanca or Valladolid. Indeed, the city's name was Valladolid until 1828, when it was changed to honour local-born Independence hero José María Morelos.

Morelia has always been a city of Spaniards. It was one of the first they founded after the Conquest – two Franciscan friars, Juan de San Miguel and Antonio de Lisboa, settled here among the native inhabitants in 1530 and first laid claim to the city. Ten years later, they were visited by the first viceroy of New Spain, Antonio de Mendóza, who was so taken by the site that he ordered

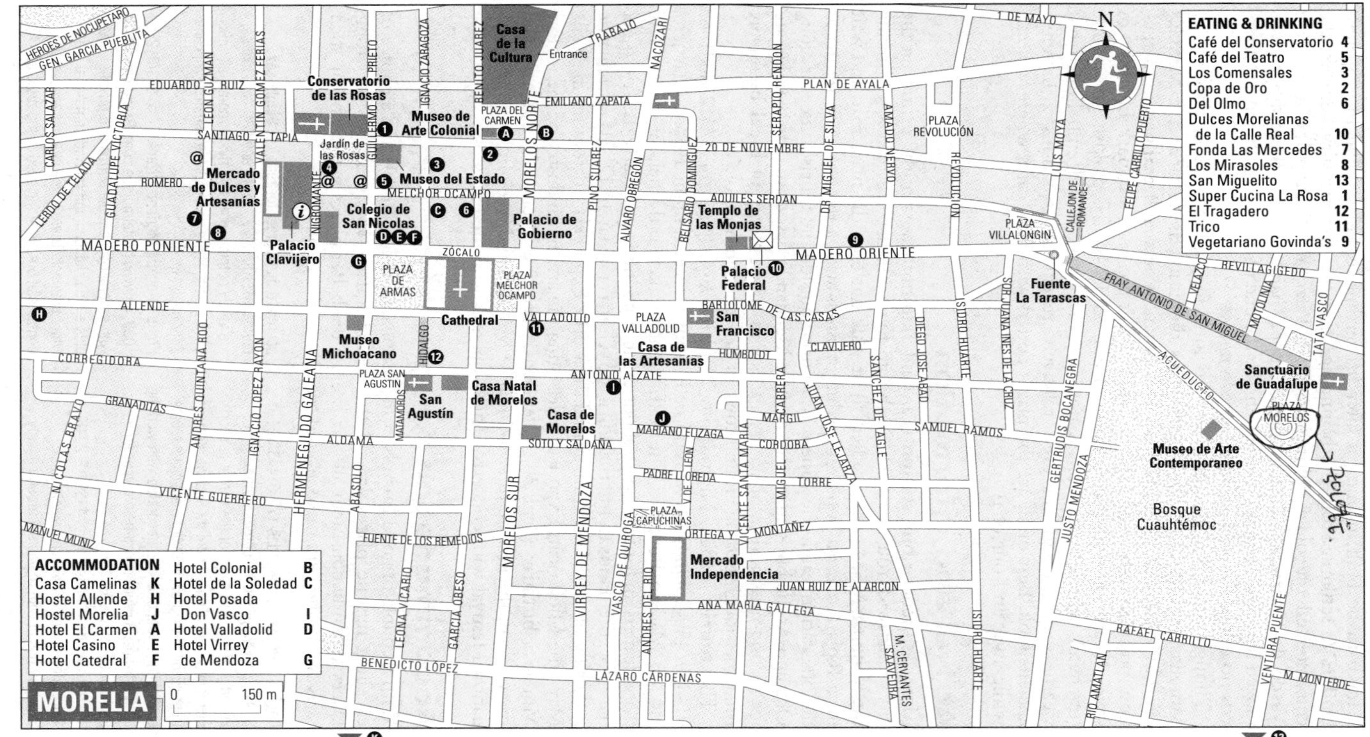
MORELIA
0 150 m
N
EATING & DRINKING
Café del Conservatorio 4
Café del Teatro 5
Los Comensales 3
Copa de Oro 2
Del Olmo 6
Dulces Morelianas de la Calle Real 10
Fonda Las Mercedes 7
Los Mirasoles 8
San Miguelito 13
Super Cucina La Rosa 1
El Tragadero 12
Trico 11
Vegetariano Govinda's 9
ACCOMMODATION
Casa Camelinas K
Hostel Allende H
Hostel Morelia J
Hotel El Carmen A
Hotel Casino E
Hotel Catedral F
Hotel Colonial B
Hotel de la Soledad C
Hotel Posada Don Vasco I
Hotel Valladolid D
Hotel Virrey de Mendoza G
Casa de la Cultura
Entrance
Conservatorio de las Rosas
Jardín de las Rosas
Museo de Arte Colonial
Plaza del Carmen
Museo del Estado
Mercado de Dulces y Artesanías
Colegio de San Nicolas
Palacio Clavijero
Palacio de Gobierno
Zócalo
Plaza de Armas
Cathedral
Plaza Melchor Ocampo
Museo Michoacano
Plaza San Agustín
San Agustín
Casa Natal de Morelos
Casa de Morelos
Templo de las Monjas
Palacio Federal
Plaza Valladolid
San Francisco
Casa de las Artesanías
Plaza Capuchinas
Mercado Independencia
Plaza Revolución
Plaza Villalongín
Fuente La Tarascas
Sanctuario de Guadalupe
Plaza Morelos
Museo de Arte Contemporaneo
Bosque Cuauhtémoc
Acueducto
Madero Poniente
Madero Oriente
Morelos Norte
Morelos Sur
Fray Antonio de San Miguel
Virrey de Mendoza
Vasco de Quiroga
Hermenegildo Galeana
Justo Mendoza
Isidro Huarte
Lázaro Cárdenas
Ventura Puente
Rafael Carrillo
Tata Vasco

a town to be built, naming it after his birthplace and sending fifty Spanish families to settle it. From the beginning, there was fierce rivalry between the colonists and the older culture's town of Pátzcuaro. During the lifetime of **Vasco de Quiroga**, Pátzcuaro had the upper hand, but later the bishopric was moved here, a university founded, and by the end of the sixteenth century there was no doubt that Valladolid was predominant.

Though there are specific things to look for and to visit in present-day Morelia, the city as a whole outweighs them: it was declared a UNESCO World Heritage site in 1991 and city ordinances decree that all new construction must perfectly match the old, such that it preserves a remarkable unity of style. Nearly everything is built of the same faintly pinkish-grey stone (trachyte), which, being soft, is not only easily carved and embellished but weathers quickly, giving even relatively recent constructions a battered, ancient look. Best of all are the plazas dotted with little cafés where you can while away an hour or two.

## Arrival and information

Morelia's modern **bus station** is around 3km northwest of the centre on the city's ring road. You can catch a cab into town (fixed-price tickets sold inside the terminal; M$24 to the cathedral) or walk out onto the main road and wait for a Roja 1 *colectivo* (look for a white minibus with a red band). To return to the bus station, catch the same *colectivo* from outside the tourist office or along Ocampo. At the bus station, Sala A is predominantly first class, salas B and C are for second-class and local services. Once in town, plenty of **local buses** ply Madero, though getting around town is easy enough on foot.

The **tourist office**, Nigromante 79 (daily 9am–7pm; ⓣ443/312-8081 or 01-800/450-2300, ⓦwww.visitmorelia.com), is located in the Palacio Clavijero, just off Madero Poniente. The staff, friendly and mostly helpful, have a few maps, leaflets and information about exhibitions, films and **festivals**. Try to get here for the Festival Internacional de Guitarra (March 17–21), a fantastic gathering of musicians from around the world; Expo Feria (dates vary in April/May), the Michoacán Expo Fair celebrating the arts and industry of the region; Morelos's birthday (Sept 30), celebrated with civic events, fairs, dances and fireworks; or the Festival Internacional de Música (third week in Nov), an international festival with concerts, recitals, operas and conferences.

## Accommodation

With a couple of good **hostels**, some reasonable budget **hotels** and a choice of excellent upscale places around the central squares you can't go far wrong. Prices are fairly consistent all year, though the better places may bump up their rates twenty percent or so around the Day of the Dead.

**Casa Camelinas** Jacarandas 172 ⓣ443/324-5194, ⓦwww.mexonline.com/casacam1.htm. Friendly B&B 1.5km south of the centre (a short taxi ride or *combi* ride – take the orange #3 from in front of the cathedral), with light, spacious rooms, each with private bath and decorated with work by local artisans. Be sure to call before your arrival, as it's not near much. ❼

**Hostel Allende** Allende 843 ⓣ443/312-2246, ⓦtravelbymexico.com/mich/hostelallende. Excellent hostel with rooms set around a leafy courtyard that's great for relaxing. Single-sex dorms (M$100; M$90 for HI and ISIC cardholders) are vastly outnumbered by private rooms, all with private bath. There's a small kitchen, free WiFi and 24hr check-in. ❹

**Hostel Morelia** Mariano Elízaga 57 ⓣ443/312-1062, ⓦwww.hostelmorelia.com. Brand new hostel with several comfortable dorms and private rooms plus a small kitchen and relaxed communal area with hammock. There's free Internet access, and Continental breakfast included in the price of dorms (M$140, HI member M$120) but not private rooms. ❹

**Hotel El Carmen** Eduardo Ruíz 63 ⓣ443/312-1725, ⓕ314-1797. Friendly budget hotel on a pretty square, with clean rooms, mostly with TV and bathroom. Some are a little small, while the better ones overlook the Plaza del Carmen. ❹

**Hotel Casino** Portal Hidalgo 229, ⓣ443/313-1328 or 01-800/450 2100, ⓦwww.hotelcasino.com.mx. Best Western hotel on the Plaza de Armas set around a covered courtyard. Rooms are a little soulless but maintain high standards with all the usual amenities. ❼

**Hotel Catedral** Ignacio Zaragoza 37 ⓣ443/313-0783, ⓦwww.hotelcatedralmorelia.com. Rooms around a restaurant in another covered colonial courtyard, although here you certainly pay for the atmosphere. Continental breakfast included. ❼

**Hotel Colonial** 20 de Noviembre 15 ⓣ443/312-1897. One of the cheaper places right in the centre with a wide range of rooms, almost all with bath (hot water all day). The nicest rooms face the street. ❹

**Hotel de la Soledad** Ignacio Zaragoza 90 ⓣ443/312-1888, ⓦwww.hsoledad.com. This spectacular colonial building, just off the Plaza de Armas, is the city's oldest inn. Breezy rooms are set around a beautiful open courtyard (M$1100); slightly lower-priced ones are in the less attractive back courtyard (M$1000). Breakfast included. ❼

**Hotel Posada Don Vasco** Vasco de Quiroga 232 ⓣ443 /312-1484, ⓔposada_don_vasco@hotmail.com. Reasonably priced colonial-style hotel is one of the best deals downtown. Some rooms are dull and modern and others a bit poky, so have a look around. Cable TV. ❹

**Hotel Valladolid** Portal Hidalgo 245, on the Plaza de Armas ⓣ443/312-0027 or 01-800/581-2212. Great position under the colonial arches. Recently upgraded, with some rooms in colonial style. These can be a bit cramped; you're better off paying the extra M$300 for one of the chic Moderne rooms, which are all blonde-wood floors and white walls. ❻–❼

**Hotel Virrey de Mendoza** Madero 310 Pte ⓣ443/312-0633, ⓦwww.hotelvirrey.com. Fantastic colonial grandeur: even if you can't afford to stay it's worth dropping by to take a look or have a drink in the courtyard. The rooms aren't as impressive as the lobby, but it is a lovely spot just the same for its history, majestic public spaces and fine service. ❾

## The Town

Everything you're likely to want to see is within easy walking distance of the **Plaza de Armas**, the heart of the colonial centre. **Avenida Francisco Madero**, which runs along the north side of Plaza de Armas and the cathedral, is very much the main street, with most of the important public buildings and major shops strung out along it.

### Around the cathedral

At the heart of the city, Morelia's massive **cathedral** boasts two soaring towers that are said to be the tallest in Mexico. Begun in 1640 in the relatively plain Herrerian style, the towers and dome were not completed for some hundred years, by which time the Baroque had arrived with a vengeance; nevertheless, component parts harmonize remarkably, and for all the cathedral's size and richness of decoration, perfect proportions prevent it from becoming overpowering. The interior, refitted towards the end of the nineteenth century, after most of its silver ornamentation had been removed to pay for the wars, is simple. A few early colonial religious paintings are preserved in the choir and the sacristy.

Flanking the cathedral, the **Plaza de Armas** (or de los Martíres) is the place to sit around and revel in the city's leisurely pace – relax with a coffee and a morning paper (you can buy a few international newspapers from the stands here) in the cafés under its elegant arcaded *portales*. On the southwestern edge of the plaza, at the corner of Allende and Abasolo, the **Museo Michoacano** (Tues–Sat 9am–4.45pm, Sun 9am–3.45pm; M$30, free on Sun) occupies a palatial eighteenth-century mansion. Emperor Maximilian lodged here on his visits to Morelia, and it now houses a collection that reflects the state's diversity and rich history: the rooms devoted to archeology are, of course, dominated by

△ Cathedral, Morelia

the **Tarascan culture**, including pottery and small sculptures from Tzintzuntzán, but also display much earlier objects, notably some obsidian figurines. Out in the patio are two magnificent old carriages, while upstairs the colonial epoch is represented in a large group of religious paintings and sculptures and a collection of old books and manuscripts.

A smaller square, the **Plaza Melchor Ocampo**, flanks the cathedral on the other side. Facing it, the **Palacio de Gobierno** was formerly a seminary – Independence hero Morelos and his nemesis Agustín Iturbide studied here, as did Ocampo, a nineteenth-century liberal supporter of Benito Juárez. It's of interest now for Alfredo Zalce's **murals** adorning the stairway and upper level of the patio: practically the whole of Mexican history, and each of its heroes, is depicted.

Immediately east along Madero are several **banks** that are among the most remarkable examples of active conservation you'll see anywhere: old mansions that have been refurbished in traditional style, and somehow manage to combine reasonably efficient operation with an ambience that is wholly in keeping with the setting.

### West and north of the plaza

One block west of the Plaza de Armas, the **Colegio de San Nicolas** is part of the University of Michoacán. Founded at Pátzcuaro in 1540 by Vasco de Quiroga, and moved here in 1580, the college is the second oldest in Mexico and hence in all the Americas – it now houses administrative offices and various technical faculties. To the side, across Nigromante in what was originally the Jesuit church of **La Compañía**, is the public library, while next to this is the beautiful **Palacio Clavijero**, now converted into government offices. Alongside the Palacio, down Gomez Farias, enclosed *portales* are home to the **Mercado de Dulces y Artesanías**, groaning with the sweets for which the city is famed, along with stalls selling leather jackets, guitars and other handicrafts, though little of much quality.

At the north end of Nigromante, on another charming little plaza – the Jardín de las Rosas – you'll come across the Baroque church of **Santa Rosa** and, beside it, the **Conservatorio de las Rosas**, a music academy founded in the eighteenth century. From time to time it hosts concerts of classical music – the tourist office should have details.

Also here, at the corner of Santiago Tapia and Guillermo Prieto, is the **Museo del Estado** (Mon–Fri 9am–2pm & 4–8pm, Sat & Sun 10am–6pm; free). Inside this eighteenth-century former home, the complete furniture and fittings of a traditional *farmacia* have been reconstructed, after which you move, somewhat incongruously, to the prehistory and archeology collections. This is mostly minor stuff, though there are some intriguing ceramic figurines and some fine, unusual Tarascan jewellery, including gold and turquoise pieces, and necklaces strung with tiny crystal skulls. Upstairs, there's one room of colonial history and various ethnological exhibits illustrating traditional local dress and lifestyles – a butterfly fishing net from Pátzcuaro plus displays on copper working and guitar manufacture.

East of here, or north from the cathedral on Juárez, is the **Museo de Arte Colonial** (Mon–Fri 9am–8pm, Sat & Sun 9am–7pm; free). Its collection of colonial art is almost entirely regional, and not of great interest, though there is an expansive display of rather gory crucifixes. Of greater interest on the north side of the plaza, entered from Morelos, the beautiful old Convento del Carmen now houses the **Casa de la Cultura** (open all day, but most exhibits Mon–Fri 9am–6pm, Sat & Sun 10am–6pm; free). It's an enormous complex, worth exploring in its own right, with a theatre, café, space for temporary exhibitions and classes scattered around the former monastic buildings.

### South of the plaza

Two blocks southeast of the cathedral, on Morelos Sur, the **Museo Casa de Morelos** (daily 9.30am–5.30pm; M$24, free Sun) is the relatively modest

## José María Morelos y Pavón

A student of Hidalgo, **José María Morelos** took over the leadership of the Independence movement after its instigators had been executed in 1811. While the cry of Independence had initially been taken up by the Mexican (Creole) bourgeoisie, smarting under the trading restrictions imposed on them by Spain, it quickly became a mass movement. Unlike the original leaders, Morelos (a *mestizo* priest born into relative poverty) was a populist and genuine reformer. Even more unlike them, he was also a political and military tactician of considerable skill, invoking the spirit of the French Revolution and calling for universal suffrage, racial equality and the break-up of the hacienda system, under which workers were tied to agricultural servitude. He was defeated and executed by Royalist armies under Agustín de Iturbide in 1815 after waging years of guerrilla warfare, a period during which Morelos had come close to taking the capital and controlling the entire country. When Independence was finally gained – by Iturbide, who had changed sides and later briefly served as emperor – it was no longer a force for change, rather a reaction to the fact that by 1820 liberal reforms were sweeping Spain itself. The causes espoused by Morelos were, however, taken up to some extent by Benito Juárez and later, with a vengeance, in the Revolution – almost a hundred years after his death.

Around Michoacán you'll see Morelos's image everywhere – notably the massive statue atop Isla de Janitzio – invariably depicted with a kind of bandana over his head. He's also pictured on the fifty-peso note, which features the butterfly-net fishers of Pátzcuaro, monarch butterflies and masks for the Danza de los Viejitos.



eighteenth-century house in which Independence hero José María Morelos y Pavón lived from 1801 (see box above). It's now a museum devoted to his life and the War of Independence. Nearby, at the corner of Corregidora (the continuation of Alzate) and García Obeso, you can see the house where the hero was born, the **Casa Natal de Morelos** (Mon–Fri 9am–8pm Sat & Sun 9am–7pm; free), which now houses a library and a few desultory domestic objects. This in turn is virtually next door to the church of **San Agustín**, from where pedestrianized Hidalgo runs up one block to the Plaza de Armas.

Walk a couple of blocks in the other direction – or take Valladolid directly from the Plaza Ocampo – to find Plaza Valladolid and the church of **San Francisco**. Its former monastery, next door, has been turned into the **Casa de las Artesanías** (Mon–Sat 9am–8pm, Sun 9am–3.30pm; free), possibly the most comprehensive collection of Michoacán's crafts anywhere, almost all of which are for sale.The best and most obviously commercial items are downstairs, while on the upper floor are a series of rooms devoted to the products of particular villages, often with craftspeople demonstrating their techniques (these are staffed by villagers and hence not always open), and a collection of historic items that you can't buy.

### Around the aqueduct

One of the most attractive parts of town to while away a few hours lies about fifteen minutes' walk east along Madero from the cathedral. Wander past the Baroque facade of the **Templo de las Monjas** and the adjacent Palacio Federal to reach tiny **Plaza Villalongin**, a small plaza through the middle of which runs the old **aqueduct**. Built on a winding course between 1785 and 1789, these 253 arches brought water into the city from springs in the nearby hills. Several roads meet here at the **Fuente Las Tarascas**, which features three bare-breasted Tarascan women holding up a vast basket of fruit.

Eastbound roads split three ways here. Madero bears slightly left and, just past the aqueduct, take a peek down the **Callejón de Romance** (Romance Lane), a pretty bougainvillea-draped alley of nineteenth-century homes running down to a couple of fountains. The second of the three roads is **La Calzada Fray Antonio de San Miguel** (named for the bishop who built the aqueduct), a broad and shady pedestrianized walkway that leads down to the wildly overdecorated **Santuario de Guadalupe**, where market stalls, selling above all the sticky local *dulces*, set up at weekends and during fiestas. The last of the three roads, Avenida Acueducto, follows the aqueduct and, 300m along, passes the small **Museo de Arte Contemporáneo** (Tues–Fri 10am–8pm, Sat & Sun 10am–6pm; free), featuring a variety of Latin American work. Behind it is **Bosque Cuauhtémoc**, in which there are some beautifully laid-out flower displays.

## Eating and drinking

On a fine day it is hard to resist the temptation of the cafés and restaurants in the *portales* around the Plaza de Armas: fairly expensive for a full meal, but good for snacks or for a breakfast of coffee and *pan dulce*. As ever, the cheapest eating as at the **market**, found just off Vasco de Quiroga, but Morelia's big Mercado Independencia is on the whole a disappointment, certainly not as large or varied as you'd expect.

Chief of Morelia's specialities are its **dulces**, sweets made of candied fruit or evaporated milk – cloyingly sweet to most non-Mexican tastes, they're very popular here. You can see a wide selection at the **Mercado de Dulces y Artesanías** (see p.385). Morelians also get through a lot of *rompope* (a drink that you'll find to a lesser extent all over Mexico) – again, it's very sweet, an egg concoction based on rum, milk and egg with vanilla, cinnamon or almond flavouring.

**Café del Conservatorio** Santiago Tapia 363. A peaceful place to enjoy local *dulces* and reasonably priced wine, facing the pretty Jardín de las Rosas.

**Café del Teatro** in the Teatro Ocampo, on Ocampo and Prieto. Its lush, almost baronial, interior makes this one of the most popular spots in town for good coffee and people watching. With breakfast for M$30–35 and sandwiches at M$20–25, it's not as expensive as it might be. Try and get a table overlooking the street.

**Los Comensales** Zaragoza 148. Daytime restaurant with a pretty, verdant courtyard setting. The comida corrida is good value at M$65; prices are a bit higher for elaborate Mexican specialities, including a tasty chicken in rich, dark *mole*.

**Copa de Oro** Juárez 194-B at Santiago Tapia. Simple place for fresh *jugos* and tortas.

**Del Olmo** Juárez 95. Sophisticated but relaxed café/bar, set around a pretty interior courtyard, with good coffee, and eggs with ham for breakfast.

**Dulces Morelianas de la Calle Real** Madero 440 Ote. Magnificent old-fashioned candy store with a café serving decadent coffees with drizzles of *cajeta*. The staff even sport colonial dress, and there's a microscopic Museo del Dulces in the back.

**Fonda Las Mercedes** León Guzmán 47. Upscale Tarascan and Mexican dishes in a swanky setting – all white linen and big wine glasses accented by giant rocks. Expect the likes of juicy steaks (M$140) and salmon *a la plancha* (M$165). Daily from 1.30pm.

**Los Mirasoles** Madero 549 Pte ⓣ443/317-5777, ⓦwww.losmirasoles.com. Inventive Mexican and international cuisine in a plush conversion of a seventeenth-century mansion – the courtyard is enchanting. There's a full range of Michoacán specialities (including trout tacos) and an Argentine *parrilla* for delicious steaks. Expect to pay around M$250 for a full meal, and reserve ahead.

**San Miguelito** Camelinas, opposite the Centro Convenciones Fracc. La Loma ⓣ443/324-2300, ⓦwww.sanmiguelito.com.mx. Superb and unpretentious Mexican dishes. Bar is a recreated bullring. Be sure to sit in the room filled with three hundred effigies of St Anthony and say a prayer for a good spouse.

**Super Cucina La Rosa** Santiago Tapia at Prieto. Filling and tasty *menú del día* for M$55.

**Trico** Valladolid 8. Excellent café in a colonial building with exposed beams, stone arches and a stained-glass skylight. It's licensed, and serves tasty breakfasts (M$42–55; until 1pm) along with soups (M$20), burgers and standard Mexican dishes (mostly M$30–40). There's a well-stocked deli and *panadería* on the ground floor.

**El Tragadero** Hidalgo 63. At this relaxed stop you're surrounded by old photos of Morelia. It's a good place for breakfast (M$28–36) or an inexpensive lunch.

**Vegetariano Govinda's** Madero 549 Ote. Good, inexpensive, vegetarian fare. Come for breakfast (M$34–44) or the *menú del día* (M$39–49), comprising meat-less versions of Mexican staples.

## Listings

**Banks and exchange** There are plenty of very grand banks with ATMs along Madero Oriente, open for exchange on weekday mornings, plus a casa de cambio at Valladolid 162-A near the corner with Vasco de Quiroga.

**Entertainment** International films are shown at the Museo Regional Michoacáno, the Casa Natal de Morelos and the Casa de la Cultura, several times a week. There are also regular organ recitals in the cathedral (check with the tourist information office), and band concerts in the zócalo (Sun).

**Internet access** Chat Room, Nigromante 132 (M$12/hr) has a cable connection and coffee bar and is open until 10pm daily; El Jardín Internet Café, Guillermo Prieto 157 (M$15/hr) is a big university hangout; and there's an unnamed place at León Guzmán 231 (M$7/hr).

**Post office** Madero 369 Ote (Mon–Fri 9am–6pm).

**Pharmacy** Farmacia Guadalajara, Morelos Sur 117, on Plaza Ocampo, stays open late.

**Telephones** Telmex, in the post office, has phone and fax offices (Mon–Fri 9am–8pm). There's also a *caseta de larga distancia* at Portal Galeana 103, opposite the front of the cathedral.

# The Monarch Butterfly Sanctuary

Each winter more than 150 million monarch butterflies (see box opposite) migrate from the northeastern US and Canada to the Oyamel fir forests in the lush mountains of Michoacán in order to reproduce. It's an amazing sight any time, but especially in January and February when numbers peak: whole trees are smothered in monarchs, branches sagging under the weight. In the cool of the morning, they dry their wings, turning the entire landscape a rich, velvety orange, while later in the day they take to the air, millions of fluttering butterflies making more noise than you'd ever think possible. As the afternoon humidity forces them to the ground, they form a thick carpet of blazing colour.

The best place to see them is in the **Sanctuario de Mariposa El Rosario** (middle weekend in Nov to third weekend in March daily 8am–5pm; M$35; Ⓦwww.turismomichoacan.gob.mx), just outside the village of El Rosario, about 120km east of Morelia. It is best to go early in the morning (and preferably on weekdays, to avoid the crowds), when the butterflies are just waking up and before they fly off into the surrounding woodlands. **Guides**, whose services are included in the entry fee, show you around the sanctuary and give a short explanation of the butterflies' lifecycle and breeding habits. For a couple of weeks on either side of the main season, those same guides run the place unofficially, still charging the entry price and offering their services for a tip. There are fewer butterflies but it is still worth the journey anytime from early November to early April. The walk to the best of the monarch-laden trees is about 2km, mostly uphill at an altitude of almost 3000 metres: take it easy if you're not acclimatized.

### The life cycle and habitat of the monarch

The sheer congregation of monarch butterflies in the hills of Michoacán is astonishing, but not as impressive as their 4500-kilometre **migration**. In the fall, when the weather starts to turn cold in the Great Lakes region of the US and Canada, the butterflies head south, taking just four to five weeks to make it to Michoacán. Here, in an area of less than 150 square kilometres, they find the unique microclimate a perfect place to spend the winter. The cool temperatures allow them to conserve energy, the trees provide shelter from the wind and precipitation and the fog-laden air prevents them from drying out. Monarchs typically have a **life cycle** of around two to five weeks, but when they fly south they go into a phase known as "reproductive diapause". The same butterflies remain in Michoacán all winter, then breed in spring in time for their caterpillars to dine on the newly emergent milkweed plants – their only food source – back in the US and Canada.

Around ten percent of all migrating monarchs get eaten by black-headed grosbeaks and black-backed orioles, but that offers no danger to species survival. The real threat is loss of this crucial mountain **habitat**. This was recognized as far back as 1986, when several key overwintering sites were protected from logging, but the local peasant families need the wood and they were never fully compensated for the loss of this resource. The Mexican government more than tripled the size of the reserves in 2000, but logging continued to a large enough extent that in early 2007 new president Felipe Calderón declared a "zero tolerance" policy against it, and increased policing. To learn more, check out the websites of the Monarch Butterfly Sanctuary Foundation (Ⓦwww.mbsf.org), the Michoacán Restoration Fund (Ⓦwww.michoacanmonarchs.org) and Monarch Watch (Ⓦwww.monarchwatch.org).



## Practicalities

Visiting the monarchs is possible on **day trips** from Morelia and Mexico City, but it is more satisfying to stay locally (probably in Angangueo) and visit at a more leisurely pace. During the season there are five direct buses a day from Mexico City (Autobuses Zincantepec from Terminal Poniente) to El Rosario, but **getting there** by public transport generally involves changing buses in Zitácuaro (see below). From Zitácuaro, buses run to Ocampo (every 15min; 30min) and continue to Angangueo (a further 20min). From Ocampo there is a minibus along a 10km cobbled road to El Rosario (every 15min; 30min). There are also minibuses from Angangueo to El Rosario (1–4 daily; 1hr) along a very rough mountain road, but it is usually more convenient to backtrack to Ocampo and take a minibus from there. Those with their own wheels can drive direct to El Rosario from Ocampo. If you are staying in Angangueo you could conceivably walk back downhill in a couple of hours.

The closest **accommodation** to the butterfly sanctuary is *Rancho Givali* (Ⓣ715/115-5236, Ⓦwww.ranchogivali.com.mx; ❼), 2km down the hill, which has comfortable rooms, tent camping and a good restaurant. There are also basic daytime restaurants that line the approach to the sanctuary. All other accommodation and dining options are in Ocampo and Angangueo (see p.390 and p.392).

For further **information**, ask at the tourist office in Morelia or the information booth on the highway outside Zitácuaro, towards Toluca.

## Zitácuaro, Ocampo and Angangueo

Most people approaching the butterfly sanctuary change buses at **Zitácuaro**, a small town prettily scattered over low hills at around 1900 metres. Being a little warmer than Angangueo makes it a potential base for visiting El Rosario. If you

## Fiestas

Both Jalisco and Michoacán preserve strong native traditions and are particularly rich in fiestas: the list below is by no means exhaustive, and local tourist offices will have further details.

### January

**New Year's Day** (Jan 1). Celebrated in Pátzcuaro (see p.370) and Uruapan (see p.364) with the Danza da los Viejitos.

**Día de los Santos Reyes** (Jan 6). Twelfth Night is celebrated with many small ceremonies and dances such as Los Sonajeros (rattles), Las Pastoras (the shepherdesses) and El Baile de la Conquista (conquest). Particularly good at Los Reyes, west of Uruapan, and Cajititlán, 25km south of Guadalajara .

**Día de San Sebastian** (Jan 20). Traditional dances in Tuxpan (see p.362).

### February

**Día de Nuestro Señor del Rescate** (Feb 1). In Tzintzuntzán (see p.379), the start of a week-long fiesta founded in the sixteenth century by Vasco de Quiroga.

**Carnaval** (the week before Lent, variable Feb–March). Celebrated everywhere.

### March

**Festival Internacional de Guitarra** (March 17–21) International Guitar Festival in Morelia (see p.382).

### April

**Palm Sunday** (the Sun before Easter Sun). Palm ornament market in Uruapan (see p.364).

**Semana Santa** (Holy Week). Observed everywhere, but especially in Tzintzuntzán (see p.379).

**Expo Feria** (variable April–May). Arts and industry show in Morelia (see p.382).

### May

**Día de la Santa Cruz** (May 3). Native dances in Angangueo (see p.392); mariachis and tequila in Tequila (see p.356).

**Día del Señor de la Misericordia** (last Sun in May). Fiesta and dances in Tuxpan (see p.362).

**Corpus Christi** (Thurs after Trinity, variable late May–early June). Traditional dances in Paracho (see p.364).

### June

**Día de San Pedro** (June 29). Mariachi and dance festival in Tlaquepaque, Guadalajara (see p.344).

### July

**Día de la Preciosa Sangre de Cristo** (first Sun in July). Torch-lit religious processions in Quiroga (see p.380).

do decide to **stay**, try the basic *Hotel México*, Revolución 22 Sur (Ⓣ715/153-2811; ❸), or the considerably more upscale *Hotel Rancho San Cayetano*, Carretera a Huetamo Km 2.3 (Ⓣ715/153-1926, Ⓦwww.ranchosancayetano.com; ❼), which has a pool and good restaurant set in its private woodland.

The nearest substantial village to the El Rosario sanctuary is **Ocampo**, 20km north of Zitácuaro. It is not an especially interesting place, but does have good

**Día de María Magdalena** (July 22). Fiesta in Uruapan (see p.364) featuring a procession of animals.

**Día de Santiago Apóstol** (July 25). Lively celebrations and fireworks in Tuxpan (see p.362) and Uruapan (see p.364).

### August

**Fiesta tradicional** (Aug 8). Ancient pre-Columbian fiesta in Paracho (see p.364).

**Feria Nacional del Cobre** (second week in Aug). National Copper Fair in Santa Clara del Cobre (see p.380), near Pátzcuaro.

### September

**Morelos's birthday** (Sept 30). Celebrated in Morelia (see p.382).

### October

**Fiestas de Octubre** (all month). Massive cultural festival in Guadalajara (see p.351).

**Día de San Francisco** (Oct 4). Saint's day celebrations in Uruapan (see p.366).

**Día de la Raza** (Oct 12). Uruapan (see p.364) celebrates Columbus's discovery of the Americas.

**Día de la Virgen de Zapopan** (Oct 12). Massive pilgrimage in Guadalajara (see p.347).

**Festival de Coros y Danzas** (Oct 24–26). Singing and dancing competitions in Uruapan (see p.364).

### November

**Día de los Muertos** (Day of the Dead; Nov 2). Celebrated everywhere, but especially around Pátzcuaro (see box, p.376). Also picturesque in Zitácuaro.

**Arrival of the monarch butterfly** (second week of Nov). *Las monarcas* start arriving in Michoacán in big numbers around now.

**Festival Internacional de Música** (third week of Nov). International Music Festival in Morelia (see p.382).

**Feria de Aguacate** (variable Nov–Dec). Three-week avocado fair in Uruapan (see p.364).

### December

**Día de La Inmaculada Concepción** (Dec 8). Celebrated in Sayula (see p.361).

**La Señora de La Salud** (Dec 8). Pilgrimage and dances in Pátzcuaro (see p.370) and Tequila (see p.356).

**Día de la Virgen de Guadalupe** (Dec 12). Large celebrations in Tapalpa (see p.360).

**Pastoral plays** (Dec 24). Performed in Tuxpan (see p.362).

connections to El Rosario, and you can stay at *Hotel San Carlos*, Zaragoza 8 (Ⓣ715/151-0212; ③), which has its own restaurant. Several small **restaurants** around the central square satisfy basic hunger.

Most butterfly visitors stay at **Angangueo**, 9km further on, a former mining town wedged into a valley at almost 2600m: it can be cool in the evenings. The name is Tarascan for "entrance to the cave", presumably an early reference to its mineral extraction potential. The mines have now closed, but with its terracotta tiled roofs, winding streets and houses stacked up the hillside it is an attractive enough place and offers the best selection of hotels and restaurants around.

Most things happen on Morelos, which becomes Nacional at the point where the minor Matamoros heads off up to the butterfly sanctuary. By far the best **place to stay** is the comfortable and very friendly *Hotel Don Bruno*, Morelos 92, 1km south of the centre (Ⓣ& Ⓕ715/156-0026; ❼), which has its own restaurant and some rooms with fireplace. Right in town, there are simple but clean rooms with bath at *Paso de la Monarca*, Nacional 20 (Ⓣ715/156-0187; ❶); and opposite, *Hotel Juarez*, Nacional 15 (Ⓣ715/1560023; ❸), with pleasant rooms set around a flower-filled courtyard. **Eating** options are limited, but *Simon's Restaurant*, on the main square, serves tasty chicken and trout dishes for around M$50. Angangueo celebrates the **Día de la Santa Cruz** (May 3) with traditional dances.



# Travel details

## Buses

What follows is a minimum of routes covering the major stops only – it should be assumed that these buses also call at the towns en route. In general the fastest and most efficient operators are Omnibus de Mexico and Tres Estrellas de Oro, though there's little to choose between the first-class companies.

**Angangueo** to: El Rosario (1–4 daily; 1hr); Ocampo (every 15min; 20min); Zitácuaro (every 15min; 1hr).

**Chapala** to: Ajijic (every 20min; 20min); Guadalajara (every 30min; 1hr).

**Ciudad Guzmán** to: Colima (every hour; 1hr); Guadalajara Central Nueva (every hour; 2hr); Guadalajara Central Vieja (every 30min; 3hr 30min); Manzanillo (3 daily; 3hr); Mexico City (2 overnight; 9hr); Sayula (every 30min; 45min); Tapalpa (4 daily, 2hr).

**Guadalajara (Central Nueva)** to: Aguascalientes (every 20–30min; 4hr); Colima (every 20–30min; 3hr); Guanajuato (hourly; 4hr); Lagos de Moreno (every 30min; 2hr 30min); Manzanillo (every 30min; 6hr); Mazatlán (every 30min; 6hr); Mexico City (every 15min; 7hr); Morelia (every 30min; 3–5hr); Pátzcuaro (2 daily; 6hr); Puerto Vallarta (hourly; 5hr); Querétaro (every 30min; 5hr); San Juan de los Lagos (hourly; 2hr); San Luis Potosí (hourly; 5hr); Tepic (10 hourly; 4hr); Tijuana (11 daily; 35hr); Toluca (every 15min; 6hr); Uruapan (18 daily; 5hr).

**Guadalajara (Central Vieja)** to: Ajijic (every 30min; 1hr); Chapala (every 30min; 1hr); Jocotepec (every 45min; 1hr 15min); Tapalpa (10 daily; 3hr); Tequila (every 15min; 1hr 45min).

**Morelia** to: Aguascalientes (4 daily; 7hr); Guadalajara (hourly; 3hr 30min); Guanajuato (hourly; 3hr 30min); León (every 20min; 4hr); Mexico City (every 30min; 4hr); Pátzcuaro (every 10min; 1hr); Querétaro (every 40min; 4hr); Toluca (hourly; 4hr); Uruapan (every 20 min; 2hr); Zitácuaro (20 daily; 3hr).

**Ocampo** to: Angangueo (every 15min; 20min); El Rosario (every 15min; 30min); Zitácuaro (every 15min; 40min).

**Pátzcuaro** to: Guadalajara (2 daily; 4–5hr); Mexico City (hourly; 5hr); Morelia (every 10min; 1hr); Quiroga (every 15min; 30min); Uruapan (every 30min; 1hr).

**Sayula** to: Ciudad Guzmán (every 30min; 1hr); Guadalajara (10 daily; 2hr 30min); Tapalpa 4 daily; 1hr).

**Uruapan** to: Guadalajara (15 daily; 4hr 30min); Lázaro Cárdenas (every 30min; 3hr 30min); Los Reyes (hourly; 1hr); Mexico City (11 daily; 6hr); Morelia (every 20min; 2hr); Paracho (every 20min; 40min); Pátzcuaro (every hour; 1hr).

**Zitácuaro** to: Angangueo (every 15min to around 9pm; 1hr); Mexico City (every 20min; 3hr) Morelia (every 30min; 2hr 40min); Ocampo (every 15min; 30min); Toluca (every 30min; 1hr 30min).

## Flights

**Guadalajara** to: Mexico City (12 daily; 1hr 10min); Puerto Vallarta (5 daily; 45min); San José del Cabo (1 daily; 1hr 30min); Tijuana (5 daily; 3hr).

**Morelia** to: Mexico City (7 daily; 50min); Tijuana (1 daily; 3hr).

5

# Mexico City and around



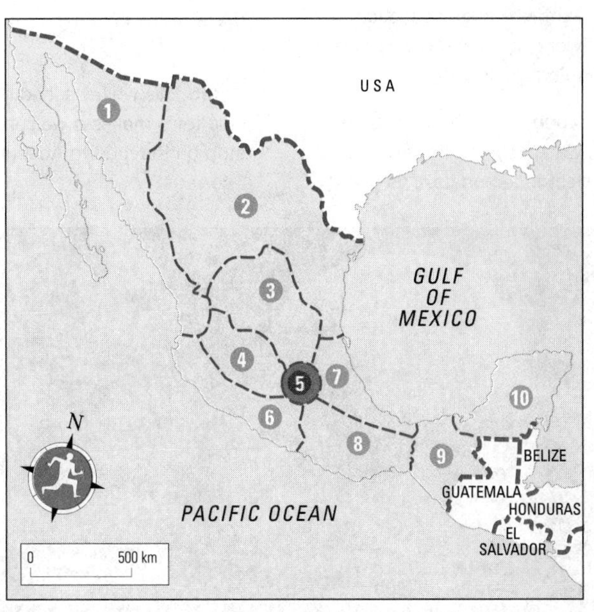

# CHAPTER 5 Highlights

* **The Zócalo** Mexico City's huge central square, surrounded by the cathedral, Aztec ruins and the Palacio Nacional. See p.413
* **Museo Nacional de Antropología** The country's finest museum, with displays on all of Mexico's major pre-Columbian cultures. See p.440
* **Museo Dolores Olmedo Patiño** A huge collection of works by Diego Rivera and Frida Kahlo. See p.459
* **Xochimilco** Ride the ancient waterways on flower-festooned boats. See p.460
* **Plaza Garibaldi** The frenetic site of massed mariachi bands. See p.473
* **La Merced** Explore Mexico City's largest and most vibrant market. See p.476
* **Teotihuacán** The largest pre-Hispanic site in the country, dominated by the Pirámide del Sol. See p.485
* **The Great Pyramid of Cholula** Mexico's most massive pyramid ruin. See p.510
* **Taxco** This whitewashed hill-side town makes a welcome stop on the road to Acapulco. See p.523

△ Olmec head, Museo Nacional de Antropología

5

# Mexico City and around



Since long before the Mexican nation actually existed, the **Valley of México** has been the country's centre of gravity. Located in this mountain-ringed basin – 100km long, 60km wide and over 2400m high, dotted with great salt- and fresh-water lagoons and dominated by the vast snowcapped peaks of Popocatépetl and Ixtaccíhuatl – were some of the most powerful civilizations the country has seen. Today the lakes have all but disappeared and the mountains are shrouded in smog, but the region continues to be the heart of the country, its physical centre and the generator of its political, cultural and economic pulse.

At the crossroads of everything sprawls the vibrant, elegant, chaotic and fascinating **Mexico City**. In population one of the largest cities in the world, with more than twenty million inhabitants, its lure is irresistible. Colonial mansions and excavated pyramids vie for attention with the city's fabulous museums and galleries, while above them tower the concrete and glass of thrusting development. But above all, the city is alive – exciting, sometimes frightening, always bewildering, but boldly alive. You can't avoid it, and if you genuinely want to know anything of Mexico you shouldn't try.

Once you've tired of the city's pace, you'll find points of interest in every direction. To the north, and the most obvious destinations for day trips, are the magnificent pyramid sites of **Teotihuacán** and **Tula**, the more dramatic legacies of the region's ancient peoples. The road to Tula passes **Tepotzotlán**, a weekend retreat from the city centred on a magnificent Baroque complex built by the Jesuits and filled with ornate treasures. To the east lies the small city of **Pachuca**, capital of Hidalgo state and a springboard for the hill country to the north, notably the attractive mountain village of **Real del Monte** with its Cornish connections.

East of Mexico City is the region's second largest city, the thriving and ultra-colonial **Puebla**. This city probably only warrants a day or two of your time, but does work as a great base for forays north to more tranquil **Tlaxcala**, and west to **Cholula** with its enormous ruined pyramid. The ancient site here offers one of the best views of central Mexico's twin volcanoes, **Popocatépetl** and **Ixtaccíhuatl**, both currently off limits due to the possible threat of eruption.

Immediately south of the capital you climb over the mountains and descend to **Cuernavaca**, full of ancient palaces, and handy for the hilltop pyramid sites

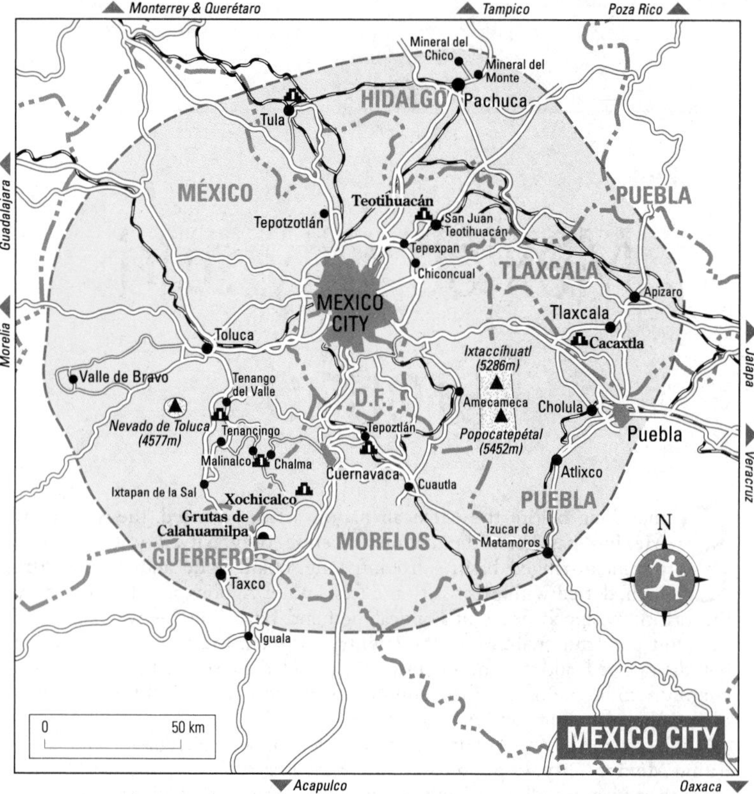


of **Tepoztlán** and **Xochicalco**. An hour further south the silver town of **Taxco** straggles picturesquely up a hillside, making it one of the most appealing destinations hereabouts. Possibly the least-visited quarter of Mexico City's environs is the west, where the city of **Toluca** offers only modest rewards, acting as a staging post for the lakeside resort town of **Valle de Bravo** and some small towns to the south, the most interesting being **Malinalco**, with yet more ancient pyramids.

All these ruins owe their existence to a long succession of pre-Columbian rulers, above all the **Aztecs**, whose warrior state was crushed by Cortés. But they were relative newcomers, forging their empire by force of arms in less than two centuries and borrowing their culture, science, arts and even language from the Valley societies that had gone before. **Teotihuacán**, whose mighty pyramids still stand some 50km northeast of the modern city, was the predominant culture of the Classic period and the true forebear of the Aztecs, a city of some 200,000 people whose influence spread throughout the country, south to the Maya lands in the Yucatán and beyond into Guatemala and Central America. Its style, though never as militaristic as later societies, was adopted everywhere: Quetzalcoatl, the plumed serpent, and Tlaloc, the rain god, were Teotihuacán deities.

For all its pre-eminence, though, Teotihuacán was neither the earliest, nor the only settlement in the valley: the pyramid at **Cuicuilco**, now in the south of the city, is probably the oldest stone structure in the country, and there were small agricultural communities all around the lakes. The Aztecs, arriving some five hundred years after the destruction of Teotihuacán, however, didn't acknowledge their debt. They regarded themselves as descendants of the **Toltec** kingdom, whose capital lay at **Tula** to the north, and whose influence – as successors to Teotihuacán – was almost as pervasive. The Aztecs consciously took over the Toltec military-based society, and adopted many of their gods: above all Quetzalcoatl, who assumed an importance equal to that of their own tribal deity, Huitzilopochtli, the god of war, who had brought them to power and demanded human sacrifice to keep them there. In taking control of the society while adopting its culture, the Aztecs were following in the footsteps of their Toltec predecessors, who had arrived in central Mexico as a marauding tribe of Chichimeca ("Sons of Dogs") from the north, absorbing the local culture as they came to dominate it.



## Health and safety in Mexico City

Mexico City comes with an unenviable reputation for overcrowding, grime and crime. To some extent this is deserved, but things are improving, and overall, Mexico City is no worse than you might expect of a city of the same size and population elsewhere in the developing world. Indeed, the frenzied atmosphere is part of its fascination.

Certainly there is **pollution**. The whole urban area sits in a low mountain bowl that tends to deflect smog-clearing winds away from the city, therefore allowing a thick blanket of haze to build up throughout the day. Conditions are particularly bad in winter, when there is no rain to wash the skies clean and pollution levels (reported daily in the English-language newspaper *The News*) tend to peak in the early afternoon. However, the city's stringent anti-emission regulations mean you'll be spared the clouds of black diesel smoke found in less developed countries all over the world. The **Hoy No Circula** ("Don't drive today") law prohibits car use from 5am to 10pm for one day in the working week for vehicles built before 1994, the day depending on the car's numberplate; rentals are exempt. Nonetheless, those prone to **respiratory problems** may have some difficulty on arrival, thanks to the combination of the city's air quality and altitude, though most suffer no ill effects.

The capital is where the Mexican extremes of wealth and **poverty** are most apparent, with shiny, valet-parked SUVs vying for space with pavement vendors and beggars. Such financial disparity fuels **theft**, but you only need to take the same precautions you would in any large city, and there is no need to feel particularly paranoid: keep your valuables – especially credit or debit cards – in the hotel safe (even cheap hotels often have somewhere secure), don't flash large wads of money around and keep an eye on your camera and the like when in busy market areas. At night, avoid the barrio known as Doctores (around the Metro station of the same name, so called because the streets are named after doctors), and the area around Lagunilla market, both of which are centres of the street drug trade, and therefore opportunist crime. The ubiquitous green-and-white **taxis** you'll see cruising the streets have a bad reputation and, though drivers are mostly helpful and courteous, there are reports of people being robbed at knife-point (often in taxis that have been stolen). If possible, it is best to get your hotel to call you a cab (more expensive), or to call one yourself from one of the firms listed on p.408. If you do have to hail a cab in the street, always take one whose registration, on both the numberplate and the side of the vehicle, begins with an L (for "libre" – to be hailed while driving around), and which has the driver's identification prominently displayed within. Better still, find a taxi rank and take a *sitio* taxi that can be tied down to it (with a number beginning in R, S or T, and again with the driver's ID prominently displayed). Do not take taxis from the airport or bus terminals other than prepaid ones, and also avoid taking those waiting outside tourist spots.

# Mexico City

Set over 2400m above sea level in a shallow mountain bowl, and crammed with over twenty million people, **Mexico City** is one of the world's most densely populated urban areas. Although it does have a high crime rate, and some terrible pollution (see box, p.397), the capital is nowhere near as intimidating as you might expect. Nonetheless, you may still prefer to take it in a couple of days at a time, taking off in between to recharge in the smaller, neighbouring colonial cities.

The city radiates out from the **Zócalo**, or main square, as much the heart of the modern capital as it was of the Aztec city that once sat here. Immediately to its west, in the streets between the Zócalo and the garden known as the **Alameda**, is the city's main **commercial area**. Beyond that, the glitzy **Zona Rosa**, with trendy **Condesa** to its south, stretches towards **Chapultepec Park** – home to the incredible **Museo Nacional de Antropología** – and the rich enclave of **Polanco**, while Avenida de los Insurgentes leads down to the more laid-back barrios of **San Ángel** and **Coyoacán**. Around the outer edges of the city are shantytowns, built piecemeal by migrants from elsewhere in the country. Hidden among these less affluent communities are a number of gems, such as the pyramids of Tenayauca, Santa Cecilia and Cuicuilco, and the canals of **Xochimilco**.

You certainly won't run out of things to do in Mexico City. In between shopping, dining and dancing, there are some excellent museums to visit, busy markets to explore, the Diego Rivera trail to follow, ancient pyramids to check out and charming old barrios to hang out in. It may be noisy and dirty, and even on occasion a little bit edgy, but it definitely isn't boring, and most of the time it's a pretty enjoyable place to be.

## Some history

**And when we saw all those cities and villages built in the water, and other great towns on dry land, and that straight and level causeway leading to Mexico, we were astounded. These great towns and cities and buildings rising from the water, all made of stone, seemed like an enchanted vision from the tales of Amadis. Indeed, some of our soldiers asked whether it was not all a dream.**

Bernal Díaz, *The Conquest of New Spain*

It's hardly surprising that Cortés and his followers should have been so taken by their first sight of **Tenochtitlán**, capital of the Aztecs. Built in the middle of a lake traversed by great causeways, it was a beautiful, strictly regulated, stone-built city of 300,000 residents. The Aztec people (or, as they called themselves, the Mexica) had arrived at the lake in around 1345, after years of wandering and living off what they could scavenge or pillage from settled communities. According to Aztec legend, their patron god Huitzilopochtli had ordered them to build a city where they found an eagle perched on a cactus devouring a snake – this they duly saw on an island in the middle of the lake. It is this legend that is the basis of the nopal, eagle and snake motif that forms the centrepiece of the modern Mexican flag and you'll see everywhere from coins and official seals to woven designs on rugs.

The lake proved an ideal site. Well stocked with fish, it was also fertile, once the Aztecs had constructed their *chinampas*, or floating gardens of reeds, and virtually impregnable, too: the causeways, when they were completed, could be flooded and the bridges raised to thwart attacks (or escape, as the Spanish found on the Noche Triste; see p.887).

The island city eventually grew to cover an area of some thirteen square kilometres, much of it reclaimed from the lake, and from this base the Aztecs were able to begin their programme of expansion: first, dominating the valley by a series of strategic alliances, war and treachery, and finally, in a period of less than a hundred years before the Conquest, establishing an empire that demanded tribute from and traded with the most distant parts of the country.

### The Conquest

This was the situation when **Cortés** and his army of only a few hundred men landed on the east coast in 1519 and began their long march on Tenochtitlán. Several key factors assured their survival: superior weaponry, which included firearms; the shock effect of horses (never having seen such animals, the Aztecs at first believed them to be extensions of their riders); the support of tribes who were either enemies or suppressed subjects of the Aztecs; and the unwillingness of the Aztec emperor to resist openly.

**Moctezuma II** (Montezuma), who had suffered heavy defeats in campaigns against the Tarascans in the west, was a broodingly religious man who, it is said, believed Cortés to be the pale-skinned, bearded god Quetzalcoatl, returned to fulfil ancient prophecies. Accordingly he admitted him to the city – fearfully, but with a show of ceremonious welcome. By way of repaying this hospitality the Spanish took Moctezuma prisoner, and later attacked the great Aztec temples, killing many priests and placing Christian chapels alongside their altars. Meanwhile, there was growing unrest in the city at the emperor's passivity and at the rapacious behaviour of his guests. Moctezuma was eventually killed – according to the Spanish, stoned to death by his own people while trying to quell a riot – and the Spaniards driven from the city with heavy losses. However, Cortés and a few of his followers were able to escape to the security of Tlaxcala, the most loyal of his native allies, to regroup and plan a new assault. Finally, rearmed and reinforced, their numbers swelled by indigenous allies, and with ships built in secret, the Spaniards laid siege to Tenochtitlán for three months, finally taking the city in the face of suicidal opposition in August 1521.

The city's defeat is still a harsh memory: Cortés himself is hardly revered, but the natives who assisted him, and in particular Moctezuma and Malinche, the woman who acted as Cortés' interpreter, are non-people. You won't find a monument to Moctezuma in the country, though **Cuauhtémoc**, his successor who led the fierce resistance, is commemorated everywhere; Malinche is represented, acidly, in some of Diego Rivera's more outspoken murals. More telling, perhaps, of the bitterness of the struggle, is that so little physical evidence remains: "All that I saw then," wrote Bernal Díaz, "is overthrown and destroyed; nothing is left standing."

### Spanish and post-colonial Mexico City

The victorious Spanish systematically smashed every visible aspect of Aztec culture, as often as not using the very stones of the old city to construct the new, and building a new palace for Cortés on the site of the Aztec emperor's palace. Until a few decades ago it was thought that everything had been destroyed; slowly, however, particularly during construction of the Metro and in the remarkable discovery of remains of the **Templo Mayor** beneath the colonial Zócalo, remains of Tenochtitlán have been brought to light.

The **new city** developed slowly in its early years. It spread far wider, however, as the lake was drained, filled and built over – only tiny vestiges remain today – and grew with considerable grace. In many ways it's a singularly unfortunate place to site a modern city. Pestilent from the earliest days, the inadequately drained waters harboured fevers, and the native population was constantly swept by epidemics of European diseases. Many of the buildings, too, simply began to sink into the soft lake bed, a process probably accelerated by regular earthquakes.

By the third quarter of the nineteenth century, the city comprised little more than the area around the Zócalo and Alameda. Chapultepec Castle, Coyoacán, San Ángel and the Basílica of Guadalupe – areas now well within city limits – were then surrounded by fields and the last of the basin's former lakes. Nonetheless, the city was beginning to take its present shape: the Paseo de la Reforma already linked Chapultepec with the city, and the colonial core could no longer accommodate the increasing population. From late 1870 through to 1911 the dictator Porfirio Díaz presided over an unprecedented, and self-aggrandizing, building programme that saw the installation of trams, the expansion of public transport and the draining of some of the last sections of the Lago de Texcoco, which had previously hemmed in the city. Jointly these fuelled further growth, and by the outbreak of the Revolution in 1910, Mexico City's residents numbered over 400,000, regaining for the first time in four centuries the population level it had held before the Conquest.

### The modern city

As many as two million Mexicans died during the Revolution and many more lost their property, their livelihood or both. In desperation, thousands fled to rapidly industrializing Mexico City in search of jobs and a better life. Between 1910 and the mid-1940s the city's population quadrupled and the cracks in the infrastructure quickly became gaping holes. Houses couldn't be built quickly enough to cope with the seven-percent annual growth, and many people couldn't afford them anyway, so up sprung **shantytowns** of scraps of metal and cardboard. Most neighbourhoods had little or no water supply and sanitation was an afterthought. Gradually, civic leaders tried to address the lot of its citizens by improving the services and housing in shanty-towns, but even as they worked a new ring of slums mushroomed just a little further out. As the city expanded, transport became impossible and the city embarked on building the **Metro** system in the late 1960s. In 2000, the 175th and most recent Metro station was completed, but plans for new stations are purportedly in the works.

### México, Mexico City and El DF

For clarity, we've referred to Mexico's capital as **Mexico City** throughout this guide, though Mexicans frequently refer to it simply as **México**, in the same way that Americans often refer to New York City as New York. It's a source of infinite confusion to visitors, but the country took its name from the city, so "México" can mean either, and in conversation it most often means the latter. To avoid misunderstandings, the nation may be referred to as La República Mexicana, or occasionally in speeches La Patria, while Mexico City may be referred to as **El DF** ("El Day Effay"), short for "Distrito Federal", the administrative zone that coincides with the city boundaries and contains most of the urban areas. The title **Ciudad de México** is used much less commonly, usually in an official context.

Urban growth continues today: some statisticians estimate that there are a thousand new arrivals each day, and the city now extends beyond the limits of the Distrito Federal and out into the surrounding state of México. Despite the spread, Mexico City remains one of the world's densest and most populated cities, with an unenviable list of major social and physical problems, including an extreme vulnerability to earthquakes – the last big one, in 1985, killed over 9000 people, made 100,000 homeless and left many of the city's buildings decidedly skewed.

# Orientation

The traditional centre of the city is the **Zócalo**, or Plaza Mayor, officially called Plaza de la Constitución. The heart of both ancient Tenochtitlán and of Cortés's city, it's surrounded by the oldest streets, largely colonial and unmodernized. To the east, the ancient structures degenerate rapidly, blending into the poorer areas that surround the airport. Westwards, avenidas **Madero** and **Juárez** lead to the **Alameda**, the small park that marks the extent of the old city centre. Here are the Palacio de Bellas Artes, the main post office and the landmark Torre Latinoamericana. Carry on west past here and you get into an area, between the ugly bulk of the **Monumento a la Revolución** and the train station, where you'll find many of the cheaper hotels. Turn slightly south and you're amid the faded elegance of the **Paseo de la Reforma**, which leads down to the great open space of **Chapultepec Park**, recreation area for the city's millions, and home of the Museo Nacional de Antropología and several other important museums. On the northwest side as you head down Reforma is a sedate, upmarket residential area, while to the southeast is the **Zona Rosa** with its shopping streets, expensive hotels and constant tourist activity. To the south, the Zona bleeds into **Condesa**, which in recent years has become *the* fashionable place to eat, drink and party. To the west, the northern flank of Chapultepec Park is lined by the flashy high-rise hotels of **Colonia Polanco**, among the city's chicest districts and home to many of the finest shops and restaurants.

**Avenida de los Insurgentes** crosses Reforma about halfway between the Alameda and Chapultepec Park. Said to be the longest continuous city street in the world, Insurgentes bisects Mexico City more or less from north to south, and is lined with modern commercial development. In the south it runs past the suburbs of **San Ángel** and **Coyoacán** to the **University City**, and on out of Mexico City by the **Pyramid of Cuicuilco**. Also in the southern extremities of the city are the waterways of **Xochimilco**, virtually the last remains of the great lagoons. In the outskirts, Insurgentes meets another important route, the **Calzada de Tlalpan**, which runs due south from the Zócalo past the eastern side of Coyoacán and a couple of fine museums.

### Finding your way in Mexico City

Remember that many **street names** are repeated over and over again in different parts of Mexico City – there must be dozens of thoroughfares called Morelos, Juárez or Hidalgo, and a good score of 5 de Mayos. If you're taking a cab, or looking at a map, be clear which area you are talking about – it's fairly obvious in the centre, but searching out an address in the suburbs can lead to a series of false starts unless you know the name of the official **colonia**, or urban district (abbreviated "Col" in addresses outside the centre), that you're looking for.

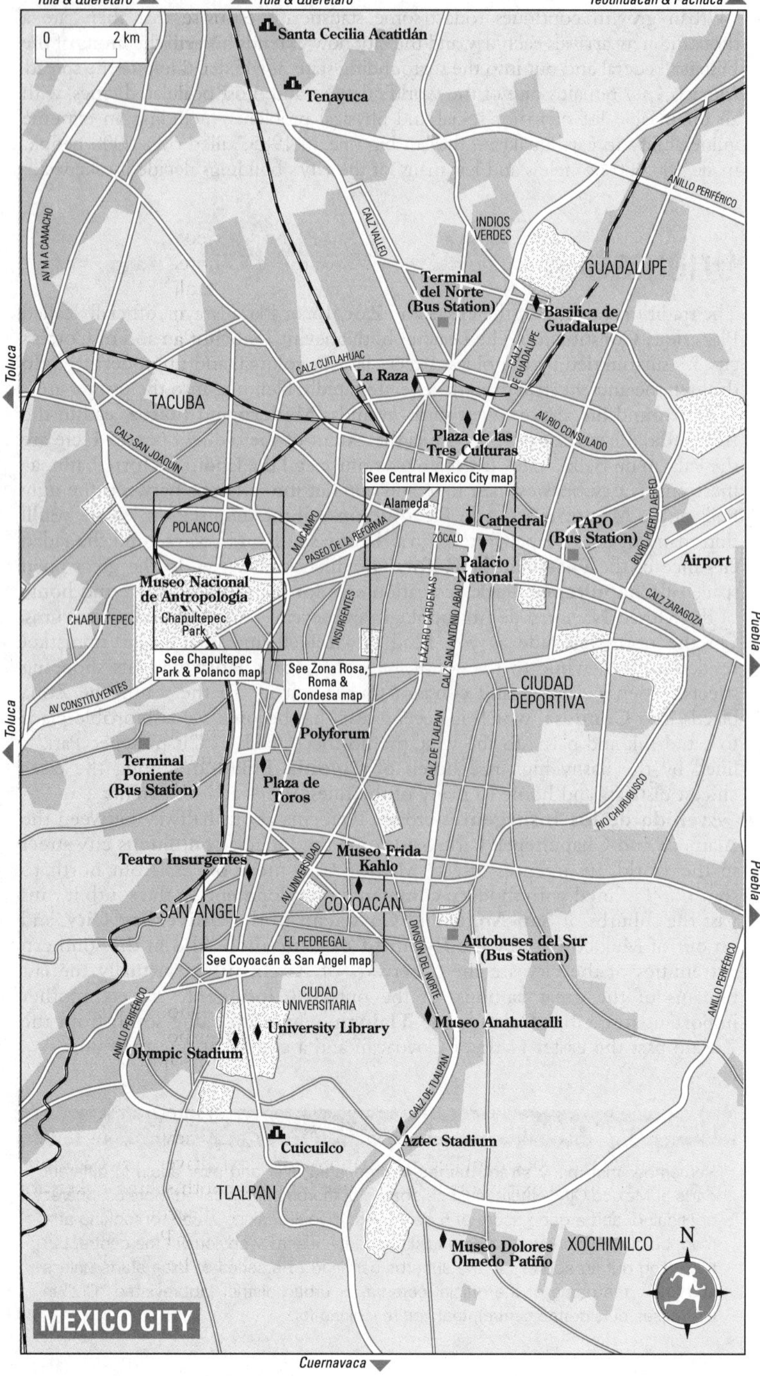

MEXICO CITY
Tula & Querétaro
Tula & Querétaro
Teotihuacán & Pachuca
Toluca
Toluca
Puebla
Puebla
Cuernavaca
0 2 km
Santa Cecilia Acatitlán
Tenayuca
ANILLO PERIFÉRICO
INDIOS VERDES
GUADALUPE
CALZ VALLEO
AV M A CAMACHO
Terminal del Norte (Bus Station)
Basilica de Guadalupe
CALZ DE GUADALUPE
CALZ CUITLAHUAC
La Raza
TACUBA
AV RIO CONSULADO
Plaza de las Tres Culturas
CALZ SAN JOAQUIN
See Central Mexico City map
Alameda
Cathedral
TAPO (Bus Station)
POLANCO
M OCAMPO
PASEO DE LA REFORMA
ZÓCALO
BLVRD PUERTO AEREO
Airport
Palacio National
Museo Nacional de Antropología
Chapultepec Park
CHAPULTEPEC
INSURGENTES
LÁZARO CÁRDENAS
CALZ SAN ANTONIO ABAD
CALZ ZARAGOZA
See Chapultepec Park & Polanco map
See Zona Rosa, Roma & Condesa map
CIUDAD DEPORTIVA
AV CONSTITUYENTES
Polyforum
CALZ DE TLALPAN
Terminal Poniente (Bus Station)
Plaza de Toros
RIO CHURUBUSCO
Teatro Insurgentes
Museo Frida Kahlo
AV UNIVERSIDAD
COYOACÁN
SAN ÁNGEL
EL PEDREGAL
DIVISIÓN DEL NORTE
Autobuses del Sur (Bus Station)
See Coyoacán & San Ángel map
CIUDAD UNIVERSITARIA
ANILLO PERIFÉRICO
ANILLO PERIFÉRICO
Museo Anahuacalli
University Library
Olympic Stadium
CALZ DE TLALPAN
Aztec Stadium
Cuicuilco
TLALPAN
Museo Dolores Olmedo Patiño
XOCHIMILCO
N

To the north, Insurgentes heads past the northbound bus station, then sweeps out of the city via the basilica of **Guadalupe** and **Indios Verdes**. The northern extension of Reforma, too, ends up at the great shrine of Guadalupe, as does the continuation of the Calzada de Tlalpan beyond the Zócalo.

# Arrival

Being dropped unprepared into the vastness of Mexico City may seem daunting, but it's not hard to get into the centre, or to a hotel, from any of the major points of arrival. The only problem is likely to be hauling large items of luggage through the invariable crowds – take a taxi if you are at all heavily laden. The airport and all four major bus terminals have a system of **authorized taxis** designed to avoid rip-offs, particularly prevalent at the airport where people will offer rides at anything up to ten times the going rate to unsuspecting newcomers. The authorized system is the same wherever it operates from – you'll find a large map of the city marked out in zones, with a standard, set fare for each; you pick where you're going, buy a ticket at the booth, then walk outside and present the ticket to one of the waiting cabs. One ticket is good for up to four people to one destination. The driver may drop you a block or two from your hotel rather than take a major detour through the one-way systems (best to accept this unless it's very late at night), and he may demand a large tip, which you're in no way obliged to pay. Most hotels are used to late arrivals, so don't be overly concerned if your flight gets in late at night, though it would be wise to have somewhere booked in advance for your first night.



## By plane

Mexico City's **airport** is surprisingly central (giving some amazing views as you come in to land, low over the buildings). Initially quite confusing, it has several **arrival** halls (salas A–F) arranged along a broad concourse.

Most international arrivals reach the concourse on the ground floor at salas E1, E2 or E3 (domestic arrivals at salas A or B). Wherever you come in, you'll find numerous **ATMs** and several **casas de cambio**, open 24 hours and with reasonable rates for US dollars (rates vary, so shop around), though not always such good rates for travellers' cheques or other currencies (they'll usually take Canadian dollars, pounds sterling, euros, Swiss francs and Japanese yen, but nothing else). There are also plenty of pricey restaurants and snack bars, **car rental** agencies (see p.483), a post office (in Sala A), a telephone *caseta* (in Sala E2), Internet offices (in Sala E2), a few bookshops and 24-hour **left luggage** lockers (in salas A and E2; M$60/day). There are several airport enquiry desks dotted around, and a small **tourist office** in Sala A (7am–9pm; ⓣ55/5786-9002), with a limited range of city information.

As you emerge from Customs and Immigration, or off an internal flight, you'll be besieged by offers of a taxi into town. You are strongly advised not to take them (tourists have been robbed by unauthorized taxi drivers on occasion); instead, by the main exit doors in Sala A you'll find a booth selling tickets for **authorized taxis** (see above), with a scale of fares posted according to where you want to go (Sitio 300 tend to be cheaper than ProTaxi or Porto Taxi): bank on roughly M$200 to the Zócalo and Alameda, M$230 to the Zona Rosa and M$260 to Polanco.

If you're travelling reasonably light you could also go in on the **Metro** (out the doors at the end of Sala A, then follow the covered walkway for 200m), or continue past the Metro station out to Bulevar de Puerto Aéreo and catch a city-bound **bus**.

If you don't fancy heading straight into the city so soon after arrival, you can get a **direct transfer to nearby cities**. There's a bus stop upstairs from Sala E1 where you can pick up first-class buses to Cuernavaca, Pachuca, Puebla, Toluca and Querétaro. There are also luxury car and van services, but they're almost ten times the price of the buses. Alternatively, there are hotels nearby (see p.413).



## By bus

Arriving in Mexico City by bus, you will probably find yourself in one of the city's four long-distance **bus stations** (details of which services use which bus station can be found on pp.480–481). All have **Metro stations** pretty much right outside, as well as authorized taxis (see p.403). They also have guarderías (left luggage offices), post and telephone offices and a tourist information kiosk.

From anywhere north of Mexico City, you will probably arrive at the **Terminal del Norte** on Avenida de los Cien Metros. There's a **Metro** station right outside the entrance (Metro Autobuses del Norte; line 5), and trolleybuses just outside, which head down the Eje Central (Lázaro Cárdenas) to Bellas Artes and on to the Central de Autobuses del Sur. Alternatively, if you head four blocks east, you come to Insurgentes, where you can catch the **Metrobús** (see p.407) south, across Reforma and on to the edge of the Zona Rosa. If you want to get a **taxi**, go to the kiosk selling tickets for authorized taxis (about M$85 to the Zócalo and Alameda, M$70 to the Zona Rosa and M$80 to Polanco, all plus M$15 surcharge 10.30pm–6.30am). If you arrive late at night and don't want to search for a hotel in town, there are places nearby (see p.413).

Buses from points east, including a number of places that you may think of as south (such as Chiapas or the Yucatán), will probably drop you at the **Terminal de Autobuses de Pasajeros de Oriente**, known as **TAPO**, which is located on Avenida Ignacio Zaragoza. It has a **Metro** station (Metro San Lazaro; lines 1 and B) just down a connecting tunnel, which also leads you to the stops for city buses and *colectivos* plying Zaragoza towards the Zócalo and the Alameda. In the same tunnel, opposite the Metro entrance, is a sales desk for the authorized **taxis**, which cost M$60 to the Zócalo and Alameda, M$70 to the Zona Rosa and M$80 to Polanco (all plus M$20 10.30pm–6.30am).

Buses from the Pacific coast generally arrive at the **Central de Autobuses del Sur** (Tasqueña or Taxqeña) on Avenida Tasqueña, outside of which is a big terminus for local buses and *peseros* (see p.407) to the centre and points south of town, and a **Metro** station (Metro Tasqueña; line 2). To find the Metro, head right as you leave the terminal, and you'll see the sign. Alternatively, to your left, on Avenida Tasqueña, trolleybuses head up the Eje Central (Lázaro Cárdenas) to Bellas Artes, and on to the Terminal del Norte. Authorized **taxis** cost M$85 to the Zócalo (M$105 between 10pm and 6am), M$95 (M$115) to the Alameda and Zona Rosa and M$125 (M$145) to Polanco.

Finally, from some places to the west of Mexico City (mainly for services passing through Toluca), there's the **Terminal Poniente** (Observatorio), at the junction of calles Sur and Tacubaya. To get the **Metro** (Metro Observatorio; line 1), leave from the exit in the middle of the terminal, where it makes a bend (next to the authorized taxi kiosk), and the entrance is straight ahead, hidden behind the market stalls. Authorized **taxis** cost M$70 to Polanco, M$80 to the Zona Rosa and M$98 to the Alameda and Zócalo; from 9pm to 6am you pay M$20 more.

If you are coming into Mexico City on a local service from somewhere nearby, it is also possible that you may be dropped off at the end of one of the Metro lines such as Indios Verdes (line 3) or El Rosario (lines 6 and 7). Obviously, the best way into town from there is by Metro.

## City transport

For all its size and frantic pace, once you're used to the city, it is surprisingly easy to get around, with an efficient and very cheap public transport system as well as reasonably priced taxis (see pp.403 and 407).

You'll want to **walk** around the cramped streets of the centre, but remember the altitude – walking gets tiring quickly, especially for the first day or so. If you're heading for Chapultepec or the Zona Rosa, you're better off taking the **bus** or **Metro** – it's an interesting walk all the way down Reforma, but a very long one. As for the outer suburbs, you've got no choice but to rely on public transport. You'll save a lot of hassle if you avoid travelling during **rush hour** (about 7–9am & 6–8pm).

**Tours** that take in the city and often include the surrounding area are available from most of the more expensive hotels, and from operators such as American Express, with various locations around the city (Ⓣ55/5207-7049 or 01-800/543-3288). The government of the DF runs a one-hour city-centre sightseeing tour on buses in the style of old trams leaving from Juárez by Bellas Artes (daily 10am–6.30pm; M$35), but the commentary is in Spanish only. One of the best city tours is with Turibus (every 30–40min 9am–9pm; Mon–Fri M$100, Sat–Sun M$115; Ⓣ55/5133-2488, Ⓦwww.turibus.com.mx), whose open-top double-deckers can be hailed at the Zócalo, the Benito Juárez monument on the south side of the Alameda, El Ángel on Reforma or other stops along its route. The tour takes two and three-quarter hours, and the commentary comes in a choice of languages including English.

### The Metro and Tren Ligero

Mexico City's superb modern **Metro** system (Ⓣ55/5709-1133 ext 5051 or 5052, Ⓦwww.metro.df.gob.mx) is French-built, fast and quiet. It is crowded (though no more so than its New York or London counterparts) and at peak hours stations designate separate entries for women and children (look for the "Mujeres" signs). **Tickets** (M$2) are sold individually and there is no discount for bulk purchases, though to save time queuing and messing about with tiny quantities of change it makes sense to buy several at a time. In theory you're not allowed **luggage** of any size on the Metro (the official limit is 80cm x 50cm x 30cm), but in practice you can get away with carrying a big bag if you board at a quiet station at a calm time, and these days even a backpack seems to be tolerated at busy times. The first train leaves from each end of the line at 6am Monday to Saturday and 7am on Sunday, with the last train at half-past midnight (and an hour later on Saturday nights).

In general, there are no maps of the entire Metro system on platforms, and certainly not on the trains – you'll just find pictographic representations of the line you are on, along with the stations where you can transfer to other lines. The map on p.406 details the system; otherwise you'll need to work out before you set off which way you'll be travelling on each line, and where to change. Direction is indicated by the last station at either end of the line (thus on line 2 you'll want either "Dirección Cuatro Caminos" or "Dirección Tasqueña");

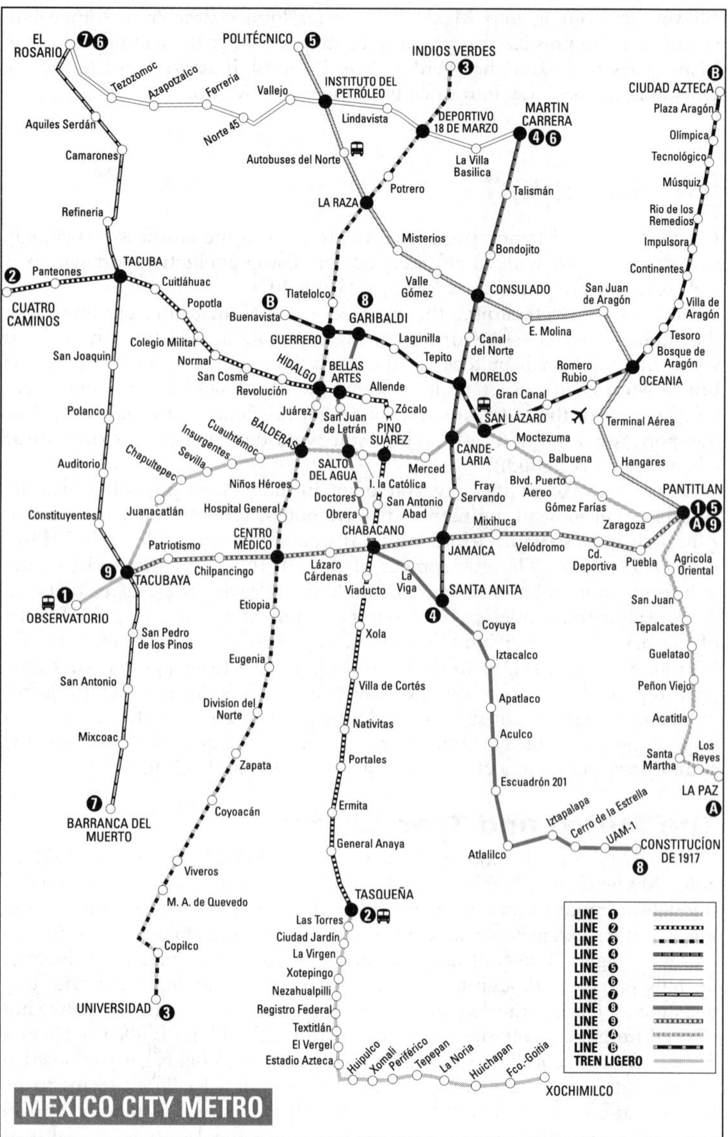


interchanges are indicated by the word "Correspondencia" and the name of the new line.

One of the most recent additions to the public transport system is the **Tren Ligero** (light rail), which runs south from Tasqueña (the southern terminus of line 2) as far as Xochimilco, entirely above ground. It requires a different ticket from the Metro system – when you change at Tasqueña you'll need to buy a

Tren Ligero ticket (good for any one-way journey) from the ticket window or the machines on the concourse (M$2).

## City buses

**Buses** in Mexico City are very efficient, if you know where you're going. **Fares** are M$2.50–5, depending on the length of your journey. Buses display their destinations in the front window, which is somewhat more helpful than looking for route numbers, since the latter are not posted up and rarely used, and some buses terminate before the end of the route. One of the most useful routes is along Reforma, and the area just by Chapultepec Metro station at the entrance to the park is also a major bus terminus, from where you can get to almost any part of the city. Note that during **rush hour** it can be almost impossible to get a bus: once they're full, they simply don't stop to let passengers on.

There are also **trolleybuses** running in both directions along Lázaro Cárdenas (the "Eje Central", or Central Axis) between Terminal del Norte and Central del Sur (Tasqueña), as well as on some other major routes. Trolleybuses charge a flat fare of M$2.50.

On Insurgentes, there is a new service called **Metrobús**, an articulated bus with its own dedicated lane, and fancy bus stops that look more like stations. The Metrobús runs all the way from Indio Verdes in the north to Doctor Gálvez in San Ángel in the south, with a flat fare of M$3.50, but in order to use it, you have to buy a card (M$8) from a machine at one of the stations, which you charge up with rides at the same machines. The machines do not always work, and there's usually a queue for them, so charge up where you can, but don't add too much as credit has been known to vanish mysteriously from the cards. To buy and charge your card, you must have the exact change. Though extremely inconvenient if you just want to take the odd journey, there is no other way to pay the fare.

## Peseros (colectivos)

Running down the major through routes, especially on Reforma and Insurgentes, you'll find **peseros** (**colectivos**), which are smaller and faster but charge more than the bus (far less than a regular taxi, however) and will let you on and off anywhere along their set route. They're mostly thirty-seater buses or VW vans, usually green with a white roof, and with their destination displayed on the windscreen – drivers of the smaller vehicles may sometimes hold up a number of fingers to indicate how many free seats they have. Like buses, *peseros* have route numbers, but routes often have branches, and a vehicle may start or finish in the middle of a route rather than at the end, so again it's more helpful to check the destination in the window. One of the most **useful routes** runs from Chapultepec Park via Avenida Chapultepec to the Zócalo.

## Taxis

Ordinary **taxis** come in a variety of forms and have a reputation for robbery at the hands of the drivers (see box, p.397). You should think twice before taking one, especially if you are on your own, but if you do take one, the most economical are the green-and-white cabs (using unleaded petrol) and the rarer yellow-and-white cabs (using leaded) that cruise the streets looking for customers. Both are usually VW Beetles, and legitimate taxis should have a meter (make sure it's switched on). The cabs that wait at *sitios* (taxi ranks), and the red-and-white radio taxis, which you have to call by phone, charge slightly more, but in general work the same way. Watch out, though, for *turismo* taxis, which lie in wait outside hotels for unsuspecting tourists and charge rates at least triple those of ordinary taxis. In the normal course of events you should avoid them, but they do have a couple of advantages, namely that they're almost always around and that many of the drivers speak some English. They can be worth it if, for example, you need to get to the airport in a hurry (for which they charge no more than an authorized airport cab would) or if you want to go on a tour for a few hours. In the latter case, with some ferocious haggling, you might even get a bargain. If you need to **phone a taxi**, try Servitaxis (Ⓣ55/5516-6020) or Taximex (Ⓣ55/9171-8880) or, to the airport, Sitio 300 (Ⓣ55/5571-9344), ProTaxi (Ⓣ55/2559-0333) or Porto Taxi (Ⓣ55/5786-8212). It can be difficult to get a taxi in the rush hour.



## Driving

**Rental cars** (see p.483 for agents' details) are available from the airport and elsewhere, but it is generally better to wait until you are ready to leave the city before renting. If you already have a car, choose a hotel with secure parking and leave it there for the duration of your stay, except possibly to do a tour of the south of the city. Driving in the city is a nightmare, compounded by confusing one-way and through-route systems, by the impossibility of finding anywhere to park and by traffic police who can spot foreign plates a mile off and know a potential "fine" when they see one. If you insist on driving, note that the "Green Angels" who operate on highways (see p.40) do not operate within Mexico City: for city **breakdown help** call the AMA (Asociación Mexicana Automovilística, equivalent of the AA or the AAA) on Ⓣ55/5424-0262.

# Information

Visitors arriving at the airport can pick up limited **tourist information** on the city at the booth in Sala A (7am–9pm), and those arriving by bus will find tourist information **kiosks** inside or just outside the terminals. Similar kiosks, run by the government of the DF, are dotted around town, none of which have much printed material to take away, though the staff are usually well versed in the ways of the city. The most central is in the **Zócalo** between the cathedral and Monte de Piedad (daily 10am–6pm; Ⓣ55/5518-1003; Metro Zócalo), and there's also one on the other side of the cathedral by the Sagrario. The **SECTUR** office at Presidente Mazaryk 172, Polanco (Mon–Fri 8am–6pm, Sat 10am–3pm; call 24/7 on Ⓣ55/3002-6300 or 078; Metro Polanco), is flush with handouts about Mexico City and the country as a whole – but inconveniently sited a long way from where you are likely to spend your time. The government of the DF also runs a tourist information **website** (Ⓦwww.mexicocity.gob.mx), in Spanish and English, with excellent background information, advice, tips and patchy listings, and you can call them toll-free on Ⓣ01-800/008-9090.

Useful local **guidebooks**, city **maps** (the best produced by Guia Roji), English-language magazines and pulp paperbacks are sold at Sanborn's, street newsstands, the airport and many big hotels.

# Accommodation

Mexico City seems to have hotels on almost every street. These range from a few budget **hostels** to some of the swankiest and most expensive **hotels** in the country. You're bound to find something to suit in between these extremes, though the best-value places can fill up quickly, so **booking ahead** is always a good idea. If you are spending a few days here or visiting more than once, you might want to lodge in a couple of different places. For example, stay near the Zócalo to see the historic sights, and then spend a few nights in the Zona Rosa, where it is easier to get back after an evening around the clubs of the Zona or the bars of Condesa.

The avenues around the **Zócalo** are awash with accommodation. Avenida 5 de Mayo is as good a place as any to begin, with a dozen or so fairly good options in close proximity. The hotels in this area are generally older than elsewhere; high ceilings and internal courtyards are common. The cheaper places often have a lot of dark rooms, but most are comfortable and, considering the location – right in the heart of the sightseeing zone – excellent value. Here, too, are the city's large backpacker hostels. The area's main drawback is its distance from any good nightlife and the better places to eat, though there are new places opening all the time.

To the west of the Zócalo is a sprawling area centred on the **Alameda** and the **Revolution Monument**. Hotels here are a mixed bag, with those nearer the Alameda tending to be more upmarket than those across Reforma near the Revolution Monument. This area is reasonably central to both the sights and the best nightlife, but neither is right on the doorstep. Note that the north of Puente de Alvarado is a red-light area and can be a little bit intimidating at night, especially for women, though it does have a number of cheap hotels.

Accommodation in the **Zona Rosa** tends to be expensive, though if you look hard you can find luxury accommodation at moderate prices. Here you'll be spoilt for choice with cafés, posh restaurants, bars and clubs, and you're also within twenty minutes' walk of the heart of Condesa. There's even more upmarket accommodation north of Chapultepec Park in **Polanco**, mostly in high-rises but with a couple of smaller (and very expensive) boutique hotels.

Most places have 24-hour reception desks and are geared for late arrivals and early departures, and with reasonably cheap taxi fares into the Zócalo or Zona Rosa it seldom makes financial sense to stay near the bus stations or airport. However, if you arrive especially late or are just in transit and need a place to rest up for a while, there are places to stay that are very handy for the **airport** and **Terminal del Norte**.

Unless otherwise noted – and except for the options around the airport and bus station – the establishments below are marked on the "Central Mexico City" map (see pp.416–417).

## Hostels

**Casa de los Amigos** Ignacio Mariscal 132 ⓣ55/5705-0521, ⓦwww.casadelosamigos.org. Involved in various community activities, the Quaker-run *Casa*, on a quiet street in the house where José Clemente Orozco spent the last decade of his life, pitches itself as a guesthouse, though it still has eight- and four-bed dorms (M$100) as well as a few singles (M$150) and doubles (❸). Clean and comfortable with a good kitchen (breakfast available), a meditation room that doubles as a library and a conference room where they show movies, it is popular with people staying in the city for a few weeks, and has a two-night minimum stay. House regulations include no alcohol and no smoking. Metro Revolución.

**Hostal Amigo** Isabel la Católica 61 ⓣ55/5512-3464 or 01-800/746-7835, ⓦwww.hostelamigo.com. Backpackers' hangout with four- to twelve-bed dorms (M$100–140), not all with outside windows, but lockers (bring your own padlock), free Internet access, a luggage deposit, a bar, a kitchen and places to hang out. Metro Isabel la Católica.

**Hostal Moneda** Moneda 8 ⓣ01-800/221-7265, ⓦwww.hostalmoneda.com.mx. Convivial hostel with only a few dorm beds (M$100), so book ahead if you want one. There are a couple of lounges (one with TV), a decent kitchen and a panoramic rooftop terrace where a buffet breakfast (included) is served. Private rooms (4) are also available. Make a reservation if you are to arrive after 11pm. Metro Zócalo.

**Hostel Catedral** Guatemala 4 ⓣ55/5518-1726, ⓦwww.hostelcatedral.com. Large, secure and efficiently run modern place in a former office right behind the cathedral. Open 24hr, it has spotless four- or six-bunk rooms, most with their own bathroom (M$130, HI members M$90, ISIC card-holders M$100; buffet breakfast included) and some private rooms (4). There's an on-site travel agency, Internet access, a café and bar and a rooftop terrace with fabulous views. About the only drawbacks are a small kitchen (though it seems little used), limited communal areas and the noise that travels through the central stairwell: bring earplugs and a lock for the lockers. Metro Zócalo.

**Hostel Home** Tabasco 303, Roma ⓣ55/5511-1683, ⓦwww.hostelhome.com.mx (see map, p.436). This small twenty-bunk hostel (called "Home" because it was originally a family house) has seen better days and is a little distant from the main sights, but has, as advertised, a "chilled atmosphere", a kitchen and free Internet access, and is open 24hr. As well as the six- and eight-bunk dorms (M$100, HI members or ISIC card-holders M$90) there's a sunny lounge and a small kitchen. Metro Sevilla.

## Hotels

### Around the Zócalo

**Azores** Brasil 25 ⓣ55/5521-5220, ⓦwww.hotelazores.com. Well-situated modern hotel with small but clean and comfy rooms around a central well, each with TV and bath. Metro Allende or Zócalo. 3

**Catedral** Donceles 95 ⓣ55/5518-5232, ⓦwww.hotelcatedral.com.mx. Very presentable mid-range place. All rooms have TV, FM stereo and telephone, and some a Jacuzzi. Internet access is available, and there's a good restaurant and a terrace overlooking the cathedral. Offers a ten percent discount for payment in cash. Metro Zócalo. 5

**Gillow** Isabel la Católica 17 ⓣ55/5518-1441 to 6, ⓔhgillow@prodigy.net.mx. Friendly and good-value mid-priced hotel with large rooms (some with a small patio), in-house travel agency and leather sofas in the public areas. Cable TV and the expected amenities in rooms. Ten percent discount for payment in cash. Metro Allende. 5

**Gran Hotel Ciudad de México** 16 de Septiembre 82 ⓣ55/1083-7700, ⓦwww.granhotelciudaddemexico.com.mx. Large hotel right on the Zócalo with sumptuous public areas (see p.421), though some of the older rooms don't match the impression given by the lobby. The remodelled suites are nice, but cost M$2230. Metro Zócalo. 8

**Isabel** Isabel la Católica 63 ⓣ55/5518-1213 to 7, ⓦwww.hotel-isabel.com.mx. Good-value hotel with services such as taxis and laundry that are normally offered only at much pricier hotels, plus an associated restaurant and bar. Rooms (with or without bath, the latter on the roof), though a little bit sombre, are quite spacious with TV and safe. It's worth booking a few days ahead. Metro Isabel la Católica. 2

**Juárez** Callejón de 5 de Mayo 17 1° ⓣ55/5512-6929, ⓔhoteljuarez@prodigy.net.mx. Very central, clean and good value, but not recommended for lone women travellers. Avoid room no. 4, which is next to the hotel's main water pump. Metro Allende or Zócalo. 2

**Majestic** Madero 73 ⓣ01-800/509-2350 (toll-free in Mexico outside the DF) or 55/5521-8600 to 09, in the US and Canada ⓣ1-800/780-7234, in the UK ⓣ0800/393 130, in Ireland ⓣ1800/709 101, in Australia ⓣ13/1779, in New Zealand ⓣ0800/237 893, in South Africa ⓣ0800/994 284, ⓦwww.majestic.com.mx. Luxury Best Western hotel on the Zócalo that has bags of character, is considerably cheaper than many of the places in the Zona Rosa and has many of the same facilities. Zócalo views from some rooms. Metro Zócalo. 8

**Montecarlo** Uruguay 69 ⓣ55/5518-1418, ⓕ5510-0081. Originally an Augustinian monastery and later inhabited briefly by D.H. Lawrence. Quiet and comfortable with a garage and a beautiful inner courtyard that is a little out of keeping with the rather small and dark en-suite rooms. Metro Zócalo. 2

**República** Cuba 57 ⓣ55/5512-9517. Old and fairly grotty but also very cheap hotel (especially for two people sharing a double bed) on a quiet street. All rooms have a bathroom and TV. ❶

**San Antonio** Callejón de 5 de Mayo 29 2° ⓣ55/5512-1625 or 6, ⓕ5512-9906. Quiet, friendly place hidden away in a side street between 5 de Mayo and La Palma. Standards are high considering the price, with light, airy, spotless rooms, good firm beds, decent sheets and free bottled water. Metro Allende or Zócalo. ❷

**Washington** 5 de Mayo 54 ⓣ & ⓕ55/5512-3502. Good-value hotel very near the Zócalo, with clean, pleasant rooms all with nicely tiled bathroom, cable TV, phone and free water. Metro Allende or Zócalo. ❸

**Zamora** 5 de Mayo 50 ⓣ55/5512-8245. One of the more basic downtown hotels, the low prices making the noise, threadbare towels and marginal cleanliness acceptable. Very popular so you may have to book ahead at busy times. Rooms are with or without bath. Metro Allende or Zócalo. ❶

## Around the Alameda

**Bamer** Juárez 52 ⓣ55/5521-9060 to 70, ⓔhbamer@prodigy.net.mx. Massive double rooms, some overlooking the Alameda, make this one of the best mid-range places in the vicinity, with TV, phone and the expected facilities, plus a few suites. Closed for renovation at last check. Metro Juárez. ❺

**Fleming** Revillagigedo 35 ⓣ55/5510-4530 or 35, ⓦwww.hotelfleming.com.mx. Modern business-style hotel with little imagination to the decor but good facilities – comfortable, carpeted rooms, cable TV, etc – at moderate prices. Metro Juárez. ❹

**Hotel de Cortés** Hidalgo 85 ⓣ55/5518-2181 to 4, in the US and Canada ⓣ1-800/780-7234, in the UK ⓣ0800/393 130, in Ireland ⓣ1800/709 101, in Australia ⓣ13/1779, in New Zealand ⓣ0800/237 893, in South Africa ⓣ0800/994 284, ⓦwww.hoteldecortes.com.mx. A Best Western hotel that manages to rise above the corporate formula, mostly because of its wonderful setting. The cool, central patio houses a restaurant and a coffee-house seemingly a million miles from the bustle of the Alameda. Facilities are good, rates include a buffet breakfast and the decor has been done with taste, though maintenance sometimes lets them down. Avoid room nos. 105 and 106, which are noisy. In quiet times rates may drop a couple of price bands, but in high season the cheapest double is at M$1614. Metro Hidalgo. ❾

**Managua** Plaza de San Fernando 11 ⓣ55/5512-1312, ⓕ5521-3062. Good-value, clean and quiet place with a cafeteria that does room service, and rooms with TV, bathroom and free bottled water, all in a restful location facing the Jardín de San Fernando. Metro Hidalgo. ❷

**Pánuco** Ayuntamiento 148 ⓣ55/5521-2916. Good-value and spotlessly clean hotel with carpeted rooms each with writing desk and TV – and a lot of fake marble – located in a drab part of town a little away from the most popular tourist areas, though tolerably close to the Zona Rosa. Parking and a restaurant on site. Tends to be full Fri and Sat. Metro Juárez. ❷

## Around the Revolution Monument

**Buenavista** Bernal Díaz 34 ⓣ55/5546-7836. Bottom-of-the-barrel option in a red-light district, where you'll need to watch your luggage and not be too picky about cleanliness. It is cheap, especially for single rooms, and even cheaper if you do without bathroom and TV. Not recommended for lone women. Metro Revolución. ❶

**Casa Blanca** Lafragua 7 ⓣ55/5096-4500 or 01-800/200-2252, in the US ⓣ1-800/905-2905, ⓦwww.hotel-casablanca.com.mx. Attractive but rather impersonal modern high-rise hotel with perfectly decent rooms at prices a good deal lower than a lot of the Zona Rosa places. There's even a rooftop pool, a gym, business facilities and a restaurant. Wheelchair friendly. Metro Revolución. ❽

**Mayaland** Antonio Caso 23 ⓣ55/5566-6066, ⓔhotelmayaland@hotmail.com. Squat and ugly from outside but tastefully decorated within. Good-value rooms all come with cable TV and purified water piped in, though you might want to spend M$65 extra for a more spacious double (with the standard two double beds) or M$60 for a Jacuzzi. Metro Revolución. ❺

**Royalty** Jesús Terán 21 ⓣ55/5566-9255. Very reasonable rates for rooms (some rather dark) with bathrooms, TV and phone. Metro Revolución. ❶

## The Zona Rosa, Roma and Condesa

The hotels listed below are marked on the "Zona Rosa, Roma and Condesa" map (see p.436).

**La Casona** Durango 280, at Cozumel ⓣ55/5286-3001, ⓦwww.hotelcasona.com.mx. Set on the edge of the Zona Rosa in an early twentieth-century building, *La Casona* has an understated, if slightly quirky, European-style elegance, with polished wooden floors, antique furniture, a piano in its lounge and quite a collection of art – including masks, original cartoons and paintings. The rooms (which start at M$2293) are all different, with an aesthete's attention to detail. On-site restaurant. Metro Sevilla. 9

**Geneve** Londres 130 ☎55/5080-0800 or 01-800/714-6549, www.hotelescalinda.com.mx. A large, century-old, but thoroughly modern hotel right in the heart of the Zona Rosa with an understated but elegant feel. Rooms are comfortable if unspectacular, with cable TV, mini-bar and the like, but the facilities are excellent, and include the lovely Salon Jardín with its stained-glass and iron roof, a restaurant, gym, spa and on-site *Sanborn's* restaurant. Metro Insurgentes. 8

**Hotel Del Principado** Londres 42 ☎55/5533-2944 to 8, www.hoteldeprincipado.com.mx. Comfortable hotel with slightly jarring decor, but reasonably large and well-kept rooms, all with TV and phone, and there are parking facilities and a laundry service. Rates include a buffet breakfast. Metro Insurgentes. 6

**Marco Polo** Amberes 27 ☎55/5511-1839 or 01-800/900-6000, in the US and Canada ☎1-800/310-9693, www.marcopolo.com.mx. Stylish small luxury hotel whose attractively furnished rooms (doubles from M$1935) come with tasteful artwork and all the amenities you'd expect, including Internet access. Complimentary fruit, coffee and purified water supplied. Metro Insurgentes. 9

**Maria Cristina** Rio Lerma 31, Cuauhtémoc ☎55/5703-1212, www.hotelmariacristina.com.mx. There's a lovely colonial feel to this stylish little hotel near the Museo Venustiano Carranza. Popular with European visitors, the rooms are bright and quiet, though without the wood panelling and blue tiles of the public areas. Metro Insurgentes. 7

**Posada Viena** Marsella 28, at Dinamarca ☎55/5566-0700 or 01-800/849-8402, in the US ☎1-888/698-0690, www.posadavienahotel.com.mx. A comfortable but unpretentious four-star hotel with rooms nicely decorated in rustic Mexican style and ceiling fans, but no a/c. Metro Insurgentes. 5

**Roosevelt** Insurgentes Sur 287 ☎55/5208-6813, www.hotelroosevelt.com.mx. The wonderful 1938 Art Deco exterior of this mid-range hotel on the edge of Condesa is not reflected by the decor within. The corridors are a bit scuffed, but the rooms are well kept, though small, and done out in a pleasing combination of pink, grey and buff, with pink granite surfaces in the bathrooms. There's a decent restaurant downstairs. Metro Insurgentes. 5

**Segovia Regency** Chapultepec 328 ☎55/5208-8454, www.hotelsegovia.com.mx. Reliable high-rise hotel with parking facilities. It's often fully booked with business regulars, so reserve ahead, especially during the week. Metro Insurgentes. 6

## Polanco

The hotels listed below are marked on the "Chapultepec Park and Polanco" map (see p.438).

**Casa Vieja** Eugenio Sué 45 ☎55/5282-0067, www.casavieja.com. Very chic ultra-deluxe small hotel in a suburban house with ten suites (junior M$3510, master M$5030, presidential M$11,110), each with the best of everything: supremely comfortable beds, Jacuzzi, kitchenette, phone and high-speed Internet, fax machine, VCR, stereo, video and music library and stacks of books and magazines. Decor is rich with mosaics and quality paintings. Every detail is taken care of, and there's a superb restaurant and bar on site. Metro Polanco. 9

**Nikko Mexico** Campos Elisos 204 ☎55/5280-1111 or 01-800/908-8800, in US and Canada ☎1-800/645-5687, in the UK ☎0800/282 502, in Australia ☎1800/622 240, www.hotelnikkomexico.com, reservations through any Japan Airlines office. Not the most expensive high-rise business hotel in the city (rooms start at M$3510) but as luxurious as you could want, with indoor pool, rooftop tennis courts, gym and acres of glass and marble. Metro Polanco. 9

## The airport and around

**Hilton** in the airport ☎55/5133-0505 or 01-800/003-1400, in the US ☎1-800/HILTONS, www.hilton.com. An elevator from Sala G (upstairs from Sala E1) takes you up to this swanky hotel which takes up much of the airport's third floor with its restaurants, bars, gym and very well-appointed, though not especially large, rooms (some with runway views). The multichannel TV even has in-house movies and flight information screens. Rack rates start at M$2230 midweek, slightly less at weekends. Metro Terminal Aérea. 9

**Hotel Aeropuerto** Blv de Puerto Aéreo 380 ☎55/5785-5888 or 5851, Ⓕ5784-1329. The cheapest of the hotels near the airport, with well-maintained, carpeted rooms; all have TV and phone, plus there's room service from the on-site restaurant. Some (soundproof) rooms have a view of the runway. The hotel is three minutes' walk from the terminal: follow signs from Sala A to the Metro, from whose entrance you can see the hotel across the busy road (use the footbridge). Metro Terminal Aérea. 5

**Ramada Aeropuerto México** Blv de Puerto Aéreo 390 ⓣ55/5133-3232 or 01-800/702-4200, ⓦwww.ramadamexico.com. Attractive business hotel with lower prices than the big airport hotels but still with most of their features and facilities. Located next to the *Hotel Aeropuerto* (see opposite), so it is barely worth using the hotel's free airport transfer. Metro Terminal Aérea. ⑨

### Terminal del Norte and around

**Acuario** Poniente 112 #100 ⓣ55/5587-2677. Institutional-looking and uninviting, but clean enough if you need a cheap bolt-hole for the night. Leaving the bus station, turn left, then at the major junction (after 100m) turn right across the main road and it's just ahead on the left. Metro Autobuses del Norte. ②

**Brasilia** Av de los Cien Metros 4823 ⓣ55/5587-8577, ⓦwww.hotel-brasilia.co.mx. Good-value business-style hotel (though sometimes a bit snooty towards backpackers) just 150m southeast of the bus station (turn left as you exit and it's straight ahead of you), where you can get a peaceful sleep in comfortable, carpeted rooms with cable TV and phone. There's a decent if slightly pricey restaurant on site, parking facilities and even room service. Metro Autobuses del Norte. ④



# Central Mexico City

The heart of Mexico City is the **Zócalo**, built by the Spanish right over the devastated ceremonial centre of the Aztec city of Tenochtitlán. Extraordinary uncovered ruins – chief of which is the **Templo Mayor** – provide the Zócalo's most compelling attraction, but there's also a wealth of great colonial buildings, among them the huge **cathedral** and the **Palacio Nacional** with its striking **Diego Rivera murals**. You could easily spend a couple of days in the tightly packed blocks hereabouts, investigating their dense concentration of museums and galleries, especially notable for works by Rivera and his "Big Three" companions, David Siqueiros and José Clemente Orozco.

West of the Zócalo the *centro histórico* stretches through the main commercial district past the **Museo Nacional de Arte** to the sky-scraping **Torre Latinoamericana** and the **Palacio de Bellas Artes** with its gorgeous Art Deco interior. Both overlook the formal parkland of the **Alameda**, next to which you'll find a number of museums, principally the **Museo Franz Mayer**, which houses an excellent Alameda-related arts and crafts collection, and the **Museo Mural Rivera**, with the artist's famed *Dream of a Sunday Afternoon in the Alameda*. Further west, the **Revolution Monument** heralds the more upmarket central suburbs, chiefly the **Zona Rosa**, long known as the spot for plush shops and restaurants, though that title has largely been usurped by swanky **Polanco** and hipper **Condesa**.

## The Zócalo

The vast paved open space of the **Zócalo** (Metro Zócalo) – properly known as the Plaza de la Constitución – was once the heart of **Aztec Tenochtitlán**, and is today one of the largest city squares in the world after Beijing's Tiananmen Square and Moscow's Red Square. The city's political and religious centre, it takes its name from part of a monument to Independence that was planned in the 1840s for the square by General Santa Anna. Like most of his other plans, this went astray, and only the statue's base (now gone) was ever erected: *el zócalo* literally means "the plinth". By extension, every other town square in Mexico has adopted the same name. It's constantly animated, with pre-Hispanic revivalist groups dancing and pounding drums throughout the day and street stalls and buskers in the evening. Stages are set up here for major national holidays and, of course, this is the place to hold demonstrations. Over 100,000 people massed here in March 2001 to support the Zapatistas after their march

△ Activity in the Zócalo

from Chiapas in support of indigenous people's rights; in July 2006 the square proved too small to contain the millions of demonstrators who gathered to challenge the result of the year's presidential election, a contest widely believed – especially in the left-leaning DF – to have been fixed. Spreading out from the Zócalo, the crowds reached as far as Reforma.

Though you're not guaranteed to see any protests, among the Zócalo's more certain entertainments is the ceremonial **lowering of the national flag** from its giant pole in the centre of the plaza each evening at sundown (typically 6pm). A troop of presidential guards march out from the palace, strike the enormous flag and perform a complex routine at the end of which the flag is left, neatly folded, in the hands of one of their number. With far less pomp, the flag is quietly raised again around half an hour later. You get a great view of this, and of everything else happening in the Zócalo, from the rooftop *La Terraza* restaurant/bar in the *Hotel Majestic* at the corner of Madero (see p.467).

The Zócalo does, of course, have its less glorious aspects. Mexico City's unemployment rate is tellingly reflected by the people who line up on the west side of the cathedral seeking work, each holding a little sign indicating their trade.

### The cathedral

The **Catedral Metropolitana** (daily 7.30am–7.30pm, discretion is required during services: Mass Mon–Fri at 9.30am, 10.30am, noon, 5pm, 6pm and 7pm, Sat same times plus 1pm, Sun 8am, 9.30am, 10.30am, noon, 1.30pm, 4pm, 5pm, 6pm and 7pm; free; Metro Zócalo) holds the distinction of being the largest church in Latin America. Like so many of the city's older, weightier structures, the cathedral has settled over the years into the soft, wet ground beneath – the tilt is quite plain to see, despite extensive work to stabilize the building. The first church on this site was constructed only a couple of years after the Conquest, using stones torn from the Temple of Huitzilopochtli, but the present structure was begun in 1573 to provide Mexico City with a cathedral more suited to its wealth and status as the jewel of the Spanish empire. The towers weren't completed until 1813, though, and the building incorporates a plethora of architectural styles throughout. Even the frontage demonstrates this: relatively austere at the bottom where work began in the years soon after the Conquest, it flowers into full Baroque as you look up, and is topped by Neoclassical cornices and clock tower.

Inside, although the size of the cathedral is striking, the chief impression is that it's a rather gloomy space, with rows of dimly lit side chapels. It is enlivened mostly by the **Altar de los Reyes**, a vast gilt reredos built of wood between 1718 and 1737 behind the main altar that features effigies of European kings and queens as well as two oil paintings, the *Assumption of the Virgin* and *Adoration of the Kings*. Fans of ornate handiwork will also appreciate the detailed work in gold and wood on the central *coro* (choir).

Next door, the **Sagrario Metropolitano** (daily 8am–8pm; free), despite its heavy, grey Baroque facade and squat, bell-topped towers, feels both lighter and richer inside, with its exuberant churrigueresque decoration and liberal use of gold paint. It was originally built as the parish church, and performs most of the day-to-day functions of a local church, such as baptisms and marriages.

### Templo Mayor

Just off the Zócalo, down beside the cathedral, lies the entrance to the site where the **Templo Mayor** (Ⓦwww.conaculta.gob.mx/templomayor; Tues–Sun 9am–5pm; M$45, plus M$30 to use a video camera; Metro Zócalo) has been excavated.

Although it had been known since the beginning of the twentieth century that Tenochtitlán's ceremonial area lay under this part of the city, it was generally believed that the chief temple, or Teocalli, lay directly beneath the cathedral. Archeological work only began in earnest in 1978 after workmen uncovered a vast stone disc weighing about eight tonnes and depicting **Coyolxauhqui**, goddess of the moon, in the streets. Coyolxauhqui was the daughter of Coatlicue, the mother goddess who controlled life and death; on discovering that her mother was miraculously pregnant, Coyolxauhqui vowed to wipe out the dishonour by killing her. Before she could do so however, Huitzilopochtli sprang fully armed from Coatlicue's womb, and proceeded to decapitate and dismember his sister (who is therefore always portrayed with her head and limbs cut off) and threw her body down a mountain. He then drove off the four hundred other brothers who had gathered to help her: they scattered to become the stars. The human sacrifices carried out in the temple – meant to feed Huitzilopochtli, the sun god, with the blood he needed to win his nightly battle against darkness – were in part a re-enactment of this, with the victims being thrown down the steps afterwards. When the disc symbolizing Coyolxauhqui's fall from the mountain was found, logic demanded that it must lie at the foot of the Temple of Huitzilopochtli, and so the colonial buildings were cleared away and excavation began.

You'll be able to see the bare ruins of the foundations of the great temple and one or two buildings immediately around it. The site is highly confusing since, as was normal practice, a new temple was built over the old at the end of every 52-year calendar cycle (and apparently even more frequently here), resulting in a whole series of temples stacked inside each other like Russian dolls – there are seven here. Look at the models and maps in the museum first (see p.417) and it all makes more sense.

Of the seven reconstructions of the temple, layers as far down as the second have been uncovered, though you can only see the top of the structure as the bottom is now well below the water table. Confusing as it is trying to work out

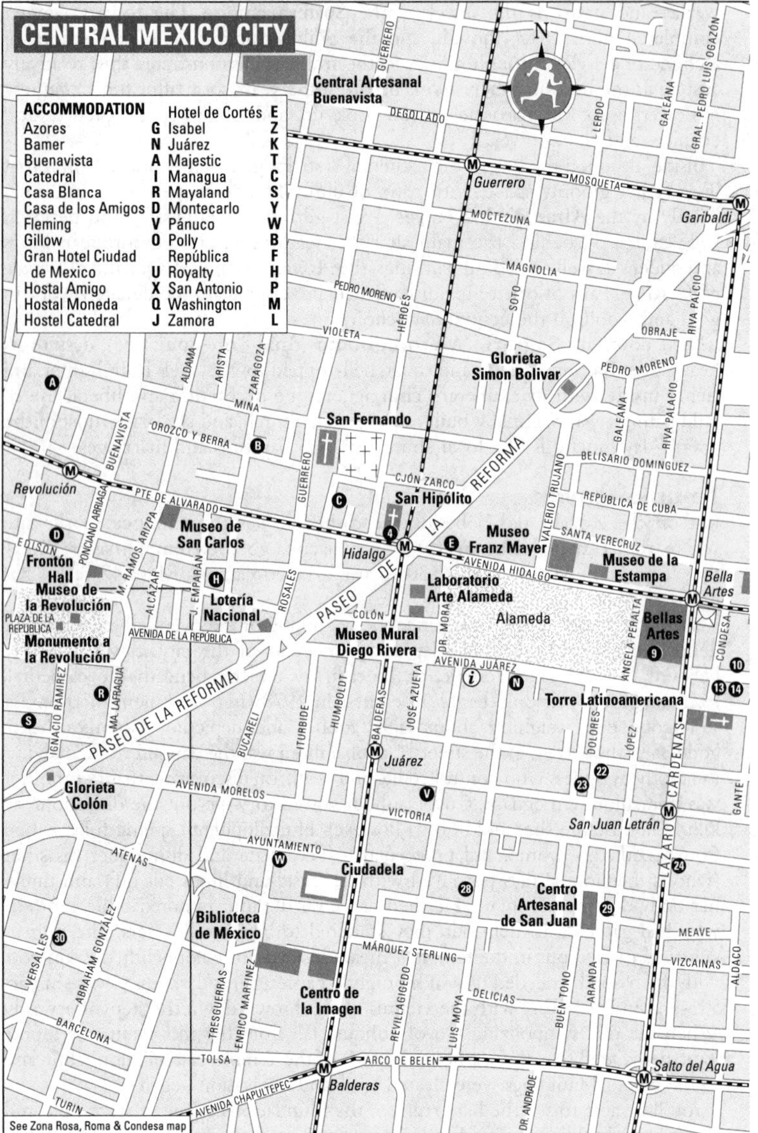


what's what, it's a fascinating site, scattered with odd sculptures, including some great serpents, and traces of its original bright paintwork in red, blue and yellow. Seeing it here, at the heart of the modern city, brings the ceremonies and sacrifices that took place rather close to home.

It is also worth calling past here in the evening when the **floodlit pyramid ruins** can be seen from the surrounding streets.

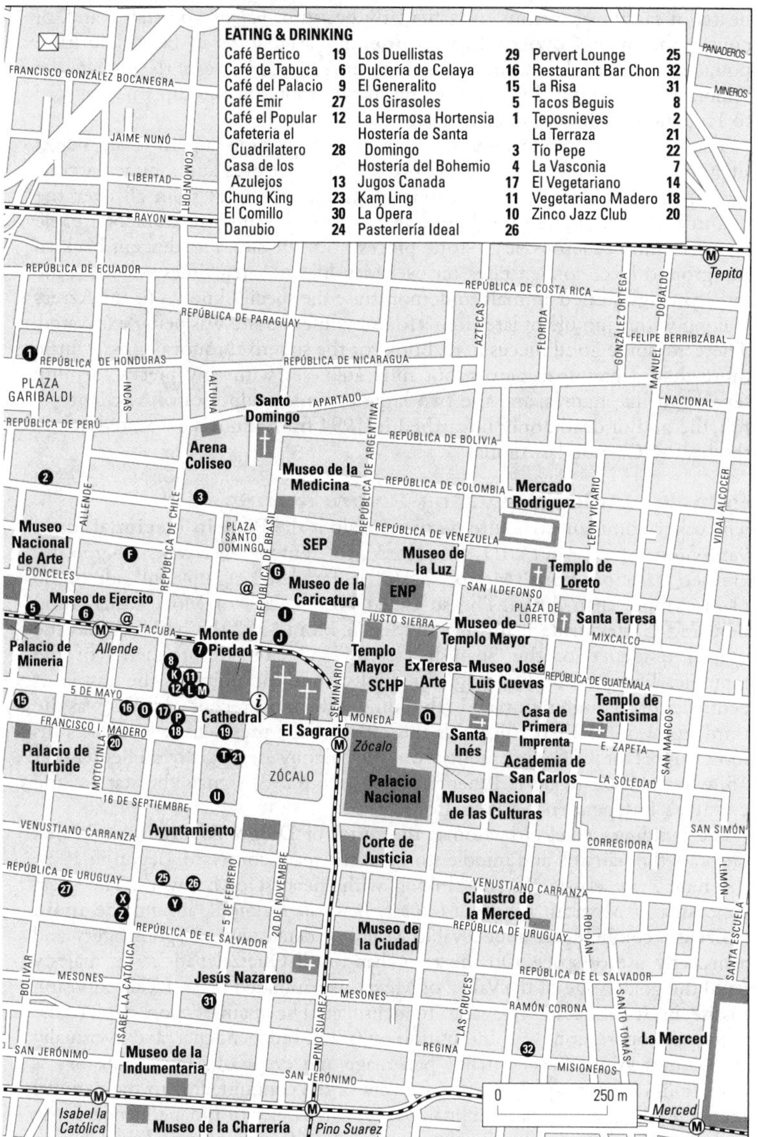


## Museo del Templo Mayor

The **museum**, entered through the site on the same ticket, helps set the temples in context, with some welcome reconstructions and models of how Tenochtitlán would have looked at its height. There are some wonderful pieces retrieved from the site, especially the replica **tzompantli** (wall of skulls) as you enter, the eagle in Room 1 with a cavity in its back for the hearts of sacrificial victims, a particularly beautiful *pulque* god statue and, of course, the huge **Coyolxauhqui stone**, displayed so as to be visible from points throughout the museum. The museum's design is meant to simulate the temple, so you climb through it to reach two rooms at the top, one devoted to Huitzilopochtli, the other to Tlaloc.

The best items are towards the top, including some superb stone masks such as the one from Teotihuacán, black with inset eyes and a huge earring, typical of the objects paid in tribute by subject peoples from all over the country. On the highest level are two magnificent, full-size terracotta eagle warriors and numerous large stone pieces from the site. The descent back to the ground level concentrates on everyday life in Aztec times – with some rather mangy stuffed animals to demonstrate the species known to the Aztecs – along with a jumble of later items found while the site was being excavated. There are some good pieces here. Look for the superb turquoise mosaic, little more than a handspan across, but intricately set with tiny pieces forming seven god-like figures; and the two large ceramic sculptures of Mictlantecihtli, the god of death, only unearthed in 1994 from tunnels excavated below the nearby Casa de las Águilas.



### Palacio Nacional and the Rivera murals

The other dominant structure on the Zócalo is the **Palacio Nacional** (daily 9am–5pm; free, but ID required to enter; ⓦwww.shcp.gob.mx/museo_palacionacional; Metro Zócalo), its facade taking up a full side of the plaza – more than 200m. The so-called New Palace of Moctezuma stood here and Cortés made it his first residence. From 1562 the building was the official residence of the Spanish viceroy, and later of presidents of the republic. The present building, for all its apparent unity, is the result of centuries of agglomeration and rebuilding – the most recent addition was the third storey, in 1927. It still holds the office of the president, who makes his most important pronouncements from the balcony – especially on September 15, when the Grito de la Independencia (see p.293) signals the start of the country's Independence celebrations.

The building's chief attraction is the series of **Diego Rivera murals** that decorate the stairwell and middle storey of the main courtyard. Begun in 1929, the murals are classic Rivera, ranking with the best of his work. The great panorama of Mexican history, *México a Través de los Siglos*, around the **main staircase**, combines an unbelievable wealth of detail with savage imagery and a masterly use of space. On the right-hand wall Quetzalcoatl sits in majesty amid the golden age of the Valley of México, surrounded by an idealized vision of life in Teotihuacán, Tula and Tenochtitlán. The main section depicts the Conquest, oppression, war, Inquisition, invasion, Independence and eventually Revolution. Almost every major personage and event of Mexican history is here, from the grotesquely twisted features of the conquistadors to the national heroes: balding, white-haired Hidalgo with the banner of Independence; squat, dark Benito Juárez with his Constitution and laws for the reform of the Church; Zapata, with a placard proclaiming his cry of "Tierra y Libertad"; and Pancho Villa, moustachioed and swaggering. On the left are post-Revolutionary Mexico and the future (as Rivera envisaged it), with Karl Marx pointing the way to adoring workers. Businessmen stand clustered over their tickertape in front of a somewhat ironic depiction of the metropolis with its skyscrapers and grim industrial wastes. Rivera's wife, the artist Frida Kahlo, is depicted, too, behind her sister Cristina (with whom Rivera was having an affair at the time) in a red blouse with an open copy of the Communist Manifesto.

△ Rivera mural, Palacio Nacional

A series of smaller panels was intended to go all the way round the upper (now middle) storey, an over-ambitious and unfinished project. The uncoloured first panel lists the products that the world owes to Mexico, including maize, beans, chocolate, tobacco, cotton, tomatoes, peanuts, prickly pears and chicle (the source of chewing gum). The remainder of the paintings that were completed reach halfway around and mostly depict the idyll of various aspects of life before the Conquest – market day, dyeing cloth, hunting scenes and so on. The last (completed in 1951) shows the arrival of the Spanish, complete with an image of La Malinche (the Indian woman widely perceived to have betrayed native Mexicans) bearing the blue-eyed baby sired by Cortés – the first Mexican *mestizo*.

## Diego Rivera

**Diego Rivera** (c.1886–1957), husband of **Frida Kahlo** (see box, pp.454–455), was arguably the greatest of Los Tres Grandes, the "Big Three" Mexican artists who interpreted the Revolution and Mexican history through the medium of enormous murals, and put the nation's art onto an international footing in the first half of the twentieth century. His works (along with those of **José Clemente Orozco** and **David Siqueiros**) remain among the country's most striking sights.

Rivera studied from the age of 10 at the San Carlos Academy in the capital, immediately showing immense ability. He later moved to Paris, where he flirted with many of the new artistic trends, in particular Cubism. More importantly, though, he and Siqueiros planned, in exile, a popular, native art to express the new society in Mexico. In 1921 Rivera returned from Europe to the aftermath of the Revolution, and right away began work for the Ministry of Education at the behest of the socialist Education Minister, poet and presidential hopeful José Vasconcelos. Informed by his own communist beliefs, and encouraged by the leftist sympathies of the times, Rivera embarked on the first of his massive, consciousness-raising **murals**, whose themes – Mexican history, the oppression of the natives, post-Revolutionary resurgence – were initially more important than their techniques. Many of his early murals are deceptively simple, naive even, but in fact Rivera's style remained close to major trends and, following the lead of Siqueiros, took a scientific approach to his work, looking to industrial advances for new techniques, better materials and fresh inspiration. The view of industrial growth as a panacea (particularly in the earlier works of both Rivera and Siqueiros) may have been simplistic, but the artists' use of technology and experimentation with new methods and original approaches often have startling results – this is particularly true of Siqueiros's work at the Polyforum Siqueiros (see p.449).

Communism continued to be a major source of motivation and inspiration for Rivera, who was a long-standing member of the Mexican Communist Party. When ideological differences caused a rift in Soviet politics, Rivera supported **Trotsky**'s "revolutionary internationalism", and in 1936, after Trotsky had spent seven years in exile from the Soviet Union on the run from Stalin's henchmen and was running out of countries that would accept him, Rivera used his influence over Mexican President Lázaro Cárdenas to get permission for Trotsky and his wife Natalia to enter the country. They stayed with Diego and Frida rent-free at their Coyoacán house before Trotsky moved down the road to what is now the **Museo Casa de León Trotsky**. The passionate and often violent differences between orthodox Stalinists and Trotskyites spilled over into the art world, creating a great rift between Rivera and ardent Stalinist Siqueiros, who was later jailed for his involvement in an assassination attempt on Trotsky (see box, p.456). Though Rivera later broke with Trotsky and was eventually readmitted to the Communist Party, Trotsky continued to admire Rivera's murals, finding them "not simply a 'painting', an object of passive contemplation, but a living part of the class struggle".

Also on the middle storey is the chamber used by the Mexican Legislature from 1845 to 1872, when it was presided over by Benito Juárez, who lived in the palace until his death. The room houses the original copy of the 1857 Constitution, which was drawn up there, but is frequently closed for renovations.

Before leaving, take a moment to wander around some of the other **courtyards** (there are fourteen in all), and through the small floral and cactus **gardens**.

### Ayuntamiento and Nacional Monte de Piedad

Clockwise round the Zócalo from the Palacio Nacional, the third side is taken up by the city and Federal District administration, the **Ayuntamiento**, while just along from there it is well worth visiting the *Gran Hotel*, 16 de Septiembre

#### Following the Rivera trail

There is a huge amount of Rivera's work accessible to the public, much of it in Mexico City, but also elsewhere around the country. The following is a rundown of the major Rivera sites organized by region and approximately ordered in accordance with their importance within that area.

**Near the Zócalo, the Alameda and Chapultepec**

**Palacio National** (see p.418). Major murals right in the heart of the capital.

**SEP** (see p.423). A large number of Rivera's early murals around the courtyards of the Ministry of Education.

**Palacio de Bellas Artes** (see p.427). Rivera's monumental *Man in Control of the Universe* (and others), as well as murals by his contemporaries.

**Museo Mural Diega Rivera** (see p.431). One of Rivera's most famous murals, *Dream of a Sunday Afternoon in the Alameda*, is on display here.

**Museo de Arte Moderno** (see p.444). Several quality canvases by Rivera and his contemporaries.

**Antiguo Colegio de San Ildefonso** (see p.423). One relatively minor Rivera mural.

**Museo Nacional de Arte** (see p.430). A handful of minor canvases.

**The southern suburbs**

**Museo Dolores Olmedo Patiño** (see p.459). A massive collection of Rivera works from almost every artistic period.

**Museo Frida Kahlo** (see p.454). Just a couple of Diego's works displayed in the house where he and Frida spent some of their married life.

**Museo Casa Estudio Diego Rivera y Frida Kahlo** (see p.451). Diego and Frida's pair of houses designed by Juan O'Gorman.

**Museo Anahuacalli** (see p.459). Large Maya-style house built by Rivera and housing his collection of pre-Columbian sculpture.

**Museo de Arte Carrillo-Gil** (see p.450). A couple of paintings from Rivera's Cubist period.

**Teatro de los Insurgentes** (see p.450). Mural depicting the history of Mexican theatre.

**Outside the capital**

**Palacio de Cortés**, Cuernavaca (see p.515). Early murals on a grand scale.

**Museo Robert Brady**, Cuernavaca (see p.517). A few paintings by both Frida and Diego.

**Museo Casa Diego Rivera**, Guanajuato (see p.285). Relatively minor works and sketches in the house where Diego was born.

82, to admire the opulent lobby with its intricate ironwork, cage-lifts and wonderful Tiffany stained-glass dome.

Around the corner, on the fourth side of the Zócalo, arcades shelter a series of shops, almost all of which sell hats or jewellery. For an unusual shopping experience, though, you can't beat the **Nacional Monte de Piedad** at the corner of the Zócalo and 5 de Mayo (Mon–Fri 8.30am–6pm, Sat 8.30am–1pm; Metro Zócalo). This huge building, supposedly the site of the palace in which Cortés and his followers stayed as guests of Moctezuma, is now the National Pawn Shop, an institution founded as far back as 1775. Much of what is put in hock here is jewellery, but there's also a wide variety of fine art and sculptures, and just about anything that will command a reasonable price. From time to time they hold major auctions to clear the place out, but it's worth coming here just to take in the atmosphere and watch the milling crowds.

## North of the Zócalo

Just a couple of blocks north of the centre the vast openness of the Zócalo gives way to a much more intimate section of small colonial plazas and mostly eighteenth-century buildings. It is still an active commercial area, and is packed with a variety of interesting sights, including ornate churches, small museums and some very fine Rivera and Siqueiros **murals**, all of which can be seen in a few hours.

### Santo Domingo and the Museo de la Medicina

Beside the cathedral, Calle Monte de Piedad runs three blocks north (becoming República de Brasil) to the little colonial plaza of **Santo Domingo** (Metro Allende). In the middle of the square, a gently playing fountain honours La Corregidora, here raised on a pedestal for her decisive role in Mexico's Independence struggle. Eighteenth-century mansions line the sides of the plaza along with the fine Baroque church of Santo Domingo, built on the site of the country's first Dominican monastery. Under the arcades you'll find clerks sitting at little desks with ageing electric typewriters, carrying on the ancient tradition of public scribes. You'll see these clerks somewhere in most large Mexican cities – their main function is to translate simple messages into the flowery, sycophantic language essential for any business letter in Spanish, but they'll type anything from student theses to love letters. Alongside them are street printers, who'll churn out business cards or invitations on the spot, on antiquated hand presses.

On the east side of the plaza the **Museo de la Medicina** (daily 9am–6pm; free, but closed for renovations at time of printing; Metro Allende) occupies grand rooms around a courtyard that was once the headquarters of the Inquisition in New Spain. It was here that heretics were punished, and although the cruelty of the Inquisition is often exaggerated, it was undoubtedly the site of some gruesome scenes. The extensive museum kicks off with interesting displays on indigenous medicine, religion and herbalism, often with reference to infirmity in sculpture. It is surprising how often skin diseases, humped backs and malformed limbs crop up in pre-Columbian art: note the terracotta sculpture bent double from osteoporosis. The progress of Western medicine from colonial times to the present is also well covered, with an intact nineteenth-century pharmacy, a complete radiology room from 1939 and an obstetrics and gynecology room filled with human embryos in bottles. A "wax room" shows full-colour casts of various skin ailments, injuries and infections – the diseased genitalia are always a hit with local schoolkids.

## SEP and Colegio de San Ildefonso

From the Plaza de Santo Domingo, República de Cuba runs a block east to the **Secretaría de Educación Pública (SEP)**, at Brasil 31, with another entrance (the only one in use at weekends) round the corner at Argentina 28 (Mon–Fri 10am–5pm, Sat 10am–4pm, Sun 10am–3pm, upper floors closed on weekends; free; Metro Zócalo). This is the Ministry of Education building, where, in 1923 and 1924, Rivera painted his first **murals** on returning from Paris.

The driving force behind the murals was **José Vasconcelos**, a revolutionary Minister of Public Education in the 1920s but better known as a poet and philosopher, who promoted educational art as a means of instilling a sense of history and cultural pride in a widely illiterate population. He is the man most directly responsible for the murals in public buildings throughout the country. Here, three floors of an enormous double patio are entirely covered with frescoes, as are many of the stairwells and almost any other flat surface. Compared with what he later achieved, Rivera's work is very simple, but the style is already recognizable: panels crowded with figures, drawing inspiration mainly from rural Mexico, though also from an idealized view of science and industry. The most famous panel on the ground floor is the relatively apolitical *Día de los Muertos*, which is rather hidden away in a dark corner at the back. Continuing clockwise, there are equally striking images: *Quema de Judas* and *La Asamblea Primero de Mayo*, for example, and the lovely *El Canal de Santa Anita*. On the first floor the work is quite plain, mostly in tones of grey – here you'll find the shields of the states of Mexico and such general educational themes as *Chemistry* or *Physics*, mostly the work of Rivera's assistants. On the second floor are heroic themes from the Revolution. At the back, clockwise from the left-hand side, the triumphant progress of the Revolution is traced, culminating in the happy scenes of a Mexico ruled by its workers and peasants.

More murals, for which Vasconcelos was also responsible, adorn the eighteenth-century **Antiguo Colegio de San Ildefonso** (also called the Escuela Nacional Preparatoria, or **ENP**; Tues–Sun 10am–6pm; M$35, free Tues; Metro Zócalo), nearby at Justo Serra 16, with its imposing colonial facade. Many artists are represented, including Rivera and Siqueiros, but the most famous works here are those of **José Clemente Orozco**, which you'll find on the main staircase and around the first floor of the main patio. As everywhere, Orozco, for all his enthusiasm for the Revolution, is less sanguine about its prospects, and modern Mexico is caricatured almost as savagely as the pre-revolutionary nation. *The Trench* depicts three Revolutionary soldiers resigning themselves to death in the battlefield, while *The Destruction of the Old Order* seems to suggest a return to a state of authoritarianism following the Revolution, rather than the ascent of any kind of free or just society.

## Museo de la Caricatura and Museo de la Luz

Half a block west of the ENP, Justo Serra becomes Doncelos, home to the **Museo de la Caricatura**, Donceles 99 (daily 10am–6pm; M$20; Metro Zócalo), located in a particularly fine example of an eighteenth-century nobleman's dwelling, complete with central courtyard. It exhibits a limited selection of work from Mexico's most famous caricaturists, but without a strong sense of Mexican history and a comprehensive grasp of Spanish much of the impact is lost. It is still worth nipping in to see a small selection of bizarre nineteenth-century prints of skeletal mariachis by José Guadalupe Posada, a great influence on the later **Muralist movement**, and to take a break in the museum coffee shop in the central patio. The most recent cartoons, many of which focus on world affairs rather than just Mexico, are also extremely sharp, and well worth a look.

A couple of minutes' walk to the northeast stands the ex-Templo de San Pedro y San Pablo, built for the Company of Jesus between 1576 and 1603. Later used as a library, military college and correctional school, it was eventually taken over by the university. The decoration here – plain white, with the arches and pilasters painted in floral designs by Jorge Enciso and Roberto Montenegro – was also influenced by Vasconcelos. The church has since been turned into the **Museo de la Luz** (Mon–Fri 9am–4pm, Sat & Sun 10am–5pm; M$20; Metro Zócalo), a kind of hands-on celebration of all facets of reflection, refraction, iridescence, luminescence and so forth. Good Spanish is essential if you want to learn anything, but it is fun just playing with the optical tricks and effects, and exploring the use of light in art.



### Plaza de Loreto and around

Just along from the Museo de la Luz, and three blocks northeast of the Zócalo, the **Plaza de Loreto** (Metro Zócalo) feels a world apart. It is a truly elegant old square, entirely unmodernized and flanked by a couple of churches. On one side is the **Templo de Loreto**, with its huge dome leaning at a crazy angle: inside, you'll find yourself staggering across the tilted floor. **Santa Teresa**, across the plaza, has a bizarre cave-like chapel at the back, entirely artificial. North of the Templo Loreto is a large and rather tame covered market, the **Mercado Presidente Abelardo Rodriguez**, inside most entrances of which are a series of large murals dating from the 1930s by an assortment of artists including Antonio Pujol and Pablo O'Higgins.

## East of the Zócalo: along Calle Moneda

**Calle Moneda**, running east from the centre, is one of the oldest streets in the city, and it's fascinating to wander up here and see the rapid change as you leave the immediate environs of the Zócalo. The buildings remain almost wholly colonial, prim and refurbished around the museums, then gradually becoming shabbier and shabbier. Within four or five blocks you're into a very depressed residential area, with street stalls spreading up from the giant market of La Merced, to the south.

### Museo de la SHCP and the Casa de la Primera Imprenta

Just a few steps from the Zócalo, the **Museo de la SHCP**, Moneda 4 (Tues–Sun 10am–5pm; M$8), occupies the former archbishop's palace and presents Mexican fine art from the last three centuries in rooms surrounding two lovely open courtyards. The building was constructed over part of Tenochtitlán's ceremonial centre, the Teocalli, and excavations have revealed a few foundation sections for the Templo de Tezcatlipoca pyramid that once stood here. Notice the short flight of stairs, a jaguar carved in high relief and a series of anthropomorphic sculptures. In the galleries, accomplished eighteenth-century canvases by Juan Correa are a nice counterpoint to the small but wonderful collection of Russian icons of the same era. Other highlights include works by Diego Rivera and the stairway mural by José Gordillo, a follower of Siqueiros and Rivera.

On the corner of Licenciado Primo Verdad, the **Casa de la Primera Imprenta** (Mon–Fri 10am–6pm, Sat & Sun 10am–5pm; free) occupies the house where the first printing press in the Americas was set up in 1535, though the only indication of this is the model of the press that sits close to the entrance. Archeological finds unearthed during restoration work are displayed in one room; other rooms house temporary exhibits.

Temporary displays are also the stock in trade next door at the **Centro Cultural Ex-Teresa Arte**, Licenciado Primo Verdad 8 (daily 10am–6pm; free), in the former temple of Santa Teresa la Antigua, which has subsided so much that false floors are needed. You can wander around the mainly video and film installations put on by a nonprofit organization funded by the National Institute of Fine Arts.

### Museo Nacional de las Culturas and beyond

Behind the Palacio Nacional, at Moneda 13, is the **Museo Nacional de las Culturas** (Tues–Sun 9.30am–6pm; free), a collection devoted to the archeology and anthropology of other countries. The museum occupies the sixteenth-century Casa de la Moneda, the official mint until 1848 and later the National Museum, where the best of the Aztec artefacts were displayed until the construction of the Museo Nacional de Antropología (see p.440). Now immaculately restored, with rooms of exhibits set around a quiet patio, it is more interesting than you might guess, though still somewhat overshadowed by so many other high-class museums in the city. One of the more intriguing aspects of the museum is the information on Mexico's historical alignment on the trade routes between Europe and Asia. Every continent is covered, with everything from Korean china to slit gongs from the Marwuasas Islands, and even a reclining nude by Henry Moore.

Just a block beyond the museum is the eye-catching blue and gold **dome** of the church of Santa Inés. The dome, though, is the church's only striking feature, and there's little else to admire apart from the delicately carved wooden doors. Painters Miguel Cabrera and José Ibarra are both buried somewhere inside, but neither is commemorated in any way. Around the corner, the church's former convent buildings have been transformed into the **Museo José Luis Cuevas**, Academia 13 (Tues–Sun 10am–5.30pm; M$10, free on Sun), an art gallery with changing displays centred on the eight-metre-high bronze *La Giganta* (The Giantess), designed by Cuevas. The only permanent collection is one room full of erotica ranging from pre-Hispanic sculpture to line drawings, some by Cuevas.

A few metres south is the **Academia de San Carlos**, Academia 22 (Mon–Fri 9am–7pm; free), which still operates as an art school, though on a very reduced scale from its nineteenth-century heyday; inside are galleries for temporary exhibitions and, in the patio, copies of classical sculptures. Further up Moneda, which by this time has become Emiliano Zapata, the **Templo de la Santísima Trinidad** boasts one of the city's finest Baroque facades. Again, the church's soft footing has caused it to slump, and plumb lines inside chart its continuing movement.

## South of the Zócalo

The area immediately south of the Zócalo warrants a brief foray, particularly if you are en route to the wonderful **La Merced** market. Right on the corner of the Zócalo itself is the colonial-style modern building housing the **Suprema Corte de Justicia** (Mon–Fri 9am–2pm; free, but ID required to enter; Metro Zócalo). Inside are three superb, bitter murals by Orozco named *Proletarian Battles*, *The National Wealth* and *Justice*. The last, depicting Justice slumped asleep on her pedestal while bandits rob the people of their rights, was not surprisingly unpopular with the judges and powers that be, and Orozco never completed his commission here.

### Museo de la Ciudad de México and around

A couple of blocks south of the Zócalo, the **Museo de la Ciudad de México**, Pino Suárez 30 (Tues–Sun 10am–6pm; M$20; Metro Zócalo), is housed in the colonial palace of the Condes de Santiago de Calimaya. This is a fabulous building, with carved stone cannons thrusting out from the cornice, magnificent heavy wooden doors and, on the far side, a hefty plumed serpent obviously dragged from the ruins of some Aztec temple to be employed as a cornerstone. The rooms are mostly given over to temporary exhibits on all manner of themes, but on the top storey is the preserved studio of the landscape artist **Joaquín Clausell**, its walls plastered in portraits and little sketches that he scribbled between working on his paintings.

Diagonally across the road from the museum a memorial marks the spot where, according to legend, Cortés first met Moctezuma. Here you'll find the church and hospital of **Jesús Nazareno**. The **hospital**, still in use, was founded by Cortés in 1528. As such, it's one of the oldest buildings in the city, and exemplifies the severe, fortress-like construction of the immediate post-Conquest years. The **church**, which contains the remains of Cortés and a bronze plaque to the left of the altar with the simple inscription "H.C. (1485–1547)", has been substantially remodelled over the years, its vaulting decorated with a fresco of the Apocalypse by Orozco.

More or less opposite Jesús Nazareno is a small open space and an entrance to a bookshop-lined subterranean walkway between the Zócalo and **Pino Suárez Metro station**, where an Aztec shrine uncovered during construction has been preserved as an integral part of the concourse. Dating from around the end of the fourteenth century, it was dedicated to Quetzalcoatl in his guise of Ehecatl, god of the wind.

Heading east from here along Salvador or Uruguay takes you to the giant **market** area of La Merced (see p.476). If you walk on Uruguay you'll pass a beautiful cloister, all that remains of the seventeenth-century **Convento de la Merced** (currently closed to the public).

Westwards you can stroll down some old streets heading towards the Zona Rosa, passing several smaller markets. Though still only half a dozen blocks south of the Zócalo, you're well outside the tourist zone down here, and it is instructive to spend a little time watching the city life go by. There's not a great deal to see but you could call in to ask if there any interesting temporary exhibitions at the **Museo de la Indumentaria Mexicana**, José María Izázaga 92 (Mon–Fri 9am–5pm, Sat 10am–2pm; free, but ID required to enter; ⓣ55/5130-3300 ext 3415; Metro Isabel la Católica), a former convent. Across the road, a handsome colonial building holds the **Museo de la Charrería**, Isabel la Católica 108 (Mon–Fri 11am–5pm; free; Metro Isabel la Católica), dedicated to all things cowboy, with a collection that includes old photographs, some of them inevitably rather camp, as well as sketches, watercolours, costumes, spurs and brands.

## West to the Alameda

The streets that lead down from the Zócalo towards the Alameda – **Tacuba**, **5 de Mayo**, **Madero**, **16 de Septiembre** and the lanes that cross them – are the most elegant and least affected by modern developments in the city, lined with ancient buildings, traditional cafés and shops and mansions converted to offices, banks or restaurants. When you reach the end of Madero, you've come to the outer edge of the colonial city centre, and should find yourself standing between two of the most striking modern buildings in the capital: the **Torre Latinoamericana** and the **Palacio de Bellas Artes**. Though it seems incredible to compare them, they were completed within barely 25 years of each other.

## Along Madero

On **Madero** you'll pass several former aristocratic palaces now given over to a variety of uses. At no. 27 stands a slightly dilapidated mansion built in 1775 by mining magnate José de la Borda (see p.523) for his wife and presided over, on the corner of Bolivar, by a statue of the Virgin of Guadalupe. Still further down Madero, at no. 17, you'll find the **Palacio de Iturbide** (Metro Allende), currently occupied by Banamex and thoroughly restored – the banks seem able to afford excellent restoration work. Originally the home of the Condes de Valparaiso in the eighteenth century, it was from 1821 to 1823 the residence of the ill-fated "emperor" Agustín de Iturbide. Nowadays it periodically houses free art exhibitions laid on by the bank. In the next block, the last before you emerge at Bellas Artes and the Alameda, the churrigueresque church of **San Francisco** (Metro Bellas Artes) stands on the site of the first Franciscan mission to Mexico.

Opposite San Francisco is the sixteenth-century **Casa de los Azulejos** (Metro Bellas Artes), now a branch of Sanborn's, with its exterior swathed entirely in blue and white tiles from Puebla that were added during remodelling in 1737. The building survived a gas explosion in 1994 – though there was quite a bit of structural damage, luckily no one was hurt, and one of the most famous features of the building, the giant Orozco mural on the staircase, suffered few ill effects. Inside you'll find a restaurant in the glassed-over patio, as well as all the usual shopping.

## Torre Latinoamericana

The distinctly dated steel and glass skyscraper of the **Torre Latinoamericana**, Lázaro Cárdenas 2 (daily 9am–10pm; M$50; Ⓦwww.torrelatino.com; Metro Bellas Artes), was completed in 1956 and, until a few years ago, was the tallest building in Mexico and, indeed, the whole of Latin America. It has now been outdone by the World Trade Center (formerly the *Hotel de México*, on Insurgentes) and doubtless by others in South America, but it remains the city's outstanding landmark and a point of reference no matter where you are. By world standards it is not especially tall, but on a clear day the views from the 139-metre observation deck are outstanding; if it's smoggy you're better off going up around dusk, catching the city as the sun sets, then watching as the lights delineate the city far more clearly. Having paid the fee, you're whisked up to the 36th floor where, another lift takes you to "El Mirador" on the 42nd floor. Here there is a glassed-in **observation area**, a small **café** on the level above and a series of coin-operated telescopes on the outdoor deck a further level up. Plans in the observation area illustrate how the tower was built, proudly boasting that it is the tallest building in the world to have withstood a major earthquake (which it did in 1985, though others may now rival the claim). The general principle of the construction appears to be similar to that of an angler's float, with enormously heavy foundations bobbing around in the mushy soil under the capital, keeping the whole thing upright.

## Palacio de Bellas Artes

Diagonally across the street there's an equally impressive and substantially more beautiful engineering achievement in the form of the **Palacio de Bellas Artes** (Ⓦwww.bellasartes.gob.mx; Metro Bellas Artes). It was designed in 1901, at the height of the Díaz dictatorship, by the Italian architect Adamo Boari and built, in a grandiose Art Nouveau style, of white marble imported from Italy. The construction wasn't actually completed, however, until 1934, with the Revolution and several new planners come

△ Palacio de Bellas Artes

and gone. Some find the whole exterior overblown, but whatever your initial impressions, nothing will prepare you for the magnificent interior – an Art Deco extravaganza incorporating spectacular lighting, chevron friezes and stylized masks of the rain god, Chac.

Much of the interior splendour can be seen any time by wandering into the foyer (free) and simply gazing around the lower floor, where there is a good arts bookshop and the *Café del Palacio* restaurant (see p.467). If you want to see more of the building, you might consider visiting the art museum on the middle two floors, the **Museo del Palacio de Bellas Artes** (Tues–Sun 10am–5.30pm; M$35, free on Tues or when there is no special exhibition on). In the galleries here you'll find a series of exhibitions, permanent displays of Mexican art and temporary shows of anything from local art-school graduates' work to that of major international names. Of constant and abiding interest, however, are the great murals surrounding the museum's central space. On the first floor are *Birth of Our Nationality* and *Mexico Today* – dreamy, almost abstract works by **Rufino Tamayo**. Going up a level you're confronted by the unique sight of murals by **Rivera**, **Orozco** and **Siqueiros** gathered in the same place. Rivera's *Man in Control of the Universe* (or *Man at the Crossroads*), celebrating the liberating power of technology, was originally painted for Rockefeller Center in New York City, but destroyed for being too leftist – arch-capitalist Nelson Rockefeller objected to Rivera's inclusion of Karl Marx, even though he was well aware of Rivera's views when he commissioned the work. This is Rivera's own copy, painted in 1934, just a year after the original. It's worth studying the explanatory panel, which reveals some of the theory behind this complex work, particularly the principal division between the capitalist world on the left, symbolized by war, disease and famine, and the socialist world on the right, all health and peace.

Several smaller panels by Rivera are also displayed; these, too, were intended to be seen elsewhere (in this case on the walls of the *Hotel Reforma*, downtown) but for years were covered up, presumably because of their unflattering depiction of tourists. The works include *Mexican Folklore and Tourism*, *Dictatorship*, the *Dance of the Huichilobos* and, perhaps the best of them, *Agustín Lorenzo*, a portrayal of a guerrilla fighter against the French. None of them was designed to be seen so close up, and you'll find yourself wanting to step back to get the big picture. *Catharsis*, a huge, vicious work by Orozco, occupies almost an entire wall, and there are also some particularly fine examples of Siqueiros's work: three powerful and original panels on the theme of *Democracy* and a bloody depiction of *The Torture of Cuauhtémoc* and his resurrection. The uppermost floor is devoted to the **Museo de la Arquitectura** (same ticket and hours), which has no permanent collection, but frequently has interesting exhibits.

Bellas Artes is also the headquarters of the National Institute of Fine Arts, and the venue for important performances of classical music, opera or dance – you should try to see the **Ballet Folklórico** (see p.473) here. Some of the finest interior decor in the building is generally hidden from view in the main theatre, so if you are not going to a show, it's worth joining one of the free lunch-time tours (Mon–Fri 1pm & 1.30pm) to see the amazing Tiffany glass curtain depicting the Valley of México and the volcanoes, as well as the detailed proscenium mosaic and the stained-glass ceiling.

## Correo Central and Palacio de Minería

Around the back of Bellas Artes, at the corner of Tacuba and Lázaro Cárdenas, you'll find the **Correo Central** (Metro Bellas Artes), the city's main post office. Completed in 1908, this too was designed by Adamo Boari, but in a style much more consistent with the buildings around it. Look closely and you'll find a wealth of intricate detail on the facade, while inside it's full of richly carved wood. On the first floor is the small **Museo Postal** (Tues–Fri 10am–5pm, Sat & Sun 10am–2pm; free, but ID required to enter), housing a rather uninspiring collection of old mailboxes, a few old documents and objects relating to the postal service and a giant picture made of postage stamps. On the fourth floor (same hours, also free), naval buffs will enjoy the **Museum of Naval History** (with explanations in Spanish only), featuring models of old ships, a reconstruction in miniature of Cortés's waterborne battle against the Aztecs on the Lake of Texcoco, plus photos and artefacts of the 1914 US occupation of Veracruz.

Directly behind the Correo on Tacuba is the **Palacio de Minería**, a Neoclassical building completed right at the end of the eighteenth century and designed by Spanish-born Manuel Tolsá, who is the subject of the devotional **Museo Manuel Tolsá** (daily 10am–6pm; M$10) within – just a couple of rooms of paintings and architectural drawings, strictly for fans only. The palacio also houses another museum, the more macabre **Torture Museum** (daily 10am–6pm; M$40), which holds instruments of torture and execution from the time of the Inquisition onwards. The exterior of the palacio makes an interesting contrast with the post office and with the Museo Nacional de Arte (formerly the Palacio de Comunicaciones) directly opposite, the work of another Italian architect, Silvio Contri, in the first years of the twentieth century.

Around the corner on Filomeno Mata is the small Convento de las Betlemitas, a seventeenth-century convent that now houses the **Museo del Ejército y Fuerza** (Tues–Sat 10am–6pm, Sun 10am–4pm; free), with a small exhibition of antique arms, and explanations mostly in Spanish.

### Museo Nacional de Arte

The **Museo Nacional de Arte**, Tacuba 8 (Tues–Sun 10.30am–5.30pm; M$30, free on Sun), is set back from the street on a tiny plaza in which stands one of the city's most famous sculptures, **El Caballito**, portraying Carlos IV of Spain. This enormous bronze, the work of Manuel Tolsá, was originally erected in the Zócalo in 1803. In the intervening years it has graced a variety of sites and, despite the unpopularity of the Spanish monarchy (and of the effete Carlos IV in particular), is still regarded affectionately. The latest setting is appropriate, since Tolsá also designed the Palacio de Minería (see p.429). The open plaza around the sculpture is now often the scene of intense pre-Columbian drumming and dancing, which usually draws an appreciative crowd.

Though the museum is the foremost showcase of Mexican art from the 1550s to the 1950s, with a collection of over a thousand pieces, its interest is mainly historical. Most of the major Mexican artists are represented, but with essentially mediocre examples spiced only occasionally with a more striking work. It's worth coming here to see something of the dress and landscape of old Mexico, and also some of the curiosities, but not the masterpieces.

Temporary displays take up the lower floor (along with a good bookshop and café), leaving the two floors above for the permanent collection. To follow the displays in chronological order, start on the **upper floor**, which covers work up to the end of the eighteenth century. Vast religious canvases take up whole walls, but seldom hold your interest for long, though Miguel Cabrera is particularly well represented with half a dozen works, notably *La Virgen del Apocalipsis*. In the same room there are some fine polychrome sculptures, particularly the diminutive Nativity scene in the glass case. You could hardly miss eighteenth-century painter Francisco Antonio Vallejo's masterwork, the four-canvas *Glorificación de la Inmaculada*, with the heavenly host borne by clouds above the court of Carlos IV.

The museum really comes to life, and modern Mexico begins to express itself, on the **middle floor**, where traditional oils are supplemented by lithographs, sculpture and photography: note the images of nineteenth-century Mexican railways, *pulqueros* tapping the maguey cactus and cattle grazing in the fields of Chapultepec Park. Elsewhere there are a couple of photos by Henri Cartier-Bresson and several by Hungarian-born Katy Horna, who worked in Mexico from 1939 until her death in 2000. The half-dozen Rivera works are mostly minor, though it is instructive to see early works, such as *El Grade de España* from 1914 when he was in Braque mode. Notice too how Rivera's technique influenced many of the other painters of the time, especially Saturnino Herrán and Olga Costa, and look out for the landscapes of the Valley of México by José María Velasco (one of Rivera's teachers).

## The Alameda

From behind Bellas Artes, Lázaro Cárdenas runs north towards the **Plaza Garibaldi** (see p.473) through an area crowded with seedy cantinas and eating places, theatres and burlesque shows. West of the Palacio de Bellas Artes lies the **Alameda**, first laid out as a park in 1592, and taking its name from the *alamos* (poplars) then planted. The Alameda had originally been an Aztec market and later became the site where the Inquisition burned its victims at the stake. Most of what you see now – formally laid-out paths and flowerbeds, ornamental statuary and fountains – dates from the nineteenth century, when it was the fashionable place to stroll. It's still popular, always full of people, particularly at weekends, but it's mostly a transient population

– office workers taking lunch, shoppers resting their feet, messengers taking a short cut and street vendors selling T-shirts.

### Museo de la Estampa and Museo Franz Mayer

On the north side of the Alameda, Avenida Hidalgo traces the line of an ancient thoroughfare, starting from the Teatro Hidalgo, right opposite Bellas Artes. To the west, the church of Santa Vera Cruz marks the **Museo de la Estampa** (Tues–Sun 10am–5.45pm; M$10, free on Sun), which concentrates on engraving, an art form that is taken seriously in Mexico, where the legacy of José Guadalupe Posada (see p.274) is still revered. There is no permanent collection, but you may expect anything from engravings and printing plates from pre-Columbian times to the modern age, including works by Posada.

Immediately next door, the **Museo Franz Mayer**, Hidalgo 45 (Tues & Thurs–Sun 10am–5pm, Wed 10am–7pm; M$30, free on Tues; Ⓦwww.franzmayer.org.mx), is dedicated to the applied arts, and occupies the sixteenth-century hospital attached to the church of San Juan de Dios. It's packed with the personal collection of Mexican arts and crafts of Franz Mayer, a German who settled here in 1913: colonial furniture, textiles and carpets, watches, Spanish silverwork, religious art and artefacts, a valuable collection of sculpture and paintings and some fine colonial pottery from Puebla. There is also much furniture and pottery from Asia, the result of Mexico's position on international trade routes, as well as a library with rare antique editions of Spanish and Mexican authors and a reference section on applied arts. Even if this doesn't sound like your thing, it's well worth seeing. The building is lovely and beautifully furnished, and offers a tranquil escape from the crowds outside. The coffee bar, too, is a delight, facing a courtyard filled with flowers and a fountain – there's a charge of M$5 for those not visiting the museum.

### Laboratorio Arte Alameda and Museo Mural Diego Rivera

Almost at the western end of the Alameda, duck down Calle Dr Mora to the **Laboratorio Arte Alameda**, at no. 7 (Tues–Sun 9am–5pm; M$15, free on Sun), an art museum built into the glorious seventeenth-century monastery of San Diego. The cool, white interior is filled with temporary exhibitions of challenging contemporary art. They're all superbly displayed around the church, chapel and cloister of the old monastery, a space also occasionally used for evening concerts – mostly chamber music or piano recitals.

One of the buildings worst hit by the 1985 earthquake was the *Hotel del Prado*, which contained the Rivera mural *Dream of a Sunday Afternoon in the Alameda*. The mural survived the quake, and was subsequently picked up in its entirety and transported around the Alameda – it can now be seen in the **Museo Mural Diego Rivera** (Tues–Sun 10am–6pm; M$15, free on Sun), at the western end of the Alameda, at the corner of Balderas and Colón. It's an impressive work – showing almost every famous Mexican character out for a stroll in the park – but one suspects that its popularity with tour groups is as much to do with its relatively apolitical nature as with any superiority to Rivera's other works. Originally it included a placard with the words "God does not exist", which caused a huge furore, and Rivera was forced to paint it out before the mural was first displayed to the public.

A leaflet (available at the entrance; M$8) explains every character in the scene: Cortés is depicted with his hands stained red with blood, José Guadalupe Posada stands bowler-hatted next to his trademark skeleton, *La Calavera Catrina*, who holds the hand of Rivera himself, portrayed as a 9-year-old boy. Frida Kahlo stands in motherly fashion, just behind him. There's a rather unenlightening **sound-and-light show** (*luz y sonido*; Tues–Fri 11am & 4pm, Sat & Sun 11am, 1pm, 4pm & 5pm), narrated in Spanish by voices representing Rivera, Kahlo and *La Calavera*. Around the walls there are also displays on the history of the Alameda and its place within the city as a whole.

### Centro de la Imagen and Biblioteca de México

A short detour south of the Alameda takes you past the excellent **artesanía market** of Ciudadela to a shady open space of the same name. Along the south side are the **Centro de la Imagen** (Tues–Sun 11am–6pm; free; Ⓦwww.conaculta.gob.mx/cimagen), with changing photographic exhibits and, next door, the **Biblioteca de México** (Mon–Fri 8.30am–7.30pm, Sat & Sun 8.30am–2.30pm & 3.30–7.30pm; free), an extensive library also containing rooms where touring art shows are displayed.



## Around the Monumento a la Revolución

Beyond the Alameda, avenidas Juárez and Hidalgo lead towards the Paseo de la Reforma. Across Reforma, Hidalgo becomes the **Puente de Alvarado**, following one of the main causeways that led into Tenochtitlán. This was the route by which the Spanish attempted to flee the city on the Noche Triste (Sad Night), July 10, 1520. Following the death of Moctezuma, and with his men virtually under siege in their quarters, Cortés decided to escape the city under cover of darkness. It was a disaster: the Aztecs cut the bridges and, attacking the bogged-down invaders from their canoes, killed all but 440 of the 1300 Spanish soldiers who set out, and more than half their native allies. Greed, as much as anything, cost the Spanish troops their lives, for in trying to take their gold booty with them they were, in the words of Bernal Díaz, "so weighed down by the stuff that they could neither run nor swim". The street takes its name from Pedro de Alvarado, one of the last conquistadors to escape, crossing the broken bridge "in great peril after their horses had been killed, treading on the dead men, horses and boxes". Not long ago a hefty gold bar – exactly like those made by Cortés from melted-down Aztec treasures – was dug up here.

### Puente de Alvarado: San Hipólito, San Fernando and the Museo San Carlos

The church of **San Hipólito**, at the corner of Reforma and Puente de Alvarado, was founded by the Spanish soon after their eventual victory, both as a celebration and to commemorate the events of the Noche Triste. The present building dates from 1602, though over the years it has been damaged by earthquakes and rebuilt, and it now lists to one side. West along Puente de Alvarado is the Baroque eighteenth-century church of **San Fernando**, by the plaza of the same name. Once one of the richest churches in the city, San Fernando has been stripped over the years. Evidence of its former glory survives, however, in the highly decorative facade and in the *panteón*, or graveyard, crowded with the tombstones of nineteenth-century high society.

At Puente de Alvarado 50 you'll find the **Museo Nacional de San Carlos** (daily except Tues 10am–6pm; M$25, free on Sun; Ⓦwww.mnsancarlos.com), which houses the country's oldest art collection, begun in 1783 by Carlos III of Spain, and comprising largely European work of the seventeenth and eighteenth centuries with some notable earlier and later additions. Major names are largely absent, but look for the delicate *San Pedro, San Andrés y San Mateo* by fifteenth-century Spanish painter Maestro de Palaquinos, portraits by Reynolds,

Rubens and Hals and a luminous canvas of Breton women by the sea (*Mujeres Bretones a la Orilla del Mar*) by another Spaniard, Manuel Benedito y Vives. Travelling exhibitions are also frequently based here.

The building itself is an attractive Neoclassical design by Manuel Tolsá. Its inhabitants have included the French Marshal Bazaine, sent by Napoleon III to advise the Emperor Maximilian – who presented the house to him as a wedding present on his marriage to a Mexican woman – and the hapless Mexican general and sometime dictator Santa Anna. Later it served for a time as a cigarette factory.

### Along Juárez to the monument

Leaving the Alameda on Juárez, you can see the massive, ugly bulk of the Monumento a la Revolución ahead of you. The first couple of blocks, though, are dull, commercial streets, heavy with banks, offices and travel agents. The junction with Reforma is a major crossing of the ways, and is surrounded by modern skyscrapers and one older one – the marvellous Art Deco **Lotería Nacional** building. In here, you can watch the winning tickets being drawn each week, although the lottery offices themselves have been moved to an ordinary-looking steel and glass building opposite. Beyond Reforma, Juárez continues in one long block to the **Plaza de la República** and the vast **Monumento a la Revolución**. Originally intended to be a new home for the Cortés (the parliament), its construction was interrupted by the Revolution and never resumed – in the end they buried a few heroes of the Revolution under the mighty columns (including Pancho Villa and presidents Madero, Carranza and Cárdenas) and turned the whole thing into a memorial. More recently the **Museo Nacional de la Revolución** (Tues–Sun 9am–5pm; M$14, free on Sun) was installed beneath the monument (entrance under the north side), with a history of the Revolution told through archive pictures, old newspapers, films and life-size tableaux. Somehow the whole area seems sidelined by the mainstream of city life and is often all but deserted.

## Reforma, Zona Rosa, Roma, Condesa and Polanco

West of the Alameda and Revolution monument the tenor of the city changes again, particularly along the grand avenue of **Reforma**, lined by tall buildings, including Mexico's stock exchange. South of here is the tight knot of streets that make up the **Zona Rosa**, one of the city's densest concentrations of hotels, restaurants and shops. The residential districts of **Roma** and **Condesa** warrant attention for their numerous small-time art galleries and, particularly in Condesa, the restaurants. The Paseo de la Reforma runs direct to Chapultepec Park, on the north edge of which lies **Polanco**, home to wealthy socialites and the stylish youth.

### Paseo de la Reforma

**Paseo de la Reforma** is the most impressive street in Mexico City. Laid out in the 1860s by Emperor Maximilian to provide the city with a boulevard to rival the great European capitals – and doubling as a ceremonial drive from his palace in Chapultepec to the centre – it also provided a new impetus, and direction, for the growing metropolis. The original length of the broad avenue ran simply from the park to the junction of Juárez, and although it has been extended in both directions, this stretch is still what everyone thinks of as Reforma. "**Reforma Norte**", as the extension towards Guadalupe is known, is just as wide (and the

△ Paseo de la Reforma

traffic just as dense), but is almost a term of disparagement. **Real Reforma**, though, remains imposing – ten lanes of traffic, lines of trees, grand statues at every intersection and perhaps three or four of the original French-style, nineteenth-century houses still surviving. Twenty or thirty years ago it was the dynamic heart of the growing city, with even relatively new buildings being torn down to make way for yet newer, taller, more prestigious towers of steel and glass. The pulse has since moved elsewhere, and the fancy shops have relocated, leaving an avenue now mostly lined with airline offices, car rental agencies and banks, and somewhat diminishing the pleasure of a stroll.

It's a long walk, some 5km from the Zócalo to the gates of Chapultepec, and you'd be well advised to take the bus – they're frequent enough to hop on and off at will. The *glorietas*, roundabouts at the major intersections, each with a distinctive statue, provide easy landmarks along the way. First is the **Glorieta Colón**, with a statue of Christopher Columbus. Around the base of the plinth are carved various friars and monks who assisted Columbus in his enterprise or brought the Catholic faith to the Mexicans. The Plaza de la República is just off to the north. Next comes the crossing of Insurgentes, nodal point of all the city's traffic, with **Cuauhtémoc**, last emperor of the Aztecs and leader of their resistance, poised aloof above it all in a plumed robe, clutching his spear, surrounded by warriors. Bas-relief engravings on the pedestal depict his torture and execution at the hands of the Spanish, desperate to discover where the Aztec treasures lay hidden. **El Ángel**, a golden winged victory atop a forty-metre column, is the third to look out for, and the place to get off the bus for the heart of the Zona Rosa. Officially known as the **Monumento a la Independencia** (daily 9am–6pm; free), and finished in 1910, the column stands atop a room containing the skulls of Independence heroes Hidalgo, Aldama, Allende and Jiménez.

## Zona Rosa

To the south of Reforma lies the **Zona Rosa** (Metro Insurgentes), a triangular area bordered by Reforma, Avenida Chapultepec and, to the west, Chapultepec Park. You'll know you're there as the streets are all named after famous cities. Packed into this tiny area are hundreds of bars, restaurants, hotels and shops, all teeming with a vast number of tourists and a cross-section of Mexico City's aspiring middle classes. Until the 1980s this was the city's swankiest commercial neighbourhood, but the classiest shops have moved to Polanco (see p.437) and many of the big international chains have relocated to the out-of-town malls that have sprung up around the Periférico. It is a process that has left the Zona Rosa in an odd situation. There's no shortage of good shopping, and the selection of restaurants, cafés, clubs and bars is respectable (see p.468 & p.472), but it has lost its exclusive feel. You're as likely to spend your time here buying cheap knick-knacks at market stalls and watching street entertainers as admiring the remaining fancy store windows. You might visit during the day to eat well, then return at night for the clubs, and may choose to stay here, but you certainly wouldn't make a special journey for the sights. The zone in general, and particularly the block of Amberes between Estrasburgo and Reforma – has become something of a centre for the city's gay scene, but otherwise, the only real attraction is the **Museo de Cera** (Wax Museum; daily 11am–7pm; M$50; Metro Cuauhtémoc), on the fringes of the Zona, at Londres 6. Thoroughly tacky, with a basement chamber of horrors that includes Aztec human sacrifices, it shares its site with the **Museo de lo Increíble** (same hours and prices; joint ticket for the two museums M$80), which displays such marvels as flea costumes and hair sculpture.

The northern side of Reforma, where the streets are named after rivers (Tiber, Danubio and the like), is a much quieter, posh residential area officially known as **Colonia Cuauhtémoc**, though it's usually just bundled in with the Zona Rosa. Here you'll find some of the older embassies, notably the US embassy, on Reforma, bristling with razor wire and security cameras. Near the much more modest British embassy is the **Museo Venustiano Carranza**, Río Lerma 35 (Tues–Sat

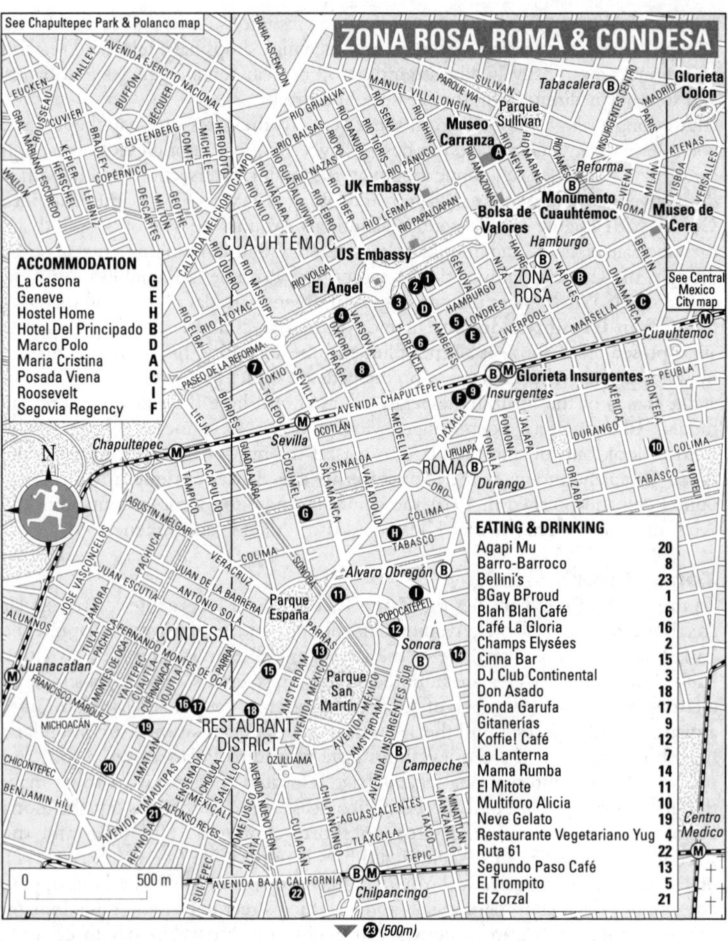


9am–6pm, Sun 11am–4pm; M$30, free on Sun; Metro Insurgentes). Carranza was a Revolutionary leader and president of the Republic who was shot in 1920. The building was his home in Mexico City and contains exhibits relating to his life and to the Revolution. Not far away, just north of the junction of Reforma and Insurgentes, the **Parque Sullivan** hosts free open-air exhibitions and sales of paintings, ceramics and other works of art every Sunday (roughly 10am–4pm); some of them are very good, and a pleasant holiday atmosphere prevails.

## Roma and Condesa

South of the Zona Rosa lie the residential districts of **Roma** and Condesa, full of quiet leafy streets once you get away from the main avenues that cut through. Both suburbs were developed in the 1930s and 1940s, but as the city expanded they became unfashionable and run-down. That all changed in the 1990s when artists and the bohemian fringe were drawn here by low rents, decent housing and proximity to the centre of the city. Small-time galleries sprang up and the first of the bars and cafés opened. **Condesa**, in particular, is now one of the best areas for good eating in the city, and definitely the place to come for lounging in pavement cafés or dining in bistro-style **restaurants** (for a rundown, see p.468). The greatest concentration is around the junction of Michoacán, Atlixco and Vicente Suárez, but establishments spread out into the surrounding streets, where you'll often find quiet neighbourhood places with tables spilling out onto the pavement. Sights in the usual sense are virtually nonexistent, but you can pass a few hours just walking the streets keeping an eye out for interesting art galleries, which seem to spring up all the time. A good starting point is **Parque México**, officially Parque San Martín, a large green space virtually in the heart of Condesa that was set aside when the owners of the horse track sold it to developers back in 1924. The streets around the park, especially Calle México, are rich in buildings constructed in Mexico's own distinctive version of Art Deco.

The Metro system gives Condesa a wide berth, with line 1 skirting the north and west while line 9 runs along the south side. Nonetheless, it is easy enough to **walk to Condesa** south from the Zona Rosa (Metro Insurgentes, Sevilla or Chapultepec); for more direct access to Condesa's main restaurant district take line 1 to Juanacatlán, and cross the Circuito Interior using the nearby footbridge. This brings you onto Francisco Marquez, which leads to the restaurants – ten minutes' walk in all.

### Polanco

High-priced high-rise hotels line the northern edge of Chapultepec Park, casting their shadow over the smart suburb of **Colonia Polanco**. Unless you've got brand-name shopping in mind or need to visit one of the district's embassies, there's not much reason to come out this way, though it is instructive to stroll along **Presidente Masaryk**, the main drag, watching the beautiful people drive by in their Porsches and Lexus SUVs on their way to the Fendi or Ferragamo stores. Polanco also has great dining and we've recommended a few places on p.469, but bad restaurants don't last long here and you can do just as well strolling along and picking any place you fancy.

The only specific destination is the **Sala de Arte Público David Siqueiros**, Tres Picos 29 (Tues–Sun 10am–6pm; M$10, free on Sun; Metro Polanco), a small but interesting collection of the great muralist's later work, including sketches he made of the Polyforum murals (see p.449). They're all displayed in his former residence and studio, donated (along with everything in it) to the people of Mexico just 25 days before his death in 1973. If it is not already playing, ask to see the hour-long **video** (in English) on his life and work made just before his death, and watch it surrounded by his murals, which cover just about every piece of wall space.

## Bosque de Chapultepec and the Museo Nacional de Antropología

**Chapultepec Park**, or the **Bosque de Chapultepec** (Tues–Sun 5am–4.30pm; free), is a vast green area, about a thousand acres in all, dotted with trees, scattered with fine museums – among them the marvellous **Museo Nacional de Antropología** – boating lakes, gardens, playing fields and a zoo. Ultimately, it provides an escape from the pressures of the city for

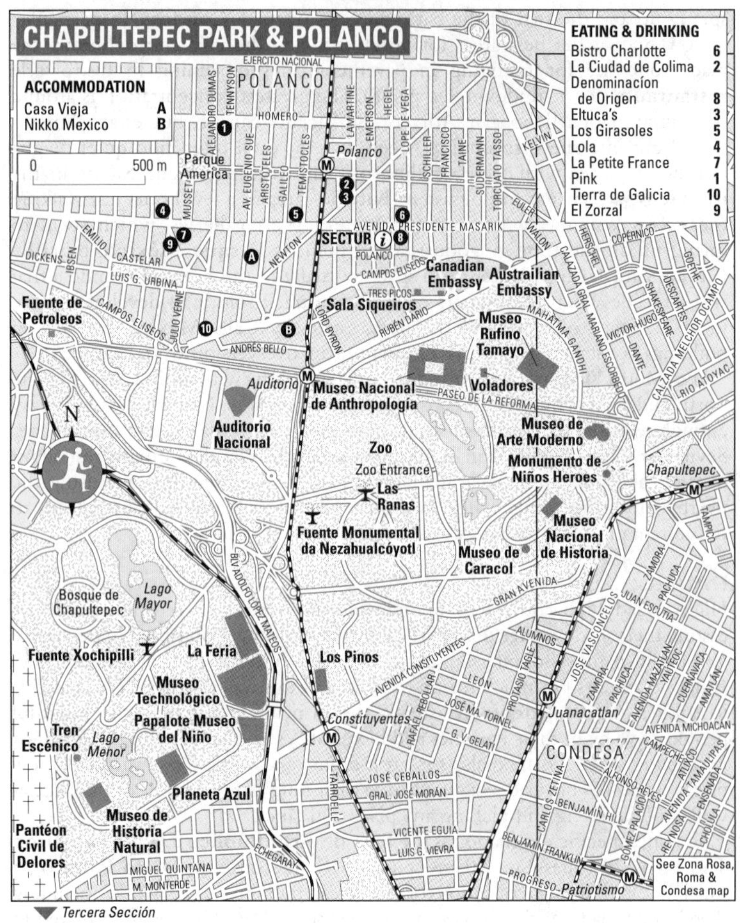


Tercera Sección

seemingly millions of Mexicans, with the result that the most visited areas get a heavy pounding and some areas are occasionally fenced off to allow the plants to recover. On Sundays, when many of the attractions are free, you can barely move for the throng, but note that on Mondays the entire park and many of the museums are closed.

The park is divided into three sections: the first and easternmost is home to the points of greatest interest, including the Anthropology, Modern Art and Rufino Tamayo museums and the zoo; the Second Section is mostly aimed at kids, with an amusement park, technology museum and natural history museum; and the Third Section contains aquatic and marine parks open at weekends.

The rocky outcrop of **Chapultepec** (Nahuatl for "hill of the locust"), from which the entire area has taken its name, is mentioned in Toltec mythology, but first gained historical significance in the thirteenth century when it was no more than an anonymous island among the lakes and salt marshes of the valley. Here the Aztecs, still a wandering, savage tribe, made their first home, though it proved to be temporary when they were defeated and driven off by neighbouring cities. Once Tenochtitlán's power was established they returned here, channelling water from the springs into the city, and turning Chapultepec into a summer resort for the emperor, with plentiful hunting and fishing around a fortified palace. Several Aztec rulers had their portraits carved into the rock of the hill, though most of these images were destroyed by the Spanish soon after the Conquest.

### Park practicalities

Chapultepec is a big place with a lot to do. You could easily spend a couple of days here and still not see everything, but if you are selective you can cover the best of it in one tiring day. Though it can be tempting to visit on Sunday, when a lot of the museums are free and the park is at its vibrant best, the Museo Nacional de Antropología and the zoo will be packed – if you want to be able to move freely it can be worth coming during the week.

How you approach the park depends on what you want to see first. The easiest access is via the Chapultepec Metro station, from where you follow the crowds over a bridge across the Circuito Interior (inner ring road). Straight ahead you'll see the Niños Héroes monument and the Castillo containing the Museo Nacional de Historia. The entrances to the Museo Nacional de Antropología and its acolytes are grouped together along Paseo de la Reforma, less than a fifteen-minute walk from the Metro station, but if that is where you are headed first it is faster to catch a *pesero* ("Auditorio", "Reforma Km 13" and others) anywhere along Reforma. Visitors with kids may want to head straight for the Second Section, either picking up a *pesero* along Constituyentes (routes 2, 24 and others) from Metro Chapultepec, or going direct to Metro Constituyentes and walking from there.

Wherever you go in the park there'll be someone selling **food and drink**, and the Museo Nacional de Antropología has a good (though pricey) **restaurant**. Nonetheless, it is as well to take some snacks (or an entire picnic lunch) and a big bottle of water: museum hopping can be thirsty work.

## Chapultepec Hill

As you approach the park from the Chapultepec Metro station you're confronted by **Chapultepec Hill**, crowned by Maximilian's very peaceful-looking "castle". As you climb the hill – and for the less able-bodied, there are land trains that'll take you up and bring you back for M$10 – you pass the modern **Museo de Caracol** (Tues–Sun 9am–4.15pm; M$45, free on Sun), devoted to "the Mexican people's struggle for Liberty". Its full name is the Museo Galería de la Lucha del Pueblo Mexicano por su Libertad, but it's colloquially known as the "shell museum" for the snail-like spiralling route through the displays. These trace the history of the constant wars that have beset the country – from Independence, through the American and French interventions to the Revolution.

At the top of the hill, in front of the castle, stands a strange, six-columned monument dedicated to the **Niños Héroes** – it commemorates the cadets who attempted to defend the castle (then a military academy) against American invaders in 1847. According to the story, probably apocryphal, the last six flung themselves off the cliff wrapped in Mexican flags rather than surrender. The **castle** itself was built only in 1785 as a summer retreat for the Spanish viceroy – until then it had been the site of a hermitage established on the departure of the Aztec rulers. Following Independence it served as a military school, but the present design was dictated by Maximilian, who remodelled it in the image of his Italian villa.

Today the castle houses the **Museo Nacional de Historia** (Tues–Sun 9am–5pm; M$45, free on Sun; Ⓦwww.mnh.inah.gob.mx). The setting is very much part of the attraction, with many rooms retaining the opulent furnishings left behind by Maximilian and Carlota, or by later inhabitants with equally expensive tastes, notably Porfirio Díaz. Rivalling the decor is a small group of carriages, including the fabulously pompous Cinderella-goes-to-the-ball state coaches favoured by Maximilian. A collection of furniture, glassware and medals leads on to the main attraction of the lower floor, a series of ornate rooms viewed from a black-and-white tiled terrace that affords great views over the park and city. Peer into Maximilian's office, games room and drawing room, all gilt and dark wood, then move on to Carlota's bedroom and a gorgeous tiled bathroom.

The upper floor is arranged around a formal rooftop garden off which you can visit yet more sumptuous rooms and a magnificent Parisian stained-glass wall imported by Díaz and depicting five goddesses in a Greco-Roman setting. There are several murals here as well, including a number of works by **Orozco** and **Siqueiros**, but the ones by **Juan O'Gorman** most directly attract attention for their single-minded political message.

## Museo Nacional de Antropología

The park's outstanding attraction – for many people the main justification for visiting the city at all – is the **Museo Nacional de Antropología** (Tues–Sun 9am–7pm; M$45 Tues–Sat, free on Sun, M$30 to bring in a video camera; Ⓦwww.mna.inah.gob.mx), one of the world's great museums, not only for its collection, which is vast, rich and diverse, but also for the originality and practicality of its design. Opened in 1964, the exhibition halls surround a patio with a small pond and a vast, square concrete umbrella supported by a single slender pillar around which splashes an artificial cascade. The halls are ringed by gardens, many of which contain outdoor exhibits. If you're rushed, the whole thing can be taken in on one visit, but it is far more satisfactory to spread your visit over two days. The museum can get rather crowded on Sundays when admission is free – it can be worth it to pay the entrance fee and come during the week.

The entrance from Reforma is marked by a colossal statue of the rain god Tlaloc – the story goes that its move here from its original home in the east of the city was accompanied by furious downpours in the midst of a drought. Just east of the museum is a large open plaza, at one end of which is a small clearing pierced by a twenty-metre pole from which **voladores** "fly". This Totonac ceremony (see box, p.620) is performed several times a day, and loses a lot of its appeal through its commercial nature – an assistant canvasses the crowd for donations as they perform – but it is still an impressive spectacle.

### Pre-Classic

The **Pre-Classic** room covers the development of the first cultures in the Valley of México and surrounding highlands – pottery and clay figurines from these early agricultural communities predominate. Notice especially the **small female figures** dated 1700–1300 BC from Tlatilco (a site in the suburbs), which are probably related to some form of fertility or harvest rites. The influence of the growing Olmec culture begins to be seen in later artefacts, including the amazing **acrobat**, also from Tlatilco. With the development of

## Museum orientation

The museum's rooms, each devoted to a separate period or culture, are arranged chronologically in an anti-clockwise pattern around the central courtyard. As you come into the **entrance hall** there's a small circular space with temporary exhibitions, usually very interesting and devoted to the latest developments in archeology; here too is the small **Sala de Orientación**, which presents an audio-visual overview of the major ancient cultures. Off to the left you'll find the **library** and a **shop** selling postcards, souvenirs, books in several languages on Mexican culture, archeology and history and detailed **guidebooks** (in Spanish, English, French and German; M$65), which provide full descriptions of most of the important pieces. The **ticket office**, and the **entrance** to the museum proper, is by the huge glass doors to the right, where you can also rent headsets, which effectively take you on a **tour** of the museum's highlights – M$50 in Spanish, M$60 in English. They're very rushed, but you do get around the whole thing with some form of explanation: labelling of individual items is mostly in Spanish, though the general introduction to each room is accompanied by an English translation.

A complete tour of the museum starts on the right-hand side with three **introductory rooms** explaining what anthropology is, the nature of and relationship between the chief Mesoamerican cultures and the region's prehistory. It's worth spending time here if only to note the clear acknowledgement of the continuing discrimination against Mexico's native people. These rooms are followed on the right-hand side by halls devoted to the **Pre-Classic**, **Teotihuacán** and **Toltec** cultures. At the far end is the vast **Mexica** (Aztec) room, followed around the left wing by **Oaxaca** (Mixtec and Zapotec), **Gulf of Mexico** (Olmec), **Maya** and the cultures of the **north** and **west**. Every hall has at least one outstanding feature, but if you have limited time, the Aztec and the Maya rooms are the **highlights**; what else you see should depend on what area of the country you plan to head on to. The upper floor is given over to **ethnography collections**, which are devoted to the life and culture of the various indigenous groups today; stairs lead up from each side. Downstairs, behind the hall given over to the cultures of the north and west, is a very welcome **restaurant**.

more formal religion, recognizable images of gods also appear: several of these, from Cuicuilco in the south of the city, depict **Huehueteotl**, the old god or god of fire, as an old man with flames on his back.

### Teotihuacán

The next hall is devoted to **Teotihuacán** (see p.485), the first great city in the Valley of México. A growing sophistication is immediately apparent in the more elaborate nature of the pottery vessels and the use of new materials, shells, stone and jewels. There's a full-scale reproduction of part of the **Temple of Quetzalcoatl** at Teotihuacán, brightly polychromed as it would originally have been. It contains the remains of nine sacrificial victims dressed as warriors, complete with their funerary necklaces: a relatively recent confirmation of human sacrifice and militarism at Teotihuacán. Nearby is a reconstruction of the inside courtyard and central temple of an apartment complex bedecked in vibrant murals representing ritual life in the city, including *The Paradise of Tlaloc*, a depiction of the heaven reserved for warriors and ball-players who died in action. Many new gods appear, too: as well as more elaborate versions of Huehueteotl, there are representations of Tlaloc, of his companion Chalchiutlicue, goddess of rivers and lakes, of Mictlantecuhtli, god of death (a stone skull, originally inlaid with gems) and of Xipe Totec, a god of spring, clothed in the skin of a man flayed alive as a symbol of regeneration.

## Toltec

The **Toltec** room actually begins with objects from Xochicalco, a city near modern Cuernavaca (see p.521), which flourished between the fall of Teotihuacán and the heyday of Tula. The large stone carvings and pottery show a distinct Maya influence: particularly lovely is the stylized stone **head of a macaw**, similar to ones found on Maya ball-courts in Honduras. Highlights of the section devoted to Tula are the weighty stone carvings, including one of the Atlantean columns from the main temple there, representing a warrior. Also of note are the **Chac-mool**, a reclining figure with a receptacle on his stomach in which sacrificial offerings were placed, and the **standard bearer**, a small human figure that acted as a flagpole when a standard was inserted into the hole between its clasped hands. This is found high up, above a large frieze. Down and to the left is a stone relief of a **dancing jaguar** and an exquisite sculpture of a **coyote's head** with a bearded man emerging from its mouth – possibly a warrior in a headdress – inlaid with mother-of-pearl, and with teeth made of bone.

Also here are reproductions of seventh-century frescoes of a birdman and jaguar from Cacaxtla (see p.502), found by a *campesino* tending his fields in 1975, and an extensive collection of rings, which served as goals in the ancient ball-game.

## Mexica

Next comes the biggest and richest room of all, the **Mexica Gallery**, characterized by massive yet intricate stone sculpture, but also displaying pottery, small stone objects, even wooden musical instruments. Two of the finest pieces here stand at the entrance: the **Ocelotl-Cuauhxicalli**, a jaguar with a hollow in its back in which the hearts of human sacrifices were placed (it may have been the companion of the eagle in the Templo Mayor museum; the two were found very close to each other, though over eighty years apart); and the **Teocalli de la Guerra Sagrada** (Temple of the Sacred War), a model of an Aztec pyramid decorated with many of the chief gods and with symbols relating to the calendar. There are hundreds of other powerful pieces – most of the vast Aztec pantheon is represented – and everywhere snakes, eagles and human hearts and skulls are prominent. Among them is a vast statue of **Coatlicue**, goddess of the earth, life and death, and mother of the gods. She is shown with two serpents above her shoulders, representing the flow of blood; her necklace of hands and hearts and pendant of a skull represent life and death respectively; her dress is made of snakes; her feet are eagles' claws. As a counterpoint to the viciousness of most of this, be sure to notice **Xochipilli**, the god of love, flowers, dance and poetry (and incidentally featured on the hundred-peso bill). You'll come across him, wearing a mask and sitting cross-legged on a throne strewn with flowers and butterflies, to the left of the entrance as you come in. Also impressive is a reconstructed version of **Moctezuma's headdress**, resplendent in bright blue quetzal feathers.

The undoubted highlight here, though, is the enormous 24-tonne **Piedra del Sol**, the Stone of the Sun or Aztec Calendar Stone. The latter, popular name is not strictly accurate, for this is much more a vision of the Aztec cosmos, completed under Moctezuma only a few years before the Spanish arrived. The stone was found by early colonists, and deliberately reburied for fear that it would spread unrest among the population. After being dug up again in the Zócalo in 1790 it spent years propped up against the walls of the cathedral. You'll pick up the most detailed description on a guided tour, but briefly: in the centre is the sun god and personification of the fifth sun, Tonatiuh, with a tongue in the form of a sacrificial knife and claws holding human hearts on each side, representing the need for human sacrifice to nourish the sun; around him are symbols for the four previous incarnations of the sun – a jaguar, wind, water and fiery rain; this whole central conglomeration forms the sign for the date on which the fifth world would end (as indeed, with defeat by the Spanish, it fairly accurately did). Encircling all this are hieroglyphs representing the twenty days of the Aztec month and other symbols of cosmic importance, and the whole thing is surrounded by two serpents.

### Oaxaca

Moving round to the third side of the museum you reach the halls devoted to cultures based away from the highlands, starting, in the corner of the museum, with the **Zapotec** and **Mixtec** people of **Oaxaca**. Although the two cultures evolved side by side, the Zapotecs flourished earlier (from around 900 BC to 800 AD) as accomplished architects with an advanced scientific knowledge, and also as makers of magnificent pottery with a pronounced Olmec influence. From around 800 AD many of their sites were taken over by the Mixtecs, whose overriding talents were as craftsmen and artists, working in metal, precious stone and clay. The best site in country for both these cultures is Monte Albán (see p.656).

The Zapotec collection demonstrates a fine sense of movement in the human figures: a reproduction of part of the carved facade of the Temple of the Dancers at Monte Albán; a model of a temple with a parrot sitting in it (in the "Monte Albán II" case); vases and urns in the form of various gods; and a superb jade mask representing the bat god. Among the Mixtec objects are many beautifully polychromed clay vessels, including a cup with a hummingbird perched on its rim, and sculptures in jade and quartz crystal. Reproductions of Zapotec and Mixtec tombs show how many of the finer small objects were discovered.

### Gulf of Mexico

Next is the **Gulf of Mexico** room, in which are displayed some of the treasures of **Olmec** art as well as objects produced in this region during the Classic period. The Olmec civilization is considered the mother culture of Mexico for its advanced development as early as 1500 BC, which provided much of the basis for the later Teotihuacán and Maya cultures. Olmec figures are delightful, but have many puzzling aspects, in particular their strikingly African features, nowhere better displayed than in some of the famed **colossal heads** dating from 1200–200 BC, long before Africa is supposed to have had any connection with the Americas. Many of the smaller pieces show evidence of deliberate deformation of the skull and teeth. The statue known as "the wrestler", with arms akimbo as if at the point of starting a bout, and the many tiny objects in jade and other polished stones are all outstanding. The later cultures are substantially represented, with fine figures and excellent pottery above all. The two most celebrated pieces are a statue of **Huehueteotl**, looking thoroughly grouchy with a brazier perched on his head, and the so-called **Huastec Adolescent**, a young Huastec Indian priest of Quetzalcoatl (perhaps the god himself) with an elaborately decorated naked body and a child on his back.

### Maya

The hall devoted to the **Maya** is perhaps the most varied of all, reflecting the longest-lived and widest-spread of the Mesoamerican cultures. In some ways it's a disappointment, since their greatest achievements were in architecture and in the decoration of their temples – many of which, unlike those of the Aztecs, are still standing – so that the objects here seem relatively unimpressive. Nevertheless, there are reproductions of several buildings, or parts of them, friezes and columns taken from them and extensive collections of jewellery, pottery and minor sculpture. Steps lead down into a section devoted to burial practices, including a reproduction of the Royal Tomb at **Palenque** (see p.740) with many of the objects found there – notably the prince's jade death mask. Outside, several small temples from relatively obscure sites are reproduced, the Temple of Paintings from **Bonampak** (see p.749) among them. The three rooms of the temple are entirely covered in frescoes representing the coronation of a new prince, a great battle and the subsequent punishments and celebrations. They are much easier to visit than the originals and in far better condition.

### Northern and western societies

As a finale to the archeological collections on the ground floor, there's a large room devoted to the north and the west of the country. **Northern** societies on the whole developed few large centres, remaining isolated nomadic or agricultural communities. The small quantities of pottery, weapons and jewellery that have survived show a close affinity with native tribes of the American Southwest. The **west** was far more developed, but it, too, has left relatively few traces, and many of the best examples of **Tarascan culture** (see box, p.363) remain in Guadalajara. Among the highlights here are some delightful small human and animal figurines in stone and clay, a Tarascan Chac-mool, a jade mask of Malinaltepec inlaid with a turquoise and red-shell mosaic and a two-storey reconstruction of the houses at Paquimé in the Chihuahua desert.

### The Ethnography Section

The **Ethnography Section** is on the upper floor. You must cross the courtyard back towards the beginning of the museum before climbing the stairs – otherwise you'll go round in reverse order. The rooms relate as closely as possible to those below them, showing the lifestyle of surviving indigenous groups today through photographs, models, maps and examples of local crafts. Regional dress and reproductions of various types of huts and cabins form a major part of this inevitably rather sanitized look at the poorest (and most oppressed) people in Mexico, and there are also objects relating to their more important cults and ceremonies.

## Around the Museo Nacional de Antropología

The enormous success of the Museo de Antropología has led to a spate of other audacious modern **exhibition halls** being set up in the park. Two are very close by, and together with the adjoining **zoo**, make this one of the finest concentrations of diversions in the otherwise sprawling city.

### Museo de Arte Moderno

Some 300m east of the Museo Nacional de Antropología on Paseo de la Reforma lies the **Museo de Arte Moderno** (Tues–Sun 10am–5pm; M$20, free on Sun). This consists of two low circular buildings dedicated to twentieth-century Mexican and Latin American art. The majority of the galleries, along with a separate gallery reached through the **sculpture garden**, are devoted to temporary and touring exhibitions, which are usually well worth inspection. The **permanent collection** is housed on the ground floor of the Sala Xavier Villaurrutia, to the right as you enter, and should not be missed.

All the major Mexican artists of the twentieth century are well represented. Among several works by Siqueiros, the most powerful is *Madre Campesina*, in which a peasant woman carries her child barefoot through an unforgiving desert of cacti. There's a whole corner devoted to Orozco, and oils by Diego Rivera, notably a portrait of his second wife, Lupe Marín, painted in 1938, long after their divorce. Look too for Olga Costa's *Vendedora de Frutas*, whose fruit-seller surrounded by bananas, sugar cane, watermelons, pumpkins, pawpaws, soursops and *mameyes*, all painted in vibrant reds and yellows, is about as Mexican a subject as you could want. The star attraction is Frida Kahlo's *Las Dos Fridas*, which stands out even among the museum's selection of haunting and disturbing canvases by Kahlo. It is one of her earliest full-scale paintings, and one whose theme she was constantly to return to. In it, Frida is depicted on the left in a white traditional dress, her heart torn and wounded, and her hand being held by a stronger Frida on the right, dressed in modern clothes and holding a locket with a picture of her husband Diego Rivera as a boy. Alongside these great paintings are works by less well-known Mexican artists: José Chávez Morado with his beautiful *Plantas y Serpientes*, and an intriguing multiple self-portrait by Juan O'Gorman.

### Museo Rufino Tamayo

Hidden among trees across the street from the Museum of Modern Art is the **Museo Rufino Tamayo** (Tues–Sun 10am–6pm; M$15, free on Sun; Ⓦwww.museotamayo.org), another fine collection of modern art – this one with an international focus. The modernist structure was built by the artist Rufino Tamayo, whose work in murals and on smaller projects was far more abstract and less political than the Big Three, though he was their approximate contemporary and enjoys a reasonable amount of international fame. There is much of his own work here, and exhibits of his techniques and theories, but also a fairly impressive collection of European and American twentieth-century art – most of it from Tamayo's private collection. Artists represented may include Picasso, Miró, Magritte, Francis Bacon and Henry Moore, though not all of these are on permanent display. First-rate contemporary international exhibits usually find their way here and sometimes take over the space of parts of the permanent collection.

### Lago Chapultepec and the Parque Zoológico de Chapultepec

On the south side of Reforma, opposite the Museo de Antropología, lies **Lago Chapultepec**, where you can rent **boats** and while away a leisurely afternoon. At the western side of the lake is the main entrance to the **Parque Zoológico de Chapultepec** (Tues–Sun 9am–4.30pm; free; Ⓦwww.cnf.org.mx), which occupies a large area in the centre of the park and is divided up into climatic zones – desert, tropical, temperate forests, etc – some of which work better than others. Enclosures are mostly open-air and tolerably large, though the animals still look bored and confined, and you wonder about their sanity on a Sunday afternoon when half of Mexico City's children seem to be here vying for their attentions. Probably the most satisfying sections are the most archetypally Mexican: the desert zone, and the enclosure of **Xoloitzcuintle**, the hairless dogs that represent the last surviving of four pre-Columbian breeds.

All the big beasts make an appearance, too: tigers, bears, lions, bison, camels, giraffes, hippos, elephants and the ever-popular **giant pandas**. The zoo is inordinately proud of these, evidenced by the posters around town that advertise new baby bears when they are born – in fact, this was the first place in the world to breed giant pandas in captivity.

## Auditorio Nacional and Los Pinos

Continuing west from the zoo, Reforma crosses Calzada Chivatito at Metro Auditorio, beyond which is the **Auditorio Nacional**, a major venue for dance, theatre and music events, with a couple of small theatres and an enormous auditorium. Further out, Reforma leaves the park via the Fuente de Petróleos, a complex of modern skyscrapers surrounding a monument to the nationalization of the oil industry, and heads into Las Lomas, an expensive suburb whose luxury villas are mostly hidden behind high walls and heavy security gates.

△ Paddleboats, Lago de Chapultepec

Heading south from Metro Auditorio, Calzada Chivatito becomes Molino del Rey, a street named after the major battle here during the Mexican–American War. There are still barracks here, along with **Los Pinos**, the president's official residence, which is strictly off-limits. A couple of footbridges lead from outside the barracks across the *periférico* (Bulevar López Mateos) to the park's Second Section.

## Nuevo Bosque de Chapultepec: Segunda and Tercera seccíónes

Over the years, new sections of parkland have been added to the west of the original Bosque de Chapultepec. These are occasionally still referred to as the **Nuevo Bosque de Chapultepec**, but are more commonly known as the **Segunda Sección**, or Second Section (marked on signs and maps as "2a Sección") and **Tercera Sección**, or Third Section (3a Sección). With very few places to cross the *periférico*, it is difficult to reach the newer parts of the park from the old. It is far better to make a separate visit (see "Park practicalities", p.439) to these sections, especially if you've got kids. There are fewer genuinely compelling reasons to visit either section for adults, though the Second Section is an enjoyable area to stroll about, and a good deal quieter than the main section of the park.

### Segunda Sección

Approaching the Second Section from Metro Constituyentes, follow Avenida Constituyentes west for a few metres and then cross it on a footbridge. Follow a short street to the *periférico*, also crossed by a nearby footbridge, to bring you to the **Museo Tecnológico** (daily 9am–5pm; free), entered on its west side, with its central building surrounded by outdoor exhibits. Despite being sponsored by some of Mexico's biggest companies, these remain unengaging affairs, at odds with the professionalism evident in the displays in most of Mexico City's museums. You can walk around a model of a geothermal power plant and another of a hydro project, as well as assorted bits of machinery and railway rolling stock all too static or inaccessible to really arouse much interest. Inside it is more accomplished, with hands-on displays, flight simulators and collections of models. It's a fun place for kids to play, but only educational if their (or your) Spanish is fairly good.

Right next door is **La Feria** (school holidays around Semana Santa, July, Aug & Dec Tues–Sun 10am–8pm, rest of the year Tues–Fri 10am–6pm, Sat 10am–7pm, Sun 10am–9pm; M$35 for entry with no rides included), the city's premier fun park. Here you'll find assorted rides and sideshows, easily the best of which is the old-fashioned wooden roller coaster (*montaña rusa*). A M$79 pass gives you access to most of the rides, but not the very top attractions including the roller coaster (M$15); a M$100 pass gives access to all the rides.

On the other side of the Museo Tecnológico lies **Papalote Museo del Niño**, Constituyentes 268 (Mon–Wed & Fri 9am–6pm, Thurs 9am–11pm, Sat & Sun 10am–7pm; M$85), a kind of cross between an adventure playground and a science experiment, with loads of fascinating hands-on experiments, plus an IMAX cinema (M$75; combination ticket with museum M$110) and a music-and-visuals dome that doubles as a planetarium (M$75; combination ticket with museum M$105; combination ticket with museum and IMAX M$145). Adults may feel as if they have entered some sort of psychotic kindergarten, but if you have kids, it will keep them entertained.

Heading west from Papalote you pass the rather tacky **Mexico Magic** fun park (Tues–Sun 10am–6pm; M$60–100, depending on what attractions are included) en route to the **Museo de Historia Natural** (Tues–Sun 10am–5pm; M$20, free on Tues, M$11.50 to bring in a camera, M$23 for a video camera), ten interconnecting domes filled with displays on nature and conservation, biology and geology, including rundowns on Mexico's mineral wealth, flora and fauna. Modern and well presented – and with the obligatory dinosaurs – it is again particularly popular with children.

Running north from here is the **Tren Escénico** (Tues–Sun 10am–4.30pm; M$5), a mini railway that will take you on a short loop around the park through some gum trees, and the ceremonial Fuente Xochipilli. From the fountain, a long pool gradually descends to a spot where you can double back past La Feria and the Museo Tecnológico, where you started.

### Tercera Sección

The newest section of the park, the **Tercera Sección**, lies yet further west, beyond the **Panteón Civil de Dolores** cemetery (daily 6am–5pm), where Diego Rivera, José Clemente Orozco and other illustrious Mexicans are buried. To get there catch a *pesero* (route #24 to "Panteón Dolores", "Rollo" or "Atlantis") from Metro Chapultepec or along Avenida Constituyentes.

The main draws in this section – open to the general public only on weekends and public holidays – are **La Ola** (formerly, and still popularly, El Rollo; Sat, Sun & public holidays 10am–6pm; M$85), a water park with all manner of chutes, slides and wave generators; and **Atlantis** (Sat, Sun & public holidays 10.30am–6pm; M$55), a kind of zoo-cum-circus with marine mammals and assorted birds, some of them trained to take part in various performances, for some of which there is an additional fee.

## South of the centre

Mexico City spreads itself furthest to the south, where a series of old villages that have been swallowed up by the urban sprawl harbour some of the most enticing destinations outside the centre. The colonial **suburbs** of **Coyoacán** and **San Ángel**, each with a couple of worthwhile museums, make a tranquil respite from the city centre's bustle, and a startling contrast to the ultramodern bravado of the architecture of the nearby National Autonomous University of Mexico (UNAM).

Out this direction you'll find echoes of ancient Mexico in the archeological site of **Cuicuilco** and **Xochimilco**'s canals, all that remains of the great valley lakes. There are also a couple of stations on the Diego Rivera trail, including his remarkable collection of antiquities in the **Museo Anahuacalli**, and a very fine collection of paintings by him and Frida Kahlo in the **Museo Dolores Olmedo Patiño**.

The residential area of **El Pedregal**, which gets its name from the vast lava flow that spreads south of San Ángel through the University City and on to the south of Coyoacán, is also south of the centre. Craggy and dramatic, it was regarded as a completely useless stretch of land, the haunt of bandits and brigands, until the early 1950s, when architect Luis Barragan began to build extraordinarily imaginative houses here, using the uneven lava as a feature. Now it's filled with an amazing collection of luxury homes, though you'll unfortunately be able to see little of what is behind the high walls and security fences even if you drive around.

## Insurgentes

**Insurgentes**, the most direct approach to the suburbs, is interesting in its own right: leaving behind the Glorieta de Insurgentes (the roundabout at Insurgentes Metro station), it runs almost perfectly straight all the way out to the university, lined the whole way with huge department stores and malls, cinemas, restaurants and office buildings. A little under halfway to San Ángel, you pass on the right the enormous **World Trade Center**, the tallest building in the city, crowned by *Bellini's*, an expensive revolving restaurant (see p.468).

Just south of the World Trade Center, and on the right (if heading south) is the garish **Polyforum Siqueiros** (daily 9am–6pm; M$15; ⓣ55/5536-4520 to 24, ⓦwww.polyforumsiqueiros.com.mx; Metrobús Poliforum). Its exterior is plastered in brash paintings by David Siqueiros and some thirty other artists. Inside, it contains what is allegedly the world's largest mural (about 4500 square metres), painted by Siqueiros alone, entitled *The March of Humanity on Earth and Towards the Cosmos*. For the full impact of the changing perspectives and use of sculptural techniques, try to see the **sound-and-light show** (in

### Getting to the southern suburbs

It's not at all difficult to get out to any of the sights outside the city centre on **public transport**, but getting from one to the other can be tricky if you're cutting across the main north–south routes. In fact, there is easily enough to see out this way to justify a couple of separate trips, thereby avoiding the slightly complicated matter of traversing the area. And while none of the connections you have to make is impossible, it's worth taking a few short taxi rides between them, from San Ángel to Coyoacán, for example, or from Coyoacán to Rivera's Anahuacalli Museum. If you want to see as much as possible in a day or even an afternoon, you might consider getting a **tourist taxi** (see p.407) to take you round the lot. If you bargain furiously, this may not be as expensive as it sounds; indeed it sometimes seems that you can barely be paying for the fuel used. Alternatively there are **coach tours** run by several of the bigger travel agencies in the Zona Rosa.

For **San Ángel and the University City**, the best approach is along Insurgentes Sur, where you'll find a constant stream of *peseros*, whose main destinations should be chalked up, or displayed on a card, on the windscreen – look for "San Ángel", "Ciudad Universitaria", "CU", or "UNAM" (for Universidad Nacional Autónoma de México). The Metrobús (see p.407) runs as far as Dr Gálvez station in San Ángel. Other terminals for heading south are the bus stands by Metro Chapultepec or at Metro Tasqueña for services along the Calzada de Tlalpan and to the southwest of the city, above all to Xochimilco. If you'd rather stick to the **Metro**, take line 3 to Miguel Ángel de Quevedo, between San Ángel and Coyoacán.

To get to **Coyoacán** from San Ángel, buses head down Altavista by the San Ángel Inn; from the centre, buses leave from Metros Chapultepec, Insurgentes or Cuauhtémoc. In each case look for "Coyoacán" or "Colonia del Valle/Coyoacán". There's also a trolleybus that runs down Lázaro Cárdenas against the flow of traffic from a stop close by Bellas Artes. Metro line 3, too, passes close by, though note that Viveros station is considerably closer to the action than Coyoacán station: from Viveros, walk south on Avenida Universidad, then turn left (east) to reach the centre. If you're coming straight from the centre of town down Cuauhtémoc or Lázaro Cárdenas, it makes sense to visit the Kahlo and Trotsky museums (see pp.454 & 456) first, in which case you'll want to get off the bus immediately after passing under Avenida Río Churubusco. The Metro stops are slightly more distant, but a good approach is to take line 2 to General Anaya and walk west from there past the Museo de las Intervenciones and the Trotsky and Frida Kahlo houses.

principle Sat & Sun noon & 2pm; M$30) with taped narration by Siqueiros. Elsewhere, the building houses visiting art exhibitions and a sizeable display of expensive crafts for sale.

Beyond this monster you shortly pass close by the **Plaza México**, the largest bullring in the world, with a capacity of 48,000. You can't actually see it from Insurgentes, but it's only a ten-minute walk along San Antonio, hard by the **Estadio Azul**, a 65,000-seat soccer stadium that is home to Cruz Azul. Finally, just before San Ángel comes the **Teatro de los Insurgentes**, its facade covered in a huge mosaic designed by Diego Rivera depicting the history of Mexican theatre, and assorted historical figures. At the top are Los Insurgentes of Mexico's War of Independence: Hidalgo, Morelos and Benito Juárez on the left, and Zapata on the right.



## San Ángel

The upmarket colonial suburb of **San Ángel** lies 12km southwest of central Mexico City, clustered around the point where Insurgentes Sur and Revolución almost meet, linked by the 200-metre-long Avenida La Paz. With its markets, ancient mansions and high-priced shops – Cartier, Italian designer furniture and the like – around flower-draped patios, San Ángel is a very exclusive place to live. It also makes an inviting place to visit, packed with little restaurants and cafés where you can sit outside and watch the crowds go by, and is especially appealing on Saturdays when the delightful **Plaza San Jacinto** is taken over by **Bazar Sábado**, a lively outdoor art market. Initially, the Saturday market was based in one of the mansions on the square, which still opens every weekend selling upmarket crafts and artworks, but nowadays there are stalls in all the surrounding streets, with fairground rides and freak shows. The plaza is surrounded by San Ángel's oldest mansions, notably the eighteenth-century **Casa del Risco**, at no. 15 (Tues–Sun 10am–5pm; free), housing a collection of antique furniture and paintings, with an extraordinary fountain in the patio made from old porcelain plates and cups, broken and unbroken.

Whether you choose to visit on Saturday or one of the quieter days of the week, consider sticking around until evening to blow an appreciable wad of cash on some of the finest dining in the city (see p.469).

### Museo del Carmen

San Ángel takes its name from the former Carmelite Convent of San Angelo Mártir, on Revolución just south of its junction with La Paz, which is now run as the **Museo del Carmen** (Tues–Sun 10am–4.45pm; M$33, free on Sun). Its three brightly coloured, tiled domes preside over this part of town and add the final touch of grace to what is a lovely example of early seventeenth-century architecture. The church is still used but the rest of the convent has become a museum where just walking through the maze of monks' cells, rooms and courtyards is pleasurable enough, though there's also an extensive collection of colonial religious paintings and furniture. Just about everyone wants to make their way to the crypt to see the dozen **mummies**, found here by troops during the Revolution and thought to be eighteenth-century nuns and monks, now displayed behind glass. Elsewhere, check out the extensive displays on daily life in New Spain and a collection of eighteenth-century oils by Cristóbal de Vallalpando.



### Museo de Arte Carrillo-Gil

Heading north along Revolución past a small flower market, you reach the **Museo de Arte Carrillo-Gil**, Revolución 1608 (Tues–Sun 10am–6pm;

M$15, free on Sun), a surprisingly good museum of modern art that seems a little incongruous in colonial San Ángel. The museum was built in 1974 to house the collection of Dr Alvaro Carrillo, a skilled painter and art critic, as well as a friend of Siqueiros and long-time supporter of the avant-garde, who had been amassing works since the 1930s. Three airy and spacious floors feature pieces by Mexicans including Rivera (a couple of Cubist canvases), Siqueiros and most importantly, Orozco, of whose work here *Zapata* and *Christ Destroying His Cross* are the most striking examples. There's also a smattering of international big names, but many are out on loan or stored away to make space for the numerous temporary exhibits and contemporary installations.

## Museo Casa Estudio Diego Rivera y Frida Kahlo and the San Ángel Inn

From the Museo de Arte Carrillo-Gil it's just over half a kilometre along Altavista to the **Museo Casa Estudio Diego Rivera y Frida Kahlo**, Diego Rivera 2 (Tues–Sun 10am–6pm; M$10, free on Sun), a pair of modernist houses built for Diego Rivera and Frida Kahlo in 1931–32 by the time's leading architect, Juan O'Gorman. Tucked behind an organ cactus fence opposite the prestigious *San Ángel Inn* restaurant (see p.470) sits a small compound with a large maroon-coloured house (Diego's) and a much smaller blue abode (Frida's), connected by a rooftop causeway. From 1933 to 1941 they both stayed here, living and working apart yet still near enough to visit each other and for Frida to deliver Diego's meals. In both buildings the walls are concrete, the floors are

### A walk from San Ángel to Coyoacán

The most enjoyable way to take in San Ángel and Coyoacán on the same day is to put an hour or so aside and **walk** between the two. The most pleasant route, through quiet streets past some of the city's prime real estate (marked on the map on p.453), starts at the main junction in the centre of San Ángel where Revolución passes the Museo del Carmen (see opposite). From here, follow La Paz northeast and cross Insurgentes to reach the **Jardín de la Bombilla**, a small park centred on a blockish concrete monument to General Alvaro Obregón, who was assassinated here in 1928 soon after being re-elected as president. Revolutionary workers (corn cob in one hand, hammer and sickle in the other) flank the monument, and you can duck inside to see the bronze statue of Obregón. On the east side of the park, cross Chimalistac and walk through the tiny Plaza Frederico Gamboa. When you reach the other side, take a left (you're now headed north) and cross Miguel Ángel de Quevedo, passing **Parque Tagle** on your left, then turn right into Arenal. This leads you across Universidad to the **Capilla de San Antonio Panzacola**, a little red chapel sited attractively next to a small stone bridge.

Continue east on the peaceful, cobbled Francisco Sosa, one of the most beautiful streets in the city, and also one of the oldest. Peer over the high walls lining the street to catch a glimpse of some gorgeous residences – the only way to get any closer to these houses is to visit the **Museo Nacional de la Acuarela**, Salvador Nova 88 (Tues–Sun 10am–6pm; free), a small museum inside one. Devoted to watercolour painting, the collection includes some architectural and graphic art as well. Look for work by Saturnino Herrán and don't miss the temporary exhibits in a separate gallery reached through a small sculpture garden.

Ten minutes' walk further along Francisco Sosa brings you to the **Plaza Santa Caterina**, a tranquil square overlooked by a mustard-yellow church and with a couple of restaurants. From here it is a short walk to Coyoacán's Plaza Central, reached through a twin-arched gateway.

wooden and many of the windows go from floor to ceiling – all very advanced for the early 1930s and especially for Mexico. Indeed, the whole set-up is in such contrast to the Blue House in Coyoacán (see p.454) that it is hard to imagine that the houses were inhabited by the same people.

Diego's studio contains some of his painting materials, along with personal items, reproductions of some of his work and some large papier-mâché skeletons. Temporary exhibits take up much of Frida's house, though there are a couple of fine portraits of her taken by photographer Nikolas Muray, with whom Frida had an affair in the late 1930s, and some of Frida's own ex-voto paintings of her debilitating accident.



## Coyoacán

Around 3km east of San Ángel lies **COYOACÁN**, another colonial township that has been absorbed by the city. Even before the Conquest it was a sizeable place. Originally the capital of a small lakeshore kingdom, it was subjugated by the Aztecs in the mid-fifteenth century. Cortés based himself in Coyoacán during the siege of Tenochtitlán, and continued to live here while the old city was torn down and construction began on the capital of Nueva España. It remains far less touristed than San Ángel, although the plazas are pretty lively, especially at weekends. The focus of the area is the spacious **Plaza Central**.

Nearby, in the small Plaza la Conchita, the **Capilla de la Concepción** has a wonderful Baroque facade. Overlooking the square, the distinctive red **Casa de la Malinche** (not open to the public) is the house in which Cortés installed his native mistress – and where he allegedly later murdered his wife shortly after her arrival from Spain. No visit to Coyoacán is complete without strolling out to the northern reaches of the suburb to the two main sights, the **Frida Kahlo** and **Leon Trotsky museums**.

### Plaza Central

Coyoacán's **Plaza Central** is one of the city's main stomping grounds for artists, artisans and musicians. It is actually made up of two adjoining plazas – **Plaza Hidalgo** and the **Jardín del Centenario**. Bars and cafés ring the plaza. On Sunday, there's a market in the Plaza Central, and the area is taken up by stalls and various rock, folk and reggae bands. It's far and away the most fun place in the city to buy your souvenirs, though most of the stuff can be found cheaper elsewhere.

The Plaza Central is also home to the sixteenth-century church of San Juan and the small Palacio Municipal (also known as the Casa de Cortés), said to have been built by Cortés himself. Inside the palacio are two **murals** by pupils of Rivera's – one by Aurora Reyes depicting the Conquest, and one by Diego Rosales showing the torture of Cuauhtémoc. The latter is particularly apposite since it was in Coyoacán that the Aztec leader was tortured and finally killed. The murals aren't open to the public, but if you ask at the **tourist office** in the same building (just inside the main entrance, on the right; daily 8am–8pm; ⓣ55/5658-0221) they might let you take a peek at Reyes's mural, in the Sala de Cabildos, a municipal office. The other mural is in the *capilla* (registry office), which is only open if there's a wedding on – should you stumble upon one you can discreetly put your head round the door for a quick look.

The **Museo de Culturas Populares** (Tues–Thurs 10am–6pm, Fri–Sun 10am–8pm; free), close to the Plaza Hidalgo at Av Hidalgo 289, has colourful

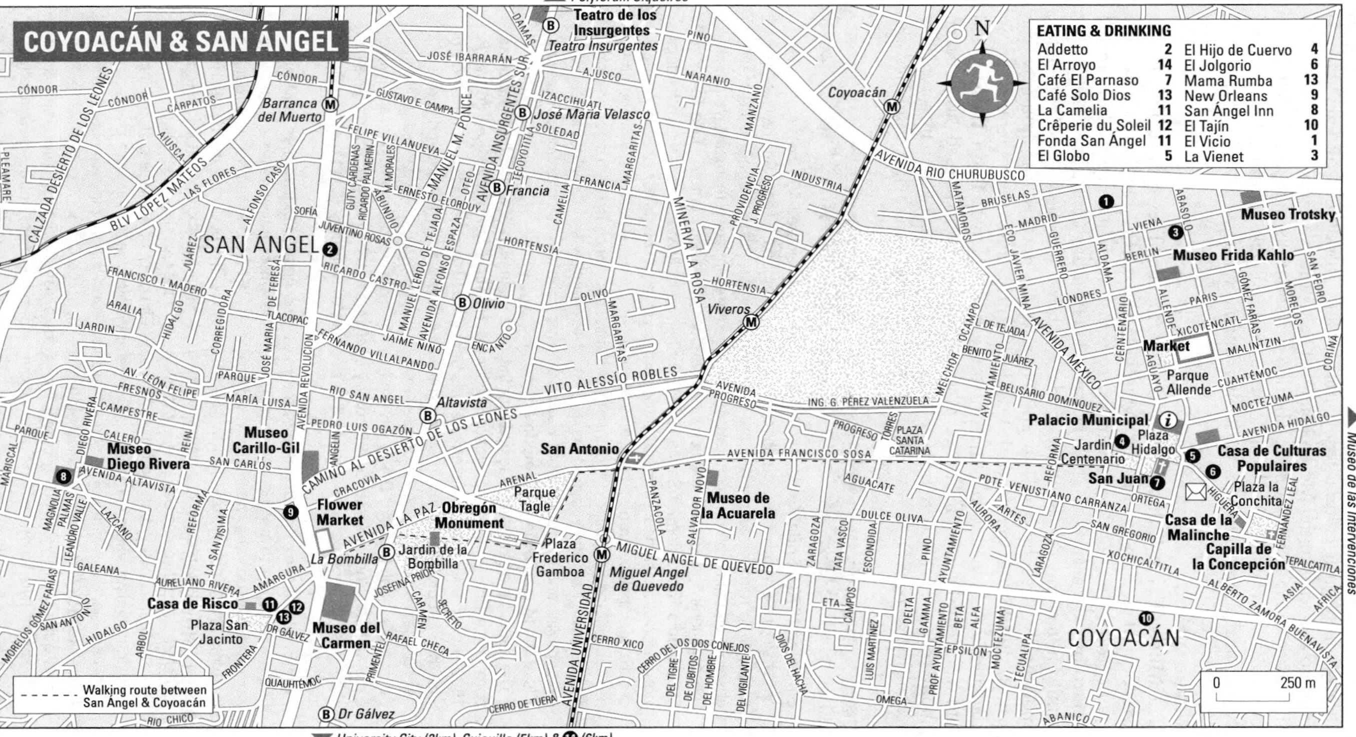
COYOACÁN & SAN ÁNGEL
EATING & DRINKING
Addetto 2
El Arroyo 14
Café El Parnaso 7
Café Solo Dios 13
La Camelia 11
Crêperie du Soleil 12
Fonda San Ángel 11
El Globo 5
El Hijo de Cuervo 4
El Jolgorio 6
Mama Rumba 13
New Orleans 9
San Ángel Inn 8
El Tajín 10
El Vicio 1
La Vienet 3
0 250 m
Walking route between San Angel & Coyoacán
Polyforum Siqueiros
Museo de las Intervenciones
University City (2km), Cuicuillo (5km) & 14 (6km)
SAN ÁNGEL
COYOACÁN
Teatro de los Insurgentes
Teatro Insurgentes
Barranca del Muerto
José María Velasco
Francia
Olivio
Altavista
Viveros
Coyoacán
Museo Trotsky
Museo Frida Kahlo
Market
Parque Allende
Palacio Municipal
Plaza Hidalgo
Jardín Centenario
San Juan
Casa de Culturas Populaires
Plaza la Conchita
Casa de la Malinche
Capilla de la Concepción
Museo Carillo-Gil
Museo Diego Rivera
San Antonio
Museo de la Acuarela
Parque Tagle
Flower Market
Obregón Monument
La Bombilla
Jardín de la Bombilla
Plaza Frederico Gamboa
Miguel Angel de Quevedo
Casa de Risco
Plaza San Jacinto
Museo del Carmen
Dr Gálvez
AVENIDA INSURGENTES SUR
AVENIDA REVOLUCION
AVENIDA RIO CHURUBUSCO
AVENIDA MEXICO
AVENIDA UNIVERSIDAD
MIGUEL ANGEL DE QUEVEDO
AVENIDA FRANCISCO SOSA
VITO ALESSÍO ROBLES
MINERVA LA ROSA
CAMINO AL DESIERTO DE LOS LEONES
AVENIDA LA PAZ
CALZADA DESIERTO DE LOS LEONES
BLV LOPEZ MATEOS
ALBERTO ZAMORA BUENAVISTA

displays on popular cultural forms, mostly dolls, masks and costumes. Avenida Hidalgo also leads to the Museo Nacional de las Intervenciones (see p.458) – to find it, continue down Avenida Hidalgo for about 300m, and bear left down General Anaya, which leads directly to the museum (crossing División del Norte on the way), a fifteen- to twenty-minute walk.

### Museo Frida Kahlo

The **Museo Frida Kahlo**, Londres 247, at Allende (Tues–Sun 10am–5.45pm; M$45, ticket also valid for Museo Anahuacalli, see p.459; Ⓦwww.museofridakahlo.org; Metro Coyoacán) is just a few minutes' walk from the centre of Coyoacán. The appropriately named Blue House was the Kahlo's family home and this is where Frida was born and spent most of her life, sporadically with husband Diego Rivera, who donated the house to the nation shortly after her death. It was during Frida and Diego's tenure here in the late 1930s that they played host to the newly arrived **Leon Trotsky** and his wife. Trotsky, ever fearful of assassins, apparently expressed his concern about the ease of access from a neighbouring property, and in a typically expansive gesture Diego simply bought the other house and combined the

#### Frida Kahlo

Since the 1970s, **Frida Kahlo** (1907–54) has been considered Mexico's most internationally renowned artist, outshining even her husband, Diego Rivera (see box, p.420), who recognized her as "the first woman in the history of art to treat, with absolute and uncompromising honesty, one might even say with impassive cruelty, those general and specific themes which exclusively affect women". Julie Taymor's 2002 biopic *Frida*, starring Salma Hayek, further consolidated her role as a feminist icon, a position earned as much through her life as through her art. Her work is deeply personal, centred on herself, her insecurities and her relations with her family, her country and her politics. "I paint myself," she said, "because I am so often alone, and because I am the subject I know best." Her relatively short painting career was never prolific and her total output was small. By far the largest collection of her work – is at the **Museo Dolores Olmedo Patiño** (see p.459).

The daughter of a *mestizo* Mexican mother and Hungarian Jewish father, Frida was born in the Blue House in Coyoacán (now the **Museo Frida Kahlo**, see above) in 1907, though she always claimed she was born in 1910, symbolically uniting her birth with the start of the Revolution. When she was 6, she battled a bout of polio that left her right leg withered. She rebounded and, as a precocious 14-year-old at Mexico City's top school, first met **Diego Rivera** (twenty years her senior) who was painting a mural there. She shocked her friends by declaring that she wished to conceive his child "just as soon as I convince him to cooperate", but they didn't meet again for many years.

At 18, and already breaking free of the roles then ordained for women in Mexico, Frida had begun to pursue a career in medicine when she suffered a gruesome **accident**. The bus she was riding in was struck by a tram, leaving her with multiple fractures and a pelvis skewered by a steel handrail. It was during the months she spent bedridden, recovering, that she first took up a paintbrush. Later in life, she reflected "I had two accidents in my life. One was the bus, the other Diego", and it was after her recovery that she fell in with a left-leaning bunch of artists, free-thinkers and Communists where she again met Rivera. Within a year they were married: she a striking, slender woman of 21; he a massively overweight man twice her age with a frog-like face and an unparalleled reputation for womanizing. Diego went about his affairs quite publicly (including briefly with Frida's sister, Cristina). With true macho jealousy, he was furious when Frida took up with other men, but her several affairs two. Continually at the centre of the capital's leftist bohemian life, Diego and Frida hosted a coterie of artist and intellectuals at this house – D.H. Lawrence visited frequently, though he had little political or artistic sympathy with Kahlo – or Trotsky, for that matter.

Several rooms have been set aside as galleries. The first features around twenty relatively minor (and less tortured) examples of Frida's work, from some of her early portraits through to her final work, *Viva la Vida*, a still life of sliced watermelons. She painted it in 1954, when the pain and trauma of her recent leg amputation had taken their toll on her painterly control, if not her spirit. Look too for a beautiful charcoal self-portrait from 1932 and the more political *Marxism Gives Health to the Sick* from 1954. A room full of Frida's signature **tehuana dresses** leads on to more paintings, including over a dozen by Rivera, such as *Paisaje de la Quebrada*, which shows a rock face at Acapulco into which Diego has painted his own face in purple. Alongside are several works by Velasco and Orozco, as well as a Klee and a Tanguy.

Other sections of the house faithfully show the artesanía style that Frida favoured. Witness the blue and yellow kitchen with "Diego" and "Frida"

with women seemed to delight him. After her death he wrote "Too late now, I realized that the most wonderful part of my life had been my love for Frida."

Encouraged by Diego, Frida pursued her **painting** career. Over half of her canvases are **self-portraits**: an unsmiling face with dark monobrow and a moustache she never tried to conceal above a body often sliced open and mutilated. Increasingly her self-portraits were imbued with sophisticated personal symbolism, with themes of abortion, broken bones and betrayed love explored through the body set in an unlikely juxtaposition of elements.

In 1932 Frida miscarried and was hospitalized in Detroit where she painted *Henry Ford Hospital*. This disturbing depiction of her grief shows her naked body lying on a bed in an industrial wasteland, surrounded by a foetus, pelvic bones and surgical implements all umbilically tied back to her. After returning to Mexico, their circle of friends expanded to include Trotsky (with whom she had a brief affair), Cuban communist Julio Antonio Mella and muralist David Siqueiros (later implicated in an attempt to kill Trotsky, see box, p.456). By now Frida and Diego were living in paired houses in San Ángel (see p.451), which allowed them to maintain relatively separate lives. In 1939 Frida and Diego **divorced**, a devastating event Frida recorded in *Self-Portrait with Cropped Hair*, in which her trademark long tresses and indigenous Tehuana dresses (both much loved by Diego) are replaced by Diego's oversized suit and cropped hair. They **remarried** a year later, with Frida insisting on financial independence and a celibate relationship. In more upbeat mood she then painted *Self-Portrait with Plait*, the shorn locks braided together and piled precariously on the head.

The injuries from her accident dogged her throughout her life, and as her physical condition worsened she found solace in her work (as well as drink and pain-killing drugs), painting *The Broken Column*, in 1944, with her crushed spine depicted as an Ionic column. Despite increasing commercial and critical success, Frida had only one **solo exhibition** of her work during her lifetime, in Mexico City just a year before she died. In her later years she was wheelchair-bound, but continued the political activism she had always pursued, and died after defying medical advice and taking part in a demonstration against American intervention in Guatemala while she was convalescing from pneumonia in July 1954. By this stage, she knew she was dying; defiantly, on her last work, she daubed the words "Viva la Vida" – "Long Live Life".

picked out in tiny ceramic mugs on the wall. Its extraordinary decoration continues with bizarre papier-mâché animals and figures, and an impressive collection of *retablos* around the stairway. This leads up to Frida's airy studio where her wheelchair is artfully set next to an easel and, of course, a mirror. Diego's influence in the house is seen more through his interest in Mexico's pre-Hispanic culture. Artefacts are scattered throughout the house and a small collection is displayed on the courtyard on a small two-step pyramid he had constructed there.

### Museo Casa de León Trotsky

Trotsky's House, or the **Museo Casa de León Trotsky**, Río Churabasco 410 (Tues–Sun 10am–5pm; M$30; Metro Coyoacán), where the genius of the Russian Revolution and organizer of the Red Army lived and worked, is about four blocks away and represents virtually the only memorial to Trotsky anywhere in the world. After Lenin's death, Trotsky was forced into exile and condemned to death, and as increasing numbers of countries refused him asylum he sought refuge in Mexico in 1937, aided by Diego Rivera (at the time an ardent Trotskyite), who petitioned President Lázaro Cárdenas on his behalf. Here Stalin's long arm finally caught up with him (see box below), despite the house being reinforced with steel gates and shutters, high walls and watch-towers. Today the fortified building seems at first a little incongruous, surrounded by the bourgeois homes of a prosperous suburb, but inside it's a human place, set up as he left it, if rather dustier: books on the shelves, his glasses smashed on the desk and all the trappings of a fairly comfortable ordinary life – except for the bullet holes.

## The University, Olympic Stadium and Cuicuilco

Around 2km south of San Ángel, Insurgentes enters the great lava field of El Pedregal, an area partly given over to plush housing, but also home to the **university campus**, the **Olympic Stadium** (Estadio Olímpico) and **Cuicuilco**, the oldest pyramid in central Mexico.

### The assassination of Trotsky

The first attempt on Trotsky's life, in his house at Coyoacán, left more than seventy scars in the plaster of the bedroom walls. At 4am on May 24, 1940, a heavily armed group led by painter David Siqueiros (who had been a commander in the Spanish Civil War and was working under the orders of the Stalinist Mexican Communist Party) overcame the guards and pumped more than two hundred shots into the house. Trotsky, his wife and son survived only by hiding under their beds. After this, the house, already heavily guarded, was further fortified. Unknown to all, though, the eventual assassin had already inveigled his way into the household, posing as a businessman being converted to the cause. Although he was never fully trusted, his arrival at the house on the afternoon of August 20, with an article that he wanted Trotsky to look over, seemed innocuous enough. Trotsky invited him into the study and moments later the notorious **ice pick** (the blunt end), which had been concealed under the killer's coat, smashed into Trotsky's skull. He died some 24 hours later, in the hospital after an operation failed to save his life. The killer, who called himself Frank Jackson and claimed to be Belgian, served twenty years in jail, though he never explained his actions or even confessed to his true identity, Jaime Ramón Mercader del Río.

**Getting to the area** is easy, as it's reached from San Ángel by just about any bus or *pesero* (route #1 or #76, for example) heading south along Insurgentes. All stop outside the Olympic Stadium, right opposite the university library, and many (try those marked "Villa Olímpica", "Cuicuilco" and "Tlalpan") continue on to the pyramid at Cuicuilco, visible on the left just after you pass under the *periférico*. The university can also be reached by Metro (line 3): Copilco is the most convenient station, Universidad much less so as it brings you out at the back of the campus, from where you have to walk all the way through – past the *frontón* courts and medical faculty – to reach the library.



## University City

To the east of Insurgentes is the **University City**. The campus is dominated by the astonishing, rectangular twelve-storey **library**, each face of which is covered in a mosaic designed by **Juan O'Gorman** – mostly natural stone with a few tiles or glass to supply colours that would otherwise have been unavailable. Representing the artist's vision of the country's progression through history, the focus of the larger north and south faces is on pre-Hispanic and colonial Mexico; on the west wall are the present and the university coat of arms; on the east, the future is ranged around a giant atom. It's remarkable how these have been incorporated as an essential feature of the building – at first it appears that there are no windows at all, but look closely and you'll see that in fact they're an integral part of the design, appearing as eyes, mouths or as windows of the buildings in the mosaic.

More or less beside the library are the long, low **administration buildings** (*rectoría*), with a giant mural in high relief by Siqueiros (or a "sculptural painting", as he called it), intended to provide a changing perspective as you walk past or drive by on Insurgentes. At the front of the *rectoría* are the university theatre and the **Museo Universitario de Ciencias y Artes** (Mon–Fri 9am–6pm, Sat & Sun 10am–6pm; free), the latter a wide-ranging general collection, with interactive scientific exhibits, plus displays on contemporary art and culture. Behind them spread out the enormous grounds of the main campus, starting with a large esplanade known as the Plaza Mayor, with sculptural groups dotted around a shallow artificial pond. Towards the back of the *rectoría* are more murals, adorning the **Faculties of Science and Medicine**; continue past these to reach another grassy area with the **Botanical Gardens** and several large walls against which the students play *frontón*.

After almost fifty years of use, the campus is beginning to show its age, and while it's no longer the avant-garde sensation it was when it opened, it remains a remarkable architectural achievement. The whole thing was built in just five years (1950–55) during the presidency of Miguel Alemán, and is now one of the largest universities in the world, with some 300,000 students and staff. It's also the oldest on the American continent: granted a charter by Philip II in 1551, the University of Mexico occupied a succession of sites in the city centre (including the Hospital de Jesús Nazareno and what is now the Escuela Nacional Preparatoria), was closed down several times in the nineteenth century and was finally awarded its status as the Universidad Nacional Autónoma de México (UNAM) in 1929.

## Estadio Olímpico

Directly across Insurgentes from the university library is the sculptured oval of the 100,000-seat **Estadio Olímpico**, its main facade decorated with a mosaic relief by Diego Rivera designed to represent the development of human potential through sport. Most taxi drivers will tell you that the stadium was deliberately designed to look like a giant sombrero, but this, sadly, is not the case; it's undeniably odd, though, half sunk into the ground as if dropped here from a great height and slightly warped in the process.

### Cuicuilco

The **Pirámide de Cuicuilco** (daily 9am–5pm; free) is dominated by the circular temple visible to the east of Insurgentes by the *periférico*, around 3km south of the Estadio Olímpico and opposite the former Olympic Village, now a housing complex. This is much the oldest construction of such scale known in central Mexico, reaching its peak around 600–200 BC before being abandoned at the time of the eruption of Xitle (the small volcano that created El Pedregal, which took place around 100–300 AD), just as Teotihuacán was beginning to develop. Not a great deal is known about the site, much of which has been buried by modern housing (completing the work of the lava). The pyramid itself, approached by a ramp and a stairway, is about 25m high by 100m in diameter and is composed of four sloping tiers (of a probable original five), the lowest one made visible only by digging away four metres of lava. A small **museum** displays objects found here and at contemporary settlements.

## Calzada de Tlalpan

Along with Insurgentes, the other main approach to the south is the **Calzada de Tlalpan**, which runs south from the Zócalo more or less in parallel with Metro line 2 (initially underground, then running down the middle of the road) and subsequently the Tren Ligero, almost all the way to Xochimilco.

The two train lines provide the easiest access to some fine museums – including Diego Rivera's Anahuacalli and the wonderful Museo Dolores Olmedo Patiño. The Tren Ligero passes the giant **Estadio Azteca** football stadium on its way to the canals of Xochimilco, and Metro line 2 also provides alternative access to the eastern end of Coyoacán.

### Museo Nacional de las Intervenciones

Travelling south on Metro line 2, the first station worth stopping at is General Anaya, from where it is a five-minute walk along 20 de Agosto (exit to the west of the Calzada de Tlalpan) to the **Museo Nacional de las Intervenciones**, 20 de Agosto and General Anaya (Tues–Sun 9am–6pm; M$33, free on Sun). This occupies the old Franciscan **Convento de Churubusco**, which owes its present incarnation to the 1847 battle in which the invading Americans, led by General Winfield Scott, defeated a Mexican force under General Anaya – another heroic Mexican effort in which the outnumbered defenders fought to their last bullet.

The building itself is a stunner, especially if you arrive at the darkening of day as the lights are coming on in the gardens. The exhibits, all on the upper floor, may not mean a great deal unless you have a reasonable grasp of Mexican history. They're labelled only in Spanish – and not very fully at that – and are dedicated to the history of foreign military adventures in Mexico: skeletons in the cupboards of Britain, Spain, France and the US are all rattled loudly. One section is devoted largely to the Mexican–American wars – with a very different perspective from that of the Alamo. Much of what's on show, however, comprises paintings of generals and flags, and unless you're a history buff you might better spend your time in the pleasant surrounding gardens. Apart from the Metro, the museum is also accessible by *pesero* ("Gral Anaya") from Coyoacán: pick it up by the market at the junction of Allende and Xicoténcatl.

The Trotsky and Frida Kahlo museums and central Coyoacán are about a fifteen-minute walk from the Museo Nacional de las Intervenciones. To reach them, take General Anaya, opposite the museum entrance, cross División del Norte and go straight ahead for about 500m, by which time General Anaya has merged into Hidalgo. For central Coyoacán and the Frida Kahlo Museum, continue straight on (see map, p.453). For the Trotsky Museum, take a right down Madero (signposted, but not easy to spot) opposite Hidalgo 62.

### Museo Anahuacalli

Metro line 2 finishes at Tasqueña, where you can transfer to the Tren Ligero and continue four stops to Xotepingo, a ten-minute walk from the bizarre **Museo Diego Rivera Anahuacalli**, Museo 150 (Tues–Sun 10am–6pm; M$45, ticket also valid for Museo Frida Kahlo, see p.454; Ⓦwww.anahuacallimuseo.org; Tren Ligero Xotepingo), designed and built by Diego Rivera to house his huge collection of pre-Hispanic artefacts. Note that during restoration (due for completion in 2008), visits are limited to guided tours, which take place at 10.30am, 11.30am, 12.30pm, 1.30pm, 3.15pm, 4.15pm and (except on Fri) 5pm. It's an extraordinary blockish structure, started in 1933 and worked on sporadically until Rivera's death, then finished off by Juan O'Gorman and opened in 1963. Inspired by Maya and Aztec architecture, this sombre mass of black volcanic stone is approached through a courtyard reminiscent of a Maya ball-court. The exquisite objects in the collection form part of a thoroughly imaginative exhibit: one small chamber contains nothing but a series of **Huehueteotls**, all squatting grumpily under the weight of their braziers, and the studio has ball-player and animal displays.

The **ground floor** is devoted to objects from the main cultures of the Valley of México – Teotihuacán, Toltec and Aztec – which provided Rivera with an important part of his inspiration. On the **middle floor**, rooms devoted to the west of Mexico (arguably the best such collection in the country) surround the huge airy space that Rivera planned to use as a studio. It's been fitted out with portraits and sketches, including preliminary studies for *Man in Control of the Universe*, his massive mural in the Bellas Artes. On the **top floor** are more Aztec objects, along with pottery and small figures from Oaxaca and the Gulf coast. Up here you can also get out onto the **rooftop terrace**, from where there are magical views of Popocatépetl and Ixtaccíhuatl, both of which seem really close here, their snowy peaks glistening on less smoggy days.

Walking through the dark recesses of the museum, note the ceilings, each with individual mosaic designs, and even the floor of the rooftop terrace, which is inlaid with snake, dog and frog forms, distinct but barely noticeable if you're not looking for them. As you leave the main museum, you'll see a low building diagonally to the left, which houses temporary exhibitions and is worth a visit if only to get a sense of the underlying volcanic rock – part of El Pedregal (see opposite) – which was hewn away to provide building materials for the museum.

**To get here** from the Xotepingo Tren Ligero station, follow the signs to the Calle Museo exit, double back at the bottom of the steps and take the first left down Museo. After 100m, cross División del Norte, and it's about 500m ahead on your right. On the way, *Antojito Berenice*, Museo 71, is a good little place to stop for a comida corrida.

### Museo Dolores Olmedo Patiño

To see a good deal more of Rivera's work (the largest private collection anywhere), and to experience one of the city's finest museums, head ten stops further along the Tren Ligero line to the **Museo Dolores Olmedo Patiño**

(Tues–Sun 10am–6pm; M$35, free on Tues; Tren Ligero La Noria). The museum sits amid peaceful and beautifully tended grounds where peacocks strut, oblivious of the busy streets outside. It is built into a seventeenth-century mansion, donated in 1994 by the elderly Dolores Olmedo, a wealthy collector and longtime friend and patron of Rivera's. Over the years she amassed over 130 of his works, all of which are on display here. They span his career, from his Cubist experimentation in the early twentieth century through self-portraits (exhibiting varying degrees of flattery) to 25 sunsets painted in Acapulco from the balcony of his patron's house. The collection is immensely varied, making this perhaps the best place to get a true sense of just how versatile a master he was. Look particularly for three large and striking nudes from the early 1940s, and sketches for his famous paintings of calla lilies.

Rivera's work is reason enough to come here, but the museum also has an outstanding collection of two dozen paintings by **Frida Kahlo**. With the works arranged in approximate chronological order, it is easy to see her development as an artist, from the Riveraesque approach of early works such as 1929's *The Bus*, to her infinitely more powerful self-portraits. Many of her finest works are here, including *Henry Ford Hospital, A Few Small Pricks, The Broken Column* and *Self-Portrait with Monkey*, the latter featuring a Xoloitzcuintle, a pre-Columbian grey-skinned, hairless dog. To see these creatures in the flesh, wander out into the garden where a few are still kept. There's also a portrait of Kahlo by Rivera elsewhere in the museum in a pastiche of her own style.

Though easily overshadowed by the Rivera and Kahlo pieces, there is also a worthwhile collection of wood-block prints done by **Angelina Beloff**, Diego's first wife, featuring scenes from Mexico and her native Russia.

**To get to the museum** from La Noria Tren Ligero station, go straight ahead from the exit and take the first left. The museum is a couple of minutes' walk on your left.

## Xochimilco

The **floating gardens** adjoining the suburb of **Xochimilco** (Tren Ligero Xochimilco) offer an intense carnival atmosphere every weekend and are likely to be one of your most memorable experiences of the city. Considerable effort has been expended in recent years to clean up the canals and maintain the water levels that had been dropping here, so Xochimilco ("place of the flower fields" in Nahuatl) looks set to remain the most popular Sunday outing for thousands of Mexicans. It's also the one place where you get some feel for the ancient city and its waterborne commerce, thriving markets and dazzling colour – or at least an idealized view of it. Rent any of the colourful boats and you'll be ferried around miles of canals, continually harangued by women selling flowers, fruit and hot food from tiny canoes, or even by larger vessels bearing marimba players and entire mariachi bands who, for a small fee, will grapple alongside you and blast out a couple of numbers. The floating gardens themselves are no more floating than the *Titanic*: following the old Aztec methods of making the lake fertile, these *chinampas* are formed by a raft of mud and reeds, firmly rooted to the bottom by the plants. The scene now appears like a series of canals cut through dry land, but the area is still a very important gardening and flower-producing centre for the city. If you wander the streets of Xochimilco town you'll find garden centres everywhere, with wonderful flowers and fruit in the **market** that enlivens the town centre for much of Saturday (though whether it's healthy to eat food raised on these dirty waters is open to question).

△ Lanchas, Xochimilco

*Lanchas* (launches) cost around M$100–120 per hour for one person, a couple or a group of up to twelve or even eighteen people. Prices should be posted up at the *embarcadero* (quay), but there's a long tradition of milking tourists here, so be certain of what you've agreed on before parting with any money. Remember that there are likely to be sundry **extras**, including the cold beers thoughtfully provided by the boatman, and any flowers, food or music you find yourself accepting on your way. You'll be encouraged to go for two hours, but try to avoid paying upfront or you're likely to get only an hour and a half, which will include a visit to the garden centre of their choice. The boatman won't like it, but you can always take your business elsewhere. Also, be clear which boat you are getting or you are liable to be shuffled to an inferior and less attractive model. You can rent a boat on any weekday for a little less-crowded cruising, but Sunday is by far the most popular and animated day; Saturdays are lively, too, partly because of the produce market. Off the huge central plaza is the lovely sixteenth-century church of **San Bernardino**, full on Sundays with a succession of people paying homage and leaving offerings at one of its many chapels; in the plaza itself there are usually bands playing or mime artists entertaining the crowds.

For the easiest **approach to Xochimilco**, take the Metro to Tasqueña station (line 2) and the Tren Ligero from there to Xochimilco (end of the line); there are also buses and *peseros* from Tasqueña as well as buses direct from the city centre, down Insurgentes and around the *periférico* or straight down the Calzada de Tlalpan. On Sundays many extra services are laid on. To get a boat, go straight ahead from the Tren Ligero station exit and follow the "embarcaderos" signs (about a 10min walk).

# North of the centre

Compared to the southern suburbs, the area north of the city centre has less to offer, but two sites of compelling interest – the emotive **Plaza de las Tres**

**Culturas** and the great **Basílica de Guadalupe** – are worth an afternoon of your attention. Further out, and harder to get to, you'll find the pyramids of **Tenayuca** and **Santa Cecilia**, the two most dramatically preserved remains of Aztec architecture in the city.

## Plaza de las Tres Culturas

Site of the ancient city of Tlatelolco, the **Plaza de las Tres Culturas** should be your first stop. Today, a lovely **colonial church** rises in the midst of the **excavated ruins**, which are in turn surrounded by a **high-rise housing complex**: all three great cultures of Mexico side by side.

Although there is a Tlatelolco Metro station (line 3), the easiest way **to get to** the Plaza de las Tres Culturas is to take Metro lines 8 or B to Garibaldi and then walk for ten minutes northwards along Lázaro Cárdenas. Alternatively, catch one of the buses headed north along Lázaro Cárdenas from near Bellas Artes, or take "La Villa" buses and *peseros* which pass within about three blocks along Reforma on their way to Guadalupe.

### The ruins

The ancient ruins of **Tlatelolco** (daily 9am–7pm; free; Metro Garibaldi – from the exit, cross Reforma and head north up Lázaro Cárdenas, where you'll find it after 400m on your right) were once the core of a city considerably more ancient than Tenochtitlán, based on a separate but nearby island in the lake. For a long time, its people existed under independent rule in close alliance with the Aztecs of Tenochtitlán, but it was by far the most important commercial and market centre in the valley; even after its annexation to the Aztec empire in 1473 Tlatelolco retained this role. When **Cortés** and his troops arrived, they marvelled at the size and order of the Tlatelolco market. Cortés himself estimated that some 60,000 people – buyers and sellers – came and went each day, and Bernal Díaz wrote:

> **We were astounded at the great number of people and the quantities of merchandise, and at the orderliness and good arrangements that prevailed . . . every kind of goods was kept separate and had its fixed place marked for it . . . Some of the soldiers among us who had been in many parts of the world, in Constantinople, in Rome, and all over Italy, said that they had never seen a market so well laid out, so large, so orderly, and so full of people.**

In 1521 the besieged **Aztecs** made their final stand here, and a plaque in the middle of the plaza recalls that struggle: "On the 13th of August 1521", it reads, "defended by the heroic Cuauhtémoc, Tlatelolco fell under the power of Hernan Cortés. It was neither a triumph nor a defeat, but the painful birth of the mixed race that is the Mexico of today". The ruins are a pale reflection of the ancient city – the original temples, whose scale can be inferred from the size of the bases – rivalled those in Tenochtitlán. The chief temple, for example, had reached its eleventh rebuilding by the time of the Conquest – what you see now corresponds to the second stage, and by the time nine more had been superimposed it would certainly have risen much higher than the church that was built from its stones. On top was likely a double sanctuary similar to that on the Templo Mayor of Tenochtitlán. The smaller structures include a square **tzompantli**, or wall of skulls, near which nearly two hundred human skulls were discovered, all with holes through the temples – presumably the result of having been displayed side by side on long poles around the sides of the building.

## The church and other buildings around the plaza

The adjacent **church** (still used and not considered part of the ruins) on the site was erected in 1609, replacing an earlier Franciscan monastery. Parts of this survive, arranged about the cloister. In the early years after the Conquest, the friars established a college at which they instructed the sons of the Aztec nobility in European ways, teaching them Spanish, Latin and Christianity. Bernardino de Sahagún was one of the teachers, and it was here that he wrote down many of the customs and traditions of the natives, compiling the most important existing record of daily Aztec life in the process.

The **modern buildings** that surround the plaza – mostly a rather ugly 1960s housing project but including the Ministry of Foreign Affairs – represent the third culture. The contemporary state of Mexico was rather brutally represented here on October 2, 1968, when troops and tanks were ordered to fire on an almost 250,000-strong **student demonstration**. It was the culmination of several months of student protests over the government's social and educational policies, which the authorities were determined to subdue with only ten days left before the Olympic Games opened in the city. Records of the death toll vary from an official figure at the time of thirty to student estimates of more than five hundred, but it seems clear today that hundreds is more accurate than tens. Mexican philosopher Octavio Paz saw the violence as part of the cycle of history – a ritual slaughter to recall the Aztec sacrifices here – but it's perhaps better seen as an example of at least one thread of continuity between all Mexico's civilizations: the cheapness of life and the harsh brutality of their rulers.

## Basílica de Nuestra Señora de Guadalupe

The **Basílica de Nuestra Señora de Guadalupe** (Metro La Villa Basílica, line 6) is in fact a whole series of churches, chapels and shrines set around an enormous stone-flagged plaza and climbing up the rocky hillock where the miracles that led to its foundation occurred. The basilica can be reached by Metro, by **buses** and **peseros** north along Reforma ("Metro La Villa"), or by **trolleybus** along Reforma from Metro Hidalgo ("Indios Verdes").

The **Virgin of Guadalupe**, Mexico's first indigenous saint, is still the nation's most popular – you'll see her image in churches throughout the country. The Virgin's banner has been fought under by both sides of almost every conflict the nation has ever seen, most famously when Hidalgo seized on it as the flag of Mexican Independence. According to the legend, a Christianized native, **Juan Diego**, was walking over the hill here (formerly dedicated to the Aztec earth goddess Tonantzin) on his way to the monastery at Tlatelolco one morning in December 1531, when he was stopped by a brilliant vision of the Virgin, who ordered him, in Nahuatl, to go to the bishop and tell him to build a church on the hill. Bishop Juan de Zumarraga was unimpressed until, on December 12, the Virgin reappeared, ordering Diego to gather roses from the top of the hill and take them to the bishop. Doing so, he bundled the flowers in his cloak, and when he opened it before the bishop he found the image of the dark-skinned Virgin imprinted into the cloth. Today the cloak hangs above the altar in the gigantic modern basilica, which takes its name from the celebrated (and equally swarthy) Virgin in the monastery of Guadalupe in Spain.

The first church here was built in 1533, but the large Baroque basilica you see now – mostly impressive for its size – was completely reconstructed in the eighteenth century and again remodelled in the nineteenth and twentieth. Around the back, the **Museo de la Basílica de Guadalupe**

(Tues–Sun 10am–6pm; M$5) contains a large collection of ex-votos and some of the church's religious art treasures, including a series of slightly insipid early eighteenth-century canvases by José de Ibarra and more powerful oils by Miguel Cabrera and Cristóbal de Villalpando.

To the left of the great plaza is the modern home of the image – a huge **church** built in 1976 with space inside for 10,000 worshippers and for perhaps four times that when the great doors all round are thrown open to the crowds, as they are pretty much every Sunday. You'll find it crowded whenever you visit, and there seems to be a service permanently in progress. The famous cloak, framed in gold and silver, hangs above the main altar. To prevent anyone lingering too long at the spot right underneath you must board a travelling walkway and admire the image as you glide respectfully by.

From the plaza you can walk round to the right and up the hill past a series of little chapels associated with the Virgin's appearance. Loveliest is the **Capilla del Pocito**, in which there is a well said to have sprung forth during one of the apparitions. Built in the eighteenth century, it consists of two linked elliptical chapels, one smaller and one larger, both with colourful tiled domes and magnificently decorated interiors. On the very top of the hill, the **Capilla de las Rosas** marks the spot where the miraculous roses grew.

Around all this, there swirls a stream of humanity – pilgrims, sightseers, priests and salesmen offering candles, souvenirs, pictures of the Virgin, snacks and any number of mementoes. On **December 12**, the anniversary of the second apparition, their numbers swell to hundreds of thousands (newspaper reports claim millions). You'll see the pilgrims on the approach roads to the capital for several days beforehand, many covering the last kilometres on their knees in an act of penance or devotion. For others, though, the day is more of a vast fiesta, with dancing, singing and drinking.

## Tenayuca and Santa Cecilia Acatitlán

In the extreme north of the city, just outside the boundaries of the Distrito Federal, lie the country's two most wholly preserved examples of **Aztec**-style architecture. They're a little hard to reach by public transport, but thoroughly repay the effort involved if you've an interest in the Aztecs. **Tenayuca** is just off the Avenida de los Cien Metros, some 6km north of the Terminal del Norte. Take the Metro to Deportivo 18 de Marzo (five blocks west of the Basílica de Nuestra Señora de Guadalupe) or La Raza and catch the "Ruta 88" *pesero* northward up Insurgentes to Tenayuca (though be warned that not all "Ruta 88" *peseros* go to Tenayuca, so check first). There are also "Tenayuca" *peseros* plying Lázaro Cárdenas anywhere north of Bellas Artes: ask the driver to drop you at the *pirámide*. *Peseros* take around forty minutes from Deportivo 18 de Marzo.

Route #88 (as well as #79) continues from Tenayuca to **Santa Cecilia Acatitlán**; alternatively, it's a twenty-minute walk, or short taxi ride, from Tenayuca. Some bus tours take both in on their way to Tula and Tepotzotlán. To return to the city from here, catch a *pesero* to Metro Deportivo 18 de Marzo (lines 3 and 6).

### Tenayuca

The twenty-metre-high **Pirámide de Tenayuca** (Tues–Sun 10am–5pm; M$30), plonked right in the main square of the suburb of the same name, is another site that predates Tenochtitlán by a long chalk. Indeed, there are those who claim it was the capital of the tribe that destroyed Tula. In this, its history closely mirrors almost all other valley settlements: a barbarian tribe from the north invades, conquers all before it, settles in a city and becomes civilized, borrowing much of its culture from its predecessors, before being overcome by the next wave of migrants. There's little evidence that Tenayuca ever controlled a large empire, but it was a powerful city and provides one of the most concrete links between the Toltecs and the Aztecs. The pyramid that survives dates from the period of Aztec dominance and is an almost perfect miniature replica of the great temples of Tlatelolco and Tenochtitlán. Here the structure and the monumental double stairway are intact – only the twin sanctuaries at the top and the brightly painted decorations would be needed for it to open for sacrifices again tomorrow. This is the sixth superimposition; five earlier pyramids (the first dating from the early thirteenth century) are contained within it and are revealed in places by excavations which took place in the 1920s. Originally there was a seventh layer built on top, of which some traces remain.

The most unusual and striking feature of Tenayuca's pyramid is the border of interlocking stone **snakes** that must originally have surrounded the entire building – well over a hundred of them survive. Notice also the two coiled snakes (one a little way up the north face, the other at the foot of the south face) known as the "turquoise serpents". Their crests are crowned with stars and aligned with the sun's position at the solstice.

### Santa Cecilia Acatitlán

A road leads north from Tenayuca to **Santa Cecilia Acatitlán** (Tues–Sun 10am–5pm; M$30), where there's another pyramid – much smaller and simpler but wholly restored and remarkably beautiful with its clean lines. When first encountered by the Spanish, this was a temple with a double staircase very similar to the others, but the outer structure was stripped away during excavation to reveal an earlier, well-preserved building inside. It's a very plain structure, rising in four steps to a single-roofed shrine approached by a ramped stairway. The studded decorations around the roof represent either skulls or stars. You approach the pyramid through a small museum in a colonial house, whose displays and grounds are both well worth a look.

## Eating

**Eating out** seems to be the main pastime in the capital, with reasonably priced restaurants, cafés, *taquerías* and juice stands on every block. As throughout the country, those on a tight budget wanting to eat well should make their main meal a late lunch-time comida. Lunch is still the biggest meal for working people and more expensive evening dining is the habit of the upper classes.

**Costs** vary enormously. You can get a decent **comida corrida** pretty much anywhere in town, even in the fancier neighbourhoods (though not in Polanco or Condesa), for M$30–60. Otherwise, there are excellent bargains to be found all over the city in small restaurants and *taquerías*, but as you move up into the mid-range places you can expect to pay something approaching what you would at home. At the top end you can soon find yourself paying big money, especially if you order something decent from the wine list.

The choice of where to eat is almost limitless in Mexico City, ranging from traditional coffeehouses to fast-food lunch counters, and taking in **Japanese**, **French**, **Spanish**, expensive **international** and rock-bottom **Mexican** cooking along the way. There's even a small cluster of **Chinese** restaurants lining Dolores, just south of the Alameda. There are also traditional food stalls in **markets** throughout the city: Merced is the biggest, but not a terribly pleasant place to eat. At the back of the Plaza Garibaldi, however, there's a market hall given over to nothing but food stands, each vociferously competing with its neighbours. Mexico City also abounds in **rosticerías**, roast chicken shops, serving tasty set meals and crispy chicken with beer in a jolly atmosphere. There are quite a few good ones on 5 de Febrero. For lighter, sweeter fare, try a **jugería** (juice bar) or a **pastelería** (cake shop). Both are good bets for flavourful and inexpensive breakfasts.

More so than anywhere else in the country, Mexico City is flooded with **chain restaurants**. American franchise establishments are well represented downtown and in the wealthier suburbs, but they're not especially cheap by Mexican standards. Slightly classier Mexican chains are found in many of the same areas. The best known is *Sanborn's*, also not particularly inexpensive, but good for a light breakfast or reasonably authentic Mexican food tailored to foreign tastes: the most interesting by far is the flagship, at Casa de los Azulejos (see below). *VIPS* is another chain restaurant that serves somewhat sanitized Mexican dishes in an American diner atmosphere. On the whole, though, you'll do better with a comida corrida.

The area **around the Zócalo** and west through to the **Alameda** is packed with places to eat, many of which cater to office workers and to tourists. The selection is fine for grabbing something while you're seeing the sights but, with a few notable exceptions, you're better off elsewhere for serious dining. Most visitors seem to end up eating in the **Zona Rosa**, where there's a huge stock of more upmarket places wedged into a few blocks. The standard is high and new places open all the time, but by far the most active area for cafés and mid-range restaurants is **Condesa**, about twenty minutes' walk south of the Zona. We've mentioned a few in this area, but they are really just starting points, and the real pleasure is in simply wandering around and seeing what grabs your fancy. Top-class restaurants are mostly concentrated in **Polanco**. The southern suburbs of **San Ángel** and **Coyoacán** are also good hunting grounds and it is worth sticking around for your evening meal after a day's sightseeing.

**Dress standards** are mostly casual, but the better the restaurant the more out of place you'll feel in sneakers and a T-shirt. A few of the very best restaurants require jacket and tie. Something else to look out for that is becoming common in the better restaurants is a **cover charge** of M$10–50 per head that is automatically added to the bill.

Unless otherwise noted, the establishments below are marked on the "Central Mexico City" map (see pp.416–417).

### Around the Zócalo

**Café Bertico** Madero 66. Spacious and friendly café specializing in pasta dishes (M$63), gelati (M$20) and even sushi (from M$45). Also good for breakfast and great coffee. Metro Zócalo.

**Café de Tacuba** Tacuba 28. Good coffee and excellent food at a price, though this doesn't deter the folk who've been packing it out since 1912. One of the country's top rock bands is sponsored by the café and thus bears its name. Metro Allende.

**Café Emir** Uruguay 45. Modernized café that's been operating since 1936 and serves good espresso, empanadas and a Mexican variation on baklava. Metro Zócalo.

**Café el Popular** 5 de Mayo 52. Cheap place serving simple food 24hr a day. It's almost always crowded, despite the perennially surly service. The turnover is pretty fast, so it's great for breakfast (M$30–43), coffee and snacks. There is a second branch called *Café la Pagoda* at 5 de Mayo 10. Metro Allende.

**Casa de los Azulejos** Madero 4. Flagship *Sanborn's* restaurant in a wonderful sixteenth-century building (see p.427), with prime seating around a fountain in an enclosed three-storey courtyard. Food is *Sanborn's* stock in trade of well-prepared Mexican staples, though a little overpriced of course for what you get. Breakfasts go for M$60–90, chicken fajitas for M$90 and comidas corridas for M$90–140. Metro Bellas Artes.

**Danubio** Uruguay 3 ⓣ55/5512-0912, ⓦwww.danubio.com. Established restaurant that has specialized in seafood since 1936. As ever, the best deals are the set lunches, in this case a full six courses for M$130, though you can also order from the menu, with most dishes priced at M$90–150. Metro San Juan de Letrán.

**Dulcería de Celaya** 5 de Mayo 39. A wonderful shop for sweet lovers, with all kinds of sticky delights including *dulce de membrillo* and candied-fruit *comates*. Metro Allende.

**El Generalito** Filomeno Mata 18. A small but nicely done-out diner, with breakfasts (M$20–30) and comidas corridas (M$40) in pleasant surroundings. Metro Allende.

**Los Girasoles** Plaza Manuel Tolsá, Tacuba 8/10, ⓣ55/5510-3281, ⓦwww.restaurantelosgirasoles.com. One of the most appealing restaurants in the centre, with Mediterranean decor, a casual atmosphere and great food served up at moderate prices. Start with the blue corn quesadillas (M$40) and perhaps follow with the turkey in tamarind sauce (M$100) served up on an ornate pewter platter bursting with sunflowers, then finish with a rose-petal pie (M$60) and espresso. Closes 9pm on Sun, midnight other days. Metro Allende.

**Hostería de Santo Domingo** Belisario Dominguez 72 ⓣ55/5526-5276. Full of character, this moderately priced restaurant in part of a former convent looks great, with decorations hanging from the ceiling, artesanía all over the walls and, usually, a pianist and singer in the corner. The food, though good, isn't quite as good as they seem to think it is; even their signature *chiles en nogada* (M$180) is better done elsewhere. Note that a compulsory tip is added to the bill. Metro Allende.

**Jugos Canada** 5 de Mayo 49. Very good torta and juice bar with decent prices, despite its central location. Metro Allende.

**Kam Ling** Cerrada de 5 de Mayo 14 ⓣ55/5521-5661. Straightforward Chinese food in seriously large proportions to eat in or take away. Set menus go for M$50–100, and there are individual dishes (M$50–80) such as squid and green pepper in oyster sauce, and chicken and vegetables, all washed down with huge pots of jasmine tea (M$20). Metro Allende.

**Pastelería Ideal** Uruguay 74. Bakery with a good range of pastries, but worth a special visit to see the huge array of outrageously ornate wedding cakes. Metro San Juan de Letrán.

**Restaurant Bar Chon** Regina 160. Eating here is almost a dare, with starters such as *mescal* worms, *escamoles* (ant eggs) or *chapulines* (grasshoppers), served with or without guacamole. If you prefer a main course from outside the insect kingdom, there's frogs' legs, armadillo in mango sauce or *chamorro al pilbil* (leg of pork barbecued in a hole in the ground). All in all, a veritable eating adventure, with main courses at M$100–180. Metro Merced.

**Tacos Beguis** Isabel la Católica 10. Bustling little restaurant serving a great range of tacos (from M$10), tortas, tostadas and breakfasts. There's also a good-value lunch-time menu at M$40. Metro Allende.

**Teposnieves** Donceles 4. Local firm selling delicious sorbets in a range of fruit flavours, plus some unlikely ones, such as peanut, rice and tequila. Metro Bellas Artes.

**La Terraza** 7th floor of *Hotel Majestic* (see p.410). Restaurant with a great terrace that's perfect for watching Zócalo life go by over a coffee or a beer (M$20–30). The buffet breakfast (7–11am; M$120) and buffet *menú comercial* (Mon–Fri 1–5pm; M$90) are also both good, and in the evening there's à la carte dining with well-prepared Mexican standards for M$100–120, with a barbecue *buffet ranchero* for lunch at weekends (Sat & Sun 1–5pm; M$160). Metro Zócalo.

**La Vasconia** Tacuba 73. One of the best bread and cake shops in the centre, with a huge range of Mexican staples at low prices. Metro Allende.

**El Vegetariano** Filomeno Mata 13. Nonsmoking vegetarian restaurant that's inexplicably decorated with mountain photos. The best deal is usually the healthy four-course *menú del día* (M$63). Metro Zócalo.

**Vegetariano Madero** upstairs at Madero 56. This sunny, spacious vegetarian restaurant lurks behind an unprepossessing stairway entrance but offers some of the best-value vegetarian food around, usually with piano accompaniment at lunch time. The four-course M$50 *menú del día* is especially good value, though they also do great breakfasts (from 8am). Metro Zócalo.

## Around the Alameda

**Café del Palacio** inside Bellas Artes. An elegant restaurant in Art Deco surroundings. Enjoy limited views of Tamayo's murals as you dine amid business lunchers and pre-theatre diners. Meals are moderately priced, especially if you go for the two-course *menú del Palacio* (available 2–5pm; M$200). Dishes include Waldorf salad, turkey breast and blue cheese sandwich, duck in hibiscus sauce, and almond and pear tart, plus there's a decent wine list. Closes 5.30pm. Metro Bellas Artes.

**Cafetería El Cuadrilatero** Luis Moya 73. Like Mexico City's other wrestling cafés, *El Cuadrilatero* ("the ring") is owned and run by an ex-wrestler whose old masks are framed on the walls along with photos of his glory days. The food's good, including standard Mexican mains, burgers and tortas (M$25–120) that are big enough for a wrestler or two mere mortals (the biggest of all comes free if you can eat it yourself in under 15min). Metro Balderas.

**Chung King** Dolores 27. Reasonable chop suey house, one of several in the city's mini-Chinatown, serving the usual standards (chop suey, chow mein, sweet and sour, etc). Set meals M$70–190. Metro Bellas Artes.

## Zona Rosa

The establishments listed below are marked on the "Zona Rosa, Roma & Condesa" map (see p.436).

**Barro-Barroco** Londres 211. Small and peaceful café a little away from the main bustle of the Zona, serving coffee, baguettes, breakfasts and light meals at prices that are modest for the area. Metro Insurgentes.

**Blah Blah Café** Londres 171, at Florencia. Café, bar and Argentine grill, where an executive steak lunch will set you back around M$140. Metro Insurgentes.

**Champs Elysées** Reforma 316 ⓣ55/5514-0450. One of the capital's finer French restaurants, this place has been reliably feeding the Mexico City elite for almost forty years. Look out on El Ángel as you feast on truly excellent food, complemented by something from the extensive wine list, delicate desserts and a great cheeseboard. Expect to pay M$500 for a full meal. Reservations required. Closed Sun. Metro Insurgentes.

**La Lanterna** Reforma 458, at Toledo ⓣ55/5207-9969. Long-standing and convivial trattoria with an intimate and suitably Italian feel, enhanced by pasta freshly made in-house and combined with some delicious sauces (M$110). The *segundi piatti* (M$140–150) are equally wonderful. Pizzas go for M$120. Metro Insurgentes.

**Restaurante Vegetariano Yug** Varsovia 3 ⓦwww.yug.com.mx. Worthy contact point for vegetarians and vegans, with set breakfasts, salads and *antojitos* in bright cheery surroundings. There's a particularly good buffet lunch upstairs (1–5pm; Mon–Fri M$70, Sat & Sun M$80) and a great comida corrida (M$60–70). Mon–Fri 7am–9pm, Sat & Sun 8.30am–8pm. Metro Insurgentes.

**El Trompito** Londres 119. If you're looking for a cheap snack amid the Zona's tourist traps, this modest little *taquería* could be the oasis you need, with tacos, tortas and *alambres* (small kebabs) at low prices in clean surroundings. Metro Insurgentes.

## Condesa

The establishments listed below are marked on the "Zona Rosa, Roma & Condesa" map (see p.436).

**Agapi Mu** Alfonso Reyes 96 ⓣ55/5286-1384, ⓦwww.agapimu.com.mx. About the best Greek restaurant in the city, but very low-key and affordable as long as you don't go too mad on the *retsina* and Hungarian wines. It's especially fun from Thurs to Sat, when there's live music and Greek dancing. Closes at 6pm on Sun and Mon. Metro Juanacatlán or Patriotismo.

**Bellini's** 45th floor, World Trade Center, Av de las Naciones ⓣ55/9000-8325 or 05. Revolving restaurant at the top of the city's tallest building (see p.449), where business people come to impress their clients, and the romantically inclined come for a candlelit dinner. Dishes from an international menu are prepared to the highest standards and service is impeccable. Obviously not the cheapest place in town, but not stupidly expensive either: even at the top end of the menu, you can start with smoked salmon, caviar and avocado for M$190, followed by red snapper in lobster and brandy sauce for M$180.

**Café la Gloria** Vicente Suarez 43. Pleasant little bistro serving pasta dishes, salads or the likes of chicken in tarragon sauce (M$88) or *filet mignon* (M$166). Tasty desserts include profiteroles, chocolate mousse or blueberry cheesecake. Metro Patriotismo or Juanacatlán.

**Don Asado** Michoacán 77 ⓣ55/5286-0789, ⓦwww.donasado.com. Wonderful char-grilled steaks (M$100–140) and *chivitos* (pork steaks; M$85–120) are the speciality of this Uruguayan restaurant. It's invariably full, with patrons spilling onto the street, so it's worth booking ahead. Metro Patriotismo or Juanacatlán.

**Fonda Garufa** Michoacán 93 ⓣ55/5286-8295. Popular Argentine and Italian restaurant with plenty of streetside tables where you can tuck into excellent steaks or something from their extensive range of inventive pasta dishes, all at moderate prices. Metro Patriotismo or Juanacatlán.

**Koffie! Café** Amsterdam 308, at Celaya. Modern café spilling out onto a quiet leafy street, making it a great spot for a M$45–60 weekend breakfast, especially if you like good strong coffee. Later on, Italian salads, pasta dishes and stuffed baguettes all come in at around M$50–70. Metro Sevilla.
**Neve Gelato** Michoacán 126. They do crepes and cakes here, but what draws the crowds is the luscious ice cream in flavours fruity (soursop, black cherry, *mamey*) or nutty (toasted almond, amaretto, hazelnut, tiramisú). One scoop for M$20, two scoops for M$35. Metro Patriotismo or Juanacatlán.
**Segundo Paso Café** Amsterdam 76, at Parras. Relaxed, low-lit corner restaurant and café, open on both sides to pavement seating. Salads, pasta dishes and mains such as chicken breast served with *al dente* vegetables are all well prepared. Most mains M$70–130. Metro Juanacatlán.
**El Zorzal** corner of Alfonso Reyes and Tamaulipas ⓣ55/5273-6023. Argentine steakhouse serving up some juicy slices of steer at M$120–200, and *alfajor* pastries or crepes filled with *dulce de leche* for dessert. Metro Patriotismo.

### Polanco

The establishments listed below are marked on the "Chapultepec Park & Polanco" map (see p.438).
**Bistro Charlotte** Lope de Vega 341, at Presidente Masaryk ⓣ55/5105-4194. Great little lunch-time bistro where they change the menu every fortnight or so and always offer an interesting and international selection (roast beef and Yorkshire pudding is not unknown). Main courses M$95–170. Only open 1–6pm, and closed Sat. Metro Polanco.
**La Ciudad de Colima** Horacio 522, at Lamartine. Smashing little *jugería* with some unusual *jugos* such as starfruit (*carambola*), kiwi, sapodilla (*zapote*) and *mamey*. Metro Polanco.
**Denominación de Origen** Hegel 406, at Presidente Masaryk ⓣ55/5255-0612, ⓦwww.denominaciondeorigendo.com.mx. Classy modern Spanish restaurant with a long bar, lots of whole hams, a whiff of cigars and dishes like *bacalao a la vizcaína* (saltfish Basque-style, in tomato sauce), confit of rabbit with cava or a superb Andalucian gazpacho. Main courses go for M$125–250. Metro Polanco.
**Eltuca's** Newton 116, at Lamartine ⓣ55/5545-8388 or 9. Forget the rubbish they sell at the international franchise chains: what you get here are proper burgers, made from sirloin steak and grilled over charcoal. You don't get them flipped in an instant, but they're worth the wait, and for non-carnivores there are salads and veggieburgers too. Home delivery available within Polanco. Metro Polanco.
**Los Girasoles** Presidente Masaryk 275 ⓣ55/5282-3981, ⓦwww.restaurantelosgirasoles.com. Polanco branch of the renowned downtown eatery (see p.467), upstairs in a swish little shopping mall. Main courses around M$150. Metro Polanco.
**La Petite France** Presidente Masaryk 360 ⓣ55/5281-0327. Swanky French restaurant whose starters include no fewer than four different snail dishes, with main courses such as *coq au vin*, fondue or roast duck in hibiscus sauce, but no frogs' legs. Main courses around M$150. Metro Polanco.
**Terra de Galicia** Alejandro Dumas 7, at Campos Elisios ⓣ55/5280-7737. Sleek, modern restaurant and tapas bar, all frosted glass and pinewood, specializing in the cuisine of Galicia, the north-western-most region of Spain. As well as great tapas and Spanish beer (should you want it – Mexican beer is frankly a lot better), there are Galician specialities such as *callos gallegos* (tripe Galician-style, M$55), or the classic Galician signature dish, *pulpo gallego* (octopus seared in olive oil with paprika, M$180). Metro Polanco.
**El Zorzal** corner of Anatole France and Oscar Wilde ⓣ55/5280-0111. Polanco branch of the Condesa Argentine steakhouse (see above). Metro Polanco.

### San Ángel and south

Establishments in San Ángel are marked on the "Coyoacán & San Ángel" map (see p.453).
**Addetto** Revolución 1382 ⓣ55/5663-5434. Smart modern Italian establishment combining a deli and spacious dining areas. It is a little inconveniently sited, but worth the journey for delightfully sticky risotto dishes (M$80–140), pasta (M$50–160) and a wide range of mains (M$100–170). There's a M$20 per head cover. Metro Barranca del Muerto.
**El Arroyo** Insurgentes Sur 4003, Tlalpan, 6km south of San Ángel ⓣ55/5573-4344. Well off the beaten path, and open only until 8pm daily, but worth the journey, this unusual restaurant comes complete with its own small bullring (used by novice bullfighters in bloodless *corridas* from April to Oct) and has almost a dozen dining areas that can jointly serve over 2500 diners. As you'd imagine, there's always a lively atmosphere, helped along by mariachis, but the Mexican food is good too, and they usually keep at least four types of flavoured *pulque*.
**Café Solo Dios** Plaza San Jacinto 2. Popular hole-in-the-wall café and takeout spot with great

espressos, frappés and the usual variations, made from fine Chiapas beans.

**Crêperie du Soleil** Madero 4-C. Small and peaceful café that's good for an espresso, cakes and, of course, crepes.

**Fonda San Ángel** Plaza San Jacinto 3 ⓣ55/5550-1641, ⓦwww.fondasanangel.com.mx. Moderately priced restaurant specializing in contemporary Mexican cuisine. Main courses M$90–120.

**San Ángel Inn** Diego Rivera 50 at Altavista ⓣ55/5616-2222. Built in the late seventeenth century, this former Carmelite monastery has been an elegant restaurant since 1915, with a sumptuous garden setting, linen tablecloths, heavy wooden furniture and a refined air (jackets required for men). Just about every visiting dignitary comes here, as do many tourists (it is included on many day-trip itineraries). The menu has some European overtones, but is predominantly Mexican, featuring some slightly less common dishes such as *huitlacoche*, a kind of fungus that grows on corn, served in crepes. Expect to pay at least M$250 per head plus wine (M$60–100 a glass). Reservations required.

### Coyoacán

The establishments listed below are marked on the "Coyoacán & San Ángel" map (see p.453).

**Café El Parnaso** (aka *Café Frida*) Carillo Puerto 2. Predominantly sidewalk café with attached bookstore; a good spot for light snacks or just a coffee.

**El Globo** corner Hidalgo and Caballocalco. Local outpost of this excellent chain of French-inspired bakeries. Pricey but very good.

**El Jolgorio** Higuera 22. Modern restaurant with an avant-garde menu, almost half of it meat-free. The imaginative combinations aren't always a success, but try one of their excellent salads (M$60–70, half-portion M$40), or one of the M$75–100 mains, including chiles stuffed with spinach and mushrooms, or some strange interpretations of Indian dishes, such as "tandoori rice" (rice with apple sauce and cashews, which are considered Indian because they're called *nueces de la India* in Spanish), or chicken breast with apple chutney, curried carrots and apple and raisin sauce. Wash your food down with one of their "spiritual" non-alcoholic cocktails.

**El Tajín** Centro Veracruzano, Miguel Ángel de Quevedo 687 ⓣ55/5659-4447. Veracruz specialities at medium to high prices; the fish dishes, such as *huachinango a la Veracruzana* and *mojarra al mojo del ajo*, are exquisite. Expect to pay around M$200 per head plus wine.

**La Vienet** Viena 112, at Abasolo. A good place for refreshments in between visits to the Kahlo and Trotsky houses, this small daytime café serves great coffee and cakes as well as breakfasts and lunch-time menus (M$110–120). Closed at weekends.

# Drinking, nightlife and entertainment

There's a vast amount going on in Mexico City, which is as much the nation's cultural and social centre as its political capital. **Bars** are dotted all over the city and range from dirt-cheap **pulquerías** and **cantinas** to upscale **lounges** and **hotel bars**, though there are unfortunately few mid-range places.

The **live music** scene has broadened appreciably in recent years, and there are venues for all kinds of bands. Two attractions are particularly worthwhile: the mariachi music in the **Plaza Garibaldi**, a thoroughly Mexican experience, and the **Ballet Folklórico**, which is unashamedly aimed at tourists but has an enduring appeal for Mexicans too.

While Mexican **theatre** tends to be rather turgid (and will of course be in Spanish), there are often excellent **classical music** concerts and **opera** or **ballet** performances by touring companies. Bellas Artes and the Auditorio Nacional are the main venues, but other downtown theatres, as well as the Polyforum and the Teatro de los Insurgentes, may have interesting shows. On most Sundays, there's a free concert in Chapultepec Park near the lake.

**Listings** for current cinema, theatre and other cultural events can be found in the weekly magazine *Tiempo Libre* (ⓦwww.tiempolibre.info), which comes out every Thursday and is available at most newsstands.

## Pulque and pulquerías

**Pulque** is the fermented sap of the maguey cactus, a species of agave that grows in the countryside north and east of Mexico City. Traditionally considered a poor man's drink, *pulque* had its heyday in the first half of the twentieth century – as beer and other drinks became more affordable, *pulque*'s stock went down. At one time there were over 1400 **pulquerías** in the capital, but today owners estimate that there are only around a hundred or so left. It's possible, however that Mexico City's *pulquerías* may yet see a revival, as the drink has seen a rise in popularity of late among young Mexicans fascinated with all things pre-Hispanic. Regardless of demand, production continues much as it has done for centuries, with barrels being shipped daily to the capital.

Unless you are looking for them, *pulquerías* are hard to spot; they're concentrated in less salubrious areas of town mostly unvisited by tourists and often have no sign, just a pair of swinging doors guarding a dark interior. Like cantinas, they are traditionally macho territory and women are more likely to receive a respectful welcome when accompanied by male friends.

These places are not set up for anything much more sophisticated than knocking back glasses of the slightly astringent, viscous white beverage, usually ladled out of barrels behind the bar. The emphasis is as much on socializing as drinking, which is a good thing since most *pulque* is only two to four percent alcohol and getting drunk requires considerable commitment. The task is made easier when pulque is blended with fresh fruit juices – pineapple, apricot, guava and many others – to form a weaker but more palatable cocktail. The most popular hunting ground is the **Plaza Garibaldi,** where *La Hermosa Hortensia* is always brightly lit and usually has several good flavours served up to a cross-section of men and women, locals and foreigners. During the day you are better off exploring the district south of Bellas Artes, where choices include *La Risa* at Mesones 71, on the corner of Callejón de Mesones (Mon–Sat 9am–9pm) and *Los Duellistas* at Aranda 30 (Mon–Sat 9am–9pm), both of which have quite a young clientele.

## Bars, clubs and live music venues

As elsewhere in the country, **cantinas** and **pulquerías** are still largely a male preserve. Though there'll often be a few women inside, most unaccompanied female tourists probably won't want to brave the back-slapping macho camaraderie. More civilized **bars**, where you might sit around and chat, are relatively thin on the ground. There are a few, but most concentrate on music, or bill themselves as **antros**, a relatively modern creation somewhere in between a bar and club where you can sit and talk (just about) or dance if the Latin pop hits get you going.

**Club**-oriented nightlife starts late, with live acts often hitting the stage after 11pm and few places really getting going before midnight. Entry can be expensive, ranging up to M$200 for men (women often get in for much less or free), though this is likely to include *bar libre*, where your drinks are free for at least part of the evening. If you stray far from your hotel and stay out after the Metro has closed for the night, be sure to get the bar or club to order a **sitio cab** for you; flagging down a cab late at night is not generally considered safe, especially if you are lost and drunk.

**Live music** venues are dotted all over town, offering anything from old-fashioned romantic ballads to cutting-edge alternative rock bands. Cuban music is particularly popular, and with Cuba just a short flight away, Mexico City provides a local but international proving ground for the island's talent.

## Around the Zócalo and the Alameda

The establishments listed below are marked on the "Central Mexico City" map (see pp.416–417).

**El Colmillo** Versailles 52. Both an *antro* and a dance club, with house, electronica, a bit of trance and other assorted beats, spread over two dancefloors and a chill-out bar area. Wed–Sat 10pm–4am. Fri M$50, Sat M$100 (often free for ladies). Metro Cuauhtémoc.

**La Hostería del Bohemio** Hidalgo 107. An alcohol-free café set around a large open courtyard of the former San Hipolito convent. Smooching couples sit at candlelit tables half-listening to romantic ballads emanating passionately from the live band in the corner. Metro Hidalgo.

**La Ópera** 5 de Mayo 10, near Bellas Artes. The best watering hole downtown, in the grand tradition of upmarket cantinas with magnificent *fin-de-siècle* decor – ornate mahogany panelling, a brass-railed bar, gilt-framed mirrors in the booths – and a bullet hole in the ceiling reputedly put there by Pancho Villa. You also can dine here, but most people come for a fairly pricey beer or cocktails in the booths or at the bar. Metro Bellas Artes.

**Pervert Lounge** Uruguay 70 ⓣ55/5518-0976. One of the centre's more cutting-edge clubs and nowhere near as sleazy as it might sound. From Thurs to Sat, the beautiful people flock here after 11pm to hear funky electronic beats, paying about M$70–100 for entry. *Club 69*, next door, is similar and equally good. Metro Allende.

**Tio Pepe** Independencia 26, at Dolores. Convivial cantina with moulded ceilings and wooden bar. Minstrels frequently drop in to bash out a few numbers, and despite the sign on the door, women are free to enter, but will probably feel more comfortable in the saloon next door. Metro Bellas Artes.

**Zinco Jazz Club** Motolina 20, at 5 de Mayo ⓣ55/5518-6369, ⓦwww.zincojazzclub.com. Small but congenial venue, really just a bar/restaurant with entertainment by local jazz bands, tucked away in the vaults beneath the Art Deco splendour of the Banco de México building. Wed–Sat 9pm–2am. Entry M$100 Thurs–Sat, free on Wed. Metro Allende.

## Zona Rosa, Condesa and Roma

The establishments listed below are marked on the "Zona Rosa, Roma & Condesa" map (see p.436).

**Cinna Bar** Nuevo Léon 67-1, at Tamaulipas, Condesa ⓣ55/5286-8456. Stylish bar with a laid-back atmosphere, Thai-ish food, chilled music and a great selection of fine tequilas, rums and flavoured vodkas. Open from 7pm. Metro Patriotismo or Sevilla.

**DJ Club Continental** Florencia 12, Zona Rosa ⓣ55/5525-6268, ⓦwww.continentaldjclub.com. Large trance and techno club featuring big-name DJs from the US, Canada and Europe. Wed–Sat 10pm–10am. M$200 entry. Metro Insurgentes.

**Gitanerías** Oaxaca 15, Roma ⓣ55/5514-2027. Flamenco club with Spanish dancer, complete with frilly skirt and castanets. Thurs–Sat from 9pm. M$120 entry. Metro Insurgentes.

**Mama Rumba** Querétaro 230, at Medellin, Roma ⓣ55/5564-6920 or 7823. Reservations are advised for this dance bar. The Hispano-Afro-Caribbean rhythms pumped out by the Cuban house band get the small dancefloor packed in no time, so come prepared to move your feet even if you don't know the steps. Open Wed–Sat 9pm–3.30am, bands come on at 11pm. Wheelchair access. Metro Insurgentes.

**El Mitote** Amsterdam 53, Condesa ⓣ55/5211-9150. Tapas bar playing Spanish and international hits to a bright, young clientele. Tues–Sat 8pm–2am. Metro Insurgentes or Chilpancingo.

**Multiforo Alicia** Cuauhtémoc 91, between Colima and Durango, Roma ⓣ55/5511-2100. "Who hasn't been to Alicia doesn't know rock music", they claim, which may be an exaggeration, but this is definitely the place to catch Mexico's latest rock *ondas*. Most of the action is on Fri & Sat, from 8.30pm, but some shows start as early as 5pm. Expect to pay M$60–70. Metro Cuauhtémoc.

**Ruta 61** Baja California 281, Condesa ⓣ55/3096-3021. Cosy little blues club with tables (reservation advised). Wed–Sat 8pm–2am; music from 10pm. M$60 entry. Metro Chilpancingo.

## Polanco

The establishments listed below are marked on the "Chapultepec Park & Polanco" map (see p.438).

**Lola** Masaryk 393 ⓣ55/5282-2297. Sleek, relaxed little discotheque playing hits of the 1980s and 1990s. Thurs–Sat 11.30pm–4am. Metro Polanco.

**Pink** Alejandro Dumas 107, at Presidente Masaryk. A fun club where the young and rich come to waggle their pretty little bottoms to the latest upbeat pop sounds. Metro Polanco.

## San Ángel and Coyoacán

The establishments listed below are marked on the "Coyoacán and San Ángel" map (see p.453).

**La Camelia** Plaza San Jacinto, San Ángel. Early evening boozing to recent US and Latin pop hits, either inside or out on the street.

**El Hijo de Cuervo** Jardín Centenario 17, Coyoacán ⓣ55/5659-5196. Dark and hip bar with seats overlooking the square and music that ranges from Latin rap to rock. There's no cover charge, and a lively evening atmosphere that runs through to 2.30am Fri night/Sat morning and Sat night/Sun morning.

**Mama Rumba** Plaza San Jacinto 14, San Ángel. Off-shoot of the popular Cuban dance bar in Roma (see opposite). Open Thurs–Sat 9pm–3.30am.

**New Orleans** Revolución 1655, San Ángel ⓣ55/5550-1908. Excellent jazz venue-cum-restaurant with very good food at moderate prices. Open Tues–Sun from 6.30pm (band on at 8.30pm), but weekends are much the liveliest unless there is some international jazz act playing. Tues–Thurs entry M$50, Fri & Sat M$75, Sun M$35.

**El Vicio** (formerly *El Hábito*) Madrid 13, Coyoacán ⓣ55/5659-1139, ⓦwww.elvicio.com.mx. Small and quirky fringe theatre and music club, mainly playing jazz.

## Plaza Garibaldi

**Plaza Garibaldi** (Metros Bellas Artes and Garibaldi) is the traditional final call on a long night around the capital's bars, and as the night wears on and the drinking continues, it can get pretty rowdy. The plaza is on Lázaro Cárdenas, five blocks north of Bellas Artes in a thoroughly sleazy area of cheap bars, grimy hotels and several brightly lit theatres offering burlesque and strip shows. Despite a high-profile police presence, **pickpockets** are always a threat and you'd be better off not coming laden down with expensive camera equipment or an obviously bulging wallet.

Hundreds of competing **mariachi** bands gather here in the evenings, all in their tight, silver-spangled *charro* finery and vast sombreros, to play for anyone who'll pay them. A typical group consists of two or four violins, a brass section of three trumpeters standing some way back so as not to drown out the others, three or four men on guitars of varying sizes, and a vocalist, though a truly macho man will rent the band and do the serenading himself. Mariachis take their name, supposedly, from the French *mariage*, it being traditional during the nineteenth-century French intervention to rent a group to play at weddings. You may also come across **norteño** bands from the border areas with their Tex-Mex brand of country music, or the softer sounds of **marimba** musicians from the south. Simply wander round the square and you'll get your fill – should you want to be individually serenaded, pick out a group and negotiate your price.

At the back of the square is a huge market hall in which a whole series of stalls serve simple food and vie furiously for customers. Alternatively, there is at least one prominent *pulquería* on the square (see box, p.471), and a number of fairly pricey restaurant/bars, which try to drown out the mariachi bands with their own canned music, and tempt customers with their no-cover entry. The last Metro leaves at midnight.

## Ballet Folklórico

The **Ballet Folklórico** (ⓣ55/5529-9320 to 22, ⓦwww.balletamalia.com.mx/eng) is a long-running, internationally famed compilation of traditional dances from all over the country, elaborately choreographed and designed, and interspersed with Mexican music and singing. Despite the billing, it isn't really very traditional – although it does include several of the more famous native dances, they are very jazzed up and incorporated into what is, in effect, a regular musical that wouldn't be out of place on Broadway.

The best place to see the Ballet Folklórico is in the original setting of the **Palacio de Bellas Artes** (see p.427), where the theatre is an attraction in itself; pressure of other events, however, occasionally forces a move to the Auditorio

△ Ballet Folklórico

Nacional in Chapultepec Park (see p.446). There are usually performances on Sunday at 9.30am and 8.30pm, and Wednesday at 8.30pm. You should try to book at least a couple of days in advance – **tickets** (M$330 for the cheap seats, M$550 for something really good) are available either from the Bellas Artes box office direct (Mon–Sat 11am–7pm, Sun 8.30am–7pm) or through Ticketmaster (ⓣ55/5325-9000) – or arrange to go with an organized tour, for which you'll pay a considerable premium.

### Cinemas

Mainstream Hollywood movies make it to Mexico just a few weeks after their release in the US and often before they get a British or European release. With the exception of movies for kids, they're almost always in their original language with subtitles, and since you'll usually only pay around M$30–50 (often reduced on Wed), a visit to the flicks can be a cheap and entertaining night out. Movies are **listed** every week in *Tiempo Libre*, as well as in most of the Spanish-language dailies.

There are **cinemas** scattered over most of city, but none near the Zócalo. One of the largest concentrations is along Insurgentes, where half a dozen multiplexes total around fifty screens in all. Handier places can be found in the Zona Rosa (Diana, Reforma 423 ⓣ55/5511-3236; Lumière Reforma, Río Guadalquivir 104, at Reforma ⓣ55/5514-0000), or in Polanco (Cinemex Casa de Arte, Anatole France 120 ⓣ55/5280-9156; Cinemark Polanco, Cervantes 397 ⓣ55/5580-0506).

## Markets and shopping

The big advantage of **shopping** in the capital is that you can get goods from all over the country and, if you are flying out of here, you don't have to lug them around the country, though of course they will usually be more expensive than at the source.

One fascinating (and occasionally frustrating) facet of shopping in the capital is the practice of devoting a whole street to one particular trade, which occurs to some extent throughout the city. There are blocks where you can buy nothing but stationery, while other areas are packed exclusively with shoe shops and still others only sell musical instruments. Due to the lack of variety in a given place – and without some luck or good directions – you can spend all day walking through markets without ever finding the items that you seek. This is a hangover from Aztec life, as their well-regulated markets were divided up according to the nature of the goods on sale, and the practice was continued by colonial planners.

Every area of the city has its own **market** selling food and essentials, and many others set up stalls for just one day a week along a suburban street. Less formal **street stalls** spring up all over the city and can take the form of anything from a New Age devotee with a sheet on the pavement selling cheap jewellery, to a relatively sophisticated stand selling pens, watches, computer hard drives and fake designer clothing and bags. The **Centro Histórico** and **Zona Rosa** are good hunting grounds, though the concentration of stalls in these areas is influenced by occasional crackdowns on this illegal but widely accepted trading. At more sensitive times you'll notice vendors alert to the presence of the authorities, and occasionally catch them packing up and sprinting off.

**Department stores** include El Palacio de Hierro at 20 de Noviembre 3, just south of the Zócalo, and Liverpool, opposite. **Sanborn's** at Madero 4, near the main post office, and with branches citywide (see Ⓦwww.sanborns.com.mx), sells books, maps and quantities of tacky souvenirs, and also has a sizeable pharmacy.

**T-shirts** and replica Mexican football shirts can be found in the *tianguis* (street stalls) on San Juan Letrán between Bellas Artes and Salto del Agua, or those in the streets north and east of the Zócalo.

For **crafts**, aside from the markets, there are the craft shops run by **FONART** (Ⓦwww.fonart.gob.mx), a government agency that promotes crafts and helps the artisans with marketing and materials. The shops are at Juárez 89 (Ⓣ55/5521-0171; Metro Hidalgo) and Reforma 116 (Ⓣ55/5328-5000 ext 53089 or 53130; Metro Cuauhtémoc). The fixed prices are usually higher than elsewhere, but it is worth visiting to check price and quality before venturing to the markets.

**Haggling** for a bargain is no longer the thrilling (or daunting) prospect it once was in Mexico City. The nation's increasing prosperity and sophistication means that most things have prices fixed. As a tourist (and especially if your Spanish is poor) you can expect people to try to bump up the price occasionally, but on the whole what you see is what you pay.

## Markets

**Bazar Sábado** Plaza San Jacinto, San Ángel. Very popular open-air art and sculpture market takes place pretty much all day Sat. On Sun it moves to Parque Sullivan, just north of the Zona Rosa (see p.436).

**Central Artesanal Buenavista** Aldama 187, just east of the former train station. Handicrafts from around the country in what is claimed to be Mexico's largest shop. Rather pricey compared to the Ciudadela and less characterful. Daily 9am–6pm. Metro Buenavista.

**Centro Artesanal de San Juan** (Mercado de Curiosidades Mexicanas) about five blocks south of the Alameda along Dolores. Modern tourist-oriented complex that's possibly the least appealing of the major artesanía markets, though there are still deals to be had (particularly in silver) provided you haggle. Mon–Sat 9am–7pm, Sun 9am–4pm. Metro San Juan de Letrán.

**Ciudadela** corner of Balderas and Emilio Donde. The best place in the capital to buy regional crafts and souvenirs from every part of the country. If you forgot to pick up a hammock in the Yucatán or some Olinalá lacquerwork in Guerrero, fear not: you can buy them here for not a great deal more. Bargaining has limited rewards. Mon–Sat 11am–7pm, Sun 11am–5pm. Metro Balderas.

**Coyoacán markets** There are two interesting markets in Coyoacán: the daily markets three blocks up from Plaza Hidalgo are typically given over to food, while on Sun a craft market converges on the plaza itself. There you can buy any manner of *típico* clothing, and lots of trendy variations. Metro Viveros.

**La Lagunilla** spreading along Rayon, a couple of blocks north of the Plaza Garibaldi. Comes closest to rivalling La Merced in size and variety, but is best visited on a Sun when the *tianguis* expands into the surrounding streets, with more stalls selling stones, used books, crafts and bric-a-brac. Get there on buses ("La Villa") heading north on Reforma, or walk from Metro Garibaldi.

**Mercado de Sonora** three blocks from La Merced on Fray Servando Teresa de Mier. This market is famous for its sale of herbal medicines, medicinal and magical plants and the various *curanderos* (indigenous herbalists) who go there. Metro La Merced.

**La Merced** corner Izazaga San Pablo and Eje 1 Ote. The city's largest market, a collection of huge modern buildings, which for all their size can't contain the vast number of traders who want to set up here. Sells almost anything you could conceive of finding in a Mexican market (and much more you'd never thought of), though fruit, vegetables and other foods take up most space. Even if you're not buying you could easily spend half a day here browsing metre-diameter columns of nopal leaves as high as a man, the stacks of dried chiles and all manner of hardware from juice presses to volcanic-stone mortars known as *molcajetes*. The Metro takes you right into the heart of things. Daily 6am–6pm. Metro La Merced.

**Palacio de las Flores** corner of Luis Moya and Ernesto Pugibet. A small market selling nothing but flowers – loose, in vast arrangements and wreaths, growing in pots, even paper and plastic. Similar markets can be found in San Ángel and Xochimilco. Metro Salto de Agua or Balderas.

## English-language books and newspapers

International weeklies are available downtown from **newspaper stands** (especially along 5 de Mayo). Sanborn's, dotted all over town, usually have a modest supply of English-language material, much of it business-oriented. The **airport** has numerous small shops partly stocked with English-language magazines and airport novels, plus a few foreign newspapers. The best bets are the Cenca store in Sala E2, and Libros y Arte between salas C and D.

**American Book Store** Bolivar 23, Centro Histórico ☎55/5512-0306. Despite the name, their stock of books in English is limited and mostly business- or computer-oriented. OK for a few paperbacks, magazines and newspapers. Mon–Sat 10am–7pm.

**Cenca** Temistocles 73, near corner of Mazaryk and Arquimedes, Polanco ☎55/5280-1666. Has a good selection of magazines, novels and even a few guidebooks, plus a good café next door for reading them all. Daily 9am–9pm. Metro Polanco.

**La Torre del Papel** Callejón de Betlemitas 6a, beside the Museo del Ejército y Fuerza, near Bellas Artes. Stocks up-to-date newspapers from all over Mexico and Latin America as well as a good showing of US, British, Spanish and Italian newspapers, plus magazines such as *National Geographic*, *The Economist*, *Entertainment Weekly* and *Paris Match*. Mon–Fri 8am–7pm, Sat 9am–2.30pm.

# Sport

**Sport** is probably the city's biggest obsession, and while **football**, **wrestling** and **bullfighting** are the three leading lights, the sporting calendar doesn't stop there. In years gone by, you could spend a moderately interesting evening watching **frontón** (*pelota vasca*, or *jai alai*) right in the city centre at the Frontón

México on the Plaza de la República. With the players on strike since 1993, in a dispute that shows no signs of being resolved, that sport – already losing popularity when play was suspended – doesn't look like making a comeback. There's **horse racing**, too, throughout the year (afternoons, especially Sat) at the Hipodromo de las Americas on Industria Militar (Ⓣ55/5387-0600, Ⓦwww.hipodromo.com.mx; Metro Cuatro Caminos); buses and *peseros* heading west on Reforma will take you there – look for "Hipodromo". More exciting horse action is involved in the *charreadas*, or **rodeos**, put on by amateur but highly skilled aficionados most weekends (often free), primarily at the Rancho del Charro, Constituyentes 500 (Ⓣ55/5277-8706, Ⓦwww.nacionaldecharros.com), close to the Third Section of Chapultepec Park; call or check their website to find out what's going on.

## Football

**Fútbol** (football, meaning soccer) is undoubtedly Mexico's most popular sport. The big games are held at the 114,000-seat Estadio Azteca (see p.458), which hosted the World Cup finals in 1970 and 1986, and is home to América (Las Águilas, or The Eagles), the nation's most popular and consistently successful club side. Elsewhere in the city, the university side, UNAM (Las Pumas), have a strong following at the Estadio Olímpico across the road from the university (see p.457); and Cruz Azul (known as Los Cementero*s* for their long-time sponsorship by a cement company) pack out Estadio Azul right by the city's main bullring (see p.450). Mexico City's other major team, Atlante (Los Potros, "the Colts") shares the Estadio Azteca with América. There are usually at least two **games** every Sunday afternoon from January to June and August to November – check local papers for fixture details – and you can almost always get a **ticket** (M$75–400) at the gate. The exceptions are the big games such as major local derbies, and "El Clásico", when América host Chivas from Guadalajara, the biggest team from the country's second largest city. Estadio Azteca can be reached by Tren Ligero or Ruta #26 ("Xochimilco") *colectivo*, both from Metro Tasqueña; Estadio Olímpico is reached by "Tlalpan" bus from Metro Chilpancingo; Estadio Azul is reached on foot from Metro San Antonio or from Metrobús station Ciudad de los Desportes on Insurgentes.

## Wrestling

Though its popularity has waned in recent years, *lucha libre*, or **wrestling**, remains one of Mexico's most avidly followed spectator sports. Over a dozen venues in the capital alone host fights several nights a week for a fanatical public. Widely available magazines, comics, photonovels and films recount the real and imagined lives of the rings' heroes and villains, though the once nightly telecasts are now a thing of the past.

Mexican wrestling is generally faster, with more complex moves, and more combatants in the ring at any one time than you would normally see in an American or British bout. This can make the action hard to follow for the uninitiated. More important, however, is the maintenance of stage personas, most of whom, heroes or villains, wear masks. The *rudos* tend to use brute force or indulge in sneaky, underhanded tactics to foil the opposition, while the *técnicos* use wit and guile to compensate for lack of brawn. This faux battle, not at all unlike the WWE on-screen antics, requires a massive suspension of disbelief – crucial if you want to join in the fun.

One of the most bizarre features of wrestling was the emergence of wrestlers as political figures – typically still in costume. The most famous of these, **Superbarrio**, arose from the struggle of Mexico City's tenant associations for fair rents and decent housing after the 1985 earthquake to become part of mainstream political opposition, even challenging government officials to step into the ring with him, and acting as a sort of unofficial cheerleader at opposition rallies.

The most famous wrestler of all time, however, was without doubt **El Santo** ("the Saint"). Immortalized in more than twenty movies, with titles such as *El Santo vs the Vampire Women*, he would fight, eat, drink and play the romantic lead without ever removing his mask, and until after his retirement, he never revealed his identity. His reputation as a gentleman in and out of the ring was legendary, and his death in 1984 widely mourned. His funeral was allegedly the second best-attended in Mexican history after that of President Obregón.

**Fights** can be seen, particularly on Fridays and Sundays, at the Arena Coliseo, Peru 77 (Metro Allende) and the Arena México, Dr Lucio 197 at Dr Lavista, Colonia Doctores (two blocks south and one east of Metro Balderas, but not a good area to be in at night).

## Bullfighting

Soccer and wrestling may be more popular, but there is no event more quintessentially Mexican than the **bullfight**. Rooted in Spanish machismo and imbued with multiple layers of symbolism and interpretation, it transcends a mere battle of man against animal. Many visitors arrive in Mexico revolted by the very idea of such one-sided slaughter, but spend an hour watching on TV and you may well find yourself hooked; if nothing else, it is worth attending a *corrida de toros* to see this integral part of the Mexican experience. It is a sport that transcends class barriers, something that is evident every Sunday afternoon during the winter season when men and women from all walks of Mexican society file into the stadium – though some admittedly end up in plush *sombra* (shade) seats while the masses occupy concrete *sol* (sun) terraces.

During the **season** (the longer *temporada grande*, late Oct or early Nov to early April, or the shorter *temporada chica*, July to early Oct) fights take place every Sunday at 4pm at the giant 48,000-seat Plaza Mexico (Ⓦwww.plazamexico.com), the largest bullring in the world. Each *corrida* lasts around two hours and involves six bulls, all from one ranch, with each of three matadors taking two bulls. Typically there will be two Mexican matadors and one from Spain, which still produces the best performers.

Each **fight** is divided into three *suertes* (acts) or *tercios* (thirds), each announced by a trumpet blast. During the first *tercio*, several *toreros* with large capes tire the bull in preparation for the *picadores* who, from their mounts atop heavily padded and blindfolded horses, attempt to force a lance between the bull's shoulder blades to further weaken him. The *toreros* then return for the second *tercio*, in which one of their number (and sometimes the matador himself) will try to stab six metal-tipped spikes (known as *bandilleras*) into the bull in as clean and elegant a manner as possible.

Exhausted and frustrated, but by no means docile, the bull is now considered ready for the third and final *tercio*, the *suerte de muleta*. The matador continues to tire the bull while pulling off as many graceful and daring moves as possible. By now the crowd will have sensed the bravery and finesse of the matador and the spirit of the bull he is up against, and shouts of "¡Olé!" will reverberate around the stadium with every pass. Eventually the matador will entice the bull to challenge him head-on, standing there with its hooves together. As it charges he will thrust his sword between its shoulder blades and, if it is well executed, the bull will crumple to the sand. However barbaric you might think it is, no one likes to see the bull suffer and even the finest performance will garner the matador little praise without a clean kill. Successful matadors may be awarded one of the bull's ears, rarely two, and perhaps two or three times a season the tail as well. An especially courageous bull may be spared and put out to stud, a cause for much celebration, but this is a rare spectacle.

Elaborate posters around town advertise **upcoming events**, as do most of the major newspapers. Look out too for the weekly coverage of the scene in the press during the season. **Tickets** can be bought at the gate and you can expect to pay as little as M$50 for general admission to sunny concrete benches far from the action. Five pesos more and you'll have the luxury of some shade, and from there prices rise rapidly the closer you get to the ring, often reaching M$500 for a front-row seat: something in the *primera tenida* (M$350–450) is close enough for most first-timers. To get there, take a Metrobús down Insurgentes to Ciudad de los Desportes, or walk ten minutes east from Metro San Antonio.



# Moving on from Mexico City

Following privatization, all passenger train services out of Mexico City have ceased to run, and the only indication that they ever did is an old steam locomotive standing outside what used to be the terminus on Buenavista. You are thus left with a choice for onward travel of either bus or plane. None of the city's four bus stations is very far from the centre of town, and the airport is surprisingly central too. All can be reached easily by the Metro.

## By plane

The **airport**, very much within the city limits, is only 5km east of the Zócalo. To get there, either take the Metro (Metro Terminal Aérea, line 5), or call the day before to one of the authorized airport taxi firms (Sitio 300 ⓣ55/5571-9344, ProTaxi ⓣ55/2559-0333 or Porto Taxi ⓣ55/5786-8212), or one of the other firms listed on p.408, to arrange a cab from your hotel. For flight enquiries, call ⓣ55/5571-3600 – you'll be offered a choice of languages, and then given the option of dialling an extension number: dial ⓣ2208 for international flight enquiries, or ⓣ2259 for domestic. For details of airport facilities, see p.403. Departure areas for domestic flights are in salas B and D; for international flights they are in Sala G, on the upper floor, poorly signposted above Sala E. For the office addresses and phone numbers of the main airlines, see p.482. For domestic flight durations and frequencies, see p.537.

## By bus

There are four chief **long-distance bus stations** in Mexico City, one for each point of the compass, though in practice the northbound terminal handles far more than its share, while the westbound one is tiny. All have Metro stations pretty much right outside.

Apart from the major terminals listed on p.482, there are large open-air bus stops at the end of all the Metro lines, with slow services to places up to an hour or so outside the city limits. For destinations in the capital's hinterland it can sometimes be quicker to leave from these.

It's rare not to be able to get onto a bus at short notice, but it can be worth booking in advance for long-distance journeys or for express services to popular destinations at busy times – that way you'll have a choice of seat and be sure of getting the fastest service. Ticket Bus (Ⓣ55/5133-2424 within the DF or 01-800/702-8000 toll-free from out of town, Ⓦwww.ticketbus.com.mx), with

## Buses to and from Mexico City

Mexico City's **bus stations** are used by hordes of competing companies, and the only way to get a full idea of the **timetable** to and from any given destination is to check each one individually – different companies may take different routes and you can sometimes waste hours by making the wrong choice, though staff are generally very helpful. The following is a list of the main services including departure and arrival times. You may find that less frequent services use other terminals.

| City/town | Bus terminal | |
|---|---|---|
| Acapulco | Sur, Norte | half-hourly 6am–11.30pm from Sur; 17 daily from Norte |
| Aguascalientes | Norte | at least half-hourly 7am–midnight |
| Amecameca | TAPO | every 20min 5.20am–11pm |
| Campeche | TAPO | 5 daily |
| Cancún | TAPO | 3 daily |
| Chalma | Poniente | every 20min 10.30am–9pm |
| Chetumal | TAPO | 3 daily |
| Chihuahua | Norte | approximately hourly 5am–11.30pm |
| Chilpancingo | Sur | hourly 6.20am–9.20pm |
| Ciudad Juárez | Norte | approximately hourly 5am–11.30pm |
| Ciudad Obregón | Norte | hourly 5.30am–11.30pm |
| Colima | Norte | 9 daily |
| Córdoba | TAPO | at least hourly 6.45am–12.45am |
| Cuautla | Sur, TAPO | every 10min 5am–11pm from Sur; every 20min 5.20am–11pm from TAPO |
| Cuernavaca | Sur | every 15min 6am–12.30am |
| Dolores Hidalgo | Norte | every 40min 5am–8pm |
| Durango | Norte | 9 daily |
| Fortín de las Flores | TAPO | 1 daily |
| Guadalajara | Poniente, Norte | 12 daily from Poniente; 14 daily from Norte |
| Guanajuato | Norte | 10 daily |
| Guaymas | Norte | 13 daily |
| Hermosillo | Norte | approximately hourly 5.30am–11.30pm |
| Ixtapa | Sur | 6 daily |
| Ixtapan de la Sal | Poniente | hourly 7am–7pm |
| León | Norte | at least hourly 6.30am–midnight |
| Los Mochis | Norte | approximately hourly 5.30am–11.30pm |
| Malinalco | Poniente | 3 daily |
| Manzanillo | Norte | 4 daily |
| Matamoros | Norte | 21 daily |
| Matehuala | Norte | 11 daily |
| Mazatlán | Norte | every 30–60min 5.30am–11pm |
| Mérida | TAPO | 5 daily |

offices at TAPO bus station; Isabel la Católica 83 in the centre; Reforma 412 in the Zona Rosa; and Masaryk with Hegel in Polanco, among other places, can book tickets for a small fee with many but not all bus lines.

The box below indicates which destination is served from which station, but if you're uncertain which bus station you should be leaving from, simply get

| | | |
|---|---|---|
| Mexicali | Norte | hourly 6am–11pm |
| Monterrey | Norte | hourly 7am–1am |
| Morelia | Poniente, Norte | 45 daily from Poniente; every 45–60min 6am–11.45pm from Norte |
| Nuevo Laredo | Norte | approximately hourly 8.45am–11.15pm |
| Oaxaca | TAPO | 25 daily |
| Orizaba | TAPO | 35 daily |
| Pachuca | Norte | every 10min 4.30am–11.30pm |
| Palenque | TAPO | 2 daily |
| Pátzcuaro | Poniente, Norte | 9 daily from Poniente; 4 daily from Norte |
| Playa del Carmen | TAPO | 2 daily |
| Puebla | TAPO Norte, Sur, | every 12–20min 4am–2am from TAPO; half-hourly 4am–10pm from Norte; every 50min 6.05am–9.40pm from Sur |
| Puerto Escondido | Sur, TAPO | 3 daily from Sur; 1 daily from TAPO |
| Puerto Vallarta | Norte | 4 daily |
| Querétaro | Norte | every 20min 5am–2.40am |
| Saltillo | Norte | 19 daily |
| San Cristóbal de las Casas | TAPO | 4 daily |
| San Luis Potosí | Norte | at least hourly 5am–1am |
| San Miguel de Allende | Norte | every 40min 5am–8pm |
| Taxco | Sur | hourly 8am–9pm |
| Tehuacan | TAPO | 13 daily |
| Tehuantepec | TAPO | 2 daily |
| Teotihuacán | Norte | every 15min 7am–4pm |
| Tepic | Norte | approximately hourly 7am–11pm |
| Tepoztlán | Sur | every 20min 7am–10pm |
| Tijuana | Norte | hourly 6am–11pm |
| Tlaxcala | TAPO | every 20min 5.40am–9pm (last departure at midnight) |
| Toluca | Poniente | every 5min 5.30am–10.30pm |
| Torreón | Norte | 10 daily |
| Tula | Norte | every 30min 6am–9.30pm |
| Tuxpan | Norte | hourly 6am–midnight |
| Tuxtla Gutiérrez | TAPO | 13 daily |
| Uruapan | Poniente, Norte | 18 daily from Poniente; 7 daily from Norte |
| Valle de Bravo | Poniente | every 20min 5am–7.25pm |
| Veracruz | TAPO | 25 daily |
| Villahermosa | TAPO | 33 daily |
| Xalapa | TAPO | 22 daily |
| Zacatecas | Norte | 18 daily |
| Zihuatanejo | Sur | 6 daily |

into a taxi and tell the driver what your ultimate destination is – he'll know where to take you. You'll find places to eat and stalls selling food and drink for the journey in all the terminals, along with ATMs, left luggage offices, post offices and newsstands.

### Terminal del Norte

The **Terminal del Norte**, Avenida de los Cien Metros 4907, is the largest of the city's four stations, handling direct routes to and from the US border, and services to every major city north of Mexico City (including the fastest services to Guadalajara and Morelia). To get to it by Metro, take line 5 to Autobuses del Norte. Alternatively, take a trolleybus heading north from Bellas Artes or anywhere along the Eje Central (Division del Norte/Lázaro Cárdenas).



### TAPO

Eastbound services use the most modern of the terminals, the Terminal de Autobuses de Pasajeros de Oriente, always referred to as **TAPO**. Buses for Puebla, Veracruz and places that you might think of as south – Oaxaca, Chiapas and the Yucatán, even Guatemala – leave from here. It is also the most central of the bus stations, most easily reached by Metro (Metro San Lazaro; lines 1 and B).

### Central de Autobuses del Sur

Buses towards the Pacific coast – Cuernavaca, Taxco and Acapulco in particular – leave from the **Central de Autobuses del Sur**, Tasqueña 1320. You can get there by Metro (Metro Tasqueña; line 2) – take the exit signposted "Autobuses del Sur", and the terminal is over to your left as you leave the station. Alternatively, you can take a trolleybus heading south anywhere along the Eje Central (Lázaro Cárdenas/Division del Norte), for example at Bellas Artes.

### Terminal Poniente

For the west, there's the **Terminal Poniente**, at the junction of calles Sur and Tacubaya. The smallest of the terminals, it basically handles traffic to Toluca, but it's also the place to go for the slower, more scenic routes to Morelia, Guadalajara and other destinations in Jalisco and Michoacán, via Toluca. Aside from the Metro (Metro Observatorio; line 1), it can be reached on buses (signed "Metro Observatorio") heading south on Reforma or from the stands by the entrance to Chapultepec Park.

# Listings

**Airlines** The main ones are Aerocalifornia, Baja California Sur s/n ☎01-800/080-9090; Aerolineas Argentinas, Amberes 1, Zona Rosa ☎55/5533-1813; Aeromar, airport Sala B ☎55/5784-1139; Aeroméxico, Reforma 445 & 155 ☎55/5133-4000 or 01-800/021-4000; Air Canada, Manuel Avila Camacho 18°, Lomas de Chapultepec ☎55/9138-0280 or 01-800/719-2827; Air France, Jaime Balmes 8, Polanco ☎55/2122-8282; Alaska Airlines, Hamburgo 213 10°, Zona Rosa ☎55/5208-6949 or 001-800/252-7522; American, Reforma 300, at Amberes ☎55/5209-1400; Aviacsa, Reforma 195, Cuauhtémoc, ☎55/5482-8280 or 01-800/284-2272; British Airways, Jaime Balmes 8, Polanco ☎55/5387-0300; Continental, Andrés Bello 45 18°, Polanco ☎55/5283-5500 or 01-800/900-5000; Delta, Reforma 381 near El Ángel ☎55/5511-0658 or 01-800/123-4710; Iberia, Ejercito Nacional 436 9°, Polanco ☎55/1101-1550; Interjet, Ejercito Nacional 843–B, Polanco ☎55/1102-5555; Japan Air Lines, Reforma 505 ☎55/5242-0150 or 01-800/024-0150; Lufthansa, Paseo de las Palmas 391, Lomas de Chapultepec ☎55/5230-0000; Mexicana, handiest offices at Juárez 82, at Balderas, and Reforma 312, at Amberes

ⓣ55/5448-0990; Northwest/KLM, Andrés Bello 45, Polanco ⓣ55/5279-5390 or 01-800/907-4700; United, Hamburgo 213, Zona Rosa ⓣ55/5627-0222; US Airways, Manuel Avila Camacho 88, Lomas de Chapultepec ⓣ55/2623-0135 or 01-800/428-4322.

**American Express** Central office and clients' mail service at Reforma 350 by El Ángel (Mon–Fri 9am–6pm, Sat 9am–1pm; ⓣ55/5207-7049 or 01-800/543-3288). Other offices at the airport and elsewhere in the city.

**Banks and exchange** ATMs are everywhere, and with the appropriate credit or cash cards you can get money throughout your stay without ever visiting a bank. Besides, many banks will only change money in the morning, and many are unhelpful for currencies other than US dollars: Banamex is your best bet. Most large hotels and shops will change traveller's cheques and cash dollars, but the quickest and easiest places to change money are casas de cambio, scattered all over town. In the *centro histórico* try Casa de Cambio Puebla, Madero 27, at Bolivar (Mon–Fri 9am–5pm, Sat 10am–2.30pm) or Cambios Exchange, at Madero 13, near Filomena Mata (Mon–Sat 9.30am–7pm, Sun 10am–6pm). You'll find several in the Zona Rosa, especially on Amberes, Londres and Liverpool, and a couple on the south side of Reforma, just south of the Monumento a la Revolución.

**Car rental** There are thousands of agencies throughout the city, and the small local operations are often cheaper than the big chains. Either way, renting a car isn't going to be cheap, and a car can be more of a liability than a help while you're in the city. Expect to pay M$600–850 a day for the cheapest car with tax, insurance and unlimited mileage, more in July and August; the usual deal for a week is that you pay for six days and get the seventh free. The major operators all have offices at the airport and in the Zona Rosa, and some of the smaller companies do too, a major boon as it saves you trawling around the city for the best deals. Local firms doing good deals from the airport include Kim Kar (ⓣ55/2599-0267), Gold Car Rental (ⓣ55/2599-0090), EconoMovil (ⓣ55/2599-0147 or 8), and Royal Rent A Car (ⓣ55/5802-8000, ⓦwww.royalrent.com). Multinational firms include: Hertz (ⓣ55/5762-8977 or 01-800/709-5000, ⓦwww.hertz.com.mx), National (ⓣ55/5786-8228 or 01-800/716-6625, ⓦwww.nationalcar.com.mx), Thrifty (ⓣ55/5785-05061, ⓦwww.thrifty.com.mx), Alamo (ⓣ55/1101-1100 or 01-800/849-8001, ⓦwww.alamo-mexico.com.mx), Budget (ⓣ55/5566-6800 or 01-800/700-1700, ⓦwww.budget.com.mx) and Avis (ⓣ55/5588-8888 or 01-800/288-8911, ⓦwww.avis.com.mx). Rental cars are exempt from the one day a week driving restriction (see p.397).

**Courier services** DHL, Madero 70, Centro Histórico (Mon–Fri 9am–6pm) and other locations (ⓣ55/5345-7000 or 01-800/765-6345, ⓦwww.dhl.com.mx); FedEx, Reforma 308, Zona Rosa (Mon–Fri 9am–7pm, Sat 9am–2pm) and other locations (ⓣ55/5228-9904 or 01-800/900-1100).

**Cultural institutes** Several countries maintain cultural institutes and libraries for their nationals within Mexico City, often allowing short-term visitors to use some of their facilities. They can also be useful places for contacts, and if you're looking for work, long-term accommodation or travelling companions their notice boards are good places to start. The US has the Biblioteca Benjamín Franklin, Liverpool 31, at Berlin (Mon–Fri 11am–7pm; ⓣ55/5080-2000, ⓦwww.usembassy-mexico.gov/biblioteca; Metro Cuauhtémoc); the UK has the British Council, Lope de Vega 316 (Mon–Fri 8am–3pm; ⓣ55/5263-1900; Metro Polanco); Canadians can use the Canadian Embassy Library (see below; Mon–Fri 9am–12.30pm).

**Embassies and consulates** Australia, Rubén Darío 55, Polanco (Mon–Thurs 8.30am–5.15pm, Fri 8.30am–2.15pm; ⓣ55/1101-2200, ⓦwww.mexico.embassy.gov.au; Metro Auditorio); Belize, Bernardo de Gálves 215, Lomas de Chapultepec (Mon–Fri 9am–1.30pm; ⓣ55/5520-1274, ⓔembelize@prodigy.net.mx); Canada, Schiller 529, Polanco (Mon–Fri 9am–1pm & 2–5pm; ⓣ55/5724-7900, toll-free emergency number for Canadians ⓣ01-800/706-2900, ⓦwww.canada.org.mx; Metro Polanco); Costa Rica, Río Po 113, at Río Lerma, Zona Rosa (Mon–Fri 9am–5pm; ⓣ55/5207-6444, ⓔconsulg@podernet.com.mx; Metro Insurgentes); Cuba, Presidente Masaryk 554, Polanco (Mon–Fri 10am–2pm; ⓣ55/5280-2453, ⓦwww.embacuba.com.mx; Metro Polanco); El Salvador, Temístocles 88, Polanco (Mon–Fri 9am–4pm; ⓣ55/5281-5723 or 5, ⓔembesmex@webtelmex.net.mx; Metro Polanco); Guatemala, Explanada 1025, Lomas de Chapultepec (Mon–Fri 9am–2pm & 3–5pm; ⓣ55/5520-9249, ⓔembaguatemx@minex.gov.gt); Honduras, Alfonso Reyes 220, at Ometusco (Mon–Fri 9am–1.30pm; ⓣ55/5211-5250, ⓔemhonmex@mail.internet.com.mx; Metro Patriotismo); Ireland, Manuel Avila Camacho 76 3°, Lomas de Chapultepec (Mon–Fri 9am–5pm; ⓣ55/5520-5803, ⓔembajada@irlanda.org.mx; Metro Polanco or Auditorio); New Zealand, Jaime Balmer 8 4°, Polanco (Mon–Thurs 8.30am–2pm & 3–5.30pm, Fri 8.30am–2pm; ⓣ55/5283-9460, ⓔkiwimexico@prodigy.net.mx; Metro Polanco); South Africa, Andrés Bello 10 9°,

Horacio 1501, Polanco (Mon–Fri 8.30am–3.30pm; ⓣ55/5282-9260 to 65, ⓔsafrica@prodigy.net.mx; Metro Polanco); UK, Río Lerma 71, at Río Sena, Zona Rosa (Mon–Thurs 8am–4pm, Fri 8am–1.30pm; ⓣ55/5207-2089, ⓦwww.embajadabritanica.com.mx; Metro Insurgentes); US, Reforma 305 at Danubio, Zona Rosa (Mon–Fri 8.30am–5.30pm; ⓣ55/5080-2000, ⓦwww.usembassy-mexico.gov; Metro Insurgentes).

**Emergencies** All emergency services (police, fire, ambulance) ⓣ060; fire department ⓣ068; Red Cross ambulance ⓣ065; Locatel, which gives information on missing persons and vehicles, medical emergencies, emotional crises and public services ⓣ55/5658-1111; tourist security ⓣ01-800/903-9200.

**Gay life** The Zona Rosa (pink zone) is increasingly becoming a gay zone, and in particular the northernmost block of Amberes between Estrasburgo and Reforma, where you'll find a whole slew of gay and lesbian bars including *BGay BProud*, *Pussy Bar* and *Boy Bar*. The listings magazine *Tiempo Libre* also has a section on gay and lesbian events and locales.

**Hospital** The American-British Cowdray Hospital (ABC) is at the junction of Observatorio and Sur 136, Col Las Américas (ⓣ55/5230-8000). Embassies should be able to provide a list of multilingual doctors if necessary (the US embassy maintains a list at ⓦwww.usembassy-mexico.gov/medical_lists.html), and American Express cardholders can make use of their Global Assist medical referral service.

**Internet access** Numerous cybercafés all over the city generally charge around M$10–15 per hour. Those in the suburbs (there are several in Xochimilco for example) tend to be slightly cheaper than those in town. In the centre, try: *Hostel Catedral* (see p.410; Metro Zócalo); Lafoel Internet Service, 1° Donceles 80, at República de Brasil (Mon–Fri 9am–8pm, Sat 10am–8pm; Metro Allende). In the Zona Rosa, there are several inside the roundabout at Glorieta Insurgentes, or try Java Chat, Génova 44 (Mon–Fri 7am–11.30pm, Sat 8am–11.30pm, Sun 9.30am–11.30pm; Metro Insurgentes).

**Laundry** Self-service launderettes are surprisingly rare in Mexico City, but most hotels should be able to point one out for you. Options include Lavandería Automática Lavajet, Danubio 123-B, at Lerma (Mon–Fri 8am–5.30pm, Sat 8am–5pm), close to the Zona Rosa; and Lavandería Automática Edison, Edison 91, at Arriaga, near the Plaza de la República (Mon–Fri 10am–7pm, Sat 10am–6pm; Metro Revolución).

**Left luggage** Most hotels will hold your bags for the rest of the day after you've checked out, and some will allow you to leave excess luggage for several days, sometimes for a small charge. At the airport there are lockers at two locations (Sala A and Sala E2) for M$60 a day. All four main bus terminals have left luggage facilities (M$40–110 a day depending on the size of your bag).

**Opening hours** Hours for most businesses in Mexico City are from 10am until 7pm. Very few now close for the traditional 2–4pm siesta.

**Pharmacies** Sanborn's offers a wide range of products at most branches, as well as dispensing some prescription drugs. Other options include El Fénix, Madero 41, at Motolinia, and Isabel la Católica 15, at 5 de Mayo. There are homeopathic pharmacies at Mesones 111-B, at 20 Noviembre, and República Guatemala 16, behind the cathedral.

**Photographic supplies** Film is available almost everywhere – pharmacies, tourist locales and so on – at reasonable prices, but for specialist needs head to Calle Donceles, between Republica de Argentina and Allende, or Foto Imagen at Juárez 56, on the south side of the Alameda (ⓣ55/5510-0240).

**Post office** The main post office is on Lázaro Cárdenas at Tacuba, across the street from Bellas Artes (Mon–Fri 8am–7.45pm, Sat 8am–3pm). Branch offices (Mon–Fri 9am–3pm, or sometimes 9am–5pm, Sat 9am–1pm) can be found at Ponciano Arriaga 11, near the Revolution Monument, and Higuera 23 in Coyoacán, among other places.

**Spanish courses** Many places run Spanish courses in the city, though most people prefer to study away from the capital in such places as Cuernavaca, San Miguel de Allende and Guanajuato. For those who prefer the metropolis, the most prestigious language school in town is the Universidad Autonomo's Centro de Enseñanza para Extranjeros, located at Universidad 3002 in the Ciudad Universitaria (ⓣ55/5622-2470, ⓦwww.cepe.unam.mx). Also worth checking out is ⓦwww.planeta.com/mexico.html, which has good links to Mexican language schools.

**Telephones** Local, domestic long-distance and international phone calls can be made from any public phone with a phonecard. Cheaper international calls can be made via the Internet, though only a few Internet locales are offering this service as yet – those which do include Java Chat at Génova 44 and Beldun at Amberes 62, both in the Zona Rosa. Otherwise, a number of shops have public phones (for international services look for the blue "Larga Distancia" signs). You can dial direct from most big hotels, but it will cost much

more. *Casetas de larga distancia* are closing down in the face of widespread use of cardphones, but you'll find them at all the bus terminals except TAPO, and at the airport, Sala E2 (all hours).
**Tourist cards** Should you lose yours, or want an extension, you apply, when your original length of stay is almost finished, to the Instituto de Migración, Ejército National 862, at the western end of Polanco (Mon–Fri 9am–1pm; ⓣ55/2581-0116; *peseros* from Chapultepec to Toreo run along Ejército Nacional). Extensions are pretty much routine if the period is two weeks or less, and should take around half an hour; go to desk D23 – "Ampliación de Estancia". Longer extensions will require copies, form filling and possibly an onward ticket or proof of sufficient funds.
**Travel agencies** A particularly good firm for youth and student fares is Mundo Joven (ⓦwww.mundojoven.com), with offices at Guatemala 4 behind the cathedral (ⓣ55/5518-1755), Eugenio Sue 342, at Homero in Polanco (ⓣ55/5250-7191), and Sala E2 in the airport (ⓣ55/2599-0155).



# Around the city

You'll find areas of interest within a couple of hours' drive of the city in any direction. The day trip that almost everyone takes is to the pyramids of **Teotihuacán**, about 50km northeast, easily the largest of Mexico's archeological sites, with enough to see to occupy a full day. Directly north of the city, on the road to Querétaro, lies **Tula**, the centre that succeeded Teotihuacán as the valley's great power. On the way you can stop at **Tepotzotlán**, which holds some of the finest Baroque and colonial art in the country.

To the east, **Pachuca** is home to the national photography museum, and nearby is **Real del Monte**, where Cornish miners introduced soccer to Mexico in the nineteenth century. Moving clockwise around the capital, **Tlaxcala** and **Cholula** were important allies of the Aztecs when Cortés marched this way from the coast. Tlaxcala is now a wonderfully quiet colonial town, while at Cholula is the rubble of the largest pyramid in Mexico. Between the two stands **Puebla**, a crowded industrial centre with aspects of colonial charm. Puebla and Cholula provide the region's best views of the twin volcanoes, **Popocatépetl** and **Ixtaccíhuatl**, the former currently off-limits after its sporadic eruptions.

South of Mexico City, **Cuernavaca** brims with colonial mansions and gardens, and also draws visitors on account of its proximity to several important archeological sites. Beyond it lies the road to Acapulco and the tourist haven of **Taxco**, renowned for its silver jewellery. **Toluca**, on the old road to Morelia, hosts a colossal market every Friday, and the surrounding country is full of mountain retreats where Mexicans go to escape city life, notably the small town of **Malinalco** with its ancient hillside ruins, and the water-sports destination of **Valle de Bravo**.

## Teotihuacán and around

It seems that every visitor to Mexico City at some stage heads out to the pyramids at **Teotihuacán** (daily 7am–5pm; M$45, M$30 to bring in a video camera): there's a constant stream of tours, buses and cars heading this way, and the ruins are always crawling with people, especially on Sunday. It is an extensive site that can easily take up most of a day. It makes sense to plan ahead: it's best to head out here as early as you can manage and do most of your exploration

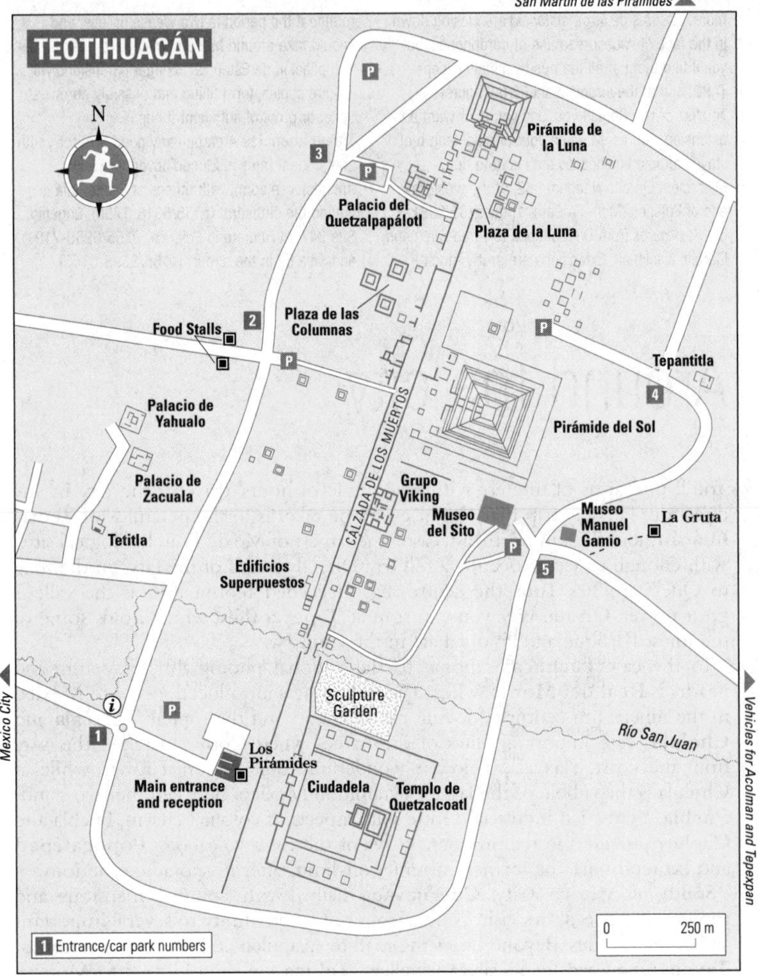


in the cool of the morning before the crowds arrive. From 11am to 3pm it can be very busy, and there is little shade, so you may want to spend that time at a restaurant or in the **museum**, returning refreshed for the photogenic light of the late afternoon. Visitors with limited Spanish will be glad to know that most of the explanatory signs are also in English.

## Site practicalities

**To get to Teotihuacán** you can catch one of the buses that leave every fifteen minutes or so (7am–4pm; 1hr) from the Terminal del Norte. Go to the second-class (left-hand) side of the bus station and look for the Autobuses Teotihuacán stand in Sala 8 (☎55/5781-1812); be aware that these buses have from time to time been targeted by bandits, so make sure you're not carrying a lot of cash. A slightly quicker alternative is to catch the Metro to Indios Verdes (line 3) and head to the northern end of Platform J, from where buses leave frequently for "Las Pirámides". A road, the Carretera de Circunvalación, provides access to the main structures through one of six gates (each with parking and lines of souvenir stalls): buses might arrive at any *puerta* (gate), though Puerta 1 and Puerta 4 are the most common. These are also the best places to wait for **buses back to Mexico City** (the last at 6pm), but late in the day most return buses make a full circuit of all gates before departing the site.

If you are on a budget it's best to bring all your **food and drink** with you, as anything bought at the site is going to be expensive. The main **restaurant** and bar, *Las Pirámides*, is at the principal entrance at Puerta 1, and has a three-course tourist menu for M$95 and some basic à la carte dishes. Prices are high considering the quality of the food, but the view of the site from the top-floor restaurant is great. Cheaper food (including comidas corridas for as little as M$30) is most easily found at the handful of small restaurants beside the ring road at Puerta 2, whose representatives will be on your case as soon as you set foot outside the gate. For something a little special, head for *La Gruta*, 200m west of Puerta 5 (ⓣ594/956-0104), a fancy restaurant set deep in an open-sided cave, with white-jacketed waiters and a live show Saturday at 3.30pm, and Sunday at 3.30pm and 5.30pm. At M$125–210 for a main course, it isn't that much more expensive than *Las Pirámides* and is much more satisfying.

## The rise and fall of Teotihuacán

The rise and fall of **Teotihuacán** is almost exactly contemporary with imperial Rome. There is evidence of small agricultural communities in the vicinity dating to around 600 BC; by 200 BC a township had been established on the present site. From then until 1 AD (the period known as the **Patlachique** phase) the population increased, and the city assumed its most important characteristics: the great pyramids of the Sun and Moon were built, and the Calzada de los Muertos laid out. Development continued through the **Tzacualli** and **Miccaotli** phases (1–250 AD) with more construction and the blossoming of artistic expression, then through the **Tlamimilolpa** phase (250–450 AD) there is evidence of the city's influence (in architecture, sculpture and pottery) occurring at sites throughout modern Mexico and into Guatemala and Honduras. From 450 to around 650 AD (**Xolalpan** phase) it reached its peak in both population and power, with much new building and addition to earlier structures. Already by the end of this period, however, there were signs of decline, and the final phase, the **Metepec**, lasted at most a century before the city was sacked, burnt and virtually abandoned. This, presumably, was the result of attack by northern tribes, probably the Toltecs, but the disaster may in the end have been as much ecological as military. Vast forests were cut down to build the city (for use in columns, roof supports, door lintels) and huge quantities of wood burnt to make the lime plaster that coated the buildings. The result was severe soil erosion that left the hillsides as barren as they appear today. In addition, the agricultural effort needed to feed so many people (with no form of artificial fertilizer or knowledge of crop rotation) gradually sapped what land remained of its ability to grow more.

Whatever the precise causes, the city was left, eventually, to a ruination that was advanced even by the time of the Aztecs. To them it represented a holy place from a previous age, and they gave it its present name, which translates as "the place where men became gods". Although Teotihuacán features frequently in Aztec mythology, there are no written records – what we know of the city is derived entirely from archeological and artistic evidence, so that even the original name remains unknown.

△ Pirámide del Sol, Teotihuacán

## The site

The ruins at **Teotihuacán** are not, on first glance, the most impressive in Mexico – they lack the dramatic hilltop settings or lush jungle vegetation of those in the south – but they reveal a city planned and built on a massive scale, the great pyramids so huge that before their refurbishment one would have passed them by as hills without a second look. At its height this must have been the most imposing city ever seen in pre-Hispanic America, with a population thought to have been around 80,000 (though 200,000 is suggested by some sources) spread over an area of some 23 square kilometres (as opposed to the four square kilometres of the ceremonial centre). Then, every building – grey hulks now – would have been covered in bright polychrome murals.

### Calzada de los Muertos

The main entrance, by Puerta 1, is at the southern end of the two-kilometre-long **Calzada de los Muertos** (Causeway of the Dead), which originally extended 1.5km further south, and formed the axis around which the city developed. A broad roadway some 40m wide and linking all the most significant buildings, it was conceived to impress, with the low buildings that flank most of its length serving to heighten the impact of the two great temples at the northern end. Other streets, leading off to the rest of the city, originally intersected it at right angles, and even the Río San Juan was canalized so as not to disturb the symmetry (the bridge that then crossed it would have extended the full width of the street). Its name is somewhat misleading, as it's more a series of open plazas linked by staircases than a simple street. Neither is it in any way linked with the dead, although the Aztecs believed the buildings that lined it, then little more than earth-covered mounds, to be the burial places of kings. They're not, and although the exact function of most remains unclear, all obviously had some sacred significance. The design, seen in the many reconstructions, is fairly uniform: low three- or four-storey platforms consisting of vertical panels (*tableros*) supported by sloping walls. In many cases several are built on top of each other – nowhere more clearly demonstrated than in the **Edificios Superpuestos** (superimposed buildings) on the left-hand side shortly beyond the river. Here you can descend a metal staircase to find excavated structures underneath the present level – these may have been the living quarters of Teotihuacán's priests.

### La Ciudadela

Directly opposite the entrance at Puerta 1 lies **La Ciudadela**, the Citadel. This enormous sunken square, surrounded by stepped platforms and with a low square altar in the centre, was the city's administrative heart, with the houses of its chief priests and nobles arranged around a vast meeting place. Across the open space stands a tall pyramid construction inside which, during excavations, was found the **Templo de Quetzalcoatl**. With the back of the newer pyramid demolished, the elaborate (Miccaotli phase) temple structure stands revealed. Pyramids aside, this is one of the most impressive sections of the whole site, rising in four steps (of an original six), each sculpted in relief and punctuated at intervals by the stylized heads of Quetzalcoatl, the plumed serpent, and **Tlaloc**, the rain god. Traces of the original paint can be seen in places. This theme – with the goggle-eyed, almost abstract mask of Tlaloc and the fanged snake Quetzalcoatl, its neck ringed with a collar of feathers – recurs in later sites throughout the country.

### Pirámide del Sol

The great **Pirámide del Sol** (Pyramid of the Sun) is Teotihuacán's outstanding landmark, a massive structure 70m high and, of Mexico's ancient buildings, second in size only to Cholula (and Cholula is a total ruin). Its base is almost exactly the same size as that of the great Pyramid of Cheops in Egypt, but the lower-angled sides and its stepped nature make it very much lower. There are wonderful views from the top nonetheless, and the bulk is all the more remarkable when you consider the accuracy of its alignment: on two days a year (May 19 and July 25), the sun is directly over the pyramid at noon, and the main west facade faces the point at which the sun sets on these days. This alignment just off the cardinal points determined the line of the Calzada de los Muertos and of the entire city. Equally remarkable is the fact that the 2.5 million tonnes of stone and earth used in its construction were brought here without benefit of the wheel or any beast of burden, and shaped without the use of metal tools. The pyramid you see was reconstructed by Leopoldo Batres in 1908, in a thoroughly cavalier fashion. He blasted, with dynamite, a structure that originally abutted the south face, and stripped much of the surface in a search for a more complete building under the present one. In fact, the Pirámide del Sol, almost uniquely, was built in one go at a very early stage of the city's development (about 100 AD), and there is only a very small older temple right at its heart. As a result of Batres's stripping of the stone surface, the temple has eroded considerably more than it might otherwise have done. He also added an extra terrace to the original four.

You approach by a short staircase leading to the right off the Calzada de los Muertos onto a broad esplanade, where stand the ruins of several small temples and priests' dwellings. The main structure consists of five sloping layers of wall divided by terraces – the large flat area at the top would originally have been surmounted by a sanctuary, long disappeared. Evidence of why this massive structure came to be raised here emerged in 1971 when archeologists stumbled on a tunnel (closed to the public) leading to a clover-leaf-shaped **cave** directly under the centre of the pyramid. This, clearly, had been some kind of inner sanctuary, a holy of holies, and may even have been the reason for Teotihuacán's foundation and the basis of its influence. Theories abound as to its exact nature, and many fit remarkably with legends handed down through the Aztecs. It's perhaps most likely that the cave was formed by a subterranean spring, and came to be associated with Tlaloc, god of rain but also a bringer of fertility, as a sort of fountain of life.

Alternatively, it could be associated with the legendary "seven grottos", a symbol of creation from which all later Mexican peoples claimed to have emerged, or to have been the site of an oracle, or associated with a cult of sacrifice – in Aztec times the flayed skins of victims of Xipe Totec were stored in a cave under a pyramid.



### Pirámide de la Luna

At the end of the Calzada de los Muertos rises the **Pirámide de la Luna** (Pyramid of the Moon), a smaller structure built slightly later (but still during the Tzacualli phase), whose top, thanks to the high ground on which it's built, is virtually on a level with that of the Pirámide del Sol. The structure is very similar, with four sloping levels approached by a monumental stairway, but for some reason this seems a very much more elegant building: perhaps because of the smaller scale, or perhaps as a result of the approach, through the formally laid-out **Plaza de la Luna**. The top of the pyramid offers the best overview of the site's layout, looking straight back down the length of the central thoroughfare. It is perfect for sunset, though as it is close to closing time the guards will soon chase you down.

### Palacio de Quetzalpapálotl and Palacio de los Jaguares

The **Palacio de Quetzalpapálotl** (Palace of the Quetzal-butterfly) lies to the left of the Plaza de la Luna, behind the low temples that surround it. Wholly restored, it's virtually the only example of a pre-Hispanic roofed building in central Mexico and preserves a unique view of how the elite lived at Teotihuacán. The rooms are arranged around a patio whose elaborately carved pillars give the palace its name – their stylized designs represent birds (the brightly coloured quetzals, though some may be owls) and butterflies. In the galleries around the patio several frescoes survive, all very formalized and symbolic, with the themes reduced almost to geometric patterns. **Mural art** was clearly very important in Teotihuacán, and almost every building has some trace of decoration, though much has been removed for restoration. Two earlier buildings, half-buried under the palace, still have substantial remains. In the **Palacio de los Jaguares**, jaguars in feathered headdresses blow conch shells from which emerge curls of music, or perhaps speech or prayers to Tlaloc (who appears along the top of the mural); in the **Templo de los Caracoles Emplumados** (Temple of the Plumed Shells), you see a motif of feathers and seashells along with bright green parrots. Other murals, of which only traces remain, were found in the temples along the Calzada de los Muertos between the two pyramids.

### Tepantitla, Tetitla and Atetelco

Mural art was not reserved for the priests' quarters – indeed some of the finest frescoes have been found in outlying apartment buildings. The famous *Paradise of Tlaloc* mural (reproduced in the Museo Nacional de Antropología, see p.441) was discovered at **Tepantitla**, a residential quarter of the old city across the road from the back of the Pirámide del Sol. Only a part of it survives here, but there are others in the complex depicting a procession of priests and a ball-game. All have great vitality and an almost comic-strip quality, with speech bubbles emerging from the figures' mouths, but their themes always have a religious rather than a purely decorative intent. More can be seen at **Tetitla**, to the west of the main site, and **Atetelco**, a little further west, just off the plan on p.486.

### Museo del Sitio

Plan to spend at least some of your time in Teotihuacán's excellent **Museo del Sitio** (site hours; entry included in site fee) situated behind the Pirámide del Sol and surrounded by a lovely sculpture and botanical garden. Artefacts from the site are well laid out and effectively lit to highlight the key features of each item in the cool interior. There's just about everything you would expect of a ritual site and living city, from sharp-edged obsidian tools and everyday ceramics to some fine polychrome vessels decorated with animal and plant designs, and a series of five ceremonial braziers or censers ornamented with appliqué flowers, butterflies and shields.

Vast windows framing the Pirámide del Sol take up one entire wall of the next room, where you walk across a glass floor – look down to see a huge relief map of the entire city as it might once have been. This area leads to a second section mostly comprising larger sculptural pieces depicting assorted gods, often bottom-lit to accentuate the gruesome features. There are some superb masks, too, along with a couple of funerary sites modelled on those found under the Templo de Quetzalcoatl.

## Around Teotihuacán

On the way to the pyramids you pass a couple of places that, if you're driving, are certainly worth a look, but barely merit the hassle involved in stopping over on the bus, though they can both be accessed easily by *combi* from a junction 500m beyond Puerta 5. At the village of **TEPEXPAN** is a **museum** (Tues–Sun 10am–5pm; free) housing the fossil of a mammoth dug up in the surrounding plain (then marshland). There's also a skeleton known as the "Tepexpan Man", once claimed to be the oldest in Mexico but now revealed as less than 2000 years old. This whole area is a rich source of such remains – the Aztecs knew of their existence, which is one of the reasons they believed that the huge structures of Teotihuacán had been built by a race of giants. The museum is a fifteen-minute walk from the village, near the motorway tollbooths, where any second-class bus will drop you; the village itself is attractive, with a good café on Calle de los Reyes, just off the main square. Buses to Metro Indios Verdes and *combis* to Teotihuacán can be picked up at the junction just outside the museum.

A few kilometres towards Teotihuacán (10min by *combi* from Tepexpan, 20min from Teotihuacán) is the beautiful sixteenth-century convent of **San Agustín Acolman** (daily 9am–5.30pm; M$30). Built on a raised, man-made terrace (probably on the site of an earlier, Aztec temple), it's a stern-looking building, lightened by the intricacy of its sculpted facade. In the nave and around the cloister are preserved portions of early murals depicting the monks, while several of the halls off the cloister display colonial religious painting and pre-Hispanic artefacts found here. If you turn right out of the gate, *combis* for Teotihuacán or Tepexpan can be picked up after 100m at the main road. **CHICONCUAC** to the south is rather more of a detour, but on Tuesdays, when there's a large market that specializes in woollen goods, sweaters and blankets, it's included in the itinerary of many of the tours to the pyramids.

Again, this is hard to get to on a regular bus, and if you want to visit the market it's easier to do so as an entirely separate trip – buses, again, leave from the Terminal del Norte.

# Tepotzotlán

**TEPOTZOTLÁN** lies en route from the capital to Tula, and it's possible to visit the two on one long day from the metropolis. Tepotzotlán is also close enough to the city to be a morning's excursion, though once you're there, you may find the town's slow place and colonial charm seduces you into staying longer. On Saturdays, with loads of Mexican visitors, the festive atmosphere is particularly enjoyable, while on Sundays a crafts market draws large crowds. In the week before Christmas, *pastorelas*, or **Nativity plays**, are staged here. Tepotzotlán's *pastorelas* are renowned, and booked up long in advance. At other times of the year, you may catch a concert in the church or cloisters.

## Museo Nacional del Virreinato

Atmosphere apart, the reason most people come to Tepotzotlán is to see the magnificent Baroque **Colegio de San Francisco Javier**, now the **Museo Nacional del Virreinato** (Viceroyalty Museum; Tues–Sun 9am–5.45pm; M$38; Ⓦwww.virreinato.inah.gob.mx). The church was founded by the Jesuits, who arrived in 1580 on a mission to convert the Otomí locals. Most of the huge complex you see today was established during the following century but constantly embellished right up to the expulsion of the Jesuits in 1767. The facade of the church – considered one of the finest examples of churrigueresque architecture in the country – was completed barely five years before this. The wealth and scale of all this gives some idea of the power of the Jesuits prior to their ousting; after they left, it became a seminary for the training of regular priests until the late nineteenth century, when the Jesuits were briefly readmitted. The Revolution led to its final abandonment in 1914.

### Iglesia de San Francisco Javier

The main entrance to the Colegio de San Francisco Javier leads into the **Claustro de los Aljibes**, with a well at the centre and pictures of the life of Ignatius Loyola (founder of the Jesuits) around the walls. Off the cloister is the entrance to the church, the **Iglesia de San Francisco Javier**. If the facade is spectacular, it's still barely preparation for the dazzling interior. Dripping with gold, and profusely carved with a bewilderment of saints and cherubim, it strikes you at first as some mystical cave of treasures. The main body of the church and its chapels house five huge gilded cedarwood *retablos*, stretching from ceiling to floor, each more gloriously curlicued than the last, their golden richness intensified by the soft yellow light penetrating through the alabaster that covers the windows. Much of the painting on the main altar (dedicated to the church's patron saint) is attributed to Miguel Cabrera, sometimes considered to be Mexico's Michelangelo, whose talents are also on display towards the main church door, which is framed by two large oils, one depicting worshippers bathing in the blood from Jesus's crucifixion wounds.

All this is still only the start, for hidden to one side is arguably the greatest achievement of Mexican Baroque, the octagonal **Camarín de la Virgen**. It's not a large room, but every inch is elaborately decorated and the hand of the native craftsmen is clearly evident in the exuberant carving – fruit and flowers, shells and abstract patterns crammed in between the angels. There's a mirror angled to allow visitors to appreciate the detail of the ceiling without straining their necks. The Camarín is reached through the **Capilla de la Virgen de Loreto**, inside which is a "house" tiled with eighteenth-century *azulejos* – supposedly a replica of Mary's house at Nazareth, in which Jesus grew up. Legend claims the original house was miraculously lifted by angels to save it when Muslims invaded the Holy Land, then deposited in the Italian town of Loreto in 1294.

### The rest of the Museo Nacional del Virreinato

Directly off the central cloister are rooms packed with a treasure of beautiful silver reliquaries and crucifixes, censers, custodia, vestments and even a pair of silver sandals; notice too the painted panel depicting the spiritual conquest of New Spain and showing the relative influence of the Franciscans, Augustinians and Dominicans in the sixteenth century, and above it the diagram of churches liberally dotted among the lakes of the Valley of México.

The **upper storey** around the cloister contains more religious painting than anyone could take in on one visit, including portraits of the Society of Jesus and others of beatific eighteenth- and nineteenth-century nuns. Here too is the **Cristo del Árbol**, a crucifix carved towards the end of the seventeenth century from a single piece of wood.

Stairs descend to the **Claustro de los Naranjos**, planted with orange and lemon trees and with a fountain in the middle. Around it are displays of wooden religious statuary – Balthazar and Caspar, two of the three Magi, are particularly fine. Other rooms contain more colonial miscellany – lacquerwork, furniture (notably an inlaid wooden desk) and clothes – and some temporary exhibition space. Outside extends the walled **Huerta**, or garden, some three hectares of lawns, shady trees and floral displays, as well as vegetables and medicinal herbs cultivated as they would have been by the monks. It is not as well tended as it could be, but makes a break from the museum and has a few architectural pieces and large sculptures dotted around, including, at the far end, the original eighteenth-century **Salto del Agua** that stood at the end of the aqueduct carrying water from Chapultepec into Mexico City (a replica of the fountain stands in the capital now, near Metro Salto del Agua).

Returning to the main cloister, you find a mixed bag, with pre-Hispanic statuary leading on to details of Spanish exploration, suits of armour, exquisite marquetry boxes and a sequence of rooms, one filled with ivory statues, another laid out for Spanish nobles to dine, and then the **Botica**, or pharmacy, with bottles, jars, pestles and mortars, and all the other equipment of an eighteenth-century healer. The **Capilla Doméstica** also opens off the cloister, a whirl of painted and gilded Rococo excess, with a magnificent gilded *retablo* full of mirrors and little figures.

## Practicalities

**To get to Tepotzotlán** from Mexico City, take a bus from Metros Cuatro Caminos or Rosario. The buses are slow, rattling their way round the suburbs for what feels like hours (though the total journey is actually little over an hour) before finally leaving the city. Alternatively, you can take an indirect ("via Refinario") Tula bus or a second-class service to Querétaro, both of which depart from the Terminal del Norte, and get off at a road junction about 200m before the first motorway tollbooths, Caseta de Tepotzotlán. From here it's about a twenty-minute walk west along a minor road to the town of

Tepotzotlán, but there's a good chance of being able to hitch, and plenty of local buses. The same road junction by the tollbooths is also the place to pick up buses on to Tula or back to Mexico City.

Tepotzotlán's only central **hotel**, the *Hotel Posada San José*, Plaza Virreynal 13 (☎55/5876-0835; ❸), has some fairly poky cells at the back and some much more appealing rooms with plaza views (❹). There's a good deal more choice when it comes to **eating and drinking**, with cheap eats around the Mercado Municipal, just west of the plaza, and numerous places around the plaza, most with outdoor seating and many hosting mariachi musicians at weekends. They're all pretty good, so peruse the menus and take your pick: favourites include *Pepe's*, below the hotel, and the slightly more expensive *Restaurant Virreyes*, on the north side of the main square, which serves a wide range of dishes for around M$100–120, special barbecues at weekends (M$125) and a Sunday paella (M$110). Less visible, but still noteworthy, is the fairly pricey *Hostería del Convento*, set beautifully in the seminary's grounds and serving excellent Mexican food for M$80–130 a dish, or M$140 if you go for the *chiles en nogada*. Not far away, the tiny Plaza Tepotzotlán shopping courtyard on the corner of Pensador Mexicano and Calle Zaragoza contains *Los Mirlos*, a lovely spot to while away half an hour over a coffee and pastry.



# Tula

The modern city of **TULA DE ALLENDE** lies on the edge of the Valley of México, 85km north of Mexico City. A pleasant enough regional centre with an impressive, if fortress-like, mid-sixteenth-century **Franciscan monastery and church**, it is most notable for the wonderful pre-Hispanic pyramid site of **Tula**, 2km north of the centre.

In legend at least, the mantle of Teotihuacán fell on Tollan, or Tula, as the next great power to dominate Mexico. The Aztecs regarded their city as the successor to Tula and hence embellished its reputation – the streets, they said, had been paved with gold and the buildings constructed from precious metals and stones, while the Toltecs, who founded Tula, were regarded as the inventors of every science and art. In reality, it seems unlikely that Tula was ever as large or as powerful a city as Teotihuacán had been – or as Tenochtitlán was to become – and its period of dominance (about 950–1150 AD) was relatively short. Yet all sorts of puzzles remain about the Toltec era, and in particular their apparent connection with the Yucatán – much of the architecture at Chichén Itzá, for example, appears to have been influenced by the Toltecs. Few people believe that the Toltecs actually had an empire that stretched so far: however warlike (and the artistic evidence is that Tula was a grimly militaristic society, heavily into human sacrifice), they would have lacked the manpower, resources or any logical justification for such expansion.

One possible answer lies in the legends of **Quetzalcoatl**. Adopted from Teotihuacán, the plumed serpent attained far more importance here in Tula, where he is depicted everywhere. At some stage Tula apparently had a ruler identified with Quetzalcoatl who was driven from the city by the machinations of the evil god Texcatlipoca, and the theory goes that this ruler, defeated in factional struggles within Tula, fled with his followers, eventually reaching Maya territory, where they established a new Toltec regime at Chichén Itzá. Though popular for a long time, this hypothesis has now fallen out of fashion following finds at Chichén Itzá that seem to undermine it (see p.819).

## The site

Only a small part of **the site** itself (daily 9am–5pm; M$33, M$30 to bring in a video camera) is of interest: though the city spreads over some considerable area only some of it has been excavated, and the outlying digs are holes in the ground, meaningful only to the archeologists who created them. The ceremonial centre, however, has been partly restored. The centrepiece here is the low, five-stepped pyramid of the **Templo de Tlahuizcalpantecuhtli** (Temple of the Morning Star, or Pyramid B), atop which stand the **Atlantes** – giant, five-metre-tall basalt figures that originally supported the roof of the sanctuary and represent Quetzalcoatl in his guise as the morning star, dressed as a Toltec warrior. They wear elaborately embroidered loincloths, sandals and feathered helmets, and sport ornaments around their necks and legs – for protection, each bears a sun-shaped shield on his back and a chest piece in the form of a stylized butterfly. Each also carries an *atlatl*, or spear-thrower, in his right hand and a clutch of arrows or javelins in his left.

Other pillars are carved with more warriors and gods. Reliefs such as these are a recurrent theme in Tula: the entire temple was originally faced in sculpted stone, and although it was pillaged long ago you can still see some remnants – prowling jaguars and eagles, symbols of the two great warrior groups, devouring human hearts. In front of the temple is a great L-shaped colonnade, where the partly reconstructed pillars originally supported a huge roof under which, perhaps, the priests and nobles would review their troops or take part in ceremonies in the shade. Part of a long bench survives, with its relief decoration of a procession of warriors and priests. More such benches survive in the **Palacio Quemado** (Burnt Palace – it was destroyed by fire), next to the temple on the western side. Its three rooms, each a square, were once covered, with a small central patio to let light in. The middle one is the best preserved, still with much of its original paint and two Chac-mools.

The main square of the city stood in front (south) of the temple and palace, with a low altar platform in the centre and the now ruinous pyramid of the Templo Mayor on the eastern side. The larger of two **ball-courts** in the central area is on the western side of the square: although also largely ruined, this marks one of the closest links between Tula and Chichén Itzá, as it is of identical shape and orientation to the great ball-court there. To the north of the temple stands the **Coatepantli** (Serpent Wall), elaborately carved in relief with images of human skeletons being eaten by giant snakes; beyond this, across an open space, there's a second ball-court, smaller but in better order.

The whole significance of the site is made much clearer if your Spanish is up to translating all the information presented in the **museum** (daily 9am–5pm; free) located by the entrance, and filled with fragments of Atlantes, Chac-mools and basalt heads along with assorted bits of sculpture and frieze.

## Practicalities

**Buses** run from Mexico City's Terminal del Norte (Autobuses del Valle de Mezquital – the desk furthest to your left when you enter the terminal). Direct buses run every thirty to sixty minutes, taking a little less than an hour and a half; slower services via a refinery – "via Refinario" – run every twenty minutes. There are also nine buses a day from Querétaro (2hr 30min). As you approach town, ask to be dropped off beside the train track by the *Hotel Sharon*, from where you should be able to walk (1km), pick up a local bus to just outside the site, or get a taxi (around M$25). Buses from Mexico City and Querétaro terminate at the bus station on Xicohténcatl close to the centre of town. From there, the **entrance to the site** is a thirty-minute walk: turn right out of the bus station to the main road (Ocampo), where you turn right again, over the river and left before the train tracks (by the *Hotel Sharon*), following signs to "Zona Arqueológica".

To get to the town centre from the bus station, turn right as you leave, take the first left (Rojo del Rio) to the end, where a right turn into Hidalgo brings you to the **cathedral** and main square (Plaza de la Constitución). On the corner of the square with Zaragoza, a small local museum, the **Sala Histórica Quetzalcoatl** (daily except Mon, 9am–5pm; free), has a small display of archeological finds, including a mammoth tusk and some Toltec artefacts. There are several reasonably priced **hotels** nearby – try the *Catedral*, Zaragoza 106 (ⓣ773/732-0813, ⓦwww.tulaonline.com/hotelcatedral; ❺), with fairly characterful old rooms all with bathroom and 24-hour hot water, but mostly without outside windows. Two other good bets are the *Hotel Cuéllar*, behind the cathedral at 5 de Mayo 23 (ⓣ773/732-0442, ⓦwww.hotelcuellar.com; ❹), with frumpy rooms and parking; and the *Casa Blanca*, Pasaje Hidalgo 11, off Calle Hidalgo by no. 129 (ⓣ773/732-1186, ⓦwww.casablancatula.com; ❹), with small but comfortable rooms, off-street parking and bottled water, plus TV for an extra M$50.

There are several good **cafés and restaurants** around the main square, particularly *La Pergola*, at no. 10 on the north side, where you can get an excellent comida corrida for M$25. A few steps up Hidalgo at no. 114, the restaurant *Casa Blanca* has a buffet and salad bar for M$110, a set menu for M$69 and breakfasts at M$40–100; *Cafetería Nevería Campanario*, beside the *Catedral*, is good for burgers, quesadillas and coffee.

# Pachuca and around

In recent years, **Pachuca**, the capital of Hidalgo state, has burst out of the ring of hills that once hemmed it in, its expansion fuelled by the need to move industry away from Mexico City. By Mexican standards, though, it remains a fairly small city, its centre easily walkable and full of colonial mansions built on the profits of the rich silver-mining country all about. If you have the time, it is worth venturing to nearby towns where the mining heritage is more apparent and the clean mountain air is refreshing.

## Arrival and information

The **bus station** is about 5km south of the centre and sees both second-class Flecha Roja and first-class ADO arrivals from Mexico City's Terminal del Norte every ten to fifteen minutes. *Colectivos* outside run frequently to Plaza de la Constitución, one of two main squares in the town centre. The other, the **Plaza de la Independencia**, two blocks away, is Pachuca's zócalo, where most of the action happens. From here, Matamoros runs south past a couple of hotels, becoming Mariano before reaching the Glorieta Revolución. There's a small **tourist office** (daily 9am–6pm; ⓣ771/715-1411) in the base of the **Reloj Monumental** on the zócalo (see opposite).

## Accommodation

Of Pachuca's **hotels**, there's nowhere especially classy near the centre, though there are several reasonable places. One good-value establishment is the colonially styled and plant-filled *Noriega*, a block south of the zócalo at

Matamoros 305 (Ⓣ771/715-1555 or 715-1569, Ⓕ715-1844; ❸), with a M$25 saving if you can manage without TV. Somewhat cheaper but not as nice, with rather dingy rooms, is *América*, Victoria 203 (Ⓣ771/715-0055; ❶), almost opposite, which has some rooms with bath (❷) and some with bath and TV (❸). The most characterful place in town is *Hotel de los Baños*, just off the zócalo at Matamoros 205 (Ⓣ771/713-0700 or 01, Ⓕ715-1441; ❸), with carpeted rooms, each with TV and bathroom around a central, enclosed courtyard. Standard rooms have attractively carved wooden furniture, and in the superior rooms (❹) the craftsmanship is decidedly over the top. For a slightly higher standard of comfort, but less character, there are two almost identical modern hotels facing each other across the zócalo, both with rooms that have plaza views: *Ciro's* (Ⓣ771/715-5351, Ⓔreservaciones@hotelciros.com; ❹), which has pleasantly furnished rooms with phone and TV; and *Emily* (Ⓣ771/715-0828 or 01-800/501-6339, Ⓦwww.hotelemily.com.mx; ❺), slightly posher, with some suites (❻).

## The Town

Nestled below the hills that once provided such a bounty, Pachuca's zócalo is dominated by the **Reloj Monumental**, a forty-metre French Neoclassical clock tower funded by the Cornish-born local mining magnate Francis Rule in 1910 to mark a hundred years of Mexican independence. There's a good deal more interest at the late sixteenth-century Ex-Convento de San Francisco, reached by walking three blocks south along Matamoros, then left for 300m along Revolución (which becomes Arista). The ex-convent now operates as the **Centro Cultural Hidalgo**, which contains the **Museo de la Fotografía** (Tues–Sun 10am–6pm; free). Drawing on over a million photographic works stored here as part of the national archive, the museum does a great job of showcasing both Mexican and foreign photographers and foreigners working in Mexico. Early photographic techniques are illustrated before you move on to the gallery space, where displays change constantly but almost always include images from the Casasola Archive. The pre-eminent Mexican photojournalist of his day, **Agustín Casasola** chronicled both the Revolution and everyday life in its wake, forming an invaluable record of one of Mexico's more turbulent periods. Look too for work by Guillermo Kahlo, father of Frida and stereoscopic plates of early railway construction, as well as photos by Tina Modotti, an Italian-born American who worked here in the 1930s and was part of the Kahlo/Rivera set.

Pachuca's other museum is the mildly diverting **Museo de Minereía** (Wed–Sun 10am–2pm & 3–6pm; M$15), which is one block south and two blocks east of the zócalo at Mina 110 (that's Calle de Javier Mina, not Calle de la Mina), and full of mineral samples and mining equipment.

## Eating and drinking

Pachuca is known in Mexico for **pastes**, which originated with the Cornish pasties once made by Cornish miners working in nearby Real del Monte (see p.498). They still come *tradicional* (or *tipo Inglés*), filled with ground meat, onion and potato, as well as with fillings such as chicken *mole* or *refritos*. Though they differ in shape, they're closely related to typical Mexican empanadas, which are usually sold in the same shops stuffed with tuna, pineapple or even rice pudding. You'll find bakeries selling *pastes* all over the region, and even at the bus station. These might sustain you for a short visit but on longer stays you'll want to visit **restaurants** such as *Reforma*, Matamoros 111, on the east side of the zócalo, which does good breakfasts (M$40–70) and typical Mexican *antojitos* (M$40–50). For espressos, croissants and burgers, pop down the street to *Mi Antiguo Café*, Matamoros 115; for something classier in the evening make for either the family-style *Mirage*, Guerrero 1210 (a block west of the zócalo and 300m south), where you might try the local *tacos mineros* (chicken tacos with salsa and cheese), or *Alex Steak*, about 500m south of the zócalo at Glorieta Revolución 102 (Ⓣ771/713-0053), where enormous and beautifully prepared steaks are served for around M$170. There's little in the way of diverting nightlife, but the *Mirage* does have a cosy **bar**.



## Around Pachuca: Real del Monte and Mineral del Chico

Fourteen kilometres north of Pachuca, draped across pine-clad hills, sits **REAL DEL MONTE** (aka Mineral del Monte), a formerly very wealthy silver-mining town, and, at over 2700m, a nice retreat from Mexico City. There's not a lot to do here, but it is a quietly appealing place where you can wander around the well-tended streets, and perhaps out into the hills all about to carefully explore mining relics. The town's architecture is largely Spanish colonial, but is given an odd twist by the almost exclusive use of red corrugated-iron roofing, and the existence of Cornish-style cottages with their double-pitched rooflines. Some 350 Cornish miners moved here after 1824 when a British company operated mines that were first opened by the Spanish in the mid-sixteenth century. The British pulled out in 1848, to be replaced by a Mexican successor firm, but many of the miners and their Cornish influence remained, resulting in surprisingly authentic Cornish pasties and the introduction of *fútbol* (soccer), which was played for the first time on Mexican soil here in Real. Indeed, this British community in Mexico went on to found Pachuca football club and the Mexican football league (see box opposite). Many of the miners, who were Methodist rather than Catholic, now rest in the British cemetery (Panteón Inglés) on the edge of town (usually locked, but the caretaker should, with luck, be somewhere nearby to open it up).

**To get to Real del Monte** from Pachuca, walk 200m north of the zócalo along Zaragoza to Calle de Julian Villagran (the northwest corner of Plaza de la Constitución) and pick up one of the very frequent **colectivos**, which drop you close to the centre of Real. Less convenient buses also run hourly from the bus station. Most likely you'll visit on a day trip from Pachuca, but there is tempting **accommodation** in the form of *Hotel Real del Monte*, just off the main square on the corner of Iturbide and García (Ⓣ 771/797-1202 or 3, Ⓦwww.hotelsecoturisticos.com.mx; ❺ midweek, ❻ weekends), beautifully decorated and furnished, with wooden floors, antique-style furniture and heaters to ward off the chilly nights. The *Restaurant D'Karla* opposite also rents out rooms (Ⓣ771/797-0709; ❸–❹). Several other small **restaurants** are located along Hidalgo, off the central plaza. *La Central* has decent food and a M$30 comida corrida. *Real de Plateros*, opposite, does the town's best *pastes* (Cornish-style potato, or Mexican-style bean) and empanadas.

### Mineral del Chico

The road between Pachuca and Real del Monte passes a road junction, 10km north of Pachuca, from where a side road winds down towards **Parque Nacional El Chico**, which is noted for its impressive rock formations and good hiking. The tiny village of **Mineral del Chico**, 4km from the road junction, is the main base for exploring the park and offers a few restaurants and

## Football in Mexico

As in much of Latin America, **fútbol** in Mexico is a national addiction, if not an obsession. Turn on the TV and often as not you'll find a match. If you can get to see a live game, it's a different experience entirely.

Football (meaning soccer, of course) was introduced to Mexico in the nineteenth century by a group of Cornish miners in Real del Monte, Hidalgo (see opposite), and it was in that state, by descendants of these Cornishmen, that Mexico's first football club, Pachuca, was founded in 1901. The football **league** was created six years later. The league follows a complicated ladder system: the first division is divided into three tables of six teams each, which are decided by the previous season's placings, with the league champions placed first in table one, second placed top of table two and so on. The top two teams of each table compete in a play-off for the league championship.

There are two **seasons** a year: Apertura (Aug–Nov) and Clausura (Jan–June). At the end of the Clausura season, the two seasons' winners (if they are different) compete to decide that year's champion of champions.

**Relegation** to a lower division is decided over a two-season (yearly) loss average, so it is, in fact, technically possible to come first in the league and be relegated in the same season. However, relegation need not be the disaster that it might seem. Take, for example, Puebla C.F., who when relegated in 1999 simply bought the team promoted from Primera B (Curtodores), changed their name to Puebla and relocated them, which is perfectly legal under Mexican financial regulations. Similarly, there are no regulations preventing anyone from owning more than one team, which can lead to a clash of interests that are never more than speculated upon; suspicion of corruption is rife but rarely, if ever, investigated.

**Matches** themselves are always exciting and enjoyed by even the most diehard "anti-futbolistas". Music, dancing and, of course, the ubiquitous Mexican Wave make for a carnival atmosphere, enhanced by spectators dressing up and wearing face paint. They're usually very much family affairs, with official salespeople bringing soft drinks, beer and various types of food at fixed prices to your seat. **Stadiums** tend to be mostly concrete, with sitting-room only, and can sometimes be dangerously overcrowded, though accidents are thankfully rare. Attendances vary depending on which team is playing, since support is less locally based than you might expect and the more successful teams naturally have the edge, to the detriment of smaller, local sides. The bigger clubs are those of Mexico City (América, Cruz Azul, Pumas – the national university side, Necaxa and Atlante) and Guadalajara (Chivas, Atlas and Tecos) and the games between any of these can draw crowds of up to 80,000, while smaller clubs like those of Puebla, Irapuato and Celaya may get no more than 10,000 or 15,000 spectators per game. The vast distances between clubs make travelling to away games impossible for many fans, another reason why smaller, more out-of-the-way clubs don't get as much support. Passion for the game means that emotions run high, but this does not usually turn into violence. Opposing fans aren't generally separated, but there's a good relationship between them and an atmosphere of self-policing prevails – part of what makes it an ideal family occasion. The greatest risk is often to the referee, who is frequently escorted from the pitch by armed riot police. The players, on the other hand, are accorded a great deal of respect and the more popular ones tend to pick up nicknames, such as "Kikín" (striker Francisco Fonseca – Kicking), "El Pajaro Humano" (goalie Oswaldo Sánchez – the Human Bird), and "Cabrito" (zippy midfielder Jesús Arellano – Little Goat).

For **national games**, of course, the whole country is united, and football has many times been shown to rise above the partisan politics of the country. In 1999, despite being outlawed by the government, the EZLN football squad even played an exhibition match against the national side in Mexico City's Estadio Azteca.

For **up-to-date information** on Mexican league teams, fixtures and tables, visit ⓦwww.futmex.com or ⓦwww.futbolmexicano.net.

a couple of luxurious **hotels**: *Posada del Amencer*, right in town at Morelos 3 (weekends only, ⓣ771/715-4812, ⓦwww.hotelesecoturisticos.com.mx; ⑥); and *Hotel El Paraíso* (ⓣ771/715-5654, ⓦwww.hotelesecoturisticos.com.mx; ⑦ midweek, ⑧ weekends), about 1km before town. There is no direct public transport from Real del Monte, but *colectivos* from Pachuca can be found on Carranza, 300m north of Plaza de la Constitución.

# Tlaxcala and around

Allied to Cortés in his struggle against the Aztecs, as well as with colonial Spain in the War of Independence, **TLAXCALA**, the capital of a tiny state of the same name, has become a byword for treachery. Because of its alliance with Cortés, the town suffered a very different fate from that of nearby Cholula, which aligned itself with the Aztecs (see p.509), and in the long run this has led to an even more total disappearance of its ancient culture. The Spanish founded a colonial town here – now restored and very beautiful in much of its original colonial glory, but whether because of its traitorous reputation or simply its isolation, development in Tlaxcala has been limited.

The town lies 100km west of Mexico City and 30km north of Puebla in the middle of a fertile, prosperous-looking upland plain surrounded by rather bare mountains. It's an exceptionally pretty and much rehabilitated colonial town, comfortable enough but also fairly dull. Most of the interest lies very close to the zócalo, with its central bandstand, where the terracotta and ochre tones of the buildings lend the city its tag of "Ciudad Roja", the Red City. Its appearance, slow pace and proximity to the nation's capital have drawn a small expat community, though the latter's impact on daily life is minimal.

## Arrival and accommodation

Frequent **buses** from Mexico City, Puebla and surrounding towns arrive at the bus station on the edge of the centre. *Colectivos* parked outside run to nearby villages and the zócalo, though it's only about a ten-minute walk: exit the bus station and turn right downhill to the next main junction, then take a right down Guerrero for five blocks and left down Juárez. To return to the bus station, take the *colectivo* that stops on the corner by the church just off the zócalo.

Behind the Palacio de Gobierno, on the zócalo, there's a helpful **tourist office** on the corner of Juárez and Lardizábal (Mon–Fri 9am–7pm, Sat & Sun 9am–6pm; ⓣ246/465-0968, ⓦwww.tlaxcala.gob.mx/turismo), where you can pick up useful free maps and book guided tours. Most other facilities – banks, post office and the like – cluster round the zócalo and along Juárez.

Tlaxcala doesn't have any really low-cost **accommodation**. The cheapest option, and good value, is *Hotel Alifer*, at Morelos 11, by the junction with Xicohténcatl (ⓣ246/466-0620 to 22, ⓦwww.hotelalifer.com; ④), which has comfy, carpeted rooms with TV. For something posher, there's *Posada San Francisco*, on the southern side of the zócalo at Plaza de la Constitución 17 (ⓣ246/462-6022, ⓦwww.posadasanfrancisco.com; ⑧), occupying a lovely old mansion with colonially furnished rooms, pool and tennis courts.

## The town and around

The entire north side of the zócalo is taken up by the **Palacio de Gobierno** (daily 8am–6pm; free; enter by easternmost door), whose patterned brick facade is broken by ornate windows and doorways. The building incorporates parts of a much earlier structure, erected soon after the Conquest, and inside boasts a series of brilliantly coloured **murals** by a local, Desiderio Hernandez Xochitiotzin, that took nearly fifty years to complete. The panels depict the history of the Tlaxcalan people from their migration from the north to their alliance with Cortés. The two most spectacular are one on the stairs depicting the Spanish Conquest and another at the bottom showing the Great Market.

To the west of the Palacio de Gobierno, and dominating a small square off the side of the zócalo, stands the tiled facade of the **Parroquia de San José**. It's an attractive building, but except for two fonts beside the door depicting Camaxtli, the Tlaxcalan god of hunting and war, the inside is a disappointment. Notice the seventeenth-century painting beside the altar that depicts the baptism of a Tlaxcalan chief, as overseen by Cortés and his mistress, La Malinche.

At the opposite corner of the zócalo, the smaller Plaza Xicohténcatl holds the **Museo de la Memoria** (Tues–Sun 10am–5pm; M$10, free on Tues), a modern museum devoted to the cultural history of the region. Its imaginative displays (some interactive) – illustrating pre-Hispanic *tianguis* (markets), Franciscan life under the Spanish and the ruling structure in Tlaxcala before and after Cortés – make up for the fact that it's light on artefacts.

At the southeastern corner of Plaza Xicohténcatl, a broad, tree-lined path leads up to a triple set of arches. Beyond them, an open area overlooking the city's pretty nineteenth-century bullring is flanked on one side by the Ex-Convento de San Francisco, started in 1537. Wrapped around the convent's cloister, the **Museo Regional de Tlaxcala** (Tues–Sun 10am–5pm; M$33) covers local life from prehistoric times to the present day – an unexceptional collection but well displayed in a series of whitewashed rooms. The **Catedral de Nuestra Señora de la Asunción** next door is also relatively plain, though it has a beautiful vaulted wooden ceiling decorated in Mudéjar style, the design elements harking back to the Moorish style then common in southern Spain. The Moors were expelled from Spain in 1492, and though their influence continued for some decades, this is only apparent in Mexican churches started immediately after the Conquest. One large chapel, more richly decorated than the rest, contains the font in which Xicohténcatl and other Tlaxcalan leaders were baptized in the presence of Cortés in 1520. Opposite, the lower walls of another chapel bear traces of ancient frescoes.

Tlaxcala's third museum is the **Museo de Artes y Tradiciones Populares**, corner of Mariano Sanchez and 1 de Mayo, three blocks west of the zócalo (Tues–Sun 10am–6pm; M$6). It focuses on traditional crafts and customs, with sections on bell making (including an example cast on the site) and has a fascinating room on the manufacture and consumption of *pulque*.

### Santuario de Ocotlán

Approaching town you will almost certainly have noticed the twin wedding-cake towers of the **Santuario de Ocotlán**, which overlook Tlaxcala on a hill to the east. There are great views over the surrounding countryside from up here, but the real interest is the church, its facade a riot of churrigueresque excess that ranks it alongside those at Tepotzotlán and Taxco. Inside, it is no less florid, the huge Baroque *retablo* seeming to spread seamlessly to the dome and along the transept in a frenzy of gilt woodwork. Such exuberance is justified by the miraculous work of the Virgin. According to legend, she appeared to a poor Indian in 1541 with instructions to cure an epidemic with waters from a stream that had miraculously sprung forth. Naturally everyone recovered. Then the Virgin asked the Indian to bring the local Franciscan monks to a forest. Once they were there, fire suddenly burst forth, but though the flames were fierce, they didn't burn the trees. The next day the monks returned, to find that one pine tree (*ocotlán*) contained a wooden image of the Virgin. Now installed on the altar, it is carved and painted very much in the style of the times. The life of Our Lady of Ocotlán is portrayed around the eight walls of the ornate **Camarín de la Virgen** (the Virgin's Dressing Room) behind the altar. In May, the church and surrounding streets host the procession of the Virgin, attended by thousands of pilgrims.

The church is about 1km from the zócalo, a fairly steep thirty minutes' walk north along Juárez, then right onto Guridi y Alcocer, which runs past the **Pocito**, a small octagonal shrine.



## Eating and drinking

For a relatively small city, Tlaxcala seems particularly well stocked with **restaurants** and **bars**, especially around the zócalo and along Juárez. Some of the most inviting are those under the *portales* on the eastern and southern sides of the zócalo, where you can sit outside and watch life go by: try *Los Portales*, Plaza de la Constitución 8 (☎246/462-5419), with its broad range of *antojitos*, burgers, salads, pasta dishes and the delicious *sopa tlaxcalteca* (M$35), made from black beans, tortilla chips, cheese, avocado and *chicharrón* (pork crackling). The *Italian Coffee Company* at Plaza de la Constitucion 4 has the best coffee in the square and a lively atmosphere. Far better value than the places in the zócalo arcades is *Mesón del Rey*, Morelos 12 at Xicohténcatl, with cobalt blue and orange decor, nicely set tables with cloths and a set menu for just M$25.

The restaurants all serve alcohol, but for a more dedicated drinking experience visit *Las Ventas*, a convivial saloon **bar** on the south side of Plaza Xicohténcatl, decorated with paintings of naked women bullfighting.

## Around Tlaxcala: Cacaxtla and Xochitécatl

Some 17km southwest of Tlaxcala lies the ancient site of **Cacaxtla** (daily 10am–5pm; M$38), where a particularly fine series of murals depicting battle scenes was discovered in 1975. They are clearly Maya in style, which would seem to indicate trade or perhaps even a Maya settlement here.

Two kilometres west of Cacaxtla, the ruins of **Xochitécatl** (same hours and ticket) have three impressive pyramids and monolithic stones. These can be reached by frequent *colectivo* ("San Miguel del Milagro") from Mariano and Lardizábal, or by bus to the nearby village of Nativitas from either Tlaxcala or Puebla. Alternatively, every Sunday the tourist office in Tlaxcala organizes **guided tours** to both sites for M$58; you're picked up in Tlaxcala from outside the post office at the southwest corner of the zócalo at 10am and dropped off at 2.30pm.

The rather less impressive archeological site of **Tizatlán** (Tues–Sun 10am–5pm; M$27), 4km north of town, can be reached by *colectivo* from 1 de Mayo and 20 de Noviembre.

# Puebla

East of the capital, the road to **PUEBLA** climbs steeply, with glorious views of the snowy heights of Popocatépetl and Ixtaccíhuatl along the way. Little more than an hour on the bus from Mexico City, this is the republic's fifth largest city

(after Mexico City, Guadalajara, Monterrey and Tijuana). The centre has a remarkable concentration of sights – a fabulous **cathedral**, a "hidden" **convent**, museums and colonial **mansions** – while the mountainous country round about is in places startlingly beautiful. Nevertheless, Puebla is unlikely to tempt you into staying particularly long and in a couple of leisurely days (or one packed day) you can see the best of the city and nearby **Cholula**.

The city was founded by the Spanish in 1531, preferred to the ancient sites of Cholula and Tlaxcala possibly because there the memories of indigenous power remained too strong. It rapidly assumed great importance as a staging point on the journey from the capital to the port at Veracruz and for the shipment of goods from Spain's Far Eastern colonies, which were delivered to Acapulco and transported across Mexico from there. Wealth was brought, too, by the reputation of Puebla's ceramics, particularly its tiles. This industry – still very much in evidence – was helped by an abundance of good clays in the region, and by settlers from Talavera in Spain, who brought traditional ceramic skills with them. The city did well out of colonial rule, and, perhaps not surprisingly, it took the wrong side in the War of Independence. As a result, it preserves a reputation for conservatism and traditional values, not dispelled even by the fact that the start of the Revolution is generally dated from the assassination of Aquiles Serdán in his Puebla home.

Military defeat seems to play a larger part in Puebla's history than it does in most of Mexico – the city fell to the Americans in 1847 and to the French in 1863 – but it isn't what's remembered. Rather, it's the greatest victory in the country's history – here, a force of some two thousand Mexicans defeated a

French army three times its size in 1872. To this day, Puebla commemorates May 5 (**Cinco de Mayo**) with a massive fiesta, and there's a public holiday throughout the country.

## Arrival and information

Puebla's **bus station**, known by the acronym CAPU (Central de Autobuses de Puebla), is 5km northwest of the city centre. There's a guardería and **authorized taxis** to the centre of town for M$40, or you can turn right outside and walk about 200m along the main road where you can hop onto one of the frequent local buses and *colectivos* that run to the centre. To get back to CAPU from town, buses can be picked up along 9 Norte or 9 Sur.

At 5 Oriente 3, near the corner of 16 de Septiembre, the **tourist office** (Mon–Sat 8am–8pm, Sun 9am–2pm; ⓣ222/777-1519; ⓦwww.sectur.pue.gob.mx) provides information and free maps; the same maps are also available at many hotels and tourist sights around town.

## Accommodation

Finding somewhere reasonable to stay in Puebla can be difficult, as accommodation fills up early, but **hotels** are easy to spot – they nearly all have a protruding "H" sign, and most are just to the west and north of the zócalo. On the whole, the closer to the zócalo, the higher the price, though there are good budget places close in.

**Colonial** 4 Sur 105 ⓣ222/246-4612, ⓦwww.colonial.com.mx. Luxurious lodgings in a beautiful colonial building next to the Autonomous University of Puebla. All rooms have TV and phone, and many have beautifully tiled bathrooms. There's also a fine restaurant on site. ❺

**Hostal de Santa Domingo** 4 Pte 312 ⓣ222/232-1671, ⓔhostalstodomingo@yahoo.com.mx. More like a budget hotel than a hostel, but still backpacker-oriented. The ten-bed mixed dorms (M$10) each has its own bathroom, and the private rooms, not deluxe by any means, are spacious and mostly en suite. There's also a lounge to hang out in, and rates include breakfast. ❸

**Mesón Sacristía de la Compañía** 6 Sur 304 ⓣ01-800/712-4028 or 222/242-3554, ⓦwww.g-networks/sacristia. Gorgeous hotel in a 200-year-old house with just nine spacious rooms and suites, each one different but all with heavy wood beams, furnished with antiques and elegantly decorated. The restaurant is also excellent (see p.509). If you can't get in here, check out the second branch (*Mesón Sacrista de Capuchinas*) at 9 Ote 16. ❾

**Palace** 2 Ote 13 ⓣ222/232-2430, ⓦwww.hotelpalacedepuebla.com. Good-value, modern three-star hotel just one block off the zócalo. The lobby area and restaurant are pretty busy, and the rooms aren't huge, but they're clean and fresh with TV, fan and good bathrooms. ❺

**Reforma 2000** 4 Pte 916, corner of 11 Nte ⓣ222/242-3363, ⓦwww.hotelreforma2000.com. Comfortable, carpeted, spacious rooms, with TV and phone. Nice bar and restaurant, plus parking facilities. ❸

**Victoria** 3 Pte 306 ⓣ222/232-8992 or 01-800/849-2793. Basic but clean and quiet rooms, each with bathroom and 24hr hot water. ❶

**Virrey de Mendoza** Reforma 538 ⓣ222/242-3903. Small hotel with big, carpeted rooms around a verdant central courtyard with its own grand staircase. Good value and one of the best of the mid-range places. ❹

## The Town

Puebla's **zócalo** is the centre of the numbering system for the ancient grid of streets (lowest numbers are nearest to the centre) and home to the great looming **cathedral** (daily 7am–12.30pm & 4.15–7.30pm; free), the second largest in the republic. Built between 1562 and the middle of the following century, the exterior is ugly and grey, but the inside improves considerably, with amazing

# Festive Mexico

**As if Mexico wasn't colourful and noisy enough on any given day, there are numerous points throughout the year dedicated especially to celebration. Everyone puts on their brightest new clothes, cranks up the music and floods the streets to commemorate a saint's birthday, a great moment in history or even the death of a loved one. Some festivities are regional – a village's annual fiesta, for instance – while others sweep up the entire nation in a wave of dancing, bright lights and *muchas cervezas*.**

▲ Holy Week procession, Iztapalapa

# Religious events

The Catholic calendar provides countless opportunities for celebrating, with many of the biggest events observed with a combination of religious fervour and all-out partying. The **Día de la Virgen de Guadalupe** (Dec 12) is one such occasion. Ringed with gold and standing on the crescent moon, this blue-robed Virgin Mary, often considered a syncretic melding of the Catholic image and the indigenous Mexican goddess Tonantzin, is an icon of Mexico. It was on December 12 in 1531 that Aztec convert Juan Diego, to whom Mary had appeared a few days earlier, tipped open his cloak to reveal a cascade of miraculous winter-blooming roses and the image of the Virgin of Guadalupe imprinted on the fabric. The cloak, with the image still visible, is on display at the Basílica de Nuestra Señora de Guadalupe in Mexico City (see p.463). The most zealous festivities take place here, with nearly a million visitors often approaching on foot or even on their knees. Similar processions can be seen during **Semana Santa**, or Holy Week (the week before Easter), when pilgrims converge on churches, and people re-enact the full Passion of Christ. The most famous staging is in Iztapalapa, outside of Mexico City, where the event involves a cast of thousands, buckets of fake blood and more than a million spectators.

Despite its religious affiliation, the week before the beginning of Lent, known as **Carnaval**, is almost purely bacchanalian: you can expect plenty of glittery costumes, elaborate parades, beauty queens and dancing in the streets at these parties in early spring (usually mid- to late February or early March). They're celebrated most vigorously in the coastal cities, including Veracruz and San Miguel on Cozumel. The city of **Mazatlán** claims to have the world's third-largest Mardi Gras party, after New Orleans and Rio de Janeiro, and the schedule includes an excellent arts and culture festival as well.

▼ Carnaval, Veracruz

## When's Mexican Independence Day?

Party-loving tourists take note: Mexicans celebrate **Día de la Independencia** on September 16 – not May 5. **Cinco de Mayo**, as that latter day is known, is actually celebrated more enthusiastically in the US, where many *gringos* (who see the date as a chance to have a theme party involving sombreros, nachos and tequila), have come to believe it's Mexico's equivalent of the US's July 4. In fact, May 5 marks the army's triumph over the French at the **Battle of Puebla** in 1862, a confrontation that put an end to European powers meddling in Mexican affairs. It's a notable date in Puebla, but barely causes a ripple elsewhere in the country. September 16, on the other hand, is a nationwide reason to take to the streets. Festivities begin at 11pm (midnight in the Yucatán) on September 15, when people gather in central plazas for the collective *grito* – the gutsy cry of "Mexicanos, viva México!", first uttered by the priest Miguel Hidalgo in 1810 as he rallied his congregation to fight the Spanish. Fireworks, dancing and, yes, tequila-drinking carry on into the next day.

# Town fiestas

Even the tiniest village in Mexico has an **annual fiesta**, usually on the name day of the town's patron saint. Depending on where you are, this often involves some blend of rodeos, bullfights, dancing, fried snacks, carnival rides, fireworks and processions around the church, often by various **gremios**, or trade guilds – everyone from plumbers to taxi drivers. Fiestas usually last at least a couple of days, to get everyone properly into the spirit. These local parties are a great opportunity to see indigenous dances – such as the **Danza de los Viejitos** (Dance of the Old Men) in **Michoacán**, or the feather-bedecked **quetzales** in Cuetzalan, **Puebla** – that the rest of the year are performed only in sterile "folkloric" stage extravaganzas.

▲ Danza de los Viejitos, Pátzcuaro

# Cultural festivals

▲ Performers, Cervantino

Not all of Mexico's festivals are in celebration of the past: the country also hosts some dazzling confabs of contemporary music, art and dance. The largest of these, Guanajuato's **Festival Internacional Cervantino** (see box, p.290), has been happening since the 1970s. Every October, it brings together Mexican marimba legends with French jazz artists, choral music from England and international dance troupes. Smaller but no less wide-ranging events grace other cities: January's **Ortiz Tirado Music Festival** in Alamos, Sonora, draws leading classical musicians and singers, while Monterrey features local rock bands, along with other eclectic musicians, in the **Festival Cultural Barrio Antiguo** every November. The best part: visitors can usually drop in to a number of performances for free, and even tickets for headlining acts can be very reasonably priced.

# Día de los Muertos

If visitors know just one Mexican holiday, it's probably the **Day of the Dead**, when families gather to honour and remember those who have died. Actually taking place over two days, November 1 and 2, it's an indigenous tradition unique to Mexico, and the least raucous religious celebration of the year. With a few exceptions (such as the beautiful torch-lighting ceremony and festive dances around Lago de Pátzcuaro), it's also usually a private rite, one that visitors don't have much chance to participate in directly. In every home and many businesses people set up *ofrendas* (altars) for the deceased: the centrepiece is always a photograph, lit by candles. In addition to the photo, the person's favourite foods are also placed on the altar, as a way of luring the soul back to this world. For the same reason, strong-scented, bright orange marigolds are often laid in a path leading to the altar, and resinous *copal* incense is lit. On the streets, market stalls brim with eggy, orange-scented *pan de muertos* and colourfully iced sugar skulls. Día de los Muertos is such an integral part of the Mexican calendar, in fact, there's even a bit of high-grade commercial kitsch on sale, from greeting cards to paper party hats decorated with skulls. Families usually gather to eat dinner the night of November 1, then go together to visit gravesites, which are also cleaned and decorated. Far from being a sad time, the Day of the Dead is an occasion for telling funny stories, bonding with family and generally celebrating life.

▼ Sugar skulls for Día de los Muertos

ornamentation in onyx, marble and gilt and a wonderful altar designed by Manuel Tolsá in 1797. The cathedral, and particularly the tower, was partly funded by Bishop Juan de Palafox y Mendoza, an illegitimate son of a Spanish nobleman who grew up with his poor mother but inherited his father's fortune. Behind the cathedral, near the tourist office, lies the old Archbishop's Palace, which was converted to a library in the seventeenth century (the Biblioteca Palafoxiana, reputed to be the oldest library in the Americas), and houses the original collection of ancient books and manuscripts on the upper floor. Downstairs there's the **Casa de la Cultura** (Mon–Sat 8am–8pm, Sun 8am–6pm; free), which hosts regular exhibitions of local arts and crafts.



## Museo Amparo

The undoubted star in Puebla's museum firmament is the modern **Museo Amparo**, 2 Sur 708 at 9 Oriente (daily except Tues 10am–6pm; M$35, free on Mon, video camera M$50; Ⓦwww.museoamparo.com), which concentrates on art from pre-Hispanic Mesoamerica, with additional material from the colonial and more recent eras. Set in a pair of modernized colonial buildings with peaceful courtyards and piped classical music, the collection is the legacy of philanthropist Manuel Espinosa Iglesias, who set up the Amparo Foundation in honour of his wife.

The historical significance of the pieces isn't glossed over, but the focus is firmly on aesthetics, with well-presented cases displaying artefacts to their best advantage. To set the tone, the entrance features an impressive glass replica of a **tzompantli skull-wall** with alternating Olmec and Totonac heads in each of the glass blocks. A room decorated with reproduction **cave paintings** from Altamira in Spain, Arnhemland in Australia, Utah, Norway and Baja California put Mexico's cultural development into some sort of context before you launch into the main collection. Though far smaller than that in Mexico City's anthropology museum, this is well chosen and a good deal more manageable. It is particularly strong on the Olmecs, a people who greatly influenced life around Puebla and left behind some strikingly beautiful pieces such as the half-metre-wide stone head on display here. Elsewhere notice the exquisite Colima jaguar, the beautiful carved conch shell from the Gulf coast and the sculpture of a kneeling woman from Nayarit with her distinctive face and body painting.

The last section of the museum is devoted to **colonial painting** and rooms set with seventeenth- and eighteenth-century furnishings. Everything in the museum is thoroughly documented at strategically located computer consoles, so you probably won't need the rental **headsets** (M$20; available in Spanish, English, French, German and Japanese) with their relatively cursory commentary. Free guided tours in English and Spanish take place at noon on Sunday.

## North of the zócalo

Head north from the zócalo along 5 de Mayo and you'll reach the church of **Santo Domingo** at the corner of 4 Poniente. The chapel here, the **Capilla del Rosario**, is, even in comparison to the cathedral, a quite unbelievably lavish orgy of gold leaf and Baroque excess; a constant hushed, shuffling stream of devotees lights candles and prays to the image of the Virgin. Three doors down, the **Museo José Luis Bello y Zetina**, 5 de Mayo 409 (Tues–Sun 10am–4pm; free), displays the paintings and furniture of the wealthy Bello family, who lived here during the nineteenth century – you'll see everything from seventeenth-century Flemish masters to a Napoleonic bedroom suite. It somehow seems too comfortless to be a home yet not

△ Capilla del Rosario, Puebla

formal enough for a museum, though the enthusiasm of your personal guide (whose services are free but not compulsory) may rub off.

Nearby, a passage leads to the glass and iron **Mercado Victoria**, at the corner of 5 de Mayo and 6 Oriente, once Puebla's main market but now a rather sanitized shopping centre. East of the market, candy stores along 6 Oriente sell *camotes*, gooey fingers of sweet potato and sugar flavoured with various fruits – a regional speciality. If you're thinking of buying any to take home, however, note that they only last a couple of weeks. Further along the street, the devotional **Museo Regional de la Revolución Mexicana**, 6 Oriente 206 (Tues–Sun 10am–4.30pm; M$10, free on Tues), records the struggles for Liberalism of the Serdán family against the dictatorship of Porfirio Díaz. The assassination of Aquiles Serdán in this house was one of the most important steps in the fall of Díaz: the date of Serdán's death, November 18, 1910, is – in the absence of any firmer indicators – generally recognized as marking the start of the Revolution. The bullet holes in the house have been lovingly preserved, and a huge smashed mirror still hangs on the wall where it appears in contemporary photos of the carnage. Revolution buffs will also enjoy the biographies of key figures in the struggle, photos of the ragtag bands of wide-hatted revolutionaries with their bandoleers and the trap door in the floor under which Serdán spent several fruitless hours trying to avoid his eventual end.

Nine blocks north of the zócalo you'll find the city's remarkable convent, now operating as the **Museo Religioso Santa Mónica**, at 18 Poniente 103 (Tues–Sun 9am–6pm; M$24, free on Sun). Here, from the suppression of the church in 1857 until their discovery in 1934, several generations of nuns lived hidden from the public gaze behind a smokescreen of secret doors and concealed passages. Just how secret they were is a matter of some debate – many claim that the authorities simply turned a blind eye – and certainly several lay families were actively supportive, providing supplies and new recruits. But it makes a good story, embellished by the conversion of the building into a museum that preserves the secret entrances along with many religious artworks and a beautiful seventeenth-century cloister. Several simple cells are also in evidence, and from the hidden chapel you can look down through a screen at the still-operating church next door.

In the same general direction, on the corner of 3 Norte, lies the **Ex-Convento de Santa Rosa**, 14 Poniente 305 (Tues–Sun 10am–5pm; M$10, free on Tues), whose main claim to fame is that the great *mole poblano* was invented here in its wonderful yellow-tiled kitchens. The kitchens are the highlight of a guided tour that includes rooms full of crafts and artesanía from the state of Puebla.

### East of the zócalo

The rest of the town's attractions are concentrated mostly to the east and northeast of the zócalo. First stop is the **Museo Casa de Alfeñique**, at the corner of 4 Oriente and 6 Norte (Tues–Sun 10am–5pm; M$15, free on Sun), located in an elaborate old mansion covered in Puebla tiles. Within, you can see period furnishings, Puebla ceramics, a small archeological section and an excellent display of colonial art.

At the end of 4 Oriente lie the **Mercado Parian** – mostly given over to rather tawdry tourist souvenirs – and the **Barrio del Artista**, traditionally the artists' quarter, now selling work aimed squarely at the tourist market. The **Teatro Principal**, nearby, is a fine eighteenth-century theatre, said to be the oldest on the continent, which still hosts occasional performances.

### West of the zócalo

Follow 4 Poniente west from the zócalo to reach **Taller Uriarte**, 4 Poniente 911 (shop open Mon–Fri 9.30am–7pm, Sat 10.30am–5.30pm, Sun 11am–4.30pm; tours of the factory half-hourly Mon–Fri 9.30am–2pm, M$50; ⓣ222/232-1598), about the best known of Puebla's pottery factories. It is a small-scale affair shoehorned into what appears to be just another urban house, but it is well set up for visitors. You can see every stage of the pottery-making process, from forming the plates and bowls to painting the intricate designs in paints whose colours are completely transformed during firing into distinctive blues and yellows.

Press on a few blocks further out to the **Museo Nacional de los Ferrocarriles**, 11 Norte at 12 Poniente (Tues–Sun 10am–6pm; free), an open-air collection of Mexican railroad cars arranged around Puebla's former train station. Pride of place is given to some menacing-looking steam locomotives, including one 285-tonne monster built in 1946, which was so heavy it could only be run on the most robust lines from Mexico City to the US border. It's amazing to think how important rail travel once was in Mexico, given its almost complete disappearance as a form of transport now.

### Cerro de Guadalupe

To the northwest of the centre, crowning the **Cerro de Guadalupe**, the site of numerous nineteenth-century battles and sieges, is the **Centro Cívico 5 de Mayo**, a collection of museums. Neither of the two forts nor any of the museums here is a match for sights downtown, but they are a decent place to spend a couple of hours away from the fumes and the noise of the centre. To get there, take a Ruta #72 *colectivo* (sometimes marked "Centro Cívico") from Heroes del 5 de Mayo, three blocks east of the zócalo.

Your first stop should be the **Fuerte de Loreto** (Tues–Sun 9am–5.30pm; M$30, free on Sun), where a moat and high walls protect a large empty parade ground and a small church containing the Museo de la No Intervención. This focuses on the events surrounding the 1862 Battle of Puebla, celebrated on Cinco de Mayo, and records 150 years of the defence of the republic through replicated battle scenes. The views of Popo and Ixta from the battlements are some of the best in Puebla.

The best of the rest of the sights out here are the modern **Museo Regional de Puebla** (Tues–Sun 10am–5pm; M$33, free on Sun), largely devoted to the state's archeology and ethnology. There's some exquisite Olmec jade sculpture and sculptural pieces along with a four-metre-high polychrome statue of San Cristóbal from the seventeenth century and sections of wider relevance, such as a detailed explanation of native migration from east Asia through Alaska. Readers with kids will want to traipse across the road to the **Museo Interactivo Imagina** (Mon–Fri 9am–1pm & 2–6pm, Sat & Sun 10am–2pm & 3–7pm; M$37, extra for some exhibits), a collection of educational interactive games, or to the adjacent **Planetarium**, with its IMAX screen, which usually has shows twice a day (M$3; times vary – call ⓣ222/235-2099 for details).

The highest point on the hill is occupied by the **Fuerte de Guadalupe** (Tues–Sun 9am–5.30pm; M$30, free on Sun), the meagre but well-tended remains of an 1862 fort – really just a few arches and roofless rooms.

## Eating and drinking

As with any large Mexican city, there's a huge range of **places to eat** in Puebla, from cheaper places around the Mercado Victoria to good mid-range options around the centre, with better places tucked away in back streets. While in town you should definitely check out the **local specialities**, particularly *mole poblano*, an extraordinary sauce made from chocolate, chiles and any number of herbs and spices. Typically served over chicken, turkey or enchiladas, it is found all over Mexico, but is nowhere better than here, where it was supposedly invented in colonial times for the viceroy's visit to the Convento de Santa Rosa. Should you want to buy some paste to take home (it lasts for ages and doesn't need to be refigerated), a good place to buy it is Abarrotes Lulu at 16 Poniente 304–A, by Mercado 5 de Mayo.

Another taste sensation is *chiles en nogada*, a dish reputedly concocted in 1821 to celebrate Mexican Independence and made to resemble the colours of the Mexican flag. Green poblano chiles are filled with ground meat, fruits and nuts, then covered with a creamy walnut sauce and doused with bright-red pomegranate seeds. It is best sampled from July to September, but can often be found at other times.

Central Puebla is mostly quiet at night and to find any **bars** you'll have to head a few blocks south to the Plazuela de los Sapos, near 6 Sur and 5 Poniente, where several lively drinking holes face each other across a small square. The city is pretty quiet until Thursday night, when you might also head around six long blocks west of the zócalo to the Zona Esmeralda, where there's a string of bars and clubs to keep you going. Otherwise, many people head out to **Cholula** to join the lively, student-heavy crowd there, though you'll have to be prepared for a fairly expensive taxi ride back: buses stop running at around 11pm, just when the clubs start warming up.

**La Batalla** 6 Sur 506. One of a handful of similar bars and *antros* on the Plazuela de los Sapos that pump out Latin and US pop hits. Take your pick from *La Boveda* at no. 503, *El Reguardo de los Angeles* at no. 504 or *D'Pasadita* at no. 501, which is more of a drinkers' bar.

**Café Aguirre** 5 de Mayo 4. Predictable and safe restaurant that's a longstanding local favourite and is always popular with business people for its range of ten breakfast combos, each with juice and coffee (M$49–61), lunch-time menus (M$50–85), *antojitos* (M$47.50–60) and tortas.

**Café Munich** corner 3 Pte and 5 Sur. Basic but reliable restaurant serving a wide range of soups and mains and a great comida in a room decorated with photos of Bavarian scenes and drawings of Einstein, Beethoven, Goethe and Wagner. Cheap (M$33) and pricier (M$59) menus are available at lunch time.

**Caldos Angelita** corner 6 Pte and 9 Nte. A popular no-nonsense diner doling out hearty bowlfuls of chicken broth (M$20) and *mole poblano* (M$28), but only until 6.30pm.

**Fonda de Santa Clara** 3 Pte 307, a couple of blocks west of the zócalo ⓣ222/242-2659, ⓦwww.fondadesantaclara.com. The best-known – and most touristy – restaurant in town, serving local food with an upmarket twist in a pretty room decorated with Mexican art. A good place to try the local specialities without breaking the bank. The weekend buffet breakfast is also worth investigating. There's a second branch at 3 Pte 920 (ⓣ222/246-1952).

**La Guadalupana** 5 Ote 605, Plazuela de los Sapos ⓣ222/242-4886. One of Puebla's most celebrated restaurants, housed in a beautiful colonial building and specializing in regional dishes, many of which are served in a *molcajete*, a kind of volcanic-rock mortar.

**Italian Coffee Company** Reforma 107. Teas, infusions, flavoured espresso coffees and cakes in convivial surroundings. Other branches around town include one at 4 Ote 202, and one at 16 Septiembre opposite the cathedral.

**Librería Cafetería Teorema** Reforma 540, at 7 Nte ⓣ222/298-0028. Combined bookstore, café and live music venue with a relaxed bohemian atmosphere and food, beer and coffee. Gigs usually start around 9.30pm, with acoustic *trova* Sun–Thurs and rock on Fri & Sat. Reservations recommended. Cover M$10–30.

**Litrox** Juárez 1305. Lively bar west of the town centre in the Zona Esmeralda (Juárez is a continuation of 7 Pte west of the Paseo Bravo) with music nightly from 8pm and no cover charge.

**Mesón Sacristía de la Compañía** 6 Sur 304 ⓣ222/242-3554. Come here for fine dining in the superb hotel's lovely enclosed courtyard. Try the house *mole* (M$85), preceded by their special soup made with fried tortilla chips, *chicharrón*, cheese and chipotle (M$45). Efficient, friendly service and a good wine list make this one of Puebla's best dining experiences.

**La Zanahoria** 5 Ote 206 ⓣ222/232-4813. A bustling vegetarian restaurant in Mexican style, with several meat dishes amid the vast array of wholesome herbivorous choices. Burgers and salads are good value, though no match for the M$58 buffet breakfasts and M$48 *menú del día* (replaced by a M$78 buffet on Sun).

## Listings

**Banks and exchange** Banamex, at Reforma 135 (between 3 Norte and 5 de Mayo) is one of several banks that will change money; there's also a casa de cambio in the arcade between the north side of the zócalo and 2 Oriente, and others at CAPU.

**Buses** You'll need to get back to CAPU for all departures except to local destinations such as Cholula, which can be reached by combi from 14 Poniente at 11 Norte, or Tlaxcala, which (in addition to buses from CAPU) is served by micros from a terminal on 10 Poniente between 11 Norte and 13 Norte, by the railway museum. There are frequent services to Mexico City's Terminal del Norte and TAPO.

**Internet access** There are a number of places around the zócalo, most charging less than M$10 per hour phone, with cheap VOIP phone calls too.

**Post office** The main post office, at 16 de Septiembre and 5 Oriente, has an efficient Lista de Correos; there's also a branch office at 2 Ote 411.

# Cholula and around

Puebla's expansion in recent years has made **Cholula**, 15km to the southwest, virtually a suburb. Nonetheless, it retains its small-town charm and has one abiding reason to visit: the **ruins of Cholula**. A rival of Teotihuacán at its height, and the most powerful city in the country between the fall of Teotihuacán and the rise of Tula, Cholula was at the time of the Conquest a vast city of some four hundred temples, famed as a shrine to Quetzalcoatl and for the excellence of its pottery (a trade dominated by immigrant Mixtecs). But it paid dearly for an attempt, inspired by its Aztec allies, to ambush Cortés on his march to

Tenochtitlán: the chieftains were slaughtered, their temples destroyed and churches built in their place. The Spanish claimed to have constructed 365 churches here, one for each day of the year. Although there are a lot of churches, the true figure certainly doesn't live up to the claim. There may well be 365 chapels within the churches, though, which is already a few hundred more than the village population could reasonably need.

One side of Cholula's large zócalo – the Plaza de la Concordia – is taken up by the ecclesiastical buildings of the **Convento de San Gabriel**, built from 1529 on the site of the temple of Quetzalcoatl. The Gothic main church is of little interest, but behind it (access at 4 Norte 401) is the great mustard-yellow **Capilla Real** (daily 10am–4.30pm), topped by 49 tiled cupolas. Moorish in conception, the interior comes with a forest of columns supporting semicircular arches and immediately recalls the Mezquita in Córdoba, Spain.



## The site

Arriving in Cholula you can't miss the Church of Nuestra Señora de los Remedios, picturesquely sited atop a hill with Popocatépetl in the background. What's not immediately apparent is that the hill is in fact the remains of the **Great Pyramid of Cholula** – the Pirámide Tepanapa – the largest pyramid ever constructed, though now it's ruined, overgrown and really not much to look at. At 66m, it is lower than the largest of the Egyptian pyramids but with each side measuring 350m it is also squatter and bulkier. As at other sites, the outer shell was built over a series of nested pyramids, constructed between 200 BC and 800 AD, something amply illustrated in the **site museum**. You can find detailed printed guides at the bookshop next to the museum, which can be useful if you have a deep interest in these ancient structures.

Cross the road to reach the **archeological site** (daily 9am–6pm; M$33, M$50 to bring in a video camera; ticket includes both museum and site), accessed through a 400-metre-long series of tunnels dug by archeologists, just a fraction of the 8km of exploratory tunnels which honeycomb the pyramid. They're well lit and capacious enough for most people to walk upright, but there's still a palpable sense of adventure as you spur off down side tunnels, which reveal elements of earlier temples and steep ceremonial stairways that appear to go on forever into the gloom. Emerging at the end of one tunnel you'll find an area of open-air excavations, where part of the great pyramid has been exposed alongside various lesser shrines with explanations of their importance in English. Though undoubtedly fascinating, the ruins are a good deal less impressive than some of the more famed sites around the Valley of México. The ring of superimposed structures around the **Patio de los Altares** are certainly worth a look and there are some fine **murals**, but these can be better appreciated in the site museum where replicas are kept.

As you leave the site, a road on the right winds up the pyramid/hill towards the church of **Nuestra Señora de los Remedios** (daily 7am–7pm; free). From the top, or from a viewpoint about halfway up, you can attempt to count the town's churches, and gaze across the countryside at Popocatépetl.

## Practicalities

**Buses** for Cholula leave the CAPU terminal in Puebla every fifteen minutes or so, and there's a constant stream of *colectivos* from 14 Poniente, between 9 and 11 Norte. In Cholula, the *colectivos* run right by the archeological site, passing en route the Estrella Roja terminal at 12 Poniente 108, from where there are services to TAPO in Mexico City until 7.50pm. Buses to Puebla's CAPU can be picked up across the street at the corner of 3 Sur until around 9pm. From the bus station, head down 5 de Mayo to get to the zócalo; from there, follow Morelos past the railway track to reach the pyramid.

There are a few **hotels** in Cholula, the most economical being the *Reforma*, Morelos and 4 Sur (ⓣ222/247-0149; ❸), which has decent enough rooms with bath, and also has parking space. Alternatively, *Hostal Chalollan*, Privada de Chalollan 2003, near 6 Norte between 20 and 22 Oriente (ⓣ222/247-7038, ⓔhostalchalollan@hotmail.com), has affordable dorm beds (M$60), but no private rooms. For large modern rooms with tiled floors and TV, try the central *Hotel Suites San Juan*, 5 Sur 103 (ⓣ222/247-0278, ⓔinfo@suitessanjuan.com; ❹–❺), or the slightly more distant *Villa Arqueológica*, 2 Poniente 601, south of the pyramid (ⓣ222/273-7900 or 001-800/514-8244, ⓔchoccrec01@clubmed.com; ❼), run by Club Med and featuring a pool, tennis courts and very comfortable rooms. If you are **camping**, head 2km out along 6 Norte to *Trailer Park Las Américas*, at 30 Oriente (ⓣ222/247-0134), where you can pitch a tent or park for M$120–160 depending on the size of the tent or the trailer.

As the home of the Universidad de las Américas campus, Cholula is often packed with students, a good number of whom seem to spend most of their time hanging out at the outdoor cafés and **restaurants** under Portal Guerrero, along one side of the zócalo. This is the place to come to eat. *Café Enamorada*, at no. 1, is eternally popular with coffee lovers, diners and those here to drink while listening to the occasional band. Along the way at no. 7, *Los Jarrones* has a wider menu, good food and a more rustic character.

Cholula is generally regarded as the **nightlife** capital of the Puebla region, but while a few bars cluster around 14 Poniente and 5 de Mayo, most of the action has moved about 3km out to Recta a Cholula, the main highway between Cholula and Puebla – thoroughly inconvenient and making taxi rides essential. Establishments also tend to be far apart from each other, making it hard to find the hottest action. The best bet is to ask locally for the current favourite and commit yourself to just one place for the night – not a bad idea when entry can cost M$100.

### Around Cholula

If you want to explore some of the churches round about, head for **ACATEPEC**, easily reached by local bus. The spectacular village church here, San Francisco, has a superb Baroque facade entirely covered in glazed bricks and *azulejos* of local manufacture. It's not particularly large but it is beautifully proportioned and quite unexpected in this setting.

Just a kilometre's walk to the northwest, in the village of **TONATZINTLA**, the plain facade of the church of Santa María conceals a remarkably elaborate Baroque treasury. Here local craftsmen covered every available inch in ornament, interspersing bird, plant and native life with the more usual Christian elements. "Chipilo" **buses** from the corner of 3 Norte and 6 Poniente run to both towns.

## Popocatépetl and Ixtaccíhuatl

You get excellent views of the snow-clad volcanic peaks of **Popocatépetl** (5452m) and **Ixtaccíhuatl** (5285m) from almost anywhere west of the capital, and viewing from afar is all most people do these days. "Popo" has been rumbling and fuming away since September 1994, and for much of the time since then the region has been on Yellow Alert, with evacuation procedures posted throughout surrounding towns. Activity was renewed in December 2000, culminating in the largest eruption on record. Though there were no devastating lava flows, the crater spat out hot rocks, dust fell on the capital and, on several occasions, Mexico City's airport (over 60km away) was closed for a few hours. Foreign media hyped the eruption excessively and fanned tourist anxiety, but the only real hardship was felt by local villagers, who, evacuated for weeks, were forced to stand idly by while their livestock trampled their fields.

While the area within a two-kilometre radius of Popo remains closed to the public, the rest of the **Parque Nacional de Volcanes** (daily 7am–10pm; M$10), which surrounds both volcanoes, has reopened – for details on the latest situation, contact the park office in Amecameca at Plaza de la Constitución 9 (Ⓣ597/978-3830, Ⓦiztapopo.conanp.gob.mx). In order to enter the park you will need to fill out and submit a formal request, using a form which can be found on the website (look for "Permisos de Aceso" on the left-hand bar of the home page). Even a visit to just the Paso de Cortés – the 3800-metre-high pass between the volcanoes – is a memorable experience, with the two giants rising high above you on either side.

"Popo" and "Ixta", as the volcanoes are affectionately known, are the nation's second and third highest peaks (after the 5700m Pico de Orizaba). Their full names come from an Aztec Romeo-and-Juliet-style legend. Popocatépetl (Smoking Mountain) was a warrior, Ixtaccíhuatl (White Lady) his lover, the beautiful daughter of the emperor. Believing Popocatépetl killed in battle, she died from grief, and when he returned alive he laid her body down on the mountain, where he eternally stands sentinel, holding a burning torch. From the west, Ixta does somewhat resemble a reclining female form and the various parts of the mountain are named accordingly – the feet, the knees, the belly, the breast and so on.

### Practicalities

If you'd just like to get as close as possible to the mountains, visit **Amecameca** (usually just Ameca), a lovely little town an hour south of Mexico City, reached by "Servicio Volcánes" buses from TAPO (every 20min; 5.20am–11pm). Dramatic views of the mountain peaks are bizarrely framed by the palms of the zócalo, around which you'll find a couple of good, inexpensive hotels. If Popo quiets down you may again be able to drive or hitch, or get a taxi from Ameca – there are no buses – along the good asphalt road up to the pine-dotted Paso de Cortés. Climbs up Ixta also begin in Ameca; this is a challenging trek for serious mountaineers only, involving a night or two with all your gear at very high altitude, and a technical three-kilometre-long ridge traverse (often requiring ropes) to reach the highest point.

## Cuernavaca and around

**CUERNAVACA** has always provided a place of escape from the city – the Aztecs called it Cuauhnahuac ("place by the woods"), and it became a favourite resort and hunting ground for their rulers. Cortés seized and destroyed the city during the siege of Tenochtitlán, then ended up building himself a palace here, the Spanish corrupting the name to Cuernavaca ("cow horn") for no better reason than their inability to cope with the original. The trend has continued over the centuries: the Emperor Maximilian and the deposed Shah of Iran both

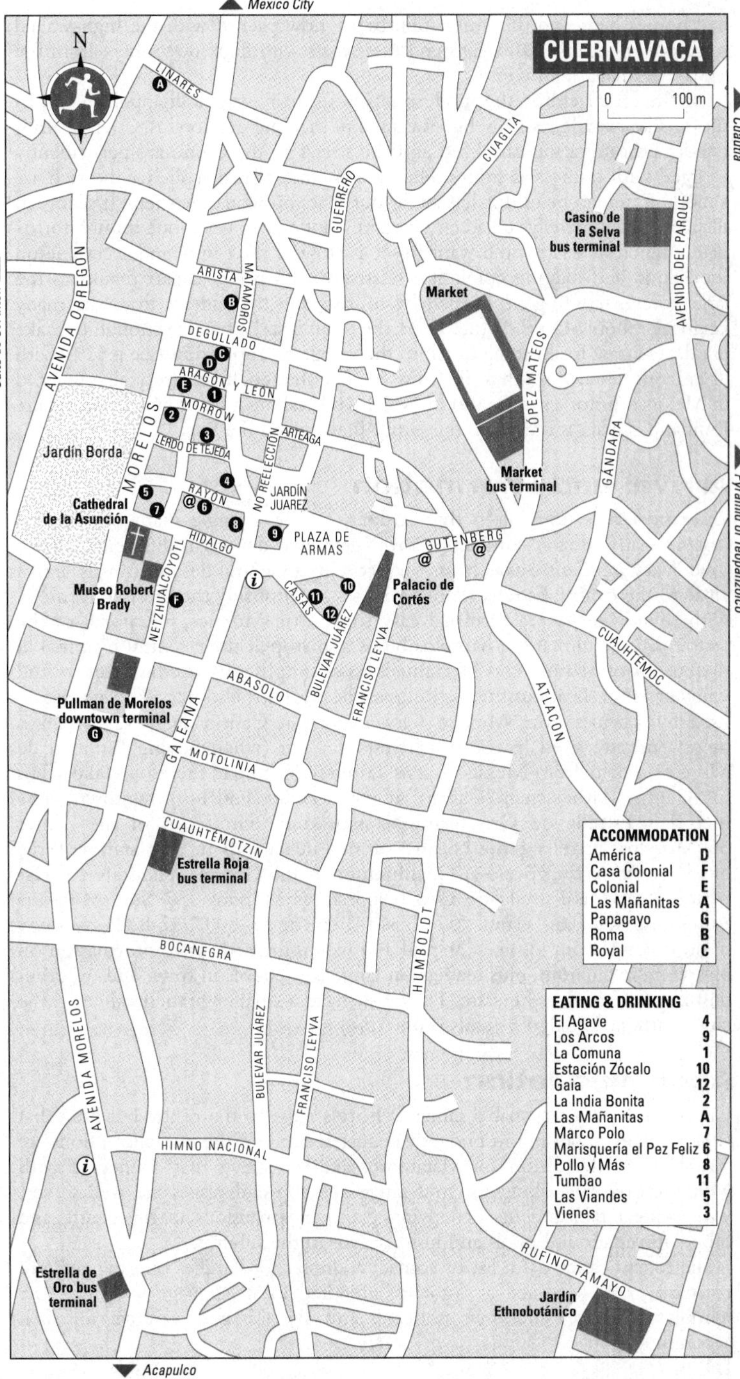
CUERNAVACA
Mexico City
Cuautla
Pyramid of Teopanzolco
Salto de St Anton
Acapulco
0 100 m
N
Casino de la Selva bus terminal
Market
Market bus terminal
Jardín Borda
Cathedral de la Asunción
Museo Robert Brady
Palacio de Cortés
PLAZA DE ARMAS
JARDÍN JUAREZ
Pullman de Morelos downtown terminal
Estrella Roja bus terminal
Estrella de Oro bus terminal
Jardín Ethnobotánico
LINARES
CUAGLIA
GUERRERO
AVENIDA DEL PARQUE
AVENIDA OBREGÓN
ARISTA
MATAMOROS
DEGULLADO
ARAGÓN Y LEÓN
MORROW
MORELOS
LERDO DE TEJEDA
ARTEAGA
NO RELECCIÓN
RAYON
HIDALGO
LÓPEZ MATEOS
GÁNDARA
GUTENBERG
CASAS
NETZHUALCOYOTL
BULEVAR JUÁREZ
FRANCISCO LEYVA
CUAUHTÉMOC
ATLACON
ABASOLO
GALEANA
MOTOLINIA
CUAUHTÉMOTZIN
BOCANEGRA
HUMBOLDT
AVENIDA MORELOS
HIMNO NACIONAL
RUFINO TAMAYO
ACCOMMODATION
América D
Casa Colonial F
Colonial E
Las Mañanitas A
Papagayo G
Roma B
Royal C
EATING & DRINKING
El Agave 4
Los Arcos 9
La Comuna 1
Estación Zócalo 10
Gaia 12
La India Bonita 2
Las Mañanitas A
Marco Polo 7
Marisquería el Pez Feliz 6
Pollo y Más 8
Tumbao 11
Las Viandes 5
Vienes 3

had houses here, and the inner suburbs are now packed with the high-walled mansions of wealthy Mexicans and the expats who flock down here from the US and Canada each winter.

For the casual visitor, the modern city is in many ways a disappointment. Its spring-like climate remains, but as capital of the state of Morelos, Cuernavaca is rapidly becoming industrialized and the streets in the centre are permanently clogged with traffic and fumes. The gardens and villas that shelter the rich are almost all hidden or in districts so far out that you won't see them. It seems an ill-planned and widely spread city, certainly not easy to get about, though fortunately much of what you'll want to see is close to the centre and accessible on foot. Food and lodging come at a relatively high price, in part thanks to the large foreign contingent, swelled by tourists and by students from the many language schools. On the other hand, the town is still attractive enough to make it a decent base for heading north to the village of **Tepoztlán** (see p.519), with its raucous fiesta, or south to the ruins of **Xochicalco**. If you are at all interested in Mexican history, it may also be worthwhile taking a trip to **Cuautla**, where Emiliano Zapata is buried in the Jardín Revolución del Sur.

## Arrival and information

**Cuernavaca** is unusual in that it doesn't have a single main bus station. Instead, half a dozen companies have their own depots in different parts of town. Very frequent **buses** from Mexico City's Central del Sur mostly arrive close to the centre: Estrella Blanca services are probably the most convenient, with their Cuernavaca terminal easy to find on Morelos, just north of the centre. Most Pullman de Morelos buses also stop at their central terminal at the corner of Abasolo and Netzahualcoyotl; simply walk up the latter to find yourself at the heart of things. Pullman de Morelos also has a second depot, used by services from Mexico City airport, at Casino de Selva, which is inconveniently sited in the northwest of town (when buying Pullman de Morelos tickets from Mexico City's Tasqueña terminal, therefore, take a bus to "Centro" rather than "Casino" if you want to end up downtown). The first-class Estrella de Oro terminus is around 2km south of the centre on Morelos. Estrella Roja coaches from Puebla pull in at a station three blocks south of the zócalo at Cuauhtémotzin and Galeana. The state **tourist office**, near the Estrella de Oro terminal, at Morelos 187 Sur (Mon–Fri 8am–5pm, Sat 10am–1pm; ⓣ777/314-3920 or 01-800/987-8224, ⓦwww.morelostravel.com), is very helpful and well informed, with information on buses and excursions, plus leaflets on language schools in town and on other destinations around the state. They also have a smaller branch office in the city centre at Hidalgo 5 (daily 9am–7pm).

## Accommodation

Cuernavaca has a reasonable range of **hotels** close to the centre but little that is particularly appealing in budget categories: many of the cheaper options are just north of the centre, on Matamoros and the streets that connect it with Morelos. Visitors looking for mid-range and top-end places are well served, with some establishments occupying grand old mansions in the centre and others spread around pools and lush gardens in the suburbs.

The tourist office has a list of contact addresses for families offering **private rooms**, a service aimed at students attending local language schools – the schools themselves and their notice boards are also good sources for such accommodation.

**América** Aragón y León 14 ⓣ777/318-6127, ⓦwww.tourbymexico.com/hotelamerica. Basic but respectable place in a street mostly full of dives; all rooms have bath, but you pay M$50 to have a TV. ❸

**Casa Colonial** Netzahualcoyotl 37 ⓣ777/312-7033, ⓦwww.casacolonial.com. Gorgeous rooms in a delightful eighteenth-century mansion close to the Museo Robert Brady. With attractive colonial public areas and a pool, this is one of the most appealing places in the centre, and prices include breakfast. TV on request, but no phones. In addition to rooms, there are suites (M$1678–1879) and junior suites (M$1295). Prices are about 15 percent higher at weekends. ❼–❽

**Colonial** Aragón y León 19 ⓣ777/318-6414. Across the street from the *América* and a bit less basic; the most comfortable hotel on Aragón y León. ❹

**Las Mañanitas** Ricardo Linares 107 ⓣ777/362-0000 or 01-800/221-5299, in the US ⓣ1-888/413-9199, ⓦwww.lasmananitas.com.mx. Beautiful luxury hotel, just a 10min walk from the zócalo. The streetfront entrance gives little clue of the oasis within, where peacocks, flamingoes and African cranes strut around a pool and lush gardens. The tiled-floor rooms come with heavy wooden furniture and all the fittings, and there's a superb restaurant on site (see p.518). ❾

**Papagayo** Motolinia 13 ⓣ777/314-1711 or 1924, ⓦwww.tourbymexico.com/hpapagayo. Large hotel close to the centre with rooms in blocks set around spacious grounds and large pool. With a family-friendly atmosphere and children's area this place can get a bit raucous on occasion, but the rooms are good value and the price includes breakfast in the on-site restaurant/bar. The remodelled rooms and suites are a little nicer than the standard rooms. ❻

**Roma** Matamoros 17 ⓣ777/318-8778 ⓦhotelroma@prodigy.net.mx. Simple but clean budget option with parking space; all rooms have bathroom, overhead fan and TV. ❸

**Royal** Matamoros 11 ⓣ777/314-4018 ⓦwww.hoteles-royal.com. One of a number of similar places along Matamoros; fairly shabby but with comfortable enough rooms with bath, and space for parking. ❸

## The Town

At the heart of the city, the **zócalo** comprises the Plaza de Armas and the smaller Jardín Juárez, with its bandstand, to the northwest. Around the twin plazas you'll find a series of cafés where you can sit outdoors under the watchful eye of a huge, black, volcanic-rock **statue of Morelos** that faces the Palacio de Gobierno, across the plaza.

### Palacio de Cortés

At the eastern end of the Plaza de Armas, behind the statue of Morelos, is the **Palacio de Cortés**, which houses the **Museo Regional Cuauhnahuac** (Tues–Sun 9am–6pm; M$33). Work on this building began as early as 1522, when, although Tenochtitlán had fallen, much of the country had yet to come under Spanish control – the fortress-like aspect of the palace's older parts reflects this period. Over the centuries, though, it's been added to and modified substantially – first by Cortés himself and later by the state authorities to whom it passed – so that what you see today is every bit a palace. The museum is a good one, spacious and well laid out with a substantial section covering local archeology, including some fine examples of stelae and a lovely seated figure from Xochicalco. In fact, the building is partly constructed over the ruins of a small pyramid, which can be seen in the courtyard and elsewhere. There's also a substantial collection of colonial art, weaponry and everyday artefacts – look for the sixteenth-century clock mechanism from the cathedral and a reproduction of a *cuexcomate*, a kind of thatched granary still found around the state.

The museum's highlight, though, is a series of **murals** around the gallery, painted by Diego Rivera in 1929 and 1930. Depicting Mexican history from the Conquest to the Revolution, they concentrate in particular on the atrocities committed by Cortés, and on the revolutionary Emiliano Zapata, who was born in nearby Cuautla, raised most of his army from the peasants of Morelos and

△ Palacio de Cortés, Cuernavaca

remains something of a folk hero to the locals. From the balcony here, there are wonderful, though sometimes hazy, views to the east with Popocatépetl in the far distance.

### The cathedral

From the plaza, Hidalgo runs three blocks west to the **Catedral de la Asunción**, located on the south side of a grassy tree-shaded compound that also contains a couple of other small churches. Founded by Cortés in 1529, the cathedral looks bulky and threatening from the outside (at one stage there were actually cannons mounted along the battlemented roof line), but it has been remarkably tastefully refurbished within. Stripped almost bare, the modernist approach here is an enormous relief if you've grown tired of the churrigueresque and Baroque flamboyance elsewhere. Most of the decor is understated, but traces of murals discovered during the redecoration have been uncovered in places – they have a remarkably East Asian look and are believed to have been painted by a Christian Chinese or Filipino artist in the days when the cathedral was the centre for missions to the Far East. At one time, the main Spanish trade route then came through here, with goods brought across the Pacific to Acapulco, overland through central Mexico and on from Veracruz to Spain. If, after viewing the interior of the cathedral you need your fix of golden exuberance, pop into the **Capilla del Santísimo**, where there's a small gilt *retablo* and Stations of the Cross done in charcoal on paper.

Until his death in December 2000, Cuernavaca's bishop was **Luis Cervantes**, one of the country's most liberal and outspoken clergymen. Apart from doing up his cathedral, he was renowned for instituting the "Mariachi Mass", something that has been continued by his disciples. Every Sunday, this service is conducted to the accompaniment of traditional Mexican music and usually attracts large crowds.

### Museo Robert Brady

South of the cathedral, at the corner of Netzahualcoyotl and 20 de Noviembre, the **Museo Robert Brady** (Tues–Sun 10am–6pm; M$30; Ⓦ www.bradymuseum.org) occupies a former sixteenth-century convent and holds the Iowa-born artist's private collection. Brady moved to Cuernavaca in the 1960s, and lived here until his death in 1986. Filled with art from around the world and decorated in an intensely colourful artesanía style, the museum is a fabulous place, with rooms arranged aesthetically, and without regard to history, geography or classification of artistic styles. As a result, what you see is more like a beautiful home than a typical museum, and is well worth a visit.

The rooms, arranged around a couple of outside patios complete with sculptures and a delightful pool, are filled with works by most of the greats of twentieth-century Mexican art. Even the bathrooms contain works by Diego Rivera and Rufino Tamayo, and there are also pieces by Frida Kahlo, Graham Sutherland, and some particularly good entries by Rafael Coronel, including a portrait of Peggy Guggenheim. Everything is labelled in English.

### Jardín Borda

Immediately west of the cathedral is the entrance to the **Jardín Borda**, Morelos 103 (Tues–Sun 10am–5.30pm; M$30, free on Sun), a large formal garden adjacent to the mansion of Taxco mining magnate José de la Borda (see p.523). Though it falls short of the grandeur Borda dreamed of when he commissioned the garden in the eighteenth century, both the garden and the mansion are a delightfully tranquil reminder of the haven Cuernavaca once was. Maximilian and Carlota later adopted Borda's mansion as their weekend home, though

Maximilian also had another retreat in Cuernavaca that he shared with his native mistress, "La India Bonita". Officially named La Casa del Olindo, this second house was popularly known as La Casa del Olvido ("House of Forgetfulness") since the builder forgot to include quarters for Carlota.

### Out from the centre

About twenty minutes' walk into the suburbs beyond the Jardín Borda is the **Salto de St Anton** (Tues–Sun 8am–6pm; free), a beautiful 36-metre cascade surrounded by vegetation and natural columns of crystallized basalt. Unfortunately, the site has been overdeveloped and is marred by concrete walkways, litter and a faint stench from the polluted water, but it's still pretty, and the road to the falls passes a number of flower shops and restaurants.

Rather more distant – 2km southeast of the centre, in the Colonia Acapantzingo – is the **Jardín Etnobotánico**, Matamoros 200 (daily 9am–5pm; free), whose grounds and collection of medicinal plants are just about worth taking a taxi (or a long walk) to see. As well as the labelled specimens – coffee, guava, roses and medicinal herbs – there is a small museum of traditional medicine.

Other sites scattered further out in the fringes of the city include the area's sole significant reminder of the pre-colonial period, the **Pyramid of Teopanzolco** (daily 9am–6pm; M$3). So effectively buried was this site that it took an artillery bombardment during the Revolution to uncover it. Located to the northeast of the centre beyond the train station (which is what the gunners were aiming at), it's a small temple in which two pyramids can be seen, one built over the other. The pyramid can be reached by city bus #6 from Degollado and Reelección.

## Eating, drinking and nightlife

You don't need to wander far from the centre to find good **places to eat**: there's a particularly fine group of restaurants around the zócalo, and you can get juices and tortas at any time around the bandstand in the Jardín Juárez. **Evening activity** mostly centres on the Plazuela del Zacate, just a couple of blocks south of the zócalo, where the corner of Galeana and Hidalgo is intersected by Fray Bartolomé de las Casas. Most nights there are large groups hanging around this small triangular area, occasionally popping into one of the fashionable cafés and bars for a beer, or sitting outside listening to someone playing on the makeshift stage. There are also free concerts from the bandstand in the Jardín Juárez every Thursday evening at 6pm.

### Restaurants

**Los Arcos** Jardín de los Héroes 4 ⓣ777/312-1510. Ever-popular restaurant and bar on the south side of the zócalo serving espresso coffee and a wide range of fairly pricey dishes catering to locals and foreign students. In the evening most people are here to drink and listen to the nightly live music, which comes in a variety of styles and abilities.

**La Comuna** Morrow 6 ⓣ777/318-2757. Small and friendly cooperatively run café, serving, in addition to coffee and beer, comidas corridas for M$25.

**Gaia** Juárez 102 ⓣ777/310-0031. Stylish restaurant known for its innovative cross-cultural cuisine. Specialities include duck in plum sauce and prawns in tamarind sauce on a bed of couscous and *amaranto* (an indigenous Mexican cereal). Main courses go for around M$170–260.

**La India Bonita** Morrow 20, just off Morelos ⓣ777/312-5021. Lovely restaurant with a pleasant outdoor patio, excellent but moderately priced food (including set breakfasts) and impeccable service. Expect to pay M$70–150 for delicious mains, or just drop in for a quiet drink at the bar.

**Las Mañanitas** Ricardo Linares 107 ⓣ777/362-0000 or 01-800/221-5299. The sort of place that people drive hours to visit, this well-known restaurant serves fine international cuisine in the sumptuous grounds of the hotel of the same name. You'll probably part with at least M$500 for a full meal but you won't regret it.

**Marco Polo** Hidalgo 30 Ⓦwww.marco-polo.com.mx. Superior Italian restaurant serving up its own fresh-made pasta (M$65–116), with main courses (if you can fit one in after the pasta) at M$120–150. Alternatively, see if you can get through one of their huge pizzas (M$65–85).

**Marisqueria el Pez Feliz** Rayon 5–C. Seafood diner where set light meals (M$30–50) feature prawn soup or prawn cocktail plus an *antojito*, or you can take a full meal (prawn soup and fish) for M$78.

**Pollo y Más** Galeana 4. Cheap snack bar opposite the zócalo, serving tasty roast chicken, enchiladas and *antojitos*.

**Las Viandas** upstairs at Teatro Morelos, Morelos 188. Stylish café overlooking the street, with a range of coffees and teas, plus juices, smoothies and good baguettes. Doubles as an art gallery.

**Vienes** Lerdo de Tejada 302. Austro-Hungarian café, patisserie and restaurant just a block from the zócalo; a great spot for Continental-style coffee and pastries.

### Bars

**El Agave** Comonfort 5. Bar/restaurant just north of the zócalo, set around a courtyard with a pretty stone fountain and offering a great range of good rums and tequilas, cheap beers during happy hour (4–6pm) and food in the form of salads and steaks. It's open until there's no one left standing.

**Estación Zócalo** Hidalgo, at southeast corner of Plaza de Armas. Night-time music bar (it doesn't open till 10.30pm) directly opposite the Palacio de Cortés, with an outdoor terrace and an upstairs balcony with views over the zócalo.

**Tumbao** Casas 11. With fluorescent tropical decor, and DJs mixing in everything from salsa to techno, this is the liveliest among a slew of good bars on Casas, which is Cuernavaca's most happening street from dusk until around 2am.

## Listings

**Banks and exchange** Casas de cambio include Gesta on the corner of Galeana and Lerdo de Tejada, plus more on Morrow at nos. 6 and 9, and Matamoros at nos. 10 and 20.

**Internet access** There are several places around the centre of town, and prices are low. You'll find the best rates (M$5/hr) at Cyber Gasso, Hidalgo 22–D and Gutenberg 8 (Mon–Fri 7.30am–9.30pm, Sat 8.30am–9.30pm, Sun 9.30am–9.30pm), and Ova-Press, Gutenberg 26–A (daily 7am–11pm).

**Laundry** Tintorería Morelos, Matamoros 28 (Mon–Sat 9.30am–8pm).

**Pharmacy** The handiest pharmacy is the 24hr Farmacia del Ahorro at the corner of Hidalgo and Galeana, just south of the zócalo.

**Post office** At the southwest corner of the zócalo (Mon–Fri 8am–6pm, Sat 9am–1pm).

**Spanish courses** The state tourist office has leaflets and brochures issued by several schools offering Spanish language courses in Cuernavaca.

## Tepoztlán

An interesting side trip from Cuernavaca is to **TEPOZTLÁN**, just 21km to the northeast and dramatically sited in a narrow valley spectacularly ringed by volcanic mountains. Until recently this was an isolated agrarian community inhabited by Nahuatl-speaking people whose life changed little between the time of the Conquest and the beginning of the twentieth century - it was on Tepoztlán that anthropologist Oscar Lewis based his classic study *Life in a Mexican Village*, in which he traced the effects of the Revolution: the village was an important stronghold of the original Zapatista movement. In recent years, though, new roads and a couple of luxury hotels have begun to change things – Tepoztlán has become a popular weekend retreat from the capital, with its good selection of restaurants and quality arts and crafts shops, though midweek it is still a peaceful spot. For now, at least, the stunning setting also survives, as does a reputation for joyously boisterous **fiestas** (especially the drunken revelry of the night of Sept 7).

Buses between Cuautla (see p.521) and Cuernavaca or Mexico City (Autobuses del Sur) leave you at a *caseta* on the highway a kilometre west of town at the end of 22 Febrero. Direct second-class buses from Cuernavaca drop you half a kilometre south of town at the end of the main street, 5 de Mayo. One block north of the junction of 22 Febrero and 5 de Mayo is the zócalo, at whose northern end you'll be dropped if you arrive by slower second-class bus from Cuernavaca. For **currency exchange**, there's a Bancomer with an ATM on 5 de Mayo opposite the zócalo.

On Sundays and Wednesdays a **market** is held in the zócalo, on whose eastern side stands the massive **Ex-Convento Dominico de la Natividad**. It was a fortress for a while during the Revolution, but is now in a rather beautiful state of disrepair with some attractive murals still surviving in the cloister. Around the back and accessed off Gonzales, part of the church has been given over to the **Museo de Arte Prehispánico** (Tues–Sun 10am–6pm; M$10), which holds a remarkably good archeological collection.

Several pre-Hispanic temples have been found on the hilltops in the area, and you can see one to the north, perched high up in impossibly steep-looking terrain. This is the **Santuario del Cerro Tepozteco** (daily 9am–5.30pm; M$30, M$30 to bring in a video camera, free on Sun), reached after an exhausting climb of an hour or so up what is little more than an upgraded dry streambed at times. If you're fit, the hike is worth it for the views from this artificially flattened hilltop, and the chance to inspect the site at close quarters. The small, three-stepped, lime-washed pyramid here was dedicated to Tepoztecatl, a god of *pulque* and of fertility, represented by carvings of rabbits. There were so many *pulque* gods that they were known as the four hundred rabbits: the drink was supposedly discovered by rabbits nibbling at the agave plants from which it is made. This one gained particular kudos when the Spanish flung the idol off the cliffs only for his adherents to find that it had landed unharmed – the big September fiesta is in his honour. Follow the example of Mexicans and reward your efforts with a picnic lunch (water and soft drinks are available at a price), but do buck the litter-dropping trend and take your empty containers away with you.

### Practicalities

Many people visit Tepoztlán as a day trip since the **hotels** are fairly expensive. The cheapest is *Posada Ali*, Netzahualcoyotl 2 (Ⓣ739/395-1971; ❼), out towards the ruins and with its lower-cost rooms tucked under the eaves. Larger rooms have sunflower-carved headboards on the beds and wood-beamed ceilings, and everyone has access to the small pool and *frontón* court. If your budget can manage it, *the* place to stay is the elegant but unpretentious *Posada del Tepozteco* at Paraíso 3 (Ⓣ739/395-0010, Ⓦwww.posadadeltepozteco.com; ❽–❾), wonderfully sited above most of the town and with views of the mountains from the manicured gardens and two outdoor pools. The rooms and suites are simple but well equipped, most with their own terrace and Jacuzzi. There are plenty of **restaurants** either close to the zócalo or out along the road towards the ruins. For reasonably priced vegetarian dishes, salads, wholemeal bread and good coffee, visit *Govinda Ram* two blocks north of the zócalo on Avenida de Tepozteco (the continuation of 5 de Mayo), or for something more upmarket get a table at *Los Colorines*, half a block south along the same street. On the zócalo at 5 de Mayo 21, *Teposnieves* (the original branch of what is now a modest chain) has ice creams and sorbets in more flavours than you can count; fig and mescal is a favourite, but if you want something more unusual, there's chile and cucumber, or carrot sorbet.

## Cuautla

Some 42km southeast of Cuernavaca, and an hour and a half by bus, lies **CUAUTLA**, really just a small regional town of limited consequence except for being the burial place of **Emiliano Zapata**. The Plazuela de la Revolución del Sur, a block south of the zócalo, surrounds a huge bronze statue of him standing in heroic pose – mustachioed, with a broad-brimmed sombrero on his head and a bandoleer across his shoulder, he clutches a rifle in one hand and a proclamation in the other that declares "Tierra y Libertad" ("land and freedom").

Back on the zócalo, there's minor interest at the **Casa de Morelos** (Tues–Sun 9am–6pm; M$24, free on Sun), a beautiful colonial mansion and gardens, formerly the home of Independence leader and local boy José Maria Morelos (see p.386), containing archeological finds and items of local historical interest. Three blocks further north along Los Bravo, Cuautla's former train station is now home to the **Museo José Maria Morelos y Pavón** (Tues–Sun 10am–6pm; M$5), which mainly traces the life and times of Morelos, and the Independence movement in this state that bears his name. For train buffs, the 1904 **steam locomotive** and carriages once used by the town's other great local hero, Emiliano Zapata, may be of interest. If you're around on the third Saturday of each month, you can take a very short ride on it, with departures every fifteen minutes from 4pm till 8.45pm (M$10; enquiries on ⓣ739/352-0495, ⓔred279@hotmail.com).

Cuautla also has something of a reputation for its thermal **spas**, and there are several large complexes a little way out from the centre. The emphasis is more on swimming than luxuriating, but for around M$50 you could easily while away an hour or two at Agua Hedionda (ⓣ739/352-6141): look for the dedicated purple-and-white buses or yellow *combis* that rumble through town and jump aboard (around a 10min trip).

### Practicalities

Cuautla has three **bus stations**, all close to each other and a couple of blocks east of the zócalo. If you can't find a map at the bus stations, ask for directions to the old train station, where there's a small **tourist office** next to the museum (Tues–Sat 8am–6pm, Sun 9am–4pm; ⓣ735/352-5221). There is little enough reason to stay the night, though **hotels** are generally good value. Right on the zócalo, the *Colón* (ⓣ735/352-2990; ❷) offers simple but clean budget accommodation – it's worth paying the M$30 extra for a larger room with a zócalo view. The *España*, at 2 de Mayo 22 (ⓣ735/352-2186; ❸), offers a little more comfort, its rooms done out in cool peppermint green and white, and equipped with a TV and fan. There's also the *Defensa del Agua*, Defensa del Agua 34 (ⓣ735/352-1679; ❹), whose more spacious modern rooms surround a patio with parking space and a small pool. The centre of town has numerous small cheap **restaurants**, but for something a little special make for *Las Golondrinas*, Nicolás Catalán 19–A, a block north of the zócalo (ⓣ735/354-1350), where fountains splash as you sink back in comfy chairs and tuck into corn and *cuitlacoche* soup (M$36), *ranchera* fish kebabs (M$89) or regional specialities such as barbecued rabbit (M$80); there's also a lunch menu for M$70.

## Xochicalco

Some 38km south of Cuernavaca lie the impressive hilltop ruins of **XOCHICALCO** (daily 9am–6pm; M$38). While not much is known of the history of this site or the people who inhabited it, it is regarded by archeologists as one of the most significant in central Mexico because of the connections it shows to both the ancient culture of Teotihuacán and the later Toltec peoples. Xochicalco flourished from around 700 AD to 900 AD – thus overlapping with both Teotihuacán and Tula – and also displays clear parallels with Maya and Zapotec sites of the era.

The setting, high on a bare mountaintop, is reminiscent of Monte Albán (see p.656), the great Zapotec site near Oaxaca. Like Monte Albán and the great Maya sites (but unlike Tula or Teotihuacán), Xochicalco was an exclusively religious and ceremonial centre rather than a true city. The style of many of the carvings, too, recalls Zapotec and Maya art. Their subjects, however, and the architecture of the temples, seem to form a transition between Teotihuacán and Tula. The appearance of Quetzalcoatl as a human is especially noteworthy, as he was to turn up in this form at Tula and almost every subsequent site, rather than simply as the feathered serpent of Teotihuacán. The ball-court is almost identical to earlier Maya examples, and similar to those that later appeared in Tula. For all these influences, however, or perhaps because there are so many of them, it's almost impossible to say which culture was dominant: some claim that Xochicalco was a northern outpost of the Maya, others that it was a subject city of Teotihuacán that survived (or perhaps precipitated through revolt) the fall of that empire.

Arriving at the site, first stop in at the **museum**, on a neighbouring hilltop, where you buy your entry **ticket**, and can take a look at some of the more portable pieces unearthed here. A carved stele that once graced one of the lower courtyards (and has now been replaced by a concrete pillar) takes pride of place in the first room, and is followed by numerous slabs of carved stone, a delicate alabaster bowl and some fine jade masks. From here it is a ten-minute walk to the ruins.

### The site

Much the most important surviving monument here is the **Pirámide de Quetzalcoatl**, on the highest part of the site. Around its base are carved extremely elaborate plumed serpents, coiling around various seated figures and symbols with astronomical significance – all clearly Maya in inspiration. On top, part of the wall of the sanctuary remains standing, though it now surrounds a large hole. In 1993 the centre of the pyramid was excavated to reveal the remains of an earlier pyramid inside.

The other main point of interest is the **Solar Observatory**, located to the northwest of the main pyramid and down the hill a little, accessed through the northern ball-court. Here you'll find the entrance to some subterranean passages, a couple of natural **caves** augmented by steps and tunnels, one of which features a shaft in the roof that is oriented so as to allow the sun to shine directly in. At astronomical midday (midway between sunrise and sunset) for around five weeks either side of the summer solstice – May 14/15 to July 28/29 – the shaft casts a hexagonal patch of light onto the cave floor. At any time, the custodian should point out the remains of frescoes on the walls.

### Practicalities

The quick and comfortable way to the site is by half-hourly first-class **bus** headed to Miacatlán from Cuernavaca's Pullman de Morelos terminal, which will take you to the Crucero de Xochicalco, 4km from the site. There is often a taxi waiting here to run you to the site for about M$25; otherwise you'll have to walk. There's also a very slow and circuitous second-class bus that leaves half-hourly from Cuernavaca's market bus station and takes you right to the site. If you're **driving**, or if you go with a **tour**, you can continue another thirty-odd kilometres down the road beyond Xochicalco to the caves of Cacahuamilpa (see p.527), from where Taxco (see below) is only a short distance.

# Taxco

**Silver** has been mined in **TAXCO** since before the Conquest. Supplies of the metal have long been depleted, but it is still the basis of the town's fame, as well as its livelihood, in the form of jewellery, which is made in hundreds of workshops here, and sold in an array of shops (*platerías*) catering mainly to tourists. The city is an attractive place, like some Mexican version of a Tuscan village, with a mass of terracotta-tiled, whitewashed houses lining narrow, cobbled alleys that straggle steeply uphill. At intervals the pattern is broken by a larger mansion, or by a courtyard filled with flowers or by the tower of a church rearing up; the twin spires of **Santa Prisca**, a Baroque wedding cake of a church in the centre of town, stand out above all. Unfortunately, the streets are eternally clogged with VW Beetle taxis and *colectivos* struggling up the steep slopes, and forming an endless *paseo* around the central Plaza Borda. Once you've spent an hour or so in the church and a few museums there's really nothing to do but sit around the plaza cafés. Still, it is a pleasant enough place to do just that if you don't mind the relatively high prices, and the profusion of other tourists.

Though it might seem a prosperous place now, Taxco's development has not been entirely straightforward – indeed on more than one occasion the town has been all but abandoned. The Spaniards came running at the rumours of mineral wealth here (Cortés himself sent an expedition in 1522), but their success was short-lived, and it wasn't until the eighteenth century that French immigrant **José de la Borda** struck it fabulously rich by discovering the San Ignacio vein. It was during Borda's short lifetime that most of what you see originated – he spent an enormous sum on building the church of Santa Prisca, and more on other buildings and a royal lifestyle here and in Cuernavaca; by his death in 1778 the boom was already over. In 1929 a final revival started with the arrival of American architect and writer **William Spratling**, who set up a jewellery workshop in Taxco, drawing on local traditional skills and pre-Hispanic designs. With the completion of a new road around the same time, a massive influx of tourists was inevitable - the town has handled it all fairly well, becoming rich at the expense of just a little charm.

## Arrival and information

You'll arrive in Taxco on Avenida de los Plateros (formerly Avenida Kennedy), the main road that contours around the side of the valley at the bottom of town. Taxco has two **bus stations**, both on Avenida de los Plateros and both with fairly frequent services to Mexico City, Cuernavaca and Acapulco. They're about 1km apart, but from either it is a steep fifteen-minute walk or M$30 taxi ride to Plaza Borda, the zócalo. To get into town from the Estrella Blanca terminal, cross the road and turn right up the hill and then left to climb even more steeply past the church of Santa Veracruz to the centre. From Estrella de Oro, head straight up Calle de Pilita, the steep alley directly across from you, until you come, to the Plazuela de San Juan, on your right; from there go down Cuauhtémoc to the zócalo.

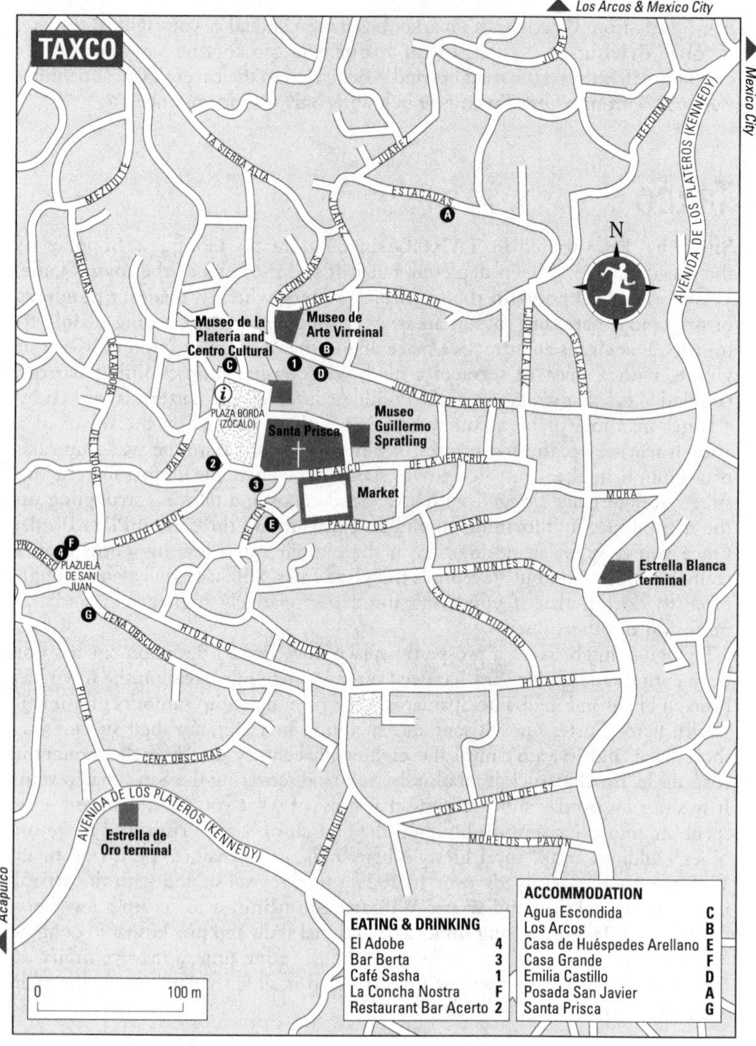


The **tourist office** (daily 9.30am–6pm; ⓣ762/622-0798) is inconveniently sited on Avenida de los Plateros at the very northern end of town, where the remains of the Los Arcos aqueduct cross the road (regular *combis* connect Los Arcos to the zócalo). Fortunately, a kiosk on the west side of the zócalo dispenses much the same information, though the staff there are sometimes a bit vague. There are several **banks** with ATMs on the streets surrounding the zócalo. Casas de cambio include Balsas, just off Plazuela de San Juan at Carlos Nibbi 2, which offers good rates and civilized opening hours (Mon–Fri 8am–5pm, Sat & Sun 8am–3.30pm).

## Accommodation

Taxco has some excellent **hotels**, and when the day-trippers have left the place settles into a calmer mode. There are plenty of inexpensive places near the zócalo, while you're swamped with choices at the higher end of the scale. Particularly nice are some lovely restored colonial buildings that now serve as comfortable hotels.

**Agua Escondida** Plaza Borda 4, on the zócalo ⓣ762/622-0726 or 36, ⓦwww.aguaescondida.com. The small frontage on the Plaza Borda gives little clue to the actual size of this rambling hotel. Hidden away are a pool, table tennis and a choice of "economic" or "remodelled" rooms, the latter with TV and telephone. Some have good views, but aren't really worth the price difference, and those at the front can be noisy due to night-time revelry in the square. ❺

**Los Arcos** Juan Ruíz de Alarcón 2 ⓣ762/622-1836, ⓔlosarcoshotel@hotmail.com. A couple of blocks east of the zócalo, this good-value hotel has large rooms in a seventeenth-century colonial building set around a pretty courtyard with trees. Book ahead if you plan to stay at a weekend. ❺

**Casa de Huéspedes Arellano** Pajaritos 23 ⓣ762/622-0215. Good-value budget hotel with three sun terraces right by the market. The higher up you get, the cheaper the rooms. ❸–❹

**Casa Grande** Plazuela de San Juan 7 ⓣ762/622-0969, ⓦwww.casagrandetaxco.com. Friendly, functional and with a slightly run-down charm, this is one of the cheapest places in town. Cheerful rooms, some with bathrooms; those on the top floor have direct access to the rooftop terrace. ❹

**Emilia Castillo** Juan Ruíz de Alarcón 7 ⓣ762/622-1396. The rooms in this lovely colonial hotel near the zócalo are decorated in bright tiles and old wood. ❺

**Posada San Javier** Estacadas 32 ⓣ762/622-3177, ⓔposadasanjavier@hotmail.com. Spacious hotel on a steep hill, with a pool and attractive gardens. Rooms are large and simply but tastefully decorated (and some have good views). It is worth paying M$30 extra for a junior suite with terracotta-tiled floors and heavy wooden furniture. No credit cards. ❺

**Santa Prisca** Cena Obscuras 1 ⓣ762/622-0080 or 0980, ⓔhtl_staprisca@yahoo.com. Attractive converted colonial building just off the zócalo, with a pleasant flower-filled patio and a variety of rooms, some of which have their own terrace. ❺

## The Town

The heart of town is the diminutive **Plaza Borda**, ringed by recently restored colonial buildings and dominated by Taxco's one outstanding sight, the church of **Santa Prisca**. Towering over the zócalo, its hyper-elaborate facade was built in a single stint between 1751 and 1759, and displays a rare unity. Inside there's a riot of gilded churrigueresque altarpieces and other treasures, including paintings by Miguel Cabrera, a Zapotec who became one of Mexico's greatest colonial religious artists. His work can be seen in the medallions of the altarpieces; lunettes of the martyrdom of St Prisca and St Sebastian; a series of fifteen scenes from the life of the Virgin in the Episcopal Sacristy behind the altar; and a collection of paintings of prominent townspeople of the age (including Borda), in a side chapel to the left. The *manifestador*, a gilt construction immediately in front of the altar, was designed to display the Holy Sacrament and comes decorated with small statues of Faith, Hope and Charity. It was thought to have been lost until rediscovered in 1988 during renovations.

In the northeast corner of the zócalo, a doorway opens onto a courtyard packed with silver shops, which in turn provides the approach to the **Museo de Platería**, Plaza Borda 1 (daily except Wed 10am–6pm; M$8). Turn left and down the stairs to reach this small but worthwhile collection of silver, including beautiful Art Deco cutlery, a coffee jug and a gorgeous teapot from William Spratling's original workshop. The rest of what's on display spans the years since Spratling's time: everything from a walking stick in the form of a snake to modern designs incorporating amethysts found in geodes hereabouts. There's even one piece with a whole geode worked into the design. Almost next door, the **Centro Cultural de Taxco** (Mon–Fri 9am–4pm, Sat 10am–5pm, Sun 9am–3pm; free) is really just a showcase for local artists and is worth a quick visit if only for the views over the town from many of the windows.

William Spratling's personal collection of antiquities is contained in the **Museo Guillermo Spratling**, Porfirio Delgado 1 (Tues–Sat 9am–6pm, Sun 9am–3pm; M$24), right behind Santa Prisca and reached down Calle del Arco at the right-hand side of the church. There are several good pieces, but overall it is disappointing, especially if you've been to the Museo Nacional de Antropología in Mexico City (see p.440): if you've yet to go, hold onto your money. Taxco's most interesting museum, the **Museo de Arte Virreinal**, Juan Ruíz de Alarcón 6 (Tues–Sat 10am–5.45pm, Sun 10am–3.45pm; M$20), is housed nearby in the beautiful colonial Casa Humboldt, an old staging inn named after an German explorer-baron who spent just one night here in 1803. Labels in Spanish and English provide detailed and diverting background to the town, its religious art and history, partly focusing on Taxco's importance on the Spanish trade routes between Acapulco and Veracruz. The life and works of José de la Borda and Humboldt both get extensive coverage too, and there's a good collection of ecclesiastical vestments and furniture, including a fine sacristy bench, a huge eighteenth-century candlestick and a kind of waffle iron for making communion wafers.

Beyond these few sights, the way to enjoy Taxco is simply to wander the streets, nosing about in *platerías* and stopping occasionally for a drink. If you're in the market for **silver** you can be fairly sure that the stuff here is the real thing (check for the mark: ".925" or "sterling"), but prices are much the same as they would be anywhere and quality and workmanship can vary enormously: there's everything from mass-produced belt buckles and cheap rings to designer jewellery that will set you back thousands of dollars. Whatever you buy, the shops off the main streets will be cheaper and more open to bargaining. A section in the **market**, down the steps beside the zócalo, is given over to silver-hawkers and is a good place to start. The bulk of the market, however, seems to specialize in rather tacky tourist goods.

There is little of interest in the immediate vicinity, though to while away an afternoon you could follow Benito Juárez to Plazuela el Minero (a small square with a statue of a miner), then head left up Avenida de los Plateros to the northern end of town (around 2km – alternatively take a *combi* from the zócalo to Los Arcos), from where you can catch the **teleférico** (daily 7am–7pm; M$30 return) up to the hilltop *Hotel Monte Taxco* for the views.

## Eating and drinking

Finding somewhere to **eat** in Taxco is no problem: there are several enticing places around the zócalo that are wonderful for watching the world go by. They do tend to be expensive, though, and by sacrificing a little atmosphere you'll do better along some of the streets that lead away from the centre. All except the cheapest of the hotels have their own dining rooms, and for rock-bottom prices, the **market** has a section of food stalls, which are better than they look. In the evening everyone gathers around the zócalo to see and be seen, to stroll or to sit outdoors with a coffee or a drink at one of the bars.

**El Adobe** Plazuela de San Juan 13. Homely restaurant where excellent Mexican food is served for moderate prices either in the cosy interior or on a balcony overlooking the square.

**Bar Berta** Plaza Borda 2. Traditional meeting place almost next to the church, and one of several places in Mexico claiming to be the original home of the margarita. Here it is a tequila and lime mixture known as a "Berta".

**Café Sasha** Juan Ruíz de Alarcón 1, opposite *Hotel Los Arcos*. Excellent upstairs café with no view to speak of, but an intimate atmosphere with comfy sofas, artesanía decor and even some English-language books for sale. Reliably good and modestly priced food, extending to pizzas, tortas, salads, falafel, garlic bread and daily specials (always including a vegetarian option). Local *músicos* turn up most evenings, making this a relaxed place to drink.

**La Concha Nostra** upstairs at Plazuela de San Juan 7. Primarily a bar with live rock on Sat (no cover), but also serving breakfasts, meals throughout the day and pizza at low prices.

**Restaurant Bar Acerto** Plaza Borda 4. Directly opposite Santa Prisca and with excellent views, especially if you can get one of the prized window seats. Formerly known as Bar Paco, it has been the place to come since 1937 and remains a nice spot for sipping a beer or dining on one of their fairly pricey but well-prepared meals.

# West of Mexico City

The terrain west of Mexico City is varied: high and flat due west around the biggest city, **Toluca**, and broken only by the occasional soaring peak, then dropping away on all sides, particularly south of Toluca, where the country becomes ruggedly hilly as you descend. Dotted with small towns of some interest, it also gets progressively warmer and more verdant. The main artery through the region is Hwy-55, which is superseded in places by a modern autopista but still used by most of the buses to the small towns.

## Grutas de Cacahuamilpa

Just 20km north of Taxco on the highway to Ixtapan de la Sal and Toluca, you pass close to the vast complex of caves known as the **Grutas de Cacahuamilpa** (open daily for guided tours only: on the hour 10am–5pm; M$30). This network of caverns, hollowed out by two rivers, extends for some 70km. The ninety-minute obligatory tour obviously takes in only a fraction of these, passing evocative rock formations, all illuminated to better illustrate their names: "the hunchback", "the bottle of champagne" and others. Among the graffiti you're shown a rather prim note from the wife of Maximilian "María Carlota reached this point". Alongside, Lerdo de Tejada, who became president in 1872, five years after Maximilian's execution, has scrawled "Sebastian Lerdo de Tejada went further". There's a restaurant and several food stalls by the entrance to the caves.

**Buses** running between Taxco and Ixtapan de la Sal pass within 1km of the entrance: ask to be dropped off at the junction and walk down the hill for fifteen minutes. *Colectivos* to the caves also leave hourly from opposite the Estrella Blanca bus terminal in Taxco.

## Ixtapan de la Sal

Continuing north on Hwy-55, the next possible stop is **IXTAPAN DE LA SAL**, not a very attractive town by Mexican standards but a long-established spa whose mineral-rich waters are supposed to cure a plethora of ills. Bathing in Ixtapan's pools is really the only reason to stop, and this can be done either among the slides and fairground-style rides at the **Spa Ixtapan**, at the very top of Juárez (pools Mon–Fri 8am–7pm, Sat & Sun 7am–7pm, M$150; aquatic park daily 9am–6pm, M$150; spa daily 8am–7pm, treatments from M$120 upwards), or more cheaply in the centre of the old town at the **Balneario Municipal**, corner of Allende and 20 de Noviembre (daily 6am–6pm; M$50), which is little more than a geothermally heated swimming pool.

The **bus station** is 3km south of town on Hwy-55, connected to the centre by taxis (M$20), but most buses also stop and pick up at the foot of Juárez, which is the town's main drag. The town gets pretty packed out at weekends, when it may be hard to find a room, but there are some very pleasant **hotels** to choose from, among them the excellent-value *Casa Sarita*, three blocks east and two north of the Balneario Municipal at Obregón 512 (Ⓣ721/143-2745; ❹), where you get nicely decorated, carpeted rooms with TV. For more luxury, try the *Avenida*, Juárez 614, towards Spa Ixtapan (Ⓣ721/143-0241, Ⓕ143-1039; ❹–❺), a three-star hotel with swimming pool whose rooms and suites all have cable TV, phone and FM radio. Ixtapan's most upmarket address is *Ixtapan Spa Hotel and Golf Resort*, next to the Spa Ixtapan (Ⓣ1-800/638-7950, Ⓦwww.spamexico.com; ❾). With the cheapest double room at M$1740, it caters mainly to gringos who've come down to take the waters; facilities include two good restaurants, a piano lounge, a golf course and even a private cinema.

There are numerous **restaurants** along Juárez, though if you're just here briefly you may be happy with the juice bar under the central bandstand and the torta shops nearby.

## Tenancingo

**TENANCINGO** is 33km north of Ixtapan de la Sal and is the next village of any size along Hwy-55. The chief reason to be here is its proximity to the Aztec ruins at **Malinalco** (see below), which can be reached by regular **buses** (every 15min; 30min), most of which continue on to Chalma. Liqueurs made from the fruits that grow in abundance on the plain surrounding the village and finely woven traditional *rebozos* (shawls) are sold here, many of them produced at the lovely monastery of **El Santo Desierto**. This is also a big flower-growing region and as you pass through you'll see whole fields devoted to one bloom, and acres of land protected by plastic greenhouses.

Most **buses** stop around the corner of Victoria and Juárez, about five blocks south of the town's tiny zócalo. You can usually change straight onto a bus for Malinalco, but if you get stuck there is acceptable **accommodation** at *Hotel Lazo*, Victoria 100 (Ⓣ714/142-0083; ❸), where rooms are a bit rough and don't have TV, though there is always hot water. Several small **cafés** serve Mexican staples cheaply.

## Malinalco and around

The village of **Malinalco**, 20km east of Tenancingo, is a lovely little place nestled in a fertile, alluvial valley at 1800m and surrounded by rich villas – many of them, complete with swimming pools, the weekend homes of the capital's privileged few. The fact that it is noticeably warmer than most of the towns hereabouts makes it a popular retreat in winter. It centres on the huge Augustinian church of **Santa Mónica** and has a vibrant Wednesday morning **market**, but the real reason to come here is to see the exemplary **Aztec ruins**.

### The site

The Aztec **site of Malinalco** (Tues–Sun 9am–6pm; M$33) sits high on a hill to the west of town (follow Guerrero west from the zócalo) and can be reached after a twenty- to thirty-minute walk up a very steep, stepped path.

Having only been started in 1501, it was still incomplete at the time of the Conquest but it is undeniably one of the most evocative sites of its kind, carved in part from the raw rock hillside of the Cerro de los Idolos. Looking back over the village and valley, the ruins may be small, but they are undeniably impressive, the main structures and the stairways up to them partly cut out of the rock, partly constructed from great stone blocks. The most remarkable aspect is the circular inner sanctuary of the main temple or **Cuauhcalli** (House of the Eagle), hewn entirely from the face of the mountain. You approach up a broad staircase on either side of which sit stone jaguars – in the centre an all but worn-away human statue would have held a flag. This was the setting for the sacred **initiation ceremonies** in which Aztec youths became members of the warrior elite, and there are images of warriors throughout: to one side of the entrance, a broken eagle warrior sits atop Quetzalcoatl, the feathered serpent; guarding the other side are the remains of a jaguar warrior, representative of the second Aztec warrior class. The doorway of the sanctuary itself, cut through a natural rock wall, represents the giant mouth of a serpent – entrance was over its tongue, and around it traces of teeth are still visible. Right in the centre of the floor lies the figure of an eagle, and on the raised horseshoe-shaped bench behind are two more eagles and the pelt of an ocelot, all carved in a single piece from the bedrock. Behind the first eagle is a hole in the ground where the hearts of human sacrificial victims would be placed, supposedly to be eaten while still beating as the final part of the initiation into warriorhood.

Other structures at the site include a small circular platform by the entrance, unfinished at the time of the Conquest, and a low pyramid directly in front of the main temple. Beyond this lie two larger temples. The first, Edificio III, again has a circular chamber at the centre, and it is believed that here Aztec warriors killed in battle were cremated, their souls rising to the heavens to become stars. Edificio IV was originally a temple of the sun; much of it was used to construct the church in the village. Below the pyramids, visible from about halfway up the steps to the ruins, you can see another prehistoric building nestling among the mountains. It's still used by local residents as a place of pilgrimage each September 29: formerly a shrine to an Aztec altar-goddess, it is now dedicated to San Miguel.

On the way to the site, you pass the **Museo Universitario Schneider** (Tues–Sun 10am–5.30pm; M$10), a well-laid-out little museum of archeological finds from the area, many donated by local residents who unearthed them while gardening or working on their homes. There's also a suit of conquistador armour, and a reconstruction of the shrine of Cuauticalli from the site.

### Practicalities

The easiest way to reach Malinalco is by **bus** or shared taxi from Tenancingo. Most buses arrive in the central plaza in front of the church of Santa Mónica, but those through to Chalma sometimes hurtle straight down Morelos, which bypasses the centre: ask to be dropped at the end of Hidalgo, which runs 200m to the zócalo. From Mexico City (Observatorio), there are only three direct daily buses to Malinalco, but departures every twenty minutes for Chalma, from where there are frequent local services. Malinalco has a virtually useless **tourist office** in the town hall at the uphill end of the main plaza (Mon–Fri 9am–3pm, Sat 9am–1pm; ⓣ714/147-0111). There are **ATMs** on Hidalgo and by the town hall.

Of the several **places to stay** in town, the best is the well-kept *Hotel Marmil*, Progreso 67 (ⓣ714/147-0916; ❸), with very pleasant country-style rooms, off-street parking, ceiling fans, a pool and cable TV. It is ten minutes' walk uphill from the zócalo (if coming by bus from Tenancingo, ask to be dropped near the hotel), and is almost always full at weekends. *Hotel Santa Mónica*, Hidalgo 109 (☎714/147-0031; ❸), near the plaza on the way to the site, is slightly less well-equipped, though its rooms are all en-suite and with TV. As a fallback, you could try *Posada Familiar Maria Dolores*, just south of the main square at Juárez 113 (☎714/147-0354; ❸), which has pleasant rooms beside a quiet garden, though maintenance and cleanliness leave something to be desired.

Come in the middle of the week and you'll find some of the **restaurants** closed, but at weekends there are at least half a dozen places catering to the weekly influx from the capital and Cuernavaca. Everything is close by so you can walk around and take your pick. *Ehecatl*, east of the main square on Hidalgo, has good food at low prices. On the square itself, *Los Placeres* is a friendly bar/restaurant with excellent food, including vegetarian dishes, lots of salads and delicious breakfasts, as well as a great ambience. One thing that's really good to eat in Malinalco is trout, fresh from a local trout farm.

### Around Malinalco: Chalma and Ahuehuete

Nestled among impressive craggy peaks 7km east of Malinalco, **CHALMA** is an important place of pilgrimage, although the town itself is a complete dump. Its filthy, muddy streets are lined with stalls offering tacky souvenirs to the pilgrims who converge here every Sunday and at times of special religious significance (especially the first Fri in Lent, Semana Santa and Sept 29), camping out for miles around: so many people come, in fact, that it's impossible to get anywhere near the church. The pilgrims flock here to take part in rituals that are a fascinating blend of Christian and more ancient pagan rites. Originally, the deity Oztocteotl, god of caves, was venerated here in a natural cave. When the first missionaries arrived, he was "miraculously" replaced by a statue of Christ, which was moved in the seventeenth century to a new church, the Santuario de Chalma. It is this church that is now the focus of pilgrimage and the site of miraculous appearances by a Christ-like figure. As well as paying their devotions to Christ, the pilgrims bathe in the healing waters that flow from the original cave.

*Colectivos* leave Malinalco's zócalo every few minutes for Chalma, from where you can continue direct to Mexico City (Terminal Poniente) passing nearby **AHUEHUETE** on the way. There's another heavily visited shrine here, at a spot where a miraculous spring issues from the roots of a huge old tree. Many people stop here before visiting Chalma, and proceed the last few kilometres to that town on foot.

## Tenango del Valle and Metepec

Half an hour north of Tenancingo you come to **TENANGO DEL VALLE**, from where you can visit the excavated remains of the large fortified Malatzinca township of **Teotenango** (Tues–Sun 9am–5pm; M$15, free on Wed) nearby. It is a fifteen-minute walk to the entrance, then a steep ten-minute hike up to the site: to get there from the centre of the village, head north along Porfirio Díaz Norte, then take a left up Roman Piña Chan Norte. There's a small museum on site.

Some 25km further north you pass **METEPEC**, famed as a **pottery**-making centre. Brightly coloured wares can be found at craft shops throughout the country; supposedly, the figures that characterize these pots were originally inspired by the saints on the facade of Metepec's sixteenth-century monastery, and in the twentieth century Diego Rivera taught the villagers new techniques of colouring and design. There's a market here on Mondays. From Metepec it is less than 10km on to Toluca (see below).

## Toluca and around

The capital of the state of México, **TOLUCA DE LERDO** is today a large and modern industrial centre, sprawling across a wide plain. At an altitude of nearly 2700m, it is the highest city in the country, and comes surrounded by beautiful mountain scenery, dominated by the white-capped **Nevado de Toluca**. It is not a place you'll want to linger, but it is the site of what is allegedly the largest single **market** in the country. Held a couple of kilometres southeast of the centre, just east of the bus station, every Friday (and to a lesser extent throughout the week), the market constitutes the overriding reason to visit. Many visitors stop over on a Thursday night (book accommodation in advance) and then move on, or even make an early start from Mexico City on Friday morning.

The market attracts hordes of visitors from the capital, but is so vast that there can be no question of its being overwhelmed by tourists; quite the opposite, many outsiders find themselves overwhelmed by the scale of the place, lost among the thousands of stalls and crowds from the state's outlying villages. Though increasingly dominated by cheap imported goods and clothing, there is still a substantial selection of **local crafts** – woven goods and pottery above all. For an idea of what quality and prices to expect, head first for the Casa de Artesanías, Paseo Tollocan 700 Ote, a few blocks east of the market.

### Arrival and orientation

An almost uninterrupted stream of **buses** leaves Mexico City's Terminal Poniente for Toluca throughout the day; the journey takes a little over an hour. Toluca's modern bus station is right by the market and a local bus will take you the last 3km into the centre. *De paso* services from Mexico City to Zitácuaro and Valle de Bravo usually stop on the bypass 500m south of the bus station. To return to the bus station, pick up a *combi* labelled "Terminal" on Juárez, just west of the *portales*. The **airport**, further out on Hwy-15, is connected to town only by taxi (M$100).

Unusually for Mexico, the heart of the city is formed not by an open plaza but by a central block surrounded on three sides by the nation's longest series of arcades, built in the 1830s and known as *portales*, lined with shops, restaurants and cafés: **Portal Madero** is to the south along Hidalgo; **Portal 20 de Noviembre** is to the east along Allende; and **Portal Reforma** is to the west along Bravo. The fourth side is taken up by the nineteenth-century **cathedral** and, to its east, the mustard-yellow church of **Santa Cruz**.

### Accommodation

In general, Toluca's **hotels** are poor value for your money, with a number of fairly grotty places clustered around the market. But even these fill up by Thursday nights, when **finding a room** can be difficult.

**Colonial** Hidalgo 103 Ote ⓣ722/215-9700, ⓕ214-7066. One of the better city-centre options, quirky and eccentric with parquet floors and an old-fashioned feel. ❺

**Rex** Matamoros 101, opposite Portal Madero ⓣ722/215-9300 or 02. Clean, functional and relatively low-priced, with fairly well-maintained rooms, all with bathroom and TV. ❸

**San Carlos** Portal Madero 210 ⓣ722/214-4336 or 214-4343. Best value in the city centre: very central, with friendly staff and large, comfortable, carpeted rooms. ❺

**San Francisco** Rayon 104 Sur ⓣ722/213-4415, ⓔsanfranciscotula@prodigy.net.mx. Business-style hotel with an atrium lobby whose canned music makes it feel rather tacky, though the rooms are fine enough, and there's a pool, bar and restaurant. ❻

**Terminal** Felipe Berriázabal 101 ⓣ722/217-4588. Fairly decent hotel despite its insalubrious surroundings right by the bus station (and with access from inside the terminal). All rooms have bathroom, 24hr hot water and TV. Those on the fifth floor upwards are carpeted and have slightly higher rates. ❷

## The Town

Most of the central sights are clustered north of the *portales* and the cathedral, close to the massive open **Plaza de los Mártires**, which dominated on the north side by the Palacio del Gobierno. To the east is the **Plaza Garibay**, rather prettier with shrubbery and fountains stretching down to the **Jardín Botánico Cosmovitral** (Tues–Sun 10am–6pm; M$10), Toluca's botanical gardens. Housed in an enormous, hundred-metre-long Art Nouveau greenhouse the garden structure was built in 1909 and served as the main market until 1975. With predominantly semi-tropical displays, small pools and even a well-tended Japanese corner, it is attractive, but the highlight is undoubtedly the amazing stained-glass panels done in the Mexican muralist style by local artist Leopoldo Flores. Coloured glass covers almost every inch of the walls and roof, the red of the flaming human figure at the west end gradually fading to blue in the east. Come early or late to catch the low sun giving a coloured cast to the plants. The northwestern corner of Plaza Garibay is occupied by the **Museo de Bellas Artes**, on Santos Degollado (Tues–Sat 10am–6pm, Sun 10am–3pm; M$10, free on Sun), which typically shows off some of the best fine arts in the state.

Back on Plaza de los Mártires, the **Museo José Maria Velasco** (Tues–Sat 10am–5.30pm, Sun 10am–3pm; M$10, free on Sun) occupies two floors of a colonial house and displays a good collection of nineteenth-century paintings, much of it by Velasco, who was born in the state of México in 1840, though he spent much of his life in Mexico City. There's a recreation of his studio, along with busts, portraits and some delightful landscapes, including a delicate rendering of the volcanoes and the Valley of México. Several rooms host temporary exhibits, often featuring work by his contemporaries from the San Carlos academy in the capital.

The state of México makes a point of honouring its artistic sons, and adjoining the Velasco museum (entrance round the corner on Nicolas Bravo) are two more museums dedicated to local painters. The **Museo Felipe Santiago Gutiérrez**, Nicolas Bravo 9 (Tues–Sat 10am–5.30pm, Sun 10am–3pm; M$10, free on Sun), fills a colonial mansion with sketches, oils and portraits of prominent nineteenth-century Mexicans; but there is more interest next door at the **Museo Taller Nishizawa** (Tues–Sat 10am–5.30pm, Sun 10am–3pm; M$10, free on Sun), where large abstract landscape canvases by Mexican-Japanese Luis Nishizawa take pride of place alongside pen-and-ink drawings and some of his more recent portraiture.

## Centro Cultural Mexiquense

Some 8km west of Toluca, the **Centro Cultural Mexiquense** harbours several museums (all Tues–Sat 10am–6pm, Sun 10am–3pm; M$20, free on Sun) scattered in park-like grounds. Among them are the **Museo Regional**, devoted to the archeology and history of the state, a small **Museo de Arte Moderno** and, perhaps the most interesting, the **Museo de Artes Populares**, a collection of local crafts, ancient and modern, in a restored hacienda. Although local buses run out there (look for "Centro Cultural Las Palomas" along Lerdo), you really need your own transport to explore the place fully.

### Calixtlahuaca and Nevada de Toluca

While in Toluca put a couple of hours aside to visit the archeological site of **Calixtlahuaca** (daily 10am–5pm; M$32). This was the township of the Matlazinca people, inhabited from prehistoric times and later subjugated by the Aztecs, who established a garrison here in the fifteenth century. Calixtlahuaca was not a willing subject, and there were constant rebellions; after one, in 1475, the Aztecs allegedly sacrificed over 11,000 Matlazinca prisoners on the **Temple of Quetzalcoatl**. This, several times built over, is the most important structure on the site. Dedicated to the god in his role as Ehecatl, god of wind, its circular design is typical, allowing the breezes to blow freely around the shrine. See also the remains of the pyramid devoted to Tlaloc, and the nearby *tzompantli* (skull wall), both constructed of the local pink and black volcanic stone. Bring something to light your way in the short dark tunnels which reveal evidence of earlier constructions; and don't worry too much about the opening hours since the site is not fenced. A small **museum** is sporadically open.

The site is on a hillside just outside the village of Calixtlahuaca, easily reached by **taxi** (roughly M$50) or by a circuitous local **bus** which takes half an hour from the stop on Santos Degollado, one block north of the main square at its junction with Nicolas Bravo.

If you've got your own vehicle – and a sturdy one at that – one trip you should make is to the crater of the extinct **Nevado de Toluca** (Xinantécatl, 4690m), which rises high enough above the surrounding plain for it to rank as Mexico's fourth highest peak. A rough dirt road – impractical during the rainy season or midwinter – leads all the way to the crater rim, from where there are numerous trails leading down to the sandy crater floor and two small lakes, the **Lagos del Sol** and **de la Luna**, right in its heart. From its jagged lip the views are breathtaking: below you the lakes; eastwards a fabulous vista across the valleys of Toluca and México; and to the west a series of lower, greener hills ranging towards the peaks of the Sierra Madre Occidental. If you do hike down into the crater, remember to take it easy in this thin, high-altitude air.

### Eating and drinking

As usual, the markets and outlying areas are the places to go for budget **food**, while around the *portales* there are some good, pricier choices. For a selection of pastries and the best coffee in town visit *Caffé Espresso*, Portal 20 de Noviembre 109; a few doors away *Hostería de las Ramblas*, Portal 20 de Noviembre 107, serves an excellent range of *antojitos* and local specialities for M$30–65 a plate (steaks for M$105–120), and breakfasts at M$45–80. On the other side of the *portales* block at Portal Reforma 108, *Las Ramblitas* has tasty and very reasonable set breakfasts (M$45–80), as well as pozole, enchiladas, *mole poblano* and a M$45 lunch-time menu.

## Valle de Bravo

**West from Toluca**, the road towards Morelia and the state of Michoacán is truly spectacular. Much of this wooded, mountainous area – as far as Zitácuaro – is given over to villas inhabited at weekends by wealthy refugees from the capital, and nowhere more so than the small colonial town of **VALLE DE BRAVO**, reached by turning off to the left about halfway. Set in a deep, pine-clad valley surrounded by low mountains, the town sits on the eastern shore of an artificial lake, **Lago Avandaro**. With terracotta-tiled roofs, iron balconies affixed to many of the older buildings and a mass of whitewashed houses all huddled together, it is an immediately appealing place, something that has drawn a coterie of artistic refugees from the big city. They mostly keep to themselves, leaving the water's edge for weekenders who descend for upmarket relaxation: boat trips, sailing, swimming, water-skiing, riding, paragliding, hiking and golf. If you indulge, it can be an expensive place, but the town itself isn't that pricey and it does make for a

## Fiestas

### January

**Día de los Santos Reyes** (Twelfth Night; Jan 6). The Magi traditionally leave presents for children on this date: many small ceremonies include a fiesta with dancing at Nativitas, a suburb near Xochimilco, and at Malinalco (see p.528).

**Bendicíon de los Animales** (Jan 17). Children's pets and peasants' farm animals are taken to church to be blessed – a particularly bizarre sight at the cathedral in México and in Taxco (see p.523), where it coincides with the fiestas of Santa Prisca (Jan 18) and San Sebastián (Jan 20).

### February

**Día de la Candelaria** (Feb 2). Widely celebrated, especially in Cuernavaca (see p.512).

**Carnaval** (the week before Lent, variable Feb–March). Especially lively in Cuernavaca (see p.512) and nearby Tepoztlán; also in Chiconcuac on the way to Teotihuacán. In Xochimilco (see p.460), for some reason, they celebrate Carnaval two weeks after everyone else.

### March

**Palm Sunday** (the Sun before Easter Sun). A procession with palms in Taxco (see p.523), where representations of the Passion continue through Holy Week.

**Semana Santa** (Holy Week). Observed everywhere. There are very famous Passion plays in the suburb of Itzapalapa, culminating on the Friday with a mock Crucifixion on the Cerro de la Estrella, and similar celebrations at Chalma and nearby Malinalco (see p.528). In Cholula (see p.509), with its host of churches, the processions pass over vast carpets of flowers.

### April

**Feria de la Flor** (early April). Cuernavaca's (see p.512) flower festival.

### May

**May Day** (May 1). A public holiday, usually marked by large marches and demonstrations in the capital. In Cuautla the same day sees a fiesta commemorating an Independence battle.

**Día de la Santa Cruz** (May 3). Celebrated with fiestas and traditional dancing, in Xochimilco (see p.460), Tepotzotlán (see p.492) and Valle de Bravo (see p.533).

**Cinco de Mayo** (May 5). Public holiday for the Battle of Puebla – celebrated in Puebla (see p.502) itself with a grand procession and re-enactment of the fighting.

**Dia de San Isidro** (May 15). Religious processions and fireworks in Tenancingo (see p.528), and a procession of farm animals through Cuernavaca (see p.512) on their way to be blessed at the church.

**Religious festival in Tlaxcala** (see p.500; third Mon in May). An image of the Virgin is processed around the town followed by hundreds of pilgrims.

### June

**Día de San Pedro** (June 29). Observed with processions and dances in Tepotzotlán (see p.492) and traditional dancing in San Pedro Actopan, on the southern outskirts of Mexico City.

very relaxing break provided you come during the week, when fewer people are about and some of the hotels drop their prices.

The zócalo, ringed with restaurants and centred on a twin-towered church, sits on a rise a fifteen-minute walk from the waterfront, where there's a small tourist office (daily 9am–5pm; ⓣ726/262-1678), and a wharf (*embarcadero*) from

**July**

**Día de la Virgen del Carmen** (July 16). Dances and a procession with flowers to the convent of Carmen, in San Ángel (see p.450).

**Día de Santiago** (July 25). Particularly celebrated in Chalco, near Amecameca. The following Sunday sees a market and regional dances at the Plaza de las Tres Culturas (see p.462) and dances, too, in Xochimilco (see p.460).

**Día de Santa Marta** (July 29). In Milpa Alta, near Xochimilco, celebrated with Aztec dances and mock fights between Moors and Christians.

**August**

**Día de la Asunción** (Assumption; Aug 15). Honoured with pilgrimages from Cholula (see p.509) to a nearby village, and ancient dances in Milpa Alta.

**September**

**Independence Day** (Sept 15–16). Celebrated everywhere, above all in the Zócalo in Mexico City, where the president proclaims the famous Grito at 11pm on the 15th, followed by the ringing of the Campana de Dolores and a huge firework display.

**Día de San Miguel** (Sept 29). Provokes huge pilgrimages to both Taxco (see p.523) and Chalma.

**October**

**Día de San Francisco** (Oct 4). A feria in Tenancingo (see p.528), with much traditional music-making, and also celebrated in San Francisco Tecoxpa, a village on the southern fringes of the capital.

**Fiesta del Santuario de la Defensa** (Oct 12). A street party that centres around an ancient church just outside Tlaxcala (see p.500).

**November**

**Día de los Muertos** (Day of the Dead; Nov 1–2). Observed everywhere. The shops are full of chocolate skulls and other ghoulish foods. Tradition is particularly strong in San Lucas Xochimanca and Nativitas, both to the south of Mexico City.

**Día de Santa Cecilia** (Nov 22). Santa Cecilia is the patron saint of musicians, and her fiesta attracts orchestras and mariachi bands from all over to Santa Cecilia Tepetlapa, not far from Xochimilco.

**December**

**Feria de la Plata** (Dec 1). The great silver fair in Taxco (p.523) lasts about ten days from this date.

**Día de la Señora de Guadalupe** (Dec 12). A massive pilgrimage to the Basilica of Guadalupe (see p.463) runs for several days round about, combined with a constant secular celebration of music and dancing.

**Christmas** (Dec 25). In the week leading up to Christmas, Nativity plays – also known as *posadas* – can be seen in many places. Among the most famous are those at Taxco (see p.523) and Tepotzotlán (see p.492).

which you can take boat rides: either rent one from M$300–400 an hour, or join a *lancha colectiva* for M$25 an hour.

### Practicalities

From Mexico City's Terminal Poniente (Observatorio), there are second-class **buses** to Valle del Bravo every twenty minutes (3hr), plus three daily first-class buses (2hr 15min). Buses from Toluca make a long circuit around town before depositing you at the **bus station** on 16 de Septiembre (no guardería). Head downhill and take a right at the end (Juárez) to get to the centre. The best of the more reasonably priced **places to stay** is the *Posada Familiar 16 de Septiembre*, 16 de Septiembre 417 (726/262-1222, posada16deseptiembre@yahoo.com.mx; ❸), which is 100m downhill from the bus station, and has prettily decorated rooms (with TV and bathroom) and a real family atmosphere; slightly upmarket, the *Posada Casa Vieja,* Juárez 101 (726/262-0318, posadacasavieja@yahoo.com.mx; ❹), has a variety of rooms, some bigger than others (so it may be worth checking a few), plus ample hot water, and a sunny veranda. Alternatives include *Posada Los Girasoles*, Plaza Independencia 1 (726/262-2967; ❹), right on the main square, clean and cool with firm beds and rooms that are spacious but a bit dark.

Valle de Bravo has a reasonable range of **restaurants**, though not many at the top end of the scale. Some of the cheapest eating is in and around the market, at the end of Juárez on Hidalgo. Another place for good cheap eats is *El Unicornio Azul*, 16 de Septiembre 402, a *comedor* that serves flavourful comida corrida for M$25. The best upmarket choice is *El Portal*, on the zócalo at Plaza Independencia 101, where you can get salads, pizzas or *antojitos*, followed by steak or chicken, or trout or octopus, at M$63–85 for a main dish. If you like trout (farmed, not from the lake), the tiny *Lonchería Trucha la Estrella* down by the *embarcadero* has trout cooked however you like it (M$60), or their own trout ceviche or smoked trout paté.

# Travel details

The capital is the centre of the nation, so any attempt at a comprehensive list of the comings and goings would be doomed to failure. What follows is no more than a survey of the major services on the main routes: it must be assumed that intermediate points are linked at least as frequently as those mentioned. Literally thousands of buses leave Mexico City every day, and you can get to just about any town in the country, however small, whenever you want. Journey times given are for the fastest services.

## Buses

**Cholula** to: Mexico City (every 20–60min; 2hr 30min); Puebla (buses every 10–15min; 20min; plus frequent *colectivos*).

**Cuautla** to: Cuernavaca (every 20–30min; 1hr 20min); Mexico City Autobuses del Sur (at least two every 15min; 1hr 40min); Mexico City TAPO (every 10min; 1hr 40min); Tepoztlán (every 15min; 40min).

**Cuernavaca** to: Acapulco (Estrella de Oro terminal, 32 daily; Estrella Blanca terminal, 7 daily; 5hr); Cuautla (Estrella Roja terminal and market terminal, every 15min; 1hr 20min); Ixtapan de la Sal (Estrella Blanca terminal, 6 daily; 3hr); Mexico City (Pullman de Morelos terminal, every 15min; 1hr 15min); Mexico City airport (Casino terminal, hourly; 1hr 30min); Puebla (Estrella Roja terminal, 9 daily; 3hr 30min); Taxco (Estrella Blanca terminal, hourly; 1hr 40min); Tepoztlán (market terminal, every 15min; 45min); Toluca (Estrella Blanca terminal, every 30min; 2hr 30min).

**Ixtapan de la Sal** to: Acapulco (3 daily; 6hr); Cuernavaca (6 daily; 3hr); Mexico City (indirect every 15min; 3hr; direct hourly; 2hr); Taxco (19 daily; 1hr 20min); Tenancingo (every 15min; 45min); Toluca (every 20min; 1hr).

**Mexico City** (N = Terminal del Norte; S = Central de Autobuses del Sur; E = TAPO; W = Terminal Poniente) to: Acapulco (S, every 30 min, N, hourly; 5hr); Aguascalientes (N, hourly; 6hr); Amecameca (E, every 20min; 1hr 15min); Campeche (E, 5 daily; 17hr); Cancún (E, 3 daily; 24hr); Chalma (W, every 20min, 2hr 30min); Chetumal (E, 3 daily; 18hr); Chihuahua (N, hourly; 18hr); Chilpancingo (S, hourly; 3hr 30min); Ciudad Juárez (N, hourly; 24hr); Ciudad Obregón (N, hourly; 26hr); Colima (N, 9 daily; 11hr); Córdoba (E, hourly; 4hr); Cuautla (S, every 10min; E, every 20min; 1hr 40min); Cuernavaca (S, every 15min; 1hr 30min); Dolores Hidalgo (N, every 40min; 4hr); Durango (N, 9 daily; 12hr); Fortín de las Flores (E, 1 daily; 4hr); Guadalajara (N, 14 daily; W, 5 daily; 7hr); Guanajuato (N, 10 daily; 5hr); Guaymas (N, 13 daily; 27hr); Hermosillo (N, hourly; 32hr); Ixtapa (S, 6 daily; 10hr); Ixtapan de la Sal (W, hourly; 2–3hr); León (N, hourly; 5hr); Los Mochis (N, hourly; 21hr); Malinalco (W, 3 daily; 2hr 30min); Manzanillo (N, 4 daily; 12hr); Matamoros (N, 21 daily; 14hr); Matehuala (N, 11 daily; 7hr); Mazatlán (N, every 30–60min; 15hr); Mérida (E, 5 daily; 28hr); Mexicali (N, hourly; 30hr); Monterrey (N, hourly; 12hr); Morelia (W, 45 daily; N, every 45–60min; 4hr); Nuevo Laredo (N, hourly; 15hr); Oaxaca (E, 25 daily; 6hr); Orizaba (E, 35 daily; 4hr); Pachuca (N, every 10min; 1hr 15min); Palenque (E, 2 daily; 13hr); Pátzcuaro (W, 9 daily; N, 4 daily; 7hr); Playa del Carmen (E, 2 daily; 22hr); Puebla (E, every 12–20min; N, every 30min; S, hourly; 2hr); Puerto Escondido (S, 3 daily; E, 1 daily; 15hr); Puerto Vallarta (N, 4 daily; 12hr); Querétaro (N, every 20min; 2hr 40min); Saltillo (N, 19 daily; 10hr); San Cristóbal de las Casas (E, 4 daily; 17hr); San Luis Potosí (N, hourly; 5hr); San Miguel Allende (N, every 40min; 4hr); Taxco (S, hourly; 2hr 30min); Tehuacán (E, 13 daily; 4hr); Tehuantepec (E, 2 daily; 10hr); Teotihuácan (N, every 15min; 1hr); Tepic (N, hourly; 12hr); Tepoztlán (S, every 20min; 1hr 15min); Tijuana (N, hourly; 42hr); Tlaxcala (E, every 20min; 1hr 40min); Torreón (N, 10 daily; 14hr); Tula (N, every 30min; 1hr 15min); Tuxpan (N, hourly; 4hr); Tuxtla Gutiérrez (E, 13 daily; 14hr); Uruapan (W, 13 daily; N, 7 daily; 5hr 30min); Valle de Bravo (W, every 20min; 3hr); Veracruz (E, 25 daily; 7hr); Villahermosa (E, 33 daily; 11hr); Xalapa (E, 22 daily; 5hr); Zacatecas (N, 18 daily; 8hr); Zihuatanejo (S, 6 daily; 9hr).

**Pachuca** to: Mexico City (every 10min; 1hr 15min); Mexico City airport (hourly; 1hr 40min); Puebla (21 daily; 4hr); Real del Monte (frequent *colectivos*; 20min); Tlaxcala (21 daily; 3hr); Tula (every 15min; 1hr 30min).

**Puebla** to: Cholula (buses every 10–15min; 20min; plus frequent *colectivos*); Cuernavaca (hourly; 3hr 30min); Mexico City TAPO (every 15min; 2hr); Mexico City Terminal del Norte (hourly; 2hr); Mexico City airport (hourly; 2hr 15min); Oaxaca (11 daily; 4hr 30min); Pachuca (every 40min; 4hr); Tlaxcala (every 8min; 40min; plus frequent micros); Veracruz (hourly; 4hr 30min).

**Taxco** to: Acapulco (14 daily; 5hr); Chilpancingo (14 daily; 3hr); Cuernavaca (hourly; 1hr 40min); Ixtapan (18 daily; 1hr 20min); Mexico City (hourly; 2hr 15min); Toluca (18 daily; 3hr 30min).

**Tenancingo** to: Ixtapan de la Sal (every 15min; 45min); Malinalco (every 15min; 30min; plus shared taxis); Toluca (every 30min; 1hr).

**Tlaxcala** to: Mexico City (every 20min; 1hr 40min); Pachuca (every 30min; 3hr); Puebla (every 8min; 40min; plus frequent micros).

**Toluca** to: Cuernavaca (every 30min; 2hr 30min); Ixtapan (every 20min; 1hr); Mexico City (every 5min; 1hr 30min); Morelia (hourly; 4hr); Querétaro (hourly; 3hr 30min); Taxco (18 daily; 3hr); Tenancingo (every 30min; 1hr); Tenango del Valle (every 4min; 30min); Valle de Bravo (every 20min; 2hr).

**Tula** to: Mexico City (every 30–60min; 1hr 30min); Pachuca (every 15min; 1hr 30min); Querétaro (9 daily; 2hr 30min); Tepotzotlán (Caseta de) (every 20min; 1hr).

## Flights

**Mexico City** to: Acapulco (9 daily; 45min); Aguascalientes (5 daily; 1hr); Bajío/León (8 daily; 50min); Campeche (3 daily; 1hr 10min); Cancún (24 daily; 2hr); Chetumal (2 daily; 1hr 50min); Chihuahua (8 daily; 2hr); Ciudad Carmen (6 daily; 1hr 25min); Ciudad Juárez (9 daily; 2hr 20min); Ciudad Obregón (3–4 daily; 2hr 15min); Ciudad Victoria (3–4 daily; 1hr 10min); Colima (4 daily; 1hr); Cozumel (1 daily; 2hr); Culiacán (9–10 daily; 1hr 45min); Durango (9 daily; 2hr); Guadalajara (34 daily; 1hr); Hermosillo (11 daily; 2hr 30min); Huatulco (3 daily; 1hr 10min); Ixtapa/Zihuatanejo (8 daily; 50min); La Paz, Baja California Sur (6 daily; 2hr 5min); Lázaro Cárdenas (1–2 daily; 1hr 10min); Los Cabos (7 daily; 2hr); Los Mochis (1–3 daily; 2hr); Manzanillo (6 daily; 1hr 40min); Matamoros (1 daily; 1hr 25min); Mazatlán (6 daily; 35min); Mérida (14 daily; 1hr 40min); Mexicali (5 daily; 3hr 15min); Monterrey (36 daily; 1hr 20min); Morelia (5 daily; 55min); Nuevo Laredo (2–3 daily; 1hr 35min); Oaxaca (7–8 daily; 55min); Puebla (6 weekly; 35min); Puerto Escondido

(1 daily; 1hr 05min); Puerto Vallarta (8–9 daily; 1hr 20min); Querétaro (2 daily except Sat; 45min); Reynosa (2 daily; 1hr 25min); Saltillo (2 daily; 1hr 25min); San Luis Potosí (9 daily weekdays, 5–6 daily weekends; 1hr 15min); Tampico (6 daily; 55min); Tapachula (3–4 daily; 1hr 35min); Tepic (2–4 daily; 1hr 55min); Tijuana (27 daily; 3hr 20min); Torreón (8–9 daily; 1hr 25min); Tuxtla Gutiérrez (11 daily; 1hr 20min); Uruapan (1 daily; 55min); Veracruz (14 daily; 50min); Villahermosa (14 daily; 1hr 20min); Xalapa (2 daily; 1hr); Zacatecas (4 daily; 1hr 15min).

**Puebla** to: Guadalajara (4–5 daily; 1hr 10min); Mexico City (6 weekly; 35min); Monterrey (2–4 daily; 2hr).

**Toluca** to: Acapulco (7 weekly; 50min); Cancún (2 daily; 2hr); Chihuahua (1–2 daily; 2hr); Ciudad Juárez (2 daily; 1hr 25min); Guadalajara (2–5 daily; 1hr); Ixtapa/Zihuatanejo (4 weekly; 50min); Los Cabos (1 daily; 1hr 55min); Monterrey (2–5 daily; 1hr 25min); Tampico (2 daily; 1hr); Tuxtla Gutiérrez (2–3 daily; 1hr 30min); Veracruz (1–2 daily; 55min).

6

# Acapulco and the Pacific beaches

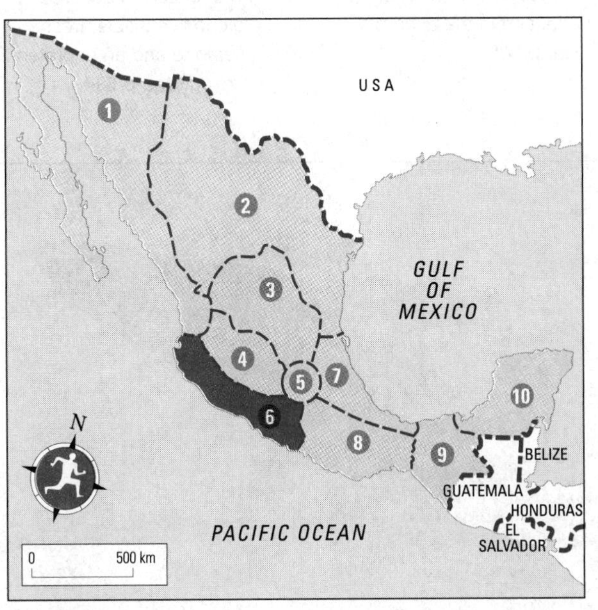

CHAPTER 6

# Highlights

* **Whale watching** Watch the humpback whales frolic in the Bahía de Banderas from December to April. **See p.554**
* **Costa Alegre** A beautiful stretch of coastline punctuated by small, low-key resorts. **See p.554**
* **Comala** Sip a beer and feast on free snacks while mariachis compete for your attention in the town plaza. **See p.568**
* **Barra de Potosí** An untouched beach where you can eat fresh fish and row through a mangrove lagoon. **See p.575**
* **Acapulco** 1950s retro glamour, romantic dining and death-defying cliff divers. **See p.577**
* **Pie de la Cuesta** Take a break from commercialism with deserted beaches, glorious sunsets, fresh seafood and an unpretentious crowd. **See p.584**

△ Humpback whale, Bahía de Banderas

6

# Acapulco and the Pacific beaches

The 800-kilometre stretch of coast between Puerto Vallarta and Punta Maldonada, where the Sierra Madre reaches out to the ocean, is lined with some of Mexico's most popular resorts. **Acapulco** – the original, the biggest, and for many, the best – is a steep-sided, tightly curving bay that, for all its excesses of high-rise development, remains breathtakingly beautiful, from a distance at least. This is the stomping ground of the wealthy, whose villas, high around the wooded sides of the bay, offer isolation from the packaged enclaves below. It's pricey, but not ridiculously so, and while tourists swarm the congested beaches the city itself retains a local feel, with the coarse characteristics of a working port.

**Puerto Vallarta**, second in size and reputation, feels altogether more manageable, with cobbled streets fanning out from a lively zócalo overlooking an oceanfront boulevard. Still, with its party ambience and unbridled commercialism, it is far removed from the tropical village it claims to be: spreading for miles along a series of tiny, rugged beaches, it's certainly a resort. However, if you travel far enough from the downtown beaches you can still find cove after isolated cove backed by forested mountains. For a less commercial experience, **Barra de Navidad**, two hours south of here, is a glorious sweep of sand, surrounded by flatlands and lagoons, with a low-key village at either end. By contrast, **Manzanillo** is first and foremost a port and naval base – despite its lively seaside boardwalk and sail fishing tournaments its pitch for tourism seems something of an afterthought. **Zihuatanejo** is an attractive, gentle resort where magnificent villas have popped up on the slopes overlooking glorious swathes of sand dotted with palms. Its purpose-built neighbour **Ixtapa**, the Pacific coast's answer to Cancún, is far less enchanting, with sterile high-rise developments, shopping malls and an international feel.

All along this coast, between the major centres, you'll find **beaches**: some completely undeveloped; others linked to a village with a few rooms to rent and a makeshift bar on the sand. The ocean breakers can be wild, even positively dangerous at times, and there are minor discomforts – unreliable or nonexistent water and electricity supplies, vicious mosquitoes – but the space and the simplicity, often just an hour's drive from a packed resort, are well worth seeking out. At the opposite end of the spectrum, a recent trend has

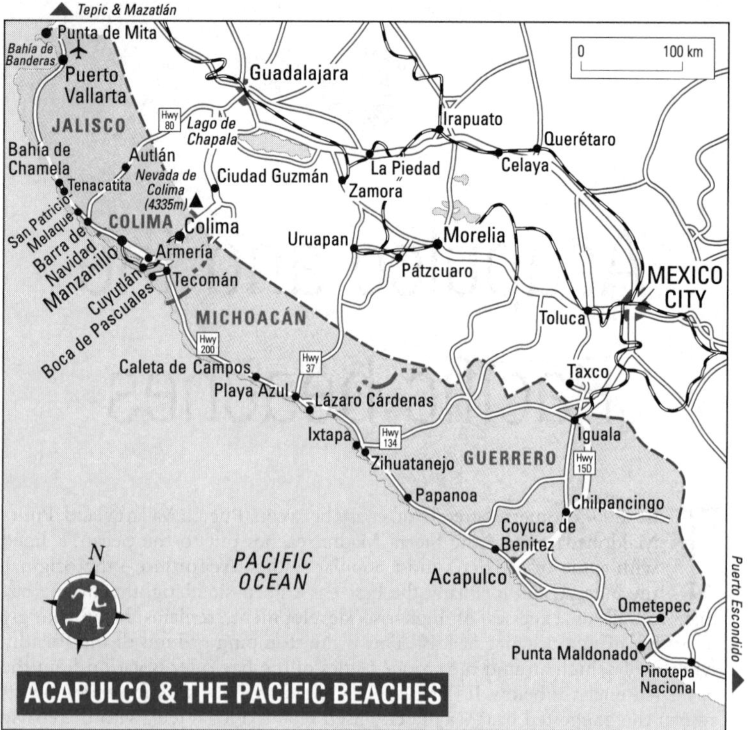


been the development of exclusive boutique hotels, designed to draw international jet-setters in search of isolation and discretion away from the congested resort compounds.

Most people arrive on the fast – and expensive – **Autopista del Sol** from Mexico City to Acapulco, but the **coast road**, whatever some old maps may say, is perfectly feasible (if a little rough in the final stretches) all the way from the US border to Guatemala. Between Puerto Vallarta and Acapulco, it's a good modern highway, unrelentingly spectacular as it forces its way south, sometimes over the narrow coastal plain, more often clinging precariously to the fringes of the sierra where it falls away into the ocean.

Most **buses** heading down from **Mazatlán** turn inland to Guadalajara, but many also continue to **Puerto Vallarta**, and from there on down Hwy-200 towards Acapulco. Guadalajara itself has very frequent bus connections with Puerto Vallarta, **Barra de Navidad** and **Manzanillo**, while from central Michoacán you can head down to the coast at **Lázaro Cárdenas**. **Zihuatanejo** has direct bus services from Mexico City, and hourly services to **Acapulco**. Plentiful buses also run between these resorts, though you may have to change if you're travelling long-distance. It's easy to get from Puerto Vallarta to Barra de Navidad and from there to Manzanillo and from Manzanillo to Lázaro Cárdenas, but there are few direct services from Puerto Vallarta all the way down. In the state of Guerrero there are occasional **military checkpoints** on the roads, where all traffic is stopped and searched. Tourists usually assume that this is for drugs, which may be at least partly true, though the check rarely amounts to more than a peremptory prod at the outside of your case. More importantly, the wild and relatively undeveloped hills retain a reputation for banditry and guerrilla activity. This is not something you need expect to come across, but travelling these roads you should keep your passport and papers handy and not carry anything you wouldn't want discovered.

**Prices** in the resorts, particularly for accommodation, are dictated largely by **season**. High season at the bigger destinations stretches from early or mid-December to after Easter or the end of April, during which time the swankier hotels can charge as much as double the off-season rates and need to be booked in advance. Budget hotels vary their prices less, but costs are still twenty to thirty percent down outside the peak season. Smaller beach towns catering exclusively to Mexicans have a shorter season, usually just December and Semana Santa (around Easter), but the same rules apply.

# Puerto Vallarta and around

By reputation the second of Mexico's beach resorts, **PUERTO VALLARTA** may be smaller and younger than Acapulco, but it is every bit as commercial – and perhaps even more so, since here tourism is virtually the only source of income. PV, as it is known, attracts a greater number of foreign visitors (mainly Americans) than does Acapulco, and thanks to its localized attractions, its vicissitudes and vices – as well as its few virtues – are more glaringly apparent.

Puerto Vallarta lies in the middle of the 22-kilometre-wide **Bahía de Banderas**, the seventh largest bay in the world, which is fringed by endless sandy beaches and backed by the jungle-covered slopes of the Sierra Madre. Until the mid-twentieth century, the town was a small fishing village located where the Río Cuale spills out into the bay. This all changed in 1954, when Mexicana airlines, their hand forced by Aeroméxico's monopoly on flights into Acapulco, started promoting the town as a resort. Their efforts received a shot in the arm a decade later, when John Huston chose Mismaloya, 10km south, as the setting for his film of Tennessee Williams's play *The Night of the Iguana*, starring Richard Burton. The scandal-mongering that surrounded Burton's romance with Elizabeth Taylor – who was not part of the cast but came along – is often deemed responsible for putting Puerto Vallarta firmly in the international spotlight: "a mixed blessing" according to Huston, who stayed on here until his death in 1987, and whose bronze image stands on the Isla Río Cuale in town. More recently, PV's standing has been bolstered by its emergence as one of the **gay** centres of Mexico.

Over the last decade, especially, frantic development has mostly overwhelmed the tropical-village atmosphere: while the historic town centre retains its charming cobbled streets and white-walled, terracotta-roofed houses – assets assiduously exploited by the local tourist authorities – the presence of tacky souvenir shops, tenacious hawkers and flashing neon have created something of an insalubrious undercurrent. Package tourists stay, on the whole, in the upmarket chain hotels – the greatest concentration of which is in **Nuevo Vallarta**, north of the town – but they are increasingly making their way into the centre to shop in pricey boutiques, to drink margaritas in the bars that face the malecón and to eat in some good restaurants. Nevertheless, what could be a depressingly expensive place to visit turns out to be liberally peppered with mid-range hotels and budget restaurants, especially during the low season (Aug–Nov).

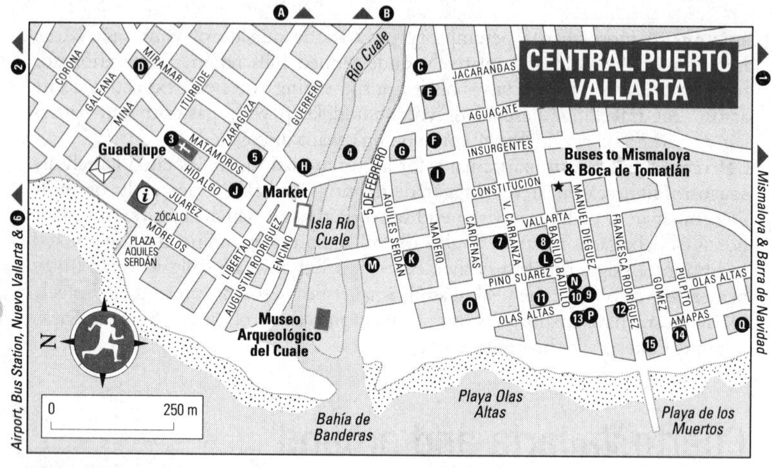


| ACCOMMODATION | | | |
|---|---|---|---|
| Azteca | C | Hotel Posada Río Cuale | K |
| Belmar | G | Lina | F |
| Blue Chairs Resort | Q | Molino de Agua | M |
| La Casa del Puente | H | Playa Los Arcos | P |
| Casa Kimberley | A | Posada de Roger | L |
| Los Cuatro Vientos | D | Vientos del Río | B |
| Escuela Cecattur | J | Villa del Mar | E |
| Hortencia | I | Yasmin | N |
| Hotel Eloisa | O | | |

| EATING & DRINKING | | | |
|---|---|---|---|
| Archie's Wok | 15 | A Page in the Sun | 9 |
| Le Bistro Jazz Café | 4 | El Palomar de los Gonzáles | 1 |
| Café de Olla | 10 | Planeta Vegetariano | 3 |
| Café des Artistes | 2 | El Torito | 7 |
| Daiquiri Dicks | 11 | Las Tres Huastecas | 12 |
| La Dolce Vita | 6 | Trio | 5 |
| Fredy's Tucán | 8 | | |
| Kaiser Maximilian | 13 | | |
| Karpathos Taverna | 14 | | |

## Arrival and information

The **Río Cuale**, spanned by two small road bridges and a pedestrianized footbridge, divides Puerto Vallarta in two. The zócalo, official buildings, market and the bulk of the shops and upscale restaurants lie on the north side. To the south of the river you'll find the town beach and the cheaper hotels. Puerto Vallarta is a very small place, hemmed in by the ocean and by the steep slopes behind – downtown, you can walk just about anywhere.

About 4km north of the town centre lies the long-distance bus station, the **Central Camionera**. Equipped with a guardería (left-luggage office) and long-distance telephones, it is served by **buses** to and from the centre – these are marked "Aeropuerto", "Ixtapa", "Juntas" or "Mojoneras". If catching a city bus from outside the entrance of the Central Camionera, be sure to ask the driver if the bus is going to the city centre, since many will be heading the other way. Frequent local buses (marked "Hoteles") run around the edge of the bay to the north, towards the hotel zone, and, slightly less frequently, south to smaller beaches such as Mismaloya and Boca de Tomatlán.

The **airport** (information on ⓣ322/221-1298) lies 2.5km north of the centre on the coastal highway, and is linked to the city by local buses (marked

### Time zones

Remember that **if you've come south** from Tepic, San Blas, Mazatlán or points north along the coast, you need to advance your watch an hour: the time zone changes at the state border, just north of Puerto Vallarta's airport.

"Olas Altas" or "Centro") that stop a few steps outside the airport's perimeter fence. Authorized airport taxis go right to the airport's main exit, and cost an exorbitant M$250 to the town centre or M$200 to the hotel zone. If you can find a *colectivo*, it should be around a third of the price of a private taxi.

The **tourist office** (Mon–Fri 8am–4pm; ⓣ322/223-2500) is in the Palacio Municipal on the zócalo; the staff can furnish you with leaflets and flyers. For up-to-date, if somewhat promotional, information on what's going on in town, pick up the English-language daily *Vallarta Today* (ⓦwww.vallartatoday.com) or the weekly *Vallarta Tribune*; both are free, and available in gringo hangouts. Puerto Vallarta is also well represented on various **websites**: ⓦwww.puertovallarta.net is the Tourism Board's official site and contains comprehensive listings of what to do and where to stay, along with news and weather reports; ⓦwww.vallartaonline.com provides travel news as well as practical information on local bus routes, money exchange, Spanish schools and the like. Should you find yourself in any trouble, or just needing advice, the **tourist police** are the people dressed in white uniforms and blue caps.

## Accommodation

With the exception of the string of package hotels along the beach north of town in Nuevo Vallarta, Puerto Vallarta's **places to stay** are all within easy walking distance of the beach and the zócalo. The more affordable options mainly lie south of the Río Cuale, though there are a couple of places worth considering to the north. The **budget accommodation** is concentrated along Madero – which can be slightly seedy at night – but remember, too, that pricier places often transform into bargains during the low season. The clean and sociable **Oasis Hostel** is at Libramiento 222 (ⓣ322/222-2636), a fifteen-minute walk from the city centre. Dorm beds are available for M$130 per night, with breakfast and Internet access included.

The closest formal **campsite** to town is the grassy *Puerto Vallarta Trailer Park* (ⓣ322/224-2828), several kilometres north of the hotel zone. Free camping on any of the more popular beaches around the middle of the bay is prohibited, but if you're reasonably well equipped and protected against mosquitoes, you could try **Punta de Mita** at the northern end of the bay or **Boca de Tomatlán** to the south (where the main road turns inland), each of which from time to time sees small communities established on the sand. At **Yelapa**, a southern beach to which there are boat trips from town (see box, p.549), you might be able to rent a hut or find somewhere to sling a hammock; otherwise there is a good hotel.

### South of the Río Cuale

**Azteca** Madero 473, at Jacarandas ⓣ322/222-2750. A longstanding, reliable choice with simple, surgically clean rooms overlooking a peaceful courtyard full of flourishing plants. Street-facing rooms are brighter but noisier. Panoramic views from the rooftop terrace. ❹

**Belmar** Insurgentes 161 ⓣ322/222-0572, ⓦwww.belmarvallarta.com. Well-located and economical, this snug, friendly hotel has clean, pleasant rooms with TV, a/c and closet-size bathrooms. Request a room with a balcony on the top floor. ❹

**Blue Chairs Resort** Almendro 4, at Playa de los Muertos ⓣ322/222-5040, ⓦwww.bluechairs.com. Gay visitors, even if not staying here, will inevitably gravitate to this gay-owned and operated landmark on the town beach. The resort has suites with or without kitchens and ocean views, as well as a rooftop bar and pool. Straight guests are welcome as well. ❽

**Hortencia** Madero 336, at Insurgentes ⓣ322/222-2484, ⓦwww.hotelhortencia.com. A variety of whitewashed, clean, spacious quarters with TV and fan in a convenient location. A/c is available for a few pesos extra. ❺

**Hotel Eloisa** Cárdenas 79 ⓣ322/222-6465, ⓦwww.hoteleloisa.com. The best of the mid-range options, this very friendly, family-run hotel with a

Mexican feel has nicely furnished, recently renovated rooms and studios (with kitchenettes), with cable TV and a/c. There is also a small rooftop pool. ❺–❻

**Hotel Posada Río Cuale** Serdán 242, at Vallarta Ⓣ & Ⓕ 322/222-0450, Ⓔ riocaule@pvnet.com.mx. One of the best-designed of the central hotels, with rooms staggered around gardens to give an open feel. Comfortable a/c rooms with balconies and a decent bar/restaurant beside the pool. ❻

**Lina** Madero 376, east of Insurgentes Ⓣ 322/222-1661. Simple, clean, but slightly gloomy rooms around a courtyard. The on-site restaurant has a fresher feel, but can occasionally be noisy for guests at the hotel. ❹

**Molino de Agua** Vallarta 130 Ⓣ 322/223-1012, Ⓦ www.molinodeagua.com. One of the most tasteful and relaxed options close to downtown. Fully in keeping with Puerto Vallarta's tropical village image, bright, spacious cabins are dotted around two swimming pools in big, tranquil gardens where the Río Cuale meets the sea. A good choice for serious pampering, there is a Jacuzzi and massage available, and two restaurants. ❼

**Playa Los Arcos** Olas Altas 380, at Diéguez Ⓣ 322/226-7102, Ⓦ www.playalosarcos.com. The best-equipped and most spacious of the beachfront hotels, with a lively social scene centred around the large pool and adjacent palapa restaurant, where live sports action and beer predominate. Well-appointed rooms with a/c, TV and safe can smell very musty in the rainy season. ❽

**Posada de Roger** Basilio Badillo 237 Ⓣ 322/222-0639, Ⓦ www.posadaroger.com. Some of the sombre rooms here have seen better days, but they all have a/c, cable TV, safe and fan, and overlook a spacious, shady courtyard where excellent breakfasts are served – the on-site *El Tucan* restaurant is considered the best breakfast spot in town. Only a couple of blocks from the beach, and with a small rooftop pool. ❺

**Villa del Mar** Madero 440, at Jacarandas Ⓣ 322/222-0785. Relaxed, long-time favourite of budget travellers. All motel-style rooms have bathrooms; the larger, more expensive "suites" also have small balconies, a/c, TV and kitchenettes. ❹

**Yasmin** Basilio Badillo 168 Ⓣ 322/222-0087. Reasonable mid-range option one block from the beach, next door to the very popular *Café de Olla*. The clean, low-slung rooms with fans have TVs and decent beds, but some are rather claustrophobic. ❺

## North of the Río Cuale

**La Casa del Puente** Insurgentes, just north of the river behind *Restaurant La Fuente del Puente* Ⓣ 322/222-0749, Ⓦ www.casadelpuente.com. A real home from home: spacious, bright, elegantly furnished apartments, a wonderful communal area with huge windows overlooking the river and an extremely friendly owner. Only two suites (with fully equipped kitchens) and one double room, so book early. ❼

**Casa Kimberley** Zaragoza 445 Ⓣ & Ⓕ 322/222-1336. Time-warp shrine-cum-hotel in the house Richard Burton bought for Liz Taylor in 1964. Except for the Liz memorabilia, the decor is little changed from when she sold it ten years later. Overpriced rooms are scruffy and in need of upgrading, but Liz fans won't care. There is a communal living room with unrivalled views over the town, a swimming pool and free breakfasts. Prices drop by fifty percent in low season. ❾

**Los Cuatro Vientos** Matamoros 520 Ⓣ 322/222-0161, Ⓦ www.cuatrovientos.com. A PV institution, with many return guests. Artistic touches and local handicrafts give the simple, spotless rooms a homely feel. There is a small pool and the terrace has wonderful views. Owner Gloria is a good resource when planning tours or dining out in the area. ❻

**Escuela Cecattur** Hidalgo at Guerrero Ⓣ 322/222-4910, Ⓔ cecati63@prodigy.net.mx. This hotel doubles as a school for those wishing to work in tourism and hospitality – students take part in the day-to-day running of the hotel. Rooms are large, if somewhat characterless. A good second choice if others are fully booked. ❺

**Vientos del Río** Cuauhtémoc 460, at the end of Guerrero across the street from *Casa Kimberley* Ⓣ 322/222-1758. Two beautiful, fully furnished suites with a small pool and big views over the river. ❼

# The Town

Apart from the **beaches**, souvenir shops and chi-chi boutiques and galleries that pack the centre of town, there's not a great deal in the way of attractions in Puerto Vallarta. This said, you can still fill a very pleasant hour or two wandering along the **malecón**, the old seafront promenade that runs adjacent to Morelos in the downtown area, and on the island in the river. The lively **zócalo**, or main square, is north of the river in the heart of town and overlooks

△Malécon, Puerto Vallarta

the oceanfront boulevard. It is the city's microcosm and has a much more cosmopolitan feel than most of its Mexican counterparts. Here, families gather in the evenings among the balloon sellers and hot dog stands, and, beneath the glowing orange neon lights of *Hooters*, tourists embark on tours of the city's restaurants, bars and clubs. The zócalo is backed by the **Church of Guadalupe**, whose tower, topped with a huge crown modelled on one Maximilian's wife, Carlota, wore in the 1860s, is a city landmark. Just down from here on the malecón is the **Plaza Aquiles Serdán**, with a strange little amphitheatre and four arches looking out over the sea, like a lost fragment of the Roman empire. With hawkers, mimes, musicians and food stands, it is one of the best places for people watching in the city. A short stroll northwards brings you to another Puerto Vallarta icon, the *Cabelleo del Mar*, by Rafel Zamarripa, a three-metre-high bronze statue of a seahorse with a naked boy riding on its back. This is a replica of the original, which ended up floating out to sea after a hurricane struck Puerto Vallarta in 2002. In between the plaza and the statue are many other fantastical sculptures by renowned Mexican and international artists, including Sergio Bustamente's *In Search of Reason* (1990), a ladder with two children climbing up and the mother beckoning them down from below.

On the **Isla Río Cuale**, in the middle of the river, a small park surrounds a clutch of shops and restaurants. At the seaward end there's a tiny, irregularly open, local **archeology museum** (Mon–Sat 10am–6pm), with half a dozen displays of local discoveries. Further inland, expensive restaurants and **galleries** line the middle of the island towards the Insurgentes Bridge. Beyond, past **John Huston's statue**, there's a park and a patch of river where women come to do the family washing, overlooked from the hillsides by the opulent villas of "Gringo's Gulch".

## Beaches in and around Puerto Vallarta

Puerto Vallarta's **beaches** vary in nature as you move round the bay: those to the north, out near Nuevo Vallarta and the airport, are long, flat stretches of creamy white sand pounded by surprisingly heavy surf; those to the south, a series of steep-sided coves, sheltering tiny, calm enclaves. The town beach, **Playa de los Muertos** (Beach of the Dead), or "Playa del Sol" as the local tourist office would prefer it known, is south of the river and falls somewhere between the two extremes: not very large, it features coarse, brown sand and reasonably calm surf, despite facing apparently open water. It's also the most crowded of the city's beaches – locals, Mexican holiday-makers and foreign tourists are packed in cheek-by-jowl during the high season. With the omnipresent hawkers selling everything from fresh fruit and tacos to handicrafts and fake jade masks, it can be a far from relaxing experience, but it's always entertaining. Just don't leave anything of value lying about. The **gay** section of this beach is at its southern end, opposite the *Blue Chairs Resort* (see p.545) – look out for the blue chairs.

**Buses** leave regularly from the junction of Constitución and Basilio Badillo and head **south** on Hwy-200. From Playa de los Muertos, **lanchas** (M$250 each way) depart three times daily (10am, 11am and 3pm) for the smaller stretches of sand to the south, including Playa las Ánimas, Quimixto and Yelapa (see box opposite). More frequent services (hourly for Yelapa) also depart for the same destinations from Boca de Tomátlan (see opposite). Some 9km out of Puerto Vallarta towards Mismaloya (see below) is Jump the Pacific Bungee, where for M$600 you can hurl yourself off a platform and plunge 40m down to the Pacific; head-dunking is optional (daily 10am–6pm).

To the **north** of the bay, the best beaches with white sand and shallower water tend to front the big hotels, but beyond Nuevo Vallarta (see p.553), where the landscape becomes drier and scrubbier, there are some lovely, deserted stretches of sand.

## Mismaloya

Some 10km south of Puerto Vallarta, the best-known and most accessible beach is **Mismaloya**. Here John Huston filmed *The Night of the Iguana*, building his set at the mouth of what was once a pristine, jungle-choked gorge on the southern side of the gorgeous bay; it's been endowed with a romantic mystique ever since. Plans to turn the set and crew's accommodation into tourist cabins never came to fruition, and now the huge and expensive *La Jolla de Mismaloya* hotel (❽) completely dominates the valley. Crowded with day-trippers and enthusiastic vendors selling everything from coconuts to sarongs, Mismaloya is not without a certain amount of seductive tropical appeal, though it is far from the "Paradise Found" pitched by the tourist office. When you tire of the beach, you can still wander out to the point and the ruins of the film set, where a handful of expensive restaurants sell beer and seafood cocktails. Boats are on hand to take you snorkelling at **Los Arcos**, a federal underwater park around a group of offshore islands, some formed into the eponymous arches. A superb array of brightly coloured fish – parrot, angel, pencil, croaker and scores of others – negotiate the deep rock walls and the boulder-strewn ocean floor. In addition to ninety-minute trips from the beach, boats are rented to groups for unlimited periods. If you're feeling adventurous, you could even rent snorkelling gear in Puerto Vallarta beforehand, get off the bus almost as soon as you see Los Arcos, and swim out to the islands; they're less than 300m offshore. Diving trips, including night dives, can also be organized from tour operators in Puerto Vallarta: Chico's Dive Shop, Díaz Ordaz 772 (Ⓣ322/222-1895, Ⓦwww.chicos-diveshop.com), and Pacific Scuba, Francisco Medina Ascencio 2486 (Ⓣ322/209-0364, Ⓦwww.pacificscuba.com.mx), run trips to Los Arcos and Las Islas Marietas (see p.554) and also rent snorkelling and scuba gear.

From behind the beach, an unpaved road, accessible by car, foot or horseback, leads up inland through a small village and after 2km (35min hike) arrives at

*Chino's Paradise*, a **restaurant** serving a small menu of seafood and steaks for lunch in a stunning setting next to a sparkling river – bring swimwear and towel.

### Boca de Tomatlán and beyond

If you're after peace and quiet, your best option is to continue along the highway for another 4km past Mismaloya until you reach the once-sleepy village of **Boca de Tomatlán**, which has become a departure point for the *lanchas* that shuttle passengers to and from the southern beaches. Still, it remains picturesque, with a small but beautiful beach in a protected cove dotted with fishing boats and surrounded by densely forested hills. The local speciality, cooked to perfection by the beachside *enramadas* (huts), is *pescado de bara*: a fish impaled on a stick and



#### Trips from Puerto Vallarta

For the more peaceful and scenic **beaches** further south – **Playa Las Animas**, **Quimixto** and **Yelapa** are the most common destinations – a boat trip is the only means of access. Travel agents all over town tout a variety of excursions, most of which leave from the marina. Miller Tours, at Paseo de las Garzas 100, between *Hotel Krystle* and *Hotel Crown Paradise* in Nuevo Vallarta (☎322/224-0585), and Vallarta Adventure, at the marina (☎322/221-0657, ⓦwww.vallarta-adventures.com), both have good reputations, though compare prices and what's on offer in the way of food and drink – if meals are not included, it's worth taking your own food along. A much cheaper way to travel is via **water taxi**. These depart from Playa de los Muertos for Quimixto, Las Animas and Yelapa at 11am, returning from all destinations at about 4pm. Alternatively, you can catch a **bus** to Boca de Tomatlán, from where about five water taxis a day, starting at 10.30am, sail to all three destinations.

Unfortunately, the once-remote beauty of many of the southern beaches has been tainted by the invasion of PV tour groups. That said, a number are still quite lovely: **Quimixto**'s crystal waters are home to a colourful profusion of exotic marine life. **Las Animas** is a larger bay and a base for a variety of water sports, including jet skiing, banana boats and parasailing. At **Yelapa** there's a small "typical" indigenous village not far from the white-sand beach, and a waterfall a short distance into the jungle. Marketed as an "untouched paradise", it's really more of a luxurious, if rustic, retreat with a contrived alternative vibe – there's no electricity, but long-distance phones, sushi and massages are all on offer. A short hike through the jungle leads to the Cascada Cola de Caballo, a small waterfall where you can swim. If you've got the time and money, stay for the night, as the beach empties as the sun sets, becoming the perfect spot for total rest and relaxation. *Hotel Lagunita* (☎322/209-5055, ⓦwww.hotel-lagunita.com; ❼) has beautiful open-air **cabañas**, a pool and beach-front **restaurant** serving Mexican and international food, but it's easy to **camp** on the beach, or with luck you might be able to rent a **hut** for very little. At **Majahuitas**, between Quiximito and Yelapa, accessed by private boat from Boca de Tomatlán, the eponymous resort is a guaranteed love-it or leave-it experience: posh tree houses have no electricity, and communal meals are served by candlelight. It's not for those who like a fluffy robe and food available at a whim (US ☎1-800/508-7923, ⓦwww.mexicanboutiquehotels.com/majahuitas; ❾).

If you want to go **snorkelling** or **scuba diving** at the southern beaches, tours are led by Chico's Dive Shop, Díaz Ordaz 772, on the malecón (daily 8am–10pm; ☎322/222-1895, ⓦwww.chicos-diveshop.com). You can rent gear here, too (M$400/day for a mask, snorkel and fins; M$790 for a two-tank dive to Los Arcos). It is usually too stiflingly humid to consider anything as energetic as **mountain biking**, but Bike Mex (☎322/223-1834), Guerrero 361, just north of the upper river bridge, rents out bikes (M$200/day, with maps of the surrounding area), but prefers you to take one of their organized tours into the jungly slopes behind the town and beyond (from M$500).

slow-cooked over a barbecue. The Río Horcones, with its thickly forested banks, empties into the sea beside the beach, so there's a choice of fresh or salt water for swimming. From Boca de Tomatlán, the main road heads inland and passes another idyllically set, if expensive restaurant, *Chico's Paradise*. Below the restaurant, the Río Horcones tumbles over a jumble of smoothed rocks or, in drier periods, forms clear pools perfect for whiling away an afternoon. There's no formal accommodation, but there are sites for fully equipped campers. Immediately upstream in the small village of **Las Juntas y Los Veranos**, Puerto Vallarta Canopy Tours offers, well… **canopy tours**, where you slide along cables up to 60m high attached only by a body harness (vertigo sufferers beware). The cables link ten treetops and carry you past coffee trees, vanilla vines and agave plants. Tours last from one and a half to two hours and cost M$800 (Ⓣ322/223-6060, Ⓦwww.canopytours-vallarta.com).

## Eating

Finding a place **to eat** in Puerto Vallarta is no problem; tourist restaurants offering cocktails by candlelight abound. Finding inexpensive places to eat requires more consideration, however. As usual, the **market** – on the north bank of the river by the upper bridge – has a few cheap *comedores* tucked away upstairs, overlooking the river, well away from the souvenir stalls that fill the rest of the building. **Taco and hot dog stands** line the streets, while vendors on the beach offer freshly caught fish, roasted on sticks. Gutiérrez Rizo Supermarket, at Serdán and Constitución, sells **picnic** supplies. South of the Río Cuale along Olas Altas, and particularly on Basilio Badillo between Suárez and Insurgentes, several **restaurants** bridge the gap between out-and-out tourist traps and plainer eating houses. Of the more **expensive places**, most offering some form of music or entertainment, or at least a good view while you eat, you can really take your pick. There are also several mid-range options serving a variety of international cuisine at the marina.

### South of the Río Cuale

**Archie's Wok** Rodríguez 130 Ⓣ322/222-0411. State-of-the-art Oriental cooking served in a stylish setting by the wife of John Huston's former personal chef. Delicious, healthful fare with an emphasis on seafood, bathed in Filipino, Thai and Chinese sauces. Expensive, but touted by fans as one of the best Asian restaurants in the Americas. There is live music at the weekend. Closed Sun and all of Sept.

**Café de Olla** Basilio Badillo 168, at Olas Altas. Good traditional Mexican food – enchiladas, *carne asado, chile relleno* – served in a lively, artful setting and delivered by cheerful, attentive waiters. Always popular and brimming with diners who come again and again. Closed Tues.

**Las Carmelitas** Camino a la Aguacatera Ⓣ322/223-2104. Phenomenal views from high up in the hills are the major draw of this small palapa restaurant – accessed by a precipitous path – where couples gaze at one another over candlelight and lights twinkle romantically in the bay below. The house speciality is hearty slabs of meat cooked on the open grill and served with freshly made tacos, but there are also decent seafood choices, salads and soups.

**Daiquiri Dicks** Olas Altas 314 Ⓣ322/222-0566. Informal beachside dining and a varied menu of generously proportioned dishes draw a gringo crowd. The signature dish – a whole grilled, seasoned fish served on a stick – is worth the 30min wait. Other crowd pleasers, including lobster tacos and chicken in marsala sauce, are as good as everyone says they are. Pricey, but not ridiculously so. Breakfast is also served.

**Fredy's Tucán** Basilio Badillo 245, at Vallarta Ⓣ322/223-0778. Bright, airy and with a tropical theme decor, this is one of the best venues for Mexican, Continental and American breakfasts: omelettes, pancakes, French toast, granola and yogurt and fresh-baked bread are served until 2.30pm in a new dining room, adjacent to the *Posada de Roger* hotel. European football matches are screened in the hotel bar on evenings and weekends.

**Kaiser Maximilian** Olas Altas 380-B, next to *Playa Los Arcos* hotel Ⓣ322/223-0760. Upscale, expensive restaurant with an old-European ambience serving traditional Austrian dishes like lamb with rosemary and sautéed squid, as well more traditional Mexican and international offerings. The restaurant's sidewalk patio is a nice spot for a gourmet coffee and an exceedingly rich pastry. Closed Sun.

**Karpathos Taverna** Gómez 110, at Playa de los Muertos ☎322/223-1562. Airy Mediterranean-style restaurant delivering a fairly standard Greek menu. The food's great, and the prices aren't too bad, though the service can be a bit slow.

**A Page in the Sun** Olas Altas 399, at Diéguez ☎322/222-3608. A sociable little corner café in a bustling part of town, with outside tables, good coffee, fresh fruit *licuados*, sandwiches, salads, cakes and a homely ambience, thanks to a stack of games and magazines. It also doubles as a used-book shop.

**El Palomar de los Gonzáles** Aguacate 425 ☎322/222-0795. Perfect for a romantic candlelit dinner, this elegant mansion carved into the hillside south of the centre has stunning views from its rooftop patio. The seafood dishes are the highlight of the menu, but the Mexican specialities are also well executed. A good wine list and exotic desserts ensure a long, indulgent evening. Expensive but memorable. Evenings only, from 6pm.

**El Torito** Vallarta 291, at Carranza ☎322/222-3784. Reasonably priced bar and restaurant for sports jocks, with satellite coverage of everything from Serie A to the Super Bowl. They do good ribs.

**Las Tres Huastecas** Olas Altas 444, at Rodríguez. No-frills, cantina-style restaurant a block from Playa de los Muertos that specializes in classic Mexican dishes such as chicken in *mole* sauce and a creative ensemble of fish tacos and enchiladas. One of the cheapest places in this part of town.

### North of the Río Cuale

**Le Bistro Jazz Café** Isla Río Cuale, just east of Insurgentes ☎322/222-0283. Come here for an upscale, predominantly seafood menu served in refined surroundings or alfresco, soothed by cool jazz. It's on the expensive side, but is a great place to wind down. Open from 9am for breakfast, too. Closed Sun.

**Café des Artistes** G. Sanchez 740 ☎322/222-3228. The epitome of Pacific coast gourmet dining. The quality of chef Thierry Blouet's French cuisine matches the sophisticated surroundings – the intriguing menu features shots of foie gras, sea bass wrapped in seaweed and served with a cod cookie and decadent desserts. Eat in the garden or dining room decorated with artwork. Live piano and flute music add to the refined atmosphere.

**La Dolce Vita** Malecón 674, at Dominguez ☎322/222-3852. Pizzas, pasta and other dishes, such as beef carpaccio and chicken cacciatore, at reasonable prices. Live jazz Thurs–Sun. Very popular.

**Planeta Vegetariano** Iturbide 270, at Hidalgo ☎322/222-3073. All-you-can-eat vegetarian buffet with a choice of main courses, salads, soup, dessert and a soft drink. The walls are painted with fantastic frescoes, and the food is reasonably priced and deliciously spiced.

**Trio** Guerrero 264 ☎322/222-2196. An elegant townhouse filled with original art and hanging plants provides the setting for Mediterranean-fusion cuisine prepared by a German and Swedish chef with Michelin credentials. In addition to dishes like rabbit with garlic sauce and braised veal with almond sauce, there are home-made pastas, Lebanese salads, sautéed calamari and an imaginatively prepared selection of seafood dishes. It's a fabulous treat, if you can afford it.

## Drinking, nightlife and entertainment

The **malecón** is the centre of Puerto Vallarta's night-time activity, lined with places that specialize in creating a high-energy party-time atmosphere – pop, techno and 1980s rock compete for the airwaves with salsa, jazz and the more gentle strumming of marauding mariachis. By midnight, revellers spill across the sidewalks, as bars, clubs and late-night coffee shops pack in young Mexican, American and European tourists. The greatest concentration of **bars** and **clubs** is along the stretch of the malecón that runs about 400m north of the Plaza Aquiles Serdán. Most of these establishments are at ground level, making it easy to wander along and take your pick of the **happy hours** and compare **cover charges**, which are sometimes nonexistent and at others around M$55–170, depending on the night and season, and almost always subject to a discount if you pick up one of the many coupons distributed liberally by the touts and tourist office. South of the river also has its share of clubs, which are generally less pretentious and more varied in character. This is also where you'll find most of the **gay nightlife**. In general, Sunday tends to be quiet – some places close

– except on the zócalo where, from around 6pm, huge crowds gather around the dozens of taco and cake stands and listen to the brass band.

For more low-key entertainment, there are two **cinemas** in town: Cine Bahía is south of the river at Insurgentes 189; and Cine Luz Maria is north of the river at México 227. Both show predominantly Hollywood films in English with Spanish subtitles. Look for listings in *Vallarta Today* and other free handouts.

### South of the Río Cuale

**Club Roxy** Vallarta 217, at Madero. A popular bar/club with bands playing blues, reggae and rock in an uplifting, if at times raucous, atmosphere that attracts locals and tourists alike.

**The Jazz House** Rodríguez at Olas Altas. First-class jazz in a tastefully decorated, sit-down venue that also serves good, if slightly pricey, food.

**Paco Paco** Vallarta 278. An unmissable experience, this is the largest and most popular gay club in town. Also drawing a straight contingent, it's a multifaceted venue with DJs playing the latest in techno, hip-hop and pop on the ground floor; Mexican music, a cantina and pool table on the first floor (open from 1pm); a rooftop bar on the second; and strippers at "The Ranch", a smaller space connected to the main club by a passageway. There are lively drag shows at 1am & 3am Thurs–Sun.

### North of the Río Cuale

**Apaches** Olas Altas 439. Popular and welcoming gay and lesbian joint where groups gather for martinis and cocktails at happy hour (5–7pm), filling up the cosy, indoor bar area and sidewalk tables. Next door, the closet-sized *Apache* bistro serves decent appetizers, steaks and seafood until midnight.

**Los Balcones** Juárez 182, at Libertad. Puerto Vallarta's oldest gay club, on three floors with a dancefloor, balconies overlooking the street and, during high season, strippers.

**La Bodeguita del Medio** Malecón 858. With graffiti blazoned across the walls, this distinctive restaurant named after the famous Hemingway haunt in Havana is as popular for its *mojitos* (ask for Havana Club 7-year-old rum), *cuba libres* and live salsa bands as it is for its Cuban and Mexican food.

**Carlos O'Brian's** Malecón 786. A gringo magnet, this is the most popular of the bar/restaurant chains serving standard issue American- and Mexican-style bar food day and night. There's a yards-long menu of alcoholic and non-alcoholic cocktails, both of which see an increasing trade as the night wears on, precipitating some intoxicated forays onto the dancefloor. Great people watching, at the very least.

**Christine's** at *Hotel NH Krystal Puerto Vallarta*, Av de las Garzas. With a state-of-the-art sound system and flashy light effects, this glitzy, expensive discotheque takes itself rather seriously. Still, if you are staying in the hotel zone north of the town centre, it's a convenient place to dance to an eclectic range of quality music.

**Hilo** Malecón 588. Popular with young, well-heeled locals, this thumping techno club with high ceilings and huge, out-of-place statues of Mexican peasants reverberates with gun-fire beats and attitude.

**Memories** Juárez 207. Sultry bar popular with dating couples who are delighted to be able to hold a conversation (a novelty in a PV bar) in between sips of coffee and speciality cocktails.

**The Zoo** Malecón 630. Leopard- and zebra-skin chairs and plastic gorillas swinging from the rafters lend a kitsch element to this club, where DJs play the latest dance tunes for a hip young clientele.

## Listings

**Airlines** Aerocalifornia ☎322/209-0643; Aeroméxico ☎322/224-2777; Air Canada ☎01-800/719-2827; Alaska ☎322/221-1350; American ☎322/221-1799; Continental ☎322/221-1025; Mexicana ☎322/224-8900; Ted ☎800/225-5833.

**American Express** Morelos 660, at Abasolo ☎322/223-2955; holds mail and changes cheques (Mon–Fri 9am–6pm, Sat 9am–1pm).

**Banks and exchange** Banamex, on the zócalo, will change cheques (Mon–Fri 9am–4pm, Sat 10am–2pm) and also has an ATM. There are branches of Banorte downtown, at Díaz Ordaz 690, and in the northern hotel zone, at Francisco Medina Ascensio 500. Other ATMs are plentiful. You can change money at the numerous casas de cambio that line the streets surrounding the zócalo: rates vary, so shop around.

**Buses** Estrella Blanca, at the station, with an office at Basilio Badillo 11, at Insurgentes (☎322/290-1014; closed Sun), has first-class services to a long list of destinations including Acapulco (3 daily; 18hr), Guadalajara (every 30min; 5hr 30min), Lázaro Cárdenas (2 daily; 12hr), Mazatlán (2 daily; 8hr) and Mexico City (3 daily; 13–14hr). Primera Plus (☎322/290-0715) runs first-class services to Barra de Navidad (4 daily; 3hr 30min), Guadalajara

(13 daily) and Manzanillo (1 daily; 5hr). They share their offices at Lázaro Cárdenas 268–9 with ETN (☎322/290-0997), who operates super-deluxe services to Guadalajara and Mexico City (1 daily; 13hr). Pacifico, at the station and with an office at Insurgentes 160, at Carranza (☎322/290-1008), also offers first-class services to a number of destinations. For second-class buses to Manzanillo (8 daily) and Barra de Navidad (6 daily), try Servicios Coordinados at Cárdenas 268 (☎322/221-0095).
**Car rental** Alamo, Díaz Ordaz 660-A ☎322/221-3030; Avis, at the airport ☎322/221-1112; and Hertz, Francisco Medina Ascencio 1602 ☎322/222-0024.
**Consulates** Canada, Obelisco Condominio, Francisco Medina Ascencio 1951 ☎322/293-0098 (Mon–Fri 9am–3pm); US, Edificio Vallarta Plaza, Zaragoza 160 ☎322/222-0069 (Mon–Fri 10am–2pm, closed every third Wed).
**Emergencies** English-speaking medics at CMQ Clinic, Basilio Badillo 365, between Insurgentes and Aguacate ☎322/223-1919; and Cruz Roja, Río Balsas y Plata ☎322/222-1533.
**Flights** Puerto Vallarta and Manzanillo (if you are heading to the Costa Alegre) are well served by flights to other Mexican cities, the US and Canada. Prices vary dramatically with season and availability. It usually works out much cheaper to buy any connecting flight tickets from Mexico City at the same time as you purchase international tickets. Contact the airlines direct (see opposite) and always check online for special promotional fares. Travel agents (see below) or any of the numerous agencies north of the river can also provide up-to-date information and advice.
**Internet access** The main Internet café is PV Net (M$10/hr) north of town, across from the *Sheraton* at Francisco Medina 1692.
**Laundry** There are facilities scattered throughout town, all charging around M$450 per load – try Lavandería Blanquita, Madero 407, east of Aguacate (Mon–Sat 8am–8pm). There's also a coin-operated laundry at hotel *Estancia San Carlos*, Constitución 210, at Cárdenas.
**Pharmacy** CMQ, Basilio Badillo 367 ☎322/222-2941, next to CMQ Clinic, is open 24hr; or try Lux, Insurgentes 169 ☎322/222-1909.
**Post office** The main post office is at Mina 188 between Juárez and Morelos (Mon–Fri 9am–5pm, Sat 9am–1pm).
**Telephone and fax services** There are various booths providing long-distance phone and fax services, such as the one on Cárdenas near Pino Suárez. Internet cafés often provide cheaper long-distance services.
**Travel agents** SAET Travel Service, in the Centro Comercial, corner of Morelos and Rodríguez ☎322/222-1886 (Mon–Fri 9am–7pm, Sat 9am–2pm).



## Nuevo Vallarta, Bucerías and Punta de Mita

North of Puerto Vallarta, over the state line in Nayarit, the Bahía de Banderas arcs out to **Punta de Mita**, some 30km away. A summer preserve for Guadalajarans and a winter retreat for motorhome vacationers from the north, these gorgeous beaches offer facilities in just a few spots – **Nuevo Vallarta**, **Bucerías** and **Punta de Mita** – leaving miles of secluded sand for camping. To get out this direction from Puerto Vallarta, your best bet is to catch any northbound local bus to the *Sheraton* hotel (a 20min walk from the zócalo), then flag down an Autotransportes Medina "Punta de Mita" bus.

**NUEVO VALLARTA**, 12km north of the airport, is a mega-resort, an ever-expanding cluster of astronomically expensive hotels. Although the beaches here are great, they are backed by ugly buildings and because the hotels tend to be all-inclusive, there's nothing much for the day-tripper to do, save **pay a visit to the dolphins** at Dolphin Adventure (☎322/297-1212 ext 25, Ⓦwww.dolphin-adventure.com), an educational centre located at Paseo de la Palmas 39. As well as swimming with dolphins (1hr 30min; M$1500), you can also spend a day with a dolphin trainer (M$2800).

You're better off pushing on to another great beach at laid-back **BUCERÍAS**, the last of the bay resorts on Hwy-200, which has wonderful views across the water to Puerto Vallarta from its seafront **restaurants**. *Adriano's* (☎329/298-0088), with bright-orange walls and an extensive range of fresh fish, is superb, if pricey. For a tea-time treat, visit the locally renowned *Pie in the Sky* **bakery** (☎322/222-8411), opposite the *De Camarón* hotel at Héroe de Nacozari 202, for heavenly chocolate brownies, Italian ice cream, bagels and exotic cheesecakes. If you want to stay, there are several **apartment**-type places in the centre of town, including *Motel Marlyn* (ⓣ329/298-0450; ④) and the *Bucerías Trailer Park* (ⓣ329/298-0265; ④).

Keeping to the coast, you leave the main highway, following the signposts for Punta de Mita, passing the beach-free fishing village of **Cruz de Huanacaxtle**, followed by **Manzanillo** and **Piedra Blanca** beaches. The Punta de Mita road continues through increasingly rocky, arid terrain, with small roads dipping down to secluded beaches. The *enramada* (a **restaurant** under palapas) at **Destiladeras** is the only one in the area, which allows them to charge rather inflated prices for the usual fare. If you've brought a picnic, several places on the beach rent out palapas, tables and chairs for the day for around M$60; boogie boards are also available for around M$20 an hour. **Camping** on the beach is great, but you need to bring everything.

**PUNTA DE MITA** is more developed than Bucerías, with bars, cafés and seafood restaurants strung along the beach. Follow the road parallel to the beach and you'll find the Sociedad Cooperativa de Servicios Turísticos (ⓣ329/291-6298), which rents out **snorkelling** and **diving gear** and organizes two-hour *panga* trips to a cluster of volcanic islands known as **Las Islas Marietas**, a wildlife sanctuary. The boats hold up to eight people and cost around M$800 – this is probably the cheapest way to get close to the **humpback whales** present in the bay from around December to April, when they come to mate and give birth before returning to the polar waters of the north. Alternatively, you can book an organized whale-watching tour from Puerto Vallarta with an operator such as Open Air Expeditions, Guerrero 339 (ⓣ322/222-3310, ⓦwww.vallartawhales.com). You can **camp** on the beach or **stay** at the pretty *Hotel Punta Mita* (ⓣ329/291-6269; ⑥) or the ultra-luxurious *Four Seasons Punta Mita* (ⓣ329/291-6000; ⑨).

# The Costa Alegre and Bahía de Navidad

The stretch of coast known as the **Costa Alegre** starts about 100km south of Puerto Vallarta. If you are heading down the coast and feel like breaking your journey, the **Bahía de Chamela** lies 130km south of Puerto Vallarta and comprises a huge, sweeping arc of superb beaches and nine islands, which are popular dive spots. Although large luxury hotels are cropping up with alarming frequency, you can still find long sections of untouched beach where you can pitch a tent. To reach **Playa Perula**, at the northern end of the bay, it's a one-kilometre walk or drive down a dusty track from Hwy-200. There's a small village and you can stay at the average, fourteen-room *Hotel Punta Perula* (ⓣ315/333-9782; ③), one block north of the main road, or, for slightly more, comfortable, clean rooms with shared kitchen and wheelchair access are available at *Hotel Vagabunda* (ⓣ315/333-9446; ⑤), two blocks from the beach at Independencia 100.

A little further south on Hwy-200 there's another unpaved road that leads to **Playa Chamela**. Here, the *Paraíso Costa Alegre* (ⓣ315/333-9778; ⑥) has attractive oceanfront cabañas surrounded by palm trees as well as full hook-ups for RVs (③). The basic *Bungalows Meyer Chamela* (ⓣ315/285-5252; ③) has palatable rooms with fan, kitchen and an on-site pool. Otherwise, it's easy to camp on the beach. At **Playa Careyes**, an upmarket beach resort around 20km further south, expensive villas and luxurious hotels nestle in the hills, including *El Careyes*, Km 53.5 Hwy-200 (ⓣ800/508-7923; ⑨), a chic resort with a spa in idyllic surroundings. Luxury, taste and style reach a zenith at *Las Alamandas*, Km 83.5 Hwy-200 (☎800/508-7923, Ⓦwww.lasalamandas.com; ⑨), where beautifully designed villas and suites overlook a breathtaking one-kilometre stretch of private beach. Also at Careyes, endangered Olive Ridley turtles lay their eggs; biologists have recruited local activists and established a conservation programme – the turtles' eggs are collected before they fall victim to predators and then the babies are released after the eggs hatch in a laboratory.

**Tenacatita**, a further 40km south along the highway, is another gorgeous beach, with the added attractions of a mangrove lagoon that teems with birdlife and still, clear waters perfect for snorkelling. Lobster- and octopus-fishing is very popular here. The town's name means "red rocks" in Nahuatl; the indigenous people used the russet rocks you'll see to make pottery, ornaments and even to build homes. The **restaurant** on the beach organizes bird-watching boat trips and you can **stay** at the *Hotel Paraíso Tenacatita* (☎314/353-9623; ④), which has a restaurant and simple rooms built round a courtyard. It's also possible to visit Tenacatita from Barra de Navidad.

Most people choose to press on to the twin towns of **Barra de Navidad** and **San Patricio-Melaque**, 30km further south and among the most enticing destinations on this entire stretch of coastline. They are not undeveloped or totally isolated – indeed, families from Guadalajara come here by the hundreds, especially at weekends – but neither are they at all heavily commercialized: just small, simple and very Mexican resorts. The entire bay, the **Bahía de Navidad**, is edged by fine sands and, if you're prepared to walk (30min along the beach), you can easily leave the crowds behind. Or, regular buses and *colectivos* connect the two communities.

## Barra de Navidad

Sitting towards the southern end of the Bahía de Navidad, where the beach runs out and curves back round to form a lagoon behind the town, **BARRA DE NAVIDAD** is easily the more appealing of the communities along the bay. San Patricio-Melaque, around 4km north and at the other end of the same beach, is scruffier, more commercial and has a more transitory feel, but if you can't find a room in Barra, it makes a good second choice, with a considerably wider range of hotels.

Activities in Barra revolve around the shelved, honey-coloured sands; you can hire surfboards, boogie boards and snorkelling gear from the Nauti Mar dive shop on the beach. Sea to Sierra, 21 de Noviembre (☎315/355-8582), runs a variety of land and water tours, including a one-hour boat trip that winds through the mangroves of the Laguna de Navidad (M$1500), horse-riding trips (M$250/hr), one-tank dives (M$850) and five- to eight-hour mountain-bike tours (M$750 for 2–4 people).

The opening of the *Wyndham Grand Bay Resort* complex across the channel from Barra de Navidad has changed things surprisingly little, not even spoiling the view from the beach or the sedate charm of the town. If you have time, it's worth taking a **boat** over to check it out – you can catch one outside the restaurant *El Manglito* near the jetty; they run across the channel every half-hour from 6am to 6pm (M$8) and, less frequently, to the beaches on the other side. **Colimilla** (M$15 return), across the Laguna de Navidad, is the most popular destination, chiefly for its seafood restaurants such as *Fortino's* (daily 9am–10pm; bring insect repellent if dining after dark), and as a base for the two- or three-kilometre walk over to the rough Pacific beach of Playa de Cocos. The *cooperativo* at the jetty also offers fishing trips, lagoon tours and day trips to **Tenacatita**.

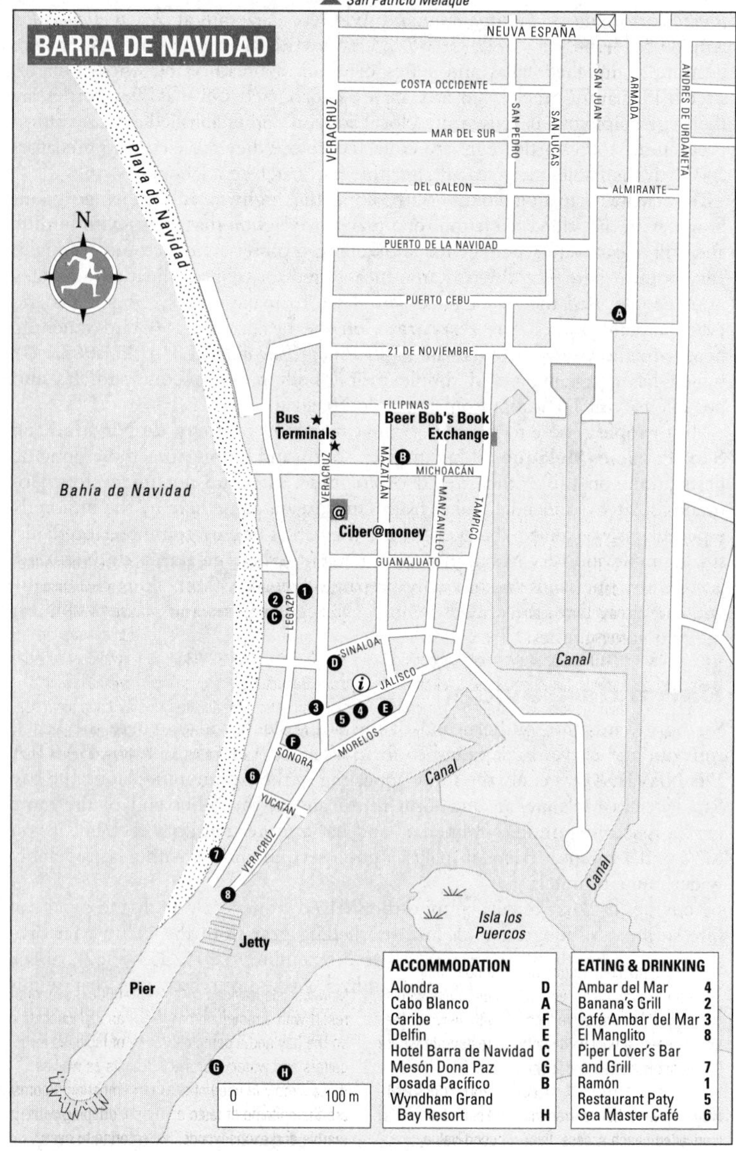




## Arrival and information

**Buses** arrive at the town's two terminals, which lie almost opposite each other on Veracruz, Barra's main drag. The services you are likely to need – post office, phones and hotels – are all close by; in any case, it only takes twenty minutes to walk around the whole town. The one shortcoming is that there is **no bank** or casa de cambio (the nearest bank is in San Patricio-Melaque; see p.558), although you can **exchange** dollars and traveller's cheques at the Ciber@ money **Internet** café at Veracruz 212 (Mon–Fri 9am–2pm & 4–7.30pm, Sat 9am–6.30pm). The **post office** is a few blocks north at Nueva España 37 (Mon–Fri 8am–3pm, Sat 9am–12.30pm).

The **tourist office**, Jalisco 67 (Mon–Fri 9am–5pm, Sat & Sun during high season; ⓣ315/355-5100), serves both Barra de Navidad and San Patricio-Melaque. The staff can advise on anything happening locally – usually not much – though you can probably obtain more useful information from the owner of Beer Bob's Book Exchange at Tampico 8 (Mon–Fri noon–3pm), two rooms absolutely packed with English-language paperbacks: bring one and take one, no charge.

## Accommodation

Although Barra has enough hotels to suit all tastes and budgets, reservations are recommended for the high season (roughly Dec–April). Free **camping** is also a possibility along the beach to the north of town. Should you want to camp, it's easiest to follow the beach, rather than the road, up to a point where you feel comfortable, as beach access is limited.

**Alondra** Sinaloa 16 ⓣ315/355-8372, ⓦwww.alondrahotel.com. The garishly decorated rooms in this modern hotel all have TV, a/c, private bath and fan. Suites don't offer any more luxury, but do have a kitchen and ocean views – the main draw here. Overpriced, but a reliable stand-by. 7–8

**Cabo Blanco** Armada, at the marina ⓣ315/355-6495 or 01-800/710-5690, ⓦwww.hotelcaboblanco.com. Best for families, this economical hotel has more facilities than the price would suggest: palapa bar/restaurant, tennis courts, games room, swimming pool, "Kid's Club" – the list goes on. Rooms come in various sizes and all have a/c, safe, fan and cable TV. Meal plans also run the gamut, from room-only to bed and breakfast to all inclusive. 6

**Caribe** Sonora 15 ⓣ315/335-5952. The best of the budget options, with clean, if rather lacklustre, rooms and a pleasant rooftop terrace with rocking chairs. 2

**Delfin** Morelos 23 ⓣ315/355-5068, ⓦwww.hoteldelfinmx.com. Bright, arcaded hotel 5min from the beach. Clean, very spacious rooms with fan lead off an attractive balcony with views of the bay. There is a pool with sundeck, restaurant where breakfast is served and a small gym. 5

**Hotel Barra de Navidad** Legazpi 250 ⓣ338/244-4043, ⓦwww.hotelbarradenavidad.com. For unrivalled beach access, this is a good-value choice. Rooms are spartan but comfortable, and with a/c; the best have wonderful sea views. There's also a pool on site. 6

**Hotel Sand's** Morelos 24 ⓣ315/355-5018. Decent rooms and a large garden, overlooking the lagoon, where you'll find a bar and a swimming pool – which non-residents can use for M$40. 5

**Mesón Doña Paz** Rinconada del Capitán ⓣ01-800/012-9887, ⓦwww.mesondonapaz.com. Beautiful, discreet colonial-style hotel with a stunning setting overlooking the bay. Each room has views of the lagoon and is richly decorated and thoughtfully appointed. An atmosphere of grace and elegance pervades the public areas, which are laden with art and antiques. The large pool has a wet bar and massages; golf and water sports can all be arranged by the superlative staff. 9

**Posada Pacífico** Mazatlán 136 ⓣ315/355-5359. A simple, friendly place with clean, airy rooms, some with balconies, around a tree-shaded courtyard. A good option in this price bracket. 4

**Wyndham Grand Bay Resort** Circuitos de los Marinos, Isla Navidad ⓣ315/331-0500. Luxurious resort with a mountain backdrop, an idyllic location on the bay and a complete range of facilities for golfers and water-sports enthusiasts as well as those simply in need of serious pampering. Rooms are the epitome of taste and style, dripping with marble and exotic woods and catering to every whim with all the expected luxuries. 9

## Eating and drinking

Of the many good **restaurants** in Barra, most are on Legazpi, or else at the junction of Veracruz and Jalisco. Here you'll find the bright yellow *Restaurant Paty* (ⓣ315/355-5907), the best of a number of similar budget places. They serve excellent *ceviche*, fresh fish, *carne asado* and barbecue chicken, as well as Mexican staples. On the beachfront at Legazpi 158, *Café Ambar del Mar*

(Ⓣ315/355-8169) is renowned for its crepes, salads and Italian and French dishes, including escargots. Slightly pricier than most, *Banana's Grill*, Legazpi 250, offers very good breakfasts (8am–12pm) and dinner (6–10pm) – chicken *mole poblano* is their signature dish. *Ramón*, opposite *Hotel Barra de Navidad* at Legazpi 260 (Ⓣ315/355-6435), is open all day and has an extensive range of Mexican and international food, including some decent fish and chips and *chiles rellenos*. **Seafood restaurants** crowd Legazpi, Morelos and the southern end of Veracruz down towards the point: *El Manglito* is one of the best, and has tables overlooking the lagoon. *Sea Master Café* (Ⓣ315/355-5845) has a relaxed vibe and takes a more inventive approach to its dishes than most of its peers: the shrimp drenched in garlic are succulent. It's also a great spot to unwind with one of their strong cocktails.

**Nightlife** is fairly limited, but you can play pool, drink, munch on snacks and listen to live rock, jazz and blues at *Piper Lover's Bar and Grill* by the beach on Legazpi. There are free-flowing cocktails and a DJ spinning nightly at *Sunset Bar*, Jalisco 140, and there's also dancing at *El Galeón* disco, next to *Hotel Sand's*.

## San Patricio-Melaque

**SAN PATRICIO-MELAQUE** seems much more of a typical Mexican town than Barra de Navidad, with a central plaza, church, largish market and substantial **bus station**, at the junction of Carranza and Gómez Farías. Opposite, in the Pasaje Comercial, you'll find the town's **casa de cambio** (which changes travellers' cheques), with a *larga distancia* **phone** and fax (Mon–Sat 9am–6pm); next door is an **Internet** café (daily 9am–2pm & 4–10pm; M$20/hr). Half a block further down Gómez Farías there's a Banamex **bank** (Mon–Fri 9am–4pm, Sat 10am–2pm) with a 24-hour ATM; you can also **exchange** travellers' cheques here; Casa de Cambio Melaque is half a block further east. The **post office** is on Orozco, around the corner from *Hotel San Patricio*. There's no **tourist office**: the office in Barra de Navidad serves both towns (see p.557).

Very cheap **camping** is an option on the patch of land at the northern end of the beach beyond the restaurants. There's a full-facility campsite right by the beach, *Playa Trailer Park*, Gómez Farías 250, at López Mateos (Ⓣ315/355-5065; ④), which charges the same for RVs and tents. If you want a roof over your head, walk along Gómez Farías, parallel to the beach, to the good-value *Hotel Los Caracoles* at no. 26 (Ⓣ315/355-7308; ③–④), a new hotel with airy, clean rooms. Further west, *Posada Pablo de Tarso*, Gómez Farías 408 (Ⓣ315/355-5117; ⑤), provides pleasant **rooms** with TV, fan and phone around a verdant courtyard, and a good pool. The cheaper, but rather down-at-the-heel *Hotel San Patricio*, opposite *Pablo de Tarso* at Gómez Farías 84 (Ⓣ315/355-5244; ④), has outside kitchens and a communal dining area; some apartments (sleeping up to eight) have kitchenettes. There's safe parking, too. At Esmeralda and Zafiro, *El Palmar Beach Resort* (Ⓣ315/355-6263, Ⓦwww.vacationinmexico.com; ⑦), is one of the more upmarket options, with spacious, brightly painted, a/c rooms with TV, kitchenette, large bathroom and sitting area. There is a nice pool, tennis courts and tropical landscaped gardens on site.

**Eating** options are fairly limited. There are plenty of identical joints along the beachfront, cheaper *comedores* on the streets beachside of the central plaza and *licuado* stalls around the market on Hidalgo and Corona. Note that during the quieter summer months many restaurants will be closed. *La Terraza*, upstairs in the courtyard of *Hotel Monterrey*, on Gómez Farías, serves generous breakfasts of freshly baked bread, granola, fruit and yogurt, as well as traditional Mexican fare in the evening. About five blocks south of the centre at Obregón 52, inventive, fusion gastronomy is served in the romantic, leafy garden at *Koala's* (from 6pm).

Across the road at Obregón 8, the Canadian-run *Ava* has good ribs and hamburgers. *Restaurant Maya*, Obregón 1 (☎315/355-6764), is arguably the best option in San Patricio for quality dining. Fresh fish dishes are prepared with an Asian or Mediterranean twist and the bountiful salads – try the roasted beet, goat cheese and candied walnut – are wholesome and inventive. Brunch is also a monumental affair.

# Manzanillo and around

Two roads head **inland to Guadalajara** from this part of the coast. The direct-looking route from Barra de Navidad is indeed reasonably fast (although any route has to tangle with the Sierra Madre), but it's also very dull, with just one town of any size: the dusty and untempting community of Autlán. The journey along the coast to Manzanillo and inland via **Colima** is considerably more interesting, not only for the towns themselves but also for the spectacular snowcapped volcanoes that come beyond.

Just ninety minutes south from the Bahía de Navidad, **MANZANILLO** is clearly a working port: tourism – although highly developed – very definitely takes second place to trade. Downtown, criss-crossed by railway tracks, rumbles with heavy traffic and is surrounded by a bewildering array of inner harbours and shallow lagoons that seem to cut the town off from the land. You

can easily imagine that a couple of hundred years ago plague and pestilence made sailors fear to land here, and it's not surprising to read in an 1884 guide to Mexico that "the climate of Manzanillo is unhealthy for Europeans, and the tourist is advised not to linger long in the vicinity". While it may still exhibit some of the same coarse characteristics, the town is healthy enough and there's even a certain shabby romance to staying in the centre. This said, few tourists do stay – most head to the hotels and club resorts of the Península de Santiago around the bay to the east – even though Manzanillo is a lot more interesting than the sanitized resort area, and cheaper, too. Buses out to the beach are frequent and efficient, but if you're kicking your heels in the centre, you could climb one of the **hills** that rise in the heart of the town in order to get a better view of the bay.



## Arrival and information

The Playa de Oro international **airport** is 30km north of Manzanillo's hotel zone. The **bus station**, the Terminal Autobuses Manzanillo, or TAMA, is about 5km from the centre, roughly halfway between Manzanillo and the beaches on the eastern side of the bay. Buses to the zócalo (marked "Jardín") and the beaches (marked "Santiago") leave from the station entrance.

Manzanillo's commercial core centres on its zócalo, the **Jardín Alvaro Obregón**, right on the harbour opposite the main outer dock and recently embellished with rose gardens and exuberant topiary. The 3.5km boardwalk dotted with palms is another recent addition, best ambled at sunset. All tourist services are a very short walk away. Banamex and Bancomer **banks** (both with ATMs) are next to each other on México, at Bocanegra; there's a *larga distancia* office with fax service (daily 9am–10pm) at Morelos 144; and the **post office** is at Galindo 30 (Mon–Fri 9am–3pm). One of the best **Internet** cafés (M$10 /hr) is on the second floor of the Centro Comercial del Puerto, on México between Quintero and Galindo. The helpful **regional tourist office** is in the Palacio Municipal on the zócalo (Mon–Fri 9am–8pm, Sat 9am–1pm), while another office with more limited hours is at the beach several kilometres out of town, at Miguel de la Madrid 1033 (Mon–Fri 9am–3pm & 5–7pm).

## Accommodation

Finding some **place to stay** is no problem in Manzanillo. Most of the budget options are close to the zócalo. **Prices** at all but the cheapest hotels drop by about 25 percent outside the high season (roughly Dec–May) and Semana Santa. In town, *Hotel Colonial*, Bocanegra 100 (☎314/332-1080; ❹), aches with faded colonial grandeur: an Andalucian mosaic-tiled courtyard with a fountain and heavy wooden furnishings add to its allure. The clean, spacious rooms, with a/c and cable TV, are perfectly comfortable. *Hotel Flamingos*, Madero 72 (☎314/332-1037; ❺), has good-sized, clean rooms (ask for an exterior room – they are lighter and not as odiferous), though the service can be a little gruff. Far better value than some of its pricier neighbors, the *Emperador*, Dávalos 69 (☎314/332-2374; ❷), has decent, small rooms with hot showers and fans, and a cheap *comedor*, too. If you want to be by the sea, but still within walking distance of the zócalo, try *Hotel San Pedrito*, Azueta 3 (☎314/332-0535; ❹), a rambling place set around a pool and tennis court, backing onto **Playa San Pedrito**, about 1km east of the centre (a 20min walk from the zócalo along the waterfront); spacious, kitchen-equipped apartments sleeping six (❼) are also available. This beach is probably your best bet for **camping**: Manzanillo has no trailer park and all the other beaches are pretty built-up.

## Eating and drinking

**Places to eat** are concentrated around the zócalo. The bustling *Chantilly*, on Juárez at Madero (☎314/332-0194; closed Sat), makes a substantial comida corrida, good *antojitos* and the best ice cream in town, while *Roca del Mar* (☎314/332-0302), diagonally opposite, serves a mind-boggling range of Mexican and international meals, top-value comidas corridas and good espresso and cappuccino. Another excellent, relaxing place for a coffee – or a frozen cappuccino – is on the shady patio of *Café Costeño*, just off the zócalo at México 69. The oversized American breakfasts are extremely popular with the gringo contingent. Heading east along Morelos, parallel to the waterfront, you come to *La Perlita*, which dishes up *antojitos* and seafood at shaded tables close to the water. At Playa Audiencia, *Vaquero Campestre* (☎314/334-1488; closed Sun & Mon), serves a hearty menu of grilled meats in a suitably cowboy-inspired palapa setting. The fruity sangria is the perfect accompaniment. The stately restaurant at the *Hotel Colonial* also grills a mean steak. If you head down México, Manzanillo's main commercial and shopping street, you'll find a whole series of other possibilities, from takeout *taquerías* to the tiny vegetarian *Yacate-cuhtli*, at no. 249 (☎314/332-5670), with its healthful foods, energy drinks, fruit salads and soya burgers. There are several very cheap places – grimy and raucous on the whole – in the market area three blocks down México and at the bottom end of Juárez by the railway tracks.

## The coast around Manzanillo

While locals might go **swimming** from the tiny harbour beach of San Pedrito and in the Laguna de Cuyutlán behind the town, both are polluted. You're far better off heading for the beaches around the bay, where the tourist hotels congregate. The nearest of these, at **LAS BRISAS**, is nearer to town than you would think – just across the entrance to the inner harbour – though it seems further away due to convoluted routes around the lagoon. Frequent **buses** from the centre (marked "Las Brisas") run all the way along the single seafront drive; it's a rather strange area, often eerily quiet and feeling more like suburbia than a resort. The six-kilometre beach shelves steeply to the ocean, causing the tide to crash upon the shore; consequently, the beach is not as conducive to swimming as those round the bay in the other direction. As the original seaside strip, Las Brisas offers a number of dated, monolithic hotels which tend to be cheaper than those in Manzanillo, except when the area is flooded by holiday-makers from Guadalajara. If you want to **stay** by the beach, take the bus out here and have a look around. *La Posada*, Lázaro Cárdenas 201, right at the end of the seafront drive towards Manzanillo (☎314/333-1899, Ⓦwww.hotel-la-posada.info; ⑥), is by far the best choice – a delightful 23-room hotel run by a very hospitable young couple a few metres from the beach. The renovated rooms (some with a/c and kitchenette) exude a retro 1950s vibe. There are excellent made-to-order breakfasts, Internet access, an honour bar and a pool included in the price. Cheaper options include *Las Brisas*, Lázaro Cárdenas 1243 (☎314/333-2716; ④), and the marginally better-equipped *Star*, Lázaro Cárdenas 1313 (☎314/333-2560; ⑤), which is on the beach side of the street and has a pool.

Better and more sheltered swimming can be found along the coast further round, where the bay is divided by the rocky Peninsula de Santiago. "Miramar" **buses** run all the way to the far side of the bay, past the settlements of **Salahua** and **SANTIAGO** and a string of beaches. The best of these are around the far edge of the peninsula (get off the bus at Santiago). Here you'll find the **hotel**

## Moving on from Manzanillo

For moving on, the **bus** station, TAMA, is northeast of town. Both Autotransportes del Sur de Jalisco and Sociedad Cooperativa de Transportes run second-class services to Colima (8 an hour between them; 1hr 30min), the former also serving Tecomán (every 20min; 1hr), Guadalajara (every 30min; 5–6hr) and **Lázaro Cárdenas** (5 daily; 7hr). La Linea runs first- and executive-class buses to **Colima** (every hour; 1hr 30min) and Guadalajara (every hour; 6hr). Primera Plus serves **Barra de Navidad** (11 daily; 1hr 30min) and Servicio Plus runs twelve buses daily to **Puerto Vallarta** (7hr). Estrella Blanca runs first-class to **Acapulco** (3 daily; 12hr), Mexico City (2 daily; 12hr) and Tijuana (2 daily; 38hr). ETN (Ⓣ315/344-1050) runs the most comfortable deluxe service from its own terminal at Carretera 200 to Barra de Navidad (3 daily; 1hr 30min), **Colima** (8 daily; 2hr) and Guadalajara (6 daily; 5hr).

*Maria Cristina*, 28 de Agosto 36 (Ⓣ314/333-0966; ④), two blocks inland from the zócalo, with a pool, a pleasant garden and some rooms that can take four and eight people. There are several restaurants here, too, both in the village and down on the beach: *Juanito's* **restaurant**, on the highway (Ⓣ314/333-1797), is a longstanding favourite with gringos and locals alike, serving mainly hamburgers and various Mexican snacks. It also has **Internet** access and *larga distancia* **phone and fax** facilities.

If you're prepared to walk a little way, you can reach the calm and tranquil waters of the beautiful cove of **La Audiencia**, on the west side of the peninsula, beneath the *Gran Costa Resort*. From here, if you're feeling reasonably energetic and looking smart enough to get past the guards, you can climb over the hill to the pseudo-private beach of *Hotel Las Hadas* (Ⓣ314/331-0101 or 01-800/713-3233, Ⓦwww.brisas.com.mx; ⑨), the amazingly flashy wedding-cake-style hotel complex where Dudley Moore and Bo Derek frolicked in the film *10*. It's worth seeing even if you can't afford a drink at any of the bars. Non-guests pay around M$250 *consumo mínimo* to use the beach and facilities. There's more glitz at the all-inclusive *Club Maeva* (Ⓣ314/331-0800 or 01-800/523-8450, Ⓦwww.clubmaeva.com.mx; ⑨), further round the bay on **Playa Miramar**, but on the whole the hotels in the vicinity are thoroughly average, and **nightlife**, such as it is, is confined to a few discos strung out along the coast road.

# South from Manzanillo

If all you need is a heaving ocean and a strip of beach backed by a few *enramadas*, then you're better off skipping Manzanillo altogether in favour of a series of tiny resorts that adorn the shoreline 50–80km beyond. Cuyutlán, Paraíso and Boca de Pascuales are easily accessible by bus and boast great beaches, but none is in any way elaborate, equipped with few facilities. To get to Cuyutlán and Paraíso from Manzanillo, you must first catch a bus (every 15min) 50km to the inland market town of **ARMERÍA**, which has a bank, a post office and a long-distance bus stop on the main street, and, should you need to stay, a clean, good-value **hotel**, *La Herradura* (Ⓣ313/328-8027; ④), at the entrance to town coming from Manzanillo. From Armería, to catch buses to Cuyutlán, 12 km west (every 30min; 20min), and Paraíso, 6km west of Cuyutlán (every 45min; 15min), walk two blocks north from the long-distance bus stop, then two blocks east to the market. To reach Boca de Pascuales (every 45min until 6pm; 25min), you'll need to take a direct bus from Manzanillo and change at the market town of

Tecomán, 20km south of Armería. Buses also run from Tecomán to Colima and Lázaro Cárdenas.

## Cuyutlán

**CUYUTLÁN**, the largest of the three coastal resorts, is also the most appealing, backed by an immense coconut grove that stretches along a narrow peninsula almost to Manzanillo. Popular with Mexican holiday-makers, the old town around the zócalo is sleepy, its inhabitants idling away the day on wooden verandas under terracotta roofs. Life in the hotels by the malecón isn't much faster, except around Christmas and Semana Santa, when things liven up considerably and you should book well ahead. In spring, the **coast** both here and further south is subject to the **Ola Verde**: vast, dark-green waves up to 10m high that crash down on the fine grey sand. Theories to explain their green hue vary widely – from the angle of the sun refracting off the wave to algae bloom – but whatever the reason, the Ola Verde has been a part of Cuyutlán lore ever since a huge tidal wave destroyed the town in 1932. At other times of the year the surf is impressive but easier to handle.

If you're staying for a couple of days, it's worth taking a trip out to the **Centro Ecológico el Tortugario**, around 4km on the road to Paraíso (Tues–Sun 8.30am–5.30pm; M$20) – catch a cab from the zócalo (M$40) or stroll south down the beach for about 45 minutes. From July to December, three **turtle** species visit the local beaches to lay their eggs and a team from the centre goes out every night to collect them before they end up as someone's dinner. The newly hatched turtles are then kept in tanks for a couple of days before being released back into the sea. Out of the egg-laying season, there's a resident turtle population and lots of information on hand. The sanctuary has a swimming pool and boats used for the three-hour **tours** (M$55) to Paraíso (see below) and back through the mangrove tunnels of the idyllic, jungly **Laguna Estero Palo Verde**, well known for its birdlife.

There's also a **Salt Museum** (daily 8am–6pm; donation) in town, two blocks east of the zócalo on Juárez, housed in an original, wooden salt *bodega*. Salt was worth more than gold in pre-Columbian times and if you're interested, the retired salt-workers who run the place will talk you through the compound's long history.

Outside the high season, **hotels** are affordable (in low season many places sell three nights for the price of two) and clustered within a block or two of the junction of Hidalgo and Veracruz. The ones to go for are *Morelos*, Hidalgo 185 (Ⓣ313/326-4013; ❹), with clean rooms (the renovated ones are the most comfortable), fans, hot water and the town's best swimming pool (M$30 for non-guests); the longstanding *Fénix*, Hidalgo 201 (Ⓣ313/326-4082, Ⓔhotelfenixcuyutlan@yahoo.com; ❸), which has some great old-fashioned rooms opening onto spacious communal verandas; and *San Rafael*, Veracruz 46 (Ⓣ313/326-4015; ❺), where some lovely rooms lead straight to the beach. All three hotels boast decent **seafood restaurants**.

## Paraíso and Boca de Pascuales

With your own vehicle you can reach **PARAÍSO** directly from Cuyutlán, or you could take the Laguna Estero Palo Verde boat tour (see above) and get off at Paraíso. However, if you're travelling by bus you'll have to return to Armería, from where it's 8km to this minute place – really just a few neglected buildings on either side of the dust-and-cobble street. The beach is peaceful though, with banks of crashing surf and a few uninspired *enramadas* serving essentially the same menu. Only at *Hotel Paraíso*, right on the seafront (Ⓣ312/312-1032; ❹), is the feeling of banality and dilapidation dispelled; the older rooms have character, but the new wing is more comfortable, and everyone uses the pool and watches the sunset from the bar. If you **camp** on the beach, they'll let you use a shower, especially if you buy a drink.

Smaller still, **BOCA DE PASCUALES**, 13km from Tecomán, is little more than a bunch of palapa restaurants and a beach renowned for huge waves and challenging surfing. Swimming can be dangerous, but otherwise it's a fine place to hang out for a few days. Beach **camping** is your best option; the uninspiring *Estrella del Surf* (no phone; ③), on the way in, offers simple and somewhat overpriced rooms. The best **restaurant**, the expensive *Las Hamacas del Mayor* (①313/324-3846), serves topnotch seafood and draws a large crowd, in spite of its remote location.

# Colima

Inland **COLIMA**, capital of the state of the same name and 100km from Manzanillo, is a distinctly colonial city, and a very beautiful one too, overlooked by the perfectly conical **Volcán de Colima** and, in the distance, the Nevado de Colima. With a handful of sights inside the city limits and interesting excursions nearby, it's a pleasant place to stop over for a night or two. In addition, Colima's Old World ambience, favourable climate – cooler than the coast, but never as cold as in the high mountains – and several good-value hotels and restaurants also make it an appealing destination.

Archeological evidence – much of it explained in the city's museums – points to three millennia of rich cultural heritage around Colima, almost all of it wiped out with the arrival of Cortés's lieutenant Gonzalo de Sandoval, who, in 1522, founded the city on its present site. Four years later Cortés decreed that Colima – named after Cilimán, a former ruler of the local Nahua people – should be the third city of New Spain after Veracruz and Mexico City. However, Acapulco's

△ Parque Nacional Nevado de Colima

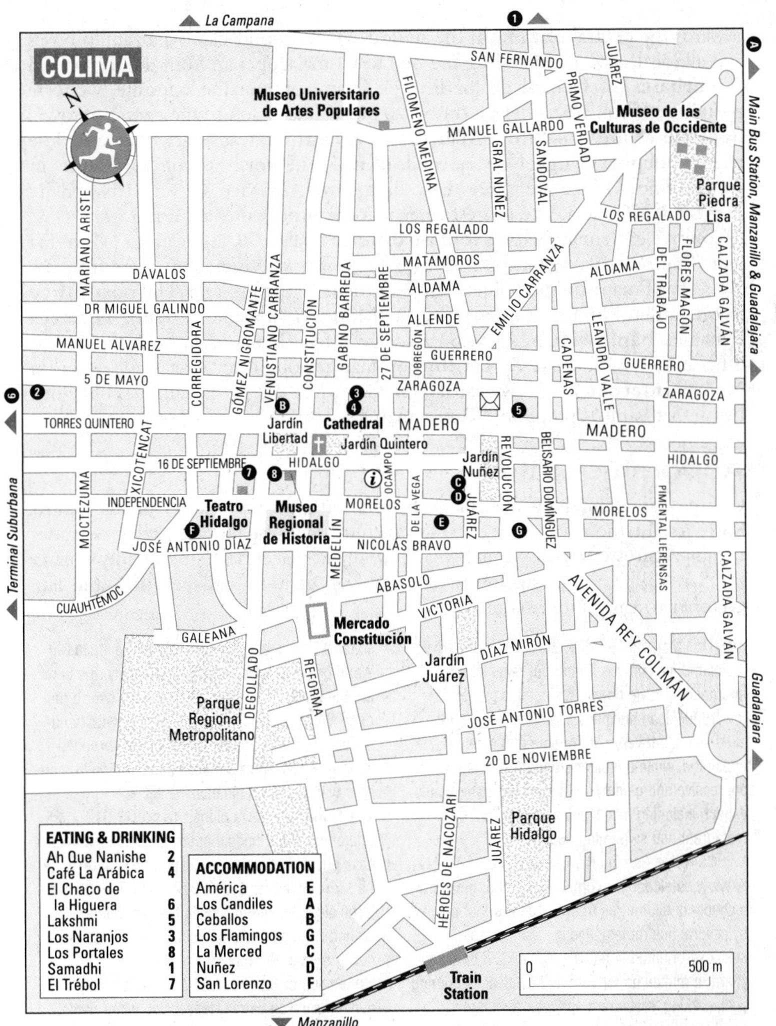




designation as the chief Pacific port at the end of the sixteenth century deprived Colima of any strategic importance; this, in combination with a series of devastating earthquakes – the most recent in 2003 – means that the city has few grand buildings to show for its former glory. It makes up for this with a chain of shady formal **plazas** called "jardíns" – Colima is known as the "City of Palms" – and a number of attractive **courtyards**, many of which are now used as restaurants and cafés and make wonderfully cool places to catch up on writing postcards.

## Arrival and information

Some 2km east of the centre, Colima's **main bus station**, the Terminal Forañea (or Central de Autobuses), handles frequent first- and second-class buses from Guadalajara and Manzanillo. **Taxis** (M$25) and **city buses** #2, #4 and #5 run towards the central plaza from the station. Many second-class Manzanillo buses and all local services, including the one to Comala, operate from the **Terminal Suburbana** (or Central de los Rojos), 1.5km out on the opposite, western, periphery. If you arrive here, a #4 or #6 bus will take you to the centre of town; from the centre, a #2 from Madero, at Revolucíon, leads back that way. The nearest **airport**, Miguel de la Madrid, is 13km northeast of the centre in Cuauhtémoc. There are three daily flights from Mexico City and two daily flights from Tijuana. The nearest international airport is Manzanillo.

Colima's extremely helpful **tourist office**, Hidalgo 96, at Ocampo (Mon–Fri 9am–8pm, Sat 10am–2pm; ⓣ312/312-4360, ⓦwww.visitacolima.com.mx), has a variety of maps and pamphlets, some of them in Spanish only. The **post office** is on Jardín Nuñez, at Madero 247 (Mon–Fri 8.30am–5.30pm). There's a Banamex **bank** with an ATM on Hidalgo, a few doors down from the tourist office, and several **casas de cambio** on Juárez, along the western side of Jardín Nuñez. **Internet** access is available at CI@, just off the zócalo at Hildago 6 (Mon–Sat 9am–10pm, Sun 10am–4pm; M$20/hr).

## Accommodation

Colima has a clutch of reasonable **hotels** within a few blocks of the centre. Sadly, for the most part they don't conform to the regal ambience that pervades the city. **Rates** don't vary much year-round, but places do fill up rapidly during the San Felipe and Todos los Santos fiestas in early to mid-February and late October to early November.

**América** Morelos 162 ⓣ312/312-0366, ⓦwww.hotelamerica.com.mx. Bland but reliable, this international-style downtown hotel is geared toward Mexican business travellers. The remodelled suites are very comfortable and nicely appointed, while the older standard rooms are oppressive and gloomy. All the facilities you would expect, including a convention centre, chi-chi restaurant and swimming pool. ❻

**Los Candiles** Camino Real 399 ⓣ312/312-3212, ⓦwww.hotelcandiles.com. Close to the university, a couple of kilometres from the centre (but passed by several bus routes), this is a comfortable, business-oriented hotel. What it lacks in personal charm it makes up for with its facilities: swimming pool, parking, restaurant and well-appointed, spacious, if rather fusty, rooms with a/c, cable TV, safe and decent bathrooms. Less expensive than its many of its downtown counterparts. ❺

**Ceballos** Portal Medellín 12 ⓣ312/312-4444, ⓦwww.hotelceballos.com. In a prime location, right on the Jardín Libertad, this characterful colonial hotel owned by Best Western exudes Old World grandeur. Rooms vary enormously; the best are the newly remodelled, deluxe ones (worth the extra M$100), which are light and airy with hand-painted furniture, French windows and wrought-iron balconies. The standard rooms are much more dour with medieval dimensions. ❻–❼

**Los Flamingos** Rey Colimán 18 ⓣ312/312-2525. One of the better budget options. Institutional rooms have private bath, good beds, balconies and TV. ❷

**La Merced** Juárez 282 ⓣ312/312-6969. Characterful old hotel with passable fan-ventilated rooms around a central patio and some less attractive, newer rooms. TV and parking. ❸

**Nuñez** Juárez 88 ⓣ312/312-7030. Reliable budget place on Jardín Nuñez, also with private parking. Large rooms with showers are almost twice the price of small ones with shared bathroom. ❷

**San Lorenzo** Cuauhtémoc 149 ⓣ312/312-2000. In a quiet part of town, but still reasonably central. Modern hotel with excellent, well-priced rooms. ❹

## The Town

As in all Mexico's old cities, life in Colima centres on the **zócalo**, where you'll find the government offices (take a quick look at the distinctly second-rate murals in the Palacio de Gobierno) and the unimpressive Neoclassical cathedral. Quite out of character for this part of Mexico, however, the town actually boasts a couple of really good **museums**.

The most central of these, Colima's **Museo Regional de Historia** (Tues–Sat 9am–6pm, Sun 5–8pm; M$35), stands across the street from the Palacio de Gobierno in a lovely old building that also houses the university art gallery. Move swiftly through the stuff on **local crafts** – though the animal and diabolical masks used in traditional dances are interesting – and make for the later rooms, chock-full of **pre-Hispanic ceramics**: gorgeous figurines with superbly expressive faces, fat Izcuintli dogs and people working on mundane, everyday tasks. Though characteristic of western Mexican culture, these examples are specific to Colima, many of them found in *tumbas de tiro* – well-like tombs up to 16m deep, more commonly found in South America and the Pacific Islands. The cultural parallel isn't well understood, but explanatory panels (all in Spanish) show the different styles.

More widely trumpeted than the regional museum, the **Museo de las Culturas de Occidente** (Tues–Sun 9am–6.30pm; M$16), 1km northeast of Jardín Nuñez, holds another substantial collection of local archeology. You'll see the same kind of things here as in the former, but more figurines: dogs with litters fighting; oversized frogs; surreal, serpent-headed deities; people blowing conch shells and dancing; even a man in a caiman mask whose dances were said to avert hurricanes. There's also a more detailed explanation of the rural agrarian society that produced the well-preserved tombs; again, all is in Spanish. In the same park as the museum, an auditorium hosts occasional concerts, plays and films. Look for posters advertising what's on.

If you've more time to spare, wander eight blocks north of the zócalo to the **Museo Universitario de Artes Populares** (Tues–Sat 10am–2pm & 5–8pm,

## Climbing the Nevado de Colima

The **Parque Nacional Nevado de Colima** comprises two beautiful volcanoes rising north of Colima. The **Volcán de Colima** (3900m), also known as Volcán de Fuego, is officially still active and smokes from time to time, though there seems little imminent danger. It is far less frequently climbed than its larger and more passive brother, the **Nevado de Colima** (4335m), which, with its pine- and oak-forested slopes, is popular with local mountaineers during the clear, dry winter months. Unless there's a lot of snow – in December and January crampons and an ice axe are essential – and provided you are fit and can get transport high enough, it's a relatively easy **hike** up to the summit. The most popular option is to ascend the Nevado de Colima from the cabin at **La Joya** (3500m), but it's also possible to walk to the microwave station a little way beyond, from where it's a stiff but non-technical walk.

You'll need to set three days aside for the climb, take a sleeping bag and waterproofs, pack enough food and water for the trip and walk from the village of El Fresnito. First, take a bus from Terminal Forañea in Colima to Ciudad Guzmán (about 1hr 30min) and from there catch a bus from stall #21 to **El Fresnito**, where there are very limited supplies. Ask for the road to La Joya – take this and keep right until the route becomes obvious. This rough service road for the microwave station leads up through cow pastures and goes right past the hut, about six to eight hours' walking (35km). You can tank up from the supply of running water here, but don't expect to stay in the hut, which is often locked, and even if open may be full, as it only sleeps six. Plan on a day from La Joya to the summit and back, then another to get back to Colima, though a very fit walker starting before dawn could make the trip back to Colima, or at least Ciudad Guzmán, in a day. Note that **hitching** isn't an option as the logging roads up here are rough, requiring high clearance or 4WD vehicles, and see very little traffic.

Sun 10am–1pm; M$10), which has an eclectic but poorly explained collection of folk art, including masks; traditional textiles and costumes modelled by enormous papier-mâché figures; shoes; ceramics; images of the Virgin; toy aeroplanes; and a small musical instrument collection – look for the violin made from scrap wood and a Modelo beer can. The workshop next door specializes in ceramic reproductions that you can buy in the museum shop.

The source of some of the museum's treasures is the **archeological site** at La Campana (Tues–Sun 9am–5pm; M$30, free on Sun), a couple of kilometres northwest of the centre, which dates back to around 1500 BC and is believed to have reached its zenith between 700 and 900 AD. Excavations have revealed some small pyramids, temple remains and one tomb. To get there, head north out of town along Gabino Barreda and take a left onto Tecnológico.

On a hot day, you can cool off in one of two parks: the **Parque Piedra Lisa** to the east – the "sliding stone" in the name referring to a rock that is said to ensure your return if you slide on it – and the **Parque Regional Metropolitano** (Wed–Sun 10.30am–5pm) to the southwest. The latter has a small, depressing zoo, a boating lake with boats for rent, hiking trails and a swimming pool.



## Eating and drinking

For a town of its size, Colima has a great range of places to eat, from restaurants serving **Oaxacan** and local specialities to the region's best **vegetarian** food.

**Ah Que Nanishe** 5 de Mayo 267, west of Mariano Arista ☎312/314-2197. The name of this surprisingly inexpensive courtyard restaurant means "how delicious" in Zapotec: appropriate, considering the tasty fare. The menu specializes in dishes from the owner's native Oaxaca: *mole*, *chapulines* (baked grasshoppers) and *tlyaduas* (large flour tortillas). Well worth the walk out from the centre. Closed Tues.

**Café La Arábica** Gabino Barreda at Madero ☎312/307-0025. A tiny, mostly takeout coffee shop where the smell of roasting *Colimense* beans heralds Americanos, espressos or cappuccinos made from excellent locally grown, roasted and ground coffee. Little else is served.

**El Chaco de la Higuera** Madero s/n, 6 blocks west of Jardín Nuñez ☎312/313-1092. Charming, friendly spot to try local delicacies including *sopitas*, *pozole* and tamales. The chicken in sesame sauce is wonderful, and local artwork is strewn across the walls.

**Lakshmi** Madero at Revolución ☎312/312-6433. Mainly a whole-food shop and bakery producing great banana and carrot breads and herbal supplements, but with a courtyard restaurant area for eat-in veggie burgers, salads, granola, yogurts and nutritious drinks.

**Los Naranjos** Gabino Barreda 34, north of Madero ☎312/312-0029. Friendly, smart restaurant where you can get a substantial comida corrida for around M$60 and a good selection of meat dishes, especially beef – try the *arrachera* (thick flank steak) The breakfasts are especially good value, with an all-you-can eat buffet for M$70 that includes *chilaquiles*, quesadillas, eggs, fruit, tea and coffee. There's a second branch on Constitución.

**Los Portales** Hidalgo, on Jardín Libertad ☎312/312-8520. Nice place on the zócalo, great for sitting outside and watching the world go by. Reasonably priced *antojitos* and seafood dishes.

**Samadhi** Juan Rulfo 458 ☎312/313-2498. Despite its inconvenient relocation to a site about 2km north of the centre, the almost entirely vegetarian menu, featuring veggie burgers, crepes and delicious *licuados*, still justifies a visit.

**El Trébol** 16 de Septiembre at Degollado ☎312/312-2952. Comfortable, cosy and inexpensive place just off the zócalo for egg dishes, snacks and light meals. Closed Sat.

## Around Colima: Comala

The best time to be in Colima is on a clear winter day when the volcanoes in the **Parque Nacional Nevado de Colima** dominate the scenery to the north. Climbing them, while not that difficult, needs some planning (see box, p.567). You can get a closer look, however, by spending an afternoon at **COMALA**, a tidy, quaint town, 10km north of Colima. Here, in the central plaza, you can sip a beer or margarita while enjoying a fantastic view of the mountains and listening to mariachi bands competing for your business. Four **restaurants** huddled together under the zócalo's southern portal each try to outdo the other by producing better *botanas* – plates of snacks, dips and tacos – free with drinks from noon until about 6pm. There's little to choose between them – the drinks are uniformly expensive (around M$20 for a beer or soft drink), but you can still get a fairly economical lunch. Friday and Saturday are the liveliest times, when you can mingle with day-tripping, predominantly middle-class Mexicans from Guadalajara; on Sundays and Mondays there are craft markets in the square. A thirty-minute stroll out of town, in the Centro Cultural Nogueras, is the **Museo Alejandro Rangel Hidalgo** (Tues–Fri 10am–2pm & 4pm–7pm, Sat & Sun 10am–5pm; M$20) which has an engaging display of the eponymous artist's work as well as pre-Hispanic artefacts from Hidalgo's personal collection. Known for his evocative book illustrations, he drew the pictures for the classic Mexican novel *Pedro Páramo,* which was written by his close friend Juan Rulfo and set in Comala. Hidalgo died in 2000 at the age of 73. **Buses** run frequently to Comala from Colima's Terminal Suburbana (every 15min; 20min; M$6).

# South to Lázaro Cárdenas

Beyond the state of Colima you run into a virtually uninhabited area: there are occasional beaches, but for the most part the mountains drop straight into the ocean – a spectacular sight, but offering little reason to stop. As you move into Michoacán, **CALETA DE CAMPOS**, some 70km short of Lázaro Cárdenas, is the first, and in many ways the best, place to stop. A small village that acts as a service centre for the area, it's friendly and unassuming, with two lovely beaches and impressive ocean views. There is something of a Wild West feel to the place: the streets are unpaved, and horses stand tied to hitching posts alongside the campers of American surfers and the fancy new cars belonging to visitors from the city. Should you need to stay, there are two **hotels** – *Yuritzi* (Ⓣ753/531-5010; ④), a modern, well-managed establishment which has its own generator and water supply, and the less expensive, more dilapidated *Arcos de Guadalupe* (Ⓣ753/531-5038; ④) – as well as a string of bar/restaurants down at the beach and a plethora of taco stands and mini-markets along the main street. For much of the year the place is virtually deserted, but in winter, when Californian beach boys come down in pursuit of sun and surf (the waves are perfect for beginners), and at weekends, when families from Lázaro Cárdenas pile in, it can take on crowds.

The beach here should definitely be seen at night, when, if the conditions are right, the ocean glows a bright, luminous green. This is not a product of the excellent local beer, or of the Acapulco Gold marijuana that allegedly grows in the surrounding mountains, but of a naturally illuminated, emerald-green plankton: go swimming in it and you'll come out covered in sparkles. The phenomenon is common along much of this coast, and also seen in Baja California – but is nowhere as impressive as here. One word of warning: the second beach, cut off by a narrow, rocky point, looks like an unspoilt paradise (which it is), but you can only get there by boat or a stiff climb over the rocks – try to swim round and you'll be swept out to sea by a powerful current. Locals are well used to picking up tourists who suddenly find themselves several hundred metres offshore.

### Playa Azul

Once a small-time, slow-moving beach surrounded by lagoons, **PLAYA AZUL** has been rather overrun by the growth of Lázaro Cárdenas, 20km away. However, there are still several reasonably priced hotels and a moderate beach, backed by scores of palapa restaurants. But, aside from lying on the sand (the surf and dangerous undercurrents make swimming unsafe) there is really nothing else to hold your attention.

Long-distance **buses** don't pass directly through Playa Azul, so ask to be dropped off at La Mira, the nearest town on the highway – from here, numerous local buses and *combis* run the remaining 7km down to Playa Azul. The road into town crosses four streets, parallel to the beach and running down to the vast plaza at the southern end. As you come in you'll pass *Hotel Playa Azul* (ⓣ753/536-0024; ⑤), where **rooms** are clustered around a leafy courtyard and have a/c and a pool view. You can also **camp** here, though the site is little more than a patch of dirt behind the hotel. The pool is a better prospect (M$20 for non-guests), and at weekends their larger pool, El Balneario, complete with water slide, costs no more. For somewhere a little cheaper, try the comfortable *María Isabela*, on the far side of the plaza (ⓣ753/536-0016; ⑤), which has pristine rooms, very friendly staff and a pool of its own. The best accommodation is *Hotel María Teresa*, also on the plaza (ⓣ753/536-0005; ⑤), which has recently renovated, attractive rooms, a decent pool and a garden bar/restaurant serving breakfast only (included in the price). **Beachfront restaurants** such as *El Pirata del Caribe* serve mainly seafood lunches and dinners, while the poolside restaurant at *Hotel Playa Azul* has a good range of international food, including pizzas and pasta dishes.

### Lázaro Cárdenas

Local buses make the trip from Caleta de Campos to **LÁZARO CÁRDENAS** several times a day. The only reason to come here, however, is if you're trying to get somewhere else – it's strictly industrial, dominated by a huge, British-funded steelworks. If you get stuck for the night, you'll find several small **hotels** in the centre. Close to the bus station, the *Hotel Reyna Pio*, Corregidora 78 (ⓣ753/532-0620; ④), is a popular inexpensive option with well-maintained, spacious rooms with fan and hot water and friendly, helpful owners. One of the tallest buildings in town, *Hotel Casablanca*, Nicolás Bravo 474 (ⓣ753/537-3480; ⑥), is a more upscale choice; rooms have phones, TV, a/c and a safe. There are three **bus stations** in town: the ones served by Sur de Jalisco and La Linea and Galeana, Ruta Paraíso and Parhikuni are opposite one another on either side of Lázaro Cárdenas; to get to the third, served by Elite, Estrella Blanca and others, walk out the front of the Galeana station, turn right, right again and second right. Buses to Caleta de Campos depart from the Galeana station. If you need information, the **tourist office** is at *Hotel Casablanca* (Mon–Sat 9am–2pm & 5–7pm, Sun 9am–2pm).

## Zihuatanejo and on to Acapulco

Some 115km south along Hwy-200 from Lázaro Cárdenas, the towns of Ixtapa and Zihuatanejo, while only 7km apart, could hardly be more different.

**IXTAPA**, a purpose-built, computer-planned "paradise" resort, is, quite simply, one of the most soulless towns imaginable, as well as one of the most expensive. Even now, thirty-plus years down the line, it hasn't yet begun to mellow or wear itself in, and its single coastal drive still runs past a series of concrete boxes of varying heights. These completely cordon off Ixtapa's admittedly lovely stretch of beach from the road, forcing those who can't afford the hotels' inflated prices to trespass, or even use the hotels' facilities. You might want to visit one of the clubs in the evening, but you will definitely not want to stay.

**ZIHUATANEJO**, on the other hand, for all its growth in recent years, has at least retained something of the look and feel of the traditional fishing village it once was – what building there has been is small-scale, low-key and low-rise. This said, it is definitely a resort town: taxi drivers are forever advertising for customers, trinket and tacky T-shirt shops are abundant and as likely as not there'll be a cruise ship moored out in the bay. Despite the proliferation of luxury hotels, though, there are at least a fair number of small, reasonably priced places to stay as well as some inexpensive restaurants. For some, Zihuatanejo is the ideal compromise – quiet by night, yet with the more commercial excitements of Ixtapa nearby. The one real problem is its popularity – with strictly controlled development, rooms can be hard to find in the centre of Zihuatanejo, a region of barely ten small blocks hemmed in by the main roads into town, the yacht marina and the beach.

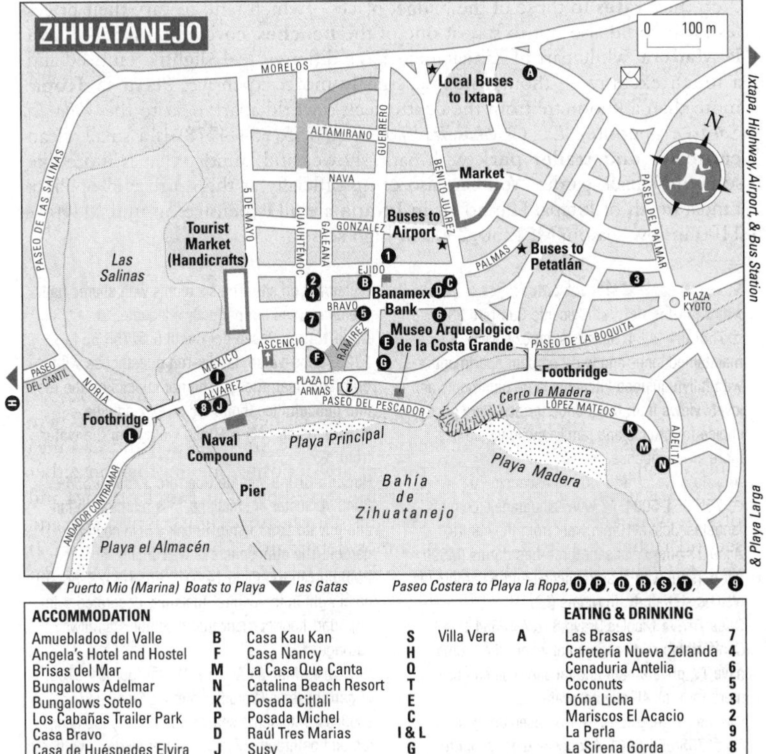

## Arrival and information

**Buses** arrive at Zihuatanejo's Central Camionera, about twenty minutes' walk from the centre of town. There are plenty of taxis outside the station, and if you walk a couple of hundred metres to the left, you can pick up passing "Zihuatanejo" buses, which will generally drop you off at the top of Juárez, where **minibuses** leave for Ixtapa every fifteen minutes (6am–10pm). Buses marked "Noria" go straight past the youth hostel and *Casa Nancy*. *Combis* making the thirty-minute run between Zihuatanejo and the **airport**, 20km south (only 2km off the highway to Acapulco), also pass by the bus station before dropping off (and picking up) just outside the market, at Gonzalez and Juárez.

The **tourist office** (Mon–Fri 8am–4pm; ⓣ755/554-2747, ⓦwww.ixtapa-zihuatanejo.com) is inconveniently located about 2km out of town in the Ayuntamiento building, Paseo Zihuatanejo 21, near the Fuente del Sol fountain. There is a smaller office on Paseo de la Bahía s/n, close to Playa La Ropa, and, in high season only, a tourist booth in the centre at Álvarez s/n. The tourist office in **Ixtapa** is at Paseo de las Gaviotas 12, behind the cinema (Mon–Fri 9am–2pm & 4–7pm; ⓣ755/553-1270).

## Accommodation

Zihuatanejo's **high season** is fairly long, from around mid-November to the end of April. Outside those times some of the slightly more expensive hotels drop their **rates** to those of the budget places – which tend to vary their prices less. You could also opt to stay at one of the **beaches**, covered on p.574. **Playa la Madera**, while part of Zihuatanejo, has a different feel, slightly removed and a touch exclusive – though not necessarily more expensive. **Playa la Ropa**, more than a kilometre from the centre, feels a world apart; next to the *Villa del Sol* (see opposite), *Las Cabañas Trailer Park* (ⓣ755/554-4718) is a small, clean **campsite and trailer park** with bath, shower and laundry that is more like someone's back garden. You can also camp officially at the north end of Playa Linda, north of Ixtapa. The hotels in **Ixtapa** are all expensive: around M$900–1100 in low season, M$1350–2300 in high season.

### Central Zihuatanejo

**Amueblados del Valle** Vicente Guerrero 33 ⓣ755/554-2084. Spacious, breezy, well-maintained, one- and two-bedroom apartments with fully equipped kitchens, large bathrooms and lovely views from the rooftop terrace. Very good choice for groups and families who would like more independence. ❺–❻

**Angela's Hotel and Hostel** Ascencio 10 ⓣ755/554-5084, ⓦwww.zihuatanejo.com.mx/angelas. Just a 10min walk from the centre, *Angela's* offers pleasant three-bed dorms (M$90 per person) with shared kitchen and bathroom, as well as some private rooms (❸).

**Casa Bravo** Nicolás Bravo 8 ⓣ755/554-2548. Comfortable mid-range hotel where the rooms have TV, private bath and fans (or you can pay more for a/c). All-day hot water. ❺

**Casa de Huéspedes Elvira** Paseo del Pescador 32 ⓣ755/554-2061. A longstanding favourite budget option with a friendly owner and very good restaurant on site. The six rooms with shared bath are unadorned but perfectly adequate. ❸

**Casa Nancy** Paseo del Cantil 6 ⓣ755/554-2123. Good-value, family-run guesthouse with drab but clean rooms. The hammocks on the roof and peaceful location lend a relaxing vibe, despite being only a 10min walk from the waterfront. ❸

**Posada Citlali** Vicente Guerrero 3 ⓣ755/554-2043. A cluster of small, no-frills rooms with fan and private bathroom overlook a lush courtyard garden. The atmosphere is welcoming. ❸

**Posada Michel** Ejido 14 ⓣ755/554-7423. Bright hotel right in the centre. Tastefully decorated, with a ground-floor corridor that resembles a railway carriage. ❺

**Raúl Tres Marias** Alvarez 214 ⓣ755/554-6706, ⓔgarroboscrew@prodigy.net.mx. Shiny and spotless, with some sea views from the top floor, a/c and bathrooms with hot water all day. Another, cheaper branch of the same hotel – with unattractive rooms – is at Noria 4, just across the lagoon footbridge (Ⓣ755/554-2191; ⑤). ⑥

**Susy** Alvarez 2 Ⓣ755/554-2339. A useful stand-by, this well-run institutional hotel has cheerless rooms with small balconies, fans and shower. ④

**Villa Vera** Morelos 165 Ⓣ755/554-2920, Ⓦwww.ixtapa-zihuatanejo.net/villavera. This four-storey modern hotel isn't the best value in town, but the rooms are nicely decorated and have shiny tiled floors, a/c and cable TV. There is a swimming pool with bar and the friendly owners run a tight ship. ⑥

**Youth Hostel** Paseo de las Salinas 50 Ⓣ755/554-2003. Compact, four-bed, single-sex rooms for M$35–80 per person or you can camp in the garden and use all their facilities for M$25.

### Playa la Madera, Playa la Ropa and Playa Larga

**Brisas del Mar** López Mateos, Playa la Madera Ⓣ755/554-2142, Ⓦwww.brisasdelmar.net. Not quite as astronomically priced as many places in these parts, this charming hotel has comfortable suites decorated with artistic flourishes and appointed with tasteful wooden furnishings. The large private terraces come complete with hammocks from which to enjoy the sea views. Other facilities include a swimming pool, volleyball court, library, fitness centre with sauna, steam room and massages. ⑨

**Bungalows Adelmar** Adelita 40, Playa la Madera Ⓣ755/554-9190, Ⓔbungalows_adelamar@hotmail.com. Immaculately clean, modern rooms, all with well-equipped kitchens – and some with small gardens – an excellent pool and tranquil location close to the beach. Up to four people in a room. ⑧

**Bungalows Sotelo** López Mateos, Playa la Madera Ⓣ755/554-6307. Comfortable apartments with a/c, satellite TV, balconies, kitchens and great sea views. The most luxurious rooms have Jacuzzis on the balcony. ⑥

**Casa Gloria María** Playa la Ropa s/n Ⓣ755/554-2055. A good option for families, these four clean, and tidy self-contained bungalows each have two twin beds, a fully equipped kitchen, a spacious bathroom and a dining area. ⑦

**Casa Kau Kan** Playa Larga s/n Ⓣ755/554-6226, Ⓦwww.casakaukan.com. The essence of good taste and discretion, this small, beachside boutique hotel has spacious, artful suites with separate living areas and plush bathrooms. Facilities create an aura of unbridled pampering in an isolated natural setting with miles of deserted beach and gorgeous gardens. The staff are efficient and unobtrusive. ⑨

**La Casa Que Canta** Playa la Ropa Ⓣ755/555-7030 or 01-800/710-9345, Ⓦwww.lacasaquecanta.com. The place to splurge. Guests rave about this beautifully designed, thatched-roof hotel draped over the hillside. The breezy rooms are luxuriously decorated with traditional Mexican artesanía and the secluded, romantic gardens are composed of labyrinthine pathways that lead to intimate hideaways. There is an excellent restaurant and a spa and fitness centre. ⑨

**Catalina Beach Resort** Playa la Ropa s/n Ⓣ755/554-2137. If you're looking for value on the beach, *Catalina* is one of the oldest and friendliest hotels in town with good facilities for the price. The rooms vary enormously – some betray their age more than others, and the new suites are well worth the extra – but the large terraces with hammocks and glorious views are the allure here. Tropical gardens, pool and an oceanfront restaurant with complimentary breakfast are perfect for relaxing. ⑦

**Villa del Sol** Playa la Ropa Ⓣ755/555-5500 or 01-888/389-2645, Ⓦwww.hotelvilladelsol.net. Lush gardens of hibiscus and bougainvillea hide spacious luxury suites all with terraces and some with small private pools. There's a large infinity pool, too, as well as a private patch of beach, a spa, a fitness centre and other creature comforts. Expensive even off-season, and there's a M$670 minimum to be spent on food per day during the winter. ⑨

## Activities

Zihuatanejo has a few things to distract you from lying on the beach. Quite apart from jet skiing, parasailing and getting dragged around on a huge inflatable banana, you could arrange to go **fishing** for dorado, yellowtail, bonito or big game. Trips, run by Lanchas de Pesca (Ⓣ755/554-2056), leave from the pier. Prices vary according to the size of your group: seven hours' fishing costs about M$1600 for four people, M$2800 for six (in a bigger boat). **Scuba-diving** courses are organized by Whisky Water World (Ⓣ755/554-0147, Ⓦwww.ixtapa-sportfishing.com) on Paseo del Pescador, next to the pier. A half-day resort course with one dive costs M$560, and one-tank reef dives for certified divers will set you back M$500. Full PADI certification takes five to six days and costs M$4500.

Just behind the beach you'll find the **Museo Arqueológico de la Costa Grande** (Tues–Sun 10am–6pm; M$7), a small and simple affair not deserving more than twenty minutes, though it does its best to tackle the history of what has always been a fairly insignificant region.

## The beaches

Four beaches surround Bahía de Zihuatanejo. **Playa Principal**, in front of Zihuatanejo, is unspectacular, with muddy water, brown sand and persistent hawkers, but is an interesting place to people-watch – the fishermen haul in their catch here early in the morning, selling much of it on the spot. A narrow footpath heads east from the end of the beach across the normally dry outlet of a drainage canal, then winds around a rocky point to the calm waters of **Playa la Madera**, a broad, moderately clean strand of dark sand that shelves softly into the ocean, making it a good option for kids. There's a handful of restaurants and hotels on the hill behind, as well as some expensive condos. Climb the steps between these to get to the road if you want to continue a kilometre or so over the headland, past the *mirador* with great views across the bay, to **Playa la Ropa**, which takes its name – "Clothes Beach" – from silks washed up here when one of the *nao de China* (trading ships from China) was wrecked offshore. This is Zihuatanejo's finest road-accessible beach, palm-fringed for more than a kilometre, with a variety of beachfront restaurants and hotels. You can walk a further fifteen minutes beyond the end of Playa la Ropa to **Playa las Gatas**, named after the nurse sharks that used to populate the waters. Las Gatas is the last of the bay's beaches, its crystalline blue water surrounded by a reef, giving it the enclosed feel of an ocean swimming pool. It's safe for kids, though the sea bottom is mostly rocky and tough on feet. The clear waters are great for **snorkelling** – you can rent gear from vendors among the rather pricey palapa restaurants. Las Gatas is directly opposite the town and, if the rocky walk doesn't appeal, it is accessible by launches (daily 9am–5pm, last return 5.30pm; 10min; M$35 return) run by Lanchas de Pesca (see p.573). Buy tickets at the entrance to the pier.

△ Beach in Zihuatanejo

The long sweep of **Ixtapa**'s main, hotel-backed **Playa de Palmar** is fine for volleyball or long walks, but often too rough for easy swimming, and plagued by jet skis. Powered water sports are also in evidence at the inappropriately named **Playa Quieta**, some 5km north of Ixtapa, which is dominated by *Club Med* and seemingly perpetual clans of inebriated spring-breakers. The water here is wonderfully clear and the surrounding vegetation magnificent, but with the exception of *Restaurant Neptuno*, which predictably specializes in fresh seafood, you won't get anything to eat or drink unless you pay handsomely to enter the confines of the three luxury resorts that dominate the beach. The next beach along, **Playa Linda**, is a huge sweep of greyish sand, with a cluster of *enramadas* at the pier end where the bus drops you off. As well as the usual trinket vendors, you can rent horses, jet skis and surfboards at the sprinkling of shacks along the beach. To find all the space you need, just keep walking away from the crowded pier end: the restaurants are supplanted by coconut groves, which in turn give way to small cliffs and an estuary with birdlife and reptiles.

Boats leave from the pier at Playa Linda for **Isla Ixtapa** (9am–5pm; M$40 return), a small island a couple of kilometres offshore with two swimming beaches, a spot reserved for diving and a few restaurants, but nowhere to stay. You can also get there on a daily launch from Zihuatanejo, which leaves at 11am and returns at 5pm (1hr; M$110 one-way).

For absolute peace and quiet, the best thing you can do is to take a day trip out of Zihuatanejo to **Barra de Potosí**, a tiny community situated at one end of an expansive, postcard-perfect, golden sandy beach that curves steeply round the bay and keeps going as far as the eye can see. The inky-blue ocean is backed by gentle hills in a gorgeous patchwork of greens and browns. To get there, board a Petatlán-bound **bus** from the station on Calle Palmas and ask the driver to drop you off at the village of Los Achotes. From here, pick-up trucks leave when full to run the final bone-rattling twenty minutes to the beach: you'll be dropped off at one end of the bay where a bunch of *enramadas* sell delicious seafood for half the price of the restaurants in town. There's not much to do out here except relax in a hammock, but if you ask at the *enramadas*, fishermen will take you on a **boat trip** through the dense mangrove forests in the lagoon adjacent to the beach, home to innumerable exotic birds. If you want to stay, you can ask to pitch a tent under a palapa, head for the only **hotel**, the *Barra de Potosí* (ⓣ755/554-8290; ⑥), which drops its rates by over fifty percent in low season, or opt for one of a handful of **B&Bs**, including the four-room, disabled-accessible *Our House* (ⓣ755/556-7310, ⓦwww.ourhouse-zihua.com; ⑧).

## Eating, drinking and nightlife

You can barely move for **restaurants** in Zihuatanejo: the waterfront Paseo del Pescador is the place for fresh fish, expensive drinks and sociable company; the cheapest place, as ever, is the **market** on Juárez. There isn't much **nightlife** in town, however: for that people head over the hill to Ixtapa, where a typical night out starts at *Señor Frog's*, in the shopping plaza opposite the *Presidente Inter-Continental* hotel, or *Carlos 'n Charlie's*, next to the *Posada Real Ixtapa* hotel, two bar/restaurant chains offering food, plenty of alcohol, loud music and dancing, before progressing to the flashy and expensive *Christine* nightclub at *Hotel Krystal*. Buses to Ixtapa run until about 10pm; after that you'll need to get a taxi (M$45).

**Las Brasas** Cuauhtémoc at Bravo. Simple but very cheap breakfasts and comidas corridas served in this cavernous and friendly restaurant.

**Cafetería Nueva Zelanda** Cuauhtémoc at Ejido ⓣ755/554-2340. This old-school, diner-style eatery serves tasty tacos, quesadillas, fajitas and tortas, as well as thick and fruity *licuados.* The American and Mexican breakfasts are bountiful and the cappuccinos the best in town.

**Cenaduría Antelia** Nicolás Bravo 14 ⓣ755/554-3091. Open since the 1970s, this snug old-time joint is a great little spot to eat unadulterated Mexican staples – tacos, enchiladas and the like – until midnight. The rich desserts are also worth the havoc they'll wreak on your midriff. The café next door has chairs and tables in a quiet alley off Nicolás Bravo.

**Coconuts** Pasaje Agustín Ramírez 1 ⓣ755/554-2518. A charming old house with a stunning patio provides the setting for moonlight dining at *Coconuts.* The food is good, with a varied menu that leans towards healthy fish, fresh poultry and creative vegetarian dishes. The overall ambience is quite romantic, especially with low-key jazz in the evenings.

**Doña Licha** Cocos 8 ⓣ755/554-3933. A wide menu of excellent and inexpensive comidas corridas (ribs, tripe and pork chops) served with mountains of rice and beans, has earned this place a loyal following. With a lackadaisical, raw atmosphere, complete with blasting TV and erratic service, the copious platters of food are undoubtedly the main attraction.

**Mariscos El Acacio** Ejido at Galeana ⓣ755/554-2087. Simple seafood restaurant, much cheaper than those on Paseo del Pescador, but still with a pleasant atmosphere as you eat at tables on a tree-shaded, pedestrianized street.

**La Perla** Playa La Ropa s/n. ⓣ755/554-2700. Chi-chi beachside dining at this palapa restaurant that dishes up excellent daily fish and seafood specials with a creative variety of sauces as well as filling *antojitos*, tacos, *ceviche* and soups. The satellite TV draws sports aficionados, who come to sip beer and hang out.

**La Sirena Gorda** Paseo del Pescador ⓣ755/554-2687. Fairly expensive but well sited, right where evening strollers can watch you dine on succulent tuna steaks and seafood cocktails, as well as a selection of American dishes, in the balmy night air. Creatively decorated with paintings of the eponymous Rubenesque mermaids. Closed Wed.

**Tamales y Atoles Any** Ejido 38, at Vicente. No prizes for what is on the menu at this good-value, bustling, beach joint that packs in locals and tourists looking for its sixteen different kinds of tamales, which range from chicken and chile to cheese and squash blossom. The signature dish is *pozole* (pork stew, traditionally eaten on Thurs). Mexican breakfasts served daily.

## Listings

**Banks and exchange** Banamex, on Ejido at Guerrero (Mon–Fri 9am–6pm; 24hr ATM), and Banorte, on Juárez at Ejido (Mon–Fri 8.30am–4pm, Sat 10am–2pm). The casas de cambio don't generally offer good rates, but Central de Cambios Guiball, on Galeana just south of Bravo, is open until 9pm daily and has a *larga distancia* phone for inexpensive collect calls.

**Buses** The two main bus companies, with services to Mexico City, Acapulco and Morelia, among other destinations, are Estrella Blanca (ⓣ755/554-3474) and Estrella de Oro (ⓣ755/554-2175). You can buy long-distance bus tickets at the downtown Estrella Blanca office on Alvárez, at Ramírez (Mon–Sat 9am–3pm & 4–8pm).

**Internet access** There are a handful of cafés along Guerrero, most of which charge M$10/hr.

**Post office** Carteros, at the northeastern corner of town (Mon–Fri 8am–5.30pm, Sat 9am–1pm).

## On to Acapulco

From Zihuatanejo to Acapulco – along Hwy-200, a fast road with regular buses – the aspect of the coast changes again, becoming flatter, more heavily populated and regularly cultivated. At **PAPANOA**, 50km on, there's a beautiful beach, some 15km long, overlooked at its far end by *Hotel Club Papanoa* (ⓣ742/422-0150; ❺). Obviously someone's plan for a luxurious, *Club Med*-style development, it never quite panned out – though there's still considerable comfort, a pool and a stairway down to the beach through manicured gardens, the place has a distinctly run-down air. It's not cheap, but nor is it in the high-luxury bracket, and double **rooms** are large enough for four. You could also easily **camp** on this stretch of sand, getting supplies in Papanoa. The hotel restaurant is also good value, and the staff friendly.

Beyond Papanoa the road leaves the coast again for a while – although with sturdy transport of your own, there are several places where you could find your way down to a beach – not to rejoin it until shortly before Acapulco. Of little interest otherwise, **Coyuca de Benitez**, the last village of any size, has some pleasant restaurants overlooking the Río Coyuca, and you can arrange boat trips downriver into the Laguna de Coyucán. Nearby you could certainly find somewhere to camp or sling a hammock at **Playa de San Jerónimo**, but again it's a windswept and wave-pounded stretch of sand. You could also get a minibus from Coyuca to the beach at **El Carrizol**, where it's possible to rent a reasonably priced bungalow.



# Acapulco

Most people – even if they've not the remotest idea where it is – have heard of **ACAPULCO**, yet few know what to expect upon arrival. Bordered by the rugged Sierra Madre to the east and beautiful Acapulco Bay to the west, the city is considered by many to be the grande dame of the Mexican tourist industry. In fact, it has played an important role in the country's development for some four centuries. The shipping route between Acapulco and the Far East was once among the most prized and preyed upon in the world: the star-shaped Fuerte de San Diego and the several freighters tied up along the city's quayside are testament to its sixteenth-century status as one of Mexico's most important ports. From Acapulco, goods were transported overland to Veracruz and then shipped onwards to Spain. Mexican Independence, Spain's decline and the direct route around southern Africa combined to kill the trade off, and in the nineteenth century Acapulco went into a long, slow decline, only reversed with the completion of a road to the capital in 1928. In the 1950s Acapulco became the poster child for exotic glitz and glamour, the playground for celebrities like Frank Sinatra and Liz Taylor. Elvis Presley immortalized the resort in the movie *Fun in Acapulco*, and JFK and Jackie O spent their honeymoon here. Since then, the city has seen its share of ups and downs; thanks to American spring-breakers getting priced out of Cancún and yet another road down from Mexico City (this time a toll highway), in recent years it has experienced something of a resurgence.

Truth is, as long as you don't yearn to get away from it all, you'll find almost anything you want here, from magnificent beaches by day to restaurants, clubs and discos by night. That said, the manicured and sanitized hotel zone, where everything is geared towards package tourists, can be thoroughly off-putting. Getting from one side of the city to the other is also a very time-consuming and frustrating experience, with perpetual gridlock, grime and choking exhaust fumes. The city's **pollution problem**, which peaks in the rainy season, sees everything from plastic bags to dead dogs get washed off the streets and back alleys into the bay. Seething humidity also adds to the oppressive atmosphere, as can the persistent **hawkers**. Most are easy enough to handle, but they can become irritating and, at times, heavy-handed. For lone women in particular, the constant pestering of would-be gigolos can be maddening, while derelict back streets can be dangerous at night for anyone. Traditionally Acapulco has been considered immune to drug-related violence – the cartels had designated the city as off-limits in order to preserve a vacation haven for themselves – but previously hidden undercurrents came to the fore in 2006, when a shoot-out in broad daylight left four traffickers dead. As evidenced by the federal police, who now patrol the streets carrying semi-automatic machine guns, Acapulco

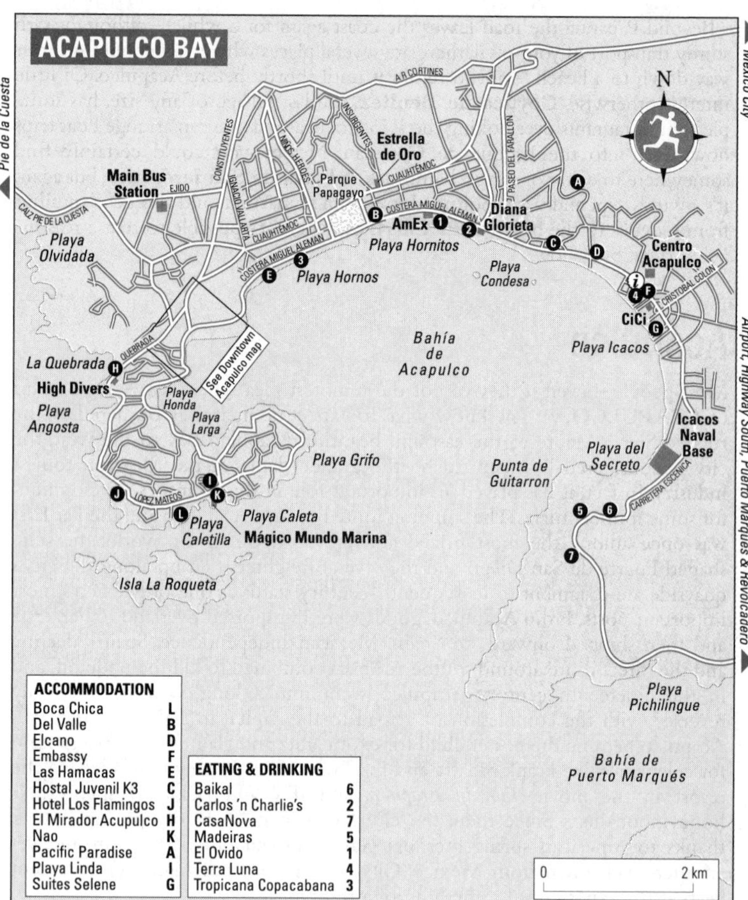


has become a battleground for several cartels aiming to control the lucrative Pacific corridor. While there have been no reported incidents involving tourists, it is advisable not to stray beyond the main tourist areas, especially at night.

What Acapulco undoubtedly has going for it, however, is its stunning **bay**: a sweeping scythe-stroke of yellow sand backed by the white towers of the high-rise hotels and, behind them, the jungly green foothills of the sierra. Even though the town itself has a population of over one and half million and hundreds of thousands of visitors come through each year, it rarely seems overcrowded. There's certainly always space to lie along the beach, partly because of its sheer size, and partly because of the number of rival attractions – everything from hotel pools to parasailing to romantic cruises.

## Orientation, arrival and information

Acapulco divides fairly simply into two halves: the **old town**, which sits at the western end of the bay, with the promontory of **La Quebrada** rising above it and curving round to protect the sheltered anchorage; and the **resort area**, a string of hotels and tourist services following the curve of the bay east. From Playa Caleta on the southern fringe of the peninsula, a single seafront drive, the **Costera Miguel Alemán** – usually just "Costera" – stretches from the old town around the bay, linking almost everything of interest. You can reach everywhere near the zócalo on foot, but to get further afield, frequent **buses** (look for "Caleta/Base", "Zócalo" or "Hornos") run all the way along Costera. From the east, "C Río" buses travel past the big hotels, then turn inland onto Cuauhtémoc, where they pass the Estrella de Oro **bus station** and the **market** before rejoining Costera before the zócalo. "Caleta" buses continue round to Playa Caleta.

Most long-distance **buses** arrive at the Central de Autobuses on Ejido, 3km northwest of the zócalo, from where you can pick up buses marked "Centro" or "Caleta" to get to the area where the cheaper hotels are located. To get to Ejido from the zócalo, look for buses marked "Mocimba". Estrella de Oro buses from Mexico City arrive at their own terminal, 3km west of the zócalo, again connected to the centre by "Caleta" city buses, or to the hotels along Costera by "Río/Base" buses. Both stations have a guardería. The busy international **airport** (information on ⓣ744/435-2060), 23km southeast of the city, is accessible by expensive taxis (M$190–225 from most points) and the Transportaciones Aeropuerto shuttle service (M$85 one-way; will pick up from hotel; ⓣ744/462-1095). Cheaper is to take a town bus to Puerto Marquéz, then another from there to the airport. Frequent flights leave Acapulco for numerous domestic and international destinations. For flight details, contact any travel agent or the airlines (see "Listings", p.587).

Acapulco's **tourist office** (daily 8am–10pm; ⓣ744/484-4416) is located in the Centro Acapulco complex, a block west of CiCi Waterpark (see p.585). Unless you strike it lucky and encounter an enthusiastic staff member, you're likely to come away with little but an armful of brochures. For more edifying reading, try the **book swaps** at some of the budget hotels or browse through the selection of magazines at the bigger hotels and Sanborn's, two blocks west of the zócalo. For 24-hour tourist information and assistance, call the **toll-free phone number** (no charge if calling from Acapulco): ⓣ744/481-1100.

## Accommodation

As with everything in Acapulco, hotel rooms are far less expensive in the **old town**. Head for the streets immediately to the west and slightly inland of the **zócalo**, to calles La Paz and Azueta, and particularly Calzada La Quebrada where it leads up the hill. In contrast to most of Mexico, many hotels in this area charge by the person rather than per room.

You won't find places as cheap out along **Costera**, but if you want to stay by the tourist beaches and the clubs there are a few reasonable options, especially off-season, when even some of the fancier hotels become quite competitively priced. The hotels at the smaller beaches of **Caleta** and **Caletilla**, a ten-minute

### Addresses along Costera

Finding places along Costera can be tricky, as the numbering system is completely meaningless: 50 could be followed by 2010, which is next door to 403. The best **landmarks**, apart from the big hotels, are (moving east from the zócalo): **Parque Papagayo**, the roundabout with the **Diana Glorieta statue** and the **CiCi Waterpark**.

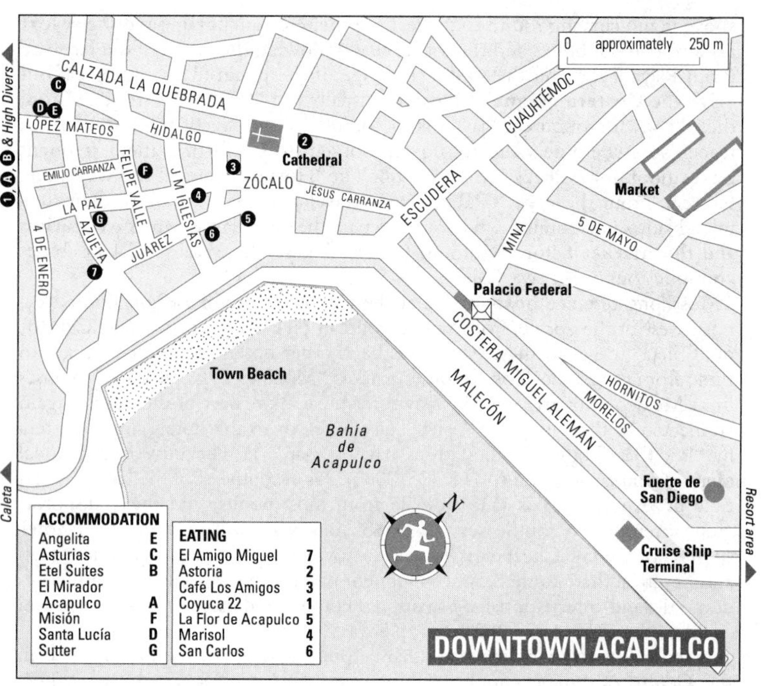




bus ride from the centre, are rather older than those along Costera, mostly patronized by Mexican families, and often booked up in advance. Still further out there's **Pie de la Cuesta**, a quiet alternative 15km north of Acapulco. This is the only place with official year-round **camping**, at *Acapulco Trailer Park* (T744/460-0010; ❹).

Acapulco's **high season** lasts longer than most, from late November or early December through to the end of April.

## In the centre

**Angelita** Calzada La Quebrada 37 T744/483-5734. One of the cheapest options. Spartan but sizeable rooms with private bath and fan lead off a courtyard. Eccentric management keeps life interesting. ❷

**Asturias** Calzada La Quebrada 45 T744/483-6548, Egerardomancera@aol.com. A welcoming budget option with clean, passable rooms around a courtyard. It is fractionally more expensive than the competition by virtue of its small pool. ❸

**Etel Suites** La Pinzona 92 T744/482-2241. This very hospitable, family-run hotel is extremely clean and well equipped, with 1950s-style three-bed rooms with kitchens, balconies and a/c nestled in lovely gardens overlooking La Quebrada. A good option for groups and long-stay guests. ❼

**El Mirador Acapulco** Plazoleta La Quebrada 74 T744/483-1155 or 01-800/021-7557. The location of this decent mid- to upper-range option – right above La Quebrada – couldn't be better. Lodging is in clean, characterless, Alpine-style rooms with kitchenettes. There are three pools and a bar/restaurant on site, from which you won't have to pay the M$140 charge to see the divers plummet. ❼

**Misión** Felipe Valle 12 T744/482-3643. The oldest hotel in town has clearly seen use, but still exudes colonial charm and is the best-value hotel in the centre. Formerly the American consulate and a Wells Fargo office, the house has attractive rooms with mosaic tiles and wooden furnishings spread out around a mango-shaded patio. Continental or Mexican breakfasts are included, and there is a book swap. ❺

**Santa Lucía** López Mateos 33 ☎744/482-0441. Basic rooms with fans and closet-size private bathrooms are cheap and unmemorable but inoffensive. ❷

**Sutter** Azueta 10 ☎744/482-0209. Although more spacious than others of a similar price, the rooms are rather plain; the ones in the back are quieter. ❹

## Along Costera

Due to the confusing nature of Costera's numbering system (see box, p.579), the following hotels are listed in order of their distance along Costera from the zócalo.

**Del Valle** Manuel Gómez 150, opposite the eastern entrance to Parque Papagayo ☎744/485-8336. *Del Valle* has a convenient location, spacious, well-maintained rooms (some with a/c), a pool and private kitchens (outside the rooms) that can be rented for M$100 a day. ❺

**Embassy** Costera 50, opposite CiCi Waterpark ☎744/481-0881. Best value in this part of town, with a small pool and a/c rooms. Some have seen better days, so look at a couple before deciding. Convenient for the nightclubs. ❻

**Elcano** Costera 75 ☎744/435-1500, Ⓦwww.hotel-elcano.com. There is a fresh feel to this renovated 1950s monolith with an all-pervasive nautical theme: spic-and-span rooms are decorated in blue and white and have a/c, TV, comfortable beds and well-proportioned bathrooms. The best rooms have terraces overlooking the ocean. Facilities include a beachside pool, Jacuzzi, gym and two bars. ❽

**Las Hamacas** Costera 239, 1km east of the zócalo ☎744/483-7709, Ⓦwww.hamacas.com.mx. Not showing its age as much as its peers, *Las Hamacas* is the closest it gets to international standard within easy reach of the centre – the only downside is that the beach here is dirty and very crowded. Bright and clean rooms are comfortable and well appointed with cable TV, a/c and spacious bathrooms. There is a swimming pool, a beachside restaurant and a gym. ❾

**Hostal Juvenil K3** Costera 116, opposite the *Fiesta Americana* hotel ☎744/481-3111, Ⓦwww.k3acapulco.com. The well-positioned hostel is a clean, friendly place with small, a/c four-bed dorms (M$195 per person), lockers, a kitchen and snack bar.

**Pacific Paradise** Punta Bruja 1, near Playa Condesa ☎744/481-1413. Mediterranean-style resort with spotless, attractive rooms on three floors. Situated a few blocks back from Costera, so nights are quieter and it's better value than many of the beachside establishments. ❻

**Suites Selene** Cristóbal Colón 175, next to CiCi Waterpark ☎744/484-2977. This snug, sociable hotel with pleasant, kitchen-equipped suites with a/c and cable TV for up to four people is recommended for families and groups. There is also a small pool and private parking, and the owners are friendly. ❺

## Caleta and Caletilla

**Boca Chica** on the point at the western end of Caletilla ☎744/483-6601. Beautifully sited resort hotel carved into the cliff face at the end of Playa Caletilla – which guests have virtually private use of – with a swimming pool and some great views (surcharges apply) of either Isla La Roqueta or the beach. ❼

**Hotel Los Flamingos** López Mateos ☎744/482-0690. A pure Acapulco retro classic, this landmark 1930s hotel was once owned by a Hollywood gang that included Tarzan (Johnny Weissmuller), Cary Grant and John Wayne. The "coco loco" cocktail was said to have been invented here, and the lush gardens and sublime sunset views from Acapulco's highest cliffs are a perfect accompaniment. The rooms have seen better days but are still spacious, characterful and comfortable. ❼

**Nao** east end of Caleta ☎744/483-8710. Faded but acceptable hotel with a pool; usually full of Mexican families. Fan-cooled rooms with shower, some much better than others. ❺

**Playa Linda** Costera 1, as you reach Caleta ☎744/482-0814. Renovated hotel with nicely decorated rooms, some with sea-view balconies. All rooms (sleeping up to four) have a/c, TV and fully equipped kitchenettes. ❻

## Pie de la Cuesta

All hotels are right by the beach and reduce their prices dramatically out of season.

**Bungalows María Cristina** ⓣ744/460-0262. Good-value suites with fully equipped kitchens and balconies for up to five people; the rooms are fine, too. ❺

**Hacienda Vayma** Base Aereo Militar 378 ⓣ744/460-2882, ⓦwww.vayma.com.mx. A low-key, arty place to hang out with hip Mexicans from the capital and *laissez-faire* Europeans. Modern bungalows with spatially challenged bathrooms (cold water) are functional, but the main attractions here are the setting, relaxed vibe and fantastic restaurant. The suites have more creature comforts: a/c, terrace and hot water. ❻

**Ukae Kim** Fuerza Aerea 536 ⓣ744/460-2187. The epitome of rustic chic, this intimate beachside enclave has colourful, breezy rooms with private bath and mosquito nets – some have a/c. There is a restaurant that serves great fresh fish, a pool and guaranteed relaxation. ❺

**Villa Nirvana** Fuerza Aerea 302 ⓣ744/460-1631, ⓦwww.lavillanirvana.com. Delightful retreat with immaculate, spacious rooms with tiled floors painted in soothing pastels and nicely furnished with local crafts, set around an attractive garden and great pool. Rooms with kitchen facilities and a little beach cottage also available. ❺

△ Cliff diver, Acapulco

## The Town

No one comes to Acapulco for the sights. By day, if people aren't at the beach, drinking cocktails with umbrellas or asleep, they're mostly scouring the expensive shops. If you only do one thing in Acapulco, though, make sure you see its most celebrated spectacle, the leap of the daredevil **high divers** (see box, p.584).

About the only place in Acapulco that gives even the slightest sense of the historic role the city played in Mexico's past is the **Museo de Acapulco** in the old town (Tues–Sun 9.30am–6pm; M$35, free on Sun). It's situated inside the **Fuerte de San Diego**, an impressive, if heavily restored, star-shaped fort built in 1616 to protect the Manila galleons from foreign corsairs but severely damaged by an earthquake in the eighteenth century. The building's limited success in defending the city against pirate attacks is charted inside the museum, where displays also extend to the spread of Christianity by proselytizing religious orders, Mexico's struggle for independence from Spain and a small anthropological collection. Air-conditioned rooms make this a good place to ride out the midday heat, and you can pop up on the roof for superb views over Acapulco. The only other cultural diversion in the centre is on Cerro de la Pinzona, near La Quebrada, where a mural by famous Mexican artist **Diego Rivera** covers the entire outside wall of the house of his former model and partner, Dolores Olmedo. The work, made of seashells and coloured tiles, depicts various figures from Aztec mythology, although the hammer and sickle in the original (Rivera was a communist) was removed on government orders.

At Costera 4834, the **Casa de La Cultura** (8am–9pm; free; ⓣ744/484-4004) has a small archeological museum, an art gallery and a crafts store, and regularly hosts a programme of cultural events with a regional bias.

## The beaches

To get to the best of the sands **around Acapulco Bay** from the centre of town, you're going to have to get on a bus; there is a tiny beach right in front of the town, but it's not in the least inviting, with grey sand made greyer by pollutants from the boats moored all around it.

### Caleta, Caletilla and La Roqueta

**Playas Caleta** and **Caletilla** (any "Caleta" bus from Costera) have a quite different atmosphere from those in the main part of the bay. Very small – the two are divided only by a rocky outcrop and breakwater – they tend to be crowded, but the water is almost always calm and the beach is reasonably clean. You can sit at shaded tables on the sand, surrounded by Mexican matrons whose kids are paddling in the shallows, and be brought drinks from the cafés behind; not particularly cheap, but considerably less than the same service would cost at the other end of the bay. There are showers here, too, and, on the rock, the **Mágico Mundo Marina** (daily 9am–6pm; M$33), a waterpark with a predictable aquarium and sea lion show, decent water slides and a choice of the pool or the bay to swim in.

From outside the waterpark, small boats ply the channel to the islet of **La Roqueta**, where there are more and yet cleaner beaches, a small zoo (daily 10am–4pm; M$3) and beer-drinking burros, one of the town's less compelling attractions. Catch one of the glass-bottomed boats (frequent, daily 8am–6pm) and keep your ticket for the return journey; it'll cost M$33 for a direct launch or M$55 for one that detours past the submerged statue of the Virgin of Guadalupe. Whether you are off to La Roqueta or only going to Caleta, leave early (especially at weekends) for the best of the sun and at least a chance of getting a beach chair or a patch of sand.

### Along Costera and on to Revolcadero

The main beaches, despite their various names – Hamacas, Hornos, Hornitos, Morro, Condesa and Icacos – are in effect a single sweep of sand. It's best to go some considerable distance round to **Playa Condesa** or **Playa Icacos**, in front of hotels (which make good points of reference) such as the *Hyatt Regency* and the *Casa Inn*, or opposite the Centro Acapulco, where the beach is far less crowded and considerably cleaner. It's easy enough to slip in to use the hotel showers, swimming pools and bars – there's no way they're going to spot an imposter in these thousand-bed monsters. The *Hyatt Regency*, at the very far end (T744/469-1234, Wwww.acapulco.regency.hyatt.com; 9), is the swankiest of the bunch. The beaches around here are also the place to come if you want to indulge in such frolics as being towed around the bay on the end of a parachute, water-skiing or sailing. Outfits offering all of these are dotted at regular intervals along the beach; charges are standard, though the quality of the equipment and the length of the trips can vary.

Beyond this end of the bay to the south are two other popular beaches: **Puerto Marqués** and **Revolcadero**. On the way you'll pass some of the fanciest hotels in Acapulco. *Las Brisas*, overlooking the eastern end of the bay (T744/469-6900, Wwww.brisas.com.mx; 9), is probably the most exclusive of all, its individual villas offering private swimming pools and pink jeeps to every occupant. Puerto Marqués (buses marked "Puerto Marqués") is the first of the beaches, a sheltered, deeply indented cove with restaurants and beach chairs right down to the water's edge, overlooked by two more deluxe hotels. You can continue by road to Revolcadero (though only an occasional bus comes this far) or get there by boat down a narrow inland channel. The beach, a long exposed stretch of sand, is beautiful but frequently lashed by heavy surf that makes swimming impossible.

### Pie de la Cuesta

**Pie de la Cuesta**, around 15km north of Acapulco, is more open to the vicissitudes of the ocean. It's definitely not for swimming – even if the waves weren't massive, there are said to be sharks offshore – but it's a good place, as you can

#### Acapulco's divers

Acapulco's famed **clavadistas** (cliff divers) plunge some 35m from the heights of La Quebrada into a rocky channel, timing their leap to coincide with an incoming wave. Mistimed, there's not enough water to stop them hitting the bottom, though the chief danger these experts seem to face is getting back out of the water without being dashed against the rocks. It could easily be corny, but it's undeniably impressive, especially when floodlit at night. The dive times – 12.45pm, 7.30pm, 8.30pm, 9.30pm and 10.30pm – are rigidly adhered to. A typical display involves four exponents, three taking the lower (25m) platform with two diving simultaneously, the fourth diving from the upper level after first asking for the Virgin's intervention at the clifftop shrine. The final diver carries a pair of flaming torches. From the road you can see the spectacle for nothing, but you'll get a much better view if you go down the steps to a **viewing platform** (M$28) more or less opposite the divers. Get here early for a good position. Alternatively, you can sit in the bar at *El Mirador Acapulco* hotel (M$140 cover includes two drinks) or watch from their expensive *La Perla* restaurant. To get there, simply climb the Calzada La Quebrada from the town centre, about fifteen minutes' walk from the zócalo.

imagine, to come and watch the sun sink into the Pacific or to ride horseback along the shore. The sand extends for miles up the coast, but at the Acapulco end, where the bus drops you, there are several rickety bars and some tranquil **places to stay**, away from the hubbub of the city.

Behind the beach, and only separated from the ocean by the hundred-metre-wide sandbar on which Pie de la Cuesta is built, lies the **Laguna de Coyuca**, a vast freshwater lake said to be three times the size of Acapulco Bay, which only connects with the sea after heavy rains. Fringed with palms, and rich in bird and animal life, the lagoon is big enough to accommodate both the ubiquitous noisy jet skiers and the more sedate **boat trips** that visit the three lagoon islands. Various outfits along the hotel strip offer tours – prices hover around M$85 per person – but it's worth checking what's on offer and how long the cruise is, as times tend to differ. Most boats stop on one island for lunch (not included in the price) and swimming. The bus ("Pie de la Cuesta") runs east every ten minutes or so past the zócalo along Costera. The last bus back leaves around 8pm.

## Activities

Acapulco Bay has a multitude of water-sport activities on offer. East along the bay from Playa Hornitos to Playa Icacos, kiosks offer everything from banana boats to jet skis, snorkelling to parasailing. The more professional outfit Fish-R-Us, Costera 100 (Ⓣ744/482-8282, Ⓦwww.fish-r-us.com) runs **sea-fishing** and **scuba-diving** tours as well as cruises around the bay. Night-time excursions (typical catch are sailfish, dorado and red snapper) are particularly appealing, illuminated by the lights of the town shining out from all around the coast. After dark, too, most of the boats lay on some kind of entertainment as they cruise. Prices vary with the length of the trip and what's on offer, but M$100–200 for a couple of hours with a free bar is typical at night, M$90–120 with no free bar during the day. Going east along Costera, at Playa Icacos, the **CiCi Waterpark** (daily 10am–6pm; M$100; Ⓣ744/484-1970, Ⓦwww.cici.com.mx) where you can splash around in swimming pools and on water slides and watch or swim with performing dolphins, makes for a welcome break from the beach. A more recent addition is the Sky Coaster, which provides a vertigo-inducing simulation of the La Quebrada cliff-diving experience. The other amusement park along Costera, the fifty-acre **Parque Papagayo**, at Playa Hornos (daily 7am–9pm; free), attracts picnicking families and joggers with its green spaces, aviary, roller-skating rink, boating lake and fairground rides. Acapulco also boasts around fifty public **tennis** courts and four eighteen-hole **golf** courses.

## Eating and drinking

Though it may not seem possible, there are even more **restaurants** than hotels in Acapulco. To eat cheaply, though, you're confined to the area around the **zócalo** where no-frills joints serve unmemorable but filling comidas corridas. Places actually on the square tend to be quite expensive, but if you can bear the ubiquitous blaring TVs, oppressive heat and lackadaisical service they are great spots to people-watch over breakfast.

Eating by the **beach** – where there's some kind of restaurant at every turn – is of course very much more expensive, and increasingly so as you head east, although the food is decent enough. Throughout the tourist zone, especially along Costera, *100% Natural*, a chain of 24-hour "healthy" eating places, serves good salads, fruit shakes, burgers and the like at grossly inflated prices, and also offers home delivery (Ⓣ744/486-2033). Alternatively, you can choose from *McDonald's*, *KFC*, the *Hard Rock Café* and several raucous Mexican bar/restaurant chains such as *Carlos 'n*

*Charlie's* and *Señor Frog's*. Heading towards Acapulco Diamante, Costera has world-class restaurants where delectable food, flawless service and goose-bump, inducing views are likely to be the highlight of your stay. Prices are, of course, on a par with upscale New York and London, but well worth the splurge.

One thing to keep an eye out for is **pozole**, a hearty pork and vegetable stew traditionally served on Thursdays and Saturdays, but available every day.

### In the centre

**El Amigo Miguel** Juárez 31 ☎744/483-6981. Two locations at the junction of Juárez and Azueta, both serving good soups, *antojitos* and seafood – sea bass, garlic shrimp and broiled Pacific lobster – at reasonable prices in clean, if institutional, surroundings.

**Astoria** inland end of the zócalo next to the cathedral ☎744/483-2944. Tucked just off the plaza under the shade of a huge tree, this is a cheap, quiet café with tables that spill out onto the pavement. The (mostly fried) dishes are predictable but satisfying – it's a good bet for a quick coffee and a giant torta.

**Café Los Amigos** La Paz 10 ☎744/482-2390. Popular shady spot just off the zócalo. Excellent breakfasts and tortas served all day, plus daily specials of spaghetti, pork chops and the like. Hawkers are actively discouraged, so it's relatively peaceful.

**Coyuca 22** Coyuca 22 ☎744/483-5030. The most chi-chi, and expensive, place to dine close to the centre, with delectable gourmet cuisine served in an unlikely, but highly atmospheric Greek theatre setting with stunning sunset views. Prime rib, veal scallopini and New Zealand lamb are the house specialities. Closed May–Oct. Reservations recommended.

**La Flor de Acapulco** on the zócalo ☎744/421-7649. With a balcony overlooking the square, this is not the cheapest option, but is a pleasant spot to linger over hearty staples including chicken *mole*, fish *pastor*, *pozole* (on a Thurs) or pork tacos. It's a popular meeting place for solo travellers.

**Marisol** one block from the zócalo on La Paz ☎744/483-1475. Offers a variety of tasty Mexican dishes, including plenty of breakfast menus, at bargain prices – understandably drawing the crowds.

**San Carlos** Juárez 5, one block from the zócalo ☎744/482-6459. Another no-frills budget restaurant in the centre, with the added allure of a breezy patio, serving good *pozole* and comidas corridas all day for M$30.

### Along Costera and beyond

**Baikal** Carretera Escénica 16 ☎744/446-6867. The best restaurant in the city, with seductive views of the bay from floor-to-ceiling windows in the classically stylish dining room. The small menu is a fusion of everything from traditional Mexican to French and Asian. Escargots sit atop jumbo seared scallops, and lobster tail is bathed in a creamy white-wine sauce and surrounded by fluffy peaks of mashed potato. Average mains are around M$250. Reservations essential (request window seating).

**CasaNova** Carretera Escénica, just south of *Las Brisas* hotel ☎744/446-6237. This is one of Acapulco's most highly regarded restaurants, as much for its spectacular location nestled in a hillside overlooking the bay as for its fine northern Italian cuisine. The menu features succulent veal chops, spaghetti with seafood and a selection of Mediterranean-prepared fish dishes.

**Madeiras** Carretera Escénica 33 ☎744/446-5636. An Acapulco institution, with a variety of set menus to choose from featuring Mexican traditional fare, simple and tasty seafood and fish dishes, and nouvelle Mexican creations. The views from the understated, but elegant, dining room are wonderful.

**El Ovido** just west of Diana Glorieta ☎744/481-0203. Upscale nouvelle cuisine, combining traditional Mexican flavours with French and Italian dishes. Good *crema quemada* (Mexican-style *crème brûlée*) and dreamy views of the bay from the dual-level, open-air dining room.

**Terra Luna** west of CiCi Waterpark, opposite the *Hard Rock Café* ☎744/484-2464. Excellent crepes as well as French/Italian dishes and imaginative salads.

## Nightlife and entertainment

If you are so inclined, and perhaps more importantly, if you are extremely rich, you could spend several weeks in Acapulco doing nothing more than trawling its scores of nightclubs and bars, discos and dinner-dances. There are people who claim never to have seen the town during daylight hours. Anywhere with music or dancing will demand a hefty **cover charge** – usually not less than M$350 in high season, though often with a free bar – before they even consider letting you in. You can reduce prices by haggling, especially on week nights and in the off-season when business is slow (this is particularly effective for larger groups), and by using the discount coupons distributed freely on the beach and along Costera. On "ladies' nights" women get a special discount.

The majority of the clubs and discos are out along **Costera** in the hotel district, beyond CiCi Waterpark. They move in and out of fashion with bewildering rapidity; look for queues outside to see what's flavour of the month. If you're not easily intimidated, you could also try some of the **downtown bars and cantinas**: you'll find a couple that aren't too heavy around the bottom of Azueta – *La Sirena*, for example – but these aren't recommended for women on their own.

There are a number of **cinemas** along Costera showing exclusively American films, in English with Spanish subtitles. More traditional entertainment can be found at the Fiesta Mexicana in the Centro Acapulco, which features two weekly performances by a troupe of the **Ballet Folklórico**. Although the admission is a bit steep, and the waiters persistent, the large-scale show – around sixty singers/dancers/musicians plus full regalia – is undeniably impressive.

**Alebrije** Costera 3308. Opposite the *Hyatt Regency*, this cavernous, rather tacky, dance hall with light shows is popular with 20-something Mexicans post-1am and couples earlier in the evening. The music runs the gamut of mainstream pop and rock and Latin tropicana.

**Baby'O** Costera, east of CiCi Waterpark. Set in an imitation cave, this is one of the more consistently popular clubs and as well as one of the most expensive (minimum cover M$800). The well-dressed, well-heeled crowd is usually high on attitude if they have managed to get in – *Baby'O* tries to maintain a spurious exclusivity by turning people away at the door. All in all a mainstream affair, with cheesy 80s music mixed with house and Latin.

**Carlos 'n Charlie's** Costera, west of the Diana Glorieta. Very popular chain bar-restaurant where you can start the evening with a bite to eat (ribs a speciality), a few drinks and a shuffle on the small, invariably crowded dancefloor before moving on to a nightclub.

**Disco Beach** Costera, Playa Condesa. A notorious hook-up beach party with all the requisite gimmicks and contests. The more casual dress code – shorts and flip-flops – draws a young, fun crowd. Wed is "ladies night".

**Enigma** Carretera Escénica, north of *Las Brisas* hotel. High-tech club complete with two waterfalls, 10m-tall statues and large windows overlooking the bay. Exclusive and luxurious, though the club's claim that "you will never have to light your own cigarette" overdoes it.

**Palladium** Carretera Escénica. It's all about the glorious bay view at this justifiably hyped club with the best music selection – techno, house and hip-hop – in the city. A slightly older and dressier, but less pretentious, crowd adds to the friendly, gregarious atmosphere. Considered the best disco in the city, and long queues testify to its kudos.

**Relax** Lomas del Mar 4, opposite *El Presidente* hotel. While not as gay-friendly as Puerto Vallarta (see p.543), Acapulco does have some gay bars and discos: this is one of the more reliable – small and a little claustrophobic, but featuring strippers and other live shows.

**Salon Q** Costera, west of CiCi Waterpark. Live Latin music that draws hard-core salsa and merengue aficionados, who come to dance all night. The reasonable cover charge (M$100; no free bar) and a slightly older clientele give it an accessible vibe.

**Tropicana Copacabana** Costera, Playa Hornos. One of a series of similar bar/restaurants that tend to play *cumbia*, merengue and salsa as much as American rock. Diners take to the dancefloor later in the evening.

## Listings

**Airlines** America West ☎744/466-9257; American ☎744/481-0161; Aviacsa ☎744/481-3240; Azteca ☎744/466-9029; Continental ☎744/466-9063; Mexicana ☎744/486-7585 or 466-9121.

**American Express** Costera, just east of Diana Glorieta ☎744/469-1100 (Mon–Fri 9am–6pm, Sat 9am–1pm). Will hold mail and exchange money.

**Banks and exchange** Banks (particularly Banamex) and casas de cambio (slightly poorer rates) are numerous along Costera. In the centre, there's a Bancomer and Santander Serfin on the zócalo and a Bital at Jesús Carranza 7.
**Buses** The first-class Estrella de Oro terminal at the corner of Cuauhtémoc and Wilfrido Massieu (city buses marked "C Río" from opposite the zócalo) handles hourly buses to Mexico City (5hr). The much larger Central de Autobuses (aka Estrella Blanca or Ejido; ☎744/469-2028; city buses marked "Ejido" or "Mocimba") handles the unified services of several companies (Elite, Turistar and Futura); don't be surprised if you find yourself on a bus that doesn't match the company named on your ticket. Buses to Mexico City leave continually day and night in five classes: the expensive *ejecutiva* has more spacious seating and free drinks, but *futuro* and *primera* are the ones to go for as they are as comfortable as *ejecutiva* – with a/c, reclining seat, TV and restroom – but almost half the price. Second-class, avoiding the autopista, is very slow, crowded and usually with no a/c. You can also get to Chilpancingo and Taxco, while first- and second-class buses run to Zihuatanejo, many of them continuing on to Lázaro Cárdenas.
**Car rental** Alamo ☎744/484-3305; Avis ☎744/466-9190; Budget ☎744/481-2433; Hertz ☎744/485-8947.
**Consulates** Canada, Centro Comercial Marbella, Diana Glorieta ☎744/484-1305; UK, Centro Acapulco ☎744/484-1735; US, next to *Hotel Continental Plaza*, Diana Glorieta ☎744/484-0300.
**Emergencies** Cruz Roja ☎744/485-4100; Emergency IMSS Hospital ☎744/445-5353; Police ☎744/486-8220; Tourist Police ☎744/434-0155; Tourist complaints ☎744/484-4416.
**Internet access** Ikernet, upstairs at Carranza 14, just off the zócalo (8.30am–12.30am; M$15/hr. There are a few Internet facilities along Costera, one of the best being on the first floor of La Gran Plaza shopping mall (M$10/hr; allows you to save your remaining time for another session).
**Laundry** Lavandería Coral, Juárez, at Felipe Valle (Mon–Fri 9am–2pm & 4–7pm, Sat 9am–5pm; M$12/kilo).
**Pharmacy** Plenty of 24hr places in the hotel zone along Costera; plus Botica de Acapulco, Carranza 3, just off the zócalo.
**Post office** At Costera 215, three blocks east of the zócalo (Mon–Fri 8am–5.30pm, Sat 9am–1pm).
**Telephones** Long-distance and collect calls can be made from Caseta Alameda (Mon–Sat 9am–8pm), west of the zócalo, on La Paz, next to *Café Los Amigos*.
**Travel agents** About the nearest to the zócalo is Las Hamacas (☎744/482-4892), at the hotel of the same name. A number of other agents are interspersed between the hotels along Costera.

# Chilpancingo

Nestled in a bowl in the Sierra Madre Occidental, 130km north of Acapulco, restful **CHILPANCINGO**, Guerrero's modest state capital, makes a cool stop-off – it's higher than 1000m – on the trip inland to the capital. Well off the tourist circuit and lent a youthful tenor by the large student population, it has a traffic-free zócalo, which is a good place to sense the town's vibe.

The modern **Ayuntamiento** and **Palacio de Gobierno** combine a harmonious blend of Neoclassical and colonial influences. The latter is adorned with a huge bronze sculpture, *El Hombre Hacia el Futuro*; there's more monumental metalwork, along with busts of famous Guerrerans, in the Alameda, three blocks east along Juárez.

Directly opposite its replacement, the former Palacio de Gobierno houses frequently changing exhibitions in the **Instituto Guerrerense de Cultura** and the excellent little **Museo Regional de Guerrero** (both Tues–Sun 10am–6pm; free). Well-laid-out displays – some labelled in English – record the history of the state's native peoples from their migration from Asia across the Bering land bridge thirty thousand years ago to the Maya and Teotihuacán influences on their pottery and stelae. With the coming of the Spaniards, the region benefited from the Manila galleons that put into Acapulco and from Chilpancingo's location on the *Camino de China* from the coast to Mexico City. But the city's most dramatic chapter – vividly depicted on murals around the internal courtyard – came with the Independence struggle. After Hidalgo's defeat in the central highlands it was left to the southern populist movement, fuelled by the spread of land-grabbing haciendas and led by the skilled tactician **José María Morelos**, to continue the campaign. With almost the whole country behind them, they forced the Spanish – who still held Mexico City – to attend the Congress of Chilpancingo in 1813, where the Declaration of Independence was issued and the principles of the constitution – chiefly the abolition of slavery and the equality of the races – were worked out. Ultimately the congress failed, and within two years the Spanish had retaken Guerrero and executed Morelos.

### Practicalities

**Buses** from Mexico City (3hr) and Acapulco (7hr) arrive at either the Estrella Blanca or Estrella de Oro terminals, opposite each other, 2km east of the zócalo on 21 de Marzo – turn right and then right again along Juárez. Minibuses run into town along Juárez and back out along the parallel Guerrero. Madero crosses these two streets just before the zócalo, and it's around here that you'll find all the essential services.

If you want to **stay** overnight, you'll be perfectly comfortable at the *Del Parque*, at Colon 5 (☎747/472-1285; ④), which has well-equipped, spacious, brightly decorated rooms and bathrooms, and a very good café/restaurant. *Hotel Paradis*, on Guerrero at 21 de Marzo, right next to the Estrella de Oro terminal (☎747/471-1122; ⑤), has clean, modern rooms and tiled floors and bathrooms. Near the zócalo, the more economical options include the colonial *Hotel Cardeña*, Madero 13 (no phone; ②), with plain, en-suite rooms and cheaper bathless ones around a courtyard.

You can **eat** light snacks or cake with an espresso at *El Portal*, beside the cathedral on Madero, or find more substantial meals at *Martita*, Guerrero 6-B, and *La Parroquia*, with shaded outdoor tables off the north side of the zócalo. The café in the Casino del Estudiantes, on Guerrero near Madero, serves good-value comidas corridas, and is the best place to ask if there is anything happening in the way of **nightlife**.

## South of Acapulco: the Costa Chica

It's hardly surprising that most tourists head straight through the stretch of Hwy-200 south of Acapulco: there's little in the way of facilities between here and Puerto Escondido – a good seven hours on the bus. However, if you have your own transport – a frustrating experience due to the illogical number of *topes* (speedbumps) – it's worth taking some time out to explore this occasionally bizarre coastline, not least for the few great **beaches**.

The people who inhabit the area towards the border of Oaxaca are for the most part either indigenous Amuzgo or black – the latter descendants of African Bantu slaves who escaped and settled here. In fact, the look of the land is vaguely reminiscent of parts of Africa – flat grazing country, many of whose villages consist of thatched huts. In **Coajinicuilapa**, the impression is reinforced by the predominance of round constructions, though these are in fact as much a local *indígena* tradition as an African one. Many African cultural traditions from food to dance to medicinal remedies are also preserved. From here a road runs some 20km down to the coast at **Punta Maldonada**, which, along with nearby San Nicolás, has some beautiful beaches but virtually no facilities, and only one

## Fiestas

### January

**New Year's Day** (Jan 1). Celebrated everywhere. In Cruz Grande, on the coast road about 120km east of Acapulco, the start of a week-long *feria*.

**Día del Senor de la Expiracíon** (second Tues in Jan). Marked in Pueblo de Coquimatlán, near Colima by a mass pilgrimage to a nearby hacienda.

### February

**Día de la Candelaria** (Feb 2). Celebrated in Colima (see p.564) and Tecomán with dances, processions and fireworks. Similar events in Zumpango del Río, on the road from Acapulco to Mexico City, and particularly good dancing in Atzacualoya, off the same road near Chilpancingo.

**Fiesta Brava** (Feb 5). A day of bullfights and horse races in Colima (see p.564).

**Carnaval** (the week before Lent; variable Feb–March). Acapulco (see p.577) and Manzanillo (see p.559) are both famous for the exuberance of their celebrations; rooms can be hard to find.

### March

**Fiesta de San Patricio** (March 10). Exuberant celebrations in San Patricio-Melaque (see p.558) continue for a week.

**Día de San José** (March 19). The excuse for fiestas in Tierra Colorada, between Acapulco and Chilpancingo, and San Jerónimo, just outside Acapulco.

**Semana Santa** (Holy Week). Widely observed: the Palm Sunday celebrations in Petatlán, just south of Zihuatanejo, are particularly fervent.

### May

**Día de la Santa Cruz** (May 3). Name-day festival in Cruz Grande.

**Cinco de Mayo** (May 5). Celebrations in commemoration of the victorious battle of Cinco de Mayo, especially in Acapulco (see p.577).

**Festival de las Lluvias** (May 8). Celebrated in Mochitlán, near Chilpancingo, the festival has pre-Christian roots: pilgrims, peasants and local dance groups climb a nearby volcano at night, arriving at the summit at dawn to pray for rain. Also a local fiesta in Azoyu, just off the coast road south of Acapulco. Manzanillo (see p.559) celebrates its **Founder's Day**.

or two buses a day. These places are famed, above all, for glass-clear water and are perfect for skin diving and snorkelling – most people come down in campers to take advantage.

If you want to break your journey in rather more comfort, there are two possibilities. **Ometepec**, an old gold-mining town a few kilometres inland of the main road before it reaches Coajinicuilapa, has several small hotels. Although it's off the highway, there are hourly buses to Acapulco, so it's easy enough to get back to the junction and pick up transport heading south from there. The second option is **Pinotepa Nacional**, across the border in the state of Oaxaca, where again there are a number of basic places to stay. Pinotepa's Sunday market is one of the best in the region, a meeting place for local Amuzgo, Mixtec and Chatino Indians.

**Día de San Isidro** (May 15). A week-long festival in Acapulco (see p.577). Celebrations also in San Luis Acatlán, south along the coast, where you might see the rare Danza de la Tortuga (Dance of the Turtle), and in Tierra Colorada.

**Founder's Day** (May 31). In Puerto Vallarta (see p.543).

### June

**Día de la Marina** (Navy Day; June 1). Celebrated in the ports, particularly Puerto Vallarta (see p.543), Manzanillo (see p.559) and Acapulco (see p.577).

**Día de San Antonio** (June 13). A *feria* in Tierra Colorada.

### August

**Día de San Bartolomé** (Aug 23). In Tecpán de Galeana, between Acapulco and Zihuatanejo, religious processions the preceding night are followed by dancing, music and fireworks.

### September

**Independence Day** (Sept 15–16). Celebrated everywhere.

**Día de Santiago** (Sept 28). Celebrated in several villages immediately around Acapulco (see p.577).

**Día de San Miguel** (Sept 29). Exuberantly celebrated in Azoyu and Mochitlán.

### November

**Feria** (first week of Nov). Colima's (see p.564) major festival runs from the last days of October until November 8.

**Día de los Muertos** (Day of the Dead; Nov 2). Widely observed, with picturesque traditions in Atoyac de Alvarez, just off the Acapulco–Zihuatanejo road.

### December

**Día de la Virgen de Guadalupe** (Dec 12). In honour of the patroness of Mexico. In Atoyac de Alvarez and Ayutla, there are religious processions and traditional dances, while Acapulco (see p.577) enjoys more secular celebrations. In Manzanillo (see p.559) the celebrations start at the beginning of the month, while in Puerto Vallarta (see p.543) they continue to the end of it.

# Travel details

## Buses

Bus services all along the coast are frequent and fast, with the possible exception of the stretch between Manzanillo and Lázaro Cárdenas, and there are almost constant departures on the major routes heading inland. The southern sector – Acapulco and Zihuatanejo – is served largely by Estrella de Oro and Estrella Blanca (deluxe and first-class) and Flecha Roja (second-class). In the north there's more competition: Primera Plus, Transportes del Pacífico and Elite are the first-class stand-bys, while Servicios Coordinados and Flecha Amarilla are the most widely seen second-class outfits. The following list covers first-class services and some local second-class services. On most routes there are as many, if not more, second-class buses, which take around twenty- to thirty-percent longer travel time.

**Acapulco** to: Chilpancingo (every 30min; 2hr); Cuernavaca (4 daily; 4hr); Guadalajara (5 daily; 17hr); Lázaro Cárdenas (5 daily; 6–7hr); Manzanillo (1 daily; 12hr); Mexico City (frequently; 6hr); Puerto Escondido (10 daily; 7hr); Puerto Vallarta (5 daily; 18hr); Salina Cruz (5 daily; 12–13hr); Taxco (5 daily; 5hr); Tijuana (2 daily; 49hr); Zihuatanejo (at least hourly; 4–5hr).

**Barra de Navidad** to: Cihuatlán (frequently; 30min); Guadalajara (every 30 min; 6–7hr);

Manzanillo (every 30min; 1hr 30min); Puerto Vallarta (18 daily; 5hr).
**Chilpancingo** to: Acapulco (every 30min; 2hr); Mexico City (hourly; 3hr 30min).
**Colima** to: Comala (every 10–15min; 20min); Guadalajara (at least hourly; 3hr); Lázaro Cárdenas (4 daily; 6–7hr); Manzanillo (frequently; 1hr 30min); Mexico City (8 daily; 11hr); Puerto Vallarta (3 daily; 6hr); Tecomán (every 15min; 45min); Tijuana (2 daily; 38hr).
**Lázaro Cárdenas** to: Acapulco (at least hourly; 6–7hr); Colima (7 daily; 6–7hr); Guadalajara (7 daily; 9hr); Manzanillo (2 daily; 6hr); Mexico City (at least hourly; 11–14hr); Morelia (6 daily; 7–8hr); Pátzcuaro (1 daily; 7hr); Puerto Vallarta (4 daily; 12hr); Uruapan (6 daily; 6hr); Zihuatanejo (every 30min; 2hr).
**Manzanillo** to: Acapulco (3 daily; 12hr); Barra de Navidad (frequently; 1hr 30min); Colima (frequently; 1hr 30min); Guadalajara (frequently; 5–6hr); Lázaro Cárdenas (7 daily; 6hr); Mexico City (4 daily; 12hr); Puerto Vallarta (at least hourly; 5–7hr); Tijuana (2 daily; 38hr).
**Puerto Vallarta** to: Acapulco (2 daily; 18hr); Barra de Navidad (9 daily; 3hr 30min); Colima (2 daily; 6hr); Guadalajara (at least every 30min; 6hr); Lázaro Cárdenas (3 daily; 12hr); Manzanillo (6 daily; 5–7hr); Mazatlán (7 daily; 8hr); Mexico City (8 daily; 14hr); Tepic (frequently; 2hr 30min).
**Zihuatanejo** to: Acapulco (hourly; 4hr); Ixtapa (continuously; 15min); Lázaro Cárdenas (hourly; 2hr); Manzanillo (3 daily; 7–8hr); Mexico City (frequently; 9hr); Morelia (6 daily; 8hr); Puerto Vallarta (2 daily; 12–13hr); Salina Cruz (2 daily; 17–18hr); Tijuana (2 daily; 40hr).

## Flights

This section of Mexico's coast is well served by flights, with services to Acapulco, Puerto Vallarta and Zihuatanejo and domestic flights to various points in between. Guadalajara and Mexico City are accessible from Manzanillo, Ixtapa/Zihuatanejo and Acapulco; Acapulco also has flights to US cities including Los Angeles, New York, Chicago, Phoenix, Dallas and Houston.
**Puerto Vallarta** is one of the busiest air hubs in Mexico, with flights to: Acapulco (3 daily); Amsterdam (1 weekly); Calgary (1 weekly); Chicago (5 weekly); Dallas (daily); Denver (4 weekly); Fairbanks (daily); Guadalajara (5–7 daily); Houston (1–3 daily); León (6 weekly); London (3 weekly); Los Angeles (2–4 daily); Los Cabos (5 weekly); Mexico City (7–11 daily); Monterrey (3–5 daily); Montreal (2 weekly); Newark (1 weekly); Oakland (6 weekly); Phoenix (2–3 daily); Portland (7 weekly); San Francisco (5 daily); Seattle (3 daily); St Louis (2 weekly); Tijuana (4 weekly); Toronto (2 weekly); Vancouver (1 weekly).

# 7

# Veracruz

7 VERACRUZ

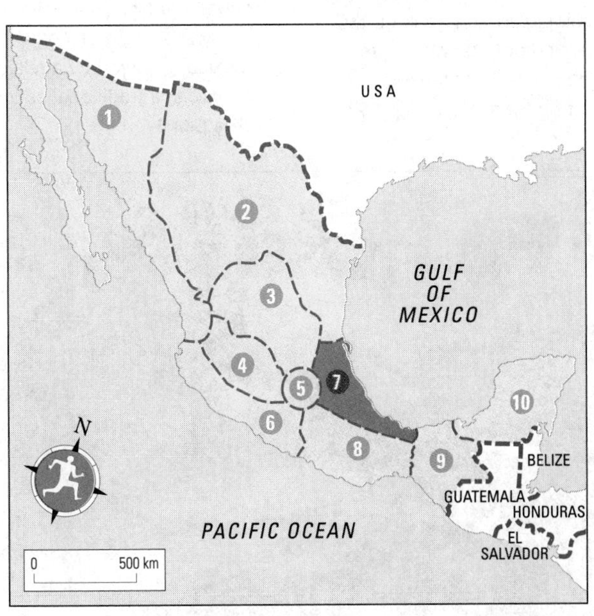

CHAPTER 7

# Highlights

* **Xalapa** Enjoy the café culture in this university town surrounded by coffee plantations. The Museum of Anthropology here is second only to Mexico City's. See p.600

* **Veracruz** Show your fiery side and salsa with divas wearing outrageous costumes at the city's exuberant Carnaval. Afterwards, relax with an ice-cold mint *julep* and soak up the sounds of marimba in the zócalo, one of Mexico's most vibrant plazas. See p.605

* **El Tajín** Explore the unique pyramids and ruins at this magnificent remnant of Classic Veracruz civilization. See p.619

* **Papantla** Witness the spectacular Voladores flying through the air at this centre of Totonac culture. See p.620

* **Catemaco** Take a boat trip across this enchanting lake, surrounded by one of the last remaining tracts of jungle in Mexico, followed by a relaxing *temazcal*, a traditional sauna. See p.626

△Marimba players, Veracruz zócalo

# 7

# Veracruz



The central Gulf coast is among the least-visited yet most distinct areas of Mexico. From Mexico City, you descend through the southern fringes of the Sierra Madre Oriental, past the country's highest peaks, to a broad, hot and wet coastal plain. In this fertile tropical zone the earliest Mexican civilizations developed: **Olmec** culture dominated the southern half of the state from 1200 BC, while the civilization known as **Classic Veracruz** flourished 250 to 900 AD in centres such as El Tajín. Today, **Huastec** and **Totonac** culture remains strong in the north. Cortés began his march on the Aztec capital from Veracruz, and the city remains, as it was throughout colonial history, one of the busiest ports in the country. Rich in agriculture – coffee, vanilla, tropical fruits and flowers grow everywhere – the **Gulf coast** is also endowed with large deposits of oil and natural gas.

The few tourists who find their way here are usually just passing through. In part, at least, this is because the area doesn't especially need them and makes no particular effort to attract them; the **weather** can also be blamed – it rains more often and more heavily here than just about anywhere else. Yet even in the rainy season the torrential downpours are short-lived, and within a couple of hours of the rain starting, you can be back on the streets in bright sunshine. Though there are long, windswept beaches all down the Atlantic coast, they are less beautiful than their Pacific or Caribbean counterparts, and many suffer pollution from the busy shipping lanes, the oil industry or even sewage outlets. Most of the coastal towns are commercial centres, of little interest to the visitor.

That said, the eastern slopes of the **Sierra Madre** hold a number of colonial cities worth a look at least in passing: **Xalapa**, seat of the Veracruz state government, is worth a longer visit, with its balmy climate and superb anthropology museum. **Veracruz** is one of the most welcoming of all Mexico's cities; it's too busy with its own affairs to create a separate life for visitors so you're drawn instead into the steamy tropical port's day-to-day workings. Only a couple of hours north lie **La Antigua** and **Villa Rica**, where Cortés established the first Spanish government on the American mainland, and **Cempoala**, ruined site of the first civilization he conquered. **El Tajín**, near the coast in the north of the state, is one of the most important archeological sites in the country, and **Filo Bobos**, only recently excavated, is also well worth a visit. To the south, **Catemaco** is a spell-binding lake set in an extinct volcanic crater, where you can see the last remaining tract of Gulf coast **rainforest**. The area is renowned as a meeting place for native *brujos* and *curanderos*, witches and healers.

The state also has some great **food** – not only local coffee, fruit and vanilla (Mexicans inevitably take home a plastic bottle of vanilla essence as a souvenir), but also seafood. *Huachinango a la Veracruzana* (red snapper Veracruz-style) is

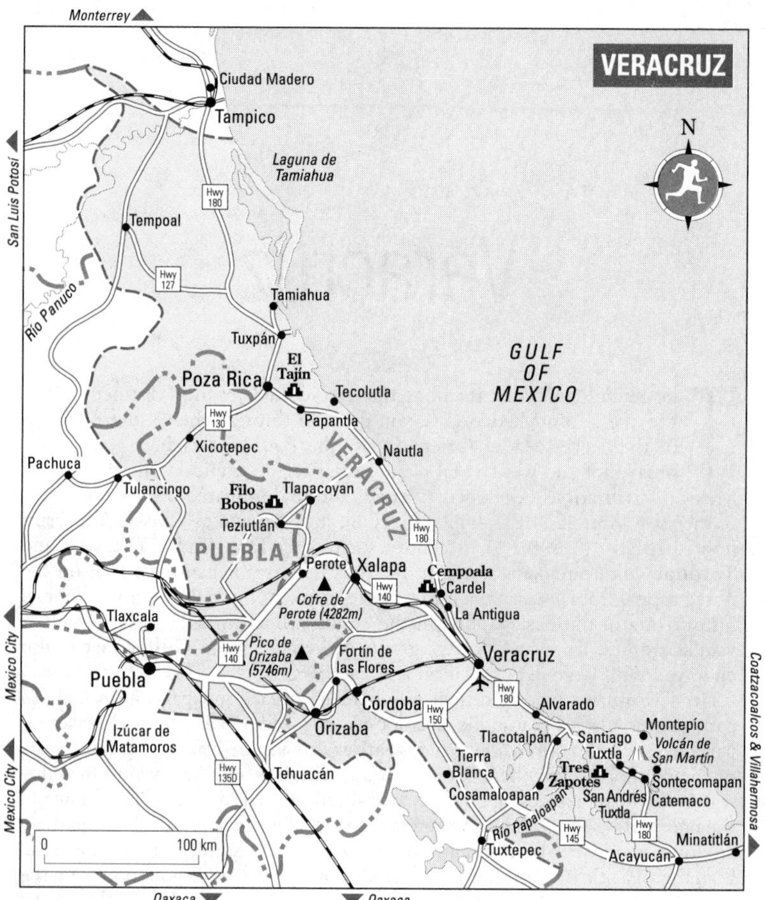


served across the country, and is of course on every menu here. But there are many more exotic possibilities, from langoustines and prawns to *jaiba*, large local crab; look out for anything made with *chile chipotle*, a hot, dark-brown chile with a very distinctive (and delicious) flavour – *chilpachole de jaiba* is a sort of crab chowder that combines the two. Sweet tamales, too, are a speciality, and to wash it all down, the local brewery at Orizaba produces several distinctive beers – less expensive and better than the big national brands.

## The route from Mexico City

If you take the direct route – the excellent Hwy-150 – from Mexico City to Veracruz, you'll bypass every major town en route; if you're driving yourself, note that the tolls along this stretch of road are extremely high (about M$400). For those pressed for time, the fast highway is a blessing –Veracruz and the coast are very much the outstanding attractions – but there are at least three cities in the mountains that merit a stop if you're in no hurry. Regardless of how fast you go or what form of transport you take, the journey is one of the most beautiful in Mexico: as Ixtaccíhuatl gradually disappears behind you, the snow on the **Pico de Orizaba** comes into view, and the plains of corn and maguey in the west are supplanted on the eastern slopes by woods of pine and cypress, and by green fields dotted with contented cows out to pasture.

It's worth noting, however, that this is the rainiest area of the country, and while the damp brings bounties in terms of great coffee and a luxuriance of flowers, downpours can become a problem. Particularly irritating – especially in October and November – is what the locals call *chipichipi*, a persistent fine drizzle caused by warm airstreams from the Gulf hitting cooler air as they reach the eastern face of the sierra.

## Orizaba

**ORIZABA**, the first major town en route, midway between Puebla and Veracruz (150km from each), is largely an uninviting industrial city. What

△ Pico de Orizaba

Orizaba lacks in charm, though, it makes up for in location, positioned at the foot of the **Pico de Orizaba** (or Citlaltépetl in Nahuatl), a perfectly formed volcano and the highest peak in Mexico, though there is a fair amount of disagreement over its exact height – a 2003 survey found it was 5636m tall.

The town is also a major brewing centre: giant Cervecería Cuauhtémoc Moctezuma produces some of the best **beer** in the republic, including globally famous brands Sol and Dos Equis – ask at the tourist office (see below) for details of tours. Even so, seeing the town need only take a couple of hours, and there are more attractive places to spend the night further down the road at Fortín and Córdoba. If, however, you plan to tackle the Pico de Orizaba – and the **climb**, detailed in R.J. Secor's *Mexican Volcanoes*, is only for serious mountaineers – you should change here for the second-class bus to the small town of Serdán (2hr). From here there are buses (1hr) to the village of **Tlachichuca**, which at 2600m is where the main trails begin. The best place to enquire for a guide is tour company Servimont (Ⓣ245/451-5009, Ⓦwww.servimont.com.mx), which runs three-day guided hikes up the mountain (Oct–May) from US$450 per person. You'll need to contact them several months in advance.

Orizaba's **tourist office** (Mon–Fri 8am–3pm & 4–8pm, Sat noon–8pm, Sun noon–4pm; Ⓣ272/728-9136), on the second floor of the ornate Palacio de Hierro, can help with further information and details of companies that arrange trekking and climbing activities in the area. The ADO **bus station** is on Oriente 6 near Sur 13, with regular onward connections to Fortín, Córdoba, Veracruz, Xalapa and Mexico City. Should you need **to stay**, *Holiday Inn*, at no. 464 on Oriente 6, near Sur 11 and the ADO bus station (Ⓣ272/724-0077; ❻), is smart and comfortable. Cheaper and further along the same street at no. 186, near Sur 5, is the colonial *Gran Hotel de France* (Ⓣ272/725-2311; ❺).

## Fortín de las Flores

**FORTÍN DE LAS FLORES**, "Fortress of the Flowers", lies on the old road to Córdoba, 15km northeast of Orizaba at a point where a beautiful minor route cuts across country to Xalapa, nearly 150km north. Its name is singularly appropriate: you'll see flowers all over the place – in the plaza, at the hotels, on the hillsides. Rain, which is frequent from May to December, and the region's constant muggy warmth ensure their growth – in particular, with the coming of the rains in May, wild orchids bloom freely. There's not a lot to do here other than enjoy the torpid atmosphere – you can fully appreciate the luxuriance of the vegetation a couple of kilometres west of town at the **Barranca del Metlac**: above the ravine flourish coffee and fruit trees, while the banks of the torrent itself are thick with a stunning variety of wild plants, which attract hummingbirds and insects of all kinds.

The town is laid out on a grid, with Avenida 1 and Calle 1 intersecting at the zócalo. This contains a small church and Palacio Municipal – buses from Córdoba drop you off here. Direct buses from Orizaba or further afield stop at the tiny ADO **bus station** on Avenida 2 at Calle 6, a short walk from the zócalo. A few blocks towards Córdoba along Avenida 2 is the stately **Hacienda de las Animas**, built in the 1880s as a coffee plantation. Behind the hacienda on Avenida 1, between calles 5 and 7, is the *Fortín de las Flores* (Ⓣ271/713-0055 or 0108; ❻). Built in 1935, this was the hotel that helped establish Fortín as a resort in the 1950s, with its pool filled with fresh gardenias every morning. The pool is still there, though minus the floral garnish, and the rooms are somewhat musty, but the flower-laden gardens make it an attractive **place to stay**. *Hotel Posada Loma*, on the eastern edge of town opposite the market on the main road to Córdoba (Ⓣ271/713-0658, Ⓔposada66@prodigy.net.mx; ⑥), has comfortable, a/c rooms around a pretty garden and includes an excellent breakfast. Cheaper accommodation is available at the *Bugambilia* (Ⓣ272/713-1350; ④), not far from the *Fortín de las Flores*, at no. 305 on Avenida 1, between calles 7 and 9, which offers motel-like rooms. Attractively situated in dense vegetation overlooking the Córdoba Valley, roughly halfway between Fortín and Córdoba, are the two bungalows of *Las Magnolias B&B* (Ⓣ272/716-4908, Ⓔfrankania@yahoo.com; ④). The owners will pick you up at either bus station. For **food**, there are several cheap cafés on the zócalo. The best place to eat breakfast is at the *Posada Loma*, where you can enjoy sweet and savoury tortillas and views of the Pico de Orizaba. There's **Internet** access at Star Internet café (9am–9pm; M$8/hr), one block behind the zócalo on Calle 3 beyond Avenida 2, and there are several **banks** around the central plaza. For **moving on**, buses depart the ADO bus station for Córdoba, Orizaba, Veracruz, Xalapa and Mexico City.

## Córdoba

Second-class buses traverse the mountain road from Fortín to Xalapa fairly regularly, but a short local bus ride covers the 7km to **CÓRDOBA**, just 129km from Veracruz and the coast. At the centre of the area's coffee trade, this is a busy modern town built around an attractive colonial centre. Founded in 1618 by thirty Spanish families – and so also known as the "City of the Thirty Knights" – its main claim to fame is that in 1821, the last Spanish viceroy, Juan O'Donoju, signed the **Treaty of Córdoba** with General Iturbide here, formally giving Mexico independence. The signing took place in the Palacio de los Condes de Zevallos, which was completed in 1687 and known as the **Portal de Zevallos**, on the northern edge of the zócalo (look for the faded sign for *Hotel Zevallos* next to the *Parroquia* café). The Portal is now filled with handicraft shops and cafés, where you can sit and sample Córdoban coffee or *julep*, a blend of various spirits and mint leaves (see p.612). Before you settle down to try one, though, check out the twin-towered **Catedral de la Inmaculada Concepción**, one of the most richly adorned religious buildings in the state – started in 1621, it contains a revered image of the Virgin Mary to the right of the altar.

### Practicalities

Central Córdoba is easy to navigate: Avenida 1 and Calle 1 intersect at the Palacio Municipal on the zócalo: avenidas run east–west, with even numbers north of the zócalo and odd numbers south. Calles run north–south, with even numbers west of the zócalo and odd numbers east. The **bus terminal** (for first- and second-class services) is 3km south of the centre at Privada 4 between calles 39 and 41, a short taxi ride to the zócalo (buy a ticket first). Alternatively, take one of the buses marked "Centro". There are frequent departures to Mexico City, Orizaba and Veracruz. Services to Fortín de las Flores leave every ten minutes from Avenida 11 and Calle 1, several blocks southwest of the zócalo, and take about fifteen minutes. The Palacio Municipal, a fine Neoclassical structure built in 1905, houses the **tourist office** (Mon–Fri 9am–7pm, Sat 9am–1pm; Ⓣ271/717-1700, Ⓦwww.mpiocordoba.gob.mx). The **post office** (Mon–Fri 8am–4pm, Sat 9am–1pm) is at the back, facing Avenida 3. For **Internet** access try *Cibermania*, in an arcade next to the *Mansur* (Mon–Sat 9am–8pm; M$10/hr).

The pricier **hotels**, such as the modern *Bello*, on Avenida 2 at Calle 5 (T271/712-8122; 6), are around the zócalo. Closest to all the action are the *Virreynal*, by the side of the cathedral on Avenida 1 at Calle 5 (T271/712-2377; 4), which also has a decent restaurant, and the quieter and marginally more expensive *Mansur*, in the same block of Avenida 1 (T271/712-6000, Wwww.hotelmansur.com.mx; 5). Here you'll find fantastic balconied rooms overlooking the cathedral in an old building full of character. There are also plenty of cheap places scattered about, especially along Avenida 2. The best of the budget hotels is the pleasant *Iberia*, a fifteen-minute walk along Avenida 2 at no. 919 (T271/712-1301; 3), with both a/c rooms and slightly cheaper ones with fan. The best **places to eat** are also around the zócalo: *El Cordobés* (T271/712-0798), opposite the cathedral, and the *Parroquia*, opposite the Palacio Municipal (breakfasts from M$40, meat dishes under M$100), have varied menus with huge comidas, as does cheaper *El Patio de la Abuela*, on Calle 1 between avenidas 2 and 4 (T271/712-0606), an ideal place for lunch (sets from M$30). There are some good seafood restaurants along Calle 15 that serve fresh fish in a variety of sauces, as well as some more unusual dishes such as black pepper casserole. For a break from Mexican food, try the sushi and other Japanese specialities at comfortable *Mikasa*, at no. 212-A on Avenida 5 (T271/712-7613), or the excellent crepes at *Los 30's* on Avenida 9 between calles 20 and 22 (T271/712-3379).

## Xalapa and around

Although it's a slower route to the coast, it's worth making a detour to **XALAPA** (or Jalapa, as some locals and bus companies occasionally spell it), 136km from Córdoba. The state capital, Xalapa is remarkably attractive despite its relative modernity and traffic-laden streets, set in countryside of sometimes breathtaking beauty. The city sprawls across a hillside below the volcanic peak of the **Cofre de Perote** (4282m), and enjoys a richness of vegetation almost the equal of Fortín's (with which it also shares a warm, damp climate). In addition to these natural advantages, Xalapa has been promoted by its civic leaders as a cultural centre, and frequent music festivals may well add to your stay. Home, too, of the **University of Veracruz** and the exceptional **Museo de Antropología**, it's a lively place, enjoyable even if you do nothing more than hang out in one of the many wonderful cafés in the centre of town, sip the locally grown coffee and watch life pass by.

### Arrival and information

Xalapa's modern **bus station**, with separate sections for first- and second-class services, is a couple of kilometres east of the centre on 20 de Noviembre. You can get to the centre by regulated taxi, booked from a booth underneath the station (follow the signs). To catch a *combi* in that direction, walk down through the shopping mall to 20 de Noviembre and look for those marked "Centro"; note that going back to the bus station, they're marked "CAXA" (Central de Autobuses de Xalapa). Xalapa's **tourist office** occupies a kiosk under the arches at the Palacio Municipal, opposite Parque Juárez (Mon–Sat 8am–2pm & 2.30am–8.30pm; T228/842-1214, Wwww.xalapa.net).

### Accommodation

There are some truly elegant hotels in Xalapa, many of which are housed in eighteenth-century haciendas loaded with historic charm.

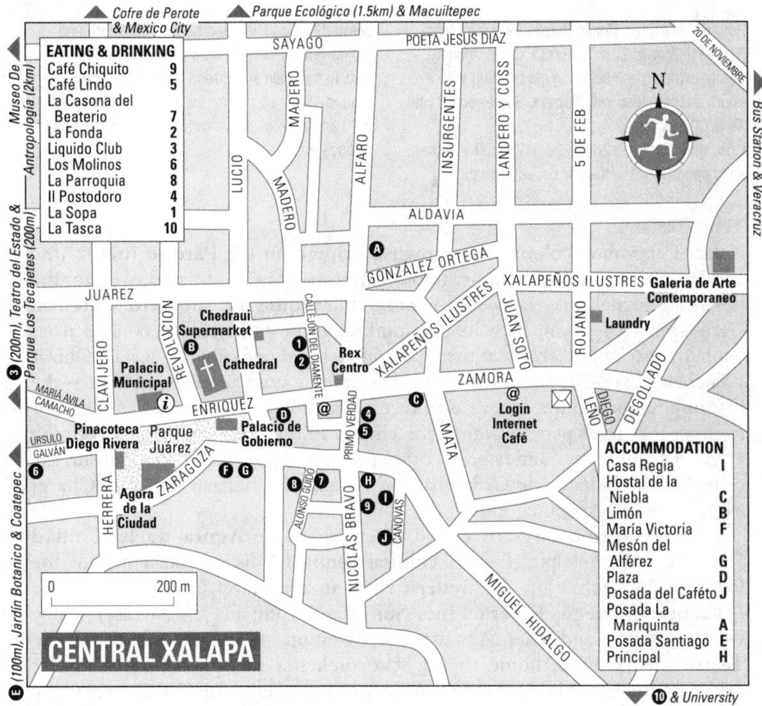


**Casa Regia** Hidalgo 12 T 228/812-0591. This brightly decorated and friendly place has peaceful, cosy rooms with TV, constant hot water and a breakfast area near the lobby. ❸

**Hostal de la Niebla** Zamora 24 T 228/817-2174, W www.delaniebla.com. Clean and friendly hostel, affiliated with YH International. There's Internet, simple breakfasts of bread and coffee (included), cable TV in the common room, hot water and large lockers. A place in a six-bed dorm costs M$115 (YHI members) or M$140 (everyone else). ISIC card holders also get a discount. Private rooms (❹) also available.

**Limón** Revolución 8 T 228/817-2204. One of the best budget options, close to the centre, with small, very clean rooms around a narrow, leafy courtyard embellished with ornate tiling. Rooms have TV and 24hr hot water, and there's a laundry. ❷

**María Victoria** Zaragoza 6 T 228/818-6011, W www.hmariavictoria.com. Comfortable, if slightly aged, rooms, each with TV and phone. Convenient, central location just east of Parque Juárez. ❻

**Mesón del Alférez** Sebastian Camacho 2 y 6, at Zaragoza T 228/818-0113, W www.pradodelrio.com. Beautiful converted colonial house, once belonging to Alférez Real de Xalapa, the last Spanish viceroy of Veracruz. Each room is unique, luxurious and charmingly decorated, and there's an excellent restaurant (*Hostería de la Candela*) with some vegetarian options. Breakfast is M$48. ❻

**Plaza** Enríquez 4 T 228/817-3310. A bit run down and basic, but clean, with TV and luggage storage. Avoid the rooms facing the street if you plan on getting any sleep. ❸

**Posada del Caféto** Canovas 8 T 228/817-0023, W www.pradodelrio.com. Rooms here are set around a pretty courtyard garden; some have balconies, all have TV and bath. The on-site café serves breakfast (included) and has books to read. ❺

**Posada La Mariquinta** Alfaro 12 T 228/818-1158, W www.lamariquinta.xalapa.net. Meticulously restored colonial hacienda with attractive, comfortable rooms equipped with cable TV and phone. There is a tranquil inner garden, a common room with a vast collection of books and an English- and French-speaking owner. More expensive extended-stay apartments are also available. Stay longer than three nights and discounts start to kick in. ❻

**Posada Santiago** Úrsulo Galván 89, 400m from Parque Juárez ☎228/818-6333. Clean, friendly, family-owned place set in an old building with a courtyard sprinkled with flowers. Some rooms with TV (M$20 extra). ③

**Principal** Zaragoza 28 ☎228/817-6400. Another solid option close to the zócalo, with clean, comfortable and light rooms with tiled bath and piping-hot showers. Rooms on the ground floor next to the main street tend to be noisy until around 10pm, so ask for those on the second or third floors, some of which are vast and have high ceilings. ④

## The Town

Xalapa's appealing colonial downtown is centred on the **Parque Juárez** (the zócalo), its trees filled with extraordinarily raucous birds at dusk. On the northeast corner, the eighteenth-century **Parroquia El Sagrario Catedral** (7am–1pm & 4–8pm), with its pale pink exterior and richly decorated nave, contains a striking Calvary at the altar and a chapel dedicated to Rafael Guízar y Valencia (1878-1938). Now St Rafael Guízar, he was canonized in 2006 – the first bishop born in the Americas to receive the honour. He is most admired for resisting the state's persecution of the church in the 1920s and 1930s, forming a "guerrilla ministry" and later becoming the Bishop of Veracruz. Opposite the cathedral, the **Palacio de Gobierno**, with murals by Chilean artist José Chaves Morado, deserves a quick look.

Xalapa's contemporary arts crowd meets up at the **Agorá de la Ciudad** (Tues–Sun 10am–10pm; free), a cultural centre in the southern half of the Parque Juárez, while on the western edge, at street level facing Herrera, the **Pinacoteca Diego Rivera** (Tues–Sun 10am–7pm; free), showcases a few works by Rivera and other Mexican artists. West on María Ávila Camacho is the **Teatro del Estado**, home to the state orchestra (see p.604). In the other direction, the **Galería de Arte Contemporáneo**, on Xalapeños Ilustres (daily 10am–6pm; free), also hosts temporary art exhibitions.

The city's outstanding sight, however, is the **Museo de Antropología** (Tues–Sun 9am–5pm; M$40), located 4km from the zócalo on the outskirts of town – take a bus marked "Museo" from Camacho, on the northwest corner of the Parque Juárez, or a taxi. Regarded by many as the second-best archeological museum in the country (only after the one in Mexico City), the collection is excellent in both scope and quality, and makes for a wonderful introduction to the various pre-Hispanic cultures of the Gulf coast. The building itself is also lovely, flowing down the hillside in a series of marble steps. Start your visit at the top of the hill, where the first halls deal with the **Olmecs**. There are several of the celebrated colossal stone heads, a vast array of other statuary and some beautiful masks. Later cultures are represented mainly through their pottery – lifelike human and animal figurines especially – and there are also displays on the architecture of the major sites: El Tajín, Cempoala and so on. Finally, with the **Huastec** culture come more giant stone statues. Some larger, less valuable pieces are displayed in landscaped gardens outside. Labels are in Spanish only, though there are a few English information sheets. There's a **café** on the first floor, and also a shop selling fantastic, though expensive, masks.

Around 200m south of the museum is the entrance to the woody **Parque Ecológico Macuiltépec**, with subalpine flora and panoramic views of the city. At 1590m, the easily climbable Macuiltépec is the highest of the hills on which the town is built, and from its *mirador* you might catch a glimpse of the Gulf. Another potential picnic spot is **Parque Los Tecajetes**, ten minutes' walk from the zócalo along María Ávila Camacho (daily 6am–6pm), a pristine public park with lush vegetation and plenty of shaded seating areas.

The **Museo Interactivo** (Mon–Fri 9am–6pm, Sat & Sun 10am–7pm; M$25, M$45 with IMAX), southeast of the centre on Murillo Vidal, is an entertaining place to take kids: along with a permanent exhibit of Mexican cars and planes and an IMAX cinema – the largest in Latin American – the museum features a planetarium and rooms dedicated to different sciences, such as space exploration, with interactive displays and impressive models. Take a taxi or a bus marked "Murillo Vidal".

## Eating

Good **food** is abundant in Xalapa. The city is home to the **jalapeño pepper**, which you'll probably taste in all main meals. Another of the great pleasures here is local **coffee** (actually grown in nearby Coatepec; see p.604), consumed in great quantities in one of the city's numerous **traditional cafés**. A particularly high concentration of these can be found along Nicolás Bravo – those listed below also have full lunch and dinner menus. Meanwhile, there are several appetizing **restaurants** and some enticing *jugo* and torta places on Enríquez and in the couple of blocks to the north and south of it. You can buy fresh food (and wine) for a picnic in the park at the Chedraui **supermarket** on Lucio, just up the hill from Enríquez; the Rex Centro supermarket and pharmacy on Enríquez, at the junction with Carillo Puerto, is open 24 hours.

**Café Chiquito** Nicolás Bravo 3, at Dr Pedro Rendón (opposite the hospital) ⓣ228/812-1122. One of the larger and most distinctive cafés, with plenty of wooden tables around a small courtyard with tiled floors. There's a reasonable menu, mostly of snacks and sandwiches (M$30–40), along with the usual range of caffeinated beverages.

**Café Lindo** Primo Verdad 21. Café with good sandwiches in addition to a full complement of Mexican-style snack foods. Lively, primarily young clientele in the large, dimly lit dining and drinking area.

**La Casona del Beaterio** Zaragoza 20 ⓣ228/818-2119. Hundreds of old photographs adorn the walls at one of the city's best eateries, which serves up fine and reasonably priced Mexican food and breakfasts from M$42. Tables are arranged around a small courtyard with running water. Live traditional music Thurs–Sun.

**La Fonda** Callejón del Diamante (aka Antonio Ma de Rivera) 1 ⓣ228/818-7287. Justifiably popular lunch-time spot (plenty of room upstairs if the street-level dining room is full) on a bustling market street. Copious and very cheap comidas corridas or an à la carte choice of chicken, meat and even some seafood dishes for M$50 and up.

**La Parroquia** Zaragoza 18 ⓣ228/817-4436. Venerable 50-year old establishment best known for its breakfast menus starting at around M$40, but whose unpretentious and busy dining room is also open for lunch and dinner. Another, smarter branch at María Ávila Camacho 42 (mains M$40 and above).

**Il Postodoro** Primo Verdad 11 ⓣ228/841-2000. All of the pasta dishes and excellent pizzas (from M$45) are made on the premises – as are the several flavours of ice cream – at this welcoming Italian restaurant. Excellent wine list, dominated by Chiantis.

**La Sopa** Callejón del Diamante (aka Antonio Ma de Rivera) 3-A ⓣ228/817-8069. Popular for its no-nonsense enchiladas, tacos and soups, almost all for under M$30, and its tranquil location – roaming mariachi bands notwithstanding – on this traffic-free street (daily 11.30am–11.30pm).

## Drinking, nightlife and entertainment

Xalapa is a city of great creative energy. A number of **bars** offer live music and occasional poetry readings or theatre, and there are **nightclubs** catering to all tastes. The loudest and hippest places tend to be along María Ávila Camacho; the *Líquido Club* (Thurs–Sat 10pm–3am) at no. 84, around half a kilometre from the zócalo, is good for dancing to mainly house and techno. One of the most innovative places is *Iguana Ranas* at 9 Oriente 406, open from 10pm with lively theme nights and regular drinks promotions. Elsewhere, *Los Molinos*, Úrsulo Galván 57 (daily 6.30pm–2am), is a restaurant/bar offering a wide selection of spirits and live entertainment and appealing to an older clientele; *La Tasca*, off

Rébsamen in the Unidad del Valle area southeast of the centre, has traditional acoustic music.

If you're in the mood for something more relaxed, the **Teatro del Estado** on María Ávila Camacho, at Ignacio de la Llave (box office ⓣ228/817-3210), hosts regular **concerts** by the Orquesta Sinfónica de Xalapa, in addition to dance and theatre. Tickets cost about M$50 for the front of the auditorium (best for watching) and M$40 for the back (best for listening). Meanwhile, the **Agorá de la Ciudad** in Parque Juárez is an arts centre with a cinema, theatre, gallery, bookshop and coffee shop. *Agorá Sky Bar* (Tues–Sun from 5pm till late), on the balcony here, is a pleasant place for an early evening drink. The Cinepolis multi-screen **cinema** is in Plaza Las Américas, on the edge of town on the highway to Veracruz.



## Listings

**Banks and exchange** There are banks and ATMs on Zamora, with HSBC on the corner of Enríquez and Clavijero, near Parque Juárez.
**Buses** Frequent services to Veracruz and Mexico City from the main bus station. You can also go direct to Cardel (for Cempoala), Fortín de las Flores and Papantla.
**Flights** Aeromar (ⓣ01-800/237-6627) operates two daily flights to Mexico City from the airstrip at Lencero, just outside the city.
**Internet access** Several places have Internet: Login (Mon–Sat 10am–11pm, Sun 2–9pm; M$12/hr) is at Zamora 18, while Ciberbazar (M$9/hr) is tucked away in the covered market off Enríquez, just east of the Parque Juárez.
**Laundry** Lavandería Diamante, Rojano 21-A (daily 9am–8pm; M$19/kilo) is one block north of the post office.
**Post office** The main post office (Mon–Fri 8am–7.30pm, Sat 9am–5pm, Sun 9am–noon) is on Zamora, at Diego Leño, and is also where you'll find a Western Union office.
**Tours and activities** A number of ecotourism companies in Xalapa offer trekking adventures, jungle tours and especially rafting trips, which tend to focus on three rivers in the area: the Río Filobobos (level II and III rapids), Río Antigua-Pescados (level II and III) and the Río Actopan (level II). Try Amigos del Río, Chilpancingo 205 (ⓣ228/815-8817, ⓦwww.amigosdelrio.com.mx); Ecco Sports, 20 de Noviembre Ote 631 (ⓣ228/812-3954, ⓦwww.eccosports.com.mx); or Veraventuras, Santos Degollado 81 (ⓣ228/818-9579, ⓦwww.veraventuras.com.mx). A half-day outing with any of these costs around M$450–480 per person, for a minimum two to four people.

## Around Xalapa

With time on your hands, a number of appealing excursions can be made into the jungly country around Xalapa. Just a couple of kilometres south of the city is the **Jardín Botánico Francisco Clavijero** (daily 9am–5pm; M$5), a collection of plants native to the state. Around 10km further out in the same direction, the small town of **COATEPEC** is a rewarding destination, mainly for its beautiful setting and the chance to spend the night at the luxurious *Posada Coatepec* (ⓣ228/816-0544, ⓦwww.posadacoatepec.com; ⑨), if you can afford it. Rooms in this wonderful old hacienda are decorated in a blend of antique and modern styles. It also has a number of good **restaurants**, including *El Tío Yeyo* (ⓣ228/816-3645), which specializes in fresh fish, particularly trout (*trucha*) served in a variety of delicious sauces. The coffee consumed in Xalapa's cafés is grown here, and in May the Feria del Café celebrates this fact.

Another 8km south is **XICO**: hop off the bus at the outskirts of the village, by a tiny church, then ask the way to the **Cascada de Texolo**, a gorgeous triple waterfall – it's 2km and forty minutes' hot walk along a paved road through banana and coffee plantations, but worth it. You can admire the falls from a modern bridge, a replacement for the crumpled iron one alongside, which was wrecked by an earthquake. Many of the scenes in the film *Romancing the Stone* were shot around these villages and waterfalls. For Coatepec or Xico take a local bus (M$6) from the Terminal Excelsiór (also known as Los Sauces, after the market next to it), 2km southwest of the zócalo, or an AU bus to Xico, from the main terminal (about 20min).

On the road to Veracruz, 10km outside Xalapa and best approached by taxi (15–20min; M$40–50), is the **Museo Exhacienda El Lencero** (Tues–Sun 10am–5pm; M$20, free Tues), a colonial hacienda that was once the property of controversial general and president Antonio López de Santa Anna. It is preserved in its full nineteenth-century splendour, and the grounds and surrounding countryside are stunning, too.

# Veracruz



**VILLA RICA DE LA VERACRUZ** was the first town founded by the Spanish in Mexico, a few days after Cortés's arrival on Good Friday, 1519. Though today's city occupies the area of coast where he first came ashore, made camp and had his first encounter with Aztec emissaries, the first development – little more than a wooden stockade – was in fact established some way to the north (see p.615) before being moved to La Antigua (see p.613) and finally arriving at its present site in 1589. The modern city is very much the heir of the original; only recently, for the first time since its foundation, has Veracruz begun to lose its position as the most important port in Mexico (to Tampico and Coatzacoalcos), and its history reflects every major event from the Conquest onwards. "Veracruz", states author Paul Theroux, "is known as the 'heroic city'. It is a poignant description: in Mexico a hero is nearly always a corpse".

Your first, and lasting, impression of Veracruz, however, will not be of its historical significance but of its present-day vitality. Its dynamic zócalo, pleasant waterfront location and relative absence of tourists make the city one of the most enjoyable places in the Republic in which simply to sit back and observe – or join – the daily round. This is especially true in the evenings, when the tables under the *portales* of the plaza fill up and the drinking and the marimba music begin, to go on most of the night. **Marimba** – a distinctively Latin-Caribbean sound based around a giant wooden xylophone – is *the* local sound, but at peak times there are also mariachi bands and individual crooners all striving to be heard over each other. When the municipal band strikes up from the middle of the square, confusion is total. Before Ash Wednesday every year (variable Feb–March), Veracruz's riotous nine-day **Carnaval** celebrations rival the best in the hemisphere, while the **Festival Internacional Afrocaribeño**, usually held in July or August, showcases dance and music performances from all over the Caribbean and Africa, film showings and art exhibitions.

## Some history

Though tranquil enough today, the port's past has been a series of "invasions, punitive missions and local military defeats . . . humiliation as history". The problems started even before the Conquest was complete, when **Pánfilo Narváez** landed here on his ill-fated mission to bring Cortés back under the control of the governor of Cuba, and continued intermittently for the next four hundred years. Throughout the sixteenth and seventeenth centuries, Veracruz and the Spanish galleons that used the port were preyed on constantly by the English, Dutch and French. In the **War of Independence** the Spanish made their final stand here, holding the fortress of San Juan Ulúa for four years after the country had been lost. In **1838** the French occupied the city, in what was

later dubbed "The Pastry War", demanding compensation for French property and citizens who had suffered in the years following Independence; in **1847** US troops took Veracruz, and from here marched on to capture the capital; in January **1862** the French, supported by Spanish and English forces that soon withdrew, invaded on the pretext of forcing Mexico to pay her foreign debt, but ended up staying five years and setting up the unfortunate Maximilian as emperor; and finally, in **1914**, US marines were back, occupying the city to protect American interests during the Revolution. These are the "Cuatro Veces Heroica" of the city's official title, and form the bulk of the history displayed in the museums here.

## Arrival and information

The ADO first-class **bus station** is about 3km from the centre at Díaz Mirón 1698, with the AU second-class terminal right behind it facing Lafragua. To reach the centre, buy a ticket for a **taxi** (M$25) from the booth on the south side of the first-class terminal (left as you exit). To take a bus (M$5), walk to the stop on Díaz Mirón to the right as you exit, and take any – most will have "Díaz Mirón" or "Centro" on the windscreen; if not, ask. These head straight to the end of Díaz Mirón, round a confusing junction at Parque Zamora, and then take a variety of routes that mostly end up on Independencia as it runs past the zócalo. The **airport** is about 10km south of the city; taxis between here and the centre cost about M$155. Buy a ticket from the taxi desk in the terminal.

Although Veracruz is a large and rambling city, the **centro histórico** (its old downtown area) is relatively small and easy to navigate – anywhere further afield can be reached by **local bus** from somewhere very near the zócalo. All trips within the city (and as far as Boca del Río) are M$5, or M$6 for the newer buses, usually marked in blue. Taxis charge according to a zone system and are pretty honest about it – trips in the centre will cost you about M$20, to the bus station M$25. If your hotel calls for one it will be more expensive (M$50 and up), though this is a generally safer option at night.

The **tourist office**, on the ground floor of the Palacio Municipal right on the zócalo (Mon–Fri 8am–8pm, Sat & Sun 10am–6pm; ⓣ229/200-2017 ext 117 or 2053 ext 653; ⓦwww.veracruzturismo.com.mx), has basic information and helpful staff on hand, though not always English speakers.

## Accommodation

There's a **hotel** right next to the first-class bus station, and several very cheap and rather grim places around the back of the second-class terminal, but unless you've arrived late at night, there's no point staying this far out. The other cheap places are mostly within a couple of blocks of the zócalo, often around the market; they're nothing to write home about, and noise can be a real problem – from the prostitutes servicing the local sailors as much as from the road – but at least you should find a clean room with a fan. The best deals in the city tend to fall in the **mid-range**, and there are some decent hotels along the malecón (María Ávila Camacho) within walking distance of the zócalo. If you want more luxury, head to the **beach**, where plenty of resort-style hotels front the *playas* of Villa del Mar, Mocambo and Boca del Río, which also has a number of **campsites** (for more on accommodation at Veracruz's beaches, see p.610).

**Amparo** Serdán 482 ⓣ229/932-2738, ⓦwww.hotelamparo.com.mx. The least sleazy of a cluster of cheap places, behind the zócalo near the market. Popular with backpackers, prices depend on three variables: the number of people (1–3), the size of the room and whether you need TV. The cheapest single with no TV is M$140; three people in the largest room with TV is M$450. ③

**Baluarte** Francisco Canal 265, at 16 de Septiembre ⓣ229/932-5222, ⓦwww.hotelbaluarte.com.mx. Well-kept hotel where the rooms have TV, a/c and, in some cases, views of the Baluarte de Santiago. Otherwise fairly characterless modern rooms. Free parking for guests. ⑤

**Colonial** Miguel Lerdo 117 ⓣ229/932-0193, ⓦwww.hcolonial.com.mx. Ageing but comfortable rooms (some with balconies) at this good-value option on the zócalo, with a swimming pool, garage and a/c. Some rooms have views over the square. ⑥

**Emporio** Paseo de Malecón 244 ⓣ229/932-2222, ⓦwww.hotelesemporio.com. Big, luxurious US-style hotel with all the associated amenities, including pool, gym and sauna. Slightly pricier rooms have sea views. ⑦

**Fiesta Inn Malecón** General Figeroa 68 ⓣ229/923-1500. Closest seafront hotel to the centre, with smart, comfortable rooms with tiled, marble floors, a gym and a decent pool with hot tub. Popular with business travellers and wealthy Mexican tourists. Most rooms have views of the harbour. ⑧

**Holiday Inn Centro Histórico** Morelos 225 ⓣ229/932-4550, ⓔhichvera@prodigy.net.mx. Charming hotel built out of the renovated half of the nineteenth-century Faro Benito Juárez, with all the modern conveniences and a pretty pool enclosed by a courtyard embellished with elegant tiling. Look out for bargain deals at the Holiday Inn website. ⑦

**Imperial** Miguel Lerdo 153 ⓣ229/932-1204, ⓦwww.hotelimperialveracruz.com. Hotel with bags of character in an eighteenth-century building with a striking stained-glass ceiling in the lobby. All of the best rooms here look right onto the plaza and church (around M$100 extra). Some of the suites are very large and decorated with colonial-style furniture. ⑥

**Mar y Tierra** Ávila Camacho at Figueroa ⓣ229/931-3866, ⓦwww.hotelmarytierra.com. One of the best mid-priced options on the seafront, about a 15–20min walk from the zócalo. A/c rooms in the old (at the front) and new buildings are very different, so look first: both buildings have some rooms with sea views. On a pleasant stretch of the malecón animated by divers street vendors in the summer, but otherwise a bit quiet. ❺

**Rias** Díaz Mirón 1242 ⓣ229/932-5399. The best place near the bus station, three blocks from the ADO first-class terminal (walk towards the city centre). Clean, modern rooms with fan or a/c. ❺

**Royalty** Abasolo 34, at Ávila Camacho ⓣ229/932-2844. Clean, friendly, quiet and good-value seafront hotel close to the centre, with a/c rooms plus some cheaper ones with a fan, TV and small balcony. Accepts credit cards (not AmEx). ❻

**Ruíz Milán** Paseo del Malecón ⓣ229/932-3777, ⓦwww.ruizmilan.com. Comfortable hotel (especially if you get a room at the front) with a/c, a small indoor pool and hot tub, plus a good restaurant. Close to both the zócalo and malecón. ❻

**Santo Domingo** Serdán 481 ⓣ229/931-6326. Opposite the *Amparo*, but much more expensive. Central and clean, with small rooms with private bath. ❺

**Veracruz Centro Histórico** Independencia 1069, at Miguel Lerdo ⓣ229/989-3800, ⓦwww.hotelescalinda.com.mx. Best hotel in the centre, with comfortable, modern rooms just off the zócalo and above Sanborn's. Big discounts available online. ❾

## The City

The attractive **zócalo**, shaded by trees and surrounded by the cathedral, the Palacio Municipal and various colonial buildings that now mainly operate as bars, cafés and hotels, is the centre of life in Veracruz – the place where everyone gathers, for morning coffee, lunch, afternoon strolls and night-time revelry. The square is physically at the heart of the **centro histórico**, and dominated by the imposing but slightly shabby **Catedral de Nuestra Señora de Asunción**. Built in typically grand Baroque style in the sixteenth century and consecrated in 1721, its most striking feature is its tiled dome. On the eastern side of the zócalo, the elegant **Palacio Municipal** was originally built between 1609 and 1627, making it one of the oldest in Mexico, though it assumed its current form in the eighteenth century. The **Fototeca de Veracruz** (Tues–Sun 10am–7pm; free) hosts beautifully presented photography exhibitions just off the southeast side of the zócalo and the **Casa Principal** (daily 10am–8pm; free), a short walk away at Mario Molina 315, is another attractive gallery of primarily modern Mexican art.

About five blocks south of the zócalo on Zaragoza, the first of some worthwhile museums occupies a former nineteenth-century orphanage. The **Museo de la Ciudad** (Tues–Sat 10am–6pm, Sun 10am–3pm; free) covers local history and folklore from the city's earliest inhabitants to the 1950s. Inevitably, given the scope of material covered, it's rather a potted version, and many of the exhibits go completely unexplained (and those that are, are done so only in Spanish), but there's some beautiful Olmec and Totonac sculpture, including one giant Olmec head; thought-provoking information on Mexico's African population, much of which was concentrated in this area after the slave trade; and enlightening sections on the social movements of the early twentieth century and the celebrated music and dance culture of the city. Upstairs you'll find temporary exhibits of modern art, usually from local artists. Just two blocks from the museum towards the sea, the facades of **Las Atarazanas** are worth a passing look. These colonial warehouses once backed onto the harbour and were built for the storage of arms and wares used by the troops that protected the city from pirates.

A short walk south from here, the **Instituto Veracruzano de Cultura**, on Francisco Canal beyond Zaragoza (Tues–Sun 9am–8pm; free), hosts modern art exhibitions in its two-floor gallery, while between 16 de Septiembre and Gómez Farías sits the **Baluarte de Santiago** (Tues–Sun 10am–4.30pm; M$35, free on Sun), a seventeenth-century fort. The Baluarte is the sole survivor of what were originally nine forts along a 2650-metre-long wall – it's hard to imagine that the sea reached this far when the fort was built in 1635 to fend off constant attacks by pirates and buccaneers. You can wander around the small museum inside, which has a few pieces of exquisite pre-Columbian gold jewellery discovered in 1976 by a local octopus fisherman. By the time the authorities got wind of his find, most of it had been melted down and sold, but what little remains is lovely. Apart from this, there's not a great deal to see.

From here, walk two blocks north to Mariano Arista, where the town's best museum, the beautifully refurbished **Museo Histórico Naval** (Tues–Sun 9am–5pm; free), takes you through Mexican naval history from the Maya and Olmec periods to the modern day, with numerous displays of weapons and models (all labelled in Spanish). Highlights include a dramatic scale model of Cortés's battle with the Aztecs on Lago de Texcoco in 1521, details of Mexico's profitable trade with the Philippines in the colonial period and some predictably hagiographical accounts of heroic exploits during the War of Independence and US attacks on Veracruz in the nineteenth and early twentieth centuries. If you follow the official route through the building, formerly the Escuela Naval, you'll pass a small hall dedicated to the **Museo Constitucionalista Venustiano Carranza**. Carranza established his Constitutionalist government in Veracruz in 1915 (with the support of US President Woodrow Wilson, whose troops then occupied the town) and inside are gathered assorted memorabilia of his government, including furnishings from Carranza's bedroom. He lived in the Castillo de San Juan while running his government – and the war against Villa and Zapata – from the old *faro* (lighthouse) alongside the huge Pemex Tower, which was built in 1952 on the malecón. There's a statue of Carranza in front of the *faro*, looking exactly as John Reed describes him in *Insurgent Mexico*: "A towering, khaki-clad figure, seven feet tall it seemed . . . arms hanging loosely by his side, his fine old head thrown back."

The **malecón** itself is worth a stroll during the day or at night, when it's particularly animated with street vendors and entertainers, and illuminated by

△ Waterfront, Veracruz

the twinkling lights of the ships in the port. There are also usually folk music and dance shows at 7pm every Wednesday. From here, the most impressive sight in Veracruz, the **Castillo de San Juan de Ulúa** (Tues–Sun 9am–4.30pm; M$35), is clearly visible across the harbour it so singularly failed to protect. In most cases this was hardly the fault of its defenders, since every sensible invader landed somewhere on the coast nearby, captured the town and, having cut off the fort by land and sea, called for its surrender. Prior to closing for refurbishment in 1997, the fortress, with its unguarded ten-metre drops and dingy, dripping corridors, was used as the location for the climactic chase scene in *Romancing the Stone*. The renovated fort – the site of Cortés's 1519 landing – and **museum** are now open to the public. The main attraction of the fortress is its prison – many political prisoners died during the rule of Díaz in three dark, unpleasant cells known as El Purgatorio, La Gloria and El Infierno (Purgatory, Heaven and Hell). Apart from the prison, the fortress is an empty ruin of battlements and stairways. The easiest way to get here is to take a taxi, which will cost M$50 if you call for one, but should be no more than M$35 if you hail one on the street – ask it to wait if you want to guarantee a lift back. Alternatively, small boats (*lanchas*) will make the trip across the harbour from the malecón for M$30.

Finally, a visit to the **Acuario de Veracruz** (Mon–Thurs 10am–7pm, Fri–Sun 10am–7.30pm; M$60, children M$30), in the Plaza Acuario shopping centre on María Ávila Camacho, is well worth your time. Designed by a Japanese architect, this modern and well-run aquarium has some large ocean fish, including sharks, barracudas and huge tarpons, as well as smaller tanks filled with a variety of saltwater, brackish and freshwater fauna. There are also some interesting educational exhibits. The undoubted highlight, however (depending on the state of your nerves), is the chance to be immersed in a tank with feeding sharks: being dunked in the **Tiburonario** is an additional M$300 for adults and M$150 for children.

## The beaches

You wouldn't make a special trip to Veracruz for its **beaches**, but for an afternoon's escape to the sea, they're quite good enough. Strips of sand hug the coast for 12km southeast of the centre, linked together by Bulevar María Ávila Camacho, which runs all the way to Boca del Río. **Villa del Mar** is the closest, but the most crowded and least clean beach. It's also the location of a cluster of hotels, including the upmarket *Hostal de Cortés* (Ⓣ229/923-1200, Ⓦwww.hostaldecortes.com.mx; ❼) at Ávila Camacho and Bartolomé de las Casas, which has a pool and a/c rooms with balconies and sea views. A bit further along the coast at the end of **Playa José Martí** is the far more enticing *Lois* (Ⓣ229/937-8290, Ⓦwww.hotellois.com; ❼), with vivid, quirky decor. The

### Veracruz water sports

To see marine life in the Gulf of Mexico at close quarters, head for one of the city's dive shops: Tridente, Ávila Camacho 165 (Ⓣ229/931-7924, tridente_ver@hotmail.com), or Scubadiver, Hernandez y Hernandez 563 (Ⓣ229/932-3994, Ⓦwww.scubaver.net), both near the *Mar y Tierra* hotel, are good. They offer guided **dive trips** to a large number of little-visited reefs and beaches within the **Parque Nacional Sistema Arrecifal Veracruzano**, along with PADI certification at better rates than you'll find in the Caribbean (around M$750 per day diving all inclusive, or M$300 snorkelling). Kayak Mexico (Ⓣ229/913-0452, Ⓦwww.kayakmexico.com) runs kayaking day trips to the **mangrove swamps** nearby.

headland beyond Playa José Martí marks the beginning of a strip of beaches that are collectively known as Boca del Río, though technically this is the name of the town at the end of the strip. The *Fiesta Americana* hotel dominates the **Playa de Oro** (229/989-8989, www.fiestaamericana.com; 8), a massive resort with giant pool and spacious rooms and balconies, all with sea views.

Five minutes' drive along Camacho from here is the beach at **Mocambo** (a local favourite and where most of the other hotels are). *Hotel Mocambo*, Ruíz Cortines 4000 (229/922-0200, www.mocambo.com.mx; 8), is a grand old hotel built in 1932 and magnificently renovated to compete with the homogenous alternatives offered in these parts. The restaurant here, *La Fragata* (same number, ext 126), is one of the best in Veracruz, serving exquisite seafood in a timbered dining room with mahogany floors, vaguely reminiscent of a Spanish galleon. For cheaper lodgings, try the *Playa de Oro*, Paseo Ejército Mexicano 23, opposite the *Mocambo* (229/921-8805; 5), where the rates include breakfast. The huge Plaza Américas shopping mall, 400m or so before the *Mocambo*, has all the **food** outlets, **shops** and **ATM** machines you might need. From the *Mocambo*, follow the street down to the wide sandy beach, where the water is warm and calm – though from time to time it can be pretty dirty (in which case you might consider paying the M$30 to use the public swimming pool next to the beach).

As its name suggests, **Boca del Río**, ten minutes or so further on by bus from Mocambo and 12km from central Veracruz, is located at the mouth of the Río Jamapa. It also has a reasonable stretch of sand, but apart from the persistent boat-trip touts, there is not much going on here. Tridente (see box opposite) owns an ecotourism site with camping and a restaurant at **Antón Lizardo**, a small village beyond Boca del Río and 28km from Veracruz. From here it runs boat trips to the best beaches and reefs near Veracruz, on the offshore coral islands. These have white sands, clean water and very few visitors. Tridente can help you get permission to stay on one of the islands if you have your own tent.

**Buses** (marked "Boca del Río", "Playas" or "Mocambo") head out from Zaragoza just next to the zócalo in Veracruz, arriving twenty minutes later at *Hotel Mocambo*. Most buses take the quick route via Ruíz Cortines; for the scenic route along the coastal road (Ávila Camacho) take buses marked "Penacho" or join the open-air **tour buses** which leave from in front of *Hotel Emporio* when they have at least ten passengers (daily 10am–10pm; M$100). They do a circuit of all the major sights in the city, also making the coastal trip to Boca.

## Eating and drinking

"**A la Veracruzana**" is a tag you'll find on menus all over the country, denoting a delicious sauce of onions, garlic, tomatoes, olives, chiles and spices, served with meat or fish. Try *pescado a la Veracruzana* (a regional fish dish), *pulpos a la marinera* (baby octopus), *arroz a la tumbada* (Veracruz-style rice) or *empanadas de camaron* (shrimp turnovers). Local liquors include the mind-wiping *toritos* (made with fruits and blended with condensed milk and a tot of brandy) and *el popo* (a beverage made of cacao and rice).

The zócalo is ringed by **bars** and **cafés**, but these are really places to drink (see p.612) and though most do serve food, or at least sandwiches, it's generally overpriced. While nowhere near as prevalent as in Xalapa, there are three decent **coffee shops** just south of the zócalo, on Mario Molina between Independencia and 5 de Mayo; the best is *Boca de Oro* at 240-A. For more substantial meals, there are a whole series of small and cheap **fish restaurants** around the market, and the top floor of the market building itself is given over to cooked-food stalls.

**El Cochinito de Oro** Zaragoza at Serdán ☎229/932-3677. This friendly, no-frills eatery has been around for fifty years, offering a reasonable selection of seafood dishes – fish, shrimp, octopus with onions – for not more than M$75. The menu is translated into English.

**La Gaviota** Trigueros 21 ☎229/932-3950. A useful address for nocturnal revellers, *La Gaviota* is open 24hr and offers fortifying, predominately meat dishes, snacks and a well-stocked bar should you wish to keep the party going. Smart place.

**Gran Café de la Parroquia** Gómez Farías 34, at Paseo del Malecón ☎229/937-2584. Comprising two vast white dining rooms and occupying nearly a whole block on the malecón this place is invariably full of hundreds of diners being served modest and comparatively pricey meat (M$100) and fish (M$50–100) meals. Check out the vintage coffee machines.

**Gran Café del Portal** Independencia at Zamora, opposite the cathedral ☎229/931-2759. The coffee (which is roasted on the premises) is undeniably good, and you can order food from a varied menu until midnight. Don't expect a tranquil afternoon – you'll be serenaded by the house marimba band all day, and will probably draw the attention of plenty of street vendors.

**Pink Panther's Food** Callejon Lagunilla ☎229/931-7982. Bar/restaurant with a satisfactory, if not outstanding, menu, recommended for its pleasant tables near a small square free from the occasionally tiresome street vendors who inhabit the zócalo. It's open 24hr, with food from 7am till the early hours of the morning.

**Samborcito** 16 de Septiembre 727 ☎229/931-4388. No-nonsense local favourite, a bit of a walk from the centre but well worth it for the *picadas* (thick tortillas with cheese), tamales and other delicious Veracruz dishes.

**Sanborn's** Independencia 1069, at Miguel Lerdo ☎229/931-0219. The Veracruz branch of the 100-year-old national department store and restaurant chain. Offerings range from Mexican snacks to filet mignon, served in an a/c dining room or the much cosier adjoining café. Hearty breakfasts from M$60–70. Daily 7am–1am.

## Nightlife and entertainment

Lots of people, locals and tourists alike, start their night off with a drink at "los portales", the arcade leading into the zócalo on its north side. In bars like *La Tasca*, *Bar Palacio* (English menu) or *Regis*, you can try traditional mint *julep* (or *jullep*) – prepared with dark rum, dry sherry, vermouth, sugar and mint. *Regis* is slightly cheaper, but *Tasca* has the best. There's usually plenty of marimba along the *portales*, and on Thursday and Saturday afternoons you'll see couples dancing *danzon*. Alternatively, find a table and in no time you'll have your very own entertainment/distractions in the form of grinning musicians or a bizarre selection of touts – from boys selling balsa toucans to fortune-tellers and uniformed nurses offering to take your blood pressure.

In the centre of Veracruz, there are a couple of **bars** on the quiet Plazuela La Lagunilla where you can listen to **live music**. *El Rincón de la Trova* has excellent

### Moving on from Veracruz

The first-class **bus station** is on Díaz Mirón, 3km from the centre. Bus tickets can be purchased at the booths lining the front of the terminal (including a special section for the luxury ADO GI and Uno services). There are numerous daily services to Alvarado, **Córdoba**, Puebla, Mexico City, **San Andrés Tuxtla** and Villahermosa. Buses to **Xalapa** depart every twenty to thirty minutes from 6am to 10.45pm. There are six buses to **Papantla** from 9am, two to Cancún in the evening, two to **Fortín** (1pm and 6pm) and eight to **Catemaco**. Second-class AU buses have their own ticket hall at the back of the terminal; get regular buses here to Córdoba, Cardel (every 30min), Xalapa (every 10min) and Orizaba (8 daily).

**Veracruz airport** (see p.606) is served by flights to several domestic destinations, including Cancún, Ciudad del Carmen, Guadalajara, Mérida, Mexico City, Monterrey, Tampico, Toluca and Villahermosa. Continental Airlines also operates flights to Houston, Texas.

Afro-Cuban sounds (Thurs–Sat 8pm–3am), and also serves food during the day. Next door, *La Casona del Trovador* is another fun place for a drink. The best places for **dancing**, both to salsa and current dance music, are out of the centre along Ruíz Cortines, a main thoroughfare of strip malls leading towards the beaches. *Carioca*, in *Hotel Lois* at Ruíz Cortines 10, is an excellent place for salsa, as is *Kachamba*, María Ávila Camacho at Médico Militar, where a Cuban orchestra plays from Thursday to Saturday from 8pm (M$80 cover). The flashiest techno clubs are *Paradise* at Ruíz Cortines 8 and *La Bertola* at Ruíz Cortines 10, also in the hotel. The best **cinema** is the multi-screen complex at the Plaza Américas mall in Mocambo (see p.611).

## Listings

**Airlines** Aero California, Ruíz Cortines 1517 ⓣ01-800/237-6225; Aerolitoral ⓣ01-800/800-2376; Aviacsa ⓣ01-800-284-2272; Click Mexicana, Ruíz Cortines 1516 ⓣ229/921-7504; Continental, at the airport ⓣ229/938-6088 or Ruíz Cortines 1600 ⓣ01-800/900-5000; InterJet, Camacho 3549 ⓣ01-800/011-2345.

**Banks and exchange** Branches of all the main banks, where you can change traveller's cheques and find ATM machines, are on Independencia, at Benito Juárez. Multiservicos Cambiarios, Morelos 343-A, has longer opening hours than the banks (Mon–Sat 9am–11pm, Sun 10am–6pm).

**Car rental** Alamo, at the airport ⓣ229/938-3700 (daily 7am–4pm & 5–11.30pm); Avis, Collado 241, Colonia Zaragoza ⓣ229/932-6032 (Mon–Fri 9am–3pm & 4–7pm, Sat 9am–3pm), and at the airport ⓣ229/934-9623 (Mon–Sat 7am–3pm & 5–11pm, Sun 7.30am–3pm & 6–11pm); Budget, *Puerta del Sol* hotel, Ruíz Cortines 3495 ⓣ229/989-0505 (Mon–Sat 9am–2pm & 4–8pm), and at the airport ⓣ229/939-2705 (daily 7am–3pm & 5–11.30pm); Dollar, Simón Bolívar 501, Colonia Zaragoza ⓣ229/935-8808 (daily 6am–midnight), and at the airport; Hertz, Fracc. Costa de Oro, Ruíz Cortines 3130-D (daily 9am–2pm & 5–8pm), and at the airport (24hr).

**Consulates** Cuba, Sierra 1014, Costa de Oro ⓣ229/922-3723; Denmark, Díaz Mirón 1500 ⓣ229/923-3434; Finland, Emparan 251 ⓣ229/931-2437; Germany, 16 de Septiembre 1383 ⓣ229/927-0656; Italy, Antonio de Mendoza 134 ⓣ229/937-5270; Netherlands, Morelos 121 ⓣ229/923-0504; Spain, Francisco Canal 264 ⓣ229/932-5829; Sweden ⓣ229/130-8501; UK, Independencia 1349-1 ⓣ229/931-1285 (Mon–Fri 9am–5pm).

**Hospital** Hospital General, 20 de Noviembre 1074 ⓣ229/932-2705.

**Internet access** There are a number of cafés near the zócalo, including two on Miguel Lerdo – one just west of 5 de Mayo (daily 9am–9pm; M$8/hr), the other between Morelos and Landero y Cos (Mon–Sat 9am–1am, Sun 10am–11pm; M$15/hr) – and two on Mariano Arista between Independencia and Clarijero (variable hours; M$12/hr).

**Laundry** Lavandería Mar y Sol, Madero 16 (Mon–Sat 8am–6.30pm; M$30/kilo).

**Pharmacies** Farmacias Del Ahorro Home Delivery Service ⓣ01-800/711-2222 (7am–10.30pm); Farmacia Torres, 20 de Noviembre 1 ⓣ229/932-0660; Farmacia del Hospital Español, 16 de Septiembre 955 ⓣ229/932-0021 ext 115 (24hr); most convenient for the centre is Farmacia Issste in the Super Issste supermarket, just south of the Monumento a los Héroes on 16 de Septiembre.

**Police** ⓣ229/938-0664.

**Post office** On the Plaza de la República, a couple of blocks north of the zócalo (Mon–Fri 8am–4pm, Sat 9am–1pm).

**Taxis** Radio Taxi ⓣ229/938-2233 or 32; Servi Taxi ⓣ229/934-6299 or 934-0620.

**Telephones** There are Ladatel phones throughout the city, and several fax and copy centres where you can make international calls – including one at Landero y Cos 41, near the zócalo.

# La Antigua and Cempoala

Heading north from Veracruz, there's a short stretch of highway as far as Cardel, at the junction of the coastal highway and the road up to Xalapa. **LA ANTIGUA**, site of the second Spanish settlement in Mexico (it's often incorrectly described as the first – Villa Rica is further north, see p.615), lies 2km off this road, 20km north of Veracruz. Although it does see an occasional bus, you'll find it much easier and quicker to take one heading for Cardel (about every 30min from the second-class terminal in Veracruz) and get off at the tollbooths. From here it's about twenty minutes' walk up a signed road.

For all its antiquity, there's not a great deal to see in La Antigua; however, it is a beautiful, broad-streeted tropical village on the banks of the **Río La Antigua** (or Río Huitzilapan). At weekends it makes a popular excursion for Veracruzanos, who come to picnic by the river and to swim or take boat rides. In the semi-ruinous centre of the village stand some of the oldest surviving Spanish buildings in the country: the **Edificio del Cabildo**, built in 1523, housed the first *ayuntamiento* (local government) established in Mexico; the **Casa de Cortés**, a fairly crude stone construction, which despite the name, was probably never lived in by Cortés and is now completely in ruins (though there are plans to restore it); and the tranquil **Ermita del Rosario**, the first Christian church built in New Spain, which also dates from the early sixteenth century, though it's been altered and restored several times since. On the riverbank stands a grand old tree – the Ceiba de la Noche Feliz – to which, according to tradition, Cortés moored his ships when he arrived here. According to local legend rubbing the trunk with your left hand is supposed to make your wishes come true.

## Cempoala

Though he first landed near the site of modern Veracruz, Cortés made camp at Villa Rica (see opposite), a move credited to the invitation he was issued by the Totonac people of **CEMPOALA** (or Zempoala), then a city of some 25,000 to 30,000 inhabitants (Cempoala was inland; Villa Rica, on the coast, was a more practical location for the Spanish). The first native city visited by the conquistadors, Cempoala quickly became their ally against the Aztecs. The city, which had existed in some form for at least eight hundred years, had been brought under Aztec control only relatively recently – around 1460 – and its people, who had already rebelled more than once, were only too happy to stop paying their tribute once they believed that the Spanish could protect them. This they did, although their leader Chicomacatl (dubbed the "Fat Chief" by conquistador Bernal Díaz del Castillo) and his people must have begun to have second thoughts when Cortés ordered the idols of their deities smashed and replaced with crosses and Christian altars.

Cortés left Cempoala in August 1519 for the march on Tenochtitlán, taking with him two hundred Totonac porters and fifty of the town's best warriors. The following May he was forced to return in a hurry by the news that Pánfilo Narváez, on a mission to bring the conquistadors back under the control of the governor of Cuba, had come after him with a large force. Cortés mounted a surprise attack on the newly arrived Spanish, who were camped in the centre of Cempoala, and despite the fact that Narváez's force was far larger and had taken up defensive positions on the great temple, Cortés won a resounding victory: Narváez was wounded (but survived), many of his generals were captured and most of the men switched sides, joining in the later assaults on the Aztec capital.

Today the ruins of the city, though not as dramatic as El Tajín further north, make for an absorbing detour – most weekdays you'll have them to yourself. The **archeological site** (Tues–Sun 9am–5.30pm; M$30, M$30 to bring in a video camera, free on Sun) is 12km north of Cardel and 4km west of Hwy-180. At the entrance you'll be able to watch regular Voladores performances, though this is a tradition more associated with Papantla (see box, p.620). The ruins date mostly from the Aztec period, and although obviously the buildings have lost their decorative facings and thatched sanctuaries, it's one of the most complete surviving examples of an Aztec ceremonial centre – albeit in an atypical tropical setting. The pyramids, grouped around a central plaza and with their double stairways, must have resembled those of Tenochtitlán, though on a considerably smaller scale. Apart from the main, cleared site, consisting of the **Templo Mayor** (the largest and most impressive structure, where Narváez made his stand), the Gran Pirámide and the Templo de las Chimeneas, there are lesser ruins scattered throughout, and around, the modern village. Most important of these are the **Templo de las Caritas**, a small temple on which a few carvings and murals can still be seen, in open country just beyond the main site, and the circular **Templo de Ehecatl** (Temple of the Wind God) on the opposite side of the main road through the village. You need a couple of hours to explore the site.



### Practicalities: Cardel

Cempoala is 42km northwest of Veracruz on Hwy-180, and though there are a few **buses** (second-class) from both Veracruz and Xalapa, it's quicker to go to **Cardel** and change there: from Veracruz, ADO services to Cardel depart every thirty minutes from 7am to 10.45pm (M$30). Coming **from La Antigua**, you can go back to the main road, get a second-class bus to Cardel and go on from there. From Cardel there are plenty of green-and-white **taxis** (M$60) to the site, but the buses marked "Zempoala" that leave from the bus station are cheaper (M$10). Cardel itself is not of much interest, but has several seafood restaurants and a couple of small **hotels** around the plaza. The mid-range *Plaza*, Independencia 25 Pte (☎296/962-0288; ❹), just opposite the ADO bus stop, may let you bargain off-season, while most tour groups stop at the smarter *Bienvenido Hotel*, just off the plaza at Sur 1 (☎296/962-0777; ❺), which has comfortable a/c rooms and a decent restaurant. From Cardel you can head 10km northeast to a good beach at **Chachalacas** (another short bus journey), a small fishing village that has transformed itself into a low-brow resort popular with domestic tourists. There's a luxury hotel, the *Chachalacas Hotel-Club* (☎296/962-5242; ❼), and some excellent seafood restaurants, and away from the built-up areas the grey-sand beaches are usually empty and quite appealing.

## North to Tuxpán

Continuing north towards Tuxpán, there's very little to see in the long coastal stretch (about 4hr on the bus) from Cardel to Papantla. About 15km north of Chachalacas is the sleepy village of **Villa Rica**, the **first Spanish settlement** in New Spain. Established by Cortés in 1519, it was abandoned in 1524 for La Antigua, and only foundations remain today, close to the normally deserted beach. Around 3km away are the similarly sparse ruins of the nearest Totonac town, **Quiahuitzlán** (daily 8am–6pm; M$20), with the great basalt outcrop known as the Peñon de Bernal looming above. What you can see today is primarily a cemetery, with over 70 small stone tombs. At **Nautla**, 153km from Veracruz, you pass the largest town en route to Papantla, surrounded by coconut groves. Although there are long, flat stretches of sand along much of the so-called "**Costa Esmeralda**" north of here, they are pretty uninviting – desolate, windswept and raked by grey surf. Only in the stretch between Nautla and Tecoluta, a low-key resort 55km north and 8km off the main road, does the beach offer much temptation, with several motels dotted along the coast. If you crave the beach you can **stay** in Tecoluta itself, and still get to Papantla and El Tajín with relative ease. *Dora Emilia* (☎766/846-0185; ❹), at Hidalgo 45, and the smarter *Albatros* (☎766/846-0002; ❹), nearby at Hidalgo 42, are both on the main street. Hotels on the beachfront are more expensive, though they do come with required ocean views – try the bright and modern *Aqua Inn* (☎766/846-0358 Ⓦhotelaquainn.tripod.com; ❻), which has cable TV and a/c. There are plenty of **places to eat**, from hotel restaurants to palapas at the beach, most of which serve seafood.

## Tlapacoyan

Some 64km southwest of Nautla, **TLAPACOYAN**, bounded to the south by the Río Bobos and to the north by the Río María de la Torre, is surrounded by forested hills and pre-Columbian ruins. Most important of these are the massive undeveloped sites of **Filo Bobos**, parts of which are over three thousand years old. In 1865 Austrian troops loyal to Emperor Maximilian captured the town, but were driven out by a small band of Mexicans led by Colonel Ferrer; after a series of fierce counter-attacks, the heavily outnumbered Mexicans were overwhelmed and Ferrer killed along with most of his troops. His statue now stands in the main square. Today the town is largely unspoilt, a friendly place going about its main business as a centre of citrus-fruit production.

**Buses to Tlapacoyan** run from Xalapa, Papantla, Puebla and Mexico City. ADO buses drop off in the centre of town: turn left at 5 de Mayo and walk up Héroes de Tlapacoyan for the zócalo. Second-class services to Nautla leave from the terminal opposite ADO. **Hotels** are thin on the ground, but in the centre there are a few quiet, good-value choices. Try the *Plaza*, on the square itself (☎225/315-0520; ❹), or the cheaper *San Agustín* (☎225/315-0023; ❸), at Héroes de Tlapacoyan 201, which also has the best restaurant in town, and organizes river trips to Filo Bobos.

### Filo Bobos

Work is ongoing at the **Filo Bobos** archeological project, which opened to the public in 1994. Thus far, you can explore two of the several pre-Hispanic sites identified along the Río Bobos valley, **El Cuajilote** and **Vega de la Peña**. Both are well worth visiting as much for the beauty of their locations, the birdlife and the serenity, as for the ruins themselves. No one yet knows for certain who occupied the Filo Bobos sites. Signs of a fertility cult suggest a **Huastec** influence, yet the other sculptures found are more Totonac in style, and the earliest buildings at El Cuajilote, which may as far back as 1000 BC, are decidedly Olmec. Archeologists are now speculating that Filo Bobos was the centre of an as yet unknown, syncretistic Mesoamerican civilization, which provided an important trade link between the Gulf coast, its environs and the central valleys.

The **trail** that leads to and links the two sites cuts through ranch land running along the sides of the Río Bobos, with steep rainforested hills rising to either side. There are unexplored mounds of rubble all along the way, and you're unlikely to see any other tourists. The first and most impressive site you come to is **El Cuajilote**, with platforms and pyramids arranged around a rectangular central plaza measuring 31,500 square metres. The surrounding buildings appear to be a series of temples dedicated to a fertility cult: a monolithic, phallic stele more than two metres tall and oriented to the stars stands in the middle of the plaza, and at Shrine A4 more than 1500 other phallic figurines were found, though none of these remain at the site today. You can also make out a ball-court and some sculptures, including one of a giant frog – it's speculated that this may also be a fertility symbol.

The trail continues 4km past El Cuajilote to the site of **Vega de la Peña**, which covers some eight thousand square metres. There's little doubt that structures buried beneath the lush greenery here extend beyond that; some archeologists believe they may have stretched as far as Nautla. If true, this would radically alter the accepted conception of Mexican and Mesoamerican pre-Columbian history, placing this coast in a far more prominent position than previously thought. What you see here today are small buildings, with more palatial dwellings than at El Cuajilote, and a small ball-court.

The complete **walk** around the two sites takes about six hours and begins at a little village called **Santiago**, reached by bus from the Terminal Regional de Tlapacoyan two blocks from Tlapacoyan's zócalo, on the corner of 5 de Mayo and Valdez. The bus driver will drop you on the edge of Santiago at the start of the road that leads to El Cuajilote, some 8km away. The walk down this road takes about an hour, though you can cut through fields to make it a little quicker, along a steep, mossy and slippery path shown as "aceite vueltos". The path is not always clear, but there are ranches along the road, and locals will point you in the right direction, and those with transport may even take you as far as Rancho Nuevo, leaving only 2km to walk. From El Cuajilote, a path leads out of the back of the site towards Vega de la Peña, and from there another leads to a manned river crossing with a small restaurant. From here it's a straightforward walk up a road lined with banana plantations to the village of **Encanto**, where you can catch local buses to Tlapacoyan. The site wardens at both El Cuajilote and Vega de la Peña are very helpful and will ensure that you are on the right path, as will the locals.

## Papantla

**PAPANTLA**, 227km from Veracruz, is by far the most attractive town on the route north, flower-filled and straggling over an unexpected outcrop of low, jungly hills. In addition to being one of the most important centres of the Mexican **vanilla** industry – the sweet, sticky odour frequently hangs over the place, and vanilla products are on sale everywhere – it's also one of the last

### El Baile de los Negritos

Popular at festivals across the state of Veracruz, the frenetic **Baile de los Negritos** is a Totonac dance dating back to colonial times, when African slaves were imported to work on local plantations, often living and labouring alongside *indígenas*. Stories abound as to the origin of the dance: the most popular version has it that a female slave and her child escaped from a plantation near Papantla and lived in the dense jungle with local indigenous groups. After her child was poisoned by a snake bite, the mother, using African folk medicine, danced herself into a trance. The Totonacs around her found the spectacle highly amusing and, it is said, began to copy her in a spirit of mockery.

The costumes of the dance are influenced by colonial dress, and the dancers wear a snake motif around the waist. The dance is directed by a "Mayordomo", the title given to plantation overseers in the colonial era. If you're in Tlapacoyan for the **Feast of Santiago** (July 25), dedicated to the town's patron saint, or the **Day of the Assumption** (Aug 15), you'll see the dance at its best and most spectacular; at other times it's held on a smaller scale in other village festivals in the area.

surviving strongholds of **Totonac** life. On the edge of the zócalo, the huge **Mural Cultural Totonaca**, created in 1979, combines sculpted images and murals of Totonac gods, myths and the pyramids of El Tajín (the tourist office has a leaflet describing each in detail), and you'll see Totonacs wandering around barefooted in loose white robes, especially in the Hidalgo market. You can also regularly witness the amazing dance-spectacle of the **Voladores de Papantla** in front of the cathedral and at El Tajín (see box, p.620). On the terrace above the murals and zócalo, the **Catedral de la Asunción**, with its beautifully maintained interior and painted *retablo*, is also worth a quick look. Established in 1570, it's been altered many times since then. East from the zócalo (walk down Enríquez and take the second left), the **Casa de Cultura** at Pino Suárez 216 has regular dance and music performances – you can check what's on at the tourist office. If you have time to kill, the **Museo de la Ciudad** is nearby, at the junction of Juárez and Madero (daily 10am–2pm & 4–8pm; free), with a small and slightly ramshackle collection of Totonac artefacts and murals. For the best **views** of the city, walk out along the road to Poza Rica to the pretty church of **Capilla de Cristo Rey**, and climb the tower.

## Practicalities

First-class **buses** use the ADO terminal on Juárez, fifteen minutes' walk from the centre; turn left when you exit and walk up Juárez (cross over the main road) until you meet Enríquez, where you turn right for the zócalo (taxis cost about M$16). **Moving on**, there are seven first-class buses daily to Veracruz, as well as frequent services to Xalapa and Tuxpán, but it can be hard to get a bus out, since most are *de paso*: book ahead, or take second-class, at least as far as Poza Rica, from where there's much more choice. The chaotic second-class Transportes Papantla terminal is on 20 de Noviembre – again, walk straight up (a couple of blocks) to the zócalo.

There's a small **tourist office** just off the zócalo (Mon–Fri 9am–8pm, Sat 9am–noon) at Azueta and Artes, opposite the Mercado Hidalgo and the Ayuntamiento – it's on the second floor, accessed via a passageway between a shoe shop and phone stall. You'll find plenty of information here, and usually an English speaker. All of the major **banks**, where you can change travellers' cheques and find ATM machines, are on Enríquez, a block or two south of *Hotel Provincia Express*. Papantla has several **Internet** cafés – the cheapest lie on 20 de Noviembre, while the one on the zócalo next to the *Hacienda* charges M$10 per hour. Walk up the metal stairs to get to the entrance.

There are several reasonably priced **hotels** in Papantla. The *Hotel Provincia Express*, on the zócalo at Enríquez 103 (ⓣ784/842-1645; ❺), has slightly worn modern rooms with cable TV and phones, as well as free Internet, while the *Tajín*, diagonally opposite and next to the cathedral at Domínguez 104 (ⓣ784/842-0121; ⓦwww.hoteltajin.com.mx; ❺), is the town's top hotel, with good views across the city. Cheaper options include the modern *Totonacapán* on Olivio at 20 de Noviembre, near the second-class bus terminal (ⓣ784/842-1220; ❹), which has a disco on Saturday nights, and the basic but good value *Hotel Pulido* at Enríquez 205 (ⓣ784/842-0035; ❸), which has rooms with fan or a/c.

Papantla has an enticing spread of **local specialities** to sample, chief of which is *sacahuil* or *zacahuilt*, a giant tamale of chicken and beans, sold at small stalls above the Mercado Juárez, opposite the cathedral. Mercados Juárez and Hidalgo are the best places to stock up on small bottles of locally produced vanilla. **Restaurants** are cheap and plentiful, though the menus differ only slightly from one place to the next. The *Plaza Pardo* on Enríquez (ⓣ784/842-0059;

daily 7.30am–11.30pm) has the best view over the zócalo, a pretty terrace, good breakfasts and reasonably priced Mexican fare. Other solid options on the zócalo include the *Sorrento* next door (daily 7am–midnight; ☎784/842-0067), and *La Hacienda*, also with a first-floor terrace on the other side of the Ayuntiamento (☎784/842-0633). *Café Catedral*, below the cathedral at Domínguez and Curato, is a more traditional place for early morning coffee, hot chocolate and pastries. Anyone on a tight budget should head for the eateries on 20 de Noviembre and around Mercado Hidalgo towards the second-class bus station.

## El Tajín

However charming and peaceful Papantla may be, the main reason anyone goes there is to visit the ruins of **EL TAJÍN**, by far the most important archeological site on the Gulf coast. The current opinion is that the principal architecture here dates from the Classic period (300–900 AD), declining in the early Post-Classic (900–1100 AD). By the time of the Conquest it had been forgotten, and any knowledge of it comes from archeological enquiries made since the accidental discovery of the site in 1785 – El Tajín remains one of the most enigmatic of all of Mexico's ancient cities. No one even knows who built it: some claim it was the Huastecs, others the Totonacs. Although "Tajín" means thunderbolt in Totonaca, experts consider it unlikely to have been built by their ancestors. Most archeologists prefer not to speculate too wildly, instead calling the civilization "**Classic Veracruz**". You'll notice many of its hallmarks at El Tajín, including niches in temple walls and complex ornamental motifs known as "scrolls", which are most prevalent on items and bas-reliefs associated with the ball-game (look at some of the stone "yokes" in the site museum). Classic Veracruz influence was widespread, and is strongly felt at Teotihuacán (see p.485), such that some believe that city may have been built by Veracruzanos.

Despite many years of effort, only a small part of the huge site has been cleared, and even this limited area is constantly in danger of being once more engulfed by the jungle: green mounds sprout from the trees in every direction, each concealing more ruins.

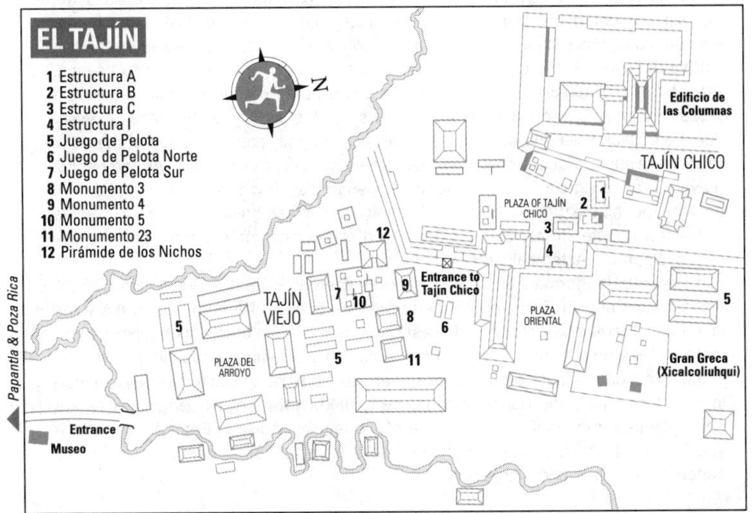

### Practicalities

The easiest way to **get to El Tajín** is from Papantla, 13km away. Buses take around fifteen minutes and can be picked up at the Pemex gas station on Madero, the main road a few blocks downhill from the zócalo (take 20 de Noviembre) – coming from the plaza, buses should be heading to your left (west). Note that any bus to Poza Rica will pass the ruins, though you'll have to walk 500m from the main highway (the junction is known as the "Desviación El Tajín"). **Taxis** to Tajín from Papantla should cost around M$50, though you can pick them up for about M$10 per person if you share. Both buses and taxis should drop you off at the collection of touristy stalls and cheap restaurants that surround the entrance.

**Moving on**, there are buses direct from El Tajín to **Poza Rica** (marked "El Chote" and "San Andrés"; 30min), from where you can connect with services to Mexico City as well as up or down the coast. Poza Rica, 21km from Papantla, is not a place of any delights – it's a dull, oil-boom city with something of a reputation for violence. You're much better off continuing north towards Tuxpán, about an hour up the coast. **Poza Rica airport** operates flights to several domestic destinations, including Mexico City, Reynosa and Villahermosa.

### The site

The site (daily 9am–5pm; M$45, M$30 to bring in a video cameras) divides broadly into two areas: **Tajín Viejo**, which centres on the amazing Pirámide de los Nichos, and **Tajín Chico**, a group of official residential buildings belonging to the city's ruling class built on an artificial terrace. The site **museum** has a small collection of the more delicate stonework salvaged from the ruins, notably murals and columns, as well as bits of pottery and some statues – displays are primarily labelled in Spanish, but there are a few English explanations. From the entrance (where, as well as the museum, there's a café and bar), a track leads

#### The Voladores de Papantla

Although the full significance of the dance of the **Voladores** has been lost over time, it has survived much as the earliest chroniclers reported it, largely because the Spanish thought of it as a sport rather than a pagan rite. It involves five men: a leader who provides music on flute and drum, and four performers. They represent the five earthly directions – the four cardinal points and straight up, from earth to heaven. After a few preliminaries, the five climb to a small platform atop a pole, where the leader resumes playing and directs prayers for the fertility of the land in every direction. Meanwhile, the dancers tie ropes, coiled tightly around the top of the pole, to their waists and at a signal fling themselves head-first into space. As they spiral down in increasing circles the leader continues to play, and to spin, on his platform, until the four hit the ground (hopefully landing on their feet, having righted themselves at the last minute). In all, they make thirteen revolutions each, symbolizing the 52-year cycle of the Aztec calendar.

In Papantla (performances in front of the cathedral Fri, Sat & Sun 11am–6pm, 4 times a day) and El Tajín (regular performances outside the entrance to the ruins starting at 11am) it has become, at least partly, a tourist spectacle, as the permanent metal poles attest. In local villages there is still more ceremony attached, particularly in the selection of a sufficiently tall tree to act as the pole, and its temporary erection in the place where the dance is to be performed. Note that all performances are nominally free, though if you catch one of the regular shows in Papantla or El Tajín you'll be expected to make a "donation" of at least M$10 per person – one of the dancers will walk round with a hat.

through a small group of buildings to **Plaza del Arroyo**, the city marketplace, and into the heart of Tajín Viejo. Before you reach the square in front of the pyramid you pass several **ball-courts**, the most prominent of which is the South Court, or **Juego de Pelota Sur**, to your left; it looks like a wide avenue between two small pyramids. There are seventeen such courts known here, and possibly more unexcavated. It's thought that the game took on a greater importance here than at any other known site. We know little of the rules, and courts vary widely in size and shape, but the general idea was to knock a ball through a ring or into a hole without the use of the hands. Clearly there was also a religious significance to the game; here at El Tajín there are indications that there it was also closely associated with human sacrifice: the superb bas-relief sculptures that cover the walls of the South Court include portrayals of a decapitated player, and another about to be stabbed with a ritual knife by fellow players, with Death waiting to his left. Bas-reliefs are a constant feature of the site, adorning many of the ball-courts and buildings, with more stacked in the museum, but these in the South Court are the most striking and best preserved.

The unique **Pirámide de los Nichos** is the most famous building at El Tajín, and indeed one of the most remarkable of all Mexican ruins. It rises to a height of about 20m in six receding tiers, each face punctuated with regularly spaced niches; up the front a steep stairway climbs to a platform on which the temple originally stood. If you tally up the niches, including those hidden by the stairs and those, partly destroyed, around the base of the temple, there are 365 in all. Their exact purpose is unknown, but clearly they were more than mere decoration: theories include each one holding some offering or sacrifice, one for each day of the year, or that they symbolized caves – the dwellings of the earth god. Originally they were painted black, with the pyramid in red, to enhance the impression of depth. Niches are also present on other buildings at the site, some bearing the attribute of Quetzalcoatl, the plumed serpent, El Tajín's most depicted god.

Around the plaza in front of the pyramid stand all the other important buildings of Tajín Viejo – note that you are not allowed to climb any of them. Opposite is **Monumento 3**, similar pyramid without niches, and behind it **Monumento 23**, a strange steep-sided bulk, one of the last structures to be built here. To the right of the Pirámide de los Nichos, Monumento 2, a low temple, squats at the base of **Monumento 5**, a beautiful truncated pyramid with a high decorative pediment broken by a broad staircase; on the left, Monumento 4 is one of the oldest in El Tajín, and only partly restored.

From the back of Monumento 4 the path continues past the **Juego de Pelota Norte** with its worn relief sculptures and up onto the levelled terrace of **Tajín Chico**, home of the city's elites. Originally this raised area was supported by a retaining wall, part of which has been restored, and reached by a staircase (which is no longer there) opposite the ball-court. Only parts of the buildings themselves now survive, making a rather confusing whole. **Estructura C** and the adjoining **Estructura B** are the most impressive remains here: Estructura C has stone friezes running around its three storeys, giving the illusion of niches. In this case, they were purely decorative, an effect that would have been heightened by a brightly coloured stucco finish. It has the remains of a concrete roof – originally a huge single slab of poured cement, unique in ancient Mexico. **Estructura A** also had a covered interior, and you can still see the entrance covered by a false arch of the type common in Maya buildings. To the left of Estructura C, **Estructura I** features internal and external murals, and was probably the residence of some major political or religious figure. On the hill above Tajín Chico stood the **Edificio de las**

**Columnas**, which must have dominated the entire city. El Tajín's most famous ruler, 13 Rabbit, lived here – bas-reliefs on columns recorded his exploits, and some of these are now on show in the museum. The building is partly restored, and bits of broken, pre-Columbian pottery litter the area, but this part of the site is closed to the public.

From the terrace of Tajín Chico you can walk down the stone path to the **Gran Greca** complex, also known as Xicalcoliuhqui, with its spiral walls containing two ball-courts and more pyramids. It's only been partially cleared of jungle, but you can stroll along the walled edges to get a sense of its vast size. Built towards the end of the city's life, it's regarded as a sign of growing crisis, Tajín's rulers becoming increasingly obsessed with monumental projects in order to maintain control over a disenchanted populace.



# Tuxpán

Straddling the river of the same name, the town of **TUXPÁN** (or Tuxpam, pronounced "Toosh-pam") offers a far preferable overnight stay to its uglier southern neighbour, Poza Rica, on the journey up the coast to Tampico (see p.222). That said, it's still fairly uninviting, with oblong concrete houses offering slim shade to barking dogs, in a landscape further marred by half-built oil platforms.

The zócalo and marketplace both spill out onto the north bank of the Río Tuxpán, but the town's most appealing spot is **Parque Reforma**, a square with plenty of trees about 200m west of the zócalo along Juárez. Small boats leave from in front of the zócalo, crossing the river to the town's single attraction, the **Museo de la Amistad México–Cuba** (Mon–Sat 9am–7pm, Sun 9am–2pm; free). Occupying the house where Fidel Castro spent a year planning his revolutionary return to Cuba, the museum, comprising one small room of unlabelled photos, and another where a video is shown, focuses on Castro, Ché Guevara and Spanish imperialism in the Americas in general. There's usually a guide around who can give you a rundown on the displays, but ask the security guard at the gate if the guide's not immediately visible. The revolutionaries sailed from Tuxpán in December 1956 in the *Granma* yacht, almost sinking on the way, and arrived in Cuba to find Batista's forces waiting. A replica of the *Granma* stands on the riverbank. To get there, walk inland a couple of blocks to Obregón and then turn right, heading back to the river at the end of the street.

The only other reason to stick around Tuxpán is some long, if mediocre, beaches at **Barra de Tuxpán**, by the river mouth some 12km east of town. **Buses** (marked "Playa) run all day along riverside Bulevar Reyes Heroles, past fishing boats and tankers, and arrive twenty minutes later at a vast stretch of grey sand. There are restaurants and changing rooms here and some palapas where you can sling a hammock.

## Practicalities

The first-class ADO **bus** terminal lies on Rodríguez near the junction with Juárez, one block from the river and some 300m east of the zócalo – follow the river along Reyes Heroles to get to the centre. Ómnibus de México (with both first- and second-class services) is further east at the junction of Reyes Heroles and Clavijero, under the huge bridge across the river. For **moving on**, there are regular ADO buses to Tampico, Veracruz and Mexico City (direct and via Poza Rica), as well as seven daily services to Papantla.

The helpful, well-stocked **tourist office** (Mon–Fri 9am–7pm, Sat 10am–6pm; ⓣ783/834-6407) is in the Palacio Municipal, at Juárez 20. There's a **laundry** at Ocampo 8, and you can **change money** or traveller's cheques at the Bancomer or Banamex, the former on Zapata two blocks west of the cathedral, the latter on Juárez at Parque Reforma. There is an **Internet** café next to Banamex, at Juárez 52.

Several of the town's **hotels** are found on Juárez between the zócalo and Parque Reforma. The best place to stay is the attractive *Reforma*, opposite the cathedral at Juárez 25 (ⓣ783/834-0210; ⓔhotelreforma@prodigy.net.mx; ❻), which has a/c rooms with TV, as well as the best restaurant in town (see below). Cheaper options include the *Posada San Ignacio*, Ocampo 29, one block north of Parque Reforma (ⓣ783/834-2905; ❸), where you can find simple rooms with fans and TV around a quiet courtyard.

With its good steaks and live music on Fridays and Saturdays, *Antonios*, at *Hotel Reforma*, is the chicest **restaurant** in town (M$60–110 for mains). Otherwise, Parque Reforma is the best place to head for. Sip natural fruit juices at tables that fan out from the centre of the square, or sit at the terrace of *El Mejicano*, Morelos 49, and enjoy dishes from its menu of Mexican food, including good guacamole and a M$45 buffet. Alternatively, *Nuevo 303*, on Pipila leading down from Juárez to the river, is popular with locals and open 24 hours.



# South of Veracruz

Leaving Veracruz to the south, Hwy-180 traverses a long expanse of plain, a country of broad river deltas and salty lagoons for nearly 150km, until it hits the hills of the volcanic **Sierra Tuxtla**. This is one of the most beautiful stretches of Veracruz state, boasting picturesque **fishing villages**, **volcanoes**, **waterfalls** and the idyllic **Lago de Catemaco**, around which the last expanse of Gulf coast **rainforest** is preserved. The region greatest claim to fame, however, is that it was the birthplace of Mexico's first civilization, the **Olmecs**. Here lies the **Volcán de San Martín**, where the Olmecs believed the earth to be created; they built a replica "creation mountain" at their city, La Venta, on the border with Tabasco (see p.764). Although archeologically significant, their second major city at **Tres Zapotes**, near Santiago Tuxtla, is little more than a mound in a maize field.

Beyond the Tuxtla mountains, there's more low, flat, dull country all the way to Villahermosa (see p.755), and though it was once part of the Olmec heartland, there are scant reminders of that past today. For most Mexicans, this part of southern Veracruz, especially around Lago de Catemaco, is best known as the "**Tierra de los Brujos**" (land of the witches or wizards). Every March a gathering takes place on Cerro Mono Blanco (White Monkey Hill), just north of Catemaco town. Mexico has thousands of practising witches, warlocks, shamans, herbalists, seers, healers, psychics and fortune-tellers, who follow a religion that blends Catholicism with ancient rites and practices. The thirteen *brujos* of Catemaco, who call themselves "the Brothers", are acknowledged as the high priests of the trade.

## Alvarado and Tlacotalpan

**ALVARADO** is the first stop on the road south, perched on a narrow strip of land between the sea and the Laguna de Alvarado, some 72km from Veracruz. It's a working fishing port and is refreshingly traditional, but though there are plenty of places to stay, it's not somewhere you'll want to hang around for long. You might, however, be tempted to stop for a meal – there are lots of good **fish restaurants** along the waterfront. Alvarado's Port Authority restaurant, especially, is famous and also cheap, being frequented by port workers and fishermen.

If you want to stay somewhere small, quiet and entirely off the tourist circuit, try **TLACOTALPAN**, some twenty minutes and 18km away from Alvarado on the winding road that heads inland towards Tuxtepec. It's best known for being where musician and composer Agustín Lara (1900-1970), whose works have been interpreted by the likes of Pavarotti, Carreras and Domingo, spent his early childhood. On the banks of the Río Papaloapan, close to the lagoon, it's a very pretty village, and you can rent boats on the river, and fish or swim. There's a small **tourist office** (Mon–Fri 9am–3pm) in the Palacio Municipal, and near the zócalo at Allegre 6 you'll find the **Museo Salvador Ferrando** (Tues–Sun 10.30am–5pm; M$10) named after one of the town's most respected painters. It operates as the town's history museum, with a mix of antique furniture and local artefacts on display. Tlacotalpan's most famous son is celebrated at the **Casa Museo Agustín Lara** (Mon–Sat 10am–5.30pm; M$10) at Beltrán 6, which has displays of Lara memorabilia, and also at the **Casa de la Cultura Agustín Lara** (Mon–Fri 9am–5pm; free) at Carranza 43, which hosts dances and shows, and upstairs, modernist paintings by Alberto Fuster, another local. The best time to visit is in early February, when the **procession of the Virgen de la Candelaria** is celebrated with bull runs, special food stalls and folk-music concerts – the main "procession" takes place on the river, where the image of the Virgin is floated downstream amongst a mass of assorted riverboats.

The upmarket *Hotel Posada Doña Lala*, by the river at Carranza 11 (Ⓣ288/884-2580; ❸ or with a/c ❹), has lovely rooms and a smart open-air restaurant serving great seafood. Otherwise, there are a couple of small hotels on the main street near where the **buses** stop. Alternatively, you can easily find a **room** in a local house for around M$100 – ask around in the restaurants and cafés near the zócalo. The **cafés** in front of the *Doña Lala* near the river have delicious, cheap seafood.

## Los dos Tuxtlas

The two townships of **Santiago Tuxtla** and **San Andrés Tuxtla** together form the hub of the attractive, volcanic hill country – known as "La Suiza Veracruzana" (the Veracruz Switzerland) – that emerges beyond Alvarado. The scenery becomes decidedly more interesting at this point, and the cooler climate is an infinite relief. The area's charms (along with Lago de Catemaco) tend to be exaggerated somewhat, aimed firmly at domestic tourists, but it can still be a rewarding place to break the journey south.

### Santiago Tuxtla and Tres Zapotes

Coming from Veracruz, you first pass the quiet and picturesque town of **SANTIAGO TUXTLA**, a place not inundated with facilities and attractions, but worth a brief look nonetheless. Buses stop on the main road a short walk from the zócalo, where a giant **Olmec head** (3.4m) known as "Rancho La Corbata" is proudly displayed – this is the largest one ever found. On the south side of the plaza is the small **Museo Tuxteco** (Mon–Sat 9am–6pm, Sun 9am–5pm; M$30), which houses an interesting collection (labelled in Spanish only) of Olmec statues, pottery and giant heads, as well as a small room dedicated to the town's colonial history and namesake Santiago Matamoros, St James the Moor Slayer (patron saint of Spain). Visiting celebrities and locals alike come here to rub their thumbs over the forehead of the Olmec head known as "El Negro" – it's supposed to provide positive energy (and miraculous cures for illness).

Around 23km and a little less than an hour away by local bus, the Olmec site of **Tres Zapotes** was one of the longest-lasting of all Olmec cities, occupied from 1200 BC to around 1000 AD. Buses to the site leave from near the main highway, and are usually marked "3 Zapotes". Frankly, the journey is barely worth it: a painfully slow ride to what is basically just a **museum** (daily 9am–6pm; M$27) containing little that is not duplicated elsewhere. Its main interest lies in a series of stelae inscribed with Olmec glyphs. Of the site itself, nearby, virtually nothing can be seen.

There are a couple of small **hotels** in town, including the remarkably good *Castellanos* (☎294/947-0300; ❺), in a distinctive circular building right on the zócalo, with 53 a/c rooms surrounding an inner atrium and a good **restaurant** serving meat dishes, seafood and salads. There are a few other restaurants and cafés, again around the zócalo, such as *Super La Joya*, where you can eat standard Mexican fare at tables outside (M$30 for comidas corridas). From back on the main road it's easy to catch frequent buses to San Andrés, 13km over the hill (20min).



### San Andrés Tuxtla

**SAN ANDRÉS TUXTLA** is the larger of the two Tuxtlas. The majority of first- and second-class **buses** stop at the top of the hill where the highway passes by – the terminal is at the top of Juárez, which leads straight down to the zócalo, a fifteen-minute walk, or M$13 by taxi.

Surrounded by tobacco fields, San Andrés is home to several **cigar factories** where you can watch *puros* being hand-rolled and then buy some. One of the top brands in Mexico, Matacapan Tobaccos, is produced here and has brought international fame to the town. The **Santa Clara** factory, established in 1830 (Mon–Fri 8am–1.30pm & 3–7.30pm, Sat 8–11am; free), on the highway one block from the ADO bus station (Catemaco direction), welcomes visitors. The tobacco export company Calidad Tobaccos (ⓦwww.calidadtobaccos.com) runs guided tours of the cultivation fields and factory, and even hands-on cigar-rolling workshops.

The other main reason to stay here is to visit the raging waters of the **Salto de Eyipantla** (M$6), a powerful waterfall 50m wide and 40m high, about 9km from San Andrés but easily reached by frequent local buses. Marked "El Salto" (M$5.50), these leave from the bus stop in the zócalo opposite *Hotel del Parque*, and drop you in the village around thirty minutes later – walk another 200m straight along the road to a car park surrounded by touristy stalls and the main entrance. From here there are 244 worn steps down to the base of the falls, which is still a magical spot despite a further collection of stalls and cafés – though it can be a bit of a carnival at weekends and the busy summer months, it's a pleasant place to have a drink.

Most **accommodation** and other facilities in San Andrés are very close to the zócalo. The *Figueroa*, at the corner of Pino Suárez and Belisario Domínguez, a couple of blocks southeast of the plaza (☎294/942-0257; ❷, TV an extra M$30), is the pick of the budget options near here, with charming rooms along a plant-strewn balcony and a good range of leaflets, brochures and maps about the region. Traditionally regarded as the town's premier hotel, the *Hotel del Parque*, Madero 5 (☎294/942-0198, ⓦwww.hoteldelparque.com; ❺), has cable TV and large but characterless rooms. You'll get better value at the *Hotel de los Pérez* (☎294/942-0777, ⓦwww.hoteldelosperez.com; ❺), around the corner at Rascón 2, which is newer and has Internet. You could also try *Hotel Posada San*

*Martin* (☎294/942-1036; ⑤), halfway to the bus station at Juárez 304, which has lovely rooms arranged around a quiet garden and a small pool.

Food and drink options include **cafés** on the zócalo: sip a coffee while people watching at *Hotel del Parque*, for instance, which has the most upmarket café in town or cheap *Café Catedral* (closed Sun) and the popular and more modern *Minni's* (M$45 *menú del día*) on the other side of the plaza. *El Pequeño Archi*, next to the *Catedral* hotel (☎294/942-4796; closed Sun) on Pino Suárez, is a cheaper option and a good spot for breakfast or tortas. There are also a number of reputable fish and seafood **restaurants**, especially along Madero west of the zócalo, past the *San Andrés* hotel – *Mariscos Chazaro* at no. 12 (☎294/942-1379) has great prawn *coctels*. For something more special, try the *Montepio*, at the end of the alley opposite the *San Andrés* hotel (☎294/942-1496), which has a steak menu (M$140–150), a good wine list and a bar that welcomes women. For self-catering, there's Super Carnicera San Miguel, opposite HSBC, which sells sumptuous roast chicken, and an excellent **market** on 5 de Mayo north of the zócalo, where you can buy superb baked goods, locally grown tropical fruits and vegetables, freshwater fish and the best selection of medicinal herbs in the region.

There are several **banks** with ATMs around the zócalo; the best for travellers' cheques is HSBC on 16 de Septiembre (which breaks of Juárez just north of the zócalo), at Carranza. The **post office** is down from the zócalo on 20 de Noviembre (beyond *Minni's*). **Internet** cafés seem to change fast in San Andrés; you could try *Bynn@r Cybercafé* (Mon–Sat 10am–midnight, Sun noon–midnight; M$10/hr) along Constitución just east of the zócalo, or the café at Juárez 421, a few blocks down from the bus station (M$10/hr) and there are also a few places along 20 de Noviembre.

For **moving on**, Catemaco is around 11km east, and Santiago is 13km to the west: both are easily accessible via frequent buses that depart in front of the Fenix store where Pino Suárez meets Constitución, two blocks east of the zócalo. There are also relatively frequent buses to Veracruz from the main terminal, but note that buses to Villahermosa tend to leave in the evening, getting you there in the early hours.

## Catemaco and around

Squatting on the western shore of wide, mountain-ringed Lago de Catemaco, (also known as Laguna de Catemaco), and by tradition a centre of native witchcraft, **CATEMACO** is a much more picturesque spot to break the journey before the long leg south. The surrounding mountains, which are volcanic in origin (though the most recent activity was in 1793), are unique on the Gulf coast, as they descend right into the sea. The nearby marshland and lagoons are also a haven for wildlife, supporting large colonies of waterbirds, including herons, cormorants, wintering ospreys and many other resident and migratory species. This said, the town, though relaxed during the week (it's more like a big village) isn't particularly attractive, with slapdash development stretching five blocks or so back from the waterfront. Veracruzanos arrive in force at weekends and holidays, when the main strip can get pretty busy, and it's the lake itself and surrounding area, particularly the beaches and *Nanciyaga* resort (see p.629), that are the primary attractions. Watch out for the touts, who'll try and persuade you to attend a native spiritual purification ceremony or to visit Playa Azul, one of the lake's several beaches and the location of an ageing resort-style hotel – it also happens to be where Sean Connery's *Medicine Man* (1992) was filmed. More recently, scenes from Mel Gibson's controversial Maya epic *Apocalypto* (2006) were filmed around the lake.

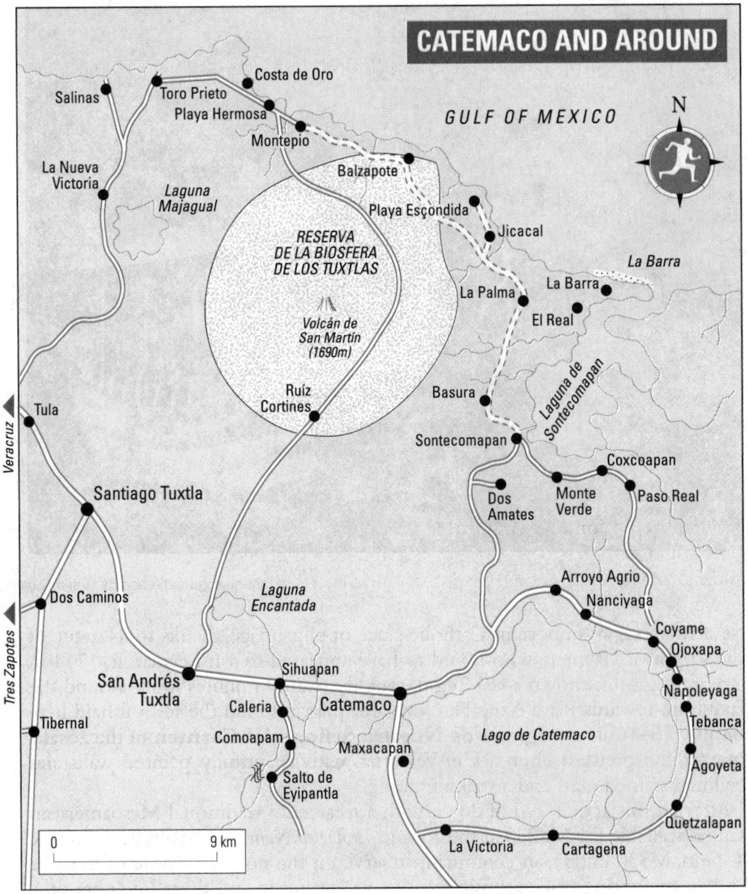

**CATEMACO AND AROUND**

A **boat trip** across the lake or to one of the islands within it is one of the highlights of southern Veracruz. The Sociedad Cooperativa de Lanchas, on the lake opposite the *Julita* hotel, one block from the zócalo, runs ninety-minute trips to all of the lake's main sights and some of its beaches for M$350 for one to six people. On **Isla de los Changos** there are stump-tailed macaques (monkeys native to Thailand, and often called, incorrectly, "baboons" by locals) that officially belong to Veracruz University – who introduced them in 1974 and have since pleaded for them to be left alone – but boat operators continue to feed them so tourists can photograph them. In 1988 endangered Mexican howler monkeys were introduced to Agaltepec Island, which is less frequently visited. Alternatively, you can just chill out on one of the lake **beaches**: Playa Espagoya is a short walk north of the town, followed by Playa Hermosa and Playa Azul. **Morelet's crocodiles**, a relatively small species (up to 3m long), live in the lake, nesting on the far bank. They're well fed on left-over fish scraps from the lakeside restaurants, and, apparently, never attack. People do swim in the lake in summer, but stick to the main beaches and ask a local if you still feel uneasy.

△ Sight-seeing boat, Lago de Catemaco

Catemaco is an important Catholic place of pilgrimage, thanks to its statue of the Virgin of Carmen, who is said to have appeared to a fisherman in 1714 in a narrow grotto known as **El Tegal**, roughly twenty minutes' walk around the lakeshore towards Playa Azul. The focus for pilgrims (and the festival held here on July 15–16) is the **Iglesia de Nuestra Señora del Carmen** in the zócalo, one of the prettiest churches in Veracruz, with beautifully painted walls and ceilings, stained glass and a striking dome.

After all this activity, wind down with a *temazcal*, a traditional Mesoamerican sauna, available for M$250 at the *Reserva Ecológica Nanciyaga* (daily 9am–2pm & 4–6pm; M$30 entry), an ecotourism reserve on the northern shore of the lake and an interesting place to visit even if you opt not to stay there (see opposite). Non-guests can rent canoes and kayaks, have mud facials, visit a crocodile pen, arrange guided walks through the forest and learn about traditional Mexican arts and crafts. From Catemaco it's only 7km by taxi to *Nanciyaga*; you can also get there by launch.

## Practicalities

From Veracruz there are several first-class **buses** daily (M$94) to Catemaco, but the town is served far less frequently from other places. The ADO first-class terminal, surely the most scenic in the country, faces the lake and is about a five-minute walk from the centre (walk along the lakefront and take the first street to your right). Some second-class buses also terminate at the ADO station, but most stop at the AU terminal on the main highway on the edge of town. If you buy tickets here, try to get them a day in advance, since seats are numbered. Buses from San Andrés Tuxtla will drop you near the zócalo at Lerdo and Revolución. In the other direction, buses make the thirty-minute trip to San Andrés from the same place, which is also the starting point for *piratas* heading to the northern beaches (see p.630). Share-taxis to San Andrés leave halfway up Carranza back towards the main highway, near the mound known as El Cerrito.

On the zócalo, two blocks from the waterfront, there's a **tourist office** in the Palacio Municipal (Mon–Fri 9am–3pm & 6–9pm) and an HSBC **ATM** machine next to the *Catemaco* hotel – note that to change traveller's cheques, you'll have to go to San Andrés. The **post office** is a short walk south of the zócalo along Carranza then left along 5 de Abril. You'll find **Internet** cafés along Carranza as you head back towards San Andrés, though they seem to turn over quickly; *Internet Yoju* is a block behind the ADO bus station.

For the most part, **hotels** right on the lake are relatively expensive, though out of season prices do drop. Otherwise, there are several places a couple of streets inland, just down from where the buses stop; people may try to accost you as you arrive to take you to a hotel, but rooms are easy enough to find without help. On the lakeside very close to the centre, *Julita*, Playa 10 (ⓣ294/943-0008; ❸), is the best value in town, with simple, clean and bright rooms with fans. Further along, at no. 14, *Juros* (ⓣ294/943-0084; ❺) boasts a fantastic rooftop swimming pool, but rooms vary in quality. *Los Arcos*, behind the *Juros* on the main street at Madero 7 (ⓣ294/943-0003, ⓦwww.arcoshotel.com.mx; ❻), has pleasant, a/c rooms with TV around an attractive pool. Some of the higher rooms have lake views. On the zócalo, the *Catemaco* (ⓣ294/943-0203, ⓔhcatemaco@yahoo.com.mx; ❻) has similar facilities, plus its own restaurant, open earlier than most. *Playa Azul Resort* (ⓣ294/943-0001, ⓦwww.playaazulcatemaco.com; ❻), further out along the lakeshore, has plenty of facilities and rooms overlooking the water, but it's getting a little worn around the edges. Finally, the most luxurious hotel is *La Finca* (ⓣ294/947-9710, ⓦwww.lafinca.com.mx; ❼), 2km west of the lake off the main highway to Acayucán, with modern, comfortable rooms with lake views and an excellent pool.

By far the most enjoyable place to stay if you want to appreciate the area's natural beauty, however, is the *Reserva Ecológica Nanciyaga* (ⓣ294/943-0199, ⓦwww.nanciyaga.com; ❺), rarely visited by Westerners and a great place to meet young Veracruzanos; **cabañas** on the lake shore (M$400 weekdays; double on weekends and holidays) have room for up to four people (no TV or phone). Many of the activities on offer at the reserve are free to guests (mud bath, guided jungle walks, massage and use of kayaks; see opposite).

Seafood **restaurants** abound on the shore and around the zócalo, most offering the local speciality, *mojarra* (small perch from the lake), best sampled when cooked *a la tachagovi* – with a delicious hot sauce. Eateries popular with locals include *Los Sauces* (ⓣ294/943-0548) and *El Pescador* (ⓣ294/943-0705), next to each other on Paseo del Malecón between the zócalo and the ADO bus terminal, open from lunch onwards; and the cheap restaurant at the *Julita* hotel. The best all-round eating option, however, is *La Casona*, an enchanting old building on the zócalo at Aldama 4 (ⓣ294/943-0813), which has plenty for seafood- and meat-lovers alike, great breakfasts, an attractive dining room looking out onto a verdant garden and a talkative parrot to boot (breakfast M$30, mains M$60–70). Another good place for breakfast is *La Casita*, a few blocks north of the plaza on Matamoros (just beyond Melchor Ocampo), which also has Mexican fare and seafood.

## Sontecomapan and the coastal beaches

From Catemaco a paved road with spectacular views of Lago de Catemaco, the rainforest and the Laguna de Sontecomapan leads through sections of ranch land only recently hacked out of the rainforest. It's 18km to the small fishing village of **SONTECOMAPAN**, where you can take a trip up the pretty **Sontecomapan canal**, which offers good **bird-watching** possibilities. From

## Fiestas

### February

**Día de la Candelaria** (Feb 2). Colourful Indian fiesta in Jaltipán, on the main road south of Catemaco, which includes the dance of La Malinche (Cortés's Indian interpreter and mistress, who is said to have been born here), recreating aspects of the Conquest. Also the final day of a week-long fiesta, complete with dances, boat races and bulls let loose in the streets, in Tlacotalpan (see p.624).

**Carnaval** (the week before Lent; variable Feb–March) is celebrated all over the region, most riotously in Veracruz (see p.605).

### March

**Fiestas de San José** (March 18–19). In Naranjos, between Tuxpán and Tampico, a fiesta with many traditional dances celebrates the local patron saint. Similar events in Espinal, a Totonac village on the Río Tecolutla, not far from El Tajín and Papantla, where with luck you can witness the spectacular Voladores.

**Semana Santa** (Holy Week). Recreations of the Passion are widespread in this area. You can witness them in Papantla (see p.617), where you'll also see the Voladores; in Coatzintla, a Totonac village near Tajín; in Cotaxtla, between Veracruz and Córdoba; and in Otatitlán. Naolinco, a beautiful village near Xalapa, stages a mock Crucifixion on Good Friday. Also celebrations in Catemaco (see p.626) – and in the port of Alvarado (see p.623) – a far more ribald Fish Fiesta following hard on the heels of the Veracruz Carnaval.

### April

**Feria de las Flores** (approx April 15–17). Flower festival in Fortín de las Flores (see p.598).

### May

**Corpus Christi** (variable; the Thurs after Trinity). The start of a major four-day festival in Papantla (see p.617), and, in particular, regular performances by the Voladores.

### June

**Día de San Juan** (June 24). Celebrated with dancing in Santiago Tuxtla (see p.624), and in Martinez de la Torre, on the road inland from Nautla, where the Voladores perform.

here it's also possible to take a *colectivo* boat up the canal to **La Barra,** 22km from Catemaco, another lovely stretch of sand and often deserted. *Lanchas* ferry passengers to here from the Sontecomapan *embarcadero* for M$20 each way, though foreigners are usually charged about M$50 (you may have to wait for a return launch) and around M$400 for a round-trip in a private launch (the boatman will wait for you at the beach or return at an appointed time). At La Barra, *Restaurant Juan Cruz* serves up tasty fresh seafood, while *Los Amigos* (Ⓣ294/943-0101, Ⓦwww.losamigos.com.mx; ❹) offers basic but clean **cabañas** or single beds in dorm-like "Ecoalbergues" with shared bathroom for M$100 (M$50 for breakfast). There's a simple restaurant here, as well as hiking trails and kayaks, and you can get a *temazcal* for M$200.

Beyond Sontecomapan the road deteriorates into an appalling state as it continues on to some of Veracruz's most alluring and least visited **beaches**: at **Playa Escondida**, a beautiful stretch of sand some 30km from Catemaco and 4km off the main road, there's *Hotel Playa Escondida* (❸), while buses terminate at **Montepio**, 39km from Catemaco, where there are a couple of posadas, the better of which, the *San José* (Ⓣ294/942-1010; ❷, with a/c ❸) is nearer the sea.

**July**

**Día de la Virgen del Carmen** (July 15–16). A massive pilgrimage to Catemaco (see p.626), accompanied by a fiesta which spills over into the following day.

**Día de Santiago** (July 25). Celebrated with fiestas in Santiago Tuxtla (see p.624) and Coatzintla; each lasts several days. In Tlapacoyan (see p.616) you can see the bizarre Baile de los Negritos (see box, p.617).

**August**

**Feria** (Aug 15). The beginning of a week-long festival in Tuxpán (see p.622) that includes dancing and the Voladores.

**Day of Assumption** (Aug 15). Commemorated in Tlapacoyan (see p.616) with El Baile de los Negritos.

**September**

**Independence Day** (Sept 15–16). Celebrated everywhere.

**October**

**Fiesta de la Virgen del Rosario** (Oct 7). In La Antigua (see p.613) the patroness of fishermen is honoured with processions of canoes on the river, while Alvarado (see p.623) enjoys a more earthy fiesta, filling the first two weeks of the month.

**November**

**Día de los Muertos** (Day of the Dead; Nov 2). Observed everywhere.

**December**

**Día de la Virgen de Guadalupe** (Dec 12). Widely observed, especially in Huatusco, Cotaxtla, and Amatlán de los Reyes, near Córdoba.

**Christmas** (Dec 25). Celebrated everywhere. There's a very famous festival in Santiago Tuxtla (see p.624) that lasts until Twelfth Night (Jan 6).

*Piratas* (converted pick-up trucks) leave Catemaco from Lerdo, at Revolución, five blocks from the lakeshore, every thirty minutes (or when full) and take up to two hours to make the journey to Montepio, and just twenty to thirty minutes to Sontecomapan.

## Acayucán and Coatzacoalcos

Travelling along the **northern shore** of the Isthmus of Tehuantepec – the narrowest part of Mexico – you'll also inevitably pass through **ACAYUCÁN**, where the coastal highway and the trans-isthmus highway meet. The enormous bus station and equally giant market cater to passing travellers; there's little otherwise but mud, dust and noise, though the **market** stalls can be a good place to stop off for provisions such as nuts, cheese, fresh pineapple and corn bread. Make your visit a short one and, if you have any choice at all, press straight on through to Villahermosa (see p.755). If you have to **stay**, go for *Hotel Plaza* (Ⓣ924/245-0088; ⑤) at Victoria 37 or *Joalicia* (Ⓣ924/245-0200; ③) at Zaragoza 4, both off the zócalo, or the more comfortable *Kinaku*, close to it at Ocampo Sur 7 (Ⓣ924/245-0410; ⑤).

The coast from here to the Tabasco border is less attractive, with a huge industrial zone stretching from the dirty concrete town of Minatitlán to **COATZACOALCOS** (formerly Puerto México, the Atlantic railway terminus), dominated by a giant oil refinery. If you have to stop in this area, Coatzacoalcos is definitely the better choice: big enough to have a real centre and with plenty of hotels and restaurants around the camionera. Coatzacoalcos also boasts a spectacular modern bridge – known as Coatzacoalcos II – by which the main highway bypasses the town. If you're on a bus heading downtown you'll cross the Río Coatzacoalcos by an older, lesser suspension bridge. In legend, Coatzacoalcos is the place from which Quetzalcoatl and his followers sailed east, vowing to return.



# Travel details

## Buses

First-class buses are mostly operated by Autobuses del Oriente (ADO) – remarkably slick and efficient. Second-class is dominated (at least on long hauls) by Autobuses Unidos (AU), more of a mixed bag. The following is a brief rundown of the routes, mainly taking into account the ADO services, and should be regarded as a minimum.

**Papantla** to: Mexico City (6 daily; 6hr); Poza Rica (frequently; 30min); Tlapacoyan (4 daily; 3hr); Tuxpán (frequently; 1hr 30min); Veracruz (7 daily; 4hr); Xalapa (7 daily; 4hr).

**Poza Rica** to: Mexico City (8 daily; 5hr); Tuxpán (frequently; 1hr); Veracruz (frequently; 4hr 30min).

**San Andrés Tuxtla** to: Catemaco (frequently; 30min); Coatzacoalcos (9 daily; 2hr 30min); Veracruz (frequently; 3hr).

**Tuxpán** to: Mexico City (9 daily; 6hr); Poza Rica (frequently; 1hr); Tampico (10 daily; 3hr); Veracruz (6 daily; 5hr 30min); Xalapa (7 daily; 6hr).

**Veracruz** to: Cardel (frequently; 30min); Catemaco (9 daily; 3hr 30min); Coatzacoalcos (8 daily; 5hr 30min); Córdoba (frequently; 1hr 45min); Mexico City (16 daily; 5hr 30min); Oaxaca (3 daily; 7hr); Orizaba (frequently; 2hr 30min); Papantla (6 daily; 4hr); Poza Rica (frequently; 4hr 30min); Puebla (frequently; 3hr 30min); San Andrés Tuxtla (12 daily; 3hr); Tuxpán (15 daily; 5hr 30min); Villahermosa (11 daily; 7hr); Xalapa (frequently; 2hr).

**Xalapa** to: Fortín de las Flores (7 daily; 3hr); Mexico City (15 daily; 5hr); Papantla (7 daily; 4hr); Veracruz (frequently; 2hr).

## Flights

**Veracruz** to: Cancún (1 daily; 1hr 35min); Ciudad del Carmen (1 daily; 1hr); Guadalajara (1 daily; 1hr 25min); Houston, Texas (1 daily; 2hr 10min); Mérida (2 daily; 1hr 15min); Mexico City (7 daily; 50min); Monterrey (3 daily; 1hr 30min); Tampico (2 weekly; 1hr); Toluca (1 daily; 55min); Villahermosa (2 daily; 50min).

**Xalapa** to: Mexico City (2 daily; 55min).

# Oaxaca



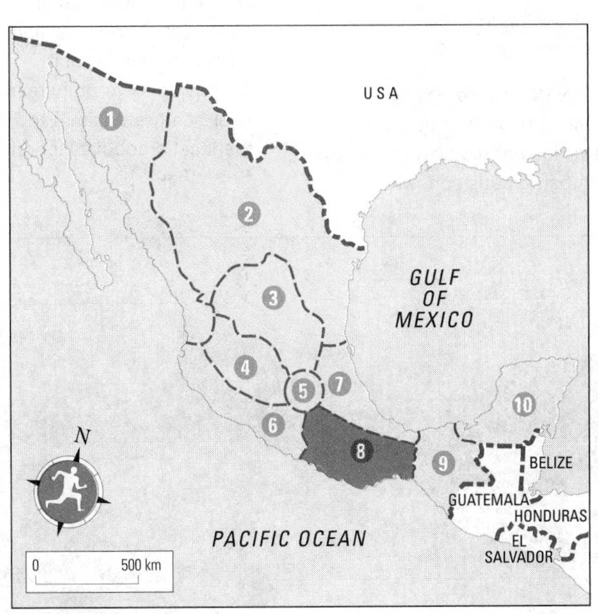
USA
1
2
3
4
5
6
7
8
9
10
GULF OF MEXICO
BELIZE
GUATEMALA
HONDURAS
EL SALVADOR
PACIFIC OCEAN
N
0
500 km

CHAPTER 8

# Highlights

* **Oaxaca** Indigenous traditions fuse with colonial grandeur in one of Mexico's most hypnotic cities. See p.638

* **Monte Albán** A potent symbol of Zapotec power, these ruins were once an astounding ancient city with a population of over twenty thousand. See p.656

* **Teotitlán del Valle** Experience the rich artisan traditions of Oaxaca's Central Valleys while shopping for iconic *tapetes* (rugs). See p.660

* **Benito Juárez** Stay in a Tourist Yú'ù cabin in this quaint village named after Oaxaca's most famous son, where you can hike in beautiful mountain surroundings. See p.660

* **Mitla** The ancient Zapotec ceremonial centre with sublime greca stonework is considered to be without peer in Mexico. See p.663

* **Puerto Escondido** Ride the Mexican pipeline – or just watch – at this world-famous surfing spot and beach destination. See p.669

* **Mazunte** See the queens of the sea, female Golfina turtles, in this tranquil oceanside town or increase your heart rate with a trip to the local crocodile lagoon. See p.684

△Monte Albán

# Oaxaca



The state of **Oaxaca** marks the break between North American central Mexico and Central America. Here the two chains of the Sierra Madre converge, to run on as a single range, through the country's narrowest point, the Isthmus of Tehuantepec, right into South America. The frequently barren landscapes of northern Mexico are left behind, replaced by thickly forested hillsides, or in low-lying areas by swamp and jungle. The striking differences of the region are compounded by the relative lack of development. Industry is virtually nonexistent, and while the city of Oaxaca and several coastal hot spots such as Puerto Escondido have thrived on tourism, the rest of the state is woefully underdeveloped – the "Mexican economic miracle" has yet to reach the south.

**Indigenous traditions** remain powerful in this area, which is home to fifteen different indigenous groups. The old languages are still widely spoken, and there are scenes in the villages that seem to deny that the Spanish Conquest ever happened. Oaxaqueño resourcefulness, pride and craft skills are manifest everywhere: nowhere else in Mexico are the markets so colourful or the fiestas so fascinating. One of Oaxaca's most rewarding and eye-opening experiences can be a stay in one of the Central Valleys' **Tourist Yú'ù** facilities, where you'll be a guest of the local indigenous community. Less enticingly, and arising out of the same traditions, the region has witnessed considerable **political disturbance** in recent years. In autumn 2006 the political situation reached its nadir when striking teachers clashed with riot police in a dispute that had begun over wages and mushroomed into protests over the alleged corruption of state governor Ulises Ruíz.

That said, the state has long been renowned for its harmonious fusion of tradition and modernity. The city of Oaxaca is the region's prime destination, close enough to Mexico City and the mainstream to attract large numbers of tourists to its fine crafts stores, markets, seemingly constant fiestas, cobbled, gallery-lined walkways and sophisticated restaurants. Here you can see one of the region's – and the whole of Iberian America's – most magnificent **Baroque churches**, notably Santo Domingo, which fuses Spanish and native influences to spectacular effect. From the earliest times the valley of Oaxaca was inhabited by the same Zapotec and Mixtec peoples who comprise the bulk of its population now. Their ancient sites – at **Monte Albán**, **Yagul** and **Mitla** – are less well known than their contemporaries in central and eastern Mexico, but every bit as important and impressive.

The Pacific resorts of **Puerto Escondido**, **Puerto Ángel** and **Huatulco** are now firmly on the map and are easily reached from the city, though their reputation for being unspoiled beach paradises is no longer justified – Escondido

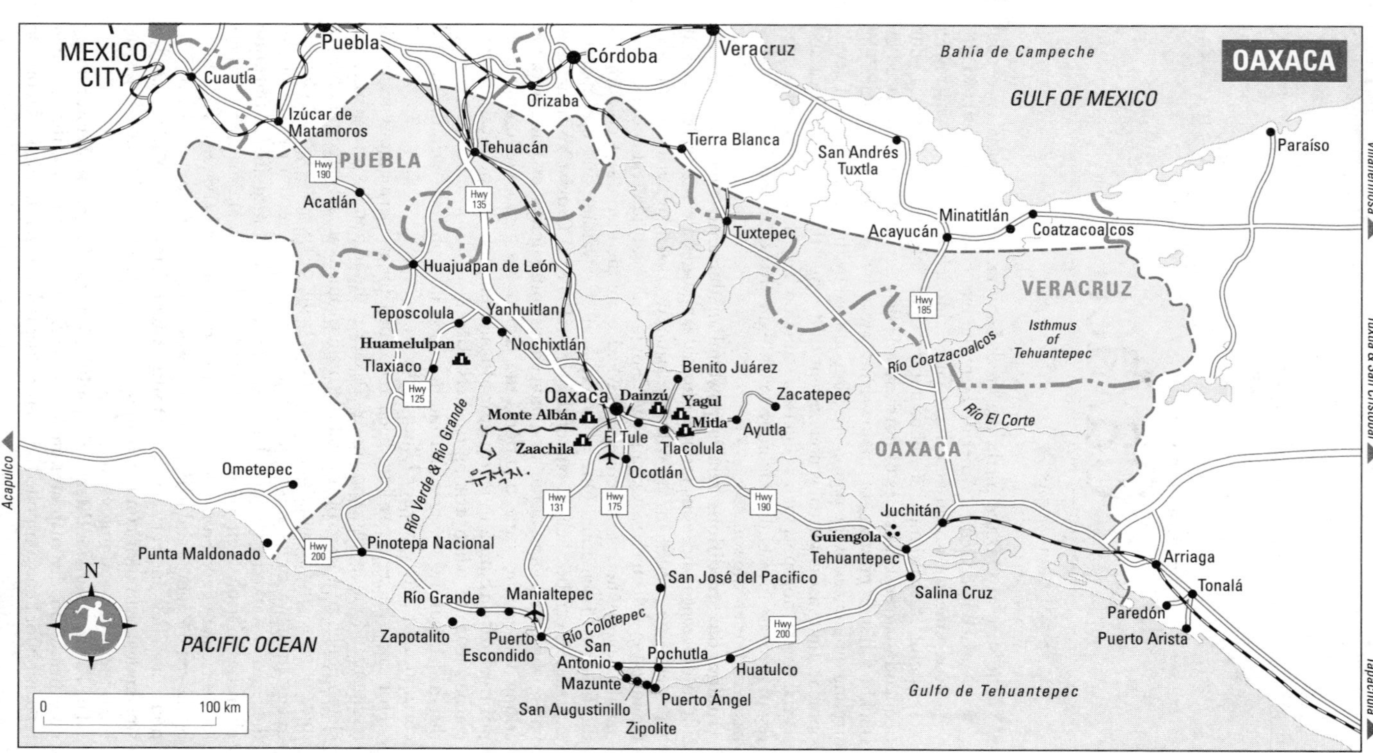
OAXACA
MEXICO CITY
Puebla
Córdoba
Veracruz
Bahía de Campeche
GULF OF MEXICO
Paraíso
Villahermosa
Cuautla
Orizaba
Izúcar de Matamoros
Tehuacán
Tierra Blanca
San Andrés Tuxtla
PUEBLA
Hwy 190
Acatlán
Hwy 135
Tuxtepec
Acayucán
Minatitlán
Coatzacoalcos
Huajuapan de León
VERACRUZ
Hwy 185
Isthmus of Tehuantepec
Tuxtla & San Cristóbal
Teposcolula
Yanhuitlan
Huamelulpan
Nochixtlán
Tlaxiaco
Río Coatzacoalcos
Benito Juárez
Hwy 125
Oaxaca
Dainzú
Yagul
Zacatepec
Monte Albán
Mitla
Ayutla
Río El Corte
Río Verde & Río Grande
Zaachila
El Tule
Tlacolula
OAXACA
Acapulco
Ometepec
Ocotlán
Hwy 131
Hwy 175
Hwy 190
Juchitán
Guiengola
Punta Maldonado
Hwy 200
Pinotepa Nacional
Tehuantepec
Arriaga
N
San José del Pacifico
Tonalá
Río Grande
Manialtepec
Salina Cruz
Paredón
Río Colotepec
Hwy 200
PACIFIC OCEAN
Zapotalito
Puerto Escondido
San Antonio
Pochutla
Puerto Arista
Huatulco
Mazunte
Gulfo de Tehuantepec
Puerto Ángel
0
100 km
San Augustinillo
Tapachula
Zipolite

in particular is a resort of some size, and Huatulco, conceived as an environmentally conscious international development, is a characterless resort with an artificial Mexican flavour. All along this coast you'll discover some of the emptiest and best **Pacific beaches** in Mexico, including tranquil **Mazunte**, accessible from the main centres. Be warned, however, that robberies have been reported on Hwy-131 and Hwy-175 to the coast (from Oaxaca to Puerto Escondido and Pochutla), and the coastal Hwy-200, but only at night. The journey takes longer than it should, as both roads to the coast are in a terrible state, with enormous potholes and a frustrating number of *topes* (speedbumps).

The resorts are all around 250km from Oaxaca, reached via spectacular mountain roads that take a minimum of six hours to traverse. Although there are regular **buses** to **Pochutla**, just inland from Puerto Ángel, and then on to Puerto Escondido, it's a slow and occasionally heart-stopping journey along winding, mountainous highways. Many people prefer to **fly** down, either with Aerotucán from Oaxaca to Escondido – an experience in itself – or with Mexicana direct from Mexico City to Escondido or Huatulco. There are also regular bus connections along the coast, from Acapulco in the north or Salina Cruz in the south, and a direct overnight service between Mexico City and Puerto Escondido.



## Getting there from Mexico City and Acapulco

There are two routes to Oaxaca **from Mexico City**. The first, via toll-road **Hwy-135**, which links to the Mexico City–Puebla–Córdoba autopista, takes only five hours and is the more travelled route. The slower, eight-hour journey on **Hwy-190** passes through the spa town of **Cuautla**, remarkable only as the birthplace of Emiliano Zapata, and **Huajapan de León**, a town of little interest but marking the beginning of mescal-producing territory, with spiny, bluish-green maguey cacti all along the road. This leads to the **Mixteca**, one of the state's most interesting regions, and home to some of the finest colonial buildings in the country. On the side road that leads from Hwy-190 to the spa town of **Tehuacán**, you pass through one of the largest and most impressive **cactus forests** in the Republic. Both routes take in some unusual mountain scenery (particularly the autopista), with cacti and scrub in the early stages giving way to thicker vegetation as you approach Oaxaca. Both routes are also well served by buses.

To reach Oaxaca **from Acapulco**, it's probably quickest to go through Mexico City, though there are relatively few buses up from the Pacific coast at **Pinotepa Nacional**; more frequent, but equally uncomfortable, are buses from **Puerto Escondido** or Pochutla, the service town for **Puerto Ángel**. However, if you are travelling along the Pacific coast, it seems a pity to miss out on the region's excellent beaches just to get to Oaxaca quickly.

# Tehuacán

If you decide to travel via the autopista from Mexico City to Oaxaca, the only place that merits a stop as you speed along is **TEHUACÁN**, the source of a good percentage of the bottled mineral water (Peñafiel, now owned by Cadbury Schwepps) consumed throughout Mexico. It's the second largest town in the state of Puebla, but despite some rapid development precipitated by the manufacture of stone-washed denim here in the 1990s, it still feels like an old-fashioned spa town: relaxed, easy-paced, temperate in every sense of the word and with a centre full of buildings from the early twentieth century. The tiled, arcade-fronted house on the zócalo, with its Moorish flourishes, was obviously designed with Vichy or Evian in mind and bears a plaque to Señor Don Joaquim Pita, who first put the water here in bottles. Take a look at the underside of the colonnade for highly graphic murals depicting the five regions that make up Tehuacán district. A more pedestrian introduction to the region fills the halls of the **Museo del Valle de Tehuacán** (Tues–Sun 10am–6pm; M$15), in the elegant Ex-Convento de Carmen at Reforma Norte 210, which features a bright tiled dome that dominates the skyline in this part of town. A tiny collection of prehistoric relics shores up the thinly illustrated story of maize in Mesoamerica and particularly in the Tehuacán valley, which was the first place to truly cultivate (rather than simply harvest) the crop some six or seven thousand years ago – ample evidence that this was one of the earliest settled areas in Mexico.



All this can be seen in a couple of hours, but if you decide to stay in town you can fill the time by heading out to the **springs** on the outskirts to sample the clean-tasting water. You might also take a dip at **Balneario San Lorenzo** (Tues–Sun 6.30am–6pm; M$35), a large complex of sun-warmed pools (including one Olympic-sized affair) that draws from local springs and is known for its relaxation-inducing high lithium content. Catch a bus from the Autobuses Unidos bus station to San Lorenzo, a suburb 5km west of the centre. Alternatively, you can pamper yourself with a *temazcal* (a pre-Hispanic steam bath), sauna and massage at the pleasant *Hotel Aldea Bazar* (Ⓣ427/272-1535; ❸–❹), a five-minute taxi ride from the centre of town at Calzada Adolfo López Mateos 3351.

## Practicalities

Most long-distance **buses** arrive at the ADO station on Independencia, two blocks west of the zócalo. Second-class buses from Mexico City, Oaxaca and elsewhere arrive at the Autobuses Unidos station near the junction of 5 Oriente and 5 Sur, on the opposite side of the centre.

The most luxurious **place to stay** in Tehuacán is the *Hotel México*, Independencia at Reforma Norte, one block west of the zócalo (Ⓣ238/382-2419, Ⓦwww.hotelmexicotehuacan.com; ❺), which has a pool, parking and clean, modern, well-appointed rooms. Budget hotels can be found near the zócalo, including the *Hotel Monroy*, Reforma Norte 217 (Ⓣ238/382-0491; ❸). **Banks** (with ATMs) and other services are mostly on Reforma.

# Oaxaca

The city of **OAXACA** sprawls across a grand expanse of deep-set valley, 1600m above sea level and some 500km southeast of Mexico City. Until recently, its colour, folklore, numerous fiestas, indigenous markets – which are known for being particularly diverse and traditional – and thoroughly colonial centre have combined to make it one of the country's most rewarding destinations. Even an increase in package tourism, an influx of American retirees and the pedestrianization of Macedonio Alcalá, the main thoroughfare from the zócalo to the cathedral, failed to dilute the city's gentle appeal. Sadly, an outbreak of violence in the summer and autumn of 2006, when teacher protests escalated into bloody conflict (see p.635), may have ruined all this, undermining Oaxaca's reputation as a vibrant, peaceful destination. Beyond the resulting cosmetic damage, including the widespread destruction of beautiful colonial buildings, an atmosphere of extreme tension has enshrouded the city. A series of arrests and a crackdown on protest marches followed Felipe Calderón's inauguration in December 2006, and an uneasy calm now prevails. The long-term impact on the city's tourist industry remains to be seen.

Once central to the **Mixtec** and **Zapotec** civilizations, the city had a limited role during the early years of the Spanish Conquest. **Cortés**, attracted by the area's natural beauty, created the title of Marqués del Valle de Oaxaca, and until the Revolution his descendants held vast estates hereabouts. For practical purposes, though, Oaxaca was of little interest to the Spanish, with no mineral



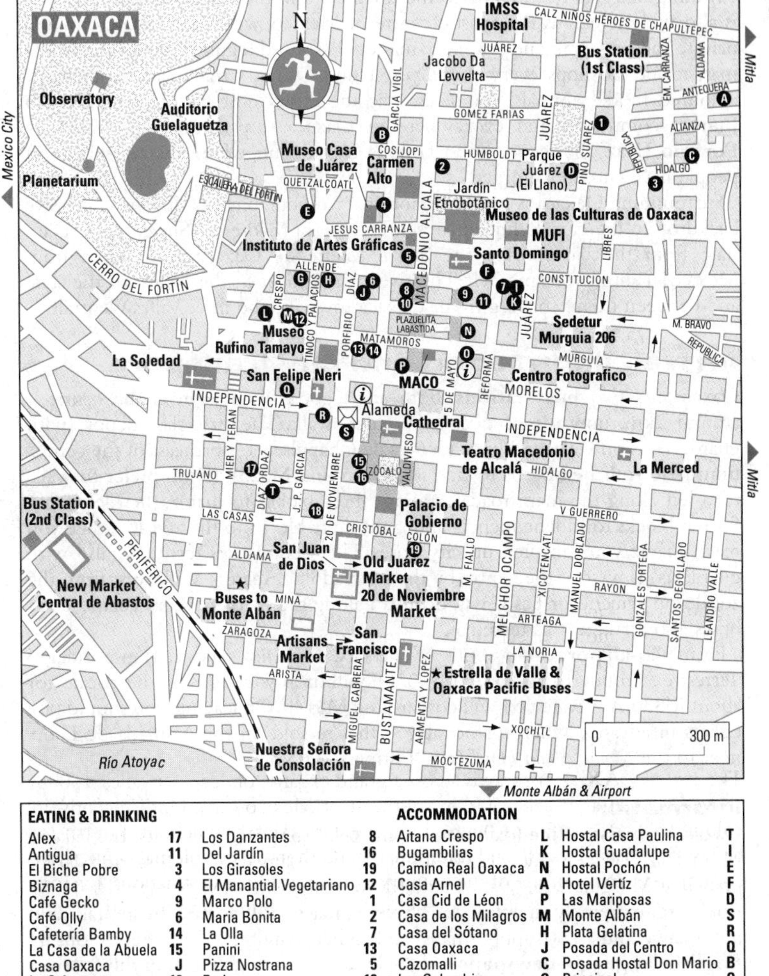


| EATING & DRINKING | | | | ACCOMMODATION | | | |
|---|---|---|---|---|---|---|---|
| Alex | 17 | Los Danzantes | 8 | Aitana Crespo | L | Hostal Casa Paulina | T |
| Antigua | 11 | Del Jardín | 16 | Bugambilias | K | Hostal Guadalupe | I |
| El Biche Pobre | 3 | Los Girasoles | 19 | Camino Real Oaxaca | N | Hostal Pochón | E |
| Biznaga | 4 | El Manantial Vegetariano | 12 | Casa Arnel | A | Hotel Vertíz | F |
| Café Gecko | 9 | Marco Polo | 1 | Casa Cid de Léon | P | Las Mariposas | D |
| Café Olly | 6 | Maria Bonita | 2 | Casa de los Milagros | M | Monte Albán | S |
| Cafetería Bamby | 14 | La Olla | 7 | Casa del Sótano | H | Plata Gelatina | R |
| La Casa de la Abuela | 15 | Panini | 13 | Casa Oaxaca | J | Posada del Centro | Q |
| Casa Oaxaca | J | Pizza Nostrana | 5 | Cazomalli | C | Posada Hostal Don Mario | B |
| La Crêpe | 10 | Red | 18 | Las Golondrinas | G | Principal | O |

wealth and, due to the rugged mountain terrain, no real agricultural value (though coffee was grown). This meant that the **indigenous** population was largely left to get on with life and did not have to deal with much outside influence beyond the interference of a proselytizing Church. Nevertheless, by 1796 it had become the third largest city in Nueva España, thanks to the export of cochineal and, later, textile manufacturing. An earthquake destroyed much of the city in 1854; the slow rebuilding process was shaken to pieces by another quake in 1931.

Today Oaxaca is well on its way to becoming an industrial city – the population is well over 250,000 and the streets are choked and noisy – yet it remains easy to navigate. In the **colonial centre**, thanks to strict building regulations, the city's provincial charm is hardly affected and just about everything can be reached on foot. It also remains parochial in its habits, as the big excitements are dawdling in a café or listening to the town band in the famous **zócalo**. Oaxaca is also widely seen as the artistic centre of Mexico, with several state-run and private galleries, craft and jewellery master classes and regular exhibitions. In the market and in shops everywhere, you'll find Oaxaca's trademark fantastically coloured model animals. You'll also see the city's most famous son, **Benito Juárez**, commemorated everywhere in Oaxaca, a privilege not shared by **Porfirio Díaz**, the second most famous Oaxaqueño, whose dictatorship most people have chosen to forget.



Surrounding Oaxaca is some extraordinary topography, making an impressive backdrop to the city skyline at sunset. The Sierra Madre del Sur enters Oaxaca state from the west, while the Sierra Madre de Oaxaca runs down from Mexico's central volcanic belt. The two ranges meet in the centre of the state and between them, converging in Oaxaca town, lie the three Valles Centrales.

## Arrival, information and city transport

Oaxaca has two **bus stations**; both are a good distance from the centre – around 2km, upwards of twenty minutes' walk. The first-class depot (with guardería) is on Calzada Niños Héroes de Chapultepec, northeast of the centre; from here your best bet is to find a taxi (around M$25). If you prefer to walk, turn left along the main road for about three blocks to Juárez, then left again for ten blocks to Independencia and right three blocks to the zócalo. Once you reach Juárez you can pick up city buses. The second-class terminal (also with guardería) is west of the centre by the Mercado de Abastos: walk west from the zócalo on Trujano or Las Casas, or north along the market. Many Pacific-coast buses also arrive at this terminal.

From the **airport**, 8km south of the city, a *colectivo* service, Transportación Terrestre Aeropuerto (Ⓣ951/514-4350), will drop you right by the zócalo for about M$30. A private taxi will cost around M$140. On leaving, you should buy tickets in advance wherever possible – they're sold on the Alameda de León, next to the *Monte Albán Hotel* (see "Listings", p.653).

### Information

Oaxaca's **tourist office** (daily 8am–8pm; Ⓣ951/516-0123) is inside the Palacio Municipal, at Independencia 607 opposite the Alameda, with a second, larger branch at Murguia 206, west of 5 de Mayo (daily 8am–8pm; Ⓣ951/516-0123). Both are extremely helpful and have contacts for apartment rentals and homestays, and can supply maps and other handouts. The free monthly **English-language newspaper**, the *Oaxaca Times,* and the monthly *Oaxaca* both carry topical features, events listings and ads for rental properties. The

## Benito Juárez

Despite the poor judgement he exhibited in his later years, **Benito Juárez** ranks among Mexico's greatest national heroes. He was the towering figure of nineteenth-century Mexican politics, and his maxim – "El respeto al derecho ajeno es la paz" ("Respect for the rights of others is peace") – has long been a rallying cry for liberals. A **Zapotec**, he strove against nineteenth-century social prejudices and, through four terms as president, successfully reformed many of the worst remnants of Spanish colonialism, earning a reputation for honesty and fair dealing.

Juárez was born in **San Pablo Guelatao** in 1806. His parents died when he was 3, and he grew up speaking only Zapotec; at the age of 12 he was adopted by priests and moved to **Oaxaca**, where he began to study for the priesthood, which included learning Spanish. Turning his talents to law, he provided his legal services to impoverished villagers free of charge, and by 1831 had earned a seat on Oaxaca's municipal council, lending his voice to a disenfranchised people. Juárez rose through the ranks of the city council to become **state governor** from 1847 to 1852, on a liberal ticket geared towards improving education and releasing the country from the economic and social stranglehold of the Church and the aristocracy. In 1853 the election of a conservative government under Santa Anna forced him into eighteen months of exile in the US.

Liberal victory in 1855 enabled Juárez to return to Mexico as minister of justice and give his name to a law abolishing special courts for the military and clergy. His support was instrumental in passing the **Ley Lerdo**, which effectively nationalized the Church's huge holdings, and bills legalizing civil marriage and guaranteeing religious freedom. In 1858 President Ignacio Comonfort was ousted by conservatives enraged by these reforms, and Juárez, as **the head of the Supreme Court**, had a legal claim to the presidency. However, he lacked the military might to hold Mexico City and retired to Veracruz, returning three years later, victorious in the War of Reform, as constitutionally elected **president** on the basis of his attempts to reduce the power of the Church. Stymied by an intractable Congress and empty coffers, Juárez suspended all national debt repayments for two years from July 1861. To protect their investments, the British, Spanish and French sent their armies in, but when it became apparent that Napoleon III had designs on the control of Mexico, the others pulled out, leaving France to install Hapsburg **Archduke Maximilian** as puppet emperor. Juárez fled again, this time to Ciudad Juárez (originally called Paso del Norte) on the US border, but by 1867 Napoleon III had buckled under Mexican resistance and US pressure, and Juárez was able to return to the capital and his army to round up and execute the hapless Maximilian.

Juárez was returned as president in the 1867 elections but alienated much of his support through unconstitutional attempts to use Congress to amend the constitution. Nevertheless, he secured another term in the 1870 elections, spending two more years trying unsuccessfully to maintain peace before dying of a heart attack in 1872.

**Spanish-language newspaper** *Noticias* also has rental ads, and can be bought from newspaper vendors around the zócalo. The city's Spanish schools (see "Listings", p.654) are another good source of rental and homestay information. You can find more on Oaxaca, including accommodation listings and language courses, **online** at ⓦwww.go-oaxaca.com, ⓦwww.oaxaca.com and ⓦwww.oaxacatimes.com.

### City transport

**Walking** is by far the best way to get around compact Oaxaca. The bus routes are Byzantine and even if you manage to hop on the right one, the traffic is so slow that you could have taken a pleasant stroll to your destination in half the time. **Taxis** are a better bet; stands can be found on Independencia at García Vígil and at the corner of Abasolo and 5 de Mayo near the cathedral, or flagged down anywhere. Cabs are not metered, so fix your price first. Expect to pay M$25–30 around town and M$40 out to the first-class bus terminal.

Getting out to the sites around the valley by **public transport** is a different matter. While taxis charge around M$35 to most of the surrounding villages and archeological sites, buses from the second-class bus station are frequent and cheap. There are also vast numbers of **colectivos** heading for destinations all over the state. These depart when full from various points around the city (ask the tourist office), mostly from Mercaderes behind the *abastos* market, and are only a little more expensive than buses. **Car rental** is as pricey here as anywhere in the country, but if you are planning extensive exploration of the valley may prove worthwhile, allowing you to trade a week of long waits for a couple of days of independence; see p.654 for details of agents. Note that poor signposting in this area can be frustrating. **Bike rental** (see p.654) may also be an effective means of exploring the city and some of the outlying villages. Several **tour** companies offer day trips to Monte Albán and other places around the city, including bird-watching, hiking and mountaineering excursions; again, see p.654 for more details.



## Accommodation

Although there are hundreds of **hotels** in Oaxaca, there are thousands of visitors, and if you arrive late in the day you may well have difficulty finding a room. Under such circumstances, it's best to take anything that's offered and look for something better the next morning. Alternatively, call at the main tourist office and consult their lists of families who take in guests on a daily basis (usually around M$50 per person), or apartments, many of them fairly central, which cost around the same. Note that at the time of writing, many hotels, especially in the streets surrounding the zócalo, had been to forced to close following the outbreak of violent protests (see p.638).

The cheapest places tend to be **south of Independencia**, especially between the old market and Calle Trujano, and along Trujano, Díaz Ordaz, Garcia and Aldama, and north of Humboldt, although they are dwindling in number as more upscale hotel offerings pop up in the touristy zone near the **zócalo** and **north of Independencia**. In this area, both prices and quality tend to be higher, though there are some surprisingly good-value establishments. In general, **rates** tend to drop by ten to thirty percent outside the Christmas, Semana Santa, July and August high seasons. It's often worth asking for a *descuenta* (discount) – the worst they can say is no.

The only **campsite** anywhere near town is the barely functioning *Trailer Park Oaxaca*, just over 3km north of the centre at Violetas 900, at the corner of Heroica Escuela Naval Militar: follow Niños Héroes east five blocks from the first-class bus station and turn left up Ruíz.

**Tourist Yú'ù** facilities are dotted around Oaxaca's valleys, offering fascinating and economical alternative accommodation (see box, p.644). These are also more conveniently located for visiting the artisan communities or the ruins at Mitla or Yugal. If you're really counting the pennies, you can even pitch a tent on their grounds.

### Around the zócalo

**Monte Albán** Alameda de León 1 ⓣ951/516-2777, ⓕ516-3265. Beautiful, if cavernous, colonial-style hotel right opposite the cathedral. Excellent value given the location, with some lovely external rooms and gloomier internal ones. Nightly *folklórico* dancing takes place in the main hall. ❹

**Plata Gelatina** Independencia 504 ⓣ951/514-9391. The best backpacker option in town. Just a stone's throw from the zócalo, this recently renovated and expanded hostel is nicely decorated and has a young, friendly atmosphere. It offers clean, airy and colourful dorms or private rooms (with shared hot showers). There are also kitchen facilities, Internet access, a pool table, a bar and a café serving excellent coffee and brick-oven pizzas. You can hang out your washing on the large terrace while enjoying great views of Santo Domingo and Monte Albán. ❷

**Posada del Centro** Independencia 403 ⓣ951/516-1874. Pleasant rooms around a tiled courtyard, most with shared bath and some with private bath; a good deal, although front rooms face a heavily trafficked street. ❹

## North of Independencia

**Aitana Crespo** Sabino Crespo 313 ⓣ951/514-3788, ⓦwww.hotelaitanaoaxaca.com. With more attention to detail than most hotels in this range, the well-managed *Aitana* has fine rooms with cable TV, safe, coffee-makers, fan and spacious bathrooms with shower, bathtub and hairdryer, all grouped around a leafy courtyard. There are panoramic views from the rooftop terrace, which has sun loungers and tables. It's five blocks west of Santo Domingo, just north of the basilica. ❺

**Bugambilias** Reforma 402 ⓣ951/516-1165, ⓦwww.mexonline.com/bugambil.htm. Peaceful, central colonial house beside *La Olla* café, just south of Santo Domingo. Eight comfortable, airy rooms (individually decorated with work by local artists) with private bath. Rates include breakfast. ❻–❼

**Camino Real Oaxaca** 5 de Mayo 300 ⓣ951/516-0611, ⓦwww.camino-real-oaxaca.com. Oaxaca's priciest hotel (from M$2000 a night), in the beautifully converted sixteenth-century Ex-Convento de Santa Catalina. Candles light the way through arcaded, flower-filled courtyards to characterful, if rather medievally dimensioned, rooms and idyllic gardens. If a night's stay is beyond your budget, a lingering coffee or cocktail in the courtyard is a worthy substitute. ❾

**Casa Arnel** Aldama 404, in Colonia Jalatlaco ⓣ951/515-2856, ⓦwww.oaxaca.com.mx/arnel. Between the zócalo and first-class bus station, and within walking distance of both, *Casa Arnel* is a popular family-run place. Reasonably priced rooms (with or without bath – some are smaller than others) sit around a leafy courtyard. Guests have access to a rooftop bar, where breakfast (additional cost) is served, as well as to Internet, laundry and a library; the management also offers tours in Oaxaca and outlying areas. There are newer rooms and apartments (around M$4000 a month) across the street. ❸

**Casa Cid de León** Morelos 602 ⓣ951/514-1893, ⓦwww.casaciddeleon.com. With just four suites, all beautifully and idiosyncratically restored by owner, poet and artist-in-residence Leticia Rodríguez, this is one of Mexico's most memorable hotels. Each spacious room is crammed with antiques, books and trinkets – a regal, timeless aura pervades every artfully conceived nook and cranny. There is a lovely terrace where breakfast is served, and the staff are charming and efficient. ❽–❾

**La Casa de los Milagros** Matamoros 500 ⓣ951/501-2262, ⓦwww.mexonline.com/milagros.htm. Justifiably a mid-range favourite, this small, family-run, colonial hotel has just three immaculate, individually styled rooms in a dream home setting. There's a beautiful communal kitchen, a dining room and a patio – the "Angeles" room even has its own waterfall. ❻

**Casa del Sótano** Tinoco y Palacios 414 ⓣ951/516-2494, ⓦwww.mexonline.com/casadesotano.htm. Just two blocks from the church of Santo Domingo, this smart, modern hotel retains a traditional feel with folk-art flourishes and comfy rooms, all with a/c. Earth tones and dark wood evoke fancy monks' quarters – some are very small, so ask to see a few first. There's an inviting terrace café and a lovely art gallery on the premises, both run by the same friendly character. Basic breakfast is included. ❼

**Casa Oaxaca** García Vígil 407 ⓣ951/514-4173, ⓦwww.casa-oaxaca.com. If you are going to splurge, *Casa Oaxaca*, the personal favourite of Gabriel García Marquéz, is the place. Seven tastefully serene, spacious rooms are set around a pristine white courtyard with a tiled pool and sumptuous restaurant. With an emphasis on intimacy and tranquillity, the service is faultless and Oaxacan artistry is woven through every immaculate detail. Delicious breakfast included. ❾

**Cazomalli** Salto 104, near Aldama ⓣ951/513-3513. Quaint little posada with comfy rooms in a colonial house with a gorgeous rooftop breakfast area, and a helpful owner. ❺

**Las Golondrinas** Tinoco y Palacios 411 ⓣ951/514-3298, ⓕ514-2126. Tidy, pristine rooms in an old colonial house, each with separate reception area and bathroom. The main draw is the gorgeous, flower-filled courtyard where breakfast is served. Very tranquil with a distinctly local flavour. ❻

**Hostal Guadalupe** Juárez 409 ⓣ951/516-6365. A short walk from the zócalo, this quiet little hostel has dorms and private rooms with tidy shared bathrooms. Luggage lockers are available. ❶–❷

**Hostal Pochón** Callejón del Carmen 102 ⓣ951/516-1322, ⓦwww.hostalpochon.com. Close to the Santo Domingo church, this is the best hostel in town. Dorms (for 2 and 4 people), double rooms and shared bathrooms are all surgically clean, and the colourfully inviting patio and common areas have an inviting traveller hangout vibe. There is cable TV, free Internet, cheap international calls, a substantial breakfast and efficient, welcoming staff. Discounts are available for group and online bookings. ❶–❷

**Hotel Angel Inn** Hidalgo 204 ⓣ951/133-6128, ⓦwww.hotelangelinn.com. Well-appointed, clean, motel-style rooms a few blocks from the zócalo. Especially good-value choice for families. Small swimming pool. ❻

**Hotel Vertíz** Reforma 404 ⓣ951/516-2525, ⓦwww.hotelvertiz.com.mx. A welcoming, cheerful place. Decent-sized, if rather sterile, rooms equipped with TV, noisy a/c, fans and sizeable bathrooms, branching off from an inviting courtyard. Slightly overpriced for what you get. ❻

**Las Mariposas** Pino Suárez 517 ⓣ951/515-5854. Delightful colonial-style hotel with spacious, thoughtful rooms, some with kitchenettes and all with private bathrooms, clustered around a vibrant courtyard complete with flowers and fish-filled fountains. The staff are very helpful and happy to provide a wealth of information on tours. Very popular with long-stay Spanish students. Breakfast and Internet access are included. ❹–❺

**Posada Hostal Don Mario** Cosijopí 219 ⓣ951/514-2012, ⓦwww.posadahostaldonmario.8m.com. The house where Rufino Tamayo, Oaxaca's most famous contemporary painter, was born is now a sociable hostel popular with language students, with bright, cheerful public areas and clean, if rather gloomy, rooms for around M$200 per night, or M$250 with private bath. Internet access, tour information and Spanish classes are available. ❸

**Principal** 5 de Mayo 208 ⓣ951/516-2535. Colonial-style place with a central courtyard and friendly owner. Simple, functional rooms with private bathrooms are grouped around a lovely garden that suggests something pricier than what it is. Rooms to the rear are quieter. Good value considering the colonial flourishes and location. ❺

### South of Independencia

**Hostal Casa Paulina** Trujano 321 ⓣ951/516-2005. Ultra-clean and white, to the point of having an institutional feel. There are separate dorm rooms for men and women, clean bathrooms and some private rooms (❷). There's also a small garden with fountains, beer for sale in the lobby and a rooftop lounge.

### Staying in local communities around Oaxaca: Tourist Yú'ù

In 1994 SEDETUR, the government agency responsible for promoting tourism, and the Secretaría de Turismo opened the first batch of **Tourist Yú'ù** (pronounced YOU) – Zapotec for "house" – small, self-contained buildings scattered through the Oaxaca valleys and designed to bring income to the local villages while minimizing the disruptive effects of mass tourism. Visitors are shown around by locals and are given the opportunity to view community life at close quarters. SEDETUR can also make reservations at a number of other locally built and run **cabins** for tourists. Some of these are equally charming and even more off the beaten track, though facilities tend to be correspondingly basic.

Either type of accommodation makes a convenient and economical base for exploring the villages and archeological sites of Oaxaca state. Many communities have their own particular handicraft tradition, such as carpet-weaving, wickerwork or pottery; others often have a museum devoted to archeological finds from the area and the life of the villagers. Some Yú'ù are in regions of outstanding natural beauty, where locals will take you horseback riding, trout fishing, biking or caving.

The Tourist Yú'ù are designed to sleep six (the cabins sleep more), with a bedroom, a fully equipped kitchen and outside shower and toilets (which can also be used by people camping in the grounds). Each facility has a custodian who collects M$90 per person, M$330 for groups of six, and M$55 for campers; some offer guides and camping equipment for rental. Reservations can be made – ideally a few days in advance, especially for the more accessible sites – through Oaxaca's tourist office, preferably the Murguia 206 location (ⓣ951/516-0984 or 4828, ⓔsedetur3@oaxaca.gob).

## The City

Simply being in Oaxaca, wandering through its streets and absorbing its life, is an experience, especially if you happen to catch the city during a **fiesta** (they happen all the time – the most important are listed in the box on pp.692–693). Nonetheless, you should definitely take time out to visit the State Museum and the Museo Tamayo, the markets (craft shopping in Oaxaca is among the best in the entire country) and the churches of Santo Domingo and La Soledad, and to get out to Monte Albán and Mitla. While you could certainly cover the city's highlights in a leisurely two days, it's easy to stay for much longer.

### Around the zócalo

The **zócalo**, closed to traffic and surrounded by *portales* (arcades) sheltering cafés, sees a steady stream of beggars, hawkers, business people, tourists and locals. In 2005 the zócalo was given an "ecorenovation" when the local government decided to uproot the gigantic imported Laurel trees planted around the square and put native cypress trees in their place. An ill-conceived plan intended to showcase Oaxaca's endemic flora, the overly manicured outcome was greeted with strong criticism and protest from Oaxaqueños. Still, despite its aesthetic shortcomings, the square continues to be Oaxaca's kaleidoscopic central reference point, a fascinating amalgam of indigenous traditions and colonial grandeur. It is usually animated, beguiling and compelling, and features some of the best free entertainment in the city – especially displays of music, song and dance. On Sundays and many weekday evenings you'll find a band playing in the centre, or else a performance or exhibition opposite the cathedral. On the south side of the square, the Neoclassical, Porfiriano **Palacio de Gobierno** features a historical mural by Arturo García Bustos. Second-rate by Mexican standards, the mural depicts the country's history: at the top are the revolutionary Ricardo Flores Magon (left), Benito Juárez and his wife Margarita Maza (centre) and José María Morelos (right). Porfirio Díaz appears below Juárez, with a sword. At the bottom right, Vincente Guerrero's execution at Cuilapan is shown, and the left wall shows ancient Mitla.

You can reach the rather inelegant **cathedral**, at the northwest corner of the square, by crossing to the Alameda de León, a more diminutive version of the main square. Begun in 1553, the cathedral's construction wasn't completed until the eighteenth century, thanks to several earthquakes. Since then it's been repeatedly pillaged and restored; as a result, despite a fine Baroque facade, it's not the most interesting of Oaxaca's churches. It is impressively large, though, with a heavy *coro* (choir) blocking the aisle in the heart of the church.

Walk past the cathedral and the Alameda, then right onto Independencia for a couple of blocks to arrive at the **Teatro Macedonio de Alcalá**, built in the French style fashionable during the dictatorship of Porfirio Díaz. Still operating as a theatre and concert hall, it's typical of the grandiose public buildings that sprang up across Mexico around 1900 – behind the Louis XV exterior, the interior (if you can see it – try going to a show, or sneaking in before one), is a magnificent swath of white marble and red plush.

### North of the zócalo

Heading north from the zócalo, Valdivieso crosses Independencia to become **Macedonio Alcalá**, the city's pedestrianized shopping street, a showcase for the best, and most expensive, Mexican and Oaxacan crafts. This is the place to come for exquisitely intricate silver designs and finely executed, imaginative textiles: check the quality of the goods here before venturing out to the villages where many of the crafts are made, and where the selection tends to include pieces of varying quality and lower prices. Heading north from the zócalo along Alcalá you'll come to **MACO**, the **Museum of Contemporary Art** (Mon & Wed–Sun 10.30am–8pm; M$11, free on Sun and holidays), housed in a seventeenth-century building widely regarded as Cortés's house although actually built after his death. Founded in 1992 with the intention of preserving Oaxaca's cultural heritage, the museum hosts temporary exhibits of national and regional contemporary art that can include anything from collections of Zapotec folk art to political caricatures to video installations focusing on the impact of Mexican immigration to the US.

A block further up Alcalá stands the church of **Santo Domingo** (daily 7am–1pm & 4–8pm; no sightseeing during Mass; free). One of the finest examples of Mexican Baroque, this sixteenth-century extravaganza is elaborately carved and decorated both inside and out, the external walls (10m thick in some places) solid and earthquake-proof, the interior extraordinarily rich. Parts were damaged during the Reform Wars and the Revolution – especially the chapels, pressed into service as stables – but most of the interior was restored during the 1950s. Notice especially the great gilded main altarpiece, and, on the underside of the raised choir above you as you enter, the family tree of the Dominican order, in the form of a vine with leafy branches and tendrils, busts of leading Dominicans and a figure of the Virgin right at the top. Most striking of all, the church drips with white and gold-leaf throughout, beautifully set off in the afternoon by the light that floods in through the window. Looking back from the altar you can appreciate the relief scenes high on the walls, the biblical events depicted in the barrel roof and the ceiling of the choir, a vision of the heavenly hierarchy with gilded angels swirling in rings around God. The adjoining Capilla del Rosario is also richly painted and carved: the Virgin takes pride of place in another stunning altarpiece, all the more startlingly intense in such a relatively small space.

Behind the church, the old Dominican monastery (the Ex-Convento de Santo Domingo) has been restored to house the **Museo de las Culturas de Oaxaca** (Tues–Sun 10am–8pm; M$47, free on Sun and holidays). Construction of the convent began in 1572, and the church held its first Mass in 1608; from then until 1812 the convent was occupied by Dominican friars. During the Revolution, the building served as barracks for the Mexican army. The damage inflicted during this period wasn't restored until the 1990s, when the exhibits were installed. One of the city's highlights, the museum traces the history of Oaxaca in an expansive and elaborately executed labyrinth of galleries that hold displays detailing the pre-Hispanic period through to the present day. The archeological finds defy hyperbole, especially the magnificent Mixtec jewellery discovered in Tomb 7 at Monte Albán (see p.656), including a couple of superb gold masks and breastplates. This lavish treasure trove constitutes a substantial proportion of all known pre-Hispanic gold, since anything the conquistadors found they melted down. The museum also owns smaller gold pieces, as well as objects in a wide variety of precious materials – mother-of-pearl, obsidian, turquoise, amber and jet among them. An interesting video shows members of each of the state's fifteen indigenous peoples speaking their own language.

Through the museum windows you'll see beautiful views of the mountains, as well as another hidden artistic masterpiece – the cactus garden, or **Jardín Etnobotánico** (visits allowed only by signing up in advance for a 1hr guided tour; English tours Fri & Sat 11am, Spanish tours Tues & Fri 10am; free). Beyond the garden's sensual appeal – specifically an ornate collection of orchids and plumeria – the tours are also extremely educational. The grounds preserve species native to Oaxaca and provide information on plants and insects, such as the *cochinilla* that dwells inside certain varieties of cactus and secretes a substance that is used to produce natural dyes for textiles.

Across the road at Alcalá 507, the **Instituto de Artes Gráficas** (Sun–Fri 9.30am–8pm; donation) is one of many cultural centres in the state sponsored by painter Francisco Toledo. Established in 1988, it displays changing exhibits of works by nationally renowned artists including José Guadalupe Posada, Rodolfo Nieto, Vicente Rojo and Toledo himself. It's worth popping in just to amble around the rooms of what was once a rather grand colonial house and to spend an hour in the excellent art library and idyllic reading room. There are also evening music recitals.

The **Museo Casa de Juárez** (Tues–Sat 10am–7pm; M$35, free on Sun), a block to the west at García Vigil 609, is where Oaxaca's most famous son, Benito Juárez, once worked for bookbinder Antonio Salanueva. The renovated house contains a small collection of the young Zapotec's possessions along with seminal historical documents. Wander through the kitchen, bedroom and dining area exhibits to get an idea of what life must have been like for the middle class in early nineteenth-century Oaxaca. The workshop displays bookbinding materials.

Oaxaca is also the proud mother of Mexico's only **philatelic museum**, housed in a sober mansion east of here at Reforma 504 (Tues–Sat 10am–7pm; free). It has a respectable permanent exhibition of Mexican stamps, letters, philatelic instruments and seals. Just around the corner at Murguia 302 you'll find the **Centro Fotográfico Alvarez Bravo** (daily except Tues 10am–8pm; free), also established by Toledo, which has three exhibition rooms displaying historical and contemporary photographs, plus an excellent reference library.

### West of the zócalo

Four blocks south along Alcalá from Santo Domingo, then three blocks west, at Morelos 503, lies the **Museo Rufino Tamayo** (Mon & Wed–Sat 10am–2pm & 4–7pm, Sun 10am–3pm; M$300), a private collection of pre-Hispanic artefacts gathered by the Oaxaqueño abstract artist. Rather than try to explain the archeological significance of its contents, the collection is deliberately laid out as an art museum, with the focus on aesthetic form, and includes some truly beautiful items from all over Mexico, with pottery and carvings from pre-Classic civilizations. Aztec, Maya and western indigenous cultures all feature strongly, though there's surprisingly little that is Mixtec or Zapotec. There are also some contemporary works.

Around the corner at J.P. García and Independencia, the church of **San Felipe Neri** is mostly Baroque, with a richly decorated proliferation of statues on the plateresque facade. It's the interior decor, though, that really makes the place of interest. The church was built in 1733 and later used as barracks during the Revolution. By the 1920s it badly needed to be repainted, which it was – in an incongruous Art Nouveau/Art Deco style. The building's other claim to fame is that it's the church in which Benito Juárez and Margarita Maza were married.

Not far to the west along Independencia, the **Basílica de Nuestra Señora de la Soledad**, built between 1682 and 1690, is one of Mexico's most important religious sites. It contains an statue of the Virgen de la Soledad – Oaxaca's patron saint, and one of the most revered in the country. The story goes that in 1620, when an statue of the Virgin was found in the backpack of a mule en route to Guatemala, the Virgin miraculously appeared. The basilica here was consequently constructed in her honour. The diamond-encrusted crown that adorns the statue of the Virgin inside the basilica is a replica of the original,

## Market days in the villages around Oaxaca

Despite Oaxaca's many craft stores, if it's quality you're after, or if you intend to buy in quantity, visiting the villages from which the goods originate is usually a far better, cheaper bet. Each has a different speciality (rugs in Teotitlán del Valle, or black pottery in San Bartolo Coyotepec, for example; see pp.660 and 665), and many have their own market each week. At these you will be able to see the craftspeople in action and you may be able to have your own design made up; quite apart from all that, a village market is an experience in itself.

**Monday** Miahuatlan: mescal, bread, leather; Ixtlan de Juárez: flowers, produce.

**Tuesday** Santa Ana del Valle: rugs; Santa Maria Atzompa: pottery.

**Wednesday** Etla: cheese, flowers.

**Thursday** Zaachila: meat, nuts; Ejutla: mescal, embroidered blouses.

**Friday** Ocotlán: flowers, meat, pottery, textiles.

**Saturday** Oaxaca: everything; Tlaxiaco: leather goods, blankets, *aguardiente* (the local firewater), baskets.

**Sunday** Tlacolula: mescal, ceramics, rugs, crafts.



which was stolen during the 1980s. The sumptuously decorated church, built in the late seventeenth century but with a more recent facade, is set on a small plaza surrounded by other buildings associated with the Virgin's cult. It's a peaceful spot to watch Oaxaqueño life unfold over an ice cream or sorbet, both of which are sold in a beguiling variety of flavours at a cluster of stands – try *tuna* (cactus) and mescal in combination. The adjoining Plaza de la Danza is the setting of outdoor concerts, *folklórico* performances and specialist craft markets. Ramshackle stalls behind the ice cream vendors sell brightly coloured religious icons. Just in back of the church there's a small **museum** (daily except Wed 10am–2pm & 4–6pm, Wed 10am–2pm only; M$3) devoted to the cult. It's a bizarre jumble of junk and treasure – native costumes displayed on permed blonde 1950s mannequins; ex-voto paintings giving thanks for miracles and cures – among which the junk is generally far more interesting.

### South of the zócalo

The only local church that compares with La Soledad, in terms of the crowds of worshippers it attracts, is the ancient **San Juan de Dios**, on 20 de Noviembre right in the heart of the old market area. Here villagers and market traders who've come to town for the day drop in to pay their devotions.

The **markets** are the main reason most travellers venture south of Oaxaca's zócalo. Traditionally, Saturday is market day, and although nowadays the markets operate daily, it's still the day to come if you want to see the old-style *tianguis* (markets) at their best. *Indígenas* flood in from the villages in a bewildering variety of costumes, and Mixtec and Zapotec dialects replace Spanish as the *lingua franca*. The majority of the activity, as well as the serious business of buying and selling everyday goods, happens at the sprawling **Mercado de Abastos**, by the second-class bus station. This is the place to go for fruit, vegetables, meat, herbs, spices and all manner of household goods, from traditional cooking pots to wooden utensils and furniture.

The most animated market is the **Mercado 20 de Noviembre**, three blocks south of the zócalo, a cacophony of sights, smells and tastes. Indigenous women wander labyrinthine corridors amidst plumes of incense, inviting you to try curious Oaxacan dishes such as *chapulines* (crunchy baked grasshoppers) and *chicharrones* (crispy pork fat). An intriguing place to eat, the market is lined with *comedores* serving inexpensive food, such as *chiles rellenos* and tamales, although the quality varies, so it's best to eat at one of the more popular spots. Surrounding the market are also clusters of mescal stores where you can, rather dangerously, taste before you commit to buying. Distilled from the sugar solution at the heart of the maguey plant, it is a locally acclaimed panacea when mixed with herbs. These days, the dead worm at the bottom is nothing more than a gimmick and a stamp of authenticity – if you get that far. The smell of Oaxacan chocolate, the food of the gods, according to Maya tradition, lingers on the corner of Mina and 20 de Noviembre, where there are a number of mills that grind cacao beans. One of the best places in this area to try a mug of hot chocolate laced with almond, cinnamon, sugar or chile is *Mayordomo*, the Willy Wonka of Oaxaca; you can also buy *mole* and other chocolate delicacies.

The old **Mercado Benito Juárez**, two blocks southwest between Flores Magón and 20 de Noviembre, is the site for village handicrafts such as *rebozas* (shawls), rag dolls and green china; plenty of fresh produce and flowers; and the infamous *chapulines*. While many of the goods here can be much cheaper than in the smaller markets, be warned that it's very touristy – you're harassed far more by the vendors and you may have to bargain fiercely to get your price. Always check the quality of the goods before you buy; *sarapes*, in particular, are often machine-made from chemically dyed artificial fibres. You can tell real wool by plucking out a thread – artificial fibres are long, thin and shiny, woollen threads short, rough and curly (and if you hold a match to it, a woollen thread will singe and smell awful; an artificial one will melt and burn your fingers). There are numerous **shops** around the zócalo and on Alcalá that will give you a good idea of the potential quality of items you can buy in the market, or try the Regional Association of Craftswomen of Oaxaca at 5 de Mayo 204 (daily 9am–8pm).

△ Market, Oaxaca

### Out from the centre

Although it's fairly easy to find your bearings in the centre of town, to get a fix on Oaxaca's relation to the rest of the valley and Monte Albán, take a hike (about 45min from the zócalo) up Cerro del Fortín, on the northwest edge of the city. It's a steep climb, but the views are rewarding and in the evening you can call at the **Planetario Nundehui** (25min shows on astronomy in Spanish only: Mon–Fri 9am–9pm, Sat noon–8pm; M$22). The road up here passes the **Auditorio Guelaguetza**, the venue for the annual festival known as Lunes del Cerro ("Monday of the Hill"), primarily because the folk dances take place on the first two Mondays after July 16. Many celebrations also take place here around Christmas.

Just three blocks north of the Iglesia de Santo Domingo, between Cosijopi and Morelos, are the **Arcos de Xochimilco**, remnants of the eighteenth-century aqueduct of San Felipe. The surrounding streets are a pleasant place to stroll with colourful, low-slung, colonial-style houses surrounded by crumbling walls draped in bougainvillea, hole-in-the-wall taco joints, snoozing dogs, street lanterns and giant cacti.



## Eating

It would be an understatement to say that the food in Oaxaca is good – it's excellent. It's also available on almost every street corner. The cheapest places to eat are in the **markets**, either in a section of the Mercado de 20 de Noviembre around 20 de Noviembre and Aldama, with rows of *comedores*, or in the *abastos* market by the second-class bus station, where you'll find excellent tamales. You'll also find a medley of stalls dotted around the **zócalo** and along its peripheral streets that serve filling staples such as *elote* (corn on the cob) and *flautas* (deep-fried, rolled tortillas filled with string cheese or meat). More formal but still basic **restaurants** are to be found in the same areas as the cheaper hotels, especially along Trujano. In addition to stalls, the zócalo is ringed by **cafés** and restaurants where you can sit outside – irresistible as ever and not as expensive as their position might lead you to expect – and there are plenty of simple places for everyday meals in the streets round about. On the pricier end, there are some colonial-style and contemporary upscale restaurants that offer nouvelle Mexican dishes that use local herbs and produce to create imaginative, and usually healthier dishes – most street food tends to be fried, often in lard. Oaxaca also provides welcome relief for **vegetarians**, especially those who have been restricted to endless *huevos* and quesadillas in other parts of the country.

### Around the zócalo

**La Casa de la Abuela** Hidalgo 616. Touristy and with erratic service, but the great views over the zócalo from the second floor are what you're paying for. Serves locally inspired takes on classic dishes, tailored to an American palette.

**Del Jardín** Portal de Flores 10, on the zócalo. One of the best cafés on the zócalo for a coffee or cocktail and some people watching. Don't go for the food, but if hunger overwhelms you there is a passable, if uninspired, menu of soups, sandwiches, enchiladas and snacks.

### North of Independencia

**Antigua** Reforma 401. Close to Santo Domingo, this café is a popular breakfast choice, with a range of American, Continental and Mexican combinations. There's also a selection of pastries and sandwiches for a quick lunch, and a lively post-dinner scene with wine, mescal and gourmet liqueur coffees.

**El Biche Pobre** Calzada de la República 600, in Colonia Jalatlaco ☎951/513-4636. A 10min walk from the centre of town, this longstanding, reasonably priced family restaurant is popular with locals and tourists alike, serving generous portions of Oaxacan favourites. The *botano surtido* is a great way to start a meal. Open lunch time only.

**Biznaga** García Vigil 512 ☎951/516-8000. Inside a lemon-walled courtyard festooned with artwork, a chalk-board outlines the daily menu, which usually ranges from wholesome salads and soups

## Food and drink in Oaxaca

Oaxaca is a wonderful city for gourmands, and you don't have to go to one of the smart restaurants serving contemporary Oaxacan cuisine to sample local specialities: worth trying are **tamales** – in just about any form, and often better from street or market vendors than in restaurants – as well as **mole Oaxaqueño**, which is not significantly different from *mole* anywhere else, but good nonetheless, and **chapulines**, crunchy seasoned grasshoppers. **Tlayudas**, giant crisp tortillas dressed with beans and a mild Oaxacan string cheese called **quesillo**, are staples of cafés and street stands after dark.

The place to go for very special home-made **ice cream** is the plaza in front of the church of La Soledad, full of rival vendors and tables where you can sit and gorge yourself while watching the world go by. Flavours are innumerable and often bizarre, including *elote* (corn), *queso*, *leche quemada* (burnt milk; even worse than it sounds), *sorbete* (cinnamon-flavoured sherbet) and exotic fruits like *mamey*, *guanabana* and *tuna* (prickly pear; a virulent purple that tastes wonderful). There are also more ordinary varieties like chocolate, peanut and coconut.

**Mescal**, the local drink of choice, is sold everywhere in bottles that usually have a dead worm in the bottom. Legend has it that the creature lives on the cactus-like maguey plant and is there to prove that the ingredients are genuine (this is debatable; these days most of the worms are farm-raised and inserted as a marketing ploy). You don't have to eat the worm, though few people are in any state to notice what they're ingesting by the time they reach the bottom of the bottle. Mescal and tequila are similar drinks – tequila is simply a speciality type of the more varied mescal. True tequila is made only from the prized blue agave species, while mescal may be a combination of a number of types of maguey. Both alcohols are made from the sugary heart of the plant, which is baked, pulverized and then distilled. These liquors were developed around the same time, when the Spaniards introduced distillation after the Conquest. Shops all around the market – try El Fornoso, J.P. García 405, and El Flor de Maguey, 20 de Noviembre 606 – sell mescal in various qualities (including from the barrel), and many places also sell it in souvenir pottery bottles, which are amazingly cheap.

On the south side of the market, your nose will lead you to Calle Mina, which is lined with **spice** vendors selling plump bags of the chile-and-chocolate powder that makes up Oaxacan *mole*. Cinnamon-flavoured chocolate powder is also available, for cooking or making into drinking chocolate.

to *pastor*-style (tomato, oil, cilantro) fish and chicken *milanesa* filled with cheese. Some of the more elaborate dishes can fall short of their adjective-heavy descriptions, but when it's good it's delicious. Service can be frustratingly slow – sip one of the excellent margaritas while you wait. Main dishes average M$100.

**Café Gecko** 5 de Mayo 412. Come here for inexpensive omelettes, yogurt and granola, coffee and snacks, which you can eat indoors or within a leafy courtyard. Open until 8pm weekdays, 11pm at weekends.

**Café Olly** García Vigil 409. Cheerful, convenient café offers good coffee, waffles, bagels, omelettes, cakes and smoothies in a bright and breezy courtyard surrounded by handicraft shops. There is also a *temazcal* sauna behind the café.

**Cafetería Bamby** García Vigil 205. Lively cafetería and *tortería* two blocks from the zócalo serving a reasonably priced comida corrida that can be hit or miss, and inexpensive beer. A good stand-by. The *panadería* next door has fresh, fragrant baked goods.

**Casa Oaxaca** García Vigil 407 ⓣ951/514-4173. Contemporary Mexican cuisine with an international twist from chef Alejandro Olmedo. Dishes such as chiles stuffed with *ceviche*, red snapper coated with *guajillo* sauce and a decadent chicken *mole* are served in the candlelit courtyard of the hotel of the same name. Service is formal and charming, entrees are upwards of M$145. Reservations must be made in advance. A sister restaurant at Constitución 104, by the church of Santo Domingo, is less romantic but with equally memorable food.

**La Crêpe** Alcalá 307. There may not be much Oaxacan flavour to the food, but the smart, lively setting – popular with locals young and old – and convenient location overlooking Alcalá make this a great international choice. Sweet and savoury crepes, fruit salads, ice creams and a range of excellent sandwiches and salads are served at decent prices. Good dessert stop-off when the music draws the pre-party crowd.

**Los Danzantes** Alcalá 403 ☎951/501-1184. A slick, nouveau-design setting, good cocktails – try the mescal margarita – and imaginative dishes like mango- and mint-infused octopus, shrimp *ceviche*, barbecue chicken strips tossed with fried cactus and Oaxacan chocolate soufflé make this one of the best choices in town. The friendly staff are efficient and graciously opinionated. Prices start from around M$120.

**El Manantial Vegetariano** Tinoco y Palacios 303. Vegetarian Mexican breakfasts, affordable veggie burgers and fruit shakes are the order of the day at this small but excellent whole-food restaurant. The Sun buffet (M$50) is a bargain.

**Marco Polo** Pino Suárez 806 ☎951/501-1184. Daily fresh seafood specials in a snug, rustic setting right by the Parque Juárez (aka El Llano). There's a lovely outdoor patio and a brick oven; very good fish dishes – refreshingly not all fried – and wonderful *ceviche* are the menu highlights. Not the best value for money in town, but certainly a very pleasant way to spend an evening.

**Maria Bonita** Alcalá 706 ☎951/516-7233. Family-run restaurant one block north of Santo Domingo, serving reasonably priced Oaxacan specialities. Start with the appetizer platter that includes *tasajo* (beef strips), fried squash blossoms, *mole* tamales, *quesillo* (string cheese) and *tlayudas* topped with lard. Average main dishes cost about M$70. Breakfasts are good, too – try the *enfrijoladas*, tortillas filled with beans and Oaxacan string cheese and then baked.

**La Olla** Reforma 402 ☎951/516-6668. Quaint, relaxed café/gallery with a reliable breakfast menu featuring enchiladas and *chilaquiles* as well as wholesome choices like wheat toast, generous fruit salads with granola and yogurt, vegetable salads and hot drinks.

**Panini** Matamoros 200-A. Closet-sized sandwich joint that serves inexpensive, fantastic *panini* made with squidgy *ciabatta* bread and oozing with all manner of fillings and flavours; the chicken *mole* is wonderful. There are also excellent home-made cakes and more virtuous salads.

**Pizza Nostrana** Allende 150. While Oaxaca's Italian culinary reputation is nonexistent, this is the best option in town for well-executed and varied pasta dishes with a vegetarian slant. The intimate, old-fashioned atmosphere and its location close to Santo Domingo lend a romantic, relaxed vibe.

### South of Independencia

**Alex** Díaz Ordaz 218, at Trujano ☎951/514-0715. Popular with locals and travellers alike, this boisterous Mexican-style diner on the corner of a noisy thoroughfare offers extensive breakfast combination menus ranging from omelettes and hot cakes to refried beans, *huevos rancheros* and fresh fruit *licuados*. Prices are fair unless you choose from the a la carte selections.

**Los Girasoles** 20 de Noviembre 102. Mid-priced, no-frills food served in generous portions at this closet-sized, upbeat restaurant close to the market. There are some inexpensive options for vegetarians, especially good breakfasts and excellent mescal.

**Red** Las Casas 101 ☎951/514-6853. A bustling, no-frills joint serving generous portions of whole fish dishes, mixed seafood soups, prawn cocktails, *ceviche* and octopus.

## Drinking and nightlife

If you're not content sitting around the zócalo over a coffee or a beer or whiling away a balmy night to the accompaniment of mariachi or brass bands, don't expect too much of evenings in Oaxaca. The *guelaguetza* **folk dances** at the *Camino Real Oaxaca* (Fri night) and *Monte Albán* (nightly) hotels are a possibility, but there's nothing much more lively even at weekends, aside from a small handful of bars, which can get packed and noisy. Week nights are also fairly quiet, though there is frequently some kind of cultural activity outside both the church of Santo Domingo and the cathedral, as well as the ubiquitous street musicians in the zócalo.

**Caffe del Borgo** Matamoros 100. Tiny, popular Italian bar where ebullient Oaxaqueños rub shoulders with language students and tourists around high tables while enjoying beers, aperitifs or coffees, all to a deafening soundtrack that ranges from soft rock to salsa and indie alternative.

**Candela** Murguia 413 ☎951/514-2010. Set in a charming colonial house, *Candela* is a restaurant by day, but the place really comes alive after 11pm when the dancefloor is packed with locals and tourists coming to practise their salsa, rumba and merengue, accompanied by a live band. Try to arrive before 10pm at the weekend in order to secure a table. M$55 cover.

**Casa del Mezcal** Flores Magon 209. Longstanding, classic Mexican cantina in the market district with cheap shots of mescal.

**La Cucaracha** Porfirio Díaz 301-A. It's hard to miss this roomy colonial-style bar with a roadhouse feel. If you want to expand your repertoire of tequila or mescal with a M$100 taster flight in a loud and often frenzied environment, this is the place. There is live entertainment and dancing at the weekend.

**Decano** 5 de Mayo 210. A folksy, cosy café, at night *Decano* is transformed into a lively bar with a varied selection of music and decent, inexpensive light meals. Full of young Oaxaqueños and foreigners, with a laid-back, bohemian feel.

**La Divina** Gurrion 104. Arguably the best bar in town, this friendly, funky space in front of Santo Domingo is decorated with masks and model animals; dripping candles on chunky wooden tables add a gothic feel. There is a good variety of beer, spirits and tequila, and unlike many other local bars, the music won't blow your ears off.

**Freebar** Matamoros 100. Dark and dingy space that becomes a packed madhouse on weekends, with locals and some foreigners dancing to alternative music and spilling into the street.

**Hipótesis** Morelos 511. A romantic, intimate little piano bar, with music starting around 10pm and small tables tucked in dark corners.

**La Nueva Babel** Porfirio Díaz 224. Loungey wine bar also serving coffee and snacks, and sometimes featuring live folk music and poetry readings. Closed Sun.

**La Sol y La Luna** Reforma 502. This restaurant by the cathedral has live jazz and occasional salsa dancing Thurs–Sat, from 9pm. M$45 cover.

**La Tentación** Matamoros 101. With just a few tables and two-for-one cocktails 5–8pm most nights, this is a good place for a happy hour cocktail. Depending on the season, there is live Latin music and rock (M$45 cover) from 9pm to midnight – it's often packed with sweaty, gyrating gringos and Mexicans.

## Listings

**Airlines and flights** Aero California, Morelos 1207 ⓣ951/514-8570; Aerocaribe, Fiallo 102, at Independencia ⓣ951/516-0229; Aeroméxico, Hidalgo 513 ⓣ9/516-1066; Aerotucán, Alcalá 201 ⓣ951/511-0532; Aviacsa, Pino Suárez 604 ⓣ951/516-4577; Mexicana, Fiallo 102 ⓣ951/516-5797, ⓦwww.mexicana.com; Aerovega, Alameda de León ⓣ951/516-2777. Prices increase dramatically during Mexican holiday times, but expect to pay around M$1100 to Mexico City, M$1200 to Puerto Escondido and M$2200 to Mérida. The airport is about 10km south of the city on the road to San Bartolo Coyotepec and Ocotlán. Buses between Oaxaca and these two towns (from the second-class bus station) pass within a kilometre or so of the airport, but it is far easier to contact Transportación Terrestre Aeropuerto (Mon–Sat 9am–2pm & 5–8pm; ⓣ951/514-4350) on the Alameda de León across from the cathedral; if you book with them the day before your flight, they'll pick you up from your hotel and deliver you for around M$20.

**American Express** Valdivieso 2, inside Viajes Mexico ⓣ9/516-2700 (Mon–Fri 9am–5pm).

**Banks and exchange** Scotiabank, on Independencia at Alcalá, has a 24hr ATM and good rates (Mon–Fri 9am–5pm, Sat 10am–2pm); Banamex, Hidalgo 821, has an ATM and Western Union service (Mon–Fri 9am–4pm, Sat 10am–2pm); Banorte is at García Vígil 103. Casas de cambio litter the centre of town – shop around, as rates vary: Casa de Cambio Puebla, García Vígil 106.

**Bike rental** Several tour operators rent bicycles (see p.654).

**Books and maps** There are a number of bookshops selling Spanish and English titles, as well as museum shops and reference libraries. Amate, Alcalá 307, has an excellent selection of new English-language books (including literature, travel, archeology and cooking) and magazines. You can get new and second-hand English books about Oaxaca, Mexico and Latin America from Librería Universitaria, Guerrero 108, just off the zócalo (Mon–Sat 9am–2pm & 4–8pm). Also try the main library, the Biblioteca Circulante de Oaxaca, Alcalá 305 (Mon–Fri 10am–1pm & 4–7pm, Sat 10am–1pm), between Matamoros and Bravo; the Instituto Welte de Estudios Oaxaqueños at 5 de Mayo 412 (for enthnography, archeology and geography); or the excellent, predominantly arts library at the Graphic Arts Institute, Alcalá 507.

**Buses** Always try to buy tickets at least one day in advance, especially for popular destinations like San Cristóbal de las Casas and Puerto Escondido. From the first-class station at Chapultepec 1036, 2km north east of the zócalo, bus companies Cristóbal Colón (first class), ADO (executive class) and UNO (deluxe class) (ⓣ951/515-1214) run regular services to Mexico City (6hr), Puebla (4–5hr), Puerto Escondido (9hr), Pochutla (6hr 30min), Huatulco (7hr), San Cristóbal (11hr), Tehuacán (2hr 30min) and Villahermosa (12hr). Ticketbus offices, one on Valdivieso by the cathedral (T 951/516-3820) and another at 20 de Noviembre 103 (Mon–Sat 8am–10pm, Sun 9am–4pm; T 951/514-6655, W www.ticketbus.com.mx) sell tickets for first-class lines. Slower, cheaper, more frequent and less comfortable services leave from the second-class bus station, 1km from the zócalo, near the new market, for Mexico City (mostly overnight), Puerto Escondido, Pinotepa Nacional, Pochutla, Salina Cruz, Tuxtla Gutiérrez and other destinations. Suburban and minivan taxis make many of the same trips; enquire at the tourist office. Autoexprés Atlántida (T 951/514-7077) also runs daily minivans along Hwy-175 to Pochutla.

**Car rental** Alamo, 5 de Mayo 203-A (T 951/514-8534), Budget, 5 de Mayo 315-A (T 951/516-4445) and Hertz, Labastida 115-4 (T 951/511-4445), are all expensive. The cheapest rates tend to be booked through their websites (W www.alamo.com, W www.budget.com, W www.hertz.com). VW Bugs start around M$450/day, including insurance. Drop-offs at a different city are very expensive – rates are calculated on the distance from the pick-up.

**Cinema** You can see international and Mexican films for free at the Cine Pochote, García Vigil 817 (for listings see the *Oaxaca Times*). The Allianza Francesca, Morelos 306, has occasional French films.

**Consulates** Canada, Pino Suárez 700 (T 951/513-3777); US, Alcalá 407 (T 951/514-3054). Other consulates in Oaxaca move regularly – check at the tourist office for the latest information.

**Emergencies** Dial T 066, or the Tourist Police are located at Independencia 607 (T 951/516-0123, 514-2155 or 01-800/903-9200).

**Internet access** Internet cafés are abundant; most have copy and printing services, and some have long-distance call booths. Open latest is Café Internet, upstairs at Valdivieso and Independencia – it closes most nights at 11pm. Café Punto, García Vigil 212, is good; towards the first-class bus station, Interactivando, Pino Suárez 804, is speedy and cheap.

**Laundry** Azteca Laundry, 404-B Hidalgo (Mon–Sat 8am–8pm, Sun 9am–2pm); Lava-Max, Bravo y Tinoco y Palacios (Mon–Sat 8am–9pm); Clin Lavandería, 20 de Noviembre 605 (Mon–Sat 9am–8pm); and Lavandería Domar, Murguia 307 (Mon–Sat 9am–9pm, Sun 10am–3pm) is the cheapest.

**Massages and saunas** Traditional *temazcal* sauna (M$250) and massage (M$250) are offered in a peaceful garden on the outskirts of town through *Bugambilias*, Reforma 402 (T 951/295-1165; reserve at least a day in advance), a short taxi or cheap bus ride from the centre of town.

**Post office** On Independencia by the Alameda (Mon–Fri 8am–7pm, Sat 9am–1pm). It has fax services and Ladatel phones for collect calls.

**Spanish courses** Language classes and courses in Latin American literature and Mexican civilization and culture can be arranged through the Centro de Idiomas at the Benito Juárez University of Oaxaca (T & F 951/515-3922; write to Centro de Idiomas, Burgoa s/n Oaxaca, Oaxaca 68000). Other courses are offered by the Instituto Comunicación y Cultura, in a restored sixteenth-century building near the zócalo at Macedonio Alcalá 307 (T 951/516-3443, W www.iccoax.com); Amigos del Sol, Libres 109 (T 951/514-3484, W www.oaxacanews.com/amigosdelsol.htm); Becari Language School, Plaza San Cristóbal, M. Bravo 210 (T & F 951/514-6076, W www.becari.com.mx); the Instituto Cultural Oaxaca, Juárez 909 (T 951/515-3404, W www.instculruraloax.com.mx); and Academia Vinigulaza, Abasolo 503 (T 951/513-2763, W www.vinigulaza.com). If you're interested in Oaxacan cuisine, you can learn to cook while practising Spanish at the Seasons of My Heart cooking school, Rancho Aurora, Admon 3 (T 951/518-7726, W www.seasonsofmyheart.com),or through Milagros Para Ti, 5 de Mayo 412 (T 951/501-2009).

**Telephones** Available in the post office (see above), with plenty more all over town.

**Tour operators** Day trips to Monte Albán and nearby villages (such as El Tule) cost around M$165. Operators include: Cantera Tours, Plaza Gonzalo Lucero, 5 de Mayo 412 (T 951/516-0512) and Turismo Marqués del Valle, *Hotel Marqués del Valle*, on the zócalo (T 951/514-6962). El Condor Jeep (T 951/514-3570) goes slightly more off the beaten track. Bicicletas Bravo, García Vigil 409-C (T 951/516-0953, W www.bikeoaxaca.com), Bicicletas Pedro Martinez, Hidalgo 100 in Colonia Jalatlaco (T 951/518-4452, W www.bicicletaspedromartinez.com) and Turismo de Aventura Teotitlán, Juárez 59 (T 951/524-4103) all rent bikes and run day trips from Oaxaca to places like Dainzú or Santa Cruz (prices vary); Pedro Martinez will design routes for those who want to ride solo, and he also runs a five-day trip to the coast. Tierra Dentro, Reforma 528 (T 951/514-9284, W www.tierradentro.com), organizes more adventurous hiking, mountain-eering and rock-climbing expeditions. Expediciones Sierra Norte, M. Bravo 210-I (T 9/514-8271, W www.sierranorte.org.mx), and Tierraventura, Abasolo 217 (T 951/501-1363, W www.tierraventura.com), lead treks to the Sierra Norte mountains outside Oaxaca City. Ecotourism companies run horse-riding, bird-watching and nature photography trips – ask at the tourist office (see p.640) for more information.

**Volunteer** The Oaxaca Street Children Grassroots project (Centro de Esperanza Infantil) aims to bring a brighter future to Oaxaca's neediest children. You can contribute to their food and medical programme, or volunteer with them in Oaxaca by visiting or contacting the centre at Crespo 308 (Ⓣ951/502-2069, Ⓦwww.oaxacastreetchildren.org).

**Western Union** A shop at Guerrero 112, as well as Banamex locations, including Valdivieso 116, behind the cathedral, offer Western Union money transfer.

**Yoga and meditation** Classes offered several times a week at La Casa del Ángel, Jacobo Dalevuelta 200, between Reforma and Juárez (Ⓣ951/545-3203). Listings for other alternative health practitioners can be found in the *Oaxaca Times*. Calypso Gym at Allende 211 and Aurobic's Fitness at Constitución 300 offer day passes for aerobic and yoga classes and their weight rooms.

# Around Oaxaca: the Zapotec and Mixtec heartland

The region around Oaxaca can be divided into two parts: the **Central Valleys**, which radiate from the state capital to the south and east, towards Mitla, Ocotlán and Zaachila; and the **Mixteca**, which extends northwest towards Puebla and arcs down to the Pacific coast via Tlaxiaco and Pinotepa Nacional. The Central Valleys include the state's most famous and frequented archeological centres, craft villages and colourful markets, while the Mixteca, rich in ruined Dominican convents and ancient towns and villages, is less visited but well worth exploring.

This area saw the development of some of the most highly advanced civilizations in pre-Hispanic Mexico, most notably the Zapotecs and Mixtecs. Their craft skills – particularly Mixtec weaving, pottery and metalworking – were unrivalled, and the architecture and planning of their cities, especially at Zapotec-built **Monte Albán**, stand out among ancient Mexico's greatest achievements. Traditional ways of life and indigenous languages are still vigorously preserved by Mixtec and Zapotec descendants in villages today.

Note that many of the towns outside Oaxaca don't observe daylight-saving time, so your watch might be an hour off local time.

## Some history

The Oaxaca valley is the cradle of some of the earliest civilizations in Mexico. The story begins here with the **Zapotecs**, who founded their first city – now called San José Mogoté and little more than a collection of mounds a few kilometres north of the state capital – some time before 1000 BC. As the city grew in wealth, trading with Pacific coastal communities, its inhabitants turned their eyes to the stars, and by 500 BC they had invented the first Mexican calendar and were using hieroglyphic writing. At this time, San José, together with smaller villages in the area, established a new administrative capital at Monte Albán, a vantage point on a mountain spur overlooking the principal Oaxaca valley. By waging war on potential rivals, the new city soon came to dominate an area that extended well beyond the main valley – the peculiar *danzante* figures carved in stone that you can see at the ruins today are widely considered to be depictions of prisoners captured in battle. By 600 BC, the population had expanded to such a degree that the Zapotecs endeavoured to level the Monte Albán spur to create more space, essentially forming a massive plateau. The resulting engineering project boggles the mind:

without the aid of the wheel or beasts of burden, millions of tons of earth were shifted to build a vast, flat terrace on which the Zapotecs constructed colossal pyramids, astronomical observatories and palaces. By the time of Christ, the city was accommodating some twenty thousand people, and Monte Albán had a sphere of influence as extensive as that of its great trading partner to the north, Teotihuacán.

Just like Teotihuacán, Monte Albán mysteriously began to implode from about 700 AD, and the Zapotec influence across the Central Valleys waned. Only Yagul and Mitla, two smaller cities in the principal valley, expanded after this date, though they never reached the imperial glory of Monte Albán. As the Zapotecs disappeared, the gap they left behind was slowly filled by the **Mixtecs**, pre-Hispanic Mexico's finest craftsmen, who expanded into the southern valleys from the north to occupy the Zapotecs' magnificent cities. Influenced by the Zapotec sculptors' abstract motifs on the walls at Mitla, the Mixtecs concentrated their artistic skills on metalwork and pottery, examples of which can be seen in the state capital's museums. By the fifteenth century, the Mixtecs had become the favoured artisans to Mexico's greatest empire, their conquerors, the **Aztecs**; Bernal Díaz recounts that Moctezuma only ate from plates fashioned by Mixtec craftsmen.



## Monte Albán

**Imagine a great isolated hill at the junction of three broad valleys; an island rising nearly a thousand feet from the green sea of fertility beneath it. An astonishing situation. But the Zapotecs were not embarrassed by the artistic responsibilities it imposed on them. They levelled the hill-top; laid out two huge rectangular courts; raised pyramidal altars or shrines at the centre, with other, much larger, pyramids at either end; built great flights of steps alternating with smooth slopes of masonry to wall in the courts; ran monumental staircases up the sides of the pyramids and friezes of sculpture round their base. Even today, when the courts are mere fields of rough grass, and the pyramids are buried under an obscuring layer of turf, even today this high place of the Zapotecs remains extraordinarily impressive . . . Monte Albán is the work of men who knew their architectural business consummately well.**

Aldous Huxley, *Beyond the Mexique Bay*

Since Aldous Huxley visited in the 1930s, little has changed at **MONTE ALBÁN**. The main structures have perhaps been cleared and restored a little more, but it's still the great flattened mountain-top (750m by 250m), the scale and overall layout of the ceremonial precinct and the views over the valley that impress more than any individual aspect of the site. Late afternoon, as the sun sinks into the valley, is the best time to see it.

It seems almost madness to have tried to build a city here, so far from the obvious livelihood of the valleys and without any natural water supply (in the dry season water was carried up and stored in vast urns). Yet that may have been the Zapotecs' point – to demonstrate their mastery of nature. Certainly, the rulers who lived here must have commanded a huge workforce, first to create the site, then later to transport materials and keep it supplied. What you see today is just the very centre of the city – the religious and political heart later used by the Mixtecs as a magnificent burial site – the dominating apex of the region between 300 and 700 AD. On the terraced hillsides below lived a bustling population of between 25,000 and 30,000 craftsmen, priests, administrators and warriors, all of who, presumably, were supported by tribute from the valleys. It's small wonder that so top-heavy a society was easily destabilized. This said, there is still much speculation as to why, just like Teotihuacán, the site had been abandoned by 1000 AD.

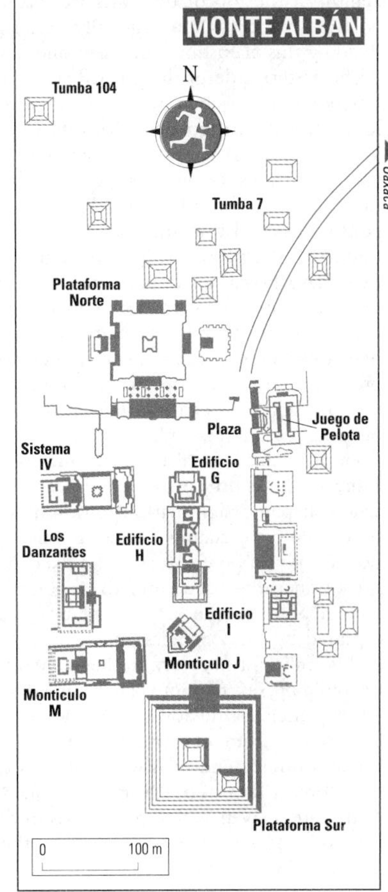


## Getting there

**Monte Albán** (daily 8am–6pm; M$40, free on Sun) is just 9km southwest of Oaxaca, up a steeply switchbacking road. Autobuses Turísticos, operating from the *Hotel Rivera del Ángel* at Mina 518, holds a monopoly on **buses from Oaxaca** to the site (M$40 return ticket). In peak season buses depart more frequently, but usually they leave at 8.30am (returning at noon), 9.30am (returning at 1pm) and hourly until 3.30pm (returning at 5pm). Apart from the one at 3.30pm, all buses give three hours at the site – enough time to see it quickly. If there's space, you can return on a later bus, but you may have to pay half the fare again. It's sometimes possible to hitch a ride or find a taxi (which for four or five people is not much more expensive than the bus), and walking back is also a realistic option: more than two hours, but downhill almost all the way – get a guard or one of the kids selling "genuine antiquities" to show you the path. The route is an eye-opening experience, veering through slum dwellings that are a far cry from the comforts of much of the city below. The **bus from Zaachila** (see p.666) passes close to the front of the site, but it's a stiff walk (about 1hr) from there. There's a car park, restaurant and souvenir shop by the entrance, and a small **museum** in the same complex: the collection is tiny, but there are good photographs of the site and its surroundings before and after clearing and restoration.

## The site

You enter the rectangular **Great Plaza** at its northeast corner. Sombre, grey and formal as it all appears now, in its heyday, with its roofs and sanctuaries intact, the whole place would have been brilliantly polychromed. The **Plataforma Norte**, to your right as you enter, may have been the most important of all the temples at Monte Albán, although now the ceremonial buildings that line its sides are largely ruined. What survives is a broad stairway leading up to a platform enclosing a square patio with an altar at its heart. This ceremonial centre was constructed between 400 and 750 AD, when Monte Albán was at its zenith. At the top of the stairs are the remains of a double row of six broad columns, which would originally have supported a roof to form a colonnade, dividing this plaza from the main one.

The eastern side of the Great Plaza consists of an almost continuous line of low buildings, reached by a series of staircases from the plaza. The first of them looks over the **Juego de Pelota** (ball-court), a simple I-shaped space with no apparent goals or target rings, obviously an early example. The ball-game was used as a means to solve conflict – it is believed that the losing team was sacrificed to the gods. Otherwise, the platforms on the east side are relatively late constructions, dating from around 500 AD onwards. Facing them from the middle of the plaza is a long tripartite building (**Edificios G**, **H** and **I**) that must have played an important role in any rites celebrated here. The central section has broad staircases by which it can be approached from east or west – the lower end temples have smaller stairways facing north and south. From here a complex of tunnels runs under the site to several of the other temples, presumably to allow the priests to emerge suddenly and miraculously in any one of them. You can see the remains of several of these tunnels among the buildings on the east side.

South of this central block, **Monticulo J**, known as the observatory, stands alone in the centre of the plaza – at 45 degrees to everything else – and its arrow-shaped design marks it out from its surroundings. Although the orientation is almost certainly for astronomical reasons, there's no evidence that this was actually an observatory; more likely it was built (around 250 AD, but on the site of an earlier structure) to celebrate an earlier victory. The carvings and hieroglyphics on the back of the building apparently represent a list of towns captured by the Zapotecs: much of the imagery at Monte Albán points to a highly militaristic society. In the vaulted passage that runs through the heart of the building, several more panels carved in relief show *danzante* figures (dancers) – these, often upside down or on their sides and in no particular order, may have been reused from an earlier building.

The southern end of Monte Albán is dominated by its tallest structure, the unrestored **Plataforma Sur**, a vast square pyramid offering the best overview of the site, as well as fine panoramas of the surrounding countryside. Heading from here back up the western side of the plaza, you'll pass **Monticulo M** and **Sistema IV**, probably the best-preserved buildings on the site. Both consist of a rectangular platform reached by a stairway from the plaza. Between Monticulo M and Sistema IV, the gallery and building of **Los Danzantes** (the Dancers), are the most interesting features of Monte Albán. A low wall extending from Monticulo M to the base of the Danzantes building forms the **gallery**, originally faced all along with blocks carved in relief of Olmec or African-featured "dancers". Among the oldest (dating from around 500 BC) and most puzzling features of the site, only a few of these *danzantes* remain *in situ*. The significance of the nude male figures is disputed: many of them seem to have been cut open and may represent sacrificial victims or prisoners; another suggestion is that the entire wall was a sort of medical textbook, or that the figures really are dancers, ball-players or acrobats. Whatever the truth, they show clear Olmec influence, and many of them have been pressed into use in later buildings throughout the site.

Several lesser buildings surround the main plaza, and although they're not particularly interesting, many contain tombs in which rich treasures were discovered (as indeed did some of the main structures themselves). **Tumba 104**, reached by a small path behind the Plataforma Norte or from the car park area, is the best preserved of these, with polychrome frescoes vividly revealing the mystical symbolism of the Zapotec gods. One of several in the immediate vicinity, this vaulted burial chamber still preserves excellent remains of murals. **Tumba 7**, where the important collection of Mixtec jewellery now in the Oaxaca Museum was found, lies a few hundred metres down the main road from the site entrance. Built underneath a small temple, it was originally constructed by the Zapotecs towards the end of Monte Albán's heyday, but was later emptied by the Mixtecs, who buried one of their own chiefs here along with his magnificent burial trove.

## The road to Mitla

**Mitla** (see p.663), some 45km from Oaxaca, just off Hwy-190 as it heads east towards Guatemala, involves a slightly longer excursion. It's easy enough to do, though: buses leave from the second-class terminal every thirty minutes or so throughout the day. On the way out here are several of the more easily accessible **native villages**, some of which have community museums. Check with the tourist office, or see the box on p.648, for which one has a market on the day you're going – there will be more buses and much more of interest once you get there. Also en route are a couple of smaller, lonelier ancient sites. If you rent a car in Oaxaca, you can take in all of this in a single day. If you want to explore the valley further, it's a good idea to stay in one of the villages, some of which have self-catering **Tourist Yú'ù** facilities (see box, p.644), which are as comfortable as many of Oaxaca's budget hotels.

### Santa María del Tule

At **Santa María del Tule**, 13km east on Hwy-190 as you head out of Oaxaca, you pass the famous **Árbol del Tule** in a churchyard by the road. This mighty tree, said to be at least 2000 years old (some say 3000), is a good 58m round, slightly fatter than it is tall, and weighs in around 500 tonnes. A notice board gives all the vital statistics: suffice to say that it must be one of the oldest living (and flourishing) objects on earth, and it's a species of cypress (*Taxodium mucrunatum*) that has been virtually extinct since the colonial era. Sadly, the tree has recently come under threat from industry and housing projects sapping its water supply. Local environmentalists are petitioning for UNESCO status in order that an integrated programme of ecological protection, including reforestation of the surrounding area, could be applied.

A tacky souvenir market takes advantage of the passing trade, and there are various food and drink stalls. If you want to avoid the tourist hype, sit on the left-hand side of the bus (heading to Mitla) and you may get a glimpse of the tree as you pass. A close-up look, for M$30, provides a better view; the tree is mightily impressive. **Buses** for El Tule (M$40) depart from Oaxaca's second-class bus terminal every thirty minutes.

### Dainzú

Seven kilometres further on Hwy-190 from the marked turn-off for Abasolo, **DAINZÚ**, the first significant archeological site, lies about 1km south of the main road (daily 8am–6pm; M$50, free on Sun). A Zapotec centre broadly contemporary with Monte Albán, around 600 BC, Dainzú stands only partially excavated in a harsh landscape of cactus-covered hills. The carvings are reminiscent in style, rather than scale, of Los Danzantes at Monte Albán, most notably **Edificio A**, a tomb adorned with a magnificently carved jaguar head; it's the first structure you come across when you enter the site, a large and rambling construction set around a courtyard and with elements from several epochs. Nearby is the ball-court, only one side of which has been reconstructed, and higher up the hill **Edificio B** is the best-preserved part of the site. Along the far side of its base a series of dancer figures can be made out, similar to the Monte Albán dancers except that these clearly represent ball-players. Barely unearthed, the main allure of Dainzú resides in its raw appeal, with few tourists or imposing facilities to detract from soulful contemplation.

### Teotitlán del Valle

Less than a thirty-minute drive northeast from Oaxaca, just before the small Zapotec archeological site of **Lambityeco** (daily 8am–6pm; M$25), a road leads 4km to **TEOTITLÁN DEL VALLE**, the most famous weaving town in Oaxaca. All over the village you see bold-patterned and brightly coloured **rugs** and **sarapes**, some following traditional designs from Mitla, others imitating twentieth-century designs, among them those of Escher. Century-old recipes are still used in the production of dyes, namely indigo, pomegranate and cochineal. The cochineal beetle secretes a substance that, when dried, creates an inimitable blood-red colour. Rugs are mainly the product of cottage industry: even if you're not buying, poke your head into the compounds with rugs hanging outside. Most weavers will be more than happy to provide a demonstration of pre-Hispanic weaving techniques. When dropped off the bus, you'll probably be pointed along a street to the left, which leads to the **mercado de artesanías**. You'll see the widest range here – ask to rummage in the back and you'll find some especially nice deals – and prices are generally cheaper than in Oaxaca. Be sure to check the quality, as some rugs are wool blends and machine-woven.

The village has an interesting **community museum** (Tues–Sun 10am–2pm & 4–6pm; M$10) with displays on pre-Hispanic artefacts and information about carpet-weaving and life in the area. Inside the local **church**, whose walls are studded with bits of Zapotec temple, worship is a syncretic fusion of Catholic and indigenous ritual.

Teotitlán has a few worthy **restaurants**. A favourite with locals as well as tour groups, *Tlamanalli*, Juárez 39 (Tues–Sun 2–5pm), serves delicious local classics such as squash-blossom soup and stewed chicken; the menu changes daily. You can also organize ecotours here to the village of Benito Juárez (see below). The less expensive *La Cúpula*, on the road into town, offers authentic Zapotec food, including hearty *pozole* soup, adjacent to a fine weaving shop. A wonderful alternative base to Oaxaca, where you can immerse yourself in the indigenous traditions of the region for a couple of days, is ★ *Casa Sagrada* (Ⓣ951/516-4275, Ⓦwww.casasagrada.com; ❼), a nature retreat that offers cosy rooms adorned with artesanía in a glorious setting and delicious food. There are cooking classes and horseback tours available, and breakfast and dinner are included. About 3.5km outside town, back towards Hwy-190, there's an inconveniently sited **Tourist Yú'ù** – check with the tourist office to see if it's open. If not, *El Descanso*, Juárez 51, also offers **accommodation** (❹). There are direct **buses** (M$45) out here every hour or so from Oaxaca, and frequent micros from Tlacolula, further east along Hwy-190.

### Benito Juárez and the Pueblos Mancomunados

Perched on a ridge overlooking the Oaxaca valleys and surrounded by pine trees, the little village of **BENITO JUÁREZ** is known for its spectacular sunsets – in clear weather you can see all the way to Mexico's highest mountain, Pico Orizaba, from the *mirador*. The village is also the starting point for more than a hundred kilometres of signposted rural **foothpaths and country roads** through the **Pueblos Mancomunados** (literally "joint villages") of the Sierra Norte towards Ixtlan (see below), suitable for hikers and mountain bikers of all abilities. All in all it's a relaxing place to spend a few days, enjoying nature and getting firsthand experience of rural Oaxacan life.

The paths have been used for centuries by local people accustomed to sharing resources with surrounding communities. The villages are an impressive example of social organization in Mexico, with eight small towns perched on common land. The landscape is spectacular – some sections of the pine forest have been classified by the World Wildlife Foundation as being the richest and most varied on earth. The biodiversity is also phenomenal, with birdlife, butterflies and mammals, including ocelot, puma and jaguar. Locals can take you on **horse** or **donkey rides** (ask at the tourist office; see below), and there's a river where you can **fish** for trout. The high-altitude footpath between the villages of Latuvi and Amatlan, which passes though mystical cloud forest, is believed to be part of a larger pre-Columbian route that connected the Zapotec cities in the Central Valleys with the Gulf of Mexico – you can still see the remains of an old road along the trail.

Don't expect one afternoon to be enough time to really see this area; a visit requires forward planning and at least a couple of days in order to be worthwhile. The most efficient way to go is through one of the tour operators in Oaxaca (see p.654). Tierraventura and Expediciones Sierra Norte organize two-day trips with guides, transport, accommodation and meals for around M$1500. If you prefer to travel independently, the small but extremely helpful **tourist information** office (Mon–Sat 9am–5pm; ⓣ951/545-9994) in Benito Juárez, next to the town square, has excellent maps which show the varying demands of each trek, and rents out reliable mountain bikes, but only with a Spanish-speaking guide (M$250 for bike and guide). Next door, the simple and friendly **restaurant** serves cheap breakfasts, comidas and hot drinks, and sells sandwiches and water.

**Basic accommodation** is limited to a pleasant Tourist Yú'ù (❶–❷), which has bunk beds and cabins with kitchens (make sure the caretaker switches on the hot water before he disappears for the night). You can reserve in advance through Oaxaca's tourist office (see p.640), although it's not strictly necessary in the low season. **Camping** is also an option in well-organized campgrounds. You can also indulge in *temazcal*, which can be arranged through the Tourist Yú'ù (see box, p.644), for about M$110. Bear in mind that this area has extremes of altitude and temperature – it's advisable to let your body acclimatize before engaging in any strenuous physical activity, to drink plenty of water and wear sunscreen. Temperatures drop dramatically at night, so take warm clothing and a sleeping bag (the Tourist Yú'ù can provide wool blankets).

### Ixtlan

**Ixtlan**, a pretty village near San Pablo Guelatao (the birthplace of Benito Juárez), is in an area of great natural beauty, and its cloud forests and pine and oak woodlands are claimed to be home to five hundred bird varieties and six thousand species of plants. As such, the place is dedicated to ecotourism, and on the main plaza you'll find the **Museo de la Bioversidad** (Mon–Fri 9am–5pm; free), which has information on the local environment and related ecoprojects, as well as examples of butterflies and animals, including ten local species of rat. Several companies offer **ecotours** of the region; try Viajes Ecoturisticos Shiaa Rua Via (ⓣ951/553-6075, ⓦwww.oaxacamex.info/ixtlan). Like the other villages nearby, Ixtlan has basic cabin **accommodation** (❷), as well as the simple *Yu Yeeva Posada* (❸). Everyone will tell you, quite rightly, that the best place to eat is *Las Truchas*, a trout farm just outside town serving fresh fish. Ixtlan is accessible either by direct **bus** from Oaxaca's second-class station (2 daily), or by *colectivo*.

### Tlacolula and Santa Ana del Valle

In the valley below Benito Juárez, just a few kilometres beyond Teotitlán del Valle, **TLACOLULA** is a scruffy and dirty village, but worth a stop to see its sixteenth-century **church**, about 1km to the south of the main road. The interior here is as ornate as Oaxaca's Santo Domingo, though less skilfully crafted. In the adjoining chapel, some gory carvings of martyrs include a decapitated St Paul. The best day to go is Sunday, when there's also a large **market**. **Buses** leave every ten minutes for Tlacolula from Oaxaca's second-class bus station (M$10).

A road leading north from the junction at Tlacolula goes to **SANTA ANA DEL VALLE**, smaller than Teotitlán but with a fine selection of locally produced **rugs**. Lucio Aquino Cruz and his younger brother Primo, at Morelos 2, make some of the most exquisite floor coverings in Mexico – it's worth visiting their house just to see them, even if they are beyond your price range. Alternatively, place orders with Lucio for your own designs – and you can see the production from beginning to end. One side of the small central square is devoted to the **Shan-Dany Community Museum** (Mon–Sat 10am–2pm & 4–6pm; M$10). Its name is Zapotec for "foot of the hill", and it marks the exact spot where a couple of **tombs** were discovered in the 1950s, though excavated more recently. Probably contemporary with Dainzú and Monte Albán, the Zapotec site here boasts some fine glyphs. Excavations have also been carried out beneath what are now basketball courts outside, enough pots and stones being recovered to fill the small but impressive co-operatively run museum. The local weaving industry is also covered and, though panels are all in Spanish, the gist is clear enough.

There's a tranquil **Tourist Yú'ù** in Santa Ana if you want to stay. The local **baker** makes delicious bread, and there's a shop where you can buy basic **provisions**. **Buses** leave every ten minutes from Tlacolula.

### Yagul

One of the least visited archaeological sites in the region, **YAGUL** (daily 8am–6pm; M$30, free on Sun) lies just to the north of the highway at about the 35-kilometre mark – just a couple of kilometres uphill from where the bus from Oaxaca stops. Its location, atop a large, cactus-dotted plateau overlooking the spectacular Tlacolula valley, is its major draw. The large site spreads expansively across a superb defensive position, and although occupied by the Zapotecs from a fairly early date, its main features are from later on (around 900–1200 AD, after the fall of Monte Albán) and demonstrate **Mixtec** influence. On the lowest level is the **Patio de la Triple Tumba**, where the remains of four temples surround an altar and the entry to the **Triple Tomb**, whose three funereal chambers show characteristically Mixtec decoration. Immediately above the patio, you'll see a large and elegantly simple ball-court, and a level above this, the maze-like **Palacio de los Seis Patios**. Probably a residential complex, this features six small courtyards surrounded by rooms and narrow passages. Climbing still higher towards the crest of the hill and the fortress, you pass several lesser remains and tombs, while from the fortress itself there are stunning views, and a frightening rock bridge to a natural watchtower.

## Mitla

The town of **MITLA** ("Place of the Dead"), where the bus from Oaxaca finally drops you, is some 4km off the main road and just ten minutes' walk from the site of the famous ruins. It's a dusty little place where you'll be harassed by would-be guides and handicraft vendors (there's also a distinctly second-rate crafts market by the ruins). **Accommodation** can be found at the *Hotel Mitla* (Ⓣ951/568-0112; ❸–❹), or *La Zapoteca* (Ⓣ951/568-0026; ❸), in town on the way to the ruins. *Restaurant Don Cenobio* (Ⓣ951/568-0330), located in the hotel of the same name, is the most stylish place to try local Oaxacan specialities at reasonable prices. On the main square, the hotel has a relaxing courtyard and thoughtfully appointed, spotless rooms (❻).

Mitla reached its apogee during the post-Classic period, when Monte Albán was in decline. Construction at the site continued up until the late fifteenth century, at which point it was finally conquered by the Aztecs. The abstract designs on the buildings seem to echo patterns on surviving **Mixtec** manuscripts, and have long been viewed as purely Mixtec in style. But more recent opinion is that the buildings were built by **Zapotecs** and that the city was a ceremonial centre occupied by the most important Zapotec high priest. This Uija-Tao, or "great seer", was described by Alonso Canesco, a fifteenth-century Spaniard, as being "rather like our Pope", and his presence here would have made Mitla a kind ofVatican City.

A few minutes by local bus from Mitla you'll find the small town of **Matatlan**, mostly dedicated to mescal, where you can visit the ateliers in which the drink is produced, enjoy free samples from the town stores, and eat the maguey plant itself. Be warned that a few samples of home-made mescal can wreak havoc with your senses.

### The site

While the **site** itself (daily 8am–6pm; M$30, free on Sun) may not have the grandiose scale and setting of Monte Albán, Mitla impresses with its superlative bas-reliefs and geometric designs, You'll see it at its best if you arrive towards closing time, when the low sun throws the patterns into sharp, shadowed relief, and the bulk of the visitors have left.

There are four main palace complexes here, each magnificently decorated with elaborate stone mosaics that are considered peerless throughout Mexico. The **Grupo de las Columnas** is the best preserved and most impressive of these, and the obvious place to head for from the entrance. The only other sites that the long, low buildings recall in any way are the two post-Classic sites of El Tajín (see p.619) and Uxmal (see p.809), which, along with other evidence, suggests that there may have been some contact between these most influential groups.

The first large courtyard in the Grupo de las Columnas is flanked by constructions on three sides – its central **Templo de las Columnas** is magnificent, precision-engineered and quite overpowering in effect. Climbing the broad stairway and through one of three entrances in its great facade, you come to the **Salón de las Columnas**, named after the six monolithic, tapered columns of volcanic stone that supported its roof. A low, narrow passageway leads from here into the small inner patio (**Patio de las Grecas**), lined with some of the most intricately assembled of the geometric mosaics; each of the fourteen different designs here are considered representative of the universe and the gods. Four dark rooms that open off the patio continue the mosaic theme. It is in these rooms that the Uija-Tao would have lived. If the

△ Mosaic, Mitla

latest theory is correct, the Zapotec architects converted the inner room of the traditional Mesoamerican temple, in which priests usually lived, into a kind of exquisitely decorated "papal flat" arranged around a private courtyard. The second courtyard of the Columns group, adjoining the southwestern corner of the first, is similar in design though less impressive in execution. Known as the **Patio de las Tumbas**, it does contain two cross-shaped tombs, long since plundered by grave-robbers. In one, the roof is supported by the **Columna de la Muerte**; legend has it that if you embrace this, the gap left between your hands tells you how long you have left to live: hand-widths translate into years remaining. At the time of writing, the column could no longer be embraced; officials at the site could not say if this is a permanent arrangement.

The **Grupo de la Iglesia**, a short distance north, is so called because the Spanish built a church over, and from, much of it. Two of its three original courtyards survive, however, and in the smaller one the mosaic decoration bears traces of the original paint, indicating that the patterns were once picked out in white from a dark-red background.

Three other groups of buildings, which have weathered the years less well, complete the site. All of them are now right in the modern town, fenced off from the surrounding houses: the **Grupo de los Adobes** can be found where you see a chapel atop a pyramid; the **Grupo del Arroyo** is near Los Adobes; and the **Grupo del Sur** lies right beside the road to the main site.

## Hierve el Agua

Before the environmental degradation worsens, you should visit **HIERVE EL AGUA** (daily 9am–6pm; M$17). Some 25km east of Mitla, down a side road that

leads to **San Lorenzo Albarradas** (Hierve el Agua lies just beyond), it's the site of the spectacular limestone **waterfalls** that you'll see in photographs all over Oaxaca city. The mineral concentration causes the water to bubble out of the ground and become petrified over the vertiginous cliff-tops, forming a stunning stalactite; it is a beautiful sight and the panoramas from above the pools, where there several stalls serving tacos and other snacks, are breathtaking. At night, the stars are also awe-inspiring – there's no electricity and the hills shield the glow from Oaxaca's populated valleys. Sadly, tourism here threatens to be more environmentally destructive than in the rest of the valley: the town can barely support the volume of visitors it receives. It is advisable to hire a car to get here; one **bus** is scheduled to make the journey from Oaxaca every day, leaving the second-class bus terminal at 8am, and returning at 2.30pm, but the service is somewhat erratic. It's a two- to three-hour drive up here from Oaxaca through some beautiful countryside. There is a **Tourist Yú'ù** (check with the Oaxaca tourist office on the status; see p.640) and some **cabins**, as well as a few **restaurants**, which close after sunset. Alternatively, tour groups in Oaxaca often take in Hierve El Agua as part of day trip that includes Mitla and Teotitlán del Valle.



## The valleys south of Oaxaca

The two roads that run almost due south of Oaxaca don't have the same concentration of interesting villages and sites as the Mitla road, but poking through the communities or admiring the beauty of the valley by bike could easily occupy a day or so. Again, you can travel around the area by **public transport** on market days – by far the best time to go – but **cycling** on rented bikes from Oaxaca isn't as arduous as it might sound, especially if you are careful about the midday heat.

### San Bartolo Coyotepec

Thirteen kilometres south of Oaxaca on the main highway to Puerto Ángel lies **SAN BARTOLO COYOTEPEC**, as unprepossessing a town as you could imagine. It is famed for its shiny black pottery, **barro negro brillante**, which can be found in crafts shops all around Oaxaca state, but is only made here. From the bus stop, a road, one side awash with pottery vendors, leads to the workshop where, in 1934, one Doña Rosa developed the manufacturing technique. The pottery may now be too weak to carry mescal to market on the back of a mule, as it did for centuries, but Doña Rosa's invention has yielded a new, purely ornamental vocation that now draws thousands of tourists every year. Although Doña Rosa died in the 1980s, her family still runs the sole operation (daily 9am–5pm; ⓣ951/551-0111), which is very tourist-oriented, with pieces ranging from beautifully simple amphorae to ghastly clocks, at Juárez 24. Prices are supposed to be fixed, and at the factory they probably are, but places down the road will haggle; just remember your piece has to get home and the stuff is fragile. **Buses** to San Bartolo Coyotepec leave Oaxaca's second-class bus station every hour.

### San Martín Tilcajete and Santo Tomás Jalieza

The same buses continue south, passing **SAN MARTÍN TILCAJETE**, a sleepy town whose main street is lined with workshops carving, painting and polishing bright copal wood figurines known as *alejibres*, which come in all manner of designs – from Day of the Dead skeletons to whimsical creatures. Although not as famous as those in Arrazola (see p.666), there are still some nice examples. It's easy to wander through the shops and observe the process.

To the east of the highway is **SANTO TOMÁS JALIEZA**, where women specialize in weaving cotton on backstrap looms. An all-women's co-operative market in the centre of town sells thick cotton tablecloths and placemats, backpacks, clothing and belts at fixed (though generally reasonable) prices.

### Ocotlán

The ride ends forty minutes from Oaxaca at **OCOTLÁN**, chiefly noted for the red **clay** figures crafted here by the Aguilar sisters. On the approach into town, look out on the right for the adjacent workshops of Guillermina, Josefina and Irene, each of whom produces slightly different items, in the distinctive Aguilar style originated by their mother. Again, you can find examples in Oaxaca, but a trip out here allows you to see the full range, including figures of animals, men and buxom women at work and play, and even Nativity scenes (apparently no subject matter is off-limits), all often gaudily decorated in polka dots or geometric patterns. Prices here also tend to be much cheaper. Try to make it on a Friday when the weekly **market** takes place not far from the **Parroquia de Santo Domingo de Guzmán**, with its newly restored facade and multiple domes richly painted with saints.

Ocotlán is also the birthplace of famous Oaxacan artist **Rodolfo Morales** (1925–2001), who set up the Fundación Cultural Rodolfo Morales here, at Morelos 108 (daily 10am–2pm & 4pm–7pm; ⓣ951/571-0952). The foundation has provided the town with its first ambulance and computer centre, as well as establishing conservation and land-restoration projects. The former jail, for example, has been turned into an art museum, featuring Morales's work in addition to sombre sacred art from the Santo Domingo church, and a restaurant.

### Arrazola, Cuilapan and Zaachila

The other major region of interest in this area is along, or beside, the road to Zaachila that runs southwest from Oaxaca past the foot of Monte Albán. **ARRAZOLA**, an easy five-kilometre cycle ride off to the right from this road, is the home of the local woodcarvers and painters who produce many of the delightful boldly patterned animals made from copal wood that you'll see for sale in Oaxaca and all over Mexico. The man responsible for transforming this local craft into an art form is octogenarian Manuel Jiménez, the village's poster child. Following on the heels of his success, entrepreneurial townspeople have turned their skills to carving, creating a thriving cottage industry that produces a fantastical profusion of spiky figures and polka-dot, hooped or expressionist styles. Carvers from other villages are catching on to the popularity but few, if any, are better than in Arrazola.

The village of **CUILAPAN**, 14km southeast from Oaxaca (frequent buses from the second-class bus station), seems insignificant beneath the immense sixteenth-century hulk of the Dominican **Ex-Convento de Santiago Apóstol**, which, though badly damaged, is still an impressive place to wander around, with a Renaissance twin-aisled nave and largely intact vaulting. The church was never finished. The original roof still remains on one section of the church, and Mass is said here amid the clangs and echoes of ongoing restoration work. The real interest, however, lies around the back in the **cloister** (daily 8am–5pm; M$20), which features a few faded frescoes on the wall. Look out for the sign pointing to the back wall, where **Vicente Guerrero** was executed by firing squad after spending his captivity here.

Buses from Oaxaca to Cuilapan continue 5km to **ZAACHILA**, which has a Thursday livestock market that makes for a very interesting spectacle. Come here then and you've got the best chance of being able to get into the **zona arqueológica** (nominally daily 9am–5pm; M$25, free on Sun), up behind the multi-domed church on the zócalo. There's not a great deal to see, but you can step down into the two opened tombs – of what is probably a much larger site – and, when your eyes become accustomed to the gloom, pick out detailed bas-relief geometric figures on the lintel and owls guarding the entrance. Two marvellous glyphs show who was interred here: Señor 9-Flower, probably a priest, depicted carrying a bag of copal for producing incense. The revered gentleman was found buried with lavish jewels that are now on displayed in the archeological museum in Mexico City; photographs are exhibited which reveal the treasures that have even been compared to those discovered in Tomb 7 at Monte Albán.

## The Mixteca

The two areas of Oaxaca's Mixteca region – the barren hills of the **Mixteca Baja** and the mountainous, pine-clad **Mixteca Alta** – are not obvious tourist destinations: the pre-Hispanic sites here are far less spectacular than those in the Central Valleys and there are no artisan centres to compare with Teotitlán or Arrazola. However, the colonial buildings are widely regarded as some of the country's most important, and the low number of visitors means that you are likely to have vast crumbling monasteries and Mixtec ruins to yourself. With restoration work under way since the 1990s, it appears that tourist traffic here is set to increase; ironically, the main appeal of the monasteries is their aching, faded glory and the spine-tingling sense that you're witnessing a scene that has remained relatively unchanged since before Cortés.

**Public transport** through the region is fairly easy. Hwy-135, one of the country's best roads, cuts through the Baja's deforested hillsides, eventually reaching Mexico City. Hwy-125 leads off Hwy-135 to the south, traversing the steeper slopes of the Mixteca Alta, eventually arriving at Puerto Escondido via a long and circuitous route. There are frequent buses and *camionetas* from Oaxaca heading out to the monasteries and the major towns.

### The Baja: Yanhuitlán, Teposcolula and Coixtlahuaca

Among the **Mixteca Baja**'s highlights are three **Dominican monasteries** – Yanhuitlán, Teposcolula and Coixtlahuaca – imposing relics of Mexico's imperial past. Once centres of mass conversion, they are now eerily deserted and in various stages of decay. Although restoration projects are under way, it will be years before they are repaired to anything resembling their former glory. All three can easily be visited as a day trip from Oaxaca if you have your own transport; less easy if you're relying on public transport, though it's possible (see p.668). If you want to stay, there are plenty of basic hotels on the route from Oaxaca.

Head out northwest out of Oaxaca on Hwy-190 for about 120km to reach the first monastery, at **Yanhuitlán**, the permanent seat of the vicarage of the Mixteca during the sixteenth century. The church is massive, built on an enormous pre-Hispanic platform overlooking the village, no doubt intended to remind the Mixtecs of the supremacy of the new religion. The vaulted ceiling is a soaring 27m tall. Inside are many original paintings and sculptures – the principal altarpiece, dating to 1570, is the work of the Spanish artist Andrés de la Concha. **Teposcolula**, south of here on Hwy-125 in the village of the same name, has one of the finest *capillas abiertas* in the Americas. These graceful open-air chapels were used for mass preaching and conversion, and are only found in the New World. The Ex-Convent of San Juan Bautista, at **Coixtlahuaca**, a couple of kilometres off Hwy-135, dates from 1576 and is one of the best preserved of the region's colonial structures. Some unusual sculptures on the facade depict grand rosettes, symbols of the Passion and John the Baptist, flanked by saints Peter and James. Red slivers of paint hint at the polychrome finish that would have glorified the sombre building during its heyday. There's an impressive churrigueresque altarpiece within the convent.

Buses to the Baja leave from the first-class bus station (ADO or Cristóbal Colón) in Oaxaca, or you can catch a **minibus** from Transportes Tlaxiaco, a small terminal on J.P. García, between Arista and Nuno del Mercado. The minibuses leave when full, approximately every hour, and take about an hour and a half to reach Yanhuitlán. You can catch the next bus, or a taxi, to Teposcolula, less than 25km away. From Teposcolula, take a cab or catch a second-class bus to **El Crucero**, at the junction of Hwy-125, Hwy-190 and Hwy-135, only about 10km from the town. Frequent first- and second-class buses heading to Mexico City or Oaxaca stop here. Catch one going towards Mexico City and get off after about 20km at the turn-off to Coixtlahuaca. The monastery is about 1.5km up a side road.



### Santiago Apoala

About 98km north from Oaxaca, reached by following Hwy-190 to the town of **Nochixtlán**, and then heading north on an unpaved road, is the rural village of **SANTIAGO APOALA**, tucked in a beautiful high valley. Here you'll find the Picturas Repuestas, 5000-year-old glyphs considered to be the oldest example of Mixtec drawing. It's a wild place, ideally located for hiking, biking and various other outdoor activities involving the nearby rivers, lagoons and falls; one rewarding hike is to follow the trail alongside the Apoala River to the sixty-metre Cola de Serpiente waterfall. Many of the trails are badly marked and it is advisable to take a guide with you. The comfortable **Tourist Yú'ù** (❷) can be reserved through the tourist office in Oaxaca, and the village ecotourism co-operative, Comité de Turismo de Santiago Apoala (Ⓣ551/151-9154), can arrange meals, organize expeditions and guides and provide general information.

Apoala can be reached by a variety of means: second-class buses make the trip daily, and minivans go to Nochixtlán, where taxi or microbus (Wed, Sat & Sun) can make the remaining climb into the mountains and into the village's lush, spring-fed valley.

### The Alta: Tlaxiaco and around

Hwy-125 climbs into the **Mixteca Alta** after Teposcolula, entering some beautiful pine forest as it gets closer to Tlaxiaco. On the way, about 50km after Teposcolula, lies **Huamelulpan**, 2km up a side road. This tiny mountain village has an extensive and mostly unexplored Mixtec archeological site, with two large plazas cut out of a hill, a ball-court and some temple complexes. Some of the sculptures found here have been embedded in the walls of the eighteenth-century colonial church. Other artefacts from the ruins are displayed in the small community **museum** (Mon–Fri 9am–5pm), which also has information about indigenous medicines – these are still used by traditional healers in the local community. The surrounding countryside is picturesque, with deer and coyotes in the woodland, and a variety of interesting plants. The friendly village residents administer a small, very basic **tourist lodge** here (book through the tourist office in Oaxaca, or just turn up, as you're likely to be the only visitor; ❷); the grocery shop on the main square can prepare **food** for you.

**TLAXIACO**, a fifteen-minute bus ride beyond Huamelulpan, is famed for its *pulque*, the lightly fermented drink made from cactus. The city once served as the economic heart of the Mixteca, and consequently its important Saturday market attracts indigenous people from across the region – many people here still wear traditional dress. An attractive town square and nearby good-value hotels could serve as a base for exploring the countryside and the Mixtec and Triqui villages nearby. The *Hotel del Portal* (Ⓣ953/552-0154; ❹), in a converted colonial house on the main plaza, is a wonderful **place to stay**, especially if you make sure you get a room in the old building. The rather grandiose **restaurant** within serves fresh juices and special dishes such as *molcajete*, a stone bowl of hot stewed meat and vegetables. Slightly less expensive are the *Hotel Colón*, Colón 11 (Ⓣ953/552-0013; ❸), and the cheery *Hotel México*, Hidalgo 13 (Ⓣ953/552-0086; ❸). The *Rincón de Gon* restaurant, next door to the *México*, has a good menu, including some vegetarian options, and puts on live music most nights.

**Camionetas** for Tlaxiaco leave from Oaxaca's Transporte Tlaxiaco (hourly; 3hr); there are also two second-class **buses** per day. For moving on from Tlaxiaco, buses leave for **Pinotepa Nacional**, where you can change for Puerto Escondido and the Pacific coast. There are also services from Tlaxiaco to Mexico City and Puebla.

## San José del Pacífico

On the route down to the coast from Oaxaca via Hwy-175, perched on the side of a pine-tree-clad mountain, enveloped in plumes of cloud, you'll find **SAN JOSÉ DEL PACÍFICO**, renowned for its hallucinogenic mushrooms. Around three hours' drive south from Oaxaca, it's the best place to break the journey, or to stay for a day or two if you want to enjoy the forest trails and cool mountain air before descending to the tropical lowlands of the coast. Many people make the short trip from nearby Zipolite, just two hours away (see p.681) for a lovely overnight stay. The *Hotel Puesta del Sol* on the main road (Ⓣ951/510-7570, Ⓦwww.sanjosedelpacifico.com) has a good **restaurant** serving comidas, dulces and mescal, plus you can stay here in wooden **cabañas** (❹) or bungalows (❺) with incredible views over the valley (try to get one of the cabañas furthest from the restaurant so that you get a clear view). Round the corner, in the centre of the village, the *Pacífico* (no phone) has equally nice cabañas that are slightly cheaper (❷), some of which also have good views, though they aren't as breathtaking as those at the *Puesta del Sol*. There is a pleasant café and small grocery store where you can stop and buy coffee, cakes and excellent *tortas de quesillo*. It gets chilly at night here in winter (although it heats up during the day), so bring warm clothing and a sleeping bag and indulge in some mescal.

# Puerto Escondido and around

The three-hundred-kilometre journey south from Oaxaca to **PUERTO ESCONDIDO** ("Hidden Port") is dramatic, passing through mountainous pine forests and descending into tropical lowlands. The air pushed in from the sea meets the air in the tropical forest, condenses and regularly rises in impressive, cold gusts up the mountainside.

Though no longer the tranquil hangout it was thirty-plus years ago, when it became the pioneer beach resort on this stretch of the coastal highway, Escondido still has a lot going for it – at least in the eyes of its surfing-oriented demographic. With direct flights from the capital and something of an international reputation, these days Escondido has firmly established itself as a destination: you'll find the standard strings of souvenir shops, crowded bars, Internet cafés and no-frills restaurants along the Adoquín (the main pedestrian strip), as well as constantly spiralling prices that for the most part do not correspond to quality. This said, there is an air that remains, against all odds, somewhat small-town, casual and uninhibited. There is still the hint of the village it once was; this is most evident in the early morning, when fishermen return to Playa Principal, their boats laden with marlin and red snapper. Beaches stretch around the bay for miles in each direction, and while there are a tremendous number of hotels to choose from, the majority tend to be on the small and basic side, catering to long-stay travellers, and most of the visitors are young, with surfing high on their agendas.

Indeed, it is along the surf beach, **Zicatela**, less than a kilometre away from the centre and divided from the main beach of Playa Principal by a rocky outcrop known as Rocas del Morro, that most of the recent changes have taken place. Where once stood just a few weather-beaten huts, there's now a thriving community with a clutch of hotels – most with pools, since the sea is almost always too rough for swimming – and open-air rustic restaurants serving everything from burgers to fresh fish and Mexican staples. Everything revolves around surfing and being outdoors: you can get your hair cut while watching the surfers paddling through the swells, or watch a video of the morning's action in one of the hotels. Non-surfers and surfer groupies have also latched onto the relaxed pace, and Zicatela is now as much a destination as Escondido town itself, especially between August and January when the weather is ideal. During the rainy season the town has a much more vacant, lacklustre air – the oppressive humidity creates a marshy, mosquito-ridden beachfront. At either end of the dry season, Escondido is packed for **surf tournaments**, including a locally sponsored event in late August and two international ones, one in August and the other in late November.

Despite Zicatela's laid-back atmosphere, **muggings** do occur and have given the entire Puerto Escondido area a bit of an overblown reputation for thievery. It's inadvisable to walk on the beach at night or along the dimly lit highway where there is a limited pedestrian footpath, but if you use the normal precautions, and are not lured into a false sense of security by the idyllic surroundings, there shouldn't be any problems.

## Orientation, arrival and information

Puerto Escondido can be loosely divided into two zones. The **old town** sprawls across the hill behind the bay, separated by Hwy-200 from the newer **tourist zone**, which spills down towards the water (the **Playa Principal**) and is concentrated along **Avenida Peréz Gasga**, the town's main thoroughfare. Half of the latter street is pedestrianized and known as **El Adoquín** – Spanish for "paving stone". **Playa Marinero** separates the main bay from **Playa Zicatela** (hidden behind rocks at the east end of the bay), which runs east and then south from here.

Puerto Escondido has four **bus stations**, all near each other in the old town on the hill near **El Crucero**, the junction where the main road between the old town and the tourist zone crosses the Carretera Costera (Hwy-200). From

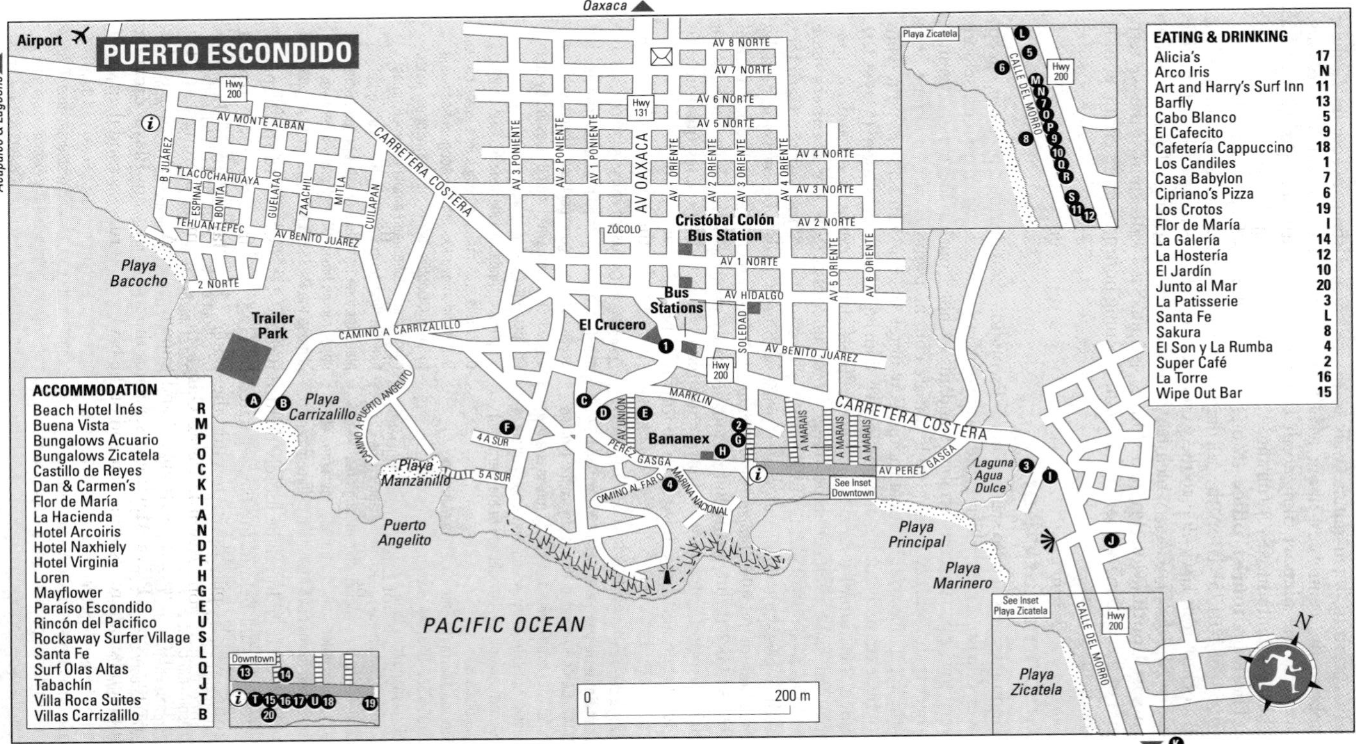
PUERTO ESCONDIDO
Airport
Acapulco & Lagoons
Oaxaca
Hwy 200
Hwy 131
CARRETERA COSTERA
AV OAXACA
AV MONTE ALBAN
B JUÁREZ
TLACOCHAHUAYA
ESPINAL
BONITA
TEHUANTEPEC
GUELATAO
ZAACHIL
MITLA
CUILAPAN
AV BENITO JUÁREZ
2 NORTE
AV 3 PONIENTE
AV 2 PONIENTE
AV 1 PONIENTE
AV 1 ORIENTE
AV 2 ORIENTE
AV 3 ORIENTE
AV 4 ORIENTE
AV 5 ORIENTE
AV 6 ORIENTE
AV 8 NORTE
AV 7 NORTE
AV 6 NORTE
AV 5 NORTE
AV 4 NORTE
AV 3 NORTE
AV 2 NORTE
AV 1 NORTE
AV HIDALGO
SOLEDAD
ZÓCOLO
Cristóbal Colón Bus Station
Bus Stations
El Crucero
Banamex
MARKLIN
AV UNIÓN
PEREZ GASGA
AV PEREZ GASGA
A MARAIS
CAMINO AL FARO
MARINA NACIONAL
4 A SUR
5 A SUR
CAMINO A CARRIZALILLO
CAMINO A PUERTO ANGELITO
Trailer Park
Playa Bacocho
Playa Carrizalillo
Playa Manzanillo
Puerto Angelito
Playa Principal
Playa Marinero
Playa Zicatela
Laguna Agua Dulce
CALLE DEL MORRO
See Inset Downtown
See Inset Playa Zicatela
PACIFIC OCEAN
0
200 m
N
Downtown
Playa Zicatela
ACCOMMODATION
Beach Hotel Inés R
Buena Vista M
Bungalows Acuario P
Bungalows Zicatela O
Castillo de Reyes C
Dan & Carmen's K
Flor de María I
La Hacienda A
Hotel Arcoiris N
Hotel Naxhiely D
Hotel Virginia F
Loren H
Mayflower G
Paraíso Escondido E
Rincón del Pacifico U
Rockaway Surfer Village S
Santa Fe L
Surf Olas Altas Q
Tabachín J
Villa Roca Suites T
Villas Carrizalillo B
EATING & DRINKING
Alicia's 17
Arco Iris N
Art and Harry's Surf Inn 11
Barfly 13
Cabo Blanco 5
El Cafecito 9
Cafetería Cappuccino 18
Los Candiles 1
Casa Babylon 7
Cipriano's Pizza 6
Los Crotos 19
Flor de María I
La Galería 14
La Hostería 12
El Jardín 10
Junto al Mar 20
La Patisserie 3
Santa Fe L
Sakura 8
El Son y La Rumba 4
Super Café 2
La Torre 16
Wipe Out Bar 15

El Crucero it's a ten-minute walk to the centre and about twenty to Zicatela; taxis to the centre cost about M$40. Flights from Oaxaca and Mexico City arrive at the **airport** 3km north of town, from where taxis (M$120) and a cheaper minibus (M$40) run into the centre.

The main **tourist office** (Mon–Fri 9am–2pm & 4–7pm, Sat 10am–2pm; ☎954/582-0175) is on the turning off to the new hotel zone (near Playa Bacocho) from Hwy-200, to the west of town, and gives away copies of the free paper *El Sol de la Costa*, which has festival and event **listings**. There's a nearer **tourist booth** (Mon–Fri 9am–2pm & 4–6pm, Sat 10am–2pm) at the western end of the walking section of Adoquín. Opening hours are more erratic outside the main season.

## Accommodation



Finding somewhere to stay in Puerto Escondido shouldn't be a problem, except over Christmas and during the major surfing contests, when **prices**, seldom very low, can rise considerably. Standards of hotel quality are generally much lower than you may be used to if you are coming from Oaxaca, and range from simple cabañas to functional rooms. Few hotels have a/c, and if they do it tends to be extremely noisy and ineffective. During the rainy season (May–Oct), when the humidity rises to oppressive levels, damp, musty sheets and mosquitoes can make even the upper-range hotels uncomfortable. For **campers** there is *Villa Relax* (☎954/582-2977), to the west of the centre, off the Carretera, with a pool and tent and trailer space, although it can be overwhelmed by busloads of people. *Trailer Park Neptune*, by the eastern end of Playa Principal (☎954/582-0327), a tatty but reasonably shady ground with cabins for the same price as pitching a tent, is more conveniently located, but rates quadruple in December, and there have been reports of robberies.

### In town

**Castillo de Reyes** Peréz Gasga 201 ☎954/582-0442. Centrally located, this roomy, castle-themed hotel with large, clean, fan-cooled rooms is a few blocks uphill from the Adoquín on a noisy street. A few artisan embellishments add to the warmth of the place. ④

**Flor de María** 1a Entrada, Playa Marinero ☎954/582-0536, Ⓦwww.mexonline.com/flordemaria.htm. With a perfect location on Playa Marinero, within easy reach of the attractions of Zicatela and the Adoquín, and offering great-value, laid-back comfort, this is a traveller favourite. All fan-cooled rooms have fresh, tiled bathrooms and a safe, and some have balconies. The omnipresent charm of the Italian owner even extends to the sharp decor. There's a rooftop pool with a very good restaurant (breakfast is included during low season) and great views. ④–⑤

**Hotel Naxhiely** Peréz Gasga 301 ☎954/582-3075. Cheery posada with plain rooms, a little café and a sprinkling of potted plants. ③

**Hotel Virginia** 4a Sur 504 ☎954/582-0176. On a quiet street three blocks from the Adoquín, with cheerful details, powerful fans and ocean views from the upper floor. ③

**Loren** Peréz Gasga 507 ☎954/582-0057. High-standard, brightly painted hotel away from the ocean but with a good pool and impressively low off-season prices, which can be slashed by up to fifty percent. ⑤

**Mayflower** Andador Libertad s/n ☎954/582-0367. This well-managed place in a lively, convenient location overlooking the Adoquín has a cult following. Double rooms and dormitories, a bar, communal kitchen and ample common areas foster a long-term traveller vibe – it's a great place for lone travellers to meet people. Some upper rooms have little balconies where you can glimpse the Pacific. A second branch, *Mayflower II*, is close by and has the added benefit of a swimming pool. ③

**Paraíso Escondido** Unión 10 ☎954/582-0444. On a flight of steps on the hill before the Adoquín, one of the better-maintained hotels in this area. Each tidy room is decorated artistically, with a smattering of kitsch, whimsical mirrors, tiles and sculptures. On the down side, the soft beds need upgrading. Each room has a balcony and there is a central, pretty pool, bar and restaurant area. The staff are very helpful, but the experience is a bit overpriced for what you get. Cash only. ⑦–⑧

**Rincón del Pacífico** Peréz Gasga 900 ⓣ954/582-0056. Can be a bargain in low season; slightly motel-like, but clean, decent-sized rooms overlooking the beach and its own stone courtyard. ④

**Villa Roca Suites** Peréz Gasga 602 ⓣ954/582-3525. The fanciest place on the Adoquín strip, with white stucco walls, palapa roofs and slightly frilly rooms backing on the Playa Principal. ⑦

## Zicatela

The hotels below are listed in order of distance from Puerto Escondido.

**Aqua Luna** Vista Hermosa s/n ⓣ954/582-1505, ⓦwww.hotelaqualuna.com Smart, minimalist hotel with neat, well-equipped rooms – about as close to a boutique hotel as you'll get in Puerto. Hospitably run by a Canadian–Mexican couple who are knowledgeable on the area, it makes for a very pleasant home base. There's also the added allure of a swimming pool, palapa bar, widescreen TV, pool table and laundry service. ④–⑤

**Dan & Carmen's** Jacaranda 14 ⓣ954/582-2760, ⓦwww.casadanycarmen.com. Very cool place with lots of character. A variety of rooms are available, each with a kitchen, terrace, great views and artfully decorated bathrooms. Larger rooms are very spacious and cost-effective for groups or families. Reservations advised in the high season. ④

**Santa Fe** Calle del Morro s/n ⓣ954/582-0170, ⓦwww.hotelsantafe.com.mx. Falsely pitching itself as Puerto Escondido's top hotel, this overpriced, rather down-at-the-heel place caters to an older, non-surfer crowd. No-frills, balconied rooms overlook the two swimming pools or have sneaking views of the ocean. Its restaurant (see p.676) redeems it. ⑨

**Buena Vista** Calle del Morro s/n ⓣ954/582-1474. This well-run, well-established hotel is set slightly off the road behind the beach up the hill. All rooms are triples, clean and spacious with mosquito nets (which you'll need) and lovely terraces with beautiful views over the bay. ④

**Hotel Arcoiris** Calle del Morro s/n ⓣ954/582-1494, ⓦwww.oaxaca-mio.com/arcoiris.htm. This is one of the better-value options if you want to be at the heart of the surfing action on Zicatela. Functional rooms set back from the shore in a modern three-storey block. They all have private baths and fans – some have kitchenettes – but are rather worn and in need of upgrading. The main draws here are the relaxing and friendly vibe, the luxuriant gardens with secluded pool and the restaurant with great views and a decent selection of fish and meat dishes. ⑥

**Bungalows Zicatela** Calle del Morro s/n ⓣ954/582-0798. A modest jumble of large rooms, most with a kitchen. The action is centred around the pool and adjacent restaurant with bar. ⑤

**Bungalows Acuario** Calle del Morro s/n ⓣ954/582-1027. A laissez-faire hotel with simple lodgings to suit low- and mid-range budgets. With an attractive pool and bar, access to a gym (M$15/day for non-guests), an Internet café with a/c and a communal vibe, there would be no need to leave if you weren't right on the beach in the centre of Zicatela. There are a lot of mosquitoes, though, and some of the furnishings are faded and musty – ask to see a few rooms before you commit. ④–⑥

**Surf Olas Altas** Calle del Morro 310 ⓣ954/582-2315, ⓦwww.surfolasaltas.com. For the more chi-chi surfer, this large, spotless, but rather banal, hotel has more creature comforts – safe, a/c, TV – modernity and order to it than the other hotels but lacks some of their organic charm. ⑧

**Beach Hotel Inés** Calle del Morro s/n ⓣ954/582-0792. With an artistic feel, a sauna and spa, the German-managed *Inés* has more facilities than you would expect in this range. Rooms are available for various budgets; it's especially economical if you share a cabaña with a group. There is access to the hotel pool and a pleasant, relaxed restaurant. ③–⑥

**La Hacienda** Atunes 15 ⓣ954/582-0279. Thanks to their gracious French owner, the six very comfortable, spacious bedrooms with kitchenettes and a/c ooze a home-spun style, including wooden furnishings and floral drapery. Outside, a colonial theme prevails, with flower-filled patios and a swimming pool surrounded by tropical foliage. A 5min walk from Playa Carrizalillo, it's not cheap, but one of the better places if you are inclined to splurge. ⑥

**Rockaway Surfer Village** Calle del Morro s/n ⓣ954/582-0668. A dedicated surfer resort. Pleasant palapa cabins with private showers flank one side of a large swimming pool while facing a newly constructed, comfortable but sterile, hotel with a/c, queen-size beds and cable TV. There is a lively on-site bar that draws the older Jimmy Buffet-style contingent in town, as well as a surf shop and a volleyball court. Very good value, especially in the low season when prices are halved. ③–④

**Tabachín** Calle del Moro s/n ⓣ954/582-1179, ⓦwww.tabachin.com.mx. Just one block from Zicatela, this eclectic cluster of studios, some with large, breezy balconies, are crammed with books, knick-knacks and vases that add to its quirky, comforting appeal. The owner is keen to help with any tours, and substantial breakfasts are included. Fans, a/c and cable TV in each room. ④–⑤

**Villas Carrizalillo** Carrizalillo 125 ⓣ954/582-1735, ⓦwww.villascarrizalillo.com. In a peaceful spot above its beautiful namesake beach, these discreet, spacious, individually designed villas with kitchens and stunning views are perfect for young couples and families who want to be away from the party scene and prefer a few more home comforts. There is free Internet access, laptops and aquatic equipment for rent and a welcoming atmosphere – enjoy it now, the area is developing rapidly. ⑧

## The beaches

Apart from shopping for international surf designs, beachwear and crafts (some tacky, some classy), Escondido offers little beyond the standard beach activities: swimming, surfing, lazing on the sand, eating, drinking and watching beautiful sunsets. The choice of **beaches**, even within a couple of kilometres of town, is impressive. Take your pick from the town strand – with the convenience of shops and bars nearby – pounding surf beaches or secluded coves ideal for snorkelling. In most places you needn't move all day, as you'll be regularly approached by ice cream carts, people trying to sell you cold drinks or hot snacks and vendors of trinkets. Note that wherever you are, the surf should be treated with respect – the waters along Zicatela, especially, have a lethal **undertow**.

There are three main beach areas: the town beach (**Playa Principal**), which stretches round to the east and south from the town centre; the surfing destination of Zicatela, to the southeast; and the trio of small coves to the west. The sand directly in front of town is perhaps a little overused, and shared, too, with the local fishermen and the activities of the port. A little to the east, beyond where the **Laguna Agua Dulce** occasionally reaches the sea, **Playa Marinero** is quieter and sometimes graced with gentle waves – it's a good place to play in the waves and to learn to surf. The real big stuff is past here, beyond the little headland, where **Zicatela** stretches for 2km. One of the world's top surf beaches, Zicatela ("place of big thorns") regularly receives beach breaks of

△ Surfer, Puerto Escondido

around 4m and can maintain the surf swell for days on end. This spot is referred to as the "**Mexican pipeline**", because the breaking waves curl into perfect cylinders – permitting expert surfers to momentarily ride inside the pipe-like tube. Surfboards and boogie boards can be rented from a number of places along Zicatela beach. When it is pumping, consider your strength and fitness (you can check the wave reports on line at one of the Internet cafés, or ask in one of the surf shops) before venturing into the water: the waves are very powerful, and occasionally even experienced surfers drown, although there are *salvavidas* (lifeguards) patrolling the beach. If the pipeline is too much for you to handle, continue east for a little over a kilometre down the beach to **La Punta** ("the point"). La Punta is a much easier break, though it can also be exceptional when the swell is up. It provides good, slower waves that are excellent for longboarding. The sheltered beach break inside La Punta is recommended as a spot to learn to surf when the waves are smaller.

Everything is much calmer in the coves to the west of the town. **Puerto Ángelito** is the closest, divided in two by a rocky outcrop, with a second beach, slightly further inland from Ángelito, called **Manzanillo**. They're about twenty minutes' walk from town, either by a track that leads to the left off Peréz Gasga, or direct from the highway on a signed road leading down opposite *El Padrino* restaurant (the two paths meet above the beach). An alternative is the recently completed concrete footpath that sets out from the western end of the town beach, dipping and turning over the coastal rocks and eventually climbing up to a road. Follow this inland, then turn left along the road signposted "Playa Manzanillo", which turns into steps going down to the beach. You can also drive or get a taxi to drop you off at the top of the steps to the beach. Both little inlets have small beaches and excellent snorkelling among the rocks (if you can avoid the boats), but you'll have to bring your own gear or rent some at great expense from the makeshift restaurants lining the beach.

The next bay, **Carrizalillo**, is reached by continuing west along the same track. At the end you have to scramble down over the rocks to reach the sand, guaranteeing that there won't be too many other people around. **Bacocho Bay** is further, following the highway out towards the airport and then cutting through the new hotel zone. There aren't a great number of hotels here yet, so the sand is still somewhat secluded, though swimming isn't considered safe – the beach is pounded by heavy surf and has a strong undertow. *Coco's Bar and Restaurant* serves decent, if pricey, **food**; you can use their pool for M$35.

It's also possible to take a **boat** (M$30) to the above beaches, and some further afield, from in front of the *Hotel Rincón del Pacífico* on the Adoquín. It should then return to pick you up at an agreed time.

## Eating, drinking and nightlife

It doesn't cost much to eat fairly well in Escondido. Many of the restaurants and cafés are laid-back, low-key affairs open to cool breezes and with plenty of natural light. The **seafood** is always fresh, and you can vary your diet with **vegetarian** food, excellent bread and cakes and **Italian** food from the inordinately large number of Italian restaurants. The classier restaurants on the Adoquín, such as the *Junto al Mar*, have terraces opening onto the main bay. There are more restaurants and cafés lining Zicatela beach that serve cheap pasta dishes, snacks and drinks.

Happy hours at the popular *Wipe Out Bar*, *3 Diablos* and *Barfly* run between 5pm and 8pm, and most of the restaurants double as **bars** too, some even hosting **live music**. Otherwise, nightlife is concentrated in the bars along Peréz Gasga.

There are arthouse **films** on show at CineMar, at the east end of Zicatela, usually in English or with subtitles. The schedule is on view at *El Cafecito* (see opposite) in Zicatela – there are two showings nightly.

## In town

**Alicia's** Peréz Gasga. No-frills, inexpensive cafeteria with a broad menu of staples, including seafood, Italian and authentic Mexican dishes. For lunch the comida corrida is a great-value option.

**Barfly** Peréz Gasga. The hub of Escondido's bar scene, this eclectic lounge with a balcony overlooking the western end of the Adoquín plays good international music and has comfy cushions for you to lie on while you sip a frosty cocktail.

**Cafetería Cappuccino** Peréz Gasga. A good place for breakfast and coffee, light lunches, pasta and snacks.

**Los Candiles** 1a Poniente, at the Carretera Costera. A good-value restaurant decorated with hand-woven tablecloths and artesanía. The chef specializes in delicious Oaxaqueña dishes and fresh seafood; the fish special of the day is a good bet.

**El Chubasco** 2a Sur 8. This simple but appealing café is one of the cheapest places in town to get a full meal; fried fish, rice and salad can be had for M$25. The TV is usually blaring and there's frequently a group of men playing cards in the corner.

**Los Crotos** Peréz Gasga. At the edge of the Playa Principal, an unassuming joint that sparkles at night and serves an unpretentious menu of extremely fresh whole grilled fish.

**Flor de María** Playa Marinero. Attached to the hotel of the same name, *Flor de María* is a nice place for a quiet meal. The menu features dishes like stuffed peppers, meat dishes and pastas.

**La Galería** Peréz Gasga. One of the best Italian joints in town, with platters of home-made tortellini, spaghetti, ravioli and gnocchi as well as delicious salads and an array of pizzas, all served in a polished setting with art strewn across the walls and exposed brick.

**La Hostería** Calle del Morro. Wood-oven pizzas and imaginative Italian and nouvelle Mexican dishes are served with flair and a decent wine selection. It's also one of the best places for creative vegetarian dishes. Substantial breakfasts are available.

**Junto al Mar** Peréz Gasga. At the western end of the Adoquín, opening onto the sea, this rustic, open-air restaurant sticks to unadulterated grilled seafood dishes that are tasty and well proportioned. With views over Playa Marinero, there is plenty of beach action to entertain at sunset.

**La Patisserie** Calle del Morro, Playa Marinero. Croissants and pastries from *Carmen's* at Zicatela, plus sandwiches, fruit salads and yogurt, served in a quiet palm hut with a book swap.

**El Son y La Rumba** Andador Mar y Sol, off Peréz Gasga. Salsa bar with a tiny dancefloor where gringos inevitably try, and fail, to imitate the locals. Live *cumbia*, merengue and reggae. Opens around 10pm.

**Super Café** up the steps above Peréz Gasga at the western end of the Adoquín. Coffee shop with scrumptious home-made breakfast specials and delicious Oaxacan bulk coffee for sale.

**La Torre** Benito Juárez 427. Just out of town (take a taxi), this smart restaurant is popular with the more gilded locals. If you have had your fill of fish, there are some delectable steaks, pork ribs and chicken dishes on offer here. There is delightful outdoor garden seating in the summertime.

**Wipe Out Bar** Peréz Gasga. This is the favourite spot on the Adoquín for surfers and travellers, so don't come here looking for a quiet drink – it gets packed and rowdy.

## Zicatela

The restaurants and bars below are listed in order of distance from Puerto Escondido.

**Santa Fe** Breezy palapa setting to tuck into seafood, pasta, vegetarian fare, *chiles rellenos* and other classic Mexican dishes at moderate to expensive prices. Don't leave without trying the wonderful chocolate cake with ice cream.

**Cabo Blanco** Hit-or-miss seafood on the beach at reasonable prices. Fish and shrimp are dressed with a more imaginative choice of sauces than at other similar restaurants: try the Thai curry or lime, wine and cream. Live music most nights draws a boisterous crowd.

**Cipriano's Pizza** Thin, crispy, cheesy pizzas, served at romantic tables wedged into the sand.

**Arco Iris** The main draw here is the elevated beachfront location, but the traditional Mexican dishes are generally very good value and tasty. An uninspired selection of international dishes include pastas and mercilessly fried fish. There are also vegetarian comidas corridas – bland, but meat free; strict vegetarians should request that their meal not be fried in animal fat.

**Casa Babylon** Arty, friendly, late-night bar next door to the *Hotel Arcoiris*. Board games, mellow music and a useful reference library with travel books and *National Geographic* magazines.

**Sakura** Though an unlikely spot for Japanese cuisine, this relaxed restaurant under an enormous palapa faces out onto the pounding surf and serves authentic Japanese fare: sushi, sashimi, tempura and sake. There are also tofu dishes for vegetarians.
**El Cafecito** A justifiably longstanding favourite. Wonderful, wholesome breakfasts, complete with the drifting aromas of freshly baked bread and coffee, are served in an open-air palapa. The menu takes a more international flavour at lunch, with burgers, whole-grain sandwiches and burritos. There are tasty, simple seafood dishes and other filling Mexican staples in the evening.
**El Jardín** Always crowded, this palapa café in front of *Hotel Olas Altas* has an extensive menu that includes home-baked sourdough bread, hummus, yogurt and granola, pasta, sandwiches, burgers, fruit smoothies, snacks and cakes, and baked pizzas in the evening.
**Art and Harry's Surf Inn** A favourite evening spot of surfers and their acolytes, who come to watch the sun go down and drink two-for-one beers, then stay on to play pool and look over that morning's surf photos on the notice board. Tasty, good-value salads, seafood and burgers served all day.

## Around Puerto Escondido: the lagoons

Unless you're a hardcore surfer or ardent sun-worshipper, a few days spent relaxing on the beach is usually sufficient before you feel the need to explore. There are a few boat excursions around Puerto Escondido that make for enjoyable, accessible day trips.

**Laguna Manialtepec**, about 15km west of the city, is cut off from the sea most of the year, forming a freshwater lake extraordinarily rich in **birdlife**. You can easily spot fifty-odd species, including parrots, hawks, falcons, ospreys, kingfishers and ibises. The most convenient way to visit is to take an organized **tour** through one of the travel agencies in Puerto Escondido. Hidden Voyages Ecotours runs trips led by a Canadian ornithologist (daily, except Thurs and Sun; 7am–noon; M$430). Contact Dimar Travel Agency, Peréz Gasga 905-B (☎954/582-1551) for additional information. If you can get enough people together it is worthwhile organizing a boat trip independently; take one of the buses that run from El Crucero to La Alejandria or El Gallo. At restaurant *Isla del Gallo* you can hire a **boat** for four passengers and captain (2hr 30min; M$350).

The **Lagunas de Chacahua**, some 75km west of Puerto Escondido, make for a more diverse venture – in order to visit independently you will need a couple of days at least. This 150,000-hectare park is a refuge of mangroves, sand dunes and forests that teem with birdlife. On the shores of the lagoon the village of Chacahua is interesting in itself, with a small Afro-Mexican population and a huge beach where you can rent basic **rooms** (❷) and cabañas (❸) by the water. The lagoon is calm enough in parts and with some good surf, though the currents are strong, so check where it's safe to swim. There's also space to **camp** and a row of outdoor seafood restaurants where you could hang a hammock. Catch a **bus** from El Crucero (every 20min) to **Río Grande**, 50km west of Puerto Escondido on Hwy-200, then change to one of the frequent minibuses to the port of **Zapotalito**. The road does continue a short way from here to the beach and palapa restaurants at **Cerro Hermoso**, but it is better to take a *lancha* to **Playa Chacahua** – you could also rent one (M$400/person) to tour the lagoon.

An ecotourism project has been established in the **Barra de Navidad**, ten minutes east of Puerto Escondido on Hwy-200 (the turning, on the right, comes just after the bridge that crosses the lagoon). For M$70, locals will take you on a tour of the local **crocodile** lagoon, and nearby deserted beach – a haven for **birdlife**; ask for Galo when you arrive. **Colectivos** run here from the main bay at Escondido – you can get more information at the tourist booth on the Adoquín (see p.672).

## Listings

**Banks and exchange** There's a casa de cambio on the Adoquín (Mon–Sat 9am–9pm, Sun 9am–5pm), although better rates are available just up the hill at the busy Banamex on Peréz Gasga near the *Paraíso Escondido* (Mon–Fri 9am–5pm, Sat 10am–2pm), which also has an ATM. There is an HSBC ATM halfway along the Adoquín. In Zicatela, there's an exchange in *Bungalows Acuario* (see p.673).

**Buses** The Central Camionera is at 3 Poniente and 10 Norte, north of town. Estrella Blanca (☎954/582-0086) has first- and second-class buses to Acapulco, Huatulco, Mexico City and Salina Cruz from here. The next best is Cristóbal Colón (☎954/582-1073), which has buses to Oaxaca, including one overnight. Estrella Roja Sur (☎954/582-3899) runs daily first-class services to Mexico City, and Estrella del Valle (☎954/582-0050) runs to Oaxaca in three classes: deluxe (10.30pm; 6hr), first-class (2 daily; 6hr) and second-class (6 daily; 8hr). Transportes Oaxaca Istmo, Hidalgo at 1 Oriente, operates second-class to Salina Cruz (5 daily; 5hr), with one a day continuing to Tuxtla Gutiérrez (10hr).

**Flights** You can get daily flights to Oaxaca with Aerotucán (☎954/582-1725) and Aerovega (☎954/582-0151); the approximate cost one way is M$1350. There are daily Aerocaribe (☎954/582-2023, Ⓦwww.mexicana.com) and Click Mexicana (☎01-800-122-5425, Ⓦwww.click.mx.com) flights to Mexico City for about the same price. You can save money on taxis by engaging the services of Transportes Aeropuerto y Turístico (☎954/582-0123), whose office is in town at the foot of the hill of Peréz Gasga.

**Internet access** There are several slightly pricey Internet cafés in Zicatela and on Peréz Gasga charging around M$20/hr. Venturing outside the tourist zone around the Adoquín leads to cheaper, M$11/hr Internet access – head north of the Carretera Costera on any major street.

**Laundry** There's the self-service Lavamatica del Centro next door to Banamex, on Peréz Gasga near the *Paraíso Escondido* (Mon–Sat 8am–8pm). Lava Max, towards the east end of the Adoquín, offers a drop-off laundry service for M$15/kilo.

**Post office** In the old town at Oaxaca Norte 7 (Mon–Fri 9am–3pm & 6–8pm, Sat 9am–1pm), though you can get stamps from postcard vendors (at a half-peso premium) and chance your luck with the mail boxes along Peréz Gasga.

**Telephones** There are several Ladatel phones (free collect calls) on the Adoquín, where there's also a *larga distancia* office. There are also pay phones in Zicatela.

**Trips and activities** Ecotourism adventures – everything from lagoon trips to cycling, camping, rock climbing, bird watching and trips to coffee plantations in Nopala and hot springs in Atonillo – are promoted here; Turismo Dimar (☎954/582-1551), Ana's Ecotours (☎954/582-2954) and other agencies on the Adoquín can arrange them. Dimar can also assist with flight bookings, ticket changes and car hire. Surfing lessons are offered at Central Surf and Mexpipe on Zicatela, and several outfits teach scuba diving, including Aventura Submarina (☎954/582-2353) on the Adoquín. Massages are offered at various places along Zicatela, including *Hotel Inés* and the gym at the *Acuario* (see p.673). Temazcalli, 10min out of town on Hwy-200 past Zicatela beach and over the bridge, at Infraganti and Temazcalli (☎954/582-1023, Ⓦwww.temazcalli.com), has a range of treatments, from shiatsu and *aqua mystical* to *temazcal*.

# Puerto Ángel and around

Some 65 km from Puerto Escondido, at the junction of Hwy-175 from Oaxaca and coastal Hwy-200, the oppressive, shabby town of **Pochutla** is the service hub for a string of beach towns and resorts that unfurl east towards the Isthmus of Tehuantepec. **Puerto Ángel**, now firmly on the tourist radar, is a dusty, rough-hewn village that draws budget travellers with its unpretentious, low-key vibe and picturesque setting with crescents of golden sand backed by craggy, jungle-covered hills. Some four miles west, the beautiful beach of **Zipolite** has gained a reputation for its liberal-minded, 1960s European hippy vibe, while just north and over the headland, attractive **San Agustinillo** has a more restrained feel. Further west, **Mazunte** is the main nesting site for Golfina turtles and, as yet, remains an unspoiled enclave where you can escape civilization on pristine beaches.

## Pochutla

Anyone visiting Puerto Ángel and the other beach communities along the coast comes through **POCHUTLA**, a rather scruffy town on Hwy-175 2km north of Hwy-200. Apart from catching a bus or changing money – there are no banks at the beaches – there's no reason to come here.

Pochutla's centre is gradually being smartened up – the main street has been resurfaced and Internet cafés have sprung up along it, catering to the transitory crowds. If you wind up stopping here, it's worthwhile stocking up on provisions at the **market**, or one of the excellent **panaderías**, north of the bus station. The main square, Plaza de las Golondrinas, is the social hub of town – families come to stroll in the evenings and local artisans sell jewellery and other knick-knacks in the pedestrianized alleys.

The **bus stations** – the second-class Estrella Blanca (Ⓣ958/584-0380), Oaxaca Pacífico (Ⓣ958/584-0349) and the first-class Cristóbal Colón (Ⓣ958/584-0274) – are close to each other on Lázaro Cárdenas, which runs from Hwy-200 into the centre of town. Daily first-class services cover Huatulco, Juchitán, Mexico City, Oaxaca, Puerto Escondido and San Cristóbal de las Casas; daily second-class buses leave for the same destinations and local villages.

Further along Cárdenas, HSBC (Mon–Fri 8am–7pm, Sat 8am–3pm) with ATM, will change travellers' cheques and dollars as well as issue cash advances. Scotiabank (Mon–Fri 9am–5pm) or Bancomer (Mon–Fri 8.30am–4pm), both with ATM, will change **money**; the Bital nearby is also open Saturdays from 8am to 3pm. Of the **hotels**, *Hotel Pochutla*, Madero 102 (Ⓣ958/584-0033; ❹), on the central plaza, is comfortable and spacious; the rather worn *Hotel Izala*, Cárdenas 59 (Ⓣ958/584-0115; ❷–❹), has unadorned rooms with cable TV, private baths and a/c grouped around a courtyard. The best option in town is the clean, well-run *Costa del Sol*, Cárdenas 47 (Ⓣ958/584-0049; ❸), while *Hotel Santa Cruz*, Cárdenas 88 (Ⓣ958/584-0116; ❶), a little nearer the bus stations, has spacious but rather noisy and dilapidated rooms, some with a/c. For **food**, the *Panificadora 7 Regiones*, a bakery across from the *Costa del Sol*, has delicious cookies and a fine selection of groceries, while *Café Café*, opposite the zócalo, has real espresso machines and excellent cold mocha cappuccinos. Just north of Puerto Ángel on Hwy-175 is the *Finca de Vaqueros* outdoor barbecue restaurant, famous with locals for grilled meats of every kind. Two cowboy brothers keep the place open every day of the year.

**Buses** head down frequently to Puerto Ángel and Zipolite, along with **colectivos** or *especial* **taxis**; one of these taxis may cost well over five times as much, so go *colectivo* – you should rarely have to wait long for fellow passengers. In Puerto Ángel, the taxis drop off at the rank by the dock. If you want to go further, over to Playa del Panteón for example, make this clear as you set out or you'll be charged an outrageous amount for the last part of the journey (you probably will be anyway, but at least you'll be prepared).

## Puerto Ángel

Though it's pretty well established as a tourist destination, **PUERTO ÁNGEL** still goes about its business as a small, scruffy fishing port with minimum fuss. Everything remains resolutely small-scale – you may very well find pigs and chickens mingling with the visitors on the streets – and locals fish off the huge concrete dock, catching yellowtail tuna and other gamefish with a simple rod and line. Though it has a nice setting – around a sheltered bay and ringed by mountains – the beaches are less than pristine. Small hotels, rooms and simple places to sling a hammock, however, are abundant, with some of the most promising on the road between the main village and the Playa del Panteón. It is a pleasant place to spend a few days, meandering and sampling the superb local **seafood**, available at every turn.

### Information

There's a **tourist information booth** (Mon–Fri 10am–noon & 4–8pm, Sat–Sun 10am–noon). The town has no bank, but there are a couple of **larga distancia** places, one just back from the pier, near the **post office**, a few shops and **Internet** access (M$20/hr) at Gel@Net (in Gambusino's travel agency, which also has a *larga distancia*).

### Accommodation

Puerto Ángel's **hotels** are a bit scattered, but the village is small enough that you should be able to find someone to mind your bags while you look around. The places listed below represent only a fraction of the total, but you'll find little better.

**Almendro** Uribe s/n ⓣ958/584-3068. A hospitable place with tidy, brightly coloured rooms, each with fan and private bathroom. The food here, courtesy of the Swiss chef (who can also arrange Spanish lessons with his Mexican wife), is one of the major draws. ❹

**Bahía de la Luna** La Boquilla beach ⓣ958/584-6186, ⓦwww.totalmedia.qc.ca/bahiadelaluna. For escape-from-it-all couples who are happy to do without creature comforts, this jungle retreat close to beautiful La Boquilla beach (wonderful snorkelling) is hard to beat. Bungalows for two to five people cling to the hillside, and a restaurant/café on the beach serves fresh fish. It also offers holistic therapy treatments, personal development workshops and yoga, and sea kayaks and scuba gear are available to rent. ❻

**Buena Vista** La Buena Compañia s/n ⓣ958/584-3104, ⓦwww.labuenavista.com. A short walk along the footpath north from Uribe, next to the Arroye River. After the fork to the left, you will find one of the nicest hotels in Puerto Ángel set back from the main road. Accommodation is arranged over three floors, with an ocean view from the top-floor restaurant terrace and a rooftop swimming pool. The quiet rooms (some with luxurious baths) may not be well equipped – not even hot water – but the Robinson Crusoe ambience is part of the appeal. The *Alta Mira* in Mazunte (see p.686) has the same owners. ❺

**Casa Arnel** José Azueta 666 ⓣ958/584-3051. This sister hotel of the *Casa Arnel* in Oaxaca (see p.643) has clean rooms with fans and bathrooms and a hammock area, all in a homely environment. ❹

**Casa de Huéspedes Gundí y Tomas** Uribe s/n ⓣ958/584-3068, ⓦwww.puertoangel-hotel.com. One of the best budget options in the village, this jungle-clad, German-run guesthouse has simple, if rather worn, rooms with fans, mosquito nets and random folksy flourishes. The atmosphere is very friendly – you'll often find travellers hanging out, exchanging tales in the open-fronted lounge area. The restaurant serves very good food, especially the bountiful breakfasts. ❸

**Casa Penelope** Uribe s/n ⓣ958/584-3073. The friendly owner offers four reasonably priced quiet, comfortable and safe rooms, with chilled-out music and laundry facilities. Try her secret-recipe margaritas. ❸

**Hotel Saroya** Vasconceles s/n ⓣ958/584-3009. A bland but efficient choice. There is little character to this modern hotel – rooms are basic and sterile rooms with frilly bedspreads, fan (some with a/c and terrace) and private bath – but it is clean and spacious and the staff are very helpful. ❸–❹

**Posada Cañon Devata** inland from the far end of Playa del Panteón ⓣ958/584-3137, ⓦwww.posadapacifico.com. Nestled on five acres of peaceful forested hillside, 90m from the beach, this artfully designed labyrinth of rooms and bungalows with lovely views is well maintained and appointed. The family-owned posada is run with an ecofriendly focus, and offers yoga classes, massage and wonderful wholesome meals in the restaurant. A perfect retreat. ❸–❻

**Puesta del Sol** Uribe s/n ⓣ & ⓕ 958/584-3096, ⓔgolfo52@hotmail.com. The pick of the cheaper hotels. Not much in the way of a view but spotless, spacious rooms (hot water for a few dollars more) around a garden with hammocks, laundry, Internet access, library, satellite TV and communal space lined with photos. ❸

### The beaches

Puerto Ángel has two, rather dirty, beaches: **Playa Principal**, is right in front of the town, and the other is opposite, beyond a rocky promontory and the mouth of a small stream. **Playa del Panteón**, the second beach, and the cleaner of the two, is reached by road or a path around the base of the cliffs to the west. Here there is some interesting snorkelling around the rocks, though the stretch of sand is not without a profusion of tenacious hawkers. By the afternoon, though, it's in shade, so most people wander round to the town beach. With just a little more effort you can visit one of the far better beaches either side of Puerto Ángel. To the west is the more primitive **Zipolite** (see below), while to the east, about fifteen minutes' walk up the Pochutla road and then down a heavily rutted track to the right, is tranquil **Estacahuite**. Here you'll find three tiny, sandy coves divided by outcrops of rock. The rocks are close in, so you can't swim far, but there's wonderful **snorkelling** (beware of sharp coral and undercurrents) and rarely more than a couple of other people around. You can rent snorkelling gear here, or hire it from cafés on the Playa del Panteón and bring it with you. In a pleasantly breezy palapa overlooking the first of the coves, the *Club Playa Estacahuite* (fancy name, simple place) serves amazingly good seafood.

There are other lovely beaches near Estacahuite, including idyllic **Playa Boquilla**, where you'll find the *Hotel Bahía de la Luna* and a **restaurant**, accessible by boat from Puerto Ángel. Boquilla is signposted from the main road to Pochutla, but it's inadvisable to drive down here, as the seven-kilometre road is in a terrible state. A better idea is to arrange a boat trip in advance to both beaches, turtle-spotting along the way.

### Eating and drinking

**Beto's** Uribe s/n, on the outskirts of town on the way to Zipolite. High-quality seafood at very good prices served in an unassuming, low-key setting. It becomes a lively spot for drinks later on in the evening.

**Buena Vista** La Buena Compañia s/n ⓣ958/584-3104, ⓦwww.labuenavista.com. People come from all over the area to this romantic hotel restaurant serving a reliable menu of Mexican and Italian classics in a lovely floral setting overlooking the bay. Reservations recommended in high season.

**Hard Times** Uribe s/n, just past *Puesta del Sol Hotel* on the way to Zipolite. Offers reliable seafood and Mexican dishes; the service is efficient and friendly.

**Posada Cañon Devata** at the hotel of the same name, inland from Playa del Panteón. Offers nightly vegetarian feasts and healthy, inspired fish dishes in a romantic jungle setting with friendly service.

**El Rincón del Mar** precariously balanced on a cliff between playas Principal and Del Panteón. Boasting windy views of the ocean, this locally renowned restaurant serves the best fish and seafood in the area. The thick, seared loins of tuna are mouth-watering, and the nightly specials menu features imaginative renditions of the daily catch – bonita, lobster, shrimp, snapper – all invariably delicious.

**Susy's** Playa del Panteón, right on the beach. The most reliable place for snacks and drinks during a day at the beach, although better seafood platters can be found elsewhere.

**La Villa Florencia** Uribe s/n. At its namesake hotel, this is a popular place with European and American travellers, serving hearty Italian staples such as antipasto, pasta *bolognese*, *arrabiata* and marinara, as well as large, leafy salads, pizzas and traditional Mexican fare.

## Zipolite

Though some people rave about Puerto Ángel for its laid-back lifestyle, others are ecstatic about **ZIPOLITE**, 3km along the road north. Everything here revolves around the beach. It is referred to by some as "sexyport" because people either come here to get high or hook up; the travellers' grapevine is alive with tales of the widely available hallucinogens, low living costs and liberal approach to **nudity** – rumours that are largely well founded, much to the chagrin of the locals. Certainly, nude bathing – predominantly at the western end of the beach – is sanctioned by the local military; keep cover handy for trips to the restaurants. As for drugs, grass, mushrooms and acid are just as illegal as – though more prevalent than – anywhere else in Mexico; unscrupulous dealers are not above setting people up. **Theft**, particularly along the beachfront at night, can be a problem, but seems in no way to detract from the lure of a few days of complete abandon.

The origin of the name "Zipolite" is uncertain – one theory is that it comes from the Nahuatl word meaning "beach of the dead", hence the constant references to it as the "playa de los muertos". The **beach** itself is magnificent, long and gently curving, pounded by heavy surf with a riptide that requires some caution – drownings are depressingly common (although there are lifeguards, as well as flags denoting danger levels up and down the beach). It is divided into three segments: Roca Blanca towards the western end, Centro in the middle and Playa del Amor at the eastern end nearest Puerto Ángel. Palapa huts line all three, catering to visitors' basic accommodation and dining needs, as do a handful of restaurants offering seafood and pasta. **Hammocks** (M$30–55) are strung from every rafter and many places rent basic **rooms**; it can be worth getting a room just to have a safe place to store your gear. **Hurricane Pauline** blew away many of the weaker structures in 1997, but since then Zipolite has grown markedly. New buildings towards the western end of the beach caused some fuss when they were built three or four storeys high, and despite a severe fire in March 2001 that wiped out virtually all of the accommodation from the *Posada San Cristóbal*, in the middle of the beach, to the lagoon close to the western end, most of the buildings have again been rebuilt.

Zipolite is a good base for **trips** to nearby places such as Mazunte or Puerto Escondido, as accommodation is abundant and inexpensive. Taxis run up and down the road behind the beach, but a better and cheaper way of getting around is by *colectivos*, which also run along the same route. All of the palapas along the beachfront advertise **boat trips** out to sea for about M$165, where you can snorkel and sometimes spot turtles, dolphins and, if you're really lucky, whales on their way up to Baja California. Scuba **diving** is also offered, but the reef isn't particularly impressive here.

### Practicalities

The main road coming into Zipolite from Puerto Ángel runs east to west, passing a grocery store and then the *Lyoban* (see opposite). A turn to the left takes you onto the road immediately behind the beach, which has a **laundry** and a few small shops with **Internet** access, long-distance **phones**, beach gear and other bare necessities, but for anything other than the simplest needs you'll have to catch the *colectivos* that run to Puerto Ángel and on to Pochutla (every 20min until around 8pm). Follow the road to the end onto a dirt track to get to the more peaceful, western end of the beach.

Most accommodation options feature shared bathrooms (cold water) and are fitted with mosquito nets; a few have fans. One of the best **places to stay**, the idyllic *Lo Cósmico* (www.locosmico.com; ❷), is at the western end of the beach. It has beautiful cabañas, some sleeping up to six people, with views of the coast, a restaurant serving delicious crepes and a secluded beach out front. Hammocks are also available for M$500 per night. Next door, the long-established and highly eccentric *Shambhala Posada* (❸) is tucked away up the side of a hill by a rocky outcrop. It boasts beautiful vistas and shares the *Cósmico*'s beach area, but it is badly in need of repair, and has slightly tatty cabañas and terrace space for hammocks. The area at the top of the hill behind the *Shambhala* seems to function as a meditation spot, and is a great place to watch the the sun rise (or set) over the bay. Below the *Cósmico*, on the sand, is *El Alquimista*, one of the best restaurants in town, which gets packed in the evenings with diners looking for seafood, chicken, steak and pizza accompanied by chilled-out music, as well as a bonfire party later on. It also offers five artfully designed cabañas with private bath and fan (⑤). Set back from the beach, *Las Casitas* (ⓣ958/585-7263; ④–⑤) is a pleasant collection of six partially open-air (mosquito nets provided) bungalows, some with kitchens, and all with private bathrooms and hammocks.

Working east down the beach, you'll find the good-value *Posada San Cristóbal* (ⓣ958/584-3191; ①–②), with private-bath cabañas and rooms with fans and safe. *Posada Mexico* (ⓣ958/584-3194; ①–②), is one of the more recent arrivals on the Zipolite scene, with functional, cheerful rooms with shared baths and an Italian restaurant; the more substantially constructed, American-run *Brisa Marina* (ⓣ958/584-3193; ③), has a range of simple, musty rooms, some with private baths. You can also try the cheap cabañas at *Palapa Katy* (②) and *Palapa Aris* (②) a little further east. The smarter *Lyoban* (ⓣ958/584-3177; ③), after that, has space to lock luggage as well as pool and ping-pong in the lounge. At the far east end of Zipolite beach is *Castillo Oasis,* with four clean, beautifully designed rooms in a leafy green oasis (ⓕ958/584-3070; ④) and *Solstice Yoga Center* (ⓦwww.solstice-mexico.com; ⑤), with colourful, thoughtfully designed bungalows and accompanying yoga and meditation programmes. *Fernando's Trailer Park* on the road to Puerto Ángel, has electrical hook-ups under shady palm trees.

Zipolite is a great place for food, with most of the popular **restaurants** along the western beachfront: *Posada San Cristóbal* covers backpacker staples such as eggs, pancakes and salads, and *Tao* and *Nueva Sol* both have seafood and Mexican dishes. *Chupón* (which serves delicious crab ravioli) and *El 3 Diciembre* (pizzas, vegetarian Mexican dishes and home-made cheesecake, and also rooms to rent), at the start of the road behind the beach, are definitely worth the short walk. *El Hongo* has a happy hour and keeps going until late, and the popular but cheesy **disco** *La Puesta del Sol* kicks off around midnight.

## San Agustinillo

Rounding the headland north of Zipolite you come to **SAN AGUSTINILLO**, another fine beach graced with good surfing waves. It has a more restrained vibe than Zipolite, with some charming places to stay and eat. The sand is backed by restaurants, which offer space for a hammock or small rooms for rent in addition to reasonably priced, fresh seafood. *Sueno* (⑤) has six tasteful, breezy cabañas with private bath at the east end of the beach. Away from the beach in the centre of town, the *Paraíso del Pescador* (⑤) offers more modern comforts, including a/c, hot water, fans and a restaurant. Cheaper options include *Palapas Olas Altas*, and *Palapa Lupita*, which have simple, rather scruffy, cabañas (②) and hammocks, right next to the beach. *Posada Dona Sol*, across the street, has rooms with bath and fan (②). The grand and slightly bizarre *Posada San Agustinillo*, set in impressive grounds at the east end of the village, looks as if it has had better days, but offers reasonable rooms looking out to sea, with balcony space (③). Your best bet among the high-end accommodation is *Rancho Cerro Largo* (ⓕ958/584-3063, ⓔranchocerrolargomx@yahoo.com; ⑦) – perched on the ridge between Zipolite (3km away) and San Agustinillo, it has spectacular views of the Pacific. The restaurant here is considered the best in the area, and the price of a double includes breakfast and dinner. Catch any Mazunte-bound *camioneta* from Zipolite to get here.

## Mazunte

Further west is the tiny village of **MAZUNTE**. Though it has grown in recent years, it remains an attractive, relaxed place with a beautiful beach. It's more peaceful than Zipolite, and lacking the hippie-party vibe. In addition, the surf is less powerful here, and at the western end of the beach, beyond the rocky outcrop, there's a smaller bay where the waves are even gentler and it's safer to swim. The village's name is derived from the Nahuatl word "maxonteita", which means "please come and spawn", a reference to the **Golfina turtles** that come here to breed, although it was once the site of an abattoir that, at its most gruesome, supposedly slaughtered three thousand of the creatures a day. In 1990 the Mexican government bowed to international pressure and effectively banned the industry overnight, removing in one fell swoop the livelihood of the villagers, who then turned to slash-and-burn agriculture. Since then, Mazunte has been declared a reserve, and more sustainable, long-term ecotourism programmes have been encouraged, including the co-op *Cosméticos Naturales* (Mon–Sat 9am–4pm, Sun 9am–2pm), which you see as soon as you enter the village, set up with help from companies such as The Body Shop and selling beauty products made from local ingredients and organic produce. *Cosméticos Naturales* also has a few, inexpensive, clean rooms (❸) to rent. The government-funded **turtle museum** (Ⓣ958/584-3035, Tues–Sat 10am–4.30pm, Sun 10am–2.30pm; M$150, guided tours in Spanish every 15min), at the east end of the village, features an aquarium with some particularly large turtles and a turtle research centre. It's well worth the visit, especially as proceeds go towards the conservation of this majestic species.

Don't leave Mazunte without following the trail next to the *Balamjuyuc* (see p.686), which runs past the remains of some unmarked **ruins** to **Punto Cometa** (a 30min walk) – a beautiful, natural park on top of the rocky headland next to Mazunte beach, and the southernmost point in Oaxaca, where you get breathtaking views at sunset. The "Jacuzzi," a rocky pool that fills with foamy surf as the waves rush in, can be accessed by scrambling down the rocks at the south end of the pool. Another nearby treat is the crocodile lagoon at **Playa Ventanilla**, about 2km to the west, where you can test your heart rate by going out on the water in a shallow boat to navigate among the scaly inhabitants. There are around four hundred in the lagoon, as well as a rich profusion of birdlife. It can be reached by *colectivo*, or by taxi (about M$40); the boat trips (M$50 person; *lanchas* accommodate 10) are arranged by the village co-operative, *Servicios Ecoturísticas*. The village co-op can also organize horse-riding tours in the area (around M$250).

### Practicalities

A makeshift **tourist booth** on the main street (Hwy-200) keeps erratic hours but is an excellent source of information on accommodation and activities – a guide named Markus mans the office, and also leads tours and boat rides to spot turtles and other wildlife. Rafting trips can be arranged at *La Empanada* restaurant, where they are a much better deal than in nearby Huatulco.

All of the palapas on the beach have **cabañas** and hammock space, along with **restaurants** serving basic breakfasts, seafood and pasta. If you are equipped and feel so inclined, you can pitch your tent right along the beach. At the western end of the sandy stretch, pass the rocks to the second small bay

△ Golfina turtle, Mazunte

for the area's best swimming, where the *Posada del Arquitecto* has hammocks and ecoconscious rooms with private bath (❹). Set discreetly up the hill, the *Alta Mira* (Ⓦwww.labuenavista.com; ❺), under the same ownership as the *Buena Vista* in Puerto Ángel (see p.680), is the most comfortable place in town, with smart bungalows with tiled bathrooms and beautiful views from the terrace restaurant. The rooms do not have electricity, but that adds to the alluring atmosphere in the evening, when the bungalows are lit with candles. The friendly *Cabañas Balamjuyuc* (Ⓣ958/584-3035; ❷–❸) next door is a more relaxed option, with impressive views of the ocean and comfy, brightly coloured shared-bath cabañas. Massages are offered, as are turtle-viewing trips and surfing lessons. In the middle of the beach, *Palapas El Mazunte* is a popular backpacker hangout, with cheap rooms (❸), hammock and tent space and a packed café. At the east end of the beach, the friendly *Cabañas Ziga* (Ⓣ958/583-9295; ❹), has a range of rooms with fan and mosquito net (the more comfortable rooms have private bathrooms), flower-filled gardens and glorious sea views from the patio restaurant, which serves decent Mexican and international fare. *Posada Ariglan* (❸–❹), between San Agustinillo and Mazunte, is one of the best places in the area, with stunning views from its charming rooms; all have private baths (some with hot water) and fan, some "suites" have a/c and king-size beds.

There are some appealing **food** options, including the excellent Italian-run restaurant *La Dolce Vita*, on the main road, which has brick-oven pizza, pastas with seafood and occasional movies in the evenings. The best place for seafood is *El Pescador*, on the beach. Breakfasts and lighter meals are available throughout the day. *La Empanada*, also on the main road, offers Asian fusion – sushi and stir-fry – as well as fillers like hearty sandwiches on home-made bread and blended juices (try the delicious cucumber and lemon); the gregarious *Tania*, further along, has good-value Mexican fare. At the western end, on the sandy path that leads down to the beach, *El Agujón* is another great snack joint with delicious fresh bread, quesadillas, tortas and pizzas.

You can find a **lavandería** on Rinconcito (the street connecting the western end of the beach to the main street through town); a pricey **Internet** café, also on Rinconcito, is open until 10pm. There are no banking facilities in Mazunte, so make sure you withdraw enough money in Pochutla or Escondido (where there are ATMs) before coming here.

You can save time and money **getting to Mazunte** from Puerto Escondido by getting dropped off at **San Antonio**, a cluster of just a few houses and a restaurant, from where you can hitch or take a taxi the 5km to Mazunte. Otherwise, the bus drags you through Pochutla and Puerto Ángel before arrival. **Colectivos from Mazunte** go to Zipolite, Puerto Ángel and Pochutla (every 30–40min), but if you can time it correctly, it makes sense also to return through San Antonio.

# Huatulco and around

Heading **east from Puerto Ángel** towards Salina Cruz, there's 170km of coast that until recently was untouched. It's a slow, hot drive – which would be enjoyable were it not for the illogical number of *topes* (speedbumps) – along a jungly coastal strip regularly cut by rivers and with tantalizing glimpses of virgin beaches. Most of these stretches of sand are extremely tough to get to, however, and few are as idyllic as they appear: quite apart from the total lack of facilities, they're marred by strong winds and currents and, as you approach Salina Cruz, an increasing amount of oil pollution.

At **HUATULCO**, some 35km from Puerto Ángel, the latest of Mexico's purpose-built resorts is well under way. FONATUR – the government tourist agency – began developing the coastline in the 1980s, with the intention of constructing an environmentally conscious resort. Of the nine bays along here, four have now been developed. The area is what it aims to be: a safe, sanitized, manicured resort with a beautiful setting. You could be anywhere – it just happens that you're in Mexico. The long-term effects of the tourism influx are still hard to predict and will largely depend on whether the infrastructure (especially the sewage treatment plants) can keep pace with the demand. With an overriding emphasis on coiffured hotels, Huatulco is certainly not the place for budget or independent travellers keen to experience the real Mexico, but if lying on the beach, snorkelling and tripping off to coffee plantations and attractive coves are your priorities, you could do much worse.

Huatulco is the all-encompassing name of this resort area, with **Santa Cruz Huatulco**, the village on the coast, as its focus. Santa Cruz was conceived as the token "Mexican village", something it patently fails to be. In fact, it feels more like the Mexican section at Epcot Centre, just dressed up with a marina, handicraft stalls, a few relatively inexpensive seafood restaurants and a handful of condos. Out of season, it's so empty as to be post-apocalyptic. Santa Cruz's **harbour**, though, is the local transport hub. From here, fishing and diving trips can be organized, or you can just catch one of the boats (on demand) that ply the coast to the more remote bays.

A couple of kilometres west from Santa Cruz, the next beach along is the attractive but busy **Playa La Entrega**, where Mexican families congregate and palapas serving fresh seafood flank the gentle surf. Just over 1km east from La Entrega is **Maguey Beach**, best accessed on one of the horseback rides that leave from the *embarcadero* in Santa Cruz. Its tranquil, blue waters curve around jungly headlands. Just beyond Maguey are the pristine sand dunes of **Bahía Cacaluta**, where the movie *Y Tu Mamá También* was filmed. It is reached by walking through the jungle from the coastal road, or for a more exhilarating route you can take one of the excellent ATV tours from Santa Cruz; contact Xpert Travel at Plaza Coyula 11, behind Banamex (☎958/587-1290). **San Agustín**, one of the more developed beaches, is 2km west of Santa Cruz and popular with Mexican holidaymakers. It has very good snorkelling, offshore reefs for diving and plenty of amenities.

To the east, the largest beach of **Chahué**, around 2km around the bay and connected by road from Santa Cruz, now sports a marina and upscale hotels. Over the headland, **Tangolunda** is by far the most developed beach, with luxury hotels, chi-chi homes and an eighteen-hole golf course. The only public access is by the road near the *Quinta Real*, a further 3km northeast from Chahué. Unless you are a guest, there is very little to do and in the restaurants you will pay upscale New York or London prices. The **tourist office** near the *Gala* in Tangolunda (Mon–Fri 9am–5pm & Sat 9am–1pm) has details of tours, rafting trips and more affordable local accommodation.

## Crucecita

The purpose-built town of **CRUCECITA**, 2km inland from Santa Cruz Huatulco, serves both of Huatulco's bays. Though designed to house the ten thousand locals needed to support and staff the bayside hotels, it is now becoming a tourist centre in its own right, probably helped along by the lack of cheap hotels elsewhere. Certainly it boasts a **zócalo** with a modern church, shops and various businesses, along with pizza joints, costly tourist shops and Internet cafés. Nevertheless, in its fifteen years of existence, it has matured well to become a friendly, functional place.

With hotel development mushrooming, finding a budget **place to stay** in Crucecita is easier than it used to be, although outside the high season (Dec, Semana Santa, July & Aug) prices can drop by up to fifty percent. Among the best of the cheaper options is the *Hotel Busanvi I*, one block from the zócalo on Carrizal 601 (Ⓣ958/587-0056; ⑤), with motel-like rooms that take up to four people and have TV, a/c, decent showers and hard beds. *Posada Michelle*, Gardenia 8 (Ⓣ958/587-0535; ③–⑤), next to the bus station, has a range of cheap, dated rooms in need of upgrading, and can help arrange tours. On the northwest side of the zócalo, also on Gardenia, *Posada Flamboyant* (Ⓣ958/587-0105; ⑥) is a charming three-storey house with pleasantly decorated a/c rooms grouped around a courtyard and an enticing swimming pool. *Misión de los Arcos*, Gardenia 902 (Ⓣ958/587-0165; ⑥), is the most polished option in town, with white stucco suites with TV and a/c. There is a restaurant, free Internet, a gym and access to a nearby pool. If you want more peace, close to the beach the best option is the Canadian-run *B&B Agua Azul* (Ⓣ958/581-0265; ⑧), which overlooks the small bay of Playa Conejos, a five-minute drive from Tangolunda. The ambience is welcoming and social, the hosts are knowledgeable, and excellent breakfasts are served in a communal palapa dining room/lounge area.

The majority of the **restaurants** surround the zócalo. American-managed *Oasis*, on the corner of Bugambilia and Flamboyán, is an animated breakfast spot that serves up reasonably priced tortas, fish, Oaxacan dishes and even reasonable sushi in the evening. For something simpler, try the tacos at *Los Portales*, on the zócalo, or the burger stand on Bugambilia and Macuitle after 8pm. For waterside dining, *Ve El Mar* on Playa Santa Cruz is the best option for fish and seafood and great cocktails; try the pineapple scooped out and filled with dorado, or the reasonably priced sweet Pacific lobster. For a splurge, head to the romantic, candlelit restaurant overlooking Tangolunda Bay at *Quinta Real*. *Picante ceviche*, tuna tartar, Chateaubriand and a wide selection of imaginative fish dishes are well prepared and the home-made ice cream makes for a fine finale. There are a few **bars and clubs** near the zócalo. The popular *Crema* is an eclectic venue with a diverse clientele, lively music and pizza, and the *Café Dublin*, a welcoming pub, serves giant, juicy hamburgers and chilled beer; both establishments are on Carrizal.

All these places, and everywhere else in Crucecita, lie within easy walking distance of the **bus stations** that line Gardenia. The **post office** is a bit further out on the road to Santa Cruz Huatulco, where you'll also find a number of **banks** (with ATMs). Hurricane Divers (Ⓣ958/587-1107), on Santa Cruz beach, offers **dive trips** in the area, along with PADI and NAUI certification. They also speak English. Copalita River Tours run **rafting and kayaking trips** from their office in the *Posada Michelle* (see above); Explora Mexico also runs class-4 rafting trips, as well as less challenging excursions, out of Huatulco (Ⓣ958/587-2058).

# The Isthmus of Tehuantepec

The **Isthmus of Tehuantepec**, where the Pacific and the Atlantic are just 210km apart and the land never rises to more than 250m above sea level, is the narrowest strip of land in Mexico. It's a hot and steamy region, long run down and not in any way improved by the trappings of the 1980s oil boom. Prior to the completion of the Panama Canal, there was talk about cutting a waterway through the isthmus. In the late nineteenth century, the coast-to-coast train was an extremely busy trade route, the chief communication link between the American continent's east and west coasts.

The Isthmus is an independent region with a fascinating and unique cultural identity. The people are descendants of various indigenous groups, principally Zapotec. Historically, the Zapotec *indígenas*, especially those in the south, have been a **matriarchal** society. Though you'll still find women dominating trade in the markets (they are renowned for their tenacious, even aggressive, sales skills) while the men work in the fields, this is a tradition that is dying faster than most others in macho Mexico. Nevertheless, some elements remain: the women exude pride, dressed in ornate hand-woven dresses and draped with gold jewellery; it's still the mother who gives away her child at a wedding (and occasionally still the eldest daughter who inherits land); and on feast days the women prove their dominance by climbing to the rooftops and throwing fruit down on the men in the Tirada de Frutas.

The best reason to stop in this region is if there's a **fiesta** going on, as they're among the most enthusiastic in the country. Otherwise, you can go straight across – from Oaxaca to **Tuxtla Gutiérrez** or **San Cristóbal** in Chiapas – in a single, very long, day. Only if you plan to go to the Yucatán is there any particular reason to cross the isthmus from the south to the north. To head into Chiapas it's considerably quicker to stick to the lowlands along the Gulf of Tehuantepec, though the inland route (leading into the Chiapas highlands) is more scenic.

## Salina Cruz

**SALINA CRUZ**, 130km east of Huatulco on the coast, was once the Pacific terminus of the trans-isthmus railway and the port through which everything was shipped. Nowadays it's exporting oil in large quantities, and is a sprawling, unattractive place with a reputation for crime and brawling violence; it also serves as a transport link to and from the Pacific coast. **Buses** arrive and leave from a central terminal at 5 de Mayo 412. If you get stuck here and need a **place to stay**, head for the large zócalo, half a block north of the bus station, which has several decent hotels nearby. One block east, at Puerto Ángel 408, is the well-appointed *Hotel Calendas* (ⓣ971/714-4574; ❺), with TV and a/c, while a block west is the bare-bones *Casa Ríos* (ⓣ971/714-0337; ❸–❹), at Wilfredo Cruz 405. At Camacho 108 lies the *Posada del Jardín* (ⓣ971/714-0162; ❸), a clean little place with a courtyard.

**La Ventosa**, the nearby beach village, reached by bus from the side of the plaza, may once have been picturesque, but it's now spoilt by the oil refinery backdrop. As windy as its name implies, and polluted too, it's a run-down place, where most of the waterfront restaurants seem in danger of dissolving into the sea. The best **hotel**, conveniently the first one you reach, is the *Posada Rustrián* (ⓣ971/714-0450; ❸), which has a courtyard and a garden.

## Tehuantepec

The modest town of **TEHUANTEPEC**, 14km north of Salina Cruz, visibly preserves many of the Isthmus's local traditions, has some of the **best fiestas** in the region and is generally an extremely pleasant place to stop, with a fine zócalo and several inexpensive hotels. In the evening, the zócalo really comes alive, with singing birds and people strolling and eating food from the stalls set up by the townswomen, who proudly wear the traditional flower-embroidered *huipil* and floor-length velvet skirt of the Zapotec. Tehuantepec is a tiny place where a walk of ten blocks in any direction will take you out into the countryside. Perhaps because the town is so concentrated, it's extraordinarily noisy considering its size and remote location. The din of passing buses is made worse by the flatbed motor tricycles (*motos*) that locals use as taxis. There's really no reason to stay long, and the number of second-class buses makes it extremely easy to leave, but if you do stop for a bit, pop into the **Casa de Cultura**, housed in the remains of the Dominican Ex-Convento Rey Cosijoní, on Callejón Cosijopí (Mon–Fri 9am–2pm & 5–8pm, Sat 9am–2pm; free). It features a random collection of archeological pieces and exhibits of local costumes and art. Sporadic dance, music and art workshops are also held here throughout the week. Construction of the convent was begun in 1544 at the behest of Cortés and it was named after the incumbent Zapotec king. You can see a few remaining frescoes by taking Hidalgo from the north side of the zócalo and following it right as it becomes Guererro. Just west of the zócalo there is an indoor market, which sells fruit, herbs, bread, flowers and other local produce.



## The ruins of Guiengola

The hilltop fortress of **GUIENGOLA**, 15km north of Tehuantepec, was the Zapotec stronghold on the Isthmus, and in 1496 its defenders successfully fought off an Aztec attempt to gain control of the area, which was never fully incorporated into their empire. It continued to be a centre of resistance during the early years of the Conquest and was a focus of Indian revolt against Spanish rule throughout the sixteenth and seventeenth centuries.

At the site you'll see remains of pyramids and a ball-court, but the most striking feature is the massive **defensive wall**. By definition, Guiengola's superb location makes it somewhat inaccessible and it's probably best to take a **taxi**, though **buses** to Oaxaca do pass the turn-off to the site, 8km from Tehuantepec on the main road (look out for the "Ruinas Guiengola" sign). From here it's a hot, seven-kilometre walk uphill. The site is open daily, and if the caretaker is around you may be asked to pay a small fee, though you'll almost certainly have the place to yourself.

## Tehuantepec practicalities

**Buses** stop at the northern edge of town on Hwy-190, a short *moto* ride or walk from the centre. There's a **post office** and bank on the north side of the square; on 5 de Mayo itself you'll find a **Bancomer** with good rates and an ATM, and a **caseta de larga distancia** (6am–9pm) as well as a Banorte with Café Internet La Frontera (9am–9pm; M$10/hr) next door. **Hotels** aren't far away: *Donaji* (ⓣ971/715-0064; ❸–❹), at Juárez 10, two blocks south of the zócalo, is one of the best, with clean rooms with TV, a/c (worth the extra few pesos) or fan overlooking the Parque Juárez. There is also a gym and pool. Just outside the centre on the road to Oaxaca (15min walk), the *Guiexhoba* (ⓣ971/715-1710; ❺) has the largest, most comfortable, motel-style rooms with a/c and fridge, convenient parking, a sizeable pool and a restaurant that serves good local and international dishes. *Hotel Oasis*, Ocampo 8 (ⓣ971/715-0008; ❸), is one block south of the zócalo and has clean rooms with a/c or fan. Calle Juana, south from the zócalo, has one of the best **places to eat**: *Café Colónial*, at no. 66, which stays open till 10pm and dishes up chicken prepared in almost every way imaginable. On the west side of the zócalo are stands offering shakes and snacks, with steaming taco carts lining the east side. *Mariscos Angel*, at the entrance to town, is good for **seafood**. Be sure to try some of the **corn bread** that local women hawk to everyone arriving on the bus. For something more colourful, try *Scaru* (north of the square next to the *Donají*), which has murals depicting Tehuantepec life and offers seafood, pasta and cocktails until 11pm.

While Tehuantepec is a major stopping point en route to Oaxaca or the Chiapas coast, few **buses** originate here, so moving on, you may find it easier to take one of the constant stream of buses to **Juchitán**, 26km away (see below), and continue from there. The main long-distance routes, operated by first-class Cristóbal Colón and Autobuses Unidos, serve Oaxaca, Mexico City, Tuxtla Gutiérrez, Coatzacoalcos and Villahermosa, and there are also buses to San Cristóbal and Puerto Escondido; you can buy **tickets** in advance. Several second-class companies also operate between the main towns on the isthmus, and there are constant departures for Salina Cruz.

## Juchitán

**JUCHITÁN**, just 26km east of Tehuantepec and the point where the road meets the railway to Guatemala, is a dusty commercial centre clogged with traffic and somewhat lacking in tourist infrastructure. Despite this, the city is culturally fascinating, offering glimpses into the matriarchal society the region is known for, with widely observed native traditions and near-constant **fiestas**, also known as **velas**. Although they take place throughout the year, in May there seem to be daily parties, where women dress in colourful *traje* and men in formal wear for all-night marathons of music and dancing. The residents are also known for strong political views and socialist leanings. The town managed to elect a reforming socialist local government in the early 1980s, which the PRI didn't take kindly to. Eventually the state governor found a pretext to remove local officials from power and replace them with party faithfuls. The political trouble – and violence – that followed has largely blown over, but local tumult still occasionally makes the front pages, and Juchitán's fiestas have a tendency to develop into political demonstrations. Another claim to fame is the region's relatively tolerant attitude towards homosexuality; it's one of the few places in Mexico where gay men live openly, sometimes even attending *velas* in drag.

The **bus** stations line the highway and you won't have long to wait, whichever direction you're heading. Unfortunately, Juchitán doesn't offer much in the way of good-value **accommodation**, and therefore Tehuantepec makes a better base. The best place to stay is the spartan but clean and comfortable *Hotel Lopez Lena* (☎971/711-1388; ❹) at 16 de Septiembre 70, which has institutional rooms. The adequate *Casa de Huéspedes Echazarreta* (no phone; ❷) is the cheapest option, and is right on the zócalo. Here you'll also find the **post office**, a **Banamex** and some good **places to eat**, notably the *Casagrande* at Juárez 12 (☎971/711-3460), which serves delicious local dishes with an emphasis on fish and seafood in an elegant cool atrium. The **Casa de Cultura**, on Belisario Domínguez beside the church, was started by Francisco Toledo (who was born in Juchitán), and offers a tiny archeological display with pre-Hispanic stone carvings and pottery shards, an art library and occasional exhibitions of local artists.

A cooling day trip from Juchitán is to the natural clear-water **spring** (M$10) in **Santiago Laollaga**, about 36km northwest of town. The concrete swimming pools by the car park can be overrun by kids, but a short walk upstream leads to natural pools by the spring's source, perfect for a refreshing dip followed by a beer in one of the streamside restaurants – although the occasional duelling

## Fiestas

**Januray**

**New Year's Day** (Jan 1). Celebrated everywhere, but particularly good in Oaxaca (see p.638) and Mitla (see p.663).

**Día de San Sebastián** (Jan 20). Big in Tehuantepec (see p.689).

**February**

**Día de la Candelaria** (Feb 2). Colourful Indian celebrations in Santa María del Tule (see p.659) and in San Mateo del Mar, near Salina Cruz.

**Carnaval** (the week before Lent; variable Feb–March). At its most frenzied in the big cities – especially Oaxaca (see p.638) – but is also celebrated in hundreds of villages throughout the area.

**March**

**Semana Santa** (Holy Week). Observed everywhere – there are particularly big ceremonies in Pinotepa Nacional and nearby Pinotepa Don Luís.

**Benito Juárez's Birthday** (March 21). Celebrated in Guelatao, near Oaxaca, the former president's birthplace.

**May**

**Día de la Santa Cruz** (May 3). In Salina Cruz (see p.689), the start of a week-long *feria*.

**Día de San Miguel** (May 8). In Soyaltepec, between Oaxaca and Huajuapan de León, festivities include horse and dog races, as well as boating events on a nearby lake.

**Día de San Isidro** (May 15). Peasant celebrations everywhere – famous and picturesque fiestas in Juchitán (see p.691).

**Corpus Christi** (Thurs after Trinity). A particularly good *feria* in Izúcar de Matamoros.

**June**

**Día de San Juan** (June 24). Falls in the midst of festivities (June 22–26) in Tehuantepec (see p.689).

**July**

**Fiesta** (first Wed in July). Teotitlán del Valle (see p.660), near Oaxaca, holds a festival with traditional dances and religious processions.

**Guelaguetza** (last two Mon in July). In Oaxaca (see p.638), a mixture of traditional

stereos can mar the peaceful atmosphere. There is nowhere to stay in town, unless you want to camp. You can get to Santiago Laollaga quickly by car, north through **Ixtepec**, or by buses on the same route in about an hour. The spring is at the northern edge of town.

# Travel details

### Buses

The following frequencies and times are for first-class services. Scores of second-class buses usually cover the same routes, taking ten to twenty percent longer.

**Huatulco** to: Acapulco (7 daily; 10hr); Oaxaca (4 daily; 7hr); Pochutla (6 daily; 1hr); Puerto dancing and rites on the Cerro del Fortín. Highly popular; tickets for the good seats are sold at the tourist office.

### August

**Fiestas** (Aug 13–16). Spectacular festivities in Juchitán (see p.691) and Tehuantepec (see p.689).

**Fiesta** (Aug 24). In San Bartolo Coyotepec (see p.665), near Oaxaca.

**Blessing of the Animals** (Aug 31). In Oaxaca (see p.638) locals bring their beasts to the church of La Merced to be blessed.

### September

**Religious ceremonies** (Sept 8). In Teotitlán del Valle (see p.660), in Putla, on the road inland from Pinotepa Nacional, and in Tehuantepec (see p.689).

**Independence Day** (Sept 16). Celebrated everywhere.

### October

**Feria del Árbol** (second Mon in Oct). Based around the famous tree in Santa María del Tule (see p.659).

**Indian fiesta** (Oct 18). Observed in Ojitlán, near Tuxtepec, with a formal, candlelit procession.

### November

**Día de los Muertos** (Day of the Dead; Nov 2). Observed everywhere, with particularly strong traditions in Xoxocotlán and in Atzompa.

### December

**Día de la Inmaculada Concepción** (Dec 8). Observed widely. There are traditional dances in Juquilla, not far from Puerto Escondido, and Zacatepec, on the road inland from Pinotepa Nacional.

**Fiesta de la Virgen de La Soledad** (Dec 18). Celebrations in Oaxaca (see p.638) in honour of the patroness of the state – expect fireworks, processions and music.

**Fiesta de los Rabanos** (Radish Festival; Dec 23). There's an exhibition of statues and scenes sculpted from radishes in Oaxaca (see p.638).

**Christmas Eve** (Dec 24). In Oaxaca (see p.638), there's music, fireworks and processions before midnight Mass. *Buñuelos* – crisp pancakes that you eat before smashing the plate on which they are served – are dished up at street stalls.

Escondido (hourly; 2hr 30min); Salina Cruz (almost hourly; 3hr); San Cristóbal (2 daily; 10hr); Tehuantepec (10 daily; 3hr 30min); Juchitlán (1 daily; 4hr).

**Oaxaca** to: Mexico City (at least two every 30min; 6hr); Pochutla (5 daily; 6hr); Puebla (hourly; 4hr 30min); Puerto Escondido (4 daily; 9hr 30min); San Cristóbal de las Casas (3 daily; 12hr); Tehuacán (3 daily; 3hr); Tehuantepec (at least hourly; 5hr); Veracruz (4 daily; 7hr); Villahermosa (5 daily; 12hr).

**Pochutla** to: Huatulco (hourly; 1hr); Oaxaca (14 daily; 7–8hr); Puerto Escondido (hourly; 1hr 30min); San Cristóbal (1 daily; 11hr).

**Puerto Escondido** to: Acapulco (3 daily; 8hr); Huatulco (hourly; 2hr 30min); Mexico City (2 daily; 18hr); Oaxaca (6 daily; 8–9hr); Pochutla (7 daily; 1hr 30min); Salina Cruz (1 daily; 5hr); San Cristóbal de las Casas (2 night buses; 14hr); Tehuantepec (1 daily; 6hr).

**Salina Cruz** to: Huatulco (10 daily; 1hr); Oaxaca (2 daily; 5hr 30min); Pochutla (5 daily; 1hr); Puerto Escondido (5 daily; 5hr 30min); Tehuantepec (every 30min; 30min).

**Tehuacán** to: Córdoba (2 daily; 2hr 30min); Mexico City (hourly; 4hr); Oaxaca (6 daily; 4hr); Veracruz (3 daily; 3hr 30min).

**Tehuantepec** to: Coatzacoalcos (10 daily; 5hr); Mexico City (at least 12 daily; 11hr); Oaxaca (hourly; 4hr 30min); Puerto Escondido (5 daily; 7hr); Salina Cruz (every 30min; 30min); Tuxtla Gutiérrez (6 daily; 5hr); Veracruz (2 daily; 7hr 30min); Villahermosa (7 daily; 7hr).

## Flights

**Oaxaca** to: Cancún via Tuxtla, Villahermosa and Mérida (daily); Huatulco (daily, through Mexico City); Mexico City (10 daily); Puerto Escondido (2 daily).
**Puerto Escondido** to: Mexico City (daily); Oaxaca (2 daily).

9

# Chiapas and Tabasco

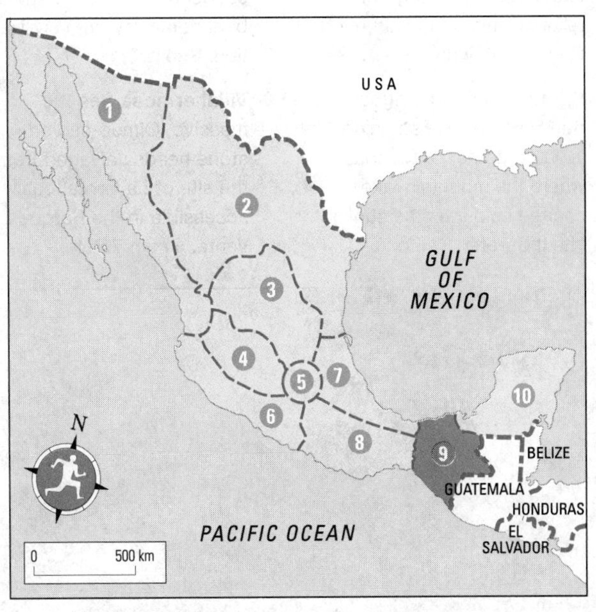

# CHAPTER 9 Highlights

* **Cañón del Sumidero** Enjoy a boat ride through this spectacular gorge, with jungle-covered cliffs soaring almost a thousand metres above the Río Grijalva. See p.716

* **San Cristóbal de las Casas** The most enchanting colonial city in Chiapas, surrounded by villages rich in indigenous culture. See p.717

* **San Juan Chamula** Witness extraordinary displays of religious faith in the haunting Iglesia San Juan. See p.728

* **Parque Nacional Lagos de Montebello** A stunning, isolated corner of Chiapas where the mountain lakes change colour as the sunlight hits the water. See p.734

* **Palenque** Visit the evocative ruins of one of the greatest Maya cities, then bathe in the crystal-clear cascades of the Río Otulúm. See p.744

* **Bonampak** Over one thousand years old, the vivid murals here provide a startling insight into ancient Maya culture. See p.749

* **Yaxchilán** For many the most magical of the Chiapas ruins, set deep in the forest and a boat ride away from civilization. See p.751

* **Villahermosa** See the massive, Olmec-carved stone heads salvaged from the site of La Venta, easily accessible in the Parque La Venta. See p.755

△ Parque Nacional Lagos de Montebello

9

# Chiapas and Tabasco

Endowed with a stunning variety of cultures, landscapes and wildlife, **Chiapas**, Mexico's southernmost state, has much to tempt visitors. Deserted Pacific beaches, rugged mountains and ruined cities buried in steamy jungle offer a bewildering choice of settings, and many **indigenous traditions** survive intact. Administered by the Spanish as part of Guatemala until 1824, when it seceded to join newly independent Mexico, today the state is second only to Oaxaca in terms of the number of Indians in its population: at least one third of its four million people are thought to be *indígenas*, mostly of Maya origin (though the official figure only counts those who speak a native language). There are eight or nine ethnic groups in the state (depending how you classify them), their numbers bolstered in 1983 after 35,000 refugees fleeing the conflicts in Guatemala settled here, many of them permanently.

The main tourist town is **San Cristóbal de las Casas**, in the geographic centre of the state, and surrounded by strongholds of **Tzotzil** and **Tzeltal** Maya culture, the largest indigenous groups. A visit to these villages is like an entry to another age, where ancient customs and religious practices survive against a backdrop of ever-present commercialism. There is, of course, a darker side to this: picturesque as their life may seem, the indigenous population has long been bypassed or ignored by the political system, their land and their livelihood under constant threat from modernization or straightforward seizure. The **Zapatista rebellion** (see box, p.700), which broke out on in this area on New Year's Day 1994, did not appear from nowhere.

One continuing legacy of the rebellion is a heavy **military** presence in what the Mexican authorities refer to as the "**conflict zone**", an area of 32 "rebel autonomous Zapatista municipalities" occupied (nominally at least) by the Zapatistas in the eastern half of the state. At its widest extent this could be anywhere east of the road from San Cristóbal via Ocosingo to Palenque, though in essence it means the **Lacandón forest region**, now encircled by the **Carretera Fronteriza** – the Frontier Highway, running roughly parallel with the Guatemalan border. Though you'll see plenty of signs announcing the fact that "you are entering Zapatista territory where the Mexican government is not obeyed" when travelling in these areas, you are extremely unlikely to stumble into trouble when visiting the main attractions, the **Parque Nacional Lagos de Montebello** or the ruins of **Yaxchilán** or **Bonampak**, and visitors are treated with respect.

The state of **Tabasco** is less aesthetically attractive than its neighbour state – steamy and low-lying for the most part, with a major oil industry to mar the landscape. Recently, however, the state has sought to encourage tourism, above all pushing the legacy of the **Olmecs**, Mexico's earliest developed civilization, as well as boundless possibilities for adventure and ecotourism. **Villahermosa**, the vibrant, modern capital, has a wealth of parks and museums, the best known of which, the **Parque La Venta**, displays original massive Olmec heads. In the extreme southwest, bordered by Veracruz and Chiapas, a section of Tabasco reaches into the mountains up to 1000m high. Here, in a region almost never visited by outsiders, a low-impact tourism initiative allows you to splash in pristine rivers and waterfalls and explore the astonishing ruins of **Malpasito**, a city of the mysterious **Zoque** culture.

# Chiapas



The state of **Chiapas** rises from the Pacific coastal plain, backed by the peaks of the Sierra Madre de Chiapas, through the mainly agricultural Central Depression, irrigated by the Río Grijalva, up to the highlands, **Los Altos de Chiapas**. Beyond the highlands, to the north the mountains drop down to the Gulf coast of Tabasco, while to the east a series of great rivers, separated by the jungle-covered ridges of the **Lacandón rainforest**, flow into the Río Usumacinta, which forms the border with Guatemala. The **climate**, like the land, varies enormously. You could spend the morning basking on the beach at **Puerto Arista**, and then a chilly night in the old colonial capital of **San Cristóbal de las Casas**. As a rule, the lowlands are hot and humid, with heavy afternoon rainfall in summer, and while days in the highlands can also be hot, by evening you may need a sweater.

Though it's a relatively small part of Mexico, Chiapas has the greatest **biological diversity** in North America. A visit to the **zoo** in the state capital of **Tuxtla Gutiérrez**, which houses only animals native to the state, will whet your appetite for the region's natural wonders. In the huge **Montes Azules Biosphere Reserve**, reached from Palenque, a section of the largest remaining rainforest in North America has been preserved. From Ocosingo you can make forays into its heart, **Laguna Miramar**, a truly isolated, pristine wilderness destination. There's **cloud forest** in the south, protected in the **El Triunfo Biosphere Reserve** and, far easier to visit, the beautiful lakes and hills of the **Parque Nacional Lagos de Montebello**.

The Classic-period Maya site of **Palenque**, on the northern edge of the highlands, is one of Mexico's finest ancient sites and has been the focus of much recent restoration work. The limestone hills in this area are pierced by crystal-clear rivers, creating exquisite waterfalls – most spectacularly at **Agua Azul**. Palenque is the best starting point for a trip down the **Usumacinta valley**, to visit the remote ruins of **Bonampak** and **Yaxchilán**. The Frontier Highway pushes south beyond these sites through the growing town of Benemérito, where you can get a boat to **Guatemala**. Buses now serve the highway day and night, enabling you to travel on to the **Lagos de Montebello** and back to San Cristóbal – passing frequent army checkpoints along the route. This remote eastern half of the state is also the home of the **Lacandón Maya**, who retreated into the forest when the Spanish arrived, and shunned all outside contact until fifty years ago.

**CHIAPAS & TABASCO**

Travelling around Chiapas is not difficult: the main cities are connected by a network of good, all-weather roads and the **Panamerican Highway** passes from west to east through some of the state's most spectacular scenery. In the south the coastal highway offers a speedy route from **Tonalá**, near the Oaxaca border, to **Tapachula**, almost on the frontier with Guatemala. In the out-of-the-way places, particularly in the jungle, travel is by dirt roads, which, though generally well maintained, can cause problems in the rainy season. These more remote places are also fairly well served by public transport, though it's more likely to be *combis* and trucks taking people and produce to and from markets than the comfortable buses of the main roads.

# The Chiapas coast

Running parallel to the coast about 20km inland, Hwy-200 provides a fast route from the Oaxaca border to Tapachula: if you're heading straight for **Guatemala**,

## Visiting Chiapas: the legacy of the Zapatista rebellion

On **January 1, 1994**, the day that NAFTA came into effect, several thousand lightly armed rebels occupied San Cristóbal de las Casas, the former state capital and Chiapas's major tourist destination. When the Mexican army recovered from the shock of the event, its immediate response was to launch a violent counter-attack. However, an unprecedented level of international solidarity with the rebels (known as **Zapatistas** after popular early twentieth-century revolutionary Emiliano Zapata) soon forced the Mexican government to halt its counter-insurgency policy. Despite a cease-fire agreed to in 1995 and years of on/off negotiations, a lasting peace treaty has yet to be signed (see Contexts, p.900, for more on the rebellion). A series of violent evictions and attacks on Zapatista communities by the army restarted the hostilities in July 2002, and though things have been quieter since then, the rebels still control dozens of villages in the southeast and tensions simmer beneath the surface, especially after the contested national elections of July 2006. **Subcomandante Marcos**, the man assumed to be the main leader of the Zapatistas (he calls himself their "chief spokesman" – the group has a collective leadership of 24), retains his role as champion of the underprivileged, and the rebels continue to benefit from immense popular support both at home and abroad. In early 2006 Marcos embarked on a tour across Mexico – titled "La Otra Campaña" – to expand his coalition for change beyond Chiapas. This, together with the large-scale disturbances in Oaxaca throughout the year, suggests that, for the moment at least, the state is no longer the country's primary focal point for social and political unrest.

Throughout the rebellion **tourists** have visited Chiapas without problems other than delays due to army checks. A word of **warning**, though, if your sympathies extend beyond giving economic assistance to the indigenous souvenir-makers: government officials, citing the "infestation of foreign activists who stir up and manipulate many indigenous groups contrary to constitutional order", claim that the presence of *simpático* foreigners influences political opposition in the state. Although there are foreign observers in "civil peace camps" in the Zapatista areas, they are not recognized as such by the Mexican authorities. Being in (or even near) the **conflict zone** invites suspicion of taking part in political activities – illegal for foreigners – and can lead to deportation.

If you do go, be as fully informed as you can: **SIPAZ**, the International Service for Peace, has a volunteer programme in Chiapas and their website – Ⓦwww.sipaz.org – provides more information. Extremely well-organized official Zapatista websites can be found at Ⓦwww.enlacezapatista.ezln.org.mx and Ⓦwww.zeztainternazional.org, though only in Spanish, while Ⓦwww.zapatistas.org has information in English.

this is the road to take. It traverses the steamy coastal plain of the **Soconusco**, once a separate province within Guatemala, but forced into union with Mexico by Santa Anna in 1842 and promptly absorbed by Chiapas. From the highway, the 2400-metre peaks of the **Sierra Madre de Chiapas**, little-visited mountains penetrated by roads only at their eastern and western extremities, are always in view. Not far from the Oaxaca border, the first point of interest is **Puerto Arista**, the only place on the Chiapas coast that even remotely resembles a resort town. The plain itself is a fertile agricultural area, mainly given over to coffee and bananas, though there are also many *ranchos*, where cattle grow fat on the lush grass. **Tapachula**, the "capital" of the Soconusco, is cut off from the rest of Chiapas by the mountains, but has frequent connections to the southern border crossings into Guatemala; on the way there you can easily visit the ancient Olmec and Maya site of **Izapa**. From Tapachula you can also take a relaxing trip up through coffee plantations to the delightful little town of **Unión Juárez**, the base for expeditions to **Volcán Tacaná**, the highest peak in Chiapas.

## Tonalá

The gateway to the main beach resorts of Chiapas, **TONALÁ** is 39km from the Oaxaca state border and just off Hwy-200. The only city in Chiapas to fight for independence, today it's a sleepy market town of 75,000, with all the basic services but not much to see. Tonalá means, quite aptly, "hot place" in Nahuatl, and you're better off pressing on to the coast, where the beachside accommodation is a lot nicer. All the **bus** companies terminate along Avenida Hidalgo, the town's main street: the main first-class companies pull in about 500m west of the zócalo; second-class to the east.

Everything you need in Tonalá (including banks) is either on the **zócalo** – Parque Central – or within a couple of blocks of it. The main feature of the park is the **Estela de Tlaloc**, a large, standing stone carved by the Olmecs, depicting the rain god Tlaloc and showing the influence of Teotihuacán. If you're stuck for something to do, the **Templo de San Francisco de Asís**, built in 1794 and a couple of blocks northeast of the zócalo, merits a quick peek for its pretty pink facade, ceiling murals and impressive gold *retablo*. Tonalá's **tourist office** (Mon–Fri 8am–7pm, Sat 9am–3pm; ⓣ966/663-1034), is just off the north side of the zócalo at 16 de Septiembre 46, and is a good source of information about beaches nearby.

The most convenient **place to stay** in Tonalá, handy for catching first-class buses in the early hours, is the *Grajandra* (ⓣ966/663-0144; ❻) at Hidalgo 204. Next door to the bus station, it offers reasonable value for your money, with large, clean, comfortable en-suite rooms with cable TV and a/c. *Galilea* (ⓣ966/663-0239; ❺) is well located in an attractive old building on the east side of the zócalo, and has clean, basic rooms with private bathrooms, a/c, TV and parking. It also has a good **restaurant** overlooking the plaza. A few other restaurants ring the zócalo; one of the best is *El Tizoncíto*, on Hidalgo, just off the western side of the plaza. Cheaper snacks can be found at the **Mercado Michael Larráinzar**, southeast of the zócalo between Matamoros and Juárez. There are plenty of **Internet** cafés around the zócalo, including *Enred@ndo* on the west side (daily 9am–11pm; M$10/hr), and several others along Hidalgo towards the first-class bus station.

**Leaving Tonalá**, most first-class buses are *de paso*, and though there are plenty of departures, in practice you can only reserve tickets for a handful of these, and none of the ADO GL buses. OCC has first-class departures every two hours to Tuxtla, 173km northeast (4am–8.40pm; 3hr) and almost hourly to Tapachula (3am–8.45pm; 3hr 30min); for Tapachula, the first bus with reserved seats departs at 9.15am. There are also a few services to Mexico City (2 daily) and Oaxaca (3 daily), and at least as many second-class buses to Tuxtla and Tapachula. In the bustling market area, red-striped shared taxis (on Matamoros beyond 5 de Mayo) leave when full for **Puerto Arista** (22km south) and **Boca del Cielo** (37km; both M$13 per person), while *combis* for Puerto Arista depart one block away on Juárez between 5 de Mayo and 20 de Marzo. The green-striped **city taxis** charge considerably more for the journey to Puerto Arista (M$80 per car).

## Puerto Arista

Although this sleepy village may not be everyone's idea of a perfect beach resort, **PUERTO ARISTA**, with its miles of grey sand, flocks of frigate birds and invigorating surf, does offer a chance to escape the unrelenting heat of the inland towns. It's a bit run-down and there's little to see, but it's a handy place to stop if you've been doing some hard travelling. While the waves are refreshing, be aware of the potentially dangerous **riptides** that sweep along the coast – never get out of your depth.

You can easily get transport from Puerto Arista 15km down the coast to **Boca del Cielo** ("Mouth of Heaven"), a cluster of houses and fishing boats on the landward side of Laguna La Joya, where you can board a *lancha* and speed across to a beautiful beach. It's best at high tide, when the water comes right up to the restaurants, and at sunset. Having said that, without your own transport you'll need to head back well before 7pm, as it's almost impossible to find a taxi after dark. Some of the palapa restaurants will let you sling a hammock for a small fee, though if you plan to sleep outdoors be prepared for mosquitoes. All of the beaches along this stretch of coast are used by **turtles** for nesting. The peak of the season is October, when the turtles emerge during the early hours of the morning to deposit their eggs beneath the sand. In June and July, the hatchlings that managed to evade egg collectors struggle to reach the sea, desperately trying to avoid being picked off by gulls, frigate birds and other predators.



### Practicalities

The road from Tonalá joins Puerto Arista's only street, Avenida Matamoros, at the lighthouse. Get off here and you're in the centre of town: walk a couple of kilometres left or right and you'll be on a deserted shoreline; ahead lies the busiest section of beach, with hotels and restaurants packed closely together. You won't feel crowded, though, unless you arrive at Christmas or Semana Santa, as there seem to be at least as many buildings abandoned or boarded up as there are occupied.

There are many **hotels** in Puerto Arista but generally few customers: you could try to bargain with a couple of the places listed here – and you can always **camp** on the beach for free. Turn right at the lighthouse (facing the beach) and the most convenient places to stay are *Lizeth*, with its clean rooms (ⓣ994/600-9038; ❹) and *La Puesta del Sol* (ⓣ994/600-9047; ❹, or ❸ without TV and a/c) on the beach itself, with old and slightly faded but clean rooms with tiled floors. Further up the road are a couple of more upmarket, but rather overpriced alternatives: *Hotel Safari* (ⓣ994/600-9036, ⓦwww.safarihoteles.com; ❾), which offers poolside suites for up to eight people; and *Arista Bugambilias* (ⓣ994/600-9044; ❻), a smart option around 500m from the lighthouse, with rooms and suites around a small pool and private garden right on the beach. Take a left at the lighthouse and accommodation is rather thinner on the ground – you'll walk a long way before you find the first decent option. It's around 1km to *Lucero* (ⓣ994/600-9042; ❻), just back from the beach, with a pool, rooms decorated with wildlife murals and suites with a/c. If you take the left turn before *Lucero* you'll soon come across signs for *José's Camping and Cabañas* (ⓣ994/600-9048; ❶, or ❷ with bath), the friendliest place in Puerto Arista and great for budget travellers. Accommodation is in sturdy thatched bungalows with electric lighting; some are en-suite, but the shared bathrooms are very clean and have a dependable water supply. There's a flower-filled patio with hammocks and a pool, and camping is also possible.

For food, there are a couple of dozen beachfront palapa **restaurants** serving seafood in the area near the lighthouse, but only five or six are ever open at once and as there's little that distinguishes them in terms of cost (M$70–100 for most dishes), menu (*mojarra*, crab and shrimp feature heavily) or quality; generally the best place to eat will be at your hotel. For Mexican staples, there are a couple of cheap places on the main road near the lighthouse.

## From Tonalá to Tapachula

It's 223km between Tonalá and Tapachula. If you have your own vehicle you can explore some of the side roads leading from Hwy-200, either up into the mountains, where heavy rains give rise to dozens of rivers and waterfalls, or down to near-deserted beaches. Around **PIJIJIAPAN**, 75km from Tonalá, a series of dirt roads lead to unspoiled beaches and lagoons with opportunities for fishing, swimming or merely relaxing in the sun. The best of these is **Playa Palo Blanco**, 20km due south of Pijijiapan. Most of the coastal villages are actually on the landward side of narrow lagoons, separated from the ocean by sand bars. These sand bars block many rivers' access to the sea, causing marshes to form and providing a superb wetland habitat, protected as the **Reserva de la Biosfera La Encrucijada**, 45km of coastline and an important wintering point for North American migrant birds. Travelling **by bus**, it's much more difficult (though still possible) to take in destinations off the main road, and you need to be prepared to hitch and camp. At **HUIXTLA**, 42km before Tapachula, Hwy-211 breaks off from Hwy-200 to snake over the mountains to join the Panamerican Highway near Ciudad Cuauhtémoc and the Guatemalan border at La Mesilla. The road offers stupendous mountain views and is traversed by buses running between Tapachula and Comitán and San Cristóbal de las Casas.

## Tapachula

Set in the imposing shadow of the 4000-metre Volcán Tacaná, **TAPACHULA** is just 16km from Guatemala and a major transit point between Mexico and Central America. A busy commercial centre and the capital of the Soconusco, it grew in importance during the nineteenth century as the demand for coffee and bananas increased. As a border city, it has a lively cultural mix, including not only immigrants from Central America, but also small German and Chinese

communities: the Germans were invited to settle here by the Mexican government in the 1880s as part of a scheme to boost the economy. They eventually established the state's coffee industry and left a legacy of fine haciendas around the city. The Chinese initially came to work on the railway, in part because the rebellious locals refused to do so; the most visible sign of their community today is the high proportion of Chinese restaurants in the city centre.

While the surrounding countryside offers some worthwhile diversions, there's not much to see in the city itself. As always, the centre of activity is the **zócalo**, a pleasant place to while away an afternoon, or an evening listening to the marimba bands. Look out for *cohetes*, strange green fruits that look like giant olives and have the flavour of sour plums, pickled in rum and sold from street stalls around the zócalo.

The main attraction here is the **Museo Arqueologico del Soconusco** (Tues–Sun 10am–5pm; M$24), in the old Palacio Municipal, recently renovated with absorbing displays of prehistoric and Olmec finds, and a decent collection of artefacts from nearby Izapa and other local sites (explanations in Spanish only).

### Arrival, orientation and information

All the main **bus stations** are north of the centre; the various second-class companies have their terminals within walking distance of the zócalo, while first-class OCC (also the terminal for Tica and Linea Dorada buses from Guatemala) is further out at 17a Calle Ote between avenidas 1a and 3a Nte. A taxi to the centre costs about M$20 and walking takes about twenty minutes. From Tapachula's **airport**, 18km south on the road to Puerto Madero, a *colectivo* into town costs M$70 per person. Buy a ticket at the Transportes Terrestre booth just outside the arrivals hall. If you are in a group it works out cheaper to take a taxi for around M$100.

The town's **layout** is a little confusing, for while the streets are laid out in the regular numbered grid common in Chiapas, the zócalo, **Parque Hidalgo**, is not at its centre. It's not too far away, though: Calle Central meets Avenida Central three blocks east and a block south of the zócalo.

The regional **tourist office** (Mon–Fri 8am–8pm, Sat 8am–2pm; ⓣ962/625-5409) is inconveniently located 2km west of the centre in Plaza Kamico on the main road to the border – with the old Palacio Municipal undergoing an ambitious restoration, the municipal tourist office has been closed, and at the time of writing its fate hadn't been decided. The main **banks** are one block east of the zócalo, with HSBC at 1a Calle Pte and 2a Avenida Nte, but for **changing cash** and travellers' cheques you'll get much quicker service from Cambio de Divisas, 2a Avenida Nte 9, between Calle Central and 1a Calle Pte (Mon–Fri 9am–5pm, Sat 9am–2pm); you can also get Guatemalan quetzales here. The **post office** (Mon–Fri 9am–3pm, Sat 9am–1pm) is a long way southeast of the zócalo at 1a Calle Ote, between avenidas 7a and 9a Nte. The Guatemalan **consulate** is at Calle Central Ote 42, at the junction with 5a Avenida Nte (Mon–Fri 10am–3pm & 4–6pm; ⓣ962/626-1525). **Visas** usually cost US$43 (transit visas US$17) but are currently not required for citizens of Europe, North America, South Africa, Australia, New Zealand and many other nations – the office is worth a visit, however, to stock up on free maps and information if you're headed over the border. There are plenty of **Internet** cafés in the centre of town: *Cyber Café Los Portales* (9am–9pm; M$10/hr) is sandwiched between the restaurants on the south side of the zócalo, while *Angelito's* (Mon–Fri 8am–8pm, Sat 8am–3pm, Sun 9am–2pm: M$10/hr) is on the way to the bus station on Avenida Central Nte, beyond 7a Calle Pte.

## Accommodation

There's no shortage of places to stay in Tapachula, with options for almost every budget. There is at least one **hotel** near any of the bus stations, but the ones around the second-class terminals are often sleazy. Your best bet is the area immediately east of the zócalo, where there are several good-value hotels along avenidas 4a Nte and 1a, 3a and 5a Pte. The cheapest places are west of the zócalo, where the market straggles down the hill, and though most are rather desperate-looking there are one or two good budget options.

**La Amistad** 7a C Pte 34, between avenidas 10 and 12 Nte ⓣ962/626-2293. The best budget hotel in the city; clean, with colourful rooms around a flower-filled courtyard. Free drinking water, but M$30 extra for TV. There's also no a/c, though rooms have fans. ❷

**Casa Mexicana** 8a Av Sur 19 ⓣ962/626-6605, ⓔcasamexicanaposada@yahoo.com. Cosy and beautifully decorated mid-range hotel arranged around a flower-laden courtyard, tastefully adorned with art and antiques. ❻

**Chelito** 1a Av Nte 107, at 17a C Ote ⓣ962/626-2428. *Chelito* has a handy location just around the corner from the OCC buses (head left out of the terminal) and clean tiled rooms (with a/c and cable TV, or cheaper rooms with fan), but no hot water. There's a small restaurant and parking for guests. ❷

**Fénix** 4a Av Nte 19, near 1a C Pte ⓣ962/625-0755, ⓦwww.fenix.com.mx. Best-value hotel in the centre, with large rooms with a/c, cable TV and decent bathrooms. There's a cooling fountain in the courtyard plus leafy gardens complete with parrots. Rooms are surprisingly tranquil given the central location, but make sure you get the better rooms at the back. ❺

**Hostal del Angel** 8a Av Nte 16 ⓣ962/625-0142. Smart new hotel just south of the zócalo. Rooms are equipped with cable TV and a/c and arranged around a courtyard. ❹

**Villa del Sol** 3a C Pte 45 ⓣ962/626-6193. This clean and friendly option offering large, bright rooms with cable TV and telephone is downhill past the market. Rooms without a/c are cheaper. ❹

## Eating and drinking

In addition to *cohotes*, you'll find plenty of cheap specialities sold from *taquito* stalls around the zócalo, as well as national favourites such as *esquites* (toasted corn). 1a Calle Pte is lined with inexpensive restaurants, most with breakfast options and a comida corrida, though some are rather better than others. As usual, there are budget places to eat and some fine *panaderías* around the market area, beginning with the row of **juice bars** on 10a Avenida Pte, just west of the zócalo. Vegetarians should make for the local outpost of *Naturalissimo* at Av Central Nte 20 near 1a Calle Pte, with a good selection of juices and healthy light meals (M$40–50). For **cafés**, *La Casa de Los Angeles*, at 8a Avenida Nte 10, is a cosy old place with wooden tables, while the *Monaco*, on the corner of 1a Calle Pte and 4a Avenida Nte is a bit smarter and also has an international telephone exchange. Los Portales, a row of restaurants on the south side of the zócalo, is the best place for drinks or standard Mexican fare, while the city's liveliest clubs are clustered in the Zonas Discotecas, 2km east on Calle Central Ote.

**Bambú** 7a C Pte 23. The most appealing of several economical Chinese restaurants along this street; also has a takeout option should the traffic fumes put you off eating in the open-fronted restaurant – a lunchbox with three dishes plus rice is M$35. *El Carboncito* next door serves great *taco pastor* (M$5).

**Los Comales** Los Portales (southwest corner). The top place to eat on the zócalo, *Los Comales* is open 24hr, serving seafood (M$100–150) and a range of Mexican favourites (M$30–40). Draught beer is M$15, coffee M$7. There's frequently live music.

**Los Jarrones** 1a C Pte 18. Classy restaurant in the *Hotel Don Miguel* with a varied, if slightly pricey, menu. Try the *tacos camarón* (M$80) or pastas (M$40–50).

**Jordan** 2a Av Nte, near Cambio de Divisas. Tranquil bookshop with small restaurant at the front, with a big menu of Mexican staples (M$30–40). Open 7am–9pm.

**La Parrilla** 8a Av Nte 20, just south of the zócalo. South American style *parillas* (grills) as well as a delicious *taquiza mixta*, with five mouth-watering

## Moving on from Tapachula

First-class **buses** (and some of the better second-class services) leave from the OCC terminal; taxis to the terminal from anywhere in the centre should be no more than M$20. Luxury ADO GL/UNO services are available to **Tuxtla Gutiérrez** (6hr), Oaxaca (12hr), Mexico City (17hr) and Veracruz (13hr). OCC has services to all the above, including at least twelve daily departures to Tuxtla Gutiérrez (6am–midnight). All buses to **Comitán** (7 daily; 6hr 30min) and **San Cristóbal** (7 daily; 9hr) are *via altos* and head over the mountains, starting at 7.30am (last one at 11.30pm). All first-class and most second-class buses to Tuxtla are *via costa*, and head up the coast via Tonalá. If you're heading directly to **Guatemala City** there are three first-class companies with daily services: Trans Galgos (6am, 10am, 3pm; ⓣ962/625-4588) which departs from its terminal at 13a Calle Ote 43, between avenidas 9a and 11a Nte; Linea Dorada (2.30pm), which is much cheaper and departs from the first-class bus station (buy tickets from the booth in the arrivals hall); and Tica Bus (daily 6am; ⓣ962/626-2880), which also runs from the OCC terminal. All of them take you right across the border (5–6hr); you'll have to get off the bus for Mexican immigration at the Talismán, walk across to the Guatemalan immigration post and then reboard.

The main **second-class bus** operators are TRF, at the corner of 16a Avenida Nte and 3a Calle Pte, and AEXA, opposite. The main **combi** terminals lie along 5a Calle Pte beyond the market, between avenidas 12a and 14a Nte. Unión y Progreso runs frequent services to Cacahoatán (for Unión Juárez) and to the Talismán Bridge for Izapa and the Guatemalan border every three to five minutes. Next door, Omnibus de Tapachula runs frequent buses to Ciudad Hidalgo, while Costenos de Chiapa, opposite, provides a virtually identical service. If you're staying on the other side of the zócalo, Gen. Paulino Navarro also offers regular *combis* to Hidalgo (every 8min 4.30am–9.45pm) from its terminal on 7a Calle Ote and Avenida Central Nte. **Shared taxis** to Hidalgo leave from 7a Calle Pte, between avenidas 2a and 4a Nte.

Tapachula's **airport** is served by several daily flights to Mexico City, operated by Aeroméxico (C Central Ote 4; Mon–Fri 9am–7pm, Sat 9am–6pm; ⓣ962/626-7757) and Aviacsa (Av Central Nte; Mon–Fri 9am–3pm and 4–7pm, Sat 9am–4pm; ⓣ962/626-1439). You can buy tickets from airline offices in town, or from helpful agent Aeropromociones y Viajes at 4a Avenida Nte 18-B (ⓣ962/625-0017).

types of supertacos (M$40–60), all served in a fast-food style diner. Cheap tortas from M$20.

**Pronto's** 1a C Pte 11. One of several good-value budget options along this street, this open-front cafeteria has the added advantage of being open 24hr. Try the *menudo sinaloense,* a typical Mexican *caldo* (broth) for M$40, or the large fried chicken (M$50).

## Ruta del Café

If you have your own transport, or don't mind splashing out on a taxi, it's worth exploring the **Ruta del Café**, a touristy designation for a series of thirteen charming old haciendas built north of Tapachula by German coffee barons in the early twentieth century. Only three currently provide accommodation and/ or tours: **Finca Irlanda** (established in 1928, it became the world's first certified organic producer in 1967); the **Argovia Finca Resort**; and **Finca Hamburgo** (ⓣ962/6251812, ⓦwww.fincahamburgo.org), which is the most absorbing and has an office in Tapachula at 9a Calle Ote 54-A, near 11a Avenida Nte. Established in 1888 by Arthur Edelmann, the hacienda and coffee plantation are still run by his family, and offer all-inclusive ecotourism packages with accommodation, meals and tours, as well as nature walks and bike rides. It's 54km from Tapachula; they'll arrange to pick you up at the airport or bus station. Otherwise, it's only accessible by car or taxi (M$300–400).

## Santo Domingo and Unión Juárez

If you're travelling by bus, the small towns of **Santo Domingo** and **Unión Juárez** offer a similar taste of the area's coffee culture as the Ruta del Café, but make for much easier targets. This said, there are still no direct buses from Tapachula, and you have to change at the town of **Cacahoatán**, approximately halfway and thirty minutes from the city (see box opposite). The route follows the road to Talismán and the border for much of the way; it's best to bring your passport in case of security checks. Once in Cacahoatán, frequent **buses** leave from the station across the street from the Unión y Progreso terminal. Shared **taxis**, which are slightly faster, also wait here. Domingo usually takes around thirty minutes, with Juárez an additional ten to fifteen minutes up the mountain. As the road climbs up the lush green valley of the Río Suchiate, which forms the border with Guatemala, the bananas and cacao give way to coffee and you begin to enjoy good views of two majestic **volcanoes**: Tacaná, at 4092m, is the highest peak in Chiapas; and the 4220-metre peak of Tajumulco, the highest mountain in Guatemala.

Around 35km from Tapachula, **SANTO DOMINGO** is a slightly shabby, sleepy village, but worth a stop for its wonderfully restored 1920s coffee-plantation house, Casa Braun, or just "**Casa Grande**" (daily 8am–8pm; free). The three-storey wooden house, set in beautiful gardens, and with balconies all around, was the home of Enrique Braun Hansen, whose German origins are reflected in the building's architectural style – early North American meets Alpine hotel, with predominately Art Nouveau interiors. Now part of a successful community-based tourism project, the house includes a good restaurant on the ground floor and the **Museo de Café** (free) above, with displays and photos charting the area's history and the coffee-making process. Opposite the main entrance, around 100m along the street and just off the main road, *Hotel Santo Domingo* (Ⓣ962/629-9073; ❸) is a good-value **place to stay**, where rooms with spacious, private baths and comfortable beds are set around a patio garden. Get off the bus at the lower end of the village, near the shop and overgrown zócalo, and you should be able to follow the signs for the "Centro Turistico" – the house is around 200m from the main road. Moving on, you can pick up buses to Juárez on the main road.

The small town of **UNIÓN JUÁREZ**, 51km from Tapachula and perched on the flank of the Volcán Tacaná (1100m), offers some of the finest hiking in southern Chiapas. There are countless waterfalls in the area and, with a guide, you can reach the summit of the volcano, where a monument symbolizes the kinship between Mexico and Guatemala. Fernando Valera Saá (Ⓔfernandao772@hotmail.com), an excellent Spanish-speaking guide, leads three-day trips up Tacaná for about M$800; the price includes government approvals and equipment. The best time to climb is between November and March, particularly December and January.

Unión Juárez has two **hotels**: the budget but comfortable *Posada Aljoad*, half a block off the west side of the plaza (no phone; ❸), which has simple but neat rooms with private bathrooms (with hot water) around a courtyard, and a decent, inexpensive restaurant; and the good-value *Hotel Colonial Campestre*, which you pass as you enter the town (Ⓣ962/647-2015; ❹). Rooms and suites here are comfortable and spacious, with en-suite bathrooms and TV. The *Campestre* has a pleasant **restaurant**, *La Suiza Chiapaneca*, and on the north side of the plaza, the *Carmelita* is an inexpensive place serving a standard menu of meat, chicken and tacos. *La Montaña*, nearby, is slightly better, with comfortable wooden tables and chairs and tasty tamales stuffed with egg, plums, chicken and olives. You can sit outside and enjoy views of Pico de Loro, a steep, rocky outcrop that actually looks like its namesake – a parrot's beak. All the coffee served in the village is organic, and can be purchased freshly roasted for about M$70 per kilo. Buses pull in on the west side of the plaza and depart for Cacahoatán from the east side (every 15min until 8pm; last bus to Tapachula 9pm from Cacahoatán).

## The ruins of Izapa

The road to the border passes right through the archeological site of **Izapa** (daily 9am–5pm; free), an important, if little-visited, group of ruins. Besides being easy to get to, the site is large – with more than eighty temple mounds – and significant for its evidence of both the Olmec and Maya cultures. Izapa culture, in fact, is seen as a transitional stage between the Olmecs and the glories of the Classic Maya period. Even though many of the best carved monuments have been removed to museums, including the Anthropology Museum in Mexico City (see p.440), you can still see early versions of the rain god Chac and other gods, many in rather sad-looking huts surrounded by barbed wire. From its founding before 1250 BC, Izapa flourished up to and throughout the Maya pre-Classic period, until around 300 AD; most of what remains is from the later period, perhaps around 200 AD.

Entry is officially free, but in practice the ruins are divided into three groups, each looked after by a family that asks M$5 from visitors to open the gates. The **northern side** of the site (left of the road as you head to the border) is the most interesting. There's a ball-court, and several stelae, which, though not Olmec in origin, are carved in a recognizable Olmec style, similar to monuments at other early Maya sites. The **southern side**, which comprises the Grupo A and B ruins, is down a track about 1km back along the main road towards Tapachula. These sections are more overgrown, but you can spot altars with animal carvings – frogs, snakes and jaguars – and several unexcavated mounds. To **get to Izapa**, take any bus or *combi* to the Talismán border and ask the driver to drop you at the site, which is signposted from the road.

## The Guatemalan border: the Talismán Bridge and Ciudad Hidalgo

Both of these southern crossing points are easy places to enter Guatemala (see box opposite) – which one you head for depends largely on your ultimate destination – but neither is a place to linger. **Talismán Bridge** is closer to Tapachula (16km) and better for onward connections if travelling by bus, especially to Quetzaltenango and the Western Highlands. Apart from a few grubby hotels and unappealing *comedores* there is nothing in Talismán; El Carmen, on the Guatemalan side, isn't much better. **Leaving Mexico**, you shouldn't have to pay departure tax of any kind: though each Mexican state seems to follow slightly different rules, the only official fee payable is the **nonimmigrant fee** of around US$20 (the exact amount in pesos changes from year to year), which should have been paid on entry to the country. Most airlines include the fee in the price of a ticket, but if you entered Mexico by land and didn't pay upon leaving the border zone, you'll have to go to a bank in Tapachula before you leave. Make sure they stamp your tourist card after you've paid – you'll need this to exit the country. **Changing money** is also best done in Tapachula; there's no shortage of moneychangers at the border but rates are unfavourable – make sure you have some idea of the official exchange rate beforehand.

## Crossing into Guatemala

There are two major **crossings** (Talismán Bridge and Ciudad Hidalgo, open 24hr) and several minor points of entry (Frontera Corozal, see p.750; Ciudad Cuauhtémoc, see p.736; Benemérito, see p.752; and El Carmen Xhan) from Chiapas into Guatemala, as well as one from Tabasco (El Ceibo; see p.773). Crossings are relatively trouble-free at the larger points these days though procedures at Frontera Corozal, Ciudad Cuauhtémoc and El Ceibo are rather more unpredictable. These are notorious entry points for illegal immigrants and the *aduanas* consist of little more than armed soldiers manning riverside tables – the soliciting of illegal fees sometimes still occurs at these crossings. Requesting a receipt is often a sufficient response to get them to waive the fee, but it may well be less hassle to pay. The only genuine tax is the nonimmigrant fee (usually around US$20), which should have been paid on your arrival (and included in the cost of most flights). If for some reason this fee was not paid, and you do not intend to return before your tourist card expires, you can make payment at any city bank before departure. If you will be returning to Mexico you will be allowed to proceed in possession of your current tourist card free of charge.

Citizens of the US, Canada, South Africa, the EU, Australia and New Zealand **do not require visas** to enter Guatemala. Citizens of other countries should check with the Guatemalan consulate in Tapachula (see p.704). Note that Mexico observes daylight-saving time, making it one hour later here during the summer than in Guatemala.

If you're heading onwards, **Guatemala City** is about five to six hours away: there's usually a bus waiting, but note that these usually travel along the Carretera al Pacifica via Tecún Umán (closer to Ciudad Hidalgo), and the fastest option is to take one of the international bus services from Tapachula direct to Guatemala City (see box, p.706). For **Quetzaltenango** and other destinations in the Western Highlands, take a shared taxi to **Malacatán** and continue from there. Travelling **into Mexico** you'll be given a tourist card at immigration, and there's plenty of *combis* to Tapachula and then first-class buses from Tapachula onwards. You'll probably have your passport checked many times along Hwy-200, so be prepared.

Further south and 37km from Tapachula, the border town of **CIUDAD HIDALGO** is a very busy road crossing, but is only useful if you're aiming for the Carretera al Pacifica (Pacific Highway; for the Guatemalan beaches) or ruins at Abaj Takalik near Retalhuleu (connected to Hidalgo's Guatemalan neighbour **Tecún Umán** with regular buses). The OCC terminal is one block from immigration, where you can pick up shuttles to Tapachula every fifteen minutes. If you get stuck (try not to), the *Mazari* (☎962/698-0098; ❸), at 3a Avenida Nte and 5 Calle Ote, is one of the better choices, with clean, comfortable rooms. Plenty of willing locals offer to pedal you across the Puente Rodolfo Robles to Umán in Guatemala, but it's an easy walk – you have to pay M$5 to cross the bridge.

# The Chiapas highlands

There is nowhere in Mexico so rich in scenery as **inland Chiapas**. Forested uplands and jungly valleys, flush with the vivid flora and fauna of the tropics – wild orchids, brilliantly coloured birds and monkeys – are studded with rivers and lakes, waterfalls and unexpected gorges. The area also has a fascinating cultural history, its isolation allowing the **indigenous population** to carry on with their lives little affected, though the pressures brought first by Catholicism and now commercialism have slowly eroded traditional ways of life in all but the most remote communities. Conversely, the customs that do survive are clung to fiercely by the older generations, and you should be extremely sensitive about **photography** – especially of anything that might have religious significance – and donning **native clothing**, the patterns on which convey subtle social and geographic meaning.

Strong and colourful as these cultures are, the economic and social lot of the *indígena* population in this region remains greatly inferior to that of *ladinos*. The oppressive exploitation of the *encomienda* (a system of forced labour under Spanish colonial rule) remained powerful here far longer than in parts of Mexico more directly in the government eye, and despite some post-Revolutionary land redistribution, most small villages still operate at the barest subsistence level. It's worth noting that many indigenous communities and some local transport operators refuse to observe the **time change** in summer, preferring *la hora vieja* – the old time.



## Tuxtla Gutiérrez

**TUXTLA GUTIÉRREZ**, the capital of the state, does its best to deny most of Chiapas's attraction and tradition – it's a fast-growing, modern, crowded city. Though not actually in the highlands, it's the main gateway from central Mexico and a major transport hub; though it's far better to press on to Chiapa de Corzo (see p.714), you may well end up having to stay the night. If you do, there's a decent **zoo** and some excellent **museums** to fill your time, and the city is the best base from which to approach the cliff-tops and *miradors* of the **Cañón del Sumidero** (see p.716), the real highlight of the area. Other day trips to surrounding attractions are better organized in San Cristóbal, two hours further east (see p.717).

### Arrival and information

Tuxtla's new airport, **Aeropuerto Angel Albino Corzo**, is inconveniently located 27km south of the city. All the major car rental companies (Alamo, Hertz and Thrifty) and top hotels have desks in the arrivals hall, but as yet there is nowhere to change money. There is a small Bancomer ATM tucked away in the departures hall upstairs, but this is often out of order. To get anywhere, you have to take a **taxi**: buy tickets at the desk in the arrivals hall. It's about M$200 to Tuxtla or Chiapa de Corzo (both take 35–45min).

First-class **buses** pull into the cramped ADO/OCC station (Ⓣ961/612-5122) on 2a Avenida Norte Pte at 2a Calle Poniente Nte. To reach the zócalo, turn left from the entrance onto 2a Avenida Norte Pte and walk two blocks. The main second-class terminal, used by Autotransportes Tuxtla Gutiérrez (ATG) and a couple of smaller companies, is on 3a Avenida Sur Ote, just before 7a Calle Oriente Sur 1km southeast of the centre: for the zócalo, walk through the small market, down to 2a Avenida Sur Ote and turn left (west); continue along here until you hit Calle Central Sur, then turn right. A confusing number of **colectivos** shoot around town, but you can walk to most of the sights. **Taxis** are easy to find: visitors are usually charged about M$30, especially arriving at the bus station.

The **municipal tourist office** (Mon–Fri 8am–8pm, Sat 8am–2pm) is on the fourth floor of the Edificio Balencio on Avenida Central between calles 4a and 5a Poniente Nte. The Chiapas **state tourist office** is a good way further

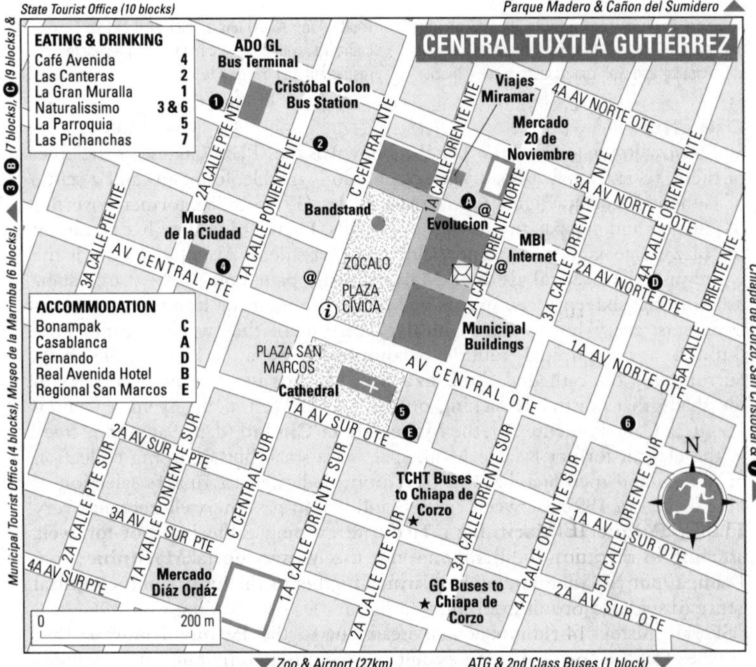


west, across from the *Hotel Bonampak* in the Edificio Plaza de las Instituciones at Blv Belisario Domínguez 950 (daily 8am–7pm; ⓣ961/617-0550), but the information there is much more comprehensive (and it's more likely to have English speakers).

## Accommodation

Tuxtla has no shortage of **places to stay**, with plenty of budget options, but compared with elsewhere in the state, they're all a bit characterless. If you want inexpensive convenience, though less noise than the area around the bus station, head a few blocks east (left out of the first-class bus station, crossing the zócalo by the underpass) to 2a Avenida Norte Ote. The city's best hotels are concentrated three to four kilometres from the centre of town, beyond the *Bonampak* along Belisario Domínguez, and are not particularly convenient unless you have a car.

**Bonampak** Belisario Domínguez 180 ⓣ961/602-5925, ⓔhotbonam@prodigy.net.mx. Fourteen blocks west of the zócalo, where Av Central Pte becomes Blv Domínguez, this upmarket business hotel is the closest of several posh options on the edge of town, but a little overpriced – make sure you get a room in the newer block. All rooms have a/c and cable TV, and there's a pool, leafy gardens, restaurant, travel agency and car hire. ❼

**Casablanca** 2a Av Nte Ote 251 ⓣ961/611-0305, ⓦwww.casablancachiapas.com. Best of the budget options, with bright blue-and-yellow rooms, most equipped with a/c and TV, facing an inner palm-fringed garden. There's luggage storage as well. ❸

**Fernando** 2a Av Nte Ote 515 ⓣ961/613-1740. The best value of the options just east of the zócalo: modern hotel with large, comfortable rooms and en-suite bathroom, wooden furniture and TV. All rooms have fans but no a/c. Parking available. ❹

**Real Avenida Hotel** Av Central Pte 1230 ⓣ961/612-2347. One of the newest hotels in town, with spotless rooms equipped with cable TV and phone – the only down side is the relatively long walk into the centre. ❻

**Regional San Marcos** 2a C Ote Sur 176, at 1a Av Sur Ote ⓣ961/613-1940, ⓔsanmarcos@chiapas.net. Popular and well-run modern hotel, a block south of the zócalo and a block east of the cathedral, with some a/c rooms, plus a decent restaurant and bar on site. ❺

## The City

Sights downtown are few: the **zócalo**, known as the "Plaza Cívica", is the chief of them, recently refurbished with ostentatious marble, fountains and a statue of General Joaquín Miguel Gutiérrez Canales (1796–1838), former governor of Chiapas and campaigner for *indígena* rights. There's often free live music on the plaza, especially at weekends. On the other side of Avenida Central is the whitewashed **Catedral de San Marcos** (daily 6am–2pm & 4–9pm). Established in the sixteenth century, its bell tower is one of the leading local entertainments: every hour a mechanical procession of the twelve apostles goes through a complicated routine accompanied by a carillon of 48 bells. Surrounding the cathedral, the **Plaza San Marcos** is a nice place to relax in the shade that's distinctly lacking on the zócalo. West along Avenida Central Pte, at 2a Calle Poniente Sur, the **Museo de la Ciudad** (daily 9am–6pm; free), in the elegant former Palacio Municipal, has a small but absorbing collection of photos and memorabilia, and one room dedicated to Tuxtla's selection as state capital in 1892. Between calles 8 and 9, you pass the well-kept and very popular **Parque la Marimba**, a favourite evening gathering spot for, well, listening to marimba. Real fans can visit the **Museo de la Marimba** (daily 10am–10pm; M$50) on the corner, which highlights the history of the musical genre (displays in Spanish only).

Slightly further afield, you could head out to the **Parque Madero**, 1km northeast of the centre, where a pedestrianized promenade leads off 5a Avenida Norte Ote, first passing the pleasant **Jardin Botánico** and less interesting **Museo Botánico** (Mon–Fri 9am–3pm, Sat 9am–1pm; free) opposite, and on to the **Museo Regional de Chiapas** (Tues–Sun 9am–5pm; M$33, free on Sun), which details the history of pre-Hispanic Chiapas and the results of the Conquest. The highlights are the intricately carved human fencers from the ruins of Chiapa de Corzo (see p.715). At the end of the promenade is the city theatre and next to it the **Museo de Paleontología** (Tues–Fri 10am–5pm, Sat & Sun 11am–5pm; M$10), with displays of fossils, lots of amber and the skeleton of a sabre-tooth tiger.

### The zoo

If you have a couple of hours to spare, it's worth heading out to the Zoológico Miguel Álvarez del Toro, or **ZOOMAT** (Tues–Sun 9am–5pm; M$20), 5km south of the city centre. There's a **bus** out there, #60, marked "Cerro Hueco" or "Zoológico", which you can catch on 1a Calle Oriente Sur between avenidas 6a and 7a Sur Ote, a bit of a walk from the centre – it's very slow and roundabout, though, and a **taxi** is a great deal easier.

Its claim to have every species native to Chiapas may be a bit inflated, but it does have quite a selection, including some of the state's more spectacular invertebrates. As far as zoos go, it's not a bad effort, with good-sized cages complete with natural vegetation, freshwater streams and a conservationist approach. A number of animals, including *guaqueques negros* (agoutis) – rodents about the size of a domestic cat – and some very large birds, are free to roam the zoo grounds. People of a nervous disposition should avoid the *vivario*, which contains a vast and stomach-turning collection of snakes, insects and spiders you might meet on your travels.

## Eating and drinking

The centre of Tuxtla has dozens of **restaurants**, and you need never wander more than a block or so on either side of Avenida Central to find something in every price range. Juice bars are everywhere, and there are also some great bakeries. The very **cheapest** places are between the second-class bus stations and the centre, where several tiny, family-run restaurants serve excellent-value comidas corridas, and in the Mercado Díaz Ordáz, Calle Central Sur, between avenidas 3a and 4a Sur Ote. Most popular for socializing and people watching are the restaurants under the arches on **Plaza San Marcos** behind the cathedral, all with outdoor seating.

**Café Avenida** Av Central Pte 230. An authentic Mexican coffee shop (they grind their own beans), where old men sip black coffee to a background of mariachi music and slow service.

**Las Canteras** 2a Av Nte Ote, one block east of the OCC terminal. *Las Canteras* provides a more refined dining experience in an open, airy restaurant serving traditional *chiapaneco* cookery, often accompanied by live marimba – don't expect a quiet meal. Mains from M$100–120, and an excellent set lunch for M$38.

**La Gran Muralla** 2a Av Norte Pte 334. Passable Cantonese restaurant near the OCC bus station, with a wide range of tasty Chinese dishes for anyone needing a break from Mexican food. Daily noon–11pm.

**Naturalissimo** 6a C Pte Nte 124, just off Av Central Pte. Bright vegetarian chain restaurant; it's inexpensive (no more than M$40 for most dishes), clean and modern, and offers a great daily special. Mon–Sat 7am–10.30pm, Sun 8am–10.30pm. There's a second branch at Av Central Ote 541.

**La Parroquia** Plaza San Marcos. Steak and *parilla* specialist, with a small terrace overlooking the plaza, a decent menu of Mexican food (M$30–40) and a good breakfast buffet (M$50).

**Las Pichanchas** Av Central Ote 837, east of the zócalo between calles 7 and 8 Ote. It's a bit touristy, but a great place for dinner, with marimba all evening, folk dancing 9–10pm and excellent *chiapaneco* food all dished up in a two-storey house with a courtyard. Try the *platón de botana regional* (a selection of local snacks: cheese, sausage, tortas). Most dishes are M$40–50. Daily noon–midnight.

### Moving on from Tuxtla Gutiérrez

ADO and OCC first-class **buses** depart from the station at the corner of 2a Avenida Norte Ote and 2a Calle Poniente Nte; the Rapidos del Sur terminal is adjacent. OCC has frequent departures for **Ocosingo**, **Palenque**, **Tonalá**, **Tapachula** and **San Cristóbal** (1hr 30min). Other destinations include Mexico City, **Villahermosa**, Cancún and Oaxaca. Buses for **Buchil** depart at 3pm and 11.30pm. ADO GL and UNO services depart the special terminal across 2a Calle Poniente Nte: Mexico City, Oaxaca (9.30pm), Palenque (2.30pm), Villahermosa (6pm), and more frequently to Tapachula, San Cristóbal and Comitán. Note that most first-class buses to Villahermosa now travel via the Puente Chiapas, which seems less direct but is much faster than going straight over the mountains. The dilapidated second-class terminal, at 3a Avenida Sur Ote and 7a Calle Oriente Sur, is used by Autotransportes Tuxtla Gutiérrez (ATG), and serves San Cristóbal, Oaxaca, Villahermosa, Mérida, Palenque and Cancún. Other local buses operate from the street outside, with frequent departures to San Cristóbal.

For **Chiapa de Corzo**, hop on one of the **microbuses** that leave from the GC terminal at 3a Calle Oriente Sur and 3a Avenida Sur Ote (every 5min 5am–10pm), or the Transportes Chiapa–Tuxtla (TCHT) station, 2a Calle Oriente Sur and 2a Avenida Sur Ote.

Tuxtla's **airport** has frequent flights to Mexico City (Aviacsa and Click Mexicana) and Cancún (Aeromar), and two to three daily flights to Toluca (InterJet) – taxis should take you to the airport for about M$200.

## Listings

**Airlines** Aviacsa, Av Central Pte 160 ⓣ961/153-6042 (airport); InterJet, Módulo Plaza Crystal, Belisario Domínguez 1081 & Belisario Domínguez 1861 ⓣ01-800-011-2345 (Mon–Sat 9am–6pm); Mexicana, Plaza Veranda 7, 8 y 9 Col Arboledes ⓣ961/602-5769.

**Banks** There are plenty of banks along Avenida Central, with a branch of HSBC right on the zócalo (C Central Nte 137).

**Car rental** Alamo, 5a Av Nte Pte 2260 ⓣ961/602-1600; Budget, Belisario Domínguez 2510 ⓣ961/615-1382; Hertz, Belisario Domínguez 1195 ⓣ961/615-5348.

**Internet access** Widely available, particularly along 2a Av Nte Ote. MBI, 2a C Ote Nte 220, just off 2a Av Nte Ote, is open daily 9am–9pm.

**Laundry** Lavandería Zaac, 2a Av Pte Ote 440 (Mon–Fri 8am–2pm & 4.30–8pm, Sat 9am–4pm; M$30/kilo).

**Post office** The main post office is at 1a Av Nte Ote, behind the Palacio de Gobierno (Mon–Fri 8.30am–4pm, Sat 8.30am–1pm).

**Travel agent** Viajes Miramar, off the northeast corner of the zócalo at 1a Av Ote Nte 310 ⓣ961/612-3930, ⓦwww.viajesmiramar.com.mx.



# Chiapa de Corzo and around

**CHIAPA DE CORZO** is an elegant little town overlooking the **Río Grijalva**, barely twenty minutes east from Tuxtla by bus. Founded by the Spanish in 1528 (their first city in Chiapas), it was already an important centre in pre-Classic times, and is the place where the oldest **Long Count date**, corresponding to December 7, 36 BC, was found on a stele. The remaining ruins are on private land behind the Nestlé plant, at the far end of 21 de Octubre on the edge of town (see opposite), but the undoubted star attraction here is the boat ride along the **Cañón del Sumidero** (see p.716).

**Buses** from Tuxtla travel along Avenida Cuauhtémoc, north of the plaza, terminating near the Nestlé plant – get off at Calle Mexicanidad, or where the driver says "parque", and turn right for the plaza. Heading back, buses cut across the top of the plaza (Avenida 21 de Octubre) and are easy to pick up. Though it's a far more appealing place to stay than Tuxtla, it's not easy to move on without doubling back to the city – buses to San Cristóbal take the new highway, which bypasses Chiapa de Corzo, and to catch one you'll have to walk or take a local bus 4km out of town. One alternative is to take a taxi from the plaza all the way to Cristóbal (about M$350). Heading to the airport however, there's little point going to Tuxtla as taxis cost the same (M$200). There's a small but helpful **tourist office** (Mon–Fri 8am–4pm; ⓣ961/616-1013) on Domingo Ruíz, just off the plaza.

The most striking feature of Chiapa de Corzo is the amazingly elaborate sixteenth-century **Fuente Colonial**, which dominates the central Plaza Ángel Albino Corzo. Built of brick in the Mudéjar style and in the shape of the Spanish crown, the fountain is one of the most impressive surviving early colonial monuments in Mexico – tribute to a painstaking restoration – and appears as the state symbol on vehicle licence plates. Just behind it, the huge tree bursting from its confines is **La Pochota**, a national monument to the suffering of the *indígenas* under the Spanish, said to have been standing here when the town was founded.

On the northwest side of the zócalo is the **Casa Museo Ángel Albino Corzo** (daily 10am–2pm & 6–9pm; free), the former residence of Ángel Albino Corzo (1816–75), the national reformer for whom the town was named. Housing an interesting jumble of period furniture and historical artefacts, it features two cannons used in the so-called Pastry War against France in 1838 (explanations in Spanish only). On the southern side of the plaza *portales* house a series of reasonably priced handicraft stores, which continue south along 5 de

△ Fuente Colonial, Chiapa de Corzo

Febrero towards the river and Embarcadero. Behind the *portales* is the lovely **Templo de Santo Domingo de Guzmán** and ex-convent, with a tall nave and timbered ceiling. Forming part of the complex, behind the main entrance to the church, is the **Centro Cultural** (Tues–Sun 10am–5pm; free), an ambitious new project that is gradually converting the old convent into a series of tasteful galleries, museums and art studios. Upstairs on the first floor, the **Museo de Laca** recounts the history of lacquer-making in Mexico, from pre-Hispanic times to the present, featuring various lacquered objects from gourds to pots and chests.

There are two good **hotels** in town: the central *Los Angeles* (Ⓣ961/616-0048; ④), on the southeast corner of the zócalo, which has small but comfortable en-suite rooms in a renovated building around a courtyard; and the newer, more upmarket ★ *Hotel La Ceiba*, Domingo Ruíz 300 (Ⓣ961/616-0389, Ⓦwww.hlaceiba.com; ⑥), three blocks west from the plaza, which encloses a tranquil palm-filled garden with a small pool and caged parrots, and offers simple but very comfortable rooms with a/c and cable TV. Several **restaurants** specialize in *chiapaneco* cuisine, though they tend to be a little overpriced: *El Campanario*, behind the municipal building on Coronel Urbina 5 (just off the plaza) is the best, with an inviting garden and courtyard, though it closes at 7pm. *Los Corredores*, at the southwest corner of the plaza at Madero 35, offers Mexican favourites. The Embarcadero along the river is a pretty spot for a drink, with plenty of live music, though the pricey seafood restaurants here are all fairly similar, and most start to wind down early.

### The ruins of Chiapa de Corzo

Strategically located on an ancient trade route high above the Río Grijalva, the ruins of **Chiapa de Corzo** comprise some two hundred structures scattered over a wide area of private property, shared among several different owners and sliced in two by the Panamerican Highway (Hwy-190). This is the longest continually occupied site in Chiapas, having begun as a farming settlement in the early pre-Classic period (1400–850 BC). By the late pre-Classic (450 BC–250 AD), it was the largest centre of population in the region. What you see today are mainly low pyramids, walls and courtyards.

There's a small example of the ruins in the middle of the road, just beyond the terminal for buses to Tuxtla on the edge of town, but to **get to the main site** from the plaza, take any microbus heading east, get off at the junction with Hidalgo and follow the signs. After about fifteen minutes, you'll come to an unmarked gate in a fence on the right; go to the house (officially closed Mon) and pay the M$10 **fee** to the family who farm among the ruins. **Walking**, it's about 3km northeast from the plaza in Chiapa de Corzo, passing the beautiful sixteenth-century church ruin of **San Sebastián** on 21 de Octubre along the way.

## Cañon del Sumidero

Driving east from Chiapa de Corzo towards San Cristóbal, you'll catch occasional glimpses of the lower reaches of the **Cañón del Sumidero**. Through this spectacular cleft the Río Grijalva runs beneath cliffs that reach almost 1000m in height in places, the rock walls sprinkled with patches of bright green vegetation. You can explore the rim of the canyon from Tuxtla, or take a mesmerizing **boat ride** along the river from Chiapa de Corzo – if you have your own transport you can also take boats from Cahuaré, where the highway crosses the river, but it's harder to get to by bus.

From Tuxtla, Autobús Panorámico (Tues–Sun 9am & 1pm; 3hr 30min) runs a bus from Parque la Marimba and the plaza along the road that borders the rim of the canyon, passing all the main *miradors* – the best views are from **La Coyota**. The buses go only when five or six people turn up; it's best to check with the Tuxtla tourist office first. More formal tours are operated by Viajes Miramar (see "Listings", p.714) and tend to be pricey (about M$450), also taking in ZOOMAT. There's no public transport otherwise.

In Chiapa de Corzo, make for the small Turistica de Grijalva office (ⓣ961/600-6402) on the west side of the plaza, where you can sign up for regular boat trips down the canyon (8am–5pm; M$100 per person). They need ten people to make the trip, but come early and you shouldn't have to wait long. Tours last a couple of hours, snaking through the whole gorge to the Chicoasén Dam, which forms a lake at the northern end, and passing several waterfalls, including the remarkable **El Árbol de Navidad**. Here bizarre calcareous formations covered with algae resemble a Christmas tree from a distance, and crocodiles are commonly seen, as well as vast numbers of pelicans, egrets and cormorants.

## Bochil and Simojovel

Just beyond Chiapa de Corzo, Hwy-195 – winding spectacularly down to the Gulf plain – cuts off to the north. Few tourists take this route, unless bound for Teapa in southern Tabasco (see p.763), since the Panamerican Highway continues to the far more enticing destination of San Cristóbal. First the road climbs through mountains wreathed in cloud to **BOCHIL**, some 60km from Tuxtla, an interesting stop on the slower route north to Villahermosa if you have your own transport (buses now bypass the mountains via the fast highway over the Puente Chiapas). A pleasant small town, Bochil is a centre for the **Tzotzil Maya**, and a good base from which to explore the surrounding hills and villages. Most people still wear the traditional dress, or *traje*: the women in white *huipiles* with red embroidery and dark blue skirts with pink ribbons in their hair, and maybe a few men in white smocks and trousers rolled up to the knee. As always, you should be *very* wary of **taking photographs**. There are a couple of simple **places to stay**, including the *Posada San Pedro* (no phone; ❸), whose basic rooms are set out around a courtyard on 1 Calle Pte Nte, a block from the plaza: to get here, head for Banamex at the top of the plaza and turn right. For onward travel, Bochil has a frequent second-class **bus** service to Tuxtla, run by Autotransportes Tuxtla–Bochil.

*Combis* run regularly up the minor road to **SIMOJOVEL**, 40km away at the head of a spectacular valley, the source of most of the amber you'll find sold in local markets. Should you want **to stay**, the *Casa de Huéspedes Simojovel* (no phone; ❷) on Independencia, a block south of the plaza, has basic rooms around a flower-filled courtyard.

### Reserva de la Biosfera El Triunfo

Cradled within the slopes of the Sierra Madre de Chiapas, on the northern edge of the Soconusco (see p.700), the **Reserva de la Biosfera El Triunfo** is most easily approached from Tuxtla, four hours to the north. The highest peaks of the reserve, a refuge for Chiapas's wildlife and hundreds of species of birds (including the rare quetzal), are covered in dense **cloud forest**.

The jumping-off point for the reserve is the town of **JALTENANGO**, also known as **Ángel Albino Corzo**, at the junction of three rivers and surrounded by coffee *fincas*. It's best to contact the reserve several weeks in advance if you intend to visit; Claudia Virgen Montesinos is the coordinator in Tuxtla, at Av Central Pte 847, responsible for tourism (ⓣ961/612-1394, ⓔclaudiavirgen@chiapas.net). Packages include one night at a hotel in Jaltenango, three to four nights in simple *Campamento El Triufo* in the mountains, a guide and porters. You'll pay around M$4000 for a minimum of two people. **Buses** to Jaltenango leave Tuxtla several times a day from the Cuxtepeques y Anexas station at Calle 10 Ote Nte and Avenida 3 Nte Ote.

## San Cristóbal de las Casas and around

Just 85km from Tuxtla Gutiérrez, **SAN CRISTÓBAL DE LAS CASAS** is almost 1700m higher – a cool place where low, whitewashed red-tiled houses huddle together on the plain, giving it an unrivalled provincial colonial charm. The town was designed as a Spanish stronghold against an often-hostile indigenous population – the attack here by Zapatista rebels in January 1994 was only the latest in a long series of uprisings. It took the Spanish, led by conquistador Diego de Mazariegos, four years to pacify the area sufficiently to establish a town here in 1528. Officially named "Ciudad Real" (Royal City), it was more widely known as "Villaviciosa" (Evil City) for the oppressive exploitation exercised by its colonists. In 1544 Bartolomé de las Casas was appointed bishop, and he promptly took an energetic stance in defence of the native population, playing a similar role to that of Bishop Vasco de Quiroga in Pátzcuaro (see box, p.363). His name – added to that of the patron saint of the town – is still held in something close to reverence by the *indígenas*. Throughout the colonial era, San Cristóbal was the capital of Chiapas (at that time part of Guatemala), losing this status in 1892 only as a result of its continued reluctance to accept the union with Mexico. This spirit of rebellion was revived by the Zapatistas in 1994, although despite being the main focus of their attack, the town was only occupied for thirty hours, and no tourists were harmed.

Today San Cristóbal remains one of the most restful and enjoyable places in the Republic to spend a few lazy days, its infrastructure catering mainly for predominantly European visitors. The city holds plenty of colonial churches and several absorbing little museums, but the true pleasure here lies in simply wandering the streets. It's also a great base for visiting nearby villages, buying inexpensive textiles, weavings and jewellery and studying at one of the numerous Spanish-language schools.

## Arrival and information

The highway from Tuxtla Gutiérrez to San Cristóbal rises quickly from the plains, breaking through the clouds into pine forests. As the modern parts of the city sprawl unattractively along the highway, first impressions of San Cristóbal itself are not the best, but in the centre there is none of this unthinking development. Whether you arrive by first- or second-class **bus**, you'll almost certainly be just off the Carretera Panamericana (Hwy-190), which becomes Bulevar Juan Sabines Gutiérrez at the southern edge of town, though if you've arrived from Bochil, you'll be just north of the market area. For the centre, turn right out of the OCC **first-class terminal**, and it's seven blocks along Insurgentes to the plaza. Most **second-class** services stop along the highway either side of the OCC terminal. The **airport** is currently closed, unable to compete with Tuxtla. **Taxis** within the centre should cost no more than M$18, though some drivers will try and charge you M$20.

The helpful **state tourist office**, just off the southwest corner of the plaza at Hidalgo 1-B (Mon–Fri 8am–8pm, Sat 9am–8pm, Sun 9am–2pm; Ⓣ967/678-1467), is one of the best in the country, with good, free city maps, up-to-date lists of hotels in all price ranges, bus times and event information. The staff know Chiapas well, and there's usually someone who speaks English. There are more bulletin boards in and around the **municipal tourist office** (daily 8am–8pm; Ⓣ967/678-0665) in the Palacio Municipal, on the northeast corner of the zócalo.

## Accommodation

Vast numbers of visitors and competition for business mean that San Cristóbal boasts some of the best-value **hotels** in Mexico. There are a few good places around the OCC terminal, but walking up Insurgentes to the plaza you'll pass more establishments in all price ranges. Most of the best **budget options** are found in the streets east of the zócalo, particularly along Real de Guadalupe and in its vicinity. An ever-larger proportion of hotels here call themselves "**posadas**", and most live up to the convivial ambience this is presumably meant to convey, but it's always worth seeing your room before you pay. Even the most basic places now have hot water, though not necessarily all of the time. Nights can be pleasantly cool in summer, but cold in winter, so make sure there are enough blankets.

For **longer stays**, check out the many notice boards in the bus stations, language schools and popular cafés, where you'll find rooms and even whole houses for rent. The closest official **campsite** is at *Rancho San Nicolás*, 2km east of the centre along the extension of Francisco León (Ⓣ967/678-0057).

**Backpackers Hostel** Real de Mexicanos 16 Ⓣ967/ 674-0525, Ⓦwww.backpackershostel.com.mx. One of the best hostels in Chiapas, with enthusiastic English-speaking owners, clean, renovated dorms (M$50; there's a separate dorm for women) and rooms (❷) and a host of extras: free Internet, breakfast, lockers, cable TV in the common room, daily use of gym (M$30), Spanish lessons (M$50/hr) and a cosy campfire in the garden (nightly 8–11pm).

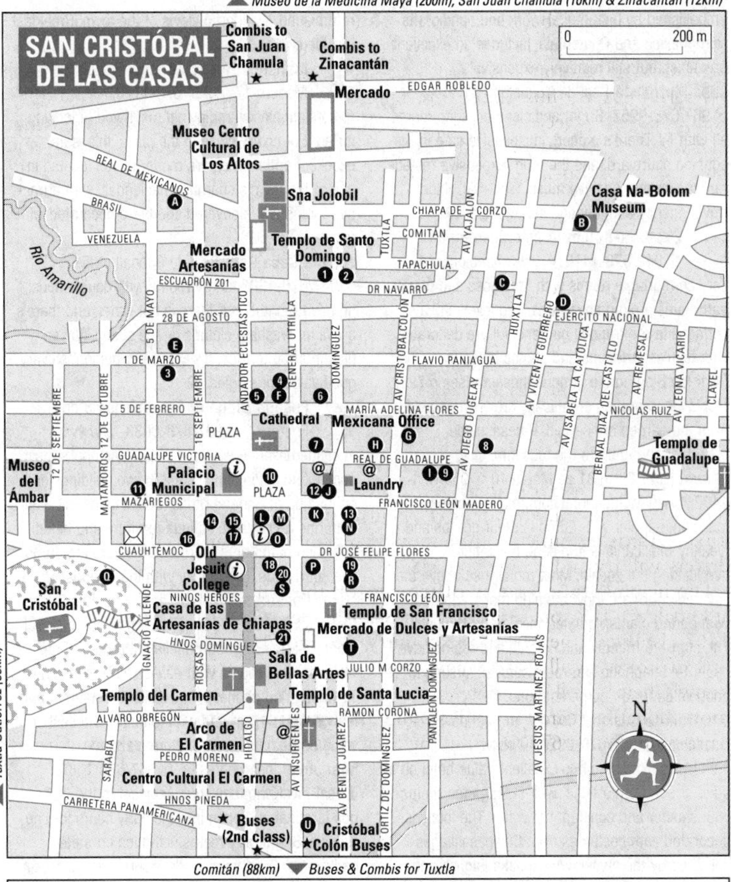


**ACCOMMODATION**

| | | | |
|---|---|---|---|
| Backpackers Hostel | A | Hotel Hacienda Los Morales | Q |
| Barón de las Casas | J | Mansión de Los Angeles | K |
| La Casa di Gladys | C | Posada Casa Real | I |
| Casa Felipe Flores | P | Posada Diego de Mazariegos | F |
| Casa Margarita | H | Posada San Cristóbal | O |
| Casa Na-Bolom | B | Real Jovel | U |
| Ciudad Real | L | Rincón del Arco | D |
| Don Quijote | G | Santa Clara | M |
| Fray Bartolome de las Casas | S | Villa Real I and II | R & T |
| Holiday Inn | E | Youth Hostel Posada Juvenil | N |

**EATING & DRINKING**

| | | | |
|---|---|---|---|
| Bar Fly | 14 | Madre Tierra | 21 |
| Bar Revolucion | 5 | Makia | 15 |
| Bar Zapata | 11 | Mare Nostrum | 3 |
| Café El Kiosco | 10 | Mayambe | 8 |
| Café El Puente | 9 | El Mirador II | 12 |
| Café Museo Café | 6 | Normita | 19 |
| Café San Cristóbal | 18 | La Paloma | 17 |
| La Casa de Pan | 2 | La Parilla | 1 |
| Emiliano's Moustache | 16 | Tequila Zoo | 4 |
| El Gato Gordo | 7 | Tuluc | 20 |
| Latinos | 13 | | |

**Barón de las Casas** Belisario Domínguez 2 ⓣ967/678-0881. Well-run, modern hotel one block east of the plaza. Rooms are simple, with spotless tiled bathrooms with plenty of hot water. TV is M$20 extra. The owners speak English. ❸

**La Casa di Gladys** 5 de Mayo 47 ⓣ967/102-0104, ⓔcasagladys@hotmail.com. Recently moved to a new location between 28 de Agosto and Escuadron 201, this is a deservedly popular, well-run travellers' hangout with both dorm beds (M$50 per person) and private rooms (❶). The clean, tiled, shared bathrooms have hot water, and there's a communal area with cable TV, kitchen and free Internet. Free pick-up from the bus station.

**Casa Felipe Flores** Flores 36 ⓣ967/678-3996, ⓦwww.felipeflores.com. Just five tastefully decorated rooms with tiled bathroom and fireplace, off two plant-filled colonial courtyards, all embellished by beautiful artwork and handicrafts from Mexico and Guatemala. Includes an excellent breakfast, but still relatively expensive. ❽

**Casa Margarita** Real de Guadalupe 34 ⓣ967/678-0957. Bright and clean en-suite rooms, all with TV. There's a good, inexpensive café in the cobbled courtyard, and the more expensive restaurant (next door) has live music Wed–Sat. Handy travel agency and luggage storage, too. ❺

**Casa Na-Bolom** Vicente Guerrero 33 ⓣ967/678-1418, ⓦwww.nabolom.org. Very comfortable rooms with fireplaces and private bathrooms around courtyards, and lovely private cottages in the tranquil gardens. All are decorated with textiles, artefacts and photos taken by Gertrude Blom in the famous museum (see p.723). Meals incorporating organically grown vegetables from the garden are served. Rates include breakfast and entry to the museum. ❼

**Ciudad Real** Plaza 31 de Marzo 10 ⓣ967/678-4400, ⓦwww.ciudadreal.com.mx. This colonial mansion, popular with European tour groups and wealthy Mexicans, is in a superb location overlooking the zócalo. Most rooms rise above the covered courtyard (now a dining room, adorned with potted plants); quieter ones are at the back. The staff are friendly and helpful, and rooms have cable TV, telephone and room service, making it good value for an upmarket hotel. ❼

**Don Quijote** Cristóbal Colón 7, at Real de Guadalupe ⓣ967/678-0920, ⓦwww.hoteldonquijote.com.mx. Excellent-value hotel on a quiet street. Comfortable, well-lit, carpeted rooms with shower and constant hot water. The lobby is decorated with costumes from Chiapas villages collected by the owner, who speaks English and French. Free morning coffee. ❺

**Fray Bartolome de las Casas** Niños Héroes 2, at Insurgentes ⓣ967/678-0932. Split into two sections, the older part of this hotel (❷) has more charm, arranged around a pretty courtyard with a central fountain, though hot water is available only 6–10am and 7–11pm. The newer section (❹) has 24hr hot water and TV, but is otherwise far less appealing.

**Holiday Inn** 1 de Marzo 15 ⓣ967/678-0045, ⓦwww.hotelesfarrera.com. Most luxurious place to stay in the centre, recently opened in an old hacienda with a gorgeous rose-walled courtyard and beautifully decorated, well-equipped rooms. ❽

**Hotel Hacienda Los Morales** Ignacio Allende 17 ⓣ967/678-1472, ⓔpanchito-sc@hotmail.com. Whitewashed stone cabins, sprawling up the hillside garden four blocks west of the plaza, each have a living room with fireplace, wood floors and a bathroom, and are all gradually being refurbished. Wonderful views of the town. Breakfast included. ❺

**Mansión de Los Angeles** Francisco Madero 17 ⓣ967/678-1173, ⓔhotelangeles@prodigy.net.mx. If you're looking for a bit of luxury close to the plaza, this is an excellent option: a smart, modern hotel located in one of the town's charming haciendas, with attractive rooms and a covered courtyard decorated with murals. ❻

**Posada Casa Real** Real de Guadalupe 51 ⓣ967/678-1303. Large rooms with double beds: no private baths, but there is hot water, and there's a *pila* for washing clothes on the sunny, flower-filled rooftop terrace. It's M$70 per person, so very good value for singles. ❶

**Posada Diego de Mazariegos** 5 de Febrero 1 ⓣ967/678-0833, ⓦwww.diegodemazariegos.com.mx. San Cristóbal's most enchanting colonial hotel, set in two buildings on either side of General Utrilla. Spacious rooms – all featuring a fireplace, antique furniture and beautifully tiled bathrooms – are arranged around attractive courtyards. Often busy with tour groups. ❼

**Posada San Cristóbal** Insurgentes 3 ⓣ967/678-6881 ⓦwww.hotelsancristobal.com. Charming, wood-panelled, three-star hotel with spacious rooms with *azulejo* bathrooms and TV (though no phones), an excellent restaurant and leafy covered courtyard with fountain; the best value of the options around the plaza. ❹

**Real Jovel** Insurgentes 66 ⓣ967/678-1668, ⓔreal-jovel@hotmail.com. Adjacent to the OCC bus terminal and open into the early hours for late arrivals. Bright, airy rooms with tiled en-suite bathrooms. Good value – it's M$60 extra for TV. ❸

**Rincón del Arco** Ejército Nacional 66, at Vicente Guerrero ⓣ967/678-1313, ⓦwww.rincondelarco.com. Well-priced luxury hotel with large rooms and suites stocked with antique furniture, fireplaces and beautifully tiled bathrooms. It's all set around a courtyard and delightful gardens, often enveloped with the scent of roasting coffee beans. About 1km northeast from the plaza, it's just a block from *Casa Na-Bolom* and affords gorgeous views of the surrounding hills, though it's a bit inconvenient if walking. Restaurant and parking on site. ❻

**Santa Clara** Insurgentes 1, at the corner of the plaza ⓣ967/678-1140, ⓦwww.hotelescoloniales.com. A former colonial mansion, known locally as "La Casa de la Sirena" after the sixteenth-century carvings of mermaids on the corners of the building. Rooms (with cable TV and phone, and some with antique furniture) are a little worn, but surround a spacious, plant-filled patio, and public areas are adorned with colonial artefacts. Facilities include a heated pool and good restaurant, though some guests find the sorry-looking caged parrots a bit off-putting. Big discounts of up to fifty percent are often available if you pay in cash. ❻

**Villa Real I and II** two locations on Benito Juárez, 8 and 24-A I ⓣ967/678-2930 & II ⓣ967/678-4485. Comfortable, well-furnished, carpeted rooms all with private bathrooms, cable TV and access to parking facilities. *Villa Real I* is the older but cheaper of the two. I ❸, II ❹

**Youth Hostel Posada Juvenil** Benito Juárez 2, near Madero ⓣ967/678-7655, ⓔyouth@sancristobal.com.mx. Friendly hostel with dorm rooms of four and six beds (M$45 per person) as well as private rooms (❶). Left luggage is M$25 per day. Not HI-affiliated.

## The City

Plaza 31 de Marzo, usually referred to simply as *el parque*, is at the heart of the city, encircled by a cluster of attractive colonial mansions and the sixteenth-century **cathedral**, which boasts an ornate, pale orange facade, impressive *artesanado* ceiling and grand *retablo*. The finest of the mansions is **La Casa de la Sirena**, now the *Hotel Santa Clara*, which is said to have been built by the conquistador Andrés de la Tovilla in the mid-sixteenth century and has a very elaborate doorway around the corner on Insurgentes. In the middle of the plaza there's a bandstand and a café, which sometimes provides piped music when no band is playing.

Cutting across the centre is the **Andador Eclesiástico**, a pedestrianized thoroughfare that connects the Templo del Carmen, 300m south of the plaza (on Hidalgo), to Santo Domingo, 400m to the north (on 20 de Noviembre). It's lined with touristy shops, cheap restaurants and ice cream parlours. The **Templo del Carmen** stands opposite the Arco del Carmen, which spans the road, and once served as the gateway to the city. Built in 1677, it shows a slight Mudéjar (Moorish) influence. The church is not particularly inspiring architecturally, but on the other side of the arch, the **Centro Cultural El Carmen** (daily 9am–5pm; free) contains a couple of galleries around gardens filled with traditional Maya plants. Considering the amount of artistic activity in and around San Cristóbal, these sights are pretty disappointing, though partly explained by a serious fire in 1993 that destroyed much of the city's artwork, including several eighteenth-century religious paintings.

### Templo de Santo Domingo Guzmán

The **Templo de Santo Domingo Guzmán**, five blocks north of the plaza, is perhaps the most intrinsically interesting of San Cristóbal's churches. Constructed between 1547 and 1551, the church's lovely pinkish Baroque stucco facade combines Oaxacan and Guatemalan styles. Inside, it's gilded everywhere, with a wonderfully ornate pulpit – if you see it in the evening, by the light of candles, you might well believe it's solid gold. To the left of the main entrance (beyond Sna Jolobil), the **Museo Centro Cultural de los Altos** (Tues–Sun 10am–2pm & 4–6pm; M$25, free on Sun), tells the story of the city, with vivid portrayals of how the Indians fared under colonial rule.

### City museums

Three blocks west of the plaza, along Diego de Mazariegos, the **Museo del Ámbar** (Tues–Sun 10am–2pm & 4–7pm; M$20; ⓦwww.museodelambar.com.mx) is in the renovated buildings of the Convento de la Merced, dating from 1774. The museum displays and sells authentic amber found in the Simojovel Valley (Spanish descriptions only, but English information sheets available). Be sure to ask museum guides for advice on how to spot fake amber (see box, p.722). Amber was

## Local crafts

It's the local crafts and indigenous culture that draw visitors to San Cristóbal, an influx not always appreciated by the *indígenas* themselves. Nevertheless, the livelihood of the town depends on the people from surrounding villages, who fill its streets and dominate its trade. Many of the salespeople who set up shop around the market are *expulsados* – converts to evangelical Protestantism expelled by village leaders and forced into shanties on the edge of town. In an effort to eke out an existence they have turned to craft-making, with tourists as their main source of income.

The plaza in front of Santo Domingo church, filled with **craft stalls**, is often the best place to buy souvenirs. Part of the former *convento* next door has been converted into a craft co-operative (**Sna Jolobil**) that sells textiles and other village products (Mon–Sat 9am–2pm & 4–6pm). The quality here is generally good, but the prices higher than elsewhere. The **Mercado de Artesanías y Dulces** on Insurgentes is another worthwhile place to look for local crafts, although traders here are less willing to barter.

Other **craft shops** are dotted around town, with the greatest concentration on Real de Guadalupe. La Pared (Ⓔlapared@prodigy.net.mex), on Hidalgo, which runs north from between the first- and second-class bus stations, sells a very good selection of genuine, good-quality amber and silver jewellery at reasonable prices. A visit to Taller Leñateros, Flavio Paniagua 54, allows you to observe the fascinating process of making paper by hand from such diverse items as banana leaves, cornstalks, coconut fibre and bamboo, mixed with waste paper and rags and coloured with natural dyes. The finished products are then printed with traditional indigenous and modern designs to become beautiful cards and notebooks. *Leñateros* is Spanish for "woodcutters", and many workers here formerly cut firewood from the pine forests surrounding San Cristóbal. Now, in addition to creative paper goods, they also produce *La jícara* (The Gourd) – a **literary magazine** in the folded-bark book design of a Maya codex; most of the original codices were destroyed by Spanish friars. At the corner of Hidalgo and Niños Héroes, the Tienda de los Artesanos de Chiapas (Tues–Sun 9am–2pm & 5–8pm) is a state-sponsored venture that provides an outlet for Chiapas's textiles and crafts at fair prices. The weaving and embroidery exhibited here are as good as what you'll find in any museum.

**Amber** is another special product of this region, sold in shops all over town, mostly in the form of jewellery – if you're serious about buying, visit the **Museo del Ámbar** first, where English-speaking staff can give you a crash course in spotting fakes and introduce the various types, as well as sell you some exquisite pieces. Real amber is exceptionally light, gives a resin-like odour when rubbed and is rarely sold with insects trapped inside it – if someone tries selling you a scorpion in amber, it's definitely a con: there are only five real pieces in existence. Tierra de Ámbar, Real de Guadalupe 16, is another trustworthy store, though you should be okay in most shops – just don't buy from street sellers, as they almost always sell fakes.

one of the most treasured decorative items in Maya society, valued both as a trade item and for its beauty and rarity. So, too was jade, something which can be found at the small **Museo del Jade** (Mon–Sat noon–8pm, Sun noon–6pm; M$30; Ⓦwww.eljade.com), two blocks north of the plaza along 16 de Septiembre. The museum contains three rooms dedicated to various pre-Hispanic cultures, with a fourth displaying a fascinating replica of the jade-enhanced tomb of Hanab (Kinich Janab) Pakal, ruler of Palenque (see p.744). Perhaps the most unusual of the city museums is the **Museo de la Medicina Maya** (daily 12.30–9.30pm; M$20), a long way north of the centre along 16 de Septiembre. It offers an absorbing journey through the world of Maya medicine, complete with medicinal plants growing in the gardens and an herbal pharmacy on site to dispense remedies.

### The market

San Cristóbal's daily market, the **Mercado Municipal**, lies beyond Santo Domingo along General Utrilla. It's an interesting place, if only because you can observe indigenous life and custom without causing undue offence. What's on sale is mostly local produce and household goods, but you'll also find good tyre-soled leather *huaraches* and rough but warm sweaters, which you might well need. The market is far bigger than it first appears, so make sure you see it all; bear in mind that the main covered area is full of stomach-churningly vile butchers' stalls that are not for the faint-hearted.

### Casa Na-Bolom

Behind Santo Domingo, Chiapa de Corzo leads east towards the **Casa Na-Bolom** (daily 10am–5pm; tours in English at 4.30pm; M$35, M$45 with tour) at Vicente Guerrero 33, also housing one of the best hotels in San Cristóbal (see p.720) and a **library** of local anthropology (daily 10am–4pm; free). This was the home of Danish explorer and anthropologist Frans Blom, who died in 1963, and his Swiss wife Gertrude (Duby), an anthropologist and photographer who died in 1993. Today it's renowned as a centre for the study of the region's indigenous cultures, particularly of the isolated Lacandón Maya, the "Hach Winik" (True People). Buy tickets in the gift shop in the **Jardín de Jaguar** across the road from the main complex, which also contains a few exhibits and information boards about the various ethnic groups in Chiapas. In one corner is a replica of a traditional highlands house, made with wooden walls covered with mud and a roof thatched with grass.

The main museum occupies rooms set around a series of beautiful courtyards – it's not particularly large (and there are English explanations), but it's a good idea to take the tour. The museum exhibits discoveries from the site of **Moxviquil** (see p.727) and explains the history and culture of the Chiapas highlands and the Lacandón forest. There's also a collection of items belonging to Frans Blom, including the detailed maps for which he is known. After the tour, you can watch a film about the life of the Bloms and specific ecological, cultural and political aspects of life in Chiapas.

The whole centre is overseen by the Asociación Cultural Na-Bolom, which arranges some small-scale volunteer cultural and agricultural projects, though you'll need to speak Spanish to participate; write or email for details (see the hotel review on p.720 for contact info).

## Guadalupe and San Cristóbal

Further afield, two churches dominate views of the town from their hilltop sites: **Templo de Guadalupe** to the east and the **Templo de Cerrito de San Cristóbal** to the west. Neither offers a great deal architecturally, but the climbs are worth it for the views – San Cristóbal, especially, is at the top of a dauntingly long and steep flight of steps. Be warned, though, that women have been subjected to harassment at both of these relatively isolated spots (especially San Cristóbal): don't climb up here alone or after dark.

## Eating

San Cristóbal has no lack of places to eat, with a huge variety of economical **restaurants** in the streets immediately east of the zócalo, especially on Madero. Where the city really scores, however, is in lively places that cater to a disparate, somewhat bohemian crowd, made up of university and language-school students, a cosmopolitan expatriate population and a constant stream of travellers. Many places are vaguely arty, with a coffeehouse atmosphere and enticing menus that feature plenty of **vegetarian** options.

### Cafés

**Café El Kiosco** in the zócalo. In a great location under the bandstand, where you can enjoy a coffee at the outdoor tables and watch the world go by. On the down side, patrons tend to be a prime target for children selling jewellery in the plaza.

**Café El Puente** Real de Guadalupe 55. Popular café serving inexpensive salads, soups, sandwiches, cakes and an inviting organic buffet (2–5pm; M$60); also acts as a cultural centre, with Internet access, live music, lectures, film shows and a good notice board. Closed Sun.

**Café Museo Café** María Adelina Flores 10. Delicious coffee (from M$10) and some of the best *chocolate con leche* (M$18) in town, served in the café of a small museum, where the walls are adorned with beautiful illustrations depicting the history of the coffee trade in Mexico. The café also sells organic beans from a co-operative of local coffee producers (one of which you can visit – ask at the museum for information) – it's M$80 per kilo. Open Mon–Sat 9am–9pm.

**Café San Cristóbal** Cuauhtémoc 2, near Insurgentes. This tiny, no-frills coffeehouse is a popular spot for locals to play chess and read the newspaper.

### Restaurants

**La Casa de Pan** Dr Navarro 10. A superb range of vegetarian food and baked goods, made with locally grown organic ingredients and at very reasonable prices, is on offer here – fresh salads go for M$35. It also serves as a shop and meeting place for expat aid-workers, and the owners are active in development projects for indigenous women and organic agriculture. Tues–Sun 8am–11pm, with live music nightly.

**Emiliano's Moustache** Cresencio Rosas 7, near Cuauhtémoc. Vast range of authentic tacos – the *combinacions* (M$50) are big enough for two – with some vegetarian choices and decent *tacos pastor* (M$5). Live music in the evening. Daily noon–1am.

**El Gato Gordo** Real de Guadalupe 20. Inexpensive and deservedly popular backpacker place serving Mexican and international dishes with great-value specials and set lunches from M$25. You can also read the newspapers, watch TV and listen to music. Closed Tues.

**Madre Tierra** Insurgentes 19, opposite the Mercado de Artesanías. European-style restaurant in a colonial house serving great, healthy food including home-made soups, salads and pastas. The upstairs terrace bar has good views of ancient walls and red-tiled roofs, and the bakery and deli next door sell whole-wheat bread and carrot cake until 8pm Mon–Sat.

**Mare Nostrum** 1 de Marzo 8 ⓣ967/678-3149. *Mare Nostrum* boasts the only rooftop dining area in San Cristóbal – it's definitely the best place to enjoy the sunset as you eat. Superb Mediterranean dishes from M$130. French and English spoken.

**Mayambe** Real de Guadalupe 66. Indian, Thai and Lebanese food in an old hacienda courtyard with fabulous hummus and chicken curry, books and Internet access. The owners speak excellent English. Mon–Sat 9am–11pm.

**El Mirador II** Madero 16. The best cheap Mexican restaurant on Madero, with good tortas and comidas corridas.

**Normita** corner of Juárez and José Flores. A great little restaurant serving Jaliscan specialities and inexpensive breakfasts from M$25. Daily 7am–11pm.

**La Paloma** Hidalgo 3, just south of the zócalo. Sophisticated restaurant in La Galería cultural centre. International food is served in the refined surroundings of an art-filled colonial mansion. Live music most evenings. Check out the hip upstairs terrace for coffee, Internet and books (mostly German).

**La Parrilla** corner Belisario Domínguez and Dr Navarro, on a tiny square adjacent to *La Casa de Pan*. Specializing in grilled meats, including *alambres*, which are similar to kebabs. Sit on one of the saddles used as bar stools and enjoy the great views. Closed Mon.

**Tuluc** Insurgentes 5. Justifiably popular, with a good comida corrida and dinner specials from M$50, mains from M$40. This is the first place in town to open in the morning (6.30am), ideal if you have to catch an early bus.

## Drinking and nightlife

Many of the city's cafés and bars host **live music** in the evenings, usually salsa or Latin, and only rarely impose a cover charge. *Madre Tierra* (see above) also has a bar and live music upstairs.

**Bar Fly** Rosas 4. Bar and club with lively theme nights featuring reggae, funky jazz and trance. Wed–Sat from 10pm.

**Bar Revolucion** 20 de Noviembre and Flavio Paniagua. Hip bar and café right on the pedestrianized Eclesiástico serving light snacks and drinks with simple Revolutionary-Cuba inspired decor. Cocktails from M$36, and two-for-one drinks daily noon–7pm.

**Bar Zapata** 5 de Mayo 2. Very popular bar and *discoteca*, with an interior blending colonial and high-tech decor, glitzy lights and a decent cocktail list. Thurs–Sat from 9pm.

**Disco Palace Olimpo Club** Crescendo Rosas 59. The only real club in town is eight long blocks south of the zócalo, with a relatively young crowd enjoying a raucous blend of Latino dance and hypnotic techno. Thurs–Sat from 9pm.

**Latinos** Madero 14. Boisterous bar and *discoteca* playing a variety of live and recorded music, from salsa and reggae to jazz and rock. Mon–Sat 8pm–3.30am.

**Makia** Andador Eclesiástico 2, at the corner of Madero and the plaza. Fashionable, dimly lit bar and club, with a good mix of locals and travellers. Thurs–Sat from 9pm.

**Tequila Zoo Karaoke Bar** María Adelina Flores 2, in lobby of *Posada Diego de Mazariegos*. Don't let the karaoke put you off – this cosy bar offers 120 different kinds of tequila (there can't be many more, surely!) and gets fairly lively at the weekends. Mon–Sat 4pm–2am, Sun 4pm–11pm.

## Listings

**Airlines** Mexicana has an office at Belisario Domínguez 2-B ☎967/678-9309 (Mon–Sat 9am–8pm, Sun 10am–3pm).

**Banks and exchange** Several bank branches (with ATMs) surround the zócalo; most will exchange dollars and give cash advances

### Moving on from San Cristóbal

**First-class buses** for destinations in the state and throughout the Yucatán leave from the OCC terminal at the end of Insurgentes, with **second-class** buses departing either side – AXA (across the highway), runs first- and second-class buses to similar destinations. You can save time by buying first-class tickets from the Ticket Bus office (Mon–Sat 7am–11pm, Sun 9am–5pm; cash only; ☎967/678-0921) at Real de Guadalupe 5, not far from the plaza. **Tuxtla Gutiérrez** (1hr 30min) is served frequently by first-class buses, and *combis* also tout for customers outside the bus stations on the main highway – for **Chiapa de Corzo** they'll drop you on the main highway, where you have to catch a local bus into town. **Villahermosa** (7hr) is not so well served, though there are a two daily first-class services daily with OCC; it's easier to get any bus to Tuxtla and change there. For **Palenque** (5hr), there are nine daily first- and second-class departures. All buses going to Palenque call at **Ocosingo** (2hr 30min), and in addition there's ample passenger-van traffic: just go to the highway and someone will call out to you. OCC has the most comfortable service to **Ciudad Cuauhtémoc** (3hr 30min; all via Comitán) on the Guatemalan border, and on the highway you'll also find any number of *combis* to **Comitán** (daily 4am–9pm). There are five daily services to **Tapachula** and there are two overnight services for Oaxaca (5pm & 10pm; 12hr); for more choice to the latter head to Tuxtla. The first-class companies all have overnight services to Mexico City (5 daily; 19hr). For Campeche (10hr) and Mérida (13hr), there's a first-class service at 6.30pm. Buses for the Yucatán coast via Chetumal (10hr), where you can catch connections to Belize, and all major stops to Cancún (16hr) depart at 12.15pm, 2.30pm and 3.50pm. Bochil buses depart from north of the market area.

Heading to Tuxtla's **airport** (the nearest in operation), you can take a direct bus organized by tour agencies (daily 9am): see Astur Viajes (☎967/678-3917) in the *portales* on the east side of the plaza. Agencies such as Trotamundos, Real de Guadalupe 26 (☎967/678-7021; English spoken) sometimes arrange buses into **Guatemala** for reasonable rates (Quetzaltenango for M$400) – worth asking about, as this will save loads of time.

(mornings only). HSBC is at Mazariegos 6. You'll get much quicker exchange, however, at good rates from the casa de cambio at Real de Guadalupe 12-A (Mon–Sat 9am–2pm & 4–8pm, Sun 9am–1pm); it changes most major currencies and usually has Guatemalan quetzales.

**Bike rental** An enjoyable way to get out to the surrounding villages. A good place to rent bikes is at the Librería Chilam Balam (see below): M$10/hr (minimum 5hr) or M$125 for guided tours. Los Pingüinos, Ecuador 4-B (Ⓣ967/678-0202 Ⓦwww.bikemexico.com), also has well-maintained bikes for M$20/hr, and takes tours to local attractions from 8.15am daily. German and English spoken.

**Books** Librería Chilam Balam (daily 9am–8pm), at General Utrilla 33 near Dr Navarro, has the best selection, including academic and educational books; also guides and topographic maps of Chiapas. Librería La Pared, Hidalgo 2, opposite the tourist office (Tues–Sat 10am–2pm & 4–8pm, Sun noon–2pm & 4–8pm), has new guidebooks (including *Rough Guides*) and the largest selection of new and secondhand books in English and other languages in southern Mexico; you can rent, trade or buy. Other useful stores are Librería Soluna, Real de Guadalupe 13-B (daily 9am–8pm), with a fair choice of books, including guides; and Casa Na-Bolom, Vicente Guerrero 33, which has an excellent library (daily 10am–2pm; free) and sells some books and maps of the Lacandón forest.

**Immigration office** Ⓣ967/678-7910. The office itself (Mon–Fri 9am–3pm) is a couple of kilometres west of the centre, at the junction of the Carretera Panamericana and Diagonal Centenario.

**Internet access** It's scarcely possible to walk a block in the centre without coming across a place. Most open 7–9am and close around 10pm – the price is usually M$10/hr. Try Fast Net, Real de Guadalupe 15-D, or Caféteria del Centro, at no. 7.

**Laundry** Lavandería Las Estrellas, Real de Guadalupe 75 (Mon–Sat 6am–9pm; M$15/kilo); Lavandería La Rapidita, Insurgentes 9 (Mon–Sat 8.30am–8pm; M$45/3 kilos); and the lavandería at Belisario Domínguez 5-B (Mon–Sat 8am–8pm; M$15/kilo).

**Post office** Corner of Ignacio Allende and Diego Mazariegos, three blocks southwest of the zócalo (Mon–Fri 8.30am–7pm, Sat 9am–1pm); in addition, most hotels have Mexipost boxes, and many of the larger ones sell stamps.

**Spanish courses** Centro Bilingüe, in Centro Cultural El Puente, Real de Guadalupe 55 (Ⓣ967/678-3723, Ⓦwww.elpuenteweb.com), is the longest-established language school in San Cristóbal; they also have courses in Maya. Centro de Lenguas Jovel, María Adelina Flores 21 (Ⓣ967/678-4069, Ⓦwww.institutojovel.com), is also recommended (Mon–Fri 8.30am–2pm & 4–8pm, Sat 9am–2pm). Both can arrange accommodation with local families.

**Telephones** Librería La Pared, Hidalgo 2, across from the tourist office (Tues–Sat 10am–2pm & 4–8pm, Sun noon–2pm & 4–8pm), has the cheapest long-distance and international rates, at M$15/min to North America and M$20 to Europe. There are Ladatel phones on the plaza, under the arches of the Palacio Municipal, and in the OCC terminal, but you need a phonecard to operate them.

**Travel agencies and tours** San Cristóbal has dozens of tour agencies, most doing the same four standard tours to local villages, the Sumidero Canyon, Lagos de Montebello and Palenque and Agua Azul. You can also arrange tours further afield to Bonampak and Yaxchilán. Horse-riding tours can be arranged at Café del Centro, Real de Guadalupe 15-B, leaving at 9am and 1pm (Ⓣ967/698273; M$100 to Chamula). One of the best local tour agencies is OTISA, Real de Guadalupe 3-C (Ⓣ967/678-1933, Ⓔotisa@otisatravel.com). For local and national adventure tours, try Viajes Pakal, Cuauhtémoc 6 (Ⓣ967/678-2818, Ⓦwww.pakal.com.mx). City tours are provided by El Coleto, a bus which leaves with at least five people (10am–1pm & 4–7pm) from outside the Mercado de Artesanías on Insurgentes.

## Around San Cristóbal: Grutas de Rancho Nuevo, El Arcotete and Moxviquil

Some organized outings go to the popular **Grutas de Rancho Nuevo** (daily 9am–5.30pm; M$10), an enormous cavern extending deep into a mountain about 10km to the southeast of San Cristóbal. It's easy enough to visit it by bus or bike, though, since they're well signed, just off the main road to Comitán. A track leads for about 1km from the road through a pine-forested park with hiking trails often used by the army. By **bike**, it's about a fifty-minute ride, uphill most of the way from San Cristóbal. There's an average restaurant here for refreshment and you can hire horses for about M$50 per hour. Although the cave system is quite extensive, only 400m of pathway are open to the public.

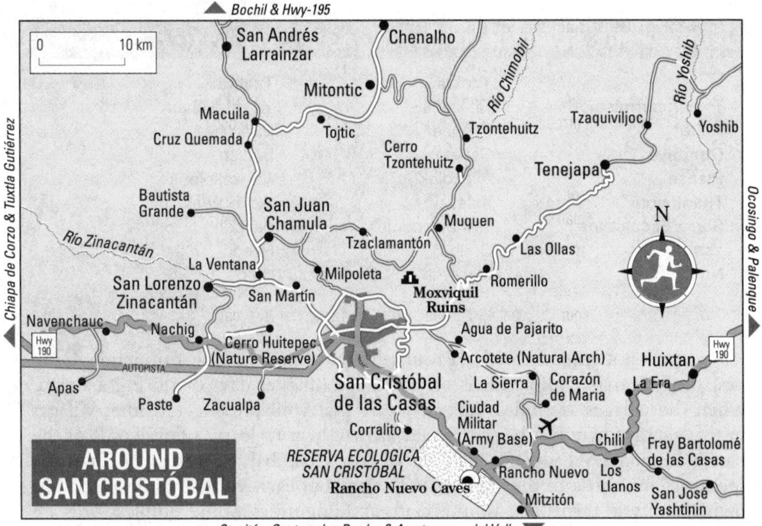


Another favourite trip is to **El Arcotete**, a natural limestone arch that forms a bridge over a river. To get there, follow Real de Guadalupe out of town, past the Guadalupe church, where it becomes the road to Tenejapa; El Arcotete is down a signed track to the right about 3.5km past the church.

**Moxviquil**, a completely deserted and ruined Maya ceremonial site, is a pleasant excursion of a few hours on foot from San Cristóbal; it's best, however, to study the plans at the Casa Na-Bolom first (see p.723), as all you can see when you get there are piles of rough limestone – in fact, the tourist office will tell you there's nothing to see at all. To reach the site, find Avenida Yajalon, a few blocks east of Santo Domingo, and follow it north to the end (about 30min) at the foot of tree-covered hills, in a little settlement called Ojo de Agua. Head for the highest buildings you can see, that is, two timber shacks with red roofs. The tracks are at times indistinct as you clamber over the rocks, but after about 300m a lovely side valley suitable for camping opens up on your left. The main path veers gradually to the right, becoming quite wide and leading up through a high basin ringed by pine forest. After 3km you reach the village of Pozeula; the ruins are ahead of you across a valley, built on top of and into the sides of a hill.

## Chamula and Zinacantán

Almost everyone that stays in San Cristóbal visits the Tzotzil Maya villages of **SAN JUAN CHAMULA** and **SAN LORENZO DE ZINACANTÁN**, the vast majority on organized tours. Though no longer pristine indigenous enclaves, both villages have retained much of their unique cultural identity, many of their traditions (especially in Chamula) a blend of traditional animist belief and Catholicism. The real highlight is the church at Chamula, one of the most moving sights in Mexico. Even if you don't visit on a tour, you'll inevitably feel a sense of intrusion here – all visits should be treated with extreme sensitivity, and definitely ask permission before taking photographs (be willing to pay for the privilege). Never take photos inside the churches.

## Useful words in Tzotzil and Tzeltal

| | Tzotzil | Tzeltal |
|---|---|---|
| **To ask permission** | Chíkhelav | Ya shka shan |
| **Hello** | Kúshee | Bish chee |
| **Goodbye** | Batkun | Bónish |
| **Please** | Avokoluk | Há wokolook |
| **Thank you** | Kalaval | Wókolawal |
| **Sorry/Excuse me** | Tsik bunjoomul | Pasbón |
| **Yes** | Chabal | Heech |
| **No** | Moo yuk | Ho'o |

If you do not intend to take a tour (though doing so is recommended), the best time to make your visit is on a Sunday (market day) or during a **fiesta**, when the villages are full of life. Be aware that your presence at other villages in the vicinity may not be welcomed. It may help to learn a few words of the native language. Villages to the west of San Cristóbal are generally **Tzotzil**-speaking, and those to the east speak **Tzeltal**, but each village has developed its own identity in terms of costume, crafts and linguistics. Some simple words are given in the box above.

### Transport and tours

Inexpensive *combis* leave frequently for Chamula, Zinacantán and other villages from Edgar Robledo, just north of the market in San Cristóbal. Though an **organized tour** (about M$140 per person) can feel a little rushed and contrived, it's usually easier, more informative and perhaps less culturally invasive to take one. Tours depart at 9.30am, go to both villages and return to San Cristóbal around 1.30pm (see "Listings", p.726, for recommendations). There is often little difference between companies (resources are often pooled) and prices tend to be standardized (hotels will charge more), with many agencies offering English-speaking guides.

### San Juan Chamula

**SAN JUAN CHAMULA** (usually referred to as just Chamula) is the closest indigenous village to San Cristóbal (10km), as well as the most frequently visited. Though thousands of residents have been expelled in recent decades for converting to Protestant faiths (most now live in shanty towns around Cristóbal), Chamula is still more like a small town than a village, with a population of 15,000 and over 90,000 in the surrounding municipality. Over the years it's been far more against change than Zinacantán, first putting up fierce resistance to the Spanish from 1524 to 1528, then from 1867 to 1870 acting as the centre of a rebellion described as the second "Caste War".

Traditional practices are maintained here, especially in religion – a visit to the 200-year-old **Iglesia de San Juan Bautista** (the first church burnt down) can be a humbling and moving experience. Before you enter, buy a ticket (M$15) from the "tourist office" in the Palacio Municipal, to the right-hand side of the plaza as you face the church. The inside is glorious, the floor covered with pine needles and the light of a thousand candles casting an eerie glow. Lining the walls are statues of the saints adorned with offerings of clothes, food and mirrors (thought to aid communication with the laity), while above the altar, San Juan, patron saint of the village, takes pride of place. The customs practised inside the church, incorporating aspects of Christian and Maya beliefs, are unique – each villager prays by clearing an area of pine needles and arranging a "message" in candles, and rituals frequently involve tearful chanting and/or singing. There are no priests, Masses or marriages here, only baptisms, and the church is open 24 hours, in part reflecting its important role as a place of healing for the sick – Tuesdays and Fridays are particularly special days for prayer.

During the annual Kinta Jimultik, the **carnival** (five days in Feb/March), representatives of all the villages in the area attend in traditional dress, marching in circles around the church and up to strategically placed crosses on the hillsides for the first four days. On the final day, which coincides with the last of the five ill-fated days of the Maya calendar, purification rites and fire-walking ceremonies take place in the plaza.

Admission to the church also grants entry to the **Museo Etnográfico** (daily 8am–7pm), behind the Palacio Municipal. Rooms with mud and straw walls

△ Iglesia de San Juan Bautista, San Juan Chamula

display artefacts of village life, musical instruments and costumes from Chamula and other villages. Remember that taking **photographs** is expressly forbidden and no foreign visitors are admitted to the church after 7pm.

### San Lorenzo Zinacantán

An easy seven-kilometre walk from Chamula and surrounded by steep, pine-forested hills, **ZINACANTÁN**, 12km from Cristóbal, is much more open than its neighbour. Far more Western in their outlook, the locals here have embraced flowers as an export crop and the hillsides are dotted with greenhouses (disappointingly, it's rare to see any flowers for sale in the village). However, traditional practices have not completely disappeared. Some older men still wear the rose-pink ponchos with silver threads (called *pok 'ul*), decorated with tassels and embroidered flowers, and the same colours and designs feature in the women's costumes. Tours include a visit to a typical house, where you'll see the family altar, women weaving beautiful table mats decorated with large embroidered flowers and the house fire where tortillas are prepared. You might also be invited to taste *posh*, the local spirit, made from sugarcane and sometimes flavoured with fruit or cinnamon. Zinacantán also has a museum, the **Museo Ik'al Ojov** ("Our Great Lord"), which has displays of costumes from different hierarchical groups and a tableau of a house interior (daily 8.30am–5pm; donation requested). The museum is a short walk downhill from the main plaza (follow the signs) and the **Iglesia de San Lorenzo**. Note that if you are visiting independently and want to visit the church, you must pay M$15 at the "Caseta de Turismo" outside the main entrance – do not take photos inside or even in the churchyard.

## San Cristóbal to Guatemala: Comitán and Montebello

Beyond San Cristóbal, the Panamerican Highway continues to the border with Guatemala through some of Chiapas's most scintillating scenery. Thirty-seven kilometres from Cristóbal it passes **Amatenango del Valle**, a Tzeltal-speaking village with a reputation for good unglazed pottery and a favourite stop for tour companies. Here, the pottery is prepared by the traditional pre-Hispanic method of building the fire around the piece, rather than placing it in an oven. **Comitán de Domínguez** (or just Comitán) is the only place of any size in this area – a jumping-off point not only for the **Guatemalan border** and for the **Parque Nacional Lagos de Montebello**, but for the Classic-period Maya site of **Tenam Puente**.

### Comitán

One of the most attractive colonial towns in Chiapas, **COMITÁN** is 88km from Cristóbal and strategically poised on a rocky hillside, surrounded by countryside in which wild orchids bloom. Once a major Maya population centre (the ruins of Bonampak and Yaxchilán, even Palenque, are not far, as the parrot flies), Comitán was originally known as Balún Canán ("Nine Stars", or "Guardians"), but was renamed Comitán ("Place of Potters" in Nahuatl) when it came under Aztec control. The final place of any note before the border (Ciudad Cuauhtémoc is no more than a customs and immigration post with a collection of shacks), today Comitán is a market and supply centre for the surrounding agricultural area populated primarily by Tzotziles and Tzeltales, a

good place to rest if you've some hard travelling through the Lacandón forest or into Guatemala ahead of you. At 1560m, it's not as high as Cristóbal but can still be milder than the sweltering lowlands.

A statue of Dr Belisario Domínguez, the city's most important historical figure, marks the gateway to Comitán and as you pass through, several more statues representing aspects of life of the various states of Mexico are placed at intervals along the central reservation of the highway.

## Arrival and information

Comitán's **airport** is currently closed, and is likely to remain that way. **Buses** stop along the Panamerican Highway (known as Blv Dr Belisario Domínguez), the hectic commercial heart of the town, but a long six or seven blocks from the historic centre. Only OCC has a terminal; all the others just pull in at the roadside. To walk to the centre, turn left out of the terminal, cross the highway, then go right along 1a Calle Sur Pte after about three blocks. The zócalo is a further seven blocks east. A booth in the terminal will call a **taxi** if required, though they are otherwise easy to find. Any journey within the city boundary costs about M$18.

The helpful **tourist office** (Mon–Fri 8am–7pm, Sat 8am–4pm; Ⓣ963/632-4047, Ⓦwww.visitacomitan.com) is on the east side of the plaza at no. 6, just along from the Palacio Municipal and within the Pasaje Morales. If you are moving on to Guatemala and need a visa, the **Guatemalan consulate** is at 1a Calle Sur Pte 26, on the corner of 2a Avenida Poniente Sur, a couple of blocks southwest of the zócalo (Mon–Fri 9am–5pm; Ⓣ& Ⓕ963/632-2979). Note that many shops and offices in Comitán observe the afternoon siesta, and much of the town shuts down between 2 and 5pm.

## Accommodation

Comitán has plenty of good-value **hotels** in all price ranges; those listed on p.732 are close to the centre. The cheapest places are just west of the zócalo, but of varying standards; we've noted the best of them. Nights here are much cooler than days, so you'll need at least one blanket.

**Hospedaje San Francisco** 1a Av Ote Nte 13 ⓣ963/632-0194, ⓔsamuel22f@prodigy.net.mx. Best of the budget options, with en-suite bathrooms and some rooms with TV. Rooms on the front courtyard are bigger and brighter. ❷

**Hotel del Virrey** Av Central Nte 13 ⓣ963/632-1811. This attractive colonial hotel has bright rooms with en-suite bathrooms, laundry service and cable TV, all arranged around a pleasant flower-filled courtyard. ❺

**Hotel Delfín** Av Central Sur 21-A, right on the plaza ⓣ963/632-0013. Pleasant, colourful and spacious, with large en-suite rooms and cable TV. There's safe parking and a quiet, flowery courtyard at the back. ❹

**Hotel Internacional** Av Central Sur 16 ⓣ963/632-0110. Smart, modern hotel with comfortable rooms, cable TV, car park and a good restaurant, *Girasoles.* ❺

**Hotel Plaza Tenam** Av Central Nte, opposite *Hotel del Virrey* ⓣ963/632-0436. One of the newer hotels in the area, with clean, modern rooms but a bit less character than the older places – not bad value though, for cable TV and telephone. ❹

**Posada El Castellano** 3a C Nte Pte 12, a couple of blocks north of the plaza ⓣ963/632-3347, ⓦwww.posadaelcastellano.com.mx. Friendly and rustic option, with a quiet courtyard containing a fountain and a horse cart laden with flowers. En-suite rooms come with telephone and cable TV, and there's a charming restaurant. ❺

## The Town

Comitán's spacious, highly manicured **zócalo** is arranged on several levels around a central bandstand. Surrounding it are a number of beautiful colonial buildings, notably the whitewashed **Palacio Municipal**, which dominates the north side, and the seventeenth-century **Templo de Santo Domingo** to the east, worth a peek for its exposed Neoclassical stone facade, spacious nave, timbered ceiling and marble-covered altar. The *portales* on the south side of the square, painted with an attractive orange and brown pattern, are teeming with souvenir shops, while to the west several restaurants have tables under the arches. On the plaza's southeast corner, the **Centro Cultural Rosario Castellanos** (Mon–Fri 8am–5pm; free), named after the respected poet and author, who grew up nearby, has a pretty courtyard featuring a mural depicting the city's history. On the same block, just off the plaza, the splendid little **Museo de Arqueología** (Tues–Sun 9am–6pm; free) offers a chronology of local Maya sites through displays of jewellery and pottery, as well as some children's skulls deliberately deformed for ceremonial purposes.

One block south of the zócalo, along Avenida Central Sur, is the most evocative of the city's museums, the **Casa Museo Belisario Domínguez** (Mon–Sat 10am–6.45pm, Sun 9am–12.45pm; M$5), once the home of the local doctor and politician who was assassinated in 1913 for his outspoken opposition to Huerta's usurpation of the presidency. Though it's packed with memorabilia (including a solemn display of the famous anti-Huerta speech that precipitated his murder), it's hard to appreciate unless you understand Spanish. Most interesting is the pharmacy, its shelves lined with diverse lotions and potions, where he would administer free treatment to the poor. A block further south, the **Museo de Arte Hermíla Domínguez de Castellanos** (Tues–Sat 10am–6pm, Sun 9am–12.45pm; M$5) is named after his wife, and houses a handsome collection of largely modern artworks by Mexican artists, many of them strikingly colourful and vibrant.

Just around the corner, the twin-towered **Templo de San José**, skirted with white and gold and featuring a blend of Gothic and Baroque architecture, is the most unusual of the city's churches. Its interior is particularly attractive, with tiled floors and stained-glass windows. Also worth seeking out is the Neoclassical **Templo de San Caralampio**, constructed in 1852 with a rich pink stucco facade, two blocks east of the plaza along 1a Calle Norte Pte, and dedicated to a martyr who became an object of devotion after cholera and smallpox epidemics decimated the town in the nineteenth century. A fiesta in his name is celebrated in mid-February.

## Eating and drinking

Apart from in the hotels, most of the best **places to eat** in Comitán are on the plaza. For really good-value Mexican food served in clean surroundings, try *Helen's Enrique*, which has tables under the arches and gets going around 9am (English menu, breakfasts from M$35), or *La Apujarra* for great pizzas and *licuados*; both are on the west side of the square. The *Café Quiptic*, on the east side next to Santo Domingo, is the smartest place to eat, serving hearty breakfasts under the stone arches from 8am, with very good coffee. Try the *desayuno Chiapanesco*, a breakfast of spicy local tamales. *La Michoacana* is the cheapest diner on the zócalo (tacos from M$5, tortas M$15), on its south side. The **market**, one block east of the zócalo, is filled with fruit stands and has some very good *comedores*.

Finally, if you're in the mood for a drink you should try **comiteco**, a rich-tasting local corn spirit flavoured with fruits (a bit like Schnappes) that's virtually unobtainable elsewhere. It's smoother than tequila, and a good deal cheaper. Most places will serve it (even if it's not on the menu) for around M$30 for a large glass, and shops sell small bottles for M$12, but the best place to buy some is *Comiteco Nueve Estrellas* (daily 9.30am–3pm, 5–9pm) on 1a Avenida Poniente Sur, near 2a Calle Sur Pte, where high-quality bottles go from M$60 and up.

## Nightlife

Comitán has a lively **nightlife** scene, with disco bars dotted around town, most of which play the standard mix of pop, salsa and dance music. Among the more popular spots is *La Jima*, a block south of the zócalo on Avenida Central Sur, which opens at 9pm Thursday to Saturday and hosts boisterous theme nights. *Jarro Café*, two blocks northwest of the plaza along 1a Avenida Poniente Nte, transforms from a quiet coffee bar by day to a rock hangout, complete with running water inside and discount drinks (Wed & Thurs), at night, while *Matisse*, opposite at no. 16, is a more stylish restaurant with

### Moving on from Comitán

**First-class buses** depart the OCC terminal regularly for **Tuxtla** and **San Cristóbal**, and there is also one ADO GL bus to Tuxtla and on to Mexico City at 3pm, and to Cristóbal at 12.30pm. There are four buses daily over the mountains to **Tapachula**, and a couple to **Palenque** (2pm & 9.15pm). Buses to **Ciudad Cuauhtémoc** on the border leave three times daily, but it's cheaper and more convenient to take the Alfa y Omega *combi* from Blv Dr Belisario Domínguez, opposite 1a Calle Sur Pte and the Transportes Balun Canan *combi* terminal, for San Cristóbal. Take the latter service for **Amatenango del Valle** – buses run from 5am to 9pm. Transportes Francisco Sarabia, on 3a Avenida Poniente Sur (between C Central Pte and 1a C Sur Pte) runs an hourly *combi* service from its ramshackle terminal to **Tenam Puente** (on the half-hour).

For the **Lagos de Montebello** and the Frontier Highway, take **combis** run by Transportes Lagos de Montebello from their terminal on 2a Avenida Poniente Sur, between calles 2 and 3 Sur Pte, about three blocks southwest of the plaza. Buses all the way to Palenque via **Benemérito** and **San Javier** (for Bonampak) start at 4am, leaving once every hour until 9.30am and take around ten hours – you might find it hard to get a bus that far later in the day. Buses to the lakes are more frequent, with services to Laguna Bosque Azul, Tziscao, Maravillas and Ixcán leaving around every thirty minutes throughout the day from 3am. Transportes Tzoyol runs buses to **Amititlán** (3hr; for boats to Laguna Miramar) from its small terminal 3km from the centre along 4a Avenida Poniente Sur, near 13a Calle Sur Pte, from 4am to 2pm.

appropriately post-Impressionist art on the walls – a fitting location for evening cocktails. Overlooking the plaza opposite San Caralampio, *Los Portales del León* opens at 8pm most nights, operating as an upmarket cantina and grill. *La Casa de Abajo*, Central Pte 31, is a smart bar in rustic surroundings. **Free** entertainment is supplied in the form of live marimba, played in the zócalo most Thursdays and Sundays from 7pm.

### Listings

**Banks and exchange** Bancomer (Mon–Fri 8.30am–4pm), on the zócalo, is useful for currency exchange and dollar cash advances, and also has an ATM. HSBC is at 2a C Sur Pte 7, just down from the zócalo.

**Internet access** Widely available throughout the city. Ciber@dictos (daily 9am–9pm; M$10/hr), at the end of pedestrianized Pasaje Morales on the north side of the plaza, has a fast connection, but there are plenty of other options on and around the plaza, including the Holanda Store on Av Central Norte, open the same hours.

**Post office** One and a half blocks south of the zócalo on Av Central Sur (Mon–Fri 8am–6pm, Sat 9am–5pm, Sun 9am–1pm).

**Tours** The Tranía Turistíco is a special tourist bus that takes in all the sights, leaving from the zócalo outside Santo Domingo six times a day (9am–8pm: M$30), but only with a minimum of five people.

**Travel agents** Viajes Tenam, Pasaje Morales 8-A (Ⓣ963/632-1654), can arrange domestic and international flights, as well as organize day trips to local attractions such as El Chiflón, a series of massive waterfalls 40km southwest of the town.

## Tenam Puente

With the Maya ruins of Junchavín, northwest of Comitán's zócalo, closed after a series of violent attacks on visitors, the much larger **Tenam Puente** (daily 9am–4pm; M$24), 14km to the south, is the now the only accessible historic site close to the city. Buses (see box, p.733) terminate in front of the ruins, 5km off the main road. A path leads up past the guard's hut and into a meadow with a huge stone terrace. The site, discovered by Frans Blom in 1925, marks a settlement which was at its peak from 600 to 900 AD and finally abandoned around 1200 AD. The most important group of ruins, the acropolis, has three ball-courts and a twenty-metre-high pyramid that affords magnificent views of the Comitán valley. To get to it, keep climbing the stone terraces until you reach the highest point.

## Parque Nacional Lagos de Montebello

The **Parque Nacional Lagos de Montebello** lies 50km southeast of Comitán, along the border with Guatemala. The park encompasses beautiful wooded country in which there are more than fifty lakes, sixteen of them very large, and many of them with small restaurants providing local food and basic cabañas. The combination of forest and water is reminiscent of Scotland or Maine, with miles of hiking potential; for the less energetic, roadside viewpoints provide glimpses of many lakes, lent different tints by natural mineral deposits and the angle of the sun. The lakes themselves are actually a series of cenotes (sinkholes) formed by the erosion of limestone over millions of years. You could see quite a bit of the park in a long day trip – buses cover the route all day from 3am, with the last bus leaving the park entrance around 7.30pm – but to really enjoy it, and to visit the small but spectacular **ruins of Chinkultic**, you're better off staying in or near the park.

The **Carretera Fronteriza** – the Frontier Highway (Hwy-307) – passes right through the national park, splitting from the Panamerican Highway 16km from Comitán at the village of La Trinitaria, from where the park entrance is a further 36km. The road roughly follows the line of the Guatemalan border and is paved all the way to Palenque. In the recent past, there were frequent **army checkpoints** along this road – you may still be asked for your passport at any time. The soldiers are invariably polite, but make sure your tourist card is valid.

### The road to the park

The most comfortable of the several **places to stay** along the road to the park is the *Museo Parador y Hotel Santa María* (Ⓣ967/678-0988, Ⓦwww.paradorsantamaria.com.mx; ❽), 22km from the La Trinitaria junction, then 1.3km along a dirt track on the right. A former hacienda, it's a lovely place, furnished with antiques and oil paintings and steeped in colonial history. There's hot water and electricity but rooms are also lit with oil lamps. A small chapel (daily 9am–6pm; M$20) in the grounds is filled with religious paintings and other ecclesiastical art from the seventeenth century.

At Km 31 on the Frontier Highway, a two-kilometre track leads off to the left to the Classic-period Maya ruins of **Chinkultic** (daily 9am–5pm; M$30). So far only a relatively small proportion of the site has been cleared and restored, but it's well worth a visit if only for the dramatic setting. Climb the first large mound as you enter the site, and you're rewarded with a view of a small lake, with fields of maize beyond and forested mountain ridges in the background. Birds, butterflies, and dragonflies abound, and small lizards dart at every step. A ball-court and several stelae have been uncovered, but the highlight is undoubtedly the view from the top of the tallest structure, **El Mirador**. Set on top of a steep hill, with rugged cliffs dropping straight down to a cenote, the temple occupies a commanding position; peaceful now, this was clearly an important hub in ancient times.

Back on the Frontier Highway, you'll find a cluster of **budget accommodation** on the left side at Km 32 – buses and *combis* stop right outside. First, just a kilometre or so past the turning for Chinkultic, there's the *Hospedaje and Restaurant La Orquídea* (❶), better known simply as *Doña María's*. Here, half a dozen simple cabins with electricity and shared cold showers sit among the pines. It's a very friendly place, run by Doña María Domínguez, who gave help to Guatemalan refugees who fled the massacres across the border in the 1980s. Next door, and a step above in comfort, *El Pino Feliz* (Ⓣ963/102-1089; ❶) has eight rooms in wooden cabins with shared, hot-water showers, and serves home-cooked meals (M$30).

### Park practicalities

The park entrance is at Km 36, with a ticket booth 1km further on (daily 9am–5pm; M$10 per person; buses will stop to let you pay), but most *combis* continue on to **Laguna Bosque Azul**, 3km left off the main highway just beyond the booth and at the heart of a series of pristine lakes. Take the dirt track beyond the car park a few hundred metres before reaching a fork. The left-hand path, signposted "Gruta San Rafael del Arco", heads into the jungle through an exquisitely forested gorge and eventually to a massive limestone arch over a river. From here the track ends up at a cave in the cliff face. On the northwest side of Bosque Azul you can rent basic **cabañas** at *Doña Josefa* (Ⓣ963/632-5971; ❶) or hire scrawny horses at the car park from local children for M$50 per person.

Buses headed for destinations further along the Frontier Highway continue from the park entrance, past turnings for several other lakes, to **Laguna Tziscao**, 9km on, where there is another checkpoint (M$5) and a tiny settlement 2km off the main highway, close to the Guatemalan border. On the lake's edge, the *Restaurant Tziscao* rents simple wooden **cabañas** (Ⓣ963/633-5244; ❶); *balsas* (**rafts**) are also available to rent for around M$50 an hour. The last buses back to Comitán from here leave at around 5pm.

### The Frontier Highway east

The main road continues through mountains with spectacular views and precipitous drops on its way around the border to Palenque. The largest settlement along the road beyond the lakes is **Las Maravillas de Tenejapa**, a pretty village with a restaurant but no accommodation, about two hours from Lake Tziscao. Beyond Maravillas the road climbs a steep limestone ridge and passes through an impressive tunnel before dropping down to the village of **Ixcán**, at the confluence of the Ixcán and Jatatė rivers. Beyond Ixcán the highway crosses the Río Ixcán on a new bridge high above the river and continues to **Benemérito** (3hr; see p.752) and **Palenque** (a further four hours), making it possible to approach Bonampak (see p.749) and Yaxchilán (see p.751) from this direction. Be aware that this route traverses the "conflict zone" (see box, p.700) where the Zapatistas, paramilitaries and Mexican army frequently clashed during the height of the rebellion: though things have been a lot quieter in recent years, you may well be stopped by any of them and questioned about your intentions.



## Ciudad Cuauhtémoc and the Guatemalan border

A visit to the Lagos de Montebello is a good introduction to the landscapes of Guatemala, but if you want to see the real thing up close, it's only another 60km or so from the La Trinitaria junction (served by plenty of passing buses) to the **Mexican border post** at **CIUDAD CUAUHTÉMOC**. There's nothing here but a few houses, the immigration post, a restaurant and the OCC bus station; the two hotels are not recommended.

The **Guatemalan border post** is at **La Mesilla**, a three-kilometre taxi ride away. As always, it's best to cross in daylight – you may not be able to get your passport stamped after 8pm. La Mesilla border post was once notorious for exacting illegal charges from tourists, though things are much improved. **Buses** onwards to Huehuetenango (2hr; US$1.50) and Quezaltenango (3hr 30min; US$4) wait just over the border, leaving at least every hour between 6am and 5pm. The **moneychangers** will give you reasonable rates for travellers' cheques or dollars, but not as good for pesos. **Getting into Mexico** is easy: the Mexican tourist card will be issued free, and vans or buses will be waiting to take you to **Comitán**.

# San Cristóbal to Palenque

If you're heading from San Cristóbal to the Yucatán, the best route takes you 203km to **Palenque** (5hr), via **Ocosingo** (88km), along Hwy-186 and then Hwy-199, a good paved road that's frequently used by buses and *colectivos*. It's an impressive and beautiful journey, as the road winds around the spectacular mountain valleys, lush with greenery, passing through several villages loyal to the Zapatistas. It's worth making a pit-stop at Ocosingo, the starting point for excursions to the **Toniná ruins** or light-aircraft trips to mesmerizing **Laguna Miramar**, deep in the pristine forests of the **Montes Azules Biosphere Reserve**. Beyond Ocosingo the road passes the pretty waterfalls at **Agua Azul**, though in practice it's easier to visit these from Palenque. If you're travelling by bus you won't have any problems, but by car or bicycle locals will occasionally try and stop you with makeshift tolls (usually under the pretext of collecting for the local church), signified by rope held across the road – you are not obliged to pay, and if you keep driving the rope will be dropped at the last minute. If you stop, they can get aggressive if you refuse to make a "donation". It's best to keep off the road at night.

## Ocosingo

**OCOSINGO**, its streets lined with single-storey, red-tiled houses and its air thick with the scent of wood smoke, makes a good place to escape the tourist crowds of San Cristóbal or Palenque. The town has stayed close to its country roots, with plenty of farmers in cowboy hats in from their ranches and local women selling *maiz* from great bubbling vats. It's also a base for visiting the captivating Maya site of Toniná. Central to town life is the **zócalo**, surrounded by *portales*, a big old country church on the east side and the *ayuntamiento*, with its thoroughly incongruous tinted glass, opposite.

**Buses** stop on the main road or at the small OCC terminal nearby. To get to the zócalo turn right out of the terminal and walk back uphill a few blocks until you reach Avenida Central. Turn left and walk down to the plaza, where you'll find pretty much everything you need within a block or two. Local **taxis** charge M$15 for trips anywhere in town.

**Accommodation** options are plentiful. The *Hotel Central* (☎919/673-0024; ❸) is hard to miss on the north side of the plaza, but though all rooms have fans, hot water and cable TV, none has a/c. *Hotel San José*, just off the northeast corner of the plaza along Calle 1 Ote Nte (☎919/673-0039; ❶), is a great budget option, with clean, comfortable rooms, some with cable TV and a/c. The best of the lot, however, is the colourful *Hospedaje Esmeralda* (☎919/673-0014, ⓔinfo@ranchoesmeralda.net), a block north of the plaza on Calle Central Norte, which has both en-suite (❹) and shared-bath rooms (❸). The friendly staff can help you book flights over the ruins (see p.738) from the airfield 3km out of town, or visits to attractions further afield: flights to **Laguna Miramar** cost about M$2500 for four people and include transport from the airfield at San Quintín to the lake and basic cabaña accommodation on the shore; a day trip to **Bonampak** and **Yaxchilán** by air is around M$6500 (for four people).

Several budget **places to eat** surround the square, most serving a standard Mexican menu. *El Campanario*, on the north side at Av Central 2, is one of the best, with an English menu, hearty plates of Mexican classics (breakfasts M$30–40, tortas M$15) and beers from M$12. The striking *El Desván*, on the opposite side of the zócalo, painted pink with green trim, is recommended for its upstairs terrace, and also serves pizza. The **food market**, or *tianguis*, is the highlight of the town, where traditionally dressed indigenous women sell fruit and vegetables and locally produced cheeses, including the round waxy *queso de bola* and the delicious creamy *queso botanero*. To get there turn right at the church for one block, then left along Calle 2 Sur Ote for another four.

There are a couple of **ATMs**, one at Banamex on the plaza, and another at Banco Santander opposite *Hospedaje Esmeralda* on Calle Central Nte. There are a few **Internet** cafés along here as well, including Compu Centro, near the zócalo (daily 9am–2pm & 4–9pm; M$8/hr), and Xanav (9am–2pm & 4–10pm; M$8/hr), which doubles as a travel agent, at no. 40-C.

**Leaving Ocosingo** by road is easy enough until mid-evening, with buses, frequent *combis* and shared taxis to San Cristóbal, and buses and regular *combis* to Palenque. The last Autotransportes Tuxtla-Gutiérrez (ATG) buses in either direction officially leave at 7.30pm – though they're *de paso* and so are likely to be later. OCC services continue after midnight, with buses to San Cristóbal at 1.40am and 6am and Palenque at 3.25am. **Taxis** to Palenque are far more expensive (around M$650), though you might be able to negotiate.

## Toniná

The Classic-period Maya site of **TONINÁ** (daily 9am–5pm; M$33, includes museum entry), some 14km east of Ocosingo, is surprisingly large, though it sees few visitors. In its heyday it controlled vast tracts of modern-day Chiapas and Guatemala, defeating Palenque in the eighth century. It's also the place where the **latest Long Count date**, corresponding to 909 AD, was recorded, and like all the major Maya centres, was abandoned not long after. It centres on the enormous grassy **Gran Plaza**, once surrounded by buildings, and a series of seven artificial terraces on the hillside above it. At the bottom are two restored ball-courts and an overgrown pyramid mound; as you climb the hill, passing corbel-arched entrances to two vaulted rooms on the right, you begin to get an impression of Toniná's vastness. From the top, 80m above the plaza, there are fine views of the surrounding country.

The most striking feature of the site is the enormous **Mural de las Cuatro Eras** (Mural of the Four Eras), on the sixth platform. This amazingly well-preserved stucco codex tells the story of Maya cosmology by following the four suns (or eras of the world) as they were created and destroyed. The worlds are depicted as decapitated heads surrounded by flowers. A grinning, skeletal Lord of Death presents a particularly graphic image as he grasps a defleshed human head. Together, the sixth and seventh terraces feature a total of thirteen temples, including the **Templo del Monstruo de la Tierra** (Temple of the Earth Monster), dedicated to one of the most powerful deities in the Maya pantheon, and sporting the best-preserved roofcomb on the site. Crowning the summit is the **Templo del Espejo Humeante** (Temple of the Smoking Mirror), built by ruler Zots-Choj in the 840s.

In ancient times Toniná was known as "the place of (celestial) captives" and in the absorbing **museum** (Tues–Sun 8am–5pm) near the entrance several carved panels and sculptures portray bound (and sometimes headless) captives. Glyphs on the panels record the place where the prisoners were captured, while those on the loincloths of the captives may tell who they were.

The **road from Ocosingo** to Toniná is traversed by *combis* which leave frequently from the bus station behind the market on 3 Calle Sur Ote, heading either for the site itself or the large army base by the turn-off to the site – look for "Predio" or "Ruinas". A taxi will cost about M$60 one-way. At the entrance to the site the *Restaurant Toniná* serves simple food, cold beer and soft drinks, and also sells quality T-shirts and postcards.

For a spectacular **flight** over the ruins (M$1000 for four people, plus guide) contact Servicios Aéreos de San Cristóbal through the *Hospedaje Esmeralda* (see p.737) or at their office on the street behind the *combi* terminal in Ocosingo (Ⓣ919/673-0188).

## Laguna Miramar

A much more remote excursion from Ocosingo is a visit to **Laguna Miramar**, in the heart of the Lacandón forest. Miramar, at 40km long the largest lake in southeast Mexico, is now part of the enchanting **Montes Azules Biosphere Reserve**, and a visit here enables you to experience the largest surviving area of rainforest in North America. The high-canopy forest is home to abundant wildlife, including howler and spider monkeys, tapirs and jaguars, and there are rivers and caves to explore. There are no settlements on the lakeshore, and no motorboats are allowed. An island in the lake has traces of a fortress, which was a Maya stronghold until it was finally conquered in 1559. It's best to avoid the rainy season (June-Oct).

You can visit Miramar on your own or as a member of an organized group. To **travel independently** takes some time and effort. By far the easiest method of transport is to **fly** to **San Quintín** in a light aircraft from Servicios Aéreos de San Cristóbal, arranged by the *Hospedaje Esmeralda* in Ocosingo (see p.737). Though they prefer to sell packages for around M$2500 (return ticket) for up to four people, you can also contact the airline directly – if they have space they might let you fly one way for M$350. Alternatively, there are several overland options. The most established route for travellers is the bone-shaking six- to seven-hour, 130-kilometre ride from Ocosingo to the *ejido* and major army base of San Quintín (M$75). Pick-up trucks known as *tres toneladas* ply the route, with passengers stuffed in the back, leaving from around 9am to noon every day (once every hour, depending on demand) from the depot behind Ocosingo market on 3 Calle Sur Ote. In theory, the journey is much faster from Comitán, where you first take a frequent *combi* to the small town of Las Margaritas, 16km northwest (M$25), then pick up another *tres toneladas* from there to San Quintín, about three to four hours away. However, this route passes through the Tojolabal community of **La Realidad**, a celebrated Zapatista stronghold, and may lead to extra hassle at military checkpoints in the area – check with the Comitán tourist office, or *Hospedaje Esmeralda*, before trying this route.

Unless your truck is going all the way, once in San Quintín you need to catch a lift or walk the 2km to the *ejido* of **Emiliano Zapata**. When you arrive, if not directed to the relevant person, ask for the *comisario* or *presidente*, either of whom will be able to organize the practicalities, charged per day: M$100 for a guide, M$50 for a porter, M$100 for use of canoe (highly recommended) and around M$30 per person to camp or sleep in hammocks in lakeside palapas. It's still a nine-kilometre hike to the lake from here. Note that although there are a few shops and simple cafeterías in San Quintín, supplies in Zapata are very basic, and it's best to bring your own food.

A more expensive but far more exciting alternative is to take a Transportes Tzoyol *combi* to Amatitlán from Comitán, and arrange a boat (M$900; 3hr) to take you up the Río Jataté to Zapata.

## North to Palenque: Agua Azul and Misol-Há

A series of magnificent **waterfalls** is the chief attraction along the winding mountain road between Ocosingo and Palenque. The dazzling cascades on the Río Shumulhá at **Agua Azul** and the exquisite falls at **Misol-Há** are more easily visited on a day trip from Palenque (see p.740), though it is possible to visit them independently and stay nearby.

### Agua Azul

The impressive waterfalls of **Agua Azul**, in the Parque Nacional Agua Azul, 58km north of Ocosingo and 4km off the main road, are now a major tour-bus destination. The main cascades lie near the car park at the end of the access road, with several smaller but equally appealing rapids stretching for 1km up the river. The whole area is certainly picturesque, though its beauty tends to be exaggerated somewhat and the river near the lower falls is lined by rows of touristy shops and restaurants. Adjust your expectations accordingly, and it still makes for a pleasant trip.

If you come **by bus** (not on a tour), you'll be dropped at the turn-off to the falls on the main highway, where you'll probably have to walk 45 minutes downhill to the waterfall (and at least an hour's sweaty hike back up) – with robberies in the area occurring fairly frequently, it's not a good idea to do this if you're alone. There are two tolls along the road: the first set up by local villagers (M$5) and the second at the official entrance (M$10). From the car park, rows of **restaurants** line the river all the way to the upper falls, serving a fairly standard mix of seafood and Mexican staples, with little to differentiate between them. If you need to stay there's a **campsite** with hammock space and simple **cabañas** (Ⓣ0155/5329-0995 ext 7002; ❷) – ask at the Modulo de Información near the car park – but neither type of accommodation is particularly good value. Make sure to keep a close eye on your belongings, and be warned that **violent attacks** on tourists have occurred away from the busy areas near the lower falls.

To escape the carnival atmosphere at the main falls, walk upstream for 2km and you'll eventually reach an impressive gorge where the Río Shumulhá explodes out of the jungle-covered mountain. At the right time of year, the river is alive with butterflies. Below the main falls, near the car park (and 1km higher up), the swimming is safe – though watch out for signs warning of dangerous currents as there are several tempting but extremely perilous spots, and people drown here every year. Heading north, it's another 64km to Palenque – some tours call at **Agua Clara**, another waterfall 10km from Azul, which is good for swimming but otherwise not as attractive.

### Misol-Há

Only 18km from Palenque, **Misol-Há** (M$10) is a much easier day trip than Agua Azul if travelling by public transport, and in many ways far more pleasant, with none of the slapdash development present at its celebrated neighbour. A 25-metre waterfall provides a stunning backdrop to a pool that's safe for swimming, and a fern-lined trail leads along a ledge behind the cascade – refreshing from the spray and mist even if you don't swim. It's an easy 1.5km walk downhill from the road (though not so much fun in the other direction), and there's inexpensive **accommodation** in some of the country's most beautiful wooden cabañas (Ⓣ0155/5329-0995, Ⓦwww.misol-ha.com.mx; ❹). The cabins, and the **restaurant** catering to tour groups, are owned and run by the San Miguel *ejido*; each cabin has a private bathroom and electricity, and some also have kitchens.

## Palenque

Set in thick jungle buzzing with insects, the ancient Maya ruins of **Palenque** offer a striking contrast to the modern town of the same name, one of the most unattractive in Chiapas. With its traffic-choked highway and uninspiring zócalo, it holds little intrinsic interest to visitors and is best viewed simply as a base for exploring the ruins and the waterfalls in the nearby hills. Alternatively, since there are a number of cabañas near the ruins, you may prefer not to stay in town at all: the Maya city, just 9km to the southwest, is a hauntingly beautiful world apart. Strongly linked to the lost cities of Guatemala, it maintained its own distinctive style, and though it once occupied a vast area, the section that's visible today is

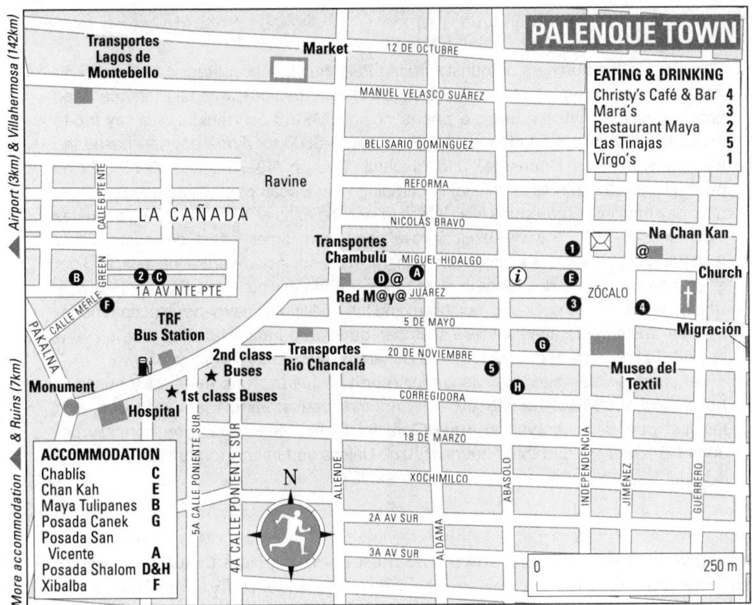


not large – you can see everything in a morning. The **site**, now a national park, was discovered by the priest Antonio Solís in 1790 and occupies the top of an escarpment marking the northern limit of the Chiapas highlands.

## Arrival and information

Arriving at any of the **bus terminals**, you'll be on Juárez, where the highway comes into the modern town of Palenque. If you plan to leave the same day, particularly on a first-class bus, get your onward or return ticket on arrival. Palenque's three main streets, avenidas Juárez, 5 de Mayo and Hidalgo, all run parallel to each other and lead straight up to the **zócalo**, the Parque Central. There is a **tourist office** (Mon–Sat 9am–9pm, Sun 9am–1pm; Ⓣ916/345-0356) in the Plaza de Artesanías on Juárez, a block below the zócalo, but all the staff can do is hand out a street map and some tour leaflets. You'll get better **information** from one of the recommended tour operators (see box, p.742) or from Palenque's own interesting and very informative website, Ⓦwww.palenquemx.com.

## Accommodation

Palenque has seen a massive boom in **hotel** construction in recent years, with the result that you'll have a choice of three different areas in which to stay. Palenque **town** is the most convenient option for onward transport and general amenities, but is fairly drab and unappealing. There are plenty of places on the streets leading from the bus stations to the zócalo, especially Hidalgo (though the traffic noise makes these best avoided) and 20 de Noviembre. **La Cañada**, a new area of development west of the town centre, is far more attractive and generally more upmarket. It's not far from the OCC bus station, but otherwise

## Tours and operators in Palenque

The surge in the numbers of tourists visiting Palenque has encouraged a dozen or so travel agencies to arrange **tours** to the surrounding attractions, with fairly standardized prices to all destinations. **Sample prices** include: M$100 per person for a day trip to **Agua Azul**, **Misol-Há** and the ruins at Palenque; M$600 for a one-day van-based trip to the Maya ruins at **Bonampak** and **Yaxchilán** (see pp.749–751); and M$1000 for an overnight trip to both sites, including camping near Bonampak. Some agencies also offer day trips into **Guatemala** (via Bethel) to visit the ruins at Tikal. Kukulcán, at Juárez 8 (ⓣ916/345-1506, ⓦwww.kukulcantravel.com), sometimes offers discounts. Other than the tours to Bonampak and Yaxchilán, most do not include entrance fees, and not all of them supply guides. Bear in mind that since the paving of the Frontier Highway, which leads to Bonampak and Yaxchilán, and the opening of inexpensive accommodation and restaurants nearby, these sites can be **visited independently**. See p.749 & pp.750–751 for details of how to get to Bonampak and Yaxchilán on your own.

Transportes Chambalú, on Allende just north of Juárez, runs three daily buses to **Agua Azul** and **Misol-Há** (M$100; entry not included) at 9am, 10am and noon, with the first bus also stopping at Agua Clara for 30min. Otherwise, you normally get 30min at Misol-Há and three hours at Azul. Unless you intend to stay the night, this is by far the most convenient way to see the falls.



a long walk from the rest of town. The most inviting places to stay line the **road to the ruins**, with several smart hotels, the deservedly popular travellers' hangout of *El Panchán* and the long-established *Mayabell* **campsite**. Taxis from the OCC bus station to these places should cost no more than M$40, but it's just as easy to flag down one of the many *combis* heading for the ruins (see p.745). Note that some places may reduce rates by as much as fifty percent in the low season.

### In town

**Chan Kah** Juárez 2, on the zócalo ⓣ916/345-0318, ⓦwww.chan-kah.com.mx. The most upmarket hotel in town, under the same ownership as the *Chan Kah Resort Village* near the ruins (see opposite). Some of the comfortable rooms, and the pleasant terrace bar, have the dubious advantage of balconies with views over the garish zócalo. ❻

**Posada Canek** 20 de Noviembre 43 ⓣ916/345-0150. One of several good budget options along this road, and great value if you're travelling alone. Dorms (M$70 per person) and huge double rooms (❸), some with private bath. Luggage storage is available, and there are views of the surrounding hills from the balconies.

**Posada San Vicente** Hidalgo 100-A ⓣ916/345-0856. A remarkably cheap budget option halfway between the zócalo and La Cañada. Rooms are clean and comfortable and have en-suite bathrooms with a fan. Just M$80 for single. ❶

**Posada Shalom** Juárez 156 ⓣ916/345-0944, and Corregidora near 20 de Noviembre ⓣ916/345-2641. Two hotels with the same name, both with clean rooms, cable TV and tiled private bathrooms. Luggage storage and laundry service available. ❸

### La Cañada

**Chablís** Merle Green 7 ⓣ916/345-0870. Large, modern doubles in spacious whitewashed rooms with a/c, cable TV and free Internet (M$25/hr for non-guests). ❹

**Maya Tulipanes** La Cañada 6 ⓣ916/345-0201, ⓦwww.mayatulipanes.com.mx. Resort-style hotel with very comfortable a/c rooms set in shady grounds with a small pool and a good restaurant embellished with Classic-Maya-themed decor. Internet access (also available to non-guests) at M$25/hr. ❼

**Xibalba** Merle Green 9 ⓣ916/345-0411, ⓔxibalbao2@prodigy.net.mx. Opposite *Chablís* (see above), offering lovely, tiled rooms with private bathrooms in an A-frame building with a wooden deck upstairs; there's a restaurant and travel agency downstairs. Cable TV and a/c available. ❺

### On the road to the ruins

**La Aldea del Halach-Uinic** 3km from town ⓣ916/345-1693, ⓦwww.laaldeapalenque.com. Series of comfortable cabañas laid out in attractive gardens with a small pool – the a/c units (❻) have private bathrooms, but there are smaller and cheaper cabins with shared bathrooms (1) that are just as well maintained.

**Chan Kah Resort Village** 3.5km from town, on the left just before the park entrance ☎916/345-0948, Ⓦwww.chan-kah.com.mx. Luxury brick and stone cabañas in a lovely forest and river setting that hums with birdlife. Extras include a fabulous stone-lined swimming pool and an open-air restaurant. 9

**Mayabell Camping and Trailer Park** 6km from town and inside the park, just before the museum ☎916/345-0597, Ⓦwww.mayabell.com.mx. A great favourite with backpackers and adventure-tour groups. In addition to palapa shelters for hammocks and tents *Mayabell* has vehicle pads with electricity and water, some very comfortable private cabañas with hot water and best of all, a decent freshwater swimming pool (with occasional fish). The tiled, shared showers have hot water as well, and the site isn't crowded, so you'll usually get a space. Lockers are available. Rates vary: hammock rental (M$15), tent camping (M$28), hooked-up RV (M$140), RV only (M$20); basic cabañas (2), with a/c (5).

**El Panchán** just inside the national park 5km from town, down a 100m track (3km from the ruins) Ⓦwww.elpanchan.com. A cluster of separate, great-value budget cabins and camping places set in the forest, with something of a New Age feel. Follow the signs to the places below. *Chato's Cabañas* (☎916/348-0520, Ⓔelpanchan@yahoo.com; 1) has neat thatched cabañas and two-storey houses, some with private bath (1). There's also a pool and an observation deck for bird-watching, and *Don Mucho's* restaurant, with excellent pasta, Mexican and vegetarian dishes, and pizza, at reasonable prices, and some live music. Nearby, *Rakshita's* (☎916/100-6908, Ⓦwww.rakshita.com; 1) has brightly painted, cosy cabañas, some with private bath and a deck with hammocks, in a lovely garden with a maze. It also has a great vegetarian restaurant and the owner offers massage and meditation. *Margarita and Ed's* (☎916/341-0063, Ⓔedcabanas@yahoo.com; 1–3) has comfortable, inexpensive thatched cabins and double rooms with private bathrooms, some with a/c. *Jungle Palace* (☎916/348-0520; 1) is the least expensive place here, with shelters for hammocks just M$20 (M$30 with lockers) and simple, shared-bath cabins (M$95), laundry and a cheap café.

## Eating and drinking

**Food** in Palenque town is fairly basic, and most restaurants serve up similar dishes, often just pasta and pizza, to customers who've really only come for the ruins; some of the best places are actually in *El Panchán* (see "Accommodation", above). The hotels in La Cañada tend to have attached restaurants and, though standards are generally fine, prices are higher than in town. **Juárez** also has several budget options between the bus stations and the zócalo, while **Hidalgo** has more Mexican-style food, with several taco places and even a couple of seafood restaurants. There's a good Mexican **bakery**, *Flor de Palenque*, on Allende next to the Chambalú *colectivo* terminal.

**Cristy's Café and Bar** 5 de Mayo 15-A, on the eastern side of the zócalo. Cosy corner café with some outdoor seating and a solid menu of Mexican and regional favourites, as well as decent breakfasts from M$35.

**Mara's** Juárez 1, on the corner of the zócalo. Smart new restaurant with bright, modern decor and menu (in English) offering classic Mexican food for under M$50. Set meals M$44–65. Open daily 7am–11pm.

**Restaurant Maya** corner of Hidalgo and the zócalo. Popular with tourists, and the food is pretty good (mains M$60–100). Set meals are better value at M$45, and refreshing margaritas are M$38.

**Las Tinajas** corner of 20 de Noviembre and Abasolo. Pleasant, family-run restaurant, deservedly popular for its large plates of hearty meats, fish, chicken and pasta in addition to the usual Mexican fare. Most dishes around M$60 and breakfast for under M$45. Daily 7am–10.30pm.

**Virgo's** Hidalgo, opposite *Restaurant Maya*. Breezy outdoor seating on the first-floor terrace and reasonable prices make this a good-value option for meats and Mexican food.

## Listings

**Banks and exchange** Several banks along Juárez will change traveller's cheques and have ATMs.

**Internet access** There are a few places along Juárez: try Red M@aya (daily 9am–10pm; M$50/hr) at no. 133 between Allende and Aldama. In La Cañada area, the hotels run something of a cartel, ripping off isolated customers with a charge of M$25/hr. *El Panchán* also has Internet access (10am–11pm; M$15/hr).

**Laundry** Several in town, including Azul Lavanderia, 2a Avenida Sur Ote, just east of the plaza (Mon–Fri 9am–2pm & 5–8pm, Sat 9am–2pm).

**Post office** On Independencia, a block from the plaza (Mon–Fri 9am–6pm, Sat & Sun 9am–1pm).

## The ruins of Palenque

Palenque's architectural style is unique. Superficially, it bears a closer resemblance to the Maya sites of Guatemala than to those of the Yucatán, but its **towered palace** and **pyramid tomb** are like nothing else, and the setting, too, is remarkable. Surrounded by hills covered in jungle, Palenque is right at the edge of the great Yucatán plain – climb to the top of any of the structures and you'll see an endless stretch of low, pale-green flatland. Founded around 100 BC as a farming village, it was four hundred years before it began to flourish, during the Classic period (300–900 AD). Towards the end of this time the city ruled over a large part of modern-day Chiapas and Tabasco, but its peak came during a relatively short period of the seventh century, under two rulers: **Hanab Pakal** (**Jaguar Shield**) and **Chan Bahlum** (**Jaguar Serpent**). Almost everything you can see (and that's only a tiny, central part of the original city) dates from this era.

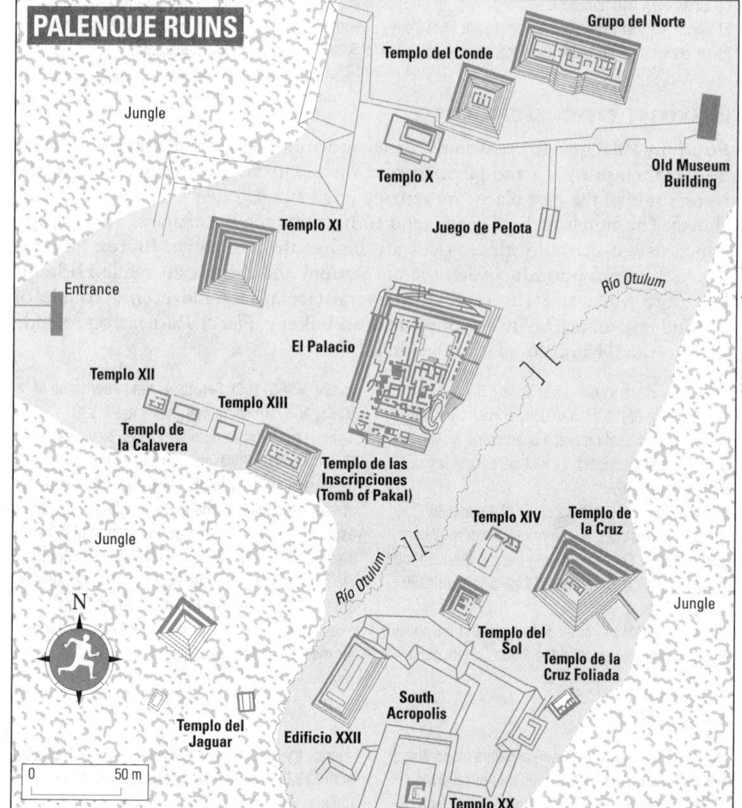

**Getting to the site** is no problem. Two *combi* services, Chambalú and Otulúm, both on Calle Allende in Palenque town, either side of Juárez, run at least every fifteen minutes from 6am to 6pm, and will stop anywhere along the road, useful if you're staying at one of the hotels or campsites near the ruins. Although they will try to sell you a return ticket, it is advisable to buy just a one-way (M$10) so you don't have to wait for the same company on the return leg. After 6pm, you'll have to either walk or take a taxi (M$50) back to town. Note that you'll have to pay an additional M$10 at the toll gate at the park entrance – if you're staying inside (at *El Panchán* or *Mayabell*) there's no need to pay again next time you pass through.

The ruins are in a **national park** (daily 8am–5pm, archeological zone daily 8am–4.30pm; M$45, includes museum) and guided tours are available from the entrance, costing around M$400 for groups of up to seven people and lasting about two hours. Ideally you'll arrive early and climb the temples in the morning mist, though with more and more tours arriving at this time, you might avoid more crowds by coming later in the afternoon, assuming you can stand the heat.

## The site

The park entrance is around 5km from Palenque, with the site museum another 2km beyond this. The museum provides a good introduction to the ruins, but if you intend to hike back through the forest, it's much easier to stay on the bus another 1.5km to the entrance to the site itself, and end up walking downhill back to the museum after you've had a good look around. There's a small **café** by the site entrance (and some expensive lockers), and a toilet by the ticket office. Here you'll also find ranks of souvenir stalls and usually a group of Lacandón in white robes (or merely people in white robes imitating Lacandón) selling arrows and other artefacts. Signs inside the site are in English, Spanish and Tzeltal, though Chol is the language spoken by most Maya living in this part of Chiapas today.

△ El Palacio, Palenque

As you enter the site, **El Palacio**, with its extraordinary watchtower, stands ahead of you. To the right, at the end of a row of smaller structures, stands the **Templo de las Inscripciones**, an eight-stepped pyramid 26m high, built up against a thickly overgrown hillside. You are not permitted to climb the pyramid, which is a shame as the sanctuary on top contains a series of stone panels carved with hieroglyphic inscriptions relating to Palenque's dynastic history. Inside the pyramid is the **tomb of Hanab Pakal** (615–83 AD). Discovered in 1952, this was the first such pyramid burial found in the Americas. Sadly, the tomb has also been closed to the general public. Some of the smaller objects found inside – the skeleton and the jade death mask – are on display at the Anthropology Museum in Mexico City, but the massive, intricately carved stone **sarcophagus** is still inside. One of the most renowned iconographic monuments in the Maya world, the sarcophagus lid depicts Pakal at the moment of his death, falling into the underworld, which is symbolized by a monster's jaws. Above the dead king rises the **Wakah Kan** – the World Tree and the centre of the universe – with **Itzam-Ye**, the Celestial Bird, perched on top representing the heavens. In order that the deified king buried here should not be cut off from the world of the living, a psychduct – a hollow tube in the form of a snake – runs up the side of the staircase, from the tomb to the temple. For now, though, you will have to be satisfied with the replica in the site museum.

In June 1994 another remarkable tomb was discovered, in **Templo XIII**, in a pyramid next to the Templo de las Inscripciones. This burial, currently the only one open to the public, is considered by archeologists to date from a similar period to that of Pakal, and its sarcophagus contains a number of jade and obsidian grave goods and food and drink vessels to sustain the deceased on the way to Xibalba, the Maya underworld.

The centrepiece of the site, **El Palacio**, is in fact a complex of buildings constructed at different times to form a rambling administrative and residential block. Its square **tower** (whose top floor was reconstructed in 1930) is unique, and no one knows exactly what its purpose was – perhaps a lookout post or an astronomical observatory. Bizarrely, the narrow staircase that winds up inside it starts only at the second level. Throughout you'll find delicately executed relief carvings, the most remarkable of which are the giant human figures on stone panels in the grassy courtyard.

To the south of El Palacio, the **Templo del Jaguar** is reached by a small path that follows the Río Otulúm upstream – a delightful shaded walk. Beyond here, more temples are being wrested from the jungle. If you want to penetrate a bit further, following the trail along the stream, you won't be permitted to pass without a guide. The path leads to the *ejido* of Naranjo, a little over an hour's walk away, and while you're on it it's easy to believe you're walking over unexcavated pyramids: the ground is very rocky and some of the stones certainly don't look naturally formed.

On higher ground south of El Palacio, on the other side of the Río Otulúm – lined with stone and used as an aqueduct in the city's heyday – lie the **Templo del Sol**, the **Templo de la Cruz** and the **Templo de la Cruz Foliada**, half-obscured by dense vegetation. All are tall, narrow pyramids surmounted by a temple with an elaborate stone roofcomb. Each contains carved panels representing sacred rites – the cross found here is as important an image in Maya iconography as it is in Christian, representing the meeting of the heavens and the underworld with the land of the living. On the right-hand side of the Templo de la Cruz, God L is depicted smoking tobacco.

From here you can walk north along the stream towards the lesser buildings of the **Grupo del Norte**, and the **Juego de Pelota** (ball-court), slightly

## Moving on from Palenque

Leaving Palenque by **bus**, there are **first-class** departures from the OCC terminal to Mérida (4 daily; 9hr): departures via Campeche are at 8am and 9pm. There are also first-class departures for Oaxaca (1 daily; 14hr) at 5.30pm; Cancún (5 daily; 12hr) at 8pm and 9.10pm, with three first-class buses going via Chetumal and Playa del Carmen at 5.30pm, 8.15pm and 9.15pm; and overnight buses to Mexico City (3 daily; 17hr) at 9pm and 9.30pm. Buses for **Tuxtla** (10 daily; 7hr) all call at **Ocosingo** (3hr) and **San Cristóbal** (5hr). The main regional transport hub is **Villahermosa** (9 daily 7am–9pm; 2hr 30min), and you may find it easier to get there and change for your onward journey. You can also book *de paso* first-class buses to Emiliano Zapata in Tabasco (see p.772) departing 8am, 8pm, 9pm and 9.10pm; for **Tenosique**; and for Guatemala. Luxury ADO GL services run to Cancún (9pm) via Chetumal, Tulum and Playa del Carmen; and at 6.30am to Tuxtla via San Cristóbal. TRF also runs **second-class** buses to Villahermosa from its terminal on the other side of the road.

Transportes Comitán y Lagos de Montebello, on Velasco Suárez, just past the market, and Transportes Río Chancala, on 5 de Mayo in Palenque, have numerous departures to destinations along the Frontier Highway, beginning at 4.30am: all go to **Benemérito** (via **San Javiér** – for Bonampak and Lacanjá) and the turn-off for **Frontera Corozal** (for Yaxchilán). Transportes Chamoan, on Hidalgo (near Allende), runs regular **minivans** to Frontera itself. The early **Montebello** departures (before 11am) continue all the way to **Comitán** via the Lagos de Montebello. You can find **taxis** at the Maya Pakal rank on the northeast corner of the plaza to: **Agua Azul** (2hr wait), **Bonampak** (2hr wait), Frontera, Ocosingo, Palenque ruins and around town.



downhill across a cleared grassy area. Further downstream, the river cascades through the forest and flows over beautiful limestone curtains and terraces into a series of gorgeous pools – the aptly named **El Baño de la Reina** (**Bathing Pool of the Queen**) is the most exquisite, with the **Grupo B** residential buildings alongside. The ruins along this section are usually much quieter, jungle-covered and even more enchanting – you might see howler monkeys in the trees. The path continues past more recently excavated buildings of the **Grupo de los Murciélagos**, and across the river over a wooden suspension bridge spanning some lovely waterfalls, eventually coming out on the main road opposite the **Museo de Sitio** (Tues–Sun 8am–4.45pm). In the museum, the map of the site shows that only a quarter of the structures have been excavated, and an intricate model of the palace complex recreates how it would have appeared in the Classic period, with the tops of the buildings adorned with roofcombs. Several carved panels removed from the archeological site are on display, as are numerous incense burners – large urns with elaborately stuccoed gods and mythological creatures – with explanations in Spanish and English. There's also a copy of Hanab Pakal's famous sarcophagus lid in the Templo de las Inscripciones.

# The Usumacinta valley and the Frontier Highway south

The Usumacinta valley and the Lacandón forest form Mexico's last frontier. Running along the edge of the forest, the **Carretera Fronteriza** (Frontier Highway) connects Palenque with Comitán, providing access to a number of new settlements whose inhabitants are rapidly clearing the trees for farmland. Note that there are several army checkpoints along the highway's length, and there remains the risk of **armed robbery** in this wild region.

Palenque is the obvious jumping-off point for the Maya ruins of **Bonampak** and **Yaxchilán**, and several agencies offer tours, by far the easiest options for visiting. If you wonder why all the buses seem to be travelling in convoy (visiting the sites at the more or less the same time, and stopping at the same restaurants) it's no coincidence – they coordinate visits for safety reasons. If you have more time it's possible to visit both of them independently, though if you're travelling alone it's not much cheaper, especially to see Yaxchilán, where hiring boats along the river can be expensive without a group. You could visit Bonampak and the **Lacandón Maya** community (see box below) of **Lacanjá Chansayab** on a day trip from Palenque – as always, it's best to get an early start: see the "Moving On" box on p.747. Accommodation is available in Lacanjá, and in several other places along the highway, convenient if you have your own transport.

If you intend to push on into **Guatemala**, you can get a boat a short distance upstream from the riverbank settlement of Frontera Corozal to **Bethél** across the border, and from the fast-expanding town of Benemérito you can occasionally take a longer trip on a trading boat upstream to **Sayaxché** (also in Guatemala), on the Río de la Pasión.

## Lacanjá Chansayab

For Lacanjá (and Bonampak), you need to get off the bus at **San Javiér** (about 3hr and 132km from Palenque), where there's an abandoned government control hut on the left and a *comedor* on the right. There's usually plenty of traffic, so you won't have to walk to Lacanjá (M$15 for a shared taxi), and several **places to stay** once you get there, though none currently

### The Lacandón

You may already have encountered the impressively wild-looking **Lacandón Maya** selling exquisite (and apparently effective) bows and arrows at Palenque. Though the wearing of their simple white robes and uncut hair is today mainly for the benefit of tourists, the Lacandón were until recently the most isolated of all the Mexican tribes. The ancestors of today's Lacandón (there are less than 700) are believed to have migrated to Chiapas from the Petén region of Guatemala during the eighteenth century. Prior to that the Spanish had enslaved, killed or relocated the original inhabitants of the forest. The Lacandón refer to themselves as "Hach Winik" (True People); "Lacandón" was a label used by the Spanish to describe any native group living in the Usumacinta valley and western Petén outside colonial control.

Appearances notwithstanding, some Lacandón families are (or have been) quite wealthy, having sold timber rights in the jungle. This change has led to a division in their society, and now most Lacandón live in one of two main communities: **Lacanjá Chansayab**, near Bonampak, a village predominantly made up of evangelical Protestants, some of whom are keenly developing low-impact tourist facilities (see p.740); and **Naha'**, where a small group still attempt to live a traditional life, and where it is possible to arrange stays in local homes. The best source of information on the Lacandón in Chiapas is Casa Na-Bolom in San Cristóbal de las Casas (see p.723), where you can find a manuscript of *Last Lords of Palenque*, by Victor Perera and Robert Bruce (Little Brown & Co, 1982). *Hach Winik*, by Didier Boremanse (University of Albany, 1998), is an excellent recent study of Lacandón life and history.

have phones. From San Javiér, a paved side road to Bonampak and Lacanjá bears right off the highway. After 3km, at a right-hand bend in the road, you'll find *Camping Margarito* (❶; 20 tents available), which also offers basic rooms with private (M$240) or shared (M$180) bathrooms and a small **restaurant**. This is where most two-day tours camp for the night; the road to Bonampak branches off left here. Lacanjá is another 2.5km; after you cross the Rio Lacanjá you'll come to a junction pointing to several purpose-built **campsites**, **cabins** and **hammock shelters** (❶–❷). Comfortable *Campamento Lacanjá* (❶–❸), which has accommodation ranging from simple cabañas to modern doubles with fans and hot water, is 2km to the south (left) and others are a kilometre ahead (west), in the main part of the village. A few places also have simple dorm **rooms** with mosquito-netted beds and electric light. The best, in a grassy area on the bank of a clear, fast-flowing river, is *Campamento Vicente Paniagua* (❷), with clean, modern rooms with bathroom, or cheaper wooden huts with shared toilets (❶). Don Vicente and his family produce some of the best artesanía in the village – clay and wood figurines and drums in addition to beautifully crafted bow and arrow sets. The villagers are eager to show you the gorgeous rivers and magical **Cascada Ya Toch Kusam** in the forest, and you can reach the **Lacanjá ruins** in less than two hours from here. You should be able to arrange knowledgeable Lacandón guides at your accommodation to lead you (around M$200 per person). If you can, pick up an information sheet in the **Casa Na-Bolom** in San Cristóbal (see p.723) before you set off.

## Bonampak

Relatively small compared to other ruined Maya cities, what makes **Bonampak** (daily 8am–5pm; M$33) utterly unique is its fascinating **murals**, evocative memorials to a lost civilization. The outside world first heard of Bonampak, meaning "painted walls", in 1946, when Charles Frey, an American conscientious objector taking refuge deep in the forest, was shown the site (but apparently not the murals) by Lacandón who still worshipped at the ancient temples there. American photographer Giles Healey was the first non-Maya ever to see these enigmatic examples of Classic Maya art, shortly after Frey's visit. The whole site dates back to at least 402 AD; it reached its heyday in the eighth century and was abandoned sometime in the ninth. Note however, the ruins themselves are not overly spectacular, and the undoubted historic importance of the murals tends to obscure the fact that they have become quite faded in parts.

At San Javiér **taxis** will probably be waiting to drive you the 12km to the ruins (return ticket M$100 or M$50 per person). After the turn-off to Lacanjá from the Frontier Highway, the paved road ends a few hundred metres past *Margarito*'s (most tours transfer to locally owned buses here), and a little further on you'll pass a mock-corbelled arch across the road and a now-abandoned visitor centre. Private vehicles cannot go further than this, and you'll need to take a local bus from here (M$70 return). You pay at the entrance to the ruins (another 9km ahead), marked by a small car park and a couple of huts (with toilets). No flash photography is allowed, and you will be charged a massive M$600 to use a video camera.

After crossing the airstrip, you enter the site at the northwest corner of **La Gran Plaza**, which is 110m long and bounded by low walls – the remains of some palace-style buildings. In the centre of the plaza **Stele 1** shows a larger-than-life **Chaan Muan II**, the last king of Bonampak, dressed for battle –at 6m, it is one of the tallest stele in the Maya world. You'll encounter other images of him throughout the site. Ahead, atop several steep flights of steps, lies the **Acrópolis**. On the lower steps, more well-preserved stelae show Chaan Muan with his wife, Lady Rabbit, preparing himself for blood-letting and apparently about to sacrifice a prisoner.

Splendid though these carvings are, the highlight of the site is the modest-looking **Edifico de la Pinturas**, halfway up the steps. Inside, in three separate chambers and on the temple walls and roof, the renowned **Bonampak murals** depict vivid scenes of haughty Maya lords, splendidly attired in jaguar-skin robes and quetzal-plume headdresses; their equally well-dressed ladies; and bound prisoners, one with his fingernails ripped out, spurting blood. Dating to around 790 AD, these paintings show the Bonampak elite at the height of their power: unknown to them, the collapse of the Classic Maya civilization was imminent. Some details were never finished, and Bonampak was abandoned shortly after the scenes in the temple were painted. Though you can't enter the rooms fully, the vantage point inside the doorway is more than adequate to absorb what's inside, and though no more than three people are permitted to enter at any one time and queues are possible, you shouldn't have to wait long. Having said that, time and early cleaning attempts have clearly taken their toll on the murals, and apart from a few beautifully restored sections, it takes some concentration and a good deal of imagination to work out what you're looking at.

In **Room 1**, an infant wrapped in white cloth (the heir apparent?) is presented to assembled nobility under the supervision of the lord of Yaxchilán, while musicians play drums, pipes and trumpets in the background. **Room 2** contains a vivid, even gruesome, exhibition of power over Bonampak's enemies: tortured prisoners lie on temple steps, while above them lords in jaguar robes are indifferent to their agony. A severed head rolls down the stairs and Chaan Muan II grasps a prisoner (who appears to be pleading for mercy) by the hair – clearly about to deal him the same fate. **Room 3** shows the price paid for victory: Chaan Muan's wife, **Lady Rabbit**, prepares to prick her tongue to let blood fall onto a paper in a pot in front of her. The smoke from burning the blood-soaked paper will carry messages to ancestor-gods. Other gorgeously dressed figures, their senses probably heightened by hallucinogenic drugs, dance on the temple steps.

Once you've seen the ruins, head back to the San Javiér junction, where you'll be able to catch a **bus** or *combi* to Palenque.

## Frontera Corozal and Yaxchilán

Fifteen kilometres beyond San Javiér is the turning for **FRONTERA COROZAL**, the gateway to **Yaxchilán**, one of the most enigmatic Maya ruins in Mexico. The ancient city can only be approached by boat along the Río Usumacinta, and though Frontera is the point of embarkation there's not much else to see in the village itself. The turn-off to Frontera is marked by a *comedor* and shop selling basic supplies, while the village centre is another 15km down the paved side road and served by regular buses and *combis* from Palenque (last one back at 4pm); there's a M$10 per person "conservation fee" payable on the outskirts. Taxis and buses should end up on the banks of the Usumacinta, where you catch the boats to Yaxchilán. There's a Mexican **immigration post** (see box, p.709, for border procedures) 400m back along the main road coming in, and on a side road beyond it and to the right, the thatched and brightly painted **cabañas** of *Escudo Jaguar* (☎0155/5329-0995 ext 8057, in Mexico City; ❶ shared bathroom, ❻ en suite), named after Shield Jaguar, a king of Yaxchilán. The spacious rooms have comfortable beds with mosquito nets, full-length windows opening onto the porch and tiled bathrooms with hot water – a touch of luxury at a bargain price. There's also a good **restaurant** here, and you can **camp** nearby for M$35. More basic accommodation is available at Corozal's two **posadas** – the *Nueva Allianza* (ⓣ0155/5329-0995 ext 8061; ❶), near to the immigration post, is marginally the better and has a good *comedor*.

To reach **Yaxchilán** you need to get a ride in a *lancha* – a narrow riverboat with benches along the side and a tin roof disguised by banana leaves for shade. Four companies now compete for business, though prices are fixed. Tickets are sold at *Escudo Jaguar* but are also available at the Officina de Contrataciones de Lanchas, next to the Museo Regional, 400m from the river, or in the building closer to the *embarcadero*. You will also have to pay your entrance fee for the site here, as cash is no longer kept at the isolated ruins. You need a group to make the trip worthwhile – boats are M$500 for up to four people, and M$600 for more, with no scope for bargaining. The journey downstream usually takes thirty to forty minutes.



### Yaxchilán: the site

A larger and more dramatic site than Bonampak, **Yaxchilán** (daily 8am–5pm; M$33, free on Sun) was an important Classic-period Maya centre dating from around 250 AD and containing over 120 major structures. From around 680 AD to 810 AD, the city's most famous kings (identified by their name-glyphs) – Escudo Jaguar (Shield Jaguar 681–742 AD), his son Pájaro Jaguar IV (Bird Jaguar 752–68 AD) and Escudo Jaguar III (772–800 AD) – began the campaign of conquest that extended Yaxchilán's sphere of influence over the other Usumacinta centres and made possible alliances with Tikal and Palenque. Today it's shrouded in jungle in an incredibly evocative setting along the river: far fewer visitors come here than go to other major sites, and the eerie moans of howler monkeys echo around the ruins.

*Lanchas* drop you at the entrance, and once inside the site the path splits, with the main route leading along level ground to the Gran Plaza, but it's more rewarding to take the narrow path that leads steeply off to the right, which climbs 50m up the hillside to the **Pequeña Acrópolis**, a set of 13 buildings. A lintel on the most prominent ruin, known as **Edificio 42**, depicts Escudo Jaguar with one of his warriors. Walk behind here to find a another narrow trail down through the jungle, over several unrestored mounds, until you reach a fork: to the right, the path climbs steeply once again, until it reaches Edificios 39–41, or the **Templos del Sur**, 90m above the river level – buildings that probably had some kind of astronomical significance. The climb is worth the effort for the view alone.

Retrace your steps back to the main path, which continues to the left from the fork, eventually emerging at the back of **Edificio 33**, which overlooks the main plaza at the top of a grand terrace and the most significant building at the site, part of a set of ruins known as the **Acrópolis**. The lintels of Edificio 33 are superbly preserved and inside one of the portals is a headless statue of Pájaro Jaguar IV. In ancient times the building was a political court, but more recently served as a religious site for the Lacandón Maya.

Descending 40m down the terrace brings you to the huge **Gran Plaza** and covered Stele I, which depicts Escudo Jaguar in a "dispersion ceremony" that took place in 761 AD. The temples here bear massive honeycombed roofs, and everywhere there are superb, well-preserved stucco carvings. These panels, on lintels above doorways and on stelae, depict rulers performing ritual events, often involving blood-letting to conjure up spirit visions of ancestors. Some of the very best lintels have been removed to the British Museum in London, but the number and quality of the remaining panels is unequalled at any other Maya site in Mexico. **Stele II**, originally sited at Edificio 41, has survived several attempts to translocate it to London and now lies at the west side of the plaza, where it shows the transfer of power from Escudo Jaguar to Pájaro Jaguar IV. When the water is low here, you can see (and climb) a pyramid built on a rock shelf on the river bed. Some archeologists suggest this was a bridge support, though this is unlikely as no corresponding structure has been found on the opposite bank, and the altar on top may indicate that it was used for religious rituals. Heading back to the entrance, be sure to pass through the **Laberinto** at the plaza's northeast corner, the most complex building on the site, where you can walk down through dim passages and eventually out onto the main path.

### On from Frontera Corozal and Yaxchilán

**Entering Guatemala** is relatively easy, with plenty of *lanchas* between Corozal and **Bethél**, a thirty-minute boat ride upstream, plus any time spent waiting for the boat to fill up. Trips across to Bethél have a set fare of M$300 for one to two people and M$400 for four. There's a Guatemalan **immigration post** (see box, p.709, for border procedures) in Bethél, from where buses normally depart at noon and 5pm for **Flores** (for Tikal; US$5), a five-hour ride, mostly along dirt roads. Alternatively, you can **stay** in the simple but comfortable *Posada Maya* cabañas (❶), on the riverbank amid the **ruins of Bethél**, or camp here (tent or hammock provided; ❶). The *lancheros* here in Bethél or in Corozal can arrange trips **downstream from Yaxchilán** to the impressive ruins of **Piedras Negras** on the Guatemalan bank, for which you'll need to get a group together as a two- to three-day trip will cost anything from US$75 to US$150 per person, depending on the number. There are rapids above the site, meaning you may well have to get out and walk along the bank at times. It's a beautiful journey, though, and well worth making if you have the time. Below the site the river speeds through two massive canyons: the **Cañon de San José**, where fearsome rapids shoot between cliffs 300m high, and the slightly less dramatic **Cañon de las Iguanas**.

## The southern Usumacinta

Following the Frontier Highway south a further 35km from Frontera Corozal brings you to **BOCA LACANTÚN**, where a bridge carries the road over the enormous Río Lacantún. You can expect any bus along this road to be stopped by immigration or army officials, so keep your passport handy. At the confluence of the Lacantún and Usumacinta rivers is an unusual Maya monument, the **Planchon de Figuras**, a great limestone slab of unknown origin carved with glyphs, birds, animals and temples. If you're travelling by river, the beautiful **Chorro cascades** are just downstream.

### Benemérito and onwards

The sprawling frontier town of **BENEMÉRITO**, 2km beyond Boca Lacantún, is the largest settlement in the Chiapas section of the Usumacinta valley, and an important centre for both river and road traffic. If you're **arriving by boat** from Guatemala you'll be met by Mexican soldiers who'll probably check your passport, though the nearest **immigration office** is at Frontera Corozal (see p.750). There's a hospital, market, shops, *comedores* and a few desperately basic **hotels**; you're better off heading on to Corozal (for

Yaxchilán), Lacanjá (for Bonampak, see p.748), or even Palenque. The highway is the town's main street, and in the centre another road splits off towards the river, less than 2km away. **Heading north** is no problem: buses from Transportes Lagos de Montebello pull in on the highway at the southern end of town. **Heading south** along the Frontier Highway, buses from Palenque pass through every couple of hours, eventually reaching the Lagos de Montebello and Comitán.

### By river to Sayaxché

If you hope to get by boat **from Benemérito to Sayaxché** in Guatemala you'll need patience, a good deal of money or both. **Trading boats** (taking at least 12hr) are the cheapest method of transport, but with no proper schedule you just have to hope there's one going when you want to. To reach Sayaxché in one day you'll need to leave early. Fast boats are now making the trip in less than three hours, stopping at the various sites en route, but you'll have to charter them at a cost of US$200–250 per boat. **Entering Guatemala**, you'll get your passport stamped at the army post at **Pipiles**, at the confluence with the Río de la Pasión. There's no Mexican immigration here; make sure you get an exit stamp in Frontera Corozal (see p.750).

# Tabasco

The state of **Tabasco**, crossed by numerous slow-moving tropical rivers on their way to the Gulf, is at last making determined efforts to attract tourists. Once the homeland of the ancient **Olmec**, **Maya** and **Zoque** cultures, the state boasts dozens of **archeological sites**. Few of these pre-Columbian cities have been excavated, though **Comalcalco**, a Maya site north of Villahermosa, and the most important Olmec site at **La Venta**, northwest of the capital, have been expertly restored and are certainly worth visiting. The Zoque site of **Malpasito**, in the remote Sierra Huimanguillo, is easily the state's most attractive ancient city, though perhaps most difficult to reach.

**Villahermosa** ("Beautiful Town"), the state capital, has undergone an amazing transformation in recent decades, with oil wealth financing the creation of several parks and museums – the city is finally beginning to live up to its name. One excellent example is the **Parque Museo La Venta**, an outdoor archeological exhibition that provides the most accessible glimpse of the Olmec civilization in the state; another is the ambitious **Yumká**, an expertly run safari park that allows you to take a step into wild Africa.

Tabasco's **coast**, alternating between estuaries and sand bars, salt marshes and lagoons, is off the beaten track to most visitors. Hwy-180 runs very close to the shore, however, enabling you to reach the deserted beaches. As yet these have somewhat limited facilities – even the main coastal town, **Paraíso**, is a tiny place. Much of inland Tabasco is very flat, consisting of the flood plains of a dozen or so major rivers; indeed, most of the state's borders are waterways. Enterprising tour operators run **boat trips** along the main rivers, the Grijalva and the Usumacinta, and these are the best way to glimpse remote ruins and the region's abundant birdlife. You can also travel by river into the Petén in **Guatemala**, leaving from La Palma, near **Tenosique**, in the far eastern corner of the state and near the Classic Maya site of **Pomoná**.

In the far south of the state, around **Teapa** and Villa Luz, the Chiapas highlands spill over into the state as the foothills of the **Sierra Puana**. Overlooking the vast Gulf coast plain, these hills offer a retreat from the heat and humidity of the lowlands. Waterfalls spill down from the mountains, and a few small spas (*balnearios*) have developed. Village tracks provide some great **hiking trails** and, despite the proximity to Villahermosa, you can enjoy a respite from the well-travelled tourist circuit.

Tabasco **cuisine** isn't especially well known, though you will come across a few local specialities. Oddly enough, **Tabasco Sauce** isn't one of them: although Tabasco peppers are named after the state, they don't grow here, and the celebrated dressing is an American product made from peppers grown in Louisiana.



## Some history

Little is known about the **Olmec culture**, referred to by many archeologists as the mother culture of Mesoamerica. Its legacy, which included the Long Count calendar, glyphic writing, a rain deity and probably also the concept of zero and the ball-game, influenced all subsequent civilizations in ancient Mexico. The fact that it developed and flourished in the unpromising environment of the Gulf coast swamps 3200 years ago only adds to its mystery. Olmec civilization began to decline around 400 BC, and over the next thousand years the plains were gradually absorbed by the great Maya cities to the east, an influence most notable at **Comalcalco** (see p.766). After the collapse of Classic Maya civilization, Tabasco became something of a crossroads, its great rivers important trade routes to the interior, though its remaining Maya communities were relatively unorganized.

When **Hernán Cortés** landed at the mouth of the Río Grijalva in 1519, he easily defeated the local Chontal Maya. However, the town he founded, Santa María de la Victoria, was beset first by indigenous attacks and then by pirates, eventually forcing a move to the present site and a change of name to "Villahermosa de San Juan Bautista" in 1596. For most of the colonial period, Tabasco remained a relative backwater, since the Spanish found the humid, insect-ridden swamps distinctly inhospitable. **Independence** did little to improve matters, as local leaders fought among themselves, and it took the **French invasion** of 1862, and Napoleon III's imposition of the unfortunate Maximilian as Emperor of Mexico, to bring some form of unity, though Tabasco offered fierce resistance to this foreign intrusion.

The industrialization of the country during the dictatorship of Porfirio Díaz passed agricultural Tabasco by, and even after the **Revolution** it was still a poor state, dependent on cacao and bananas. Though **Tomás Garrido Canabal**, Tabasco's socialist governor in the 1920s and 1930s, is still respected as a reformer whose laws regarding workers' rights and women's suffrage were decades ahead of the rest of the country, his period in office was also marked by intense **anticlericalism**. Priests were killed or driven out (a process vividly brought to life in Graham Greene's *The Power and the Glory*), all the churches were closed, and many of them, including the cathedral in Villahermosa, torn down. The region's **oil**, discovered in the 1930s but not fully exploited until the 1970s, provided the impetus to bring Tabasco into the modern world, enabling capital to be invested in the agricultural sector and Villahermosa to be transformed into the cultural centre it is today.

# Villahermosa

**VILLAHERMOSA**, the state capital, is a virtually unavoidable road junction: sooner or later you're almost bound to pass through here on the way from central Mexico to the Yucatán or back, especially if you hope to see Palenque (see p.740). It's a large and prosperous city, and at first glance it can seem to be subject

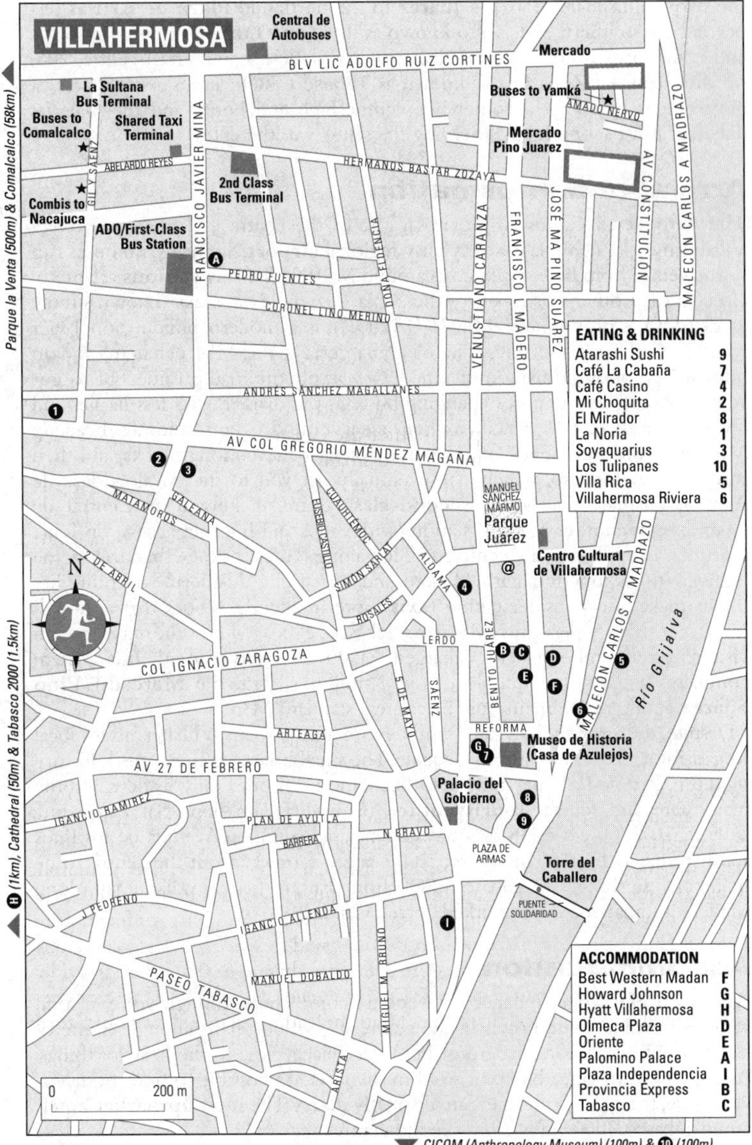

to as bad a case of urban blight as any in Mexico. The longer you stay, though, the more compensations you discover. Quite apart from the **Parque La Venta** and sudden vistas of the broad sweep of the **Río Grijalva**, there are attractive plazas, quiet ancient streets, impressive ultramodern buildings and several new art galleries and museums. In the evening, as the traffic disperses and the city cools, its appeal is heightened, and strolling the pedestrianized streets around the **Zona Remodelada** or the lively malecón, where everything stays open late, becomes a genuine pleasure. The Zona Remodelada, which encompasses the area between the two main squares, **Parque Juárez** to the north and **Plaza de Armas** just beyond the southern end, is also known as the **Zona Luz** – or simply La Zona, and is the city's historic heart. Villahermosa's modern commercial centre, 2km northwest of the Zona Luz, is known as **Tabasco 2000**, and is a smart area of government buildings, a conference centre, high-end hotels and the Galerías Tabasco, a vast shopping mall serving the state's wealthy elites.



## Arrival and information

The Aeropuerto Carlos A. Rovirosa, east of the centre at Km 13 Carretera Villahermosa–Palenque, is a very busy regional **airport**. Strangely, no buses run to the centre from here; a taxi costs around M$180. The **bus stations** are pretty close to each other northwest of the Zona Luz: the **first-class** (known simply as El ADO – pronounced El *AH-DAY-OH*), is a modern building on Javiér Mina just off Ruíz Cortines. There's a guardería (24hr; M$4 per item) and an information booth, usually unmanned. *Combis* ply the road outside, but to **get to the Zona Luz** requires changing buses at the market – it's less hassle (and less confusing) to take a taxi. Walking takes around twenty minutes: head up Merino or Fuentes, opposite the station, for six or seven long blocks, and then turn right at Madero, which will eventually get you to the zócalo (Plaza de Armas). Villahermosa's main **second-class** terminal, known as Central de Autobuses, is another modern station (with shops and Internet access) on Ruíz Cortines. To walk into the centre, turn left along Ruíz Cortines, then follow the highway to its junction with Madero and turn right. Villahermosa's humidity might make you consider taking **taxis** more frequently – note that although locals pay M$15 per trip (M$16 to Tabasco 2000) within the city, foreign visitors often end up being charged M$20. The city's **local bus** system comprises a confusing jumble of *combi* minivans, with the **Mercado Pino Suárez** acting as the main hub. Fares are a standard M$5.

Despite the growth in visitor numbers in recent years, Villahermosa's local tourist information remains inadequate. The small booths at the airport, history museum, Parque La Venta and ADO bus station can offer only leaflets, and the main state and federal **tourist office** (Mon–Fri 8am–6pm, Sat 8am–1pm; ⓣ993/310-9700 ext 5238, ⓦwww.visitetabasco.com), on Avenida de los Ríos south of Paseo Tabasco in Tabasco 2000, is too far away from the centre to be of much use. To get to Tabasco 2000 from Parque Juárez, walk north along Madero and catch a *combi* marked "Fracc Carrizal".

## Accommodation

**Accommodation** in Villahermosa doesn't come cheap, though you will find some reasonable-value hotels in the centre if you look hard enough. Some of the best options are on Madero or Lerdo de Tejada, close to the heart of things. Along Constitución, a block or so from the river, it's possible to find rooms for very little, though the cheapest are distinctly dodgy. The most **upmarket** hotels are in Tabasco 2000, away from the old centre.

**Best Western Madan** Madero 408 ⓣ993/312-1650, ⓦwww.madan.com.mx. Best value of the central hotels, in a great location with smart, modern rooms with cable TV, spacious bathrooms and popular restaurant. ❻

**Howard Johnson** Aldama 404 ⓣ993/314-4645, ⓦwww.hojo.com.mx. Not quite as upmarket as some of the newer hotels in the Zona, but still good value, with comfortable, modern a/c rooms and suites with great bathrooms, TV and phone. ❻

**Hyatt Villahermosa** Juárez 106 ⓣ800/233-1234, ⓦwww.villahermosa.regency.hyatt.com. Best luxury hotel in town, close to the Laguna de Ilusiones and on the edge of Tabasco 2000, just off Paseo Tabasco. Comfortable, well-furnished a/c rooms and suites with beautiful tiled bathrooms, and big discounts at the weekends. Also has two of the best restaurants in town. ❾

**Olmeca Plaza** Madero 418 ⓣ993/358-0102, ⓦwww.olmecaexpress.com. One of the newest hotels in the old centre, with bright, well-equipped and extremely comfortable rooms, as well as decent gym and outdoor pool. Bit pricey, but special promotions can make it more affordable. ❼

**Oriente** Madero 425 ⓣ993/312-0121. Opposite the *Olmeca*, *Oriente* has clean, tiled rooms with modern, private bathrooms, some with a/c and TV; drinking water available. ❹

**Palomino Palace** across from ADO terminal ⓣ993/312-8431. Conveniently located and usually has rooms available, but a bit overpriced considering its age – best as a last resort for late-night arrivals. Rooms, some with a/c, all have private shower and TV. ❺

**Plaza Independencia** Independencia 123 ⓣ993/312-1299, ⓦwww.hotelesplaza.com.mx. Comfortable, well-furnished rooms and suites in a quiet area just off the zócalo and handy for CICOM. Front rooms have balconies with views over the river and a safe-deposit box in every room. There's a lift, a pool, a good restaurant, a bar with live music and secure parking. ❻

**Provincia Express** Lerdo de Tejada 303 ⓣ993/314-5376. Reasonable mid-range chain hotel right in the Zona Luz. Rooms are a bit characterless, but come with a/c, private bath, TV and phone. ❺

**Tabasco** Lerdo de Tejada 317 ⓣ993/312-0077. One of the cheapest options in the Zona Luz, with spartan but functional rooms with TV and bathroom – singles are cheaper. ❸

## The City

Most visitors to Villahermosa head straight out to **Parque La Venta**, the obvious highlight of the city, but the **Zona Luz** in the old centre also warrants some exploration. The narrow streets contain several absorbing museums and galleries, particularly the **Museo de Historia de Tabasco**, housed in one of the state's most ornate buildings. Tabasco's rich archeological legacy is also showcased at the **CICOM complex** to the south, and with more time it's worth heading out to **Yumká**, an enjoyable safari park and ecological research centre.

### Zona Remodelada and the city centre

The pedestrianized **Zona Remodelada** (or **Zona Luz**) retains some vestiges of the nineteenth-century city - though most of the original colonial buildings were built of wood and have long since been torn down – and is as good a place as any to start your wandering. At its northern end the **Parque Juárez**, at the junction of Madero and Zaragoza, is lively in the evenings as crowds watch street entertainers. Opposite, on Madero, the futuristic glass **Centro Cultural de Villahermosa** (Tues–Sun 10am–8pm; free) has changing exhibits of art, photography and costume, as well as film screenings and concerts; it's also home to a good café.

In the centre of the Zona, on the corner of Sáenz and Lerdo, the distinctive pink and purple paintwork of **La Casa Siempreviva** (daily 9am–9pm; free) dating from the early 1900s, immediately catches the eye. Now a gallery with a small café, it's one of the few fully restored houses from that era, with tiled floors, arched stained-glass windows and some later Art Deco features. In the 1930s it was home to journalist and women's rights activist Isabel Rullán de Izundegui, and in the 1940s it became Villahermosa's first hotel with private bathrooms. Just around the corner at Sáenz 117 is the **Carlos Pellicer Casa Museo** (Tues–Sat 10am–7pm, Sun 10am–4pm; free), with bits and bobs related to the life of Carlos Pellicer, a poet and anthropologist born in Villahermosa and the driving force behind the rescue of the stone carvings from La Venta. The side streets here boast a number of other small **art galleries** – look around for signs of current exhibitions. The steps at the far end of Lerdo lead up past a statue of Simon Bolivar to the small, tree-shaded **Parque Los Pájaros**, where budgerigars sing in a large, globe-shaped cage and water flows through a series of blue-tiled fountains and pools.

The newly renovated (and air-conditioned) **Museo de Historia de Tabasco**, at the corner of 27 de Febrero and Juárez (Tues–Sun 9am–7pm; M$15), provides a quirky, detailed account of Tabasco's history, illustrated by such diverse objects as an early TV, the printing press for *El Disidente* (a newspaper from 1863) and a rare portrait of Porfirio Diáz signed by J.A. Vargas in 1888. The main attraction, however, is the museum building itself (completed in 1915), which used to be a hotel. Popularly known as the "**Casa de Azulejos**", it is tiled from top to bottom with blue mosaic patterns from all over Europe and the Middle East, forming an optical illusion on the lobby floor. Look up to see the statues of nymphs and classical figures perched on the railings around the roof.



The zócalo, the **Plaza de Armas**, is modern and not particularly attractive, despite its river views, but two historic buildings remain: the imposing **Palacio del Gobierno**, with its columns, turreted corners and clock tower, and at the southern end, the pretty little **Iglesia de la Concepción** (or just "La Conchita"). The first church was built here in 1799, but both this and its successor were demolished twice over – the present building dates from 1945. On the corner of the plaza the Puente Solidaridad footbridge over the Grijalva is topped by the incongruous bulk of the **Torre de Caballero** (daily 8am–4pm; free); climb up for splendid views of the city. To get a closer look at the river, walk back up to the **Corredor Turístico Malecón**, a new riverside development lined with bars and restaurants adjacent to the Zona, where the *Capitán Beuló II* offers cruises (Tues–Sun 3.30pm & 6.30pm; M$80) – check at the *Olmeca Plaza* (see p.757).

### The CICOM complex

A fifteen-minute walk south along the riverbank from the Plaza de Armas brings you to Villahermosa's cultural centre, **CICOM** – Centro de Investigaciones de las Culturas Olmeca y Maya. The complex includes the Teatro de Estado Esperanza Iris, *Los Tulipanes* restaurant (see p.761) and beyond that (the tallest building and the highlight for most visitors), the **Museo Regional de Antropología Carlos Pellicer Cámara** (Tues–Sun 9am–4.30pm; M$25). Here artefacts and models are displayed on four levels, proceeding chronologically from prehistoric times on the top floor to the Olmecs on the ground floor, though labels are in Spanish only. In addition to the exhibits of Olmec and Maya ceramics and other artefacts (including a fascinating toy jaguar with wheels), you can also view a reproduction of the Bonampak murals. Carlos Pellicer is commemorated by a bronze statue outside the museum. Further along is the mildly interesting **Centro de Estudios y Investigación de los Belles Artes** (daily 10am–2pm & 6–9pm; free), which hosts art and costume displays.

### Catedral del Señor de Tabasco

Villahermosa's original cathedral was pulled down in the 1930s, but in 1973 the first stage of this far grander replacement was completed. Visible from much of the city, the soaring towers of the **Catedral del Señor de Tabasco** are some of the highest in Mexico, and a stunning addition to the skyline. Construction started in the 1960s and is still ongoing – you can get a sense of the ambitious scale of the project from the model inside. Although the interior is impressive, with its vaults mimicking the Gothic cathedrals of Europe, the completed area is actually very small – walk behind the spires and the building looks chopped off. It's a fifteen- to twenty-minute walk up Paseo Tabasco from the river, at the junction with 27 de Febrero.

### Parque La Venta, the zoo and the Museo de Historia Natural

Discovered by Pemex engineers who were draining a marsh for oil, the Olmec site of **La Venta**, some 120km west of the city, at the border with Veracruz state, had most of its important finds transferred to the **Parque La Venta** (daily 8am–5pm, last ticket 4pm; M$40, including museum and zoo, latter closed

△ Blue heron, Parque La Venta

Mon). The entrance to this is on Ruíz Cortines, 1km west of the ADO bus station. Set inside the much larger **Parque Tomás Garrido Canabal**, the open-air museum stands on the shores of a large lake, the **Laguna de Ilusiones**, where you can also rent boats or climb the Mirador de los Águilas, a tower on its northern shore.

Although hardly the exact reproduction it claims to be, Parque La Venta does give you a chance to see a superb collection of artefacts from the earliest Mexican civilization in an appropriately jungly setting. The **Sala de Introducción**, under an enormous thatched roof just inside the entrance, allows you to familiarize yourself with the known facts of the Olmec culture and the history of the discovery of La Venta. The most significant and famous items in the park are, of course, the four gigantic **basalt heads**, which present such a curious puzzle. There's a whole series of other Olmec stone sculptures; follow the numbers as the path winds through the park. In their zeal to recreate an authentic jungle setting, the designers have introduced monkeys and coatis (members of the racoon family), which wander around freely, while crocodiles, jaguars and other animals from Tabasco are displayed in the zoo's sizeable enclosures. There's also several species of birds. The mosquitoes add an authentic but unplanned touch. Also in the park, opposite the La Venta entrance, the small **Museo de Historia Natural** (Tues–Sun 9am–5pm; M$15) has displays on the geography, geology, animals and plants of Tabasco, focusing on the interaction between humans and the environment. **To get to the park** from the centre it's easiest to take a taxi; otherwise you could take a *combi* to the market first, then catch one headed for Tabasco 2000 (or walk to Ruíz Cortines and flag one down). On weekends and holidays, buses link the entrance with Yumká at 9am, 10.30am, noon and 1.30pm.



### Yumká

Villahermosa's chief ecological attraction, **Yumká** (daily 9am–5pm, last ticket 4pm; M$50; Ⓦ www.yumka.org), is an ambitious combination of safari park and environmental studies centre 16km from the city, 4km beyond the airport. Its formal name, Centro de Interpretación y Convivencia con la Naturaleza, is a bit of a mouthful, so most people simply call it Yumká, after the Chontal Maya god, a dwarf who looks after forests. The park is large, covering more than six square kilometres, and divided into three zones: after a guided walking tour of the Tabasco jungle section, complete with monkeys, you board a train for a tour round enormous paddocks representing the savannas of Africa and Asia. Elephants, rhinos, giraffes and antelopes are rarely displayed in Mexico and almost never in such spacious surroundings. After a stop at the restaurant and souvenir shop, you can take a boat tour of the lagoon, where you'll see hippos and a number of species of birds.

*Combis* leave regularly from 9am along Amado Nervo near the market at the top end of Constitución (the last one leaves Yumká at 5pm). A taxi will set you back about M$150.

## Eating and drinking

Villahermosa's most famous dish is *pejelagarto,* or freshwater gar, a green-fleshed, pike-like fish barbecued and served with chile and lime. Other than that, the city doesn't have much in the way of culinary specialities. There are plenty of food joints and juice bars around the bus station – and the *tacos pastor* and *tacos barbacoa* along Madero are sublime – but for the most part the Zona Remodelada boasts only cheap *comedores*. The **Corredor Turístico Malecón** on the riverfront has improved things somewhat, with a decent selection of restaurants and bars, but for better quality and more cosmopolitan flavours you're better off heading towards Tabasco 2000, where the hotel restaurants are among the best in the city and you'll find plenty of international chains. **Mercado Pino Suárez**, several blocks northeast of the Zona Remodelada at the top end of Constitución, is good for fruit, bread and cheap tacos. There are a couple of **cafés** at opposite ends of Juárez: *Café La Cabaña*, at the south end opposite the Casa de los Azulejos, is slightly smarter, while the fifty-year old *Café Casino*, at the north end near the corner with Zaragoza, is almost as good but much cheaper, and a local hangout.

**Atarashi Sushi** Vázquez Nte 203. Relatively authentic sushi restaurant with the usual Japanese fare along with a selection of steaks. Rather pricey, but the *sushi combinación especial* allows you to sample ten different types of sushi without breaking the bank (M$120). Mon–Sat noon–midnight.

**Mi Choquita** Javiér Mina 304-A. No-frills local place with plastic tables and chairs offering good breakfasts from M$25 and regional dishes in a typical Tabascan style as well as Spanish/Castilian classics like roast lamb – there's a decent *menú del día* for M$43.

**El Mirador** Madero 105. Classy seafood restaurant with river views and not unreasonable prices. Try the delicious *róbalo* (bass).

**La Noria** Gregorio Méndez 1008. Lebanese and Middle Eastern restaurant with very cheap prices and a menu containing items you are unlikely to find anywhere else in the state: excellent *gyros* (M$55) and *kafta* (M$70). Open 12.30–7.30pm, later at the weekends; closed Thurs and holidays.

**Soyaquarius** Javiér Mina (opposite Choquita), with branch at Zaragoza 410, near Parque Juárez. Vegetarian food and health-food shop that, bizarrely, also sells hamburgers and fried chicken (M$20–30). Delicious fresh sandwiches and daily set lunch (M$55).

**Los Tulipanes** CICOM complex. For Tabasco cuisine, it's hard to beat this attractive riverside restaurant in the heart of the Cultural Centre, with a menu featuring local specialities such as *pejelagarto* empanadas (mains from M$70) and a popular buffet on Sun (M$140). Daily 1–9pm.

**Villa Rica** Corredor Turístico Malecón (end of Zaragoza) ☎993/312-1801. One of the best options on the waterfront, with excellent seafood, prawns and shellfish and a smart riverside setting (mains from M$100). Handy for a post-dinner bar crawl along the malecón.

**Villahermosa Riviera** Constitución 104 ☎993/312-4468. Classy and expensive – main courses start from M$120 – but the food is fantastic. Puts on frequent live music, and Thurs–Sat the fifth floor turns into a lounge bar and club with various theme nights (M$30 cover on Sat). The views along the river at sunset are magical. Daily 1pm–2am.

## Nightlife

Villahermosa's clubs and bars are scattered all over the city, but unless you're staying near Tabasco 2000 your best bet is to head for the malecón. Most places get going at around 7pm, and close around 3am: *Embarcardo* (Tues–Sun 1pm–3am), at the southern end of the promenade, is a good place for an early drink, with a big video screen showing major sports events. *Aqa Oyster Bar* is further up and turns into a fashionable club with guest DJs and various covers (Tues–Sun 9pm–4am; cover M$30–100). *Fiesta Río* (Tues–Sun 6pm–3am) next door focuses more on Latin pop and local music. Over on the landward side of the malecón, across the street and just north of Reforma, *El Jarro Café* offers salsa and *son Cubano* (Thurs–Sat), while *La Malinche* at no. 652 serves M$10 beers in an upmarket cantina. Hotel bars such as *El Barzón* in the *Best Western*, host live music and happy hours most evenings.

## Listings

**Airlines** Aeroméxico, Carlos Pellicer Cámara 511 ☎993/314-9262; Aviacsa, Vía 3 no.120 Local 8 Plaza D'Atocha Mall, in Tabasco 2000 ☎1800-284-2272; Mexicana, Vía 3, no.120 Local 5 y 6 Plaza D'Atocha Mall, in Tabasco 2000 ☎993/316-3132.

**Banks and exchange** There are branches of all major banks at the airport and in the centre, on

## Moving on from Villahermosa

Villahermosa is a major regional transport hub, with excellent air and bus connections to every corner of the country and state. From the **airport**, there are flights to Mexico City, Guadalajara, Ciudad del Carmen, Monterrey, Tampico, Veracruz, Cancún, Mérida and Reynosa (via Poza Rica). Express Jet Airlines, a Continental subsidiary, also flies to Houston, Texas once a day.

To get to the **ADO bus station** from the centre, catch a *combi* from the malecón heading for "Chedraui". Between them, ADO and OCC operate dozens of services to all major destinations: Campeche (20 daily), Cancún (21 daily), Mérida (20 daily), Mexico City (27 daily), Oaxaca (3 daily), **Tuxtla** (11 daily) and Veracruz (15 daily). There are several departures to Palenque, usually leaving in the morning, and two buses to San Andrés Tuxtla (2.40am & 10.15am), as well as ADO GL services to Tuxtla (7.30am) and other major cities – note that most buses into Chiapas now travel via Puente Chiapas, which seems circuitous but knocks several hours off the journey through the mountains. Buses to **Tenosique** are not so frequent. There are a few daily services to **Emiliano Zapata** and three to **Frontera**, the most convenient leaving at 7.55am. For **San Cristóbal**, there are few direct services; it's often easier to change at either Tuxtla or **Palenque**. First-class buses to **Coatzacoalcos** usually stop at La Venta, and there are second-class buses every thirty minutes from the Central de Autobuses.

The **Central de Autobuses** (the main second-class terminal) has buses to virtually everywhere in the state and all the main cities beyond, including Malpasito, which is served by one bus daily (2.30pm). Otherwise you can take regular services to Tuxtla, which will drop you off at the junction 5km from the village. There's another, more dilapidated second-class terminal near the ADO, off Eusebio Castillo near Zozaya, with frequent buses to Emiliano Zapata, Frontera, Paraiso and Huimanguillo. Several companies run buses to **Comalcalco**, the best of which is Comalli Bus, on Gil y Saenz above Abelardo Reyes, not far from the ADO (5am–10pm). Just south of here on Gil y Saenz, *combis* run to Nacajuca. Just to the north, off Ruíz Cortines, La Sultana runs a comfortable service to Teapa (5am–10.30pm, every 30min). **Shared taxis** are usually faster and not that much more expensive: the terminal is behind the ADO on Abelardo Reyes. Taxis leave when full for Huimanguillo, Paraíso, Frontera and Tacotalpa, taking four to five people, but you won't have to wait long, especially for Huimanguillo.

Madero or Juárez, and you can easily change cash and traveller's cheques. Most banks have ATMs.

**Internet access** Internet cafés are a bit thin on the ground in the Zona Luz. Try Ciberware at Aldama 521 (M$5/hr) or G&C on Zaragoza overlooking Parque Juárez (daily 9am–1am; M$10/hr). Opposite the ADO station Blue Network Internet is open similar hours (M$5/hr).

**Laundry** Lavandería Top Klean, Madero 303-A, between Reforma and 27 de Febrero (Mon–Sat 8.30am–8pm; M$25/kilo).

**Post office** The main post office is in the Zona Luz at Sáenz 131 on the corner of Lerdo (Mon–Fri 9am–3pm, Sat 9am–1pm).

**Travel agents and tours** There's no shortage of travel agencies in the Zona Luz, and all the big hotels have a tour desk to arrange domestic flights and trips to Palenque. Creatur, Paseo Tabasco 1404, on the right just beyond Ruíz Cortines (T 993/310-9900, W www.creaturviajes.com), is the best in the region, with multilingual staff.

# South of Villahermosa

South of Villahermosa is an area of exceptionally beautiful highland. The foothills here are heavy with banana plantations, but the surrounding hillsides retain the thick forest characteristic of the area, and the roadside pools and wetlands – unsuitable for cultivation – are as wild as ever. The highlights of this region include numerous **caves and grottoes**, as well as several accessible spas, created by tectonic activity, in the main town of **Teapa**. From here there are a couple of daily first-class buses to Tuxtla Gutiérrez, making it a good place to break the journey over the mountains into Chiapas.

## Teapa and the southern hills

Fifty-nine kilometres to the south of Villahermosa, the small, friendly town of **TEAPA** is a lovely base for the spas and caves nearby. Most buses pull in at the **market** near the edge of town: to get to the centre, walk a couple of blocks down the hill and turn left at the green clock onto Méndez, which takes you past the hotels and on to the plaza. The **tourist office**, Plaza Independencia 128 (☎932/322-0083), provides information about the area. Teapa's **hotels** are good value: try the *Quintero* (☎932/322-0045; ❹) at Eduardo Rosario Bastar 108, which has comfortable modern rooms.

There's swimming in the Río Teapa here, but it's better at the **Balneario Natural Río Puyacatengo** (open daily; free, vehicles M$5) 3km east (walk or take the bus for Tacotalpa; taxis charge M$15). Two-bed cabañas here cost M$200. Eight kilometres west of Teapa, almost on the Chiapas border, the **Hacienda Los Azufrés spa** has a classy hotel (☎932/327-5806; ❺) with a huge pool, spa baths and a restaurant serving local specialities, including *pejelagarto*. Besides taking the glorious spa waters, you can organize guided walks, rent bikes and camp here, and fishing rods are also available for hire – non-guests pay M$30 for access to the pools. Again, you can get here on foot, or catch a second-class bus towards Pichucalco.

*Colectivos* run from behind the church near the plaza in Teapa to the spectacular **Grutas del Coconá** (Tues–Sun 9am–5pm; M$20), 4km northeast. Eight chambers are open to tourists, and others for potholing only. A stroll through the caves, which also contain a small museum displaying pre-Hispanic artefacts found inside, takes about 45 minutes. They're surprisingly humid, lined with oddly shaped stalactites and stalagmites. You could also walk to the caves from Teapa (45min): from Méndez, head for the Pemex station and turn right, following the sign. When you get near the forested hills, the road divides; head left over the railway track.

## The Sierra Puana: Tapijulapa and Oxolotán

If you want to escape the humidity of the lowlands, try taking day trips up the valley of the Río Oxolotán to Tabasco's "hill country". This is an extraordinarily picturesque area, with unspoiled colonial towns set in beautiful wooded valleys, and a turquoise river laden with sulphur. You'll need to make a fairly early start to get the most out of the day. Buses to **Tacotalpa** from the OCC terminal on Méndez in Teapa (every 30min; 20min) connect with those to **TAPIJULAPA**, the main settlement (hourly; 45min) – the last bus back leaves at 7pm. The town is celebrated for its **wicker craftsmen** – the weekend market at the Parque Central is the best place to buy their products. It's a compact place, with narrow cobbled streets, red-tiled roofs and, unfortunately, no accommodation.

Turn right at the end of the main street, Avenida López Portillo, where steps lead down to the Río Oxolotán. Here you may find boats to take you five minutes upstream to visit the **Parque Natural Villa Luz** (daily 8am–5pm; free), with its spa pools, cascades and caves. You can also take an easy 3km **walk** to the park: cross the tributary river on the suspension bridge, head left on the concrete path, across the football field, then follow the track over the hill, keeping close to the main river – about 35 minutes in all. The park's outstanding feature – not least for its powerful aroma – is the stream running through it, which owes its cloudy blue-ish white colour to dissolved minerals, especially sulphur. The stream exits from the **Cueva de Villa Luz** and meanders for 1km or so until it reaches the cliff marking the valley of the Río Oxolotán. Here it breaks up into dozens of cascades and semicircular pools. Thousands of butterflies settle on the riverbanks, taking nourishment from dissolved minerals, and jungle trees and creepers grow wherever they find a foothold – a truly primeval sight.

If you arrive by boat, signed trails lead around 1.5km to the waterfalls, passing the **Casa Museo Tomás Garrido Canabal** (daily 8am–5pm; free), the country retreat of Canabal, the controversial former governor of Tabasco, which contains a few of his personal effects as well as Zoque artefacts and handicrafts from the area. You take another path to the cave, also known as **Cuevas de las Sardinas Ciegas** – the caves of "blind sardines", sightless cavefish with translucent scales that somehow survive in the cave's sulphur-rich waters. To go inside you'd need oxygen, the gases are so powerful, but you can peer into their precipitous entrances. In Maya cosmology the openings are believed to lead to the underworld (Xibalba) and abode of the Lords of Death. During Semana Santa the cavefish are caught and dedicated to Maya rain god Chac by the local Zoque people. Beyond the caves are a couple of open-air **swimming pools** said to have therapeutic properties.

Trucks and *combis* frequently make the trip (25min) from Tapijulapa to **OXOLOTÁN**. Here the ruins of a seventeenth-century Franciscan monastery house the colonial pieces, oil paintings and wooden sculptures of the small **Museo de la Sierra** (daily 10am–5pm; free). It occasionally also hosts performances by the Teatro Campesino y Indígena (The Peasant and Indian Theatre), a company that has taken part in cultural festivals throughout Mexico and abroad. **To get there** from Tapijulapa, climb the hill to the church, then descend to the road beyond, where there's a bus stop. The last bus back leaves at 6pm, but you're probably better off catching the 3pm bus if you're heading to Teapa.

## West of Villahermosa

West of Villahermosa the main attractions are a series of isolated ruins, the most famous being the Olmec site at **La Venta**, although the best pieces now reside in Villahermosa. The mysterious Zoque culture also flourished in this area, and the Zoque ruins at **Malpasito** are quite unique.

### La Venta

The small town of **LA VENTA**, on the border between Tabasco and Veracruz, 128km from Villahermosa, would be of little interest were it not for the nearby **archeological ruins** (daily 10am–5pm; M$30, free Sun). The town is served by a steady stream of **buses** from Villahermosa and Coatzalcoalcos (see box, p.762), so there's no need or real reason to stay. The ancient city, the name of which remains unknown, was occupied by the Olmecs between 1200 BC and 400 BC and is regarded as their most important centre. Most of the finest pieces found here, including the famous **basalt heads** – extraordinary because the material from which they were hewn does not occur locally in the region and must have been imported from what is now Veracruz, Oaxaca or Guatemala – were transferred to Villahermosa's Parque La Venta in 1957 and 1958. The **museum** at the entrance to the site (800m north of the bus station) has a model of the grounds, as well as glass cases with rather confusing displays of unlabelled pottery. The site itself retains some replicas of the sculptures and heads now displayed in Villahermosa, and few weathered stelae and monuments, but the highlight is the huge grass-covered mound, about 30m high, clearly a pyramid, with fluted sides believed to represent the ravines on the flanks of a sacred volcano. The climb up is worth the effort for the views and the breeze. Paths below take you through the jungle – fascinating for its plants and butterflies, but haunted by ferocious mosquitoes.

## Malpasito

Some 100km southwest of Villahermosa, between the borders of Veracruz and Chiapas, a narrow triangle of Tabasco thrusts into mountains known as the **Sierra Huimanguillo.** These rugged peaks are not that high, only up to 1000m, but in order to fully appreciate them, you'll need to do some hiking: not only to canyons and waterfalls, but also to the **Zoque ruins of Malpasito**, with their astonishing **petroglyphs**. The ruins are not difficult to reach, but you'll need to spend the night or camp when you get there.

Second-class buses from Villahermosa to Tuxtla Gutiérrez drop you at the junction 5km east of the *ejido* of **MALPASITO** (around 3hr) – there may be a *combi* or a truck going to the village, but otherwise you have to walk. By this point you should be able to see the peaks, with the great jungle-covered plateau of El Mono Pelón ("the bald monkey") dominating the skyline. This is the highest point in Tabasco, and the sheer sides look impossible to climb. In Malpasito you can stay at the small *Albergue* (Ⓣ55/5151-5229; ❶), which has a few cabañas with bathroom (cold water) and provides simple meals from M$40. The *Albergue* can also arrange guides (M$140) but you can also ask for Guillermo Perez in the village; he can offer advice about the ruins, and might also have a room to rent.

### The site

A walk of just over 1km from the village of Malpasito brings you to the post-Classic **Zoque** ruins of the same name (daily 9am–5pm; M$24, free Sun), overlooked by jagged, jungle-covered mountains. Though the ruins bear certain resemblances to those at Palenque (see p.744), the Zoque were not a Maya group – one of the few things known about them. On the way into the site you pass terraces and grass-covered mounds, eventually arriving at the unique **ball-court**. At the top of the stone terraces forming the south side of the court, a flight of steps leads down to a narrow room, with stone benches lining either side. Beyond this, and separate from the chamber, is a square pit more than two metres deep and 1.5m wide. This room may have been used by the ball-players, or at least one team, to effect a spectacular entrance as they emerged onto the top of the ball-court. Beyond the ball-court a grass-covered plaza leads to two flights of wide steps with another small plaza at the top, from where you'll have stunning views of mountains all around.

Perhaps the most amazing features of this site are its **petroglyphs**. More than three hundred have been discovered so far: animals, birds, houses and what are presumably religious symbols, etched into the rock. One large boulder has the most enigmatic of all: flat-topped triangles surmounted by a square or rectangle, and shown above what look like ladders or steps – stylized houses or launching platforms for the chariots of the gods, depending on your viewpoint. Beyond the ruins, a trail heads on to a clear pool beneath a twelve-metre waterfall, which is too good to miss if the hike around the ruins has left you hot and dirty. More trails lead up into the mountains; a relatively easy one heads to the base of **La Pava**, an almost perpendicular pillar of rock, the top of which is said to resemble the head of a turkey.

Higher up the valley, the **La Pava waterfalls** are an hour's hike along the side of a gorge, during which you'll step between moss-covered boulders and cross the river on a suspension bridge. This is an utterly beautiful, tranquil place, perfect for enjoying the abundant wildlife.

# Comalcalco and the north coast

The journey from Villahermosa along **the coast**, either west to Veracruz or east to Campeche, is extraordinarily beautiful. The road hugs the shore so closely that in some places it's been washed away (you may have to cross by boat) and it's never hard to find deserted beaches and lagoons. New bridges have replaced the ferries that used to cross the broad river mouths.

Attractive as the coastal route is, it's undeniably slow and almost no tourists travel it, preferring the inland route to the Yucatán in order to stop by Palenque on the way. Even if this is your intention, you'll be well rewarded by spending a day north of Villahermosa, at the ruins of **Comalcalco**.

## Nacajuca and Cupilco

On the road north from Villahermosa to Comalcalco, you wind through the heart of the **cacao-growing region**, with a few minor diversions along the way. Twenty kilometres on, just beyond the village of **NACAJUCA**, is the **Centro de Reproducción de Tortugas de Agua Dulce** (or simply Granja de Tortugas – Turtle Farm). A breeding centre for seven local species of freshwater turtle, it is the only one of its kind in Latin America (Tues–Sun 9am–6pm; free, but donations welcome; ⓣ914/279-6471). Ten kilometres beyond here the main road passes through **CUPILCO**, notable for its roadside church, the **Templo de la Virgen de la Asunción**. Decorated in gold and blue with floral patterns, it's the most beautiful church in Tabasco. In the area around Comalcalco several **cacao haciendas** have opened their doors to visitors. The first you will pass, 2km before Comalcalco, is Hacienda de la Luz (ⓣ933/334-1126, ⓦwww.chocolatour.com.mx), which runs a **chocolate museum** (M$30), while Hacienda Cholula (ⓣ933/334-3815) is a further 3km beyond the ruins.

## Comalcalco

The Classic-period site of **Comalcalco** (daily 9am–5pm; M$33, including museum, free Sun), 58km north of Villahermosa, is an easy, very worthwhile trip from the city. The westernmost Maya site, Comalcalco was occupied around the same time as Palenque (250–900 AD), with which it shares some features. The area's lack of building stone forced the Chontal Maya to adopt a distinctive form of construction – kiln-fired brick. As if the bricks themselves were not sufficient to mark this site as different, the builders added mystery to technology: each brick was stamped or moulded with a geometric or representational design before firing, with the design face placed facing inwards, so that it could not be seen in the finished building.

Most **buses from Villahermosa** (see box, p.762) take an hour and a quarter; once in Comalcalco you'll likely be dropped off at or near the ADO terminal on the main highway, a short walk east of the town centre. Green *combis* (M$5),

△ Comalcalco

found outside the ADO terminal, ply the route to the ruins, but any bus heading north will pass by. Ask the driver for "ruinas", or get off after about five minutes, when you see the sign. The ruins are on the right along a long straight paved road; some *combis* go all the way there, but otherwise it's a fifteen-minute walk. Taxis charge M$20. There's a small **restaurant** and toilets at the site, and plenty of buses back to Villahermosa or on to Paraíso (20min), running along the main road.

### The museum and the site

You can see the astonishing designs on the bricks in Comalcalco's marvellous **museum**, though the labels are in Spanish only. Animals depicted include crocodiles, turtles, frogs, lizards, dogs and mice, while those portraying the sculpted faces of rulers display an advanced level of artistic development. The most amazing figure, however, is that of a skeleton – it appears to leap out at you from the brick. The abundant clay that proved such a versatile medium for architects and artists here also formed the basis for many more mundane artefacts: Comalcalco means "place of the *comales*" – fired-clay griddles for cooking tortillas – in Nahuatl, and these and other clay vessels have been found in great numbers. Some of the largest jars were used as **funerary urns** and several are on display here, including one with an intact skeleton.

Though the accessible area is not large, exploring the site can be tiring as the humidity is often extremely high and you'll need to take plenty of water with you – insect repellent will also come in handy. Though there are dozens of structures, only around ten or so of the larger buildings have been subjected to any restoration. Due to the fragile nature of the brickwork you're not allowed to climb many of the buildings, but you can follow a path that passes several of the more interesting structures.

The first one you come to is the main building of the **North Plaza Cluster**: **Templo I**, a tiered pyramid with a massive central stairway. Originally, the whole building (along with all of the structures here) would have been covered with stucco made from oyster shells, sculpted into masks and reliefs of rulers and deities and brightly painted. Only a few of these features remain – the exposed ones protected from further erosion by shelters, while others have been left buried. Opposite Temple I is the **Gran Acrópolis**: it's 80m long, with more buildings being excavated, and there's a fine stucco mask of Kinich Ahau, the Maya sun god. In front of the Acrópolis, Templo V has a small, corbelled side room containing stucco reliefs of nine half-life-size figures in conversation or even argument – they may represent the **Lords of Xibalba**, the Maya underworld.

At the far end of the site and above Templo V you'll come to **El Palacio**, where you can climb the mound and get a close view of the brickwork. There's a series of massive brick piers and arches here that once formed an enormous double corbelled vault, 80m long and over 8m wide – one of the largest enclosed spaces the Maya ever built.

## The north coast

Skirting the coast and passing through areas of wetland teeming with wildlife, the little-travelled **north coast** road is a treat. Mangroves and lagoons are covered with flocks of feeding waterbirds, and if you look hard enough you may spot the odd crocodile. However, if it's beaches that you've come for, you are likely to be disappointed – the sand is grey-brown and, though generally clean, you've always got the oil refinery in sight to the east. There are few hotels along this stretch, but plenty of spaces for camping – if you can stand the swarms of mosquitoes and sandflies.

### Paraíso

If you want to travel on to the coastal route, catch one of the frequent buses passing the Comalcalco turn-off to **PARAÍSO**, 17km away on the banks of the Río Seco. It's a sleepy place, with some beaches nearby – pleasant enough if you need to wind down. Paraíso's ADO **bus station** is inconveniently located 1km south of the centre along Benito Juárez, the main road. Turn right out of the station and keep walking: eventually you'll see the town's most distinctive monument – the twin-towered colonial church – across the river up ahead. The main second-class station, with departures for points along the coast, is fifteen minutes' walk north of the centre and well served by *combis*. If you're walking from the second-class station to the centre, head south (left) and aim for the church towers, which is visible from just about everywhere. Most **hotels** here are not up to much: *Hotel Hidalgo* (Ⓣ933/333-0007; ❹), on the river at Degollado 206, at 2 de Abril, is the exception, with clean rooms with fan or a/c, private bathrooms with hot water and drinking water. There are plenty of juice bars around the zócalo and a couple of decent, moderately priced **restaurants**: *Real de la Costa* on the east side is perhaps the best, with a wide selection of Mexican food, meats, pastas and seafood dishes. The nearest beach, **Playa Limón**, is a twenty-minute *combi* ride north of Paraíso. **Taxis** to the beaches cost M$20–30, and there are a couple of daily first-class buses to Frontera.

### Puerto Ceiba and the coast road east

Ten kilometres east of Paraíso, the road passes through **PUERTO CEIBA** on the shores of the **Laguna de Mecoacán**. There's a *parador turístico* here offering boat trips (M$280 for up to 14 people) and a restaurant serving regional dishes and fish straight out of the lake. The road then crosses **Laguna Santa** to the east, and there are turn-offs for several good beaches before it meets Hwy-180, 50km or so north of Villahermosa. The first is **Playa Azúl**, a favourite of water-sports enthusiasts; **Playa Pico de Oro**, 6km or so further on, is more tranquil. If you're travelling light you could easily camp at any of these and get back to the main road in the morning.

### Frontera and the Reserva de la Biósfera Pantanos de Centla

About 50km beyond Paraíso the bus will drop you in **FRONTERA**, a pleasant, if uninspiring, working town and port. Visited and written about by Graham Greene in 1938, it is little changed since then. If you **arrive** by second-class bus, turn left out of the bus station and walk two blocks along Madero to get to the zócalo or, from the first-class bus station, left along Zaragoza, then right, and walk three blocks down Madero from the other direction. **Buses** for Villahermosa or Ciudad del Carmen leave every one or two hours during daylight hours, and four buses daily go to Veracruz. Everything you'll need is around the tastefully modernized zócalo, including a couple of nondescript **hotels**; the renovated *Marmor Plaza* (Ⓣ913/332-0001; ❺) at Juárez 202 is the best option, with great-value rooms equipped with a/c and smart new bathrooms. For tasty shrimp or a hearty comida corrida, try *El Conquistador*, in an old colonial building, at Juárez 8.

The main reason to stay in Frontera is to visit the **Reserva de la Biósfera Pantanos de Centla**, an unspoilt wetland area positively teeming with wildlife: five hundred types of flower and 523 species of animal, including storks, crocodiles and tortoise. The Desarrollo Ecoturístico **Punta Manglar** (daily 9am–5pm; ⓣ993/315-4491), 10km south of the town along the Jonuta road, offers guided walks, pricey boat trips (M$900 for up to 10 people), and other educational activities as well as a small restaurant for refreshment. Around 2.5km further along the road is the **Centro de Interpretación Uyotot-Ja** ("House of Water"; Tues–Sun 9am–5pm; free), with displays and information about the whole reserve as well as a twenty-metre observation tower overlooking the entire area. You can catch *combis* (M$10) for both sites along Madero (south of the zócalo) in Frontera.

## Fiestas

The states of Chiapas and Tabasco are extremely rich in festivals. Local tourist offices should have more information on what's happening.

### January

**New Year's Day** (Jan 1). San Andrés Chamula and San Juan Chamula (see p.728), both near San Cristóbal, have civil ceremonies to install a new government for the year.

**Día de San Sebastián** (Jan 20). In Chiapa de Corzo (see p.714) a large fiesta with traditional dances lasts several days, with a re-enactment on Jan 21 of a naval battle on the Río Grijalva. The event is big, too, in Zinacantán (see p.730), near San Cristóbal.

### February

**Día de la Candelaria** (Feb 2). Colourful celebrations at Ocosingo (see p.737).

**Fiesta de San Caralampio** (Feb 11–20). In Comitán (see p.730), celebrated with a parade to San Caralampio church, where elaborate offerings are made and dances held in the plaza outside.

**Carnaval** (the week before Lent; variable Feb–March). Celebrated in hundreds of villages throughout the area, but at its most frenzied in the big cities, especially Villahermosa (see p.755). San Juan Chamula (see p.728) also has a big fiesta.

### March

**Anniversary of the foundation of Chiapa de Corzo** (March 1).

**Semana Santa** (Holy Week). Widely observed. There are particularly big ceremonies in San Cristóbal de las Casas (see p.717). Ciudad Hidalgo (see p.709), at the border near Tapachula, has a major week-long market.

### April

**Feria** (April 1–7). Festival in San Cristóbal de las Casas (see p.717) celebrating the town's foundation. A Spring Fair is generally held here later in the month.

**Feria** (second half of April). Villahermosa (see p.755) hosts its annual festival, with agricultural and industrial exhibits and the election of the queen of the flowers.

**Día de San Pedro** (April 29). Celebrated in several villages around San Cristóbal, including Amatenango del Valle (see p.730) and Zinacantán (see p.730).

### May

**Día de la Santa Cruz** (May 3). Celebrated in San Juan Chamula (see p.728) and in Teapa (see p.763), between Villahermosa and San Cristóbal.

**Día de San Isidro** (May 15). Peasant celebrations everywhere – famous and picturesque fiestas in Huistán, near San Cristóbal. Also, there's a four-day nautical marathon (variable dates) from Tenosique to Villahermosa, when watercrafts from all over the country race down 600km of the Río Usumacinta.

# East to the Usumacinta and Guatemala

Heading east from Villahermosa, the toll road Hwy-186 (cars M$25) cuts across northern Chiapas before swinging north into Campeche to Francisco Escárcega, then east again as the only road across the base of the Yucatán peninsula to Chetumal. At Catazajá, in Chiapas, 110km from Villahermosa, is the junction for **Palenque**. If you've already been there and want to see Tikal in Guatemala's Petén, you can go via **Tenosique** and **La Palma** (see p.772), although it's

### June

**Día de San Antonio** (June 13). Celebrated in Simojovel (see p.717), near San Cristóbal, and Cárdenas (Tabasco), west of Villahermosa.

**Día de San Juan** (June 24). The culmination of several days' celebration in San Juan Chamula (see p.728).

### July

**Día de San Cristóbal** (July 17). Celebrated enthusiastically in San Cristóbal de las Casas (see p.717) and in nearby villages such as Tenejapa and Amatenango del Valle (see p.730). This is just one highlight in over a week of festivities.

**Día de Santiago** (July 25). Provokes widespread celebrations, especially in San Cristóbal de las Casas (see p.717).

### August

**Fiesta de San Lorenzo** (Aug 10). Celebrated in Zinacantán (see p.730), with much music and dancing.

**Día de Santa Rosa** (Aug 30). Celebrated in San Juan Chamula (see p.728), when the locals don traditional garb and play Tzotzil harps and instruments outside the church.

### September

**Independence Day** (Sept 14–16). In Chiapas, independence celebrations are preceded by those in honour of the state's annexation to Mexico.

### October

**Día de la Virgen del Rosario** (first Sun in Oct). Celebrated in San Juan Chamula and Zinacantán (see p.728 & p.730) with Tzotzil folk music and dances, locals wearing traditional costume. There's also a special craft market.

**Día de los Muertos** (Day of the Dead; Nov 1–2) The most captivating celebration of the Day of the Dead in Chiapas takes place in Comitán (see p.730), where the cemeteries overflow with flowers and ornate altars. Families make offerings and hold dances, to the accompaniment of traditional music.

### December

**Día de la Virgen de Guadalupe** (Dec 12). An important day throughout Mexico. There are particularly good fiestas in Tuxtla Gutiérrez (see p.710) and San Cristóbal de las Casas (see p.717), and the following day another in nearby Amatenango del Valle (see p.730).

**Feria and cheese expo** (Dec 17–22). Held in Pijijiapan (see p.703), on the coast highway to Tapachula.

quicker and cheaper to go from Frontera Corozal (see p.750); if you go this way, however, you could visit the nearby ruins of **Pomoná**. You'll pass through the town of **Emiliano Zapata** on the way, though there's little reason to stop unless you're coming from Palenque, in which case you'll probably need to change buses here.

## Tenosique

The Río Usumacinta is crossed by the road and railway at Boca del Cerro, 8km southwest of **TENOSIQUE**, where the now placid river leaves some pretty impressive hills. **Buses** arrive at a small terminal close to the highway, 2.5km out of town. Inexpensive *colectivos* and shared taxis (M$15) run frequently to the centre; get off when you see a large white church with red trim on the right of the main street, Calle 26 (also known as "Pino Suárez"). Navigation around town can be difficult. Streets are numbered rather than named, and in no logical order. Calle 26 leads up to the zócalo, decorated with ridiculous giant fibreglass macaws, and Calle 28 runs parallel; pretty much everything you will need will be located along these two streets.

As it's primarily a staging post on the route to the Guatemalan border, there's not a lot to do in Tenosique, whose main claim to fame is as the birthplace of Mexican national hero Pino Suárez (born here on September 8, 1869). His former house is on Calle 26, the blue and white building across the road from the church towards the zócalo. It now houses offices of Telcel, the Mexican telecom provider. If you have **to stay**, *Hacienda Tabasqueña*, Calle 26 no. 512 (☎934/342-2731; ❷), is easily the best option, with comfortable, spacious en-suite rooms, some with a/c (❹). Calles 26 and 28 are also the main areas for shopping and **eating**. Most of the restaurants around here are unimpressive and cheap, and have similar menus. A row of inexpensive *comedores* lines the front of the market, just off the northwest corner of the plaza, while *Los Tulipanes*, on the corner of calles 27 and 22, is better than most, under a large palapa and featuring live marimba in the afternoons, though it tends to close in the early evening. Several places with **Internet** access are found along Calle 28, charging around M$10 an hour.

If you are going **to Guatemala** you'd be wise to stock up on provisions here: there's a good **bakery** opposite the *Hotel Roma* and there are fruit stalls everywhere. The **banks** in Tenosique aren't interested in changing money, but Bancomer on the plaza has an ATM; for Guatemalan quetzales ask around in the shops on Calle 28, where you should find someone who will give better rates than the boatmen. For **moving on**, there are at least fifteen daily bus services to Villahermosa. For the Yucatán, there are a few buses to Escárcega and points east in the evening up to 8pm, but otherwise it's best to get a frequent bus to **Emiliano Zapata** and change there.

## The ruins of Pomoná and Reforma, and the Reserva Ecológica Cascadas de Reforma

On the road from Emiliano Zapata, about 30km west of Tenosique, the ruins of **Pomoná** (daily 10am–5pm; free) are reached 4km down a signed track. Although the site, located in rolling countryside with views of forested hills to the south, makes a pleasant diversion, a visit is really only for the dedicated. The restored structures date from the Late Classic period; the site's largest building is a stepped pyramid with six levels. Pomoná was a subject of the much larger city of Piedras Negras in Guatemala, further up the valley of the Usumacinta.

The modern little **museum** houses some interesting carved panels and stelae, made even more mysterious by the omission of any explanations as to what you're seeing.

North of Tenosique a road heads about 70km through the **Reserva Ecológica Cascadas de Reforma** (daily 8am–6pm; M$20) where the Río San Pedro forms four pretty waterfalls. There's a *balneario* here with restaurants, toilets and swimming opportunities in the naturally formed pools. A further 2km beyond here are the ruins of **Reforma** (daily 10am–5pm; M$30, free Sun), which feature six Maya stelae, seven large buildings and a ball-court, as well as several other smaller and more minor constructions.

### El Ceibo and the Río San Pedro to Guatemala

It's now much more convenient to enter Guatemala at the border crossing of **EL CEIBO**, 60km southeast of Tenosique, rather than the town of La Palma, cutting travel time to Flores to around six hours in total. **Buses** leave Tenosique every hour from 6am to 5pm behind the market on the corner of calles 45 and 16, and take an hour to reach the border, where pick-up trucks drive you to the Río San Pedro for the **boat trip to El Naranjo** in Guatemala. *Lanchas* depart frequently until around 5pm, charging M$35 for the thirty-minute trip.

Opposite the dock at **EL NARANJO** are some large, overgrown **ruins**, where the bigger pyramids are surmounted by posts bristling with machine guns. At least eight daily **buses** leave El Naranjo for **Flores** (3hr); most will pass by the dock but if you get stuck here it's only a ten-minute walk to the main road and a number of rather desperate hotels and *comedores*.

## Travel details

### Buses

Departures given are for direct first-class services; there are likely to be at least as many second-class buses (and often *combis* as well) to the same destinations. See also the "Listings" sections of larger city accounts.

**Palenque** to: Campeche (3 daily; 6hr); Cancún (5 daily; 12hr); Mérida (4 daily; 9hr); Mexico City (2 daily; 17hr); San Cristóbal (10 daily; 5hr); Tuxtla Gutiérrez (10 daily; 7hr); Villahermosa (15 daily; 2hr 30min). Plenty of second-class buses run along the Frontier Highway for the junctions to Bonampak and Yaxchilán.

**San Cristóbal** to: Ciudad Cuauhtémoc, for Guatemala (at least 8 daily; 3hr 30min); Comitán, for Lagos de Montebello or the Guatemalan border (at least hourly; 2hr); Mexico City (5 daily; 18hr); Palenque (9 daily; 5hr); Tapachula (4 daily; 9hr); Tuxtla Gutiérrez (constantly; 2hr); Villahermosa, some direct, otherwise via Tuxtla or Palenque (6 daily; 8–9hr).

**Tapachula** to: Guatemala City (4 daily; 5–6hr); Mexico City (12 daily; 18hr); Oaxaca (1 daily; 12hr); San Cristóbal (2 daily; 9hr); San Salvador (1 daily; 12–13hr); Tonalá (hourly; 3hr 30min); Tuxtla Gutiérrez (15 daily; 7hr); Veracruz (1 daily; 14hr); Villahermosa (2 daily; 13hr).

**Tuxtla Gutiérrez** to: Ciudad Cuauhtémoc, for Guatemala (6 daily; 6hr); Comitán, for Lagos de Montebello or the Guatemalan border (7 daily; 4hr); Mérida (1 daily; 14hr); Mexico City (7 daily; 16hr); Palenque (hourly; 7hr); San Cristóbal (15 daily; 2hr); Tapachula (15 daily; 7hr); Tonalá (every 2hr; 3hr); Villahermosa (9 daily; 7hr, or 5hr via Puente Chiapas).

**Villahermosa** to: Campeche (15 daily; 6hr); Cancún (11 daily; 12hr); Chetumal (9 daily; 7hr); Mérida (18 daily; 9hr); Mexico City (27 daily; 11hr); Palenque (11 daily; 2hr 30min); San Andrés Tuxtla (5 daily; 5hr 30min); San Cristóbal, some direct, otherwise via Tuxtla or Palenque (3 daily; 8–9hr); Tapachula (1 daily; 13hr); Tuxtla Gutiérrez (10 daily; 7hr, or 5hr via Puente Chiapas); Veracruz (15 daily; 7hr).

## Ferries

**Frontera Corozal** (Yaxchilán) to: Bethél, Guatemala (several daily, no schedule; 30min).
**El Ceibo** (near Tenosique) to: El Naranjo, Guatemala (frequent; 30min).

## Flights

Villahermosa is the main regional airport, with international services to the US (Houston, TX) as well as direct flights all over Mexico. Only Tapachula and Tuxtla Gutiérrez airports currently host commercial flights in Chiapas, though Servicios Aéreos San Cristóbal, based in Ocosingo (☎919/673-1088), operates light aircraft to Bonampak and San Quintín (for Laguna Miramar).
**Tapachula** to: Mexico City (4 daily).
**Tuxtla Gutiérrez** to: Cancún (1 daily); Mexico City (4 daily); Toluca (2–3 daily).
**Villahermosa** to: Cancún (1 daily); Ciudad del Carmen (2 weekly); Guadalajara (1 daily); Houston (1 daily; 2hr 15min); Mérida, (2 daily); Mexico City (9 daily); Monterrey (2 daily); Reynosa via Poza Rica (1 daily); Tampico (1 or 2 daily); Veracruz (4 daily).

10

# The Yucatán

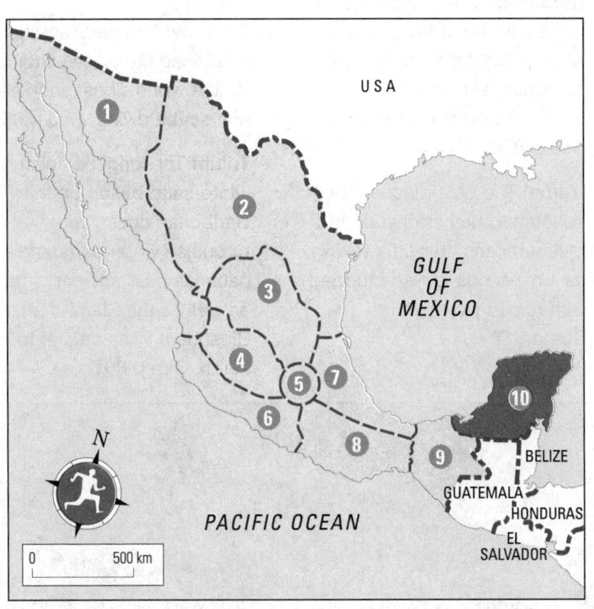

# CHAPTER 10 Highlights

✱ **Campeche** This lovely walled city with narrow streets and pastel-coloured houses is kept immaculate by its proud citizens. **See p.781**

✱ **Mérida** Although the "White City" is the largest on the peninsula – alive with music and Sunday markets – it retains a tranquil charm. **See p.793**

✱ **Ruta Puuc** See the distinctive sculpture at the Maya sites in this area (the largest is Uxmal), and visit (or stay at) one of the quiet towns nearby. **See p.808**

✱ **Izamal** The best place in the Yucatán to buy craftwork and meet artisans, this little town east of Mérida is also studded with ruined pyramids. **See p.817**

✱ **Chichén Itzá** Visit the best known of the Maya sites, with its vertiginous temple, Chac-mool figures and dramatic, snail-shaped observatory. **See p.819**

✱ **Cenotes** On a peninsula with no rivers and few lakes, these underground oases played an essential role in Maya survival and spirituality. Their clear waters make for a refreshing swim. **See p.827**

✱ **Cozumel** The reefs around this island are on the shortlist for the world's best snorkelling and scuba diving. **See p.854**

✱ **Tulum** The longest, finest white-sand beach on the Caribbean coast, with turquoise water and candlelit cabañas near ancient ruins, as well as the Sian Ka'an Biosphere Reserve just to the south. **See p.861**

△ Sian Ka'an Biosphere Reserve

10

# The Yucatán

The three states that comprise the Yucatán peninsula – Campeche, Yucatán and Quintana Roo – are among the hottest and most tropical parts of Mexico, though they lie further north than you might imagine: the capital of Yucatán state, **Mérida**, is actually at a higher latitude than Mexico City. Until the 1960s, when proper road and rail links were finally completed, the Yucatán lived out of step with the rest of the country and had almost as much contact with Europe, Cuba and the US as with central Mexico, resulting in a very distinct culture. Tourism has since made major inroads, especially in the north around the great **Maya sites**, such as Chichén Itzá, and on the **Quintana Roo coast**, where development has centred on the "super-resort" of **Cancún** and the islands of **Mujeres** and **Cozumel**, but is now shifting to the so-called Riviera Maya, the stretch of beachfront that includes **Playa del Carmen** and **Tulum**. But away from the big centres, especially in the south, where towns are sparsely scattered in thick jungle, there's still a distinct pioneering feel.

In northern Yucatán state, the landscape is relatively spare: shallow, rocky earth gives rise to stunted trees, and underground springs known as cenotes are the only source of water. Campeche state, by contrast, boasts a huge area of **tropical forest**, the Calakmul Biosphere Reserve – though the forest is being thinned in spots for cattle ranching and timber. The entire peninsular coastline is great for spotting **wildlife** – notably turtles at the Sian Ka'an Biosphere Reserve in Quintana Roo and flocks of flamingoes at Celestún and Río Lagartos in Yucatán – but the most spectacular, white-sand **beaches** line the Caribbean coast, where magnificent offshore **coral reefs** form part of the second largest barrier reef system in the world.

## Some history

The peninsula's modern boom is, in fact, a reawakening, for this has been the longest continuously settled part of the country, with evidence of Maya inhabitants as early as 2500 BC. The **Maya** are not a specifically Mexican culture – their greatest cities were in the lowlands of modern Guatemala, Belize and Honduras. They did, however, produce a unique style in the Yucatán and continued to flourish here long after the collapse of the earlier, grander civilizations to the south. This was done in spite of natural handicaps – thin soil, heat and lack of water – and invasions from central Mexico. Indeed, the Maya still live in the Yucatán, both in the cities and in rural villages, in many cases remarkably true to their old traditions and lifestyle, despite the hardships of the intervening years: ravaged by European diseases, forced to work on vast colonial *encomiendas* or, later, subjected to the semi-slavery of debt peonage.

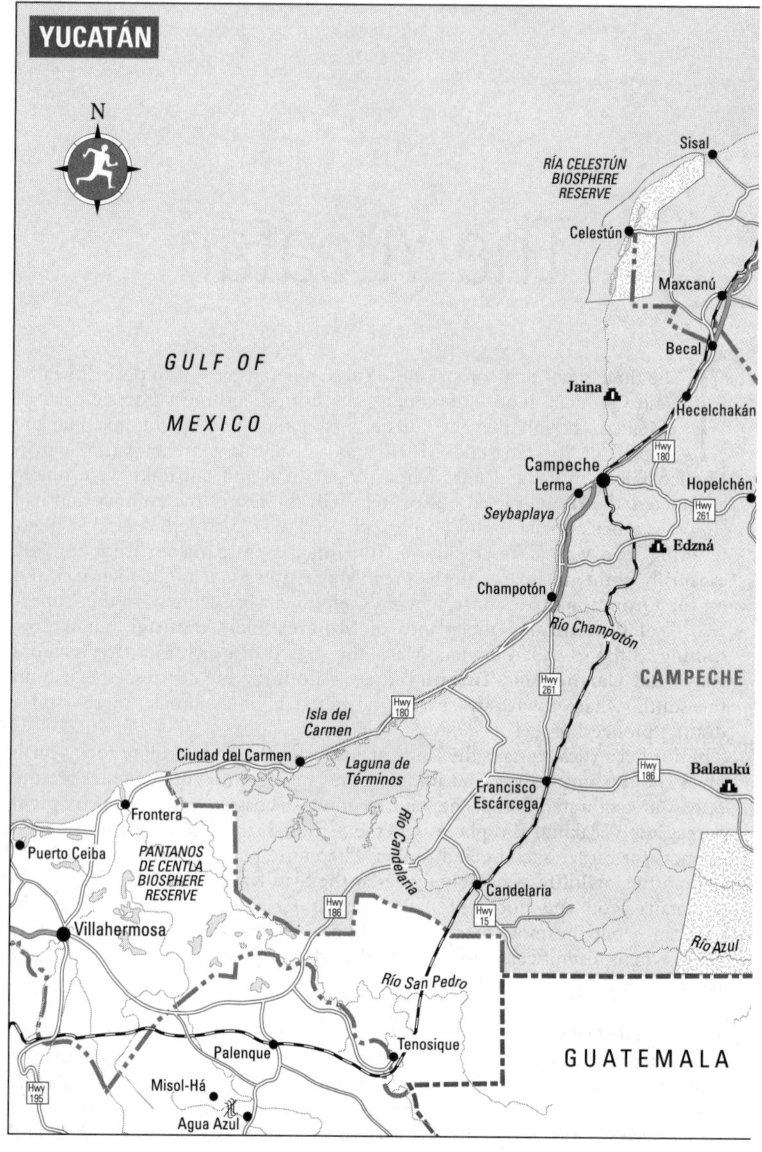




The florescence of Maya culture, throughout its extensive domain, came in the **Classic period**, from around 300 to 900 AD, an age in which the cities (most over the border to the south) grew up and Maya science and art reached their height. The Maya calendar, a complex interaction of solar, lunar, astral and religious dates, was far more complex and accurate than the Gregorian one. Five hundred years before the European Renaissance, the

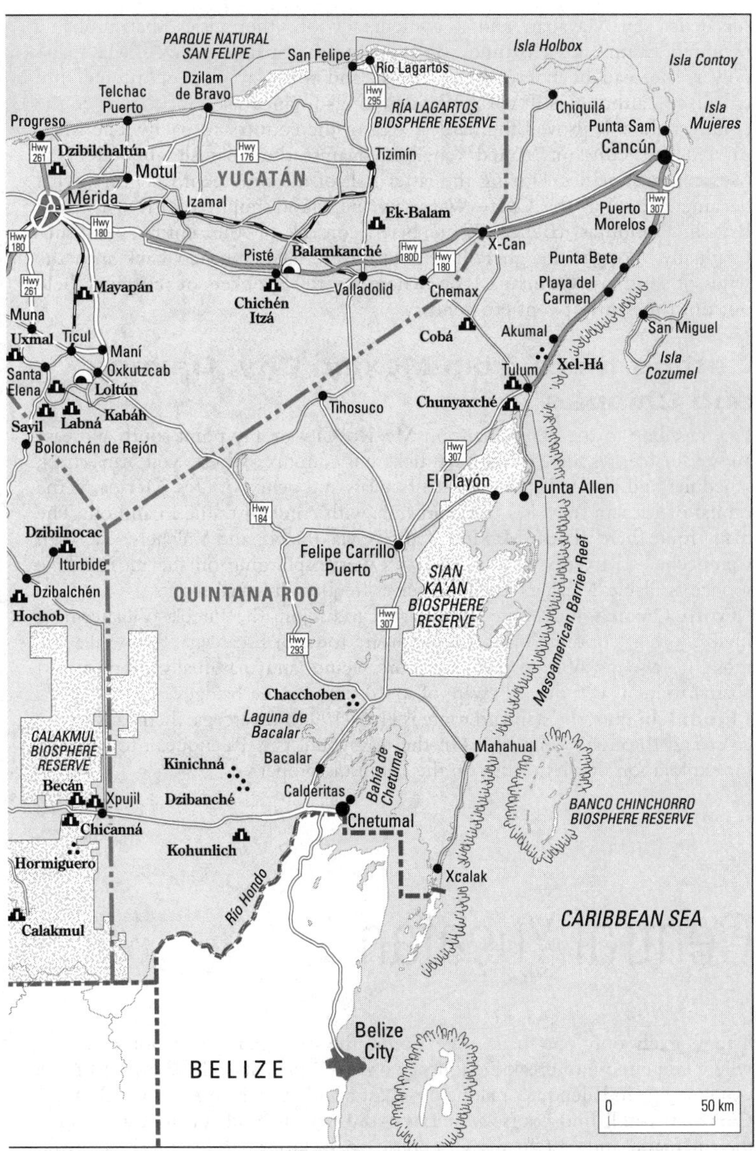


Maya had already developed a sophisticated perspective in art and an elaborate mathematical and hieroglyphic system. In the early ninth century AD, growing military tension and a prolonged drought saw the abandonment of many of the southern lowland cities (Tikal and Calakmul among them), while the cities of the north – such as Chichén Itzá, Uxmal and the Puuc sites – began to flourish. These in turn collapsed around 1200 AD, to be succeeded by Mayapán and a confederacy of other cities that probably included Tulum and Cozumel. By the time the Spanish arrived, Mayapán's power, too, had been broken by revolt, and the Maya had splintered into tribalism – although still with cities and long-distance sea trade that awed the conquistadors. It proved the hardest area of the country to pacify. The Maya carried out constant armed rebellion against the Spanish and later the Mexican authorities. During the latter half of the nineteenth century, what became known as the **Caste Wars** saw the Maya, supplied with arms from British Honduras (Belize), gain brief control of the entire peninsula. Gradually, though, the guerrilla fighters were again pushed back into the wilds of southern Quintana Roo, where the final pockets of resistance held out until the early twentieth century.

## Getting there from Mexico City, Oaxaca and Chiapas

For travelling to the peninsula from Mexico City or any point south and east, an invaluable resource is Ⓦwww.ticketbus.com.mx, where you can check schedules and buy tickets for most first-class and deluxe routes. Mérida, as the capital of Yucatán state, is a transport hub, with constant traffic in and out. The main route here **from Mexico City** is via Puebla and Villahermosa, then Campeche – a twenty-hour ride, so it's worth splurging on the most deluxe service available. Mérida's airport receives frequent internal flights.

**From Oaxaca**, most buses head north and rejoin the Puebla–Villahermosa highway, then continue on to the lacklustre town of Escárcega. From Villahermosa, it's also possible to take the more scenic (and marginally more direct) coastal route. If you drive, beware of speed traps on the bridges.

**From Chiapas**, the standard route is Hwy-199 to Escárcega, then back to the coast and through Campeche. On the way you'll pass Palenque, a touchstone for exploration of Maya ruins on the peninsula proper.



# Central Yucatán

There's really only one main route around the Yucatán; the variation comes in where you choose to break the journey or make side trips off the trail. Whether you come from Palenque or along the coast from Villahermosa and **Ciudad del Carmen**, you'll find yourself on **Hwy-180**, which heads up to **Campeche**, then **Mérida** and east to the Caribbean coast. From Mérida the best of the **Maya sites**, including **Uxmal** and **Chichén Itzá**, as well as a trove of smaller, less visited ruins, are in easy reach.

The road that runs across **the south** of the peninsula from **Escárcega** to **Chetumal** (Hwy-186) was laid in the early 1980s in an attempt to better define the border with Guatemala; it passes through jungle territory dotted with ruins, many of which have been open to the public only since the mid-1990s. The star attraction is the enormous site of **Calakmul**, located deep in a reserve near the border with Guatemala; from the top of its main pyramid, the tallest in the Maya world, the tropical forest stretches like a green sea. You can get accommodation and arrange tours to all of the ruins at **Xpujil**, on the border between Campeche and Quintana Roo states.

# Campeche

**CAMPECHE**, capital of the state of the same name, is one of the country's colonial gems. At its heart, relatively intact, lies a port town surrounded by defensive **walls and fortresses** built when pirates were a threat and the wealth of the Americas flowed through the city on its way to Spain. The centre's streets, laid out around an immaculately groomed garden plaza, are lined with elegant eighteenth- and nineteenth-century houses painted in pastel shades. Ringing the centre are the trappings of an up-and-coming modern city, while the **seafront** is a bizarre mixture of centuries-old monuments and twentieth-century concrete follies. In the past, tourists have just swept by en route to Palenque or Villahermosa, but gradually more are discovering the place – less lively than Mérida, it's also cleaner and more tranquil. For now, though, Campeche remains unblighted by tourist overkill.

A crew of Spanish explorers under Francisco Hernández landed outside the Maya town of Ah Kin Pech in 1517, only to beat a hasty retreat on seeing the forces lined up to greet them. Not until 1540 did second-generation conquistador **Francisco de Montejo the Younger** found the modern town. Until the nineteenth century, Campeche was the peninsula's chief port, exporting mainly **logwood** (source of a red dye known as hematein) from local forests. It was an irresistible target for **pirates** until locals prevailed upon the Spanish authorities to fortify the city: construction of the walls, with eight massive *baluartes* (bulwarks), began in 1686 after a particularly brutal massacre. Although large sections of the walls have been replaced by a ring road, two major sections survive, along with seven of the eight *baluartes*.

## Arrival and information

Campeche has two main **bus stations**, one each for first- and second-class services, as well as a separate terminus for local and rural buses. The **first-class** station is about 5km from the centre on Avenida Central; taxis line up outside (M$30 to the centre), as do buses and *colectivos* (look for "Mercado" or "Centro"). The **second-class** terminal is 2km east of the centre on Gobernadores; to get downtown, cross the street in front of the station and take a city bus, also marked "Centro" or "Mercado". Virtually all of these buses will head to the market, just outside the city wall on the landward side. To get back to the bus stations, look for "Av Central or "ADO" (first-class) or "Gobernadores", "Universidad" or "Terminal Sur" (second-class). Buses from Edzná, Champotón and other **local destinations** use Sur's terminal on Republica, a block inland from the Puerta de Tierra, alongside the market. If you arrive at the **airport** (Ⓣ981/816-6656), about 10km southeast of town, you'll have to take a taxi (M$80).

Within the city, even-numbered **streets** run parallel to the sea, starting with Calle 8, just inside the ramparts; odd-numbered streets run inland. The central **Plaza de la Independencia**, or Plaza Principal, is bordered by calles 8, 10, 55 and 57. Outside the ring of the old city wall, the grid system is less strict; the **market**, just outside the wall by the Puerta de Tierra, is as far as you're likely to need to venture into the modern city.

Campeche's **state tourist office**, in the Plaza Moch Couoh on Avenida 16 de Septiembre opposite the Palacio de Gobierno (daily 9am–8pm; Ⓣ981/811-9229, Ⓦwww.campechetravel.com), is helpful, and there's usually someone there who speaks English. Although this is officially the tourism department for the whole state, specifics on activities outside the city are somewhat limited. It does have a list of **guides** (speaking various languages) who lead tours of the city and archeological zones, though you might be expected to provide transport; try to make reservations a day ahead. The more convenient but slightly less equipped **city tourist office** is on the Plaza Principal, on Calle 55 next to the cathedral (see opposite).

## Accommodation

Campeche's **hotels** are only just beginning to match tourist demand – there are relatively few to choose from, and those at the budget end can be shockingly shabby. The few decent ones are within a few blocks of the Plaza Principal; a couple more upmarket choices are just outside the old city walls. In any case, avoid rooms overlooking the street, as Campeche's narrow lanes magnify noise. There are several good **hostels** and one luxury hotel; in this latter category, you might also consider the lavish eighteenth-century *Hacienda*

*Uayamón* (ⓣ981/829-7257, ⓦwww.starwoodhotels.com/luxury; ⑨), 21km outside town on the way to Edzná.

**Baluartes** 16 de Septiembre 128, between C 59 and C 61 ⓣ981/816-3911, ⓦwww.baluartes.com.mx. Bland but modern, with spacious rooms with a/c, a pool and an inexpensive breakfast café. Request one of the sea-view rooms, which are bigger but cost the same. ⑥

**Colonial** C 14 no. 122, between C 55 and C 57 ⓣ981/816-2630. The only attractive budget place (book ahead, as it's often full). The owners keep the place immaculate. Optional a/c in a few of the thirty rooms, which are painted in Easter-egg hues and in an airy courtyard building. ②

**Hostal Parroquia** C 55, between C 10 and C 12 ⓣ981/816-2530, ⓦwww.hostalparroquia.com. Next door to the restaurant of the same name, this converted colonial home has a good mix of attractive dorms (M$100 per bed) and private rooms with high ceilings (③) around a very pleasant courtyard. Somewhat limited kitchen, but laundry services available; rates include Continental breakfast.

**López** C 12 no. 189, between C 61 and C 63 ⓣ981/816-3344, ⓦwww.hotellopezcampeche.com. Clean rooms (all recently redone, with a/c and TV) in an elegant apartment building – missing a colonial courtyard, but generally good value, with wireless Internet available. ⑤

**Maya Campeche** C 57 no. 14, between C 14 and C 16 ⓣ800/561-8730, ⓦwww.mayacampechehotel.com.mx. This new hotel is a good, if spare, mid-range choice, with a/c in the fifteen high-ceiling rooms, which are done up with pink bedspreads; bathrooms can be a bit small. ⑤

**Monkey Hostel** C 57 at C 10 ⓣ981/811-6605 or 1-800/CAMPECHE, ⓦwww.hostalcampeche.com. In a prime location on the west side of the plaza, this long-established backpacker haven has a helpful staff, clean rooms and a host of services, from laundry to local tours. Breakfast is included. Single-sex dorm beds are M$80; basic double rooms (②) are also available.

**Pirate Hostel** C 59 no. 47, between C 14 and C 16 ⓣ981/811-1757, ⓔpiratehostel@hotmail.com. The public areas and general vibe are nice at this hostel, though the dorms (M$80) and private rooms (②) are in a utilitarian new building in the backyard, behind the colonial place that overlooks the street; all other facilities match the competition, and the location is quieter.

**Plaza Campeche** C 10 at Circuito Baluartes ⓣ981/811-9900, ⓦwww.hotelplazacampeche.com. Immediately outside the old wall on the north side, the *Plaza Campeche* is a higher-end place with some character and friendly service – attractive, antique-look furniture fills the large rooms, which have luxe marble baths (including tubs). There's also small pool, a bar and wireless Internet. The same management's *Plaza Colonial*, on C 12 just inside the walls, has smaller rooms, but the same bathroom fixtures, for a bit less. ⑦

**Puerta Campeche** C 59 no. 61, between C 16 and C 18 ⓣ981/816-7508, ⓦwww.starwoodhotels.com/luxury. Located just inside the Puerta de Tierra, this extraordinary place occupies the shell of a colonial home and warehouse that sprawls down most of the block, all restored to maximize the romance of the past – the pool winds through crumbling walls, and the restaurant has a formal elegance that local business lunchers like, but anyone will feel comfortable on the breezy terrace. All the expected amenities at what is far and away Campeche's finest hotel. ⑨

**Regis** C 12 no. 148, between C 55 and C 57 ⓣ981/816-3175. Seven very large rooms, all with a/c, arranged around a small patio – a reasonable alternative to the *Colonial* or the *López*, and about halfway between the two in price. ④

## The City

One of the greatest pleasures to be had in Campeche comes from simply wandering the streets or **malecón** – especially in the early evening, when the heat lessens and locals also come out to stroll. You'll come across churches, mansions and fortresses along the way, though only the **archeological museum** in the Fuerte de San Miguel can be described as a "must-see".

A good starting point for a walk is the **tourist information office**, on the north side of the Plaza Principal – its side room contains a scale model of the city, which can help you get your bearings. Next door is the **cathedral**; founded in 1540, it's one of the oldest churches on the peninsula. The bulk of the construction, though, took place much later, and what you see now is a

△ Baluarte de San Carlos, Campeche



wedding-cake Baroque structure; look inside (daily 10am–2pm & 5–7pm; free) for a seventeenth-century body of Christ, interred in a dark wood and silver catafalque, among other relics. Across the plaza is the **Centro Cultural Casa Seis** (daily 9am–9pm; free), which has an elegant permanent display of Baroque interiors and hosts art shows and performances, including musical *serenatas* most Thursdays. On the seaward side of the plaza, the Baluarte de la Soledad, just south of the public library, houses the **Museo de la Escultura Maya** (Tues–Sat 8am–8pm, Sun 8am–6pm; M$24), where columns and faded stelae taken from Edzná and other local Maya sites depict religious and civil ceremonies. From here, you can head southwest along the line of the wall to the **Baluarte de San Carlos**, which has cannons on the battlemented roof and, underneath, the beginnings of a network of ancient tunnels that runs under much of the town. Sealed off now, the tunnels provided refuge for the populace during pirate raids, and before that were probably used by the Maya. The *baluarte* houses Campeche's **Museo de la Ciudad** (daily 9am–8pm; M$24), a tiny but rather lovely collection of local memorabilia that includes models of ships, with Spanish commentary.

The other remaining chunk of wall is on the inland side of the old city – hence the name **Puerta de Tierra** (daily 8am–9pm; M$10 for access to the wall and a small museum), for the massive gate that pierces it. From the gate, you can walk along the top of the wall in either direction, looking off the **Baluarte de San Francisco** over the busy new town and the **Alameda Francisco de Paula Toro**, the Havana-inspired promenade next to the market, or off the **Baluarte de San Juan**, where you can peer into the warren of old colonial houses – and see that quite a lot of them lie derelict behind their facades. Every Tuesday, Friday and Saturday, this section of the wall hosts an enjoyable **sound-and-light show** (8.30pm; M$40).

On a steep hill on the southwest side of town, about 4km from the centre, the **Fuerte de San Miguel** houses Campeche's impressive **Museo Arqueológico** (Tues–Sun 8am–8pm; M$25). Plaques are in Spanish only, but the beautiful relics from all over the peninsula speak for themselves. Maya artefacts from Edzná and Jaina make up much of the collection; highlights include delicate Jaina figurines, many of which are cross-eyed – a feature that the Maya considered a mark of beauty. There's also some fine sculpture and pre-Hispanic gold, but the best part of the collection is the treasure from the tombs at Calakmul, including the first mummified body to be found in Mesoamerica, unearthed in 1995. The jade death masks are mesmerizing. Enjoy the view over the ramparts, too, which is wonderful at sunset. To get here, you can take a city bus along the coast road (look for "Lerma" or "Playa Bonita"), but that will leave you with a stiff climb up the hill to the fort. An easier alternative is to take the *tranvía* tour (see "Listings", p.786) or a taxi here, then walk down and take the bus back.

On the north side of the city, the **Fuerte de San José** (Tues–Sun 8am–8pm; M$25) is home to a museum of armaments and a collection of items from the colonial era. It's at the top of an even steeper hill than the southern fort; buses to look for are marked "Morelos" or "Bellavista".

If you're desperate for **beaches**, take one of the buses along the waterfront marked "Playa Bonita" or "Lerma", two seaside destinations just south of Campeche; Playa Bonita is the better of the two, with palapas for shade, but it can be rather dreary and empty on weekdays.

## Eating and drinking

Restaurants abound in the centre of Campeche, especially along calles 8 and 10. **Seafood**, available almost everywhere, is a good bet; try the *pan de cazón* (a kind of lasagne made with tortillas and shredded shark meat) or shrimp (*camarónes*) in spicy sauce. For breakfast, the cafés along Calle 8 near the government offices offer everything from tacos to fresh juices and pastries. Later in the day, the café in the centre of the plaza serves excellent coffee and home-made ice cream. The blocks around the Instituto Campechano (C 10 at C 63) hold numerous snack joints catering to students, and Campeche's **market**, just east of the walled city, is surrounded by *comedores* offering cheap and tasty lunches. Another local favourite is the stretch of *paradores de cockteleros* on the malecón – these seafood-vending kiosks are open until around 4pm. At **night**, not much is open late, but definitely stop by the rooftop terrace bar at *Puerta Campeche* (Fri & Sat only) for the gorgeous view.

**Café Tulum** C 59, between C 10 and C 12. Baguette sandwiches, crepes and fruit plates are on the menu at this casual spot that doubles as a gallery; the courtyard is a quiet place to relax, and it's open until 10pm.

**Casa Vieja** C 10 no. 319, on the Plaza Principal. Cuban-owned restaurant with well-appointed balcony overlooking the main square that serves tasty international cuisine. Prices match the classy setting, but if your budget doesn't stretch to a full meal, you can just stop in for one of the excellent rum cocktails.

**Marganzo** C 8 no. 267, between C 57 and C 59. Somewhat touristy but pleasant nonetheless, and not as expensive as it looks. The varied menu includes tasty crab quesadillas and generous *botanas* (bite-size snacks).

**La Palapa** Resurgimento, a 30min walk south along the malecón from the city centre. Large bar right on the water, where delicious *botanas* are served with every drink.

**La Parroquia** C 55 no. 8, between C 10 and C 12. Traditional, family-run café with high ceilings, echoing with the clink of dishes and buzz of conversation. The excellent-value *pan de cazón* and other local dishes are very popular with locals. Open 24hr.

**La Pigua** Alemán 179-A. Follow C 8 north to find one of the city's most legendary restaurants, a pretty, somewhat elegant lunch spot with exceptionally delicious seafood. Daily 12.30–6pm.

**El Zaguán** C 59, between C 10 and C 12. Small, friendly restaurant/bar, with tables in wooden booths, serving inexpensive but good local and Mexican specialities, including *pan de cazón* and *mole poblano*.

## Listings

**Airlines** Aeroméxico (ⓣ981/816-3109 or 01-800/021-4010) operates a variety of internal flights.

**American Express** Inside the VIPS travel agency, C 59 between Ruíz Cortines and 16 de Septiembre behind the *Hotel del Mar* (Mon–Fri 9am–8pm, Sat 9am–1pm; ⓣ981/811-1100, ⓕ816-8333).

**Banks and exchange** HSBC, C 10 at C 55, is just off the main square and has an ATM; Banorte is on the plaza.

**Bicycle rental** Aventura (ⓣ981-811-9191 ext 405), on C 59 in the *Hotel del Mar* parking lot, rents cruisers with baskets (M$25/hr) and leads tours around town. Rentamar (ⓣ981/811-6461, ⓔrentamar@aol.com), across the street, rents mopeds (M$100/hr).

**Buses** Separate terminals for first-class services from ADO, ATS and OCC, and second-class Sur, ATS and others (see p.782). For stops along Hwy-180, or for Escárcega, Hopelchén, Bolonchén de Rejón and Iturbide (for the Chenes sites), you'll need the second-class terminal. You can buy first-class tickets at the Ticketbus office on Circuito Colonias at C 8. First-class buses leave for Chetumal via Escárcega and Xpujil (1 daily at noon; 5hr); Ciudad del Carmen on semi-deluxe ADO GL (1 daily at 6.40am; 3hr) and ADO or ATS (hourly; 3hr); Mérida (every 30min; 2hr 30min); and Villahermosa on semi-deluxe ADO GL (1 daily at 4pm; 5hr 30min) and ADO or ATS (hourly; 6–7hr). There are also services to San Cristóbal de las Casas (via Palenque), Playa del Carmen, Veracruz, Mexico City and Coatzalcoalcos (for southern Veracruz), and second-class buses to Uxmal (5 daily; 1hr 30min). For Edzná, look for buses outside the Sur terminal near the market (see opposite) in the mornings.

**Car rental** Try Maya Car Rental (ⓣ981/816-0670), in the *Hotel del Mar*, Localiza (ⓣ981/811-3187), in the *Hotel Baluartes*; or one of the tour operators listed below.

**Internet access** There are Internet cafés on every street in the centre of Campeche, most charging approx M$10/hour. You can send a fax from Ah-Kim-Tel *caseta*, C 10 between C 57 and C 59.

**Laundry** Good ones include Klar, C 16 no. 305 at C 61, and Lave Klin, Circuito Baluartes Norte between C 14 and C 16. They charge by weight – about M$10/kilo (though Klar has a three-kilo minimum).

**Post office** In the Palacio del Gobierno Federal, 16 de Septiembre at C 53 (Mon–Fri 8.30am–3.30pm, Sat 9am–1pm).

**Shopping** Casa de Artesanías Tukulná, C 10 no. 333 between C 59 and C 61, is a particularly well-stocked craft shop.

**Taxis** Within the city, they are inexpensive, and usually waiting at the bus stations and at taxi stands throughout the centre. To call a cab, try ⓣ981/816-2363.

**Tours** For a concise overview of the city, the *tranvía* tour, with commentary in Spanish and English, departs from the Plaza Principal. The city route (9am–1pm & 5–9pm) visits the main sights and a few other neighbourhoods, while another goes south to Fuerte de San Miguel (10am–1pm & 6–9pm). Both cost M$70, with departures every hour on the hour. For destinations outside town, Servicios Turísticos Xtampak, C 57 no. 14, between C 10 and C 12 (Mon–Sat 8am–3pm & 5–9pm; ⓣ981/811-6473), runs trips to Edzná (M$150 half-day, transport only; or M$750 with guide, lunch and other stops), as well as Calakmul, the Chenes sites and Champotón for kayaking and bird watching. Other operators include the *Monkey Hostel* (see "Accommodation", p.783) and IMC, in the lobby of the *Hotel Baluartes* (ⓣ981/811-7263, ⓦwww.travel2mexico.com).

## Around Campeche: Edzná and the Chenes sites

Some 50km east of Campeche lie the impressive ruins of **EDZNÁ** (daily 8am–5pm; M$33), the only local site accessible by bus (and even then, with a bit of trouble). Though this is an area where the so-called **Chenes** style of architecture (*chen* means "well" and is a fairly common suffix to place names hereabouts) dominated, Edzná is far from a pure example of it, also featuring elements of Río Bec, Classic Maya and Puuc design. At the height of its power, between 250 BC and 150 AD, it was a large city, on the main route between the Maya communities of the highlands and the coast. The ruins show evidence of a complex drainage and irrigation system that probably supported a large agricultural project and more than a thousand people.

The most important structure here is the great **Templo de los Cinco Pisos** (Temple of the Five Storeys), a stepped palace-pyramid more than thirty metres high. Unusually, each of the five storeys contains chambered "palace" rooms: while solid temple pyramids and multistorey "apartment" complexes are relatively common, it is rare to see the two combined in one building. At the front, a steep monumental staircase leads to a three-room temple, topped by a roofcomb. It's a hot climb, but the view is fine, taking in the dense greenery and the hills that mark this side of the peninsula. As you look out over two plazas, the further of which must have been capable of holding tens of thousands of people, it is easy to imagine the power that the high priest or king commanded. Beyond lie the unexcavated remains of other large pyramids, and behind them, the vast flat expanse of the Yucatán plain. Inside the west-facing temple, a stele of the god of maize was illuminated by the sun twice a year, on the dates for the planting and harvesting of the crop.

Lesser buildings surround the ceremonial precinct. The **Nohochná** (Casa Grande, or Big House), a palace on the northwest side, is some 55m long and contains a room used as a *temazcal* (sauna), with stone benches and hearths over which water could be boiled. Over in the **Pequeña Acrópolis**, the **Templo de los Mascarones** contains two eerie masks representing the sun god, rising on the east (left-hand) side and setting on the west.

**Buses** leave from Campeche in front of the Sur terminal on Republica south of the market (see p.782) in the mornings; the last ride back to Campeche is at 3.30pm, but check with the driver on the way there. You may also be able to get a **combi** along Gobernadores north of the market. A **sound-and-light show** was scheduled to begin in December 2006; it ends after the last bus, so you'll need your own transport back. Alternatively, you could join an **organized trip** from Campeche (see opposite).

## Other Chenes sites

Ruins that exhibit undiluted Chenes style (marked by colonnaded facades and monster-mouth doorways, evolved from the Río Bec further south) are accessible only with a car or exceptional determination. You could take one of the near-hourly buses from Campeche's second-class terminal to **HOPELCHÉN**, about 90km east of Campeche, but the sites are buried in the jungle quite a ways off the road that runs southeast. If you drive, fill your gas tank in Campeche, as there are no services. In the village, which has been home to a Mennonite community since the 1980s, the woodcarvings in the eighteenth-century church of San Antonio de Padua are worth a visit. To **stay** the night in Hopelchén, the only option is *Los Arcos* (Ⓣ982/822-0123; ❸), Calle 23 on the corner of the plaza, near where the buses stop.

**Hochob** (daily 8am–5pm; M$24), just southwest of the village of Dzibalchén (follow signs to Chencoh), has an amazing three-room temple (low and fairly small, as are most Chenes buildings), with a facade richly carved with stylized snakes and masks. The central chamber is surmounted by a crumbling roofcomb, and its decoration, with fangs, eyes and ears, creates the effect of a huge face, with the doorway as a gaping mouth. The remains of **Dzibilnocac** (daily 8am–5pm; free) demonstrate the ultradecorative facades typical of the Chenes style – its restored western temple pyramid is quite pretty. This one is relatively accessible by **bus**, as it's 1km east of the village of Iturbide (or Vicente Guerrero, according to many road signs), which gets regular second-class service from Hopelchén and Campeche; to be on the safe side, arrive early and check return times. If you're driving, you can continue south on this route to Xpujil – it's a good back route that avoids a lot of the truck traffic that plagues Hwy-186.

# South of Campeche: the coast

Continuing south from Campeche, Hwy-180 splits into free (*libre*) and toll (*cuota*) roads. The old *libre* route winds between hills fuzzy with sea grass and reeds, with striking vistas of the green Gulf waters; the only flaw is the likelihood of tailing an underpowered delivery truck. The toll highway (M$51) is less remarkable, but straight and fast to **Champotón**, a port town renowned for its delicious and cheap shrimp cocktails and *ceviche*. It's also where most travellers turn inland, following Hwy-261 southeast towards Escárcega for Chetumal (via Hwy-186) or Palenque, but if you're heading to Villahermosa in your own car, opt for Hwy-180 via **Ciudad del Carmen**. Although this city isn't really a compelling destination (nor worth pausing at during a longer bus trip), the drive down the coast is fast and pretty, with the road just a few feet from the water most of the way. At **Isla Aguada**, the Puente de la Unidad (M$45 toll) crosses the eastern entrance to the **Laguna de Terminos**, linking **Isla del Carmen** to the mainland. Be careful not to exceed the 50-kph speed limit; traffic cops posted at either end of the bridge are notorious for demanding heavy fines on the spot.

## Ciudad del Carmen

The only town of any size on 35-kilometre-long Isla del Carmen, midway between Campeche and the state border with Tabasco, **CIUDAD DEL CARMEN** doesn't merit a special trip except perhaps during its lively **fiesta** in the second half of July, when the town's namesake, Our Lady of Carmen, is celebrated. If you do wind up here, you'll find a crowded, dilapidated historic centre surrounded by modern sprawl, and exceptionally terrible traffic. The conquistadors landed here in 1518, but the first real settlers, in 1633, were pirates who used the island as a base of operations. Nowadays the money's in shrimp (an enormous bronze prawn presides over one central traffic circle) and oil, with many rigs just off shore in the Gulf. That industry has forced prices up, so you won't find many bargains.

### Practicalities

Ciudad del Carmen is a very big place, but once you find your way downtown, you won't need to stray more than a few blocks. ADO (first-class) and Sur (second-class) **buses** use the same station on Avenida Periférica Oriente, a very long way out. To get to the centre, take a taxi or *colectivo* (5am–11pm; about 20min and M$60). There's a downtown ADO ticket office on Calle 24, next to the *Hotel Zacarias*. You can pick up a map from the **tourist office** – really, just a desk in the modern building jutting toward the water from the malecón in front of the central Parque General Ignacio Zaragoza (Mon–Fri 8am–3pm). The **post office** (Mon–Fri 9am–3pm) is on the corner of calles 22 and 27, while Banamex, on the corner of Calle 24 at the edge of the park, and Bancomer, Calle 24 at the corner with Calle 29B, both have **ATMs**. A handy **Internet** café is in the Plaza Delfin, on Calle 20 across from the Plaza de Artesanías y Gastronomía, on the malecón.

Most of the budget **accommodation** in town is around the plaza near the waterfront. At fiesta time places fill up, so book ahead. *Hotel Victoria* (Ⓣ938/382-9301; ❺) and *Hotel Zacarias* (Ⓣ938/382-3506; ❺), both on Calle 24, are comfortable and clean enough; marginally more luxurious is the *Hotel del Parque*, on Calle 33 between the park and the waterfront (Ⓣ938/382-3046; ❺), where all rooms have a/c, TV and phone, and some have balconies. **Food** in Ciudad del Carmen is a mixture of specialities from the Yucatán peninsula and spicier flavours from Tabasco, with a stress on shellfish. Many enjoyable and low-priced **restaurants** are grouped together in a couple of complexes on the malecón just north of the park. Away from the water, *Los Pelicanos,* Calle 24 between calles 29 and 29-A, has an attractive courtyard and a Tex-é menu popular with American oilmen.

## Escárcega to Xpujil



Heading south from Champotón on the inland route, Hwy-261 meets the east–west Hwy-186 at **ESCÁRCEGA** (officially Francisco Escárcega, though the full name is seldom used), a hot, dusty town straggling along the road and old train tracks for a couple of kilometres. Generally known as the region's ugliest town, it's not an ideal stopover; however, Escárcega does serve as a jumping-off point for a number of **Maya sites** that opened to tourists only in the 1990s. Known as the **Río Bec sites**, many of them are in the **Calakmul Biosphere Reserve**, a vast area of tropical forest once heavily populated by lowland Maya, which stretches all the way into the Petén region of Guatemala. Though the most famous ruins lie over the border at Tikal, those within Mexico are every bit as exciting as the sites of the northern Yucatán.

The ADO **first-class bus station** is at the west end of town, at the junction of Hwy-261 and Hwy-186; from there, it's 1.5km east – a long walk or a short taxi ride – to the east end of town and the Sur **second-class bus station** (though you can buy tickets for all services at ADO). You'll find an **ATM** opposite the Sur station, as well as some basic places to eat; the **food** options are a little better closer to the ADO station (try *La Teja*). If you need to **stay**, the gaily painted *Hotel Escárcega*, on the town's main drag (Ⓣ982/824-0186, Ⓔhotelescarcega@hotmail.com; ❸–❹), has tidy enough rooms with a/c or fan, but if you definitely want a/c, *Gran Hotel Colonial del Sureste*, a bit further east (Ⓣ982/824-1908; ❹), is much better value. **Getting out of town** is relatively easy: there are more than a dozen buses daily to Mérida (4hr 30min) and even more to Campeche (2hr); five run to Palenque (though all depart in the middle of the night or early morning; 3hr 30min), and three to San Cristóbal de las Casas (8hr). Services to Xpujil (2hr 30min) go nine times daily, though only three of those buses depart during daylight hours; express service to Chetumal (4hr 30min) is somewhat more frequent.

The ramshackle village of **XPUJIL**, 150km west, on the border with Quintana Roo, is a slightly better base for exploring the region. Basically a one-street town straddling Hwy-186, it offers nothing more remarkable than the ancient Maya site it's named for, though it does have an unofficial **tourist information** office (Ⓣ983/871-6064; daily 9am–2pm, 9am–8pm during Aug and Semana Santa) at the east end. Of the two main **places to stay**, *Hotel Calakmul*, about 500m west of the bus station (Ⓣ983/871-6029; ❸–❺), is marginally preferable, with tidy a/c rooms or a few very rustic wood cabins with shared bath. *Mirador Maya*, 500m further (Ⓣ983/871-6005, Ⓔmirador_maya@hotmail.com; ❺), has marginally cheaper digs in the form of cabins with porches and private baths. Both have decent **restaurants** that are better bets than the dodgy ones across from the bus station. There's a touch-and-go **Internet** café (two blocks south of the highway at the western end of town – look for signs for "La Selva Ciber Estancia"), several Ladatel **phones** and a small **post office**. A **gas station** is 5km east of town.

A far better accommodation option is 10km north of Xpujil in the tranquil village of **Zoh-Laguna**. *Cabañas and Restaurant Mercedes* (Ⓣ983/871-6054, Ⓕ871-6055; ❷) offers spotless cabins with private baths, and the kindly owners can fix tasty meals on request. You might fall asleep to the sound of your neighbour's satellite TV, but you'll wake up to the sound of turkeys, pigs and other roaming village livestock. If you don't have your own car, you can hire a taxi from Xpujil for M$30 one way, or hop on a *colectivo* if your timing is right – though this will drop you about 700m from the hotel itself.

**Leaving Xpujil**, there are four **buses** a day to Chetumal, and seven to Escárcega, though you may not always be able to secure a seat, as first-class buses can be packed with through travellers. The schedule in the station does not include several second-class Caribe buses – enquire about these if you're in a pinch. **Colectivos** gather in front of the station, but don't run frequently. It's also possible to catch a second-class bus running north out of town; this route takes you through the Calakmul Biosphere Reserve, past the Chenes sites and eventually to Mérida via Dzibalchén, Hopelchén and the Ruta Puuc – a handy back route for those **driving from Campeche**.

## The Río Bec sites

The Río Bec style, characterized by long buildings with matching towers (really, dramatically elongated pyramids) at each end and narrow roofcombs, can be seen at a number of sites in this region. The most accessible, though also the smallest, of these sites is **Xpuhil** (the site is spelled according to the traditional Maya name), less than 300m west along the highway from the bus station (daily 8am–5pm; M$30). Dating from the Classic period, it is in excellent shape, and its three ersatz pyramids, with almost-vertical and purely decorative stairways, are very striking.

The easiest way of visiting the other sites in the Río Bec region is via **taxi**, arranged from either of the tourist hotels in Xpujil – though you may be able to negotiate a better rate if you discuss directly with the drivers gathered at the crossroads in town. Expect to pay at most M$600 per head to go to Calakmul and Balamkú or to Kohunlich and Dzibanché (see p.876), and M$300 for Chicanná and Becán (see opposite), including waiting time (this latter option always includes Xpuhil as well, even though you can walk there); all prices go down significantly if you have more people in the car. Alternatively, you could take an organized **tour** to Calakmul from Campeche (see "Listings", p.786, for details) or, if your Spanish is up to it, with the experienced team at Servidores Turísticos de Calakmul (Ⓣ983/871-6064, Ⓔservidoresturisticos@yahoo.com.mx), which runs the unofficial tourist office in Xpujil. Tours may costs more, but a good guide can really make the area come alive, as many of the more recently opened sites have no signage.

For groups, **renting a car** in Campeche or Chetumal is an economical option, though the drive to Calakmul is tedious, down a winding one-lane road that requires frequent braking for wild turkeys. It can be worth paying a little extra for taxis or a tour, just to leave the driving to someone else.

## Becán

**BECÁN** (daily 8am–5pm; M$33), 6km west of Xpujil and then 500m north on a signed track, is unique among Maya sites in being entirely surrounded by a dry moat, sixteen metres wide and four metres deep. This moat and the wall on its edge form one of the oldest-known defensive systems in Mexico, and have led some to believe that this, rather than present-day Flores in Guatemala, was the site of Tayasal, an early capital of the Itzá, who later ruled at Chichén Itzá. First occupied in 600 BC, Becán reached its peak between 600 and 1000 AD. Unlike the sites in the northern Yucatán, many of the buildings here seem to have been residential rather than ceremonial; in fact, the tightly packed structures – with rooms stacked up and linked by internal staircases – create a strong sense of urbanism, akin to modern apartment blocks.

## Chicanná and Balamkú

The buildings at **CHICANNÁ** (daily 8am–5pm; M$30), 2km west from Becán and just south of the highway, are the precursors of the Chenes style, with their elaborate decoration and repetitive masks of Chac; the gaping, square-carved doorway at the impressive Structure II gives the site its name ("House of the Serpent Mouth"). The rest of the building is covered in smaller masks of hook-nosed Chac, made up of intricately carved mosaic pieces of limestone, many still painted with red stucco.

After visiting the site, stop across the highway for a drink and a dip in the pool at *Chicanná Ecovillage Resort* (ⓣ983/871-6075; ❽), which also offers the most comfortable rooms around (though the "eco" label isn't really accurate). A bit further west on the highway, *Rio Bec Dreams* (ⓣ983/834-2516, ⓦwww.riobecdreams.com; ❺–❻) is a smaller **lodging** option (with cosy cabins), as well as a great travellers' resource: the owners are archeology buffs who can advise on the latest site openings and arrange good tours. Non-guests can stop in at the **restaurant**, with its varied (non-Mexican) menu.

The main draw at **BALAMKÚ** (daily 8am–5pm; M$24), 50km beyond Chicanná and 5km west of the turn-off to Calakmul, is the elaborate, beautifully preserved seventeen-metre-long stucco frieze. It's inside the central palace; ask the caretaker to let you in. The embellished wall, crawling with toads, crocodiles and jaguars, seems to undulate in the dim light, and the rolling eyes of the red-painted monster masks, though smaller than those at Kohunlich (see p.876), are perhaps more alarming here.

## Hormiguero and Río Bec

**HORMIGUERO** and **RÍO BEC** (the latter gives its name to the region's dominant architectural style) are accessible only by dirt road – and Río Bec is rarely even reachable by that. At Hormiguero (daily 8am–5pm; M$25), 22km south from the main crossroads in Xpujil, excellently preserved carved monster mouths adorn the two excavated buildings, which are topped with impossibly steep towers. It's a small site, but the decoration and the wild jungle setting make it a particularly transporting one. Keep your eyes on the forest floor here as you explore – Hormiguero has its name ("anthill") for good reason.

The scattered buildings of the city of Río Bec, 10km east of Xpujil and south of the *ejido* of 20 de Noviembre, are usually closed to visitors, though some years it opens for a few months in the spring. If you do visit, you will see the most extreme example of the Río Bec false-pyramid style: as at Xpujil, the "steps" on the twin towers were never meant to be climbed – the risers actually angle outward. Ask at the tourist office in Xpujil about arranging an expedition on horseback.

### Calakmul

The ruined Maya city of **CALAKMUL** (daily 8am–5pm; M$33, plus M$40 per car and M$40 per person for the biosphere reserve) is one of the best places for quiet contemplation of the culture's architectural legacy. Though the complex is only partially restored and a long drive south of Hwy-186 (down a signposted road midway between Escárcega and Xpujil), its location in the heart of the jungle and its sheer size make it irresistible. Probably the biggest archeological area in Mesoamerica, it has nearly seven thousand buildings in the central area alone and more stelae and pyramids than any other site; the great pyramid here is the largest Maya construction in existence, with a base covering almost five acres. The view of the rainforest from the top is stunning, and on a clear day you can even glimpse the tip of the Danta pyramid at El Mirador in Guatemala. Arrive early (the gate to the biosphere on Hwy-186 opens at 7am) to look for wildlife such as wild turkeys, peccaries, toucans and jaguars. Even if you don't spot anything, you'll likely hear booming howler monkeys and raucous frogs.

During the Classic period, the city had a population of about 200,000 and was the regional capital. A *sacbé* (Maya road) running between Calakmul and El Mirador (another leads on to Tikal) confirms that these cities were in regular communication. Calakmul reached its zenith between 500 and 850 AD but, along with most other cities in the area, it was abandoned by about 900 AD. Excavations begun in the 1980s have so far uncovered only a fraction of the buildings, the rest being earthen mounds.

Some of Calakmul's treasures are on display in the archeological museum at Campeche (see p.785), including two hauntingly beautiful jade masks. Another mask was found in a tomb in the main pyramid as recently as January 1998. At the site, ask about a huge interior stucco **frieze**, substantially larger and more ornate than the one at Balamkú (see p.791).

A few kilometres inside the reserve, Servidores Turísticos Calakmul, an excellent ecotourism organization, maintains *Yaxche* (Ⓣ983/871-6064, Ⓦwww.servitourcalakmul.com), a **campsite** with basic cabins (❸) and space for tents (M$50). It also rents gear, and will point you to **nature trails** within the reserve. You can try stopping in for a **meal**, but as the kitchen uses all local products, it may not have provisions on hand in slow seasons. In that case, you could try the **lodge** *Puerta Calakmul*, down a dirt road just after the entrance gate to the reserve; it also rents pretty private cabins and has a pool (Ⓣ998/884-3278, Ⓦwww.puertacalakmul.com.mx; ❽).



## From Campeche to Mérida

From Campeche north to Mérida there's a choice of two routes. First-class buses and all *directo* services take **Hwy-180**, once the colonial Camino Real. The highway bypasses most of the towns along the way, but signposts direct you to two worthwhile detours: **Hecelchakán**, about 80km from Campeche, which has a small **archeology museum** on the main square (Mon & Tues 8am–4pm, Wed–Sun 8am–7pm; M$24) with figures from Jaina and objects from other nearby sites; and **Becal** (35km further), one of the biggest centres for the manufacture of baskets and the ubiquitous Yucatecan **jipis**, or "Panama" hats (the original Panama hats came from Ecuador). Shops throughout town sell them, and it's interesting to see a village so consumed with a single cottage industry – a fountain made of concrete hats even graces the town square. This area has two special **accommodation** possibilities: *Hacienda Blanca Flor*

# Ancient Mexico

**When the Spanish arrived in what is now Mexico in 1519, they were astonished to find a thriving, previously unknown civilization. In fact, the Aztecs, still expanding their sphere of influence from their base at Tenochtitlán, were then just the latest in a string of Mesoamerican cultures to impact the region – the last in a rich, two thousand-year history. Centuries later, our understanding of these cultures continues to develop, even as physical remains further decay. New theories constantly emerge, and the worlds of the ancient Olmecs, Toltecs, Maya, Zapotecs and Aztecs remain as fascinating, if cryptic, to us as they were to the conquistadors.**

# The Olmecs

The earliest known civilization in all of Mesoamerica, the **Olmecs** flourished in the jungles of southern Veracruz and Tabasco as long ago as 1150 BC. Very little Olmec physical culture has survived since the society died out around the fourth century BC, though what has is enormous: seventeen colossal **basalt heads**, the largest around three metres tall and weighing more than twenty tonnes. Unearthed in the 1930s at **San Lorenzo Tenochtitlán** and **La Venta**, these boulders are all carved with strikingly realistic features, as well as handy dates. Archeologists, who had previously credited the Maya with being the first culture in these regions, were forced to readjust their timeline of Mesoamerican development. The details of Olmec society remain unclear, but its artistic and religious influences can be seen in its pottery, which has been found as far away as Oaxaca, and in its worship of the feathered serpent and a god of rain, figures that evolved into the Aztec Quetzalcoatl and Tlaloc, and the Maya Kukulcán and Chac.

# Teotihuacán and the Toltecs

◀ Templo de Quetzalcoatl, Teotihuacán

The first of the powerful cultures in Mexico's central plain, the rulers of **Teotihuacán** (see p.485) built the largest city in ancient Mesoamerica. At the height of its dominance, between 150 and 450 AD, it was home to nearly 100,000 people. Yet these rulers and their subjects have never been clearly identified – they are known only through reverential descriptions by later civilizations.

The **Toltecs**, who held sway over the same region from their capital of **Tula**, in Hidalgo (see p.494), during the Classic period (900–1200 AD), are nearly as inscrutable a group – or perhaps not a single group at all, as one theory goes. According to this line of thought, "Toltec" simply means "artist", and references to Toltecs in later Aztec texts refer to people in any number of cities in central Mexico. Whatever the case, the Toltec period did see the dissemination of many consistent design elements, including terraced pyramids, Atlantean warrior columns and a grisly fixation on decoration with skulls and sacrificial hearts.

▲ Uxmal ruins

# The Maya

While Teotihuacán dominated the middle of the country, an even more impressive society ruled over much of what is now southeastern Mexico, Guatemala and Belize. At its height, the **Maya** population is thought to have been roughly two million, spread around at least forty substantial cities, including **Chichén Itzá**, **Calakmul** and **Uxmal** (see p.819, p.792 and p.809). More than any other Mesoamerican culture, the Maya have been subject to the fantasies of explorers, who

## The art of ancient Mexico

Outside of the ruined buildings you'll find all over Mexico, the most famous Mesoamerican artwork is probably the **Jaina figurines**, a collection of clay animals and people found at the Maya burial ground of Isla Jaina, off the coast of the Yucatán Peninsula. The statuettes depict a broad range of individuals – everyone from queens to weavers – and their expressive features give a clear impression of the Maya as people, rather than just pyramid-builders. Other types of artwork are **plaster sculpture** and **fresco painting** – but because these mediums are so fragile, little has survived, and even less can still be seen at ruins, as they require careful preservation. The elaborate plaster figures at **Ek-Balam** (see p.828) and the red stucco masks at **Kohunlich** (see p.876), both in the Yucatán, and especially the lurid murals of sacrifice and war at the Chiapas ruins of **Bonampak** (see p.749) are a reminder that the ancient world was much more ornate and colourful than the grey stone we see today.

▲ Jaina figurine

have credited them with everything from creating a pacifist utopia (a theory unravelled when the bloody murals at Bonampak were brought to light) to being enlightened extraterrestrials. After 1200 AD, the Maya empire splintered into a loose confederation of city-states, then, in the fifteenth century, independent trade centres, but despite the best efforts of the Conquest, the culture was not completely obliterated, and even helped fuel a rebellion in the nineteenth century.

# The Zapotecs

Often overshadowed by the larger empires to the north and east of them, the **Zapotecs**, who ruled from **Monte Albán** (see p.656) in Oaxaca, were actually one of the more influential groups: it's believed that they developed the first full writing and calendar systems in Mesoamerica. Like the Toltecs and the Maya, they reached the height of their power in the Classic period. The Zapotecs were one of the few cultures that managed to resist being overtaken by the Aztecs; they were subdued only by the Spanish.

▲ Monte Albán, Oaxaca

▲ Tzompantli, Museo del Templo Mayor, Mexico City

# The Aztecs

Ruling from **Tenochtitlán** (see p.398), the **Aztecs** were the last and most successful of the empires in central Mexico – their influence is still felt today, with more than a million people speaking the Aztec language of Nahuatl, countless images of Aztec warriors in popular culture and the very name México, derived from the name the Aztecs used for themselves, Mexica. When the Aztec empire's development was interrupted by the Spanish invasion, it had existed for less than a hundred years, yet had already grown to dominate an area equal to that of any of its predecessors.

## Active archeology: five alternate perspectives on Mexico's ruins

From beautiful beaches to exotic wildlife, you'll find that there's much more to do at Mexico's ancient sites than simply look at dusty historical relics.

**➤ Measure time at Chichén Itzá**
The great pyramid of El Castillo is a numerological puzzle – trek to the top to unravel it, and enjoy the amazing view once you get there. See p.819.

**➤ Bask on the beach at Tulum**
Built on sea trade, this late Maya settlement still commands a breathtaking spot overlooking the water. Climb down the cliffs at the site, or just stroll south to reach even wider sands. See p.864.

**➤ Spot wildlife at Calakmul**
In the heart of a biosphere reserve, this massive site is the country's most remote, and one of the more rewarding for nature lovers. See p.792.

**➤ Take a dip at Palenque**
A series of pools and waterfalls provides cool refreshment at the end of a stroll around this site in Chiapas. See p.744.

**➤ Stay with the Maya at Lacanjá**
To really appreciate the heritage of the ruins here – as well as nearby Bonampak and Yaxchilán – spend the night in this traditional Lacandón village. See p.748.

▲ Tulum

(Ⓣ999/925-8042, Ⓦwww.mexonline.com/blancaflor.htm; ⑧), near the village of Poc-Boc, is a great opportunity to stay in a rambling, antiques-crammed old house for a relatively low price; it has somewhat dated decor in the rooms, but a wonderful feeling of overgrown decay. Just over the border of Yucatán state near the town of **Granada** (turn off Hwy-180 at Maxcanu) is the small but markedly more luxurious *Hacienda Santa Rosa* (Ⓣ999/910-4875, Ⓦwww.starwood.com/luxury; ⑨); you can also **eat** here, but it's a good idea to call ahead and tell the staff you're coming.

The longer route to Mérida goes via Hopelchén and Muna, passing the great sites of **Sayil**, **Kabáh** and **Uxmal** (see p.809), and is much better if you have the time. With a car you could easily visit all three, perhaps stopping also at **Bolonchén de Rejon**, a pretty village of stone houses, rolling hills and nine wells in the plaza, and the nearby **Grutas de Xtacumbilxunaan** (daily 9am–5pm, M$50), 3km south, and still get to Mérida within the day. By bus it's slightly harder, but with a little planning – and if you set out early – you should be able to get to at least one site. Kabáh is the easiest because its ruins lie right on the main road.



# Mérida

Even if practically every road didn't lead to **MÉRIDA**, it would still be an inevitable stop. Nicknamed "La Ciudad Blanca" after its white limestone buildings (now covered in peeling layers of gem-coloured paint), the capital of Yucatán state is in every sense the leading city of the peninsula, with a calm, small-town geniality despite its population of nearly one million. It draws thousands of visitors, both Mexican and foreign, and has seen a rash of expat investment since 2000, leading some to speculate that it may succeed San Miguel Allende as the country's prime artsy expat haven. But even as the buzz increases, the city retains its grace and manners: every street in the centre boasts a well-maintained colonial church or museum, and locals still ride in little horse-drawn taxis, which gather by the plaza in the evenings. Not only can you live well here, but you can also find good beaches nearby, and it's a great base for excursions to the Maya sites of Uxmal and Chichén Itzá (see pp.809 & 819).

## Arrival and information

Mérida is laid out on a simple **grid**: even numbered streets run north–south and odd from east to west, with the central **Plaza Grande** bounded by calles 60, 61, 62 and 63. Mérida has two main **bus stations**, both on the southwest side of town. The **Terminal CAME**, reserved for express and first-class services from ADO, ADO GL and UNO, is on Calle 70 between calles 69 and 71. You'll arrive here if you're coming directly from Cancún, Campeche or Chichén Itzá. The **Terminal de Segunda Clase**, across the street on Calle 69 between calles 68 and 70, deals with Mayab, ATS, Mayab, Sur and some Oriente buses. The latter station has **luggage-storage** service (also a window outside, facing the CAME entrance). Some deluxe buses from Cancún arrive at the **Fiesta Americana** hotel, north of the centre off Paseo de Montejo at Colón. City buses don't go all the way from the bus stations to the Plaza Mayor; a **taxi** costs about M$30, or it's a twenty-minute walk.

Mérida's Manuel Crecencio Rejón **airport** (Ⓣ999/946-1372) is 7km southwest of the centre. It has a tourist office (daily 8am–8pm), post office, long-distance phones and car-rental desks. To get downtown, buy a ticket for a

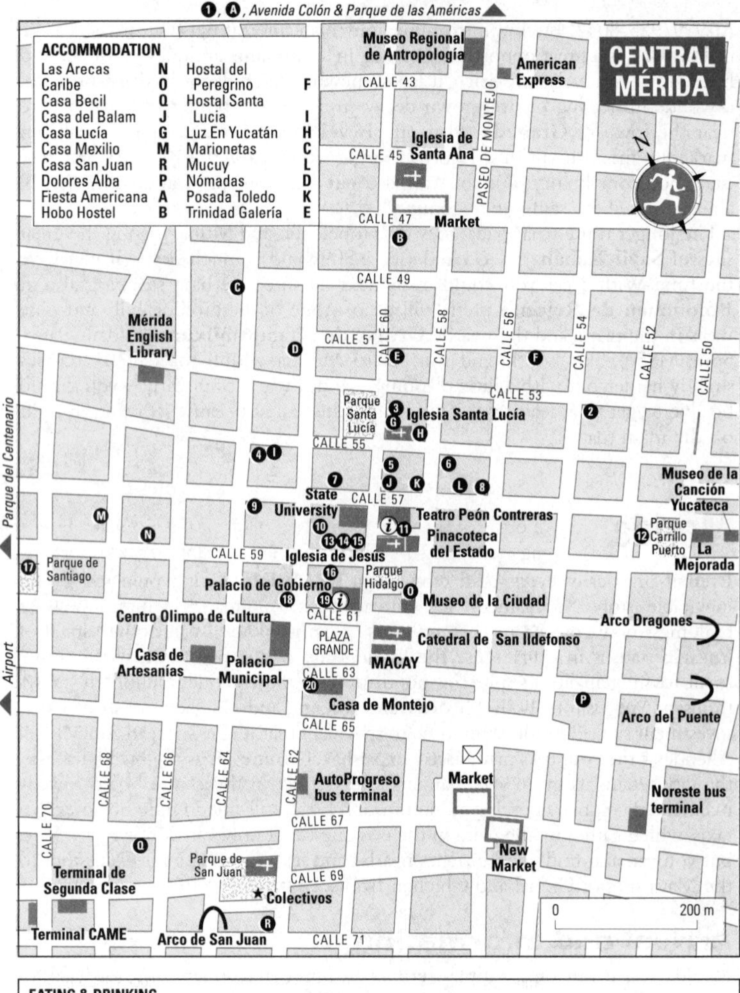


**EATING & DRINKING**

| | | | | | |
|---|---|---|---|---|---|
| Alberto's Continental Patio | 9 | Café Peón Contreras | 11 | El Marlin Azul | 10 |
| Los Almendros | 12 | Cafetería Pop | 7 | Pan Montejo | 20 |
| Amaro | 14 | La Casa de Todos | 4 | Pancho's | 13 |
| Azul Picante | 5 | El Cumbanchero | 1 | Pizzería de Vito Corleone | 16 |
| El Burladero | 15 | Dulcería y Sorbetería El Colón | 19 | La Reina Itzalana | 17 |
| Café Alameda | 6 | Los Henequenes | 8 | Restaurante D'Al | 2 |
| Café Lucía | G | Ki'bok | 3 | El Trapiche | 18 |

taxi at the transport desk outside (M$135). You could also take bus #79 ("Aviación"), which goes to the Parque San Juan, but the stop is a very long walk from the terminal, and it runs infrequently.

Mérida's main **tourist office**, usually staffed with at least one English-speaker, is in the Teatro Peón Contreras, on the corner of Calle 60 and Calle 57A (daily 8am–8pm; ⓣ999/924-9290, ⓦwww.merida.gob.mx/turismo). Pick up a copy of the excellent *Yucatán Today* (Ⓦwww.yucatantoday.com), in English and Spanish. Other **tourist information booths** are in the Palacio de Gobierno on the Plaza Mayor and on Paseo de Montejo at Colón, just south of the *Fiesta Americana* hotel.

Generally, you won't need to use **city buses**, which run on a very convoluted system. But in general, northbound buses run up Calle 56. For Paseo de Montejo, look for #17 on Calle 59 between calles 56 and 58, or #18 on Calle 56 at Calle 59. You can flag buses down at any corner; fares are posted on the doors. **Taxis** can be hailed all around town and from ranks at Parque Hidalgo, the post office and Parque de San Juan. The ones at ranks can charge what they like – usually M$30 around the centre, and up to M$70 to the outskirts – but many of the cars roving the streets (marked "Radio Taxi") use meters, and are usually cheaper.

## Accommodation

Although Mérida can get crowded at peak times, you should always be able to find a good, reasonably priced **hotel** room. Unless you have a brutally early bus to catch, there's not much point in staying in the grimier area near the **main bus stations**, nor in the generic upmarket hotels along **Paseo de Montejo**; the far more desirable options are all within a few blocks of the central plaza – which is still just a long walk or a short cab ride from the furthest transport and sights. In addition to the usual hotels, Mérida now has a glut of excellent **B&Bs**, smaller inns and even **hostels**, all housed in converted old homes complete with vintage tile floors and lofty ceilings. The hostels (some of which also have space to **camp** or sling up a hammock) are booming, but some of the newer ones have not proven completely reliable; try to at least call ahead to confirm whether your top choice is open.

A glamorous but more rural alternative is to stay outside of town in a **hacienda**. The closest one, and one of the best, is *Xcanatun*, 12km north of the city on the way to Progreso (Ⓣ999/941-0213, Ⓦwww.xcanatun.com; ❾), but if you're happy to go further afield, check the state tourism website (Ⓦwww.mayayucatan.com) for a full list – you'll find everything from ramshackle ruins to ultra-deluxe resorts.

### Hostels

**Hobo Hostel** C 60 no. 432, at C 47 Ⓣ999/928-0880, Ⓦwww.hotelhobo.com.mx. This converted warehouse is absolutely cavernous, with lots of space for hanging hammocks (M$50). Beds are only M$60. Unlike other hostels, no breakfast is offered.

**Hostal del Peregrino** C 51 no. 488, between C 54 and C 56 Ⓣ999/924-5491, Ⓦwww.hostaldelperegrino.com. At M$130 per bed, it's a bit more expensive than others, but set in a quiet, beautifully redone house, with an especially nice outdoor kitchen. Private rooms (❺) have choice of a/c or fan.

**Hostal Santa Lucia** C 55 no. 512, between C 62 and 64 Ⓣ999/928-9070, Ⓦwww.hostalstalucia.com. Nice converted house, but arranged a bit awkwardly, with men's dorm beds surrounding the women's section. Choice of fan (M$75) or a/c (M$90) in dorm.

**Nómadas** C 62 no. 433, at C 51 Ⓣ999/924-5223, Ⓦwww.nomadastravel.com. Longest-running and most reliable hostel, with co-ed and single-sex dorms (M$79), space for hammocks (M$59), private rooms (❸) and plenty of helpful advice.

### Hotels

**Caribe** C 59 no. 500, Parque Hidalgo Ⓣ999/924-9022, Ⓦwww.hotelcaribe.com.mx. One block from the plaza, on a pretty, small square of its own. Rooms (fan or a/c) don't have any particular flair, but the views of the cathedral and plaza from the rooftop pool are lovely. There's also a travel agency and parking on site. ❻

**Casa Becil** C 67, between C 66 and C 68 Ⓣ999/924-6764, Ⓔcasabecil@hotmail.com. This small hotel may need a fresh coat of paint, but the staff are very friendly and helpful, and it's close to the main bus stations; a few rooms have a/c. If you don't need this proximity, though, you can find better value closer to the plaza. ❷–❹

**Casa del Balam** C 60 no. 488, at C 57 ⓣ999/924-2150, ⓦwww.hotelcasadelbalam. Good combo of colonial-house style – tiled floors, dark-wood furniture – with all the amenities of a large hotel. Rooms have extra perks like fridges and bathtubs, and there's a shady pool and cosy, wood-panelled bar. Breakfast included. ❽

**Casa Lucía** C 60 no. 474-A, between C 53 and C 55 ⓣ999/928-0740, ⓦwww.casalucia.com.mx. A small, artfully restored hotel across from Parque Santa Lucía that combines European antiques, Persian rugs and typically Méridan details, like heavy wood doors from the original building. ❽

**Dolores Alba** C 63 no. 464, between C 52 and C 54 ⓣ999/928-5650, ⓦwww.doloresalba.com. Popular mid-range place situated around two courtyards (one colonial-style, and one sporting a dazzling array of mirror glass) and a large swimming pool. Rooms in both sections have TV, phone and a/c. With parking, laundry facilities and more, you get a lot for your money, but the place is a bit out of the way. ❺

**Fiesta Americana** C 56, at Colón ⓣ999/942-1111, ⓦwww.fiestaamericana.com. Just off Paseo de Montejo, Mérida's top business-class hotel is often booked with tour groups, but it's a bit of a hike from the centre. It's mentioned here primarily as a landmark: the lobby houses a number of travel and car agencies, as well as a terminal for express buses. ❽

**Mucuy** C 57 no. 481, between C 56 and C 58 ⓣ999/928-5193, ⓦwww.mucuy.com. Quiet and well run, with clean, good-value rooms (choice of fan or a/c), a small pool and a truly hospitable owner. English-speaking staff and a laundry on the premises. ❸

**Posada Toledo** C 58 no. 487, at C 57 ⓣ999/923-1690, ⓔhptoledo@finred.com.mx. Grand, well-kept colonial building with beautiful tile floors and heaps of antique furniture. Single rooms can be a little small, but the "honeymoon suite" is an amazing confection of French antiques and gold trim. ❹

**Trinidad Galería** C 60 no. 456, at C 51 ⓣ999/923-2463, ⓦwww.hotelestrinidad.com. Wonderfully eccentric hotel crammed full of bizarre artefacts, sculptures and paintings. Rooms upstairs are lighter and more spacious, but all are individually decorated (some have a/c). Also has a pool, a small breakfast café and two art galleries. The *Trinidad* (C 62 at C 55), under the same ownership, has several cheaper rooms with shared bath (❸), and guests can use the pool at the *Galería*. ❹

### B&Bs and inns

**Las Arecas** C 59 no. 541, between C 66 and C 68 ⓣ999/928-3626, ⓦwww.lasarecas.com. Small, colonial-style guesthouse (one of the few run by a *meridano*) that's a fantastic bargain. Of the five modestly furnished rooms, two have kitchenettes and one has a/c. ❹

**Casa Mexilio** C 68 no. 495, between C 59 and C 57 ⓣ999/928-2505, ⓦwww.casamexilio.com. One of Mérida's real treasures, this very attractive B&B, in a restored colonial townhouse, is a fascinating labyrinth of individually decorated rooms, tranquil gardens, sun terraces and a pool. The full breakfast (included) is delicious. ❻

**Casa San Juan** C 62 no. 545-A, between C 69 and C 71 ⓣ999/986-2937, ⓦwww.casasanjuan.com. Eight reasonably priced rooms, some with a/c and all furnished in a very homely style, in a landmark house midway between the bus station and the plaza. ❺

**Luz En Yucatán** C 55 no. 499, between C 58 and C 60 ⓣ999/924-0035, ⓦwww.luzenyucatan.com. Delightful studio rooms and apartments in a rambling house, all done in rich colours, plus a pool and plenty of comfortable public space. The owner can arrange excellent Ayurvedic massages, Spanish lessons and more, but service is generally hands-off. Rates are negotiable for longer stays. ❺

**Marionetas** C 49 no. 516, between C 62 and 64 ⓣ999/928-3377, ⓦwww.hotelmarionetas.com. No antique clutter in this fully renovated colonial home – rooms are sunny, sparely furnished and spacious. The owner designed many of the traditional-style floor tiles herself, and the breakfasts here (included) are memorable. Pool and free parking. ❼

## The City

Founded in 1542 by conquistador Francisco de Montejo the Younger, Mérida is built over, and partly from, the ruins of a Maya city known as **Tihó** or Ichcansihó. Like the rest of the peninsula, it had little effective contact with central Mexico until the 1960s and looked to Europe for influence. This is especially evident in the architecture of the older houses, built with French bricks and tiles that were brought over as ballast in ships that exported **henequen**, the rope fibre that was Yucatán's "green gold" from early in its colonization to World War I.

Trade was interrupted in the spring of 1849, when, early in the Maya uprising that became known as the Caste Wars, rebel armies laid siege to Mérida. They were within a hair's breadth of capturing the city and thus regaining control of the peninsula, when, legend has it, the Maya peasant fighters could no longer neglect their fields and left the siege to plant corn. Thus spared, the Yucatecan elite quickly arranged a deal with the central Mexican government ceding the peninsula's independence in exchange for support against future Maya rebellions, which ground on for some fifty years.

By 1900, Mérida had become an extraordinarily wealthy city – or at least a city that had vast numbers of extremely rich *haciendados* (estate owners). Much of this wealth was poured into grandiose mansions on the outskirts of town (especially along Paseo de Montejo) and European educations for upper-class children. Today, though the henequen trade is all but dead (it petered out around World War II, when nylon became the rope-making material of choice), Mérida remains elegant, prosperous and intellectual – it's said to have Mexico's highest number of PhDs per capita. The streets are filled with a vibrant mix of Maya, *mestizos*, Lebanese (who emigrated here in the early twentieth century) and more recent transplants from Mexico City and abroad, all drawn by the city's mellow yet cosmopolitan feel.

### Plaza de la Constitución

Any exploration of Mérida begins naturally in the **Plaza de la Constitución**, also called the Plaza Grande or Playa Mayor. It's the hub of city life, particularly in the evenings, when couples meet on park benches and trios of *trovadores* wait to be hired for serenades. The plaza is ringed by some of Mérida's oldest buildings, including the simple **Catedral de San Ildefonso** (daily 6am–noon & 5–8pm), built in the second half of the sixteenth century. Most of the church's valuables were looted during the Mexican Revolution. One object that was destroyed, the **Cristo de las Ampollas**, has been recreated and is the focal point of a **fiesta** from mid-September through mid-October. According to legend, this "Christ of the Blisters", which is in a chapel to the left of the main altar, was carved from a tree in the village of Ichmul, which had burned for a whole night without showing the least sign of damage; later, in 1645, the church at Ichmul burned down, and the crucifix survived, though blackened and blistered.

Beside the cathedral, the former bishop's palace has been converted into shops, offices and the **MACAY** (Museo de Arte Contemporáneo Ateneo de Yucatán; 10am–6pm daily, closed Tues; M$20), which has the best modern art collection in the region, with permanent displays featuring the work of internationally acclaimed Yucatecan painters Fernando Castro Pacheco, Gabriel Ramírez Aznar and Fernando García Ponce.

On the south side of the plaza stands the **Casa de Montejo**, a palace built in 1549 by Francisco de Montejo, the first conquistador to attempt to bring the peninsula under the control of Spain. His initial effort, in 1527, failed, as did several later forays; however, his son, Francisco de Montejo the Younger, did what the father could not, and secured the northern part of the peninsula in the 1540s. The building now belongs to Banamex, and most of it is used as office space. Visitors are welcome to see the lavishly restored wood-panelled dining room, off the back right corner of the Moorish-feeling courtyard. Above a staid doorway of Classical columns, the facade is decorated in the manically ornate Plateresque style (probably the first instance of it in the New World), with conquistadors depicted trampling savages underfoot.

Across the plaza from the cathedral, the **Palacio Municipal** is another impressive piece of sixteenth-century design, with a fine clock tower. Next door, the modern **Centro Olimpo de Cultura** contains an auditorium, a planetarium and an art gallery showing local works and travelling exhibits.

Completing the square, the nineteenth-century **Palacio de Gobierno** (daily 8am–10pm) is a must-see; enormous, aggressively modernist murals by Fernando Castro Pacheco cover the walls on the ground floor and in the large front room on the second floor. They powerfully depict the violent history of the Yucatán and the trials of its indigenous people, though it's interesting to note that the images are don't always tell quite the same story as the accompanying texts in Spanish, English and Maya. One block east on Calle 61, the small but informative **Museo de la Ciudad** (Tues–Fri 10am–2pm & 4–8pm, Sat & Sun 10am–2pm; free) traces city history from ancient Maya times through the henequen boom.

## North and east of the Plaza de la Constitución

Most of the remaining monuments in Mérida lie north of the plaza, bordering Calle 60 and Paseo de Montejo. Calle 60 is one of the city's main commercial streets, lined with fancy hotels and restaurants. It also boasts a series of colonial buildings, starting one block north of the plaza with the seventeenth-century Jesuit **Iglesia de Jesús**, on the corner with Calle 59. It was built using stones from the original Maya city of Tihó, and a few pieces of decorative carving are visible in the wall on Calle 59. In the same block of Calle 59, the **Pinacoteca del Estado Juan Gamboa Guzmán** (Tues–Sat 8am–8pm, Sun 8am–2pm; M$28) houses a collection of nineteenth-century portraits of prominent Yucatecans and Mexican leaders – Emperor Maximilian, who was executed less than three years into his reign, looks particularly hapless among the crowd of presidents. Back on Calle 60, continuing north, you reach **Teatro Peón Contreras**, a grandiose Neoclassical edifice built by Italian architects in the heady days of Porfirio Díaz. Across the street stands the **Universidad Autónoma de Yucatán**, a highly respected institution that has existed, under various names, since 1624.

To the east, behind the former monastery of La Mejorada, on Calle 57 between calles 50 and 48, the **Museo de la Canción Yucateca** (Tues–Fri 9am–5pm, Sat & Sun 9am–3pm; M$20) details the diverse musical influences on the local *trovadores*, from pre-Columbian traditions to Afro-Cuban styles. The gift shop is an excellent place to pick up some romantic tunes.

Returning to Calle 60, one block north of the Teatro Peón Contreras the sixteenth-century **Iglesia Santa Lucía** stands on the elegant plaza of the same name – a small square that was once the town's stagecoach terminus. Three blocks further on, the **Plaza Santa Ana** is a modern open space. From here, turn right, then take the second left to reach Paseo de Montejo.

## Paseo de Montejo and beyond

**Paseo de Montejo** is a broad boulevard lined with trees and modern sculptures. It's also lined with the magnificent, pompous mansions of the henequen-rich grandees who strove to outdo one another around the end of the nineteenth century. One of the most striking, the Palacio Cantón, at Calle 43, houses Mérida's **Museo Regional de Antropología** (Tues–Sat 8am–8pm, Sun 8am–2pm; M$33). The Beaux Arts palace, grandly trimmed in wrought iron and marble, was built at the beginning of the twentieth century by Francisco Cantón Rosado, the railway tycoon, state governor and general who was a key supporter of dictator Porfirio Díaz. The walk **to the museum** from the plaza takes about thirty minutes; you can also get there on a "Paseo de

△ Museo Regional de Antropología, Mérida

Montejo" bus running up Calle 56, or in a horse-drawn **calesa** taxi (about M$100 straight from the centre to the museum).

The collection is short on actual relics, but it's a useful introduction to the sites and Maya culture nonetheless, with displays covering everything from prehistoric stone tools to modern religious practice and an informative emphasis on ancient Maya daily life and belief. Upstairs, temporary exhibits examine Mérida's history and specific archeological sites. Most displays are in both Spanish and English. The **bookshop** offers leaflets and guidebooks in English for dozens of ruins in the Yucatán and the rest of Mexico.

Another fifteen minutes' walk north on Paseo de Montejo, past scores of mansions, brings you to the **Monumento a la Patria**, covered in neo-Maya sculptures relating to Mexican history. You could also visit **Parque de las Américas**, west on Colón, which is planted with a tree from every country on the American continent. Travellers with children – or anyone who wants to see modern Mérida at leisure – can head to the green space of **Parque del Centenario**, west of the plaza (head straight out Calle 59 to Avenida Itzáes). It contains a **zoo** (free admission), with a miniature train running through it.

## Markets and craft shops

Mérida's main **market** – really, two connected halls that create a huge complex between calles 65, 69, 54 and 56 – is for most visitors a major attraction. A scrum of consumer goods, you'll find everything from fresh beef to hand-tooled belts to more varieties of bananas than you can count. For **crafts**, though, you're almost always better off buying in a shop; prices in the market are no great shakes, unless you're an unusually skilled and determined haggler. Before buying anything, head for the **Casa de Artesanías** (Tues–Sat 9am–8pm, Sun 9am–1.30pm), in the Casa de la Cultura on Calle 63 two blocks west of the plaza. Run by a government-sponsored organization, the shop sells consistently high-quality crafts, including a selection of delicate silver filigree jewellery; the clothing options are somewhat limited, though.

One of the most popular souvenirs of Mexico is a **hammock** – and Mérida is probably the best place in the country to buy one. If you want something you can realistically sleep in, exercise a degree of care and never buy from street vendors or even a market stall – their products are invariably of poor quality. Comfort is measured by the tightness of the weave and the breadth: because you're supposed to lie in a hammock diagonally to be relatively flat, the distance it stretches sideways is as crucial as the length (although obviously the woven portion of the hammock, excluding the strings at each end, should be at least as long as you are tall). A decent-size hammock (*doble* at least, preferably *matrimonial*) with cotton threads (*hilos de algodón*, more comfortable and less likely to go out of shape than artificial fibres) will set you back about M$200. "Sisal" hammocks are generally fraudulent; this material is seldom used today. For a **specialist dealer**, head to Tejidos y Cordeles Nacionales, very near the market at Calle 56 no. 516-B, just north of Calle 65. More a warehouse than a shop, it has hundreds of hammocks stacked against every wall, sold by weight rather than by size; a high-quality, dense-weave *doble* weighs about a kilo. Buy several and you can enter into serious price negotiations. Similar stores include El Campesino and El Aguacate, both on Calle 58, and La Poblana, at Calle 65 no. 492, near Calle 60.

Other good buys include men's *guayabera* shirts, which both Cubans and *meridanos* claim to have invented, Panama hats (known here as *jipis*) and *huipiles*, which vary wildly in quality, from factory-made, machine-stitched junk to hand-embroidered, homespun cloth. Even the best, though, rarely compare with the **antique dresses** that you can occasionally find: identical in style (as they have been for hundreds of years) but far better made and very expensive. Mérida's distinctive *trova* **music** is available in many gift shops on CD; it's especially cheap at the weekly serenade on Parque Santa Lucía, where vendors sell remastered classics or newer songs in the same vein. You can also try the gift shop at the Museo de la Canción Yucateca (see p.798).

## Yucatecan cuisine

Though it varies across the peninsula, food in the Yucatán has a few unifying elements, most based on **traditional Maya combinations** and accented with many earthy **spices**. One standard is *puchero*, a mutable stew that often includes chicken, beef, pork, squash, cabbage and sweet potato in a broth seasoned with cinnamon and allspice, all garnished with radish, coriander and Seville orange. *Poc-chuc*, a combination of pork with tomatoes, onions and spices, is widely considered the region's signature dish, while *sopa de lima*, chicken broth with lime and tortilla chips, is the most popular appetizer or evening snack. Maya tradition pervades *pollo* or *cochinita pibil*, chicken or suckling pig wrapped in banana leaves and cooked in a *pib*, basically a pit in the ground – the shredded meat is then utilized in many other snacks. Also look out for *papadzules*, tacos filled with hard-boiled eggs and covered in a very rich red and green pumpkin-seed sauce, and anything *en relleno negro*, a black, burnt-chile sauce. *Salbutes*, crisp corn tortillas topped with shredded turkey, pickled onions, avocado and radish, are ubiquitous at dinner time; *panuchos* are nearly identical but for an added dab of beans. For breakfast, start with a refreshing blend of pineapple and *chaya* – a spinach-like green that's reputed to cure everything that ails you – and perhaps *huevos motuleños*, an interesting sweet-savoury mix of fried eggs and beans on a crisp tortilla, topped with mild salsa, ham, cheese, peas and fried banana slices. Little of this is hot, but watch out for the *salsa de chile habañero* that most restaurants have on the table – pure fire.

## Eating

Good **restaurants** are plentiful in the centre of Mérida, though the best (and some of the least expensive) are open only for lunch. Dinner restaurants are typically operated by hotels and frequented by out-of-towners; prices are high and most menus verge on international-bland. Nonetheless, evening is the perfect time to visit the sidewalk cafés on the **Parque Hidalgo**, along Calle 60 between calles 61 and 59. Around the Plaza de la Constitución several wonderful **juice bars** – notably *Jugos California*, on the southwest corner, and *La Michoacana*, on calles 61 and 56 – serve all the regular juices and *licuados*, as well as more unusual local concoctions such as home-made root beer. Combine these with something from the **bakery** *Pan Montejo*, at the corner of calles 62 and 63, to make a great breakfast.

**Alberto's Continental Patio** C 64 no. 482, at C 57 ☎999/928-5367. Old-world Mérida, with a beautiful courtyard and formal service. The food, which blends Mexican and Middle Eastern flavours, is erratic in quality and ungodly expensive, however; better to go just for snacks and a drink, and a chat with the charming Lebanese owner.

**Los Almendros** C 50 between C 57 and C 59, in the Plaza Mejorada. One of Mérida's most venerable Yucatecan restaurants is marred by inconsistency, but when it's on, it serves delicious, moderately priced food. The dressier wing, *Gran Almendros*, with a separate entrance around the corner, has slightly higher prices, but can be fun on a busy Sunday afternoon.

**Amaro** C 59 no. 507, between C 60 and C 62. *Amaro* is set in a lovely tree-shaded courtyard with a fountain and a romantic guitarist Wed–Sat. The food is a little overpriced, but there are lots of veggie options, such as *crepas de chaya* – though many are heavy on cheese.

**Café Alameda** C 58 between C 55 and C 57. This old-fashioned lunch café, a popular Lebanese hangout, serves *garbanzos* (hummus) and other Middle Eastern standards.

**Café Lucía** in the *Casa Lucía* hotel, C 60 no. 474-A. The good Italian and international menu isn't too steep, considering the upscale clientele and excellent collection of modern Latin American art on the walls (at least go for a drink to admire this). Also has outdoor seating on Parque Santa Lucía.

**Café Peón Contreras** C 60, adjacent to the Teatro Peón Contreras. One of the more pleasant outdoor spots in the city, right in the midst of Calle 60's bustle. Serves passable Mexican food and pizza.

**Cafetería Pop** C 57 between C 60 and C 62. A good breakfast joint with vintage 1960s decor that also serves hamburgers, spaghetti and Mexican snacks. Close to the university, it's a favoured hangout for students and older intellectuals. Daily 7am–midnight.

**Dulcería y Sorbetería El Colón** C 61, on the north side of the plaza. Popular spot for exotic fruit sorbets. There's another branch on Paseo de Montejo, between C 39 and C 41, a good place to stop after the archeology museum.

**Ki'bok** C 60 no. 468, between C 53 and C 55. Modern, stylish coffee bar, restaurant and lounge serving a varied dinner menu, which includes delicate treats like crepes with squash blossoms. Closed Mon.

**El Marlin Azul** C 62 between C 57 and C 59. Longtime local favourite for seafood, including great fish tacos and perfect fresh *ceviche*. Note that it closes at 4.30pm, however, and there's no sign on the blue awning.

**Pizzería de Vito Corleone** C 59 no. 508, at C 62. Inexpensive joint that also does takeout. Head for tables on the upstairs balcony if you don't want to get roasted by the wood-burning oven.

**La Reina Itzalana** Parque de Santiago, C 59 between C 70 and C 72. This and a couple of other basic restaurants in the same market are some of the few places in the centre to get a casual, super-cheap dinner of *panuchos, salbutes* and *sopa de lima*. Packed with families until 10pm at least.

**Restaurante D'Al** C 54 at C 53. A typical *cocina económica* serving hearty, stick-to-your-ribs daily specials (about M$30), but open into the evenings. Also, beer is served – a rarity at this type of hole-in-the-wall restaurant.

**El Trapiche** C 62, between C 59 and C 61. Basic, budget-friendly Yucatecan restaurant, open for every meal, from fresh juices for breakfast to *poc-chuc* for dinner.

## Entertainment, drinking and nightlife

Mérida is a lively city, and nearly every evening you'll find the streets buzzing with revellers enjoying a variety of **free entertainment**. Venues include the plazas, the garden behind the Palacio Municipal, Teatro Peón Contreras (next to the tourist office) and the Casa de la Cultura, Calle 63 between calles 64 and 66. Expect to see energetic **jaranas**, vibrant Yucatecan folk dances to a distinctive local rhythm (Plaza Mayor, Mon); Glen Miller–style **big band** music (Parque de Santiago, Tues); and the very popular **Serenata Yucateca**, a performance of traditional *trova* songs at the Parque Santa Lucía (Thurs). More free culture – often with an international bent – can be had at the **Centro Olimpo de Cultura** on the northwest corner of the plaza; the schedule of lectures, films and performances is posted outside.

Perhaps the best time to see the Plaza de la Constitución and the surrounding streets is Sunday, when vehicles are banned from the area and music, dancing, markets and festivities take over for the day – a real pleasure after the usual traffic rumble. Food and crafts stalls set up all along Calle 60, and there's a **flea market** in the Parque Santa Lucía.

There's plenty to do of a more commercial nature too, from **mariachi nights** in hotel bars to **salsa dancing** in nightclubs. The best of the more touristy events is the **Ballet Folklórico de la Universidad de Yucatán**, a colourful performance of traditional Mexican and Maya ceremonies at the Centro Cultural Universitario, Calle 60 at Calle 57 (Fri 9pm; M$30).

Apart from hard-drinking cantinas (and there are plenty of these in the city, including a couple on Calle 62, just south of the plaza), many of Mérida's **bars** double as restaurants, with relatively early closing times to match.

**Azul Picante** C 60, between C 55 and C 57. This small salsa club caters more to tourists than some of the other ones listed here, but it offers free lessons early in the evenings, as well as Mexican- and Caribbean-themed nights. A couple of other bars are in adjacent buildings.

**El Burladero** C 59, between C 60 and C 62. A raucous atmosphere, live music and a mixed crowd, as well as a full menu – a good, unpretentious hangout that's not as gritty as a standard men-only cantina.

**La Casa de Todos** C 64 at C 55. Very small student bar – more of a clubhouse, really – with a strong leftist bent. Most nights there's a rousing folksinger or two on the tiny stage; other nights, young punk bands.

**El Cumbanchero** Paseo de Montejo at C 39. More convenient than *Mambo Café*, this small salsa bar is owned by the son of the late Rubén González, of Buena Vista Social Club. Dancing starts around dinner time, with an older crowd at first, who then give way to younger dancers around 10pm. Also open for brunch on Sun.

**Los Henequenes** C 56 at C 57. A modern reinvention of a traditional bar serving *botanas* (snacks) and beers, set in an old house and generally busy in the late afternoon. It's perhaps a little *too* modern, but it does have a local clientele, two-for-one beer specials and live music.

**Mambo Café** In the Plaza Las Américas mall. Worth the cab ride (about M$50) if you're looking to mingle with salsa-mad locals in what's considered the city's best nightclub. Touring Dominican and Cuban bands often play here. Free on Wed; otherwise, cover is about M$50. Wed–Sat 10am–3am.

**Pancho's** C 59, between C 60 and C 62. A restaurant with a pricey but interesting modern-Mexican menu and a lively, if tiny, dancefloor, *Pancho's* is a magnet for hip young *meridanos*. The revolutionary theme, with bandolier-draped waiters in sombreros, is ridiculously over-the-top. Try to hit the daily happy hour (6–9pm).

## Listings

**Airlines** Aerocaribe/Mexicana Internacional, Paseo de Montejo 500 ⓣ999/928-6790; Aeroméxico, Plaza Americana, *Hotel Fiesta Americana* ⓣ999/920-1260, at the airport 946-1400; American, at Nice Trip travel agency, C 62 no. 309-D, at Colón ⓣ999/925-9643; Continental, Paseo de Montejo 437, at C 29 ⓣ999/926-3100; Mexicana, C 56 no. 493 ⓣ999/924-7421.

**American Express** Paseo de Montejo 492, between C 41 and C 43 ⓣ999/942-8200, ⓕ942-8210 (Mon–Fri 9am–5pm, Sat 9am–noon).

## Moving on from Mérida

As the biggest travel hub in the Yucatán, Mérida has a profusion of **bus stations**, each theoretically dedicated to certain bus companies and regions; in practice, however, the different terminals duplicate routes and services. If you want the fastest long-distance service, go via ADO, semi-deluxe ADO GL or deluxe UNO service at the first-class **Terminal CAME** or the **Fiesta Americana** terminal on Paseo de Montejo (which handles only deluxe service to Cancún). You might, however, be able to find a comparably fast trip at a lower price at the **Terminal de Segunda Clase** across the street from the CAME; also come here if you're looking for a bus to any town between Mérida and Campeche, or a town on the Ruta Puuc.

Slow buses to small towns leave from the **Noreste** terminal, on Calle 67 at Calle 50: visit here for coastal towns east and west of Progreso (such as Chelem, Dzilam de Bravo or San Felipe) and some points on the Ruta de los Conventos southeast of Mérida (such as Mayapán). The Dzibilchaltún and Progreso service runs from the **AutoProgreso** bus station on Calle 62 between calles 65 and 67. Additionally, **colectivos** often provide more frequent service to destinations an hour or two outside the city, and to smaller villages. These, as well as small buses to Dzibilchaltún, Oxkutzcab and Ticul, congregate on **Parque de San Juan** (Calle 62 at Calle 69). For Progreso, colectivos leave from the east side of Calle 60 between calles 65 and 67.

Bus services from Mérida include (C=Terminal CAME; SC=Terminal de Segunda Clase; N=Noreste; AP=AutoProgreso): **Celestún** (N: hourly 5.15am–10.30pm; 2hr); **Chetumal** (C: 5 daily; SC: 7 daily; 6–8hr); **Chichén Itzá** (C: 3 daily; SC: hourly 6am–midnight; N: hourly 5.20am–10.20am; 1hr 30min–2hr); **Chiquilá/Holbox** (SC: 1 daily at 11.30pm; 6hr); **Ciudad del Carmen** (C: hourly 4am–12.30pm; SC: 7 daily, 2 of which are deluxe; 5hr 30min–7hr); **Dzibilchaltún** (AP: hourly; 30min); **Dzilam de Bravo** (N: 8 daily; 4hr); **Escárcega** (C: 6 daily; SC: 3 daily; 4hr 30min–6hr); **Felipe Carrillo Puerto** (SC: 8 daily; 2hr 30min); **Izamal** (N: every 45min 4am–9pm; 1hr 30min); **Mayapán** (N: 2 daily; 1hr 15min); Mexico City (C: 6 daily; 18–20hr); Oxkutzcab (SC: hourly 6am–6pm; N: hourly 5.30am–8pm; 2hr); Palenque (C: 4 daily; 7hr 30min–9hr); **Playa del Carmen** (C: 15 daily; SC: 1 daily via Cobá at 5am; 5–7hr); Progreso (AP: every 30min; 45min); Río Lagartos (N: 3 daily; 6hr); **San Felipe** (N: 1 daily at 5.30pm; 6hr 30min); Santa Elena (SC: 5 daily; 1hr); **Tizimín** (N: hourly 5.30am–8.20pm; 4hr); **Tulum** (C: 4 daily; SC: 6 daily, plus 1 daily via Cobá at 5am; 5hr 30min–7hr); **Valladolid** (C: 10 daily; SC: hourly 6am–midnight; N: hourly 5am–10:20pm; 2–3hr); Villahermosa (C: hourly 7.15am–12.30pm; SC: 3 daily; 7hr 30min–10hr).

**Flights** depart from Lic. Manuel Crecencio Rejón airport (☎999/946-1372) for Mexico City, Cancún, Ciudad del Carmen and Villahermosa, as well as some international destinations; to get to the airport, catch bus #79 ("Aviación") going east on C 67. A taxi from the centre costs about M$80.

### The Ruta Puuc bus

Infrequent buses make the more out-of-the-way ruins on the **Ruta Puuc** (see p.808) difficult to visit without your own car, but the Autotransportes del Sur (ATS) company offers a day-trip service for tourists that's budget-friendly, if a bit rushed. The trip costs M$120 and leaves at 8am every day from the Terminal de Segunda Clase, visiting Uxmal, Sayil, Kabáh and Xlapak. You get just long enough at each site to form a general impression, and there's no guide or lunch included in the price.

**Banks and exchange** Most banks are around C 65 between C 60 and C 64, have ATMs and are open 9am–4pm. The most centrally located is Banamex, in the Casa de Montejo on the south side of the plaza; it also has an ATM.

**Books** Librería Burrel, C 59 between C 60 and C 62, is good for maps; Librería Dante across the street sells guidebooks (another Dante branch is on the west side of the plaza). The Conaculta bookstore adjacent to Teatro Daniel Ayala, C 60 just north of the plaza, carries a good stock of art books, guides and music. Alternatively, borrow English-language books from the extensive Mérida English Library, C 53 between C 66 and C 68, which also functions as a meeting point for the city's expat community.

**Car rental** Family-run Mexico Rent a Car, with offices at C 57-A, between C 58 and C 60, and at C 62 no. 483-A, is friendly, with very good rates that include all types of insurance (ⓣ999/927-4916, ⓔmexicorentacar@hotmail.com). All the international agencies have offices at the *Fiesta Americana* on Paseo de Montejo.

**Consulates** Belize, C 53 no. 498, at C 58 ⓣ999/928-6152, ⓔdutton@sureste.com; Cuba, C 1-D no. 320, at C 42 ⓣ999/944-4216, ⓔconsulcuba@yuc1.telmex.net.mx; US, Paseo de Montejo 453, at Colón ⓣ999/925-5011.

**Internet access** There are Internet cafés on every street in central Mérida, with rates between M$15 and M$20/hr; try Chandler's, in the shopping complex on the north side of the plaza.

**Hospitals** Clinica de Mérida hospital, Itzáes 242, at Colón (ⓣ999/920-0411, ⓦwww.clinicademerida.com.mx), is accustomed to dealing with foreigners.

**Laundry** If your hotel doesn't do laundry, try Lavandería La Fe, C 61 between C 62 and C 64, which is open seven days a week.

**Post office** C 65 between C 56 and C 56-A (Mon–Fri 8am–4.30pm, Sat 9am–1pm).

**Telephones** A small *caseta* in the *Fiesta Americana* mall has better-than-usual prices for calls to the US and Europe.

**Tourist police** This special squad, dressed in white shirts and brown pants, roams the plaza giving directions and otherwise helping visitors (ⓣ999/925-2555 ext 260).

**Travel agents and tours** Mérida's tourism bureau gives a free walking tour every day but Sunday at 9.30am; reserve at the office in the Palacio de Gobierno. Horse-drawn carriages (*calesas*) are M$150 for a 1hr trip around the centre and up Paseo de Montejo, or M$250 to the out-of-the-way Parque de las Américas. Two bus tours go further afield than you'd walk: avoid the eyesore red double-deckers in favour of the festive open-sided one that departs from Parque de Santa Lucía (ⓣ999/927-6119; Sun 10am & 1pm, Mon–Sat 10am, 1pm, 4pm & 7pm; M$75). To get out of town, student travel agency Nómadas (ⓣ999/948-1187, ⓦwww.nomadastravel.com) has good-value excursions to Uxmal and Chichén Itzá. Ecoturísmo Yucatán (ⓣ999/920-2772, ⓦwww.ecoyuc.com) runs a day trip to three nearby cenotes. With Yucatan Trails, C 62 no. 482, between C 57 and C 59 (ⓣ999/928-2582, ⓔyucatantrails@hotmail.com), tours include a handy one-way Mérida–Chichén Itzá–Cancún package; Cuba trips are also available. The knowledgeable Canadian owner offers luggage storage for M$10/day.

## North of Mérida: the coast

A wide, fast road (Hwy-261) connects Mérida with the coast to north, first passing the ancient Maya complex of **Dzibilchaltún**, then arriving after 36km in the port of **Progreso**, on which *meridanos* descend en masse in summer. The drive out of the city follows Paseo de Montejo through miles of suburbs and shopping malls before reaching the countryside, where the henequen industry still operates on a small scale.

It's easy enough to visit both Dzibilchaltún and Progreso from Mérida: **combis** leave for the village adjacent to the ruins (also called Dzibilchaltún) from Parque San Juan (calles 62 and 69) about every thirty minutes. From the site, you can walk or hitch a ride back to the main highway, where you can flag down a Progreso- or Mérida-bound bus or *combi*. *Combis* return to Mérida from the corner of calles 80 and 31 near the post office, on the north side of Progreso's Parque Central (note that leaving on Sunday evenings in the summer, with the rest of the weekend crowds, you'll have a very long wait). To go straight to the coast from Mérida, **buses** leave from the terminal dedicated to Progreso services on Calle 62 between calles 65 and 67.

Due west of the city, the little village of **Celestún** offers a very different coastal experience, as it's surrounded by a large nature reserve. In fact, most people hit the beach only after taking a boat tour around a long inlet that's home to a massive flamingo colony.

## Dzibilchaltún

The archeological importance of the ruins of the ancient city of **DZIBILCHALTÚN** (daily 8am–5pm; M$58) is hardly reflected in what you actually see. What it lacks in grandiosity, though, it makes up for in the excellent small **Museo del Pueblo Maya** (Tues–Sun 8am–4pm), which examines the persistence of Maya culture until modern times. There's also a very pretty **cenote**, in which you can swim, and the area is part of an **eco-archeological park**, where birders can catch the rough-winged swallow and the Yucatán woodpecker. Allow about two hours to see everything.

The place was settled from 1000 BC right through to the Conquest, the longest continuous occupation of any known site. More than eight thousand structures have been mapped, but unfortunately, little has survived, in particular because the ready-dressed stones were a handy building material, used in several local towns and in the Mérida–Progreso road. There is virtually no descriptive labelling on the buildings, so it's worth hiring a **guide** (M$200 for up to six people) at the main entrance.

From the museum at the entrance, a meandering nature trail leads to the **Templo de las Siete Muñecas** (Temple of the Seven Dolls). The temple was originally a simple square pyramid, subsequently built over with a more complex structure. Later still, a passageway was cut through to the original building and seven deformed clay figurines (dolls) were buried, with a tube through which their spirits were meant to commune with the priests. The structure is remarkable for being the only known Maya temple to have windows, and for having a tower in place of the usual roofcomb. On the **equinoxes**, the sun shines straight through the tower doors, in a display of ancient astronomical savvy that draws crowd of tourists.

One of the ancient causeways that linked the city's major points runs straight from the temple to another cluster of ruins. The centre of the grassy field is dominated by the shell of a Franciscan chapel. A little further west, **Cenote Xlacah**, in addition to providing the ancient city with water, was of ritual importance to the Maya: more than six thousand offerings – including human remains – have been discovered in its deeper end. It's also home to a species of spiny fish found only in the Yucatán.

## Progreso and around

First glimpses of **PROGRESO** – a working port with a six-kilometre-long concrete pier – can be uninspiring, especially at the end of a summer weekend when crowds of day-trippers have pulled out, leaving beer bottles and food wrappers in their wake. But the beach, really the only reason to visit, is long and broad, with fine sand (though, like the rest of the Gulf coast, the water's not very clear), and it makes for a pleasant day out from Mérida. If you're here in the winter, the beach will be empty, except perhaps for a few intrepid tourists from one of the cruise ships that dock here occasionally.

Progreso is a small place, and it's not difficult to find your way around. The **bus station** is on Calle 29 (running east–west, four blocks south of the water) at the corner of Calle 82. Calle 80, one block east, is the main street, running north–south and dead-ending at the beach. You'll find the **tourist office** (Mon–Fri 8am–2pm, Sat 8am–1pm; ⓣ969/935-0114) here, in the Casa de la Cultura at Calle 27; it has only a free map and a couple of flyers. On cruise-ship days, the courtyard in front hosts a craft market. Also on Calle 80 is the lively city **market** (the fruit and veg vendors are usually shut by 2pm), along with a few **banks** with ATMs, and a couple of **Internet** cafés.

**Hotels** in town range from very seedy to somewhat overpriced, but Progreso is a popular family destination, so many have large rooms ideal for groups. The high season is July, August and Semana Santa; outside of that, prices drop considerably. Best bets include the *Hotel Progreso*, Calle 29 no. 142, at Calle 78 (☎969/935-0039; ❸), several blocks back from the beach with clean, a/c rooms, and *Casa Isidora*, on Calle 21 between calles 58 and 60 (☎969/935-4595, Ⓦwww.casaisidora.com; ❹). The latter is in a grand old house a little east of the centre and has a small pool. The *Hotel Embajadores*, on Calle 64 at Calle 21 (☎969/935-5673, Ⓦwww.progresohotel.com; ❷), is a blessedly spotless option at the bargain end. It's run by a veteran of the hostel scene who always has a hot pot of coffee and a story to tell.

For **eating**, try the lively *Eladio's*, on the malecón at Calle 80, where you can make a meal of the tasty *botanas* that come free with beers. Equally popular is *Sol y Mar*, across the street, for seafood snacks, and *Le Saint Bonnet*, a family restaurant on calles 19 and 78 that serves more elaborate seafood specialities and has a pool. All of these places also set out tables on the beach. For cheap comidas corridas, the town's small market has several good stalls.



### Beaches around Progreso

**Heading east from Progreso**, the shorefront behind the beach is built up all the way to the village of **Chicxulub Puerto** some 5km away, where the excellent *Restaurante Moctezuma* (aka "Los Barriles", for the giant wood barrels that form its front entrance) is a favourite destination for a late seafood **lunch**. After this, you're shunted away from the beach and onto Hwy-27, which runs a bit further inland. At Km 15 on the highway, a **viewing platform** (free; follow signs for the *mirador turístico*) over the Uaymitún inlet is a great place to see flocks of **flamingoes** – not in such great numbers as at Celestún (see opposite), but impressive considering the proximity to the busy road. Go at sunset, but before the 6pm closing time (7pm in summer), for your best chance of spotting them; the caretakers rent binoculars for M$10.

The road continues to **Telchac Puerto**, a laid-back seaside village popular in the summer with escapees from Mérida. A couple of nice small hotels, *Posada Liz* (☎991/917-4125, Ⓔposadaliz_telchac@hotmail.com; ❸) and *Hotel Principe Negro* (☎991/917-4004; ❹), are west of the plaza (a bit of a hike from the bus stop). The plaza has several good seafood **restaurants**.

With more time, it's possible to get even further east along an ever-narrowing road to where the coast reverts to a wild state. In the village of **Santa Clara** (really just a few buildings between the sea and the salt flats), the beach is tranquil and seafood fresh. At the end of the road, **Dzilam de Bravo** has a sea-defence wall rather than a beach; *Jean Lafitte* (☎991/102-1543; ❸) is the only **hotel**, but a decent one, with a pool that's sometimes full. The real draw here is **Bocas de Dzilam**, a state nature reserve in the Parque Natural San Felipe. Set in 620 square kilometres of coastal forests, marshes and dunes, the *bocas* (Spanish for "mouths") are freshwater springs on the seabed. The water's minerals encourage wide biological diversity: you may see turtles, tortoises, crocodiles, spider monkeys and dozens of bird species. To arrange a tour, walk east from the plaza to the fishing port, where a few boat captains are equipped to take you out; expect to pay about M$400 for three or four hours. A more direct way to the town is a second-class **bus** in Mérida from the Autobuses del Noreste terminal (see p.803).



Venturing **west from Progreso** is not as promising, though in the 19km of coast road you will find a few more beach villages. The small resorts of **Yucalpetén, Chelem** and **Chuburná**, respectively fifteen, twenty and thirty minutes from Progreso and easy day trips from Mérida, have clean, wide beaches, and some **accommodation** and restaurants. *Hotel Sian Ka'an* (Ⓣ969/935-4017, Ⓦwww.hotelsiankaan.com; ❻), in Yucalpetén, is one good option, offering oceanfront rooms ideal for groups or families, with balconies and kitchenettes. *Costa Azul*, just down the road in Chelem, is a highly recommended fish **restaurant**.

Beyond Chuburná, the coast road, which was damaged by Hurricane Isidore in 2002, is no longer negotiable, and you'll have to turn inland again. It's not worth making a detour back to the coast at **Sisal**; unbelievably, this was Mérida's chief port in colonial times (and gave its name to the henequen fibre exported from here), but now it's quite shabby and practically deserted.

## Celestún

Were it not for its amazing flamingo-filled lagoon, **CELESTÚN** – 93km west of Mérida, at the end of a sandbar on the peninsula's northwest coast – would be little more than a one-boat fishing village. To see the birds – most numerous from November to May, when blue-winged teal and shovellers also migrate – in the warm waters of the 146,000-acre **Ría Celestún Biosphere Reserve**, hire a boat at the official *parador turístico*, just past the bridge on the main road into town. Ask the bus driver to drop you here, as it's a twenty-minute walk back from the main square.

The ticket system here is so complex, you might suspect you're being scammed. In fact, it *is* a system, and you should work out the math in advance to know what you're getting into. The pricing is essentially designed to deter people from crowding together in a single boat, as there are plenty of captains and not always a lot of custom. For the standard tour (approx 1hr), stopping at the flamingo feeding grounds and a fresh-water spring amid mangroves, groups of four or fewer need to purchase a group ticket (M$500), then individual tickets (M$40) – this works out to M$165 per person for four. If, however, you're with a group of five or six (the maximum boat capacity), the rate is simply M$140 per person. None of this includes an additional M$40 in taxes per person, or an optional M$200 per boat for a dedicated guide. A two-hour trip, which also visits a "petrified forest" (really, a spooky swath of salt-choked trees), is M$1000 for the boat plus M$40 per person up to four (M$240 per person for groups of five or six); a guide is M$400. These prices may fluctuate, but the basic system should stay the same. If you would like to join a larger group, show up around 10am, as that's when most people arrive, usually on the 8am bus from Mérida.

You may be approached by unlicenced captains outside the *parador*; they will offer a competitive price, but their deep-keel boats are not designed for the inlet, and some passengers have even found themselves pushing their craft out of the mud. These captains drive too close to the birds in order to give visitors a spectacular flying display; happily, the official captains no longer do this.

For extended **bird-watching** tours, contact Alberto Rodriguez Pisté (Ⓔx2rodriguez@hotmail.com), one of the expert guides at the *parador turístico*; a fluent English-speaker and longtime birder, he can sometimes be found at *Restaurant Celestún*, on the waterfront.

**Buses** for Celestún depart 17 times daily from Mérida's Noreste terminal (see p.803) beginning at 5.15am; the trip takes about two hours. The village has half a dozen **places to stay**: beachfront *María del Carmen*, Calle 12 no. 111, at Calle 15 (Ⓣ988/916-2170, Ⓔmcrodriguez@hotmail.com; ❹), is the best bet, with balconies overlooking a wide beach (a/c is an option), while the *Ría*

*Celestún* **hostel**, on Calle 12 at Calle 13 (Ⓣ988/916-2219, Ⓔhostelriacelestun@hotmail.com), has decent dorm beds (M$70). At the upper end, *Hotel Manglares* (Ⓣ988/916-2156, Ⓦwww.hotelmanglares.com.mx; ❼) is a comfortable little hotel on the northern edge of town. If you really want to escape, the remote and lovely *Eco Paraíso Xixim* (Ⓣ988/916-2100, Ⓦwww.ecoparaiso.com; ❾) is 10km north of town. Operating primarily on wind and solar power, it offers well-appointed cabañas, excellent showers and a deserted beach; rates include breakfast.

Of the several **seafood restaurants** along the beach, *La Palapa* is the biggest and priciest, but unfortunately one of the only reliable ones. For home cooking, visit the *loncherías* by the market (just off the inland side of the plaza). There's also a bakery, a bank (but no ATM) and a petrol station.

# South of Mérida: Uxmal and the Ruta Puuc

About 80km south of Mérida in the Puuc hills lies a group of the peninsula's most important archeological sites. **Uxmal** is chief of them, second only to Chichén Itzá (see p.819) in size and significance, though greater in beauty and harmony of extraordinary architectural style. The so-called **Ruta Puuc** carries on from Uxmal along Hwy-261 to the lesser sites of **Kabáh**, down the main road not far beyond; **Sayil**, nearby on a road running east; and **Labná**, further along, past Sayil. From Labná you could continue to the farming town of **Oxkutzcab**, on the road from Muna to Felipe Carrillo Puerto, and head back to Mérida via **Ticul** and Muna, or follow the **Ruta de los Conventos** north to Maní and its Franciscan monastery then past other fortified churches and the Maya ruins of **Mayapán**.

The distinctive Puuc sites clearly evolved from themes in the Río Bec and Chenes regions: you'll see the same gaping monster mouths and facades decorated in mosaic-like Xs and checkerboards. In both cases, though, the techniques reflect a new strategy of mass production – the mask-covered front of the Codz Poop at Kabáh, for instance, is dotted with hundreds of consistently round carved eyes that form both a regular decorative pattern and individual images of the rain god Chac. A new core-and-veneer style of construction, rather than stone blocks stacked with mortar, yielded sounder buildings with a smoother appearance, which is highlighted by the tendency to leave the lower registers of buildings unadorned. However, though related architecturally, each site is actually quite distinct from the others.

### Getting to the sites

The sites are far enough apart that it's impractical to visit more than a couple by bus, unless you're prepared to spend several days. The cheapest and most practical – if also the most rushed – way to visit the sites is to take the "**Ruta Puuc**" **day-trip bus** (M$120) from Mérida (see p.803). Though you don't get much time at the ruins, Uxmal is the last visited and it is possible to stay later here and pay for a different bus back. Scores of Mérida travel agencies offer pricier Puuc-route trips that include meals and a guide.

It's better to **rent a car**: in two days you can explore all of the key sites, either returning to Mérida in the evening or finding a room at Uxmal or in Santa Elena or Ticul. For details of car rental agencies, see p.804.

## Uxmal

Meaning "thrice-built", **UXMAL** (OOSH-mal) represents the finest achievement of the **Puuc architectural style**, in which buildings of classical proportions are decorated with broad stone mosaic friezes of geometric patterns, or designs so stylized and endlessly repeated as to become almost abstract. As in every Maya site in the Yucatán, the face of **Chac**, the rain god, is everywhere. Chac must have been more crucial in this region than almost anywhere, for Uxmal and the other Puuc sites have no cenotes or other natural sources of water, relying instead on *chultunob*, jug-shaped underground cisterns, to collect and store rainwater (most have been filled in, to prevent mosquitoes breeding, but Kabáh has an extant one).

Little is known of the city's history, but the chief monuments, which marked its peaks of power and population, were erected around 900 AD. Sometime after that, the city began to decline, and by 1200 Uxmal and the other Puuc sites, together with Chichén Itzá, were all but abandoned. The reasons are unknown,

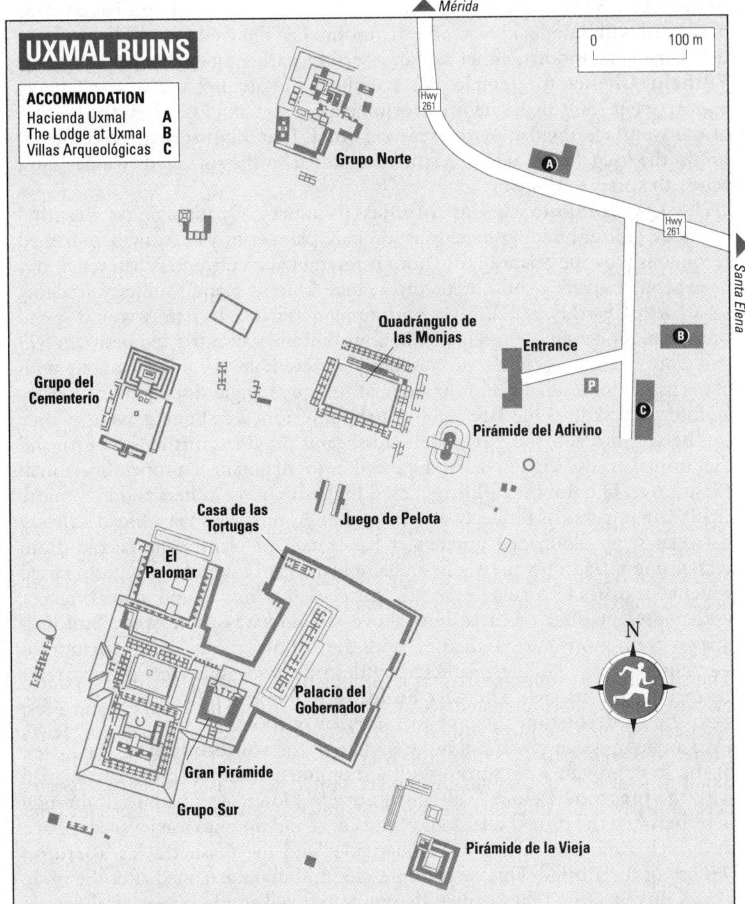

although political infighting, ecological problems and loss of trade with Tula, near Mexico City, may have played a part. Later, the **Xiu dynasty** settled at Uxmal, making it one of the central pillars of the League of Mayapán (see p.816), but a rebellion in 1441 overthrew that alliance and put an end to centralized Maya authority over the Yucatán.

## The site

Entering the site, the back of the great **Pirámide del Adivino** (Pyramid of the Magician) rises before you. The most remarkable of all Mexican pyramids, it soars at a startling angle from an oval base to a temple some 30m above the ground, with a broad but steep stairway up either side. The structure takes its name from a legend that it was constructed in a single night by a magical dwarf, though in fact at least five stages of construction have been uncovered – six if you count the modern restoration, which may not correspond to any of its earlier incarnations.

Visitors are no longer permitted to climb the pyramid, but from the base of the rear (east) stairway you can see a tunnel that reveals **Templo III**, one of the earlier levels. Surrounded by a platform, the temple at the summit has a facade decorated with interlocking geometric motifs. On the west face of the pyramid, the stairway runs down either side of a second, earlier sanctuary. Known as the **Edificio Chenes** (or Templo IV), it reflects the architecture of the Chenes region (see p.786), the entire front forming a giant mask of Chac. At the bottom of the west face, divided by the stairway, you'll find the first stage of construction – the long, low facade of a structure similar to the so-called Nunnery, just across the grass to the west.

The **Quadrángulo de las Monjas** (Nunnery Quadrangle), a beautiful complex of four buildings enclosing a square plaza, is one of many here named erroneously by the Spanish, to whom it resembled a convent. Whatever it may have been, it wasn't a convent; theories range from its being a military academy to a sort of earthly paradise where intended sacrificial victims would spend their final months in debauchery. The four buildings, constructed between 895 and 906 AD, are each set on a slightly different level and decorated with patterns of stone reliefs. All four sides of the quadrangle display refined Maya architectural skills – the false vaults of the interiors are about as wide as they can be without collapsing (wooden crossbeams provided further support), and the frontages are slightly bowed in order to maintain a proper horizontal perspective. The **north building**, raised higher than the others and even more richly ornamented, is probably also the oldest. Approached via a broad stairway between two colonnaded porches, it has a strip of plain stone facade (from which doors lead into the vaulted chambers) surmounted by a slightly raised panel of mosaics featuring geometric patterns and human and animal figures, with representations of Maya huts above the doorways. The **west building** boasts even more varied themes, and the whole of its ornamentation is surrounded by a coiling, feathered rattlesnake with the face of a warrior emerging from its jaws. The **east building** is almost a reflection of the west, with similar decoration and an equal number of rooms.

An arched passageway through the middle of the **south building**, the lowest of the four, provided the square with a monumental entrance directly aligned with the **Juego de Pelota** (ball-court) outside. Nowadays a path leads through here, between the ruined side walls of the court and up onto the levelled terrace on which stand the Palacio del Gobernador and the **Casa de las Tortugas** (House of the Turtles). This very simple, elegant building, named after the stone turtles carved around the cornice, demonstrates well another constant theme of

△ Quadrángulo de las Monjas, Uxmal

Puuc architecture: stone facades carved to appear like rows of narrow columns. These probably represent the building style of the Maya huts still in use today, consisting of bamboo or thin branches lashed together to form walls. The plain bands of masonry that often surround them mirror the cords that tie the hut walls in place.

Despite all this, it is the **Palacio del Gobernador** (Governor's Palace) that marks the finest achievement of Uxmal's builders. Explorer and writer John L. Stephens, who arrived at the site in June 1840, had no doubts as to its significance: "If it stood this day on its grand artificial terrace in Hyde Park or the Garden of the Tuileries," he later wrote, "it would form a new order . . . not unworthy to stand side by side with the remains of the Egyptian, Grecian and Roman art." The palace faces east, away from the buildings around it, probably for astronomical reasons – its central doorway aligns with the column of the altar outside and the point where Venus rises. Long and low, it is lent a remarkable harmony by the architect's use of light and shade on the facade, and by the strong diagonals that run through its broad band of mosaic decorations, particularly in the steeply vaulted archways that divide the two wings from the central mass, like giant arrowheads aimed at the sky. Close up, the mosaic is equally impressive, masks of Chac alternating with grid-and-key patterns and stylized snakes. Inside, the chambers are narrow, gloomy and unadorned, but the great central room, 20m long and entered by three close-set openings in the facade, is grander than most. At the back, the rooms have no natural light source at all.

Behind the palace stand the ruined buildings of the **Grupo Sur** (South Group). You can climb the rebuilt staircase of the **Gran Pirámide** to see the temple on top, decorated with macaws and more masks of Chac, and look across at the rest of the site. **El Palomar** (Dovecote) was originally part of a quadrangle like that of the Nunnery, but the only building to retain any form is this, topped with the great wavy, latticed roofcomb that gives it its name.

After you've taken in the main site, the outlying structures are a little anticlimactic. The **Pirámide de la Vieja** (Pyramid of the Old Woman), probably the site's earliest surviving building, is little more than a grassy mound with a clearly man-made outline. The **Grupo del Cementerio** (Cemetery Group) is also unrestored, though traces of carved hieroglyphs and human skulls are visible on the low altars in the middle of this square.

### Practicalities

Several **buses** a day run direct from Mérida to Uxmal, and any bus heading down the main road towards Hopelchén (or between Mérida and Campeche on the longer route) will drop you just a short walk from the entrance. **Driving** from Mérida is very easy, with wide Hwy-261 heading straight south and bypassing all the towns on the way. There's a pay car park at the modern **entrance to the site** (daily 8am–5pm; M$95, M$50 on Sun), where the **visitor centre** includes a small museum, a shop with guides to the site, a snack bar, phones and an ATM. Uxmal's **sound-and-light show** (daily; M$30, or included in price of day entrance ticket) starts at 7pm in winter and 8pm in summer. The commentary is in Spanish (translation equipment M$25) and of dubious historical accuracy, but the lighting effects highlight the relief decorations beautifully. Note that no buses run late enough to get you back to Mérida after the hour-long show.

Several **hotels** can be found close to the site, none of them in the budget category. All are subject to sudden arrivals of huge tour groups, which can make quality of service and food erratic, but are likely to offer good deals when not full. Club Med's *Villas Arqueológicas* (Ⓣ in the US 1-800/258-2633; ❼) is the best value, with a pool and tennis courts; *The Lodge at Uxmal* (Ⓣ998/887-2450, Ⓦwww.mayaland.com; ❾) has bigger rooms and a breezy restaurant and its bar, *La Palapa*, is a convenient spot for a cool drink. The most attractive option is the colonial-style *Hacienda Uxmal* (Ⓣ998/887-2450, Ⓦwww.mayaland.com; ❾), which is slightly further away on the main Mérida–Uxmal road and marginally less expensive. Further still, but much more lavish, the ultra-luxurious *Hacienda Temozón* (Ⓣ999/923-8089, Ⓦwww.starwoodhotels.com/luxury; ❾), on the sprawling grounds of which are two cenotes, a dramatic swimming pool and a restaurant that's not terribly expensive for **breakfast**. It's located in Temozón Sur, just off Hwy-261, about 45km south of Mérida and a half-hour drive from Uxmal.

For **lunch** after visiting the site, head to *Restaurante Cana-nah*, in the otherwise dumpy *Rancho Uxmal* hotel, about 1.5km back towards Mérida on the main road. It's tasty and inexpensive, and restaurant guests are welcome to use the swimming pool.

## Santa Elena

A small town at a convenient point on the road between Uxmal and Kabáh, the village of **SANTA ELENA** is a handy base for exploring further south, with two exceptionally nice **places to stay**. They're both on the highway as it bypasses the village centre (coming from Mérida, ask the bus driver to drop you at the junction after you've passed through the town). The *Flycatcher Inn* (no phone, Ⓦwww.flycatcherinn.com; ❺) is a B&B with two suites and three rooms decorated with local crafts. Just down the road toward Kabáh is *Sacbé Bungalows* (Ⓣ997/978-5158 or 985/858-1281, Ⓦwww.sacbebungalows.com.mx; ❸), where a hospitable Mexican–French couple offer spotless, basic rooms with porches, dotted among shady fruit trees; breakfast is available for an additional charge. They also rent a large bungalow with a full kitchen (❺). Between the hotels are two **restaurants**, *El Chac Mool*, which does decent local fare (closes at 8pm), and the Canadian-owned *Pickled Onion*, with an international menu. You may be able to hitch a ride to Santa Elena with Uxmal's workers after the sound-and-light show (though you should arrange your room ahead of time, as these two places can fill up).

Santa Elena is itself worth visiting for the magnificent view from its large **church**, built atop a hill that is actually a tumbledown pyramid; ask for the sacristan, who will open the door to the spiral staircase that leads to the roof. Beside the church is a morbidly interesting small **museum** (daily 8am–6pm; M$10) that serves as a home for the 200-year-old mummified remains of four children that were discovered under the church floor in 1980.

## Ticul

Eighty kilometres south of Mérida on Hwy-184, **TICUL** is another good base for exploring the Puuc region, although not particularly scenic. The town is an important centre of Maya shamanism as well as a pottery- and shoe-producing centre. Its streets are full of shoe shops and stores selling reproduction Maya antiquities; visitors are welcome to watch the manufacturing processes at the *fábricas*. On what used to be the main road between Mérida and the Quintana Roo coast (the upgraded highway via Mayapán now takes most of the traffic), Ticul is also well served by **buses**.

The centre of town is around the junction of calles 25 and 26, with a large plaza on either side, plus a massive church and several **hotels** in the immediate vicinity. Simplest of these is the friendly *Sierra Sosa*, Calle 26 no. 199-A (Ⓣ & Ⓕ997/972-0008; ❸), where basic rooms have a shower and fan (upstairs is better), and newer a/c rooms, a TV. A smarter alternative is the *Plaza*, overlooking the main square at Calle 23 no. 202 (Ⓣ997/972-0484, Ⓦwww.hotelplazayucatan; ❹), with TV, telephone and a/c in all rooms. But it pays to go a little further afield, to *Posada Jardin*, Calle 27 no. 216 between calles 28 and 30 (Ⓣ997/972-0401, Ⓦwww.posadajardin.com; ❹), which has four excellent-value cabins with separate sleeping and sitting areas, a/c and fridge, set in a garden with a small pool.

Ticul's best-known **restaurant**, *Los Almendros*, claims to have invented *poc-chuc* and other Yucatecan dishes – unfortunately that's no guarantee you'll get a great meal. It's on Calle Principal heading out of town towards Oxkutzcab, in a glitzy building complete with a pool, which is packed with families at weekends. Back in the centre, for an inexpensive comida try *Lonchería Carmelita*, two doors up from the *Plaza* on Calle 23 at Calle 26, or, as is usual, the *loncherías* near the bus station. For night-time dining, don't miss the tortas at the front of the market on Calle 23 between calles 28 and 30.

**Buses** from Mérida arrive at a station behind the church, on the corner of calles 24 and 25-A. **Colectivos** and **trucks** for Oxkutzcab and surrounding villages set off when they're full from spots along Calle 25-A alongside the church; **combis** for Mérida leave from around the corner of calles 24 and 25. Other practicalities are also central: a **bank** facing the plaza on Calle 26 just off Calle 25 has an ATM; directly opposite is a good **Internet** café. A small, locally run **tourist information office** (Ⓣ997/972-2350) is at the corner of calles 23 and 26, above *Lonchería Carmelita*.

## Kabáh

The extensive site of **KABÁH** (daily 9am–5pm; M$30), which means "Mighty Hand", stretches across the road about 25km from both Uxmal and Ticul. Much of it remains unexplored, but the one great building, the **Codz Poop**, or Palace of Masks, lies not far off the highway to the east, near the main entrance. The facade of this amazing structure is covered all over, in ludicrous profusion, with goggle-eyed, trunk-nosed masks of Chac – to get into the doorways, you need to tread over the mask's noses. Even in its present state – with most of the long, curved noses broken off – this remains one of the strangest and most striking of all Maya buildings, decorated so intricately and repetitively that it seems the product of an insane mind. The back of the building, which at other sites is usually left plain, displays two standing figures, some geometric designs and a few badly worn bas-relief portraits. Directly in front of the Codz Poop stands a rare working *chultun*, with a concave stone floor to gather water in an underground chamber.

On the other side of the road is an unusual circular pyramid – now simply a green conical mound that, once you spot it, is so large you can't believe you missed it. It is believed that the building, erected on a natural elevation, functioned as a place where priests offered sacrifices or interpreted divine messages. Just beyond, a sort of triumphal arch marks the point where an ancient thirty-kilometre causeway, or *sacbé*, from Uxmal entered the city.

**Leaving Kabáh**, you may have to literally lie down in the road to persuade a bus to stop for you – ask the guards at the site for the bus times. Hitching a ride with other visitors, though, might work, and with luck you may even meet someone touring all the local sites.

## Sayil

A sober, restrained contrast to the excesses of Kabáh, the site of **SAYIL** (daily 8am–5pm; M$30) lies some 5km along a smaller road heading east off the highway, from a junction 5km beyond Kabáh. Once one of the most densely populated areas in the Puuc region, Sayil was home to an estimated 17,000 people from 700 AD to 1000 AD. It is dominated by one major structure, the extensively restored **Gran Palacio** (Great Palace), built on three storeys, each smaller than the one below, and some 80m long. Although several large masks of Chac adorn a frieze around the top of the middle level, the decoration mostly takes the form of bamboo-effect stone pillaring – seen more extensively here than at any other Puuc site. The interiors of the middle level, too, are lighter and airier than usual, thanks to the use of broad openings, their lintels supported on fat columns.

Few other structures have been cleared, and those that have been are widely scattered in the forest – a walk to these remote spots is a long, hot one, but it gives you a better sense of the scale of the old city, as well as a chance to view wildlife like hummingbirds. From the Gran Palacio a path leads through the forest to the small temple of **El Mirador**, and in the other direction to a stele, carved with a phallic figure and now protected under a thatched roof. The path (in fact, a former ceremonial *sacbé*) carries on to the **Palacio Sur**, a large, little-restored structure with another characteristic bamboo facade.

## Xlapak and Labná

The minor road continues from Sayil past tiny **XLAPAK** (daily 8am–5pm; free), the smallest and least-visited of the Puuc sites. If you have the time, stop to see the one restored building, a small, elegant palace with huge Chac masks above its doorways and geometric patterns on the facades. Three kilometres after Xlapak, the ancient city of **LABNÁ** (daily 9am–5pm; M$30) is comparable in size to Sayil. Although it was historically less important, it is more impressive today. There has been more excavation here, so the main buildings can all be seen as part of a harmonious whole. **El Palacio**, near the entrance, bears traces of sculptures including the inevitable Chac, and a crocodile-snake figure with a human face emerging from its mouth – thought to symbolize a god escaping from the jaws of the underworld. Remnants of a *sacbé* lead from here to the **Arco de Labná**. Originally part of a complex linking two great squares, like the Nunnery at Uxmal, it now stands alone, richly decorated on both sides: on the east with geometric patterns, on the west (the back) with these and niches in the form of Maya huts or temples. Nearby is **El Mirador**, a temple with the well-preserved remains of a tall roofcomb. An inner passageway at one time led to the site's principal temple.

## Grutas de Loltún

Just before you reach Oxkutzcab on the road from Labná, the **Grutas de Loltún** (daily 9am–5pm, by guided tour only at 9.30am, 11am, 12.30pm, 2pm, 3pm & 4pm; M$20, plus M$30 for tour), are the most impressive caves in the Yucatán, at least among those that are developed for visitors. The hour-long tour (for which you can request an English guide) concentrates on strange rock formations and patterns in giant stalactites and stalagmites. The caves were revered by the Maya as a source of water. At the entrance, a huge bas-relief warrior guards the opening to the underworld, and throughout are traces of ancient paintings and carvings on the walls. The surrounding jungle is visible through the collapsed floor of the last gallery, and ten-metre-long tree roots find an anchor on the cavern floor.

Outside are two decent, though pricey, **restaurants**, *El Guerrero* and *Los Aluxes de Loltún*, both with tasty *panuchos* and other standards. If you're coming from Oxkutzcab, just up the road, you can take a **colectivo** or truck; they leave from Calle 51 next to the market, and if you get there by 8.30am you may be able to catch the truck taking the cave employees to work. Getting back is less easy, as the trucks are full of workers and produce, but if you wait something will turn up. The short taxi ride from the village will cost you approximately M$50.

## Oxkutzcab and around

From Labná, you can head back to Mérida on the fast Hwy-18 (look for signs just north of the Grutas de Loltún), or you can stop off in the village of **OXKUTZCAB**, 25km northeast from Labná. It's a decent rest stop after completing the Ruta Puuc, with a huge **fruit market**. Calles 51 and 50 edge the main park and the mercado, with a Franciscan church between them.

**Buses** to Mérida via Ticul (2hr) leave about every hour from the **bus station** at the corner of Calle 56 and Calle 51; *colectivos* come and go from beside the mercado on Calle 51. One clean, basic **hotel**, *Hospedaje Duran* (Ⓣ997/975-1748; ❷), is centrally located on Calle 51 opposite the fruit market, but the *Hotel Puuc*, on Calle 55 at Calle 44 on the way out of town towards Labná (Ⓣ997/975-0103, Ⓔchachi9639h9@hotmail.com; ❸), is much preferable and costs only marginally more for bright, clean rooms with a/c and TV, and has a good restaurant next door. The Banamex **bank** on Calle 50, opposite the park, has an ATM, and there's an **Internet** café at the corner of calles 51 and 52. **Restaurants** and cafeterias skirt the market, but if you fancy a long, lazy lunch, try a few blocks back towards the bus station at *Al Rincón Isleño*, Calle 54 no. 101, between calles 51 and 49, where comidas are served in a spacious open-sided palapa.

### Maní and Mayapán

Twelve kilometres north of Oxkutzcab is the small town of **MANÍ**. Founded by the Xiu after they abandoned Uxmal, at the time of the Conquest it was the largest city encountered by the Spanish in the Yucatán, though almost no trace now survives. Avoiding a major confrontation, Maní's ruler, Ah Kukum Xiu, converted to Christianity and became an ally of the Spanish. In 1548 one of the earliest and largest **Franciscan monasteries** in the Yucatán was founded here. This still stands, surrounded now by Maya huts, and just about the only evidence of Maní's past glories are the ancient stones used in its construction and in walls around the town. In front of the church, in 1562, Bishop Diego de Landa held his infamous auto-da-fé, in which he burned the city's records (because they "contained nothing in which there was not to be seen the superstitions and lies of the devil"), destroying virtually all surviving original Maya literature. Méridans often come down here on day trips to dine at *El Príncipe Tutul-Xiu*, Calle 26 between calles 25 and 27 (Tues–Sun 11am–7pm), a festive palapa-roof **restaurant** that has been serving Yucatecan standards for more than thirty years – it can be an absolute zoo on Sundays, but the food is always delicious.

Roughly halfway between Maní and Mérida, the ruins of **MAYAPÁN**, the most powerful city in the Yucatán from the thirteenth to the fifteenth century, sit right beside the road. According to Maya chronicles, it was one of the three cities (the others being Chichén Itzá and Uxmal) that made up the **League of Mayapán**, which exercised control over the entire peninsula from around 987 to 1185. The league broke up when the **Cocom** dynasty of Mayapán attacked and overwhelmed the rulers of an already declining Chichén Itzá, establishing themselves as sole controllers of the peninsula. However, archeological evidence suggests that Mayapán was not a significant settlement until the thirteenth century. The rival theory has Mayapán founded around 1263, after the fall of Chichén Itzá.

Whatever its history, Mayapán was a huge city by the standards of the day, with a population of some 15,000 on a site covering five square kilometres, in which traces of more than four thousand buildings have been found. Rulers of subject cities were forced to live here, perhaps even as hostages, where they could be kept under control. This hegemony was maintained until 1441, when Ah Xupan, a Xiu leader from Uxmal, finally led a rebellion that succeeded in overthrowing the Cocom and destroying their city – thus paving the way for the tribalism that the Spanish found on their arrival and facilitating considerably the Conquest.

What can be seen today is in some ways a disappointment – the buildings were crude and small by Maya standards, at best poor copies of what had gone before, and only a few have been restored (a visit doesn't take long). This less-than-grand architecture has led to the society being dismissed as decadent and failing, but a case can be made for the fact that it was merely a changing one. As the priests no longer dominated here (hence the lack of great ceremonial centres), what grew instead was a more genuinely urban society: highly militaristic, no doubt, but also far more centralized and more reliant on trade than previous Maya culture.

## East of Mérida: Aké and Izamal

The land east of Mérida and north of Hwy-180 is particularly dense with Maya towns and villages. All laid out according to the same orderly Spanish plan, around a central plaza and church, they are uniformly pretty, but the excellent regional crafts centre of **Izamal** in particular merits a detour. It's easy enough to come from Mérida on a day trip, but don't leave before sunset, when the place takes on a perfect golden glow, thanks to the striking ochre-yellow that covers all of the buildings. You may even consider staying a night or two and making this a base for day trips, if you want a break from cities. On the scenic, slow route to Izamal (via the hammock-weaving town of Tixkokob and Cacalchén), you also pass **Aké**, an intriguing Maya ruin now inextricable from a neighbouring henequen factory. Public transport runs frequently to Izamal, but Aké requires a car, or at least a taxi south from Hwy-180, where the closest second-class bus runs about every 45min.

## Aké

Halfway between Mérida and Izamal on the back road via Cacalchén, the Maya city of **AKÉ** (daily 9am–5pm; M$24) was probably in alliance with Izamal and is linked to it by one of the peninsula's largest *sacbeob* (Maya roads). One of the most impressive buildings here is a large platform topped with more than twenty stone pillars, resembling something from central Mexico or even Greece more than anything typical of the Yucatán. A working henequen **hacienda**, San Lorenzo de Aké, intermingles with the Maya rubble, and you're welcome to wander through to see the fibre-making process. North of the henequen plant, a church has been built on top of one of the old Maya temples. To reach the ruins, turn south off the main road just before Tixkokob; this smaller road peters out after 10.5km, a little way past the village of Ekmul, and the entrance is to the far right, beyond an overgrown plaza and the main hacienda building.

## Izamal

The exceptionally scenic town of **IZAMAL**, 72km east of Mérida, was formerly an important religious centre for the Maya, where they worshipped **Itzamná**, mythical founder of the ancient city and one of the gods of creation, at a series of huge pyramid-temples. Most of these are now no more than low mounds in the surrounding country, but several survive in the town itself, and are fascinating to see right in the middle of the residential grid. The largest, **Kinich Kakmo** (daily 8am–8pm; free), dedicated to the sun god, has been partly restored. It's just a couple of blocks north of the two adjacent central plazas – ask for directions from the roving brown-clad tourist police.

In 1552 Fray Diego de Landa (later responsible for a vicious Inquisition and auto-da-fé in Maní) lopped the top off a neighbouring pyramid and began building the grand **Convento de San Antonio de Padua** (daily; free), which now anchors the main squares. The porticoed atrium is particularly beautiful in the late afternoon. Inside the complex is a statue of Nuestra Señora de Izamal (usually in a small chapel behind the main altar, reached through a side hall and stairs), the patroness of the Yucatán. The statue brings pilgrims from all over the peninsula, especially during the fiesta dedicated to her in August, when penitents climb the convento's broad staircase on their knees. A few evenings a week, a **sound-and-light show** (Tues, Thurs & Sat 8.30pm; M$45) is projected on the facade of the main church.

### Practicalities

Izamal is also renowned as a refined **crafts centre**. A free **map**, available from most hotels and businesses, identifies artisans' workshops; be sure to visit Don Esteban, on Calle 26 at Calle 45, whose jewellery made from henequen spines

△ Convento de San Antonio de Padua, Izamal



is striking and modern, and whose effusive character is memorable. As a complement, a **folk-art museum** (Mon–Sat 9am–5pm; free) on the plaza highlights local artists as well as others from around the country, in an excellent collection, thanks to its generous funding from Banamex.

Of the very few **hotels** in town, *Posada Flory*, on Calle 30 at Calle 27 just off the plaza (ⓣ988/954-0562; ❸), is a bargain, with ten homely rooms with a/c, operated by a chatty, hospitable woman. For a bit more, *Macan Ché B&B*, Calle 22 between calles 33 and 35 (ⓣ988/954-0287, ⓦwww.macanche.com; ❹–❻), is an assortment of comfortable cottages tucked among rambling gardens east of the plaza; rates include breakfast, and other meals are available as well. Also look for *San Miguel Arcangel*, on the plaza (ⓣ988/954-0109, ⓦwww.sanmiguelhotel.com.mx; ❹), a twelve-room hotel furnished with art and antiques; out back, there's a hot tub perched atop a ruined pyramid. A few kilometres south, near the town of Sudzal, and well worth the drive if you have your own transport, is the rambling, artfully decorated *Hacienda San Antonio Chalanté* (ⓣ999/908-0726, ⓦwww.haciendachalante.com; ❺); the owner is a champion horsewoman, and offers riding around the expansive grounds.

Back in town, the palapa-roof *Kinich*, on Calle 27 between calles 28 and 30, is a popular spot for **lunch**, while *El Toro*, on Calle 30 just east of the convent, is open for **dinner**, with a hearty Yucatecan menu of dishes like *chaya* tamales and *queso relleno*. You can enjoy coffee or ice cream at *La Estación*, a small courtyard **café** in the arcade leading to *Posada San Miguel*; in the same building, Hecho a Mano, a particularly good craft and folk-art **shop**, is stocked with everything from Mexican wrestling masks to Huichol yarn paintings from Nayarit, as well as excellent photography by one of the owners; note that the hours (Mon–Sat 10am–2pm & 4–7pm) can be erratic.

**Buses** arrive at a small station one block off the main plaza. Services run back to Mérida nearly every thirty minutes, and nearly as frequently east to Valladolid and Cancún (though the faster buses go only five times daily); three buses run to Tizimín. In the north plaza you'll find a Banorte **bank** with ATM, while on the main plaza is a **post office** (Mon–Fri 8am–2.30pm) and the **tourist office** (daily 9am–6pm; ⓣ988/954-0692). An **Internet café** is on Calle 30 just off the plaza, and a **laundry** is one block further. **Horse-drawn buggies** lined up around the plaza will take you for a pleasant *paseo* around the town (20min; M$50).

# Chichén Itzá

**CHICHÉN ITZÁ**, the most famous, the most extensively restored and by far the most visited of all Maya sites, lies conveniently along Hwy-180 from Mérida to Cancún, about 120km from Mérida and a little more than 200km from the Caribbean coast. A fast and very regular bus service runs all along this road, making it perfectly feasible to visit as a day's excursion from Mérida, or en route from Mérida to the coast (or even as a day out from Cancún, as many tour buses do). The site, though, deserves better, and both to do the ruins justice and to see them when they're not utterly trammelled by tourists, an overnight stop is well worth considering – either at the site itself or, less extravagantly, in the nearby village of **Pisté** or in Valladolid, which is both convenient and inexpensive (see p.825).

## Arrival and practicalities

Arriving at Chichén Itzá, Hwy-180 *libre* curves around the site to the north, making an arc that merges with the site access road (the original highway straight through) at both ends. Buses should drive right up to the site entrance, though there's a slim chance they'll drop you at the junction with the bypass road on the west side; they also stop in neighbouring Pisté.

The main **entry to the site** (daily winter 8am–5pm, summer 8am–6pm, though the process of getting everyone out starts at least an hour earlier; M$95) is on the west side. A huge **visitor centre** (open until 10pm) houses a museum, restaurant, **ATM** and shops selling souvenirs, film, maps and guides. **Guided tours** of the ruins can be arranged here: private tours in one of four languages (Spanish, English, German or Italian) cost approximately M$480 and last ninety minutes; group tours cost a little less. You can also buy tickets and get in at the **smaller eastern gate** by the *Hotel Mayaland* (see p.821), where there are fewer facilities. You can book two-hour **horseback-riding trips** around the wilder, southern part of the site, Chichén Viejo, at the hotel reception area (M$500 with guide). A **sound-and-light-show** in Spanish runs nightly (7pm in winter, 8pm in summer; M$30, or included in price of day entrance ticket); it's a bit of a yawn, but it does recreate the shadow-serpent effect (see p.822) on the stairs of El Castillo. It's worth seeing only if you're staying nearby, as there's nothing else to do in the evening.

About a thirty-minute walk west from Chichén Itzá, **Pisté** is an unattractive village straddling the road. Its main function is providing visitors with accommodation (see p.821), so they can get up early enough to beat the buses that arrive at the ruins around 10.30am. There's an **Internet** café here, opposite the **bus station**, at the east end of town.

## Accommodation

Visitors to Chichén Itzá have a choice of staying in a handful of more expensive **hotels** immediately **east of the ruins** (all but one are on the short

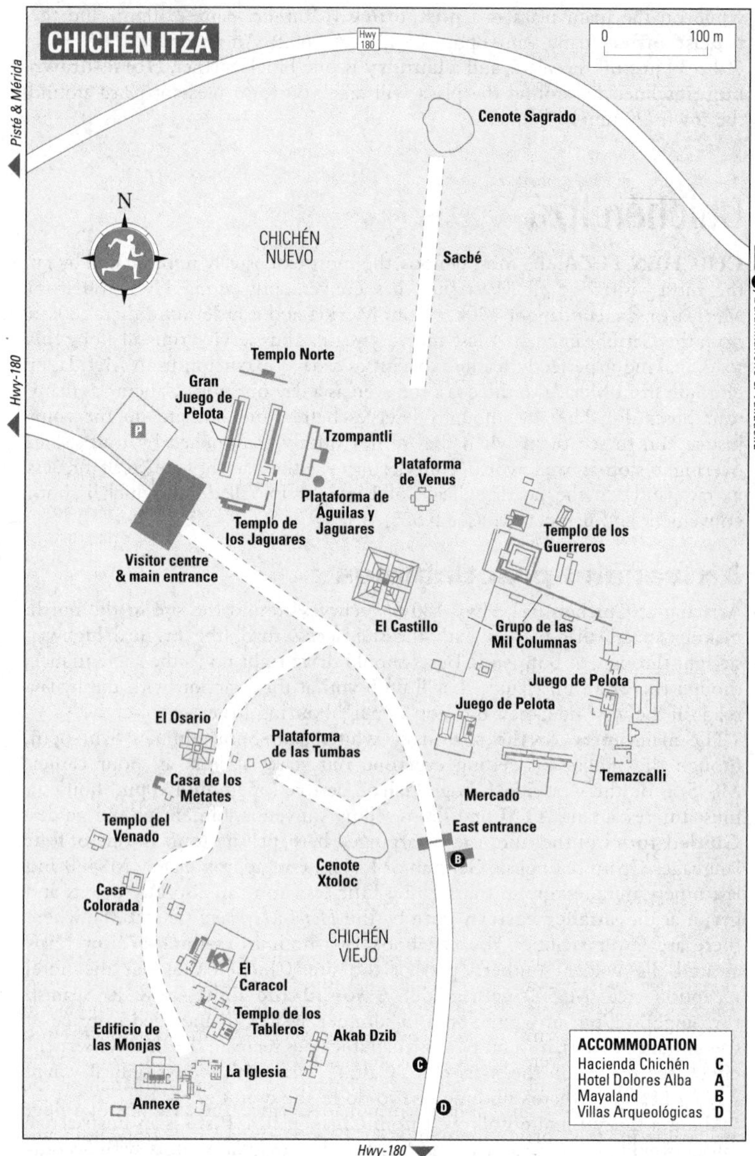




access road off Hwy-180, signposted "Zona Hotelera"), or along the main street in the town of **Pisté**, to the west of the site. In Pisté, most hotels are on the main road, between the village and the ruins, so it's easy to shop around for the best deal – though quality can be low and occupancy high; the reliable *posadas* have only a few rooms apiece. You can **camp** or sling up a hammock at the *Pirámide Inn* (M$45).

### Near the ruins

**Dolores Alba** Km 122 Hwy-180 *libre*, 2km east of Chichén Itzá east entrance ⓣ999/928-5650, ⓦwww.doloresalba.com. The best-value hotel on either side of the ruins, with clean, colourful rooms, a good restaurant (see below) and two swimming pools, one built out of a natural spring. Transport is provided to the site in the morning. ❺

**Hacienda Chichén** off Hwy-180 *libre*, near the east entrance to the ruins ⓣ985/924-2150, ⓦwww.haciendachichen.com. This place has a gracious old-colonial feel, with wrought-iron furniture and plenty of greenery, as well as a couple of small ruins within its grounds. Rooms, in individual cottages, aren't quite as attractive as the public spaces, though. ❾

**Mayaland** off Hwy-180 *libre*, at the east entrance to the ruins ⓣ985/851-0100, ⓦwww.mayaland.com. High-end resort with a gorgeous hacienda-style dining room and luxurious thatched-hut suites dotted about the gardens. ❾

**Villas Arqueológicas** off Hwy-180 *libre*, near the east entrance to the ruins US ⓣ1-800/258-2633. Not as lavish as its neighbours, but certainly comfortable. Rooms are set round a patio enclosing a pool and cocktail bar. By night, its library full of archeological tomes doubles as a disco, which is usually empty. ❼

### In Pisté

**Pirámide Inn** Hwy-180 *libre* at the west end of town, next to the bus station ⓣ985/851-0115, ⓦwww.chichen.com. Conveniently situated near the main entrance to the ruins, with a pool, *temazcal* sauna, extensive gardens and a somewhat New Age clientele. ❹

**Posada Chac-Mool** Hwy-180 *libre* about 200m west of the bus station ⓣ985/851-0270. No frills, just nine small, sparkling-clean rooms, with choice of fan or a/c. ❸

**Posada Olalde** On C 6, south of the main road ⓣ985/851-0086. The basic rooms, with fans and hot water, can be a bit dim, but they're very clean. This is one of the quieter spots, since it's off the main road. Calle 6 is about two-thirds of the way through town coming from the bus stop; turn left across from *Posada Carrousel*. ❹

## Eating

For refreshment near the ruins, or if you're staying overnight, the **restaurant** at the *Dolores Alba* is good and affordable, and guests can use the pool. Across the road is the somewhat ritzy Parque Ikkil (daily 8am–6pm; M$60), which is more appealing for its large Sagrado Azul **cenote** than its massive buffet restaurant. In Pisté, the best dining options are *El Carrousel*, for cheap beers and snacks, and *Las Mestizas*, which does some good regional cuisine, such as *poc-chuc* and *brazo de reina*. At the west end of town, in front of the small plaza, a short row of *loncherías* serve comida corrida for about M$30, and are also open in the evenings, with lighter fare.

## The site

Though in most minds **Chichén Itzá** represents the Maya, it is in fact the site's divergence from Maya tradition that makes it archeologically so intriguing. Experts are fairly certain that the city was established around 300 AD, and began to flourish in the Terminal Classic period (between 800 and 925 AD); the rest of its history, however, as well as the roots of the Itzá clan that consolidated power in the peninsula here after 925, remain hotly disputed. Much of the evidence at the site – an emphasis on human sacrifice, the presence of a huge ball-court and the glorification of military activity – points to a strong influence from central Mexico. For decades researchers guessed this was the result of the city's defeat by the Toltecs, a theory reinforced by the resemblance of the Templo de los Guerreros to the colonnade at Tula, near Mexico City (see p.494), along with Toltec-style pottery remains and numerous depictions of the Toltec god-king, the feathered serpent Quetzalcoatl (Kukulcán to the Maya).

Work since the 1980s, however, supports a theory that the Itzá people were not Toltec invaders, but fellow Maya who had migrated from the south (an explanation for their subjects referring to them as "foreigners" in texts). The

Toltec artefacts, this view holds, arrived in central Yucatán via the Itzás' chief trading partners, the **Chontal Maya**, who maintained allegiances with Toltecs of central Mexico and Oaxaca.

### Chichén Nuevo

The old highway that used to pass through the site is now a path dividing the ruins in two: the Itzá-era **Chichén Nuevo** (New or "Toltec" Chichén) to the north and Terminal Classic **Chichén Viejo** (Old Chichén) to the south. If it's still reasonably early, head first to the north and **El Castillo** (also called the Pyramid of Kukulcán), the structure that sits alone in the centre of a great grassy plaza. It is a simple, relatively unadorned square building, with a monumental stairway ascending each face (though only two are restored), rising in nine receding terraces to a temple at the top. The simplicity is deceptive, however, as the building is in fact the **Maya calendar** rendered in stone: each staircase has 91 steps, which, added to the single step at the main entrance to the temple, amounts to 365; other numbers relevant to the calendar recur throughout the construction. Most remarkably, near sunset on the spring and autumn equinoxes, the great serpents' heads at the foot of the main staircase are joined to their tails (at the top of the building) by an undulating body of shadow – an event that lasts just a few hours and draws spectators, and awed worshippers, by the thousands.

Inside El Castillo an **earlier pyramid** survives almost wholly intact. An entrance has been opened at the bottom, through which you reach a narrow, dank and claustrophobic stairway (formerly the outside of the inner pyramid) that leads steeply to a temple on the top. In the temple's inner sanctuary, now railed off, stands one of the greatest finds at the site: an **altar**, or perhaps a throne, in the form of a jaguar, painted bright red and inset with jade "spots" and eyes. The inner stairs are open from 11am to 3pm, and from 4pm to 5pm (last entrance at 4.45pm).

#### The "Toltec" plaza

El Castillo marks one edge of a **plaza** that formed the focus of Chichén Nuevo, and in addition to a *sacbé* leading to **Cenote Sagrado**, all its most important buildings are here, many displaying a strong Toltec influence in their structure and decoration. The **Templo de los Guerreros** (Temple of the Warriors), lined on two sides by the **Grupo de las Mil Columnas** (Group of the Thousand Columns), forms the eastern edge of the plaza. These are the structures that most recall the great Toltec site of Tula, both in design and in detail – in particular the colonnaded courtyard (which would have been roofed with some form of thatch) and the use of Atlantean columns representing battle-dressed warriors, their arms raised above their heads. The temple is richly decorated on its north and south sides with carvings and sculptures of jaguars and eagles devouring human hearts, feathered serpents, warriors and, the one undeniably Maya feature, masks of the rain god Chac, with his curling snout. On top (now visible only at a distance, as you can no longer climb the structure) are two superb examples of figurines called **Chac-mools**, once thought to be introduced by the Toltecs: offerings were placed on the stomachs of these reclining figures, which are thought to represent the messengers who would take the sacrifice to the gods, or perhaps the divinities themselves. The "thousand" columns alongside originally formed a square, on the far side of which is the building known as the **Mercado**, although there's no evidence that this actually was a marketplace. Near here, too, is a small, dilapidated ball-court.

Walking west across the plaza from El Castillo, you pass the **Plataforma de Venus**, a raised block with a stairway up each side guarded by feathered serpents. Here, rites associated with Quetzalcoatl when he took the form of Venus, the morning star, would have been carried out. Slightly smaller, but otherwise identical in design, the adjacent **Plataforma de Águilas y Jaguares** features reliefs of eagles and jaguars holding human hearts. Human sacrifices may have been carried out here, judging by the proximity of a third platform, the **Tzompantli**, where victims' heads likely hung on display. This is carved on every side with grotesque grinning stone skulls.

### Gran Juego de Pelota and the Templo de los Jaguares

Chichén Itzá's **Gran Juego de Pelota** (ball-court), on the west side of the plaza, is the largest known in existence, with walls some 90m long. Its design is a capital "I" surrounded by temples, with the goals, or target rings, halfway along each side. Along the bottom of each side runs a sloping **panel** decorated with scenes of the game. Although the rules and full significance of the game remain a mystery, it was clearly not a Saturday afternoon kick-about in the park. On the panel, the players are shown proceeding from either side towards a central circle, the symbol of death. One player, just right of the centre (whether it's the winning or losing captain is up for debate) has been decapitated, while another holds his head and a ritual knife. Along the top runs the stone body of a snake, whose heads stick out at either end. The court is subject to a whispering-gallery effect, which enables you to be heard clearly at the far end of the court, and to hear what's going on there.

The **Templo de los Jaguares** overlooks the playing area from the east side. At the bottom – effectively the outer wall of the ball-court – is a little portico supported by two pillars, between which a stone jaguar stands sentinel. The outer wall panels, the left and the right of the interior space, are carved with the images of Pawahtuns, the gods who supported the sky and who are thought to be the patrons of the Itzá people. Inside are some worn but elaborate relief carvings of the Itzá ancestors inserted in the Maya creation myth – a powerful demonstration of their entitlement to rule.

## Cenote Sagrado

The **Cenote Sagrado** lies at the end of the *sacbé* that leads about 300m off from the north side of the plaza. It's an almost perfectly round hole in the limestone surface of the earth, some 60m in diameter and more than 30m deep, the bottom third full of water. It was thanks to this natural well (and perhaps another in the southern half of the site) that the city could survive at all, and it gives Chichén Itzá its name (literally "at the edge of the well of the Itzá"). The well was regarded as a portal to the underworld, called Xibalba, and the Maya would throw offerings into it – incense, statues, jade and especially metal disks (a few of them gold) engraved and embossed with figures and glyphs – as well as human sacrificial victims. People who were thrown in and survived were believed to emerge with the power of prophecy, having spoken with the gods.

## Chichén Viejo

The **southern half of the site** is the most sacred part for contemporary Maya, though the buildings here are not, on the whole, in such good condition. They were built for the most part prior to 925 AD, in the indigenous architectural styles used in the Puuc and Chenes regions. A path leads from the south side of El Castillo to the major structures, passing first the pyramid **El Osario** (the Ossuary; also called the High Priest's Grave), the only building in this section that shows any Toltec-style detail. Externally it is very similar to El Castillo, but inside a series of **tombs** was discovered. A shaft, first explored at the end of the nineteenth century, drops down from the top through five crypts, in each of which was found a skeleton and a trap door leading to the next. The fifth is at ground level, but here too was a trap door, and steps cut through the rock to a sixth chamber that opens onto a huge underground cavern: the burial place of the high priest.

Follow the main path and you arrive at **El Caracol** (the Snail, for its shape; also called the Observatory), a circular, domed tower standing on two rectangular platforms and looking remarkably like a modern-day observatory. The roof has slits aligned with various points of astronomical significance. Four doors at the cardinal points lead into the tower and a circular chamber. A spiral staircase leads to the upper level, where observations were made.

Immediately to the south, the so-called **Monjas** (Nunnery) palace complex shows several stages of construction. Part of the facade was blasted away in the nineteenth century, but it is nonetheless a building of grand proportions. Its **annexe**, on the east end, has an elaborate facade in the Chenes style, covered in small heads of Chac that combine to make one giant mask, with the door as a mouth. By contrast, **La Iglesia**, a small building standing beside the convent, is a clear demonstration of Puuc design, its low band of unadorned masonry around the bottom surmounted by an elaborate mosaic frieze and roofcomb. Masks of Chac again predominate, but above the doorway are also figures of the four mythological creatures that held up the sky – a snail, a turtle, an armadillo and a crab.

South of Las Monjas, a path leads, after about ten minutes, to a further group of ruins that are among the oldest on the site, although they are unrestored; this is a good area for bird watching, with few people around to disturb the wildlife. Just east of Las Monjas, is the **Akab Dzib**, a relatively plain block of palace rooms that takes its name ("Obscure Writings") from undeciphered hieroglyphs found inside. Red palm prints – frequently found in Maya buildings – adorn the walls of some of the chambers. Backtrack along the main path to the building opposite El Osario, the **Plataforma de las Tumbas**, a funerary structure topped with small columns; behind it is a jungle path that heads back to the main east–west road via the site's other water source, Cenote Xtoloc.



## Around Chichén Itzá: Grutas de Balamkanché

Just 1.6km east of the *Dolores Alba* hotel (see p.821), the **Grutas de Balamkanché** are a somewhat creepy complement to Chichén Itzá's sun-lit grandiosity, and a refreshingly cool way to pass an hour. These caverns were reopened in 1959, when a sealed passageway was discovered, revealing a path to an underground altar to Chac. Tours with taped commentary (in English daily 11am, 1pm & 3pm; M$50) lead you past an underground pool, stalagmites and stalactites to a huge rock formation that resembles a ceiba, the Maya tree of life.

### Moving on from Chichén Itzá

To make your way **to the Caribbean coast** from Chichén Itzá, it's best to take any **bus** you can as far as **Valladolid**, and if necessary change there for first-class service. You can bypass Cancún by taking a second-class bus to **Tulum** via Cobá (3 daily; 3hr). From the site entrance or the bus station in Pisté (on the east end, near the *Pirámide Inn*), first-class buses run three times daily to **Mérida**, four times to Valladolid and once (4.30pm) to **Cancún**; second-class services are at least hourly in both directions.

Around its base lie many of the original Maya offerings, such as clay pots in the shapes of gods' faces. In places the caves can be damp and claustrophobic, despite the heavy-handed use of coloured lights.

## Valladolid and around

The second town of Yucatán state, **VALLADOLID** is around 40km east of Chichén Itzá, still close enough to beat the crowds to the site on an early bus, and of interest in its own right. Although it took a severe bashing in the nineteenth-century Caste Wars, the town has retained a strong colonial feel and exudes the unpretentious attitude of a rural capital, catering to the farmers and ranchers who live in the surrounding counties, while village women gather in the plaza to sell hand-embroidered *huipiles* and other crafts.

The most famous of the churches to have survived the wars is the sixteenth-century **Iglesia de San Bernardino de Siena**, 1km southwest of the plaza (Wed–Mon 9am–noon & 5–8pm; Mass daily 6pm). Franciscan missionaries began work on it shortly after the Spanish established Valladolid as an outpost in 1545. In 1848 Maya rebels sacked the church; despite this, a fine Baroque altarpiece from the eighteenth century remains, as do some striking seventeenth-century paintings on the side walls.

Closer to the plaza, on Calle 41 between calles 38 and 40, the **Museo de San Roque** (Mon–Sat 9am–9pm; M$20) displays objects from the site of Ek-Balam (see p.828), embroidery and other craftwork. Valladolid is a good place to shop for crafts: the main **market** is on Calle 44 at Calle 39. If you need to cool down after a morning spent wandering, **Cenote Zací**, on the block formed by calles 34, 36, 37 and 39 (daily 8am–6pm; M$20) has broad stairs leading down into a huge cavern, with an open-air restaurant at the top. Unlike at many cenotes, swimming is not permitted.

## Arrival and information

Many first-class buses between Mérida and Cancún don't actually enter Valladolid, but stop at **La Isleta**, a small bus station on the toll highway where you transfer to a shuttle bus for the ten-minute ride into town; Valladolid's main **bus station** is on Calle 39 at Calle 46, just a block and a half west of the plaza. First-class buses run from here (via the same shuttle system) 12 times daily to Mérida and five times daily to Cancún, and there are eight daily departures for Playa del Carmen (most of which are via Cancún) and three to Cobá and Tulum. All local second-class buses begin their journey here too, for the above destinations as well as Chichén Itzá and Tizimín. Most **colectivos** depart from Calle 44. You can catch one to Chichén Itzá for M$15, or a taxi for M$150.

The plaza is bounded by calles 39, 40, 41 and 42. The **tourist office**, on the southeast corner of the plaza (Mon–Sat 9am–8.30pm, Sun 9am–1pm), has plenty of information, including free maps of Valladolid and details of in-house **tour operator** Viajes Valladolid (Ⓣ985/856-1857), though it's a pretty casual set-up, and the office is often unattended; however, most hotels and souvenir shops on the plaza also have **maps**. The **post office** (Mon–Fri 9am–3pm) is also on the plaza, on Calle 40 near the corner of Calle 39, as is Bancomer, which changes travellers' cheques and has an **ATM**. In Supermaz, a shopping plaza on Calle 39 between calles 48 and 50, you'll find a supermarket and **laundry**. A Ladatel *caseta* on the plaza has phones and is also an **Internet** café (daily 7am–10pm). You can **rent bikes** from the Rey de Béisbol sports shop, Calle 44 no. 195, between calles 39 and 41, owned by Antonio "Negro" Aguilar, a one-time professional baseball star who is also a great source of local information.

## Accommodation

Valladolid's budget hotels are serviceable, but in general prices are low enough that you might want to spring for perks like a swimming pool or a mansion setting. An excellent **hostel**, *La Candelaria*, on the edge of Parque de la Candelaria, on Calle 35 between calles 44 and 42 (Ⓣ985/856-2267, Ⓔcandelaria_hostel@hotmail.com; M$88), offers spotless dorms and private rooms, a garden, Internet access and bike rental. Also note that *Genesis Retreat* (see p.829) is only about twenty minutes outside town.

**Casa Quetzal** C 51 no. 218 Ⓣ985/856-4796, Ⓦwww.casa-quetzal.com. A pleasant alternative to the plaza hotels, *Casa Quetzal* is a very comfortable guesthouse with a big pool near the San Bernardino church. ❻

**Lili** C 44 no. 192, between C 37 and C 39 Ⓣ985/856-2163. One block off the plaza, this small, homely hotel rents 21 basic rooms (upstairs ones get a little more light) at reasonable rates. ❷

**María de la Luz** C 42, between C 39 and C 41 Ⓣ985/856-2071, Ⓦwww.mariadelaluzhotel.com. The best value on the plaza, *María de la Luz* offers clean, comfortable rooms with (somewhat noisy) a/c, all arranged around a small pool. ❺

**María Guadalupe** C 44 no. 198, between C 39 and C 41 Ⓣ985/856-2068. The best of Valladolid's cheapies, with well-kept rooms featuring private baths and a/c in a small two-storey 1960s building with a little curvy flair. *Colectivos* for Cenote Dzitnup leave from outside. ❸

**El Mesón del Marqués** C 39 no. 203, on the plaza ⓣ985/856-2073, ⓦwww.mesondelmarques.com. Lovely hotel in a former colonial mansion, overlooking a courtyard with fountains and lush plants. There's a wonderful palm-fringed pool, and one of the best restaurants in town (see below). Rates include full breakfast. ❻

**Zací** C 44 no. 191, between C 37 and C 39 ⓣ985/856-2167. Pleasant, modern, three-storey hotel with a quiet courtyard and small pool; the big rooms have a fan, or, for a few dollars more, a/c and TV. ❸

## Eating and entertainment

Whatever your budget, to eat well in Valladolid you don't have to stray from the plaza, where you can get inexpensive **snacks** or treat yourself at a refined **restaurant**. As for **nightlife**, there's not much beyond people watching on the plaza, where there's usually some live music on Sundays.

**El Bazar** northeast corner of the plaza. Houses a dizzying selection of inexpensive, always busy *loncherías* and pizzerias. It's also about the only place in town aside from *Hostería El Marqués* where you can eat after 9pm.

**La Casa del Café Kaffè** C 44, on Parque la Candelaria. This place serves organic coffee, juices and little snacks to hostel guests from across the square as well as members of the local arts scene.

**Hostería El Marqués** C 39 no. 203, in *El Mesón del Marqués*. Valladolid's best (and quite reasonably priced) restaurant is set in an interior courtyard on the plaza. Don't be put off if you see it packed with a tour group – the excellent menu features Yucatecan classics such as *sopa de lima* and *poc-chuc*, along with city specialities like *escabeche de Valladolid* (chicken in a spicy vinegar broth).

**María de la Luz** C 42, on the plaza. This popular terrace restaurant has a basic Mexican and Yucatecan menu. Good-value (M$50) breakfast buffet with American and Mexican dishes offered daily.

**Restaurante San Bernardino de Siena** C 49 no. 227. Locally known as *Don Juanito's* and frequented mostly by city residents, this family-run restaurant with decent prices is a great place for a lazy lunch or dinner, two blocks behind Iglesia de San Bernardino. Grilled fish and meat are the specialities.

**Yepez II** C 41, between C 38 and C 40. Friendly open-air bar and restaurant opposite the Museo de San Roque with live music after 9.30pm, as well as very cheap Mexican snacks (*queso fundido* for M$20). Families come for dinner, but the crowd becomes predominantly male (not too rowdy, though) once the music starts. Open daily till 2am.

## Around Valladolid

From Valladolid, the vast majority of traffic heads straight to Cancún and the Caribbean beaches. A few places merit taking time out to explore, however – whether the beautiful sculpture at the ruins of **Ek-Balam**, the cenotes of **Dzitnup** and **Samula** or, further afield, the flamingo colony at **Río Lagartos** or the beach at **San Felipe**. If you want to go all the way to the coast as a day trip, you'll need to make an early start – the last bus from Río Lagartos for Tizimín leaves at 5pm. You'll have to return at least to Tizimín to continue on to Mérida or Cancún.

### Cenotes Dzitnup and Samula

Perhaps the most photogenic swimming hole in the Yucatán, the remarkable **Cenote Dzitnup**, also called X'Keken (daily 7am–6pm; M$25), is 7km west of Valladolid on Hwy-180 *libre*. Visitors descend through a cramped tunnel into a huge vaulted cave, where a nearly circular pool of crystal-clear turquoise water glows under a shaft of light from an opening in the ceiling. A swim in the ice-cold water is a fantastic experience, but take a sweater – the temperature in the cave is noticeably cooler than outside. Across the road, at the equally impressive (but smaller and less developed) **Cenote Samula** (daily 8am–5pm; M$25), the

△ Cenote Dzitnup



roots of a huge tree stretch down into the pool. While Dzitnup is frequently crowded and plagued by small children asking for tips, you may well find yourself alone at Samula.

**Colectivos** run direct to Dzitnup from outside the *María Guadalupe* hotel in Valladolid (M$10; see p.826). Alternatively, any westbound second-class **bus** will drop you at the turn-off, 5km from Valladolid; then it's a walk of 2km down a signed track. You could also take a taxi or, best of all, **cycle** from Valladolid on the paved bike path; the most scenic route is down Calle 41A to San Bernardino, then along Calle 49, which eventually connects to Avenida de los Frailes, then the old highway and the *ciclopista*.

## Ek-Balam

Little visited but well excavated, **Ek-Balam** (daily 8am–5pm; M$24) is notable for the high quality and unique details of its sculpture. Check to see if Oriente is running a 9am bus to the site, about 20km north of Valladolid, from the main station (a scheme that was being debated in late 2006); if not, it's just as easy to catch a **colectivo** on Calle 44 just west of the plaza (M$40). The compact site, enclosed by a series of defensive walls, is really only the ceremonial centre; the entire city, which was occupied from the pre-Classic period through to the Spanish Conquest, spreads out over a very wide area, punctuated by *sacbeob* leading out in all directions.

The entrance is along one of these ancient roads, leading through a freestanding four-sided arch. Beyond are two identical temples, called **Las Gemelas** (the Twins), and a long **ball-court**. The principal building, on the far side of the plaza, is the massive **Acrópolis**, the stones along its two-hundred-metre-long base adorned with bas-reliefs. Thatched awnings at the top protect the site's finest treasure, an elaborate stucco frieze fully uncovered only recently; 85 percent of what you see is original plaster from the ninth century that didn't even require retouching once the dirt was brushed away.

A staircase leads up the centre of the building. On the first level, two doorways flanking the steps display near-matching designs of twisted serpents and tongues; in the right-hand carving, the snake's tongue is emblazoned with a glyph thought to represent the city. Just below the summit, a **Chenes-style doorway** in the form of a giant gaping mouth is studded with protruding teeth. This is the **entrance to the tomb** of Ukit-Kan-Lek-Tok, Ek-Balam's king in the mid-ninth century. The lower jaw forms the floor, while skulls, lilies, fish and other symbols of the underworld carved below reinforce its function as a tomb gateway. Back on the ground, in the plaza, an exceptionally well-preserved **stele** depicts a king receiving the objects of power from Ukit-Kan-Lek-Tok, the smaller seated figure at the top of the stele. Given the rich detail at the site, it's worth hiring a **guide** for about M$250 for a small group. Juan Canul, who has worked on many excavations, is recommended; ask for him at the ticket desk.

In the parking lot at the ruins, you'll find someone selling tickets to a nicely maintained **cenote**, which can be a great afternoon refresher. Entrance is M$30, or M$150 for rappelling and a guide.

In the nearby village of Ek-Balam, ⭑ *Genesis Retreat* (Ⓣ985/852-7980, Ⓦwww.genesisretreat.com; ❺) is a beautiful **ecolodge** with a big garden and a bio-filtered pool; the hospitable Canadian owner, who built the place herself, can arrange tours and activities, such as tortilla-making, hammock-weaving or language lessons, with the local Maya. The **café** (daily 1–3pm) makes a great stop after the ruins, with treats like avocado ice cream, chocolate-chile cookies and rich *chaya* crepes. If you take a taxi there, be aware that some drivers may attempt to take you to another, less savoury lodge around the corner – *Genesis* has a doghouse labelled "Concierge" out front.

### Tizimín and Río Lagartos

Travelling by bus from Valladolid north to Río Lagartos, you have to transfer in **TIZIMÍN**, the unofficial capital of Yucatán's cattle country, 51km from Valladolid. It's a pleasant enough city, but of little interest to travellers except during Epiphany in early January, when the Feria de los Tres Reyes draws both Catholic pilgrims and cowboys. If you're hungry, though, it's worth making time in your bus schedule for a meal at a great **restaurant**, ⭑ *Tres Reyes*, where you get generous free *botanas*, hand-made tortillas and delectable food like *pollo en pipian* (chicken in a pumpkin-seed broth) or local steak, all served with heartfelt enthusiasm. It's on the plaza, which is bounded by calles 50, 51, 52 and 53 – a ten-minute walk from the two bus stations, around the corner from each other at Calle 46 and Calle 47. Should you wind up staying, the best of the modest **hotels** in the centre, *Hotel San Jorge*, on the plaza at Calle 51 (Ⓣ986/863-2037; ❹–❻), has a pool and a/c, but its prices can vary wildly depending on how full it is. *Posada María Antonia* (Ⓣ983/863-2384; ❸) is always budget-priced. Tizimín also has direct **bus** services to and from Mérida and Cancún.

The village of **RÍO LAGARTOS**, 100km north of Valladolid, is protected from the Gulf of Mexico by a long barrier island; it's on a small spit surrounded on three sides by water and inhabited much of the year by tens of thousands of **pink flamingoes** (Nov–May most migrate to Celestún, on the west coast). The flamingoes alone make a visit worthwhile, as the town itself is somewhat dreary. It's manageable to visit on a day trip from Valladolid, but if you want to **stay the night**, the large rooms at *Posada Leyli* (Ⓣ986/862-0106; ❹), on Calle 14 at the north end of town, are about the only option; if possible, push on to San Felipe, a short drive or bus ride east (see p.830).

As soon as you arrive at the **bus station** (on Calle 19 just east of the main north–south street through town), or get out of your car, you're likely to be swamped by offers to take you out to see the flamingoes. If not, the best place to start is the friendly *Restaurante Isla Contoy*, on the waterfront on the west side, where you can arrange a **boat** to visit the many feeding sites; an hour-long tour usually costs about M$350, with a maximum of seven people. (There is **no bank or ATM** in town, so plan accordingly.) As well as flamingoes, you're likely to see fishing eagles, spoonbills and, if you're lucky, one of the very few remaining crocodiles after which Río Lagartos was (mis)named. Make sure that your guide understands that you don't want to harass the flamingoes, as some will get too close if they think their passengers would prefer to see some action.

### San Felipe

If it's beaches you're after, head to the tidy town of **SAN FELIPE**, where an offshore spit is lined with white sand. The town, which is also a popular destination for sport-fishing, is 12km west of Río Lagartos; many of the buses from Tizimín to Río Lagartos come out here as well. There's one good **hotel**, *San Felipe de Jesús,* Calle 9 between calles 14 and 16 (Ⓣ986/862-2027, Ⓔhotelsf@hotmail.com; ❺), which also has a decent restaurant. To get to the beach, take a boat (M$15/person) from the east end of the malecón, where you can also get basic **tourist information**. At Mexican holiday times – July, August and Semana Santa – the beach is crowded; the rest of the year, though, it's quite deserted, and you can set up **camp** here. If you do, be sure to bring protection against mosquitoes.

# Isla Holbox

Although most traffic between Mérida and the coast heads directly east to Cancún, it is possible to turn north at Valladolid (on the bus) or at the small town of El Ideal (if you're driving) to reach **Chiquilá**, where you can board the ferry for **ISLA HOLBOX**, a small island near the northeasternmost point of the Gulf coast. The sand-street village of Holbox is still relatively unspoilt, with a genuinely warm feel, and though the Gulf waters here do not have the same glittering clarity as the Caribbean, they're warm and clean. Development is on the rise, but a good part of the island is remains wild, as is the long spit from the mainland that runs east of the island. All manner of **birds**, including flamingoes, thrive along this stretch of coast, but the main attraction, though, is the huge pod of rare **whale sharks** that congregate just off the cape July to mid-September. Tours to see and swim with the gentle animals take the better part of a day (M$800 and up per person, including lunch and snorkel gear), and can be arranged through any number of guides in town; Mosquitours (Ⓣ984/875-5126) and Mextreme Travel (Ⓦwww.holboxdmc.com) are recommended. A dive shop at *Posada Mawimbi* (see opposite) does **snorkelling** excursions. The whale shark season unfortunately overlaps with the absolutely fearsome mosquitoes that arrive at the end of the summer and stay until the rains stop – be prepared.

## Arrival and information

The direct **bus for Chiquilá** leaves Mérida (6hr) and Valladolid (3hr) in the middle of the night and arrives in time for the 6am ferry. Transferring in Tizimín (3hr) is a little easier, with a choice of three day-time buses. Coming from the east, the easiest route to Chiquilá is from Cancún (3hr), on an early-morning Mayab bus or a 1.45pm Noreste bus. If you're **driving**, don't take the toll highway, as there's no convenient exit; turn north off Hwy-180 *libre* at the tiny town of El Ideal.

The **Chiquilá ferry** for Holbox leaves nine times daily, the first run at 6am and the last at 7pm (30min; M$40). Secure parking is available near the pier (set the price before you leave – usually about M$30 for any portion of a day). If you're with a group or arrive between ferries, you might want to hire a *lancha* (about M$500). But don't miss the last ferry: Chiquilá is not a place you want to get stranded. There's a restaurant, a basic hotel, a store and a gas station, but little else. Although a couple of restaurants on Holbox take credit cards, there's **no ATM** there, nor in Chiquilá – plan accordingly, particularly if you intend to take a trip to the whale sharks.

When you arrive on the island, you'll be greeted by *triciclo* taxis, which can spare you the slightly long trek to the plaza, straight ahead from the ferry dock; the maximum charge is M$50, to the very farthest hotels. On the main square, which locals call the *parque*, is an **Internet** café and a **money-exchange**. Very few people have cars; locals use the *triciclos* and electric **golf carts**. The latter are available to rent from several outlets near the *parque*.

## Accommodation

Low-key hotel development stretches east of Holbox town for a couple of kilometres; only one property lies far to the west. Out of season (early summer and before Christmas), rates for some of the upscale rooms can fall by almost half; August, however, can be priced as high as Christmas and Easter weeks. All of the hotels on the **beachfront** are mid-range to luxury, but there are a few decent cheaper options away from the water, as well as the excellent *Ida y Vuelta* **campground**, with screened shelters for tents or hammocks, clean bathrooms and a shared kitchen (Ⓣ984/875-2358, Ⓦwww.camping-mexico.com; M$80). It's on the eastern edge of town, just 200m from the beach, right behind *Xaloc*.

**Casa las Tortugas** on the beach adjacent to *Mawimbi* Ⓣ984/875-2129, Ⓦwww.holboxcasalastortugas.com. Very similar to *Mawimbi* in architecture; rates are a little higher, but breakfast is included and rooms have a more mod feel, with polka-dot fabrics. ❻

**Faro Viejo** Benito Juárez, at the beach Ⓣ984/875-2217, Ⓦwww.faroviejoholbox.com.mx. Modern, a/c rooms directly on the beach (the only stretch in town that's free of fishing boats), plus a few suites ideal for groups, with kitchenettes and porches; full breakfast included. ❽

**Posada Los Arcos** west side of the plaza Ⓣ984/875-2043. Clean, basic rooms, some with kitchenettes, around a small courtyard. Choice of a/c or fan. ❹

**Posada Mawimbi** on the beach three blocks east of the plaza Ⓣ984/875-2003, Ⓦwww.mawimbi.com.mx. A great little collection of round, two-storey cabañas with high ceilings, beautifully decorated and tucked among dense greenery. ❻

**Villas Chimay** on the beach 1km west of town Ⓣ984/875-2220, Ⓦwww.holbox.info. A wonderful hideaway, and the only lodging on the western beach. Self-sufficient with wind and solar power, and plenty of space between the well-designed bungalows. ❼

**Villas Los Mapaches** on the beach two blocks west of the plaza Ⓣ984/875-2090, Ⓦwww.losmapaches.com. Spotless, comfortable bungalows with kitchenettes, ideal for longer stays; a larger rental house can accommodate groups or families. ❻

**Xaloc** on the beach at the east edge of town Ⓣ984/875-2160, Ⓦwww.holbox-xalocresort.com. Eighteen cabañas with rough-hewn wood canopy beds and particularly well-appointed bathrooms. The property is smartly divided into areas for families and adults only, with a pool in each section. Free kayaks and snorkel gear. ❽

## Eating and drinking

The island's village has several very good restaurants, and most hotels have their own offerings as well. There's very little nightlife to speak of – locals generally lounge around on the plaza.

**Azul** one block north of the plaza, off the northeast corner. Tiny blue-lit spot with a range of well-priced items, from meaty lasagne to milkshakes.

**La Cueva del Pirata** on the west side of the plaza. Wonderful Italian restaurant, complete with hand-made fresh pasta. A little expensive compared with other island options, but very much worth the splurge. Dinner only.

**La Isla de Colibri** on the southwest corner of the plaza. Come for delicious fresh fruit juices and other healthy options, or in the evening for a drink (the dinner menu is pricey and not so satisfying, though).

**Pizzas y Mariscos Edelín** on the east side of the plaza. Basic wood-panelled joint where inexpensive pizzas dominate the menu, but you're better off with the *mariscos* selection, and guacamole.

**Villamar** On the beach straight north from the plaza. Good laid-back, local-owned restaurant with inexpensive seafood and Mexican dishes.

**Viva Zapata** just west of the northwest corner of the plaza. Great fresh fish in banana leaves and chipotle shrimp, as well as pasta and even chop suey. The second-floor palapa is a good place to watch the sun go down. Dinner only.

# Quintana Roo and the Caribbean coast



The coastal state of **Quintana Roo** was a forgotten frontier for most of modern Mexican history, its tropical forests exploited for their mahogany and chicle (from which chewing gum is made), but otherwise unsettled, a haven for outlaws, pirates and Maya living beyond the reach of central government. In the 1970s, however, the stunning palm-fringed white-sand **beaches** of the Caribbean coast and its magnificent offshore **coral reefs** began to be developed for **tourism**: the first highways were built, new towns were settled, and the place finally became a full state (as opposed to an externally administered federal territory) in 1974.

The stretch of **coast** between **Cancún** and **Tulum**, known as the Riviera Maya, is the most visited, and the focus of much recent hotel construction. Cancún and **Playa del Carmen**, along with the islands of **Mujeres** and **Cozumel**, have become desirable package-tour destinations, and are overdeveloped as a result. Images of the Maya appear everywhere, but the foreign-owned, all-inclusive resort companies make sure little of their profit ever goes to Mexico, much less to the indigenous villages that dot the jungle.

Further south things have remained quieter: sea turtles nest on the beaches within the **Sian Ka'an Biosphere Reserve**, while the inlets shelter manatees and the mangrove swamps clamour with bird life. The coast south of the

### Prices on the Caribbean coast

Because Cancún, Cozumel and the big towns in the Riviera Maya cater largely to tourists, local businesses often quote **prices** in US dollars, and accept payment in that currency. Moreover, prices for major attractions, tours and the like are often pegged to the exchange rate, so a US$70 hotel room could be M$700 one week and M$770 the next. As elsewhere in the guide, prices here are given in Mexican pesos, but note that they may be a bit different when you visit.

biosphere – dubbed the Costa Maya – is on its own development trajectory, but bus service is infrequent, so it's still your best bet for hammock camping. The vast, beautiful **Laguna de Bacalar** is known primarily as a vacation destination among Mexicans – it's quiet, rich in wildlife and an affordable alternative to the beaches. **Chetumal**, the state capital and a duty-free border town, is chiefly important as a gateway to and from Belize.

**Inland** Quintana Roo is barely populated, let alone visited. There are some **Maya sites**, though they are not as accessible or as restored as the pristine open-air museums of Yucatán state. **Cobá**, a lakeside ruin between Tulum and Valladolid, has some of the Maya world's tallest temples, but is only partially excavated, hidden in jungle swarming with mosquitoes. The early Classic site of **Kohunlich**, famous for its giant sculpted faces of the Maya sun god, lies in the heart of the Petén jungle that stretches into Guatemala and Belize.

# Cancún

If nothing else, **CANCÚN** is proof of Mexico's remarkable ability to get things done in a hurry, so long as the political will exists. Between 1970 and 1974, a near-deserted stretch of beach was transformed into a viable resort destination, as the Mexican government built city infrastructure from scratch. International hotel chains flocked to the area, workers and tourists arrived in droves and now Cancún has a resident population of more than half a million and hosts almost two million visitors a year. In 2005 the beachfront was flattened by two hurricanes, just a few months apart. Foreign media coverage painted the second, Hurricane Wilma, as an overwhelming disaster, but within a year this industrious city had made short work of the mess, and Cancún's hotels are now, if anything, even more splendid and the twenty-plus kilometres of white sand even more beautiful than before the storms.

The place has a lot to offer the active vacationer – striking modern hotels, hectic nightlife and high-energy entertainment – and from here much of the rest of the Yucatán is easily accessible. For independent travellers, though, the beachfront pleasures can be expensive, and, for anyone who has been out in the rest of the Yucatán or is eager to get there, the abundance of concrete and apparent lack of local culture can be very off-putting. However, a night spent here on the way in or out doesn't have to be wasted time, so long as you appreciate the city as an energetic, successful frontier experiment, rather than lament its lack of history. A closer look reveals lively salsa clubs, bare-bones beach bars and inexpensive taco stands, all frequented by *cancunenses* who are friendly and proud of their city's prosperity.

The city has two parts: the *zona comercial* downtown – the shopping and residential centre which, as it gets older, is becoming genuinely earthy – and the *zona hotelera*, a narrow, 25-kilometre-long barrier island connected to the mainland at each end by causeways and lined with hotels and tourist amenities. It encloses a huge lagoon, so there's water on both sides.

## Arrival, information and city transport

Charter flights from Europe and South America, along with direct scheduled flights from dozens of domestic cities and cities in North and Central America, land at **Cancún International Airport** (Ⓦwww.cancun-airport.com), 20km south of the centre. Past customs, you'll find **ATMs** and **currency exchange** desks, as well as luggage **lockers**. A **bus** (M$35) runs every thirty minutes to

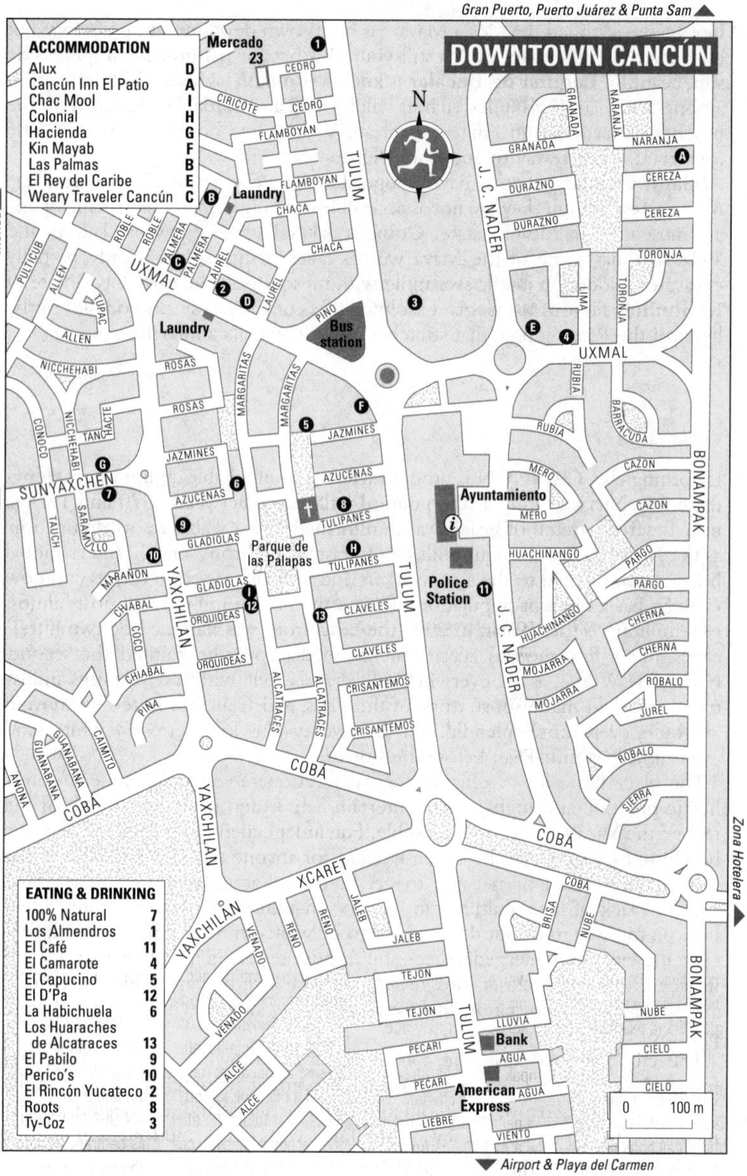

Gran Puerto, Puerto Juárez & Punta Sam

## DOWNTOWN CANCÚN

Mérida

Post office & Mercado 28

Zona Hotelera

Airport & Playa del Carmen

| ACCOMMODATION | |
|---|---|
| Alux | D |
| Cancún Inn El Patio | A |
| Chac Mool | I |
| Colonial | H |
| Hacienda | G |
| Kin Mayab | F |
| Las Palmas | B |
| El Rey del Caribe | E |
| Weary Traveler Cancún | C |

| EATING & DRINKING | |
|---|---|
| 100% Natural | 7 |
| Los Almendros | 1 |
| El Café | 11 |
| El Camarote | 4 |
| El Capucino | 5 |
| El D'Pa | 12 |
| La Habichuela | 6 |
| Los Huaraches de Alcatraces | 13 |
| El Pabilo | 9 |
| Perico's | 10 |
| El Rincón Yucateco | 2 |
| Roots | 8 |
| Ty-Coz | 3 |

the main terminal downtown, while **colectivos** take you to any part of the hotel zone for a fixed price (M$85); buy tickets at the respective desks outside customs. **Taxis** cost considerably more. Arriving by bus, you'll pull in at the city's main **bus station**, in the heart of downtown, just by a roundabout at the major junction of avenidas Tulum and Uxmal.

**Avenida Tulum**, downtown Cancún's main north–south street, is lined with shops, banks, restaurants and travel agencies, as well as many hotels – up side streets, but in view. The **tourist office** is half a block south of the bus station, inside the city hall at Tulum 26 (daily 9am–8pm; ⓣ998/884-8073). The friendly bilingual staff will help with even the smallest enquiries. They also dish out free maps and leaflets and copies of ubiquitous promotional listings **magazines**, the glossiest of which is *Cancún Tips* – all information that you can also pick up at just about every travel agency and hotel reception. Other "tourist information" **kiosks** are usually pitching time-shares or tickets to the big nature parks down the coast.

Most attractions in the downtown area are within walking distance, but you need some sort of transport to get to and around the *zona hotelera*, about a thirty-minute ride away. **Buses** marked "Tulum–Hoteles, Ruta 1" run along Tulum every few minutes; the fare is M$4.50 for downtown and M$6.50 to anywhere in the hotel zone. Alternatively, **taxis** are plentiful and can be hailed almost anywhere – the trip between downtown and Punta Cancún in the *zona hotelera* costs around M$110, based on a complex zone system (they're just M$15 within the downtown area). A **car** isn't necessary within the city, but it affords you more scope and makes day trips to destinations as far away as the ruins at Cobá perfectly feasible.

## Accommodation

Cancún has a dizzying number of hotels, but most are very expensive for the casual visitor. **Downtown** holds the only hope of a true budget room; in the **zona hotelera**, you can stay on the lagoon side for far less than in the glittering beachfront palaces, with their expansive pools and lavish restaurants (though it's worth checking for low-season deals at these). If you're interested in staying at an all-inclusive resort, book ahead and don't skimp: cheaper places may seem like a bargain on paper, but the facilities are often run down and the meals border on inedible.

If you're on a tight budget, several places downtown have dorm accommodation; in addition to those **hostels** recommended below, *Villas Juveniles* hostel (ⓣ998/883-1337), at Paseo Kukulcán Km 3.2 in the *zona hotelera*, has been renovated, and is a bargain option on the beach.

### Downtown

**Alux** Uxmal 21 ⓣ998/884-6613, ⓦwww.hotelalux.com. Popular, good-value hotel, if a little dated with its mirror-clad decor; all rooms have a/c, TV and telephone. Travel agency next door and street café on site. ❺

**Cancún Inn El Patio** Bonampak 51 ⓣ998/884-3500, ⓦwww.cancuninn.com. A hands-off staff and a location in a residential neighbourhood make this small hotel feel more like a private apartment complex. The thirteen simple rooms ring a quiet garden courtyard. Easy walk to downtown. ❺

**Chac Mool** Gladiolas 18 ⓣ998/887-5873, ⓔchacmoolhostel@hotmail.com. Small four-bed dorms (M$120) as well as a few private rooms (❷), and the option of a/c. The cool rooftop lounge, with a grand view over the Parque de las Palapas, serves cheap drinks.

**Colonial** Tulipanes 22 ⓣ998/884-1535, ⓦwww.hotelcolonialcancun.com. Well-lit rooms are simple and modern, with TV and a choice of a/c or fan; not much character, but good value. ❺

**Hacienda** Sunyaxchen 39 ⓣ998/884-3672, ⓕ884-1208. Quiet location a little out of the densest tourist area; rooms all have a/c and TV and there's a big pool, a pretty garden and a café. ❺

**Kin Mayab** Tulum 75, at Uxmal ⓣ998/884-2999, ⓦwww.hotelkinmayab.com. This centrally located hotel is clean and secure, with the most comfortable rooms and best pool in its price range (book ahead). Request the back section, by the pool and away from the street noise. ❻

**Las Palmas** Palmera 43 ⓣ998/884-2513, ⓔhotelpalmascancun@hotmail.com. This quiet family operation caters as much to Mexican workers as to backpackers, so there's less of the

10 THE YUCATÁN | Cancún

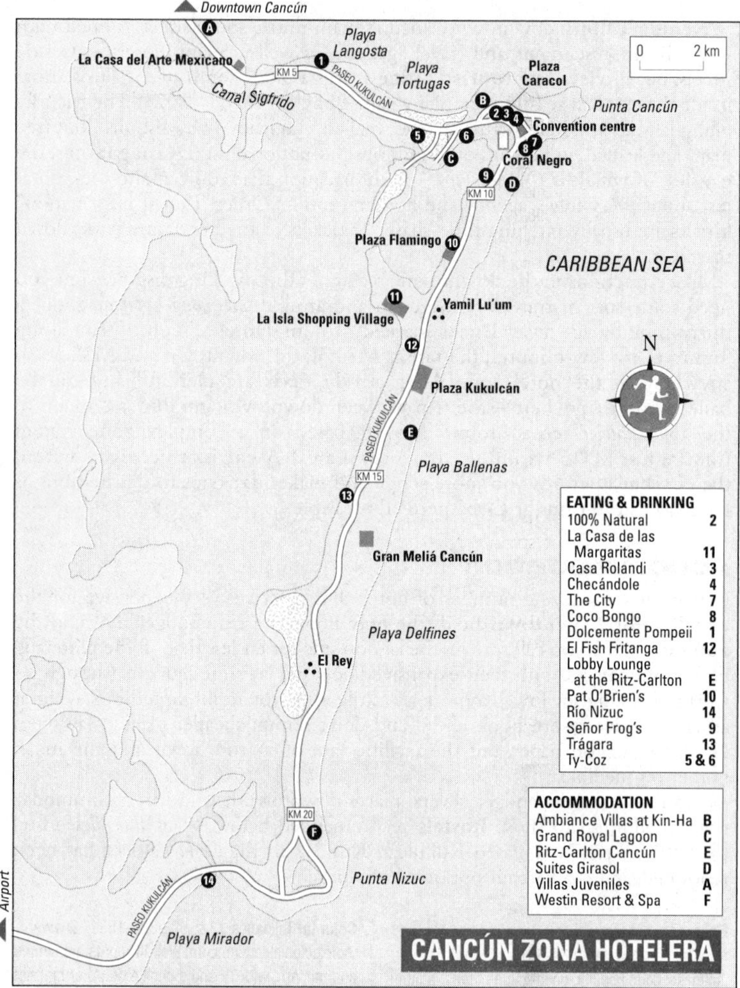




typical hostel party atmosphere. The real draw: the cheapest a/c beds in town (M$100), in big single-sex dorms, and a few huge private rooms (4). Continental breakfast included.

**El Rey del Caribe** Uxmal 24, at Nader ⓣ998/884-2028, ⓦwww.reycaribe.com. Sunny yellow rooms with kitchenettes, plus a pool, spa services and generous breakfast at this casual hotel that feels like it should be on a beach in Tulum. The only place in Cancún with a real ecofriendly sensibility. 6

**Weary Traveler Cancún** Palmera 30, at Uxmal ⓣ998/887-0191. The oldest and most popular Cancún hostel with young backpackers, maintaining several dorms (M$95) and a rooftop terrace where you can hang a hammock. Internet access, bike rental and laundry available.

## Zona hotelera

**Ambiance Villas at Kin-Ha** Paseo Kukulcán Km 8.5 ⓣ998/891-5400, ⓦwww.ambiancevillas.com. Big, tastefully furnished double-bed rooms, studios with kitchenettes and full suites with one, two or three bedrooms. Every room has a terrace or balcony, and the beach is one of the best of those facing the bay. A very good deal for families or groups. 8

**Grand Royal Lagoon** Quetzal 8-A, near Km 7.5 on Paseo Kukulcán ⓣ998/883-1270, ⓦwww.grlagoon.com. Facing the lagoon, this is the cheapest option in the *zona hotelera*. Thirty-six small but spotless rooms done in cheerful colours are set around an equally small pool. A few studio rooms have kitchenettes. ❼

**Ritz-Carlton Cancún** Retorno del Rey 36, near Paseo Kukulcán Km 14 ⓣ998/881-0808, ⓦwww.ritzcarlton.com. The last word in luxury in Cancún: all chandeliers, oil paintings and deep carpeting. Even if it doesn't seem particularly Mexican, it's still an impeccably run hotel. Prices can drop by half in the low season. ❾

**Suites Girasol** Paseo Kukulcán Km 9.5 ⓣ998/883-5045. The entry and public areas of this condo high-rise don't look promising, but the rooms are surprisingly large and clean, and all have kitchenettes. The pool is nothing special, but the beach out front is gorgeous. ❼

**Westin Resort & Spa Cancún** Paseo Kukulcán Km 20 ⓣ998/848-7400, ⓦwww.westin.com. Striking, minimalist accommodation with pillow-top beds, deluxe showers and impressive views. An additional west-facing beach and pool on the lagoon get afternoon sun. Isolated (and quiet), but a free shuttle runs up to sister hotel the *Sheraton*, closer to the action. ❾

## The town and beaches

There's little in the way of sights in **downtown Cancún**, though it is a pleasant place to stroll in the evenings, particularly around the central **Parque de las Palapas**, which is ringed with food stalls and often serves as a venue for live music; smaller parks in the neighbourhood host craft or art shows.

Most visitors head straight for the *zona hotelera* and the **beaches**. You're free to lie on the sand anywhere, but hotel staff will move you off beach furniture if you're not a guest. To avoid being eyed suspiciously by hotel heavies, head for one of the half-dozen or so designated **public beaches** squeezed between the hotels. The beaches on the north coast of the *zona hotelera* – playas Tortugas, Linda and Langosta – face a bay, so the water is calm and very good for swimming; they can be crowded, however, and all have loud bars nearby. On the east coast, playas Ballenas, Delfines and others have more surf (and occasionally,

△ Playa Tortugas, Cancún

dangerous currents), but fewer people and services. All are free, but you may have to pay a small charge for a shower.

To catch a bit of culture while you're out here, visit **La Casa del Arte Mexicano** in the Embarcadero complex at Paseo Kukulcán Km 4 (daily 9am–9pm; M$55), a really high-quality folk-art museum crammed with musical instruments, children's toys and colourful traditional costumes. If you admire an item, chances are you'll find something similar in the well-stocked **gift shop**. You can also see a small Maya ruin on the grounds of the *Sheraton* opposite La Isla Shopping Village, as well as at **El Rey**, at Paseo Kukulcán Km 18, overlooking the Nichupté Lagoon (daily 8am–5pm; M$30). Those at El Rey are the largest Maya remains in Cancún, but that's not saying a lot. There's very little information available to explain them, but the area is peaceful and good for spotting birds and iguanas.

The best **snorkelling** in Cancún is at Punta Nizuc, at the far southern point of the peninsula. Its coral has been damaged by unchecked crowds, but the array of fish is impressive. When you visit by boat, a M$20 national-park fee is charged (though tour operators often don't include this in the price they quote). The typical outing is the so-called **jungle tour**, which entails riding two-passenger speedboats through lagoon mangroves, then out to the reef. Aquaworld (Ⓣ998/848-8326, Ⓦwww.aquaworld.com.mx) is the main operator, offering trips for M$500, though you can book something similar through hotels, or directly at any of the numerous docks on the lagoon side.

Elsewhere on the water, **jet skiing** (M$500 for 30min) and **parasailing** (M$400 for 10min) are very popular, and operators are dotted at frequent intervals in front of the big hotels on the beach. For something mellower, head for the winding walkway along **Canal Sigfrido**, opposite the Embarcadero complex at Paseo Kukulcán Km 4. Especially nice at sunset, you can get an up-close view of the mangroves. Though you might occasionally see kids swimming here, don't be tempted: crocodiles are still plentiful in the lagoon.

## Eating

Cancún is home to a plethora of restaurants. Downtown, the most popular eating-places line Tulum and its side streets. Though seafood and steak are menu mainstays, you can also eat Middle Eastern, Yucatecan, Italian, Chinese, French, Cajun and Polynesian fare, not to mention international fast food and items from local chains.

For **budget food**, follow the locals and make for the downtown markets. The biggest in Cancún is **Mercado 28**, close to the city's main post office at the western end of Avenida Sunyaxchen, where two rows of stalls form a sort of pan-Mexican food court, with specialities from Monterrey, Mexico City, Guadalajara and elsewhere. **Mercado 23** is much smaller but makes a peaceful venue for a decent lunch; from the bus station, walk a few blocks north along Tulum and then turn left on Calle Flamboyan or Calle Cerdo. For dinner, food stalls at **Parque de las Palapas** serve open-face *huaraches* and quesadillas with an array of toppings; they're open until about 11pm.

Almost all of the restaurants in the **zona hotelera** are geared towards one thing only: parting tourists from their money. The few recommended here are worth a splurge, or are rare bargains. If you're staying on the beach, you're often better off taking a cab or bus downtown, where you'll find more satisfying food at reasonable prices, plus a congenial mix of people.

## Downtown

**100% Natural** Sunyaxchén 26, at Yaxchilán. As the name implies, the menu at this largely vegetarian restaurant is decidedly wholesome, with fruit salads and veggie burgers, as well as fresh Mexican dishes. Breakfasts are especially nice, with inventive combos like poached eggs over nopal leaves with spinach and an almond cream sauce.

**Los Almendros** Tulum 66. The original restaurant in the town of Ticul (see p.813) is credited with inventing the emblematic Yucatecan pork dish *poc-chuc.* This branch is somewhat stiff, with bright lights and white tablecloths, but the food is well prepared and reasonably priced. Nightly specials on Mon, Wed, Thurs and Sun.

**El Café** Nader 5, behind the city hall. A buzzing terrace frequented by Cancún's journalists. Good coffee and *pan dulce* for breakfast, plus a simple, reasonably priced lunch and dinner menu with basics like steak and fries and *enchiladas de mole.*

**El D'Pa** Alcatraces, at the southwest corner of Parque de las Palapas. Typical French crepes, both sweet and savoury, and decent wine by the glass. Choose a sidewalk table or sit inside among plush furniture. Closed Mon.

**La Habichuela** Margaritas 25, in front of the park ⓣ998/884-3158, ⓦwww.lahabichuela.com. Long-established, elegant restaurant set in a walled garden. The featured *cocobichuela* (half a coconut filled with lobster and shrimp in a curry sauce; M$325), draws raves, but less expensive Caribbean concoctions are equally good. The sommelier is attentive and enthusiastic. Neighbouring *Labná,* under the same ownership, applies similar elegant flair to Yucatecan specialities, with somewhat lower prices.

**Los Huaraches de Alcatraces** Alcatraces 31 (or enter on Claveles). This sparkling cafeteria-style restaurant serves up hearty breakfasts and hot lunches as well as lighter snacks like *huaraches* and quesadillas. Everything's very fresh, and the staff are happy to explain the various dishes. Closed Mon.

**El Pabilo** Yaxchilán 31, in the *Xbalamqué* hotel. Mellow literary coffee shop (a "*cafébrería*") with very good cappuccino, espresso and snacks. Live guitar music or readings at night.

**Perico's** Yaxchilán 61 ⓣ998/884-3152, ⓦwww.pericos.com.mx. A phantasmagoria of strolling magicians, crooning mariachis and stilt-walkers – so over the top that even sceptics may be swayed, and the food (tasty steaks and enchiladas; M$140–250) holds its own.

**El Rincón Yucateco** Uxmal 24. In business since 1981, this stalwart specializes in simple cuisine such as *panuchos* and *brazo de reina*, a hearty tamale-like dish, all washed down with cold beers. Closed Sun.

**Ty-Coz** Tulum behind *Comercial Mexicana.* A sandwich shop where French and Mexican tastes mix: the warm ham-and-cheese *baguette económico* is slathered with garlic-herb mayo and studded with pickled jalapenos. Coffee and croissants for breakfast. Open till 10pm. Also branches in the *zona hotelera* at Paseo Kukulcán Km 7 and Km 7.5.

## Zona hotelera

**100% Natural** Paseo Kukulcán Km 8.5. A branch of the veggie-friendly café that's also downtown, in a strip mall just west of Plaza Caracol. There's also a branch in the Plaza Kukulcán mall at Km 13.

**La Casa de las Margaritas** in La Isla Shopping Village, Paseo Kukulcán Km 12. Upscale Mexican restaurant with decent regional specialities such as Oaxacan *tlayudas* (chewy corn cakes with assorted toppings; M$90) that isn't quite as over-decorated as some. The live music, a wider variety than the usual blaring mariachi, doesn't dominate the room. The Sun buffet (noon–5pm; M$140) is a good deal.

**Casa Rolandi** in Plaza Caracol, Paseo Kukulcán Km 8.5 ⓣ998/831-1817, ⓦwww.rolandi.com. This Cancún fixture serves northern Italian specialities, many done in a wood-burning oven, in a candle-lit, white-tablecloth setting. Expensive (mains M$125–530), but suitable for a romantic splurge.

**Checándole** Plaza El Parián, Paseo Kukulcán Km 8.7. One of the few spots in the hotel zone for satisfying, inexpensive local grub like *tacos al pastor.* Daily 2–8pm.

**Dolcemente Pompeii** Pez Volador 7, near Paseo Kukulcán Km 5 ⓣ998/849-4006. A rare casual restaurant catering to Mexican families and hotel-zone residents with mammoth portions of hearty Italian food, from hand-made pastas (M$90 and up) to gelato. Hard to find because it's not affiliated with a mall or hotel: turn north in front of the giant Mexican flag. Closed Mon.

**El Fish Fritanga** Paseo Kukulcán Km 12.5. Hidden behind a *Domino's*, this lagoon-side seafood specialist is inexpensive, laid-back and frequented by residents – there's even a bit of beach, so you can stick your feet in the sand while you eat.

**Río Nizuc** off Paseo Kukulcán near Km 22. *Ceviche* and *tikin-xic* fish grilled in banana leaves are popular with locals at this casual place tucked among the mangroves near the opening to the lagoon. Daily 11am–5pm.

## Drinking, entertainment and nightlife

As Cancún's goal is to encourage some two million visitors a year to have fun, the **zona hotelera**'s array of huge dance clubs, theme bars and top-volume everything is lavish – or remorseless, depending on how you look at it. **Downtown**, people often dance at weekends at the Parque de las Palapas to traditional Mexican music, and the stretch of Avenida Yaxchilán north of Sunyaxchen is quite lively – a few touts push menus at tourists, but the clientele at the open/terrace restaurant/bars is mostly Mexican, and the entertainment limited to TVs, karaoke and roving *trovadores*. Cancún's hipper population can be spotted at a string of little bars on Avenida Nader, just behind the city hall and the Ki-Huic market. In addition to the bars and clubs listed below, you may find interesting touring bands, as well as the city's chamber orchestra, playing at El Teatro de Cancún (☎998/849-4848), at El Embarcadero in the hotel zone.

### Downtown

**El Camarote** In the *Plaza Kokai* hotel, Uxmal 26 ☎998/884-3218. Older gentlemen play backgammon and cards at this nautical-themed terrace bar. In the back, a small stage hosts crooners of sad ballads (M$30 cover).

**El Capucino** Margaritas near Azucenas. Local reggae and jam bands play for a mixed clientele of students and bohemians.

**Roots** downtown on Tulipanes 26. Funky little live jazz and blues club that also serves dinner.

### Zona hotelera

**The City** Paseo Kukulcán Km 9. Mega-club with great sound and a mesmerizing laser show, frequented by cool locals. Music ranges from European techno to Mexican hip-hop.

**Coco Bongo** in the Forum by the Sea shopping centre, Paseo Kukulcán Km 9.5. Vast state-of-the-art rock and pop disco popular with US college kids, but with more diverse music than competitor *Dady O* across the street. Open till 5am; cover charge at weekends only.

**Lobby Lounge at the Ritz-Carlton** Retorno del Rey 36, near Paseo Kukulcán Km 14. Soak up the ersatz Continental feel while sitting in overstuffed chairs and listening to the tinkling piano. The giveaway you're in Cancún: the sea view, exhaustive tequila menu and *ceviche* bar.

**Pat O'Brien's** in Plaza Flamingo, Paseo Kukulcán Km 11. Live rock, blues and jazz in a larger-than-life version of the famous New Orleans establishment. Three rooms: a piano bar, a video lounge and an outdoor patio. Open until 2am daily.

**Señor Frog's** Paseo Kukulcán Km 9.5. Practically synonymous with the name Cancún, the *Frog* is the first stop off the plane for the spring-break hordes. Go for live reggae or karaoke night, or just as an anthropological experience.

**Trágara** Paseo Kukulcán Km 15.6. Velvet couches, numerous aquariums and mosaic trim on every surface set a super-cool mood in this breezy lagoon-front lounge – the perfect spot for a sunset drink and a snack from the Asian-fusion finger-food menu.

## Listings

**Airlines** Aeroméxico ☎998/884-1097; American ☎800/904-6000; Aviacsa, Cobá 37 ☎998/887-4211, at the airport 886-0093; Delta ☎800/902-2100; Mexicana ☎998/881-9090; Northwest/KLM ☎800/907-4700.

**American Express** Tulum 208, at Agua ☎998/884-4000 (Mon–Fri 9am–5pm).

**Banks** Most banks (usually Mon–Fri 9.30am–3pm, Sat 9.30am–1pm) are along Tulum between Uxmal and Cobá and in the biggest shopping malls – Kukulcán, Plaza Caracol – in the *zona hotelera*. The HSBC, Tulum 192, stays open until 7pm on weekdays.

**Car rental** Available at most hotels and at the airport, or try Buster Rent a Car, in Plaza La Hacienda, Paseo Kukulcán Km 7 (☎998/883-0510, Ⓦwww.busterrentacar.com), or Budget (☎998/886-2949), which provides shuttle pick-up at the airport, but doesn't charge additional airport location fees.

**Consulates** Canada, Plaza Caracol, Paseo Kukulcán Km 8.5 ☎998/883-3360; Germany,

## Moving on from Cancún

If you're heading west **by car** to Valladolid, Chichén Itzá and Mérida, you have a choice between the old free road (*libre*) or the new toll highway (*cuota*), which runs a few kilometres north of the old road for most of its length. From the bus station, drive north on Tulum about 1km, then turn onto Avenida López Portillo. After a few kilometres you will have the choice of which road to join; just south of the Cancún airport, there's also an entrance to the *cuota* only. For the toll road, you pay in advance for the sections you intend to travel along at the booths on the highway. The drive to Mérida costs M$340.

First- and second-class **buses** both go from the terminal at the corner of Tulum and Uxmal. Destinations include **Campeche**, on ADO GL (2 daily; 7hr) and first-class (5 daily; 7hr); **Chetumal**, on ADO GL (2 daily; 5hr 30min), first-class (hourly 5am–12.30am; 6hr) and second-class (6 daily; 7hr); Mahahual (2 daily; 5hr); **Mérida**, on deluxe UNO (2 daily; 4hr 15min), semi-deluxe ADO GL (9 daily; 4hr 15min) and standard first-class (hourly round-the-clock; 4hr 30min); Mexico City, on ADO GL (1 daily; 26hr) and first-class (4 daily; 26hr); **Playa del Carmen** via Puerto Morelos (every 10min; 1hr 15min); **Tizimín** on first-class (5 daily; 4hr) and second-class (at least 2 daily; 5hr); **Tulum**, on first-class (hourly 6am–midnight; 2hr 15min) and second-class (hourly 4am–12.15pm; 3hr); and **Valladolid** (8 daily; 3hr). For Playa del Carmen, you can also take a **colectivo**, which is marginally cheaper - one service leaves from the parking lot in front of the bus station.

International and domestic **flights** leave regularly from Cancún; from downtown and the *zona hotelera* a taxi to the airport costs about M$200, and the bus from downtown costs M$35.

### The ferry to Isla Mujeres

Passenger **ferries** (15min; M$35) for Isla Mujeres leave from Gran Puerto and, about 250m further north, Puerto Juárez, every thirty minutes (6.30am–10.30pm). To get to the ferry terminals, catch a bus ("R-13" or "R-1 – Pto Juárez"; M$4.50) heading north from the stop on Tulum opposite the bus station (15min), or take a taxi from Avenida Tulum (around M$40). There's also a less frequent ferry service from Playa Tortugas in the *zona hotelera* (30min; M$100).

The car ferry (M$185 per car with one driver, M$14 per extra person) leaves from Punta Sam, a few kilometres north of Puerto Juárez; however, it isn't really worth taking a car to the island, which is quite small and has plenty of bicycles and mopeds for rent.

Punte Conoco 36 SM 24 downtown ⓣ998/887-2127; UK, *Royal Sands*, Paseo Kukulcán Km 13.5 ⓣ998/848-8229; US, Plaza Caracol, Paseo Kukulcán Km 8.5 ⓣ998/883-0272.

**Hospital** The largest hospital close to the *zona hotelera* is AmeriMed, Tulum Sur 260, behind Plaza las Américas ⓣ998/881-3400 or 881-3434 for emergencies, ⓦwww.amerimedcancun.com.

**Internet access** Immediately across from the bus station and northwest on Uxmal are several Internet cafés; some are *casetas* as well. In the *zona hotelera*, Web access is significantly more expensive; in a pinch, try the Internet cafe in La Isla Shopping Village.

**Laundry** Lavandería Uxmal, on Uxmal opposite *Hotel Alux*, or Lavandería Martinez, across the street from *Las Palmas* hotel.

**Post office** Sunyaxchén at Xel-Ha (Mon–Fri 8am–6pm, Sat 9am–1pm); has a reliable Lista de Correos (postcode 77501).

**Travel agencies and tours** Most hotels in the *zona hotelera* have in-house agencies that can arrange day trips to the chief Maya sites or other attractions along the coast. Otherwise, the student-friendly agency Nómadas has a branch at Cobá 5 (ⓣ998/892-2320, ⓦwww.nomadastravel.com) and leads affordable tours to Chichén Itzá and other nearby attractions.

# Isla Mujeres

Just a few kilometres off the easternmost tip of Mexico in the startlingly clear Caribbean, **ISLA MUJERES** is substantially mellower than Cancún, drawing people for long stays despite the lack of tourist attractions and wild nightlife. A hippie hangout in the 1970s, the tiny island still retains an air of bohemian languor, with wild-haired baby-boomers passing on travel wisdom to a new generation of young backpackers.

Physically, however, Mujeres is hardly the desert island it was thirty years ago, and its natural attractions have been developed considerably. Thousands of day-trippers visit from Cancún, and the once beautiful **Garrafón coral reef** off the southern tip is now almost completely dead. Prices, too, have risen. All that said, the island can still seem a respite to those who've been slogging their way from Maya pyramid to Maya pyramid, or to anyone who is overwhelmed by Cancún – the wooden buildings and narrow streets have a genuine Caribbean feel.

The attractions here are simple: first there's the beach, then there's the sea. And when you've tired of those, you can cruise around the island to more sea, more beaches and the tiny Maya temple full of female figures that the conquistadors chanced upon, which gave the place its name. But you'll want to be back under the palms on **Playa Norte**, the big west-facing beach, by late afternoon: Isla Mujeres is one of the few places along Mexico's eastern shoreline where you can enjoy a glowing sunset over the water.

## Arrival, information and island transport

Passenger **ferries** arrive at Isla Mujeres town at two adjacent piers; the car ferry comes in further southeast on Avenida Medina, at the end of Calle Bravo. From the piers, it's about a twenty-minute walk to the opposite side of the island and the most distant hotels.

The **tourist office** (Mon–Fri 8am–8pm, Sat & Sun 9am–2pm) is on Medina just northwest of the passenger ferry piers. Here you can pick up leaflets, maps and copies of the free *Islander* magazine (in Spanish and English). The **post office** (Mon–Thurs 9am–4pm) is on Guerrero at Mateos. There is a **caseta** on Madero between Hidalgo and Juárez and an **Internet** café on Hidalgo at Abasolo. The only **bank**, HSBC, is on Medina opposite the ferry piers. A couple of **lavanderías** are on Abasolo.

The best way of getting around the island is by **moped** (M$100/hr) or **bicycle** (M$100/day), as the island is a very manageable size with few hills; alternatively, hire a **golf cart** (M$150/hr). Virtually every other storefront rents out all three forms of transport for approximately the same rates. There are several **dive shops** on the island – recommended is Coral, Matamoros 13-A (Ⓣ998/877-0763, Ⓦwww.coralscubadivecenter.com), which offers a range of trips, including some to the "Cave of the Sleeping Sharks", where tiger, bull, grey reef, lemon and nurse sharks are regularly encountered. You can also take **snorkelling** trips with a couple of *lancheros* co-operatives, which are set up on the piers (M$200; 2hr). The main day outing, to which scores of touts devote their efforts, is a boat trip to the island bird sanctuary of **Contoy** (with special permission, you may stay overnight). You can see colonies of pelicans and cormorants and occasionally more exotic sea birds, as well as a sunken Spanish galleon. The experienced captains at La Isleña Tours, on Morelos one block back from Medina, run a relaxed *faux*-castaway trip, with lunch caught straight from the sea, for M$480.

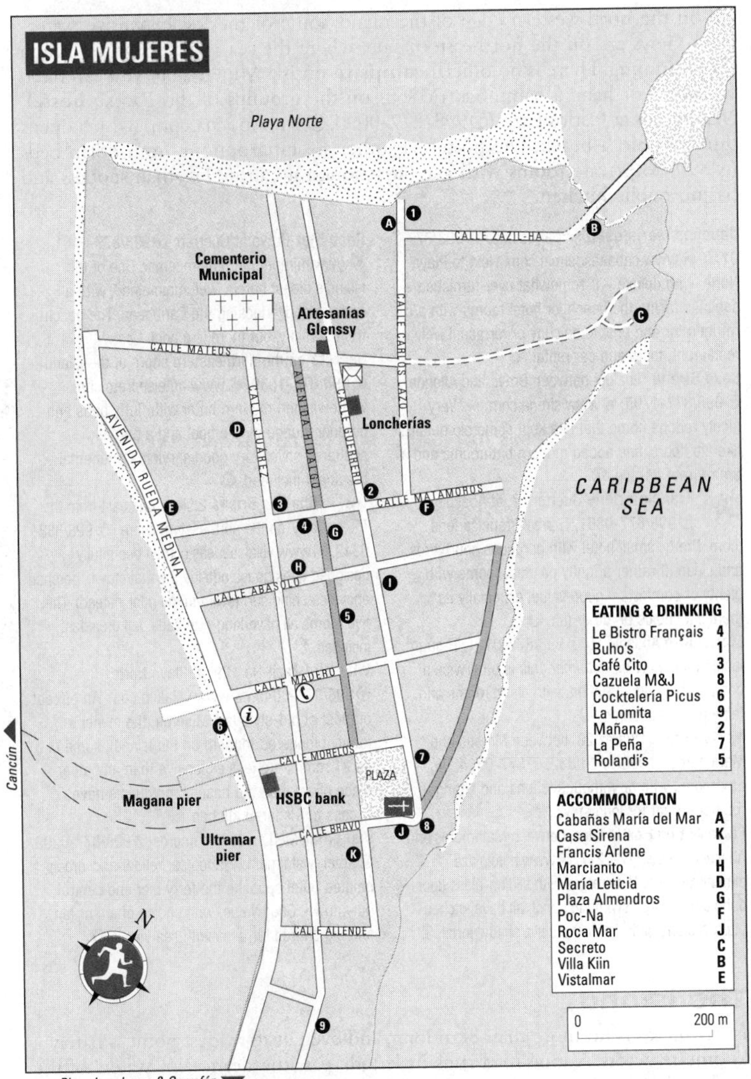




In recent years, the *lancheros* have begun offering tours to see the **whale sharks** that gather off the coast in August and September – a trip more commonly taken from Isla Holbox (see p.830). Going from Isla Mujeres costs slightly more (about M$1250) and takes longer, but it's easier to get here than to Holbox.

## Accommodation

Isla Mujeres is short on good **budget places to stay**, and, though rates are lower than in Cancún, so is the quality. Most of the reasonably priced options are on the northwestern edge of the island; some of the less expensive waterfront views are on the northeastern side, where the sea is generally too rough for swimming. There is no official **campsite** on Isla Mujeres, but you can pitch your tent or hang a hammock (M$65) on the grounds of the *Poc-Na* **hostel**, Matamoros at Carlos Lazo (ⓣ998/877-0090, ⓦwww.pocna.com), which opens directly onto a beach. The hostel has other sleeping options, from dorm beds (M$90) to private rooms with a/c (❹), though it can be less than spotless and has no public kitchen.

**Cabañas María del Mar** Carlos Lazo ⓣ998/877-0179, ⓦwww.cabanasdelmar.com. Next to Playa Norte, with deluxe – if somewhat over-furnished – cabañas facing the beach, or hotel rooms with a/c, refrigerator and private balcony or terrace. Lively restaurant, tours and car rental. ❽

**Casa Sirena** Hidalgo, between Bravo and Allende ⓣ998/877-1705, ⓦwww.sirena.com.mx. Very nicely redone home that has kept some old details, like tile floors, and added modern bathrooms and a breezy roof terrace. ❽

**Francis Arlene** Guerrero 7, at Abasolo ⓣ998/877-0861, ⓦwww.francisarlene.com. Pretty, small hotel with gorgeous courtyards and clean (if rather brightly painted) rooms with plenty of comforts – good value, especially as there's a choice of a/c or fan. ❻

**Marcianito** Abasolo 10 ⓣ998/877-0111. Though lacking the view of *Vistalmar*, this is otherwise a comparable budget option, with clean rooms and fairly new bathrooms. ❺

**María Leticia** Juárez 28, between Mateos and Matamoros ⓣ998/877-0832, ⓕ877-0394. Big, airy rooms with or without kitchens and sitting rooms – great for long stays. ❺

**Plaza Almendros** Hidalgo, between Matamoros and Abasolo ⓣ998/877-1217, ⓦwww.hotelplazaalmendros.com. New rooms with sliding-glass doors open onto a large swimming pool; all have kitchenettes, a/c and sitting areas under a shady portal. ❺

**Roca Mar** Bravo at Guerrero ⓣ998/877-0101, ⓦwww.mjmnet.net/hotelrocamar. One of the island's oldest hotels, well maintained, with a restaurant overlooking the Caribbean. The beachfront is rocky, but there is a pool. ❻

**Secreto** on the northeastern shore of the island ⓣ998/877-1039, ⓦwww.hotelsecreto.com. Whitewashed modern hotel with fluffy beds and outdoor lounge by the pool and a partially sheltered cove. Very good service; Continental breakfast included. ❾

**Villa Las Brisas** 2.5km southeast from the ferry, on the northeastern shore ⓣ998/888-0342, ⓦwww.villalasbrisas.com. A beautifully designed guesthouse outside the main town, perched above crashing surf (swim in the pool instead). The five rooms all have king-size beds; full breakfast included. ❽

**Villa Kiin** Zazil-Há 129, at Playa Norte ⓣ998/877-0045, ⓦwww.villakiin.com. An offbeat outpost of old-style Isla Mujeres (the owner's family pioneered tourism on the island), some of its 21 rooms are less expensive than any other place directly on the beach, and guests have access to a shared kitchen. ❼

**Vistalmar** Medina at Matamoros ⓣ998/877-0209, ⓔhotel_vistalmar1@yahoo.ca. Yellow-and-green-painted hotel opposite the ferry pier and central downtown. Good value, with choice of a/c or fan and big shared terraces with sea views. ❹

## The island

Isla Mujeres is no more than 8km long, and even at its widest point is barely a kilometre across. A lone road runs its length, past the dead-calm waters of the landward coast; the other side, northeast-facing, is windswept and exposed. There's a small beach on this side in the town, but even here the currents can be dangerous. The most popular beach, just five minutes' walk from the town plaza, is **Playa Norte** – at the northern tip of the island, but protected from the open sea by a promontory on which stands a large resort.

If you've had enough of the beach, windsurfing and wandering round town (the grand tour takes little more than 30min), rent a bike or moped to explore the south of the island. The **Garrafón** reef at the southern end is now a pricey nature park (daily 9am–6.30pm; ⓦwww.garrafon.com), with a zip-line and "snuba" (swim underwater with an oxygen line attached to a raft) set-up, all for exorbitant fees; for snorkelling, you're much better off going on a trip with the *lancheros* (see p.842).

## Reef etiquette

**Coral reefs** are among the richest and most complex ecosystems on earth, but they are also very fragile. The colonies grow at a rate of only around 5cm per year, so they must be treated with care and respect if they are not to be damaged beyond repair. Follow these **simple rules** – and advise your guide to do so as well – while you are snorkelling, diving or in a boat:

**Never** touch or stand on corals, as the living polyps on their surface are easily damaged.

**Avoid** disturbing the sand around corals. Quite apart from spoiling visibility, the cloud of sand will settle over the corals and smother them.

**Don't** remove shells, sponges or other creatures from the reef, and avoid buying reef products from souvenir shops.

**Don't** use suntan lotion in reef areas, as the oils are pollutants and will stifle coral growth; look for special biodegradable sunscreen for use while snorkelling.

**Don't** anchor boats on the reef: use the permanently secured buoys instead.

**Don't** throw litter overboard.

**Check** ahead of time where you are allowed to go fishing.

**Review** your diving skills before you head out to the reef, especially if you are a new or out-of-practice diver.

The entrance to the park is almost at the southern tip of the island – beyond, the road continues to the old lighthouse, surrounded by faux-Caribbean houses containing shops and a restaurant. From there you can visit a somewhat gratuitous sculpture park and the **Templo de Ixchel**, at the southeastern tip (M$30; free with Garrafón ticket). It's not much of a ruin (the fertility figures the Spanish spotted here have been removed), but it is very dramatically situated on low rocky cliffs, and you can often spot large fish basking below.

On the way back north, stop at **Playa Lancheros**, a small, palm-fringed beach that is virtually deserted except at lunch time, when day-trippers pile in. There's a restaurant here, specializing in seafood, and a clutch of souvenir stalls. Just north and inland lurk the barely visible remains of the **Hacienda Mundaca** (daily 9am–5pm; M$20), to which scores of romantic – yet quite untrue – pirate legends are attached. The place has been criss-crossed with a few too many concrete paths, but the jungly shade in the back garden makes for a prime picnic spot. Across the traffic circle, another road leads to a government-run **turtle farm** and research centre (daily 9am–5pm; M$20), which breeds endangered sea turtles for release in the wild. Entrance helps fund the preservation project.

## Eating and drinking

The area along and around Hidalgo between Morelos and Abasolo is lined with **restaurants** and **bars**. For inexpensive, basic Mexican food and great fruit salads, head for the **loncherías** on Guerrero between Mateos and Matamoros. At night, food vendors set up on the main plaza.

**Le Bistro Français** Matamoros 29, at Hidalgo. Vaguely French café with a varied, inventive and delicious menu (fish with fennel and capers, for instance) at reasonable prices. Good breakfasts too.

**Buho's** Playa Norte at Carlos Lazo, in front of *Cabañas María del Mar*. In high season, this beach bar tends to be the liveliest in town, with loud rock music, swinging hammock chairs and a well-attended happy hour.

**Café Cito** Juárez at Matamoros. Visit this colourful, cheery restaurant for healthful yogurt-granola breakfasts or more decadent crepes and waffles, along with very good coffee.

**Cazuela M&J** Bravo at the ocean, past the *Rocamar* hotel. Enjoy fine ocean views at this casual café serving inexpensive (mostly Mexican) breakfasts. Big glasses of green *chaya* juice are a healthful option. Daily 7am–2pm.

**Cocktelería Picus** Medina just north of the ferry piers. Small beachfront hut serving fresh and inexpensive *ceviche* and shrimp cocktails. Lunch only in the low season.

**La Lomita** Juárez 25-B, two blocks southeast of the plaza. Home cooking that's worth the hike up the hill, and the wait: locals line up for a helping of the daily lunch special.

**Mañana** Matamoros at Guerrero. Brightly painted breakfast and lunch café serving everything from falafel to *churrascos* (Argentine-style steak sandwiches). A secondhand book shop occupies one corner.

**La Peña** Guerrero, on the main plaza. An upstairs bar-lounge popular with younger visitors, with a view of the Caribbean, cocktails, DJs and a big movie screen.

**Rolandi's** Hidalgo, between Madero and Abasolo. Part of a small family-run chain serving great wood-oven pizza, lobster, fresh fish and other northern Italian dishes with salads.

# The east coast: Cancún to Playa del Carmen



Resort development along the spectacular white-sand beaches south from Cancún to the ruins of Tulum has snowballed as the region, now known as the Riviera Maya, has become nearly as large a tourist draw as Cancún itself. The **Mesoamerican Barrier Reef**, which extends all the way to Honduras, begins off **Puerto Morelos**, a quiet town with excellent restaurants. Further south, the phenomenal growth of **Playa del Carmen**, once known only as the departure point for boats to Cozumel, has transformed a fishing village into a major holiday destination renowned for its chic nightlife.

Finding a relatively deserted stretch of beach is increasingly difficult, though not impossible, and many visitors based in Cancún rent a car to explore the coast. Bus and *colectivo* service along Hwy-307 is cheap and efficient, but be prepared for at least a 500m walk, or a longer taxi ride, towards the water.

## Puerto Morelos and around

Leaving Cancún behind, the first town south along the coast is **PUERTO MORELOS**, 20km away. The only remaining working fishing village in this area, it's a good place to hang out for a while, as it's less style-conscious than Playa del Carmen and has some lovely beaches. The reef offshore is also near-pristine, making it a good base for **dive trips**. Inland, on the dirt road to Central Vallarta, are some beautiful cenotes that are only just beginning to receive visitors. With direct bus service from the Cancún airport (9 daily, 8.30am–6.45pm), it's easy for visitors to bypass Cancún altogether, making Puerto Morelos their first stop along the Riviera Maya.

### Arrival and information

**Buses** going down the coast leave Cancún's bus station every ten minutes and drop you at the highway junction, where taxis wait to take you the 2km into town (about M$25). On the plaza, you'll find several **long-distance telephones**, an **Internet** café, a supermarket, a couple of **casas de cambio** and an **ATM**, though no actual bank. Marand Travel (Ⓦwww.puertomorelos.com.mx), on the southwest corner of the plaza, is the unofficial tourist info spot, dispensing maps and advising on hotels. There's a **laundry** just south of the plaza, across from *Posada Amor*.

## Accommodation

Beachfront hotels in Puerto Morelos are significantly cheaper than in Playa del Carmen or Cancún, so this might be a place to splurge if your budget allows. If you want to **camp**, your only option is the pleasantly ramshackle *Acamaya Reef Park* (Ⓣ987/871-0132, Ⓦwww.acamayareef.com; M$90 per person), on the beach 5km north of town – from the highway, look for a signposted turn near the entrance to the Crococun zoo, or head up the coast road from Puerto Morelos. Cabañas, with shared or private bath, are also available (❻), and the French owner cooks good food.

**Amar Inn** on the seafront 500m north of the main plaza Ⓣ998/871-0026, Ⓔamar_inn@hotmail.com. Bohemian, family-run hotel with eight large, well-furnished rooms and cabañas, some with kitchenettes. Delicious Mexican breakfast included in rates. ❻

**Hacienda Morelos** on the waterfront just south of the plaza Ⓣ998/871-0448. Huge, bright rooms strung out in a row, motel-style, all with kitchenettes and bathtubs (a rare treat at this price), plus terraces opening onto a pool area, then the beach. ❻

**Inglaterra** Niños Héroes 29, 200m north of the plaza and two blocks back from the sea Ⓣ987/871-0418. Basic rooms, a little dark, but the lowest rates in town (and, yes, the owner is British). ❹

**Maya Echo** C 2 in the *zona urbana*. Ⓣ998/208-9148, Ⓦwww.mayaecho.com. An expat with strong ties to the Maya community offers one cabaña with your choice of bed (M$220) or hammock (M$170) on her forested property on the inland side of the highway. Tell the cab driver "Casa Cacahuate, Calle Dos".

**Ojo de Agua** on the seafront 400m north of the plaza Ⓣ987/871-0027, Ⓦwww.ojo-de-agua.com. Bright, sunny rooms (some have a/c) with colourful decor, most overlooking a giant pool; beyond lies a clean beach. The restaurant/bar occasionally hosts a live band. One added perk: ocean-view rooms don't cost more. ❻

**Posada Amor** Rojo Gómez, just south of the plaza Ⓣ998/871-0033, Ⓔpos_amor@hotmail.com. Not on the beach, but friendly, and one of the longest-running hotels in town, and still some of the lowest rates. Rooms are quirky and individually decorated – ask to see a few. ❺

**Posada El Moro** Rojo Gómez 17, just north of the plaza Ⓣ987/871-0159, Ⓦwww.posadaelmoro.com. Ten clean, relatively new rooms, some with kitchens, in a pretty little garden; rooms in the back are preferable, as the bar across the street can be noisy at night. Amenities are excellent for the price: there's a small pool, and Continental breakfast is included. ❻

**Sak Ol** 1km south of the plaza, beyond the car ferry dock Ⓣ998/871-0181, Ⓦwww.ranchosakol.com. Two-storey thatched cabañas in a tranquil garden that leads into a deserted-feeling beach. Rates include large breakfasts with fruit and cereal. Kitchen facilities and massage available to guests. ❼

## The Town

The turn-off from Hwy-307 ends at the small, modern **plaza** in the centre of Puerto Morelos. The only proper streets lead north and south for a few blocks, parallel to the beach. The plaza has a small church, a baseball court and a taxi rank, and hosts a produce market on Wednesdays. It's also home to the wonderful Alma Libre (Oct–April Tues–Sat 9am–noon & 6–9pm), probably Mexico's most extensive secondhand English-language **bookshop** (you can also get your digital photos transferred to CD here, and pick up a copy of the handy *Sac-Be* English newspaper). Ahead lies the **beach**, a wooden **dock** and a **lighthouse**, knocked askew years ago by a hurricane, and now kept as a local icon. Very attractive and reasonably priced **craftwork** can be found at Hunab-Ku Artesanía, two blocks south of the plaza on Rojo Gómez. Here you can often see the artisans at work.

With a healthy stretch of reef only 600m offshore, Puerto Morelos is a great place to learn to **dive**. Long-established Almost Heaven Adventures, on the square (Ⓣ987/871-0230, Ⓦwww.almostheavenadventures.com), offers certification courses and one- and two-tank dives (M$450–650) and snorkelling trips (M$350 per person; 2hr), as well as sport-fishing charters. It also leads tours to some inland **cenotes**, accessible via a turn-off from the main highway, marked by a modern concrete Maya arch. Strung along this dirt road are a number of swimming holes, developed to various degrees. If you just want to go swimming, you can take a taxi (M$450 for 2hr) to **Boca del Puma**, about 16km inland, where the owner has installed a long zip-line ride and an observation tower, or **Verde Lucero**, immediately up the road on the left; both charge M$50 admission, and Boca del Puma asks an additional M$50 for its zip-line.

On the east side of the highway, opposite the turn for the cenote route, the **Jardín Botánico Dr Alfredo Barrera Marín** (also signposted as Yaax Ché; Mon–Sat 9am–5pm; M$70) provides a good overview of the Yucatán's flora. A three-kilometre path leads through medicinal plants, ferns, palms, some tumbledown Maya ruins and a mock-up *chiclero* camp, where you can see how the sap of the *zapote* (sapodilla) tree is tapped before being used in the production of gum.

For more information on indigenous flora, and the Maya traditions surrounding it, contact **Sandra Dayton** (Ⓣ998/208-9148, Ⓦwww.mayaecho.com), who arranges visits to cenotes and tours with the local people. She also organizes a very small-scale **craft market** at which members of a women's co-op sell their wares (winter only, Sun 10.30am), which include great food as well as handicrafts. It's on the inland side of the highway – tell the cab driver "Jungle market, zona urbana, Calle Dos".

## Eating and drinking

For a town of its size, Puerto Morelos has a disproportionately high number of great **places to eat**, offering a mix of local flavours and things brought in by various expats (expect higher prices at the latter, of course). Most places are on the plaza, where everyone seems to convene at night. The bar at *Hacienda Morelos* occasionally hosts **live music**, as do a few restaurants. The tastiest snacks can be found at *Triny's*, a taco stand on the northwest corner of the plaza, and *El Tío*, just north of the plaza on Avenida Melgar, which does shrimp tacos in the morning and tortas and *panuchos* at lunch; also look out for a few informal eateries run out of people's front yards.

**Bodo's** south of the plaza in *Hacienda Morelos*. German-run spot with an international menu – good food, and a great terrace on the water. Closed Wed.

**Don Pepe Olé** Rojo Gómez north of the plaza. A sometimes rowdy local bar scene, which starts in the afternoon. Karaoke is the entertainment of choice once the sun goes down, and the Mexican dinner menu is quite good.

**Hola Asia** south side of the plaza. Get your fix of General Tso's chicken, or sample other Asian delicacies such as Thai fish with tamarind or Indonesian-style coconut shrimp. The rooftop tiki bar is nice at sunset – and the main expat hangout in town. Closed Tues.

**John Gray's Kitchen** Niños Héroes north of the plaza Ⓣ998/871-0665. Visitors from Cancún often make the short drive down for dinner at this small, casually elegant restaurant with combos like pan-roasted duck breast with chipotle, tequila and honey, or mac-and-cheese with shrimp and truffle oil. Closed Sun.

**Mama's** Rojo Gómez, one block north of the plaza. Homely American-owned breakfast and lunch joint, offering breakfast burritos with veggie chorizo, oatmeal, fruit smoothies and a wide range of baked goods. Closed Mon.

**Le Marlin Bleu** south side of the plaza. French dishes are on the menu, but this place is also good for tacos in all forms, from shrimp to *arrachera*. Closed Sun.

**La Petita** Melgar, half a block north of the plaza. This small wooden house is a fishermen's hangout and a local favourite for enjoying the catch of the day, sold by the kilo and available fried, grilled or in *ceviche*.

**Spaghettino** Rojo Gómez north of the plaza. An informal, inexpensive Italian place with a Euro café feel. Pizza, panini and hand-made pastas are on the menu. Closed Sun.

## Punta Bete

Tucked away between the more touristed resorts of Puerto Morelos and Playa del Carmen, the sedate **PUNTA BETE** is little more than a beach, several basic restaurants and a few small hotels. The beach is a bit rocky and nowhere near as beautiful as those in Cancún or Playa del Carmen, though it does have the advantage of being uncrowded. Punta Bete is some 4km east of the highway, with the turn-off signposted just south of the Cristal/Coca-Cola bottling plant around Km 62. Follow the road to the entrance to hip luxury hideaway *Ikal del Mar* (Ⓣ984/877-3000, Ⓦwww.korhotelgroup.com; ❾), where it forks: to the left (north) you'll eventually find *Los Piños* (Ⓣ984/873-1506; ❺), a small, somewhat dull beachfront concrete block, and, a bit back from the sea, the more charming *Coco's Cabañas* (Ⓣ998/874-7056, Ⓦwww.cocoscabanasplaya.com; ❹), with five individual cabañas, a small pool and a restaurant. The right-hand road (south) leads to Playa Xcalacoco and *Petit Lafitte* (US Ⓣ1-800/538-6802, Ⓦwww.mexicoholiday.com; ❽). Should you be looking to splurge, head 10km south of Punta Bete to one of the finest luxury hotels on the coast, *Maroma* (Ⓣ998/872-8200, Ⓦwww.orient-expresshotels.com; ❾). Elegant yet informal, and with a strong Mexican style, the white-washed hotel has a wonderful spa and an exceptionally personal feel.

## Playa del Carmen

**PLAYA DEL CARMEN** (known simply as Playa), once a soporific fishing village, has mushroomed in recent years to become, for tourists anyway, a trendy place touted as the next Miami Beach – from a local's perspective, a goldmine of employment in construction. Not only do Mexico City's elite pop in, but so do day-trippers from Cancún and passengers from cruise ships. As a result, the town's main centre of activity, Avenida 5 (also called **La Quinta**), a long, pedestrianized strip one block back from the sea, is often packed to capacity with tourists rapidly emptying their wallets in pavement cafés, souvenir outlets and designer-clothes shops. Nonetheless, Playa does retain a rather chic European atmosphere, due to a high number of Italian- and French-owned businesses, and compared with hyperactive, Americanized Cancún, it seems positively cosmopolitan and calm. The **nightlife** in particular is excellent, and you'll also find sophisticated cuisine, hotels for most budgets and diverse shops. Everywhere visitors will want to go is compact and very pedestrian-friendly – even a walk to the better **beach** on the north side of town, a broad expanse of silky sand, is an easy one.

The stretch of the reef offshore is almost as spectacular here as the coral in Cozumel. Of the scores of **scuba-diving** operations in Playa, recommended is Tank-Ha, Avenida 5 between calles 8 and 10 (Ⓣ984/873-0302, Ⓦwww.tankha.com), which offers one- and two-tank dives (M$400–600) and twice-daily snorkelling tours (9am & 1.30pm; M$300; 3hr), as well as **cave diving** in the inland cenotes (M$1000), and cave-diving training courses.

### Arrival, information and city transport

Playa del Carmen has two **bus stations**: the central depot is at the corner of Avenida 5 and Avenida Juárez, the main street running east–west from the highway to the beach, and deals with short-haul buses between Cancún and Tulum; the other station, on Avenida 20 between calles 12 and 14, is primarily for ADO and affiliated companies handling some local services as well as destinations further afield. From the international **airport** in Cancún, buses runs hourly to Playa between 8.30am and 8.45pm (M$80), or you can

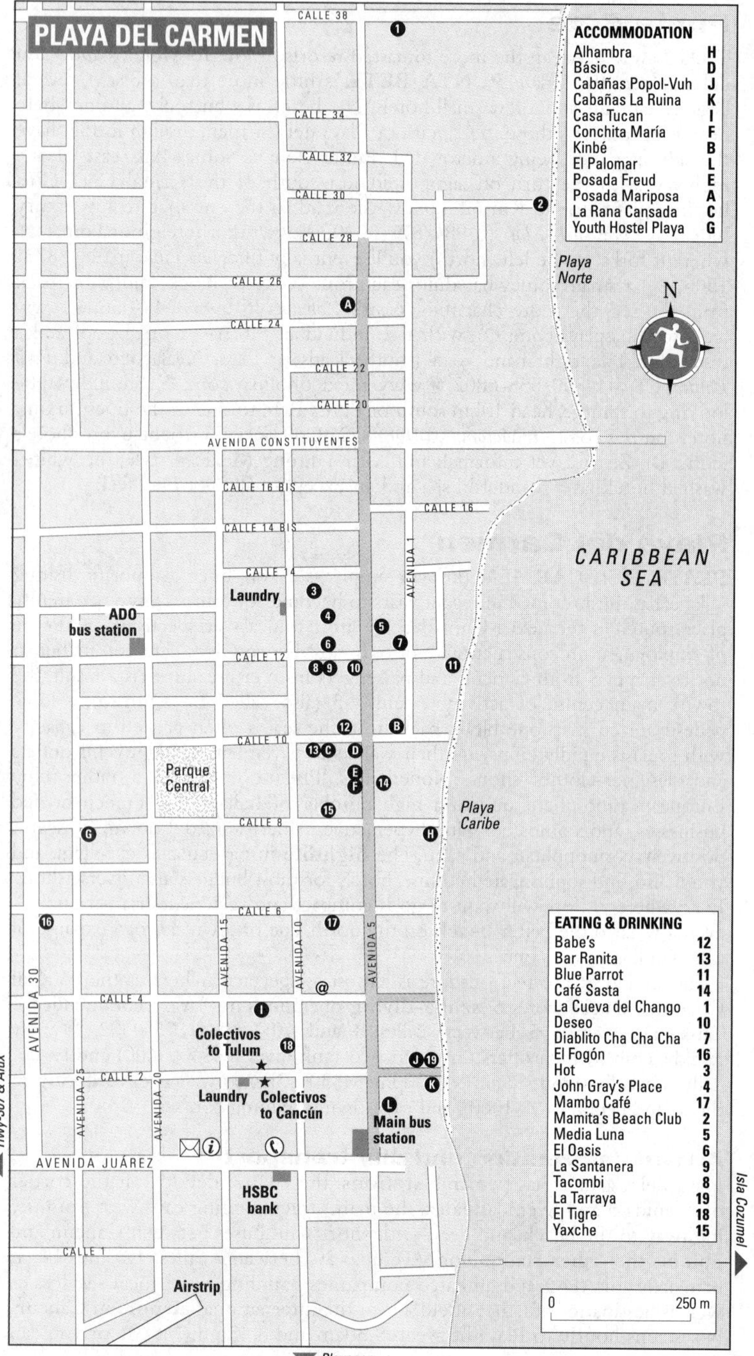
PLAYA DEL CARMEN
ACCOMMODATION
Alhambra H
Básico D
Cabañas Popol-Vuh J
Cabañas La Ruina K
Casa Tucan I
Conchita María F
Kinbé B
El Palomar L
Posada Freud E
Posada Mariposa A
La Rana Cansada C
Youth Hostel Playa G
EATING & DRINKING
Babe's 12
Bar Ranita 13
Blue Parrot 11
Café Sasta 14
La Cueva del Chango 1
Deseo 10
Diablito Cha Cha Cha 7
El Fogón 16
Hot 3
John Gray's Place 4
Mambo Café 17
Mamita's Beach Club 2
Media Luna 5
El Oasis 6
La Santanera 9
Tacombi 8
La Tarraya 19
El Tigre 18
Yaxche 15
CALLE 38
CALLE 34
CALLE 32
CALLE 30
CALLE 28
CALLE 26
CALLE 24
CALLE 22
CALLE 20
AVENIDA CONSTITUYENTES
CALLE 16 BIS
CALLE 16
CALLE 14 BIS
CALLE 14
CALLE 12
CALLE 10
CALLE 8
CALLE 6
CALLE 4
CALLE 2
AVENIDA JUÁREZ
CALLE 1
AVENIDA 1
AVENIDA 5
AVENIDA 10
AVENIDA 15
AVENIDA 20
AVENIDA 25
AVENIDA 30
Playa Norte
N
CARIBBEAN SEA
Laundry
ADO bus station
Parque Central
Playa Caribe
Colectivos to Tulum
Laundry
Colectivos to Cancún
Main bus station
HSBC bank
Airstrip
Hwy-307 & Alux
Isla Cozumel
Playacar
0 250 m

arrange a spot on a passenger van (approx M$150 per person). Coming by **ferry** from Cozumel, you'll arrive at a pier at the end of Calle 1, the southern edge of Playa's public beachfront – the rest of town extends north and inland from here.

The **tourist information centre**, on Juárez at Avenida 15 (daily 9am–9pm; ⓣ984/873-2804, ⓔturismo@solidaridad.gob.mx), is very helpful, with bilingual staff who do their best to answer any enquiries you may have. Pick up a copy of the useful *Playa del Carmen*, which has a quality map and hotel and restaurant listings. Online, you can prep for your trip or get news on upcoming events at ⓦwww.playa.info.

The best way to reach smaller towns or beaches just north and south of Playa is by **colectivo**; Cancún service departs frequently from Juárez in front of the main bus station, and vans heading south to Tulum leave from Calle 2 between avenidas 5 and 10. **Taxis** can also take you anywhere you need to go along the coast – they're more expensive than *colectivos*, but far cheaper than any tour company, even when you pay for waiting time.

## Accommodation

**Hotels** are being built all the time in Playa, so you'll have no difficulty finding a room. Competition keeps prices relatively low, but it's still virtually impossible to get something for less than M$350 in high season – which here includes the European vacation months of July and August, as well as mid-December through April. In general, the further from the water, the cheaper the accommodation; the central beach is somewhat eroded, so seafront hotels are not good value. Hotels on Avenida 5 can be noisy due to the bars, but at the time of writing, noise from construction was an issue almost everywhere in town – request an interior room when possible.

The town has one place for **camping**, beachfront *Cabañas La Ruina* (M$100; see below), and two recommended **hostels**, *El Palomar*, Avenida 5 between Juárez and Calle 2 (ⓣ984/803-2606, ⓦwww.elpalomarhostel.com), with beds in very large dorms for M$100, and the big, groovy *Youth Hostel Playa*, Avenida 25 at Calle 8 (ⓣ984/803-3277, ⓦwww.hostelplaya.com), which is further from the beach but more comfortable, with dorm rooms (M$110) and a variety of private options.

**Alhambra** on the beach at C 8 ⓣ984/873-0735, ⓦwww.alhambra-hotel.net. With gleaming white a/c rooms and a small pool, this is the strongest beachfront option. The exotic, Moorish-looking building seems a bit out of place, but the pristine white hotel is a great locale for the daily yoga classes and treatments offered by the resident massage therapist. ❽

**Básico** Av 5 at C 10 ⓣ984/879-4448, ⓦwww.hotelbasico.com. Cool industrial design meets an equally cool clientele – the rooftop pools (converted water tanks) are a hot spot. Also look for the same owners' *Deseo* hotel, at C 12: equally sharp style, and marginally quieter. ❾

**Cabañas Popol-Vuh** C 2, on the seafront ⓣ984/803-2149, ⓔpdcpopol_vuh@hotmail.com. Across the street from *La Ruina*, and a good option if that place is full – no camping, but basic, shared-bath cabañas with cement floors, plus some nifty bi-level ones with private bath. ❸

**Cabañas La Ruina** C 2, on the seafront ⓣ984/873-0405. Playa's most sociable and economical place to stay, giving backpackers a slice of the good life on the beach despite large hotels all around. Hang a hammock for M$100, or choose from the cabañas, the cheapest of which have shared bath. ❹

**Casa Tucan** C 4, between Av 10 and Av 15 ⓣ984/873-0283, ⓦwww.casatucan.de. A Playa institution, this is still one of its best bargains. The cheapest rooms have palapa roofs and shared bath; the studios are excellent value. Swimming pool. Book well in advance. ❺

**Conchita María** Av 5, between C 8 and C 10; no phone. Surprising budget operation on a prime block – fifteen fan-only rooms, a couple with a small kitchenette and terrace. Top-floor rooms are best, though they're reached by a dodgy staircase. ❺

**Kinbé** C 10, between Av 1 and Av 5 ⓣ984/873-0441, ⓦwww.kinbe.com. Small, friendly Italian-run hotel with comfortable rooms (all with a/c) and a small pool; guests get discounts at the hip *Mamita's Beach Club* in Playa Norte. 7

**Posada Freud** Av 5, between C 8 and C 10 ⓣ984/873-0601, ⓦwww.posadafreud.com. Pretty rooms with colourful details smack in the middle of the action at reasonable (and often negotiable) rates. Ground-floor rooms can be a little loud – it may be worth springing for a back, upstairs room or, if you have a big group, the three-bedroom penthouse. 6

**Posada Mariposa** Av 5, between C 24 and C 26 ⓣ984/873-3886, ⓦwww.posada-mariposa.com. Quiet hotel filled with overgrown greenery in the Playa Norte area; apartments with balconies and full kitchens are also available. 6

**La Rana Cansada** C 10 no. 132, between Av 5 and Av 10 ⓣ984/873-0389, ⓦwww.ranacansada.com. One of the oldest hotels in Playa, "The Tired Frog" is friendly, sparkling clean and laid-back. It has communal kitchen facilities and various room options, including a smart two-level suite with beer delivery by bucket from the bar downstairs. 6

## Eating

Playa del Carmen is heaving with **restaurants** of every kind, and even the traditional Mexican places stay open late. The quality of food is often very good (particularly at the **Italian** places), with correspondingly high prices. The pedestrianized section of **Avenida 5** is lined with tables at which you can eat all sorts of cuisine – but if you're on a **budget** you'll need to search out where locals go: try the taco carts on Juárez close to the beach or the inexpensive comida and grilled-chicken places starting around Avenida 10. One warning: the turnover in restaurants in Playa is so high as to make a guidebook writer despair – half these places may have closed by the time you go looking for them; the good news is that new places will have opened.

**Babe's** C 10, between Av 5 and Av 10. This Swedish-owned Thai noodle house – which also serves a fine Cuban *mojito* – typifies Playa's international hodgepodge. Dishes like *pad thai* start at M$45.

**Café Sasta** Av 5, between C 8 and C 10. Pastries and espresso are the main items at this Italian coffeehouse, and the sidewalk tables are an ideal spot for watching the fashion parade along La Quinta.

**La Cueva del Chango** C 38, between Av 5 and the beach. Local favourite for lazy breakfasts and lunches, perfect after a morning stroll up the beach. Good granola, tasty empanadas and house-roasted coffee served in a big garden. Closes at 2pm on Sun.

**El Fogón** Av 30 at C 6. A basic, brightly lit taco joint that's generally mobbed with locals; anything off the grill is recommended. No booze is served, but you can wash down all the meat with a big selection of *aguas frescas*. There's another branch on Av 30 near C 28.

**Hot** C 12 Bis north of Av 5. Stop by this bakery-café for fresh muffins, bagels, brownies and giant cinnamon rolls. Heartier eaters can choose from omelettes and sandwiches and, on the weekend, eggs Benedict.

**John Gray's Place** Corazón, north of Av 5, between C 12 and C 14 ⓣ984/803-3689. An outpost of an excellent restaurant in Puerto Morelos (see p.848), with the same varied, tasty menu. In the cosy bar area, try the signature "smoky margarita" made with mescal. Closed Sun.

**Media Luna** Av 5, between C 12 and C 14. Eclectic veggie and seafood restaurant with big healthful sandwiches and salads, as well as delicious breakfasts. Prices look a little steep on paper, but portions are enormous.

**El Oasis** C 12, between Av 5 and Av 10. There's a full menu of seafood dishes, but the star attraction is the batter-fried shrimp tacos, served with *pico de gallo* and a smear of mayonnaise – cheap for this part of town, and tasty. Closed Sun.

**Tacombi** C 12, between Av 5 and Av 10. Clubbers flock to this 24-hour taco vendor built in a groovy VW bus – you'll pay more, but the variety is good, and its breakfast combos are tasty too.

**La Tarraya** on the seafront at C 2. This local institution has been open for more than thirty years, well before Playa was a gleam in a developer's eye. It still serves standard beach fare like *ceviche* and *pescado frito* (M$90/kilo) with plenty of cold beer.

**Yaxche** C 8, between Av 5 and Av 10 ⓣ984/873-2502. Haute Maya cuisine is the agenda at this gracious restaurant: (very) hot peppers stuffed with *cochinita pibil* (shredded roast pork), a Yucatecan shrimp gratin or lobster flambéed in *xtabentun*, a local liqueur. With main dishes between M$120 and M$200, it's very reasonably priced, considering the level of service and presentation.

## Drinking and nightlife

At night, La Quinta becomes one long street party, and you can find any sort of music in the array of **bars**, though most people will wind up around the intersection with Calle 12, which has the highest concentration of cool **clubs** and **lounges**. If you're looking for a mellower atmosphere, head north of Calle 16, even as far up as Calle 40. Drinks aren't cheap, but don't let that stop you from going out, as it's easy to meet people, and happy-hour specials can ease you into the night without depleting funds too rapidly.

**Alux** Juárez, 400m west of Hwy-307 ⓣ984/803-0713. It's expensive and a trek from the main drag (tell the cab driver "ah-LOOSH"), but how often do you get to party in a Technicolor-lit cave? French-tropical dinner menu starts at 8pm; a DJ or a floor show of belly dancers and jazz musicians begins around 10pm. Usually no cover; drinks are M$70 and up.

**Bar Ranita** C 10, between Av 5 and Av 10. A crew of regulars – mostly expats – hang out at the horseshoe-shaped bar in this snug and mellow wood-panelled spot. A welcome break from Playa's generally top-volume scene.

**Blue Parrot** on the beach at C 12. As the rest of Playa goes upscale, this longtime beach haunt, also known as the *Dragon Bar*, stays true to its casual, anything-goes vibe, with tables in the sand, a young crowd and two-for-one drinks 7–10pm.

**Deseo** Av 5 at C 12. The poolside bar at the stylish hotel draws its inspiration from Miami Beach, with beds to lounge on, over-the-top cocktails and bartenders as attractive and ostentatious as the crowd.

**Diablito Cha Cha Cha** C 12 at Av 1. Mexico-goes-rockabilly is the loose theme at this retro-cool lounge – you can fuel up on Asian snacks, or just go straight to vanilla martinis and the like.

**Mambo Café** C 6, between Av 5 and Av 10 ⓣ984/803-2656. A smaller version of the popular Cancún club, this space has an excellent sound system and a roster of big-name Cuban and Dominican bands. Wed is ladies' night, with open bar from 10pm till midnight. Cover is usually M$50. Closed Mon.

**Mamita's Beach Club** on the beach at C 30. The single coolest place to be during the day, with a hip but not overbearing party atmosphere, complete with a live DJ. Chairs and umbrellas are for rent, but you can spread a towel at the water's edge and still get waiter service. Occasionally hosts blow-out night-time dance parties.

**La Santanera** C 14, between Av 5 and Av 10. Super-stylish club with a comfortable, breezy lounge area, diverse music and good strong drinks. The scantily clad party crowd – equal parts visitors and residents – usually staggers out around 5am. No cover.

**El Tigre** Av 10, between C 2 and C 4. Good local spot for beers, *ceviche* and ridiculously generous *botanas*. Women will probably feel more comfortable accompanied by a man; the billiards area upstairs is men-only. Closes by 5pm.

## Listings

**Banks and exchange** HSBC, Juárez between Av 10 and Av 15 (Mon–Fri 9am–7pm); Bancomer, Juárez between Av 25 and Av 30 (Mon–Fri 9am–4pm). Both have ATMs.

**Buses** The distinction between Playa's two bus stations is somewhat fluid; typically, long-haul ADO-run trips go from Av 20 between C 12 and C 14, and short-haul services leave from the central station, Juárez at Av 5. In any case, you can buy tickets for all routes at the central station – just ask which terminal the bus will leave from. Routes include Cancún (every 10min; 1hr); Cancún airport (9 daily; 1hr); Chetumal (hourly 5.30am–1.45am; 4–6hr); Mérida (hourly 6.30am–12.30am; 5hr); San Cristóbal de las Casas via Palenque (12 daily; 16–19hr); Tulum (hourly; 1–2hr); Valladolid (5 daily; 3hr); and Villahermosa (16 daily; 11hr 30min–15hr).

**Car and bike rental** All the large car-rental companies have outlets in Playa – most are situated on the main coastal highway at the turn-off into town or in Plaza Marina near the Cozumel ferry pier at C 1 Sur. Try Localiza, Juárez between Av 5 and Av 10 (ⓣ984/873-0580). Isla Bicycleta, C 8 at Av 10 (ⓣ984/879-4992), rents mountain and road bikes (M$160/day).

**Internet access and telephones** The streets off Av 5 hold numerous Internet cafés; one on C 4 between Av 5 and Av 10 doubles as a *caseta*. There's also a Telmex *caseta* on Juárez between Av 10 and Av 15.

**Laundry** Giracaribe Laundry, Av 10 between C 12 and C 14; Lavandería Lua, C 2 between Av 10 and Av 15.

**Post office** Juárez, between Av 15 and Av 20 (Mon–Fri 8am–2pm); geared to dealing with tourists. The Lista de Correos (postcode 77710) keeps mail for ten days.

# Isla Cozumel

A forty-kilometre-long island directly off the coast from Playa del Carmen, **ISLA COZUMEL** caters primarily to the mainstream tastes of the cruise-ship passengers that put ashore here – during the high season, up to twenty liners a week dock at the piers south of the main town of **San Miguel** (often called just Cozumel). But you can escape to the wild, windy eastern shore – or underwater, as the island offers the best **diving** in Mexico, with spectacular drop-offs, walls and swim-throughs, some beautiful **coral gardens** and a number of little-visited remote reefs where you can see larger pelagic fish and dolphins. The island is also good for **bird watching**, as it's a stopover on migration routes and has several species or variants endemic to Cozumel.

Before the Spanish arrived, the island appears to have been a major Maya centre, carrying on sea trade around the coasts of Mexico and as far south as Honduras and perhaps Panama. This ancient community – one of several around the Yucatán coast that survived the collapse of Classic Maya civilization – is usually dismissed as the remnant of a moribund society, but that theory is being revised. Architecture might have declined, but large-scale trade, specialization between centres and even a degree of mass production are all in evidence. A US air base, built during World War II, has erased the ancient city, however, and the lesser ruins scattered across the roadless interior are mostly unrestored. (The airfield did bring a degree of prosperity: converted to civilian use, it remains the means by which most visitors arrive.)

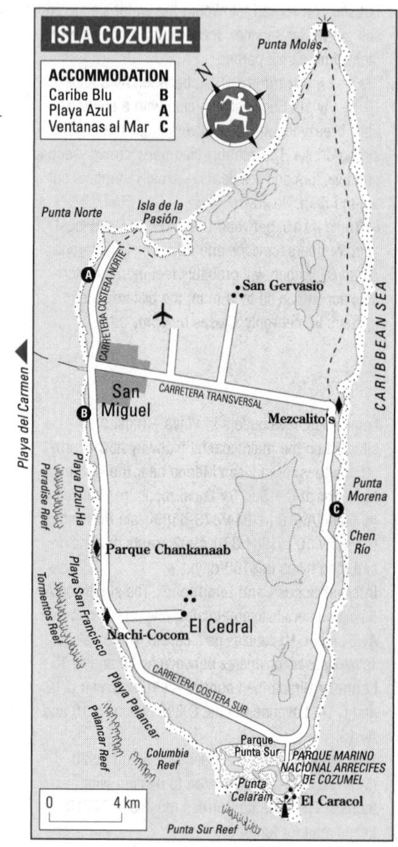


After about 1600 Cozumel was virtually deserted. In the mid-nineteenth century, though, as the Caste Wars made life on the peninsula unstable, the island became a place of refuge, and by the 1880s, the town of San Miguel was established as a home for the growing population. Over the years, island culture has developed distinct from that of the mainland, with *cozumeleños* relishing their lifestyle, which is somehow even more easy-going than on the rest of the coast; San Miguel hosts a particularly colourful celebration of **Carnaval**, the decadent week prior to Lent.

## Arrival and information

**Ferries** depart from Playa del Carmen nearly every hour (6am–11pm; M$110); they return between 5am and 10pm. You can leave your car in the secure car park behind the bus station. (There is also a car ferry from Puerto Calica; see "Listings", p.860.) **Arriving by boat**, you'll be right in the centre of San Miguel, with the plaza directly across the street. From the **airport** a *combi* service (about M$50) makes the short trip to town.

A branch of the **tourist office** (Mon–Sat 8.30am–5pm; ⓣ987/872-7585, ⓦwww.islacozumel.com.mx) is in a kiosk on the plaza, facing the ferry dock, and you can get a range of maps and brochures from the helpful staff. There are dozens of **dive shops** in town – Deep Blue, Salas at Avenida 10 (ⓣ987/872-5653, ⓦwww.deepbluecozumel.com), is one of the best, offering tailor-made small-group tours to the more interesting and remote reefs off the island (Las Palmas and Cedral Wall are popular advanced dive spots, while Palancar Shallows is good for novices); a two-tank dive is M$680. It also runs a full range of certification courses and can help find accommodation, including longer-term house rental.

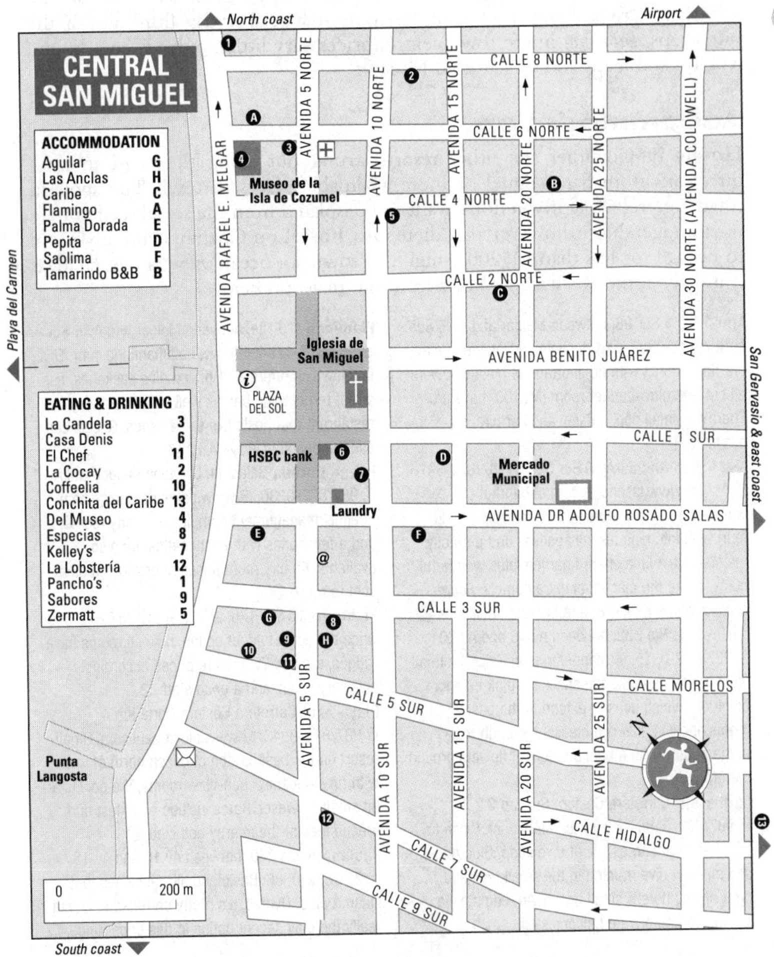

**Snorkelling** and **sport-fishing** tours are both available as well. If you want to snorkel you'll need to organize a boat ride out to the reef – all of the dive shops in town should be able to take you (approximately M$450 for several hours in the water). The best spots are Palancar Shallows and Colombia Shallows – a little further south, but a good way of judging your tour operator, if they're willing to make the extra effort.

## Island transport

**San Miguel** is easy enough to get around on foot, but blocks are quite a bit larger than in Playa del Carmen – if you have substantial luggage, you'll want a **taxi** for any hotel east of Avenida 10. They're plentiful and operate on a zone system, starting at M$15. Buses are distinctly lacking, however, so to get outside of town, you'll have to go on a tour, take a taxi or rent a vehicle. **Mopeds** are a popular choice, though roads can be dangerously slick in the rain, while **jeeps** are available from numerous outlets, but all contracts specify that the vehicles can't be taken on dirt roads. All you really need is a regular **car** – old-school VW Bugs are still the most common option here. Per day from any of the numerous *rentadoras* in the town centre (prices vary little), mopeds cost around M$300 and jeeps and cars around M$550.

## Accommodation

**Hotels** in Cozumel are either resorts strung out along the coast in both directions from San Miguel or more affordable places in town. The spots in town are preferable if you don't want to be isolated from the social scene or are on a budget. Note, however, that there's **no hostel** on Cozumel, nor any room to be had for less than M$200 a night. In town, an ocean view is overrated, as it usually comes with traffic noise from the malecón below.

**Aguilar** C 3 Sur 98, between Melgar and Av 5 Sur ⓣ987/872-0307, ⓦwww.hotelaguilar.com. Clean, tile-floor rooms with no shortage of plastic flowers; all but one ultra-budget room (M$100) have a/c. There's a small pool on site, and car hire is available. ❺

**Las Anclas** Av 5 Sur 325 ⓣ987/872-5476, ⓦwww.lasanclas.com. A handful of well-designed two-storey suites (sleeping up to four) with kitchenettes, all spotless and perfectly maintained. A little shared garden, plus wonderful hosts, make the place feel extra homely. *Rough Guides*' readers receive a ten percent discount. ❼

**Caribe** C 2 Nte 332, between Av 15 and Av 20 ⓣ987/872-0325, ⓔmanuelbrito_estrella@hotmail.com. If you can take the shocking-pink exterior paint job (which doesn't extend to the pastel rooms, luckily), this is a pleasant enough mid-range option, with a pool and lots of flowers around the grounds. ❺

**Caribe Blu** Carretera Costera Sur Km 2.2 ⓣ987/872-0188, ⓦwww.caribeblu.net. Close to town, and with an excellent dive shop, Blue Angel, and shallow dive training in the small pool and right off the hotel's small beach. All rooms have sea views and private balconies. ❼

**Flamingo** C 6 Nte, between Melgar and Av 5 Sur ⓣ987/872-1264, ⓦwww.hotelflamingo.com. This hotel, which offers well-priced dive packages, has a roof terrace and bar, as well as a Cuban-fusion restaurant that hosts live salsa bands. Guests can use the beach at *Playa Azul*. ❼

**Palma Dorada** Salas 44, between Melgar and Av 5 ⓣ987/872-0330, ⓦwww.palmadoradainn.com. Friendly management complements tidy rooms, and a few suites with kitchenettes are also available. An airy rooftop lounge provides a nice spot to relax. ❻

**Pepita** Av 15 Sur 120, at C 1 Sur ⓣ987/872-0098. Once the go-to budget option, now all rooms have fridges, a/c and TV and are priced accordingly – still, very clean, and a good staff. ❺

**Playa Azul** Carretera Costera Norte Km 4 ⓣ987/872-0043, ⓦwww.playa-azul.com. Small resort on the best stretch of beach north of town, with fifty elegant ocean-view rooms; the pool is a bit small, however. Rates include breakfast and greens fees at the nearby golf club. ❾

**Saolima** Salas 260, between Av 10 and Av 15 ⓣ987/872-0886. Basic and old-fashioned, but clean rooms. Overall, it's pretty unremarkable, but really the only decent option in this price range. ❹

**Tamarindo B&B** C 4 Nte 421, between Av 20 and Av 25 ⓣ987/872-6190, ⓦwww.tamarindoamaranto.com. Run by a friendly French–Mexican couple who take good care of the five pretty rooms with whimsical details. You can also use the outdoor grill in the huge yard, and a full breakfast is included. ❺

**Ventanas al Mar** on the east coast, 5km south of *Mezcalito's* beach bar and the intersection with the Carretera Transversal ⓦwww.cozumel-hotels.net/ventanas-al-mar. The only hotel on the empty east coast has gigantic rooms with terraces overlooking the crashing surf. Rates include a full breakfast; for other meals, you get a discount at the neighbouring beach bar, or stock up on groceries for the kitchenette in your room. ❼

## The island

Along the malecón, **downtown San Miguel** is devoted to tourism, packed with restaurants, souvenir shops, tour agencies and jewellery stores – all designed to lure in the huge cruise-ship clientele. As a result, it's all too often uncomfortably crowded and you may be hassled by aggressive salespeople. The weekends, though, are blissfully free of cruise ships – none generally stop on Cozumel on Sunday, and only a couple arrive on Saturday and Monday (to check the ships' schedules, visit ⓦwww.cruisecal.com).

If you decide to shop, try not to do it on a cruise-ship day (prices may rise), and don't buy **black coral**, an endangered and beautiful type of sea life which is unfortunately sold everywhere. Cozumel used to have one of the largest colonies of this rare, slow-growing species, but it has been severely depleted since the tourist trade started here in the 1960s. Don't, under any circumstances, go breaking it off the reefs.

The attractive **Museo de la Isla de Cozumel** (Mon–Sat 9am–5pm, Sun 9am–4pm; M$33) on the malecón between avenidas 4 and 6, has small displays of the flora, fauna and marine life of the island, as well as a good collection of Maya artefacts and old photos. It occasionally hosts live music and theatre events – check with the tourist office.

Cozumel's rugged, windy eastern shoreline remains undeveloped because, as on Isla Mujeres, it faces the open sea and is usually too rough for **swimming**. On the more placid west coast, which is additionally protected by a string of reefs, the easiest **beaches** to get to are north of the town in front of the older resort hotels. It's far more fun, though, to rent a vehicle and head to the more isolated places in the other direction.

Going **south** out of San Miguel, you pass first a clutch of modern hotels; the reef here is very close to shore, with accessible **snorkelling** off the pier at *Caribe Blu*; the hotel's dive shop rents equipment. The next good place to snorkel is **Playa Dzul-Ha** (Mon–Sat 8am–5pm, Sun 9am–5pm), a popular but not totally mobbed spot where you can wade out to the coral gardens from the shore. The beach bar rents gear; there's a M$50 drink minimum to use its pool. Most visitors to the island are steered right to the **Parque Chankanaab**, or "Little Sea" (ⓦwww.cozumelparks.com.mx; daily 7am–5pm; M$170); it's a lovely lagoon, but overdeveloped, and you'll probably want to skip it unless you have kids, as there's a protected children's beach. Further south, **Playa San Francisco** is the best free beach for lounging and swimming, but if you're willing to pay, the quieter **Nachi-Cocom** club (M$100 minimum) has very fine facilities, including a swimming pool – but note that there's no reef for snorkelling.

If you turn inland here, you reach the village of **Cedral**, the only other population centre on the island. It has a tiny Maya site near the old Spanish church; enquire here about visiting several **cenotes** on horseback (M$250; 2hr). In May, the village hosts a huge fiesta.

The least crowded of the leeward beaches, with a laid-back, castaway vibe to match, is **Playa Palancar** (daily 9am–6pm), at Km 19. There's no entertainment other than the restaurant, which serves seafood specialities like *tikin-xic*. You can also arrange a boat out to the Palancar Reef just offshore.

The southernmost point of the island is a protected reserve for diverse wildlife, the **Parque Punta Sur** (Ⓦwww.cozumelparks.com.mx; daily 9am–5pm; M$100). The site contains several lovely beaches, the Punta Celarain **lighthouse** and the **Templo El Caracol**, which may have been built by the Maya as a lighthouse, and is worth visiting to hear the sounds produced when the wind whistles through the shells encrusted in its walls. You can climb to the top of the lighthouse for amazing views over the coast, or visit the adjacent **museum of navigation** (daily 10am–4pm; same ticket) in the former lightkeeper's house, which has a series of displays on maritime history. A bus transports visitors between various sites (or you can rent bicycles), including viewing towers over a network of lagoons and a beach restaurant serving good fried fish. This is also a prime spot for **bird watching**, as the mangroves host a number of both migratory and endemic species.

You can complete a circuit of the southern half of the island by following the road up the windswept eastern shoreline. There are a couple of good, if basic (no running water or electricity), restaurants at **Chen Río** and **Punta Morena** – the latter is popular with kitesurfers. The beaches here are often deserted, but swim only where you see others, as currents can be dangerous. The main road cuts back across the middle of the island to town.

Midway along this road, called the Carretera Transversal, then 6km north, **San Gervasio** (daily 7am–5pm; M$50) is the only excavated Maya site on the island. Built to honour Ixchel, the goddess of fertility and weaving, and apparently modelled on Chichén Itzá, with several small temples connected by *sacbeob*, or long white roads, San Gervasio was, between 1200 AD and 1650 AD, one of the most important centres of pilgrimage in Mesoamerica – though it's not particularly impressive now. As part of a larger nature reserve, however, the site is worth

△ Templo El Caracol, Isla Cozumel

a visit for the numerous birds and butterflies you can spot early in the morning or late in the day.

## Eating and drinking

Many of San Miguel's **restaurants** are tourist traps catering to a dull palate, but if you look hard you can find some quality local flavour. In general, you're better off sticking to casual cafés, rather than the more formal restaurants. The cheapest snacks of all can be at the city **market**, on Salas between avenidas 20 and 25. And if you really want to ditch civilization, you can enjoy lazy lunches in the palapa bars dotted every few kilometres along the southwestern and eastern coasts. Evening entertainment centres on the Plaza del Sol, which is ringed with party-hearty **bars** blasting classic rock and dance hits. On Sunday evenings the crowd is a little more mellow and mixed, as local families come out to chat and listen to strolling musicians.

**La Candela** Av 5 at C 6 Nte. Really friendly home-cooked breakfast and lunch place, with a selection of hot dishes – just point at what looks good. Fresh fish specials and breezy terrace seating.

**Casa Denis** C 1, between Av 5 and Av 10. A little wood-frame house, this is the best bet for eating near the plaza. Bigger meals can be bland, so best to stick with a beer and some *panuchos* and watch the action from your sidewalk table.

**El Chef** Av 5 at C 5 Sur. Charming, personal place where the chef-owner devises new specials every day, such as various pizzas, grilled fish and, for lunch, fresh sandwiches.

**La Cocay** C 8, between Av 10 and Av 15. The best place in town for a splurge, with formal service and inventive dishes such as pork in currant sauce – plus very rich desserts. Closed Sun.

**Coffeelia** C 5 Sur 85, between Melgar and Av 5. The proud local owner presides over breakfast and lunch from her homely kitchen in this sweet café with outdoor space. The menu mixes fresh Mexican dishes, smoothies and huge Dutch-style pancakes.

**Conchita del Caribe** Av 65, between C 21 and C 23. This locally famous seafood spot in a converted garage is worth the cab ride. The *ceviche*, served in generous portions, is particularly good. Closes at 6pm.

**Del Museo** Melgar, between C 4 and C 6, at the Museo de la Isla de Cozumel. Enjoy a quiet breakfast or early lunch on the upstairs balcony of the museum with a view of the sea. The food – from *huevos rancheros* to club sandwiches – is fresh and filling. Closed Sun.

**Especias** C 3 Sur at Av 5 ⓣ987/876-1558. Inexpensive Argentine, Mexican and even occasionally Thai meals, served by an exceptionally friendly husband and wife team. The breezy rooftop is a good place for a sunset beer. Closed Sun.

**Kelley's** Av 10, between Salas and C 1 Sur. A big open-air bar with a pool table and live music on weekends – you might see your divemaster or tour guide in their off-hours. Tasty American food during the day.

**La Lobstería** Av 5 at C 7. As the name suggests, lobster *al gusto* (choose from several classic preparations) is the main draw at this restaurant. But the rest of the menu is equally appetizing, with each dish receiving a special touch; big green salads available. Closed Sun.

**Pancho's** Melgar 27 at C 8 Norte ⓣ987/872-2141. By no means "authentic" Mexican – especially at lunch, when it's a favourite with cruise-ship passengers – but the best service on the island. Very good margaritas, tortilla chips hot out of the fryer and fresh-tasting, slightly dressed-up Mexican entrées; strong veggie selection too. Closed for lunch Sat & Sun.

**Sabores** Av 5 between C 3 Sur and C 5 Sur. Real home cooking – in an actual house – at this lunch-only *cocina económica* – walk through the living room and kitchen and out to the huge shady garden. Unfortunately, there have been reports of a waiter trying to overcharge – know that the set price (M$45) includes a choice of mains, soup and an all-you-can-drink jug of *agua de jamaica*.

**Zermatt** C 4 Nte at Av 5. Bakery serving delectably light sugar doughnuts, among other sweet treats.

## Listings

**Banks** HSBC (Mon–Fri 9am–7pm) is on Av 5 at C 1 Sur.

**Car rental** Posted rates are the same everywhere, but you may be able to negotiate. Aguilar, in the lobby of the *Aguilar* hotel, C 3 Sur 98 (ⓣ987/872-0307), also rents scooters and bicycles.

**Consulate** US, Plaza Villamar ⓣ987/872-4574.
**Ferries** Two companies, Mexico Waterjets and UltraMar, provide passenger service to Playa del Carmen, roughly 5am–10pm, though schedules can change. Transpordadores del Caribe (ⓣ987/872-7688, ⓦwww.transcaribe.com.mx) operates a car ferry to Cozumel from Puerto Calica (also called Punta Venado), 7km south of Playa del Carmen. It runs seven times daily, with a crossing time of about 1hr 15min; at M$504 per car and M$70 per passenger, it's recommended only if you'll be staying on the island more than a few days.
**Internet access** The Crew Office, Av 5 no. 201-A between Salas and C 3 Sur, can also download images from digital cameras.
**Laundry** Lavandería Express, Salas between Av 5 and Av 10.
**Post office** 15min walk south from the centre, on Melgar at the corner with C 7 Sur (Mon–Fri 9am–4pm, Sat 9am–1pm); for Lista de Correos use postcode 77600.

## From Playa del Carmen south to Tulum

Like the beaches to the north, much of the seafront **south of Playa del Carmen** has been developed into resorts or condominium villages, and their access gates line the east side of Hwy-307, leaving little or no access to the sea for non-guests. There are only a few places worth investigating along the coast, but inland you'll find some of the best **cenotes** in the peninsula.

First you have to get past the massive tourist attraction that is **Xcaret** (daily 9am–9pm in winter, 9am–10pm in summer; M$600, or M$450 at night; ⓦwww.xcaretcancun.com), 6km south of Playa del Carmen. With a museum, tropical aquarium, "Maya village", beach, some small authentic ruins, pools and more than a kilometre of subterranean rivers down which you can swim, snorkel or float, it's like having all of the Yucatán's attractions in one handy place – and it's remarkably un-tacky for what it is. Anyone on a longer trip can happily skip the place, though.

Twenty-five kilometres further south, **Xpu-ha** is an especially lovely stretch of beach, curving around in a gentle arc. An all-inclusive resort, *Hotel Copacabana*, breaks up the view, but serves as a landmark for smaller **accommodation** options. Along the north wall of the resort a narrow road marked "X-4" leads to *Villas del Caribe* (ⓣ984/873-2194, ⓦwww.xpuhahotel.com; ❻), a small hotel adjacent to the excellent *Café del Mar* **restaurant** and bar (closed Mon), which serves a tasty international menu all day. If you're on a budget you can stay in basic cabañas or **camp** (M$40) on the beach at *Bonanza Xpu-ha* (no phone; ❹) – look for the second narrow dirt road south of the *Copacabana* (*not* the road to Playa Xpu-Ha Beach Club). Also at Xpu-Ha, at the other end of the price spectrum, is the luxurious *Esencia* (US ⓣ1-877/528-3490, ⓦwww.hotelesencia.com; ❾); rare for this type of beach property, kids are welcome.

Another 10km south (turn at "Playa Akumal"), **Akumal** is primarily a condo community, but its bay offers beautiful snorkelling, and the chummy *Turtle Bay* **restaurant** is delicious. For more entertainment, head up the coast road to *La Buena Vida* beach **bar**, a funky place bedecked with fish skeletons. Aquatech Divers (ⓣ984/875-9020, ⓦwww.cenotes.com), one of the most respected **cave-diving** operations in the Yucatán, also has its offices in Akumal. A few kilometres south of Akumal, **Xcacel** is a sea-turtle research station and pristine beach where visitors are welcome between 8am and 6pm; there are no services. It's only 500m from the highway, if you're walking.

The next big landmark is **Parque Xel-ha** (daily 8.30am–5.30pm in winter, till 6pm in summer; M$350, or M$660 including all food and drink; ⓦwww.xelha.com.mx), a natural water park built around a system of lagoons, inlets and caves. It's a beautiful place, but like Xcaret, it's nothing you won't see elsewhere.

## Exploring the cenotes

The area north and west of Tulum has one of the largest concentrations of **cenotes** on the peninsula. First-time visitors to these freshwater sinkholes are strongly encouraged to stop off at Hidden Worlds (see below), a cluster of cenotes and caverns where tours are led by guides who explain the geological processes by which the caves were formed, as well as put tentative snorkellers at ease. Once in the cool, crystal-clear water, you'll have the surreal experience of floating above stalagmites and other rock formations – all the fun of cave exploration, with none of the scrabbling around.

If you'd prefer to explore on your own, you can just rent gear here or at a number of the other cenotes that see a lot of visitors, such as those on the Tulum–Cobá road. **Divers** must have open-water certification for **cavern diving** (in which you explore within the reach of daylight), while **cave diving** (in which you venture into closed passageways and halls) requires rigorous training – veteran diver Steve Gerrard is one specialist (Ⓣ984/873-5037, Ⓦwww.deephorizon.info).

When diving, snorkelling or just swimming, wear only **biodegradable sunscreen; do not touch** the surprisingly delicate stalactites; never break off anything as a souvenir; **mind your flippers**, as it's easy to kick up silt or knock into the rocks; and be very careful climbing in and out of the water – use the provided paths and ladders.

Across the highway, the small and only partly excavated **ruins of Xel Há** (daily 8am–5pm; M$30) are notable for the stucco paintings in the Grupo Pájaros and miniature, chest-high temples that resemble ones found at Tulum.

Just south of the ruins, **Hidden Worlds** (tours daily 9am–3pm; Ⓣ984/877-8535, Ⓦwww.hiddenworlds.com.mx) is a park area encompassing some exceptionally beautiful cenotes and caverns. Guided group snorkelling (M$250–450) and diving (M$500 for one tank) trips run several times a day. You can also visit glimmering **Dos Ojos** cenote on your own, for M$50 paid at a separate entrance.

# Tulum

To visitors, **TULUM** can mean several things. First, it's one of the most picturesque of all the Maya sites, poised on fifteen-metre-high cliffs above the impossibly turquoise Caribbean. Tulum also refers to a stretch of broad, white beach that's the finest in the Riviera Maya, dotted with lodging options that range from bare-bones to ultra-swank; many of them, as well as many ultra-casual beach bars, still show their backpacker-friendly roots in style, if no longer in price. Finally, it's a booming town (often called Tulum Pueblo to distinguish it from the beach) that has evolved from roadside waystation to real population centre, where visitors can arrange tours into the Sian Ka'an Biosphere Reserve (see p.867), among other things.

## Arrival and information

Coming into the Tulum area on Hwy-307 from the north (it's 130km from Cancún), you arrive first at the well-marked pedestrian and bus entrances to the **ruins** – the site itself is on the water, 1km east. There's a dedicated long-haul bus stop here, so you don't have to double back from town.

Another kilometre or so south along the highway is the turn for the **beach**, where most of the local accommodation is strung along a narrow but paved road running north–south along the water. To reach the water, first turn left (east) at the stoplight with signs for "Boca Paila–Punta Allen"; after 3km, it dead-ends at the beach road. To the left are many of the cheaper cabañas, and, after 2km, the back side of the ruins. To the right, many of the nicer hotels dot 7km of road; after that, you're at the border of the Sian Ka'an Biosphere Reserve and the road reverts to dirt.

Back on Hwy-307 (here called Avenida Tulum), the centre of **town** is just a little further south. The **bus** station, open 24 hours, is near the southern end; luggage storage is available, but expensive (M$10/hr). To get to the beach hotels, you will probably need a **taxi** from here (starting at M$40); a **town bus** runs to the beach, but its schedule is erratic, and it doesn't pass the hotels to the south. Tulum's taxi drivers have a reputation for denying the existence of hotels that don't pay them commission; if you have planned on a particular hotel, insist on being taken there.

Just south of the bus station is the *Weary Traveler* hostel, also the unofficial information centre (see below), as the owners publish good free maps. An HSBC **bank** with an **ATM** is in the middle of town, about 300m north of the bus station on the eastern side of Avenida Tulum. A good **laundry** service is Lavandería Burbujas, two blocks east of the main drag on Jupiter, which runs south of the bus station. The **post office** is on the north side of town, just south of the first small traffic circle on the inland side of the street. You can **rent a car** from Buster (Ⓣ984/133-9111, Ⓦwww.busterrentacar.com), opposite the bus station and a little south. On the north edge of town, near the entrance to the ruins and *El Crucero* hotel, Sian Ka'an Info Tours (Ⓣ984/871-2499, Ⓦwww.siankaan.org) is one of the most reputable companies leading **nature tours** into the reserve. The excellent Iguana Bike Shop, on Satélite at Andrómeda (Ⓣ984/119-0836, Ⓦwww.iguanabike.com), runs **bicycle tours** to nearby cenotes and Playa Xcacel; this place also has the best-maintained **rental bikes** (M$50/24hr).

## Accommodation

Although Tulum's beach is an obvious draw, you may want to stay in **town** if you arrive late in the day, have a limited amount of time or prefer hot water round-the-clock. Hotel owners in the *zona hotelera* along the **beach road** do not have permanent electricity, relying instead on varying combinations of solar panels, windmills and diesel generators; most have power for only about six hours in the evening. Depending on your point of view, the candle-lit ambience is rustic charm or expensive primitivism. The few remaining hotels that made this area famous with hippie backpackers provide sand- or cement-floor **cabañas** with shared bathrooms and often little to no security (though this seems to be improving), and you'll also find quite a few ritzier places (including a small all-inclusive resort) with prices to match. Unfortunately, though, there are very few mid-range beds on the beach, and, like Playa del Carmen, most hotels also charge high-season rates in the European holiday period of July and August.

For **hostel** accommodation, *The Weary Traveler* (Ⓣ984/871-2390, Ⓦwww.intulum.com; M$120), opposite the bus station, is a well-run, longstanding destination for budget travellers; *Hostel Tulum*, Jupiter 20, east of Avenida Tulum (Ⓣ984/871-2089, Ⓔtulumhostel@hotmail.com; M$100), and *El Crucero* (see opposite; M$85) also offer some dorm beds. Alternatively, you can **camp** at *Camping Santa Fe*, 2.4km north on the beach road (M$100), or *Camping Oasis Piedra del Sol*, 4km south of the junction with the road in from town (M$90).

### In town

**El Crucero** east side of Hwy-307, at the first stoplight in town, by the pedestrian entrance to the ruins ⓣ984/871-2610, ⓦwww.el-crucero.com. Fun, friendly hotel convenient for visiting the archeological site. Choose dorm beds, standard rooms or deluxe rooms with a/c and distinctive murals painted by a local artist. The bar/restaurant is extremely hospitable. 4

**Don Diego de la Selva** west side of Hwy-307, south of town ⓣ984/114-9744, ⓦwww.dtulum.com. Quiet French-owned hideaway set back from the highway, with a pool and big, white rooms with terraces; two have fans, while the other six have a/c. 7

**Posada Addy** Polar Oriente, between Satélite and Centauro ⓣ984/871-2423. The very clean rooms in this bright-green concrete building are basic Mexican modern, with limestone floors and polyester bedspreads; one giant room has four beds. Parking available. 4

### On the beach

**Cabañas Copal** On the coast road, 700m south of the junction with the highway access road; reservations in the US on ⓣ1-877/532-6737, ⓦwww.cabanascopal.com. The round, cement-floor cabañas are crowded in a little close, but they're relatively well priced; if you're looking to go cheap, try to nab one of two shared-bath cabins. There's electricity only in public areas but plenty of hot water, and a clothing-optional beach. Book at sister hotel *Zahra* if you'd like more comfort. Good spa on site. 5–8

**Cabañas El Mirador** 2.6km north of the junction ⓣ998/874-6019, ⓦwww.hotelstulum.com/mirador. Just south of where the coast road dead-ends against the ruins, this backpackers' stand-by offers basic cement-floor cabañas with beds or hammocks and shared bathrooms with cold water. The restaurant sits atop a cliff, with a wonderful view and cooling breezes. 3

**Cabañas Zazil-Kin** 2.4km north of the junction; no phone, ⓦwww.hotelstulum.com/zazilkin. Cement-floor cabañas with shared or private bath (cold water only). One "ecologic room" has hot water and a/c at night (M$1200). Perennially popular, with a lively bar scene. Reserve, or arrive early – rooms go fast. 6

**Dos Ceibas** 5.5km south of the junction ⓣ984/877-6024, ⓦwww.dosceibas.com. Small, attractive hotel in front of a turtle-hatching beach. Yoga and meditation classes offered. The cheapest cabaña has a bathroom outside; all are spacious and colourful. 6–8

**Papaya Playa** 400m south of the junction ⓣ984/804-6444, ⓦwww.papayaplaya.com. New management has given this large, party-friendly place a facelift, but fortunately kept the wide selection of rooms, from sand-floor, shared-bath cabañas to deluxe villas (good value for groups), nearly all of them with sea views. A small restaurant and bar, set on a cliff above the beach, plays chilled-out lounge beats. 5–9

**Piedra Escondida** 1.5km from the road junction ⓣ984/100-3826, ⓦwww.piedraescondida.com. Solid, comfortably furnished two-level cabañas with tiled floors; each room has its own balcony and a view of the beach, a lovely sheltered cove. Full breakfast is included. 9

**La Posada del Sol** 1km south of the junction ⓣ984/876-6206, ⓦwww.laposadadelsol.com. The four artfully designed, high-ceiling "jungle" rooms on the wooded side of the road are exceptionally well priced for their size and attractiveness; three beachfront bungalows cost a bit more, but are quite nice as well. There's an excellent jewellery shop in the lobby. The same owners run the equally attractive *Posada Lamar*, a little to the south. 7

**Las Ranitas** 5.4km south of the junction ⓣ984/877-8554, ⓦwww.lasranitas.com. This understated but comfortable French-owned hotel has well-designed breezy rooms and two suites for families, plus tennis courts, a pool and an excellent library. The biggest perk: 24hr electricity. 8

**Zamas** 1.2km south of the junction; US ⓣ1-415/387-9806, ⓦwww.zamas.com. Enormous, comfortable rooms, some right on one of the prettiest stretches of beach in Tulum. Hot water and electricity are plentiful, but the style remains bohemian. Good restaurant on site (see p.866). 8

## The town and the beaches

Tulum **town** offers all the basic tourist services and an increasing number of good dinner restaurants and bars, but it's devoid of typical attractions. The place is generally empty of visitors by day because they've all decamped to the **beach**, the longest, most impeccable stretch of sand outside of Cancún. The most popular spot is **El Paraiso Beach Club**, about 2km north from the junction with the road to town, with a fully stocked bar and friendly vibe. For solitude, head immediately north along the sand to Playa Maya, a public beach that's generally empty. It's followed by **Mar Caribe Beach Club**, which is more of a locals' hangout where you can get super-fresh *ceviche*. You can also pop into the sea anywhere else, as long as you don't use the lounge chairs maintained by hotels.

### The ruins

On a sunny day, with the turquoise sea glittering behind the weather-beaten grey stones, your first glimpse of the **Tulum ruins** (Nov–April daily 7am–6pm, May–Oct 8am–7pm; M$45) can be quite breathtaking, despite the small scale of its buildings, all clustered in a compact mass. When the Spanish first set eyes on the place in 1518, they considered it as large and beautiful as Seville. They were, perhaps, misled by their dreams of El Dorado and the brightly painted facades of the buildings, for architecturally Tulum is no match for the great Maya cities. On closer inspection, the buildings, most built after 1200, seem a bit haphazard because walls flare outward and doorways taper in – not the effect of time, but an intentional design, and one that is echoed in other post-Classic sites along the coast like El Rey in Cancún and San Gervasio on Cozumel.

Tickets are sold at the site **entrance**, about 1km from the main highway and parking lot, where there's also an enormous warren of souvenir shops; a shuttle bus (M$20) runs between the parking lot and the ruins. The site is less than 500m long and takes only an hour or so to see, though you may want to allow time to **swim** at the tiny, perfect beach that punctuates the cliffs. Arrive in the early morning or late afternoon to avoid the worst crowds.

You walk into the site through a breach in the wall that surrounded the city on three sides; the fourth faced the sea. This wall, some 5m high with a walkway around the top, may have been defensive, but more likely it delineated the ceremonial and administrative precinct (the site you see today) from nearby residential enclaves. If you walk straight towards the sea, you reach the **Casa del Cenote**, a square structure straddling a water-filled cave; a small tomb occupies its central portion. On the bluff above and to the right are the **Templos Miniaturas**, several scale-model temples, complete with tiny lintels and mouldings, which were probably shrines.

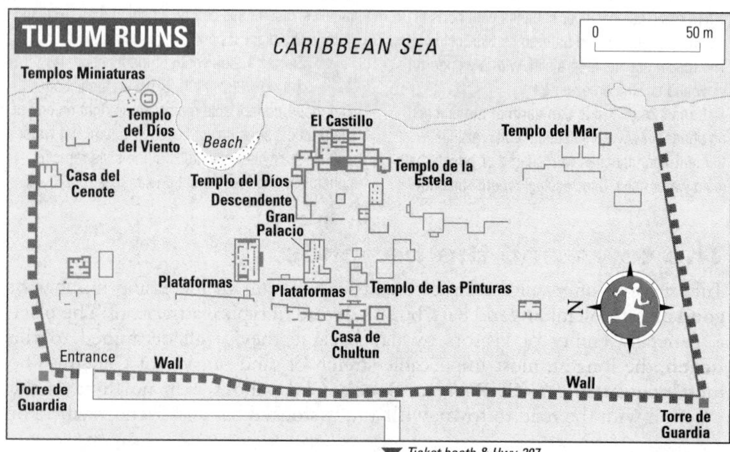

Skirt the small beach to get to the north side of the main promontory and the **Templo del Díos Descendente**, in which the flared walls of the small temple at the top are emphasized by moulding that juts out at an opposite angle. The diving (or descending) god, carved in stone above the narrow entrance of the temple, is one of Tulum's quirks: the upside-down winged figure appears all over the city, but in only a handful of places elsewhere in the Maya world. His exact meaning is unclear – he may represent the setting sun, or rain or lightning, or he may be the bee god, since honey was one of the Maya's important exports.

Adjacent to the temple, on the highest ground, the imposing **Castillo** commands fine views in every direction, but to protect the worn stones, visitors may now only look up at the building. The fortress-like pyramid, flanked by steep staircases, may have served not just as a temple, but also as a beacon or pseudo-lighthouse; even without a light, it would have been an important landmark for mariners along an otherwise featureless coastline.

Turning away from the sea, you face a cluster of buildings arranged on a city-like grid, with the chief structures set on stone platforms along parallel streets. The most fascinating of these – and what used to be the main attraction here, before it was closed to visitors – is the colonnaded **Templo de las Pinturas** (Temple of the Paintings). The murals, actually painted on the exterior of an older temple, have been preserved by the surrounding gallery you see now, which is decorated with masks of the rain god Chac. One remarkable mural, done at a later date than the others, shows Chac seated on a four-legged animal – clearly inspired by the conquistadors' horses.

If you want to take time out for a **swim**, you can plunge into the Caribbean right in front of the ruins. Limitless further possibilities for a dip are strung out down the long beach road that leads off the southern edge of the site. The beginning of the road has been blocked to cars, but you can walk out this way, and straight to a beachfront lunch at one of the hotels.



## Eating and drinking

Because the accommodation in Tulum is spread over 10km and the town is so far from the beach, almost every hotel has its own restaurant – ranging from cheap to very chic. Guests tend to stick to the restaurants in their own hotels, but a few **places to eat** along the beach road merit a special trip. In the village, a number of inexpensive **cafés** serve comida corrida and rotisserie chicken, and there's an increasing number of cheerful, mid-range places run by European expats. As for nightlife, *Mezzanine* hosts a beach party every Friday, while *El Paraiso Beach Club* often has some kind of event around the full moon; otherwise, some hotel **bars** expand into a dancing scene.

**La Casa del Buen Pan** Sagitario Pte at Alfa, in town. Savour the a/c along with organic coffee and a flaky croissant at this bakery that does both Mexico and European treats. Nice shaded garden area, too.

**Don Huacho** west side of Av Tulum, between Beta and Osiris, in town. The town's longtime Mexican seafood specialist features the mysteriously spiced *pescado a la Don Huacho*, very fresh *ceviche* and tasty shark empanadas, which are great with beer.

**Gaudí Café** west side of Av Tulum, opposite the bus station, in town. Good for inexpensive set-price breakfast specials, Spanish sandwiches and really strong coffee.

**Hechizo** 7.5km south of the junction with the road to town, on the beach road ⓣ984/100-0170, ⓔhechizo_tulum@yahoo.com. This gem of a restaurant is owned by a former *Ritz-Carlton* chef and features a short, sophisticated international menu that changes frequently. Call or email to reserve one of the eight tables. Closed Mon and parts of the low season.

**Hola Primo** two blocks east of Av Tulum on Acuario, in town. This palapa-roof kitchen on the "Cancha Maya" (the plaza around the ceiba tree where the town was founded) caters to locals with *sopa de lima*, *panuchos* and *salbutes*. You can fill up on savoury snacks for just a few pesos.

**Mezzanine** 1.5km north of the junction, on the beach road. Channelling Ibiza chic, this super-cool bar-lounge does excellent cocktails and Thai snacks; it's the only place on the beach where you can regularly find a dance scene in high season. Helpfully, its morning menu includes, next to the smoothies, a special of coffee, cigarettes and a shot of tequila.

**La Nave** east side of Av Tulum between Orion and Beta, in town. A busy hangout with fresh-fruit breakfasts, inexpensive pizza from a wood-fired oven (M$45 and up) and Italian staples like fresh gnocchi.

**Posada Margherita** 2.5km south of the junction, on the beach road, at *Posada Margherita* hotel ⓣ984/100-3780. Fantastic Italian restaurant with great seafood; the antipasto platter, served on a slice of a tree trunk, is a bounty of piquant cheeses, cured meats and olives. Prices are higher than the sand-floor setting might suggest (around M$140 for mains), but the food is worth it.

**Qué Fresco** 1.2km south of the junction, on the beach road, at *Zamas*. Very popular mid-range restaurant with fresh salads, pastas and some of the healthier Mexican dishes. Its beachside setting makes it a great way to start the day, too.

**La Vita è Bella** 1.6km north of the junction, on the beach road. Reasonably priced sandwiches and wood-oven pizzas are served until 11pm; a cocktail bar opens at 9.30pm, and a European party crowd often gets dancing later under the big palapa.



# Cobá

Set in muggy rainforest 50km northwest of Tulum, the crumbling ancient city of **COBÁ** (daily 7am–6pm; M$45) is a fascinating and increasingly popular site. The clusters of buildings are spread out over several kilometres, so the area can absorb lots of visitors without feeling crowded, and you can ramble through the forest in peace, looking out for toucans, egrets, coatis and myriad tropical butterflies, including the giant iridescent blue morpho. A visit here requires at least a couple of hours; renting a **bicycle** just inside the site entrance (M$25) is highly recommended. Although the ruins aren't as well restored as those at Tulum, their scale is much more impressive, and the dense greenery and wildlife make a good counterpoint to the coast.

Ceramic studies indicate that the city was occupied from about 100 AD up until the advent of the Spanish – the site is even mentioned in the *Chilam Balam* of Chumayel, a book of Maya prophecy and lore written down in the eighteenth century, well after the city had been abandoned. The city's zenith was in the Late Classic period, around 800 AD, when most of the larger pyramids were built and its wealth grew from links with the cities of Petén, in lowland Mexico and Guatemala. These cities influenced Cobá's architecture and use of stelae, typically seen only in the southern Maya regions. Cobá also prospered later through its connections with coastal cities like Tulum, and several structures reflect the style found at those sites.

The centrepiece of the site is the giant pyramid **Nohoch Mul**, taller than El Castillo at Chichén Itzá and, in its narrow and precipitous stairway, resembling the pyramid at Tikal in Guatemala; at the top, a small temple, similar to structures at Tulum, dates from around 1200. The view takes in nearby lakes, as well as the jungle stretching uninterrupted to the horizon.

If you're feeling intrepid, head 1km down a shady *sacbé* to **Grupo Macanxoc**, a cluster of some twenty stelae, most carved during the seventh century AD. Stele 1 shows part of the Maya creation myth and the oldest date recorded in the Maya Long Count calendar system, which tracks the days since the moment of creation. Other stelae depict a high number of women, suggesting that Cobá may have had female rulers. Clambering between the carvings, you're crossing not natural hills, but unreconstructed buildings; in a way, these offer a more palpable sense of the civilization that thrived here than some of the more immaculately rebuilt structures.

If you turn right at the traffic circle a few kilometres before Cobá (follow signs for Nuevo X-Can), after 18km kilometres you will reach the **Reserva de Monos Arañas de Punta Laguna**, which since 1994 has been a site for the observation of one of the northernmost populations of spider monkeys. From the reserve's entrance kiosk, you're required to hike with a guide (M$30 per person, plus M$150 for a guide for a group of up to ten people) to where the monkeys usually congregate – there's no guarantee you'll see them, but they're at their liveliest in the early morning and late afternoon.

### Practicalities

Four **buses** a day run to Cobá from Tulum and continue on to Valladolid. The first one leaves Tulum at 7.30am (arriving at 8.30am), and the next, which continues to Chichén Itzá after stopping in Valladolid, arrives in Cobá at 11am – you could therefore theoretically cover both sites via public transport from Tulum, though you would be very rushed. Five buses run back to Tulum from Cobá, the last leaving at 6.30pm. A taxi from Tulum to Cobá costs about M$250 each way.

The **village** of Cobá, where the bus stops, is little more than a cluster of houses and cabañas a few hundred metres from the site entrance, which fronts a small lake (it's filled with crocodiles; don't swim). **Hotels** are few, but two are quite comfortable: *Villas Arqueológicas* (US ⓣ1-800/258-2633; ❼), overlooking the lake, offers a modest bit of luxury, complete with a swimming pool and an archeological library; the *Hotelito Sac-bé* (ⓣ984/879-9340; ❸), on the south side of the main street through the village, is leagues better than the other budget option in town, with five clean rooms offering various amenities (one has a/c). Enquire at the post office across from the bus stop if no one's at the hotel. There's a good **restaurant** in front of the lake, *La Pirámide*, which serves Yucatecan specialities.

## The Sian Ka'an Biosphere Reserve

Sian Ka'an means "the place where the sky is born" in Maya, which seems appropriate when you experience the sunrise in this beautiful part of the peninsula. Created by presidential decree in 1986 and made a World Heritage Site in 1987, the **Sian Ka'an Biosphere Reserve** is a huge, sparsely populated region sprawling along the coast south of Tulum. One of the largest protected areas in Mexico, it covers 1.3 million acres. Only about a thousand permanent inhabitants are found here, mainly fishermen and subsistence farmers gathered in the village of **Punta Allen**.

It contains all three of the principal ecosystems found in the Yucatán Peninsula and the Caribbean: the area is approximately one-third **tropical forest**, one-third fresh- and saltwater marshes and **mangroves** and one-third marine environment, including a section of the Mesoamerican Barrier Reef. All five species of Mexican **wild cat** – jaguar, puma, ocelot, margay and jaguarundi – live in the forest, along with spider and howler monkeys, tapir and deer. More than three hundred species of **birds** have been recorded (including fifteen types of heron and the endangered wood stork, the largest wading bird to breed in North America) and the coastal forests and wetlands are important feeding and wintering areas for North American migratory birds. The Caribbean beaches provide nesting grounds for four endangered **marine turtle** species, while extremely rare West Indian manatees have been seen in the inlets. Morelets and mangrove **crocodiles** lurk in the lagoons.

Although you can enter the park unaccompanied (M$20), on the road south from Tulum's beach hotels, you will benefit more from an organized tour, which is easily arranged in Tulum. One of the best operators is Sian Ka'an Info Tours, part of a non-profit group called Centro Ecológico de Sian Ka'an (CESIAK), which funds its research and educational programmes with several **tours**: one by day through the ancient Maya canals that criss-cross the marshy areas here, and a late-afternoon excursion that takes in sunset inside the reserve (M$700 each); half-day kayaking trips are also an option (M$500). These are great trips around the fringes of the reserve's vast open spaces, with excellent opportunities for bird watching, especially on the sunset tour. You can reserve a spot at the office in Tulum (see p.862).

CESIAK also offers **accommodation** at its rigorously ecofriendly *Boca Paila Camps* (Ⓣ984/871-2499, Ⓦwww.siankaan.org; ❻), hidden among the trees in a prime location near the beach; guests share bathrooms (with composting toilets), but there is hot water, thanks to solar and wind power. The staff are very well informed about the reserve, and the inexpensive **restaurant** is worth the long drive from Tulum for its sunset view across the jungle. Note that although there are many enticing stretches of sand along the road from Tulum, biosphere regulations **prohibit camping** on the beach to control erosion – which is not to say it's not done, unfortunately.



## Muyil (Chunyaxché)

The little-visited ruins of **MUYIL** (daily 8am–5pm; M$24), also known as **CHUNYAXCHÉ**, lie on the north border of the reserve, about 20km south of Tulum. Catch any second-class **bus** from Tulum to Chetumal and ask to be dropped at the gate to the ruins. A sign on the west side of the highway points across to the entrance, with just a ticket booth and restrooms. Despite the size of the site – probably the largest on the Quintana Roo coast – and its proximity to Hwy-307, you're likely to have the place to yourself, as most visitors to the Yucatán don't travel further south than Tulum.

Archeological evidence indicates that Muyil was continuously occupied from the pre-Classic period until after the arrival of the Spanish in the sixteenth century. There is no record of the inhabitants coming into direct contact with the conquistadors, but they were probably victims of depopulation caused by European-introduced diseases. Most of the buildings you see today date from the post-Classic period, between 1200 and 1500 AD. The tops of the tallest structures, just visible from the road, rise 17m from the forest floor. There are more than one hundred mounds and temples, none of them completely clear of vegetation, and it's easy to wander around and find buildings buried in the jungle; climbing them is forbidden, however.

The centre of the site is connected by a *sacbé* to the small **Muyil lagoon** 500m away. This is joined to the large Chunyaxché lagoon and ultimately to the sea at **Boca Paila** by an amazing **canalized river** – the route used by ancient Maya traders. At the end of the boardwalk leading through the mangroves to the lagoon, you will probably encounter a representative from the local fishing co-operative (Ⓣ984/806-0860, Ⓦwww.muyil.com) offering a **boat tour** down the river (M$300 per person; 2hr), where you'll come across even less explored sites, some of which appear to be connected to the lagoon or river by **underwater caves**.

**Leaving the site**, particularly if you're making your way up to Tulum, should be easy enough, provided you don't leave too late; continuing south could prove a little more difficult, as buses to Chetumal run only every two hours and *colectivos* are often full when they pass.

## Punta Allen

Right at the tip of a narrow spit of land, with a lighthouse guarding the northern entrance to the **Bahía de la Ascensión**, the remote fishing village of **PUNTA ALLEN** is not the kind of place you stumble across by accident. With a population of just five hundred, it's the largest village inside the reserve. Bonefish and tarpon in the bay are a draw for active travellers; layabouts will appreciate the sandy streets and the feeling of being entirely cut off from the larger world. Telecommunications are almost completely absent, and the most noise you'll hear is the creak of your hammock and the rustle of palm fronds in the breeze.

The road south from Tulum has helped maintain Punta Allen's special quality: it's famously rutted and flooded in the rainy season, and is still slow going during the dry months, typically requiring at least three hours for the 50km drive. Even if you have your own car, it can be better to leave the driving to someone else: a **colectivo** (daily at 2pm; M$150) runs from next to the taxi syndicate in Tulum (don't fall for the *taxistas*' claim that the van isn't running; you can call ⓣ984/879-8040 in the morning to reserve a seat). Another goes from Felipe Carrillo Puerto (see p.870) via an alternate route through the reserve, at the end of which you get a launch across the bay to the village (M$50 for 2–3 people). In any case, the trip is so time-consuming that you will use half a day just getting there, so take plenty of cash (there's **no bank**), and plan to spend at least a couple of nights to recover from the jarring trip and prepare for the return.

Entering Punta Allen from the north, past the naval station on the right and beached boats on the left, the first and cheapest of the **accommodation** options is *Posada Sirena* (ⓣ984/877-8521, ⓦwww.casasirena.com; ④), where you can choose from three comfortable sleeping options. *Cuzan Guesthouse* (ⓣ983/834-0358, ⓦwww.flyfishmx.com; ⑥), a bit further south, specializes in **bonefish tours** and rents cabañas and tepees, some with hot water. In the off season, prices are cut by almost half. Its **restaurant** is the best in town, though you should request meals ahead of time if you're not staying. Next door, *Serenidad Shardon* (US ⓣ1-248/628-7217, ⓦwww.shardon.com; ③–⑨) has the most developed, comfortable beach houses, as well as dorm beds (M$100) and **camping** space (M$150); it's also the only place in the village that takes credit cards.

A **mobile shop** in a truck travels the length of the peninsula on Wednesdays and Saturdays, selling fresh items you can't get in the few village *tiendas*, reaching Punta Allen sometime in the afternoon or evening, depending on the condition of the road. Although there's no dive shop, the hotels generally have some form of **water-sports equipment** for their guests and allow non-residents to rent. Fishermen can be persuaded to take you into the reserve for a fee: for instance, a three-hour snorkelling tour, during which you might see some of the local loggerhead turtle population, costs about M$1200 for a boat. Victor Barrera is a recommended local guide who takes people **fishing** in the flat waters of Bahía de la Ascensión (ⓣ998/893-1063, ⓦwww.macabimarch.com).

**Leaving** requires a little forethought. The Tulum *colectivo* departs at 5am. For the launch and *colectivo* to Carrillo Puerto, boats go at 6am – sign up beforehand at Tienda Caamal to reserve your space. The last launch leaves around 5pm.

# From Tulum to Chetumal

The road from Tulum to Chetumal skirts the Sian Ka'an Biosphere Reserve and heads inland amid ever-denser low jungle, past **Felipe Carrillo Puerto**, a major crossroads on the routes to Valladolid and Mérida; through Limones, where there's a turn-off to the region known as the **Costa Maya** (the coastal towns of Mahahual and Xcalak); along the beautiful **Laguna Bacalar**, as scenic as any Caribbean beach; and on to **Chetumal**, the gateway to Belize and a good point from which to explore **Kohunlich** and other Maya sites.

## Felipe Carrillo Puerto

A slow-paced agricultural town with a population of about 15,000, **FELIPE CARRILLO PUERTO** doesn't look like much on the surface; however, following its role as capital of the independent "Zona Maya" during the nineteenth-century Caste Wars (when it was called Chan Santa Cruz), it is still an important cultural and spiritual centre for the modern Maya. In the 1850s rebels from the north gathered forces here and took guidance and inspiration from a miraculous talking cross that told them to fight on against their oppressors – you can still visit the **Santuario de la Cruz Parlante**, built on the site of the Talking Cross (the remnants of which have been moved to a smaller town nearby); turn west off the main street at the Pemex, and the complex is four long blocks down on the right. Back on the plaza, the Franciscan-style **church** was in fact built by the rebel Maya as a temple – using the slave labour of captured white fighters, no less; it was consecrated as a Catholic church in 1948. If you're interested in exploring the Maya villages in this area, visit the small **tourist office** (Mon–Fri 8am–2pm & 6–9pm), six blocks south of the **bus station** and one block east. The **colectivo to Punta Allen** (1 daily at 9am; 3hr) leaves from the first block east out of the main traffic circle. There are several reasonable **hotels** around the main plaza (where the **bus station** is also located) – try *Chan Santa Cruz*, just off the plaza (Ⓣ983/834-0021; ❸), where high-ceilinged rooms overlook a little green courtyard. The best **place to eat** in the evenings is taco specialist *La Placita Maya*, two blocks south of the bus station.

## The Costa Maya: Mahahual and Xcalak

South of Carrillo Puerto, a dead-straight road turns east to the beaches that line the 250km of coast between the southern edge of the Sian Ka'an reserve and the Belize border. The **Costa Maya**, as the area is known, still has a very end-of-the-world feel – though even that is changing (the area got its name when the glitzy cruise-ship pier Puerto Costa Maya opened here in 2001). Divers will also want to make the trek to **Banco Chinchorro**, a coral atoll littered with shipwrecks that was designated a biosphere reserve in 2003.

Puerto Costa Maya is out of sight north of **MAHAHUAL** (60km east of Hwy-307), but its influence is felt on cruise-ship days, when the tiny village springs to life with souvenir stands, jet-ski rental and the like. Generally, though, the pace is still more akin to the Playa del Carmen of twenty years ago, and has attracted a small European expat community; there's **no bank** or **ATM**. If you prefer quiet, check out Ⓦwww.cruisecal.com for the ship schedules, or just head down the bumpy dirt beach road south of town. The main **dive shop**, Dreamtime Diving (Ⓣ983/834-5818, Ⓦwww.dreamtimediving.com), runs trips to Banco Chinchorro.

For **accommodation**, seek out the wonderfully secluded and very comfortable *Mayan Beach Garden*, 20km north of town (Ⓦwww.mayanbeachgarden.com; ❽). In Mahahual proper, *Los 40 Cañones* (Ⓦwww.los40canones.com; ❼) is recommended; if you want quiet, head south 5.5km to the white stucco cottages at *Balamku* (Ⓣ983/839-5332, Ⓦwww.balamku.com; ❺), built to stringent ecofriendly guidelines. The best cheap option is *Travel In'*, at Km 6 on the beach road, which offers **camping** (M$60) on the beach or two simple rooms with shared bath (no phone; ❷); if it's full, head a bit further south to *Kabah-Na* (Ⓣ983/838-2195, Ⓦwww.kabahna.com; ❹). *Travel In*'s **restaurant** (closed Sun) is excellent, serving home-made bread and eclectic meals in the evenings. In town, head for *Casa del Mar*, among the strip of restaurants on the beach, for its delicious beer-batter shrimp tacos.

**XCALAK**, less than 20km south of Mahahual, can only be reached by a paved road that runs a bit inland. Once the largest town in Quintana Roo, today it's a desolate village that still hasn't recovered from being flattened by a hurricane in 1955; steady electricity was restored only in 2004. As it has no real beaches, the main reason to visit is its superb **snorkelling**, **diving** and **fishing**. For more information on Xcalak, check out the good website, Ⓦwww.xcalak.info, maintained by relocated American and Canadian residents. The best place to **stay** here is *Tierra Maya* (Ⓣ983/831-0404, Ⓦwww.tierramaya.net; ❼), a welcoming guesthouse a short drive north of town; it also has a bit of a sandy beach. Back in town, the **dive shop** XTC (Ⓦwww.xtcdivecenter.com) runs snorkelling trips (M$300; 2hr), offers open-water certification courses (M$3750) and has a licence to dive at Banco Chinchorro. For **eating**, plan to be in town on the weekend, when the extremely casual yet supremely delicious *Leaky Palapa*, on the seafront, is open to serve fresh-caught fish (closed in the low season).

So far, infrequent transport to this area has helped keep the tourist droves at bay. Two direct **buses** to Mahahual leave Cancún daily at 7am and 11.30pm, or you can take a bus to Limones and transfer to a bus coming from Chetumal. This latter service departs Chetumal at 4am, 6am and 4pm daily from the main bus terminal (though only the second two go down the beach road to the hotels and on to Xcalak); to connect, you should be in Limones by 5.30am, 7.30am and 5.30pm respectively.

Note that on the way out on the main highway from Mahahual, a military **checkpoint** conducts very thorough searches for drugs and other contraband – as long as you haven't got any of that stuff, the soldiers are perfectly pleasant.

## Laguna Bacalar

Back on Hwy-307, some 35km north of Chetumal, the gorgeous **Laguna Bacalar** stretches along the east side of the road. It resembles the Caribbean Sea, sparkling clear and ranging in colour from palest aqua to deep indigo. About 45km and 1km wide, it's the second largest lake in Mexico (after Laguna de Chapala, south of Guadalajara). The small town on its edge was once a key point on the pre-Columbian trade route, and unexcavated **Maya remains** surround the lake. The *Chilam Balam* of Chumayel, one of the Maya's sacred books, mentions it as the first settlement of the Itzá, the tribe that occupied Chichén Itzá. All this is detailed in the interesting **Museo de San Felipe Bacalar** (Tues–Thurs & Sun 9am–7pm, Fri & Sat 9am–8pm; M$50), set in a restored fort built by the Spanish for protection against pirates from Belize (then British Honduras), and later used as a Maya stronghold in the Caste Wars. In town, you can go **swimming** at the *balneario municipal* El Aserradero, down the hill from the fort and right (south) along the lakeshore drive (10am–6pm; free). Or head further south along this road to the inky-blue "bottomless" **Cenote Azul** (daily 8am–8pm; free), which is busy with swimmers, dive-bombing teens and live musicians at weekends. Several **restaurants** capitalize on the lake view, but more reliable is the basic yet satisfying *Orizabas*, one block off the northwest corner of the town's plaza.

If you want to **spend the night**, check out *Casita Carolina* (Ⓣ983/834-2334, Ⓦwww.casitacarolina.com; ❹), a guesthouse on the lakeshore with a spacious back garden. At the south end of the road along the water, the wonderfully kitsch and comfortable *Hotel Laguna* (Ⓣ983/834-2206, Ⓦwww.hotellagunabacalar.com; ❻) is done up with seashell-encrusted lacquer countertops and plaster pillars galore.

The lake harbours a wide variety of **birdlife**, and a couple of places outside of town are good nature havens: *Villas Ecotucan* (Ⓣ983/834-2516, Ⓦwww.villasecotucan.info; ❻), 5km north, has comfortable cabañas on attractively landscaped grounds between the lake and acres of uncleared forest. The very groovy *Botadero San Pastor* (Ⓣ983/831-3494, Ⓔbotadero@yahoo.com; ❷), 10km south, has a few fixed tents and space for **camping** (M$50), as well as kayaks for guests' use. *Colectivos* and second-class buses can drop you on the highway near the entrances to both places.

# Chetumal and around

If you're heading south to Belize or Guatemala, you can't avoid the capital of Quintana Roo, **CHETUMAL**, 15km from the Belize border – the neighbouring country's influence is reflected in everything from the language (many people speak English) to the clapboard houses. Obliterated by Hurricane Janet in 1955, the city is a hodgepodge of modern concrete buildings (some even exuding a bit of 1960s flair) and a few old wooden houses with porches that remain from the settlement's earliest days. With almost no notable "sights" to speak of, Chetumal is largely oblivious to tourists – which can be refreshing after the hedonism of the Riviera Maya. Moreover, everything is cheaper here, from hotels to food to Internet cafés. Mexicans come to visit the **duty-free zone** between the two countries, a mini-mall where shops flog everything from Dutch cheese to Taiwanese hi-fis. Despite these modern details, Chetumal retains a certain old-fashioned graciousness, especially palpable in the evenings, when the bay boulevard is filled with lovers and families. Although it can't really be praised as a destination for its own sake, Chetumal does make a decent one- or two-day stop for resting and restocking, as everything's relatively cheap. You could also take day or overnight trips to the Río Bec archeological sites west from here, though car rental is the one thing in Chetumal that's not a great deal.

## Arrival and information

Chetumal's main **bus station** is on the north side of town, a short taxi ride from the centre (about M$20). A **bus ticket office** in town, on Belice between Gandhi and Colón, handles long-haul services. The central part of Chetumal is strung along **Avenida de Niños Héroes**, the town's main street, which runs south to the waterfront. The **tourist information** office, on 5 de Mayo at Carmen Ochoa (Mon–Fri 8.30am–4pm; Ⓣ983/835-0500), is happy to provide information on buses, hotels and tours; they can also advise on nearby attractions in Belize.

## Accommodation

Most of Chetumal's **hotels** are on or near Niños Héroes in the few blocks back from the malecón. One **hostel**, the *Villa Deportiva*, in the local sporting club on Escuela Naval (Ⓣ983/833-0019) is clean enough, with basic but very small beds (M$50); you'll probably have the place to yourself unless a sports team is in town.

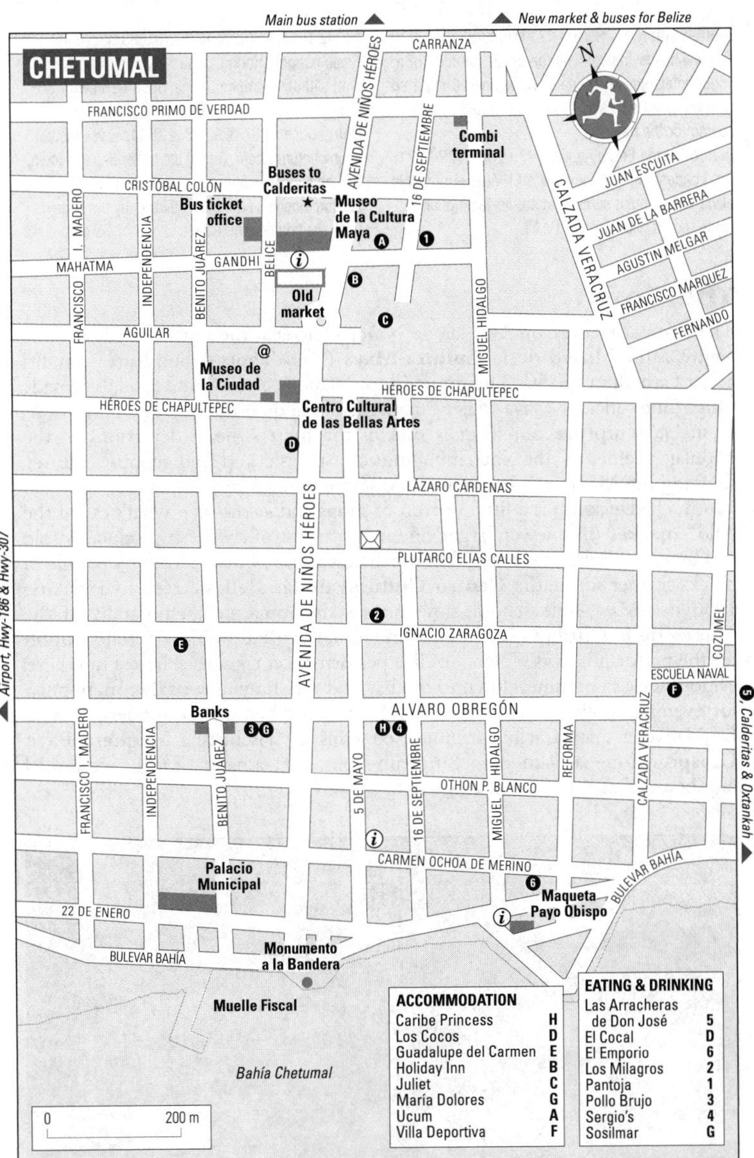


**Caribe Princess** Obregón 168 ⓣ983/832-0520, ⓔcaribe_princess@hotmail.com. One step up from the real budget places – rooms are clean and all have a/c. Free parking. ④

**Los Cocos** Niños Héroes 134 ⓣ983/832-0544, ⓦwww.hotelloscocos.com.mx. A better deal than the *Holiday Inn*, with large, comfortable rooms (the recently redone "premier" category is worth the upgrade), a pool and a sprawling terrace bar and restaurant. ⑦

**Guadalupe del Carmen** Zaragoza 226 ⓣ983/832-8649. Exceptionally clean and tidy two-storey hotel, and a little roomier than budget competitor *María Dolores*; some rooms have a/c. ③

**Holiday Inn** Niños Héroes 171 ⓣ983/835-0400, ⓦwww.holidayinn.com. All the usual comforts of a chain hotel, plus an onsite travel agency. Compared with the giant suites at *Los Cocos*, though, you're paying for the name. ❽

**Juliet** Privada Efraín Aguilar 171 ⓣ983/129-1871. On a pedestrian walkway just off Niños Héroes, this place has clean, if somewhat sterile-feeling, all-white rooms with fan and TV. ❹

**María Dolores** Obregón 206 ⓣ983/832-0508. Basic budget offering, popular with backpackers, with slightly cramped rooms, but an excellent restaurant downstairs. ❸

**Ucum** Gandhi 167 ⓣ983/832-0711, ⓦwww.hotelucumchetumal.com. One of the better deals in town, though it looks unpromising from the motel-like front section. Rooms in the back building, by the huge pool, are brighter and have a choice of a/c or fan. ❸

## The Town

The main attraction, on Avenida de Niños Héroes at the northern edge of the centre, is the **Museo de la Cultura Maya** (Tues–Thurs & Sun 9am–7pm, Fri & Sat 9am–8pm; M$50). The numerous interactive displays and models provide insight into ancient Maya society, mathematics and cosmology. The *Alegoría del Mestizaje* **sculpture** out front is one of the most striking depictions of the popular theme of the intermingling of Spanish and indigenous cultures, showing the Mexican born of a conquistador and a Maya woman.

Immediately south is a little warren of shops and *loncherías* – what's called the "old" **market** (the newer, larger one, where most of the fresh produce is sold and buses for Belize gather, is 1km northwest along Niños Héroes). A couple of blocks further south, the **Centro Cultural de las Bellas Artes**, in a striking 1936 neo-Maya-style school, now houses the romantic memorabilia of the **Museo de la Ciudad** (Tues–Sun 9am–7pm; M$10) as well as the state schools for the performing arts – plenty of live performances take place here. From here, Niños Héroes continues down to the bay and the shiny new **malecón**, popular for evening strolls and fishing. A few blocks east, behind the modern Palacio Legislativo, a small Caribbean house contains the fascinating **Maqueta Payo Obispo** (Mon–Sat 9am–8pm, Sun 9am–2pm; free), a hand-carved scale model of Chetumal as it looked in the 1920s.

△*Alegoría del Mestizaje*, Museo de la Cultura Maya, Chetumal

## Eating and drinking

The intersection of Niños Héroes and Obregón has the highest concentration of restaurants, while the **market stalls** south of the Museo de la Cultura Maya have good, inexpensive fare at lunch. **Nightlife** isn't particularly vibrant, but on weekend evenings the plaza has food stalls, and residents flock to the bar/restaurants strung along the seafront east of the plaza.

**Las Arracheras de Don José** east on the malecón, where it turns north. The speciality of this sprawling terrace restaurant, very popular on weekend nights, is meat tacos, from plain old pork to ostrich (*avestruz*), served with a fantastic array of fresh salsas.

**El Cocal** in *Los Cocos* hotel. Not the cheapest food in town, but Mexican dishes at this open terrace restaurant are served with more care. A mix of tourists and dressed-up locals makes for a convivial scene. Open till 1am Fri and Sat.

**El Emporio** Merino, between Hidalgo and Reforma. An excellent Uruguayan restaurant in a historic wooden house – great for a splurge, and even then, the steaks, served with lashings of garlicky *chimichurri*, are relatively cheap. The good selection of South American wines isn't too expensive, either.

**Los Milagros** Zaragoza, between Niños Héroes and 5 de Mayo. Tasty, inexpensive breakfasts at this little sidewalk café.

**Pantoja** Gandhi at Av 16 de Septiembre. Good *comida corrida*, a favourite with the locals, and hearty dishes like *mondongo* (tripe) and *chilaquiles* for breakfast. Closed Sun.

**Pollo Brujo** Obregón, between Juárez and Niños Héroes. Roast chicken and nothing else, served fast and hot.

**Sergio's** Obregón 182. This upscale but reasonably priced restaurant (most mains are less than M$100) has a few veggie options, such as soups, pizzas and salads.

**Sosilmar** Obregón, in the *María Dolores* hotel. One of the best budget options in town, with good meat and fish and a few splurgy items like *camarones al diablo* for M$90. Closed Sun.

## Listings

**Airlines** Mexicana and Aviacsa run daily flights to Mexico City; Aviacsa has offices on 5 de Mayo at Cardenas (☎983/832-7676).

**Buses and combis** Long-haul buses leave from the main bus station. Other services include Campeche via Escárcega and Xpujil (3 daily; 7hr); Cancún via Tulum and Playa del Carmen (hourly; 5hr 30 min–7hr); Escárcega (13 daily; 4–5hr); Mahahual (3 daily; 3hr 30min); Mérida (9 daily; 6hr 30min–8hr); Mexico City (2 daily; 21hr); San Cristóbal de las Casas via Palenque (4 daily; 12hr); Villahermosa (7 daily; 8–9hr); Xcalak (2 daily; 4hr 30min); Xpujil (12 daily; 2hr). Buses to Flores in Guatemala (1 daily; 12hr) also leave from here; for Belize, see box below. For Bacalar (every 30min; 30min), it's easier to catch *combis* in town, at the Terminal de Combis on Hidalgo at Primo de Verdad.

### Moving on to Belize

Buses run frequently between Chetumal and **Corozal** (1hr), the closest town on the Belize side, though you must get off the bus and walk across the bridge at the official border at Subteniente Lopez, 8km west of Chetumal. Citizens of the UK, US, Canada, Australia and New Zealand do not need a visa to enter Belize; if you are planning to return to Mexico, make sure to keep your tourist card, or you will have to purchase another.

The cheapest, very rattle-trap buses leave from Lázaro Cárdenas market (called the "mercado nuevo"), on the north side of town on Calzada Veracruz, between 10am and noon; you can get over the border for about M$20 – a few of these buses continue on to **Orange Walk** (2hr 30min) and **Belize City** (5hr). The first-class service on better-outfitted vehicles departs from the main bus station (4 daily; 3hr to Belize City). Note that cars rented in Mexico cannot typically be driven into Belize. Likewise, there's no air travel straight from Chetumal; you have to cross to Corozal and take an internal flight.

**Car rental** Aventura Maya in *Hotel Los Cocos* Ⓔaventuramaya@hotelloscocos.com.mx. Sacbe Tours (see "Tour operators", below) also has a few cars for rent.

**Internet access** Web Center, in the new market just south of the Maya culture museum, is cheap and has fast connections.

**Post office** Plutarco Elias Calles at 5 de Mayo (Mon–Fri 8am–6pm, Sat & Sun 9am–12.30pm).

**Tour operators** Are not plentiful in Chetumal, and often need several days' advance notice to arrange something for you. On the plus side, because there are not yet many fixed routes, you can often tailor a trip precisely to your tastes. Sacbe Tours (Ⓣ983/833-2080, Ⓦwww.sacbetours.com) runs day trips to Kohunlich.

## Around Chetumal

Near Chetumal are any number of refreshing escapes. At weekends, the town descends en masse on **CALDERITAS**, a small seaside resort just 6km north around the bay; there's only one **place to stay**, the *Yax-Há* RV park (Ⓣ983/834-4127, Ⓔyax_ha1@yahoo.com; ❼), which has nice rooms and a large picturesque garden with swimming pool right on the seafront. You can hire a **boat** at the adjacent *El Rincón de las Tortugas* bar (Ⓣ983/834-4220) for various day outings: to the beaches on the nearby empty island of Tamalcab (M$300 for 6–8 people); a tour around the bay to look for manatees (3hr; M$1500); or to several other nature spots. **Buses** to Calderitas leave frequently from Cristóbal Colón west of Héroes, behind the museum.

Seven kilometres north of Calderitas, **OXTANKAH** (daily 8am–5pm; M$30, free Sun) is a small Maya site with the remains of a maritime city occupied principally in the Classic period (200–600 AD) and developed to exploit ocean resources – specifically salt. Allegedly, it was also the site of the first *mestizaje*, where shipwrecked Gonzalo Guerrero married into a Maya family and fathered mixed-blood children. What remain are the ruins of several buildings around two squares, with an architectural style similar to that of the Petén region, and a chapel built by the Spanish conquerors. It's a peaceful wooded place with trees – *ceiba, yaxche* – and other flora neatly labelled. You'll need your own transport to get there (follow the shoreline north through Calderitas) or a taxi (M$200 round-trip with waiting time).

### Kohunlich and other Maya sites in the south

The only way from Chetumal back towards central Mexico is across the bottom of the peninsula along Hwy-186. Though the road enters the forests of the Calakmul Biosphere Reserve in Campeche state, in Quintana Roo a lot of the trees have been felled to make way for farming and ranching. The main reason to stop anywhere along here is for the seldom-visited ruins – together with the archeological sites in Xpuhil and further east (see p.790), they represent a fascinating period of architectural decoration, which is only enhanced by the dense jungle that surrounds some of them. If you stop for only one, make it the Classic Maya city of **KOHUNLICH**, set some 60km from Chetumal, then another 9km off the road from the village of Francisco Villa (daily 8am–5pm; M$38).

The ruins, seldom visited by anyone other than enormous butterflies and wild parrots, are beautifully situated, peering out above the treetops. The buildings date from the late pre-Classic to the Classic periods (100–900 AD) and the majority are in the Río Bec architectural style. Foliage has reclaimed most of them, except for the **Templo de los Mascarones**, which is named after the five two-metre-high stucco masks that decorate its facade. Disturbing enough now, these wide-eyed, open-mouthed images of the sun god, Kinich Ahau, once stared out from a background of smooth, bright-red-painted stucco. Also look for an elite residential area called the **27 Escalones**, worth the detour to see the great views over the jungle canopy from the cliff edge on which it is built (prime real estate was just as valuable 1400 years ago, it seems).

A few kilometres east along Hwy-186 is the turn to **Dzibanché** and **Kinichná** (8am–5pm; M$33); set in a drier area with sparse trees, these two neighbouring ruins are an interesting contrast to Kohunlich. Kinichná's hulking pyramid, built layer upon layer by successive leaders, does *not* actually afford a great view – spare yourself the climb up metre-high stones.

There is no public transport from Chetumal to these sites, and they are too far off the highway for you simply to get off the bus and walk. If you're without a car, the easiest way to visit this area is to take a taxi tour from **Xpujil** (see p.789). It's also possible to start off from Chetumal by taking a *combi* to the town of Nicolás Bravo, then hiring a taxi from there (about M$450), ending by flagging down a second-class bus back to Chetumal or onward to Xpuhil.

# Travel details

## Buses

The most useful bus services are those between Mérida and Cancún and those provided by Mayab and Riviera, which run at least every thirty minutes between Cancún and Playa del Carmen. First-class buses don't serve some places, but second-class buses and *combis* or *colectivos* will get you around locally and to the nearest major hub. The following frequencies and times are for both first- and second-class services, but you can also check Ⓦwww.ticketbus.com.mx for up-to-date schedules on major routes in the peninsula and to buy tickets from a number of different bus companies, including ADO, ATS, Sur and Mayab.

**Cancún** to: Campeche (7 daily; 7hr); Chetumal (hourly 5am–12.30am; 6hr); Chiquilá (2 daily; 3hr); Mahahual (2 daily at 7am and 11.30pm; 5hr); Mérida (hourly; 4hr 30min); Mexico City (5 daily; 26hr); Playa del Carmen (every 10min; 1hr 15min); Puerto Morelos (every 10min; 30min); Tizimín (at least 7 daily; 4hr); Tulum (hourly; 2hr 15min); Valladolid (8 daily; 3hr); Villahermosa (14 daily; 12hr).

**Chetumal** to: Bacalar (every 30min: 30min); Belize City via Orange Walk (4 daily; 3hr); Campeche via Escárcega and Xpujil (3 daily; 7hr); Cancún via Tulum and Playa del Carmen (hourly; 5hr 30 min–7hr); Escárcega (13 daily; 4–5hr); Flores, Guatemala (1 daily; 12hr); Mahahual (3 daily; 3hr 30min); Mérida (9 daily; 6hr 30min–8hr); Mexico City (2 daily; 21hr); San Cristóbal de las Casas via Palenque (4 daily; 7–12hr); Villahermosa (7 daily; 8–9hr); Xcalak (2 daily; 4hr 30min); Xpujil (12 daily; 2hr).

**Mérida** to: Celestún (hourly 5.15am–10.30pm; 2hr); Chetumal (12 daily; 6–8hr); Chichén Itzá (hourly 5.20am–midnight; 1hr 30min–2hr); Chiquilá/Holbox (1 daily at 11.30pm; 6hr); Ciudad del Carmen (hourly 4am–12.30pm; 5hr 30min–7hr); Dzibilchaltún (hourly; 30min); Dzilam de Bravo (8 daily; 4hr); Escárcega (9 daily; 4hr 30min–6hr); Felipe Carrillo Puerto (8 daily; 2hr 30min); Izamal (every 45min 4am–9pm; 1hr 30min); Mayapán (2 daily; 1hr 15min); Mexico City (6 daily; 18–20hr); Oxkutzcab (hourly 5.30am–8pm; 2hr); Palenque (4 daily; 7hr 30min–9hr); Playa del Carmen (15 daily via Cancún, 1 daily via Cobá at 5am; 5–7hr); Progreso (AP, every 30min; 45min); Río Lagartos (3 daily; 6hr); San Felipe (1 daily at 5.30pm; 6hr 30min); Santa Elena (5 daily; 1hr); Tizimín (hourly 5.30am–8.20pm; 4hr); Tulum (10 daily via Cancún, 1 daily via Cobá at 5am; 5hr 30min–7hr); Valladolid (hourly 5am–10.20pm; 2–3hr); Villahermosa (hourly 7.15am–12.30pm; 7hr 30min–10hr).

**Playa del Carmen** to: Cancún (every 10min; 1hr 15min); Cancún airport (9 daily; 1hr); Chetumal (hourly 5.30am–1.45am; 4–6hr); Cobá (2 daily; 2hr); Mérida (hourly; 5hr); San Cristóbal de las Casas via Palenque (12 daily; 16–19hr); Tulum (hourly; 1–2hr); Valladolid (5 daily; 3hr); Villahermosa (16 daily; 11hr 30min–15hr).

**Tulum** to: Cancún (frequently; 2hr); Chetumal via Felipe Carrillo Puerto and Bacalar (hourly; 3–4hr); Cobá (4 daily; 1hr); Mahahual (2 daily; 3hr); Mérida (12 daily; 4–8hr); Playa del Carmen (frequently; 1hr); San Cristóbal de las Casas via Palenque (2 daily; first-class: 15hr; second-class: 24hr); Valladolid (8 daily; 2hr).

## Ferries

Ferry services run frequently to **Isla Mujeres, Cozumel** and **Isla Holbox**. Although there are car ferries to all three islands, it's not worth taking a vehicle to Holbox and Mujeres; for Cozumel, the trip

## Fiestas

### January

**New Year's Day** (Jan 1). Beginning of the Fiesta de los Tres Reyes in the cow town of Tizimín (see p.829), an important religious and secular gathering during which lots of steak is consumed.

**Fiesta de Polk Keken** (Jan 6). Celebrated in Lerma, near Campeche, with many traditional dances.

**Día de la Virgen de Santa Inés** (Jan 16–21). An ancient festival with roots in Maya tradition celebrated in Dzitas, north of Chichén Itzá.

### February

**Día de la Candelaria** (Feb 2). Candlemas: colourful celebrations and candlelight processions at Tecoh and Kantunil. The whole week before (beginning Jan 25) is a fiesta in Valladolid (see p.825).

**Carnaval** (the week before Lent; variable Feb–March). At its most riotous in the big cities – especially Mérida (see p.793) – but is also celebrated in Tixkokob, Campeche and Chetumal (see p.781 & p.872), as well as on Isla Mujeres and Cozumel (see p.842 & p.854) with particularly Caribbean flair. The village of Hocaba adds a sombre note, with re-enactments of the Inquisition of the Maya in the sixteenth century.

### March

**Feria de las Hamacas** (March 20). In Tecoh, a hammock-producing village near Mérida.

**Equinox** (March 21). Huge gathering to see the serpent shadow at Chichén Itzá (see p.819).

### April

**Semana Santa** (Holy Week). Celebrated with particularly colourful Passion plays in Mérida (see p.793) and Maní (see p.816).

**Festival of honey and corn** (April 13–17). Traditional celebrations in Hopelchén (see p.787).

**Fiesta de San Telmo** (April 14–22). Progreso (see p.805) celebrates the patron saint of fishermen.

### May

**Día de la Santa Cruz** (May 3). The excuse for another fiesta in Hopelchén (see p.787); also celebrated in, among other towns, Celestún (see p.807) and Felipe Carrillo Puerto (see p.870).

**Feria del Jipi** (May 20). In Becal (see p.792), celebration of the Panama hat, which is the major industry in the town.

**Sport-fishing tournament** (last weekend in May). Occasion for a town-wide party in Puerto Morelos (see p.846).



might make sense if you'll be spending more than a few days there.

### Passenger ferries

**Chiquilá** to: Isla Holbox (9 daily; 30min).
**Playa del Carmen** to: Cozumel (hourly 6am–11pm; 30min).
**Puerto Juárez** and **Gran Puerto**, Cancún to: Isla Mujeres (every 30min 6.30am–10.30pm; 15min).

### Car ferries

**Chiquilá** to: Isla Holbox (2 daily; 1hr).
**Puerto Calica**, Playa del Carmen to: Cozumel (7 daily; 1hr 15min).

### June

**Fiesta de San Pedro y San Pablo** (June 26–30). Celebrated on Cozumel (see p.854) and in Panaba, north of Tizimín.

### July

**Fiesta de Nuestra Señora del Carmen** (July 15–30). Festival for the patron saint of Ciudad del Carmen (see p.788). Motul also celebrates, with lots of dancing.

**Feria** (July 31). On Holbox (see p.830).

**Maya ceremony** (dates variable). Held in Edzná (see p.786) to the god Chac, to encourage, or celebrate, the arrival of the rains.

### September

**Día de San Roman** (Sept 14). In Dzan, near Ticul, the end of a four-day festival with fireworks, bullfights, dances and processions. In Campeche (see p.781), the **Feria de San Roman** lasts until the end of the month. Also marks the beginning of the season of "Los Gremios", the workers' processions to honour the Cristo de las Ampollas at the cathedral in Mérida; daily pilgrimages begin in earnest on Sept 27 and continue until Oct 17.

**Equinox** (Sept 21). Another serpent spectacle at Chichén Itzá (see p.819).

**Día de San Miguel** (Sept 29). Celebrated with a major festival in Maxcanú, as well as on Cozumel.

### October

**Pilgrimage** (Oct 18). Centred on Izamal (see p.817), in honour of the miraculous Black Christ of Sitilpech, it starts ten days of celebration, culminating in dances on the night of Oct 28.

### November

**Feria del Estado de Yucatán** (first two weeks of Nov). Typical thrill rides, agriculture exhibits and fried foods at the fairgrounds south of Mérida (see p.793).

**Día de los Muertos** (Day of the Dead; Nov 1–2). Celebrated everywhere.

### December

**Día de la Inmaculada Concepcíon** (Dec 8). Widely celebrated, but especially in Kantunilkin, Izamal (see p.817) and Champotón, each of which has a fiesta starting several days earlier. Izamal's and Kantunilkin's fiestas include bullfights.

**Día de la Virgen de Guadalupe** (Dec 12). Celebrated everywhere, but look for runners on the roads around Mérida (see p.793) in the days prior; church groups organize days-long relays as penance. On Isla Mujeres (see p.842), the week prior celebrates the church's statue of the Virgin.

**Día de Nuestra Señora de la Estrella** (Dec 27). Peto celebrates until Jan 2 with a trade fair, bullfights and dancing.

**Punta Sam** to: Isla Mujeres (5 daily).

## Flights

Cancún and Cozumel both have busy international airports with several daily flights to Mexico City and regular connections to Miami and Houston. Mérida's airport also receives a few international flights, from Atlanta and Houston, and Chetumal has daily direct services to Mexico City. Around the Caribbean coast various small companies fly light planes – frequently between Cancún and Cozumel, less often from these places to Isla Mujeres, Playa del Carmen and Tulum.

# Contexts

# Contexts

History .......... 883

Chronology .......... 905

Ball-games and sacrifice: the pre-Columbian belief system .......... 907

Environment and wildlife .......... 913

Mexican music .......... 924

Books .......... 934

# History

The nation of Mexico, with its current borders, has only existed for about 150 years. The loose political entity known as Mexico can be traced to the Spanish Conquest. Anything pre-dating that, however, is largely a matter of histories recorded long after the events or of archeological conjecture, as the Spanish did their best to erase all traces of the cultures that preceded them.

These earlier cultures were not confined to present-day Mexico, but spread throughout the area referred to as **Mesoamerica**, which extends from the northern part of Mexico well into Central America. The north of this region was occupied by native peoples who never abandoned their nomadic, hunter-gatherer existences; the south was ruled by a succession of powerful empires, including the Aztecs and the Maya, who at one time spread all the way from southeastern Mexico into what is now Honduras. Some of the world's most extraordinary societies flourished in this region, creating – without the use of metal tools, draught animals or the wheel – vast cities, intricate statuary and a mathematical and calendar system more advanced than those known in the "civilized" world.

The **framework** set out below is based on archeological theories that are generally, but by no means universally, accepted. There are still major gaps in modern knowledge – especially concerning the extent and nature of the contact between the societies and their influence on each other – which, should they ever be filled, may overturn many existing notions.



## The framework

The exact date when human beings first crossed the Bering land bridge into the Americas is debatable (as is the very theory of the migration from North Asia), but the earliest widely accepted date is around 13,000 years ago. Successive waves of nomadic Stone Age hunters continued to arrive until around 6000 BC, pushing their predecessors gradually further south.

The first signs of settled habitation in Mexico – the cultivation of corn, followed by the emergence of crude pottery, stone tools and even some trade – seem to come from the **Archaic** period, around 8000 to 2000 BC. The first established civilization did not appear until the **pre-Classic** or **Formative** era (2500 BC to 250 AD) with the rise of the Olmecs.

Still the least understood of all the ancient societies, the **Olmecs** thrived in the low-lying coastal jungles of Tabasco and Veracruz. Many of their political, cultural, artistic and architectural innovations can be observed in later Mesoamerican cultures. What you see of them in the museums today is a magnificent artistic style, exemplified in their sculpture and famous colossal basalt heads. These, with their puzzling "baby-faced" features, were carved from monolithic blocks and somehow transported over ninety kilometres from the quarries to their final settings – proof in itself of a hierarchical society commanding a sizeable workforce.

# Classic civilizations

By the end of the **pre-Classic** period, the Olmec civilization was already in decline – La Venta, the most important cultural centre, seems to have been abandoned around 400 BC, and the other towns followed over the next few hundred years. As the Olmec weakened, new civilizations grew in strength and numbers, establishing cities throughout central Mexico. However, these sites, such as Monte Albán, near Oaxaca, were obviously influenced by the earlier Olmec. To the north, in the Valley of México (where Mexico City now stands, an area then known as Anahuac), many small cities expanded. Tlatilco, one of the towns in this region, hoarded Olmec objects, suggesting significant contact with Monte Albán to the south – at least through trade. Meanwhile, there were hints of bigger things to come: Cuicuilco (now in the capital's suburbs) was an important city until it was buried by a volcanic eruption around the beginning of the first century AD; at the same time, the first major buildings of Teotihuacán were being constructed.

The city of **Teotihuacán** rose in central Mexico, ruling the area during the **Classic Period** (250–900 AD) as the first truly urban society. Its architectural and religious influences reached as far south as the Maya heartland of Guatemala. Even today, the ruins of the city, with the great Pyramids of the Sun and Moon, are an impressive testimony to the civilization's strength. Very little is known about Teotihuacán, including details about its people or rulers, or even its true name (Teotihuacán was coined later by the Aztecs – it means "the place where men became gods"). What is certain is that the city's period of dominance ended between 500 and 600 AD, and that within a century it had been abandoned altogether. Mysteriously, several societies throughout Mesoamerica, particularly the Maya, seem to have been disrupted at around the same time.

The great **Maya** centres also reached the peak of their artistic, scientific and architectural achievements in the Classic period, above all their cities in the lowlands of Guatemala and Honduras. These survived longer than Teotihuacán, but by around 800 AD had also been abandoned. In the Yucatán the Maya fared rather better, their cities revived from about 900 by an injection of ideas from central Mexico and, archeologists now propose, new leaders from the south. The famous structures at Chichén Itzá mostly date from this later phase, around 900 to 1100 AD.

In general, the Classic era saw development everywhere – other important centres grew up on the Gulf coast at El Tajín and in the Zapotec areas around Monte Albán – but was followed by rapid decline. There are numerous theories to account for this, but none is entirely convincing, although the fall of Teotihuacán must have affected its trading partners throughout Mexico. In all likelihood, once started, the disasters – probably provoked by some sort of agricultural failure or ecological disaster – led to a loss of faith in rulers and perhaps even rebellion, and had a knock-on effect.

# Toltecs and Aztecs

The start of the **post-Classic** era (900–1520 AD) saw the beginning of a series of invasions from the north which must have exacerbated any existing problems. Wandering tribes would arrive in the fertile Valley of México, like what they saw, build a city adopting many of the styles and religions of their predecessors in the area, enjoy a brief period of dominance and be subdued in turn by a new wave of invaders, or Chichimeca. All such marauding tribes were known as Chichimec, which implies barbarian (even if many of them were at least semi-civilized before they arrived), and all claimed to have set out on their journeys from the legendary seven caves of Chicomoztoc. In connection with the many cities founded in the Valley in this bellicose era, two names stand out – the Toltecs and the Aztecs.

The **Toltec** people, who dominated the central valleys around 950–1150 AD, were among the first to arrive – indeed, some say that it was a direct attack by them that destroyed Teotihuacán. Later, they assumed a mythical significance for the Aztecs, who regarded them as the founders of every art and science and claimed direct descent from Toltec blood. In fact, it appears that the Toltecs borrowed most of their ideas from Teotihuacán.

Nevertheless, there were developments under the Toltecs. In particular, the cult of **Quetzalcoatl** assumed new importance: at Tula, the Toltec capital, the god is depicted everywhere, perhaps embodied as a king or dynasty of kings, and it was from here that he was driven out by the evil god Texcatlipoca. (The prediction of his return was later to have fatal consequences for the Aztecs.) The structure of Toltec society was at least as militaristic as it was religious, and human sacrifice was practised on a far larger scale than had been previously recorded.

When the **Aztecs** (or Mexica) arrived in central Mexico around the end of the twelfth century they found numerous small city-states, with none in a position of dominance. They spent some years scavenging and raiding until about 1325 – when legend has it that they saw the prophesied sign (an eagle perched on a cactus devouring a snake) telling them to build their own city.

The new city, **Tenochtitlán**, was to become the heart of the most formidable of all Mexican empires, but its birth was not easy. The chosen setting, an island in a lake (now Mexico City), was hardly promising, and the city was at first a subject of its neighbours. The Aztecs overcame the lack of arable land by growing crops on floating reed islands that they fashioned in the lake. This agricultural success led to self-sufficiency and a burgeoning population. They became the most powerful civilization in the Valley, and around 1428 formed the so-called Triple Alliance with neighbouring Texcoco and Tlacopán, establishing the **Aztec empire**. The empire's achievements were remarkable – in less than a hundred years the Aztecs came to control, and demand labour tribute and taxes from, the whole of central and southern Mexico. Tenochtitlán grew huge – the invading Spanish could not believe its size and grandeur – but even as it expanded, the gods continued to demand more war: to suppress rebellious subjects, and to capture fresh victims for the constant rituals of human sacrifice.

Meanwhile, other societies had continued much as they had before the Aztec rise. In present-day Oaxaca, the Zapotecs were subjected to invasions by **Mixtecs** from the mountains. By war and alliance the Mixtecs came eventually to dominate this region – developing the trades of the potter and goldsmith as never before – and fell to the Aztecs only in the last years before the Spanish Conquest. In the Yucatán, the **Maya** were never conquered, but their civilization was in decline and any form of central authority had broken down into city-states. Nevertheless, they carried on trade all around the coasts, and Christopher Columbus himself (though he never got to Mexico) encountered a heavily laden boat of Maya traders, plying the sea between Honduras and the Yucatán. On the Gulf coast Aztec supremacy was total by the time the Spanish arrived, but they were still struggling to subdue the west.

# The Spanish Conquest

**Hernán Cortés** landed on the coast near modern Veracruz in the spring of 1519. With him there were just 550 men, a few horses, dogs and a cannon; yet less than three years later the Spaniards had defeated the Aztecs and effectively

△ *Disembarkation of the Spanish at Veracruz* (Diego Rivera mural)

established control over most of Mexico. Several factors enabled them to do so. First was Cortés himself, as ruthless a leader as any in history: he burned the expedition's boats within days of their arrival, so that there was literally no turning back. In addition, his men had little to lose and much to gain, and their metal weapons and armour were greatly superior to anything the Aztecs had (although many Spaniards adopted Aztec-style padded cotton, which was warmer, lighter and almost as protective). Their gunpowder and cannon could also wreak havoc on opposing armies, both physically and psychologically. The horses and attack dogs, too, terrified the Aztecs. None of these, though, in the end counted a fraction as much as Cortés's ability to form alliances with tribes who were fretting under Aztec subjugation and whose numbers eventually swelled his armies tenfold.

**Moctezuma**, the Aztec leader, could certainly have destroyed the Spanish before they left their first camp, since his spies had brought news of their arrival almost immediately. Instead he sent a delegation bearing gifts of gold and jewels which he hoped would persuade them to leave in peace. This served only to inflame the greed of the Spanish. By all accounts Moctezuma was a morose, moody and indecisive man, but his failure to act against Cortés had deeper roots: he was heavily influenced by religious omens, and the arrival of Cortés coincided with the predicted date for the return of **Quetzalcoatl**. The invaders were fair-skinned and bearded, as was Quetzalcoatl, and they had come from the east, where the deity had vanished. Moreover, it seemed they bore a peaceful message like that of the god, for one of their first acts when they conquered a city was to ban human sacrifice. So although he put obstacles in their way, even persuading his allies to fight them, when the Spanish finally reached Tenochtitlán in November 1519, Moctezuma welcomed them as his guests. They promptly repaid his hospitality by taking him prisoner within his own palace.

This first phase of the Conquest, during which Spanish troops skirmished with a number of other Indian tribes and made allies of many – most significantly the **Tlaxcalans** (or Tlaxcalteca) – lasted for about a year. In April 1520 news came of a second Spanish expedition, led by Pánfilo de Narváez, who was under orders to capture Cortés and take him back to Cuba (Cortés's mission had always been unofficial, and many others hoped to seize the wealth of Mexico for themselves). Again, though, Cortés proved the more decisive commander – he marched back east, surprised Narváez by night, killed him and persuaded most of his troops to switch allegiance.

Meanwhile, the Spaniards left behind in Tenochtitlán had finally provoked their hosts beyond endurance by killing a group of priests during a religious ceremony, and were under siege in their quarters. Cortés, with his reinforcements, fought his way back into the city on June 24, only to find himself trapped as well. On June 27, Moctezuma (still a prisoner) was killed – according to the Spanish, stoned to death by his own people while attempting to appeal for peace. Finally Cortés decided to break out on the night of June 30 – still commemorated as **Noche Triste** – when the Spanish lost over half their number on the causeways across the lake. Most of them were so weighed down with gold and booty that they were barely able to move, let alone swim in the places where the bridges had been destroyed.

Once more, though, the Aztecs failed to follow up their advantage, and the Spanish survivors managed to reach their allies in Tlaxcala, where they regrouped. The final assault on Tenochtitlán began in January 1521, with more supplies and fresh troops, tens of thousands of whom were Tlaxcalteca and other Indians. The city, besieged, was also ravaged by an epidemic of smallpox, among whose victims was Moctezuma's successor, Cuitláhuac. The Aztecs held out for several more months under **Cuauhtémoc** – in Mexican eyes the only hero of this long episode – but on August 13, 1521, Tenochtitlán finally fell to the Spanish.

Although much of the country remained to be pacified, the defeat of the Aztec capital made it inevitable that it would be.

# Colonial rule

By dint of his success, Cortés was appointed governor of this new territory, although in practice he was watched over by minders from Spain, and therefore never had much real freedom of action. In 1535 **Nueva España** (New Spain) was formally established. There followed nearly three centuries of direct Spanish rule, under a succession of 61 viceroys responsible to the Spanish king. By the end of the sixteenth century the entire country had been effectively subjugated, its boundaries stretched by exploration from Panama to the western states of the US (although the area from Guatemala south, including the Mexican state of Chiapas, was soon under separate rule).

When the Spanish arrived, the **native population** of central Mexico was at least 25 million; by the beginning of the nineteenth century the total population of Nueva España was just six million, and at most half of these were pure-blooded natives. Some had been killed in battle, a few as a result of ill-treatment or simply from being left without homes or land to live on, but the vast majority died as a result of successive epidemics of European diseases to which the New World had no natural immunity. The few survivors found the burden of labour placed on them ever-increasing as their numbers dwindled – for certainly no European man came to Mexico to do manual work – and became more and more like slaves.

The first tasks, in the Spanish mind, were reconstruction, pacification and conversion. Tenochtitlán, destroyed in the war, had been subsequently pillaged and burned, its population dispersed. In a deliberate policy of destroying all reminders of Aztec power, the remaining stones were used to construct the new city, **México** (Mexico City). At first there was quite remarkable progress: hundreds of towns were laid out according to a plan drawn up in Spain, with a plaza surrounded by a grid of streets. Thousands of churches were built (by 1800, the count reached 12,000), often in areas that had been sacred to the Indians, or on top of their pyramids. And when the first Franciscan monks arriving in 1524, mass conversions were the order of the day. In a sense the indigenous peoples were used to all this – the Aztecs and their predecessors had behaved in a similar manner – but they had never experienced a slavery like that which was to follow.

**The Church**, which at first championed indigenous rights and attempted to record native legends and histories and educate the children, grew more and more concerned with money. Any attempt to treat the Indians as human was, in any case, violently opposed by Spanish landowners, to whom they were rather less than machines (in fact, cheaper than machinery, and therefore more expendable). By the end of the colonial era, the Church owned more than half of all the land and wealth in the country, yet most native villages would be lucky to see a priest once a year.

In a sense Mexico was a wealthy nation – certainly the richest of the Spanish colonies – but its riches were confined to the local elite and the imperialists in Spain. The governing philosophy was "what's good for Spain is good for

Mexico", and it was towards this end that all **trade**, industry and profit were exclusively aimed. No local trade or agriculture that would compete with Spain was allowed, so the cultivation of vines or the production of silk was banned; heavy taxes on other products – coffee, sugar, tobacco, cochineal, silver and other metals – went directly to Spain or to still poorer colonies. Since the "Spanish Galleon" (actually more of a convoy) sailed from Veracruz just once a year and was even then subject to the vagaries of piracy, this was a considerable handicap.

It didn't prevent the growth of a small class of extraordinarily wealthy **hacendados** (owners of massive estates) and **mine-owners**, whose growing confidence is shown in the architectural development of the colonial towns, from fortress-like huddles at the beginning of the colonial era to the full flowering of Baroque extravagance by its end. However, it did stop the development of any kind of realistic economic infrastructure, even of decent roads linking the towns: just about the only proper road in 1800 was the one that connected Acapulco with Mexico City and Veracruz, by which goods from Spain's colonies in the Far East would be transported cross-country before being shipped on to Spain.

Even among the wealthy Spanish-descended landowners there was growing **resentment**, fuelled by the status of those among them born in Mexico: only **gachupines**, Spaniards born in Spain, could hold high office in the government or Church. Out of the six million people in Mexico in 1800, only 40,000 of them were *gachupines* – the rest were **criollos** (creoles, born in Mexico of Spanish blood) who were generally educated, wealthy and aristocratic, and **mestizos** (of mixed race) who dominated the lower ranks of the Church, army and civil service, or lived as anything from shopkeepers and small ranchers to bandits and beggars.



## Independence

By the beginning of the nineteenth century Spain's status as a world power was in severe decline. In 1796 British sea power had forced the Spanish to open their colonial ports to free trade. At the same time, new political ideas were transforming the world, and memories of the French Revolution and the American War of Independence were still fresh. Although the works of such political philosophers as Rousseau, Voltaire and Paine were banned in Mexico, the opening of the ports made it inevitable that their ideas would spread – especially since it was traders from the new US who most took advantage of the opportunities. Literary societies set up to discuss these books quickly became centres of **political dissent**.

The spark, though, came when the French invaded Spain in 1808, and Napoleon placed his brother Joseph on the throne. Colonies throughout Latin America refused to recognize the Bonaparte regime (and the campaigns of Bolívar and others in South America began). In Mexico, the *gachupine* rulers proclaimed their loyalty to Ferdinand VII (the deposed king) and hoped to carry on much as before, but creole discontent was not so easily assuaged. The literary societies continued to meet, and from one, in Querétaro, emerged the first leaders of the Independence movement: **Father Miguel Hidalgo y Costilla**, a creole priest, and **Ignacio Allende**, a disaffected junior army officer.

When their plans for a coup were discovered, the conspirators were forced into premature action, with Hidalgo issuing the famous "Grito de Dolores"

(*Á Méxicanos, viva México!*) from his parish church in Dolores on September 16, 1810. The mob of Indians and *mestizos* who gathered behind the banner swiftly took the towns of San Miguel, Guanajuato and others to the north of the capital, but their behaviour – seizing land and property, slaughtering the Spanish – horrified the wealthy creoles who had initially supported them. In spring 1811 Hidalgo's army, huge but undisciplined, moved on the capital, but at the crucial moment Hidalgo threw away a clear chance to overpower the royalist army. Instead he chose to retreat, and his forces broke up as quickly as they had assembled. Within months, Hidalgo, Allende and the other ringleaders had been captured and executed.

By this time most creoles had rejoined the ranks of the royalists. However, many *mestizos* and much of the indigenous population remained in a state of revolt, with a new leader in the *mestizo* priest **José María Morelos**. Morelos was not only a far better tactician than Hidalgo – instituting a highly successful series of guerrilla campaigns – he was also a genuine radical. By 1813 he controlled virtually the entire country, with the exception of the capital and the route from there to Veracruz, and at the **Congress of Chilpancingo** he declared the abolition of slavery and the equality of the races. The royalists, however, fought back with a series of crushing victories. Morelos was executed in 1815, and his forces, led by **Vicente Guerrero**, were reduced to carrying out the occasional minor raid.

Ironically, it was the introduction of liberal reforms in Spain, of just the type feared by the Mexican ruling classes, which finally brought about **Mexican Independence**. Worried that such reforms might spread across the Atlantic, many creoles pre-empted a true revolution by assuming a "revolutionary" guise themselves. In 1820 **Agustín de Iturbide**, a royalist general but himself a *mestizo*, threw in his lot with Guerrero; in 1821 he proposed the **Iguala Plan** to the Spanish authorities, who were hardly in a position to fight, and Mexico was granted independence. With it, though, came none of the changes which had been fought over for so long – the Church retained its power, and one set of rulers had simply been changed for another, local set.

# Foreign intervention

In 1822 Iturbide proclaimed himself emperor; a year later he was forced to abdicate and a year after that he was executed. It was the first of many such events in a century which must rank among the most confused – and disastrous – in any nation's history. Not only had Independence brought no real social change, it had left the new nation with virtually no chance of successful government: the power of the Church and of the army was far greater than that of the supposed rulers; there was no basis on which to create a viable economy; and if the state hadn't already been bankrupted by the Independence struggle, it was to be cleaned out time and again by the demands of war and internal disruption. There were no fewer than 56 governments in the next forty years. In what approaches farce, the name of **General Antonio López de Santa Anna** stands out as the most bizarre figure of all – the man became president or dictator on eleven separate occasions and masterminded the loss of more than half of Mexico's territory.

Santa Anna's first spell in office immediately followed Iturbide – he declared Mexico a **republic** (although he himself always expected to be treated as a king, and addressed as His Most Serene Majesty) and called a constitutional convention. Under the auspices of the new constitution, the republic was confirmed, the country divided into thirteen states, and **Guadalupe Victoria**, a former guerrilla general, elected its first president. He lasted three years, something of a record. In 1829 the Spanish attempted a rather half-hearted **invasion**, easily defeated, after which they accepted the fact of Mexican Independence. In 1833 Santa Anna was elected president (officially) for the first time, the fifth man to hold the post thus far.

In 1836 a rather more serious chain of events was set in motion when Texas (Mexican territory but largely inhabited by migrants from the US) declared its independence. Santa Anna commanded a punitive expedition that besieged **the Alamo** in the famous incident in which Jim Bowie and Davy Crockett, along with 150 other defenders, lost their lives. Santa Anna himself, though, was promptly defeated and captured at the battle of San Jacinto, and rather than face execution he signed a paper accepting **Texan independence**. Although the authorities in Mexico refused to accept the legality of its claim, Texas was, de facto, independent. Meanwhile, in 1838, the French chose to invade **Veracruz**, demanding compensation for alleged damages to French property and citizens – the "Pastry War" (so called on acound of one of the French claimants, who owned a *patisserie* in Mexico City) lasted about four months, during which Santa Anna lost a leg.

In 1845 the US annexed Texas, and although the Mexicans at first hoped to negotiate a settlement, the redefinition of Texas to include most of Arizona, New Mexico and California made yet another war almost inevitable. In 1846 clashes between Mexican troops and US cavalry in these western zones led to the declaration of the **Mexican–American War**. Following defeats for the Mexicans at Palo Alto and Resaca, three small US armies invaded from the north. At the same time General Winfield Scott took Veracruz after a long bombardment, and commenced his march on the capital. Santa Anna was roundly defeated several times, and in September 1847, after legendary resistance by the Niños Héroes (cadets at the military academy), Mexico City itself was captured. In 1848, by the **Treaty of Guadalupe Hidalgo**, the US paid $15 million for most of Texas, New Mexico, Arizona and California, along with parts of Colorado and Utah; in 1854 the present borders were established when Santa Anna sold a further strip down to the Río Grande for $10 million under the **Gadsden Purchase**.

## Reform

Mexico finally saw the back of Santa Anna when, in 1855, he left for exile in Venezuela, but the country's troubles were by no means at an end. A new generation had grown up, knowing only an independent Mexico in permanent turmoil and espousing once more the liberal ideals of Morelos. Above all, this generation saw its enemy as **the Church**: immense, self-serving and far wealthier than any legitimate government, it had further sullied its reputation by refusing to provide funds for the American war. Its position enshrined in the constitution, it was an extraordinarily reactionary institution, bleeding the peasantry for the most basic of sacraments (few could afford official marriage, or burial) and failing to provide it with the few services with which it was charged. All education was in Church schools, which for 95 percent of the population meant no education at all.

**Benito Juárez**, a Zapotec Indian who had been adopted and educated by a priest and trained as a lawyer, led this liberal movement through several years of civil war. When the **liberals** first came to power following Santa Anna's exile they began relatively mild attempts at **reform**: permitting secular education, liberating the press, attempting to distance the Church from government and instituting a new democratic constitution. The Church responded by threatening to excommunicate anyone co-operating with the government. In 1858 there was a conservative coup, and, for the next three years, **internal strife** on an unprecedented scale. With each new battle the liberals proclaimed more drastic reforms, churches were sacked and priests shot, while the conservatives responded by executing anyone suspected of liberal tendencies. In 1861 Juárez emerged triumphant, at least temporarily. Church property was confiscated, monasteries closed, weddings and burials became civil affairs and set fees were established for the services of a priest.

It wasn't until 1867 that most of these **Reform Laws** were fully enacted, though, for the conservatives had one more card to play. At the end of the civil war, with the government bankrupt, Juárez had suspended payment of all foreign debts, and in 1861 a joint British, Spanish and French expedition occupied Veracruz to demand compensation. It rapidly became clear, however, that the French were after more than mere financial recompense. Britain and Spain withdrew their forces, and Napoleon III ordered his troops to advance on Mexico City. Supported by Mexican conservatives, the aim was to place **Maximilian**, a Habsburg archduke, on the throne as emperor.

Despite a major defeat at **Puebla** on May 5, 1862 (now a national holiday), the French sent for reinforcements and occupied Mexico City in 1863. The new emperor arrived the following year. In many ways, Maximilian was a pathetic figure. He came to Mexico with almost no knowledge of its internal feuds (having gleaned most of his information from a book on court etiquette), and expecting a victorious welcome. A liberal at heart – he refused to repeal any of Juárez's reforms – he promptly lost the support of even the small group of conservatives that had initially welcomed him. While his good intentions seem undeniable, few believe that he would have been capable of putting them into practice even in the best of circumstances. And these were hardly ideal times. With Union victory in the **US Civil War**, the authorities there threw their weight behind Juárez, providing him with arms and threatening to invade unless the French withdrew (on the basis of the Monroe doctrine: America for the Americans). Napoleon, already worried by the growing power of Bismarck's Prussia back home, had little choice but to comply. After 1866 Maximilian's position was hopeless.

His wife, the Empress Carlota, sailed to Europe to win fresh support, but Napoleon had made his decision, and the Vatican refused to contemplate helping a man who had continued to attack the Church. The constant disappointments eventually drove Carlota mad; she died, insane, in Belgium in 1927. Maximilian, meanwhile, stayed at the head of his hopelessly outnumbered troops to the end – May 15, 1867 – when he was defeated and captured at **Querétaro**. A month later, he faced the firing squad.

Juárez reassumed power, managing this time to ride through the worst of the inevitable bankruptcy. The first steps towards **economic reconstruction** were taken, with the completion of a railway from Veracruz to the capital, encouragement of industry and the development of a public education programme. Juárez died in office in 1872, having been re-elected in 1871, and was succeeded by his vice-president, **Sebastián Lerdo de Tejada**, who continued on the same road, though with few new ideas.

# Dictatorship

Tejada was neither particularly popular nor spectacularly successful, but he did see out his term of office. However, there were several Indian **revolts** during his rule and a number of plots against him, the most serious of them led by a new radical liberal, **Porfirio Díaz**. Díaz had been a notably able military officer under Juárez, and in 1876, despite the re-election of Tejada, he proclaimed his own candidate president. The following year he assumed the presidency himself, then consolidated power to effectively become dictator for the next 34 years. At first his platform was a radical one – including full implementation of the Reform Laws and a decree of no re-election to any political office – but this was soon dropped in favour of a brutal policy of **modernization**. Díaz did actually stand down at the end of his first term in 1880, but he continued to rule through a puppet president, and in 1884 resumed the presidency for an unbroken stretch until 1911.

In many ways the **achievements** of his dictatorship were remarkable: some 16,000km of railway were built, industry boomed, telephones and telegraph were installed and major towns, reached at last by reasonable roads, entered the modern era. In the countryside, Díaz established a police force – the notorious *rurales* – which stamped out much of the banditry that had plagued the nation. Almost every city in Mexico seems to have a grandiose theatre and elegant public buildings from this era. But the costs were high: rapid development was achieved basically by handing over the country to **foreign investors**, who owned the majority of the oil, mining rights, railways and other natural resources. At the same time, there was a policy of massive land expropriation, in which formerly communal village holdings were handed over to foreigners or simply grabbed by corrupt officials.

**Agriculture**, meanwhile, was ignored entirely. The owners of vast haciendas could make more than enough money by relying on the forced labour of a landless peasantry, and had no interest in efficiency or production for domestic consumption. By 1900 the whole of Mexico was owned by some three to four percent of its population. Without land of their own, peasants had no choice but to work on haciendas or in forests, where their serfdom was ensured by wages so low that they were permanently in debt to their employers. The rich became very rich indeed, while the poor had lower incomes and fewer prospects than they had a century earlier.

Once the *rurales* had done their job by making the roads safe to travel, they became a burden – charging for the right to travel along roads they controlled and acting as a private police force for employers. In short, slavery was reintroduced in all but name, and up to a quarter of the nation's resources came to be spent on internal security. The press was censored, education strictly controlled and **corruption** rife.

# Revolution

By the onset of the **twentieth century**, Díaz was old and beginning to lose his grip on reality. While he had every intention of continuing in power until his death, a real middle-class opposition began to develop, concerned above all by the racist policies of their government (which favoured foreign investors above native ones) and by the lack of opportunity for themselves – the young educated classes. Their movement popularized the slogan of "no reelección", and in 1910 **Francisco Madero** stood against Díaz in the presidential election. The dictator responded by imprisoning his opponent and declaring himself victor. Madero, however, escaped to Texas, where he proclaimed himself president, and called on the nation to support him.

This was an entirely opportunist move, for at the time there were no revolutionary forces, but several small bands immediately took up arms. Most important were those in the northern state of Chihuahua, where **Pancho Villa** and **Pascual Orozco** won several minor battles, and in the southwest, where **Emiliano Zapata** began to arm Indian guerrilla forces. In May 1911 Orozco captured the major border town of Ciudad Juárez, and his success was rapidly followed by a string of Revolutionary victories. By the end of the month, hoping to preserve the system, if not his own role in it, Porfirio Díaz had fled into exile. On October 2, 1911, Madero was elected president. Like the originators of the Independence movement before him, Madero had no conception of the forces he had unleashed. He freed the press, encouraged the formation of unions and introduced genuine **democracy**, but failed to do anything about the condition of the peasantry or the redistribution of land. Zapata prepared to act again.



Emiliano Zapata was perhaps the one true revolutionary in the whole long conflict to follow. His battle cry of "**¡Tierra y libertad!**" ("Land and liberty!") and his insistence that "it is better to die on your feet than live on your knees" still make him a revered figure among the peasants – and revolutionaries – of the present day. By contrast, the rest were mostly out for personal gain: Pancho Villa, a cattle rustler and bandit in the time of Díaz, was by far the most successful of the more orthodox generals, brilliantly inventive, and ruthless in victory. But his motivation seems to have been personal glory. He appeared to

△ Statue of Pancho Villa, Zacatecas

love fighting, and at one stage, when a Hollywood film crew was travelling with his armies, allegedly arranged his battles so as to ensure the best lighting conditions and most impressive fight scenes. (The result was the silent film *Life of Villa*, released in 1912.)

In any case, Madero was faced by a more immediately dangerous enemy than his own erstwhile supporters: US business interests. **Henry Lane Wilson**, US ambassador, began openly plotting with **Victoriano Huerta**, a government general, and **Felix Díaz**, a nephew of the dictator, who was held in prison. Fighting broke out between supporters of Díaz and those of Madero, while Huerta refused to commit his troops to either side. When he did, in 1913, it was to proclaim himself president. Madero was shot in suspicious circumstances (few doubt an assassination sanctioned by Huerta) and opponents on the right, including Díaz, either imprisoned or exiled. The new government was promptly recognized by the US and most other foreign powers, but not by Madero's erstwhile supporters within the country.

## Constitution versus Convention

Villa and Zapata immediately took up arms against Huerta, and in the north Villa was joined by **Alvaro Obregón**, governor of Sonora, and **Venustiano Carranza**, governor of Coahuila. Carranza was appointed head of the **Constitutionalist** forces, though he was always to be deeply suspicious of Villa, despite Villa's constant protestations of loyalty. At first the Revolutionaries made little headway – Carranza couldn't even control his own state – although Obregón and Villa did enjoy some success raiding south from Chihuahua and Sonora. But almost immediately the new US president, **Woodrow Wilson**, withdrew his support from Huerta and, infuriated by his refusal to resign, began supplying arms to the Revolution.

In 1914 the Constitutionalists began to move south, and in April of that year US troops occupied Veracruz in their support (though neither side was exactly happy about the foreign presence). Huerta, now cut off from almost every source of money or supplies, fled the country in July, and in August Obregón occupied the capital, proclaiming Carranza president.

Renewed fighting broke out straight away, this time between Carranza and Obregón, the Constitutionalists, on one side, and the rest of the Revolutionary leaders on the other, the so-called **Conventionalists** whose sole point of agreement was that Carranza should not lead them. The three years of fighting that followed were the most bitter and chaotic yet, with petty chiefs in every part of the country proclaiming provisional governments, joining each other in factions and then splitting again, and the entire country in a state of anarchy. Each army issued its own money, and each forced any able-bodied men it came across into joining. It was reckoned that about 900,000 people were killed between 1910 and 1921, out of a total population of 15 million.

Gradually, however, Obregón and Carranza gained ground – Obregón defeated Villa several times in 1915, and Villa withdrew to carry out raids into the US, in the hopes of provoking an invasion (which he nearly did: US troops led by General "Black Jack" Pershing pursued him across the border but were never able to catch up, and withdrew following defeat in a skirmish with Carranza's troops). Zapata, meanwhile, had some conspicuous successes – and occupied Mexico City for much of 1915 – but his troops tended to disappear back to their villages after each victory. In 1919 he was tricked into a meeting with one of Carranza's generals and assassinated. Villa retired to a hacienda in his home state and was murdered in 1923.

## The end of the Revolution

Meanwhile, Carranza continued to claim the presidency, and in 1917 he set up a constitutional **congress** to ratify his position. The document it produced – the present constitution – included most of the Revolutionary demands, among them workers' rights, a mandatory eight-hour working day, national ownership of all mineral rights and the distribution of large landholdings and formerly communal properties to the peasantry. Carranza was formally elected in May 1917 and proceeded to make no attempt to carry out any of its stipulations, certainly not with regard to land rights. In 1920 Carranza was forced to step down by Obregón, and was shot while attempting to escape the country with most of the contents of the treasury.

Obregón, at least, was well intentioned – but his efforts at land reform were again stymied by fear of US reaction: in return for American support, he agreed not to expropriate land. In 1924 **Plutarco Elias Calles** succeeded him and initiated some real progress towards the ideals of the Revolutionary constitution. Work on large public-works schemes began – roads, irrigation systems, village schools – and about eight million acres of land were given back to the villages as communal holdings. At the same time, Calles instituted a policy of virulent **anticlericalism**, closing churches and monasteries and forcing priests to flee the country or go underground.

These moves provoked the last throes of a backlash, as the **Catholic Cristero** movement took up arms in defence of the Church. From 1927 until about 1935 isolated incidents of vicious banditry and occasional full-scale warfare continued, eventually burning themselves out as the stability of the new regime became obvious, and religious controls were relaxed. In 1928 Obregón was re-elected, but was assassinated three weeks later in protest at the breach of the "no reelección" clause of the constitution. He was followed by **Portes Gil**, **Ortíz Rubio** and then **Abelardo Rodríguez**, who were all controlled behind the scenes by Calles and his political allies, who steered national politics to the right in the bleak years of the 1930s Depression.

## The road to modern Mexico

By 1934 Mexico enjoyed a limited degree of peace. A new culture had emerged – seen nowhere more clearly than in the great murals of **Diego Rivera** and **José Clemente Orozco** that began to adorn public buildings throughout the country – in which native heroes like Hidalgo, Morelos, Juárez and Madero replaced European ideals. Everyone in the Republic claimed Indian blood – even if the Indians themselves remained the lowest stratum of society – and the invasion of Cortés was seen as the usurpation of the nation's march to its destiny, a march which resumed with Independence and the Revolution. At the same time, there was a fear in these early days that Calles was attempting to promote a dynasty of his own.

With the election of **Lázaro Cárdenas** in 1934, such doubts were finally laid to rest. As the spokesman of a younger generation, Cárdenas expelled Calles and his supporters from the country, simultaneously setting up the single broad-based party that was to rule for the next 71 years, the **PRI** (Party of the Institutional Revolution). He set about an unprecedented programme of reform, redistributing land on a huge scale (170,000 square kilometres during his six-year term), creating peasant and worker organizations to represent their interests at national level and incorporating them into the governing party. He also relaxed controls on the Church to appease internal and international opposition.

In 1938 Cárdenas nationalized the **oil companies**, an act which has proved one of the most significant in shaping modern Mexico and bringing about its industrialization. For a time it seemed as if yet more foreign intervention might follow, but a boycott of Mexican oil by the major consumers crumbled with the onset of **World War II** (apart from Neville Chamberlain, who cut off diplomatic relations and lost Great Britain an important investment market as a result), and was followed by a massive influx of money and a huge boost for Mexican industry as a result of the war. By the time he stood down in 1940, Cárdenas could claim to be the first president in modern Mexican history to have served his full six-year term in peace, and to have handed over to his successor without trouble.

Through the war industrial growth continued apace under **Manual Ávila Camacho**, and Mexico officially joined the Allies in 1942. **Miguel Alemán** (1946–52) presided over still faster development, and a further massive dose of public works and land reform – major prestige projects, like the University City in the capital, were planned by his regime. Over the next thirty years or so, massive oil income continued to stimulate industry, and the PRI maintained a masterly control of all aspects of public life. Though it is an accepted fact that governments will line their own pockets first – a practice which apparently reached its height under **José López Portillo** (1976–82) – the unrelenting populism of the PRI, its massive powers of patronage and, above all, its highly visible and undoubted progress maintained it in power with amazingly little dissent.

This is not to say there were no problems. The year **1959** saw the repression of a national railway strike during which ten thousand workers lost their jobs and their leaders were jailed. In **1968** hundreds of students were massacred in Tlatelolco Square in Mexico City in the government's heavy-handed attempt to stem the pro-democracy student movement that threatened Mexico's image as the Olympic Games neared (Mexico's were the first Olympics to be held in the "Third World" and were seen as an opportunity to promote the regime). The PRI was unable to buy off the students due to their rotating leadership, and unwilling to negotiate for fear of losing face. Although the massacre did put an end to student unrest, or at least any public manifestation of it, after Tlatelolco the opposition gradually saw fewer reasons for working within the system; guerrilla movements sprang up in Guerrero state, for example. The PRI was still very much in control, however, and snuffed these movements out by the mid-1970s.

## Economic crisis

All this said, the PRI seemed to be losing its populist touch: the years between 1970 and 1982, later dubbed the "**Docena Trágica**" (tragic dozen), saw flourishing corruption and economic mismanagement destroy the hopes brought about by the development of the oil industry, and by 1982 Mexico had run up a foreign debt of almost $100 billion. As a result, the government of **Miguel de la Madrid** (1982–88) found itself faced with economic crisis on a national and international scale. A US-educated financier, he adopted **austerity measures** imposed by the World Bank. Such policies won acclaim from international bankers, but at home they produced massive unemployment and drastically reduced standards of living (the average wage-earner lost fifty percent of his or her purchasing power), and inflation was barely held down to one hundred percent a year. An exploding population only added to the country's problems, and the huge level of illegal **emigration** to the US had little impact. The business community suffered too, with the nationalization of the banks in 1982, then a series of bankruptcies and a devaluation of the peso by 55 percent, which made imported materials almost impossible to afford. With no sign of economic recovery, some of the wide panoply of interests covered by the PRI – from the all-powerful unions to the top businessmen – began to split off.

This movement against the PRI was exacerbated in 1985, when a huge **earthquake** hit the capital. The quake, which had a magnitude of 8.1 on the Richter scale, revealed widespread corruption, as the government tried to hide the inadequacy of official rescue efforts by preventing ordinary people from organizing their own. Furthermore, many of the buildings that collapsed were government-owned and turned out to have been constructed using inferior materials. Grass-roots organizations sprang up in response, marking the beginning of a modern civil society, as they pressed the government for specific rebuilding programmes as well as on questions of broader social concerns such as lack of housing and police corruption.

Opposition also grew outside the capital. The right-wing party **PAN** (National Action Party), which had been established in 1939 in support of Catholic rebels and in opposition to what would become the PRI, won a string of minor elections in the north (and were cheated out of the state governorship of Chihuahua by blatant fraud in 1986), while in the south a socialist/peasant alliance held power for a while in Juchitán (Oaxaca) before being ousted by strong-arm tactics. These episodes highlighted the increasing polarization of the country. In the north, where life was heavily influenced by the US, business and ranching interests held sway. In the south, where peasants continued to press for more land redistribution, opposition was far more radical and left-wing, alternately inspired and intimidated by events in Central America.

In this climate, the **1988 election** was certainly dramatic – even though, predictably, the PRI candidate, **Carlos Salinas de Gortari**, won. Into the contest between PRI, PAN and a number of splinter groups, however, a formidable new challenger emerged in the form of **Cuauhtémoc Cárdenas**, son of the much-loved Lázaro. Cárdenas split from the PRI a year before the election and succeeded in uniting the Mexican left behind him (under the banner of the National Democratic Front, or **FDN**) for the first time since the Revolution. Cárdenas officially won 31 percent of the vote, although the results took a week to appear after the "breakdown" of the electoral computer at a point when Cárdenas was clearly in the lead. Salinas emerged from the tarnished contest with 50.48 percent of the vote, while the PAN leader, **Manuel Clouthier** (previously the only serious challenger), came third with 17 percent. Opposition parties won seats in the Senate for almost the first time since the PRI came to power.

Salinas undertook to pave the way for a new multiparty democracy in Mexico. As a relatively young, internally chosen candidate, he had little following either within the PRI itself or the country as a whole, and began by announcing a clean-up **campaign against corruption**, starting with the arrest of the notorious head of the PEMEX oil workers' union. Salinas also created a human rights commission to investigate abuses, and ended direct government control over PIPSA, the official monopoly newsprint supplier. Early signs were thus encouraging. Despite PAN leader Manuel Clouthier's death in suspicious circumstances in 1989 and controversial victories by the PRI in various state elections, Salinas managed to secure widespread support through the radical nature of his **economic policy**, in which he was able to reduce the foreign debt by almost half in three years. He also continued to privatize state-owned companies (with the choicest ones, such as TelMex, going to hand-picked bidders). The compliant **television media** helped foster the image of the president. This was not a new phenomenon, but the backing of media barons, who benefited from Salinas's deregulation of the media, helped the PRI sweep the board during the 1991 mid-term elections.

In the meantime, Cuauhtémoc Cárdenas was able to harness his success in 1988 by forming the **PRD** (Party of the Democratic Revolution). Its radical platform opposed privatization and any tinkering with the *ejido* system (see below), though in the following years, this stance has been tempered significantly. The PAN, with the PRI moving to the right, found its support base being eroded, although it enjoyed unprecedented electoral gains.

Within a few years, it was clear that the long-term effects of Salinas's economic policy were not positive. By 1993, nearly forty million Mexicans were living below the official **poverty** line (about half the population), while 24 were listed in the Forbes list of the 500 wealthiest men in the world, most grown rich on privatized utilities. Salinas was committed to reducing the public debt and encouraging private investment, which he achieved by drastically cutting public spending. To boost foreign investment, Salinas expanded the "**maquiladora**" programme, which allowed foreign companies to set up assembly plants along the US–Mexican border while enjoying substantial tax concessions. He also pushed through the North American Free Trade Agreement (**NAFTA**; **TLC** in Spanish), which created a free market between Canada, the US and Mexico. Theoretically, a free market, with each country benefiting from its own comparative advantage, should increase trade levels to a degree in which all the participants would gain. In this case, the Mexican economy would be spurred to expand to the level of its partners, allowing Mexico to enter the "First World". Most Mexicans, with significant foresight, suspected that the agreement would provide little benefit, allowing US companies to offload polluting industries to Mexico and take advantage of cheap labour – Mexico's "comparative advantage".

Additional upheaval came from Salinas's modifications to the Revolutionary legacy. Diplomatic relations with the Vatican, severed during the Revolution, were re-established, and the pope visited Mexico for the first time. The national oil company, **PEMEX**, was split into smaller units to improve productivity, and foreign oil companies were allowed to prospect for deposits. The most important change, however, was the amendment of Article 27 of the constitution. This article had been written to protect communal village landholdings, known as **ejidos**; under Salinas, their status shifted from state property to private property, allowing them to be sold.

Despite, and maybe because of, these unpopular moves, Salinas began to be seen as a strong presidential figure who had given the PRI a new lease on life. The crisis and upheavals of earlier days finally seemed to have been left behind.

## The Chiapas uprising

All this changed on New Year's Day 1994, when NAFTA took effect and an armed guerrilla movement known as the **Zapatista Army of National Liberation** (EZLN) took control of San Cristóbal de las Casas and four other municipalities in the state of Chiapas. The guerrillas were mainly indigenous villagers; they demanded an end to the feudal system of land tenure in Chiapas, free elections, the repeal of NAFTA and the restoration of Article 27 of the constitution. The government reacted with a predictable use of force, committing numerous human-rights abuses along the way, including the bombing of civilians and the torture and murder of prisoners, particularly in the town of Ocosingo. Long hidden from the world, the repressive side of the Mexican state – together with the plight of the country's indigenous peoples – was front-page news throughout the world. To Salinas's credit, he prepared the ground for peace negotiations by ordering a cease-fire within twelve days.

At the beginning, **negotiations** progressed with remarkable speed. The government representative, Manuel Camacho Solís, ex-mayor of Mexico City, made concessions to the guerrillas, upstaging the PRI presidential candidate, Luis Donaldo Colosio, who remained silent about the conflict. Camacho Solís was assisted by the bishop of San Cristóbal, Samuel Ruíz, a champion of Indian rights in Chiapas and an advocate of liberation theology (many on the right have since accused the diocese of San Cristóbal of fostering the subversion, though with little apparent evidence; the Vatican even attempted to recall Ruíz to explain himself in the middle of negotiations). The real star of the talks was **Subcomandante Marcos** of the EZLN, the main spokesman for the Zapatistas. The Balaclava-clad, pipe-smoking guerrilla became a cult hero, his speeches and communiqués full of literary allusions and passionate rhetoric. Negotiations ended in March, when an accord was drawn together. The EZLN then sent the accord back to its community bases for them to vote on it. The decision to fight or negotiate was not made easy by the different languages and dialects spoken and the inaccessibility of many villages. While the accord was being considered, the army and the guerrillas maintained an uneasy truce, and Mexicans were given ample time to dwell on events in Chiapas.

The results of the accord were not to be ready for months, but in the meantime, the saying "Nothing happens in Mexico . . . until it does", was proved true on March 23, when **Luis Donaldo Colosio** was shot dead while campaigning in the border city of Tijuana. It was the first **assassination** of such a prominent government figure since 1928. Despite the presence of Colosio's bodyguards, the shooter, a former policeman, managed to fire from point-blank range, fuelling conspiracy theories similar to those surrounding the assassination of John F. Kennedy.

One such theory proposed a connection to Tijuana's **cocaine cartels** – a situation not without precedent, as the previous year the archbishop of Guadalajara had been shot dead, reportedly caught in the crossfire between warring drug gangs. Others speculated that both these murders had been carried out from within the PRI itself: the so-called party "**dinosaurs**", those committed to maintaining the status quo, felt threatened by moves to democratize the political system, which had been galvanized by the Chiapas negotiations. According to this theory, Colosio had been planning democratic reforms, and his murder was calculated to remove the threat he posed. When another prominent reformer, PRI general secretary José Francisco Ruíz Massieu, was gunned down in Mexico City in 1994, suspicions of a ruling-party plot were only strengthened. Colosio's successor as presidential candidate, **Ernesto Zedillo Ponce de León**, was a minor PRI apparatchik, and in this climate of insecurity and violence the **elections of August 1994** did not augur well.

In June the EZLN rejected the accord with the government, and in July a leftist candidate for the governorship of Chiapas, Amado Avendaño Figueroa, met with a suspicious "accident" when a truck with no numberplates collided with his car, killing three passengers; Avendaño lost an eye. It was no surprise, then, that the PRI again triumphed: Zedillo gained 48 percent of the vote for president; Diego de Cevallos, the PAN candidate, 31 percent; and Cuáhtemoc Cárdenas for the **PRD** (the radical Party for the Democratic Revolution he'd founded six years earlier), only 16 percent. The PRI also won all the senatorial races and the governorship of Chiapas. The scale of the vote (75 percent voter participation) and the presence of foreign observers at an election for the first time left little doubt that the PRI had managed yet again to defy all attempts to remove it.

Once the results were announced, the situation began almost immediately to deteriorate. In **Chiapas** Avendaño declared himself "rebel governor" after denouncing the elections as fraudulent; as many as half the municipalities in the state refused to pay taxes. Both the PRD and the EZLN supported his move. The EZLN warned that if the PRI candidate, Eduardo Robledo, was sworn in, the truce with the government would be at an end. By this point Chiapas was essentially in a state of **civil war**. Ranchers and landowners organized paramilitary **death squads** to counter a mobilized peasantry. Land seizures and roadblocks were met with assassinations and intimidation, and a build-up of federal troops in the state exacerbated the situation.

On January 8, 1995, Zedillo attended the swearing-in of the PRI governor of Chiapas. Ten days later, the EZLN deployed its forces, breaking the army cordon surrounding its positions and moving into 38 municipalities (it had previously been confined to four). That this was accomplished, as was their later retreat, virtually undetected, even under the watchful eyes of government troops, showed their familiarity with the terrain, their discipline and the folly of the "surgical strike" tactic that many in the military had been contemplating.

The EZLN's timing could not have been worse for the government. The previous month had seen Salinas's term ending in a sudden, surprise slide in the economy, with the **peso devalued** by almost half and wages plummeting (the period was later dubbed "the December Mistake"). Following the Chiapas action, what little foreign capital remained was yanked out, resulting in further cuts in salaries. In the meantime, unemployment rose drastically, and IMF austerity measures were again imposed to pay for a debt run up by the government. Public anger turned on Salinas, who was now said to have kept the peso artificially high to hide economic problems. On this tide of discontent, the PAN prosecutor arrested **Raúl Salinas**, brother of the president, in February; later in the year, Ruíz Massieu's brother Mario was caught in the US with millions of dollars of suspected drug money. Both were accused of complicity in the 1994 murder of José Francisco Ruiz Massieu. Although the two were never convicted (Mario committed suicide in 1999, while fighting extradition; Raúl was acquitted in 2005, though inextricably linked to money laundering for drug cartels), it was clear that the most cynical conspiracy theorists had been closest to the mark.

In March 1995, apparently under pressure from the US, Zedillo launched an offensive against the EZLN. Thousands of peasants, terrified by the army and by right-wing landowners' paramilitary groups, left their villages, becoming internal refugees. Exercising the military option was a high-risk strategy for Zedillo: the EZLN enjoyed considerable public sympathy, especially in view of its largely non-violent methods. Even unmasking Subcomandante Marcos as (allegedly) **Rafael Guillén**, a philosophy professor educated in Mexico City, failed to affect his popularity – indeed, cries of "Guillén for president" became common at opposition rallies. In a rapid U-turn, the government called off the army and set up **new negotiations**.

These proved to be even more protracted than the 1994 talks, but eventually resulted in the **San Andrés Accords on Rights and Indigenous Cultures** (named after the village near San Cristóbal where the talks took place), signed in February 1996. The accords guaranteed indigenous representation in national and state legislatures, but their implementation required constitutional and legislative changes that Zedillo failed to push through Congress. Relations between the Zapatistas and the government negotiators, characterized by mutual distrust, were strained to breaking point, and in September the EZLN suspended talks.

The remorseless increase of the military presence on the Zapatistas' perimeter appeared to give the paramilitary groups even greater freedom to operate. This culminated in the December 1997 **Acteal Massacre**: 45 displaced Tzotzil Indians, 36 of them women and children, were murdered at a prayer meeting by forces linked to PRI officials. The killings brought worldwide condemnation, and Zedillo had to act to show that the federal government still ran Chiapas. He announced an official investigation into the massacre and ordered the arrest of those suspected of taking part. The next month, Interior Minister Emilio Chuayffet and the governor of Chiapas, César Ruíz Ferro, resigned.

More troops were sent to the state, and the army even entered Zapatista strongholds on the pretext of searching for paramilitary arms. Emboldened by the weak EZLN response to these incursions, the army began to move against the municipalities set up by the Zapatistas. This betrayal of the principles of a negotiated settlement finally provoked Bishop Ruíz to resign as mediator in June 1998, causing the dissolution of the National Mediation Commission (CONAI). Negotiations broke down completely, leading some observers to conclude that the government had opted for a military strategy to overcome the Zapatistas.

One consequence of the increased international interest in Chiapas was the Mexican government's active campaign against *simpático* **foreigners**, whom it accused of instigating political unrest in the state. Several dozen foreign journalists, Church workers, human-rights observers and even scientists were detained and deported, and immigration officials subjected anyone they suspected of being a Zapatista sympathizer to questioning and harassment.

# The new millennium

Despite the crisis in Chiapas, Mexico's **political reforms** continued, with limits on campaign spending and the establishment of a federal electoral body in 1996. Subsequently, the PRI lost its majority in the Chamber of Deputies (the lower house of Congress) and as well as control of Mexico City. But the biggest change of all came on July 2, 2000, when **Vicente Fox Quesada**, the PAN candidate, was voted in as president. It was a landmark event: not only was he the first opposition candidate ever to have been democratically placed in power, it was also the first peaceful transition between opposing governments since Independence. Most remarkably, though, it was the end of seven decades of PRI rule – in fact, since the collapse of Communism in the Soviet Union, Mexico had been living under the world's longest-lasting one-party dynasty.

A former Coca-Cola executive and governor of Guanajuato, the media-savvy, fiscally conservative Fox had wooed the business sector and wowed the general public with his campaign promise of *cambio* ("change"), encouraging hopes that he would shake up the system of political patronage and corruption. However, little of the much-vaunted *cambio* was realized: Fox's ambitions for constitutional and structural reforms were hampered by the fractured nature of PAN and by the PRI, which still controlled Congress, more than half the state governorships and most of the bureaucracy. In spite of his political shortcomings, the president for the most part retained his popularity, and set the stage well for the July 2006 election – which, in many ways, was even more crucial than the previous one, as it would either prove the PAN victory a fluke or help consolidate the party's power.

Unfortunately, it is still not clear whether PAN passed its test. Fox's would-be successor was **Felipe Calderón**, the former energy secretary (who actually quit his post in protest against Fox). His campaign started easily enough, with polls showing him well ahead of his main opponent, the PRD's **Andrés Manuel López Obrador** (AMLO to his supporters), the very popular leftist former mayor of Mexico City. For the first time, the PRI was a negligible factor. But Obrador drew attention to Calderón's association with Fobaproa, a somewhat suspect government organization that had bailed out banks after the 1994 economic crisis, as well as participating in some other questionable financial dealings.

At the same time, the Zapatista movement had resurfaced in a broader form: Subcomandante Marcos had proclaimed himself "Candidate Zero" and was leading the **Otra Campaña** ("other campaign"), a tour through every state in the country, endorsing no candidate but drumming up fervour for workers' rights and other populist issues. Another unexpected factor in the election was a teachers' strike for higher wages in **Oaxaca**, which began in May 2006 when the PRI-affiliated governor, Ulises Ruíz Ortíz (who had been previously accused of rigging his 2004 election), attempted to evict the teachers' sit-in with rubber bullets and gas. The ad-hoc **APPO** (Popular Assembly of the Peoples of Oaxaca), a collection of community organizations, had mobilized around the teachers and claimed leadership of the state to gain greater rights for the poor and the indigenous (largely the same, in this case).

These two left-leaning movements helped boost Obrador's standing, and the election **results**, officially delivered on July 6 (after four days of review) showed Calderón with 35.89 percent and Obrador with 35.31 percent – a difference of 0.58 percent, or 243,934 votes. The numbers told the story of a divided Mexico – every state north of the capital (for the most part, the wealthier part of the country) supported Calderón, while Obrador took all of the poor, southern states with large indigenous populations. The only exception in the south was Yucatán state, not coincidentally home to a substantial upper class. The gulf between the two blocs was vast: many derided the leftist as "Loco Obrador" and "AM-Loco" (just plain crazy), while Obrador's fiery speeches and meetings with Venezuela's Hugo Chávez seemed like throwbacks to an era of Latin American Communism that Mexico had managed to largely avoid.

With the decision so close, the battle immediately went to the courts. Obrador alleged irregularities and demanded a complete recount. Millions of his supporters took to the streets, occupying the Zócalo in Mexico City and scores of other cities. After the electoral court confirmed Calderón's victory in late

August, Obrador declared himself head of an **alternative government**, and urged his followers to continue their resistance.

Meanwhile, the confrontation in Oaxaca had grown violent – another uncomfortable reminder that Mexico had not completely shed its "Third World" image. As the APPO continued to occupy Oaxaca's main square and run roadblocks to shut down transport, PRI-sponsored paramilitary groups tried to intimidate the protesters (the same strategy used in Chiapas a decade earlier). When an American freelance activist/journalist was shot in late October, Fox (still president at this point) finally sent in the federal police, which led to additional deaths and alarming images of heavily armed *federales* facing down rock-throwing protesters amid the rubble that once was a gem of a colonial plaza. By the end of November, most of the APPO leaders had been arrested, and Governor Ruíz was still in place.

Many Mexicans were simply relieved when Calderón was sworn in to the presidency peacefully on December 1, 2006. The fallout from the battle in Oaxaca and the fight for the election remains to be seen – the coming years will test whether Mexico's democratic structures are strong enough to weather this kind of internal dissent. Police corruption and the drug cartels are ongoing problems, as is the country's relationship with the US – the 370-mile **border fence** proposed by President Bush in 2006 was a rather brutal symbol of how intractable the debate over **illegal immigration** has become. Overall, though, Mexico has swelled into the world's twelfth largest economy and now exports more than all other Latin American countries combined; if that progress can be maintained, the future looks bright.

# Chronology

**11,000 BC ▸** First waves of Stone Age migrants from the north. Earliest evidence of humans in the central valleys.

**8000–2000 BC ▸** Archaic period. First evidence of settlement – cultivation, pottery and tools in the Valley of México.

**2000 BC–250 AD ▸** Pre-Classic period. The first simple pyramids and magnificent statuary at the Gulf coast sites – San Lorenzo, La Venta and Tres Zapotes. Rise and dominance of the Olmecs. Olmec influence on art and architecture everywhere, especially Monte Albán. Early evidence of new cultures in the Valley of México – Cuicuilco (buried by volcano) and Teotihuacán.

**250–900 AD ▸** Classic period. Teotihuacán dominates central Mexico, with evidence of its influence as far south as Kaminaljuyu in Guatemala. Massive pyramids at Teotihuacán, decorated with stucco reliefs and murals. Monte Albán continues to thrive, while El Tajín on the Gulf coast shows a new style in its Pyramid of the Niches. Maya cities flourish in the highlands of Guatemala and Honduras, as well as the Mexican Yucatán: all the great sites – Uxmal, Palenque, Chichén Itzá, Edzná, Kabáh – are at their peak, with Puuc, Chenes and Río Bec styles as perhaps the finest pre-Hispanic architecture.

**900–1520 AD ▸** Post-Classic. In central Mexico, a series of invasions by warlike tribes from the north. Toltecs make their capital at Tula (c.900–1150); new use of columns and roofed space – Chac-mools and Atlantean columns in decoration.

**987 ▸** New Toltec–Maya synthesis (through trade or invasion) especially evident at Chichén Itzá.

**C10 ▸** Mixtecs gain control of Oaxaca area. Mixtec tombs at Monte Albán, but seen above all at Mitla.

**C11 ▸** League of Mayapán, a confederation of city-states in the Yucatán. Maya architecture in decline, as Mayapán itself clearly demonstrates.

**C13 ▸** Arrival of the Mexica in central Mexico. Many rival cities in the Valley of México, including Tenayuca, Texcoco and Culhuacán.

**1345 ▸** Foundation of Tenochtitlán – rapid expansion of the Aztec empire and growth of all the great Aztec cities, especially Tenochtitlán itself. In the east, cities such as Cholula and Zempoala fall under Aztec influence, and in the south the Mixtecs are conquered. To the west, Purépecha (or Tarascan) culture is developing, with their capital at Tzintzuntzan. Maya culture now concentrated in coastal cities such as Tulum.

**1519 ▸** Cortés lands in present-day Veracruz.

**1521 ▸** Tenochtitlán falls to the Spanish, who destroy many ancient cities. Early colonial architecture is defensive and fortress-like; churches and mansions in Mexico City and elsewhere; monasteries with huge atriums for mass conversions. Gradually replaced by more elaborate Renaissance and Plateresque styles – seen best in churches in the colonial cities north of the capital.

**1524** ▶ First Franciscan monks arrive.

**1598** ▶ Conquest officially complete.

**C17–C18** ▶ Colonial rulers grow in wealth and confidence. Baroque begins to take over religious building – great cathedrals at Mexico City and Puebla, lesser ones at Zacatecas, for example. Towards the end the still more extravagant churrigueresque appears: magnificent churches around Puebla and at Taxco and Tepotzotlán.

**1810** ▶ Hidalgo proclaims Independence. Development of the Neoclassical style through the influence of the new San Carlos art academy, but little building in the next fifty chaotic years.

**1821** ▶ Independence achieved.

**1836** ▶ Texas declares independence – battles of the Alamo and San Jacinto.

**1838** ▶ Brief French invasion.

**1845** ▶ Texas allies with the US in the Mexican–American War.

**1847** ▶ US troops occupy Mexico City.

**1848** ▶ Half of Mexican territory ceded to US by treaty.

**1858–61** ▶ Reform Wars between liberals under Benito Juárez and Church-backed conservatives. Many churches damaged or despoiled.

**1861** ▶ Juárez triumphant; suspends payment of foreign debt. France, Spain and Britain send naval expeditions.

**1862** ▶ Spain and Britain withdraw – invading French army defeated on May 5.

**1863** ▶ French take Mexico City. Maximilian becomes emperor. Brief vogue for French styles. Paseo de la Reforma and Chapultepec Castle built in the capital.

**1866** ▶ French troops withdraw.

**1867** ▶ Juárez defeats Maximilian.

**1876** ▶ Porfirio Díaz accedes to power. Porfiriato period sees an outbreak of Neoclassical and grandiose public building. Palacio de las Bellas Artes and Post Office in Mexico City. Theatres and public buildings throughout the country.

**1910** ▶ Francisco Madero stands for election, sparking the Revolution. Another period of destruction.

**1911** ▶ Díaz flees into exile.

**1911–17** ▶ Vicious revolutionary infighting continues.

**1920 on** ▶ Modern Mexico. Modern architecture in Mexico is among the world's most original and adventurous, combining traditional decorative colours with streamlined forms and technology. Vast decorative murals are one of its constant themes. The Museo Nacional de Antropología and University City in the capital are among its most notable achievements.

# Ball-games and sacrifice: the pre-Columbian belief system

The Spanish Conquest and subjugation of Mesoamerica saw the destruction of more than just the physical culture of some of the most advanced societies in the world at the time. More important for the Spanish were the suppression of "alien" cultures and the propagation of Catholicism. All traces of traditional religion and culture were to be rooted out. In their attempts to do these things, hundreds of thousands of books were burnt, priests executed and temples overturned. Such is the tenacity of traditional beliefs, though, that even five hundred years of effort have not been enough to eradicate them entirely, as anyone who has entered a rural Mexican church or witnessed the rituals of the Day of the Dead can attest.

Much of our knowledge of ancient Mesoamerican beliefs is derived from the surviving traditions of contemporary indigenous groups, which have been handed down through the generations. Further fragments are gleaned from various Spanish accounts, from hieroglyphs and images carved into ruined buildings, from sculpture and pottery, from jewellery retrieved from tombs and from the few surviving written records.

## Shamanism: the root of Mesoamerican culture

By all appearances, the great **Mesoamerican civilizations** comprised some of the purest **theocracies** the world has known. Every aspect of life was a part of a cosmic interplay between the material world and the dreamlike spirit world. This spirit world was home to a pantheon of gods and the souls of dead ancestors. The priests and kings who governed Mesoamerica had privileged access to this realm, communicating with its denizens while in a state of trance, predicting the effect of the spiritual on the material from the motion of the stars, and maintaining the balance between the two worlds, thus avoiding misfortune or disaster. Every part of life was sacred, as were the days of the week and the cardinal points with their associated deities and spiritual properties. Every event, from the planting of crops to the waging of war, had to occur at the correct spiritual time.

This elaborate belief system had its roots in **shamanism**, whose origins pre-date agriculture and settled village life. This is still the religion of the nomadic communities of Siberia, whose ancestors were the first to populate the Americas. In the shamanic universe everything is alive, not only in the material world but, more truly, in the spiritual. A rock has a soul every bit as much as a jaguar or a human being, and this soul can be separated from the physical form, a feat achieved by spiritually adept individuals known as shamans. The shaman's soul is able to travel through the spirit world, communing with gods, demons or ancestors or even appearing in the material world in another form, such as an animal. But the spirit world is an ambivalent place, containing both paradise, populated by the good, and its opposite, inhabited by gods and demons and the souls of the evil.

These malevolent and benevolent forces make the relationship between the **material and spiritual worlds** a delicate one. Disease, for instance, is not merely a physical condition; it is also a spiritual one which may result from the imprisoning of a soul by an evil spirit, or some other imbalance. The shaman, in a state of trance, can correct imbalances – journeying to free the soul, and thus making the material person well again. But in the shamanic universe, you rarely get something for nothing, and if a powerful spirit or a god is involved, sacrifice may be required to recompense that spirit.

The legacy of the shaman can still be found in Mexican religion. The Day of the Dead celebrations have their roots in a shamanic conception of the universe, as do the rituals of modern Mexican witchcraft. The best contemporary examples, though, are the belief systems of the tribes of northern Mexico, such as the **Yaqui** (whose shamanic traditions have been immortalized by Carlos Castaneda) or the **Huichol**. It is worth taking a more detailed look at the practices and beliefs of the latter for the light they throw on ancient belief systems.



## Huichol shamanism

In the province of Nayarit in the desert of northern Mexico, the **Huichol** have survived the dominance of the Aztecs, the Spanish Conquest of western Mexico, subsequent exploitation, the Revolution and the technological leaps of the twentieth century. More than any other people in Mexico, they have remained faithful to the spiritual beliefs of their ancestors, and their way of life has changed little in thousands of years.

Like all shamanic communities, the Huichol see the material and spirit worlds as two poles of one universe. The border between the two is blurred: the communities are in regular communication with their dead ancestors, most of who live in the underworld, and who often sneak back into the world of the living to steal their maize beer. The spirit world is used as a constant reference for occurrences in the material, with shamans, known as **maracames**, providing the readings that inform the community. However, two facets of Huichol cosmology – the orientation of their sacred buildings to the four cardinal points and a belief in a "first place" where their ancestors had been gods – stand out as distinctly Mesoamerican.

The most important Huichol structures, **xirikis**, are precisely aligned with north, south, east and west, each of which has a particular spiritual connotation. Each *xiriki* is home to a disembodied ancestral shaman whose soul inhabits a quartz crystal attached to a ceremonial arrow lodged in the roof. Contemporary shamans use the spiritual strength of these crystals to travel to the Huichol spirit world.

The centre of this spirit world is called **Wirikuta**. In the everyday, physical world, this is a dull stretch of desert in northwest Mexico, some 500km from Nayarit. In the spiritual world it is the Huichol womb of creation – the ground from which the sky and the stars emerged at the beginning of time, and the paradise where humans were created by the gods, and where for a while they lived with them as equals. The Huichol frequently visit Wirikuta in pilgrimages that involve taking peyote to induce trance-like states. A shaman guide orchestrates key rituals throughout the journey to protect the pilgrims from deceitful spirits, and interprets the landscape along the way: a waterhole becomes a spiritual gateway; shreds of cactus, the bones of ancestors. Plants, animals, rivers and mountains all have associated spirits and an individual, symbolic, sacred meaning.

Every aspect of Huichol life is filled with symbolism. Their bright weavings and intricate beaded masks reflect the spiritual reality behind the material, often depicting the three most sacred symbols of all – **corn**, the substance of creation; **deer**, hunted for food but also revered; and **peyote**, the trance-inducing cactus. Gourds covered in brightly coloured beads, spelling out the wishes of their maker, are offered to the gods as sacrifices.

## The Olmecs: the roots of Mesoamerican shamanism

Archeological research at **Olmec** sites tells us that many of the Huichol's beliefs were common to the first great Mesoamerican civilization, whose cities and preoccupations formed a template traced by subsequent cultures. The Olmecs were the first Mesoamerican civilization literally to set their cosmology in stone, making a record of their rulers, and the gods and spirits with whom they communed. Like the Huichol, they had a place of creation: the mighty volcano of **San Martín** in the south of modern Veracruz state. They built a replica – a sacred artificial mountain, complete with fluted sides – in their city at **La Venta**. This was the original Mesoamerican **pyramid**, a feature that recurred in virtually every society that followed: the Classic Maya conceived of their cities as a living landscape of artificial mountains and trees, while the Aztec Templo Mayor was a dual pyramid representing the two sacred mountains of Coatepec and Tonacatepetl.

Into the base of their volcano pyramid the Olmecs embedded huge stone **stelae**, one portraying ruling dignitaries communicating with gods and spirits – shamans, who, because of their crucial role in maintaining the balance between the material and spiritual, had come to govern Olmec society. Such stelae (which perhaps shrank to become the Huichol rooftop arrowheads), seem to have been regarded as embodiments of the gods or kings they represented – spiritual telephones to the dead and the divine, whose users operated them in a trance state. These were the first stelae in Mesoamerica, and later versions fill the plazas of ruined cities all over Mexico and Central America.

One stele at La Venta depicts a **World Tree**, a symbol of the "axis mundi" at the centre of the Mesoamerican universe: its roots in the earth, its branches in the heavens, linking the underworld with the earth and sky. Though this was perhaps the first such representation, World Trees have been found in cities all over Mesoamerica and are portrayed in Teotihuacán mythology and in the **Codex Borgia**, one of the most beautiful of the few surviving Aztec books. At Maya Palenque there are several, including one on the lid of a ruler's sarcophagus: symbols and events of Maya mythology are written in the patterns and motion of the stars, and the ruler is shown falling through a World Tree inscribed in the night sky – the Milky Way.

Opposite Mexico's first pyramid, the Olmecs built a **gateway** to the shamanic spirit world in the form of a sunken, court-shaped plaza with an enormous pavement of blocks made of the mineral serpentine. They added two large platforms on either side of the entrance into the court and deposited huge quantities of sacred serpentine inside. These two platforms were topped with mosaics and patterns depicting aquatic plants, symbols of a gateway to the spirit world. Such symbols appeared all over Mesoamerica in the ensuing centuries, often decorating ball-courts or ceramics.

Other surviving artefacts speak of stranger shamanic aspects to Olmec religion. **Statuettes** of half-jaguar, half-human babies probably depict the awakening of latent shamanic powers and associations with spirit animals – in the Mesoamerican pantheon each soul has its companion spirit animal. **Mirrors** found at Olmec cities – made of highly polished minerals such as hematite – were symbols of portals to the spirit world, an idea developed by the Aztecs, whose god, Tezcatlipoca ("Smoking Mirror") governs shamans and sorcerers in the Toltec and Aztec pantheon. In the Aztec creation myth, Tezcatlipoca assisted Quetzalcoatl in the creation of the world.

The Olmec shaman-rulers also recompensed the gods and spirits through whom they kept the crucial balance between the material and the spiritual world. They probably developed human **sacrifice** and ritual blood-letting for this purpose. And though there were different emphases, the basic structure of Olmec society – a theocracy ruled over by a priestly and regal elite who communicated with and propitiated the spirit world through sacrifice – would change little throughout Mesoamerica until the advent of Cortés. But there were some important developments. An increasing preoccupation with divining and balancing the material and the spiritual led to the invention of the calendar and writing, and the ball-game and sacrifice became ever more crucial, particularly in central Mexico, where the appetites of the malevolent and bloodthirsty Mesoamerican gods increased with each new civilization.



## The calendar

The Mesoamericans believed that the relationship between the spirit and material worlds was recorded in the stars, and that certain astronomical configurations were ominous. For both the Maya and Aztecs, the stars were embodiments of gods and the constellations re-enactments of cosmic events. This preoccupation led to the invention of the **calendar**, probably by the Zapotecs of Monte Albán around 600 BC. Subsequent depictions of calendars can be seen across the spectrum of Mesoamerican art, notably on the Aztec Piedra del Sol (Sun Stone), now in the Museo Nacional de Antropología in Mexico City, and in the paintings in Maya codices.

By the time of the Classic Maya (250–900 AD), a 260-day calendar had become the fundamental map of the relationship between the spirit and material worlds, and the highest tool of prediction and divination outside the trance state itself. Every number and day had its own significance; each of the twenty day names was connected with a specific god and a particular direction, passing in a continuous anticlockwise path from one day to the next until a cycle of time was completed. This calendar was used alongside a 365-day calendar, roughly matching the solar year, but lacking the leap days necessary to give it real accuracy. This was divided into eighteen groups of twenty days plus an unlucky additional five days. Each twenty-day grouping and each solar year also had a supernatural patron. When the two calendars were set in motion and were running concurrently, it took exactly 52 years for the cycle to repeat. In addition to these two calendars, the pre-Classic Maya developed what is known as the **Long Count**, recording the total number of days elapsed since a mythological date when the first great cycle began (August 11, 3114 BC, to be exact). For Mesoamerican civilizations, the ending of one cycle and the beginning of another heralded apocalypse and, afterwards, a new age and a reassertion of the ordered world from the disordered and demonic; one symbol of this new age

△Piedra del Sol (Sun Stone)

was the construction of new temples over the old every 52 years. The Maya Long Count will end on December 23, 2012, and there are many who believe that this date will herald the end of the world that others predicted for the millennium.

## Sacrifice

At the beginning of the 365-day cycle, the Aztecs extinguished all fires and smashed all ceramics throughout their empire. At midnight, if the stars passed overhead, priests ripped out the heart of a warrior and started a new fire in his chest – for the Aztecs, **sacrifice** was crucial in maintaining harmony and the continuance of cosmic events. If the forces of the spirit world were not kept in balance, chaos and death would reign.

The ruling shaman-priests were vital to the continued existence of the world, and sacrifice was one of their main tools: Mesoamericans believed that they were not so much living on borrowed time, but on time won by trickery from the gods of death. Maya vases, buried with the dead, often depict scenes from the *Popul Vuh*, the creation epic of the Quiché Maya, in which the Hero Twins defeat the **Lords of the Underworld** through a series of shamanic tricks and their skill at the ball-game. Central Mexican mythology went still further: life is not won from death, it is quite literally stolen. In one story, Quetzalcoatl and Xolotl descend to the underworld, where they trick the god of death, Mictlantecuhtli, into giving them sacred bones left over from a previous creation. These bones are taken to the paradise of **Tamoanchán** – the central Mexican equivalent of the Huichol Wirikuta, or the Olmec San Martín – where they are ground into meal. The gods then let their blood into the ground meal, and humans are born. After the creation of people, the gods convene in darkness at Teotihuacán, where they decide to create a new sun. This, too, depends on sacrifice, and the two gods hurl themselves into a fiery furnace to become the sun and the moon.

The bloody creation mythology of central Mexico is filled with the presence of the Lords of the Underworld trying to regain the life that was stolen from them; none was more preoccupied with this than the Aztecs. The Aztec empire was enslaved to the Lords of the Underworld's seemingly insatiable appetite for **human hearts** – the price of continuing life and order. The conquistador Bernal Díaz recounts the sacrifice of fattened children, women and captured warriors with horror, and concludes that the Aztec priests were slaves of the powers of darkness, an idea suggested even in their own mythology. The great Toltec prince **Topiltzin Quetzalcoatl**, renowned for his wisdom and holiness and founder of the great city of Tula, decided to make an end to human sacrifice and attempted to convince the inhabitants of Tula to give it up. He was unsuccessful, however, as the shamanic god, Tezcatlipoca, tricked the Toltecs and forced Topiltzin Quetzalcoatl into exile. Topiltzin Quetzalcoatl built a raft and left "for the east" from the Gulf coast, promising to return one day to banish false rulers and reinstate a higher order, where human sacrifice would play no part. It is a well-known irony that Cortés landed on the Gulf coast, whence Topiltzin Quetzalcoatl was said to have left, at the time predicted for his return.

## The ball-game

The Mesoamerican **ball-game**, once played all over pre-Hispanic Mexico and Central America, and still played in some villages in Oaxaca and the northwest, seems to have been imbued with shamanic symbolism and the Mesoamerican mythology of death.

Like so much of Mesoamerican religious tradition, the game was developed by the Olmecs, probably from an earlier prototype. A carving dating back to 900 BC, found at the Olmec city of **San Lorenzo**, depicts a ball-player kneeling to receive a ball; ball-players were depicted at Dainzú, outside Oaxaca, sometime after 150 BC, and ball-courts appear in the pre-Classic Maya city of Izapa in Chiapas. The game was usually played in a ball-court shaped like the letter I. The players, in teams of two or three, would score points by hitting the ball with their upper arms or thighs, through hoops or at markers embedded in the court walls. Heavy bets were placed by supporters, and the penalty for losing the most important games was death (though there have been suggestions that the winners were sacrificed in some cities).

The Classic Veracruz civilization was obsessed with the ball-game – there are more than seventeen courts in their most important city, **El Tajín**. Most are covered with superb bas-reliefs showing all aspects of the game, including sacrifice: one depicts a player having his chest cut open while a grinning skeleton rises from a pot. This figure appears in many of the carvings at Tajín, and is almost certainly an underworld lord – a personification of death. In Maya mythology, the ball-game is played against the Lords of the Underworld, most famously by the Hero Twins of the *Popul Vuh*. The largest court at **Chichén Itzá** is covered in bas-reliefs of aquatic plants, which are traditionally associated with an opening to the underworld. Still more depict the death rituals that were associated with the game. One shows a player holding the severed head of a captive. The stump of his neck spouts serpents – symbols of the spiritual life force contained in blood – which transform into water lilies, showing how the sacrifice opens the way to the spirit world.

# Environment and wildlife

Mexico is one of the world's most biologically diverse countries, with the second highest number of mammal species (about 450, after Indonesia), more than a thousand species of birds, at least 30,000 species of higher plants (including half of the world's pines) and more reptile species (700) than anywhere else on the globe. Many of these are endemic, and this diversity, combined with the country's vast size (1,960,000 square kilometres) and tremendous range of natural environments, make Mexico an ideal location for the visiting naturalist, irrespective of expertise.

Unfortunately, as in many developing countries, much of Mexico's natural beauty is under threat either from direct hunting or from the indirect effects of **deforestation** and **commercialization**. It is imperative that we, as paying visitors, show a responsible attitude to the natural environment, and endeavour to support the educational programmes that are seeking to preserve these remnants. It should be stressed that not only is it extremely irresponsible to buy, even as souvenirs, items that involve wild animals in their production, but it is also generally **illegal** to bring them back to the UK or the US. This applies specifically to tortoiseshell; black coral; various species of butterfly, mussels and snails; stuffed baby crocodiles; cat skins; and turtle shells. Trade in living animals, including tortoises, iguanas and parrots (often sold as nestlings) is also illegal, as is the uprooting of cacti.

## Geography and climate

The distinct geographical pattern seen in Mexico, in conjunction with the climatic variation from north to south, creates a series of isolated **biomes**, each with its individual flora and fauna. The **Tropic of Cancer** divides the country laterally, technically placing half the country inside and half outside the tropics.

The predominant geographical features tend to be southward continuations of formations in the US: the **Sierra Madre Oriental**, which lies to the east is an extension of the Rocky Mountain range, and the **Sierra Madre Occidental**, which lies to the west and is an extension of the **Sierra Nevada** range. The highlands between and the intermontane basins form the lofty **Northern Plateau**, which extends from Mexico City to the western tablelands of the US. Further south (between latitudes 18 and 20 degrees north) is the range of volcanoes known as the **Sierra Volcánica Transversal**, which rises in altitude towards its southern edge and runs from the Pacific coast almost as far as the Gulf of Mexico. The lands south of this range are coastal plains and plateaus – the low-lying Yucatán, for one – with intermittent higher ranges, such as the **Oaxaca** and **Chiapas uplands**.

Most of the landmass is subject to the prevailing **trade winds** that blow from the northeast out across the Gulf of Mexico. Cool currents keep the Pacific coastal waters colder and the air drier than the Atlantic coast, while the sharp escarpments of the Sierra Madre Oriental, creating a vast rain shadow, contribute to the aridity of the Northern Plateau. Rainfall is variable, scant in the arid deserts of the north Pacific and interior sierras and extremely heavy in the tropical cloud forests and rainforests of the southeastern slopes of the **Sierra Madre del Sur** and sections of the Gulf coast (the **rainy season** itself extends from late May to Oct or Nov).

# Vegetation

The influence of long-term **deforestation** for charcoal or slash-and-burn agriculture has substantially denuded the forest that originally covered large areas of Mexico. Today the northern mountains contain tracts of conifer, cedar and oak, especially around Durango, where the largest **pine forest** reserves are found. At lower altitudes, grass-covered **savannas** are interrupted by the occasional palm or palmetto tree, and the riverbanks are graced with poplar and willow. **Tropical rainforests**, which border the Gulf of Mexico, form a band that extends southwards from Tampico across the base of the Yucatán Peninsula and northern Oaxaca. They contain mahogany, cedar, rosewood, ebony and logwood. **Seasonal tropical forest** and **dry scrub** cover the remaining areas of the Gulf coast and the lowlands of the Pacific coast. One particularly notable tree is a single **ahuehuete** (Montezuma cypress) in the state of Oaxaca, which measures 36m around; it's alleged to be at least 1200 years old.

Extensive **mangrove forests** once lined much of the Gulf coast and the Caribbean, and grew along sheltered reaches of the Pacific shore, but tourism growth along the coasts has eaten away at the swamps – a short-sighted move, as runoff from the trees' root systems nourish the coral reefs that draw tourists in the first place. Laws are in place to protect these zones, but there always seems to be room to squeeze in one more hotel.

The flatter lands of the north, the north Pacific and portions of central Mexico are characterized by dry scrub and grassland – better known as the **Sonoran** and **Chihuahuan Deserts**, though they are hardly the empty sands that the term "desert" conjures. The most conspicuous vegetation here is the **cacti**. Various species adorn these flatlands: the **saguaro** is a giant, tree-like growth which can exceed 15m in height, whereas the columns of the **cereus** cactus stand in lines, not dissimilar to fence posts, and can reach 8m. Another notable variety is the **prickly pear** (*nopal*) which produces a fruit (*tuna*) that can be eaten raw or used in the production of sweets. Other harvested varieties include the pulpy-leaved **maguey cactus** (a member of the agave family), whose fermented juice forms the basis of tequila, mescal and *pulque*, and **henequen** (another agave), which is grown extensively on the Yucatán Peninsula and used in the production of rope. The temperate grasslands are composed primarily of clumped bunch grass and wiry, unpalatable **curly mesquite**. Low-lying shrubs found amongst these grassy expanses include spindly ocotillo, **creosote** bush and palm-like **yucca**, with **mesquite** and **acacia bushes** in the more sheltered, damper areas.

Flowers are commonplace throughout Mexico and form an integral part of day-to-day life. Once, **frangipani** and **magnolia** were considered to be of such value that they were reserved for the Aztec nobility. Today the blue blossoms of **jacaranda** trees and purple and red **bougainvillea** still adorn the walls of cities and towns during the spring and summer. Even the harsh arid deserts of the north are carpeted with wild flowers during the brief spring that follows the occasional rains; the cacti blooms are particularly vivid. Many of these floral species are indigenous to Mexico, including **cosmos**, **snapdragons**, **marigolds** and **dahlias**. In the wetter areas, several species of **wild orchid** are endemic, while more than eight hundred other species have been classified from the forests of Chiapas alone.

The tropical forests of Mexico provide supplies of both **chocolate** (from the cacao trees of the Chiapas) and **vanilla**. Also harvested are **chicle**, used in the preparation of chewing gum, from the latex of the **sapodilla** tree, and **wild**

**rubber** and **sarsaparilla**. Herbs, used in the medicinal or pharmaceutical industries, include **digitalis** from wild **foxgloves** and various **barks** used in the preparation of purges and disinfectants. One plant, unique to Mexico, is **Discorea composita**, which is harvested in Veracruz, Oaxaca, Tabasco and Chiapas, and is used in the preparation of a vegetable hormone that forms an essential ingredient of the contraceptive pill.

## Insects

Insect life is abundant throughout Mexico, but numbers and diversity reach their peak in the tropical rainforests. Openings in the tree canopy attract a variety of colourful **butterflies**, **gnats** and **locusts**. For the most part, insect life makes itself known through the variety of bites and sores incurred whilst wandering through these areas: **mosquitoes** are a particular pest, with malaria still a risk in some areas. The **garrapata** is a particularly tenacious tick found everywhere livestock exists, and readily attaches itself to human hosts. A range of **scorpions**, whose sting can vary from extremely painful to definitively lethal, is found throughout the country.

In the forests, long columns of **leafcutter ants** crisscross the floor in their search for tasty bits of fungus on tree bark, and surrounding tree trunks provide ideal shelter for large nests of **termites**. Carnivorous **army ants** also sweep through in waves, devouring grasshoppers and other pests but leaving greenery untouched. One species of ant, local to Tlaxcala, provides for seasonal labour twice each year: first, during the egg stage, when it is harvested for a highly prized form of caviar, and secondly during the grub stage, when it is an equally loved food source. The most spectacular insect migration can be seen in winter in eastern Michoacán, where thousands of **monarch butterflies** hatch from their larval forms en masse, providing a blaze of colour and movement (see p.388).

## Fish, reptiles and amphibians

The diversity of Mexican inland and coastal habitats has enabled large numbers of both marine and freshwater species to remain mostly undisturbed. Among the freshwater species, **rainbow** and **brook trout**, **silversides** and **catfish** are particularly abundant (as are European **carp** in certain areas, where it has been introduced). The most highly regarded is a species of **whitefish** found in Laguna de Chapala and Lago de Pátzcuaro, where it forms the basis of a thriving local fishing industry.

Offshore, Mexican waters contain over one hundred marine species of significance, including varieties of tropical and temperate climates, coastal and deep waters, surface and ground feeders and sedentary and migratory lifestyles. Among the most prevalent species are **goliath grouper** (which can grow up to 5m), **swordfish**, **snapper**, **king mackerel**, **snook**, **tuna**, **mullet** and **anchovy**. **Shrimp**, **crayfish** and **spiny lobster** are also important commercial species. The marine fishing grounds on the Pacific coast are at their best off the coast of Baja California, where the warmer southern waters merge with subarctic currents from the north. Similarly, deep ocean beds and coastal irregularities provide rewarding fishing in the waters of the Campeche bank on the Gulf of Mexico.

Reptiles are widely represented throughout Mexico. The lower river courses that flow through the southern forests are frequented by **iguana**, crocodile and its close relative, the **caiman**. Lizards range from tiny **nocturnal lizards** along the Gulf coast to **tropical iguanas**, which can reach up to 2m in length. **Marine turtles**, including the loggerhead, green, hawksbill and leatherback, are still found in many stretches of undeveloped waters and shores on both the Atlantic and Pacific coasts, though several species are endangered. Hunting of both adults and eggs is now illegal, and a number of official and unofficial turtle sanctuaries have been established along the coastlines, with positive results on the population. Several kinds of **rattlesnake** are common in the deserts of northern Mexico, and further south the rainforests hold a substantial variety of other snakes, including the **boa constrictor**, **fer-de-lance**, **bushmaster** and the small **coral snake**. Amphibian life includes salamanders, several types of **frog** and one marine toad that measures up to 20cm in length.

## Birds



More than five hundred species of tropical birds live in the rainforests and cloud forests of southern Mexico alone. Among these are resplendent **macaws**, **parrots** and **parakeets**, which make a colourful display as they fly amongst the dense tree canopy. The cereal-feeding habits of the parrot family have not endeared them to local farmers, and for this reason (and their continuing capture for sale as pets) their numbers have been seriously depleted in recent times. Big-billed **toucans** perch on lower branches and a few larger game birds, such as **curassow**, **crested guan**, **chachalaca** and **ocellated turkey** can be seen on the ground, amid the dense vegetation.

Particularly rare are the brilliantly coloured **trogons**, including the resplendent **quetzal**, which inhabit the cloud forests of the Sierra Madre de Chiapas (in El Triunfo Reserve). The ancient Maya coveted its long, emerald-green tail feathers, which were used in priestly headdresses; its current status is severely endangered. To the east, the drier tropical deciduous forests of northern Yucatán, the Pacific coastal lowlands and the interior lowlands provide an ideal habitat for several predatory birds including **owls** and **hawks**. The most familiar large birds of Mexico, however, are the carrion-eating **black** and **turkey vultures** – locally *zopilote* – often seen soaring in large groups. The Yucatán is also one of the last remaining strongholds of the small **Mexican eagle**, which features in the country's national symbol.

Large numbers of coastal lagoons provide both feeding and breeding grounds for a wide variety of aquatic birds – some of them winter visitors from the north – including **ducks**, **herons** and **grebes**. Foremost amongst these are the substantial flocks of graceful **flamingoes** which can be seen at selected sites along the western and northern coasts of the Yucatán peninsula. In the north of Mexico, where the harsher and drier environment is less attractive, outlying towns and villages form a welcome sanctuary for a variety of **doves** and **pigeons**, and the areas with denser cover have small numbers of **quail** and **pheasant**. Any water feature in these drier zones, in addition to wetland areas further south, provides attractive migration stopover sites for large flocks of North American species, including **warblers**, **wildfowl** and **waders**.

# Mammals

Zoologists divide the animals of the Americas into two categories: the **Nearctic** region of the mid-latitudes, in which the native animals are of North American affinity, and the **Neotropical** region of the lower latitudes, in which the fauna is linked to that of South America. The Isthmus of Tehuantepec marks the border between these two regions, serving as a barrier to many larger mammalian species.

The Nearctic region is predominantly composed of open steppe and desert areas and higher-altitude oak and pine forests. Relatively few large mammals inhabit the highland forests, although one widespread species is the **white-tailed deer**, which is still hunted as a source of food. The northern parts of the Sierra Madre Occidental mark the southernmost extent of several typically North American mammals, such as **mountain sheep** and **black** and **brown bears**, though the latter are near extinction. Bears live in the Cumbres de Monterrey National Park, and wild horned **sheep** can be seen at the San Pedro Mártir National Park in Baja California. Other mammals include **deer**, **puma**, **lynx**, **marten**, **grey fox**, **mule sheep**, **porcupine**, **skunk**, **badger**, **rabbit** and **squirrel**. A large array of smaller **rodents**, and their natural predators, the **coyote** and the **kit fox**, are also widespread throughout the forests. Nowadays the extensive grassland plains are frequented only by sporadic herds of white-tailed deer; the days of the pronghorn and even the bison have long passed under the burden of overhunting. Within the desert scrub, the **peccary** is still widely hunted, and rodents, as ever, are in abundance, forming an ample food supply for the resident **bobcats**, **ocelots** and even the occasional **jaguar** – more commonly associated with the country's jungle regions, but also at home in the drier areas and known to roam across the US–Mexico border.

Baja California forms an outstanding wildlife sanctuary for marine mammals, harbouring nearly 40 percent of the world's species. Isla Guadalupe is one of the few remaining breeding sites of the endangered **elephant seal**, and the only known mating and nursery sites of the **grey whale** are around Guerrero Negro.

Although some southern species (notably the opossum and armadillo) have succeeded in breaching the Tehuantepec line, and now thrive in northern Mexico and the southern US, on the whole the Neotropical region holds a very different collection of mammals. The relationship between these species and the lush vegetation of the tropical rainforest and the highland cloud forests is particularly apparent. Many species are arboreal, living in the tree canopies: these include **spider** and **howler monkeys**, **opossums**, **tropical squirrels**, the racoon-like **coati** and the gentle **kinkajou**.

Because of the paucity of grass on the shaded forest floors, ground-dwelling mammals are relatively scarce. The largest is the **tapir**, a distant relative of the horse, with a prehensile snout, usually never found far from water. Two species of **peccary**, a type of wild pig, wander the forest floors seeking their preferred foods (roots, palm nuts and even snakes), and there's the smaller **brocket deer**. The **agouti** and the spotted **cavy** are large rodents living along the numerous streams and riverbanks. These are hunted by the resident large cats, including **jaguar**, **puma** and **ocelot**.

The drier tropical and subtropical forests of northern Yucatán, the Pacific coastal lowlands and the interior basins produce a more varied ground cover of shrubs and grasses, which supply food for the **white-tailed deer** and abundant small rodents, including the spiny tree **rat** and the **paca**, which in turn provide food for a variety of predators such as the **coyote**, **margay** and **jaguarundi**. Other large mammals which can still be found in small numbers are **anteaters**,

**opossums** and **armadillos**. The reefs and lagoons which run along the Quintana Roo coast have small colonies of the **manatee**, or sea cow, a docile creature which feeds on sea grass.

## Wildlife sites

It would be almost impossible to compile a comprehensive list of sites of wildlife interest in Mexico, particularly as so much can be seen all over the country. The following is a selection of some of the outstanding areas, particularly ones that are easily accessible or close to major tourist centres. The few zoos that exist in Mexico are generally depressing places, but there is one outstanding exception – the conservation-oriented **Zoológico Miguel Álvarez del Toro** in Tuxtla Gutiérrez.

### Baja California



The peninsula of **Baja California** is a unique part of the Mexican landmass. Its coastline provides sanctuary for a wide variety of marine mammals, including the major wildlife attraction of the area, the migratory **grey whale** (see box opposite). The lagoons where these whales gather can also offer views of other species of whales, including blue, humpback, fin, minke, sperm and orca (killer whales). Dolphins and sea lions and a variety of sea birds, including pelicans, ospreys, plovers and sanderlings, inhabit the lagoons as well. The sparse vegetation provides roosting sites for jaegers and peregrines, and the occasional coyote may be seen wandering the shores.

Offshore, several small islands with protected status have been colonized by highly diverse animal communities. Furthest north is the island of **Todos Santos**, where the sandy beaches, festooned with the remnants of shellfish, are used as occasional sunning spots by the resident harbour seals. The atmosphere is ripe with an uncommon blend of guano, kelp and Californian sagebrush. The Pacific swell frequently disturbs the resting cormorants, which bask in the hot sunshine, and the skies are filled with wheeling western gulls (similar to the European lesser blackback gull).

Further south lies the island of **San Benito**, just northeast of the much larger Isla Cedros. San Benito provides ideal nesting grounds for migrating ospreys, which travel south from the US. The hillsides are covered by tall agave (century plants) whose brief, once-in-a-lifetime blooms add an attractive splash of colour to the slopes. These towering succulents produce a broad rosette of golden florets, which are a welcome supply of nectar for resident hummingbirds, and ravens soar above, searching for carrion. The island, along with Isla Cedros and the distant **Isla Guadalupe** (now a biological reserve), also provides a winter home to thousands of elephant seals, now happily recovering after years of overhunting. The large adult males arrive in December, and the pebbly coves are soon crammed with the noisy and chaotic colony of mothers, calves and bachelor bulls, all ruled by one dominant bull (or beach master) which can weigh up to two tonnes. The males make a terrifying spectacle as, with necks raised and heads thrown back, they echo their noisy threats to any would-be rivals.

The interior of the peninsula has several areas of wildlife interest, many of which now have the protected status of nature reserve. Most significant are the national parks of the **Sierra San Pedro Mártir** and the **Desierto Central**. Here the chaparral-covered hills cede to Jeffrey pine forests and high meadows,

## Grey whale migration and breeding

Each year **grey whales** and their migrations off the west coast of Baja California attract an estimated 250,000 visitors. The whales' **migratory route** runs the length of the American Pacific seaboard, from Baja to the Bering Sea and back; this is a round trip of some 20,000km – the longest recorded migration undertaken by any living mammal. They remain in the north for several months, feeding on the abundant krill in the high Arctic summer and building up body reserves for the long journey south to the breeding lagoons. The migration begins as the days shorten and the pack ice thickens, sometime before the end of January.

Nowadays human interest in the whales is purely voyeuristic, though times have not always been so peaceful for these graceful leviathans; less than 150 years ago, the secret breeding grounds of the whales were discovered by **Charles Melville Scammon**. The Laguna Ojo de Liebre (renamed in recent times after the infamous whaler) was rapidly emptied of almost all of these magnificent beasts, and it wasn't until the establishment of **Scammon's Bay** as the world's first whale sanctuary in 1972 that their numbers began to rebound. The population in the area is currently estimated at about 20,000 – a dramatic recovery in a relatively short time span. In 1988 the Mexican government extended the range of the protected area to include nearby San Ignacio Lagoon, forming an all-embracing national park, the Biosfera El Vizcaíno. San Ignacio Lagoon offers a daunting entrance of pounding surf and treacherous shoals, but once inside, its calmer waters flatten and spread inland for 15km towards the distant volcanic peaks of the Santa Clara mountains. Accessible points for land-based observation lie further north in the Parque Natural de Ballena Gris ("Grey Whale Natural Park"), 32km south of Guerrero Negro.

interspersed with granite *picachos* (peaks) and volcanic mesas. The **Parque Nacional Constitución de 1857** is another green oasis in the arid lowlands, where the coniferous woodlands form a picturesque border to the central **Laguna Hanson**. These sierras are renowned for the numerous palm-filled canyons which cut deep into the eastern escarpment; they make spectacular hiking areas with their miniature waterfalls, ancient petroglyphs, caves, hot springs and groves of fan palms.

## Durango

**Durango** lies within a dry, hilly area where the intermittent oak and pine woodland is surrounded by large expanses of low-lying scrub. These areas are frequented by large numbers of birds, whose presence is an extension of their North American range. Typical species include red-tailed hawk, American kestrel and mockingbird. The denser, wooded areas provide the necessary cover for several more secretive varieties such as Mexican jay, acorn woodpecker, hepatic grosbeak and the diminutive Mexican chickadee. This is also an occasional haunt of the mountain lion (or puma) and the coyote. In the dry scrub, scorpions abound. Other nearby sites worthy of investigation include **El Salto** and **El Palmito**.

## The Teacapán estuary

South of Mazatlán on the Pacific coast, the **Teacapán estuary** is an extensive area of sands with marshy margins: ideal feeding grounds for a variety of waders and wildfowl, including marbled godwit, greater yellowlegs and willet. Large numbers of herons and egrets feed in the shallow waters (including little green and Louisiana heron and snowy and cattle egret), while further out to sea passage birds include laughing gull, gull-billed tern and olivaceous cormorant. Most spectacular of all are the magnificent, aptly named frigate birds, which make a dramatic sight as they skim over the water's surface in their search for fish, with their long wings (sometimes more than 2m across), forked tails and hooked bills.

The rocks offshore provide a suitable breeding site for both brown- and blue-footed boobies, and the pools at the northern end of the town, behind the large hotels, have some interesting water birds, including jacana, ruddy duck and canvasback.

## San Blas

Immediately around **San Blas** are lagoons with wildlife very similar to that found in the estuary near Mazatlán; boat tours from San Blas take you out to see herons, egrets and much more, with the possibility of seeing a caiman being the big attraction. Deeper in the wetlands the landscape forms areas of thicker scrub and at higher altitudes dense forest. Amongst the lower-lying scrub, it is possible to see the purplish-backed jay, Gila woodpecker and tropical kingbird, while the skies above have the patrolling white-tailed kite. At higher altitudes, the birdlife includes the locally named San Blas jay, white-crowned parrot and cinnamon hummingbird. The town itself provides sufficient scraps for scavengers such as black and grey hawks and various rodents.

## Veracruz and the Gulf coast

The eastern coastline of Mexico has attractions of its own, and none is more rewarding to the visiting naturalist than the final remaining tract of rainforest on the Mexican **Gulf coast**, southeast of **Veracruz**. The vegetation is lush, the tended citrus orchards yielding to rolling tropical forest, with its dense growth of ficus, mango and banana trees and the occasional coconut palm. These trees provide cover for a colourful underlying carpet, including orchids, lemon trees, camellias, fragrant cuatismilla and gardenias. The roadsides are lined with banks of hibiscus, oleander and the pretty, white-flowered shrub known locally as *cruz de Malta*. At the centre of the whole area, **Lago de Catemaco** is outstandingly beautiful.

The surrounding forest has suffered much in recent times, and many of the larger mammals that once resided in this region are no longer to be found. One sanctuary which remains amidst this destruction is the ecological research station of **Los Tuxtlas**. Although the institute's holding is fairly small, it adjoins a much larger state-owned reserve of some 25,000 acres on the flank of the **San Martín volcano**. Despite problems of poaching and woodcutting, the area has the last remaining populations of brocket deer, black howler monkey, ocelot, jaguarundi, kinkajou and coati. It also boasts 92 species of reptile, fifty amphibians, thousands of insects and over three hundred species of birds. With patience, it is possible to see such outstanding avian varieties as keel-billed toucan, black-shouldered kite, gold-crowned warbler, red-throated ant tanager, plain-breasted brush finch, red-lored parrot, ivory-billed woodpecker and the magnificent white hawk.

## The Chiapas uplands and Palenque

In the **Chiapas uplands**, the absence of climatic moderation and coastal breezes creates dense, lush vegetation that makes it truly worthy of the name of tropical rainforest. The **Sierra Madre de Chiapas** is of particular interest, particularly the Pacific slopes at altitudes between 1500m and 2500m, as these are the last sanctuary of the endangered horned guan and azure-rumped tanager, and even the quetzal. **El Triunfo Reserve**, at 1800m in the very southeastern corner of the country, less than 50km from the Guatemalan border, makes an excellent base camp for exploration of the area. The cloud forest here is dense, and the tall epiphyte-laden trees grow in profusion on the slopes and in the valleys, in the humid conditions which occur after the morning fogs have risen (generally by early afternoon).

Another area of interest in eastern Chiapas is the **Parque Nacional Lagos de Montebello**, where more determined bird watchers may be rewarded with views of the azure-hooded jay and the barred parakeet. Human encroachment has substantially reduced the population of large mammals in the area, but small numbers of howler monkey, tapir and jaguar (known locally as *el tigre*) are a reminder of bygone days. Another speciality of the region is a vivid and diminutive tree frog, whose precise camouflage ensures that it is more often heard than seen.

At the archeological site of **Palenque** you're back among the tourists (and the howler monkeys), but the birding is unrivalled, and local species include the chestnut-headed oropendola, scaled ant pitta, white-whiskered puffbird, slaty-tailed trogon and masked tanager. In the area of marshland around the **Río Usumacinta**, about 25km east of the junction between the main Palenque road and Hwy-186, pinnated bittern, everglade kite and the rare lesser yellow-headed vulture have all been recorded.

## The Yucatán Peninsula

The vegetation of the **Yucatán Peninsula** is influenced by its low relief and the ameliorating effects of its extensive coastline, which bring regular and fairly reliable rain along with year-round high temperatures. In the north it's predominantly dry scrub and bush, although large areas have been cleared for the cultivation of crops such as citrus fruits and henequen. To the south is lusher tropical and subtropical forest, where the effects of agriculture are less obvious and the dense forest of acacia, albizia, gumbo limbo and ceiba is in parts almost impenetrable. These form an ideal shelter for scattered populations of both white-tailed and brocket deer.

The **birdlife** on the peninsula is particularly outstanding. The abundant and spectacular birds which fill the treetops include squirrel cuckoo, citreoline trogon and Aztec parakeet, while circling in the skies above are the resident birds of prey such as the bat falcon, snail kite and the ever-present black and turkey vultures (these can be distinguished, even at great heights, as the wings of the latter are clearly divided into two bands – the darker primaries and the lighter secondaries being quite distinct). It is also possible to see all three species of Mexican toucan: collared aracari, emerald toucanet and the spectacular keel-billed. The denser areas of forest also hold small remnants of the original black howler and spider monkey populations.

Two specific sites worthy of thorough investigation are the archeological sites of Cobá and Chichén Itzá. The village of **Cobá** borders a lake with extensive reed margins along its eastern edge, which attracts a variety of water birds. Typical visitors, either migratory or resident, include the grebe, the elusive spotted rail, ruddy crake, northern jacana and the occasional anhinga – a cormorant-like bird which captures fish by spearing them with its dagger-like bill. The reed beds provide cover for several more-secretive species, including mangrove vireo, ringed kingfisher and blue-winged warbler, as well as several varieties of hirundine such as mangrove swallow and grey-breasted martin.

The ruins of **Chichén Itzá** are a must on the list of any visitor, but save a little time at the end of the day for an exploration of the forested areas which lie to the south of the "Nunnery". The drier climate and lower altitude in this part of the peninsula encourage a sparser vegetation, where the oaks and pines are less obvious. The colours amongst the greenness come from a variety of splendid flowers, such as the multicoloured bougainvillea, the aromatic frangipani and the blue and mauve blooms of the jacaranda tree. Occasional splashes are added by the red bracts of the poinsettia (Christmas flower) and the brilliant yellows of golden cups. The resident birds appear oblivious to the tourist traffic, and in the quieter areas to the south and southwest of the main site, the abundant birdlife includes plain chachalaca (surely a misnomer), ferruginous pygmy owl, cinnamon hummingbird, turquoise-browed motmot and numerous brilliant vireos, orioles and tanagers.

## Cancún, Cozumel and the Caribbean coast

Even the mega-resort of **Cancún** has wildlife possibilities: the lagoons that line the outskirts have a variety of birds (such as great-tailed grackle and melodious blackbird). These wetlands form an ideal breeding ground for a number of brilliantly coloured dragonflies and damselflies.

More importantly, the longest **barrier reef** in the Americas begins just south of the city, off the coast of **Puerto Morelos**, where the scuba diving and snorkelling are quite stunning. Formed by the limey skeletons of dozens of species of coral, the reefs show spectacular diversity, with varieties such as star, lettuce, gorgonian, elkhorn and staghorn being particularly widespread. The reefs provide food and shelter for more than four hundred species of fish alone, including several varieties of parrotfish, butterfly fish, beau gregories, rock beauties and porkfish; the blaze of colour is unforgettable. The coral also provides protection for several other residents, including spiny lobster, sea urchins, crabs and tentacled anemones, but this fragile environment requires cautious exploration if the effects of snorkellers and boat anchors are not to destroy the very thing that they seek to enjoy.

A series of offshore islands and coastal sites in Yucatán state are worthy of special mention. Natural parks and nature reserves include **Celestún**, on the west coast, and **Río Lagartos**, to the north. Both have spectacular flocks of migratory flamingoes, which winter here in the milder climate. The **Isla Contoy** bird sanctuary off the northeastern tip of the peninsula is a worthwhile and popular day trip from Cancún (via Isla Mujeres), and **Isla Holbox**, off the north coast, is the closest point to an annual gathering of more than one hundred whale sharks. To get acquainted with flora, the largest **botanic garden** in Mexico is near Puerto Morelos.

**Playa del Carmen** is frequented by various wetland species including American wigeon, and the ferry trip to **Cozumel** island produces sightings of sea birds such as royal and Caspian terns, black skimmer, frigate birds and Mexican sheartails. On the island, the most rewarding sites are a couple of kilometres inland on the main road that runs across the island. The sparse woodland and hedgerows provide shelter for many typical endemics, such as Caribbean dove, lesser nighthawk, Yucatán and Cozumel vireo, the splendid bananaquit and a variety of tanagers. Elusive species which require more patient exploration (best through the mangroves which lie 3km north of **San Miguel**

along the coast road) are the mangrove cuckoo, yellow-lored parrot, Caribbean ealania and Yucatán flycatcher. Cozumel, though, is better known for the **coral reefs** that ring the island, which are ranked among divers' favourites, for their colour and varied life.

The highlight of the peninsula's protected areas is the magnificent **Sian Ka'an Biosphere Reserve**, which includes coral reef, mangroves, fresh- and salt-water wetlands and littoral forest – possibly the widest range of flora and fauna in the whole of Mexico.

# Mexican music

The international boom in Mexican music took place in the 1940s and 1950s, when classic songs like "Besame Mucho" and "Cielito Lindo" warbled from cinema screens and radios and were played by "Latin-style" orchestras all over the world. This "golden age" had died out by the 1960s, when that same era in Mexican cinema came to an end. In Mexico, though, live music continues to thrive, whether performed by romantic trios or twenty-piece dance orchestras, responding to a country that loves to dance and sing.

As Luís Buñuel was making cinema history in the capital, **Celia Cruz** came from Cuba to seek her fortune along with **Beny Moré**, **Bienvenido Granda** and **Damasio Pérez Prado**, the last of whom developed the mambo rhythm between shifts as a session pianist at the Churrubusco film studios. These musicians were attracted by the bright lights of a city that didn't sleep: cosmopolitan and bohemian, Mexico City had long welcomed musicians from all over Latin America and taken their styles of music to heart. It's now the international capital of both **danzón**, originally from Cuba, and **cumbia**, from Colombia. Go to the Salón Los Ángeles in the old centre of Mexico City on a Tuesday evening at 7pm, and you'll find seven hundred couples dancing. Sunday is the biggest night, however, when the enormous wooden floors carry the scent of shoe polish and perfume, and three different fourteen-piece orchestras play *danzones* old and new.

## Son

Compared with Mexican **son**, however, *danzón* is just a fad. Still an inspiration to artists today, *son* is a traditional music that grew out of the eighteenth-century encounter between Spanish, indigenous and African cultures. Though the same encounter produced Cuban *son* and other Latin American styles like the Venezuelan *joropo*, Mexican *son* fast developed its own distinct sound.

Mexican *son* actually describes eight or nine different styles of music, all of which share certain aspects. These country styles rely on the participation of the public to add counter-rhythms through **zapateado** (foot-stamping dancing), but more importantly, are all incredibly creative. A *son* musician has to be able to make up lyrics on the spot in response to a comment from the dancefloor. He must also be able to create new flights on the violin or guitar to satisfy an audience that demands nothing less than inspiration. *Son* is almost always played by a string band, with lyrics, sung in four-line *coplas*, that are witty, more sexual than sensual, poetic and proud.

Most internationally famous are the **sones jaliscienses**, those from Jalisco, birthplace of **mariachi**. Mariachi became nationally and internationally popular following the cinema boom, when regional music was recorded by major labels, notably RCA. A few of these treasures can be found on cassettes in markets, and there's a healthy trade among collectors looking for the original vinyl, but only the biggest names have been re-released on CD. Sadly, few commercial bands now play this original repertoire, preferring the simpler ballads and *cumbias* that the public knows from the radio and TV. To hear the bands who still master the original *sones*, it's best to skip Mexico City's infamous Plaza Garibaldi and head off to southern Jalisco, where incredible twelve- or

△ Mariachis



fourteen-piece mariachis, like **Los Reyes del Aserradero** and **Mariachi Tamazula**, offer spectacular violins, plenty of trumpet and vocal harmonies in a sophisticated version of the country *sones* that were originally played on a harp and three guitars.

Apart from the *sones* from Jalisco, the **sones jarochos** from Veracruz also received a lot of attention. Many Jarocho musicians like **Andrés Huesca**, **Nicolás Sosa** and **Lino Chávez** tasted the big time in Mexico City before – as in the case of Nicolás Sosa – returning to the main square of Veracruz. Today, there is a new interest in *son jarocho*, and the first lady of this style is without doubt **Graciana Silva**, "La Negra Graciana", who was offering her *sones* for ten pesos apiece to the people drinking beers Veracruz's zócalo until one such drinker turned out to know more than she had expected about *son jarocho*. Eduardo Llerenas invited her to record for his staunchly independent label, Discos Corason, and the CD generated great interest in Europe when it was released in 1996. La Negra set off to play her *sones* at the Barbican Centre and Royal Festival Hall in London, the Théâtre de la Ville in Paris and the Harbourfront Centre in Toronto.

Around the port of Veracruz, and in villages like Medellín de Bravo, where La Negra was born, the **African** influence has left its imprint on *son jarocho*, although further south the **indigenous** presence is much stronger, and the harp virtually never played. Instead, the line-up consists exclusively of *requinto* and *jarana* guitars of different sizes and tunings. The *sones* are played more slowly and with a melancholy that is not so evident around the port. In the south of Veracruz, several young, experimental bands gather annually on February 2 for the spectacular **Fiesta de la Candelaria** in Tlacotalpan. They set up a stage, and band after band plays, several of whom invite the old *soneros* of the region to join their line-up. Leading this younger generation of *jarocho* musicians is **Gilberto Gutiérrez** and his band, Mono Blanco, who have recorded with the Mexican label Urtext.

Perhaps most vibrant today is the **Huastecan** style of *son*, in which a virtuoso violin is accompanied by a *huapanguera* and a *jarana* guitar, with the two guitarists singing falsetto vocals between flights of the violin. Each *son huasteco* is reinvented every time it's played: the singers compose new verses, and the violinist creates new flourishes. There are literally hundreds of Huastecan *son* trios, the most outstanding being **Los Camperos de Valles**, **Trio Tamazunchale** and the relative youngsters **Dinastia Hidalguense**. Lesser-known bands play in cantinas and at fiestas throughout the Huastecan region and participate in festivals in towns like Pahuatlán, Huejutla, Amatlán and Xilitla. In the cafés of Mexico City's Coyoacán barrio, trios sell their *sones* by the piece, offering impressive versions of "La Huasanga", "El Llorar" and "El Fandanguito", to name but a few.

Seldom heard in the city but enormously popular back home in the villages of the Sierra Gorda, the **arribeño** style is the most poetic form of *son*. Here, the *trovador* – who seems to be the natural successor of the medieval troubadour – is a country poet, often with no formal education, who composes verses about local heroes, the planets, the earth and the continuing struggles for land. Usually two *trovadores*, both playing the *huapanguera* guitar and each accompanied by two violins and the small *vihuela* guitar, confront each other on tall bamboo platforms that are erected on two sides of the village square. The poets enter into musical combat, improvising verses which are interspersed with *zapateado* dancing. Each year on December 31, probably the greatest living *trovador*, **Guillermo Velázquez**, organizes a festival in his village, paying homage to the old musicians before starting the *topada* musical combat that lasts all night.

Based in the Mexican west, in the Tierra Caliente (hot land) of the Río Balsas basin, the violinist **Juan Reynoso** won the prestigious National Prize for Arts and Science, never before given to a country musician. Rebaptized by a local poet as "The Paganini of the Hotlands", Reynoso, who turned 90 in 2003, is an extraordinary violinist, even within the local tradition of *sones calentanos*, which are known for their complex melodies on the violin. Musicians find it hard to follow Don Juan, whose flights take unexpected turns and whose genius, fortunately, has been recognized during his lifetime with books, videos, concerts and tours.

Further west, in a region where the heat is so intense that it's known as "Hell's Waiting Room", **sones de arpa grande** (*sones* of the big harp) are one of Mexico's best-kept musical secrets. These bands – made up of a big harp, one or two violins and two guitars – don't thrive as they used to, but it's still possible to track down some great harp by masters such as **Juan Pérez Morfín**, who plays with esteemed violinist **Beto Pineda**. In the brothels of Apatzingán and in the region's country fairs, the sound boxes of the big harps are beaten in counter-rhythm by one of the band members or by a fan who pays for the privilege. The harpist, meanwhile, must hold onto the melody with vocals that can sound something like a shout from the soul. Concerts are often organized by stable-owners who pride themselves on their dancing horses: *norteño* music may be popular in this region, but the horses only dance to the big harp music, and they do so on wooden platforms, beating out the rhythm and counter-rhythm with their hooves.

Although *son* is basically *mestizo* music, several indigenous cultures play instrumental *sones* to accompany their ritual dances. **Sones abajeños** are the frenetic party music of the Purépecha of Michoacán, played on guitars, violins and a double bass. Between *abajeños*, the same musicians sing the hauntingly beautiful **Purépecha** love songs, *pirecua*. Outstanding Purépecha *son* bands include **Atardecer** (Sunset), from the lake village of Jarácuaro, and **Erandi** (Dawn). In the southern state of Oaxaca, the vibrant Zapotec culture has produced some of the country's great love songs and inspired mainstream Mexican romantic singers along the way. Sung in both Zapotec and Spanish, the **sones istmeños**, as they are known, are played to a slower 3/4 rhythm and are more melancholy than the *mestizo sones*. They boast some great solo passages on the *requinto* guitar and uniquely Zapotecan vocals, which together have created a very beautiful repertoire that has tempted some of Mexico's greatest urban vocalists to learn the Zapotecan lyrics and perform them in the big-city venues. **Lila Downs**, half-Mixtecan, half-American, is among the most successful and, typically, her repertoire also includes *rancheras*, *boleros* and jazz.

## Ranchera

It's interesting that the great divas of Latin American music have turned to Mexican traditional and country music to develop their own repertoire. Singers like **Tania Libertad** and **Betsy Pecanins**, enormously popular throughout the 1980s as **nueva canción** (new song) protest singers, are now singing their own versions of *norteños*, mariachi, *sones istmeños* and Mexican *boleros* to a more mature public. Outstanding among this illustrious company is **Eugenia León**, whose vocal range and passion encompasses a broad range of music styles. The diva tradition has a direct line back to the early days of *ranchera* music, an urban style that emerged alongside the new towns and cities in the early twentieth century and that became massively popular with the growth of film and radio.

"Ranchera" comes from the word *rancho* (farm) although the music was composed in the towns and cities for a public that wanted to remember how it used to be. The wit and freshness of the original *son* lyrics were replaced by bitter words about loss and betrayal, while musically the intensity shifted from the complex melody and rhythms of *son* to a more melodramatic style.

The first great diva of *ranchera* music was **Lucha Reyes**, whose emotionally charged voice hinted at her own inner turmoil. She died tragically, but her work was resuscitated by the great Mexican cabaret singer **Astrid Hadad**, who offered a postmodern take on Reyes in the early 1990s, carried off so successfully by a blend of humour and a very fine voice. Although Astrid now includes a breadth of Latin cabaret music in her repertoire, her great moments were captured in her 1995 CD of *ranchera* songs called, quite simply, *¡Ay!*.

Of the classic *ranchera* singers, since the death of **Amalia Mendoza**, the great **Lola Beltrán** and **María de Lourdes**, the divas are now few and far between. Today, fame and fortune have passed to a younger generation of male singers and, in particular, to **Alejandro Fernández**, a superstar who has left his father, *ranchera* star Vicente Fernández, in the shade. Although musically there's little of the original *ranchera* left in Alejandro's repertoire, the melodrama and the association with ranch culture still exist – the mariachi trousers and sombrero hat are still in place; nonetheless Alejandro represents a different generation, more in the style of the new rock idols.

## Norteño

Apart from *ranchera*, the style that has had most popularity throughout the country is probably **norteño**. Known north of the border as **Tex-Mex**, *norteño* has its roots in the *corrido* ballads that retold the battles between Anglos and Mexicans in the early nineteenth century. The war turned out badly for Mexico, which lost half its territory, and many people living in what is now California, Arizona, New Mexico and Texas found themselves with a new nationality.

## El Gato Félix (Felix the Cat)

I'm going to sing a *corrido*
About someone who I knew
A distinguished journalist
Feared for his pen
From Tijuana to Madrid

They called him Felix the Cat
Because the story goes that
He was like those felines
He had seven lives
And he had to see them through

He came from Choix, Sinaloa
That was the place he was born
He stayed in Tijuana
Because it took his fancy
And he wanted to help in some way
With what he wrote in the paper

He made the government tremble
He went right through the alphabet
A whole rosary of threats
He made his paper *Zeta* popular
With his valiant pen
He pointed to corruption
He always helped the people
And more than two presidents
Had their eyes on him
In a treacherous way
The Cat met his end
Death, mounted on a racehorse
A real beast
Rode him down

Now Felix the Cat is dead
They are carrying him to his grave
He will be another one on the list
Of brave journalists
That they've wanted to silence

Candles burn for Felix Miranda
To you I dedicate my song
But don't you worry
There will be other brave people
To take your place

*Enrique Franco*
*(Los Tigres del Norte, 1989)*

The late 1920s were the golden age of the **corrido**, when songs of the recent Revolution were recorded in San Antonio, Texas, and distributed on both sides of the border. The accordion, which had arrived with Mennonite immigrants in the late nineteenth century, was introduced into the originally guitar-based groups by **Narciso Martínez** and **Santiago Jiménez** (father of the famous Flaco) in the 1930s, and the sound that they developed became the essence of *corrido* ensembles on both sides of the border.

Along with the **accordion** came the polka, and by the 1950s this had blended with the traditional duet-singing of northern Mexico and with salon dances like the waltz, mazurka and the *chotis* (the central European *schottische* that travelled to Spain and France before arriving in northern Mexico) to produce the definitive *norteño* style. The accordion pepped up the songs with lead runs and flourishes between the verses, but the *conjuntos norteños* needed to round out their sound to keep up with the big bands and so added bass and rolling drums – the basis of today's **conjuntos**.

Unlike most other regional styles, *norteño* is popular throughout the country. At a party in an isolated mountain community in central Mexico, the host takes out his accordion and plays *corridos norteños* until the dawn breaks. In an ice-cream parlour on the Pacific coast, the piped music is a *norteño* waltz. And waiting for darkness to cross the border at Tijuana, *norteños* are again the musical backdrop.

This countrywide popularity is most likely due to the **lyrics**. *Norteño* songs speak to people in words more real and interesting than the cosy pseudo-sophistication of Mexican pop music. The ballads tell of anti-heroes: small-time drug runners, illegal "wet-back" immigrants, a thief with one blond eyebrow who defied the law. *Norteño* reflects the mood of a country that generally considers the government to be big-time thieves and hence has a certain respect for everyday people with the courage to stand up to a crooked system.

Groups like **Los Tigres del Norte** and **Los Cadetes del Norte** take stories from the local papers and convert them into ballads that usually begin "Voy a cantarles un corrido" ("I'm going to sing you a *corrido*") before launching into a gruesome tale sung in a deadpan style as if it were nothing to go to a local dance and get yourself killed. One of the most famous *corridos*, "Rosita Alvírez", tells the story of a young girl who struck lucky: only one of the three bullets fired by her boyfriend hit and killed her.

Los Tigres are without a doubt the superstars of *norteño*, having won a Grammy and subsequently been adopted by Televisa. They record in both the US and Mexico, and have achieved superstardom on both sides of the border. Quite early in their career, the band modified the traditional line-up by adding a sax and mixed the familiar rhythms with *cumbias*; however, their nasal singing style and the combination of instruments identifies the music very clearly as *norteño*.

## The banda boom

The enormous success of Los Tigres del Norte and their updated *norteño* sound resulted in a phenomenon that changed the face of Mexican music in the 1990s: **banda** music. This is a fusion of the *norteño* style with the brass bands that have played at village fiestas all over the country for the last century. There are now hundreds of *bandas* in Mexico – ranging in size from four to twenty musicians – all playing brass and percussion, with just an occasional guitar. Their repertoire includes *norteño* polkas, *ranchera* ballads, *cumbia*, merengue and salsa.

## Discography

Mexican recordings are widely available in the US – less so in Europe. For the more traditional music, a label to look out for is **Corason**, which in the 1990s recorded and released consistently excellent CDs and cassettes of traditional sounds from all over the country; the recordings are now out of print, but can often be found secondhand. Also check the excellent online shop **Global Sound** (ⓦwww.globalsound.org), maintained by Smithsonian Folkways; here you can purchase either CDs or MP3 files from the American institution's vast trove of Mexican folk music, which includes many of the artists listed below.

### Compilations

**Anthology of Mexican Sones** (Corason, Mexico). The definitive survey of Mexican traditional music, featuring wonderful recordings of rural bands. Excellent accompanying notes plus lyrics in Spanish and English.

**Mexico – Fiestas of Chiapas & Oaxaca** (Nonesuch Explorer, US). Recordings from village festivities in southern Mexico. Marimba *conjuntos*, brass bands, some eccentric ensembles and great fireworks on the opening track. The next best thing to being there.

**The Rough Guide to the Music of Mexico** (World Music Network, UK). This set examines a wide variety of both traditional and contemporary music, including *rancheras*, *corridos*, *boleros*, indie rock and various stylistic fusions.

### Sones and mariachi

**Los Camperos de Valles** *Sones de la Huasteca* and *El Triunfo* (Corason, Mexico). The Huasteca *sones* are considered by many to be the most beautiful music in Mexico. Played on violin, guitar and the small *vihuela* guitar, an important element is the falsetto singing of love songs that are both rowdy and romantic.

**Conjunto Alma Jarochos** *Sones Jarochos* (Arhoolie, US). A fine disc, the first in a series of regional Mexican releases, featuring *sones* from Veracruz with harps and *jarana* guitars.

**Juan Reynoso** *El Paganini de la Tierra Caliente* (Corason, Mexico). The title is fair dues: Reynoso is Mexico's greatest country violinist, in fine form on this recording, backed by vocal, guitars and drum.

**Mariachi Coculense de Cirilo Marmolejo** *Mexico's Pioneer Mariachis Vol 1* (Arhoolie, US). Wonderful archive recordings from the 1920s and 1930s of one of the seminal groups.

**Mariachi Reyes del Aserradero** *Sones from Jalisco* (Corason, Mexico). An excellent mariachi band from Jalisco state play the original *sones* from the region where mariachi was born.

**Mariachi Tapatío de José Marmolejo** *The Earliest Mariachi Recordings: 1906–36* (Arhoolie, US). Archive recordings of a pioneer mariachi band, featuring the great trumpet playing of Jesús Salazar.

**Mariachi Vargas** *20 Exitos* (Orfeon, Mexico). Big-band style mariachi from Silvestre Vargas, who has managed to stay at the top of his field for over fifty years. Always flexible, his band released one disastrous album of mariachi-rock but has otherwise had hits all the way. They work much of the year in the US.

**La Negra Graciana** *Sones Jarochos* (Corason, Mexico). The first lady of Mexican harp plays solo and accompanied by her brother and sister-in-law.

**Los Pregoneros del Puerto** *Music of Veracruz* (Rounder, US). Rippling *sones jaroches* from the Veracruz coast, where harp and *jarana* guitars still dominate. An enchanting album.

### Ranchera and norteño

**Flaco Jiménez** *Ay Te Dejo en San Antonio y Más* (Arhoolie, US). The best of Flaco's many recordings; he's a huge name in the Tex-Mex world north of the border.

**José Alfredo Jiménez** *Homenaje a José Alfredo Jiménez* (Sony Discos, US). Jimenez was the king of *ranchera* and embodied the best and worst of Mexican machismo. As he predicted in one of his songs, everyone in Mexico missed him when he died.

**Linda Ronstadt** *Canciones de Mi Padre* and *Más Canciones* (Asylum, US). *Ranchera* classics sung very convincingly by the Mexican-American vocalist, accompanied by Mariachi Vargas.

**Los Lobos** *La Pistola y El Corazón* (Warner, US). The East LA band's brilliant 1988 tribute to their Mexican roots, with David Hidalgo pumping the accordion on their blend of *conjunto* and rock and roll.

**Los Pingüinos del Norte** *Conjuntos Norteños* (Arhoolie, US). This album pairs up Tex and Mex *conjuntos*: Los Pingüinos, singing *corridos* live in a cantina in northern Mexico, and Fred Zimmerle's Trio from San Antonio, Texas, performing typical polkas and *rancheras*.

**Santiago Jiménez Snr** *Santiago Jiménez Snr* (Arhoolie, US). One of the great accordion players, recorded in 1979 with his son Flaco on *bajo sexto*. Earthy, authentic sound.

**Los Tigres del Norte** *Corridos Prohibidos* (Fonovisa, US). A collection of *corridos* about Mexican low life and heroism from one of the best *norteño* groups in the business.

### Cumbia

**Los Bukis** *Me Volví a Acordar de Ti* (Melody, Mexico). The sound of soft *cumbia* – probably the most popular Mexican record ever.

**The Rough Guide to Cumbia** (World Music Network, UK). The tunes on this compilation show why *cumbia* is such an infectious groove in Mexico and other regions of Latin America. The songs are licensed from the Sonolux label and date from the 1960s to the 1990s. Compulsively danceable, this is an essential party album and a solid overview of the genre.

**Sonora Dinamita** *Mi Cucu* (Discos Fuentes, Colombia). Mexican *cumbia* performed by a breakaway group of artists who took the name of the Colombian originals. Their lyrics, full of double entendres, are performed with a zest that has brought huge success in Mexico.

### Rock and miscellany

**Agustín Lara** *Agustín Lara* (Orfeon, Mexico). The legendary crooner, a man who idolized prostitutes and married for love twelve times. One of Mexico's greatest composers of popular music, specializing in *bolero* ballads and music from Veracruz.

**Café Tacuba** *Re* (Warner Music Mexico). The Monterrey band's second album is addictively buzzy and rhythmically complex. Harder to find, but worth the hunt is the double-disc *Revés/Yo Soy*, which critics have likened to Radiohead's *Kid-A* in scope.

**Molotov** *Dónde Jugarán las Niñas?* (Universal Latino). This aggressive, political rap album was banned in Mexico for obscenity (and possible use of an underage model on its cover). Needless to say, it was a mammoth hit, and the band's "Gimme Tha Power" perfectly captures a moment in Mexican youth culture.

**Nortec Collective** *Tijuana Sessions Vol 3* (Universal Latino). More so than Vol 1 (which errs on the side of generic techno), this album shows off the funky potential of remixing blaring Mexican horns for the dancefloor.

The most exciting of these groups is a fiery orchestra from Mazatlán, the **Banda El Recodo**. This is not a new band; indeed, its former leader, Don Cruz Lizárraga, had been in the business for half a century, starting out in a traditional *tambora* marching band (the *tambora* is the huge, carried side drum) that played a straight repertoire of brass-band numbers. However, Don Cruz had always had an eye for musical fashions, adapting his material to merengue, *ranchera* or whatever anyone wanted to hear. His great *banda* hit was a version of Cuban bandleader Beny Moré's classic "La Culebra".

The *banda* boom dominated the national airwaves in the 1990s. Outside of the big cities, it is still the *bandas* that fill the stadiums and village halls, and it's their names you'll see painted in enormous multicoloured letters on patches of white wall along the roads. The craze brought with it a series of new dances, too, particularly the *quebradita* – a gymnastic, very intimate combination of lambada, polka and even a little bit of swing and hip-hop, which is danced with particular skill in points north of Guadalajara.

In 1995, during a successful two-month tour of Europe, Cruz Lizárraga died, and the Banda del Recodo passed into the hands of two of his musician sons, Germán, now in his late fifties, and the young Alfonso. Changes were afoot. The band left the independent label where they had made about a hundred records and signed to the Televisa media empire. Several of the older musicians have been replaced with younger ones, and the original sound has suffered, although, ironically, record sales have never been better.

## Cumbia

Although the *banda* line-up dates back to the village band tradition and the *tambora* music of northwest Mexico, today's *bandas* rely heavily on **cumbia** for their repertoire, the simple dance music that came originally from Colombia but has taken deep root across Mexico.

*Cumbia*, now more popular in Mexico than in its native Colombia, has become simpler in its new home, more direct and danceable. For most of the 1980s, a national radio station used to call out "ÁTropi. . .Q!" – the last letter a "coooooh" that seemed to momentarily clear the smog in the DF – and then launch into the latest *cumbia* hit, which was played without reprieve for a month and then forgotten. A song about cellular telephones replaced "No Te Metas con Mi Cucu" (Don't Mess With My Toot-toot), which in turn had taken over from a song about fried chicken and chips – a thinly disguised treatise on how a macho likes his bird.

The flirtatious *cumbia* was the most popular music in Mexico until *bandas* came along, and it remains a force throughout the country. Outside the capital, it tends to take on a more mellow, romantic tone, a sound closely associated with the band **Los Bukis**, who, before splitting up in the mid-1990s, made several albums, among them *Me Volví a Acordar de Ti*, which sold 1.5 million legal copies and an estimated four million more bootleg.

In the same line, an insipid mixture of *cumbia*, *norteño* and *ranchera*, which is sometimes known as **grupera** (or **onda grupera**), emerged in the late 1980s and continues to be popular in small towns and villages, where populations have been known to swell four or five times over when a band like the **Yonics**, **Banda Machos** or the (now defunct) **Bronco** come to play. These musicians, like the *bandas* who share the same audience, arrive in a fleet of well-equipped coaches – one for them, one for the generator, one of lights and equipment and lavish leather suits and, quite often, one for their families. This music was despised by the media executives who, for many years, thought it common and continued to plug the familiar pretty faces of the pop idols that they manufactured. However, beginning in the 1990s, the phenomenal commercial success of the self-made *grupera, banda* and *norteño* musicians forced the entertainment business to rethink. Groups like **Limite** are now regularly featured on TV shows and are invited to play in the hallowed halls of Mexico City's Auditorio Nacional, once the stronghold of protest singers and foreign ballet companies.

## Rock en español

One reason that traditional forms such as *son* have flourished in Mexico is that the country was closed to **rock** music until the late 1980s, when the government finally lifted import regulations and laws banning rock concerts. These had been in place since a chaotic 1971 festival dubbed the "Mexican Woodstock" scandalized the nation, and the country's modern music culture was effectively driven underground. When international rock music finally flooded in on the free market, Mexican rock began to flourish. The boom began in Mexico City (fostered by an ongoing record swap-meet there), with middle-class rockers like **Los Caifanes** playing to middle-class audiences who knew about the outside scene because they, or their parents, travelled regularly to Europe and the US. Ironically, the Caifanes' massive hit was a 1988 cover of a traditional Cuban *son*, "La Negra Tomasa", which appealed to a public that understood *son* and salsa better than the British punk referenced in other songs. A little later, the eclectic **Café Tacuba** began to reach a bigger audience, with an interest, to some extent, in exploring Mexican roots and reinterpreting Mexican *son* in their own way. Then came **Maná**, from Guadalajara, and Mexican rock – now rather slickly produced – entered the superstar level (albeit after a decade of labouring in obscurity).

In the late 1990s the scene began to splinter into subcultures. The industrial town of Monterrey, home to a prestigious university and a lot of English-speaking, US-oriented youth, was a seemingly bottomless well of talent that drew comparisons to Seattle in the grunge years. Funky mix-masters **Plastilina Mosh**, ska band **El Gran Silencio** and **Control Machete**'s hip-hop went from here to Latin MTV. In Tijuana, meanwhile, **Nortec Collective** helped create an international club scene with its remixes of classic *norteño* sounds with techno beats. Accordion-playing **Julieta Venegas**, also of Tijuana, won a Latin Grammy in 2004 for her gutsy singing and songwriting.

But never mind record sales and radio airplay. Perhaps the best indicator that the modern sound of rock (and hip-hop, ska and electronica) has finally arrived in Mexico is that so many of these artists now perform sold-out shows at Mexico City's legendary Salón Los Ángeles, the same club where *danzón* fans still gather on other nights.

Mary Farquharson

# Books

Mexico has attracted more than its fair share of famous foreign writers, and has inspired a vast literature and several classics. Until very recently, however, Mexican writers had received little attention outside the country; what translations exist are published by small US presses, and few authors are well known north of the border. Most big US bookstores will have an enormous array of books about, from or set in Mexico, plus a few novels. In the rest of the English-speaking world there's far less choice, though the best-known of the archeological and travel titles here should be available almost anywhere. In the lists below, the UK publisher is followed by the US one; where only one publisher is listed it's the same in both places, or we've specified; o/p means a book is out of print, but may still be found in libraries or secondhand bookshops. Books with a ★ symbol are highly recommended.

In London you can freely visit Canning House Library, 2 Belgrave Square, SW1X 8PJ (☎020/7235 2303, ext. 208, Ⓦwww.canninghouse.com), which has the UK's largest publicly accessible collection of books and periodicals on Latin America. If you're travelling to the **Maya** areas, visit the library and resource centre at The Guatemalan Maya Centre, 94 Wandsworth Bridge Rd, London SW6 2TF (call ☎020/7371 5291 for opening times, Ⓦwww.maya.org.uk; closed Jan, Easter & Aug). Members (£5 annually) have use of the reference library and video collection. There is also a particularly fine textile collection. The Centre's founder, Krystyna Deuss, is the acknowledged English authority on Guatemalan life, dress and contemporary Maya rituals.

# Travel

**Sybille Bedford** *A Visit to Don Otavio* (Eland/Counterpoint). An extremely enjoyable, often hilarious, occasionally lyrical and surprisingly relevant account of Ms Bedford's travels through Mexico in the early 1950s.

**Jeff Biggers** *In the Sierra Madre* (University of Illinois). Biggers juxtaposes the history of the Copper Canyon region – with all its indigenous tribes and foreign treasure-hunters – with his present-day experiences living there amid the Rarámuri, the drug-runners and other colourful characters. Really lively story-telling from someone with an obvious love of the place.

**Frances Calderón de la Barca** *Life in Mexico* (University of California). The diary of a Scotswoman who married the Spanish ambassador to Mexico and spent two years there in the mid-nineteenth century.

**Tony Cohan** *Mexican Days: Journeys into the Heart of Mexico* (Broadway, US). Cohan, an American novelist, relocated to San Miguel de Allende in the 1980s; this is a travelogue of his explorations into small towns after some twenty years in Mexico – a perspective that's both respectful and informed, and without the gee-whiz tone that his earlier work about rebuilding his house, *On Mexican Time*, sometimes displayed.

**Charles Macomb Flandrau** *Viva Mexico!* (Eland, o/p). First published in 1908, Flandrau's account of life on his brother's farm is something of a cult classic. Though attitudes are inevitably dated in places, it's extremely funny in others.

**Thomas Gage** *Thomas Gage's Travels in the New World* (University of Oklahoma Press, o/p). Unusual account by an English cleric who became a Dominican friar chronicling his travels through Mexico and Central America in the early seventeenth century, including fascinating insights into colonial life and some great attacks on the greed and pomposity of the Catholic Church abroad.

**Graham Greene** *The Lawless Roads* (Penguin Classics). In the late 1930s Greene was sent to Mexico to investigate the effects of the persecution of the Catholic Church. The result (see also his novel on p.938) was this classic account of his travels in a very bizarre era of modern Mexican history.

**Katie Hickman** *A Trip to the Light Fantastic: Travels with a Mexican Circus* (Flamingo/HarperCollins, o/p). Enchanting, funny and uplifting account of a year spent travelling (and performing) with a fading Mexican circus troupe.

**Aldous Huxley** *Beyond the Mexique Bay* (Flamingo/Academy Chicago, o/p). Only a small part of the book is devoted to Mexico, but the descriptions of the archeological sites around Oaxaca, in particular, are still worth reading.

**D.H. Lawrence** *Mornings in Mexico* (Fredonia). A very slim volume, half of which is devoted to the Hopi Indians of New Mexico, this is an uncharacteristically cheerful account of Lawrence's stay in southern Mexico, and beautifully written – although his characterizations of native culture will likely strike modern readers as condescending.

**John Lincoln** *One Man's Mexico* (Century, o/p). Lincoln – the pen name of British Council officer Maurice Cardiff, whose identity was only revealed after his death in 2006 – travelled through the Mexican jungles in the late 1960s, producing an entertaining and offbeat read that you'd never guess was the product of a civil servant. Graham Greene called it the best book about Mexico of the twentieth century.

**John Lloyd Stephens** *Incidents of Travel in Central America, Chiapas, and Yucatán* (Dover). Stephens was a classic nineteenth-century traveller. Acting as American ambassador to Central America, he indulged his own enthusiasm for archeology. His journals, full of superb Victorian pomposity punctuated with sudden waves of enthusiasm, make great reading, especially as companions to the great Maya ruins, many of which he helped uncover. The best editions, such as this one, include the fantastic original illustrations by Frederick Catherwood; you won't have trouble finding inexpensive paperback editions in Mexico.

**Paul Theroux** *The Old Patagonian Express* (Penguin). The epic journey from Boston to the tip of South America by train spends just three rather bad-tempered chapters in Mexico, so don't expect to find out too much about the country. A good read nonetheless.

**John Kenneth Turner** *Barbarous Mexico* (University of Texas, o/p). Turner was a journalist, and this account of his travels through nineteenth-century Mexico exposing the conditions of workers in the plantations of the Yucatán, serialized in US newspapers, did much to discredit the regime of Porfirio Díaz.

**Ronald Wright** *Time Among the Maya* (Abacus/Grove). A vivid and sympathetic account of travels from Belize through Guatemala, Chiapas and Yucatán, meeting the Maya of today and exploring their obsession with time. The level of detail makes this a complex read – best for readers with a specific interest in ancient Maya culture.

# Mexican fiction

**Mariano Azuela** *The Underdogs* (Hackett/Modern Library). The first novel of the Revolution (finished in 1915), *The Underdogs* is told through the eyes of a group of peasants who form a semi-regular Revolutionary armed band. The story concerns their escapades, progress and eventual betrayal and massacre. Initially fighting for land and liberty, they end up caught in a cycle of violence they cannot control and descend into brutal nihilism. The novel set many of the themes of post-Revolutionary Mexican writing.

**Carmen Boullosa** *The Miracle Worker* (Jonathan Cape, o/p). One of Mexico's most promising contemporary writers, Boullosa focuses on traditional Mexican themes, often borrowing characters from history or myth. *The Miracle Worker* explores Mexican attitudes to Catholicism through the eyes of a messianic healer and her followers. The story can be seen as a parable about the Mexican political system, where ordinary Mexicans petition a distant government for favours, which are granted or refused in seemingly arbitrary decisions. You may be able to find Boullosa's novel *Leaving Tabasco* more readily; it's not as strong a work, but an interesting vision of small-town life (and trauma) through the eyes of a child.

**María Amparo Escandón** *Gonzalez & Daughter Trucking Co.* (Three Rivers). A story within a story, told with gusto by an inmate at a women's prison in Mexicali – borderline pulp, with cliffhangers and campy drama, but heartwarming and funny in its treatment of loyalty and freedom. Escandón's earlier work, *Esperanza's Box of Saints* (Picador/Touchstone), is a charming, quick-read tale of female emancipation.

**Laura Esquivel** *Like Water for Chocolate* (Black Swan/Anchor). Adapted to film, Esquivel's novel has proved a huge hit in Mexico and abroad. The book is even better: funny, sexy, sentimental (schmaltzy, even), it deals with the star-crossed romance of Tita, whose lover marries her sister. Using the magic of the kitchen, she sets out to seduce him back. The book is written in monthly episodes, each of which is prefaced with a traditional Mexican recipe. The author's 2006 novel, *Malinche* (Simon & Schuster/Atria), is not nearly as successful, but presents a sympathetic version of Cortés's courtesan and translator, whose name is synonymous with "traitor" in Mexico.

**Carlos Fuentes** *The Death of Artemio Cruz* (Farrar, Straus & Giroux) and *The Old Gringo* (Farrar, Straus & Giroux). Fuentes is by far the best-known Mexican writer outside Mexico, influenced by Mariano Azuela and Juan Rulfo, and an early exponent of magical realism. In *The Death of Artemio Cruz*, the hero, a rich and powerful man on his deathbed, looks back over his life and loves, from an idealist youth in the Revolution through disillusion to corruption and power. *The Old Gringo* takes place during the Revolution, imagining that vanished American writer Ambrose Bierce has joined Pancho Villa's army; it's shorter, but no less carefully crafted. Fuentes examines contemporary issues in *The Crystal Frontier* (Bloomsbury/Harvest), a collection of interwoven stories examining the way personal contact colours Mexicans' unequal relationship with the US.

**Jorge Ibargüengoitia** *The Dead Girls*, *Two Crimes* and others (all Chatto & Windus/Avon, o/p). One of the first modern Mexican novelists translated into English (and unfortunately now left to languish), Ibargüengoitia was killed in a plane crash in 1983. These two, published just before his death, are both blackly comic thrillers, superbly told, the first of them based on real events.

**Mónica Lavín** (ed) *Points of Departure: New Stories from Modern Mexico* (City Lights, US). A collection of short stories from some of the country's most respected writers – the selection is a little uneven, but it may be interesting and refreshing to read stories that *don't* involve magical realism.

**Octavio Paz** (ed) *Mexican Poetry* (Grove). Edited by Paz (perhaps the leading man of letters of Mexico's post-Revolutionary era) and translated by Samuel Beckett, this is as good a taste as you could hope for of modern Mexican poets. Some of Paz's own poetry is also available in translation.

**Elena Poniatowska** *Here's to You, Jesúsa!* (Penguin). One of Mexico's best-known essayists and journalists lightly fictionalizes the life story of her cleaning lady to create a lively "autobiography" covering her marriage, involvement in the Revolution and the postwar period. Some of Poniatowska's other excellent works available in English include *Massacre in Mexico* (University of Missouri), a collage of testimonies of those present at the 1968 massacre of students in Tlatelolco, and *Tinisima* (University of New Mexico), a portrait of communist organizer and photographer Tina Modotti, who also moved in Diego Rivera's circles.

**Juan Rulfo** *Pedro Páramo* (Serpent's Tail/Grove). First published in 1955, this is widely regarded as the greatest Mexican novel of the twentieth century and a precursor of magical realism. The living and spirit worlds mesh when, at the behest of his dying mother, the narrator visits the deserted village haunted by the memory of his brutal father, Pedro Páramo. Dark, but ultimately very rewarding. Rulfo's short-story collection, *The Burning Plain and Other Stories* (University of Texas), is rated by Gabriel García Márquez as the best in Latin America.

# Foreign fiction

There must be hundreds of novels by outsiders set in Mexico, all too many in the sex-and-shopping genre. Apart from those below, others to look out for include a whole clutch of modern Americans, especially **Jack Kerouac**'s *Desolation Angels* (Flamingo, o/p) and several of Richard Brautigan's novels. And of course there's **Carlos Castaneda**'s *Don Juan* series (Arkana/University of California) – a search for enlightenment through peyote.

**Tony Cartano** *After the Conquest* (Secker & Warburg, o/p). An extraordinary fictional account of a fictional author who believes he is Bruno Traven's son and sets out to discover the truth about his father (see p.938). A psychological thriller that is also full of Mexican history and politics.

**Eduardo Galeano** *Genesis* and *Faces & Masks* (both W.W. Norton). The first two parts of a trilogy by a Uruguayan writer, these anthologies of Indian legends, colonists' tales and odd snatches of fictionalized history illuminate the birth of Latin America. Not specifically Mexican, but wonderful, relevant reading nonetheless.

**Graham Greene** *The Power and the Glory* (Penguin). Inspired by his investigative travels, this story of a doomed whisky priest on the run from the authorities makes a great yarn. It was a wonderful movie too.

**Gary Jennings** *Aztec* (Tor). Sex and sacrifice in ancient Mexico. The narrator travels around the Aztec empire in search of his fortune, chancing upon almost every ancient culture along the way, and sleeping with most of them, until finally the Spanish arrive. Perfect beach or bus reading, and informative too; if you're hooked, there are two more gripping instalments in the trilogy.

**D.H. Lawrence** *The Plumed Serpent* (Dodo). One of Lawrence's own favourites, the novel reflects his intense dislike of the country that followed on from the brief honeymoon period of *Mornings in Mexico* (see p.935). Fans of his heavy spiritualism will love it.

**Haniel Long** *The Marvellous Adventure of Cabeza de Vaca* (Bear & Co.). Two short stories in one volume – the first the account of a shipwrecked conquistador's journey across the new continent, the second the thoughts and hopes of Malinche, Cortés's interpreter.

**Malcolm Lowry** *Under the Volcano* (Penguin/Harper Perennial). A classic since its publication, Lowry's account of the last day in the life of the British consul in Cuernavaca – passed in a mescal-induced haze – is totally brilliant. His *Dark as the Grave Wherein My Friend Is Laid* (Picador, o/p) is also based on his Mexican experiences.

**James A. Michener** *Mexico* (Fawcett). Another doorstop from Michener. Fans will love it.

**Bruno Traven** various works. In the 1920s and 1930s, the mysterious Traven – allegedly American, naturalized Mexican but perhaps a German revolutionary – wrote a whole series of compelling novels set in Mexico. Among the best known are *Treasure of the Sierra Madre* (Prion/Hill & Wang) and *The Death Ship* (Chicago Review/Lawrence Hill), but of more direct interest if you're travelling are such works as *The Bridge in the Jungle* and the other six books in the *Jungle* series: *Government*, *The Carreta*, *March to the Monteria*, *Trozas*, *The Rebellion of the Hanged* and *General from the Jungle* (all Ivan R. Dee, o/p). These latter all deal with the state of the peasantry and the growth of revolutionary feeling in the last years of the Díaz dictatorship, and if at times they're overly polemical, as a whole they're enthralling. Will Wyatt's *The Secret of the Sierra Madre: The Man Who Was B. Traven* (Doubleday/Harcourt, o/p) is the best of the books on the quest for the author's identity.

# History

The sources below are all entertaining and/or important references; more standard **general histories** include *A History of Mexico*, by Henry Bamford Parkes (Mariner, o/p); *Fire and Blood: A History of Mexico*, by T.R. Fehrenbach (Da Capo); *A Concise History of Mexico from Hidalgo to Cárdenas*, by Jan Bazant (Cambridge UP, o/p); and *The Course of Mexican History*, by Michael Meyer, William Sherman and Susan Deeds (Oxford UP).

**Inga Clendinnen** *Ambivalent Conquests: Maya and Spaniard in Yucatán 1517 to 1570* (Cambridge UP). A product of meticulous research that documents the methods and consequences of the Spanish

Conquest of the Yucatán. The ambivalence in the title reflects doubts about the effectiveness of the Conquest in subjugating the Maya, and the book provides insights into the rebellions that followed: more than three hundred years later, the Maya rose in revolt during the Caste Wars, and almost succeeded in driving out their white overlords. This revised edition also comments briefly on the 1994 Chiapas uprising.

**Hernán Cortés** *Letters from Mexico* (Yale UP). The thoughts and impressions of the conquistador, at first hand. Less exciting than Díaz, though.

**Bernal Díaz** (trans. J.M. Cohen) *The Conquest of New Spain* (Penguin). This abridged version is the best available of Díaz's classic *Historia Verdadera de la Conquista de la Nueva España*. Díaz, having been on two earlier expeditions to Mexico, accompanied Cortés throughout his campaign of conquest, and this magnificent eyewitness account still makes compelling reading.

**Adolfo Gilly** *The Mexican Revolution* (New Press). Written in Mexico City's notorious Lecumberri jail (Gilly was later granted an absolute pardon), this is regarded as the classic work on the Revolution. Heavy going and highly theoretical though.

**Brian Hamnett** *A Concise History of Mexico* (Cambridge UP). The book kicks off with a brief examination of contemporary issues and then jumps back to the time of the Olmecs. A combined chronological and thematic approach is used to analyse the social and political history of Mexico from then up until the present day. Some fairly large chunks of history are glossed over, but key events and issues are explored in greater detail, making for a good general introduction.

**John Mason Hart** *Empire & Revolution: Americans in Mexico* (University of California). Hart's detailed history of the Mexican Revolution proposes that it was not so much an internal upheaval as an uprising against exploitation by American business interests. A massive work, but worth skimming for his unique take on this period in history.

**Enrique Krauze** *Mexico: Biography of Power* (HarperCollins). First published in Spanish, this sprawling history covers most of the nineteenth and twentieth centuries – the biography format makes it very readable, and easier to dip into if you can't weather all 896 pages. Street names and public holidays will make a lot more sense, at the very least.

**William Prescott** *History of the Conquest of Mexico* (Cooper Square Press). Written in the mid-nineteenth century, and drawing heavily on Díaz, Prescott's history was the standard text for more than a hundred years. It makes for pretty heavy reading and has now been overtaken by Thomas's account – but as a classic history (written by someone who had never even visited Mexico) it's a fascinating work of scholarship, ranking with Gibbon's *The Decline and Fall of the Roman Empire*.

**John Reed** *Insurgent Mexico* (International Publications). This collection of his reportage of the Mexican Revolution was put together by Reed himself. He spent several months in 1913 and 1914 with various generals of the Revolution – especially Villa – and the book contains great descriptions of them, their men and the mood of the times.

**Nelson Reed** *The Caste War of the Yucatan* (Stanford UP). Reed's book is the authority on this tumultuous and defining era in Yucatán history, with great detail on the Talking Cross movement. A must-read for anyone intrigued by this period.

**Jasper Ridley** *Maximilian & Juárez* (Weidenfield & Nicholson/Phoenix). This comprehensive, highly readable account of one of "the great tragicomedies of the nineteenth century" charts the attempt by Napoleon III to establish Archduke Maximilian as the emperor of Mexico. The colourful narrative brings to life an unmitigated political disaster with huge consequences, including the execution of Maximilian, the insanity of his wife Carlota and the emergence of the US as a world power.

**Hugh Thomas** *Conquest: Montezuma, Cortés, and the Fall of Old Mexico* (Simon & Schuster); *The Conquest of Mexico* (Pimlico). Same book, different title, but either way a brilliant narrative history of the Conquest by the British historian previously best known for his history of the Spanish Civil War. A massive work of real scholarship and importance – much of the archive material was unearthed only in the 1980s and 1990s – but also humorous and readable, with appendices on everything from Aztec beliefs, history and genealogy to Cortés's wives and lovers.

# Ancient Mexico



There are thousands of studies of **ancient Mexico**, many of them extremely academic and detailed, plus any number of big, highly illustrated coffee-table tomes on individual sites. Those below are of more general interest, and any of them will have substantial **bibliographies** to help you explore further.

**Ignacio Bernal** *Mexico Before Cortez* (Dolphin, o/p). The leading Mexican archeologist of the twentieth century, and one of the inspirations behind the Museo Nacional de Antropología (see p.440), Bernal did important work on the Olmecs and the restoration of Teotihuacán, and has written many important source works. This book covers much the same ground as Davies's, though in less detail, and is more dated, but it has the advantage of being widely available in Mexico. A more scholarly version is available in *A History of Mexican Archeology: The Vanished Civilizations of Middle America* (Thames & Hudson/ W.W. Norton, o/p).

**Warwick Bray** *Everyday Life of the Aztecs* (Peter Bedrick). A volume full of information about Aztec warfare, music, games, folklore, religious ritual, social organization, economic and political systems and agricultural practice. Although the book is now showing its age, and some of its conclusions are a bit dubious, its attractive comprehensiveness more than makes up for this. An excellent general introduction.

**Inga Clendinnen** *Aztecs: An Interpretation* (Cambridge UP). A social history of the Aztec empire that seeks to explain the importance – and acceptance – of human sacrifice and other rituals. Fascinating, though best to know something about the Aztecs before you start.

**Michael D. Coe** *The Maya* (Thames & Hudson). The best available general introduction to the Maya: concise, clear and comprehensive. Coe has also written several weightier, academic volumes. His *Breaking the Maya Code* (Thames & Hudson), a history of the decipherment of the Maya glyphs, owes much to the fact that Coe was present at many of the most important meetings leading to the breakthrough that demonstrated how the glyphs actually did reproduce Maya speech. Aside from anything else, it is a beautifully written, ripping yarn, though the slagging-off of Eric Thompson gets a bit wearisome.

**Nigel Davies** *The Ancient Kingdoms of Mexico* (Penguin). Although no single text covers all the ancient cultures, this comes pretty close, covering the central areas from the Olmecs through Teotihuacán and the Toltecs to the Aztec empire. An excellent mix of historical, archeological, social and artistic information, but it doesn't cover the Maya. Davies is also the author of several more-detailed academic works on the Aztecs and Toltecs, including *The Aztecs, A History* (University of Oklahoma, o/p).

**M.S. Edmonson** (trans.) *The Book of Chilam Balam of Chumayel* (University of Texas, o/p). The *Chilam Balam* is a recollection of Maya history and myth, compiled by the Maya over centuries; this version was written in Maya in Latin script in the eighteenth century. Although the style is not easy, it's one of the few keys into the Maya view of the world.

**George Kubler** *Art and Architecture of Ancient America* (Yale UP). Exactly what it says: a massive and amazingly comprehensive work, covering not only Mexico but Colombia, Ecuador and Peru as well. It's rather old-fashioned, however, and fails to take into account the ground-breaking epigraphic findings in Maya scholarship.

**Diego de Landa** *Yucatán Before and After the Conquest* (Dover). A translation by William Gates of the work written in 1566 as *Relación de las Cosas de Yucatán*. De Landa's destruction of almost all original Maya books as "works of the devil" leaves his own account as the chief source on Maya life and society in the immediate post-Conquest period. Written during his imprisonment in Spain on charges of cruelty to the Indians (remarkable itself, given the institutional brutality of the time), the book provides a fascinating wealth of detail. Various other translations are widely available in Mexico.

**Maria Longhena** *Splendours of Ancient Mexico* (Thames & Hudson, o/p). Sumptuously illustrated coffee-table tome, with better than average text (translated from the Italian original) and excellent pictures and plans of all the major ancient sites.

**Simon Martin and Nikolai Grube** *Chronicle of the Maya Kings and Queens* (Thames & Hudson). A more graphic approach to Maya history, replete with photo illustrations, timelines, hieroglyphics and the like, making the complex dynasties a little easier to grasp.

**Mary Ellen Miller** *Maya Art and Architecture* (Thames & Hudson, UK). An excellent survey of the artisanship of the Maya, organized by media, from stelae to pottery. Her *The Art of Mesoamerica: From Olmec to Aztec* (Thames & Hudson) gives a broader view.

**Mary Ellen Miller and Karl Taube** *The Gods and Symbols of Ancient Mexico and the Maya: An Illustrated Dictionary of Mesoamerican Religion* (Thames & Hudson, o/p). A superb modern reference on ancient Mesoamerica, written by two leading scholars. Taube's *Aztec and Maya Myths* (British Museum Press/University of Texas, o/p) is perfect as a short, accessible introduction to Mesoamerican mythology.

**Chris Morton and Ceri Louise Thomas** *The Mystery of the Crystal Skulls* (HarperCollins). Intriguing, if somewhat sensationalist investigation into an ancient Amerindian legend that tells of a number of life-size crystal skulls said to contain vital information about the destiny of mankind. Following the discovery that such a skull actually exists, film-makers Morton and Thomas set off on a journey through Mexico and Central America, meeting experts in Maya culture, archeologists and modern-day shamans and finally coming to their own conclusions.

**Jeremy A. Sabloff** *Cities of Ancient Mexico* (Thames & Hudson, o/p). An easy-to-digest introduction to ancient Mexico, with excellent photos by Macduff Everton – the main text focuses on daily life, with the end of the book explaining how these conclusions are deduced from the archeological record. Thoroughly up-to-date and easy to digest. Also worth checking is his *New Archaeology and the Ancient Maya* (Scientific American Library, o/p).

**Linda Schele, David Freidel et al.** The authors, at the forefront of the "new archeology", have been personally responsible for decoding many Maya glyphs, revolutionizing and popularizing this field. Although their writing style, which frequently includes recreations of scenes inspired by their discoveries, is controversial to some colleagues, it has also inspired a devoted following. *A Forest of Kings: The Untold Story of the Ancient Maya* (William Morrow/Harper Perennial), in conjunction with *The Blood of Kings*, by Linda Schele and Mary Ellen Miller (Thames & Hudson/George Braziller), shows that far from being governed by peaceful astronomer-priests, the ancient Maya were ruled by hereditary kings, lived in populous, aggressive city-states and engaged in a continuous entanglement of alliances and war. *Maya Cosmos: Three Thousand Years on the Shaman's Path* (William Morrow, US), by Schele, Freidel and Joy Parker, is perhaps more difficult to read, dense with copious notes, but continues to examine Maya ritual and religion in a unique and far-reaching way. *The Code of Kings* (Scribner, US), written in collaboration with Peter Matthews and illustrated with Justin Kerr's "rollout" photography of Maya ceramics, examines in detail the significance of the monuments at selected Maya sites.

**Robert Sharer** *The Ancient Maya* (Stanford UP). The classic, comprehensive (and weighty) account of Maya civilization, now in its sixth edition. Required reading for archeologists, it provides a fascinating reference for the non-expert.

**Dennis Tedlock** (trans.) *Popol Vuh* (Simon & Schuster/Touchstone). Translation of the Quiché Maya bible, a fascinating creation myth from the only ancient civilization to emerge from rainforest terrain. The Maya obsession with time can be well appreciated here, where dates are recorded with painstaking precision.

**J. Eric S. Thompson** *The Rise and Fall of Maya Civilization* (Pimlico/University of Oklahoma, o/p). A major authority on the ancient Maya during his lifetime, Thompson produced many academic works; *Rise and Fall*, originally published in 1954, is one of the more approachable. Although researchers have since overturned many of Thompson's theories, his work provided the inspiration for the postwar surge of interest in the Maya, and he remains a respected figure.

**Ptolemy Tompkins** *This Tree Grows Out of Hell* (HarperSanFrancisco, o/p). An interesting attempt to piece together the mystery of Mesoamerican religion, synthesizing and making readable many of the late twentieth-century findings in the area. The latter half of the book is a thoroughly unconvincing apology for the brutality of the Aztecs.

**Richard F. Townsend** *The Aztecs* (Thames & Hudson). Companion in the series to Coe's *Maya* book (see p.940), this attempts to be an introduction to all aspects of Aztec history and culture, but if you haven't done some prior reading, the details of names and battles may be overwhelming. That said, it's a comprehensive reference.

## Society, politics and culture

**Taisha Abelar** *The Sorcerer's Crossing* (Penguin). The extraordinary true story of an American woman who joins an all-female group of sorcerers in Mexico and undergoes a rigorous physical and mental training process, designed to enable her to breach the limits of ordinary perception.

**Rick Bayless** *Rick Bayless's Mexican Kitchen* (Scribner/Prentice Hall). Aimed at the ambitious chef, this weighty tome has more than 150 recipes but no photos. The country's gastronomic heritage is explored in detail with a special focus on the myriad types of chile that form the heart of Mexican cuisine. More accessible is his *Mexico One Plate at a Time* (W.W. Norton, US), which focuses on the classics of the cuisine, with careful instructions and thorough coaching, including a testimony in favour of lard.

**Fernández de Calderón Candida** *Great Masters of Mexican Folk Art* (Harry N. Abrams). An ambitious and gorgeously photographed coffee-table book produced by the cultural wing of Banamex, with portraits of the artisans alongside their works.

**Miguel Covarrubias** *Mexico South* (KPI, o/p). The people and popular culture of Veracruz and the Isthmus of Tehuantepec, as depicted by the well-known Mexican artist and anthropologist. A good read, well illustrated.

**Augusta Dwyer** *On the Line* (LAB, o/p). A painstakingly detailed account of conditions on the US/Mexico border, where many of the most environmentally damaging factories on the continent poison lands and people on both sides of the frontier. The "line" is the only place in the world where the rich north directly borders the poorer south, and Dwyer documents the consequences of this economic discrepancy in case studies of *maquila* workers, legal and illegal immigrants and both victims and members of the US Border Patrol.

**Macduff Everton** *The Modern Maya: A Culture in Transition* (University of New Mexico). Everton's black-and-white photographs document Maya village life with affection and dignity, with an eye to socioeconomic issues.

**Clare Ferguson** *Flavours of Mexico* (Ryland, Peters & Small, o/p). All the classics are here: tortillas, enchiladas, empanadas, *flautas* and tamales, along with party-food suggestions and a few vegetarian recipes. A colourful and straightforward cookbook that will inspire you to keep feasting on Mexican cuisine once back home.

**Judith Adler Hellman** *Mexican Lives* (The New Press, US). A compilation of interviews with fifteen Mexicans on the eve of the signing of NAFTA, offering poignant insight into how rich and poor alike cope with life on the brink of enormous political and social change. The voices of the interviewees themselves speak so clearly that their personalities and emotions stand out from the pages. Underlying all the accounts is the reality of institutional corruption, which affects every sector of society but falls most heavily on the poor. Although published in 1994, still worth reading by anyone who wants to understand what modern Mexico is like behind the headlines.

**Hayden Herrera** *Frida: The Biography of Frida Kahlo* (Bloomsbury). This mesmerizing bio brings to life a woman of extreme magnetism and originality. Starting with her childhood in Mexico City, the account goes on to describe the crippling accident she had as a teenager that left her in chronic pain, her tempestuous marriage to Diego Rivera and the various men with whom she had affairs including, most notoriously, Leon Trotsky. The book contains numerous colour reproductions of her paintings.

**Diana Kennedy** *From My Mexican Kitchen: Techniques and Ingredients* (Crown/Clarkson Potter). Kennedy was a pioneer in bringing the multi-faceted cuisine of Mexico to the attention of Americans, when she published her first cookbook in 1972. This book is a good starting point for anyone new to Mexican cooking. Also look out for *My Mexico: A Culinary Odyssey with More Than 300 Recipes* (Clarkson Potter, US), which has a great travelogue element as well – though the recipes are geared only to American kitchens.

**Dan La Botz** *Democracy in Mexico* (South End, US). Examines the political landscape of modern Mexico and puts it into historical context by equating the rise of civil society and political consciousness with the major defining events of recent decades – the 1968 student massacre, the 1985 earthquake and the 1994 Zapatista uprising, among others.

**Peter Laufer** *Wetback Nation: The Case for Opening the Mexican–American Border* (Ivan R. Dee, US). An impassioned argument for revision of the current US immigration system, first published in 2004, even before the contentious border-fence proposal.

**Daniel C. Levy and Kathleen Bruhn** *Mexico: The Struggle for Democratic Development* (University of California). A bit academic, but one of the more up-to-date analyses of Mexico's political and economic situation – this revised edition was published in 2006.

**Oscar Lewis** *The Children of Sanchez* (Random House). These oral histories of a working-class family in the Mexico City of the 1940s are regarded as a seminal work in modern anthropology. The book is totally gripping, and doesn't read in the least like an anthropological text. Lewis's other works, including *Five Families* (Basic/HarperCollins), use the same first-person narrative technique. All are highly recommended.

**Patrick Marnham** *Dreaming with His Eyes Open: A Life of Diego Rivera* (Bloomsbury/University of California). A gripping account of the extraordinary life of the great Mexican muralist in which truths are revealed and myths are unravelled.

**Octavio Paz** *The Labyrinth of Solitude* (Penguin/Grove). An acclaimed series of philosophical essays exploring the social and political state of modern Mexico. Paz, who died in 1998, won the Nobel Prize for literature in 1990 and was universally regarded as the country's leading poet.

**Sam Quiñones** *True Tales from Another Mexico: the Lynch Mob, the Popsicle Kings, Chalino and the Bronx* (University of New Mexico). Snappy, absorbing essays and reporting about Mexican popular culture and heroes, from an Oaxacan basketball team to the scrappy force behind the Michoacana ice-cream shops.

**Gregory G. Reck** *In the Shadow of Tlaloc* (Waveland). Reck attempts a similar style to that of Oscar Lewis in his study of a Mexican village, and the effects on it of encroaching modernity. Often seems to stray over the border into sentimentality and even fiction, but interesting nonetheless.

**John Ross** *Rebellion from the Roots* (Common Courage, US).

A fascinating early account of the build-up to and first months of the 1994 Zapatista rebellion, and still the definitive book on the subject. Ross's reporting style provides a detailed and informative background, showing the uprising was no surprise to the Mexican army. His *Zapatistas: Making Another World Possible: Chronicles of Resistance 2000–2006* (Thunder's Mouth/Nation Books) brings the ongoing saga up to the present day.

**Guiomar Rovira** *Women of Maize* (LAB). Rovira, a Mexican journalist, witnessed the Zapatista uprising in Chiapas on New Year's Day, 1994. This book, which interweaves narrative, history and the personal recollections of numerous women involved in the rebellion, provides an extraordinary insight into the lives of indigenous people. The women interviewed reflect on how their previously traditional lifestyles were transformed when they joined up with the Zapatista National Liberation Army and gained access to education and other opportunities they'd never even dreamt of.

**Chloë Sayer** *Arts and Crafts of Mexico* (Thames & Hudson/ Chronicle). Sayer is the author of numerous books on Mexican arts, crafts and associated subjects, all of them worth reading. *The Skeleton at the Feast* (University of Texas), written with Elizabeth Carmichael, is a wonderful, superbly illustrated insight into attitudes to death and the dead in Mexico.

**Joel Simon** *Endangered Mexico* (LAB/Sierra Club). Eloquent and compelling study documenting the environmental crisis facing Mexico at the end of the twentieth century. Essential reading for those wanting to know how and why the crisis exists – and why no one can offer solutions.

**David Rains Wallace** *The Monkey's Bridge* (Sierra Club Books, o/p). When the Panama Bridge formed between North and South America three million years ago, plants and animals surged back and forth across it in an evolutionary intermingling that created one of the world's richest natural environments. This engaging account of Central America's role as an evolutionary link between the two continents cleverly interweaves natural history, human history, travel writing and personal reflection.

**Mariana Yampolsky** *The Traditional Architecture of Mexico* (Thames & Hudson). The enormous range of Mexico's architectural styles, from thatched peasant huts and vast haciendas to exuberant Baroque churches and solid yet graceful public buildings, is encompassed in this inspired book. While most of Yampolsky's superb photographs are in black and white, a chapter on the use of colour emphasizes its importance in every area of life; the text by Chloë Sayer raises it above the level of the average coffee-table book. (For guides to ecclesiastical architecture in Mexico see Perry, p.946.)

## Other guides

In Mexico, the best and most complete series of guides is that published by **Guías Panorama** – they have small books on all the main archeological sites, as well as more general titles ranging from *Wild Flowers of Mexico* to *Pancho Villa – Truth and Legend*.

**Carl Franz and Lorena Havens** *The People's Guide to Mexico* (Avalon Travel). Not a guidebook as such: more a series of anecdotes and words of advice for staying out of trouble and heading off the beaten track. Perennially popular (2006 saw the publication of the thirteenth edition), and deservedly so.

**Joyce Kelly** *An Archaeological Guide to Mexico's Yucatán Peninsula* (University of Oklahoma, o/p). Detailed and practical guide to more than ninety Maya sites and eight museums throughout the peninsula, including many little-known or difficult-to-reach ruins; an essential companion for anyone travelling purposefully through the Maya world. Kelly's "star" rating – based on a site's archeological importance, degree of restoration and accessibility – may affront purists, but it does provide a valuable opinion.

**Richard and Rosalind Perry** *Maya Missions* (Espadaña, US). One in a series of expertly written guides to the sometimes overlooked treasures of Mexico's colonial religious architecture. *More Maya Missions* covers Chiapas. Both are illustrated by the authors' simple but beautiful drawings. These specialist offerings, ideal for travellers who want more information than most guidebooks can provide, are not widely available, though you can sometimes find them in tourist bookshops in the areas they cover.

**R.J. Secor** *Mexico's Volcanoes* (Mountaineers). Detailed routes up all the big volcanoes, and full of invaluable information for climbers.

**Jules Siegel** *Cancun User's Guide 2005*. Siegel, a freelance journalist, moved to Mexico in 1981, then worked for the tourism ministry in the nascent resort city. His self-published tome is as much an ode to this under-appreciated city and the people who built it as it is a practical guide, with shopping and eating recommendations. Affectionate, opinionated and guaranteed to change your outlook on Cancún, as well as Mexico as a whole. (Purchase online at www.lulu.com.)

## Wildlife

**Rosita Arvigo** *Sastun: My Apprenticeship with a Maya Healer* (HarperCollins). The author established an organic herb farm in Belize, then studied with the region's best-known medicine man for five years. Her story is fascinating for anyone interested in herbal treatments; more detail can be found in her *Rainforest Home Remedies*.

**Les Beletsky** *Tropical Mexico: The Ecotravellers' Wildlife Guide* (Academic, o/p). An excellent field guide, with colour plates of not just birds but also reptiles and mammals found through the Yucatán and Chiapas.

**Steve Howell** *Where to Watch Birds in Mexico* (Christopher Helm). One for the enthusiast – more than a hundred sites are listed, where some 950 bird species can be seen. General information on the recommended regions is also provided, along with tips on how to spot birds and identify them.

**Steve Howell and Sophie Webb** *A Guide to the Birds of Mexico and Northern Central America* (Oxford UP). A tremendous work, the result of years of research, this is the definitive book on the region's birds. Essential for all serious birders, though a bit hefty to use in the field.

**Paul Humann and Ned DeLoach** *Snorkeling Guide to Marine Life: Florida, Caribbean, Bahamas* (New World). A handy, spiral-bound field guide to corals, fish, plants and other underwater life off the Caribbean coast, with 280 colour photos.

**Eugene H. Kaplan** *Coral Reefs of the Caribbean and Florida* (Houghton Mifflin). Part of the Peterson Field Guide series, a useful handbook on the abundant wildlife off the coasts of the Yucatán peninsula.

**R.T. Peterson and E.L. Chalif** *Mexican Birds* (Houghton Mifflin). The classic ornithological guide to Mexico. The text is excellent, but drawings are limited to indigenous examples only. For migratory species, you'll have to consult something like the *Sibley Field Guide to Birds* (Knopf), which comes in editions for both Western and Eastern North America.

**Victoria Schlesinger** *Animals and Plants of the Ancient Maya: A Guide* (University of Texas). More than a field guide, this book also examines the cultural significance of more than a hundred species in the ancient Maya world.

# Language

# Language

Rules of pronunciation ........ 951

Useful words and phrases ........ 951

Food and drink terms ........ 954

Terms and acronyms ........ 958

Art and architectural terms ........ 960

# Mexican Spanish

Once you get into it, **Spanish** is actually a straightforward language, and in Mexico people are eager to understand and to help even the most faltering attempt. **English** is widely spoken, especially in heavily visited areas, but you'll get a far better reception if you at least try to communicate with people in their own tongue. You'll be helped by the fact that Mexicans speak relatively slowly, at least compared with Spaniards.

## Rules of pronunciation

Relative to English, the rules of **pronunciation** are clear-cut and, once you get to know them, strictly observed. Unless there's an accent, words ending in d, l, r and z are stressed on the last syllable, all others on the second last. All vowels are pure and short.

**A** is between the A sound of "back" and that of "father".
**E** as in "get"
**I** as in "police"
**O** as in "hot"
**U** as in "rule"
**C** is spoken like S before E and I, hard otherwise: *cerca* is pronounced "SER-ka".
**G** is a guttural H sound (a little softer than the ch in "loch") before E or I, a hard G elsewhere: *gigante* becomes "hi-GAN-te".
**H** is always silent.
**J** is the same sound as a guttural G: *jamón* is pronounced "ham-ON".
**LL** sounds like an English Y: *tortilla* is pronounced "tor-TEE-ya".
**N** is as in English unless it has a tilde (accent) over it, when it becomes NY: *mañana* sounds like "ma-NYA-na".
**QU** is pronounced like an English K.
**R** is rolled; RR, doubly so.
**V** sounds more like B, *vino* becoming "BEE-no".
**X** has an S sound before consonants; between vowels in place names, it has an H sound, like México ("MEH-hee-ko") or Oaxaca ("wa-HA-ka"). In many place names from indigenous languages, the X is pronounced as S – as in Xochimilco ("so-chee-MIL-co") and Xalapa ("sa-LA-pa"); in Maya, however, X sounds like SH – Xel-Ha is pronounced "shel-ha".
**Z** is the same as a soft C, so *cerveza* becomes "ser-VAY-sa".

## Useful words and phrases

Although we've listed a few essential words and phrases here, if you're travelling for any length of time some kind of **dictionary** or **phrasebook** is obviously a worthwhile investment: the *Rough Guide to Mexican Spanish* is the best practical guide, correct and colloquial, and will have you speaking the language faster than any other phrasebook. One of the best small Latin American Spanish dictionaries is the University of Chicago version (Pocket Books), widely available in Mexico, although the Langenscheidt pocket dictionary is also handy because its yellow plastic cover holds up well. If you're using an older dictionary, bear in mind that CH, LL and Ñ are traditionally counted as separate letters and are listed after the Cs, Ls and Ns respectively; most current dictionaries, however, follow more familiar alphabetizing procedures, though Ñ retains its own section.

## Basics

| | |
|---|---|
| **Sí, No** | Yes, No |
| **Abierto/a, Cerrado/a** | Open, Closed |
| **Por favor, Gracias** | Please, Thank you |
| **Empujar, Tirar** | Push, Pull |
| **¿Dónde?, ¿Cuándo?** | Where?, When? |
| **Con, Sin** | With, Without |
| **¿Qué?, ¿Cuánto?** | What?, How much? |
| **Buen(o)/a, Mal(o)/a** | Good, Bad |
| **Aquí or Acá, Allí or Allá** | Here, There |
| **Gran(de), Pequeño/a** | Big, Small |
| **Éste, Eso** | This, That |
| **Más, Menos** | More, Less |
| **Barato/a, Caro/a** | Cheap, Expensive |
| **Hoy, Mañana** | Today, Tomorrow |
| **Ayer** | Yesterday |
| **Ahora, Más tarde** | Now, Later |

## Greetings and pleasantries

| | |
|---|---|
| **¡Hola!, Adiós** | Hello, Goodbye |
| **Buenos días** | Good morning |
| **Buenas tardes/ noches** | Good afternoon/night |
| **¿Qué tal?** | How do you do? |
| **Hasta luego** | See you later |
| **Lo siento/ disculpeme** | Sorry |
| **Con permiso/ perdón** | Excuse me |
| **¿Cómo está (usted)?** | How are you? |
| **De nada/por nada** | Not at all/You're welcome |
| **(No) Entiendo** | I (don't) understand |
| **¿Habla (usted) inglés?** | Do you speak English? |
| **(No) Hablo español** | I (don't) speak Spanish |
| **Mande?** | What (did you say)? |
| **Me llamo...** | My name is... |
| **¿Cómo se llama usted?** | What's your name? |
| **Soy inglés(a)** | I am English |
| **...americano(a)** | ...American* |
| **...australiano(a)** | ...Australian |
| **...canadiense(a)** | ...Canadian |
| **...irlandés(a)** | ...Irish |
| **...escosés(a)** | ...Scottish |
| **...galés(a)** | ...Welsh |
| **neozelandés(a)** | ...New Zealander |

*Mexicans are from the Americas too, so describing yourself as American can occasionally cause offence. Another option is "estadounidense" (or, more simply, "de Los Estados Unidos", from the United States) if you are a US American.

## Needs: hotels, transport and directions

| | |
|---|---|
| **Quiero...** | I want... |
| **Quisiera...por favor** | I'd like... |
| **¿Sabe...?** | Do you know...? |
| **No sé** | I don't know |
| **(¿)Hay...(?)** | There is... (Is there...?) |
| **Deme... (uno así)** | Give me... (one like that) |
| **¿Tiene...?** | Do you have...? |
| **...la hora** | ...the time |
| **...un cuarto** | ...a room |
| **...con dos camas/ cama matrimonial** | ...with two beds/ double bed |

| | |
|---|---|
| Es para una persona (dos personas) | It's for one person (two people) |
| ...para una noche (una semana) | ...for one night (one week) |
| ¿Está bien, cuánto es? | It's fine, how much is it? |
| Es demasiado caro | It's too expensive |
| ¿No tiene algo más barato? | Don't you have anything cheaper? |
| ¿Se puede...? | Can one...? |
| ¿...acampar (cerca) aquí? | ...camp (near) here? |
| ¿Hay un hotel cerca aquí? | Is there a hotel nearby? |
| ¿Por dónde se va a...? | How do I get to...? |
| Izquierda, derecha, derecho | Left, right, straight on |
| Por acá, por allá | This way, that way |
| ¿Dónde está...? | Where is...? |
| ...la camionera central | ...the bus station |
| ...la estación de ferrocarriles | ...the railway station |
| ...el banco más cercano | ...the nearest bank |
| ...el cajero automático | ...the ATM |
| ...el correo (la oficina de correos) | ...the post office |
| ...el baño/sanitario | ...the toilet |
| ¿De dónde sale el bus parav...? | Where does the bus to . . . leave from? |
| ¿Es éste el tren para Chihuahua? | Is this the train for Chihuahua? |
| Quisiera un boleto (de ida y vuelta) para... | I'd like a (return) ticket to . . . |
| ¿A qué hora sale (llega en...)? | What time does it leave (arrive in...)? |
| ¿Qué hay para comer? | What is there to eat? |
| ¿Qué es eso? | What's that? |
| ¿Cómo se llama éste en español? | What's this called in Spanish? |

## Numbers and days

| | |
|---|---|
| 1 | un/uno/una |
| 2 | dos |
| 3 | tres |
| 4 | cuatro |
| 5 | cinco |
| 6 | seis |
| 7 | siete |
| 8 | ocho |
| 9 | nueve |
| 10 | diez |
| 11 | once |
| 12 | doce |
| 13 | trece |
| 14 | catorce |
| 15 | quince |
| 16 | dieciséis |
| 17 | diecisiete |
| 20 | veinte |
| 21 | veintiuno |
| 30 | treinta |
| 40 | cuarenta |
| 50 | cincuenta |
| 60 | sesenta |
| 70 | setenta |
| 80 | ochenta |
| 90 | noventa |
| 100 | cien(to) |
| 101 | ciento uno |
| 200 | doscientos |
| 500 | quinientos |
| 700 | setecientos |
| 1000 | mil |
| 2000 | dos mil |

| | |
|---|---|
| first | primero/a |
| second | segundo/a |
| third | tercero/a |
| fifth | quinto/a |
| tenth | decimo/a |

| | |
|---|---|
| Monday | Lunes |
| Tuesday | Martes |
| Wednesday | Miércoles |
| Thursday | Jueves |
| Friday | Viernes |
| Saturday | Sábado |
| Sunday | Domingo |

# Food and drink terms

## On the table

| | |
|---|---|
| **Azúcar** | Sugar |
| **Cuchara** | Spoon |
| **Cuchillo** | Knife |
| **Cuenta** | Bill/check |
| **Mantequilla** | Butter |
| **Pan** | Bread |
| **Pimienta** | Pepper |
| **Queso** | Cheese |
| **Sal** | Salt |
| **Salsa** | Sauce |
| **Servilleta** | Napkin |
| **Tenedor** | Fork |

## Cooking terms

| | |
|---|---|
| **A la parilla** | Grilled over charcoal |
| **A la plancha** | Grilled on a hot plate |
| **A la tampiqueña** | Strips of grilled meat served with guacamole |
| **A la veracruzana** | Stewed with tomatoes, onions and green olives |
| **Al horno/horneado** | Baked |
| **Asado/a** | Broiled |
| **Barbacoa/pibil** | Wrapped in banana leaves and steamed/ baked in a pit |
| **Con mole** | In a thick, rich sauce of chiles, nuts, spices and (often) bitter chocolate |
| **Empanizado/a** | Breaded |
| **En mojo de ajo** | Fried with slow-cooked garlic |
| **Frito** | Fried |
| **Poco hecho/a punto/bien cocido** | Rare/medium/ well-done |

## Breakfast

| | |
|---|---|
| **Huevos…** | Eggs |
| **…a la Mexicana** | scrambled with tomato, onion and chile |
| **…con jamón** | with ham |
| **…con tocino** | with bacon |
| **…motuleños** | fried, served on a tortilla with beans, ham, cheese, tomato sauce, peas and fried sweet plantains |
| **…rancheros** | fried, on a tortilla, smothered in a red chile sauce |
| **…revueltos** | scrambled |
| **…tibios** | lightly boiled |
| **Pan dulce** | Pastries |

## Soups (sopas) and starters

| | |
|---|---|
| **Caldo** | Broth (with bits in) |
| **Ceviche** | Raw fish pieces, marinated in lime juice |
| **Entremeses** | Hors d'oeuvres |
| **Sopa…** | Soup |
| **…de arroz** | …with rice |
| **…de fideos** | …with noodles |
| **…de lentejas** | …with lentils |
| **…de verduras** | …with vegetables |

## Tortilla and corn dishes (antojitos)

**Burritos** Wheat-flour tortillas, rolled and filled

**Chilaquiles** Tortilla chips stewed with meat and tomato sauce

**Enchiladas** Rolled-up tacos, covered in chile sauce and baked

**Enchiladas suizas** As above, with green chile and cheese

**Flautas** Small rolled tortillas filled with red meat or chicken and then fried

**Gorditas** Small, fat, stuffed corn tortillas

**Machaca** Shredded dried meat scrambled with eggs

**Molletes** Split roll covered in beans and melted cheese

**Quesadillas** Toasted or fried tortillas topped with cheese

**Queso fundido** Melted cheese, served with tortillas and salsa

**Sincronizadas** Two flour tortillas sandwiched together with melted cheese and ham

**Sopes** Like bite-size tostadas, with a thicker, chewier base

**Tacos** Soft corn tortillas with filling

**Tacos al pastor** With spicy pork and a slice of pineapple

**Tacos dorados** Deep-fried tacos

**Tamales** Corn-meal paste, stuffed with meat and steamed in corn husks or banana leaves

**Tlacoyo** Fat tortilla stuffed with beans

**Torta** Bread roll filled with meat, lettuce and avocado

**Tostadas** Flat crisp tortillas piled with meat and salad

## Fish and seafood (pescados y mariscos)

**Anchoas** Anchovies

**Atún** Tuna

**Cabrilla** Sea bass

**Calamares** Squid

**Camarones** Prawns

**Cangrejo** Crab

**Caracol** Conch

**Corvina** Sea bass

**Filete entero** Whole, filleted fish

**Huachinango** Red snapper

**Langosta** Rock lobster

**Merluza** Hake

**Ostión** Oyster

**Pezespada** Swordfish

**Pulpo** Octopus

**Robalo** Bass

**Sardinas** Sardines

**Trucha** Trout

## Meat (carne) and poultry (aves)

**Alambre** Kebab

**Albóndigas** Meatballs

**Arrachera** Skirt steak

**Barbacoa** Barbecued meat

**Bistec** Steak (not always beef)

**Cabeza** Head

**Cabrito** Kid

**Carne (de res)** Beef

**Carne adobado** Barbecued/spicily stewed meat

**Carnitas** Pork cooked with garlic until crispy

**Cerdo** Pork

| | |
|---|---|
| **Chivo** | Goat |
| **Chorizo** | Spicy sausage |
| **Chuleta** | Chop (usually pork) |
| **Codorniz** | Quail |
| **Conejo** | Rabbit |
| **Cordero** | Lamb |
| **Costilla** | Rib |
| **Filete** | Tenderloin/fillet |
| **Guisado** | Stew |
| **Hígado** | Liver |
| **Lengua** | Tongue |
| **Lomo** | Loin (of pork) |
| **Milanesa** | Breaded escalope |
| **Pata** | Foot (usually pig's) |
| **Pato** | Duck |
| **Pavo/Guajolote** | Turkey |
| **Pechuga** | Breast |
| **Pierna** | Leg |
| **Pollo** | Chicken |
| **Salchicha** | Sausage |
| **Salpicón** | Shredded meat with vinegar |
| **Ternera** | Veal |
| **Tripa/Callos** | Tripe |
| **Venado** | Venison |

## Vegetables (verduras)

| | |
|---|---|
| **Aguacate** | Avocado |
| **Betabel** | Beetroot (often as a juice) |
| **Calabacita** | Courgette (zucchini) |
| **Calabaza** | Squash |
| **Cebolla** | Onion |
| **Champiñones/hongos** | Mushrooms |
| **Chícharos** | Peas |
| **Col** | Cabbage |
| **Coliflor** | Cauliflower |
| **Elote** | Corn on the cob |
| **Espárragos** | Asparagus |
| **Espinacas** | Spinach |
| **Flor de calabaza** | Squash blossoms |
| **Frijoles** | Beans |
| **Huitlacoche** | Corn fungus, "Mexican truffles" |
| **Jitomate** | Tomato |
| **Lechuga** | Lettuce |
| **Lentejas** | Lentils |
| **Nopales** | Cactus leaves, often pickled |
| **Papas** | Potatoes |
| **Pepino** | Cucumber |
| **Rajas** | Strips of mild green *poblano* pepper |
| **Zanahoria** | Carrot |

## Fruits (fruta) and juice (jugo)

| | |
|---|---|
| **Albaricoque/chabacano** | Apricot |
| **Cherimoya** | Custard apple (sweetsop) |
| **Ciruela** | Plum |
| **Coco** | Coconut |
| **Durazno** | Peach |
| **Frambuesa** | Raspberry |
| **Fresa** | Strawberry |
| **Guanábana** | Soursop, like a large custard apple |
| **Guayaba** | Guava |
| **Higo** | Fig |
| **Limón** | Lime |
| **Mamey** | Like a large zapote, with sweet pink flesh reminiscent of sweet potato |
| **Melón** | Melon |
| **Naranja** | Orange |
| **Papaya** | Papaya |
| **Piña** | Pineapple |
| **Pitahaya** | Dragonfruit, a type of cactus fruit |
| **Plátano** | Banana/plantain |
| **Sandía** | Watermelon |
| **Toronja** | Grapefruit |
| **Tuna** | Prickly pear (cactus fruit) |
| **Uva** | Grape |
| **Zapote** | Sapodilla, fruit of the chicle tree |

## Sweets (dulces)

| | |
|---|---|
| **Ate** | Quince paste |
| **Cajeta** | Caramel confection often served with... |
| ...crepas | ...pancakes |
| ...churros | ...cinnamon-covered fritters |
| **Ensalada de frutas** | Fruit salad |
| **Flan** | Crème caramel |
| **Helado** | Ice cream |
| **Nieve** | Sorbet |

# Glossaries

## Terms and acronyms

**Ahorita** diminutive of *ahora* (now) meaning "right now" – but seldom applied as literally as a visitor might expect.

**Alameda** city park or promenade; large plaza.

**Ayuntamiento** town hall/government.

**Aztec** the empire that dominated the central valleys of Mexico from the thirteenth century until defeated by Cortés.

**Barrio** area within a town or city; suburb.

**Camino blanco** unpaved rural road, so called because it is paved with limestone gravel.

**Camioneta** small truck or van.

**Cantina** bar, usually men-only.

**Cenote** underground water source in the Yucatán, a natural sinkhole in the limestone surface.

**Chac** Maya god of rain.

**Chac-mool** recumbent statue, possibly a sacrificial figure or messenger to the gods.

**Comal** large, round flat plate made of clay or metal used for cooking tortillas.

**Comedor** cheap restaurant, literally dining room; also called a *cocina económica*.

**Convento** either convent or monastery.

**CTM** central union organization.

**Cuauhtémoc** the last Aztec leader, commander of the final resistance to Cortés, and a national hero.

**Descompuesto** out of order.

**Don/Doña** courtesy titles (sir/madam), mostly used in letters or for professional people or the boss.

**Ejido** communal farmland.

**Enramadas** palapa-covered restaurants.

**EPR** Ejército Popular Revolucionario, the Popular Revolutionary Army. Guerrilla group, not allied to the Zapatistas; their first appearance was in Guerrero in 1996.

**EZLN** Ejército Zapatista de Liberación Nacional, the Zapatista Army of National Liberation. Guerrilla group in Chiapas.

**Feria** fair (market).

**Finca** ranch or plantation.

**FONART** government agency to promote crafts.

**Fonda** simple restaurant or boarding house.

**FONATUR** government tourism agency.

**Fray** Spanish word for friar.

**Gringo** not necessarily insulting, though it does imply North American – said to come from invading US troops, either because they wore green coats or because they sang "Green grow the rushes oh!..."

**Guayabera** embroidered Cuban-style shirt, usually for men.

**Güera/o** blonde – very frequently used description of Westerners, especially shouted after women in the street; again, not intended as an insult.

**Hacienda** plantation estate or the big house on it.

**Hacendado** plantation owner.

**Henequen** a variety of agave cactus grown mainly in Yucatán, the fibres of which are used to make rope.

**Huipil** Maya women's embroidered white smock dress or blouse, worn over a white petticoat, usually with a small checkered scarf.

**Huitzilopochtli** Aztec god of war.

**I.V.A.** fifteen percent value-added tax (VAT).

**Kukulkán** Maya name for Quetzalcoatl, the plumed serpent god.

**Ladino** applied to people, means Spanish-influenced as opposed to Indian; determined entirely by clothing (and culture) rather than physical race.

**Licensio** A common title, literally meaning "graduate" or "licensed"; abbreviated Lic.

**Malecón** seafront promenade.

**Malinche** Cortés's Indian interpreter and mistress, a symbol of treachery.

**Mariachi** quintessentially Mexican music, with lots of brass and sentimental lyrics.

**Marimba** xylophone-like musical instrument, also used of the bands based around it; derives from northern Mexico.

**Maya** people who inhabited Honduras, Belize, Guatemala and southeastern Mexico from earliest times, and still do.

**Mestizo** mixed race, of Indian and Spanish descent.

**Metate** flat stone for grinding corn; used with a *mano*, a grinding stone.

**Milpa** a small subsistence farm plot, usually tended with slash-and-burn agricultural practices.

**Mirador** lookout point.

**Mixtec** people from the mountains of Oaxaca.

**Moctezuma** Montezuma, the leader of the Aztec empire when the Spanish arrived in Mexico.

**Muelle** jetty or dock.

**NAFTA** the North American Free Trade Agreement including Mexico, the US and Canada; see also TLC below.

**Nahuatl** ancient Aztec language, still the most common after Spanish.

**Norteño** literally northern – style of food and music.

**Palacio** mansion, but not necessarily royal.

**Palacio de Gobierno** headquarters of state/federal authorities.

**Palacio Municipal** headquarters of local government.

**Palapa** palm thatch. Used to describe any thatched/palm-roofed hut.

**Palenque** cockpit (for cockfights).

**PAN** Partido de Acción Nacional (National Action Party), conservative party that first took power when Vicente Fox became president in 2000.

**Paseo** a broad avenue, but also the ritual evening walk around the plaza.

**PEMEX** the Mexican national oil company.

**Planta baja** ground floor – abbreviated PB in lifts.

**Porfiriato** the three decades of Porfirio Díaz's dictatorship.

**PRD** Partido Revolucionario Democrático (Party of the Democratic Revolution), the left-wing opposition formed and led by Cuauhtémoc Cárdenas; has the second largest number of seats in Congress.

**PRI** Partido Revolucionario Institucional (Party of the Institutional Revolution), the ruling party for eighty years, until the PAN upset in the 1999 elections.

**PT** Partido del Trabajo (Workers' Party), small party but with opposition seats in Congress.

**PVEM** Partido Verde Ecologista de México (Green Party), small opposition party.

**Quetzalcoatl** the plumed serpent, most powerful, enigmatic and widespread of all ancient Mexican gods.

**Romería** procession.

**Sacbé** ancient Maya road, paved with limestone; plural *sacbeob*.

**Stele** freestanding carved monument; plural *stelae*.

**Tenochtitlán** the Aztec capital, on the site of Mexico City.

**Teotihuacán** ancient city north of the capital – the first major urban power of central Mexico.

**Tianguis** Nahuatl word for market, still used of particularly varied marketplaces.

**Tlaloc** Toltec/Aztec rain god.

**TLC** Tratado de Libre Comercio, the Spanish name for NAFTA.

**Toltec** tribe which controlled central Mexico between Teotihuacán and the Aztecs.

**Tope** speed-bump or other barrier on rural roads for slowing traffic.

**Trova** Romantic Yucatecan song style popular in the early twentieth century, still played by *trovadores*.

**Tula** the Toltec capital.

**Tzompantli** Aztec skull rack or "wall of skulls".

**Virreinal** from the period of the Spanish viceroys – ie colonial.

**Wetback** derogatory term for illegal Mexican (or any Hispanic) in the US; *mojado* ("wet") is the Spanish slang term, without the negative connotations.

**Zapotec** tribe which controlled the Oaxaca region to about 700 AD.

**Zócalo** the main plaza of any town.

# Art and architectural terms

**Alfiz** decorative rectangular moulding over a doorway.

**Arabesque** elaborate geometric pattern of Islamic origin.

**Artesonado** intricate ceiling design, usually of jointed, inlaid wood.

**Atlantean** pre-Hispanic column in the form of a warrior – examples found at Tula and Chichén Itzá.

**Atrium** enclosed forecourt of churchyard or monastery; *atrio* in Spanish.

**Azulejo** decorative glazed tile, usually blue and white.

**Camarín** room in a church used for storing and dressing sacred statues.

**Churrigueresque** highly elaborate, decorative form of Baroque architecture (usually in churches), named after the seventeenth-century Spanish architect.

**Convento** monastery residence which includes the cloister.

**Dado** ornamental border on the lower part of an interior wall.

**Escudo** shield-shaped decoration.

**Espadaña** belfry, usually on top of the front wall of a church.

**Fluting** vertical grooves in a column.

**Fresco** technique of painting on wet or dry plaster.

**Garita** ornamental pinnacle or battlement which looks like a sentry box.

**Grotesque** ornamental style depicting fantastic birds, beasts and foliage.

**Herrerian** imperial style named after sixteenth-century Spanish architect Juan de Herrera.

**Lunette** crescent-shaped space above a doorway or beneath a vault.

**Merlón** decorative pyramidal battlement.

**Mudéjar** Spanish architectural style strongly influenced by Moorish forms.

**Ogee** curved, pointed arch.

**Pila** font or water basin; also commonly found in domestic buildings.

**Pilaster** flattened column used as decorative element.

**Pinjante** glove-shaped decorative pendant, popular in eighteenth-century architecture.

**Plateresque** elaborately decorative Renaissance architectural style.

**Porfirian** referring to the elaborate, eclectic architecture of the Porfirio Díaz period (also *Porfiriano*).

**Portales** arcades.

**Portería** entry portico to a monastery.

**Predella** base panel of an altarpiece.

**Purista** severe Renaissance architectural style, originating in sixteenth-century Spain.

**Retablo** carved, painted wooden altarpiece.

**Tecali** translucent onyx, also called Mexican alabaster.

**Tequitqui** early colonial style of sculpture using pre-Conquest techniques.

**Zapata** wooden roof beam, often decoratively carved.

# Travel store

Hacienda
San Antonio
Chalanté
a rural inn near
Izamal, Yucatan
Come stay with us and enjoy a beautiful natural setting on our 800 acre estate. Sleep in centuries old rooms, ride out on horseback, enjoy our exceptional cuisine, or just laze by the pool. Venture to the near-by colonial town of Izamal, the world heritage site of Chichen Itza or the many other haunts of the mysterious Maya.
info@haciendachalante.com
www.haciendachalante.com

Eco Adventure in the
Maya World
Sian Ka'an
Lodge
EcoColors
Phone: 52 998 884 3667
www.ecotravelmexico.com

COLUMBUS
Travel Insurance

ROUGH
GUIDES

ROUGH GUIDES Complete Listing

**UK & Ireland**
Britain
Devon & Cornwall
Dublin **D**
Edinburgh **D**
England
Ireland
The Lake District
London
London **D**
London Mini Guide
Scotland
Scottish Highlands & Islands
Wales

**Europe**
Algarve **D**
Amsterdam
Amsterdam **D**
Andalucía
Athens **D**
Austria
Baltic States
Barcelona
Barcelona **D**
Belgium & Luxembourg
Berlin
Brittany & Normandy
Bruges **D**
Brussels
Budapest
Bulgaria
Copenhagen
Corfu
Corsica
Costa Brava **D**
Crete
Croatia
Cyprus
Czech & Slovak Republics
Denmark
Dodecanese & East Aegean Islands
Dordogne & The Lot
Europe
Florence & Siena
Florence **D**
France
Germany
Gran Canaria **D**
Greece
Greek Islands
Hungary
Ibiza & Formentera **D**
Iceland
Ionian Islands
Italy
The Italian Lakes
Languedoc & Roussillon
Lanzarote & Fuerteventura **D**
Lisbon **D**
The Loire Valley
Madeira **D**
Madrid **D**
Mallorca **D**
Mallorca & Menorca
Malta & Gozo **D**
Menorca
Moscow
The Netherlands
Norway
Paris
Paris **D**
Paris Mini Guide
Poland
Portugal
Prague
Prague **D**
Provence & the Côte D'Azur
Pyrenees
Romania
Rome
Rome **D**
Sardinia
Scandinavia
Sicily
Slovenia
Spain
St Petersburg
Sweden
Switzerland
Tenerife & La Gomera **D**
Turkey
Tuscany & Umbria
Venice & The Veneto
Venice **D**
Vienna

**Asia**
Bali & Lombok
Bangkok
Beijing
Cambodia
China
Goa
Hong Kong & Macau
Hong Kong & Macau **D**
India
Indonesia
Japan
Kerala
Laos
Malaysia, Singapore & Brunei
Nepal
The Philippines
Rajasthan, Dehli & Agra
Singapore
Singapore **D**
South India
Southeast Asia
Sri Lanka
Taiwan
Thailand
Thailand's Beaches & Islands
Tokyo
Vietnam

**Australasia**
Australia
Melbourne
New Zealand
Sydney

**North America**
Alaska
Baja California
Boston
California
Canada
Chicago
Colorado
Florida
The Grand Canyon
Hawaii
Honolulu **D**
Las Vegas **D**
Los Angeles
Maui **D**
Miami & South Florida
Montréal
New England
New Orleans **D**
New York City
New York City **D**
New York City Mini Guide
Orlando & Walt Disney World® **D**
Pacific Northwest
San Francisco
San Francisco **D**
Seattle
Southwest USA
Toronto
USA
Vancouver
Washington DC
Washington DC **D**
Yellowstone & The Grand Tetons
Yosemite

**Caribbean & Latin America**
Antigua & Barbuda **D**
Argentina
Bahamas
Barbados **D**
Belize
Bolivia
Brazil
Cancùn & Cozumel **D**
Caribbean
Central America
Chile
Costa Rica
Cuba
Dominican Republic
Dominican Republic **D**
Ecuador
Guatemala
Jamaica
Mexico
Peru
St Lucia **D**
South America
Trinidad & Tobago
Yúcatan

**Africa & Middle East**
Cape Town & the Garden Route
Dubai **D**
Egypt
Gambia
Jordan

**D**: Rough Guide **DIRECTIONS** for short breaks

Kenya
Marrakesh **D**
Morocco
South Africa, Lesotho & Swaziland
Syria
Tanzania
Tunisia
West Africa
Zanzibar

**Travel Specials**
First-Time Africa
First-Time Around the World
First-Time Asia
First-Time Europe
First-Time Latin America
Travel Health
Travel Online
Travel Survival
Walks in London & SE England
Women Travel
World Party

**Maps**
Algarve
Amsterdam
Andalucia & Costa del Sol
Argentina
Athens
Australia
Barcelona
Berlin
Boston & Cambridge
Brittany
Brussels
California
Chicago
Chile
Corsica
Costa Rica & Panama
Crete
Croatia
Cuba
Cyprus
Czech Republic
Dominican Republic
Dubai & UAE
Dublin
Egypt
Florence & Siena
Florida
France
Frankfurt
Germany
Greece
Guatemala & Belize
Iceland
India
Ireland
Italy
Kenya & Northern Tanzania
Lisbon
London
Los Angeles
Madrid
Malaysia
Mallorca
Marrakesh
Mexico
Miami & Key West
Morocco
New England
New York City
New Zealand
Northern Spain
Paris
Peru
Portugal
Prague
Pyrenees & Andorra
Rome
San Francisco
Sicily
South Africa
South India
Spain & Portugal
Sri Lanka
Tenerife
Thailand
Toronto
Trinidad & Tobago
Tunisia
Turkey
Tuscany
Venice
Vietnam, Laos & Cambodia
Washington DC
Yucatán Peninsula

**Dictionary Phrasebooks**
Croatian
Czech
Dutch
Egyptian Arabic
French
German
Greek
Hindi & Urdu
Italian
Japanese
Latin American Spanish
Mandarin Chinese
Mexican Spanish
Polish
Portuguese
Russian
Spanish
Swahili
Thai
Turkish
Vietnamese

**Computers**
Blogging
eBay
iPhone
iPods, iTunes & music online
The Internet
Macs & OS X
MySpace
PCs and Windows
PlayStation Portable
Website Directory

**Film & TV**
American Independent Film
British Cult Comedy
Chick Flicks
Comedy Movies
Cult Movies
Film
Film Musicals
Film Noir
Gangster Movies
Horror Movies
Kids' Movies
Sci-Fi Movies
Westerns

**Lifestyle**
Babies
Ethical Living
Pregnancy & Birth
Running

**Music Guides**
The Beatles
Blues
Bob Dylan
Book of Playlists
Classical Music
Elvis
Frank Sinatra
Heavy Metal
Hip-Hop
Jazz
Led Zeppelin
Opera
Pink Floyd
Punk
Reggae
Rock
The Rolling Stones
Soul and R&B
Velvet Underground
World Music (2 vols)

**Popular Culture**
Books for Teenagers
Children's Books, 5-11
Conspiracy Theories
Crime Fiction
Cult Fiction
The Da Vinci Code
His Dark Materials
Lord of the Rings
Shakespeare
Superheroes
The Templars
Unexplained Phenomena

**Science**
The Brain
Climate Change
The Earth
Genes & Cloning
The Universe
Weather

For more information go to www.roughguides.com

# Small print and Index

## A Rough Guide to Rough Guides

Published in 1982, the first Rough Guide – to Greece – was a student scheme that became a publishing phenomenon. Mark Ellingham, a recent graduate in English from Bristol University, had been travelling in Greece the previous summer and couldn't find the right guidebook. With a small group of friends he wrote his own guide, combining a highly contemporary, journalistic style with a thoroughly practical approach to travellers' needs.

The immediate success of the book spawned a series that rapidly covered dozens of destinations. And, in addition to impecunious backpackers, Rough Guides soon acquired a much broader and older readership that relished the guides' wit and inquisitiveness as much as their enthusiastic, critical approach and value-for-money ethos.

These days, Rough Guides include recommendations from shoestring to luxury and cover more than 200 destinations around the globe, including almost every country in the Americas and Europe, more than half of Africa and most of Asia and Australasia. Our ever-growing team of authors and photographers is spread all over the world, particularly in Europe, the USA and Australia.

In the early 1990s, Rough Guides branched out of travel, with the publication of Rough Guides to World Music, Classical Music and the Internet. All three have become benchmark titles in their fields, spearheading the publication of a wide range of books under the Rough Guide name.

Including the travel series, Rough Guides now number more than 350 titles, covering: phrasebooks, waterproof maps, music guides from Opera to Heavy Metal, reference works as diverse as Conspiracy Theories and Shakespeare, and popular culture books from iPods to Poker. Rough Guides also produce a series of more than 120 World Music CDs in partnership with World Music Network.

Visit www.roughguides.com to see our latest publications.

Rough Guide travel images are available for commercial licensing at www.roughguidespictures.com

## Rough Guide credits

**Text editor**: Ella Steim
**Layout**: Umesh Aggarwal
**Cartography**: Karobi Gogoi, Maxine Repath
**Picture editor**: Sarah Smithies
**Production**: Aimee Hampson
**Proofreader**: Jennifer Speake
**Cover design**: Chloë Roberts
**Photographer**: Paul Whitfield
**Editorial**: **London** Kate Berens, Claire Saunders, Ruth Blackmore, Polly Thomas, Richard Lim, Alison Murchie, Karoline Densley, Andy Turner, Keith Drew, Edward Aves, Nikki Birrell, Alice Park, Sarah Eno, Lucy White, Jo Kirby, Samantha Cook, James Smart, Natasha Foges, Róisín Cameron, Joe Staines, Duncan Clark, Peter Buckley, Matthew Milton, Tracy Hopkins, Ruth Tidball; **New York** Andrew Rosenberg, Steven Horak, AnneLise Sorensen, Amy Hegarty, April Isaacs, Anna Owens, Joseph Petta, Sean Mahoney
**Design & Pictures**: **London** Scott Stickland, Dan May, Diana Jarvis, Mark Thomas, Jj Luck, Harriet Mills, Chloë Roberts, Nicole Newman; **Delhi** Ajay Verma, Jessica Subramanian, Ankur Guha, Pradeep Thapliyal, Sachin Tanwar, Anita Singh, Madhavi Singh, Karen D'Souza
**Production**: Vicky Baldwin
**Cartography**: **London** Ed Wright, Katie Lloyd-Jones; **Delhi** Jai Prakash Mishra, Rajesh Chhibber, Ashutosh Bharti, Rajesh Mishra, Animesh Pathak, Jasbir Sandhu, Amod Singh, Alakananda Bhattacharya, Athokpam Jotinkumar
**Online**: **New York** Jennifer Gold, Kristin Mingrone; **Delhi** Manik Chauhan, Narender Kumar, Rakesh Kumar, Amit Kumar, Amit Verma, Rahul Kumar, Ganesh Sharma, Debojit Borah
**Marketing & Publicity**: **London** Liz Statham, Niki Hanmer, Louise Maher, Jess Carter, Vanessa Godden, Vivienne Watton, Anna Paynton, Libby Jellie, Rachel Sprackett, Lenalisa Fornberg; **New York** Geoff Colquitt, Megan Kennedy, Katy Ball; **Delhi** Reem Khokhar
**Editorial Coordinator**: Emma Traynor
**Manager India**: Punita Singh
**Series Editor**: Mark Ellingham
**Reference Director**: Andrew Lockett
**PA to MD and Publishing Director**: Helen Phillips
**Publishing Director**: Martin Dunford
**Commercial Manager**: Gino Magnotta
**Managing Director**: John Duhigg

## Publishing information

This seventh edition published July 2007 by **Rough Guides Ltd**,
80 Strand, London WC2R 0RL
345 Hudson St, 4th Floor,
New York, NY 10014, USA
14 Local Shopping Centre, Panchsheel Park,
New Delhi 110017, India
**Distributed by the Penguin Group**
Penguin Books Ltd,
80 Strand, London WC2R 0RL
Penguin Group (USA)
375 Hudson Street, NY 10014, USA
Penguin Group (Australia)
250 Camberwell Road, Camberwell,
Victoria 3124, Australia
Penguin Books Canada Ltd,
10 Alcorn Avenue, Toronto, Ontario,
Canada M4V 1E4
Penguin Group (NZ)
67 Apollo Drive, Mairangi Bay, Auckland 1310,
New Zealand
Cover concept by Peter Dyer.
Typeset in Bembo and Helvetica to an original design by Henry Iles.
Printed in Italy by LegoPrint S.p.A.

984pp includes index
A catalogue record for this book is available from the British Library
ISBN: 978-1-84353-843-1

1 3 5 7 9 8 6 4 2

## Help us update

We've gone to a lot of effort to ensure that the seventh edition of **The Rough Guide to Mexico** is accurate and up to date. However, things change – places get "discovered", opening hours are notoriously fickle, restaurants and rooms raise prices or lower standards. If you feel we've got it wrong or left something out, we'd like to know, and if you can remember the address, the price, the time, the phone number, so much the better. We'll credit all contributions, and send a copy of the next edition (or any other Rough Guide if you prefer) for the best letters. Everyone who writes to us and isn't already a subscriber will receive a copy of our full-colour thrice-yearly newsletter. Please mark letters: "**Rough Guide Mexico Update**" and send to: Rough Guides, 80 Strand, London WC2R 0RL, or Rough Guides, 345 Hudson St, 4th Floor, New York, NY 10014. Or send an email to **mail@roughguides.com**
Have your questions answered and tell others about your trip at
**www.roughguides.atinfopop.com**

## Acknowledgements

**Daniel Jacobs** would like to thank Armida Durán for looking after him and for her help in preparing Chapter 5, and Ella Steim for her super-efficient editing.

**Zora O'Neill** would like to thank: Madeline Parmet of Luz en Yucatán, Lee Christie at Genesis, Jim Conrad (aka "the Backyard Naturalist"), Sofi at Marionetas, Jim and Ellen from YucatanLiving.com, Rob and Joanne Birce at Alma Libre Books, Rick Bertram at Rio Bec Dreams, and Jules Siegel and Anita Brown, for sharing invaluable information and general hospitality; Laura Perez, Lydia Gregory, Aimee Szparaga and Audra Poole, who opened doors at the best hotels; the very understanding staff at Budget Rent-a-Car in Cancún (the Punta Allen road is no joke!); "my companion" Tamara Reynolds and Peter "Chofer" Moskos, for making the trip livelier; Ella Steim for her attentive editing; and especially all the readers who took the time to send in corrections, tips and criticism.

**Paul Whitfield** would like to thank the people of Mexico for making his travels there so enjoyable. In particular, thanks to Ernesto for opening my eyes to Zacatecas, Ricardo for similar enlightenment in San Miguel de Allende, and the helpful staff at visitor centres all over. This update would only have been half what it is without the helpful hints and shared experiences of people met along the way, especially bar hopping with Alexandre Munhoz and a Day of the Dead all-nighter with Kara.

**Richard Arghiris** would like to thank Terri Wright, Peter McCallan and Lina Spyrou for their support; "Mexico Mike" Nelson and Nicky for their kindness and hospitality; Caro Monza and Ruben Carrizales for the conversation, on and off the road. Thanks to the tireless staff of Mexico's tourist offices, especially Adolfo in Hermosillo. Most of all, thanks to the countless kind strangers who supplied helpful advice and information, or simply pointed him in the right direction.

**Jason Clampet** would like to thank his wife Veronica Chambers for being the first person to tell him about Baja California's fish tacos and long roads. His work is dedicated to her and their daughter Flora Victoria, whose first solid food will be ceviche.

**The editor** would like to thank Daniel, Zora, Paul, Richard, Jason, Stephen and Caroline for all their hard work. Many thanks also to Umesh Aggarwal for putting it all together; the indefatigable cartographers – Karobi and everyone at RG Delhi, Maxine, Katie and Ed – for their patient mapmaking; Sarah Smithies for picture research; Jennifer Speake for proofreading; Todd Obolsky for the index; Seph Petta for reading the colour; and AnneLise Sorensen and Andrew Rosenberg for guidance throughout.

## Readers' letters

Thanks to all the readers who have taken the time to write in with comments and suggestions (and apologies if we've inadvertently omitted or misspelt anyone's name):

Lola Reid Allin, Juliana Barrett, Eugene and Erika Chen, Mary Duncan, Giorgio Genova, Julian Gilbey, Jonathon Gore, Joshua Gottlieb, Caroline Grinsted, Geoff Holden, Nat Hill, Kara Iselin, Ken Kageyama, Paul and Kathy Kester, Dominic Laurie, John Molteno, Matthew Monahan, Brian Mulligan, Ken Nawrocki, Ronald Roskell, Dan Smith, Wim Sparenburg, Joy Stonor, Susan Warrington, Graham Williams, Anya Wilson, Colin Wright, Tony Wright, Siye Wu, Niki Young, Jim Zosel

## Photo credits

All photos © Rough Guides except the following:

**Title page**
Zócalo, Mexico City © Walter Bibikow/Jon Arnold Images

**Full page**
Chac-mool, Cancún © Schmid Reinhard/SIME/4Corners

**Introduction**
Wool table cloth, Teotitlán del Valle © age fotostock/SuperStock
Bahía Concepcíon, Baja California Sur © Mark Lewis/Alamy
Women at market in Oaxaca state © Brian Atkinson/Alamy
Ruins of Palenque © Gordon Sinclair/The Travel Library

**Things not to miss**
**01** Copper Canyon © Bruce Herman/Photolibrary.com
**03** Hammocks © Walter Bibikow/Index Stock Imagery/Photolibrary.com
**05** Bahia de Concepcíon, Baja California Sur © Lalage Johnstone/Eye Ubiquitous/Corbis
**07** Football match, Mexico City © AFP/Getty Images
**08** Zócalo, Mexico City © Angelo Cavalli/SuperStock
**11** Bonampak, Chiapas © age fotostock/SuperStock
**12** Coffee © age fotostock/SuperStock
**13** Temple of the Sun, Palenque © Angelo Hornak/Corbis
**15** Downtown Playa del Carmen © Bertrand Gardel/Hemis.fr
**17** El Castillo, Chichén Itzá © Larry Dunmire/SuperStock
**20** Market, Oaxaca © Pixtal/SuperStock
**21** Cenote Dzitnup © James May/Stock Connection/Alamy
**22** Tulum © Carlos Sánchez Pereyra/Mauritius Die Bildagentur/Photolibrary.com
**24** Cowboys at a rodeo © SuperStock
**25** Ruins of Calakmul © T.C. Middleton/Photolibrary.com
**26** Restaurant Tacuba, Mexico City © Bertrand Gardel/Hemis/Alamy
**27** Sian Ka'an Biosphere Reserve © Robert Fried/Alamy
**28** Mariachis in Plaza Garibaldi, Mexico City © Oliviero Olivieri/Robert Harding Picture Library/Photolibrary.com
**30** Grey whale, Laguna San Ignacio © Mark Newman/FLPA
**32** Acapulco cliff divers © Thom Lang/Corbis
**35** Yucab divesite, Cozumel © Chris A Crumley/Alamy

**Colour section: Mexican food and drink**
Woman making tortillas © Gary Moss/Jupiterimages
Salsa cups © Claudia Uribe Touri/Jupiterimages
Jose Cuervo tequila © Wesley Hitt/Alamy

**Colour section: Festive Mexico**
Boy dressed for the Quetzal dance, Cuetzalan © Sergio Dorantes/Corbis
Re-enactment of Jesus carrying the cross, Iztapalapa © Henry Romero/Reuters/Corbis
Carnaval, Veracruz © Lindsay Hebberd/Corbis
Mexican Independence Day celebrations © Jack Kurtz/ZUMA/Corbis
Dance of the Old Men, Pátzcuaro © Xela/Alamy
Chinese Folk Arts Performance Troupe, Cervantino Arts Festival © Keith Dannemiller/Alamy

**Colour section: Ancient Mexico**
Olmec head © Chris Sharp/South American Pictures
Ruins of Uxmal © Gordon Sinclair/The Travel Library
Jaina figurine © Werner Forman/Corbis
Monte Albán © Macduff Everton/Corbis
Skull wall, Templo Mayor Museum © Danny Lehman/Corbis
Tulum, Quintana Roo © Stuart Black/Corbis

**Black and whites**
**p.76** Harbour, Guaymas © Kevin Schafer/Alamy
**p.85** Centro Cultural Tijuana © Kevin Foy/Alamy
**p.95** Mercado Negro, Ensenada © Thomas Shjarback/Alamy
**p.106** Whale-watchers, Laguna San Ignacio © Fleetham Dave/Pacific Stock/Photolibrary.com
**p.154** Cathedral, Alamos © age fotostock/SuperStock
**p.165** Playa Olas Altas, Mazatlán © Dave G. Houser/Houserstock
**p.180** Paquimé ruins © Danny Lehman/Corbis
**p.191** Copper Canyon railway © Gerald French/Corbis
**p.201** Cathedral, Chihuahua © Hubertus Kanus/SuperStock
**p.210** Villa del Oeste, Durango © Walter Bishop Verlade
**p.228** Fuente de Neptuno, Macroplaza, Monterrey © age fotostock/SuperStock

**p.326** Eduardo Ruíz National Park © Danny Lehman/Corbis
**p.414** Aztec rituals in the Zócalo, Mexico City © Janet Jarman/Corbis
**p.474** Ballet Folklórico, Mexico City © Nik Wheeler/Danita Delimont/Alamy
**p.506** Capilla del Rosario, Puebla © age fotostock/SuperStock
**p.540** Humpback whale breaching, Puerto Vallarta © Gerard Soury/Photolibrary.com
**p.547** Malecón, Puerto Vallarta © Walter Bibikow/Index Stock Imagery/ Photolibrary.com
**p.564** Colima Volcano © Roger Ressmeyer/ Corbis
**p.574** Beach in Zihuatanejo © Franz-Marc Frei/ Corbis
**p.582** Cliff diver, Acapulco © Steve Vidler/ SuperStock
**p.597** Pico de Orizaba, Veracruz state © SAS/ Alamy
**p.628** Boat with the egrets, Lago de Catemaco © Michal Cerny
**p.634** Ruins of Monte Albán © age fotostock/ SuperStock
**p.649** Mercado de Abastos, Oaxaca © Prisma/ SuperStock
**p.664** Detail of decoration at Mitla ruins © age fotostock/SuperStock
**p.674** Surfer, Puerto Escondido © Michele Falzone/Alamy
**p.685** Olive Ridley (Golfina) Sea Turtle © Tomas Bravo/Reuters/Corbis
**p.696** Lagos de Montebello National Park, Chiapas © age fotostock/SuperStock
**p.715** Colonial fountain, Chiapa de Corzo © Alison Wright/Corbis
**p.729** Church, San Juan Chamula © Sergio Pitamitz/SuperStock
**p.745** Palenque © Jtb Photo/Photolibrary.com
**p.759** Blue Heron, Parque La Venta, Villahermosa © age fotostock/SuperStock
**p.767** Ruins of Comalcalco © age fotostock/ SuperStock
**p.776** Punta Allen, Sian Ka'an Biosphere Reserve © PCL/Alamy
**p.784** Baluarte de San Carlos, Campeche © TUT/Alamy
**p.799** Museum of Anthropology, Mérida © Dave G. Houser/Corbis
**p.811** Nunnery Quadrangle, Uxmal © Eric Nathan/Alamy
**p.818** Convento de San Antonio de Padua, Izamal © Fabienne Fossez/Alamy
**p.828** Cenote X-Keken, Dzitnup © Macduff Everton/Corbis
**p.837** Playa Tortugas, Cancún © Ian Dagnall/ Alamy
**p.874** Stone sculpture, Museo de la Cultura, Chetumal © Eric Nathan/Alamy
**p.925** Mariachis, Plaza Garibaldi, Mexico City © Hemis/Alamy

# Index

Map entries are in colour.


## A

**ACAPULCO** ........ 577–588
Acapulco Bay ............. 578
Acapulco, downtown ................................ 580
- accommodation ............. 579
- activities ......................... 585
- addresses along Costera ................................ 579
- airport ............................ 579
- arrival .............................. 578
- beaches ........................... 583
- boat trips ......................... 585
- buses .............................. 579
- CiCi Waterpark ................ 585
- cliff divers ........................ 584
- drinking ........................... 585
- eating .............................. 585
- entertainment ................... 586
- information ...................... 579
- La Roqueta ....................... 583
- Laguna de Coyuca ............ 585
- listings ............................ 587
- Mágico Mundo Marina ..... 583
- Museo de Acapulco ......... 583
- nightlife ........................... 586
- Parque Papagayo ............ 585
- Pie de la Cuesta .............. 584
- Playa Caleta .................... 583
- Playa Caletilla ................. 583
- Playa Condesa ................ 584
- Playa Icacos .................... 584
- Puerto Marqués ............... 584
- Revolcadero ..................... 584
- scuba-diving .................... 583
- sea-fishing ....................... 585

**Acapulco and the Pacific beaches** ........... 539–592
Acapulco and the Pacific beaches .................... 542
Acatepec ....................... 511
Acayucán ....................... 631
accommodation ............. 42
Acteal massacre ........... 902
addresses ...................... 41
Agua Azul ...................... 739
Agua Prieta .................... 145
**Aguascalientes** ... 270–275
Aguascalientes ............ 271
Ahuehuete ..................... 530
airlines ........................... 32
airpasses ........................ 28
Ajijic ............................. 358
Aké ................................ 817
Alamo ............................ 891
**Alamos** ................ 151–155
Alamos ........................... 152
alcohol ............................ 48
Alemán, Miguel ............. 897
Algodones ..................... 150
altitude, problems with ... 54
Alvarado ........................ 623
Amatenango del Valle ... 730
Amecameca ................... 512
American Express .......... 66
Angahuan ...................... 369
Angangueo .................... 389
Angeles Verdes .............. 40
Armería ......................... 562
Arrazola ......................... 666
*arribeño son* ................ 926
Atenquique .................... 362
Aticama ......................... 173
ATMs ............................... 68
Aztecs .......... 885 & *Ancient Mexico* colour section

## B

Bahía Concepción ........ 111
Bahía de Chamela ........ 554
Bahía de Kino ............... 147
Bahía de Los Ángeles ................................ 101
Bahía de Mantanchén ................................ 173
Bahía de Navidad ......... 555
Bahía Magdalena ......... 102
Baile de los Negritos, El ................................ 617
**Baja California** ...... 79–136
Baja California and the Pacific Northwest ....... 78
**Bajío, the** ............ 239–323
Bajío, the ............ 242–243
Balamkú ........................ 791
Ballet Folklórico ... 474, 802
ball-game, Mesoamerican ................................ 912
Balneario Natural Río Puyacatengo ............ 763
Banco Chinchorro ........ 870
*banda* .......................... 929
bandits ............................ 40
banks .............................. 68
bargaining ....................... 61
Barra de Navidad ......... 555
Barra de Navidad ........ 556
Barranca de Oblatos .... 348
Barranca del Cobre ...... 190
Basaséachic Falls ......... 196
Batopilas ....................... 196
Becán ............................ 791
beer ................................ 48
Benemérito ................... 752
Benito Juárez ............... 660
Bernal ............................ 315
birds .............................. 916
Boca de Pascuales ...... 564
Boca del Cielo ............. 702
Boca Lacantún ............ 752
Bocas de Dzilam .......... 806
Bochil ............................ 716
Bolonchén de Rejon ..... 793
Bonampak ... 749 & *Ancient Mexico* colour section
**books** .................. 934–947
border checks ................ 84
border crossing, Tijuana ................................ 84
border formalities .......... 30
border posts ................... 30
Bucerías ........................ 553
bullfights ......................... 58
buses
- to Mexico ......................... 28
- within Mexico ............ 35–38

butterflies, monarch ..... 389

## C

cabañas .......................... 43
**Cabo San Lucas** ........................... 125–130
Cabo San Lucas .......... 126
Cacaxtla ........................ 502
Calakmul ...... 792 & *Ancient Mexico* colour section
Calakmul Biosphere Reserve ........................ 792
Calderitas ..................... 876
calendar, Mesoamerican ................................ 910
Caleta de Campos ....... 569
Calexico ........................ 138
calling card numbers ...... 70
**Campeche** ........... 781–786
Campeche .................... 781
camping card ................. 43

campsites 43
**Cancún** 833–841
Cancún 834
Cancún Zona Hotelera 836
Cañon del Sumidero 716
cantinas 49
cape beaches (Baja) 132
car rental agencies 40
Cardel 615
Cárdenas, Lázaro 897
Carnaval 56 & *Festive Mexico* colour section
casas de cambio 68
Caste War 728
Cataviña 100
**Catemaco** 626–629
Catemaco and around 627
Catholic Cristero 896
cave-painting tours 103, 107, 110
caving 58
Celestún 807
cell phones 69
Cempoala 614
Cenote Azul 871
Cenote Dzitnup 827
Cenote Samula 827
cenotes 861
Cerocahui 193
Chachalacas 615
Chalma 530
Champotón 788
Chamula 728
Chapala 357
Chelem 806
chemists 55
Chetumal 872
Chetumal 873
Chiapa de Corzo 714
**Chiapas** 698–753
Chiapas 699
Chicanná 791
**Chichén Itzá** 819–824
Chichén Itzá 820
Chicomoztoc 269
Chicxulub Puerto 806
**Chihuahua** 198–203
Chihuahua 199
children, travelling with 71
chiles 45 & *Mexican food and drink* colour section
Chilpancingo 588
Chinkultic 734
Chiquilá 830
chocolate *Mexican food and drink* colour section
cholera 54
Cholula 509
CHP 191
chronology 905
Chuburná 806
Chunyaxché 868
Chupaderos 209
Ciudad Acuña 211
Ciudad Cuauhtémoc 736
Ciudad del Carmen 788
Ciudad Guzmán 361
Ciudad Hidalgo 709
**Ciudad Juárez** 183–187
Ciudad Juárez 184
Ciudad Obregón 150
Ciudad Tecún Umán, Guatemala 709
Ciudad Valles 322
Ciudad Victoria 221
cliff divers 584
climate 12, 913
Coajinicuilapa 589
Coatepec 604
Coatzacoalcos 631
Cobá 866
cocaine cartels 900
Cocom dynasty 816
Codz Poop 814
coffee 48
Coixtlahuaca 668
*colectivos* 41
**Colima** 564–568
Colima 565
collect calls 69
Comala 569
Comalcalco 766
**Comitán** 730–734
Comitán de Domínguez 731
Concordia 168
Congress of Chilpancingo 890
consulates 64
Conventionalists 895
Copala 168
**Copper Canyon** 188–192
Copper Canyon and around 189
Copper Canyon railway 188–192
copper mines 109
coral reefs 845
Córdoba 599
Corridor, the 130
Corridor, the 131
Cortés, Hernán 399, 886
Costa Alegre 554
Costa Chica 589
costs 61
cowboy boots 198
**Cozumel** 854–860
crafts 60, 722
credit cards 68
Creel 193
Creel 194
crime 49
Crucecita 687
cruises 30
Cuauhtémoc 190
Cuautla 521
**Cuernavaca** 512–519
Cuernavaca 513
Cueva Pintada, La 101
Cuilapan 666
Culiacán 160
*cumbia* 932
Cupilco 766
currency 67
Cusárare 196
customs 64
Cuyutlán 563

# D

Dainzú 659
Danza de los Viejitos 364 & *Festive Mexico* colour section
Danza del Venado 151
*danzón* 924
Day of the Dead *see* Día de los Muertos
de Quiroga, Vasco 363
death squads 901
dengue fever 53
Día de la Virgen de Guadalupe *Festive Mexico* colour section
Día de los Muertos 57, 376, & *Festive Mexico* colour section
dialling codes 70
diarrhoea 52
Díaz, Felix 895
Díaz, Porfirio 893
disabled travellers 62
discography 930
discount agents 33
discrimination 59
divers 584
diving 58, 112
Divisadero 192
Docena Trágica, La 897
Dolores Hidalgo 292

drinking......... 47 & *Mexican food and drink* colour section
driving
car rental ........................... 40
in Mexico........................38–40
to Mexico ........................... 29
drugs ............................50
**Durango**..............205–209
Durango .......................206
Dzibalchén....................787
Dzibilchaltún.................805
Dzibilnocac...................787
Dzilam de Bravo...........806

# E

earthquake,1985 ..........898
eating.......................44–47 & *Mexican food and drink* colour section
ecotourism, Baja Sur....102
Edzná...........................786
*ejidos* ............................899
Ek-Balam ......................828
El Arcotete....................727
El Ceibo.........................773
El Crucero.....................668
El Fuerte........................158
El Naranjo, Guatemala ...............773
El Paso, Texas..............185
El Pinacate Biosphere Reserve.....................143
El Rosario .....................100
El Rosario butterfly sanctuary...................388
El Saltito........................210
El Tajín ..........................619
El Tajín...........................619
electricity........................62
email ..............................65
embassies ......................64
emergency numbers.......70
Encanto .........................617
**Ensenada**...............91–97
Ensenada...............92–93
entry requirements.........62
Escárcega......................789
exchange offices ............68
EZLN.............................900

# F

*farmacias* .........................55
Felipe Carrillo Puerto....870
ferries..............................38
Ferrocarril de Chihuahua al Pacifico.............191
ferry, from La Paz .........122
Festival Internacional Cervantino... 290 & *Festive Mexico* colour section
Fiestas ........... 56 & *Festive Mexico* colour section
Acapulco and around....... 590
Baja California................. 174
Bajío, the......................... 320
Chiapas and Tabasco ...... 770
Jalisco and Michoacán .... 390
Mexico City..................... 534
Monterrey and the north ... 234
Oaxaca............................ 692
Veracruz ......................... 630
Yucatán........................... 878
Filo Bobos ....................616
fish.................................915
fishing, Baja California ..................................112
flights
from Australia, New Zealand and South Africa............ 31
from the UK and Ireland .... 30
from the US and Canada... 27
within Mexico.................. 38
food ......44 & *Mexican food and drink* colour section
**food and drink terms** ..........................954–957
food poisoning ..............52
football..................58, 499
Fortín de las Flores.......598
Fox, Vicente..................902
Frontera ........................769
Frontera Corozal...........750
frontier posts ..................30
fuel..................................39

# G

Gadsden Purchase.......891
Garrido Canabal, Tomás ..................................754
gas..................................39
gay and lesbian travellers .......................59
geography ....................913
**glossaries** ...........958–960
Gómez Palacio............203
Gran Desierto, El .........137
Granada........................793
Grito de la Independencia ..................................293
Grutas de Balankanché ..................................824
Grutas de Cacahuamilpa ..................................527
Grutas de Coconá........763
Grutas de Garcia..........233
Grutas de Loltún ..........815
Grutas de Rancho Nuevo ..................................726
Guachochi ....................197
**GUADALAJARA**.... 330–353
Guadalajara..................331
accommodation .............. 335
arrival.............................. 331
Barranca de Oblatos....... 348
Biblioteca IberoAmericana Octavio Paz ................ 343
bus routes ....................... 334
Capilla Tolsa................... 342
Central Guadalajara ........ 333
Centro Histórico ............. 338
cathedral ........................ 338
drinking .......................... 350
eating ............................. 348
entertainment ................. 351
fiestas............................. 351
haciendas....................... 337
history ............................ 331
Hospicio Cabañas........... 341
information ..................... 334
listings ............................ 352
Mercado Libertad............ 342
murals ..................... 339, 341
Museo Regional .............. 339
nightlife........................... 350
orientation ...................... 332
Palacio de Gobierno ........ 339
Parque Agua Azul ........... 342
Plaza de Armas............... 339
Plaza de la Liberación...... 340
Plaza Guadalajara ........... 338
Plaza Tapatía.................. 341
sport ............................... 352
Tlaquepaque................... 344
Tlaquepaque .................. 345
Tonalá............................. 346
Tonalá............................. 347
transport.................. 332, 334
university........................ 343
Zapopan.......................... 347
Zoológico Guadalajara..... 348
Guadalupe ....................269
**GUANAJUATO**..... 277–292
Guanajuato .......... 278–279
accommodation .............. 280
Alhóndiga de Granaditas ................................. 285
arrival.............................. 278
Cerro de Cubilete............ 288
Cristo Rey ...................... 288
drinking .......................... 289
eating ............................. 288
entertainment ................. 289
frogs ............................... 282
Ex-Hacienda de San Gabriel de Barrera..................... 287
Festival Internacional Cervantino ................... 290

INDEX

information ........ 279
Jardín de la Reforma ........ 282
Jardín de la Unión ........ 283
La Compañia ........ 284
La Valenciana ........ 287
listings ........ 291
Mercado Hidalgo ........ 282
Monumento al Pípila ........ 284
Museo Casa Diego Rivera ........ 285
Museo de la Mineralogía ........ 286
Museo de las Momias ........ 286
Museo del Pueblo de Guanajuato ........ 284
Museo Iconográfico del Quijote ........ 284
Museo Olga Costa-José Chávez Morado ........ 287
nightlife ........ 289
orientation ........ 280
Pípila, El ........ 285
Plaza de la Paz ........ 283
Presa de la Olla ........ 287
Salón del Culto a la Muerte ........ 286
Spanish, learning ........ 291
Teatro Juárez ........ 283
Templo de San Cayetano de Valenciana ........ 288
Guatemala
border ........ 708
bus to Guatemala City ........ 706
crossing into ........ 709
trading boats to ........ 752
Guaymas ........ 148
Guaymas ........ 148
Guerrero Negro ........ 103
Guiengola ........ 690

# H

hammocks ........ 43
health ........ 51
heatstroke ........ 54
Hecelchakán ........ 792
hepatitis A & B ........ 54
Hermosillo ........ 145
Hernández, Francisco ........ 782
Hidalgo del Parral ........ 204
Hierve el Agua ........ 664
**history** ........ 883–904
hitchhiking ........ 40
Hochob ........ 787
holidays ........ 69 & *Festive Mexico* colour section
Hopelchén ........ 787
Hormiguero ........ 791
hotels ........ 42
hostels ........ 44
Huamelulpan ........ 668
Huastecan *son* ........ 926
Huatulco ........ 686
Huerta, Victoriano ........ 895
Huichol Centre for Cultural Survival and Traditional Arts ........ 176
Huichol shamanism ........ 908
Huichol, the ........ 170
Huixtla ........ 703

# I

Iguala Plan ........ 890
Ihuatzio ........ 378
Independence Day ........ 57 & *Festive Mexico* colour section
independence ........ 889
insects ........ 915
insurance ........ 64
Internet ........ 65
ISIC card ........ 62
Isla Ángel de la Guarda ........ 101
**Isla Cozumel** ........ 854–860
Isla Cozumel ........ 854
Isla de la Piedra ........ 164
Isla del Rey ........ 173
Isla Holbox ........ 830
**Isla Mujeres** ........ 842–846
Isla Mujeres ........ 843
Isthmus of Tehuantepec ........ 688
Iturbide ........ 788
Ixtaccíhuatl ........ 511
Ixtapa ........ 571
Ixtapan de la Sal ........ 527
Ixtlan ........ 661
Ixtlán del Río ........ 176
Izamal ........ 817
Izapa ruins ........ 708

# J

**Jalisco, northern** ........ 330–362
Jalisco, northern ........ 328–329
Jaltenango ........ 717
James, Edward ........ 318
Janitzio ........ 377
Jerez... ........ 270
Jiménez ........ 203
Juárez, Benito ........ 641, 892
Juchitán... ........ 691
*jugos* ........ 47
Junchavín ........ 734

# K

Kabáh ........ 813
Kahlo, Frida ........ 418, 445, 451, 454–455, 460, 517
kayaking ........ 103
Kohunlich ........ 876 & *Ancient Mexico* colour section

# L

La Antigua ........ 613
La Bufa ........ 196
La Contadoría ........ 172
La Mesilla ........ 736
La Palma ........ 773
**La Paz** ........ 115–122
La Paz ........ 117
La Tovara Springs ........ 173
La Tzaráracua ........ 368
La Venta ........ 764
Labná ........ 814
Lacandón Maya, the ........ 748
Lacanjá Chansayab ........ 748 & *Ancient Mexico* colour section
Lago de Pátzcuaro ........ 376
Lago de Pátzcuaro ........ 377
Lagos de Moreno ........ 276
Laguna Bacalar ........ 871
Laguna de Chapala ........ 356
Laguna Miramar ........ 738
**language** ........ 951–960
Las Brisas ........ 561
Las dos Tuxtlas ........ 624
Las Maravillas de Tenejapa ........ 736
Las Playitas ........ 149
Las Pozas ........ 319
laundry... ........ 65
Lázaro Cárdenas ........ 570
League of Mayapán ........ 816
left-luggage offices ........ 37
León ........ 277
lesbian and gay travellers ........ 59
*licuados* ........ 47
lobster... ........ 91
Loreto ........ 113
Los Barriles ........ 136
Los Cabos ........ 123
Los Mochis ........ 155
Los Mochis ........ 157

# M


Madero, Francisco ....... 894
Madrid, Miguel de la .... 898
Mahahual ..................... 870
mail ................................ 66
malaria ........................... 53
Malinalco ..................... 528
Malpasito ..................... 765
mammals ..................... 917
Maní ............................. 816
**Manzanillo** .......... 559–562
Manzanillo ................... 559
maps .............................. 67
*maquiladora* programme ............................ 220, 899
Marcos, Subcomandante ................................... 900
mariachi ....... 473, 924, 930
markets .......................... 61
**Matamoros** .......... 216–219
Matamoros .................. 217
Matehuala .................... 244
Maximilian, Emperor .... 641, 892
Maya, the ............ 884, 885, 909, 910, 912 & *Ancient Mexico* colour section
Mayapán, League of ..... 816
**Mazatlán** ............. 161–168
Mazatlán ...................... 162
Mazunte ....................... 684
media ............................. 55
medical resources .......... 55
Mennonites .................. 191
**MÉRIDA** ............. 793–804
Mérida ......................... 794
accommodation ............... 795
arrival ................................ 793
Ballet Folklórico de la Universidad de Yucatán ..................................... 802
Casa de Artesanías .......... 799
Casa de Montego ............ 797
Cathedral of San Ildefonso ..................................... 797
eating .............................. 801
entertainment .................. 801
Iglesia de Jesús ............... 798
Iglesia Santa Lucía ........... 798
listings ............................. 802
MACAY ............................ 797
markets ............................ 799
Monumento a la Patria .... 799
Museo de Antropología ... 798
Museo de Arte Contemporáneo Ateneo de Yucatán ........................ 797
Museo de la Canción Yucateca ...................... 798
Museo de la Ciudad ......... 798
nightlife ............................ 801
Palacio de Gobierno ........ 798
Palacio Municipal ............. 798
Parque de las Américas ... 799
Paseo de Montejo .... 795, 798
Pinacoteca del Estado Juan Gamboa Guzmán ......... 798
Plaza Mayor ..................... 797
Plaza Santa Ana ............... 798
shopping .......................... 799
tourist information ........... 795
transport ................. 795, 803
mescal ............................ 48
Metepec ....................... 530
Mexcaltitán .................. 176
Mexicali ........................ 137
**Mexican Spanish** ........................... 951–957
Mexican-American War ............................... 891
**MEXICO CITY** ...... 398–485
Mexico City ................. 402
Academia de San Carlos ..................................... 425
accommodation .............. 408
airport ..................... 403, 479
Alameda .......................... 430
Antiguo Colegio de San Ildefonso ..................... 423
arrival .............................. 403
Atlantis ............................ 448
Auditorio Nacional .......... 446
Ayuntamiento .................. 421
Ballet Folklórico ....... 429, 473
banks .............................. 483
bars ........................... 470–473
Basílica de Nuestra Señora de Guadalupe ................... 463
Biblioteca de México ....... 432
Bosque de Chapultepec ..................................... 437
bullfighting .............. 450, 478
buses ....... 403, 407, 479–482
Calle Moneda .................. 424
Calzada de Tlalpan .......... 458
car rental ......................... 483
Casa de la Primera Imprenta ..................................... 424
Casa de los Azulejos ....... 427
Casa del Risco ................. 450
Catedral Metropolitana .... 414
Central Mexico City ......... 413
Central Mexico City ... 416–417
Centro Cultural Ex-Teresa Arte ............................. 425
Centro de la Imagen ........ 432
Centro de Autobuses del Sur ..................................... 482
Chapultepec .................... 438
Chapultepec Park ............ 437
Chapultepec Park ............ 438
cinema ............................ 474
*colectivos* ......................... 407
Condesa .......................... 437
Condesa .......................... 436
consulates ....................... 483
Correo Central ................. 428
Cortés .............................. 399
Coyoacán ........................ 452
Coyoacán ........................ 453
Coyolxauhqui stone ......... 418
Cuauhtémoc ............. 399, 435
DF, El ............................... 400
drinking ..................... 470–473
driving .............................. 408
eating ........................ 465–470
El Rollo ............................ 448
embassies ........................ 483
emergencies .................... 484
entertainment .................. 470
Estadio Olímpico ............. 457
floating gardens .............. 460
football ............................ 477
gay life ............................. 484
Glorieta Colón ................. 435
health .............................. 397
history ............................. 398
hostels ............................. 409
hotels .............................. 410
information ...................... 408
Insurgentes ...................... 449
Internet ............................ 484
Kahlo, Frida ............. 454, 460
La Feria ............................ 447
Laboratorio Arte Almeda ... 431
Lago Chapultepec ........... 445
light rail ........................... 406
listings ............................. 482
Los Pinos ......................... 446
Lotería Nacional .............. 433
Madero .................... 401, 427
markets ........... 424, 425, 475
Metro ............................... 405
Metro ............................... 406
Monumento a la Revolución ..................................... 433
Museo Anahuacalli .......... 459
Museo Casa de Leon Trotsky ..................................... 456
Museo Casa Estudio Diego Rivera y Frida Kahlo ..... 451
Museo de Arte Carrillo-Gil ..................................... 450
Museo de Arte Moderno .. 444
Museo de Caracol ............ 439
Museo de Cera ................ 435
Museo de Historia Natural ..................................... 448
Museo de la Arquitectura ..................................... 429
Museo de la Caricatura ... 423
Museo de la Ciudad de México ........................... 425
Museo de la Estampa ...... 431
Museo de la Indumentaria Mexicana ...................... 426
Museo de la Luz .............. 424
Museo de la Medicina ..... 422
Museo de la SHCP .......... 424
Museo de lo Increíble ...... 435
Museo del Carmen .......... 450
Museo del Ejército y Fuerza ..................................... 429

Museo del Templo Mayor ........ 417
Museo Dolores Olmedo Patiño ........ 459
Museo Franz Mayer ........ 431
Museo Frida Kahlo ........ 454
Museo José Luis Cuevas ........ 425
Museo Manuel Tolsá ........ 429
Museo Mural Diego Rivera ........ 431
Museo Nacional de Antropología ........ 440
Museo Nacional de Historia ........ 440
Museo Nacional de la Revolución ........ 433
Museo Nacional de las Intervenciones ........ 458
Museo Nacional de las Culturas ........ 425
Museo Nacional de San Carlos ........ 432
Museo Nacional del Arte ........ 430
Museo Rufino Tamayo ........ 445
Museo Tecnológico ........ 447
Museo Venustiano Carranza ........ 435
Nacional Monte de Piedad ........ 422
Niños Héroes ........ 439
Nuevo Bosque de Chapultepec ........ 447
Ola, La ........ 448
Olympic Stadium ........ 456
orientation ........ 401
Orozco, José Clemente ........ 423
Palacio de Bellas Artes ........ 427
Palacio de Minería ........ 429
Palacio Nacional ........ 418
Papalote Museo del Niño ........ 447
Parque México ........ 437
Parque Sullivan ........ 436
Parque Zoológico de Chapultepec ........ 445
Paseo de la Reforma ........ 433
*peseros* ........ 407
pharmacies ........ 484
Pirámide de Cuicuilco ........ 458
Plaza de la Constitución ........ 413
Plaza de la Republica ........ 433
Plaza de las Tres Culturas ........ 462
Plaza de Loreto ........ 424
Plaza Garibaldi ........ 473
Plaza México ........ 450
Polanco ........ 437
Polanco ........ 438
Polyforum Siqueiros ........ 449
Puente de Alvarado ........ 432
*pulque* ........ 471
Reforma ........ 433
restaurants ........ 465–470
Rivera, Diego ........ 420, 459
Rivera murals ........ 418, 421, 422, 428
Rivera Trail ........ 421
Roma ........ 436
Roma ........ 436
safety ........ 397
Sala de Arte David Siqueiros ........ 437
San Ángel ........ 450
San Ángel ........ 453
San Fernando ........ 432
San Hipólito ........ 432
Santa Cecilia ........ 465
Santo Domingo ........ 422
SECTUR ........ 408
Segunda Sección ........ 447
SEP ........ 423
shopping ........ 474
sport ........ 476
TAPO ........ 404
taxis ........ 397, 407
telephones ........ 484
Templo Mayor ........ 399, 415
Tenayuca ........ 464
Tenochtitlán ........ 398
Teotihuacán ........ 441
Tercera Sección ........ 448
Terminal del Norte ........ 482
Terminal Poniente ........ 482
Tlatelolco ........ 462
Torre Latinoamericana ........ 427
Torture Museum ........ 429
tourist information ........ 408
transport ........ 405
tren ligero ........ 405
Trotsky, León ........ 456
university ........ 457
wrestling ........ 477
Xochimilco ........ 460
Zócalo ........ 413
Zona Rosa ........ 435
Zona Rosa ........ 436
zoo ........ 445

Mexico City, around ........ 396
**Michoacán, northern** ........ 362–392
Michoacán, northern ........ 328–329
Mineral del Chico ........ 498
Miramar ........ 150
Misión Mulegé ........ 110
Misol-Há ........ 740
Mitla ........ 663
Mixteca Alta ........ 668
Mixteca Baja ........ 667
mobile phones ........ 69
*mole* ......45 & *Mexican food and drink* colour section
Monarch Butterfly Sanctuary ........ 388
Monclova ........ 212
money ........ 67
monkey reserve ........ 867
Monte Albán ........ 656 & *Ancient Mexico* colour section
Monte Albán ........ 657
**Monterrey** ........ 224–233
Monterrey ........ 225
Montes Azules Biosphere Reserve ........ 736
Montezuma (Moctezuma II) ........ 399, 887
**Morelia** ........ 380–383
Morelia ........ 381
Morelos y Pavón, José María ........ 386
mosquito bites ........ 53
Moxviquil ........ 727
mugging ........ 49
Mulegé ........ 109
**music** ........ 924–933
Muyil ........ 868


## N


Nacajuca ........ 766
NAFTA ........ 220, 899
Navojoa ........ 151
Nevado de Colima ........ 362
newspapers ........ 55
Noche Triste ........ 887
Nocoh Mul ........ 867
Nogales ........ 144
Nopoló ........ 115
*norteño* music ........ 927
**north, the** ........ 179–238
north, the ........ 182
Nueva España ........ 888
Nuevo Casas Grandes ........ 187
Nuevo Laredo ........ 213
Nuevo Laredo ........ 214
Nuevo Vallarta ........ 553


## O


**OAXACA** (city) ........ 638–655
Oaxaca (city) ........ 639
accommodation ........ 642
Arcos de Xochimilco ........ 650
arrival ........ 640
Basílica de Nuestra Señora de la Soledad ........ 647
drinking ........ 652
eating ........ 650
folk dances ........ 652
Instituto de Artes Gráficas ........ 647

Jardín Etnobotánico......... 646
listings............................ 653
MACO............................. 646
Macedonio Alcalá............ 645
markets........................... 648
mescal............................. 651
Museo Casa de Juárez
....................................... 647
Museo de las Culturas de
Oaxaca............................ 646
Museo Rufino Tamayo..... 647
Museum of Contemporary Art
....................................... 646
nightlife........................... 652
Palacio del Gobierno....... 645
Planetario Nundehui........ 650
San Juan de Dios............ 648
tourist information........... 640
Tourist Yú'ù..................... 644
transport.......................... 641
**Oaxaca (state)**..... 633–694
Oaxaca (state)...............636
Oaxacan cuisine...........651
Obregón, Alvaro...........895
Ocampo.......................390
Ocosingo.....................737
Ocotlán........................666
older travellers...............70
Olmec culture...........909 & *Ancient Mexico* colour section
Ometepec....................590
opening hours................68
Orizaba........................597
Orozco, José Clemente
........ 339, 341, 423, 425, 427, 448, 451, 896
Orozco, Pascual..........894
Ortiz Tirado Music Festival
.................................152
Oxkutzcab...................815
Oxolotán.......................764
Oxtankah......................876

# P

Pachuca.......................496
**Palenque**.............740–747
Palenque......................741
Palenque ruins.............744
Palenque ruins............744
Palenque tours and operators..................742
PAN...........................898
Papanoa......................576
Papantla......................617
Paquimé......................187
Paracho.......................364
Paraíso (Acapulco).......563
Paraíso (Tabasco)........769
Paricutín......................368
parking...........................39
Parque Internacional del Río Bravo.................211
Parque Nacional de Volcanes...................512
Parque Nacional de la Ballena Gris..............104
Parque Nacional El Chico
.................................498
Parque Nacional Eduardo Ruíz............367
Parque Nacional Lagos de Montebello................734
Parque Nacional Nevado de Colima.....568
Parque Nacional San Pedro Mártir.........99
Parque Natural del Desierto Central de Baja California
.................................101
Parque Natural Villa Luz
.................................763
Parque Xel-ha.............860
Parral..........................204
**Pátzcuaro**...........370–376
Pátzcuaro....................371
PEMEX.......................899
pesos............................67
petroglyphs, Zoque......765
petrol.............................39
peyote.........................246
pharmacies...................55
phones..........................69
Piedras Negras............212
Pijijiapan.....................703
Pinacate Biosphere Reserve, El...............143
Pinotepa Nacional........590
*pirecua*.........................926
Pisté............................819
Playa Azul....................570
Playa Chamela............554
**Playa del Carmen**
.........................849–853
Playa del Carmen.......850
Playa Olas Altas...........164
Playa Perula................554
Playitas, Las................149
Pochutla......................679
police............................50
Pomoná ruins...............772
Popocatépetl................511
Portillo, López..............897
Posada, José Guadalupe
.................................274
Pozos...........................294
PRD.............................899
prickly heat....................54
Progreso......................805
public holidays...............69
public transport........38, 41
**Puebla**.................502–509
Puebla.........................503
Puebla defeat...............892
**Puerto Ángel**.......679–681
Puerto Arista................701
Puerto Ceiba...............769
**Puerto Escondido**
.........................669–678
Puerto Escondido........671
Puerto Morelos............846
Puerto Peñasco...........141
**Puerto Vallarta**....543–553
Puerto Vallarta............544
*pulque*.....................48, 471
Punta Allen..................869
Punta Bete...................849
Punta de Mita..............553
Punta Maldonada.........589
Purépechan, the..........363
Puuc Hills....................808

# Q

**Querétaro**...........307–315
Querétaro....................308
Quesada, Vicente Fox...902
Quetzalcoatl................489
Quiahuitzlán Nautla......615
Quija............................734
Quintana Roo..............832
Quiroga.......................380

# R

rabies............................55
radio..............................56
*ranchera* music............927
Real de Catorce..........245
Real de Catorce..........245
Real del Monte............498
Recohuata hot springs
.................................196
reefs...........................845
reform laws..................891
Reforma ruins..............773
*refrescos*.......................47
reptiles........................915
Reserva de la Biosfera Patanos de Centla.....769
Reserva Ecológica Cascadas de Reforma
.................................773

Reynosa 216
Ría Celestún Biosphere Reserve 807
Río Bec 791
Río Bec sites 790
Río Lagartos 829
Río Urique 188
Rivera Trail 421
Rivera, Diego 274, 285, 418–422, 428, 429, 431, 448, 450, 451, 455, 459, 583, 896
rock art 107
rodeos 58, 477
Rosarito 89
Ruta Puuc 808

## S

sacrifices 911
safety 49
Salahua 561
Salina Cruz 689
Salinas de Gortari, Carlos 898
salsa 45 & *Mexican food and drink* colour section
Saltillo 235
San Agustinillo 683
San Andrés Accords on Rights and Indigenous Cultures 902
San Andrés Tuxtla 625
San Bartolo Coyotepec 665
**San Blas** 170–176
San Blas 171
San Carlos 150
**San Cristóbal de las Casas** 717–726
San Cristóbal de las Casas 719
San Cristóbal de las Casas and around 727
San Felipe (Baja California) 140
San Felipe (Yucatán) 830
San Ignacio 105
San Ignacio Mission 195
San Jorge Island 143
San José del Cabo 132
San José del Cabo 134
San José del Pacífico 669
San José Iturbide 294
San Juan Chamula 728
San Juan Cosalá 359
San Juan de los Lagos 276
San Juan del Río 317
San Lorenzo Zinacantán 730
San Luis de la Paz 293
**San Luis Potosí** 250–256
San Luis Potosí 251
San Luis Río Colorado 141
San Martín Tilcajete 665
San Miguel 855
**San Miguel de Allende** 295–305
San Miguel de Allende 296
San Patricio-Melaque 558
San Quintín 97
Santa Ana 141
Santa Ana del Valle 662
Santa Anna, General 890
Santa Clara 806
Santa Clara del Cobre 380
Santa Cruz Huatulco 687
Santa Elena 812
Santa María del Tule 659
Santa Rosalía 108
Santiago 561
Santiago Apoala 668
Santiago Ixcuintla 176
Santiago Tuxtla 624
Santo Domingo 707
Santo Tomás 99
Santo Tomás Jalieza 666
Santuario de Atotonilco 306
Sayil 814
Sayula 361
Scammon's Lagoon 104
scorpions 53
sea kayaking 103
Semana Santa 57 & *Festive Mexico* colour section
senior travellers 70
sexual assault 49
sexual harassment 59
shamanism 907
Sian Ka'an Biosphere Reserve 867
Sierra de San Francisco 107
Sierra Tarahumara 195
siestas 69
Simojovel 717
Sinaloa 155
SIPAZ 700
Siqueiros, David 343, 429, 449, 451, 457
Sisal 807
snakes 53
soccer 58, 477, 499
*son* 924
Sonoita 141
Sontecomapan 629
Spanish conquest 886
sport 58
study programmes 66
Sumidero canyon 716
sun, problems with 54
surfing 58, 95, 124, 132, 674

## T

**Tabasco** 753–774
Tabasco 699
Talismán Bridge 708
Tamayo, Rufino 428, 445
Tampico 222
Tangolunda 687
**Tapachula** 703–706
Tapachula 703
Tapalpa 360
Tapatío cuisine 348
Tapijulapa 763
Tarascans, the 363
**Taxco** 523–527
Taxco 524
taxis 41
Teapa 763
Tehuacán 637
Tehuantepec 689
Tehuantepec, Isthmus of 688
Tejada, Lerdo de 892
Telchac Puerto 806
telegrams 67
telephones 69
Tenacatita 555
Tenam Puente 734
Tenancingo 528
Tenango del Valle 530
Tenochtitlán 398 & *Ancient Mexico* colour section
Tenosique 772
Teotihuacán 485–491 & *Ancient Mexico* colour section
Teotihuacán 486
Teotitlán del Valle 660
Tepexpan 491
Tepic 169
Teposcolula 667
Tepotzotlán 492
Tepoztlán 519

tequila....................48, 356
& *Mexican food and drink* colour section
Tequila (town)...............354
Tequila Express...............355
Tequisquiapan...............316
tetanus...............54
Texan Independence...891
Tex-Mex...............927
theft...............49
Ticul...............813
**Tijuana**...............80–89
Tijuana, Central.......82–83
Tijuana, Downtown.......86
time...............71
timeline, historical.........905
Tinganio...............370
tipping...............60
Tizimín...............829
Tlacolula...............662
Tlacotalpan...............624
Tlapacoyan...............616
Tlaquepaque...............344
Tlaquepaque...............345
Tlaxcala...............500
Tlaxiaco...............669
Todos Santos...............123
toilets...............71
Toltecs...............885 & *Ancient Mexico* colour section
Toluca de Lerdo...............530
Tonalá (Chiapas)...............701
Tonalá (Jalisco)...............346
Tonalá...............347
Tonatzintla...............511
Toniná...............738
Topolobampo...............155
Torreón...............203
tortillas..........45 & *Mexican food and drink* colour section
tour operators...............33
tourist card...............62
tourist information...............71
tourist offices, Mexican overseas...............64
Tourist Yú'ù...............644
Tovara Springs, La........173
trains
- to Mexico...............28
- within Mexico...............38

Transpeninsular Highway...............100
transport...............38
travel insurance...............64
travellers' cheques.........68
Treaty of Guadalupe Hidalgo...............891
Tres Zapotes...............623
Trotsky, Leon.......420, 454, 456
Tula...............494
**Tulum**...............861–866
Tulum Ruins...............864
turtles........563, 591, 684, 766, 845, 860, 867, 916
Tuxpan...............362
Tuxpán...............622
**Tuxtla Gutiérrez**....710–714
Tuxtla Gutiérrez...........711
TV...............56
typhoid...............54
Tzeltal language...........728
Tzintzuntzán...............379
Tzotzil language...........728

# U

Unión Juárez...............707
**Uruapan**...............364–368
Uruapan...............365
**Uxmal**...............809–812
Uxmal Ruins...............809

# V

vaccinations...............54
Valladolid...............825
Valladolid...............825
Valle de Bravo...............533
Valle de Guadalupe........97
Vasco de Quiroga...........363
Vasconcelos, José........423
vegetarian food...............46
vegetation...............914
**Veracruz** (city)......605–613
Veracruz (city)...............606
**Veracruz (state)**...595–632
Veracruz (state)...........596
Victoria, Guadalupe......891
Villa del Oeste...............209
Villa Garcia...............234
Villa Rica...............615
Villa, Pancho...............894
**Villahermosa**.......755–762
Villahermosa...............755
visas...............63
Voladores de Papantla....620
voluntary work...............66

# W

Wadley...............250
water, safety of...............52
whale migration...............919
whale watching...102, 107, 917, 919
whales..........102, 107, 917, 919
**wildlife**...............915–923
wildlife sites...............918
work programmes..........66
wrestling...............58

# X

**Xalapa**...............600–604
Xalapa...............601
Xcalak...............871
Xcaret...............860
Xico...............604
Xilitla...............319
Xlapak...............814
Xochicalco...............521
Xochimilco...............460
Xochitécatl...............502
Xpu-ha...............860
Xpujil...............789

# Y

Yagul...............662
Yanhuitlán...............667
Yaqui, the...............151
Yaxchilán...............751
youth hostels...............44
**Yucatán**...............775–879
Yucatán...............778–779
Yucatán, history...........777
Yucatecan cuisine........800 & *Mexican food and drink* colour section
Yumká...............760

# Z

Zaachila...............666
**ZACATECAS**.......257–268
Zacatecas...............258
- accommodation...............259
- arrival...............259
- cable car...............265
- cathedral...............262
- Casa de la Moneda..........263
- Centro Platero de Zacatecas...............268
- Cerro de la Bufa.......257, 265

drinking .......................... 267
eating .......................... 265
Eden Mine .......................... 264
entertainment .......................... 267
Feria de Zacatecas .......................... 259
festivals .......................... 259
Guadalupe .......................... 268
history .......................... 257
International Folk Festival .......................... 259
La Morisma .......................... 259
Mausoleo de los Hombres Ilustres .......................... 265
Mina El Edén .......................... 264
Museo de Arte Abstract Manuel Felguérez .......................... 263
Museo de la Toma de Zacatecas .......................... 265
Museo Francisco Goitia .......................... 264
Museo Pedro Coronel .......................... 262
Museo Rafeo Coronel .......................... 264
Museo Zacatecano .......................... 263
Parque Enrique Estrada .......................... 264
San Agustín .......................... 263
Santo Domingo .......................... 262
teleférico .......................... 265
tourist information .......................... 259
Zacatecas en la Cultura .......................... 259
Zamora de Hidalgo .......................... 364
Zapata, Emiliano .......................... 739
Zapatista Army of National Liberation .......................... 900
Zapatista rebellion .......................... 700
Zapopan .......................... 347
Zapotecs .......................... 656 & *Ancient Mexico* colour section
**Zihuatanejo** .......................... 570–576
Zihuatanejo .......................... 571
Zinacantán .......................... 730
Zipolite .......................... 681
Zitácuaro .......................... 389
Zona Dorada .......................... 164
Zoológico Miguel Álvarez del Toro (ZOOMAT) .......................... 712
Zoque ruins .......................... 765

INDEX